THE INSURANCE OF
COMMERCIAL RISKS:
LAW AND PRACTICE

THE INSURANCE OF COMMERCIAL RISKS: LAW AND PRACTICE

Third Edition

DIGBY C. JESS

BSc (Hons) (Aston), LLM (Manch.), PhD (Manch.)
F.C.I.Arb., F.R.S.A., Chartered Arbitrator
Barrister of Gray's Inn and the Northern Circuit

LONDON
SWEET & MAXWELL

To Bridie, Piers and Francesca

Published in 2001
by Sweet and Maxwell Limited
of 100 Avenue Road, Swiss Cottage
London NW3 3PF.
(http://www.sweetandmaxwell.co.uk)
Typeset by J&L Composition Ltd, Filey, North Yorkshire.
Printed in England by MPG Books Ltd, Bodmin, Cornwall

No natural forests were destroyed to make this product; only farmed timber was used and replanted.

A CIP catalogue record for this book is available from the British Library.

ISBN 0421 824409

T   1002469766

FOREWORD

In today's world of increasing business complexity and litigiousness, the insurance of commercial risks assumes greater importance than ever before. This is demonstrated daily in London's Commercial Court, where insurance claims form a greater proportion of the diet of cases than they once did. Moreover, market demands and the ingenuity of underwriters have created new forms of cover.

In this third edition of his work Dr Jess has rewritten and expanded a volume which succinctly covers the ground set out in his title "The Insurance of Commercial Risks: Law and Practice". As there indicated, the work is both learned and practical. In between a concise restatement of general principles in Part I and a helful synopsis of the legal and practical considerations of the making and defence of claims in Part IV, are to be found analysed chapter by chapter the major forms of commercial risk—both those arising out of the incurring of liabilities and those arising out of the protection of property. The treatment of each of such risks is clear and straightforward, with plentiful illustrations from the facts and decisions of reported cases.

An especially helpful addition to the work are the Appendices, which bring together specimen policies, the critical sections of relevant statutes, the regulations enacted in important statutory instruments, and other pertinent documents.

This volume is not intended to reproduce other more general works on insurance law, but focuses, as its chapter headings demonstrate, on the individual types of risk concerned. As such, I am confident that practitioners, underwriters and businessmen alike will find it of interest and assistance.

In his first inaugural address, almost exactly 200 years ago as I write, Thomas Jefferson spoke of "Peace, commerce and honest friendship with all nations . . .". It is perhaps no surprise that commerce finds itself in such good company. Insurance makes that commerce possible.

Bernard Rix
June 2001

PREFACE

I am delighted that the 3rd edition of this book now enters the fold of Sweet & Maxwell, and the more so that it becomes part of the "Insurance Practitioner's Library". My belief that this subject deserves a specific text is borne out by this new edition. I have taken the opportunity to totally revise and reorganise the material within this new edition. Many readers have commented that they found the previous arrangement easy to use, and my aim has been to increase that ease of use, as well as increase the practical use of this work. I believe that I have achieved this. Readers will also find that, not only is the material brought up to date from the last edition in 1993, but it has also been expanded. There is a new Chapter 4, dealing with the duties and liabilities of insurance brokers and intermediaries. Secondly, there is a new Chapter 22, where I have sought to discuss many of the necessary matters that require consideration in the conduct of litigation involving commercial insurance contracts. Finally, I have now introduced credit insurance into Chapter 14. Otherwise, the book's arrangement remains the same:

Part I — General;
Part II — Liability Insurances;
Part III — Property and Other Insurances; and
Part IV — Claims.

The Appendices include some current specimen policy forms, and I am most grateful to the Co-operative Insurance Society Ltd and the Royal & Sun Alliance Insurance plc for their kind permission to reproduce those forms. I am also grateful to the new General Insurance Standards Council for permission to include their *Commerical Code* within Appendix 15. It will be seen that the Appendices now include statutory and subordinate materials for ease of reference. Finally, I must thank Lord Justice Rix for kindly writing the Foreword to this new edition.

The work remains very much one man's labour, but I am grateful to Professor David Milman of Manchester University for reading the draft Chapter 8 on Director's and Officer's Liability Insurance and making suggestions thereon.

I have strived to reflect the law as at March 21, 2001.

Digby C. Jess
8 King Street Chambers,
Manchester, M2 6AQ.

CONTENTS

Chapter 3 — Concealment of Material Facts

Chapter 4 — The Duties and Liabilities of Insurance Brokers and Intermediaries

APPENDICES

Specimen Policies
1. The Co-operative Insurance Society ("CIS") Commercial Combined Policy
2. The Co-operative Insurance Society ("CIS") Shopkeeper's Policy
3. The Co-operative Insurance Society ("CIS") Contract Works Policy
4. The Co-operative Insurance Society ("CIS") Contractors' "All Risks" Policy
5. The Co-operative Insurance Society ("CIS") Motor Vehicle Policy
6. Royal & Sun Alliance Insurance plc ("RSA") Contractors' "All Risks" — Annual Policy
7. Royal & Sun Alliance Insurance plc ("RSA") Fidelity Policy
8. Royal & Sun Alliance Insurance plc ("RSA") Directors' and Officers' Insurance Policy
9. Royal & Sun Alliance Insurance plc ("RSA") Commercial Vehicle Policy
10. Royal & Sun Alliance Insurance plc ("RSA") Premier Transit — Haulage

Statutes
11. Fires Prevention (Metropolis) Act 1774, s. 83
    Marine Insurance Act 1906, ss. 6, 17–20, 27, 28, 33–35, 52, 53, 55–57, 67–72, 74, 75, 77, 79–81, 84.
    Third Parties (Rights Against Insurers) Act 1930
    Employers' Liability (Compulsory Insurance) Act 1969
    Insurance Brokers (Registration) Act 1977
    Insurance Companies Act 1982, ss. 94B and 96A, and Sched. 3A, Part I.
    Road Traffic Act 1988, ss. 143–154, 157–162, 197
    Contracts (Rights of Third Parties) Act 1999

Statutory Instruments
12. Employers' Liability (Compulsory Insurance) Regulations 1998 S.I. 1998 No.2573
    Motor Vehicles (Third Party Risks) Regulations 1972 S.I. 1972 No.1217
    Motor Vehicles (Compulsory Insurance) (No. 2) Regulations 1973 S.I. 1973 No.2143
    Motor Vehicles (Compulsory Insurance) Regulations 1992 S.I. 1992 No.3036
    Motor Vehicles (Compulsory Insurance) Regulations 2000 S.I. 2000 No.726
    Insurance Brokers Registration Council (Code of Conduct) Approval Order 1994, S.I. 1994 No.2569

TABLE OF CASES

TABLE OF STATUTES

TABLE OF STATUTORY INSTRUMENTS

PART I

GENERAL

CHAPTER 1

THE NATURE OF INSURANCE CONTRACTS

1. DEFINING CONTRACTS OF INSURANCE

It has been said that the insuring of ships is as old as the laws of Oleron   **1–01**
and Rhodes, whose inhabitants were long ago the great traders of the
world,[1] but, in any event, marine insurance was introduced into England
in the fifteenth century, and, about a century later, insurances upon lives
arose.[2] The earliest form of non-marine property insurance, buildings' fire
insurance, developed after the Great Fire of London in the Cities of
London and Westminster, subsequently spreading across the country
during the early part of the eighteenth century, at the same time being
extended to the insurance of goods against loss or damage from fire.[3] It
will be understood that the majority of liability and other insurances that
are considered in this work are of comparatively recent origin, *e.g.*
employers' liability insurance developed about a century ago, whilst directors' and officers' insurance has been introduced within the past decade
only.

Despite the large number of cases that have come before the courts   **1–02**
upon insurance contracts, there is but comparatively scant judicial discussion of a definition of a "contract of insurance". Lord Mansfield C.J.'s
statement in 1766 that insurance is "a contract upon speculation" hardly
suffices,[4] particularly when the court is faced with many of these newer
forms of insurances. Over a century later the Court of Appeal considered
a suitable definition of a contract of insurance providing an indemnity
against loss and Cotton L.J. said[5]:

> "The policy is really a contract to indemnify the person insured for the loss
> which he has sustained in consequence of the peril insured against which has
> happened, and from that it follows, of course, that as it is only a contract of
> indemnity, it is only to pay that loss which the assured may have sustained
> by reason of the (peril) that has occurred."

That statement was rather more imprecise than the definition given   **1–03**
sometime earlier by Lawrence J., that an insurance is a contract by which
the one party in consideration of a price paid to him adequate to the risk
becomes security to the other that he shall not suffer loss, damage, or
prejudice by the happening of the perils specified to certain things which

---

[1] *Sadler's Co. v. Badcock* (1743) 2 Atk. 554 at 556, *per* Lord Hardwicke L.C.

[2] Crawley, *The Law of Life Insurance* (1982), p. 2.

[3] See the report of *Lynch v. Dalzell* (1729) 4 Bro. Parl. Cas. 431, HL, which also states that
the Sun Fire Office was the first insurance office to insure the loss of goods, as well as houses,
against fire in 1709.

[4] *Carter v. Boehm* (1766) 3 Burr. 1905 at 1909.

[5] *Castellain v. Preston* (1883) 11 Q.B.D. 380 at 386, CA.

may be exposed to them.[6] The first attempt at a comprehensive definition of a contract of insurance was probably that of Channel J. in *Prudential Insurance Co. v. I.R.C.*[7] where he determined that there are three criteria necessary to constitute a contract of insurance[8]:

> (i) it must be a contract whereby for some consideration, usually but not necessarily for periodical payments called premiums, one secures for oneself some benefit, usually but not necessarily the payment of a sum of money, upon the happening of some event;
> (ii) the event should be one which involves some amount of uncertainty there must be either uncertainty whether the event will ever happen or not, or if the event is one which must happen at some time there must be uncertainty as to the time at which it will happen;
> (iii) the insurance must be against something, *i.e.* the uncertain event which is necessary to make the contract is prima facie adverse to the interest of the insured.[9]

1–04   An alternative three criteria were more recently postulated by Megarry V.-C. in *Medical Defence Union Ltd v. Department of Trade*[10]:

> (i) the contract must provide that the insured will become entitled to something[11] on the occurrence of some event;
> (ii) the event must be one which involves some element of uncertainty (perhaps with the addition of the words "outside the control of the insurer");
> (iii) the insured must have an insurable interest in the subject matter of the contract.

In proffering this definition, though, Megarry V.-C. doubted whether a satisfactory definition of a "contract of insurance" will ever be evolved, it being a matter of considerable difficulty. It is a concept which it is better to describe than to attempt to define.[12]

Insurers

1–06   Subject to detailed exceptions concerning members of Lloyd's and certain other bodies, section 2 of the Insurance Companies Act 1982 (as amended) provides that no person can carry on business in the United Kingdom unless he is authorised to do so. Authorisation is now carried out by the Financial Services Authority pursuant to section 3 of the Insurance Companies Act 1982. To carry on insurance business without the

---

[6] *Lucena v. Craufurd* (1806) 2 Bos. and P.N.R. 269 at 301, HL.

[7] [1904] 2 K.B. 658.

[8] *ibid.* at 663; followed *Department of Trade and Industry v. St Christopher Motorists Association Ltd* [1974] 1 W.L.R. 99.

[9] This element of adversity, whilst existing in indemnity insurances, may not truly exist in life assurances. See *Gould v. Curtis* [1913] 3 K.B. 84 at 95, *per* Buckley L.J., CA.

[10] [1980] Ch. 82 at 89–90.

[11] *ibid.* at 97, "money or money's worth" is "probably on the right lines".

[12] *ibid.* at 95.

required authorisation, unless exempted, is an offence under sections 2(1) and 14 of the 1982 Act, and this includes the process of soliciting business and issuing an invitation to treat, as well as effecting insurance contracts.[13] Directors of a company which commits such an offence may themselves be prosecuted under section 91(1) of the 1982 Act if the company's offence was committed with their consent or connivance or neglect. Authorisation will be restricted to specific categories of insurance business, which, for the insurances covered by this book will be the following classes of "general business" set out in Part I of Schedule 2 to the 1982 Act:

    (3) land vehicles;
    (7) goods in transit;
    (8) fire and natural forces;
    (9) damage to property;
    (10) motor vehicle liability;
    (13) general liability;
    (14) credit;
    (16) miscellaneous financial loss.

With the exception of individuals who are members of Lloyd's of London, **1–06** insurers will, in practice, be limited companies registered in the United Kingdom under the Companies Acts, or companies registered in a member State of the European Union with a representative resident in the United Kingdom,[14] or companies registered elsewhere which have lodged sufficient deposits and have a United Kingdom representative.[15] There are extensive provisions in the Financial Services Act 1986 dealing with the regulation of authorised insurance companies. As regards insurers who are members of Lloyd's of London, they are called "underwriters", and do not deal directly with the general public, but only effect insurance through Lloyd's brokers (who are also members of Lloyd's) who submit proposals for insurance to them on "slips". Underwriters tend to combine into "syndicates" and their affairs are usually looked after by "managing agents". The regulation of the operation of Lloyd's underwriters is largely by the Corporation of Lloyd's within a framework established by the Lloyd's Act 1982. The insured cannot look to any other member of Lloyd's, or the Corporation of Lloyd's, to make payment of an indemnity due under a policy, as only the subscribing members are liable upon it.[16]

The premium
The consideration paid by the insured to the insurer in exchange for the **1–07** undertaking to pay an indemnity in the event insured against,[17] is known

---

[13] *R. v. Wilson* [1997] 1 W.L.R. 1247, CA.
[14] The Insurance Companies Act 1982, s.10(5), requires that representative to be authorised to act generally, and to accept service of any document, on behalf of the authorised insurance company in its capacity as representative of that insurer.
[15] *ibid.*, s.9.
[16] *Industrial Guarantee Corp. v. Lloyd's Corp.* (1924) 19 Ll. L. Rep. 78.
[17] *Sun Insurance Office v. Clark* [1912] A.C. 443 at 460, *per* Lord Atkinson, HL.

as the "premium", and may be paid in one instalment, or several instalments during the period of insurance. The amount of the premium will be determined by the insurer in this first instance, but in the case of commercial insurances, that first offer may be the subject of negotiation between the insurer and the insurance intermediary acting on behalf of the person seeking the insurance (the "proposer"). The amount of the premium will obviously depend on such matters as the insurer's assessment of the risk, for instance, commercial properties may by "surveyed" on behalf of the insurer to determine the theft and fire risks, and various improvements may be required before the insurer is prepare to offer cover. It will further depend on the precise terms of the cover and the exclusions to cover, the risks to be insured, and the sums to be insured. That premium may be subject to later adjustment, as with employers' liability insurance where the premium is largely "rated" on the employers' wages bill and the insurance policy may require a declaration from the insured employer at the end of the period of insurance of the actual wages bill for that period, upon which the premium is adjusted up or down from the estimated wages bill given at the inception of the insurance. Further, upon renewal of the insurance, an insurer may offer a "no claims discount" on the normal premium rate, but this is not common in the case of commercial insurances as against, for example, domestic household insurance or private motor insurance.

1–08   The failure to fix a premium will lead to the result that there is no concluded and enforceable contract of insurance, unless the premium is otherwise capable of ascertainment. This can lead to difficulty. A valid contract can be made where the premium, or an additional premium, is "to be arranged" on the basis that in default of an arrangement, a reasonable sum is payable.[18] This sum will be one calculated in accordance with the prevailing market rate,[19] so the fact that there is no available market for a particular risk will, in that case, prevent the formation of an enforceable contract of insurance.[20]

1–09   In principle, provided the premium is agreed or ascertainable, the contract of insurance is effective and the insured is liable to pay the premium, rather than the insurance being ineffective until such time as the insured makes payment of the premium.[21] However, the terms of the insurance contract, as set out in the policy, may provide that the insurance will not come into force until the premium has been paid,[22] or that the insurer will not be liable for any loss occurring before payment of the premium.[23] If there is such a precondition set out in the policy, the mere fact that the policy also recites, incorrectly, that the premium has been received, does not prevent the insurers relying on the non-payment of the premium.[24] If

---

[18] Applying the Marine Insurance Act 1906, s.31(1) and (2).
[19] *Hyberabad (Deccan) Co. v. Willoughby* [1899] 2 Q.B. 530; F. *Gliksten and Son Ltd v. State Assurance Co. Ltd* (1922) 10 Ll. L. Rep. 604; *Banque Sabbag S.A.L. v. Hope* [1972] 1 Lloyd's Rep. 253.
[20] *Liberian Insurance Agency v. Mosse* [1977] 2 Lloyd's Rep. 560.
[21] *Roberts v. Security Co. Ltd* [1897] 1 Q.B. 111, CA.
[22] *General Accident Insurance Co. v. Cronk* (1901) 17 T.L.R. 233.
[23] *Tarleton v. Staniforth* (1796) 1 Bos. and P. 471.
[24] *Equitable Fire and Accident Office Ltd v. Ching Wo Hong* [1907] A.C. 96, PC.

the insured cancels the policy during its currency, he will generally be able to recover (but is not entitled to recover, unless the policy provides otherwise[25]) some part of the premium to reflect the fact that the insurance has not run its full course. Such returnable premium will not be in proportion to the unexpired term, and is really a matter of discretion for the insurer, unless the policy provides otherwise. In the case of payment of the premium by instalments, it will be necessary to refer to the precise terms in order to determine whether non-payment of a single instalment causes the insurance to lapse automatically, or entitles the insurer to cancel the insurance upon notice to the insured, or merely entitles the insurer to sue for the outstanding premium.

Where the insurer seeks, in one condition, to make the due payment of **1–10** all premiums due a condition precedent to his liability under the policy, but, in the following condition, provides a right to terminate the policy, the question arises of whether the insured can recover in respect of losses that arose before the failure to submit a monthly declaration of amounts due near the end of the policy period. This question arose in the credit insurance case of *Kazakstan Wool Processors (Europe) Ltd v. Nederlandsche Credietverzekering Maatschappij N. V.*[26] where the insured had failed to declare the amounts due in respect of all goods despatched or services invoiced for June 1998, under a policy commencing July 1, 1997, and ending on August 31, 1998. The premium was calculated for each £100 declared. The insured also failed to pay the May 1998 premium when it ceased trading. The insured submitted claims in August 1998, and, in September 1998, the insurer gave notice of termination of the policy under the following provision:

> "In the event of any breach of any condition precedent we also have the right to retain any premium paid and give notice terminating the policy and all liability under it."

Toulson J. held that such notice did not have effect of rescission *ab initio*, **1–11** but only discharged the insurer of further liability under the policy from the date that the termination was effective. Accordingly, the notice of termination could not, and did not, extinguish liabilities under the policy that had already arisen. He rejected the insurer's argument that the condition made the due payment of monthly premiums a condition precedent to the insurer's liability in respect of all claims, whether or not they arose before the default. Such a construction would produce results which would seem most unreasonable and would thus be rejected in preference for a construction that was more consistent and reasonable.[27]

Insurable interest

Section 1 of the Life Assurance Act 1774 prohibits the making of insur- **1–12** ance contracts on events where the insured has no interest, and renders all

[25] *Wolenburberg v. Royal Co-operative Collecting Society* (1915) 84 L.J.K.B. 1316.
[26] [1999] Lloyd's Rep. I.R. 596.
[27] *ibid.* at 601.

such contracts null and void. The Act applies to all insurances on real property, but not to insurances on goods and merchandise.[28] Quite apart from this Act, all contracts of insurance where the insured has no interest in the event insured against are invalid at common law.[29] It used to be thought that an insurable interest had to comprise a legal or equitable possessory or proprietary interest in property,[30] but recently the courts have been prepared to recognise a wider concept of the person being materially adversely affected by loss or damage to the insured property by reason of the incidence of any of the perils insured against,[31] or the fact that the person might incur legal liability for negligently causing damage to the insured property.[32] Insurable interests in real property and on goods are further considered in Chapters 11 and 12 respectively. As for liability insurances and insurances against financial loss, the very nature of the indemnifying provisions of the insurance will require the insured to have sustained the insured loss.

1–13   As regards the time at which the insured must have an insurable interest, this need only exist at the time the insured peril occurs in order that the insured suffers a loss which can be indemnified,[33] except in the case of insurances on houses, buildings and the like, because the Life Assurance Act 1774, s.1 (above) would seem to require the insured also to have an insurable interest in that property when the insurance is taken out.

Formation of a contract of insurance

1–14   There are no formalities to the formation of a contract of insurance, and the general rules of the law of contract apply. These require the five elements of offer, acceptance, certainty of terms, consideration, and an intention to create legal relations. The Unfair Contract Terms Act 1977 does not apply to contracts of insurance, nor do the Unfair Terms in Consumer Contracts Regulation 1999[34] have any application to the commercial insurances in this book. Regulations do apply, however, to the content of the two compulsory insurances of employers' liability insurance and motor vehicles insurance which are dealt with in Chapters 5 and 10 respectively, below. Thus a contract of insurance can be made orally, for example, by the telephone acceptance of an insurer's quotation by either the proposer or his authorised agent, provided there is agreement on the material terms, although not all terms.[35]

---

[28] Life Assurance Act 1774, s.4.

[29] *Castellain v. Preston* (1883) 11 Q.B.D. 380 at 379, *per* Bowen L.J., CA.

[30] *Lucena v. Craufurd* (1806) 2 Bos. and Pul.N.R. 269 at 321, *per* Lord Eldon L.C., HL; *Macaura v. Northern Assurance Co.* [1925] A.C. 619, HL.

[31] *Stone Vickers Ltd v. Appledore Ferguson Shipbuilders Ltd* [1991] 2 Lloyd' s Rep. 288 at 301 (reversed on other grounds [1992] 2 Lloyd's Rep. 578).

[32] *Petrofina (U.K.) Ltd v. Magnaload Ltd* [1983] 2 Lloyd's Rep. 91; *National Oilwell Ltd v. Davy Offshore (U.K.) Ltd* [1993] 2 Lloyd's Rep. 582 at 611, *per* Colman J.; applied in *Hopewell Project Management Ltd v. Ewbank Preece Ltd* [1998] 1 Lloyd's Rep. 448 at 456.

[33] *Sadler's Co. v. Badcock* (1743) 2 Atk. 554.

[34] S.I. 1999 No. 1956.

[35] *Allis-Chalmers Co. v. Maryland Fidelity and Deposit Co.* (1916) 114 L.T. 433, HL; *Murfitt v. Royal Insurance Co.* (1922) 38 T.L.R. 334; *Rust v. Abbey Life Assurance Co. Ltd* [1979] 2 Lloyd's Rep. 334, CA.

Discrimination

As regards the insurances dealt with in this book, it is illegal for an insurer to discriminate against a woman,[36] or against any person on the grounds of his colour, race, nationality, or ethnic or nationality origins,[37] or against disabled persons.[38] Discrimination for these purposes means refusing or deliberately omitting to provide any insurance facilities, or to provide those facilities in quality, manner or terms that are different to those provided to male, or other, members of the public.

1–15

Cover notes and written policy documents

Temporary insurance cover may be provided by a "cover note" pending full consideration of the proposal form. Such may be issued by an authorised agent of the insurer,[39] or an insurance intermediary authorised for that purpose. It has even been held that an agent[40] or insurance intermediary[41] can have implied authority to enter into oral temporary insurance contracts in certain circumstances. The cover note will usually expressly incorporate the terms of the insurer's usual form of policy, provide for the insurer to cancel the cover note upon notice, and state that the policy when issued will retrospectively replace the cover note. The cover note will lapse after the stated period of its duration (usually 30 days) so that all cover ceases unless the insurer issues a fresh cover note, or accepts the proposal and issues a policy.[42] The "policy" is simply the term given to the written document issued by the insurer to the insured incorporating the full terms, conditions, warranties, endorsements and limitations of the contract of insurance. The policy document combined with the insurance "schedule", which identifies the insured, the period of insurance, the operative parts of the policy, and the sums insured, together comprise the contract of insurance. The policy will usually expressly incorporate the completed proposal form. The only other insurance documents will be, in the case of compulsory motor insurances and employers' liability insurances, the issue of the appropriate Certificates of Insurance in the statutory form.

1–16

2. PRINCIPLES OF CONSTRUCTION OF POLICIES

Words to be given ordinary meaning within their context

The court applies the same principles of construction to insurance contracts as are applicable to any commercial document.[43] In common with other contracts, a contract of insurance will be construed by a court adopting the principle of objective interpretation that words will be given

1–17

---

[36] Sex Discrimination Act 1975, s.29.
[37] Race Relations Act 1976, ss.3(1) and 20.
[38] Disability Discrimination Act 1995, s.19.
[39] *Mackie v. European Assurance Association* (1869) 21 L.T. 102.
[40] *Murfitt v. Royal Insurance Co. Ltd* (1922) 38 T.L.R. 334.
[41] *Stockton v. Mason* [1978] 2 Lloyd's Rep. 430, CA.
[42] *Levy v. Scottish Employers' Insurance Co.* (1901) 17 T.L.R. 229.
[43] *Cementation Piling and Foundations Ltd v. Aegon Insurance Co. Ltd* [1995] 1 Lloyd's Rep. 97 at 101, *per* Sir Ralph Gibson, CA.

their ordinary meaning, unless there is good reason to consider a special meaning to particular words used by the parties to the insurance contract. This reflects the common sense proposition that a reasonable person will not easily accept that people have made linguistic mistakes, particularly in formal documents.[44] This proposition deserves to be given great weight, so that the clearer the language, the less easily should the court be persuaded that the parties intended it to bear something other than its natural meaning.[45] Equally, no more importance will be placed on words written or printed in larger letters than on all other legible words.[46] This first rule of construction was clearly stated by Lord Ellenborough C.J. as long ago as 1803[47]:

> "In the course of argument it seems to have been assumed that some peculiar rules of construction apply to the terms of a policy of assurance which are not equally applicable to the terms of other instruments and in all other cases: it is therefore proper to state upon this head, that the same rule of construction which applies to all other instruments applies equally to this instrument of a policy of insurance, *viz.* that it is to be construed according to its sense and meaning, as collected in the first place from the terms used in it, which terms are themselves to be understood in their plain, ordinary, and popular sense, unless they have generally in respect to the subject-matters, as by the known usage of trade, or the like, acquired a peculiar sense distinct from the popular sense, of the same words; or unless the contract evidently points out that they must in the particular instance, and in order to effectuate the immediate intention of the parties to that contract, be understood in some other special and peculiar sense. The only difference between policies of assurance, and other instruments in this respect, is, that the greater part of the printed language of them, being invariable and uniform, has acquired from use and practice a known and definite meaning, and that the words superadded in writing (subject indeed always to be governed in point of construction by the language and terms with which they are accompanied) are entitled nevertheless, if there should be any reasonable doubt upon the sense and meaning of the whole, to have a greater effect attributed to them than to the printed words, in as much as the written words are the immediate language and terms selected by the parties themselves for the expression of their meaning, and the printed words are a general formula adopted equally to their case and that of all other contracting parties upon similar occasions and subjects."

1–18   Whilst the meaning of words is a matter of dictionaries and grammars, and the meaning of the document is what the parties using those words against the relevant background would reasonably have been understood to mean,[48] there are many examples of the interpretation of particular words. For instance, where the peril insured against is "fire", that is, unless

---

[44] *Investors Compensation Scheme Ltd v. West Bromwich Building Society* [1998] 1 W.L.R. 896 at 913, *per* Lord Hoffmann, HL.

[45] *Charter Reinsurance Co. Ltd v. Fagan* [1997] A.C. 313 at 384, *per* Lord Mustill, HL; *Kingscroft Insurance Co. Ltd and others v. Nissan Fire and Marine Insurance Co. Ltd (No.2)* [1999] Lloyd's Rep. I.R. 603 at 614, *per* Moore-Bick J.

[46] *Koskas v. Standard Marine Insurance Co. Ltd* (1927) 137 L.T. 165, CA.

[47] *Robertson v. French* (1803) 4 East. 130 at 135–136.

[48] *Investors Compensation Scheme Ltd v. West Bromwich Building Society* [1981] 1 W.L.R. at 912, *per* Lord Hoffmann.

the context suggests otherwise, to be understood in its normal meaning, and therefore has to be construed as meaning that there must be an ignition or burning or incandescence of insured property not intended to be ignited.[49] If the peril is "storm", the ordinary meaning of the word means something more prolonged and widespread than a gust of wind[50]; it connotes some sort of violent wind usually accompanied by rain or hail or snow, not merely persistent bad weather, or heavy or persistent rain by itself.[51] In *Thompson v. Equity Fire Insurance Co.*,[52] the Privy Council was concerned with interpreting an exclusion of liability where gasoline was "stored or kept" in the insured building, the circumstances being that the fire was caused by the ignition of a small quantity of gasoline in a stove used for cooking. Lord Macnaghten considered that the words were[53]:

> "common English words with no precise or exact signification. They have a somewhat kindred meaning and cover very much the same ground. The expression as used in the . . . condition seems to point to the presence of a quantity not inconsiderable or at any rate not trifling in amount, and to import a notion of warehousing or depositing for safe custody or keeping in stock for trading purposes. It is difficult, if not impossible, to give an accurate definition of the meaning, but if one takes a concrete case, it is not very difficult to say whether a particular thing is 'stored or kept' within the meaning of the condition. No one probably would say that a person who had a reasonable quantity of tea in his house for domestic use was 'storing or keeping' tea there, or (to take the instance of benzine, which is one of the prescribed articles) no one would say that a person who had a small bottle of benzine for removing grease spots or cleaning purposes of that sort was 'storing or keeping' benzine.
> Some meaning must be given to the words 'stored or kept'. Their Lordships think those words must have their ordinary meaning. So construing them their Lordships come to the conclusion that the small quantity of gasoline which was in the stove for the purpose of consumption was not being 'stored or kept' within the meaning of the . . . condition at the time when the loss occurred."

Commercial contents insurances and goods-in-transit insurances gener-   **1–19**
ally provide cover in respect of goods held "in trust or on commission" by the insured in addition to the insured's own goods, and in construing these words in such a policy where the insured was a warehouseman, Lord Campbell, C.J. was not convinced that a restricted technical sense should be attached to those words[54]:

[49] *Fleming v. Hislop* (1886) 11 App. Cas. 686 at 692, *per* Lord Selborne, HL; *Tempus Shipping Co. Ltd v. Louis Dreyfus and Co. Ltd* [1930] 1 K.B. 699 at 708, *per* Wright J. (unaffected by [1931] 1 K.B. 195, CA); *Harris v. Poland* [1941] 1 K.B. 462 at 468, *per* Atkinson J. (as he then was).
[50] *S. and M. Hotels Ltd v. Legal and General Assurance Society Ltd* [1972] 1 Lloyd's Rep. 157 at 165, *per* Thesiger J.
[51] *Oddy v. Phoenix Assurance Co. Ltd* [1966] 1 Lloyd's Rep. 134 at 138, *per* Veale J. See also *Glasgow Training Group (Motor Trade) Ltd v. Lombard Continental plc* [1989] S.L.T. 375.
[52] [1910] A.C. 592, PC.
[53] [1910] A.C. 592 at 594.
[54] *Waters and Steel v. Monarch Fire and Life Assurance Co.* (1856) 5 E. and B. 870 at 880–881; see also *Hepburn v. A. Tomlinson (Hauliers) Ltd* [1966] A.C. 451 at 467 *per* Lord Reid, HL; *John Rigby (Haulage) Ltd v. Reliance Marine Insurance Co. Ltd* [1956] 2 Q.B. 468, CA.

"The first question is whether, upon the construction of the contract, those goods were intended to be covered by the policy . . . What is meant in those policies by the words 'goods in trust'? I think that means goods with which the assured were entrusted; not goods held in trust in the strict technical sense, so held that there was only an equitable obligation in the assured enforceable . . . in Chancery, but goods with which the assured were entrusted in the ordinary sense of the word. They were so entrusted with the goods deposited on their wharfs; I cannot doubt the policy was intended to protect such goods. . ."

1–20   Similarly, if the policy insures goods "whilst in warehouse", these words do not embrace goods on a lorry parked in an open space, albeit within a locked compound enclosed by a high bricked wall topped with barbed wire, because that compound will not be within the ordinary and popular meaning of the word "warehouse".[55] Burglary policies on, e.g. stock in trade, often state that the loss must occur by theft "following upon actual forcible and violent entry upon the premises". Where a jeweller held such an insurance for the stock of his shop and a theft occurred one morning when the front door of the shop was shut, but not locked or bolted, and the shop was unattended, and someone opened the door by turning the handle and entering the shop, the Court of Appeal held that the theft had occurred without "forcible and violent entry upon the premises".[56] On the other hand, those words do include a theft perpetrated by using an instrument to slide back the catch of a lock on a door to the insured premises.[57] Any attempt to expand the meaning or further to define common words in everyday use, having a perfectly ordinary and clear meaning, is to be deprecated.[58]

Technical meaning of particular words

1–21   It has long been recognised that terms of art or technical words must be understood in their proper sense, unless the context controls or alters their meaning; ancient words may be explained by contemporaneous usage; and words which have acquired a particular sense by usage in particular districts, occupations or trades, must be read in their acquired sense.[59] The principle is that where words used by the parties to the insurance contracts have a particular meaning, the court will assume that the parties intended that particular understanding of the words to be applied in construing the contract.[60]

1–22   The application of this principle is perhaps most readily illustrated where the peril insured against is identified by a word which has a specific

---

[55] *Leo Rapp Ltd v. McClure* [1955] 1 Lloyd's Rep. 292; see also *Barnett and Block v. National Parcels Insurance Co. Ltd* [1942] 2 All E.R. 55n, CA.

[56] *Re George and Goldsmiths and General Burglary Insurance Association Ltd* [1899] 1 Q.B. 595, CA.

[57] *Re Calf and Sun Insurance Office* [1920] 2 K.B. 366, CA; see also *Dino Services Ltd v. Prudential Assurance Co. Ltd* [1989] 1 All E.R. 422, CA.

[58] *Starfire Diamond Rings Ltd v. Angel* [1962] 2 Lloyd's Rep. 217 at 219, *per* Upjohn L.J., CA.

[59] *Cliff v. Schwabe* (1846) 3 C.B. 437 at 469, *per* Parke B.

[60] *L. Schulder A.C. v. Wickman Machine Tool Sales Ltd* [1947] A.C. 235 at 263, *per* Lord Simon, HL.

meaning in the general body of the criminal law, as Lord Sumner emphasised in a case concerning the interpretation of an insurance exclusion of loss or damage caused by "riot"[61]:

> "It is true that the uninstructed layman probably does not think under the word 'riot', of even such a scene, as is described in the case stated. How he would describe it I know not, but he probably thinks of something, if not more picturesque, at any rate more noisy. But there is no warrant here for saying that when the proviso uses a word which is emphatically a term of art, it is to be confined, in the interpretation of the policy, to circumstances which are only within the popular notions on the subject and are not within the technical meaning of the word. That clearly must be so with regard to martial law; that, I think, must be so with regard to acts of foreign enemies; and I see no reason at all why the word 'riot' should not include its technical meaning as clearly as burglary. . ."

So, also will the words "embezzlement",[62] "fraud",[63] and "theft"[64] be   **1–23**
construed in accordance with the criminal law. Thus, where an insurance covers the insured in respect of loss by "theft" whilst the goods are on their premises, the insured must show a prima facie case that the person who steals the goods forms an intention to steal them and dishonestly appropriates those goods whilst on the premises. Where goods are handed over to a driver for delivery elsewhere, and are driven away never to be seen again, it will not be an easy task to establish theft on the premises for the theft may have occurred when the driver, at some later time, decided to deviate from his route and dishonestly dispose of the goods.[65] Equally, if there is an exception in regard to thefts by the insured's customers, a theft by a person who is not a customer is not excepted.[66] The plain and ordinary meaning of "theft" includes robbery.[67]

On the other hand, it must not be forgotten that those who aid or abet,   **1–24**
e.g. thieves, are, under criminal law, equally as guilty of theft as the principal offender(s). Therefore, where there is a policy exception relating to theft by members of the insured's staff, that exception will operate in circumstances where, e.g. the insured's employee admits the thieves to the insured premises even though he departs before the insured goods are physically removed by the thieves.[68] Evidence of complicity in the crime may be admitted even though it might be of a type that would be excluded from a criminal trial.[69]

---

[61] *London and Lancashire Fire Insurance Co Ltd v. Bolands Ltd* [1924] A.C. 836 at 847, HL.

[62] *Debenhams Ltd v. Excess Insurance Co. Ltd* (1912) 28 T.L.R. 505.

[63] *Excess Life Assurance Co. Ltd v. Firemen's Insurance Co. of Newark New Jersey* [1982] 2 Lloyd's Rep. 599; *Ravenscroft v. Provident Clerks' and General Guarantee Association* (1888) 5 T.L.R. 3.

[64] *Grundy (Teddington) Ltd v. Fulton* [1983] 1 Lloyd's Rep. 16, CA; *Lake v. Simmons* [1927] A.C. 487, HL; see also *Dobson v. General Accident Fire and Life Assurance Corp. plc* [1990] 1 Q.B. 274, CA.

[65] See *Grundy (Teddington) Ltd v. Fulton* [1983] 1 Lloyd's Rep. 16, CA.

[66] *Lake v. Simmons* [1927] A.C. 487, HL.

[67] *Hayward v. Norwich Union Insurance Ltd, The Times*, March 8, 2001, CA.

[68] *Saqui and Lawrence v. Steams* [1911] 1 K.B. 426, CA.

[69] *Hurst v. Evans* [1917] 1 K.B. 352.

1-25   The context in which even terms of art or technical words are found may, however, make it appropriate to disregard their technical meaning. For example, where an insurance policy is issued in England and is governed by English law, and yet is to cover events in a foreign country, with the insured being unfamiliar with which words have a technical meaning, nor what that meaning might be under English law, then the words will not be restricted to their technical sense. This was the view of the Court of Appeal in *Algemeene Bankvereeniging v. Langton*[70] where Maugham L.J. said[71]:

> "I do not doubt that the law of the contract is English, but I do think under the circumstances that the loss which is intended to be covered by the policy is a loss which must be incurred in Belgium; that it is quite wrong in principle to construe the words which have been so much discussed here, 'fire, burglary, theft, robbery, or hold-up' as if those words could only be construed in a technical sense according to English law. The Belgian bank, of course, do not know what the precise technical meaning, for instance, of the word 'larceny' is, if the word 'larceny' had been used in England . . . I am content with this, that in my opinion, the phrase 'lost, destroyed, or otherwise made away with by fire, burglary, theft, robbery or hold-up, whether with or without violence, and whether from within or without,' is a phrase which has to be construed as ordinary commercial men would construe it, or rather would understand it, and in particular I object to the notion that ordinary commercial men in this country, giving a policy containing that phrase, would intend that the phrase should be read as if it were drawn in the form that it was applicable only to crimes which would be treated as burglary, theft, robbery or hold-up, if the crime were being investigated in this country. It is apparent that the theft, robbery or hold-up must be a crime committed in Belgium, and that the perpetrator, if he escapes here, is going to be extradited to Belgium for the purpose of investigating the crime; and accordingly, in my opinion, the policy is obviously to be construed as if it related to a loss by crimes or misdemeanours perpetrated in that foreign country, and to be punished, if punished at all, according to the laws of the foreign country.
>
> I would add this, that there is nothing in the phrase which leads me to suppose that it is intended to have a very technical significance, because it contains some phrases which are not known to English law as technical phrases. It runs: 'lost, destroyed or otherwise made away with'. I do not think you will find the words 'made away with' in a statute or even in an ordinary book on criminal practice."

Particular trade usage

1-26   An example of the application of this principle is provided by *Anglo-African Merchants Ltd v. Bayley.*[72] The claimant insured 412 bales of 20-year-old unused army surplus leather jerkins against "all risks" with Lloyd's underwriters under the description "New Men's Clothes in Bails for Export". During the period of cover, 245 bales disappeared and the claimants sought recovery of an indemnity under the policy. Whilst Megaw J. (as he then was) accepted that in the clothing trade goods were never described at that time as "new" unless they were government surplus

---

[70] (1935) 40 Com. Cas. 247, CA.
[71] *ibid.* at 259.
[72] [1970] 1 Q.B. 311.

goods, no matter what its age, that particular trade meaning of "new" will not be applied by the court in construing the insurance contract where one party, the insurer in this case, was not aware of that particular trade meaning. His lordship pointed out that it was not a question of the meaning of the word "new" in isolation, but a question of its meaning in the context of a request for insurance of goods which were described as being "New Men's Clothes in Bales for Export".

The *ejusdem generis* rule

The *ejusdem generis* canon of construction is that where general words, **1–27**
e.g. "or other", follow specifically enumerated things, the general words must be confined in their interpretation as being restricted in meaning to things of the same type or genus as those preceding things specifically enumerated. Whether the rule applies at all, and if so, what effect should be given to it, must in every case depend upon the precise terms, subject matter and context of the clause under construction,[73] for, being a rule of construction, it cannot be more than a guide to enable the court to arrive at the true meaning of the parties[74] to the insurance contract.

Thus, "stock-in-trade, household furniture, linen, wearing apparel and **1–28**
plate" covered by a fire policy, has been held to include household linen but not linen drapery goods bought on speculation by the insured who was not a draper by trade.[75] Similarly, where a policy specified that "jewellery, watches, field glasses and other fragile or specially valuable articles must be separately declared and valued", Rowlatt J. said[76]:

> "The question I have to ask myself is whether furs are specially valuable articles in the same son of sense as jewellery, watches, field glasses and cameras are fragile or specially valuable articles. I think that is the modern and plain English translation of the doctrine of *ejusdem generis*. In other words, are they specially valuable articles in the sense exemplified by the particular instances named? That is the natural way of putting it. I do not think they are. Furs are a commonplace article of dress in the case of nearly every woman of any sort of comfortable means at all. The circumstance that they afford great scope for extravagance and vanity, so that you can get furs of fantastic price, does not, to my mind, show that being commonplace articles of dress they are specifically valuable in the same sort of way that jewellery, watches, field glasses and cameras are."

Binding precedent

The doctrine of binding precedent pervading all English law will be **1–29**
applied by the court, but it is only applicable in exactly the same circumstances. In other words, "if a construction has already been put on a clause precisely similar in any decided case, we should defer to that authority".[77] Decisions upon the construction and meaning of words in

---

[73] *Sun Fire Office v. Hart* (1889) 14 App. Cas. 98 at 103, *per* Lord Watson, PC.
[74] *Chandris v. Isbrandtsen-Moller Co. Inc.* [1951] 1 K.B. 240 at 244, *per* Devlin J. (as he then was).
[75] *Watchorn v. Longford* (1813) 3 Camp. 422.
[76] *King v. Travellers' Insurance Association Ltd* (1931) 41 Ll. L. Rep. 13 at 15.
[77] *Glen v. Lewis* (1853) 8 Exch. 607 at 618, *per* Parke B.

previously decided cases must, therefore, only be taken as authoritative if the language and the circumstances are substantially identical.[78] Put another way, authorities may determine principles of construction, but a decision upon one form of words is no authority upon the construction of another form of words.[79] Whilst higher tribunals need not consider themselves bound by decisions of inferior tribunals, it is a salutary rule that the courts should be chary in interfering with the interpretation given to a well-known document and acted on for any considerable period of time.[80] As one past Lord Chancellor has said[81]:

> "where the same words have for many years received a judicial construction it is not unreasonable to suppose that parties have contracted upon the belief that their words will be understood in what I will call the accepted sense. And it is to be remembered that what Courts have to do in construing all documents is to reach the meaning of the parties through the words they have used."

1–30   Where there is no English decision upon the exact form of words in question, a court may have regard to decisions upon those words in a similar context determined in other common law jurisdictions, but how much weight will be given to such decisions will depend upon the status of that other court, and the quality of the reasoning behind the judgment. Thus, in *Hitchens (Hatfield) Ltd v. Prudential Assurance Co. Ltd*,[82] the Court of Appeal considered and approved the decision of the High Court of Australia in construing the wording of a contractor's policy.

Construing the contract as a whole

1–31   In its task of construing a contract of insurance so as to give a reasonable interpretation to it, as well as to particular words or phrases, the court may only give effect to the intention of the parties as evidenced by the written words of the policy, and any other document incorporated with it,[83] *e.g.* commonly the proposal form. Like any contract, a contract of insurance must be construed by reference to all that it contains.[84] The general rule is that the background must always be considered to determine if something is wrong with the language used by the parties, because

[78] *Re Calf and Sun Insurance Office* [1920] 2 K.B. 366 at 382, *per* Atkin L.J. (as he then was), CA.
[79] *Re Coleman's Repositories Ltd and Life and Health Assurance Association* [1907] 2 K.B. 798 at 812, *per* Buckley L.J. (as he then was), CA.
[80] *Re Hooley Hill Rubber and Chemical Co. Ltd and Royal Insurance Co. Ltd* [1920] 1 K.B. 257 at 269, *per* Bankes L.J., CA.
[81] *Thames and Mersey Marine Insurance Co. Ltd v. Hamilton Fraser and Co.* (1887) 12 App. Cas. 484 at 490, *per* Lord Halsbury L.C., HL.
[82] [1991] 2 Lloyd's Rep. 580, CA. The case is discussed in detail in Chapter 16, below.
[83] *South Staffordshire Tramways Co. v. Sickness and Accident Assurance Association* [1891] 1 Q.B. 402, DC; *Yorkshire Insurance Co. Ltd v. Campbell* [1917] A.C. 218, PC; *Bensuade v. Thames and Mersey Marine Insurance Co.* [1897] A.C. 609 at 612, *per* Lord Halsbury L.C., HL.
[84] *Cementation Piling and Foundations Ltd v. Aegon Insurance Co. Ltd* [1995] 1 Lloyd's Rep. 97 at 101, *per* Sir Ralph Gibson, CA.

the law does not require judges to attribute to the parties an intention which they plainly could not have had.[85] As Lord Greene M.R. has said[86]:

> "The true construction of a document means no more than that the Court puts on it the true meaning which the party to whom the document was handed or who is relying on it would put on it as an ordinarily intelligent person construing the words in the proper way in the light of the relevant circumstances."

In the case of ambiguity or inconsistency between particular terms or clauses of the insurance contract, the court will have regard to the whole policy to reconcile the ambiguity or inconsistency, but the grammatical interpretation of the operative insuring clauses will prevail over recitals,[87] though if unclear, the policy recital may provide assistance in the interpretation of operative insuring words.[88] A reasonable construction must be given to each clause in order to give effect to the plain and obvious intention of the parties as collected from the whole policy,[89] and it is to be assumed that the parties intended the same words to have the same meaning throughout the policy.[90] If there is an inconsistency between the wording of the policy and that in the proposal or other earlier document, when reconciling the inconsistency the court will consider that the policy wording's interpretation prevails, it being the later document.[91]

1–32

Commercial efficacy

The court should construe the words according to the understanding of business people so as to make their meaning realistic and such as to give business efficacy to the agreement between the parties.[92] If detailed semantic and syntactical analysis of words in a commercial contract is going to lead to a conclusion that flouts business commonsense, it must yield to business commonsense.[93] Thus, where a policy requires the insured to do something "immediately", that is construed as meaning, not instantaneously, but "with all reasonable speed considering the circumstances of the case".[94] Similar reasoning applies to "as soon as possible".[95]

1–33

---

[85] *Investors Compensation Scheme Ltd v. West Bromwich Building Society* [1998] 1 W.L.R. 896 at 913, *per* Lord Hoffmann, HL.

[86] *Hutton v. Walling* [1948] Ch. 398 at 403, CA.

[87] *Anglo-International Bank Ltd v. General Accident Fire and Life Assurance Corp. Ltd* (1934) 48 Ll. L. Rep. 151, HL.

[88] *Blascheck v. Bussell* (1916) 33 T.L.R. 74, CA.

[89] *Borradaile v. Hunter* (1843) 5 Man. and G. 639 at 657, *per* Erskine J.

[90] *South Staffordshire Tramways Co. v. Sickness and Accident Assurance Association* [1891] 1 Q.B. 402 at 407, *per* Bowen L.J., CA; unless context demands otherwise, *Andrews v. Patriotic Assurance Co. (No.2)* (1886) 18 L.R. Ir. 355.

[91] *Izzard v. Universal Insurance Co. Ltd* [1937] A.C. 773 at 780, *per* Lord Wright, HL; *Kaufmann v. British Surety Insurance Co. Ltd* (1929) 45 T.L.R. 399.

[92] *J. Lowenstein and Co. Ltd v. Poplar Motor Transport (Lymm) Ltd* [1968] 2 Lloyd's Rep. 233 at 238, *per* Neild J.

[93] *Antaios Compania Naviera SA v. Salen Rederierna A.B.* [1985] A.C. 191, at 201, *per* Lord Diplock, HL.

[94] *Re Coleman's Repositories Ltd and Life and Health Assurance Association* [1907] 2 K.B. 798 at 807, *per* Fletcher-Moulton L.J., CA; followed *Farrell v. Federated Employers Insurance Association Ltd* [1970] 1 W.L.R. 1400, CA.

[95] *Farrell v. Federated Employers Insurance Association Ltd* [1970] 1 W.L.R. 1400, CA.

1–34   In the same way, the usual condition in liability policies that the insured should take reasonable care to avoid accidents must be construed bearing in mind the commercial efficacy of the contract of insurance. Where the condition appears in an employers' liability policy one of the main foundations of an employee's action against his employer if he suffers injury in the course of his work will be an allegation of negligence, *i.e.* the employer's failure to take reasonable care in regard to the safety of his employees. To construe that condition as excluding an indemnity wherever the insured employer is proved to have been negligent, would not be giving commercial effect to the obvious intention of the parties. This was explained by Lord Greene M.R. in *Woolfall and Rimmer Ltd v. Moyle* as follows[96]:

> "In approaching the construction of that condition, it is important to remember the context in which it is found. A duty to take care is a duty which arises by virtue of the relationship between the person on whom such a duty lies and the person towards whom it is to be discharged. That relationship may arise by contract, or it may arise by mere operation of law, by reason of the fact that two persons are thrown into a particular relationship with one another. In the present case, the duty that this condition purports to impose is a contractual duty imposed on the insured towards the underwriters, who are indemnifying the insured against a variety of risks, a very important proportion of which arises in cases of negligence either by the insured himself or by persons for whose negligence he is vicariously responsible to his employees. Of course, in the many classes of risks which are covered, there are some, and no doubt very important ones, in respect of which a workman can recover from the employer without the necessity of establishing negligence. On the other hand, there are a multitude of risks covered in which the workman must establish negligence if he is to succeed. The argument which was presented to us with great skill and ingenuity for the [insurers] was based on the contention that the condition in question is imposing upon the insured a duty to take care co-terminous with, and similar in quality to, the obligation to take care which lies on the employer *vis-à-vis* his workmen. In my judgment that is the wrong method of approach to this question. The effect of the argument of counsel for the [insurers] would be to exclude from the scope of the indemnity which the policy purports at the outset to give a very large and important class of case which in the body of the policy is expressed to fall within it."

1–35   The matter was considered again by Diplock L.J. (as he then was) in *Fraser v. B.N. Furman (Productions) Ltd*[97]:

> "Obviously the condition cannot mean that the insured must take measures to avert dangers which he does not himself foresee, although the hypothetical reasonably careful employer would have foreseen them. That would be repugnant to the commercial purpose of the contract, for failure to foresee dangers is one of the commonest grounds of liability in negligence. What in my view is reasonable' as between the insured and the insurer, without being repugnant to the commercial object of the contract, is that the insured should not deliberately court a danger the existence of which he has recognised, by refraining from taking any measures to avert it. Equally the condition

---

[96] [1942] 1 K.B. 66 at 72, CA.
[97] [1967] 1 W.L.R. 898 at 905, CA.

cannot mean that, where the insured recognises that there is a danger, the measures which he takes to avert it must be such as the hypothetical reasonable employer, exercising due care and observing all the relevant provisions of the Factories Act, 1961, would have taken . . .

In other words, it is not enough that the employer's omission to take any particular precautions to avoid accidents should be negligent; it must be at least reckless, *i.e.* made with actual recognition by the insured himself that a danger exists, not caring whether or not it is averted. The purpose of the condition is to ensure that the insured will not refrain from taking precautions which he knows ought to be taken because he is covered against loss by the policy."

The same principle of construction may be regarded as being put into effect where a burglary policy, with a condition precedent to liability that "the burglar alarm installed at the premises . . . is kept in efficient working order", was held as not requiring the burglar alarm to be in efficient working order at the time of loss. Woolf J. (as he then was) held[98]: **1–36**

"The burglar alarm is not required to be in efficient working order; it is required to be kept in efficient working order. The insertion of the word 'kept' in my view, implies within it a requirement that before there can be a breach of that condition by an insured, he must be aware of the facts which give rise to the alarm not being in efficient working order, or if he is not aware of those facts he should at least be in a position where exercising common care, he should have known of those facts. Furthermore, in my view, he must be given (having been acquainted with those facts or being in a situation where he must be deemed to be aware of those facts) a sufficient opportunity to have the alarm installed once more restored to proper working order. Were the situation otherwise, the consequences would be as follows. The burglar alarm is obviously only intended to be in operation when the premises are unattended. Yet the way the clause is drawn, even if the premises were attended so there would be no requirement for the burglar alarm to be in operation, because the burglar alarm was not in efficient working order, a person would have no right to recover. What is more, as I have indicated, the efficiency of the burglar alarm could be through no fault of the insured, it could be through no fault of the maintenance company but through some sort of latent defect which nobody could protect themselves against. Yet, in such circumstances, because of the wording of this clause, were it to be construed other than I have indicated, an insured could find himself without any form of cover whatsoever . . .

However, in order to interpret this clause, it is necessary to gather the intent from the words used by the parties to the policy and I am satisfied that the Norwich Union could not have intended that the policy should have been interpreted in that way, and equally that the insured would not have intended it to be interpreted in this way. Therefore, the situation here is that the word 'kept' has the effect of treating this clause as being similar to a clause in a lease setting out an obligation of a landlord to keep the premises in repair. The obligation is one to repair promptly on notice, but not one that is in absolute terms."

Ambiguity and the *contra preferentem* rule

Where the words of a document are genuinely ambiguous in that there are two reasonable interpretations, it is a rule of construction that the **1–37**

---

[98] *Victor Melik and Co. Ltd v. Norwich Union Fire Insurance Society Ltd and Kemp* [1980] 1 Lloyd's Rep. 523 at 530.

interpretation least favourable to the party who drew up the document shall prevail (*contra preferentem*).[99] As it is generally the insurer who drafts the policy, the result is that an ambiguous clause must be construed against, rather than in favour of, the insurer.[1] This general rule of construction has been applied to an exception in a motor policy whilst the car is "conveying any load in excess of that for which it was constructed" is limited to situations where a weight load is specified in respect of the insured motor vehicle, rather than squeezing in one extra passenger to the normal seating capacity.[2] Similarly, an exception in a motor policy for death or injury to "any member of the assured's household" was held not to exclude a claim by the young insured's sister injured whilst he was driving, because it was to be construed as referring to any member of the same household of which the insured was the head, not of which he was simply a member.

1-38   Similarly, in *W. and J. Lane v. Spratt*,[3] Roskill J. (as he then was) considered that the following clause in a goods in transit insurance was ambiguous as to the extent of the following condition:

> "The insured shall take all reasonable precautions for the protection and safeguarding of the goods and/or merchandise and use such protective appliances as may be specified in the policy and all vehicles and protective devices shall be maintained in good order."

Accordingly, it was to be construed *contra proferentem*, against the insurer who had drafted the policy[4]:

> "I think there is force in Counsel's arguments, first, that this is a clause for the benefit of the underwriters, and therefore if underwriters wish to say that it is to extend not merely to what I have called physical precautions but is to cover selection of staff, the clause ought to say so in express terms."

1-39   An ambiguity was also held to exist in the interpretation of another goods-in-transit policy in *Metal Scrap and By-Products Ltd v. Federated Conveyors Ltd*[5] where the main operative insuring words stated that:

> "all and every risk of loss and/or damage whilst in course of transit per the vehicles owned or hired by the assured or by any sub-contractors."

It was held by Croom Johnson J. that the policy would be construed *contra proferentem*, and, on that basis, the cover provided would be interpreted to

---

[99] *Tarleton v. Staniforth* (1794) 5 Term Rep. 695 at 699, *per* Lord Kenyon C.J.; *Youell v. Bland Welch and Co. Ltd* [1992] 2 Lloyd's Rep. 127 at 134, *per* Staughton L.J., CA.

[1] *Re Etherington and Lancashire and Yorkshire Accident Insurance Co.* [1909] 1 K.B. 591 at 596, *per* Vaughan Williams L.J., CA; *Metal Scrap and By-Products Ltd v. Federated Conveyors Ltd* [1953] 1 Lloyd's Rep. 221 at 227, *per* Croom Johnson J.; *Anderson v. Fitzgerald* (1853) 4 H.L. Cas. 484 at 507, *per* Lord St Leonards; *English v. Western* [1940] 2 K.B. 156 at 165, *per* Clauson L.J., CA.

[2] *Houghton v. Trafalgar Insurance Co. Ltd* [1954] 1 Q.B. 247, CA.

[3] [1970] 2 Q.B. 480.

[4] *ibid.* at 486.

[5] [1953] 1 Lloyd's Rep. 221.

include all and every risk of loss occurring during such time as the insured were liable to their customers.

It must be emphasised that the *contra preferentem* rule only comes into operation in a case of real ambiguity,[6] remaining after the court has considered the whole policy[7] and adopting one meaning does not make the rest of the policy clear.[8] Thus, in *de Maurier (Jewels) Ltd v. Bastion Insurance Co. Ltd and Coronet Insurance Co. Ltd*,[9] Donaldson J. (as he then was) found that there was no ambiguity surrounding the meaning of the word "locks" in the following warranty in a jewellers' all risks policy: **1–40**

> "road vehicles . . . fitted with locks and alarm system (approved by underwriters) and in operation."

> "'Locks' in my judgment in the context of this contract . . . must at least mean locks having a greater security than that provided by those supplied by the manufacturers of cars on ordinary production models."[10]

Oral evidence upon interpretation is inadmissible

Oral evidence concerning the background to the making of the document is admissible to assist the court, but oral or other evidence of the parties' subjective intentions behind the meaning of words and phrases in an insurance contract is not admissible to either contradict or vary what is plain.[11] On the other hand, oral evidence is admissible to explain more fully what the risk was (when that evidence is consistent with the language of the policy),[12] or to prove a term in the policy was used in a peculiar sense differing from its ordinary meaning[13] (*e.g.* technical trade meaning[14]) if the meaning is doubtful,[15] or to introduce a matter upon which the policy is silent.[16] The boundaries of this exception to the admission of evidence are accepted as being unclear in some respects.[17]   **1–41**

Oral (parol) evidence has been admitted to determine the identity and extent of the premises insured under a fire policy which contained a latent, rather then patent, ambiguity, *i.e.* where the street number was incorrect.[18] Oral evidence is also admissible to show the circumstances under which   **1–42**

---

[6] *Hare v. Barstow* (1844) 8 Jur. 928 at 929, *per* Lord Denman C.J.; *Alder v. Moore* [1961] 2 Q.B. 57, CA.

[7] *Passmore v. Vulcan Boiler and General Insurance Co. Ltd* (1935) 154 L.T. 258 at 259, *per* du Parcq J.

[8] *Yorkshire Insurance Co. Ltd v. Campbell* [1917] A.C. 218 at 223, *per* Lord Sumner, PC.

[9] [1967] 2 Lloyd's Rep. 550.

[10] *ibid.* at 560; see also *Marzouca v. Atlantic and British Commercial Insurance Co. Ltd* [1971] 1 Lloyd's Rep. 449, PC; *Jaglom v. Excess Insurance Co. Ltd* [1972] 2 Q.B. 250.

[11] *Beacon Life and Fire Assurance Co. v. Gibb* (1862) 1 Moo. PCCNS 73, PC.

[12] *Hunting and Son v. Boulton* (1895) 1 Com. Cas. 120; *Kaufmann v. British Surety Insurance Co. Ltd* (1929) 45 T.L.R. 399; *Moss v. Norwich and London Accident Insurance Association* (1922) 10 Ll. L. Rep. 395, CA.

[13] *Beacon Life and Fire Assurance Co. v. Gibb*, above.

[14] *Crofts v. Marshall* (1836) 7 C. and P. 597.

[15] *Hall v. Janson* (1855) 4 E. and B. 500 at 509–510, *per* Lord Campbell C.J.

[16] *Blackett v. Royal Exchange Assurance Co.* (1832) 2 Cr. and J. 244 at 249, *per* Lord Lyndhurst C.B.

[17] *Investors Compensation Scheme v. West Bromwich Building Society* [1998] 1 W.L.R. 896, at 912, HL.

[18] *Hordern v. Commercial Union Insurance Co.* (1887) 56 L.J.P.C. 78, PC.

the contract was made so that the court may construe the words of the policy in context.[19] For instance, in *Simon Brooks Ltd v. Hepburn*,[20] oral evidence was admitted to show that an exclusion in an all risks shop policy in respect of theft from "shop portion of Louisette Ltd" was a reference to the premises of Louisette Ltd at the time that the policy was effected, so that a loss which had occurred at other premises at which Louisette Ltd subsequently carried on business was not excluded. Finally, an alleged act of waiver by the insurer may be proved by oral evidence, *e.g.* that an agent of the insurer had authority to waive written conditions of a policy.[21]

3. ASSIGNMENT

Assignment of a contract of insurance

1-43   Property and liability insurances are personal contracts,[22] and do not run with the property if it is sold or otherwise disposed of or with a transfer of liabilities of the insured. Therefore, both in common law and equity, an assignment of a policy of insurance can only be valid if the insurer consents to this course,[23] whereby, in truth a new contract of insurance is effected between the assignee and the insurer, and that between the assignor (the original insured) and the insurer lapses.[24] Such an invalid assignment will not automatically avoid the insured's contract of insurance with the insurer, it only renders the policy avoidable at the election of the insurer.[25] In practice, policies often contain express provisions relating to assignment of the policy, varying from express consent, *e.g.* including in the description of the "insured" all assigns of the insured, to an expression of the requirement of consent.

1-44   As a corollary of the foregoing, there can be no valid assignment of an insurance contract without a contemporaneous assignment of the subject matter of the insurance, for the assignee must have an insurable interest to be indemnified by the insurer.[26] In the case of death or bankruptcy of the insured, any policy effected by the insured may be enforced by the personal representatives or the trustee in bankruptcy, for the benefit of his estate (subject, in the case of liability insurances, to the protection afforded to the injured third party under the Third Parties (Rights against Insurers) Act 1930), both in respect of claims prior to the insured's death or bankruptcy[27] or subsequently.[28] This assignment of the policy and the subject matter of the insurance by operation of law extends, during the currency of the policy, to any transfer of the policy and subject matter thereof to a

---

[19] *Bawden v. London, Edinburgh and Glasgow Assurance Co.* [1892] 2 Q.B. 534, CA.
[20] [1961] 2 Lloyd's Rep. 43.
[21] *Brook v. Trafalgar Insurance Co. Ltd* (1946) 79 Ll. L. Rep. 365 at 368, *per* Tucker L.J., CA
[22] *Sadlers' Co. v. Badcock* (1743) 2 Atk. 554 at 556, *per* Lord Hardwicke.
[23] *Lynch v. Dalzell* (1729) 4 Bro. Parl. Cas. 431, HL.
[24] *Peters v. General Accident Fire and Life Assurance Corp. Ltd* [1938] 2 All E.R. 267, CA.
[25] *Doe d. Pitt v. Laming* (1814) 4 Camp. 73 at 75, *per* Lord Ellenborough C.J.
[26] *Lloyd v. Fleming* (1872) L.R. 7 Q.B. 299 at 302, *per* Blackburn J.
[27] *Marriage v. Royal Exchange Assurance Co.* (1849) 18 L.J. Ch. 216; *Hood's Trustees v. Southern Union General Insurance Co. of Australasia* [1928] Ch. 793, CA.
[28] *Jackson v. Forster* (1859) 1 E. and E. 470.

beneficiary[29] or purchaser.[30] Where there is a valid assignment of the policy and the subject matter of the insurance, the assignee takes the policy subject to any rights of the insurer to avoid the policy by reason of acts or omissions of the assignor, and must himself comply with all the terms and conditions (*e.g.* notification of claims) of the policy.[31] The assignee may sue the insurer in his own name.[32]

Assignment of the benefit of a contract of insurance

An assignment of the benefit of a policy of insurance is made by operation of law in the case of a contract for the sale of land or goods, the subject of the insurance, until such time as the sale is completed, *i.e.* the property in the land or goods has been transferred from the vendor to the purchaser. This is the effect of section 47 of the Law of Property Act 1925 which provides that where, after the date of any contract for sale or exchange of property, money becomes payable under any policy of insurance maintained by the vendor in respect of any damage to or destruction of property included in the contract, the money shall, on completion of the contract, be held by or receivable by the vendor on behalf of the purchaser and paid by the vendor to the purchaser on completion of the sale or exchange, or as soon thereafter as the same shall be received by the vendor. Because there is no question of the assignment of the policy itself, any consideration of consent of the insurer is irrelevant for the insured remains the same person, and the property has not yet become vested in the purchaser. The important words in this statutory provision are "money becomes payable under any policy of insurance . . ." in that the purchaser can only receive moneys to the extent that the policy indemnifies not his, but the insured's interest in the property conveyed, and, more importantly, no moneys at all may be payable. The latter circumstances may arise through no fault of the purchaser, *e.g.* the insurer becoming entitled to avoid the policy for breach of warranty or non-disclosure by the insured vendor, or a failure to comply with a notification provision which is a condition precedent to the liability of the insurer. **1–45**

Section 47(2) of the 1925 Act also provides that the statutory assignment of the benefit of the policy in these circumstances only takes effect where there is no stipulation to the contrary in the contract of sale, that any express requisite consent of the insurer is obtained, and that the purchaser reimburses the vendor the proportionate part of the policy premium from the date of the contract of sale. **1–46**

Assignment of the subject matter of a contract of insurance

A purchaser of property insured under a policy does not by the mere fact of purchase acquire a right to the insurance moneys upon the happening of **1–47**

---

[29] *Mildway v. Folgham* (1797) 3 Ves. 471; *Durrant v. Friend* (1852) 5 De G. and Sm. 343.
[30] *Re Birkbeck Permanent Benefit Building Society, Official Receiver v. Licenses Insurance Corp.* [1913] 2 Ch. 34.
[31] *Re Carr and Sun Fire Insurance Co.* (1897) 13 T.L.R. 186, CA.
[32] *Manchester Fire Assurance Co. v. Wykes* (1875) 33 L.T. 142, CA.

the insured event.[33] On the other hand, once an insured has completely divested himself of an insurable interest in the subject matter of the insurance, he no longer has an insurable interest and the relevant policy will automatically lapse,[34] or, at least, the insured can suffer no loss[35] and can therefore recover nothing on general principles. Certain aspects require further examination in relation to the retention by the insured of an insurable interest in the subject matter assigned.

1–48   First, if property is lost or damaged after the insured has made a contract for its sale, but prior to completion of that sale, the insured remains fully entitled to an indemnity under the policy even though the risk has passed to the purchaser. This is the clear effect of the decision in *Collingridge v. Royal Exchange Assurance Corp.*[36] where certain premises were insured under a fire policy and were in the process of being compulsorily purchased by the Metropolitan Board of Works when the premises were damaged by fire. Lush and Mellor JJ. held that the insured had an insurable interest that required indemnifying under the policy. *Per* Lush J.[37]:

> "The [insured] is in the position of a person who has entered into a contract to sell his property to another. The fact that the vendee is so important a corporation as the Board of Works can make no difference. The contract will no doubt be completed, but legally the buildings are still his property. The [insurers] by their policy undertake to make good any loss or damage to the property by fire. There is nothing to show that any collateral dealings with the premises, such as those stated in the case, are to limit this liability. If the [insured] had actually conveyed them away before the fire, that would have been a defence to the action, for he would then have had no interest at the time of the loss. But in the present case he still has a right to the possession of the property, and the [insurers] are bound to pay him the insurance money. . ."

1–49   This view was subsequently upheld by the Court of Appeal in *Castellain v. Preston*[38] where Brett L.J. explained the insurable interest of the insured vendor thus[39]:

> "The [insured] were the owners of property consisting partly at all events of a house, and the [insured] had made a contract of sale of that property with third persons, which contract upon the giving of a certain notice as to the time of payment would oblige those third persons, if they fulfilled the contract, to pay the agreed price for the sale of that property, a part of which was a house, and according to the peculiarity of such a sale and purchase of land or real property the vendees would have to pay the purchase money, whether the house was, before the date of payment, burnt down or not. After the contract was made with the third persons, and before the day of payment, the house was burnt down. The vendors, the [insured], having

[33] *Poole v. Adams* (1864) 4 New Rep. 9; *Rayner v. Preston* (1881) 18 Ch.D. 1, CA.
[34] *Rayner v. Preston* (1881) 18 Ch.D. 1 at 7, *per* Cotton L.J.
[35] *Ecclesiastical Commissioners for England v. Royal Exchange Assurance Corp.* (1895) 11 T.L.R. 476.
[36] (1877) 3 Q.B.D. 173.
[37] (1877) 3 Q.B.D. 173 at 177.
[38] (1883) 11 Q.B.D. 380, CA.
[39] *ibid.* at 385.

insured the house in the ordinary form with the [insurance] company, it is not suggested that upon the house being burnt down the [insured] had not an insurable interest. They had an insurable interest, as it seems to me, first, because they were at all events the legal owners of the property; and, secondly, because the vendees or third persons might not carry out the contract, and if for any reason they should never carry out the contract, then the vendors, if the house was burnt down, would suffer the loss."

Secondly, property belonging to the insured, albeit being the subject of **1–50** a legal claim of ownership by another person, remains the valid subject matter of the insured's insurance until such time as that third person has established that the property is under his ownership and not the insured's. This must follow from the preceding discussion, in that until the disposition of the ownership in the property is complete (*i.e.* until the insured admits ownership does not vest in him, or is declared to be the property of the third person by a court) the insured's possession of the property gives him an insurable interest in it. The decision of Diplock J. (as he then was) in *Thomas v. National Farmers Union Mutual Insurance Society Ltd*[40] would appear, however, to be against this proposition.

The facts were that the insured was the tenant of an agricultural hold- **1–51** ing which he quit on October 5, 1956, and on the holding when he quit he had left a crop of hay and straw which were produce of the preceding twelve months. This crop was the subject of a claim by the landlord to be entitled to it by reason of the Agricultural Holdings Act 1948, particularly sections 12(1) and 47(1), as being crops left on the holding, but entitling the insured tenant who quit to the right of compensation from the landlord. Diplock J. (as he then was) approached the problem of insurable interest of the tenant insured not from the proposition as suggested above, but by determining ownership retrospectively to the date of the quitting of the holding, and held that the insured had no insurable interest in the hay and straw after October 5, 1956[41]:

"It seems to me quite clear that at some point, either on or after the tenant quitting the holding, the property which he undoubtedly had before that date is divested from him and vested in the landlord. [Counsel] has argued that that does not occur until the amount of the compensation has been fixed by one method or another under the Act. I cannot accept that argument. It seems to me that once the tenant has quit the holding, or, in the words of section 47 'on the termination of the tenancy, on quitting the holding', the tenant is divested of all rights in respect of the crops left on the holding pursuant to section 12 of the Act, and is granted instead, the right to obtain compensation under the Act. He is not entitled to go on to the holding; he is not entitled to remove the hay and straw from the holding, and it seems to me that the clear scheme of the Act is that property passes in the crops left pursuant to section 12 on the termination of the tenancy, on quitting the holding, as is stated in section 47; the property then passes to the landlord, and the tenant, instead, acquires the right to obtain compensation under the Act through the machinery which I have already dealt with. It follows, therefore, that I accept the contention of the

[40] [1961] 1 W.L.R. 386.
[41] [1960] 2 Lloyd's Rep. 444 at 448.

> [insurers] that after he had quit the holding on 5 October 1956, the claimant had no property in the hay or straw, the subject matter of the insurance, nor had he any insurable interest therein."

1-52   Thirdly, where property is sold and paid for, but the risk contractually remains with the seller, any insurance effected by the seller covering the property remains in force so long as the seller bears the risk on that property. This proposition stems from the decision in *Martineau v. Kitching*[42] which concerned a floating fire policy on sugar stored, both before and after sale, in the insured's premises, although, on the facts, the insured in that case no longer had an insurable interest on sugar sold to a customer that was damaged by fire after the contractual period of two months during which time the risk of loss fell on the insured seller.

1-53   Fourthly, even where property is sold and ownership and risk vest in the purchaser, the insured seller has a beneficial interest in the nature of a vendor's lien, which is on insurable interest, until such time as he has been paid the whole of the purchase-money.[43]

4. PARTNERSHIPS

1-54   Where the insured is a partnership, a change in partners means that a new partnership is formed and the former partnership is dissolved, so what is the effect of such a change in the constitution and identity of the insured partnership, bearing in mind the personal nature of an insurance contract? This problem has been raised in only one English case, *Jenkins v. Deane*[44] which concerned the third party liability part of a motor vehicle policy issued to a partnership, and where an accident occurred after a change in the partnership. Goddard J.'s judgment was as follows, dealing at first, *obiter*, with the case of property insurances, and then liability insurances[45]:

> "It is curious that there is no authority in English law dealing with the effect on a policy of the assured taking in a fresh partner without the knowledge or consent of the insurers, even one to whom no objection in fact could be taken . . . Bearing in mind that a contract of insurance is essentially a personal contract, where property is insured and lost, it would in my judgment be a good defence for the insurers to prove that a new partner had been admitted without their consent. The assured cannot be changed by assignment, but only by novation.
>
> In the present case, however, there was only one insurance, namely, against third party risks . . . This is, of course, an insurance against a liability in tort. In deciding whether the addition of a member to an assured firm avoids this insurance, as distinct from insurances against damage to or loss of the vehicle itself, it seems to me that the fundamental question is whether the insurers' risk in this respect has been enlarged or altered.

---

[42] (1872) L.R. 7 Q.B. 436.
[43] *Castellain v. Preston* (1883) 11 Q.B.D. 380 at 405, *per* Bowen L.J., CA.
[44] (1933) 103 L.J.K.B. 250.
[45] (1933) 47 Ll. L. Rep. 342 at 347.

Now, a liability in tort is a several liability ... If more than one is sued, execution may be levied on the property of the firm, but equally it may be levied against the goods of one partner only. If therefore a policy insures A and B against third party claims in respect of the negligent driving of a car that they own jointly, it insures each severally against the whole claim, because either A or B may be called upon alone to pay. How, then, is the insurers' risk enlarged or altered if C is taken into partnership? If C alone is called upon to pay, he can get nothing from the insurers, for he was never insured. But if A or B or both called upon to pay, I do not see on what principle the insurers should not indemnify him or either of them against the claim. I do not think that the principles applicable to an insurance on property must necessarily apply to an insurance against liability for tort. . .

In my judgment, therefore, the fact that a new partner is admitted to a firm without obtaining the consent of the insurers does not relieve the latter from indemnifying those who were partners at the time when the policy was affected from a liability to a third party claim, provided always that the partner claiming retains as he ordinarily would, his undivided interest in the insured [item causing the third party liability]."

5. THE DUTY OF GOOD FAITH

Mutual duty

Unlike the vast majority of contracts, contracts of insurance are generically contracts in respect of which both the insurer and the insured owe the other a duty to act with utmost good faith (*uberrimae fidei*). One of the main aspects of this is that the insured owes the insurer a duty to disclose, and not to misrepresent, all facts material to the risk being insured, and this is subject of Chapter 3, below. The duty of the insurer in this respect has only been dealt with in one reported case, that of *Banque Financière de la Cité SA v. Westgate Insurance Co. Ltd*[46] where the House of Lords held that the insurers' duty was to disclose facts known to them which were material to the risk and to the recoverability of a claim by the insured. The test of materiality was whether the fact was one which a prudent insured would take into account in deciding whether or not to place the risk with that insurer. The case concerned credit insurance, and the insurers had discovered the fraud of the claimant bank's broker which meant that the bank had a substantial gap in its credit insurance supporting very large loans it had made. The insurers did not tell the insured bank of this fact. The remedy was held, however, not to sound in damages, but only the equitable remedy of rescission of the contract of insurance and return of the premium paid. It is unlikely that this remedy will attract itself to many insureds, so little litigation can be anticipated on this duty of good faith owed by insurers to their insureds.

1–55

Continuing nature of the duty

Recently, there has been an exploration of the concept of the insured's continuing duty of good faith in respect of the presentation of the claim

1–56

---

[46] [1991] 2 A.C. 249, HL.

under the insurance first recognised by Lord Ellenborough nearly two hundred years ago.[47] Hoffmann L.J. (as he then was) put the matter in this way in *Orakpo v. Barclays Insurance Services Ltd*[48]:

> "I do not see why the duty of good faith on the part of the assured should expire when the contract has been made. The reasons for requiring good faith continue to exist. Just as the nature of the risk will usually be within the peculiar knowledge of the assured, so will the circumstances of the casualty; it will rarely be within the knowledge of the insurance company. I think that the insurance company should be able to trust the assured to put forward a claim in good faith. Any fraud in making the claim goes to the root of the contract and entitles the insurer to be discharged. One should not readily infer fraud from the fact that the insured has made a doubtful or even exaggerated claim."

Fraud required

1–57   The House of Lords has now held in *Manifest Shipping Co. Ltd v. Uni-Polaris Shipping Co. Ltd*[49] that it is wrong for an insurer to seek to defend claims on the ground of breach of a supposed duty of good faith which continued after inception of the insurance. The proper and only defence to a claim under an insurance policy is that of fraud in presentation of the claim.[50] The decision is also important, because the House of Lords pointed out that once an insured and his insurer are in hostile litigation, any concept of a duty to act in good faith falls away, and the parties' relationship and rights become governed by the rules of procedure and the orders which the court makes during the litigation. Thus, the insurers cannot rely on the non-fraudulent failure of the insured to make disclosure of documents during litigation as constituting some breach of a suggested continuing duty of good faith owed by the insured to the insurer in presenting a claim.[51]

Fraudulent conduct must be relevant to the claim

1–58   To claim for a total loss, knowing it to be false, and to later seek to claim for a partial loss, is fraudulent conduct in relation to a claim.[52] So is the deliberate over-valuing of lost items.[53] The relevant test must be honest belief.[54] The insurers have to show that a fraudulent claim has been made or maintained by the insured.[55] There is no relevant fraudulent conduct, however, by an act in relation to a claim which does not have relevance to

---

[47] *Shepherd v. Chewter* (1808) 1 Camp. 274 at 275; *Boulton v. Houlder Bros. and Co.* [1904] 1 K.B. 784 at 791–792, *per* Mathew L.J., CA; *Manifest Shipping Co. Ltd v. Uni-Polaris Insurance Co. Ltd ("The Sea Star")* [1997] 1 Lloyd's Rep. 360, *per* Leggatt L.J., CA.

[48] [1995] L.R.L.R. 443 at 451, CA.

[49] [2001] UKHL/1; [2001] 2 W.L.R. 170, HL.

[50] *ibid.* at [72], *per* Lord Hobhouse.

[51] *ibid.* at [75].

[52] *Dome Mining Corp. Ltd v. Drysdale* (1931) 41 Ll. L. Rep. 109.

[53] *London Assurance v. Clare* (1937) 57 Ll. L. Rep. 254.

[54] *Piermay Shipping Co. S.S. v. Chester, The Michael* [1979] 2 Lloyd's Rep. 1 at 21–22, *per* Roskill L.J. (as he then was), CA.

[55] *Manifest Shipping Co. Ltd v. Uni-Polaris Shipping Co. Ltd* [2001] UKHL/1; [2001] 2 W.L.R. 170, at [70] and [72], *per* Lord Hobhouse, HL.

the insurer's liability to pay under the policy. This is illustrated by the unusual case of *K/S Merc-Scandia XXXXII v. Underwriters of Lloyd's Policy 25T 1054 and others*,[56] where the insured has the benefit of a liability policy and, after the claim has arisen, the insured contests the jurisdiction of the English courts over the third party's claim by use of a forged letter, this fraudulent act does not give the insurer any ground to rescind or avoid the insurance policy. That misrepresentation was irrelevant to the insurer's liability to indemnify the insured against his liability to the third party because the use of the forged letter on that application would not have influenced the outcome of the issue of the insured's liability to the third party.

All benefit lost

The Court of Appeal held in *Galloway v. Guardian Royal Exchange (U.K.) Ltd*[57] that fraud, once established, taints the whole of the insured's claim, so that he cannot recover anything, not even the honest part of his claim. The bar to the insured's recovery if fraud is discovered in relation to a claim affects not only the claims under one section of a combined insurance policy, but to all claims under all sections of the insurance policy.[58] The House of Lords have now affirmed that all benefit is lost in *Manifest Shipping Co. Ltd v. Uni-Polaris Shipping Co. Ltd.*[59]   **1–59**

The difficulty is determining what amounts to fraud in the presentation   **1–60** of a claim. Lord Woolf M.R. in *Galloway* considered that where a dishonest £2,000 claim was made as part of a total claim of just over £18,000, that was "an amount which is substantial and therefore an amount which taints the whole".[60] Millett L.J., with whose judgment Mummery L.J. agreed, gave rather fuller guidance on the approach that the courts should take[61]:

> "... I reject the submission that this is to be tested by reference to the proportion of the entire claim which is represented by the fraudulent claim. That would lead to the absurd conclusion that the greater the genuine loss, the larger the fraudulent claim which may be made at the same time without penalty. In my judgment, the size of the genuine claim is irrelevant. The policy is avoided by breach of the duty of good faith which rests upon the insured in all his dealings with the insurer. The result of a breach of this duty leaves the insured without cover. In the present case the insured took advantage of the happening of an insured event to make a dishonest claim for the loss of goods worth £2,000 which, to his knowledge, had not occurred. In my view the right approach in such a case is to consider the fraudulent claim as if it were the only claim and then to consider whether, taken in isolation, the making of that claim by the insured is sufficiently serious to justify stigmatising it as a breach of his duty of good faith so as to avoid the policy.

---

[56] [2000] Lloyd's Rep. I.R. 694.
[57] [1999] Lloyd's Rep. I.R. 209, CA.
[58] *Insurance Corp. of the Channel Islands Ltd v. McHugh and the Royal Hotel Ltd* [1997] L.R.L.R. 94; applied *Nsubuga v. Commercial Union Assurance Co. Ltd* [1998] 2 Lloyd's Rep. 682.
[59] [2001] UKHL/1; [2001] 2 W.L.R. 170, HL.
[60] [1999] Lloyd's Rep. I.R. 209 at 214, CA.
[61] *ibid.*

> The making of dishonest insurance claims has become all too common. There seems to be a widespread belief that insurance companies are fair game, and that defrauding them is not morally reprehensible. The rule which we are asked to enforce today may appear to some to be harsh, but it is in my opinion a necessary and salutary rule which deserves to be better known to the public. I for my part would be most unwilling to dilute it in any way."

Pleading and proof of fraud

1–61   Counsel is professionally prohibited by paragraph 606 of the Bar Code of Conduct from pleading any allegation of fraud without reasonably credible evidence before him to substantiate the allegation. The Court of Appeal has said that this means that such material has to be evidence which could be put before the court to make good the allegation. If there was material before counsel which could not be used in court, its existence cannot justify counsel in putting his name to the allegation. The same applied to pleading any other dishonest or dishonourable conduct. A breach will expose counsel to the wasted costs jurisdiction of the court.[62] As for the standard of proof placed on the insurer who alleges fraud on the part of the insured, this standard must reflect the seriousness of the allegation.[63] The civil standard of proof must be flexibly applied, so that the court is satisfied that the allegation is made out, but will not require proof to the criminal standard of proof (*i.e.* proof beyond reasonable doubt).[64]

[62] *Medcalf v. Mardell* [2001] T.L.R. January 2, CA.
[63] *Hornal v. Neuberger Products Ltd* [1957] 1 Q.B. 247 at 263–264, *per* Hodson L.J., and at 266, *per* Morris L.J., CA.
[64] *Khawaja v. Secretary of State for the Home Department* [1984] A.C. 74 at 112–114, *per* Lord Scarman, HL; applied *Baghbadrani v. Commercial Union Assurance Co. Ltd* [2000] Lloyd's Rep. I.R. 94; but see *Nsubuga v. Commercial Union Assurance Co. plc* [1999] 2 Lloyd's Rep. 682, where the court was satisfied to the criminal standard.

CHAPTER 2

CONDITIONS AND WARRANTIES

1. CONDITIONS AND WARRANTIES DIFFERENTIATED

Introduction

Unfortunately, there is no complete consistency within the general body **2–01** of insurance law, particularly in older cases, upon the interpretation of the words "condition" and "warranty", and the effect of breaches of them. It is generally accepted now, though, that in contradistinction to the use of the terms in the general law of contract, in insurance law "condition" is used to describe a term of the insurance contract which is not fundamental, and breach of which will not give the insurer any right to repudiate the contract of insurance as a whole. Breach by the insured may only prevent the insured's recovery of an indemnity under the insurance contract in three circumstances:

(i) where performance of the condition is expressly made a condition precedent to the liability of the insurer to indemnify the insured.

(ii) as only recently established by the Court of Appeal in *Alfred McAlpine plc v. BAI (Run-off) Ltd*,[1] where a breach of a condition is, "so serious as to give a right to reject the claim albeit it was not repudiatory in the sense of enabling [the insurer] to accept a repudiation of the whole contract."[2]

(iii) where the proximate cause of the relevant insured loss was a breach of a condition, *e.g.* failing to take reasonable precautions to prevent accidents occurring.[3]

The term "warranty" is used in insurance law to describe a funda- **2–02** mental term of the contract, breach of which will render the insurer discharged from further liability from the date of breach, rather than render the insurance contract void *ab initio*.[4] In the case of facts warranted to be correct at the time of proposing for the insurance, the avoidance arises on the ground that the risk never attached.[5] In relation to statements of facts expressly warranted to be true, irrespective of whether those facts are material to the risk, which are true at the time of the proposal for insurance and which are also required to remain true, or things which the insured agrees to carry out throughout the

---

[1] [2000] 1 Lloyd's Rep. 437, CA.

[2] *ibid.* at 443, col.1, *per* Waller L.J. It is a factual test, *K/S Merc-Scandia XXXXII v. Ocean Marine Insurance Co. Ltd* [2000] Lloyd's Rep. I.R. 696 at [87]–[89].

[3] *W. and J. Lane v. Spratt* [1970] 2 Q.B. 480 at 493–495, *per* Roskill J. (as he then was).

[4] *Barnard v. Faber* [1893] 1 Q.B. 340, CA.

[5] *Thomson v. Weems* (1884) 9 App. Cas. 671, HL.

duration of the insurance, (both termed promissory warranties), the insurer is automatically discharged from further liability when those facts become no longer true, subject to any express policy term, or waiver.[6] The modern trend is for terms which used to be called warranties to be called conditions precedent in order to convey the importance of the term, and the consequence of breach, more easily to the insured. Pressure from government and consumer lobbies are probably largely responsible for this trend.

Construction of insurance policies

2–03   The same rules of construction apply to insurance contracts (and the policy document which usually embodies the terms and conditions and limitations of that contract) as to all other contracts, as discussed in Chapter 1. It is therefore always important to bear in mind those principles when construing the policy term, and those principles of construction have recently been restated by Lord Hoffmann to be as follows[7]:

> "(1) Interpretation is the ascertainment of the meaning which the document would convey to a reasonable person having all the background knowledge which would reasonably have been available to the parties in the situation in which they were at the time of the contract;
>
> (2) The background was famously referred to by Lord Wilberforce as the 'Matrix of fact', but this phrase is, if anything, an understated description of what the background may include. Subject to the requirement that it should have been reasonably available to the parties and to the exception to be mentioned next, it includes absolutely anything which would have affected the way in which the language of the document would have been understood by a reasonable man.
>
> (3) The law excludes from the admissible background the previous negotiations of the parties and their declarations of subjective intent. They are admissible only in an action for rectification. The law makes this distinction for reasons of practical policy and, in this respect only, legal interpretation differs from the way we would interpret utterances in ordinary life. The boundaries of this exception are in some respects unclear. But this is not the occasion on which to explore them.
>
> (4) The meaning which a document(or any other utterance) would convey to a reasonable man is not the same thing as the meaning of its words. The meaning of words is a matter of dictionaries and grammars; the meaning of the document is what the parties using those words against the relevant background would reasonably have been understood to mean. The background may not merely enable the reasonable man to choose between the possible meanings of words which are ambiguous but even (as occasionally happens in ordinary life) to conclude that the parties must, for whatever reasons, have used the wrong words or syntax. . .

[6] *Bank of Nova Scotia v. Hellenic Mutual War Risks Association (Bermuda) Ltd* [1992] 1 A.C. 233, HL, applying s.33(3) of the Marine Insurance Act 1906; *Hussain v. Brown* [1996] 1 Lloyd's Rep. 627, CA; *Printpak v. AGF Insurance Ltd* [1999] Lloyd's Rep. I.R. 542, CA.
[7] *Investors Compensation Scheme Ltd v. West Bromwich Building Society* [1998] 1 W.L.R. 896 at 912–913.

(5) The 'rule' that words should be given their 'natural and ordinary meaning' reflects the common sense proposition that we do not easily accept that people have made linguistic mistakes, particularly in formal documents. On the other hand, if one would nevertheless conclude from the background that something must be wrong with the language, the law does not require judges to attribute to the parties an intention which they plainly could not have had. Lord Diplock made this point more vigorously when he said in *Antaios CompaniaNaviera SA v. Salen Rederierna A.B.*[8]:

> 'if detailed semantic and syntactical analysis of
> words in a commercial contract is going to lead to
> a conclusion that flouts business commonsense, it
> must yield to business commonsense.'"

2. WARRANTIES

Determining existence of a warranty

It is a question of construction of the policy as a whole whether a term **2–04** is a warranty or condition,[9] but it has been said some time ago that, prima facie, the use of the word "warranty" or "warranted" shows that the parties understood that a breach of it will debar the insured's right to recover.[10] As will be seen below, the modern approach of the courts may be to ameliorate the effect of warranties, with a reluctance to find continuing warranties rather than simply a warranty as to existing fact. In this regard, see for instance, *Hussain v. Brown*[11] discussed below under "Promissory or future warranties".

Implication of a warranty **2–05**

It has been said that words qualifying the subject matter of the insurance are prima facie words of warranty that must be complied with.[11] Thus, in *Newcastle Fire Insurance Co. v. Macmorran and Co.*,[13] a cotton mill was insured under a fire policy where the insured warranted that the mill constituted a building having a particular description, and Lord Eldon L.C. said[14]:

> "It is a first principle in the law of insurance, on all occasions, that where a representation is material, it must be complied with — if immaterial, that immateriality may be inquired into and shown; but that if there is a warranty, it is part of the contract that the matter is such as it is represented to be. Therefore the materiality or immateriality, signifies nothing. The only question is as to the mere fact."

[8] [1985] A.C. 191 at 201.
[9] *Ellinger and Co. v. Mutual Life Insurance Co. of New York* [1905] 1 K.B. 31, CA; *Union Insurance Society of Canton Ltd v. George Wills and Co.* [1916] 1 A.C. 281, HL.
[10] *Palatine Insurance Co. Ltd v. Gregory* [1926] A.C. 90, PC; but see *de Maurier (Jewels) Ltd v. Bastion Insurance Co. Ltd and Coronet Insurance Co. Ltd* [1967] 2 Lloyd's Rep. 550.
[11] [1996] 1 Lloyd's Rep. 627, CA.
[12] *Yorkshire Insurance Co. Ltd v. Campbell* [1917] A.C. 218, PC.
[13] (1815) 3 Dow. 255, HL.
[14] *ibid.* at 262.

In the event, the House of Lords held that the facts showed that the warranty freed the insurers from liability.

2–06   Similarly, in *Sillem v. Thornton*[15] a policy was executed on April 7 to insure certain premises for a year from the preceding February 1. The premises were described in the policy as:

> "a brick building used as a dwelling house and store (described in the paper attached to this policy)."

The paper attached gave a minute description of a two-storeyed house, with what purported to be a certificate that the description was accurate, signed on the preceding October 30. The description was in fact accurate up to a month before the policy was effected, when the insured altered the house by adding a third storey. This was not known by the insurers, and when, in May, the building was destroyed by fire, the insurers denied liability. It was held that the description in the policy amounted to a warranty that the insured would not, during the term of insurance, voluntarily do anything to make the condition of the premises vary from that description, so as to increase the insurer's liability. This warranty was broken so the insured could not recover.

2–07   The implied warranty so given when describing the subject matter of the insurance only relates, however, to an alteration in the premises which increases the insurer's risk as is illustrated by *Stokes v. Cox.*[16] Here, included in the description of the insured building, was a statement:

> "No steam engine employed on the premises. The steam from the said boiler being used for heating water and warming the shops."

Subsequently, during the currency of the policy, the insured erected a steam engine on the premises and supplied it with steam from the boiler, but gave no notice of this to the insurer. It was held that, as there was no increase in the risk insured by reason of the erection of the steam-engine, the implied warranty was not breached.

Promissory or future warranties

2–08   Express warranties can be rather more extensive in their scope than implied warranties. In *Beauchamp v. National Mutual Indemnity Insurance Co. Ltd*[17] a builder took out an employers' liability insurance to cover the work of demolition of a mill. A question in the proposal form asked if explosives would be used and the insured replied "no", and Finlay J. held that this amounted to a warranty which, on the facts, was breached so that the insurer was not liable.[18]

---

[15] (1854) 3 E. and B. 868.
[16] (1856) 1 H. and N. 533.
[17] [1937] 3 All E.R. 19.
[18] *ibid.* at 22.

"I think that the true view to take is that he was insuring what I may conveniently call. . . a non-explosive demolition. . . It is, perhaps, significant that [the insured] made it quite clear to me that, but for one circumstance, as to which he was clearly mistaken, he would have thought it right to inform the insurance company with reference to the use of explosives. That point was this. He seemed to think that it was not necessary to do because the explosives were not being used by him, but by a gentleman whom he had employed for the purpose. I cannot resist the view that, in the first place, this was, as I think, a warranty."

The question of whether there was a continuing warranty arising from **2–09** a commercial contents insurance proposal form asking : "Are any inflammable oils or goods used or kept on the premises?" was similarly construed as an implied continuing warranty in *Hales v. Reliance Fire and Accident Insurance Corp. Ltd.*[18] The court held that the question referred to the situation throughout the whole currency of the policy, and was not confined to the time that the proposal form was completed. Accordingly, the introduction of inflammable goods into the insured premises amounted to a breach of that continuing warranty. This decision has been criticised,[20] though, because the judge was not referred to the Court of Appeal's decision in *Woolfall and Rimmer Ltd v. Moyle*[21] which is discussed below.

Where the warranty, correctly construed, only relates to the quality **2–10** of the subject matter of the insurance (*i.e.* the risk of injury to employees) existing at the time the insurance is proposed for or effected, rather than for the duration of the insurance contract, this may also involve interpreting a proposal form question, as was the circumstance in *Woolfall and Rimmer Ltd v. Moyle*[22] where the proposal form contained the question:

> "Are your machines, plant and ways properly fenced and guarded and otherwise in good order and condition?"

The insured answered in the affirmative and Lord Greene M.R. gave the opinion of the Court of Appeal that this did not constitute a warranty relating to anything other than present facts[23]:

> "It is said that the question does not merely relate to the moment of time at which the proposer is answering it, but extends to the future condition of the machinery, plant and ways during the currency of the policy. In my opinion, there is not a particle of justification for reading into that perfectly simple question any element of futurity whatsoever . . . The value of the question, as I construe it, to the underwriters is that it enables them to find out what sort of person they are dealing with, *i.e.* whether he is the sort of person who keeps his machinery, plant and ways properly fenced and guarded and otherwise in good order and condition . . . If the underwriters

[19] [1960] 2 Lloyd's Rep. 391.
[20] *Hussain v. Brown* [1996] 1 Lloyd's Rep. 627 at 629, *per* Saville L.J. (as he then was), CA.
[21] [1942] 1 K.B. 66, CA.
[22] [1942] 1 K.B. 66, CA.
[23] [1941] 3 All E.R. 304 at 306–307, CA.

in fact intended that this question should carry the meaning which they now suggest, nothing would have been easier than to say so . . . In my judgment, the meaning of this question is perfectly clear, and there is no evidence on the facts of this case that the particular plank which was the cause of this accident was not in good order and condition at the time when the question was answered . . ."

2–11   The Court of Appeal has recently stated in *Hussain v. Brown*[24] that there is no special principle of insurance law that requires answers in proposal forms to be read, prima facie or otherwise, as importing promises to the future. Whether or not they did depends on the ordinary rules of construction, namely consideration of the words used, in the light of the context of that meaning which seemed most closely to correspond with the presumed intention of the parties.

2–12   The facts in that case were that the claimant insured completed and signed a proposal form for a Lloyd's fire policy in respect of his commercial premises in Bury, Lancashire. Question 9 of the proposal form asked:

"Are the premises fitted with any system of intruder alarm? If YES give name of installing company. (Please provide a copy alarm specification if applicable.)"

The claimant answered the question "Yes" and "See specification". That specification was correct at the time that the risk was presented to the underwriters. The proposal form also contained the usual following declaration:

"I/We the Proposer warrant that the above statements are true and that they shall be the basis of the contract between me/us and the Underwriters and will be incorporated into such contract."

2–13   The underwriters accepted the proposal and issued an insurance certificate which stated that the proposal and declaration were to be the basis and form part of the certificate. A few months later there was a fire at the insured premises and the insured claimed under the insurance. The insured admitted that the alarm system was inoperative before and at the time of the fire, and the underwriters relied on this to defend liability, alleging that the answer given to question 9 amounted to a continuing warranty that the premises were fitted with an intruder alarm which was operational and/or would be habitually set by the claimant when the premises were unattended.

2–14   Both the judge in the Mercantile Court in Manchester, and the Court of Appeal, held that the answer to question 9 did not amount to a continuing warranty as contended for by the underwriters. The Court of Appeal came to this conclusion in applying the ordinary rules of construction mentioned above, for a number of reasons:

---

[24] [1996] 1 Lloyd's Rep. 627 at 629, col.1, *per* Saville L.J. (as he then was), CA.

(i) the question posed was in the present tense;
(ii) it did not seek on its face any information as to the practice of the proposer with regard to the alarm, for example, whether it was set when the premises were left unoccupied;
(iii) there was nothing in the words of the simple question posed, or to be gleaned from the context, which began to suggest that what an affirmative answer entailed was an undertaking as to the future; and
(iv) if underwriters wanted protection from a continuing warranty, which was a draconian term, then it was up to them to stipulate for it in clear terms.

State of repair

Where the insured answers "yes" to the question "Are the buildings kept   **2–15**
in a good state of repair?" in a proposal for fire insurance in respect of those buildings, it has been held that the question is whether, on the balance of probability, the building is kept in a good state of repair as at the date of the proposal form. The issue of whether such question and answer amounted to a warranty confined to that time, or was a continuing warranty, was left undecided given the fact that there was no evidence that the building was not kept in a good state of repair throughout the period of insurance.[25]

Occupation of buildings

In relation to the occupation of insured buildings, the proper way to   **2–16**
regard the questions and answers concerning occupation is to treat them as being an indication of the state of affairs which existed at the time the answers were given, or is going to exist within the immediate future thereafter, and is going to continue so far as the insured is concerned for the period of the policy, but they do not amount to a continuing warranty that no change will occur.[26] Moreover, where the insured premises are warranted to be always occupied, or occupied at night, an insured is not to be considered in breach of that continuing warranty by reason of his temporary absence from the premises, either by reason of an emergency,[27] or even simply because the insured chooses to go out for a few hours.[28]

Insurance history

The courts tend not to give questions in proposal forms extended mean-   **2–17**
ings. Thus it has been held that there was no breach of warranty where a proposer for insurance does not reveal his own personal insurance history when the following question was inserted in a proposal form for a commercial insurance of his business premises: "Are you or have you been insured in this or any other office?" That question is to be construed as referring only to the particular premises to be insured[29] and will not be

[25] *Hair v. Prudential Assurance Co. Ltd* [1983] 2 Lloyd's Rep. 667.
[26] *ibid.* at 672, col.2.
[27] *Winicofsky v. Army and Navy General Assurance Association Ltd* (1919) 88 L.J.K.B. 1111.
[28] *Simmonds v. Cockell* [1920] 1 K.B. 843.
[29] *Golding v. Royal London Auxiliary Insurance Co. Ltd* (1914) 30 T.L.R. 350.

construed beyond its ordinary meaning.[30] However, such questions will be construed as referring to previous forms of the business to be insured, *e.g.* a former partnership business now constituted as a limited company.[31] The matter of the extent of the duty of disclosure is more fully considered in Chapter 3, below.

Procedures to be followed

2–18   On the other hand, no warranty, promissory or otherwise, was held to exist where a fidelity insurance proposal contained the following questions and replies in *Hearts of Oak Building Society v. Law Union and Rock Insurance Co. Ltd.*[32]:

> "**Q:** How often are they [the named employees] required to send statements of cash received?
> **A:** Daily.
> **Q:** How often do you require them to pay over to you and is he allowed to retain a balance in hand? If so, how much? And do you see that they have the amount in their possession?
> **A:** McMurdy should not retain and should pay over as received."

2–19   In fact, McMurdy dishonestly appropriated mortgage moneys coming into his hands, but Goddard J. (as he then was) rejected the insurers' contention that the answers in the proposal form amounted to promissory warranties that such duties would be performed by McMurdy. His lordship determined that the questions and answers were directed to stating what the duties of the employee were, in other words, the terms of employment of their employee, and did not amount to a promissory warranty that those duties would be carried out by the employee[33]:

> "In this case it seems to me that it is quite impossible , especially when one remembers that this is a fidelity guarantee policy, to construe these undertakings as a promise that during the currency of the policy McMurdy would faithfully carry out his duties, which is what the argument comes down to, because that is the very thing against which the insurance is being taken out, and it cannot be said that this was a promise that McMurdy would never retain and would always pay over the money as received and that he would always send statements of cash daily, because, of course, if McMurdy always did that and the claimants could always say that he did that, there would be no point at all in insurance. I think these questions are merely directed to finding out what was the system in force in the [claimant's] office, so that the insurers could see whether the [claimant's] office system was such that they could accept the risk."

2–20   Likewise, in *Benham v. United Guarantee and Life Assurance Co.*[34] the insurers granted the claimant, the treasurer of a literary institution, a

---

[30] *Locker and Woolf Ltd v. Western Australian Insurance Co. Ltd* [1936] 1 K.B. 408, CA.
[31] *ibid.* See also *Arthrude Press Ltd v. Eagle Star and British Dominions Insurance Co. Ltd* (1924) 18 Ll. L. Rep. 382.
[32] [1936] 2 All E.R. 619.
[33] *ibid.* at 624.
[34] (1852) 7 Exch. 744.

fidelity insurance in respect of losses occasioned by the want of integrity of W, the secretary of the institution. One of the questions and answers declared to be true by the claimant in the proposal was:

> "**Q:** The checks, which will be used to secure the accuracy in his accounts, and when and how often they will be balanced and closed?
> **A:** Examined by finance committee every fortnight."

It was held that that statement did not amount to a warranty, but was a mere representation of the intention of the claimant, and, consequently, he was entitled to recover in respect of a loss arising from the want of integrity of W, although such loss was occasioned by the neglect to examine the accounts in the manner specified.

Casual non-observance of continuing warranty

Even outside the context of fidelity insurance, where a set procedure is expressly warranted, it has been said that a casual non-observance of it by one of the insured's minions will not amount to a variation of procedure amounting to breach of the warranty. This view was expressed by Staughton J. in *Mint Security Ltd v. Blair, Thos R. Miler and Son (Home) Ltd and E. C. Darwin*.[35] The facts were that the insured security firm, which was in the business of transporting cash to banks and post offices, had answered the following questions in the proposal form, it being warranted that equipment/personnel/procedures as described would not be varied:　　2–21

> "14. Do you undertake not to entrust cash or other valuables to a crew member unless at least one member, driver or guard, has been in your employ for at least a year?
>
> Answer: Yes
>
> [. . .]
>
> 16. State briefly the period of regular training required to produce a fully trained member and the minimum you require new staff to complete before using them on operations?
>
> Answer: Fully trained two months. Minimum period one month.
>
> [. . .]
>
> 20. What will be the maximum value which will be at risk any one time outside the armoured vehicle i.e. pavement risk?
>
> Answer: £10,000."

The insured claimant sought to recover under the cash in transit policy in respect of a robbery when the facts were that no member of the crew had been in the claimants' employment for at least one year; at least one member of the crew had not been trained before embarking on operations; the crew's references had been inadequately checked; and more than £10,000 was outside the vehicle at the time. Staughton J. held that[36]:　　2–22

---

[35] [1982] 1 Lloyd's Rep. 188.
[36] *ibid.* at 197.

"the action of the crew in taking more than £10,000 outside the vehicle at any one time was not a variation of procedures, merely non-observance by them of the plaintiffs' rule. But in respect of the other breaches alleged ... I find that there had been a variation in procedures; these were not casual breaches, but the result of decision at some level of management or administration. Indeed, it was the plaintiffs' case that with the change in the nature of the business, it was no longer practicable to comply with the old procedures. To some extent at least — in relation to the minimum employment period — this was proved. So a breach of warranty is made out."

2–23   Similarly, in *Shaw v. Robberds*[37] the insured building was described as "a kiln for drying corn in use", but on an isolated occasion it was used to dry bark from a vessel which was sunk in a river near the premises, as an act of kindness. Unfortunately, during the process of drying that bark, a fire had taken hold and the insured building was destroyed. It was held by Lord Denman C.J. that the description of use amounted to neither an express warranty, or an implied warranty, that nothing but corn was ever to be dried in the kiln. The description of the user of the building merely served, in the court's view, to identify the premises, and to enable the insurers to determine whether the risk was singly or doubly hazardous for rating purposes at the time of proposal.

2–24   The casual non-observance of express warranted procedures, however, may well leave a court with less room to manoeuvre, as illustrated by *A. Cohen and Co. Ltd v. Plaistow Transport Ltd.*,[38] where a goods-in-transit policy contained an express warranty that all vehicles were garaged in a locked garage at night. On the night of the alleged theft of goods, the insured's employees had unusually left the loaded lorry in the insured's locked yard and not in the garage, because another lorry was being repaired there. MacKenna J., in dismissing the insured's claim for failing to prove that the goods were stolen, however, stated his view, *obiter*, that if this was an express warranty, it was breached.[39] Another approach to non-compliance which attracted itself to MacKenna J. is non-attachment of the risk whilst the warranty is not being complied with, in other words, treating the warranty as defining or delimiting the risk, and this is discussed below.

Ambiguous interpretations

2–25   Finally, it must be emphasised that in the case of real ambiguity between two reasonable interpretations of an express term, one being favourable to the insured, the other favourable to the insurer, the words will be construed *contra proferentem,* that is against the insurer being the person who drafted the wording.[40] Thus, where an insurer inserted a recital in a buildings and contents fire policy that:

---

[37] (1837) 6 Ad. and El. 75.
[38] [1968] 2 Lloyd's Rep. 587.
[39] *ibid.* at 592.
[40] See Chapter 1.

"buildings brick-built and slated; warmed exclusively by steam, lighted by gas, etc, worked by the steam engine above-mentioned; in the tenure of one firm only, standing apart from all other mills, and worked by day only."

It was held that the words "worked by day only" were to be construed as referring only to the mill, and not to the steam engine, both being reasonable interpretations, but that least favourable to the drafter of the policy being applied.[41]

Consequence of breach of warranty in combined policy

If there is truly a warranty, and the insured breaches it, there may be circumstances where the insurer is not discharged from further liability under the whole policy, but only in relation to the section of, or cover in, a combined policy. This was recognised in *Printpak v. AGF Insurance Ltd.*[42] Under an express warranty in the policy, numbered P17, the claimant warranted that the burglar alarm to the insured premises was fully operational at all times when the premises were closed for business. It was common ground that the warranty had been incorporated into the policy. It was also common ground that the warranty had been broken, as the alarm was not working during the currency of the policy and had been switched off, according to the claimant, as building work was going on.

    2–26

In the usual way of combined policies, each type of insured risk was dealt with in a separate section. Section A, which was relevant for present purposes, provided cover in respect of loss or damage by fire. Section B provided cover against theft, and other lettered sections provided cover in relation to money, business interruption, employers' liability, public liability, goods in transit and computer protection. The claimant had selected a section of cover from those available under the policy.

    2–27

Again, as is often the case, the nature of each type of cover and the terms and conditions applicable were stipulated in separate sections of the policy. The precise terms of each individual insurance contract, and the extent to which individual sections were incorporated, were set out in the schedule to the issued policy which was tailor-made to fit the particular cover provided to the insured. Certain "general conditions" were specifically prescribed to be applicable to the whole of the policy. By contrast, the standard forms of endorsement (headed "section endorsements") each of which was prefixed by the letter "P", were expressed to be "operative only as stated in the policy schedules", *i.e.* applicable to a section of the policy only if expressly incorporated into that section by cross references to them. A number of "P" endorsements had been incorporated into Section A (Fire), but the alarm warranty, P17, was incorporated only into section B of the policy (Theft). General Condition 5, which applied to the whole policy, provided:

    2–28

---

[41] *Whitehead v. Price* (1835) 2 Cr. M. and R. 447; see also *Provincial Insurance Co. Ltd v. Morgan* [1933] A.C. 240 at 253–256, HL, where Lord Wright emphasised that a warranty must be strictly complied with, but the warranty must be strictly and reasonably construed.
[42] [1999] Lloyd's Rep. I.R. 542, CA.

> "Any Warranty shall, from the time it is applied, continue to be in force during the whole currency of this Policy. Failure to comply with any Warranty shall invalidate any claim for loss, destruction, damage or liability which is wholly or partly due to or affected by such failure to comply."

2–29   The defendant insurers argued that as the insurance contract was a single contract and there had been an admitted breach of warranty P17, it automatically followed that they were discharged from all liability under the contract of insurance. They relied on the common law rule enshrined in section 33(3) of the Marine Insurance Act 1906. As a fall-back argument, the insurers contended that General Condition 5, above, provided a defence by invalidating any claim brought about by the failure to comply with warranty P17. The Court of Appeal rejected both arguments, observing that the insurers' second argument really amounted to General Condition 5 disapplying the normal consequence of breach of a warranty. As regards the insurers' main argument, the Court of Appeal held that the mere fact that the policy was a single contract did not mean that "it is to be treated as a seamless contractual instrument".[43] On the contrary, the court held that the whole structure of this commercial combined policy was based on its division into sections, and explicitly wrote warranty P17 into section B, and not section A. Accordingly, P17 would only be operative in relation to a claim under section B, which happened to also expressly exclude loss or damage caused by fire or explosion, and the present claim under section A must be paid by the insurers.

Composite insurance policies

2–30   Where there is a composite, rather than a joint, insurance of various insureds' separate interests, as discussed in Chapter 17, below, a breach of warranty by one insured will not bar claims by, or affect the validity of the insurance for the other insureds. This is on the basis that such a composite insurance should be treated as a bundle of separate contracts.[44]

Express term dealing with a breach

2–31   As mentioned above, an express provision may show that the parties to the insurance contract have agreed that the normal consequence of breach of warranty, that of the insurers' discharge from further liability, will not apply. Such was held to be the case in the solicitors' professional indemnity insurance case of *Kumar v. AGF Insurance Ltd*,[45] where the insurance policy stated that the insurers would "not avoid repudiate or rescind this insurance upon any ground whatsoever including in particular non-disclosure or misrepresentation". Thomas J., in the special circumstances of the case regarding the background of solicitors' indemnity insurance, and the fact that the policy was issued at a time when the consequence of breach

---

[43] *ibid.* at 546, col.2, *per* Waller L.J.
[44] *New Hampshire Insurance Co. Ltd v. M.G.M. Ltd.* [1997] L.R.L.R. 24, CA, *Arab Bank plc v. Zurich Insurance Co. Ltd* [1999] 1 Lloyd's Rep. 262; *First National Commercial Bank plc v. Barnet Devanney (Harrow) Ltd* [1999] Lloyd's Rep. I.R. 43.
[45] [1999] 1 W.L.R. 1747.

of warranty was regarded as being the insurers' right to elect to avoid the policy, held that this provision had to be interpreted as extending to the insurers agreeing that a breach of warranty could not be relied on by them to deny liability.

3. CONDITIONS

Introduction

As a generalisation it can be said that whilst terms of the contract of insurance which relate directly to the risk insured, or to statements of facts, are often found to be warranties, other terms which relate to other matters, *e.g.* the procedure to be adopted when the insured suffers a loss and wishes to make a claim under the policy, are lesser terms, called "conditions". The use of the words "warranty" and "condition" in insurance law, it must be remembered, are directly opposite to their respective meanings in the general body of contract law, which can be confusing. It is now clear that, in accordance with normal contractual principles, an insurer does not have to show any prejudice to be entitled to rely on a breach of condition by the insured.[46]

2–32

Consequence of breach of a condition that is not a condition precedent to liability

Where a condition in a policy is construed as not being precedent to the commencement of the policy, the liability of the insurer, or recovery, the insurer's remedy on breach of the condition by the insured, is usually to counterclaim for damages for that breach upon the insured's action for recovery under the policy. Breach of such a condition does not entitle the insurer to repudiate the insurance contract upon the breach, but may be "so serious as to give a right to reject the claim".[47] This will be a factual test.[48] If the breach of the condition is causative of the loss, it may be that the insurer can deny liability on this ground.[49] Subject to an express reversal of the burden of proof in policy terms,[50] it is for the insurers who wish to rely on a breach of condition to prove it.[51]

2–33

Determination of whether a condition is a condition precedent

The mere fact that the policy recites that a particular condition is a condition precedent to the insurers' liability to the insured under the policy is not conclusive that the condition is, indeed, to be construed as a condition precedent when the policy is considered as a whole. In *London Guarantee*

2–34

[46] *Pioneer Concrete (U.K.) Ltd v. National Employers Mutual General Insurance Association Ltd* [1985] 2 All E.R. 395; *Kier Construction Ltd v. Royal Insurance (U.K.) Ltd* (1993) 30 Con. L.R. 45.

[47] *Alfred McAlpine plc v. B.A.I. (Run-off) Ltd* [2000] 1 Lloyd's Rep. 437, CA.

[48] *K/S Merc-Scandia XXXXII v. Ocean Marine Insurance Co. Ltd* [2000] Lloyd's Rep. I.R. 694.

[49] *W. and J. Lane v. Spratt* [1970] 2 Q.B. 480 at 493–495, *per* Roskill J. (as he then was).

[50] *Re Hooley Hill Rubber and Chemical Co. and Royal Insurance Co.* [1920] 1 K.B. 257 at 273, CA.

[51] *Bond Air Services Ltd v. Hill* [1955] 2 Q.B. 417 at 428, *per* Lord Goddard C.J., CA.

Co. v. Fearnley,[52] the House of Lords held that a term in a fidelity policy that the insured employer should, at the company's request, assist in suing the defaulting employee for reimbursement "of any money which the company shall have become liable to pay" under the policy, could not be construed as being a condition precedent to the insurer's liability despite it being expressed as such in the policy wording. The provision came into effect on a true construction only after liability of the insurer had been established.

2–35   Similarly, in *Re Bradley and Essex and Suffolk Accident Indemnity Society*,[53] an employers' liability policy contained a section headed "conditions" and there was also a general declaration that compliance with all conditions of the policy was a condition precedent to the society's liability under the policy. Condition 5 of the policy read:

> "The first premium and all renewal premiums that may be accepted are to be regulated by the amount of wages and salaries and other earnings paid to employees by the insured during each period of insurance. The name of every employee and the amount of wages, salary and other earnings paid to him shall be duly recorded in a proper book. The insured shall at all times allow the society to inspect such books, and shall supply the society with a correct account of all such wages, salaries, and other earnings paid during any period of insurance within one month from the expiry of such period of insurance, and, if the total amount so paid shall differ from the amount on which premium has been paid, the difference in premium shall be met by a further proportionate payment to the society or by a refund by the society, as the case may be."

2–36   The insured only employed one person, his son, and paid him a fixed sum each year, but kept no wages book as required by Condition 5. When the insured made a claim under the policy, the society claimed this breach of a condition precedent to their liability relieved them of any liability. The Court of Appeal, by a majority, though, construed the purpose of Condition 5 as being solely to provide for the adjustment of premiums and held that, as such, it was not, on its true construction, a condition, compliance with which was precedent to the society's liability. Accordingly, the insured was entitled to recover.

2–37   Certainly, where a stipulation in a policy is not even expressed as being a condition precedent, the court is unlikely to construe it as anything other than a mere condition. This happened in *Stoneham v. Ocean Railway. and General Accident Insurance Co.*[54] where a policy provided that "notice must be given to the company within seven days" of an insured event. Notice was not given within that time, but the court held the insured entitled to recover, breach of this mere condition only giving the insurance company a right in respect of any extra expense that might be incurred in investigating the claim upon late notification.

---

[52] (1880) 5 App. Cas. 911, HL.
[53] [1912] 1 K.B. 415, CA.
[54] (1887) 19 Q.B.D. 237.

Similarly, in *W. and J. Lane v. Spratt*,[55] Clause 9 of a carriers' insurance   **2–38**
provided:

> "The Insured shall take all reasonable precautions for the protection and
> safeguarding of the goods and/or merchandise and use such protective
> devices as may be specified in the Policy. . ."

Roskill J. (as he then was) held that this clause did not amount to a condition of the contract for breach of which the insurer would be entitled to
repudiate the policy, but pointed out that where the proximate cause of the
relevant loss was a breach of that clause, the insurer would then be able to
argue that he was not liable for the loss.[56]

Notice to the insured of conditions precedent to liability or express warranties

Whilst it is generally the case that the proposal states that the proposer   **2–39**
will accept insurance in the insurers' usual form for that risk, the question
of whether the insured is given due notice of conditions that may deprive
him of a recovery under the insurance arises. For instance, the insured may
not receive a copy of a policy until after an insured loss has occurred and
the insurers defend the claim relying on the breach by the insured of a
warranty, or condition precedent, of which the insured was completely
unaware at the time of breach.

This problem was recognised ninety years ago by Farwell L.J. *obiter* in   **2–40**
Re Bradley and Essex and Suffolk Indemnity Society[57] when he said:

> "Contracts of insurance are contracts in which *uberrima fides* is required,
> not only from the assured, but also from the company assuring. It is the
> universal practice for the companies to prepare both the form of proposal
> and the form of policy: both are issued by them on printed forms kept ready
> for use; it is their duty to make the policy accord with and not exceed the
> proposal, and to express both in clear and unambiguous terms, lest (as
> Fletcher Moulton L.J., in quoting Lord St. Leonards, says in *Joel v. Law
> Union and Crown Insurance Co.*[58]) provisions should be introduced into policies
> which:
>
>> 'unless they are fully explained to the parties, will lead a vast number of
>> persons to suppose that they have made provision for their families by an
>> insurance on their lives, and by a payment of perhaps a very considerable
>> portion of their income, when in point of fact, from the very commence-
>> ment, the policy is not worth the paper upon which it is written.'
>
> It is especially incumbent on insurance companies to make clear, both in
> their proposal forms and in their policies, the conditions which are prece-
> dent to their liability to pay, for such conditions have the same effect as
> forfeiture clauses, and may inflict loss and injury to the assured and those
> claiming under him out of all proportion to any damage that could possibly
> accrue to the company from non-observance or non-performance of the
> conditions. . .

[55] [1970] 2 Q.B. 480.
[56] *ibid.* at 493–495.
[57] [1912] 1 K.B. 415 at 430.
[58] [1908] 1 K.B. 863 at 886.

They receive a printed form of proposal, and it is reasonable to assume that they read and rely on it, and they receive in exchange for the form so supplied to and required from them a policy which they are entitled to assume and do assume, in most cases without careful perusal of the document, to accord with the proposal form. It is, in my opinion, incumbent on the company to put clearly on the proposal form the acts which the assured is by the policy to covenant to perform and to make it clear in the policy the conditions, non-performance of which will entail the loss of all benefits of the insurance. It is contended that it is of the utmost importance to insurance companies that they should be able to defend themselves against frauds by inserting conditions precedent, such as keeping wages books, and the like. Be it so; there is no objection whatever to the insertion of such conditions, so long as the intending assurer [sic] has full and fair notice of them and consents to them. This can easily be done by stating them shortly in the proposal forms with the addition that payment may be refused if they or any of them are not complied with; but it is, in my opinion, scarcely honest to induce a man to propose on certain terms, and then to accept the proposal and send a policy as in accordance with it when such policy contains numerous provisions not mentioned in the proposal, which operate to defeat any claim under the policy, and all the more so when such provisions are couched in obscure terms."

2–41   It is submitted that these very valid remarks have not been fully heeded in the ensuing period. Whilst it is the case that proposal forms invariably now state that a copy of the standard policy for that type of insurance can be sought from the insurer, neither insurance companies, nor Lloyd's underwriters, generally go so far as to give an explanation of the conditions precedent, or continuing warranties, which will lead to the insured losing the benefit of the insurance cover upon breach. The only warning in this regard will be in relation to the non-disclosure of material facts, and the only amelioration of the need for correctness of proposal form answers where those answers are made the basis of the contract, is that they are true and correct to the proposer's "knowledge and belief". Agreement to the terms of the insurer's usual form of policy for the risk proposed, by the insured submitting a completed proposal stating expressly that he will accept such a policy, will form a contract of insurance on those terms of the standard policy for the agreed period and at the agreed premium.[59] That does not resolve, however, the question of whether the insurer is entitled to rely on all the terms of the policy in defence of a claim by the insured, where the insured has had no opportunity to examine the issued form of policy.

2–42   The general law of contract has been the subject of recent development in this general area of the right of a party who has issued a standard form contract to rely on onerous or unusual conditions contained within that document. Most recently, in *Lacey's Footwear (Wholesale) Ltd. v. Bowler International Freight Ltd*,[60] a case concerning carrier's standard terms of trading with its customers, in a minority judgment which held that the defendant carrier could not rely on the incorporated term, Brooke L.J.

---

[59] *Adie and Sons v. Insurances Corp.* (1898) 14 T.L.R. 544.
[60] [1997] 2 Lloyd's Rep. 369, CA.

referred to the Court's earlier decision in *Interfoto Picture Library Ltd v. Stiletto Visual Programmes Ltd.*[61] In that case it was held that where clauses incorporated into a contract contained a particularly onerous or unusual condition, the party seeking to enforce that condition had to show that it had been brought fairly and reasonably to the attention of the other party. Brooke L.J. pointed out that two members of the Court had there differed on the precise effect of inadequate notice. Dillon L.J. had held that the onerous condition never became a part of the contract at all, whilst Bingham L.J. (as he then was) had held that the defendant, against whom the claimant was seeking to enforce the onerous condition, was relieved from liability under it. Brooke L.J. went on to approve the three-fold test relied on by Bingham L.J. in the *Interfoto* case,[62] namely:

   (i) to look at the nature of the transaction in question and the character of the parties to it;
   (ii) to consider what notice the party alleged to be bound was given of the particular condition said to bind him;
   (iii) to resolve whether in all the circumstances it is fair to hold him bound by the condition in question.

It is submitted that an insured may well be able to rely on this line of **2–43** authority to overcome an insurer's reliance on a breach of a condition precedent, or a promissory warranty, in circumstances where the insured loss is sustained prior to the insured's receipt of the policy document, and there was no prior notification of that condition precedent, or promissory warranty. Such prior notification might be in either the proposal form, or any related information provided by the insurer about the available cover. An express condition stating that the insured forfeits all benefit under the policy if he makes a fraudulent claim has been held in *Nsubuga v. Commercial Union Assurance Co. plc*[63] to be a common provision in fire policies for over 100 years and, therefore, did not need to be specifically brought to the insured's attention in order to be validly incorporated in the issued policy of insurance. Thomas J. also regarded the proposal form declaration, which expressly stated that the proposer "agrees to accept insurance subject to the terms and conditions of the Company's Policy", as sufficient to incorporate the policy's terms and conditions.[64] This may, however, be an area of insurance law ripe for future development.

There is also the situation where special terms have been added, **2–44** unknown to the proposed insured, to the standard form of policy by the insurer. Correctly analysed, this is a counter-offer by the insurer, and the

---

[61] [1989] 1 Q.B. 433, CA.
[62] *ibid.* at 445B.
[63] [1998] 2 Lloyd's Rep. 682.
[64] *ibid.* at 685.

contract of insurance will therefore not be complete until the proposer has by words or conduct accepted that counter-offer.[65]

Condition precedent to commencement of insurance

2–45   Insurers sometimes insert clauses to the effect that the insurance will not commence until the premium has been received, and such provisions have been held to be conditions precedent to the commencement of the policy or the attaching of the risk, *e.g.* "No assurance can take place until the first premium is paid"[66]; "The risk of the company will not commence until receipt of the first premium"[67]; "No insurance shall be held to be effected until the premium due thereon shall have been paid."[68] It is, however, a matter of law for the court to decide in any particular case[69] whether a policy issued subject to such a condition precedent is a fully concluded contract of insurance, so that the insurer is bound to accept the premium once it is paid, or only constitutes a counter-offer which may be accepted by the proposer for insurance by his paying the premium and thereby concluding the contract.

Condition precedent regarding notification of claims

2–46   Conditions relating to a notification of claims are commonly stated in the policy to be conditions precedent to the liability of the insurer, as are conditions regarding assistance to the insurer and non-admission of liability to a third party claimant. These conditions relating to notification of claims are more particularly considered, below, in Chapter 18.

Condition precedent regarding burglar alarms

2–47   In insurances of stock-in-trade where burglary risk is covered, it is generally provided in the policy that a fully-maintained burglar alarm installed at the relevant premises which is put into operation whenever those premises are unattended, shall be a condition precedent to the liability of the insurer. The insurer may properly defend a claim and thereby escape liability if the insured breaches such a condition precedent.[70]

2–48   The wording is unlikely to be construed, though, as requiring the insured to do more than that which it is in his own power to do to maintain the alarm in efficient working order, *e.g.* there is no breach of the condition if the telephone line to the police station is not working through no fault of the insured and he cannot interfere with the telephone line which is not his property.[71] This type of condition precedent, or warranty, is considered more fully in Chapter 12, below.

---

[65] *Allis-Chalmers Co. v. Maryland Fidelity and Deposit Co.* (1916) 114 L.T. 433 at 434, *per* Lord Loreburn L.C., HL.

[66] *Canning v. Farquhar* (1886) 16 Q.B.D. 727, CA; *Harrington v. Pearl Life Assurance Co. Ltd* (1914) 30 T.L.R. 613, CA.

[67] *Looker v. Law Union and Rock Insurance Co. Ltd* [1928] 1 K.B. 554.

[68] *Sickness and Accident Assurance Association v. General Accident Assurance Corp.* (1892) 19 R. 977, Ct of Sess.

[69] *Tarleton v. Staniforth* (1796) 1 Bos. and P. 471, Ex. Ch.

[70] *Roberts v. Eagle Star Insurance Co. Ltd* [1960] 1 Lloyd's Rep. 615.

[71] *Victor Melik and Co. Ltd v. Norwich Union Fire Insurance Society Ltd and Kemp* [1980] 1 Lloyd's Rep. 523.

Condition precedent regarding reasonable precautions against loss

It is often the case that insurers will provide for the insured's exercise **2–49** of reasonable precautions to be a condition precedent to their liability.[72] For instance, in relation to carriers' insurance, the failure to lock all locks on a vehicle when it is unattended will probably show a failure to take all reasonable precautions against loss.[73] Such a condition precedent does not, however, require the insured to take every practicable precaution, and the court has to look at all the circumstances in any given case in order to determine whether a precaution is a reasonable precaution. The test is whether the insured courted danger, in effect acted recklessly,[74] in other words, whether the insured had actual recognition that a danger existed, but did not care whether or not it is averted.[75] That test applies whether the condition is within a property insurance[76] or a liability insurance.[77] The condition means reasonable as between the insured and the insurer having regard to the commercial purpose of the contract of insurance.[78] Thus, under a contents insurance, even though it is known that a burglar alarm link to a control centre is not working, but the alarm is otherwise functioning, it is not reasonable to expect the insured to keep the premises attended all night, every night.[79] In the case of a corporate insured, its authorised agents and employees will be responsible for the insured's compliance with this contractual duty owed to the insured.[80]

Condition precedent regarding notification of dishonest employees

If there is a condition precedent to liability in a fidelity policy to the **2–50** effect that the insured employer must notify the insurer of the discovery of dishonest conduct of an employee which is covered by that insurance, that condition will not be breached if the insured has unsubstantiated suspicions of such misconduct rather than actual proof.[81] The particular wording must be carefully scrutinised, however, in every instance.

---

[72] *J. Lowenstein and Co. Ltd v. Poplar Motor Transport (Lymm) Ltd* [1968] 2 Lloyd's Rep. 233; *Ingleton of Ilford Ltd v. General Accident Fire and Life Assurance Corp. Ltd* [1967] 2 Lloyd's Rep. 179.

[73] *Princette Models Ltd v. Reliance Fire and Accident Insurance Corp. Ltd* [1960] 1 Lloyd's Rep. 49 at 55, *per* Pearson J.

[74] *Sofi v. Prudential Assurance Co. Ltd.* [1993] 2 Lloyd's Rep. 559 at 565–566, *per* Lloyd L.J. (as he then was), CA.

[75] *Victor Melik and Co. Ltd v. Norwich Union Fire Insurance Society Ltd and Kemp* [1980] 1 Lloyd's Rep. 523 at 531, *per* Woolf J. (as he then was).

[76] *Lambert v. Keymood Ltd* [1999] Lloyd's Rep. I.R. 80.

[77] *Sofi v. Prudential Assurance Co. Ltd* [1993] 2 Lloyd's Rep. 559 at 566, *per* Lloyd L.J. (as he then was), CA.

[78] *Fraser v. B.N. Furman (Productions) Ltd* [1967] 1 W.L.R. 898 at 906, CA.

[79] *ibid.*

[80] As conceded in *Devco Holder Ltd v. Legal and General Assurance Society Ltd.* [1993] 2 Lloyd's Rep. 567, CA.

[81] *Ward v. Law Property Assurance and Trust Society* (1856) 27 L.T.(o.s.) 155, this case is discussed in Chapter 14, below; *Byrne v. Muzio* (1881) 8 L.R. Ir. 396.

4. CLAUSES DELIMITING THE RISK

Introduction

2–51   There is a further category into which a particular provision may properly be regarded as falling. This is a clause that, in its proper construction, is to be regarded as neither a warranty nor condition, but a clause delimiting the insured risk in a particular area. This means that the insurance is to be regarded as effective and valid when the provisions of the clause are being complied with, but that if they are not, the insurance is to be treated as not attaching at that point in time and the insurers are not liable for losses arising at times of non-compliance. Such clauses have also been described as being descriptive of the risk. The importance of this distinction from a warranty is that the policy will not automatically come to an end upon breach of the provision, and the insurance continues to run until its expiry, but will only cover future losses whilst the policy requirement is being met.

Examples of clauses defining or delimiting the risk

2–52   Such clauses have been found to be present in motor policies. In *Farr v. Motor Traders Mutual Insurance Society Ltd,*[82] the insured owned two taxi-cabs and insured them against damage caused by accidental external means. In answer to a question in the proposal form, the insured stated that each cab was to be driven in one shift per 24 hours. At the foot of the proposal form the insured stated that the above statement was true, and the policy itself provided that the statements in the proposal were to be the basis of the contract and to be considered as incorporated therein. Due to repairs to one cab, for a short time the other cab was used for two shifts each day, but then the routine reverted to one shift for each cab. A few months later, the cab that had earlier been used twice a day during the repair of the other, sustained damage. The insurers denied liability under the policy on the ground that the policy had become void upon the insured's breach of warranty when he used one cab for two shifts a day. The Court of Appeal refused to construe the proposal question and answer as a warranty, determining that they amounted to a description of the risk insured, *i.e.* if in any one day of 24 hours the cab was driven in more than one shift, the risk was no longer covered.

2–53   An attempt by insurers to overcome that decision by introducing an express term seeking to introduce a promissory warranty failed in *Roberts v. Anglo-Saxon Insurance Association.*[83] A motor policy incorporated a proposal to be used for commercial motor vehicles or trade vehicles, the material parts of which were as follows:

> "State clearly the purposes for which the vehicles are to be used.   (Answer) Commercial.
>
> State nature of goods to be carried.   (Answer) Textile goods.

[82] [1920] 3 K.B. 299, CA.
[83] (1927) 96 L.J.K.B. 590, CA; see also *Provincial Insurance Co. Ltd v. Morgan* [1933] A.C. 240, HL.

I warrant the above statement and particulars are true, and I agree that this declaration shall be held to be promissory and shall form the basis of the contract between me and the Anglo-Saxon Insurance Association Limited . . ."

The policy contained, in the schedule, particulars of the motor car **2–54** which was insured, followed by the words in print: "warranted used only for the following purposes", then, written in, were the following words: "commercial travelling". In the event, the insured car was destroyed by fire whilst it was being used to carry passengers. The Court of Appeal held that this was not a warranty, despite the words used, but as defining or delimiting the risk covered by the insurance. It made no practical difference to the insured, however, in that he could not recover an indemnity for the loss of the car, because he was not complying with the risk as defined by the description of commercial travelling, but the policy was not avoided.

Scrutton L.J. considered that it amounted to a promissory declaration **2–55** as to the risk by the insurer that he would insure the insured in certain circumstances, but only in certain circumstances. He pointed to it being the same as the well-known warranty or promise in marine insurance "warranted no St Lawrence between October 1 and the March 31," which means that if the ship goes into the St Lawrence and is lost between those dates, the insured cannot recover under the policy because it is not the risk that the insurer has undertaken. It was also similar to clauses in life policies at that time that if the insured died outside the United Kingdom, or within dangerous latitudes or longitudes in certain dangerous countries, he was not insured, because that was not the risk the insurer had undertaken.[84]

Clauses of this type are also to be found in carriers' insurance. For **2–56** instance, in *A. Cohen and Co. Ltd v. Plaistow Transport Ltd (Graham. Third Party)*[85] there was a provision in a goods in transit policy that stated "warranted vehicles garaged in locked garage at night, except when employed on night journeys, but then never left unattended". MacKenna J. stated, *obiter*, that his "strong inclination" would have been to accept the insured's argument that this was not a true warranty, but rather that the words merely defined the risk, *i.e.* that it was a delimiting or descriptive provision. Similarly, in *de Maurier (Jewels) Ltd v. Bastion Insurance Co. Ltd and Coronet Insurance Co. Ltd*,[86] there was a provision in a jewellers' all risks policy that "warranted" that all the insured's road vehicles would be fitted with locks and alarm systems approved by the underwriters. Donaldson J. (as he then was) regarded a loss occurring before approved locks had been fitted to the relevant vehicle as not being covered by the insurance, on the ground that the risk had not attached until the correct locks had been fitted.

More recently, the significance of a breach of this type of provision not **2–57** being the automatic ending of the whole policy was highlighted in *C.T.N.*

[84] *ibid.* at 593.
[85] [1968] 2 Lloyd's Rep. 587 at 592.
[86] [1967] 2 Lloyd's Rep. 550.

Cash and Carry Ltd v. General Accident Fire and Life Assurance Corp. Ltd.[87] The insured had covered its two cash and carry premises by a composite liability and material damage policy with the defendant insurers. The cover was set out in 12 sections embracing such risks as compulsory employers' liability insurance and public liability insurance. Cover number 5 referred to burglary insurance and number 12 referred to money insurance. Both these sections were subject to this provision:

> "It is warranted that the secure cash kiosk shall be attended and locked at all times during business hours".

2–58   During the opening hours of the Burnley premises, just before closing, the kiosk attendant left the secure kiosk and a robbery occurred. The insurers denied liability because the secure kiosk was not attended in accordance with the provision. The insured argued that as this was a warranty the insurers should have repudiated the whole policy, and this they had failed to do and were therefore bound by the policy to indemnify the insured. This contention was rejected by Macpherson J., who held that notwithstanding the use of the word "warranty" attaching to this clause, it was really a risk delimiting clause dealing with the special circumstances discussed by both parties beforehand as to manning of the kiosk. If it had been held otherwise, the insured business would have been totally uninsured for both locations and under all covers, from the time that the kiosk was unattended on the day of the robbery.

5. "BASIS OF THE CONTRACT" CLAUSE

2–59   A third category of term relevant to this discussion of conditions and warranties, is the "basis of the contract" clause that can appear in a variety of forms, either only in the proposal form, or in the policy (usually in a recital wording), or in both of these documents. Alternatively, other wordings amounting to the same legal effect may be found, *e.g.* a declaration that if any statement in the proposal is untrue, the policy shall be null and void. The essential characteristic is that the courts will give the insurer the full benefit of any provision that is construed as rendering the accuracy or truth of statements made, in or about the obtaining of the insurance, as the fundamental basis of the contract of insurance. It will be seen that various avenues have been followed by the courts to achieve this result that can often produce what may be considered by many to be a harsh ruling against an insured seeking to enforce a policy.

2–60   The first reported case concerning a "basis of the contract" wording, *Duckett v. Williams*[88] was a reinsurance case. The primary insurer, having reinsured part of his risk on a life policy granted to John Stephenson with the defendant reinsurer, had paid out under that policy and sought to recover under the reinsurance. The defendant reinsurer relied on a "basis"

---

[87] [1989] 1 Lloyd's Rep. 299.
[88] (1834) 2 Cr. and M. 348.

clause in the plaintiff insurer's proposal for reinsurance, and claimed the policy was null and void because of untrue statements contained therein. There had been no incorporation of this proposal form into the contract of reinsurance, and the court gave effect to its provisions apparently on the ground that the proposal form declaration formed a collateral agreement providing for the avoidance of the separate contract of insurance. The language of the proposal declaration is beautifully archaic and is therefore quoted in full:

> "We, Scrope Bernard Morland and George Duckett, trustees of the Provident Life Office, do hereby declare and set forth, that the herein-named John Stephenson is now in good health, and has not laboured under gout, dropsy, fits, palsy, insanity, affection of the lungs or other viscera, or any other disease which tends to shorten life, and that his age does not exceed forty-one years; that we have an interest in the life of the said John Stephenson to the full amount of £5000; and we agree that the declaration or statement hereby made shall be the basis of the agreement between ourselves and the [reinsurer]; and that if any untrue averment be contained herein, or if the facts required to be set forth in the above proposal be not truly stated . . . the assurance itself [shall] be absolutely null and void."

In giving judgment for the reinsurer, Lord Lyndhurst C.B. also dealt with the question of whether the truth of statements was to be construed as meaning true within the knowledge of the proposer, or absolutely true, and preferred the latter construction[89]:   **2–61**

> "We have come to the conclusion, that, at the time when the policy was effected, Mr. Stephenson had upon him a disease which tended to shorten life. It follows, that the facts set forth in the proposal were not truly stated, and the question then turns entirely on the construction of the declaration and agreement. It was contended, on behalf of the plaintiffs, that the words must mean 'truly' or 'untruly', within the knowledge of the party making the statement; and that if the party insuring ignorantly and innocently makes a misstatement he is not to forfeit the premiums under the clause in question. We are of opinion, however, that this is not the real meaning of the clause. A statement is not the less untrue because the party making it is not apprised of its untruth; and looking at the context, we think it clear that the parties did not mean to restrict the words in the manner contended for. Two consequences are to follow if the statement be untrue . . . the other, that the assurance is to be void."

In the subsequent case of *Anderson v. Fitzgerald*,[90] which again concerned a life insurance, the House of Lords considered the effect of the policy recital which provided: **2–62**

> "if . . . any false statements are made to [the insurer] in or about the obtaining or effecting of this insurance, this policy shall be null and void."

Incorrect answers had been given by the insured to two questions on his medical history in the proposal form and the insurers argued that the

---

[89] *ibid.* at 350–351; followed *Thomson v. Weems* (1884) 9 App. Cas. 671 at 682 *per* Lord Blackburn, HL.
[90] (1853) 4 H.L. Cas. 484, HL.

policy was therefore null and void under this provision. The House of
Lords accepted that submission, holding that the parties, in effect, agreed
to make non-material facts material for the purposes of that policy. Lord
Cranworth L.C. delivered the leading judgment[91]:

> "Whether certain statements are or are not material, where parties are enter-
> ing in a contract of . . . assurance, is a matter upon which there must be a
> divided opinion. Nothing, therefore, can be more reasonable than that the
> parties entering into that contract should determine for themselves what
> they think to be material, and if they choose to do so, and to stipulate that
> unless the assured shall answer a certain question accurately, the policy or
> contract which they are entering into shall be void, it is perfectly open to
> them to do so, and his false answer will then avoid the policy.
>
> Now it appears to me, my Lords, that this is precisely what has been done
> here . . . The question . . . to decide was simply whether it was false or not.
> In that narrow compass the whole case lies."

2–63   Lord Cranworth L.C. also expressly differentiated this type of contractual provision from the principle relating to breach of an insurance
warranty,[92] but this decision was distinguished in *Thomson v. Weems,*[93]
where the House of Lords found that a proposal form declaration,
together with the policy recital that that declaration was the "basis" of the
contract, operated as an express warranty that the proposal answers were
true. The declaration signed by the insured read:

> "the foregoing statements . . . and other particulars are true . . . And I . . . do
> hereby agree that this declaration shall be the basis of the contract . . . and
> that if any untrue averment has been made . . . the assurance [shall] be
> absolutely null and void."

The policy recited that:

> "[The Insured] having subscribed or caused to be subscribed and deposited
> at the office of the said Company . . . a declaration . . . which is hereby
> declared to be basis of this contract . . . Provided also, that if anything
> referred to shall be untrue, this policy shall be void."

2–64   Whilst holding that the parties made the accuracy of the statements and
other particulars material facts, the House considered that their truth
therefore became warranted. *Per* Lord Blackburn[94]:

> "It is competent to the contracting parties, if both agree to it and sufficiently
> express their intention so to agree, to make the actual existence of anything
> a condition precedent to the inception of any contract; and if they do so the
> non-existence of that thing is a good defence. And it is not of any impor-
> tance whether the existence of that thing was or was not material; the parties
> would not have made it part of the contract if they had not thought it material

---

[91] *ibid.* at 503; Lords Brougham and St Leonards concurring at 505 and 507.
[92] *ibid.* at 504.
[93] (1884) 9 App. Cas. 671, HL.
[94] *ibid.* at 683, and *per* Lord Watson at 687.

and they have a right to determine for themselves what they shall deem material. . .

I think when we look at the terms of this contract, and see that it is expressly said in the policy, as well as in the declaration itself, that the declaration shall be the basis of the contract, that it is hardly possible to avoid the conclusion that the truth of the particulars . . . is warranted."

In *Yorkshire Insurance Co. Ltd v. Campbell*,[95] another variation in form **2–65** was found. Here, the insured did "warrant and declare the truth" of the statements in the proposal and agreed that that declaration was to be "the basis of the contract", and this proposal was incorporated in the policy by its recital. There was no express provision as to the effect of an untrue statement as in the previous cases, and the Privy Council had to determine, therefore, the legal consequence of an untrue statement. It was held that the insured had warranted the truth of the statement, and breach of that warranty accordingly entitled the insurers to avoid the policy:

"effect must be given to the words in question by holding that the assured warranted their truth, in accordance with the intention expressed in the form of words employed, and, as the words turn out to be unfounded, in fact, the policy is avoided."[96]

An even briefer policy recital wording was considered in *Dawsons Ltd v.* **2–66** *Bonnin*[97] where there was no declaration in the proposal form, the policy merely reciting:

". . .which proposal shall be the basis of this contract and be held as incorporated herein."

An untrue answer having been made in the proposal, the insurer argued that the policy was void under this "basis" provision, and the House of Lords, by a bare majority of three to two, upheld this contention. The reasoning of the majority was not, however, consistent. Viscount Haldane construed the provision as rendering the accuracy of the answers in the proposal form a warranty (although using the description "condition") exact fulfilment of which became by the stipulation foundational to the policy's enforceability.[98] On the other hand, Viscount Cave and Lord Dunedin considered the "basis" clause as something separate from a warranty, but a provision which nevertheless resulted in the policy becoming void *ab initio* upon breach. Viscount Cave explained his conclusion thus[99]:

"I cannot think that [the wording] amounts to nothing more than a statement that the proposal initiated the transaction and led to the grant of the policy. That fact sufficiently appears from the recital in the proposal; and the addition of an express stipulation that the proposal shall be treated as incorporated in the policy and shall be the basis of the contract, is plainly

---

[95] [1917] A.C. 218, PC.
[96] *ibid.* at 225–226, *per* Lord Sumner.
[97] [1922] 2 A.C. 413, HL.
[98] *ibid.* at 423–425.
[99] *ibid.* at 432–433.

intended to have some further effect. 'Basis' is defined in the Imperial
Dictionary as 'the foundation of a thing; that on which a thing stands or
lies'; and similar definitions are to be found elsewhere. The basis of a thing
is that upon which it stands, and on the failure of which it falls; and when a
document consisting partly of statements of fact and partly of undertakings
for the future is made the basis of a contract of insurance, this must (I think)
mean that the document is to be the very foundation of the contract, so that
if the statements of fact are untrue or the promissory statements are not
carried out, the risk does not attach. No doubt the stipulation is more concise in form than those contained in the policies which fell to be construed
in *Anderson v. Fitzgerald* [1] and *Thomson v. Weems*[2], in each of which cases
the policy contained an express provision to the effect that if anything stated
in the proposal was untrue, the policy should be void; but I think that the
effect is the same as if those words had been found in the present policy. . .
    Upon the whole, it appears to me, both on principle and on authority that
the meaning and effect of the 'basis' clause, taken by itself, is that any untrue
statement in the proposal, or any breach of its promissory clauses, shall
avoid the policy."

Lord Dunedin said[3]:

"I think that 'basis' cannot be taken as merely pleonastic and exegetical of
the following words 'and incorporated therewith'. It must mean that the
parties held that these statements are fundamental — *i.e.* go to the root of
the contract — and that consequently if the statements are untrue the
contract is not binding. And therefore I come to the same conclusion . . . for
essentially the same reasons."

2–67   The truth of the answers given was expressly warranted in a proposal
form by a declaration, and the whole proposal form was incorporated into
the issued policy, which included a recital that the proposal was "the basis
of the contract", in *Paxman v. Union Assurance Society Ltd*[4] McCardie J.
found no difficulty in holding that the insurer could avoid the policy
because certain untrue answers had been given by the insured.

2–68   In *Provincial Insurance Co. Ltd v. Morgan*[5] another variation in form was
considered by the House of Lords. Here, both a declaration in the proposal
and a recital in the policy stated that the proposal would be the "basis of the
contract". The policy further stated, however, that the giving of true
answers in the proposal form was a condition precedent to the liability of
the insurer, rather than that the untruth of answers would give rise to the
policy being avoided. The case concerned a motor policy issued after the
insured had answered the following questions in the proposal form:

"**Q:** State   (a) the purpose in full for which the vehicle will be used; and

A: . . . Delivery of coal.

            (b) the nature of the goods to be carried

A: . . . Coal."

[1] (1853) 4 H.L. Cas. 484, HL.
[2] (1884) 9 App. Cas. 671, HL.
[3] *Dawsons Ltd v. Bonnin* [1922] 2 A.C. 413 at 435, HL.
[4] (1923) 39 T.L.R. 424.
[5] [1933] A.C. 240, HL.

Just before the relevant accident which formed the basis of the claim   **2–69**
under the policy, the insured's employees had been carrying timber as well
as coal on the lorry and the insurers therefore contended that by so doing
the answer became untrue, and accordingly, they were not liable in respect
of the claim.

The House of Lords held that the insured could recover on the ground
that, on the true construction of the question and answer, it was not the
intention of either party to exact or to give a warranty that the lorry
should never be used for any purpose other than the carriage of coal.
Rather, the questions and answers were intended to ascertain the intentions of the insured with regard to the use of the lorry and the goods to be
carried therein. On this construction, the answers were true, correct and
complete.

This case, therefore, turned entirely on the construction of the particu-   **2–70**
lar wording adopted by the parties to the contract of insurance and the
proposal which was incorporated into the policy. From the speeches, however, it is unclear whether this provision, if it had applied on the facts of
the case, would have applied because of breach of a "basis of the contract" clause[6] itself, or breach of a continuing warranty relating to the user
of the lorry, or breach of a condition precedent to liability of the insurer
regarding the truth of the answers given.[7]

In *Mackay v. London General Insurance Co. Ltd,*[8] answers in the pro-   **2–71**
posal were recited in the policy to be the "basis of the contract". Two
answers were inaccurate, and Swift J. came to a finding in favour of the
insurers on a different ground. This fourth avenue of the defeat of an
insured who provides inaccurate answers to questions in the proposal form
was that the inaccuracy gives the insurers a common law right to "repudiate their liability under [the] policy".[9]

In conclusion, it can only be said that an insured must approach the
answering of proposal questions which are to be "the basis of the contract", or are expressed to be "warranted" as true and correct, with
extreme care.

6. ONUS OF PROOF OF BREACH

The burden or onus of proof regarding an alleged breach of a term of the   **2–72**
contract, whether it be a condition or warranty,[10] or a "basis" clause,[11] lies
upon the insurer in the absence of contrary agreement. In *Stebbing v.
Liverpool and London and Globe Insurance Co. Ltd,* Viscount Reading
C.J.,[12] in giving judgment upon whether the burden lay on the insurer to

---

[6] [1933] A.C. 240 at 246, *per* Lord Buckmaster.
[7] *ibid.* at 249, *per* Lord Russell.
[8] (1935) 51 Ll. L. Rep. 201.
[9] *ibid.* at 202.
[10] *Barrett v. Jermy* (1849) 3 Exch. 535.
[11] *Thomson v. Weems* (1884) 9 App. Cas. 671 at 684 *per* Lord Blackburn, HL.
[12] [1917] 2 K.B. 433 at 437, DC.

prove a breach of a declaration regarding the truth of answers in a proposal for burglary insurance, said:

> "The proposal form contains a question, 'Have you ever proposed for
> burglary insurance?' The claimant has answered 'No' and his answer is
> challenged by the company. He has been asked about another policy signed
> by him, and he has given an explanation. The arbitrator is in doubt whether
> the answer to the question is true, and he asks the Court on whom is the
> burden of proof; whether on the claimant to prove that the answer is true or
> on the company to prove that it is false. The burden of proof, in the first
> instance at all events, lies on that party against whom judgment should be
> given if no evidence were adduced upon the issue. Assuming in this case that
> a loss was established and the policy put in evidence, then the claimant
> would be entitled to recover. If he is met by the company with the objection
> that his answer to a question is not true, they must establish that the answer
> is not true. If they fail to establish that, their objection fails. That is to say,
> the burden lies on the company to prove that the claimant's answer is
> untrue."

2–73   This principle has been followed on numerous occasions,[13] the *Stebbing*
decision in particular being referred to and followed in *Bond Air Services
Ltd v. Hill.*[14] This case concerned an alleged breach of a condition precedent to the insurer's liability, and Lord Goddard C.J. stated[15]:

> "I cannot find . . . doubt on what I think is axiomatic in insurance law, that,
> as it is always for an insurer to prove an exception, so it is for him to prove
> the breach of a condition which would relieve him from liability in respect
> of a particular loss. The [insurer's] contention, no doubt, is that, by provid-
> ing that the observance of conditions is to be a condition precedent to his
> liability to pay, the policy has shifted the onus on to the claimants. It is
> enough to say that in this court *Stebbing v. Liverpool and London and Globe
> Insurance Co. Ltd.*[16] concludes the matter . . . The learned arbitrator in the
> present case has held that the effect of the provision as to the observance of
> the claimants' undertakings is to give to them the quality of warranties, so
> that a breach would absolve the [insurer] of liability for a loss occurring
> when the claimants were in breach but has held that the onus of proof is not
> affected; and I agree with him."

Express shifting of burden to the insured required

2–74   Whilst the parties to a policy can use words which place the onus of
proof onto the insured to prove that he has not breached a condition or
warranty, Lord Goddard C.J. continued his judgment in *Stebbing*, above,
by emphasising that very clear words will be necessary to change this
fundamental principle of insurance law.

---

[13] See, *e.g. Bonney v. Cornhill Insurance Co. Ltd* (1931) 40 Ll. L. Rep. 39; *W. and J. Lane v.
Spratt* [1970] 2 Q.B. 480.
[14] [1955] 2 Q.B. 417.
[15] *ibid.* at 427.
[16] [1917] 2 K.B. 433, DC.

7. AFFIRMATION OF THE CONTRACT OF INSURANCE BY WAIVER

Rather than treat the contract of insurance as having been determined   **2–75**
by a breach of warranty or "basis" provision, or, indeed, as not rendering them liable to pay an indemnity to an insured who is in breach of
a condition precedent, insurers may treat the contract or, respectively,
their liability, as subsisting notwithstanding the breach by the insured.
This election to continue with the policy being in full force despite a
breach by the insured has been described both as an act of "waiver"[17]
and as conduct preventing the insurer from relying on a defence relating to the breach under the equitable doctrine of estoppel,[18] but, in any
event, the term "affirmation" of the policy is, perhaps, best utilised for
the purposes of this discussion. The essential elements necessary to constitute an affirmation of the policy and liability thereunder are the
insurer's knowledge of the breach, combined with some express or implied
conduct leading a reasonable insured to conclude that the policy subsists
in full.

Issue of the policy with knowledge of breach

The knowledge of the breach need not be the knowledge of the directors   **2–76**
of the insurance company. It is sufficient if an agent or employee of the
company has received the facts of the breach whilst carrying out his duties
within the ordinary scope of his employment. This is demonstrated by
Bawden v. London, Edinburgh and Glasgow Assurance Co.[19] which concerned an untrue fact being written in a proposal form, which was the subject of a "basis of the contract" provision, but the local agent/canvasser of
the insurance company knew the true facts were not as written and forwarded the proposal to head office to be processed. A policy was duly
issued, which the company later argued was avoided by the untrue statement in the proposal form.

Upon the important finding of fact that the local agent/canvasser had   **2–77**
the company's authority to "negotiate and settle the terms of the proposal",[20] the Court of Appeal held that the company were liable under the
policy because they accepted the proposal, knowing through their agent of
the true facts.[21] As Kay L.J. explained[22]:

> "That knowledge was obtained by him when he was acting within the scope
> of his authority, and it must be imputed to the Company. This is an answer
> to the argument that the policy is to be treated as void, because the

---

[17] See, *e.g. Evans v. Employers Mutual Insurance Association Ltd* [1936] 1 K.B. 505 at 514, *per* Greer L.J. CA; *Ayrey v. British Legal and United Provident Assurance Co.* [1918] 1 K.B. 136 at 140, *per* Lawrence J.
[18] See, *e.g. Bentsen v. Taylor Sons and Co. (No.2)* [1893] 2 Q.B. 274 at 283 per Bowen L.J., CA.
[19] [1892] 2 Q.B. 534, CA.
[20] *ibid.* at 539, *per* Lord Esher M.R.
[21] *ibid.* at 540, *per* Lord Esher M.R.
[22] *ibid.* at 541–542.

statements in the proposal are not accurate. In my opinion, the condition that the statements in the proposal are to form the basis of the contract does not apply at all, because knowledge is to be imputed to the company of the [true facts]."

2–78   There is no imputation to the insurance company of facts learned by their agent or employee whilst not acting within the ordinary scope of his duties or authority.[23] The decision in *Bawden's* case has been criticised in so far as it is an authority for the proposition that knowledge gained by an agent or employee whilst himself carrying out his duties carelessly or fraudulently, should always be imputed to the insurance company, and as an authority covering a case where the proposer has requested the agent or employee to fill up the proposal form.[24]

2–79   The question of affirmation of the policy by reason of knowledge to be imputed to the insurance company through their agent's or employee's knowledge, was raised more recently, in *Stone v. Reliance Mutual Insurance Society Ltd.*[25] Here there was even a declaration in the proposal that any part of the proposal filled in by an agent of the insurance company was completed on the insured's instructions. In fact the case turned on two incorrect answers filled in by the agent without seeking any information from the insured, although the completed form had been signed by the insured's wife. Lord Denning M.R. approved the *Bawden's* case, and held that the agent had been acting within the scope of his duties, so binding the company. As a further ground to finding in the insured's favour, Lord Denning M.R. considered that the agent had innocently misrepresented to the insured's wife that he had filled in the proposal form correctly, because of his mistake, and she trusted him. This innocent misrepresentation leading to her mistake could give rise to relief other than a cancellation of the contract, the relief in this case being to prevent the insurance company from relying on the untruth of the answers.[26]

2–80   Megaw L.J. did not follow this line of reasoning, but considered the matter simply resolved by the fact that the area inspector had done as his company required him, *i.e.* he filled in the proposal form, and, as the incorrect answers came about through his fault, the company could not rely upon non-disclosure.[27] Finally, Stamp L.J. considered that the insurance company could not raise in defence a matter that arose by reason of their agent's failure to do his job properly.[28] Whilst the defence in *Stone* was on the general ground of non-disclosure, rather than any breach of the "basis" clause, there seems no reason to suspect that the reasoning or outcome would have been any different.

---

[23] *Biggar v. Rock Life Assurance Co.* [1902] 1 K.B. 516.
[24] *Newsholme Bros. v. Road Transport and General Insurance Co. Ltd* [1929] 2 K.B. 356 at 376, *per* Scrutton L.J, CA; see also *Stoneleigh Finance Ltd v. Phillips* [1965] 2 Q.B. 537 at 572, *per* Davies L.J., CA.
[25] [1972] 1 Lloyd's Rep. 469, CA.
[26] *ibid.* at 474–475.
[27] *ibid.* at 476.
[28] *ibid.* at 477.

Knowledge of breach and subsequent receipt of premium

A second instance of circumstances where the insured may not be pre-   **2–81**
vented from recovering because of the insurer's affirmation of the policy,
is where the insurer has accepted payment of the premium after being
made aware of the true facts. In *Ayrey v. British Legal and United Provident Assurance Co. Ltd,*[29] Lawrence and Atkin J.J. held that an insured
could recover where, although the written answers in the proposal form
were incomplete, the insured had informed the insurance company's district manager of the full facts. He in turn had said the additional information was "immaterial" and had accepted payment of the premium. The
subsequent attempt of the insurance company to avoid the policy because
of the incomplete information in the written answers was rejected.
Lawrence J. said that it was not necessary that the communication should
have been made direct to the head office or to the company's general
manager, the receipt of premium payment with full knowledge of the facts
was a waiver by the company of their objection.[30] Atkin J. (as he then was)
felt the knowledge of the district manager had to be imputed to the
company — who else could reasonably be supposed to be given the information than the district manager?[31]

Similarly, in the earlier case of *Wing v. Harvey,*[32] a policy condition had   **2–82**
stated that the policy would be rendered void in certain circumstances.
One such circumstance occurred, but the local agent was informed of this
by the assignee of the policy, and he subsequently accepted further premium payments. It was held that the company could not rely on this
breach of condition by receiving those payments of premium with
imputed knowledge of the breach.[33] It was the local agent's duty to communicate the circumstances under which the premiums had been paid and
received to head office, not the insured's.[34]

The insurers were unsuccessful in their effort to avoid the policy for   **2–83**
breach of a "basis of the contract" clause in a proposal form where the
insured was inaccurately described as a "joiner", rather than a "joiner and
builder", in *Holdsworth v. Lancashire and Yorkshire Insurance Co.*[35] An
agent of the insurers had filled in the proposal form for the employers'
liability insurance and had placed therein the incomplete description of
the insured's business. The facts were rather special because, when the policy
arrived, and prior to the insured paying any premium, the insured asked the
agent to alter the description in the policy to "joiner and builder". The
agent obtained the sanction of the chief clerk of the local branch office of
the insurers, and then the first premium was paid. The head office of the
insurers were never informed of this alteration of description of the
insured. When he subsequently made a claim for indemnity, the insurers

---

[29] [1918] 1 K.B. 136.
[30] [1918] 1 K.B. 136 at 140.
[31] *ibid.* at 142.
[32] (1854) 5 De G. M. and G. 265.
[33] *ibid.* at 270, *per* Knight Bruce L.J.
[34] *ibid.* at 271, *per* Turner L.J.
[35] (1907) 23 T.L.R. 521.

successfully pleaded that the description "joiner" was the "basis of the contract", and because this condition was breached, they were entitled them to avoid the policy.

2-84 Bray J. was firmly of the view that the insurers were unable to treat the policy as avoided, and were liable to indemnify the insured, upon the grounds that:

> (i) by receiving the premiums, the insurers were precluded from denying the agent's authority to alter the contract;
> (ii) in those circumstances the knowledge of the agent was the knowledge of the insurance company; and
> (iii) even if the policy had not been altered, the company would have been liable, because the contract must be treated as having been negotiated by the agent with a joiner and builder, and the knowledge of the agent must be treated as the knowledge of the company.

2-85 Very recently the courts have considered two cases where affirmation with knowledge of a breach, by reason of receipt of premium, was pleaded by the insured. First, in *Container Transport International Inc. and Reliance Group Inc. v. Oceanus Mutual Underwriting Association (Bermuda) Ltd,*[36] the Court of Appeal held, *inter alia*, that there can be no waiver of material information unless it would and should have been disclosed by an inquiry by the insurer which common prudence demanded and no affirmation of the contract unless the insurer entered into it, or carried it out, after he had full knowledge of the information. Although this case concerned a waiver of a breach of the duty of disclosure, rather than breach of a warranty or condition, the situation is similar and the principle must logically apply to both instances. The facts were very complicated, but it is sufficient here to say that the insured raised the argument that information had been disclosed whereby the insurers should have been put on inquiry. As they did not make those inquiries, it was contended that the insurers were estopped from raising the defence of breach of the duty of disclosure by reason of this waiver of inquiry together with their subsequent acceptance of premiums and payment of other claims prior to their purported avoidance of the policy.

The Court of Appeal held that this type of waiver, or affirmation of the contract as the court termed it, only applies to circumstances where the insurer elects to affirm the policy after he has acquired full knowledge of the material facts (or, it is submitted, the breach of an express warranty or "basis" clause) which would have entitled him to avoid it. Having the means of knowledge, or having been put on inquiry, is not enough.[37]

2-86 In *Hadenfayre Ltd v. British National Insurance Society Ltd,*[38] an insurer's affirmation of the insurance contract by virtue of that insurer's

[36] [1984] 1 Lloyd's Rep. 476.
[37] *ibid.* at 498, *per* Kerr L.J., and at 530, *per* Stephenson L.J.
[38] [1984] 2 Lloyd's Rep. 393.

acceptance of a single premium payment on an annual policy was pleaded by the insured. The facts were that a contract of insurance was concluded on March 28, 1983, but on April 7 the insured's broker telephoned the office of the insurer's authorised agent and spoke to someone there. That person was told of a change in the circumstances affecting the risk after having told the caller that the office principal was not available. The broker asked that the message be passed on to the office principal.

The defendant insurers argued that only an office principal was autho-   **2–87**
rised to receive any notice in relation to the policy and, therefore, there was no affirmation of the contract by reason of the subsequent acceptance of the payment of the premium and issue of the policy after that telephone conversation. Lloyd J. (as he then was) considered the decision of the Court of Appeal in the *Container Transport International* case (above) and said[39]:

> "Here, by accepting the premium and issuing the policy, the defendants were undoubtedly carrying out the contract. So the question is whether they did so with full knowledge of the relevant facts. Constructive notice is not, of course, enough; it is not enough that the defendants were put on inquiry ... What is required is actual knowledge. But what does actual knowledge mean in this context?"

In relation to the defendants' contention that only an office principal at   **2–88**
their agent's office was strictly their agent, and therefore no other of the office staff were authorised to receive the information in relation to the policy, Lloyd J. rejected that argument and expounded the modern legal view of the imputation of an agent's knowledge to his principal[40]:

> "I cannot accept so narrow a view. It seems to me that it would make business almost unworkable. Suppose a letter were delivered by hand to [the agent's] office, properly addressed to [the principal]. Suppose that by mistake it were opened by one of [the principal's] assistants and accidently not passed on. It would in my view be hopeless to argue that [the principal] had no actual notice or knowledge of the contents of the letter. So here, I have found as a fact that the person who answered the telephone call said, 'OK' or 'I will tell him'. Once that had been said, it seems to me that [the principal] had sufficient actual notice or knowledge for the purpose of affirmation. It was argued that nobody in the office was authorised to receive any message at all relating to underwriting matters, other than the [principals] themselves, and further that there is no evidence that the message was ever in fact passed on.
>
> As to the first point, I find it difficult to accept the evidence, unanimous though it was, that nobody in the office, except [the two principals], had actual authority within the office to accept even the simplest message relating to an underwriting matter. But even if that be wrong, I would hold that the person who answered the telephone had ostensible authority to accept the message and pass it on. It might have been different if the person who answered the telephone had been an office cleaner. But there was no question of that here.
>
> As to the second point, there is, at the very least, a presumption of fact that a notice to an agent will be passed on to his principal: see *A/S Rendal v.*

---

[39] *ibid.* at 400–401.
[40] *ibid.* at 401.

Arcos Ltd.[41] Of course, like any other presumption of fact it can be rebutted
by evidence . . . The notice which was received in the office in the present
case, being a notice which was intended for and so to speak addressed to [the
principal], was the equivalent of actual notice to [the principal] himself.
With the knowledge derived from that notice, [the principal] accepted the
premium and issued the policy. In my judgment the defendants have,
through [the principal], affirmed the contract with full knowledge of the
alteration. They cannot now disaffirm the contract. . .
   Can they be heard to say that the plaintiffs are in breach? Clearly not. If with
full knowledge of the breach whether of condition or warranty, insurers
elect to affirm the contract, they cannot afterwards rely on the breach as a
defence to a claim. Thus the answer to the defence based on breach of warranty
is the same as the answer to the defence based on a variation of the risk."

Renewal of the insurance contract

2–89   Commercial insurances are generally annual contracts, and any renewal
of the policy in consequence is a fresh contract of insurance.[42] Thus, any
breach of condition precedent, warranty or "basis" clause of which the
insurer has actual knowledge by reason of an earlier year's insurance, and
known to continue to apply to the renewal insurance contract, must also
be waived and the renewal contract be affirmed by acceptance of the
renewal premium.

Failure to treat the whole contract of insurance as determined

2–90   If the insurers fail to repudiate the whole policy upon learning of a
breach of warranty or the "basis" clause entitling them to treat the contract of insurance as repudiated, then such conduct will be regarded by the
courts as an election to affirm the validity of the policy. This results from
the Court of Appeal's decision in *West v. National Motor and Accident
Insurance Union Ltd.*[43] where the Court unanimously held that breach of a
"basis" clause gave rise to a right to repudiate the policy as a whole, and
not a right to reject any particular claim whilst regarding the policy as
remaining in force.

2–91   The insured had signed a "basis of the contract" declaration in the
proposal form and the policy recital incorporated that proposal into the
contract of insurance and repeated that it should be the "basis of the contract". When Mr West, the insured, subsequently made a claim, the insurers sent loss assessors to investigate the claim and they discovered that the
value of the building and contents as declared in the proposal form were
incorrect in that the value was understated. The insurers, on learning of
this, wrote to the insured in terms that they repudiated liability on the
claim only, the policy itself otherwise remaining in force. The Court of
Appeal rejected that submission for the defendant's insurers had not taken
advantage of the fact that the contract had lost its basis, but had proceeded on the footing that the basis remained. Accordingly, they could not
resist the claim on the ground of that understatement of value.[44]

[41] [1937] 3 All E.R. 577.
[42] *Stokell v. Heywood* [1897] 1 Ch. 459.
[43] [1955] 1 W.L.R. 343, CA.
[44] [1955] 1 W.L.R. 343 at 348, *per* Hodgson L.J., CA.

This decision must apply whenever the insurers become aware of their   **2–92**
right to treat the policy as determined, *e.g.* in the case of a breach of warranty. The decision will not, however, apply to situations where there is a
breach of a mere condition, or of a condition precedent to liability or
recovery. In those latter instances, the nature of those conditions are such
that the intention of the parties will be construed by the courts to be that
the contract of insurance subsists and only the right to pursue a particular claim, or the measure of that claim, are to be affected by a breach by
the insured.

Delay in a decision on a claim following breach

Delay on the part of the insurer in deciding whether or not to treat the   **2–93**
breach as having determined the policy, or avoiding liability in the case of
a condition precedent, may amount to affirmation of the policy and liability under it. Insurers are entitled to delay their decision upon whether
to affirm or avoid, and in *Allen v. Robles*[45] a delay of some four months
was held by the Court of Appeal not to be of such length as to be evidence
that they had in truth decided to affirm their liability under the relevant
insurance in circumstances where the insured had breached a condition
precedent to their liability. Although the court also stated that affirmation
of their liability could be construed in circumstances where either in some
way the rights of third parties intervened, or prejudice was suffered by the
insured.[46]

Waiver of future performance of warranty or condition

The principle was explained by Scrutton J. (as he then was) in *Toronto*   **2–94**
Railway Co. v. National British and Irish Millers Insurance Co. Ltd[47]:

> "Conditions precedent may be waived by a course of conduct inconsistent
> with their continued validity, even though the contracting party does not
> intend his conduct to have that result. This is especially so if the course of
> conduct leads the other party to spend time and incur expense in a proceed-
> ing which he would not have undertaken had he not been led, by the action
> of the other party, to think that he was relieved, by concurring in those
> proceedings, from the other course of conduct and conditions prescribed by
> the policy."

The facts of the case were that it was a condition precedent in a fire   **2–95**
insurance policy that the loss should not become payable until 60 days
after notice, ascertainment, estimate, and satisfactory proof of the loss
had been received by the insurance company, and that a magistrate or
notary public should, if the company required it, certify that he had examined the circumstances and believed the insured had honestly sustained the
loss as appraised. The insured, having suffered a loss of fire, served notice
of claim on the insurance company and appointed an adjuster to ascertain

[45] [1969] 1 W.L.R. 1193, CA.
[46] [1969] 2 Lloyd's Rep. 61 at 63, *per* Atkinson L.J.
[47] (1914) 111 L.T. 555 at 563, CA; applied *Burridge and Son v. F. H. Haines and Sons Ltd*
(1918) 87 L.J.K.B. 641.

the loss. The adjuster was appointed with the assent of the company and he provided a full report and this was forwarded to the company. After a long correspondence, the company requested to be supplied with a certificate of a magistrate as provided by the above stipulation, expressed as being a condition precedent to the insured's right of recovery under the policy. In an action brought by the insured for recovery, the Court of Appeal held that the defendant company had, by agreeing to the appointment by the insured of a loss adjuster, waived their right to insist on the stipulation regarding the requirement of a magistrate's certificate.

2–96   A further example is to be found in *Yorkshire Insurance Co. Ltd v. Craine*[48] which concerned a contents fire policy in which a condition precedent to the insured's right to recover was that he must give notice of any loss or damage covered by the policy "forthwith", and deliver detailed particulars within 15 days. Under the provisions of a further clause of the policy, the insurance company were granted power to take possession of the insured premises and any goods therein at the date of the fire, and sell the goods, so long as the claim was not adjusted. After a fire, the insured gave notice of claim forthwith, and the insurers took possession of the premises of goods before the time limit for delivery of the detailed particulars of claim had expired. In total, the insurers remained in possession for some four months, during which time they did not sell any of the goods. The insured served detailed particulars after the expiration of the period stipulated in the condition, and the Privy Council held that, in the circumstances of the taking of possession of the premises and goods before the expiry of the stipulated period for delivery of detailed particulars, the insurers, by that conduct, had waived the requirement of the insured to deliver those particulars within the remaining period of the specific time. The reference to "adjustment" in the possession clause had to be construed as referring to the completion of all the requirements of a valid claim. Accordingly, as the insurers had expelled the insured from the premises before they were entitled to take possession, they could not be permitted to say that the circumstances legalising their action (*i.e.* the waiver of the requirement to serve the detailed particulars within the 15-day period) did not, in fact, exist.

2–97   A waiver of the need for future compliance with a policy provision was also held to have taken place by reason of the conduct of the insurers in *Barrett Bros. (Taxis) Ltd v. Davies*.[49] A clause of a liability policy contained a notification provision that full written particulars should be given to the insurers as soon as possible after the relevant event, and that any notice of intended prosecution, etc. should be forwarded immediately. An accident covered by the policy occurred on May 17, but the insured gave no notice to the insurers, nor did he forward the notice of intended prosecution received by him. The insurers, however, were told of the intended prosecution by the prosecuting authority, and thereafter wrote to the insured that:

---

[48] [1922] 2 A.C. 541, PC.
[49] [1966] 1 W.L.R. 1334, CA; see also *Kier Construction Ltd v. Royal Insurance (U.K.) Ltd* (1993) 30 Con. L.R. 45.

"We understand that proceedings are being taken against you on 2 July . . . It would be appreciated if you would let us know why you have not notified us of these proceedings since we will wish to arrange your defence."

The Court of Appeal held that the insured was entitled to recover under   **2–98** the policy for the insurers had led him to believe, as any reasonable person receiving the letter would,[50] that the requirement was no longer being relied upon. Accordingly, the insurers could not at a later stage seek to rely on that failure to comply with the strict policy requirements.

On the other hand, no waiver of compliance with a policy requirement was considered to exist where the insured had not complied with its requirements, and the third party claiming against the insured notified the insurers of his claim and the insurers wrote back to the third party, not the insured, in terms that they had no objection to the third party serving proceedings upon the insured.[51]

It must be pointed out that a waiver of compliance with a warranty,   **2–99** condition, or "basis" clause, may not be absolute. For instance, an express waiver of strict compliance may be conditional, as in *Re Carr and Sun Fire Insurance Co.*[52] where the insurers permitted an extension of the time permitted for submission of full details of a fire claim, but only for the purpose of enabling specified persons to compute the loss. The Court of Appeal held that this was not a complete waiver of the need to comply with the requirement for full details, nor did it act as a waiver of the need to provide the details within any specific period at all. Rather, the extension of time was a waiver but only for the actual period of time that it in fact took those specified persons to make the necessary calculations.

In connection with the question of future compliance of provisions of   **2–100** the policy, the decision in *E. Hulton and Co. Ltd v. Mountain*[53] is worth discussing for the Court of Appeal considered the effect of the common provision in liability insurances regarding the incurring of costs in defence or settlement of the claim against the insured. Once the insurer has acceded to the insured's initial request for the incurring of costs, does this act as a waiver of any further requirement to seek the insurer's consent to the incursion of all further costs in the defence or settlement of the claim? Banks L.J. said[54]:

"In my view, the words of the policy, 'no costs shall be incurred without the consent of the underwriters', literally construed, mean that at every stage of the proceedings involving costs the consent of the underwriters must be applied for. A clause, however, must be construed reasonably. Application for consent was a necessary condition precedent, and it must be shown either that an express application was made and express consent given, or that the necessity for making it was waived, or that the consent was implied."

[50] *ibid.* at 1339, *per* Salmon L.J.
[51] *Farrell v. Federated Employers Insurance Association Ltd* [1970] 1 W.L.R. 1400, CA.
[52] (1897) 13 T.L.R. 186, CA.
[53] (1921) 8 Ll. L. Rep. 249, CA.
[54] *ibid.* at 250.

2–101   The application for the consent of the underwriters should be made at every important stage of the proceedings. When the consent was applied for and given for defending an action, if the action resulted in favour of the assured and there was an appeal it would be necessary to apply and obtain consent to oppose the appeal, and if the appeal resulted in a new trial being ordered, application and consent would be necessary before proceeding to defend the new trial.

8. *EX GRATIA* PAYMENTS BY INSURERS

2–102   Finally, it must be stated that the mere fact that the insurers have made an *ex gratia* payment of a claim on an earlier loss, despite an entitlement to treat either the policy, or their liability under it, as avoided, that *ex gratia* payment does not act as an affirmation of the insurance contract such that subsequent claims must be met by the insurers. No act of waiver is constituted by such earlier payment and no estoppel arises thereby, either in relation to past, existing, or future breaches of warranty, condition precedent, or "basis" clause.[55] The premise of an *ex gratia* payment is, of course, that the insurer makes no admission of his liability to meet the claim in law.

---

[55] *London and Manchester Plate Glass Co. Ltd v. Heath* [1913] 3 K.B. 411, CA.

CHAPTER 3

CONCEALMENT OF MATERIAL FACTS

1. THE DUTY OF DISCLOSURE

Introduction

There is no class of documents as to which the strictest good faith is **3–01** more rigidly required in courts of law than policies of insurance,[1] and this resulting duty to disclose facts material to the running of the risk, is not based upon an implied term of the contract, but arises outside the contract.[2] That said, it is conceptually possible for a clause in a contract of insurance to completely exclude the duty of disclosure.[3] Full disclosure is of the very essence of a contract of insurance, and it has been for centuries in England the law in connection with insurance of all sorts — marine,[5] fire, life, guarantee and every kind of policy[6] — that, as the underwriter knows nothing and the man who comes to him to ask him to insure knows everything, it is the duty of the insured, the man who desires to have a policy, to make a full disclosure to the underwriter without being asked all the material circumstances. This is expressed by saying that it is a contract of the utmost good faith — *uberrima fides*.[7] The duty to disclose also applies to the insurer, *e.g.* to correctly represent the period during which the risk will be covered,[8] although primarily this duty affects the insured rather than the insurer.[9]

The doctrine has been expounded in many learned judgments, one of **3–02** the most cited being that of Lord Mansfield C.J., given in 1766[10]:

> "Insurance is a contract upon speculation. The special facts, upon which the contingent chance is to be computed, lie more commonly in the knowledge of the insured only: the underwriter trusts to his representation, and proceeds upon confidence that he does not keep back any circumstance in his

---

[1] *Mackenzie v. Coulson* (1869) L.R. 8 Eq. 368 at 375, *per* James V.-C.

[2] *March Cabaret Club & Casino Ltd v. London Assurance* [1975] 1 Lloyd's Rep. 169 at 175, *per* May J.

[3] *H.I.H. Casualty & General Insurance Ltd v. Chase Manhattan Bank* [2001] 1 Lloyd's Rep. 30 at 42, paras 24–26, *per* Aikens J.; *Svenska Handelsbanken v. Sun Alliance & London Insurance plc* [1996] 1 Lloyd's Rep. 519 at 551, *per* Rix J. (as he then was); *Sumitomo Bank Ltd v. Banque Bruxelles Lambert SA* [1997] 1 Lloyd's Rep. 487 at 495, *per* Langley J.

[4] *Lee v. British Law Insurance Co. Ltd* [1972] 2 Lloyd's Rep. 49 at 57, *per* Karminski L.J., CA.

[5] Marine Insurance Act 1906, s.17.

[6] *London Assurance Co. v. Mansel* (1879) 11 Ch. D. 363 at 367, *per* Jessel M.R., CA.

[7] *Rozanes v. Bowen* (1928) 32 Ll. L. Rep. 98 at 102, *per* Scrutton L.J., CA; *London Assurance v. Mansel* (1879) 11 Ch. D. 363 at 367, *per* Jessel M.R.

[8] *Duffell v. Wilson* (1808) 1 Camp. 401.

[9] See Chapter 1, above, for discussion of the insurer's duty and for consideration of the other aspect of the insured's duty of good faith in relation to the presentation of claims honestly.

[10] *Carter v. Boehm* (1766) 3 Burr. 1905 at 1909.

knowledge, to mislead the underwriter into a belief that the circumstance does not exist, and to induce him to estimate the risk as if it did not exist. The keeping back of such a circumstance is fraud, and therefore the policy is void. Although the suppression should happen through mistake, without any fraudulent intention; yet still the underwriter is deceived, and the policy is void; because the risk run is really different from the risk understood and intended to be run at the time of the agreement . . . Good faith forbids either party by concealing what he privately knows, to draw the other into the bargain, from his ignorance of that fact, and his believing the contrary."

Knowledge of the insured subject to the duty

3–03   The duty is to make full disclosure of all knowledge possessed by the proposer (applicant) that is material to the risk.[11] This has two aspects, one relating to the knowledge of the proposer, and the second relating to what is material to the risk, which were settled in relation to marine insurance by 1832,[12] and codified by section 18 of the Marine Insurance Act 1906 (see below). With regard to the other limb concerning the knowledge of the proposer, the duty covers the actual knowledge of the proposer for insurance, and facts which the proposer ought to know in the ordinary course of his business.[13] In any event, the insured is not generally under a duty, unless the proposal form requires it, to conduct a special investigation or otherwise reorganise his business practices to discover all possible material facts.[14] This has been explained by McNair J., thus[15]:

> "The [insurers'] submission that the board of the [insured] company ought to have known the material facts because they would have known them if they had made such inquiries as to [material facts] as a reasonable, prudent board of such company in the ordinary course of business would have made, in my judgment fails both in law and on the facts. I have been referred to no authority to suggest that the board of a company proposing to insure owe any duty to carry out a detailed investigation as to the manner in which the company's operations are performed, and I know of no principle in law which leads to that result. If a company is proposing to insure wages in transit, I cannot believe that they owe a duty to the insurers to find out exactly how the weekly wages are in fact carried from the bank to their premises, though clearly they must not deliberately close their eyes to defects in the system and must disclose any suspicions or misgivings they have. To impose such an obligation upon the proposer is tantamount to holding that insurers only insure persons who conduct their business prudently, whereas it is a commonplace that one of the purposes of insurance is to cover yourself against your own negligence or the negligence of your servants."

---

[11] *Joel v. Law Union & Crown Insurance Co.* [1908] 2 K.B. 863 at 885, *per* Fletcher Moulton L.J., CA; *Economides v. Commercial Assurance Co. Ltd* [1998] Q.B. 587 at 607, *per* Peter Gibson L.J., CA.

[12] *Elton v. Larkins* (1832) 8 Bing. 198.

[13] *Simner v. New India Assurance Co. Ltd* [1995] L.R.L.R. 240; *Lee v. British Law Insurance Co. Ltd* [1972] 2 Lloyd's Rep. 49 at 56, *per* Davies L.J., CA; Marine Insurance Act 19086, s.18(1).

[14] *Simner v. New India Insurance Co. Ltd,* [1995] L.R.L.R. 240.

[15] *Australia & New Zealand Bank Ltd v. Colonial & Eagle Wharves Ltd* [1960] 2 Lloyd's Rep. 241 at 252, *per* McNair J.

Imputation of agent's knowledge

The knowledge of the insured's agents will be imputed to the insured **3–04** himself if the agent or agents in question could be expected to have passed on that information to their principal, the proposer, in the ordinary course of events.[16] This has particular importance in the case of corporate insured bodies. Imputation of knowledge from a defaulting agent to his principal will not be assumed by the court, however, in so far as the knowledge in question concerns that agent's defaults; for it is contrary to common sense to impute to a principal an agent's knowledge of an irregularity or impropriety for which the agent himself is responsible.[17] The Court of Appeal in *P.C.W. Syndicates v. P.C.W. Reinsurers*[18] has applied that principle, but also pointed out that there are real difficulties in applying the tests of both actual knowledge, and matters which ought to be known, by a company when applying for insurance[19]:

> "I can see no reason to restrict the knowledge of a company under section 18 to what is known at a high level, by the directing mind and will. I would have thought that knowledge held by employees whose business it was to arrange insurance for the company would be relevant, and perhaps also the knowledge of some other employees. . .
> By section 18 the person seeking insurance must first disclose what is known to him. If he is a natural person, that means known to him personally; if a company, known to a director or employee at an appropriate level. Secondly, the person must disclose everything which in the ordinary course of business ought to be known to him. That is a quite sufficient test to deal with the knowledge of agents and others to whom he may have entrusted all or part of the running of his business. There is no need to create some doctrine by which others become the company's directing mind or will, or the agents of the company to know things."

Certainly, though, Mance J. (as he then was) in *Insurance Corp. of the Channel Islands v. The Royal Hotel Ltd*,[20] found no difficulty in attributing to the insured the conduct of its director and company secretary in creating false hotel occupancy rates and trading records for presentation on renewal of the hotel's insurance.

Duration of the duty

Apart from an express duty being cast on the insured in the policy, the **3–05** insured's common law and equitable duty to make full and accurate disclosure of material facts only applies up to the moment when a binding

---

[16] *ibid.* at 254; *Hadenfayre Ltd v. British National Insurance Society Ltd, Trident General Insurance Co. Ltd & Lombard Elizabethan Insurance Co. Ltd* [1984] 2 Lloyd's Rep. 393 at 401, per Lloyd J.

[17] *Stoneleigh Finance Ltd v. Phillips* [1965] 2 Q.B. 537 at 572, *per* Davies L.J., CA; *J. C. Houghton and Co. v. Nothard, Lowe & Wills Ltd* [1928] A.C. 1 at 15, *per* Viscount Dunedin, HL; *Re Hampshire Land Co.* [1896] 2 Ch. 743 at 749, *per* Vaughan Williams L.J.; *Newsholme Bros. Road Transport & General Insurance Co. Ltd* [1929] 2 K.B. 356 at 374, *per* Scrutton L.J., CA.

[18] [1996] 1 W.L.R. 1136, CA.

[19] *ibid.* at 1142–1143, *per* Staughton L.J.

[20] [1998] Lloyd's Rep. I.R. 151 at 156.

contract of insurance is concluded.[21] There is no duty upon an insured when presenting a claim to disclose all facts material to the decision of insurers whether or not to meet the claim.[22] The rationale for the rules relating to the duration of the duty of disclosure is that the material time for assessing materiality is the time the contract of insurance is made, as explained by Lord Esher M.R. in *Canning v. Farquhar*[23]:

> "In this case [there] was a representation which was true at the time, but the material time is the moment when the insurance is made, and the representations ought to be true then. If there had been a material change, there ought to be an alteration of the representation, and the ground for entering into the contract is altered."

3–06   An interesting illustration of this principle is afforded by *Allis-Chalmers Co. v. Maryland Fidelity and Deposit Co.*,[24] where a fidelity policy premium was arranged on 7 March, and the policy was drawn up on 8 March reciting that the policy indemnity was to run from March 8 to March 7 in the following year. On March 9, the policy was sent to the claimant's Paris office, but was returned with a request to send it to the claimant's London office, where it was delivered on March 18. At that time, the claimant's manager was absent and the claimant resolved to leave the matter till his return, which transpired to be April 18, when the manager arranged for payment of the premium. On April 13, the employee in respect of whom the fidelity policy had been arranged had left his office and, without explanation, had not returned by April 18. When it was later discovered that the employee had stolen the claimant's money on April 13, the insurers argued that the policy was avoided by the non-disclosure of the fact that the employee had gone missing. The House of Lords held that there was no concluded contract of insurance until April 18, and as the employee's absconding had been known, but not disclosed to the insurers on that date, the insurers were entitled to avoid the policy. *Per* Earl Loreburn[25]:

> "I therefore come to the conclusion that there was no completed agreement . . . at any rate before April 18, and that prior to April 18 either party could have refused to proceed with this business of the insurance. When the policy was delivered and the premium paid on April 18, there was knowledge of a state of facts upon the part of the assured which admittedly ought to have been communicated to them; and it is agreed that in that state of facts it is impossible to recover upon the policy."

3–07   Sometimes, an express term in the dealings between the proposer and insurer makes it quite clear that no insurance will take effect until the premium has been paid,[26] and the duty of full disclosure thus continues until

---

[21] *Harrington v. Pearl Life Assurance Co. Ltd* (1914) 30 T.L.R. 613, CA.
[22] *Manifest Shipping and Co. Ltd v. Uni-Polaris Insurance Co. Ltd* [1997] 1 Lloyd's Rep. 360, CA.
[23] (1886) 16 Q.B.D. 727 at 731, CA.
[24] (1916) 114 L.T. 433, HL.
[25] *ibid.* at 434.
[26] See Chapter 2, above.

the premium has been paid.[27] The reason is that the express term intimates to the proposer that any subsequent acceptance by the insurer of the premium and risk would be subject to the condition that the material facts disclosed should remain meanwhile unaffected, as Acton J. has explained[28]:

"The second point . . . was that there was here a failure to discharge a duty incumbent upon all proposers of contracts of insurance such as these . . . namely a duty to inform the insurers of any material change in the nature of the risk to be undertaken by them . . . In my opinion, the contention of the insurance company on this point also is a sound one."

The law in this area can be harsh to honest proposers unaware of the legal situation, as occurred in *Re Yager and Guardian Assurance Co.*[29] Here, the insured had obtained a fire-policy with L company, renewable on September 29 the following year. In August of the following year, the insured arranged with the Guardian Assurance Co. a top-up insurance, *i.e.* an additional sum above the primary layer insured with L company, which was also to expire on September 29. It was then arranged that the Guardian Assurance would insure the full sum for the following year, running from September 29. On September 21, the Guardian Assurance sent the insured a statement showing the premium payable, and at the side were the words "held covered". Underneath was a note in print that "No insurance is in force until the premium is paid." On September 27, the insured became aware that L company had refused to continue the existing policy, but this fact was not communicated to the Guardian Assurance. On September 28, the Guardian Assurance executed the policy to run from September 29, and the next day the premium was paid and the policy forwarded. Channell J., upon the finding of fact that the refusal to renew their policy by L company was a material fact, held that when this fact became known to the insured on September 27, there was no concluded contract of insurance, and it was still the duty of the insured to disclose that fact to the Guardian Assurance. Having omitted so to do, the insured was not entitled to treat the policy as a valid policy[30]:

3–08

"The time up to which it must be disclosed is the time when the contract is concluded. Any material fact that comes to his knowledge before the contract he must disclose . . . There still was a time at which any circumstance coming to his knowledge material to be disclosed would have to be disclosed. I quite agree that in this case it is rather hard upon the assured because I do not see anything to throw doubt upon [his] bona fides . . . or anything to show that he had the least idea that he was bound to disclose the fact which had come to his knowledge as to the refusal of the [L] company, to renew the insurance; and, if so, it was rather hard upon him, but that is the effect of this clause in the policy, which undoubtedly sometimes does work hardship to one of the parties . . . that, however, is the consequence of this law of insurance which upon the whole does justice between the parties and is rather necessary for the protection of insurers."

[27] *Canning v. Farquhar* (1886) 16 Q.B.D. 727, CA.
[28] *Looker v. Law Union & Rock Insurance Co. Ltd* [1928] 1 K.B. 554 at 558.
[29] (1912) 108 LT 38, DC.
[30] *ibid.* at 44.

3–09   That case may be contrasted, however, with *Whitwell v. Autocar Fire and Accident Insurance Co. Ltd*[31] where the insurers made no conditional acceptance of the proposal. The proposal form contained a question about any refusal, etc. to renew the proposer's insurance, which the proposer correctly answered in the negative. On May 1, the defendant insurance company accepted the proposal, but the insured gained no knowledge until after that date that the previous insurers had declined to renew the insurance. There being a concluded contract of insurance on May 1, by which time the insurance company were unable to prove to the court that the proposer had knowledge of the refusal, Clauson J. held that the defendants could not avoid the policy and their liability thereunder.

Renegotiation of policy terms

3–10   Upon any renegotiation of the policy terms a limited duty of disclosure again arises and continues until the new contract of insurance is concluded[32]:

> "Suppose the policy were actually executed, and the parties agreed to add a memorandum afterwards, altering the terms: if the alteration were such as to make the contract more burdensome to the underwriters, and a fact known at the time to the assured were concealed which was material to the alteration, I should say that the policy would be vitiated. But if the fact were quite immaterial to the alteration, and only material to the underwriter as being a fact which showed that he had made a bad bargain originally, and such as might tempt him, if it were possible, to get out of it, I should say that there would be no obligation to disclose it."

Renewal of insurance

3–11   The renewal of an annual policy is the entering into of a fresh contract of insurance[33] by the parties. The duty of disclosure accordingly again applies until the conclusion of each renewal. Although it has been held that the renewal of a policy is impliedly made on the basis that the statements in the original proposal are still accurate,[34] it is, perhaps more accurate to state the proposition that the statements made initially must still be accurate so far as the insured is aware. *Hearts of Oak Building Society v. Law Union and Rock Insurance Co. Ltd*[35] supports this latter proposition. The facts were that the claimants had insured the fidelity of their employed solicitor who handled the daily cash, and although at the time of renewal the claimants had known that the solicitor had once not accounted immediately for money received by him, that did not amount to the claimants' knowledge of his defalcation.

---

[31] (1927) 27 Ll. L. Rep. 418.

[32] *Lishman v. Northern Maritime Insurance Co.* (1875) L.R/ 10 C.P. 179 at 182, *per* Blackburn J.

[33] *Stokell v. Heywood* [1897] 1 Ch. 459.

[34] *Re Wilson and Scottish Insurance Corp.* [1920] 2 Ch. 28; *Pim v. Reid* (1843) 6 Man. and G. 1 at 25, *per* Cresswell J.

[35] [1936] 2 All E.R. 619.

Insurer's remedy for concealment by the insured

Quite apart from any remedy that the insurer has for breach of condition **3–12**
precedent, warranty, or under the Misrepresentation Act 1967 in respect of
the remedies of rescission or damages for a misrepresentation, dependent
upon whether it be fraudulent, innocent or negligent, equity regards any
misrepresentation or non-disclosure of material facts by an insured as
entitling the insurer to rescind the contract of insurance *ab initio*:

> "If there is information given, be it quite innocent which is not a matter of
> contract, and never becomes a matter of contract, yet, nevertheless, if it is
> inaccurate, it can be used to avoid the policy or policies in question."[36]

This right arises from the court's inherent jurisdiction to prevent hard- **3–13**
ship and unfair dealings,[37] thus the insurer cannot rescind for concealment
of a fact which only diminishes the risk proposed.[38] The House of Lords,
in *Pan Atlantic Insurance Co. Ltd v. Pine Top Insurance Co. Ltd*,[39] has reaffirmed the remedy, with the proviso that the insurer must be able to show
that the misrepresentation or non-disclosure of material facts induced him
to enter into the particular contract of insurance. This is discussed below.
The result is that the contract is treated as never having been made, with
the result that the insured is entitled to the return of any premium paid,
and the insurer is entitled to repayment of any indemnities previously paid
under the rescinded policy of insurance.[40] The remedy in relation to composite, rather than joint, contracts of insurance is modified, and the
insurer can only rescind the insurance in so far as it affects a co-insured
who has been guilty of a material concealment.[41] This can be justified by
treating a composite insurance as a bundle of contract with the separate
co-insureds.[42] However, a clause in a contract of insurance could exclude
the right of an insurer to rescind for breach of the duty of disclosure, even
if the non-disclosure amounted to deliberate concealment provided the
wording of the contract clearly reflected an intention of the parties to
exclude the right of rescission in those circumstances.[43] Such a wording
was held to achieve that in *Kumar v. A.G.F. Insurance Ltd*.[44]

[36] *Graham v. Western Australian Insurance Co. Ltd.* (1931) 40 Ll. L. Rep. 64 at 66, *per* Roche J.; *Everett v. Hogg Robinson & Gardner Mountain (Insurance) Ltd* [1973] 2 Lloyd's Rep. 217; *Versicherungs und Transports A.G. Daugava v. Henderson* (1934) 48 Ll. L. Rep. 54 at 58, *per* Roche J.; *Merchants & Manufacturers Insurance Co. Ltd v. Hunt* [1941] 1 K.B. 295 at 318, *per* Luxmore L.J., CA; *Herman v. Phoenix Assurance Co. Ltd* (1924) 18 Ll. L. Rep. 371 at 372, *per* Scrutton L.J., CA.
[37] *Merchants & Manufacturers' Insurance Co. Ltd v. Hunt and Thorne and Thorne* [1941] 1 K.B. 295 at 318, *per* Luxmore L.J., CA; *Everett v. Desborough* (1829) 5 Bing. 503.
[38] Marine Insurance Act 1906, s.18(3)(a).
[39] [1995] A.C. 501, HL.
[40] *Cornhill Insurance Co. Ltd v. Assenheim* (1937) 58 Ll. L. Rep. 27 at 31, *per* MacKinnon J.
[41] *Woolcott v. Sun Alliance & London Insurance Co. Ltd* [1978] 1 W.L.R. 493.
[42] See *New Hampshire Insurance Co. Ltd v. M.G.M. Ltd* [1997] L.R.L.R. 24, CA; *Arab Bank plc v. Zurich Insurance Co. Ltd* [1999] 1 Lloyd's Rep. 262; *First National Bank plc v. Barnet Devanney (Harrow) Ltd* [1999] Lloyd's Rep. I.R. 43.
[43] *H.I.H. Casualty & General Insurance Ltd v. Chase Manhattan Bank* [2001] 1 Lloyd's Rep. 30 at 42–43 and 48, *per* Aikens J.
[44] [1999] Lloyd's Rep. I.R. 147.

2. THE TEST OF MATERIALITY

3–14 It is clear since the House of Lords' majority decision in *Pan Atlantic Insurance Co. Ltd v. Pine Top Insurance Co. Ltd*[45] that the common law test of the alleged materiality of a fact concealed by the proposer for insurance was codified by the Marine Insurance Act 1906, s.18(2), which provides:

> "Every circumstance is material which would influence the judgment of a prudent insurer in fixing the premium, or determining whether he will take the risk."

This test therefore contains three elements[46]:

(i) "would" looks to a consequence which is, within the civil standard of proof, definite rather than speculative (as in the case of the word "might");

(ii) "influence the judgment of a prudent insurer" only requires "influence", and this does not mean "decisively influence", or "conclusively influence" or "determine the decision";

(iii) "determining whether he will take the risk" denotes an effect on the thought processes of the insurer in weighing up the risk, which is quite different from weighing up whether to take the risk proposed.

3–15 Lord Mustill explained how he came to this view as follows[47]:

> "My Lords, this conclusion accords with what I regard as the practicalities. Looking at the matter through the eyes of a court, called upon to rule after the event on whether an undisclosed circumstance was material, the proposition that 'influence' means 'decisively influence' takes as its point of reference a hypothetical underwriter personifying the generality of those who know their job and perform it carefully, without exceptional timidity or boldness; it assumes that this underwriter has had before him all the material which was before the actual underwriter; it also assumes that after weighing up the conflicting factors which enter into a decision of this kind the hypothetical underwriter has decided that the balance comes down in favour of writing the risk on the terms on which it was actually written; and then on these assumptions requires a firm conclusion on whether or not the undisclosed facts would (not might) have tipped the balance the other way and caused him to reach a different decision. Even looking at the matter after the event, this exercise presents great difficulties, for the reasons given by Parker L.J. in the *C.T.I.* case[48]. . . . But the point is that it is not the court after the event, but the prospective assured and his broker before the event, at whom the test is aimed; it is they who have to decide, before the underwriter has agreed to write the risk, what material they must disclose. I am bound to say that in all but the most obvious cases the 'decisive influence' test faces them with an almost impossible task. How can they tell whether

---

[45] [1995] 1 A.C. 501, HL.

[46] *ibid.* at 531, *per* Lord Mustill, with whom Lord Goff agreed.

[47] *ibid.* at 531–532.

[48] *Container Transport International Inc. v. Oceanus Mutual Underwriting Association (Bermuda) Ltd* [1984] 1 Lloyd's Rep. 476 at 510–511, CA.

the proper disclosure would turn the scale? By contrast, if all that they have to consider is whether the materials are such that a prudent underwriter would take them into account, the test is perfectly workable."

The test, therefore, is an objective test to be applied by the court, it being **3–16** irrelevant that the insured did not consider the fact to be material.[49] Moreover, the question for the court is whether a prudent insurer would wish to know the fact in the formation of his opinion, *i.e.* be aware of it in reaching his decision upon whether to take the risk and, if so, the terms to apply. The defendant insurers do not have to prove that a prudent insurer's final decision on these matters would in fact have been different if he had known of the concealed fact. In the words of Lord Mustill in *Pan Atlantic*,[50] a circumstance may be material even though a full and accurate disclosure of it would not in itself have had a decisive effect on the prudent underwriter's decision whether to accept the risk and if so at what premium. A fact may be material if it increases the risk, or increases the risk in some respects but diminishes it in others, or even only diminishes the risk, although an insurer cannot rescind the contract on this last ground.[51] The line of authority[52] suggesting that the test is whether a reasonable man in the position of the insured, with the knowledge of the allegedly material facts, ought to have realised that they were material to the risk, has now been overruled. All matters are material which would have been taken into account by the prudent underwriter when assessing the risk which he was consenting to assume.[53]

3. PROOF OF MATERIALITY

Onus of proof on insurer

The onus of proof is on the insurers to prove the materiality of the fact **3–17** or facts,[54] and, accordingly, they must prove that the fact alleged to be material would have affected the judgment of a prudent insurer, and not merely might possibly have done so. Whilst expert evidence may well be called by the parties to prove or disprove the alleged materiality of the fact or facts in question,[55] the House of Lords has pointed out that sometimes it will be obvious to the court that the fact is material[56]:

[49] *Lindenau v. Desborough* (1828) 8 B. and C. 586 at 592, *per* Bayley J.; *Bates v. Hewitt* (1867) L.R. 2 Q.B. 595 at 608, *per* Mellor J.; *Re Yager & Guardian Assurance Co.* (1912) 108 L.T. 38 at 44, *per* Channell J.; *Godfrey v. Britannic Assurance Co. Ltd* [1963] 2 Lloyd's Rep. 515 at 529, *per* Roskill J.

[50] *ibid* at 550.

[51] *St Paul Fire & Marine Insurance Co. (U.K.) Ltd v. McConnell Dowell Constructors Ltd* [1996] 1 All E.R. 96 at 107, *per* Evans L.J., CA; Marine Insurance Act 1906, s.18(3)(a).

[52] *Joel v. Law Union & Crown Insurance Co.* [1908] 2 K.B. 863 at 884–885, *per* Fletcher Moulton L.J., CA; *Roselodge Ltd v. Castle* [1966] 2 Lloyd's Rep. 113; *Anglo-African Merchants Ltd v. Bayley* [1969] 1 Lloyd's Rep. 268 at 277, *per* Megaw J. (as he then was).

[53] *St Paul Fire & Marine Insurance Co. (U.K.) Ltd v. McConnell Dowell Constructors Ltd* [1996] 1 All E.R. 96, *per* Evans L.J., CA.

[54] *Insurance Corp. of the Channel Islands v. The Royal Hotel Ltd* [1998] Lloyd's Rep. I.R. 151 at 156, *per* Mance J. (as he then was).

[55] *Yorke v. Yorkshire Insurance Co. Ltd* [1918] 1 K.B. 662; *Horne v. Poland* [1922] 2 K.B. 364.

[56] *Glicksman v. Lancashire and General Assurance Co. Ltd* [1925] 2 K.B. 593 at 609, *per* Scrutton L.J., CA; affirmed. [1927] A.C. 139 at 143, *per* Viscount Dunedin, HL.

"[It was argued] that it cannot be held that a fact was material unless some-body gave evidence for the materiality. That is entirely contrary to the whole course of insurance litigation, it is so far contrary that it is frequently objected that a party is not entitled to call other people to say what they think is material; that is a matter for the court on the nature of the facts. I entirely agree [with the court below] that the nature of the facts may be such that you do not need anybody to come and say, 'This is material'. If a shipowner desiring to insure his ship for the month of January knew that in that month she was heavily damaged in a storm, it would, with deference to counsel who has suggested the opposite, be ridiculous to call evidence of the materiality of that fact; the fact speaks for itself."

Expert evidence

3–18   Even where expert evidence is called, the court does not have to unques-tioningly accept that evidence as representing an accurate portrayal of the views of a prudent underwriter. Thus, in a case concerning a jeweller's insurance, McNair J. rejected the evidence of the defendant's expert wit-ness that a prudent insurer would have wanted to know that an employee had been convicted of bribing a police officer some 12 years earlier.[57] Forbes J. extensively reviewed this area of the role of expert underwriting evidence when a court is considering the test of materiality[58]:

"Before coming on to the evidence itself I should consider one further pre-liminary point. In this branch of the law it is permissible for either side to adduce evidence relating to what would be regarded as material. The ques-tion at once arises, what is the nature of such evidence and what are the pow-ers and duties of the Court in relation to it? [Counsel for the insurance company] maintains that the Court's only duty is to listen to the evidence, decide whether the witness is telling the truth and, if he is, go on to decide whether he is a reasonable and prudent underwriter. If both decisions are favourable then the Court must act on that evidence. Now I should say at once that I am satisfied that all the insurance witnesses (and such witnesses are called by both sides) were truthful in so far as they dealt with factual questions and also that they all appeared to me to be at any rate prudent underwriters. So far as the word 'reasonable' is concerned [Counsel] says this merely means [rational] and has none of the connotations of the word as used in the term of the 'reasonable man'. Apparently underwriters never ride on the Clapham omnibus.

Now I do not accept these arguments. In the first place the evidence of insurers called in this way is expert evidence in the sense that such witnesses are assisting the Court in deciding what a reasonable and prudent under-writer would or would not do. They are not to give evidence of what they themselves would do, because their evidence is expert, that is opinion evi-dence and not factual. They are to give evidence of what, in their opinion, having regard to the general practice of underwriters, a reasonable under-writer would do. There is a world of difference between saying — 'A reason-able underwriter, in my opinion, would do so and so: I would do so myself; and saying — 'I would do so and so, and because I am a reasonable under-writer, it must follow that that is what a reasonable underwriter would do.' The former is unobjectionable expert evidence; the latter is not only logically fallacious but also not really acceptable evidence at all; see for instance *per*

[57] *Roselodge Ltd v. Castle* [1966] 2 Lloyd's Rep. 113.
[58] *Reynolds & Anderson v. Phoenix Assurance Co. Ltd* [1978] 2 Lloyd's Rep. 440 at 457–459.

Mr Justice Rush in *Horne v. Poland*.[59] The test of such a witness is not whether he is telling the truth, but whether he is giving an honest opinion.

Further, in giving expert evidence such witnesses are only assisting the Court not deciding the matter.

> 'Their duty is to furnish the judge or jury with the necessary scientific criteria for testing the accuracy of their conclusions so as to enable a judge or jury to form their own independent judgment by the application of these criteria to the facts proved in evidence. The parties have invoked the decision of a judicial tribunal and not an oracular pronouncement by an expert [*per* Lord President Cooper in *Davie v. Edinburgh Magistrates*.'[60]

It seems to me therefore that although I may derive assistance from such expert testimony as has been put before me, I am not bound to regard it as conclusive of what a reasonable and prudent underwriter would do . . .

Now the first general impression of the evidence of these gentlemen (apart from one) was that they were telling me that they would want to know, and all underwriters would want to know, everything which by any stretch of the imagination be regarded as indicating any moral hazard, in order that the insurer might himself decide whether what was disclosed could properly be regarded as material. Within that envelope might be matters which, once stated, would not cause the insurer a moment's uneasiness; others which might require further investigation before the risk was accepted; and others still which might result in refusal or the grant of temporary cover only. I have no doubt that every insurer would like to have the most complete information about the moral makeup of each proposer, but that is not the test. The test is whether the circumstances in question would influence his judgment in determining whether he will take the risk. The insurer's thirst for knowledge, however understandable, is not therefore the required criterion. A good example of what I have in mind is that many of the witnesses maintained that any allegation of fraud made against a proposer must be disclosed even though it has no foundation; the reason being that it must be for the insurer to investigate such allegations and decide on their truth . . .

There is one other matter to which I should advert in relation to these witnesses and that is their general attitude to the role of the insurer. This again varied from, at the one end, Mr D., and, at the other, Mr F. For Mr D. the attitude of the first class insurance company was that you had to take the rough with the smooth, and it was not fair to the community to take only the first-class business — *i.e.* that with minimal risk. For Mr F. the reverse was the case; he said that there was a substantial amount of business about with persons against whom no allegations had been made and it was better to decline business than to get involved in whether an allegation was true or false. A breath of suspicion, however unfounded, would be enough for him to decline, and his staff had instructions to that effect. In between, perhaps, was Mr W., who considered that an underwriter's first duty was to make a profit, and increase in business was a secondary matter.

[Counsel for the insurance company] argues that the correct attitude is that of Mr F. He constantly reiterated that no one is entitled to insurance as, apparently, a justification for any arbitrary behaviour on the part of the insurers. That is why he maintains that the reasonable insurer is only a rational insurer, the word 'reasonable' bearing none of the overtones appropriate to the reasonable man. I feel I must reject this argument and any evidence that suggests that this is the practice of underwriters generally. I prefer to rely on Mr D.'s evidence . . . I do not think that a reasonable or prudent insurer is entitled to or would in fact adopt an arbitrary attitude."

[59] [1922] 2 K.B. 364 at 365.
[60] [1953] S.C. 34 at 40.

The correct approach

3–19   Shortly after the House of Lords delivered its judgment in *Pan Atlantic*, the Court of Appeal were faced with the practical application of the materiality test in the Contractors All Risks insurance case of *St Paul Fire and Marine Insurance Co. (U.K.) Ltd v. McConnell Dowell Constructors Ltd*[61] Briefly, the works were presented to the insurers as being new buildings with piled foundations, which was the original scheme. Before acceptance of the risk, however, the defendant insured had changed the foundation design to the cheaper option of spread foundations, believing that the ground conditions allowed this as a viable alternative. In the event, the ground did not support even the part-built buildings, and the insured claimed under the policy for subsidence damage. Upon disclosure of the actual plans for the works, and an earlier comprehensive ground report which stated spread foundations would require additional safeguards, the insurers successfully sought a declaration that they were entitled to rescind the insurance contract because of non-disclosure or the implied misrepresentation of the site's ground conditions. The court stated that the correct approach on materiality was to simply compare the representation made with the representation that would have been made, if all material facts had been disclosed, and determine if that would have affected the prudent underwriter's assessment of the risk.[62]

4. INDUCEMENT

3–20   The second vital matter that the insurer must establish in order to be entitled to rescind the contract of insurance, is that he was induced to enter into that insurance contract by the proposer's (by this time, the insured) concealment of the fact which is the subject of the above objective test of materiality.[63] If the misrepresentation or non-disclosure of a material fact did not in fact induce the making of the contract (in the sense in which that expression is used in the general law of misrepresentation) the underwriter/insurer is not entitled to rely on it as a ground for rescinding the contract of insurance.[64] In the general law of misrepresentation, "inducement" means that the fact misrepresented "should have operated on the mind of the representee".[65] There is, thus, no requirement for the insurer or underwriter to prove that he would not have written the insurance at all if he had known the true facts, nor even that the terms upon which he wrote the risk, or the premium, were in any way different than they would have been if he had known the true facts. Given the practical difficulty of an insured being able to get expert underwriting evidence at all in many cases, the insurers are in a very powerful position wherever they choose to rescind an insurance policy on the grounds of concealment of a material fact. The insurer need only call the actual underwriter who

---

[61] [1996] 1 All E.R. 96, CA.
[62] *ibid.* at 110–111, *per* Evans L.J.
[63] *Pan Atlantic Insurance Co. Ltd v. Pine Top Insurance Co. Ltd* [1995] 1 A.C. 501, H.L.
[64] *ibid.* at 550, *per* Lord Mustill.
[65] *Chitty on Contracts* (28th ed., Sweet & Maxwell, London), para. 6–034.

wrote the risk at the trial to establish, on the balance of probabilities, that the information relating to the concealed facts "did form part of his consideration in deciding on what terms he would write the risk".[66] It has to be borne in mind, also, that discloseable facts are not limited to those which are seen as increasing the risk, because the risk may be increased in some respects but decreased in others by the fact.[67]

Actual underwriter called

Where the actual underwriter is called to give evidence, and is cross-examined, the court will be able to make up its own mind on the question of inducement. In cases where he is called, and the court genuinely cannot make up its mind on the question of inducement, the insurer's defence of disclosure should fail because he will not have been able to show that he had been induced by the non-disclosure to enter into the insurance on the relevant terms. At the end of the day it is for the insurer to prove that the non-disclosure did induce the writing of the risk on the terms on which it was written. If it can be shown that the actual underwriter was careless in the writing of the very risk itself, any presumption of the causative effect of the concealed fact will be much diminished.[68]

3–21

Actual underwriter not called

In *Pan Atlantic*, above, Lord Mustill referred to a presumption of inducement of the causative effect of a concealed material fact upon the underwriter. He said[69]:

3–22

> "As a matter of common sense . . . the assured will have an uphill task in persuading the Court that the withholding or misstatement of circumstances satisfying the test of materiality had made no difference."

This is probably better expressed by saying that inducement cannot be inferred in law from proved materiality, although there may be cases where the materiality is so obvious as to justify an inference of fact that the representee was actually induced, but, even in such exceptional cases, the inference is only a prima facie one, and may be rebutted by counter-evidence.[70] Longmore J. has now twice asserted that any such presumption

[66] *Sirius International Insurance Corp. v. Oriental Assurance Corp.* [1999] Lloyd's Rep. I.R. 343 at 352, *per* Longmore J.; however, in *St Paul Fire & Marine Insurance Co. (U.K.) Ltd v. McConnell Dowell Constructors Ltd* [1996] 1 All E.R. 96 at 108, CA, where it is recorded that it was common ground between the parties that the insurer had to establish that he entered into a contract which he would not have accepted if all the material facts had been made known to him.

[67] *St Paul Fire & Marine Insurance Co. (U.K.) Ltd v. McConnell Dowell Constructors Ltd* [1996] 1 All E.R. 96 at 107, *per* Evans L.J.

[68] *Marc Rich and Co. A.G. v. Portman* [1996] 1 Lloyd's Rep. 430 at 442, *per* Longmore J., unaffected on appeal, [1997] 1 Lloyd's Rep. 225, CA.

[69] [1995] 1 A.C. 501 at 551. The rest of the House of Lords did not concur with this proposition. Followed *Aneco Reinsurance Underwriting Ltd v. Johnson & Higgins Ltd* [1998] 1 Lloyd's Rep. 565 at 590.

[70] 31 *Halsbury's Laws* (4th ed., Butterworths, London), para. 1067; approved in *St Paul Fire & Marine Insurance Co. (U.K.) Ltd v. McConnell Dowell Constructors Ltd* [1996] 1 All E.R. 96 at 112, *per* Evans L.J., CA.

will only come into play where the actual underwriter is not called "for good reason",[71] and where there is no other reason to suppose that the actual underwriter acted other than prudently in writing the risk. The extent of this possible proviso to the presumption has yet to be explored.

3–23   As for the operation of the presumption, it was applied by the Court of Appeal in *St Paul Fire and Marine Insurance Co. (U.K.) Ltd v. McConnell Dowell Constructors Ltd.*[72] The circumstances were rather special in that the three underwriters who had been called at the original trial, had only given evidence directed towards the views of the notional prudent underwriter. This was because at the time of the trial, the House of Lords had not yet introduced the requirement of actual inducement. In these circumstances, the Court of Appeal was prepared to apply the presumption to the fourth insurance company which had chosen not to call their underwriter at trial to give evidence about a prudent underwriter although he was available. Giving the judgment of the court, Evans L.J. explained[73]:

> "Here, the evidence of the three underwriters who did give evidence and of the expert witnesses was clear. If the underwriters had been told the true state of the ground conditions, as revealed in the 1982 report, and of the conflicting views expressed by the authors of the report and by Worleys, then they would have called for further information and in all probability either refused the risk or accepted it on different terms. In fact, all four underwriters including Mr Earnshaw [who was not called] accepted it without any relevant inquiries. There is no evidence to displace a presumption that Mr Earnshaw like the other three was induced by the non-disclosure or misrepresentation to give cover on the terms which he did. In my judgment, these insurers also have discharged their burden of proof."

3–24   Cresswell J. in *Aneco Reinsurance Underwriting Ltd v. Johnson and Higgins Ltd*[74] has also applied the presumption to following insurers who were not called to give evidence at trial, but the lead underwriter was called. This was in circumstances where he was satisfied that those following insurers would have very largely followed the leading underwriter in assessing the risk, and that lead underwriter had been induced to write the risk upon the misrepresented facts. He was satisfied that there was no evidence to displace the presumption.[75] And in *Insurance Corp. of the Channel Islands v. The Royal Hotel Ltd,*[76] Mance J. (as he then was) accepted that the presumption applied to satisfy the burden of proof on the insurer, where the insurer only called two underwriters to give evidence at court, but, without explanation, only produced written statements from the other two relevant underwriters.

---

[71] *Marc Rich and Co. A.G. v. Portman* [1996] 1 Lloyd's Rep. 430 at 442; *Sirius International Insurance Corp. v. Oriental Insurance Corp.* [1999] 1 Lloyd's Rep. 343 at 351.
[72] [1996] 1 All E.R. 96, CA.
[73] *ibid.* at 112.
[74] [1998] 1 Lloyd's Rep. 565.
[75] *ibid.* at 597.
[76] [1998] Lloyd's Rep. I.R. 151 at 158–160.

5. FACTS OUTSIDE THE DUTY OF DISCLOSURE

Facts covered by a warranty or "basis of the contract" clause

The right of the insurer to elect to rescind the policy *ab initio* for non-   **3–25**
disclosure or misrepresentation of material facts, is wholly independent of
the principles relating to a breach of warranty, or a "basis of the contract"
clause, which automatically discharges the insurer from liability upon
breach (although it can be affirmed by the insurer). It has therefore been
held that where the facts alleged to be material were the subject of warranties, recourse to the law relating to non-disclosure is superfluous, the
insurer being adequately protected by the law relating to warranties,[77]
unless information upon the subject be particularly called for.[78] The materiality of facts warranted or declared to be true and/or subject to a "basis
of the contract" clause is irrelevant, the insurer only has to establish the
breach by the insured. This can be very harsh on the insured, but there is
no code of practice or statutory restriction on insurers relying on any
breach, no matter how immaterial, in the case of commercial insurances,
unlike personal domestic and consumer insurances.[79] The harshness in the
commercial field has been ameliorated in recent years, because many
insurers follow the domestic insurance practice of only requiring the declaration of truth to be to the best of the proposer's knowledge and belief. If
the proposer answers such questions honestly, in good faith, there is no
breach of the declaration, and there is no further implied requirement that
the proposer should have had objectively reasonable grounds for his belief.[80]

Facts which diminish the risk

It has long been understood that an insurer does not need to be told of   **3–26**
facts which lessen the risk agreed and understood to be accepted by the
express terms of a contract of insurance. Thus, if the insured obtains an
insurance for one year and yet the risk is only going to run for six months,
although this will usually be a material fact (*i.e.* it would influence the fixing of a premium) there is no breach of the duty of disclosure if the
insured does not inform the insurer of this fact.[81]

Facts within the knowledge of the insurer   **3–27**

> "An underwriter cannot insist that the policy is void because the insured
> did not tell him what he actually knew; what way soever he came to the
> knowledge."[82]

---

[77] *Ross v. Bradshaw* (1761) 1 Wm. Bl. 312; *de Maurier (Jewels) Ltd v. Bastion Insurance Co Ltd & Coronet Insurance Co Ltd* [1967] 2 Lloyd's Rep. 550 at 557, *per* Donaldson J.; Marine Insurance Act 1906, s.18(3)(d).

[78] *Haywood v. Rodgers* (1804) 4 East. 590.

[79] The Statement of General Insurance Practice applicable to members of the Association of British Insurers.

[80] *Economides v. Commercial Assurance Co. plc* [1998] Q.B. 587, CA.

[81] *Carter v. Boehm* (1766) 3 Burr. 1905 at 1910, *per* Lord Mansfield C.J.; Marine Insurance Act 1906, s.18(3)(a).

[82] *ibid.* at 1910, *per* Lord Mansfield C.J.; Marine Insurance Act 1906, s.18(3)(b).

The insurer is presumed to know matters of common notoriety or knowledge,[83] and which an insurer in the ordinary course of business as such ought to know.[84]

> "It is also true that when a fact is one of public notoriety, as of war ... the party proposing the insurance is not bound to communicate what he is fully warranted in assuming the underwriter already knows ...
>
> [The proposer] is not bound to communicate facts or circumstances which are within the ordinary professional knowledge of an underwriter. He is not bound to communicate facts relating to the general course of a particular trade, because all these things are supposed to be within the knowledge of the person carrying on the business of insurance, and which, therefore, it is not necessary for him to be specially informed of."[85]

3–28   As regards presumed knowledge of particular trades that the insurer is insuring, in *Hales v. Reliance Fire and Accident Insurance Corp. Ltd,*[86] where the insured was a retail shopkeeper who obtained a composite insurance policy from the defendant insurers, McNair J. considered, *obiter*, the question of whether the insured should have disclosed the annual stocking of fireworks for a period round Guy Fawkes' Day[87]:

> "I am not satisfied that there was any obligation upon the proposer for this particular class of shop to disclose to the underwriters the fact that fireworks would be, or might be, on the premises at this short season, because I think on the evidence that is a matter which the underwriters must be taken to have known. On the other hand, I am far from saying that I would not feel that it was a material fact to disclose that the fireworks were not kept as required by law in a secure place. I am quite clear in my mind that if it had been disclosed that fireworks were being stored in the shop under conditions not permitted by (that would normally be a matter which would have to be disclosed) it clearly, I should have thought, would have resulted either in the insurance not being proceeded with, or, more probably, would have resulted in the fireworks being properly protected ..."

3–29   Again, in *Anglo-African Merchants Ltd v. Bayley,*[88] the plaintiffs insured army surplus leather jerkins, over 20 years old, under an "all risks" insurance, having given the description of the property to be insured in the proposal form as being; "New Men's Clothes in Bales for Export". The insurer subsequently contended that this description amounted to non-disclosure or misrepresentation of a material fact, whilst the insured argued that the term "new" was a trade term with which the insurer should have been familiar. Megaw J. (as he then was) rejected that contention by the insured[89]:

---

[83] *Leen v. Hall* (1923) 16 Ll. L. Rep. 100.
[84] *ibid.*; *Foley v. Tabor* (1861) 2 F. and F. 663 at 672, *per* Erle C.J.; Marine Insurance Act 1906, s.18(3)(b).
[85] *Bates v. Hewitt* (1867) L.R. 2 Q.B. 595 at 605 and 611, *per* Shee J.
[86] [1960] 2 Lloyd's Rep. 391.
[87] *ibid.* at 397.
[88] [1970] 1 Q.B. 311.
[89] [1970] 1 Q.B. 311 at 320.

"Much evidence was given and argument offered as to the meaning of the word 'new', with particular reference to the clothing trade. Of course, it is not a question of the words in isolation: it is a question of its meaning in the context of a request for insurance of goods which are described as being 'new men's clothes in bales for export'. The defendant contended that to describe 20-year-old leather jerkins as 'new' was a misdescription; a corollary, as it were, of the non-disclosure that the goods were 20 years old. The plaintiff contended on the other hand, that, so far from being a misdescription, the use of the word 'new' in this context indicated that the clothes were government surplus clothes and that they were not of recent manufacture . . .

The gist of the evidence is that in the clothing trade goods are never described as 'new' (for example, in invoices or advertisements or other trade documents) unless they are government surplus goods. If they are government surplus goods, and are unused, they may be described as 'new', despite the fact that they are not of recent manufacture. I accept that evidence, but I do not, on the whole of the evidence, accept the proposition that this special connotation of the word 'new', whether with or without the addition of the words 'in bales', ought to have brought it to the attention of an ordinary prudent underwriter that the goods which he was asked to insure under the description of 'new men's clothes in bales for export' were, or might reasonably be expected to be, government surplus clothes, or old clothes, in the sense that they were manufactured at least 20 years previously."

The principle of knowledge negating the duty of disclosure extends to **3-30** circumstances where the insurer had abundant means of knowing the facts in question from his previous knowledge coupled with the particulars given by the insured.[90] Further, the normal rule relating to agent and principal — that knowledge gained by the agent in pursuance of his agency and which should be passed on to his principal in the normal course of business — will result in knowledge being imputed to an insurer, even if his agent has not, in fact, passed on that information.[91] Employees, of course, are agents of their employers and thus, in *Anglo-Californian Bank Ltd v. London and Provincial Marine and General Insurance Ltd*[92] where the claimant bank had arranged insurance with the defendant insurers to cover the solvency of a third party, and the secretary of the insurance company knew of the financial difficulties of the third party, it was held that the defendants could not claim non-disclosure of this fact which was within their knowledge.

Waiver of disclosure

Lord Esher M.R. once explained the operation of the aspect of waiver **3-31** of disclosure of material facts thus[93]:

"The assured is bound to disclose every material fact within his knowledge, which is not fairly to be taken as being within the knowledge of the underwriters, and, if he fails to do so — he is guilty of what is called in insurance

---

[90] *Bates v. Hewitt* (1867) L.R. 2 Q.B. 595.
[91] *Woolcott v. Excess Insurance Co. Ltd* [1979] 1 Lloyd's Rep. 231 at 240, *per* Megaw L.J., CA.
[92] (1904) 20 T.L.R. 665.
[93] *Asfar and Co. v. Blundell* [1986] 1 Q.B. 123 at 129, CA; applied *Mann Macneal & Steeves Ltd v. Capital & Counties Insurance Co. Ltd* [1921] 2 K.B. 300, CA; also Marine Insurance Act 1906, s.18(3)(c).

law — concealment . . . But it is not necessary to disclose minutely every material fact; assuming that there is a material fact which he is bound to disclose, the rule is satisfied if he discloses sufficient to call the attention of the underwriters in such manner that they can see that if they require further information they ought to ask for it."

3–32   It has been said, though, that waiver of disclosure of material facts will not be inferred too readily, or else the obligation to disclose would be destroyed.[94] Thus, where a proposer wishes to insure a building, and he provides the insurer with a value which he believes to be a reasonable prospect upon appreciation, there are no grounds for arguing waiver of further disclosure, *i.e.* that the value is speculative rather than immediate, in the absence of anything to put the insurer on inquiry.[95] A similar plea in *Anglo-African Merchants Ltd v. Bayley*[96] discussed above, was rejected on the facts by Megaw J. (as he then was)[97]:

> "the plaintiffs seek to assert that a reasonable underwriter would have been put on enquiry by the description 'new men's clothes in bales for export'; that such enquiry would have revealed that the goods were army surplus; that [the underwriter], though he made other enquiries, failed to make any enquiry as to the precise nature of the goods and that the defendants thus 'waived further information on the precise nature of the goods.' Let me assume in favour of the plaintiffs that an insurer waives his right to complain of non-disclosure, if he has received information which would put an ordinarily careful insurer on enquiry and nevertheless fails to enquire. That is put by Sargant L.J., as the minimum required for a successful plea of waiver in *Greenhill v. Federal Insurance Co. Ltd*[98] Scrutton L.J. in his judgment in the same case[99] clearly regards the law on this point as much more favourable to insurers. Even on the assumption of the most lenient test, I cannot hold on the evidence that a normally prudent insurer would have been put on enquiry as to the precise nature of the goods by reason of seeing them described as 'new men's clothes in bales for export.' Some underwriters might be alerted by the word 'new' to make enquiries, because they would realise that it is an unusual adjective to apply to clothes. More underwriters, I think, would take the attitude which (the underwriter here) took: the goods are described as 'new'; they are new; they are not clothes which were manufactured years ago; they are not government surplus, which is normally some distance away from having been newly manufactured when it is sold as surplus. I do not think that that attitude can properly be said to show any lack of care or prudence; or that failure to enquire could give rise to valid claim of waiver. The claim therefore fails."

3–33   More recently, in *Marc Rich and Co. A.G. v. Portman,*[1] the Court of Appeal has reaffirmed the caution required by the courts as put by Parker L.J. in *Container Transport International Ltd v. Oceanus Mutual Underwriting Assoc. (Bermuda) Ltd*[2]:

---

[94] *Greenhill v. Federal Insurance Co. Ltd* [1927] 1 K.B. 65 at 85, *per* Scrutton L.J., CA.
[95] *Hoff Trading Co. v. Union Insurance Society of Canton Ltd* (1929) 45 T.L.R. 466, CA.
[96] [1970] 1 Q.B. 311.
[97] *ibid.* at 320.
[98] [1927] 1 K.B. 65 at 89, CA.
[99] *ibid.* at 85–86.
[1] [1997] 1 Lloyd's Rep. 225 at 233–234, *per* Legatt L.J., CA.
[2] [1984] 1 Lloyd's Rep. 476 at 511, CA.

"In *Harrower v. Hutchinson*[3] and in *Greenhill v. Federal Insurance Co. Ltd*[4] it was made clear that there could be no waiver merely because the insurer was aware of the possibility of the existence of other material circumstances. If this were to be permitted the duty of disclosure would be emasculated to the point of extinction and waiver would become an instrument of fraud. In the present case, for example, it was submitted before the Judge and accepted by him that the insurer had waived disclosure of earlier experience because he was aware that there had been such experience and asked no questions about it. I cannot accept this. As the Judge stressed, regard must be had to the commercial realities. Thus it is permissible for the assured to present a summary of previous experience. So long as this summary is fair, the insurer cannot complain that the full details of the experience were not disclosed. He must however be entitled to assume that the summary is fair. From this it follows that, if he then proceeds to negotiate on the basis of the summary without enquiry as to its accuracy, he waives nothing. He can assume both that it is accurate as far as it goes and that, if it covers only part of the past experience, there is nothing in the part omitted which would vitiate the summary. In order to establish waiver by implication from non-enquiry the insurer must be put on enquiry by the disclosure of facts which would raise in the mind of a reasonable insurer at least a suspicion that there were other circumstances which would or might vitiate the presentation made to him."

Where the proposer is asked by the insurer to complete a proposal form, **3–34** and an answer is left obviously incomplete by the proposer, the insurer may be deemed to have waived disclosure of the remaining part of the answer. For example, if the proposal form requests the proposer to provide his name, address and profession or occupation, and he only fills in his name and address, the insurers may preclude themselves from raising non-disclosure of his occupation or profession.[5] Whether a waiver arises from the non-answering of a proposal form question depends upon the nature of the question, and whether the insurer is put on inquiry by the lack of an answer.

Two cases, though, show how difficult a task the insured may have to **3–35** prove waiver by the insurer where a question in the proposal requests information about previous losses. First, in *Roberts v. Avon Insurance Co. Ltd*,[6] the proposal relating to contents insurance included a declaration in the following terms:

"I have never sustained a loss in respect of any of the contingencies specified in this proposal except
....
....
NOTE: Give date, amount and name of insurers in respect of such loss."

The proposer left this blank, although he had recovered from a different insurance company in respect of a previous loss from burglary. Barry J. held that the insurers were not put on inquiry by the answer being left blank in these circumstances[7]:

[3] (1870) L.R. 5 Q.B. 584.
[4] [1927] 1 K.B. 65.
[5] *Perrins v. Marine & General Travellers' Insurance Society* (1860) 2 E. and E. 324.
[6] [1956] 2 Lloyd's Rep. 240.
[7] *ibid.* at 249.

"The inference to be drawn from leaving blank the two lines provided for the purpose of stating any exception can, to any reasonable applicant and to any reasonable insurer, have only one meaning, namely, that no exception exists . . . It seems to me perfectly clear that any applicant for insurance, completing this form, would appreciate without any doubt or ambiguity that the insurers required particulars of any previous loss in respect of contingencies specified to be set out on the two blank lines left for that purpose, with the date, amount and name of the insurers who were concerned in respect of each of those losses. If that information is clearly required, it seems to me that the only inference, and the obvious inference, is that the applicant intended the blank lines to represent what I think has been described as a negative answer. As this statement is in a declaration, the obvious inference to be drawn from the applicant leaving those lines blank is there was in fact no exception to his categoric statement that he has never sustained any loss in respect of any of the categories specified."

3–36   Similarly, in *Arterial Caravans Ltd v. Yorkshire Insurance Co. Ltd*[8] the insurers had accepted a proposal for fire insurance from the insured where a question in the proposal form, requesting information about any previous fire losses, had been left blank. Chapman J. rejected the claim of waiver of non-disclosure by the insurer, emphasising that it is the duty of the insured to disclose material facts and not of the insurer to elicit material facts from the insured.[9]

The whole issue of non-disclosure and misrepresentation of material facts becomes more complicated where an insurer has provided a proposal form for the proposer for the insurance to fill in, and later seeks to avoid the policy then issued on the ground on non-disclosure or misrepresentation of a material fact, no question having been asked about this fact in the proposal form. Although there is a presumption that matters dealt with by questions in the proposal form are material, with no corresponding presumption that matters not so dealt with are not,[10] and though the proposer is always under a duty to disclose material facts even if no question is asked,[11] the insurer runs the risk of the court doubting the alleged materiality of the fact.[12] Equally, where the insured has correctly answered the particular question asked, the insurer may be precluded from arguing non-disclosure of other, related facts. A few examples will illustrate the situation.

3–37   In *Krantz v. Allan and Faber*,[13] a question in a proposal form for burglary insurance asked "Have you ever sustained a loss?" and Bray J. held that non-disclosure of an earlier *ex gratia* payment by a previous insurer was not a material fact. In *Golding v. Royal London Auxiliary Insurance Co. Ltd*,[14] the proposer was seeking insurance of his business premises against

[8] [1973] 1 Lloyd's Rep. 169.

[9] *ibid.* at 180–181.

[10] *Schoolman v. Hall* [1951] 1 Lloyd's Rep. 139, CA.

[11] *Dawsons Ltd v. Bonnin* [1922] 2 A.C. 413, HL; *Glicksman v. Lancashire & General Assurance Co.* [1927] A.C. 139, HL.

[12] *McCormick v. National Motor & Accident Insurance Union Ltd* (1934) 40 Com. Cas. 76 at 78, *per* Scrutton L.J., CA; *Newsholme Bros. Ltd v. Road Transport & General Insurance Co. Ltd* [1929] 2 K.B. 356 at 363, *per* Scrutton L.J., CA.

[13] (1921) 9 Ll. L. Rep. 410 at 412, *per* Bray J.

[14] (1914) 30 T.L.R. 350.

fire. The proposal form asked "Are you or have you been insured in this or any other office?" and he did not disclose that he had insurance on his own dwelling house, that there was no non-disclosure or misrepresentation of a material fact.

Similarly, in *Ewer v. National Employers' Mutual General Insurance Association Ltd*[15] the fact that another insurance company had refused to transfer to the proposer a different policy in relation to other property, was held not to be an undisclosed material fact where the proposal question was "Has any other office declined to accept or renew your insurance" and the proposer had answered "No", because the question related to the risk proposed.

Waiver was established in *Roberts v. Plaisted*[16] where it was held that the insurers had waived any right which they might have had to repudiate on the basis that the insured had failed to disclose that he was operating a discotheque at the insured motel. This was because the proposal form asked only if the premises were used as a hotel or an inn, with specific questions as to whether any club or casino was operated in any part of the premises, plus a general question as to whether the premises were occupied for any other purpose. The Court of Appeal held that at the time the proposal was filled in, in 1985, it was generally accepted that hotels obviously catering for a clientele beyond those residing in the hotel, could well provide a discotheque to be enjoyed by non-residents, and the particular question could only be construed as referring to exceptional risks. The decision, it was indicated, may have been different if the question had referred to "the premises or any part thereof" being used for any other purpose.

3–38

6. PARTICULAR ASPECTS OF THE DUTY OF DISCLOSURE

Proposals by partnerships and limited companies

Questions in the proposal form relating to the history of the business will probably be construed as being concerned with the history and claims record of the pervading business operation, rather than the particular legal formation or constitution of the proposing partnership or limited company. For example, in *Arterial Caravans Ltd v. Yorkshire Insurance Co. Ltd*[17] the court considered that the business was essentially the same throughout its history, namely, manufacturing and selling caravans, and, therefore, the sole director of the insured company should have disclosed the loss suffered by a separate company when it had been operating this same business. The facts were that S., a businessman, had set up the insured company to sell caravans manufactured by him, but this company became dormant within two years. S. incorporated his manufacturing business in 1956, acting as its sole director, and this company traded until 1968, having in 1965 suffered severe damage at the manufacturing

3–39

---

[15] [1937] 2 All E.R. 193.
[16] [1989] 2 Lloyd's Rep. 341, CA.
[17] [1973] 1 Lloyd's Rep. 169.

premises, caused by a fire. In 1968, S. reactivated the insured company
and recommenced trading from the same premises, and in due course
proposed for fire insurance from the defendant insurers. The insurers'
representative and then their district manager had interviewed S., and the
district manager had asked whether the business had had any experience
of losses or claims in the past; but S., on behalf of the company, had
made no disclosure of the fire at the premises in 1965 when they were
owned by his other company. Chapman J. held that the failure to inform
the insurer of that previous fire suffered by the insured company's predecessor in the business amounted to a material non-disclosure entitling the
insurers to avoid the policy.

3–40   A similar finding was made by the Privy Council in *Marene Knitting
Mills Ltd v. Greater Pacific Insurance Ltd.*[18] The business had always been
technically operated by the claimant company, which had disclosed to the
defendant insurers that they had suffered a fire in 1973 at their premises.
The insurers sought to avoid the policy for non-disclosure on learning that
the insured company had suffered four fires within the preceding 15 years,
at their previous premises. The company argued that those earlier fires
were immaterial on a number of grounds — that the premises were at a
quite different location, that the management had changed, and that the
labour force had changed — all to the effect of diminishing the fire risk.
The Privy Council refused to find that the physical migration of the business rendered the fact of the earlier fires immaterial, and gave judgment to
the defendant insurers.

3–41   Another example is *Locker and Woolf Ltd v. Western Australian Insurance Co. Ltd*[19] where the recently formed plaintiff company had answered
"no" to the following question in the proposal for fire insurance: "Has this
or any other insurance of yours been declined by any other company?"
The company had been formed by two persons who had previously carried
on the business in partnership, and the partnership, two years earlier, had
sought insurance on a business vehicle that had been declined by another
insurance company. The Court of Appeal held that this amounted to non-
disclosure of a material fact. Another question in the proposal had asked:
"Have you ever suffered loss by fire?" and the company replied, "Yes, £5,
Sea". The insurers argued that the company should also have disclosed
that one of the partners, when trading on his own account, had suffered a
loss by fire several years before. The Court of Appeal found that this fact,
also, was material and should have been disclosed as Slesser L.J.
explained[20]:

> "The word 'Sea' there does not as one might imagine, mean a loss of fire
> at sea, but refers to a loss by fire on land of £5 which was paid by the Sea
> Insurance Company. That statement, [Yes, £5, Sea] as we shall see when we
> come to examine the findings of the learned arbitrator, is either untrue or
> a considerable economy of the truth, because in reality one of these partners

[18] [1976] 2 Lloyd's Rep. 631, PC.
[19] [1936] 1 K.B. 408, CA.
[20] *ibid.* at 413.

had suffered, at a date which is stated by the arbitrator in his award, a very serious loss by fire, a loss which involved not only a serious destruction of goods but actually caused the death of a person who was present in the warehouse. Now, as regards that matter that loss was incurred by one only of the partners, and for that reason the learned arbitrator has found that in answer to the question 'Have you ever suffered loss by fire?' the answer 'Yes, £5, Sea' was not an untrue answer because 'you' collectively had not suffered that loss, but only one of the partners. Whether that is a right view or not it is not necessary for us to decide. It is very arguable, in my personal opinion, that even that use of the word 'you' did not justify necessarily the answer to the question, but we need not determine it, because he has found, as I have indicated, in the alternative, that the non-disclosure of the fact that one of the partners had suffered a grievous loss by fire, though not possibly an untrue answer to this question, was a non-disclosure of a material fact."

Slesser L.J.'s doubts upon the arbitrator's interpretation of "you" in the proposal question no doubt sprang from earlier decisions, such as that of the Court of Appeal in *Arthrude Press Ltd v. Eagle Star and British Dominions Insurance Co. Ltd*.[21] The company had just been formed by a man who, up to the time of incorporation, had carried on the string and paper merchant and printing business on his own account. He had been refused fire insurance on the premises by a different insurance company, and, on behalf of the company, he answered "No" to the following question in the proposal form: "Has your insurance ever been declined by any office?" On learning of this earlier refusal, the defendant insurance company sought to avoid the policy for non-disclosure, and were successful. *Per* Banks L.J.[22]:   **3–42**

"reading this proposal and asking oneself what this means: 'Has your insurance ever been declined by any office?', that is not referring to the individual who happens to put forward the policy. It is perfectly obvious the question was and ought to have been understood as meaning: 'Has this risk ever been declined by any office?'"

Finally, there is the decision in the House of Lords in *Glicksman v. Lancashire and General Assurance Co. Ltd*[23] where two persons in partnership sought to effect a burglary policy on their stock-in-trade. A question in the proposal asked: "Has any company declined to accept, or refused to renew, your burglary insurance?" and they answered, "Yorkshire accepted, but proposers declined." The House of Lords upheld the arbitrator's finding that the questions should be construed as being directly to the partners jointly and severally, so that one partner should have disclosed that he had been refused a proposal for burglary insurance on a former occasion when he was carrying on the same business upon the same premises, but without a partner.   **3–43**

[21] (1924) 19 Ll. L. Rep. 373, CA.
[22] *ibid.* at 374.
[23] [1927] A.C. 139, HL.

Key personnel

3–44   As explained by Slesser L.J. in *Locker and Woolf Ltd v. Western Australian Insurance Co. Ltd*[24] the facts of which have already been given, the insurer is entitled to look to the key personnel of the proposing business in order to assess whether there is an acceptable level of "moral hazard" associated with those persons who will actually operate the business:

> "It is elementary that one of the matters which may be considered by an insurance company in entering into contractual relations with a proposed insured is the question of his moral integrity — what has been called in the cases 'moral hazard' — and I do not think it necessary to cite authority to the effect that once the conclusion arises that had certain knowledge been in the minds of the insurance company, they might have taken a different course in agreeing to or declining a particular proposal of insurance, and that it might have affected the conditions and the rates on which they would take it, this 'moral hazard' is one of the incidents which do become directly material.
>
> In my view, it is quite impossible in the present case to say that the non-disclosure of the fact that the person proposing to take out an insurance policy for fire (on behalf of the plaintiff company) has had a motor policy declined on the grounds of misrepresentation, untrue answer, and non-disclosure, is not one which is very material for the . . . insurance company to know. It is, in fact, a non-disclosure of the fact that the person who seeks to enter into the insurance has already been overtly discovered to be a person who tells untruths, conceals matters material, and is a person who at any rate the . . . insurance company, whatever view they took, might reasonably have come to the conclusion was a highly undesirable person with whom to have any contractual relations whatever. It is unarguable, in my opinion, that such an answer was not a material matter, and was a non-disclosure of something which was essential."

3–45   In *Gallé Gowns Ltd v. Licenses and General Insurance Co. Ltd*[25] the claimant company, which owned a costumiers business, insured their stock against fire. A Mr Hershorn, chairman of the company, had completed the proposal on behalf of the company and answered a question regarding previous losses for similar risks with "See previous records Hershorn." Those records did not reveal a considerable number of facts to the insurer.[26] First, that he, when trading with his brother as Pinkus, Goldstein and Co., had suffered a fire and recovered on a fire policy. Secondly, that he should have signed himself as Abraham Gergshorn or Gersghorn, a person who had a "hectic financial past", who had been found guilty of misfeasance, stemming from a number of previous business ventures. Thirdly, that he had some 30 years before been adjudicated bankrupt under the name of Goldstein and had not obtained his discharge for 11 years. Fourthly, that some 10 years before, a receiving order had been made against him resulting in his again being adjudicated bankrupt, that time under the name of Gergshorn, and a discharge was not obtained for a period of five years. Fifthly, that some 11 years before, when director of

---

[24] [1936] 1 K.B. 408 at 414.
[25] (1933) 47 Ll. L. Rep. 186.
[26] *ibid.* at 191–192.

a company called Louvre (London) Ltd and using the name Jacobs, that company having gone into liquidation, he was proceeded against in the county court and had been found guilty of breach of trust and misfeasance and had been ordered to pay a considerable sum of money back to the receiver of the company in respect of his actions in that connection. Sixthly, that he had been chairman of Devonport Ltd and that company had gone into liquidation. Seventhly, that a judgment had been obtained against him when trading under the name of Philip Abbott, and, finally, that he had been director of another failed company, Hershorn and Murray Ltd Perhaps not surprisingly, there was a finding that there had been non-disclosure or misrepresentation, and the insurers were held entitled to avoid the policy issued to Galle Gowns Ltd.

The cases show that not only the character of the company chairman **3–46** should be disclosed, but other key personnel as well. Thus, in *O. and R. Jewellers Ltd v. Terry and Jardine Insurance Brokers Ltd*[27] it was accepted by all parties and the expert witnesses called, that the serious criminal convictions of a director of a parent company, who had some involvement in the management of the subsidiary company proposing for insurance, needed to be disclosed to the insurer. In *Roselodge Ltd v. Castle*,[28] the insurer alleged non-disclosure concerning criminal convictions of the insured company's principal director and its sales manager (the case being heard prior to the Rehabilitation of Offenders Act 1974). The principal director had been convicted of attempting to bribe a police officer some 18 years earlier, when he received a fine of £75, the case centring on a parking offence which the director had sought to avoid being reported by the officer. The insurer's defence as regards the director only failed on the question of the materiality of the concealed fact. McNair J. said[29]:

> "I have come to the conclusion that it is not established to my satisfaction that Mr Rosenberg's offence and conviction on a matter which has no direct relation to trading as a diamond merchant was a material fact which would have influenced a prudent underwriter."

On the other hand, the second fact relied on by the insurer was the **3–47** undisclosed conviction of the insured's sales manager for smuggling diamonds into the United States some eight years earlier. That person had been employed for some six years by the insured company since his return to this country upon his release, after serving part of his sentence of three years' imprisonment. McNair J. was satisfied that this was a material fact which would have influenced the mind of a prudent underwriter when considering the jewellery company's proposal for an "all risks" policy in respect of diamonds held in pursuit of the business.[30]

---

[27] [1999] Lloyd's Rep. I.R. 436.
[28] [1966] 2 Lloyd's Rep. 113.
[29] *ibid.* at 132.
[30] *ibid.* at 133.

3–48   In a similar vein, in *Reynolds and Anderson v. Phoenix Assurance Co. Ltd*,[31] Forbes J. was not satisfied that a partner's 11-year-old conviction for receiving stolen goods was material to the business partnership's proposal for fire insurance where the conviction only resulted in a fine, "the size of which might quite properly have been designed to reflect not the gravity of the offence but, the fact that Mr Reynolds was a man of considerable means".[32] But in *Regina Fur Co. Ltd v. Bossom*,[33] Pearson J. (as he then was) was satisfied on the evidence that an isolated conviction of one of the two directors, more than 20 years before, for receiving stolen goods, was material to the "moral hazard" of insuring the claimant company against burglary.

3–49   Another case where materiality was not proved was *Ewer v. National Employers' Mutual General Insurance Association Ltd*,[34] in which the facts were that the claimant had carried on business in partnership until two years prior to his proposing for the fire policy on his sole account. His erstwhile partner remained joint owner of the business premises, and occasionally lent the claimant money to carry on the business. After six renewals of the policy the claimant made a claim which was defended by the insurance company on the ground of, *inter alia*, non-disclosure of his ex-partner's insurance history, but MacKinnon J. (as he then was) rejected that contention in the absence of the insurers having asked any questions about the matter.

Disclosure of crimes and dishonesty

3–50   When seeking insurance, the proposer must disclose his criminal record[35] for it shows the type of person he has been,[36] and, if a limited company, as has been discussed above, the criminal record of key personnel may equally affect the "moral hazard" which the insurer is entitled to regard as a material fact. It is always a matter of fact and degree in each individual case whether the offence committed is one which would influence the mind of an insurer in deciding whether to take the risk. Where the case is one of dishonesty, the amount involved, and the length of time since the commission of the offence are the most important factors to be considered.[37]

3–51   Whilst it was doubted by McNair J. in *Roselodge Ltd v. Castle*[38] whether very minor offences not resulting in prosecutions and convictions would constitute material facts for disclosure, the defendant insurers in *Reynolds*

---

[31] [1978] 2 Lloyd's Rep. 440.

[32] *ibid.* at 461.

[33] [1957] 2 Lloyd's Rep. 466; affirmed [1958] 2 Lloyd's Rep. 425, CA.

[34] [1937] 2 All E.R. 193.

[35] *Woolcott v. Sun Alliance & London Insurance Ltd* [1978] 1 All E.R. 1253 at 1257, *per* Caulfield J.; *Regina Fur Co. Ltd v. Bossom* [1957] 2 Lloyd's Rep. 466; *Schoolman v. Hall* [1951] 1 Lloyd's Rep. 139, CA.

[36] *Woolcott v. Excess Insurance Co. Ltd* [1978] 1 Lloyd's Rep. 633 at 638, *per* Caulfield J.; retrial ordered without affecting this point [1979] 1 Lloyd's Rep. 231, CA; reported [1979] 2 Lloyd's Rep. 210.

[37] *Reynolds & Anderson v. Phoenix Assurance Co. Ltd* [1978] 2 Lloyd's Rep. 440 at 459, *per* Forbes J.

[38] [1966] 2 Lloyd's Rep. 113 at 133.

and Anderson v. Phoenix Assurance Co. Ltd[39] contended that a mere allegation of fraud against one of the insuring partners was a material matter for disclosure irrespective of whether the allegation was true or false. The authority relied on was an *obiter dictum* of May J. in *March Cabaret Club Ltd v. London Assurance Ltd*[40] where he said:

> "There is one thing however which I would like to add; had it been material I would have been prepared to hold in this case that in any event Mr Scolding ought to have disclosed the fact of his arrest, charge and committal for trial at the date of renewal even though in truth he was innocent."

In his discourse upon consideration of this contention, Forbes J. **3–52** admirably explained what may be regarded as the true foundation of the requirement to disclose criminal convictions and the like[41]:

> "With the greatest respect to Mr Justice May I must decline to follow him in this suggestion. The object of requiring disclosure of circumstances which affect the moral risk is . . . to discover whether the proposer is a person likely to be an additional risk from the point of view of insurance. The most relevant circumstance for disclosure is therefore that he has actually committed an offence of a character which would in fact influence the insurer's judgment. The proposer is bound to disclose the commission of that offence even though he has been acquitted or even if no one other than he has the slightest idea that he committed it: the material circumstance is the commission of the offence. A conviction of a criminal offence is itself, it seems to me, also material (if the commission of the offence is itself material) even though the proposer may protest his innocence or in fact has not committed the offence; for a responsible insurer is himself entitled to assume that prima facie the proposer was rightly convicted and has therefore in fact committed the offence. If therefore an allegation of a relevant criminal offence is made and the allegation is true the proposer must disclose it not because the allegation has been made but because the offence has in fact been committed; it is not then the allegation which must be disclosed but the underlying fact that a crime has been committed. This seems to me to be trite law . . . In my view the [criminal] allegation which the defendants made no attempt to suggest had any basis in fact, was not a material fact to be disclosed. This also disposes of another of the defendants' submissions namely that there is some cumulative effect where there is a conviction followed some time later by an allegation of dishonesty. If the later allegation is an unfounded one and therefore not a matter for disclosure, it can add nothing to any previous disclosable behaviour nor could it in any way affect the moral hazard."

The Rehabilitation of Offenders Act 1974 has abrogated the duty of **3–53** disclosure by an insured to a considerable extent, providing as follows:

> "Effect of rehabilitation
>
> **4.** — (1) Subject to sections 7 and 8 below, a person who has become a rehabilitated person for the purposes of this Act in respect of a conviction shall be treated for all purposes in law as a person who has not committed or been charged with or prosecuted for or convicted of or sentenced for the offence

[39] [1978] 2 Lloyd's Rep. 440.
[40] [1975] 1 Lloyd's Rep. 169 at 177.
[41] [1978] 2 Lloyd's Rep. 440 at 460.

or offences which were the subject of that conviction; and, notwithstanding the provisions of any other enactment or rule of law to the contrary, but subject as aforesaid —

   (a) no evidence shall be admissible in any proceedings before a judicial authority exercising its jurisdiction or functions in Great Britain to prove that any such person has committed or been charged with or prosecuted for or convicted of or sentenced for any offence which was the subject of a spent conviction; and

   (b) a person shall not, in any such proceedings, be asked, and, if asked, shall not be required to answer, any question relating to his past which cannot be answered without acknowledging or referring to a spent conviction or spent convictions or any circumstances ancillary thereto.

(2) Subject to the provisions of any order made (by the Secretary of State) where a question seeking information with respect to a person's previous convictions, offences, conduct or circumstances is put to him or to any other person other wise than in proceedings before a judicial authority —

   (a) the question shall be treated as not relating to spent convictions, and the answer thereto may be framed accordingly; and

   (b) the person questioned shall not be subjected to any liability or otherwise prejudiced in law by reason of any failure to acknowledge or disclose a spent conviction or any circumstances ancillary to a spent conviction in his answer to the question.

(3) Subject to the provisions of any order made (by the Secretary of State) —

   (a) any obligation imposed on any person by any rule of law or by the provisions of any agreement or arrangements to disclose any matters to any other person shall not extend to requiring him to disclose a spent conviction or any circumstances ancillary to a spent conviction (whether the conviction is his own or another's);

   (b) [. . .]

(4) For the purposes of this section . . . any of the following are circumstances ancillary to a conviction, that is to say —

   (a) the offence or offences which were the subject of that conviction;

   (b) the conduct constituting that offence or those offences; and

   (c) any process or proceedings preliminary to that conviction, any sentence imposed in respect of that conviction, any proceedings (whether by way of appeal or otherwise) for reviewing that conviction or any such sentence, and anything done in pursuance of or undergone in compliance with any such sentence.

Rehabilitation periods for particular sentences

5. — (1) The sentences excluded from rehabilitation under this Act are —

   (a) a sentence of imprisonment for life;

   (b) a sentence of imprisonment or corrective training for a term exceeding thirty months;

   (c) a sentence of preventive detention; and

   (d) a sentence of detention during Her Majesty's pleasure or for life, . . . and any other sentence is a sentence subject to rehabilitation under this Act.

(2) [. . .]"

Section 5 goes on to specify the relevant period after which time, the **3–54** conviction becomes "spent". In particular, custodial sentences of over 30 months never become "spent", those of six to 30 months become "spent" after 10 years, and those of lesser periods after seven years. Other sentences are generally "spent" after five years, except conditional discharges and probation orders which are spent one year after the end of the discharge or order, and a period of six months for absolute discharges. However, the Act further provides in section 7(3):

> ". . . If at any stage in any proceedings before a judicial authority in Great Britain the authority is satisfied in the light of any considerations which appear to it to be relevant including any evidence which has been or may thereafter be put before it that justice cannot be done in the case except by admitting or requiring evidence relating to a person's spent convictions or to circumstances ancillary thereto, that authority may admit or as the case may be require the evidence in question notwithstanding the provisions of sub-section 1 of section 4 above and may determine any issue to which the evidence relates in disregard, so far as necessary, of those provisions."

Although in *Reynolds and Anderson v. Phoenix Assurance Co. Ltd*   **3–55** Forbes J. found that an isolated conviction for receiving 11 years old was an immaterial fact in relation to the proposal for fire insurance in 1972, he went on to express his views, *obiter*, upon the effect of the 1974 Act, in this case where the insurers alleged non-disclosure of a "spent" criminal conviction[42]:

> "The provisions of section 4(1) are those which prohibit the giving of evidence relating to a spent conviction or the fact that the person so convicted committed the offence with which he had been charged. It is the reference to the evidence which I have emphasised in section 7(3) which seems to me to make it incumbent upon a Judge of first instance to deal with this matter. Had I considered that the defendants had proved that the conviction was a material fact it would have been because I would have accepted the evidence of those of the expert witnesses who maintained that the conviction was material. This in its turn would be because I accepted that it was the general practice among insurance companies to require such matters to be disclosed, to consider themselves entitled to refuse cover in such circumstances, and this is important, to avoid a policy on the ground of material non-disclosure in cases where no such disclosure was made. It would be against that background that I would have had to have judged whether or not I was satisfied that justice could not be done in the case except by admitting or requiring evidence of the spent conviction. It seems to me on those hypotheses that there is really only one conclusion to which I could have come. If the universal practice of insurance companies would involve the probable refusal of cover if the fact of a previous conviction had been disclosed . . . then there would be no real injustice to the plaintiffs in requiring the conviction to be disclosed now because on this view they were bound to disclose it in 1972, did not do so, and therefore obtained a policy which otherwise they would probably never have obtained. On the defendants' side on the other hand there would be the gravest injustice because they would be prevented from avoiding a policy, which on this view of the evidence it would be the universal practice of insurers to avoid in such circumstances, and would be bound

[42] [1978] 2 Lloyd's Rep. 46 at 461–462.

> to pay insurance moneys on a policy relating to a risk which, again on this view of the evidence, they would, by universal practice, have been entitled to decline."

3–56   It is submitted that this *obiter dictum* should be understood within its confines of dealing with a case coming to trial after the 1974 Act had come into force, concerning an allegation of non-disclosure of a previous conviction (now "spent" under the Act) taking place prior to the Act's coming into force. This passage should not be considered as creating any doubt that evidence of "spent" convictions is not, without leave, to be adduced in court where an insurer alleges non-disclosure of that conviction since the 1974 Act has come into force. Any contrary view, it is submitted, would be ignoring that the primary purpose of the Act, as provided in section 4, is to have "spent" convictions treated "for all purposes in law" as though they had never happened, and the person who has the "spent" conviction, or convictions, is to be treated as though he had not committed or been charged with the offence in question. The Court of Appeal's decision in this same case that it was a matter for the trial judge whether to admit the evidence under section 7(3) is wholly consistent with this view.[43]

Gender, race or disability

3–57   As mentioned in Chapter 1, above, the Sex Discrimination Act 1975, the Race Relations Act 1976 and the Disability Discrimination Act 1995, provide that it is unlawful for persons, *inter alia* providing insurance cover[44] to the public, to discriminate on the grounds of sex or race against any person seeking cover by failing to provide that cover on the same terms as those on which they are available to other members of the public. The 1976 Act defines "racial grounds" as referring to colour, race, nationality or ethnic or national origins.[45] In view of these statutory changes, the decision in *Horne v. Poland*[46] that the nationality of the proposer was a material fact cannot be said to represent a view that a court is now entitled to find.

Previous refusals

3–58   It is not possible to lay down a general rule as to the materiality of the fact that other insurers have refused to insure the insured on previous occasions, other than that a previous refusal in respect of the same risk is virtually bound to be material, but a refusal in respect of a different risk may or may not be material. The whole issue may also be affected by the construction and effect to be given to specific questions put by the insurer to the insured. Thus, in *Locker and Woolf Ltd v. Western Australian Insurance*

[43] [1978] 2 Lloyd's Rep. 22, CA.
[44] Sex Discrimination Act 1975, s.29(2)(c); Race Relations Act 1976, s.20(2)(c); Disability Discrimination Act 1995, s.19.
[45] Race Relations Act 1976, ss.1 and 3.
[46] [1922] 2 K.B. 364; see also *Becker v. Marshall* (1922) 12 Ll. L. Rep. 413, CA; *Lyons v. J. W. Bentley Ltd* (1944) 77 Ll. L. Rep. 335.

Co. Ltd,[47] the proposal question asked "Has this or any other insurance of yours been declined by any other company?" and this was, not surprisingly, because of its wide form, held to require disclosure of a refusal of a motor insurance even though fire insurance was being sought. However, merely because an insurer asks a question about a particular fact does not mean that non-disclosure of that fact will give rise to the insurer's right to rescind the policy,[48] the insurer must always prove that such fact was a material fact and that he was induced to enter into it (see above). The proof of the materiality of the fact of the previous refusal can be satisfied under the ground of the "moral hazard" of the proposers.[49] Even in the absence of any question in the proposal form, it has been held that the fact that a previous insurer has declined to renew an insurance on the same risk, is a material fact that the insured is under a duty to disclose.[50]

Where a proposal question seeks facts of a previous refusal of insurance,[51] and, by its construction, serves to define the extent of disclosure of material facts, then the insurer may be regarded as dispensing with the need for the insured to meet the full rigours of his common law duty of disclosure. As has been said by the Court of Appeal[52]:   **3–59**

> "It is unquestionably plain that questions in a proposal form may be so framed as necessarily to imply that the underwriter only wants information on certain subject-matters, or that within a particular subject-matter their desire for information is restricted within the narrow limits indicated by the terms of the question, and, in such a case, they may *pro tanto* dispense the proposer from what otherwise at Common Law would have been a duty to disclose everything material."

Similarly, in a different case, again in the Court of Appeal, it was said[53]:   **3–60**

> "I think also that the insurance office may, by the requisitions for information of a specific sort, which it makes of the proposer, relieve him partially from the obligation to disclose by an election to make enquiries as to certain facts material to the risk to be insured against . . ."

Thus, if the proposal question asks for information about refusals, etc., by other insurers "within the last five years", refusals made earlier in time may well not give the insurer a right to avoid the policy if they are not disclosed.[54] Where a proposal question relates to previous refusals to

---

[47] [1936] 1 K.B. 408, CA.
[48] *cf. Glicksman v. Lancashire & General Assurance Co. Ltd* [1925] 2 K.B. 593 at 609 *per* Scrutton L.J., CA, though this view was not specifically affirmed [1927] A.C. 139, HL.
[49] *ibid.*
[50] *Re Yager & Guardian Assurance Co.* (1912) 108 L.T. 38; *Ascott v. Cornhill Insurance Co. Ltd* (1937) 58 Ll. L. Rep. 41.
[51] See, *e.g. Arthrude Press Ltd v. Eagle Star & British Dominions Insurance Co. Ltd* (1924) 19 Ll. L. Rep. 373, CA; *Glicksman v. Lancashire & General Assurance Co. Ltd* [1927] A.C. 139, HL.
[52] *Schoolman v. Hall* [1951] 1 Lloyd's Rep. 139, at 143, *per* Asquith L.J., CA.
[53] *Joel v. Law Union & Crown Insurance Co. Ltd* [1908] 2 K.B. 863 at 878, *per* Vaughan Williams L.J., CA.
[54] *Jester-Barnes v. Licences & General Insurance Co. Ltd* (1934) 49 Ll. L. Rep. 231 at 237, *per* McKinnon J. (*obiter*).

"accept" or "renew" the insured's insurances, it has been held that the insurers did not require information about refusals by other insurers to transfer an insurance to be insured upon the same peril.[55] An offer by a previous insurer only upon special terms may also amount to a material fact.[56]

Previous losses

3–61   A question in a proposal form seeking information about previous "losses" of the proposer, will not be construed as referring only to losses that the proposer has suffered which were not covered by insurance, but also to losses which were indemnified by insurers,[57] or where property was stolen but later returned by the police.[58] Insurers invariably ask questions in their proposal forms about the previous losses suffered by the insured.[59] Being a material fact, the insured will, of course, be under a duty to disclose that fact of a loss under the same type of insurance even in the absence of any proposal question, unless, in the circumstances, the insurers can be considered to have waived that duty of disclosure. It is too wide a proposition, though, simply to say that a proposer for any insurance must disclose the fact that he has had, during the course of his life, claims on other policies of every kind.[60]

Unusual risk of loss

3–62   Special facts which render the risk of loss unusually greater should be disclosed to the insurer as they are likely to be material facts. Thus it has been held that where it was desired to effect an "all risks" insurance in respect of pictures and objets d'art stored in premises, it was material to know that those premises would be unoccupied outside normal business hours.[61] Where the premises to be insured under a fire policy were very close to some other premises that have recently caught fire, that fact has also been held to be a material fact requiring disclosure,[62] although normal risks incidental to the normal trade user of the premises will be presumed to be known to the insurer.[63] Believable threats or attempts, e.g. to set fire to premises or other property the subject of insurance against fire or relating to other losses being covered by the relevant insurance, have been proven to be material facts which must be disclosed unless those threats, attempts, or other facts can be said to be unnecessary to disclose,

---

[55] *Golding v. Royal London Auxiliary Insurance Co. Ltd* (1914) 30 T.L.R. 350.

[56] *Dent v. Blackmore* (1927) 29 Ll. L. Rep. 9.

[57] *Roberts v. Avon Insurance Co. Ltd* [1956] 2 Lloyd's Rep. 240.

[58] *Morser v. Eagle Star & British Dominions Insurance Co. Ltd* (1931) 40 Ll. L. Rep. 254.

[59] See, *e.g. Krantz v. Allan & Faber* (1921) 9 Ll. L. Rep. 410; *Rozanes v. Bowen* (1928) 32 Ll. L. Rep. 98, CA; *Farra v. Hetherington* (1931) 47 T.L.R. 465; *Condogianis v. Guardian Assurance Co. Ltd* [1921] 2 A.C. 125, PC; *Arterial Caravans Ltd v. Yorkshire Insurance Co. Ltd* [1973] 1 Lloyd's Rep. 169; *Marene Knitting Mills Pty Ltd v. Greater Pacific General Insurance Ltd* [1976] 2 Lloyd's Rep. 631, PC.

[60] *Ewer v. National Employers' Mutual General Insurance Association Ltd* [1937] 2 All E.R. 193 at 200, *per* McKinnon J.

[61] *Haase v. Evans* (1934) 48 Ll. L. Rep. 131.

[62] *Bufe v. Turner* (1815) 6 Taunt. 338.

[63] *Hales v. Reliance Fire & Accident Insurance Corp. Ltd* [1960] 2 Lloyd's Rep. 391.

e.g. by reason of common notoriety.[64] Indeed, where premises are being insured, it may be material for the insurers to be informed of the nature of the goods kept or other contents of those premises, particularly if they would otherwise be led to think that the premises were empty.[65]

Where the general nature of the goods insured is disclosed, but not in more particular terms, that may or may not be a non-disclosure or misrepresentation of a material fact. It may simply give rise to the insurer contending that he was not insuring what was actually there, but what he was told was to be insured. This occurred in *A.F. Watkinson and Co. Ltd v. Hullett*,[66] where the insurers were able to successfully defend the claim upon the ground that they were insuring the stock of the insured paperboard merchants, as proposed to them, and not the hazardous stock of 500 tons of waste paper which was actually at the insured's premises. No argument on non-disclosure of the actual stock of waste paper was necessary. In contrast, in *Herman v. Phoenix Assurance Co. Ltd*[67] the claimant merchant insured some furs under a fire policy, giving the description of the goods to be insured as "general merchandise". Whilst the Court of Appeal in fact held that the claim was fraudulent, Scrutton L.J. commented *obiter*, as follows as regards the defence of misrepresentation[68]:

> "I think [the claimant] would have failed on misrepresentation if he had not failed on fraud. Personally, I am extremely doubtful whether, if you insure general merchandise, and the nature of the greater part is valuable furs, you are not guilty of concealment in not stating what you know of the nature of the goods. I do not wish to be taken as agreeing with the view the [trial] Judge has taken that, if you go to insure general merchandise and know that two-thirds of the value insured are furs of a very valuable nature, you are not guilty of concealment if you say nothing to the underwriter except that it is general merchandise."

Similarly, in *Anglo-African Merchants Ltd v. Bayley*[69] where the claimants had insured 20-year-old army surplus leather jerkins under the description "new men's clothes in bales for export", Megaw J. (as he then was) held that the facts that the clothes were war surplus and of old manufacture were material facts to be disclosed when they insured those goods under the "all risks" insurance[70]:

> "In particular, in relation to the fact of war surplus, I am satisfied that underwriters, rightly or wrongly, but not unreasonably, regard war surplus goods, at any rate war surplus clothing, as being goods which they classify as 'hot'; that is, involving an abnormally high risk of theft. In relation to the age of the goods underwriters would normally and reasonably be concerned with the possibility of defects, such as staining, in respect of which claims

3–63

3–64

---

[64] *Leen v. Hall* (1923) 16 Ll. L. Rep. 100; *Pimm v. Lewis* (1862) 2 F. and F. 778.
[65] *Versicherungs und Transport A.G. Daugava v. Henderson* (1934) 48 Ll. L. Rep. 54 at 58, *per* Roche J.; affirmed (1934) 49 Ll. L. Rep. 252, CA.
[66] (1938) 61 Ll. L. Rep. 145.
[67] (1924) 18 Ll. L. Rep. 371, CA.
[68] *ibid.* at 372.
[69] [1970] 1 Q.B. 311, other aspects of the case are discussed above.
[70] *ibid.*

might be made and it might be a matter of great difficulty and dispute to ascertain when the damage was in fact sustained; unless, of course, a pre-insurance inspection were to be required as a condition of accepting the risk."

3–65   The structure and locality of the premises in which insured goods are kept may also in themselves be material if they are likely to increase the chance of the occurrence of an insured peril, or the chance of reducing the loss on the occurrence of the peril.[71] On the other hand, it has been said that insurers should only count on the insured disclosing to them unusual attributes of the risk which could not ordinarily be appreciated from the facts given by the insured.[72]

Over-valuation of the subject matter

3–66   Whilst an insured is allowed to insure goods at a price which includes an element of anticipated profit without being guilty of a material overvalu-ation of the subject matter insured,[73] an excessive valuation given for the purpose of a valued policy may be proved by the insurers to be a material fact[74] because it changes the character of the risk from a business risk to a speculative risk.[75] Thus, in *Hoff Trading Co. v. Union Insurance Society of Canton Ltd*[76] it was found that some bearer shares, insured against loss in transit, were given an excessive valuation based on optimistic expectations of their future value, and excessive valuation of negative films was shown in *Fournier v. Valentine*,[77] when the films had cost £500 but were insured for £12,000 under a burglary policy. Again, in *Haase v. Evans*[78] it was found that paintings and objets d'art were given an excessive valuation. The giving of inflated trading figures when proposing for fire and business interruption insurance affects the "moral hazard" of the proposed risk and thus amounts to a material fact which should be disclosed.[79] Wilful misrepresentation of the value of property destroyed when making a claim under an indemnity insurance is not concealment of a material fact, but may well amount to a breach of the insured's continuing duty of good faith entitling the insurer to avoid the policy.[80]

Existence of other insurances

3–67   The general principle with regard to all insurances of indemnity is that the fact of other insurances held by the insured covering the same risk and subject matter will not be material, because the liability of the insurer is likely to be lessened rather than increased upon the application of the

---

[71] *Dawsons Ltd v. Bonnin* [1922] 2 A.C. 413 at 429, *per* Lord Finlay, HL; see also *Johnson and Perrot Ltd v. Holmes* (1925) 21 Ll. L. Rep. 330.
[72] *Greenhill v. Federal Insurance Co. Ltd* [1927] 1 K.B. 65 at 85, *per* Scrutton L.J., CA.
[73] *Mathie v. Argonaut Marine Insurance Co. Ltd* (1925) 21 Ll. L. Rep. 145, HL.
[74] *Ionides v. Fender* (1874) L.R. 9 Q.B. 531.
[75] (1874) L.R. 9 Q.B. 531 at 538–539, *per* Blackburn J.
[76] (1929) 45 T.L.R. 466, CA.
[77] (1930) 38 Ll. L. Rep. 19.
[78] (1934) 48 Ll. L. Rep. 131.
[79] *Insurance Corp. of the Channel Islands v. The Royal Hotel Ltd* [1998] Lloyd's Rep. 151.
[80] *Britton v. Royal Insurance Co.* (1866) 4 F. and F. 905.

doctrine of contribution.[81] Over-insurance may reach such a level as to amount to a material fact, though,[82] its materiality, perhaps, being in relation to the questionability of the insured's honest intentions and the "moral hazard" associated with insuring that risk.

Facts affecting the insurer's rights of subrogation

It is probably trite to point out that if the insurer's prospects of recouping some of the insurance moneys paid under a policy are reduced by particular circumstances, those circumstances must be related to the insurer by the person proposing for insurance, for they are material to the risk being run by the insurer if he decides to accept the risk. This is illustrated by the case of *Tate v. Hyslop*[83] where the insured did not make known to the insurers that, contrary to the normal practice, he had agreed with the carrier of his goods that the carrier should only be liable for damage to or loss of the goods carried in the case of carrier's negligence. It was held that this fact should have been disclosed to the insurer, because it affected his rights of subrogation[84] against the carrier.

3–68

Interest in the subject matter

English law only requires the proposer for insurance to disclose his interest in the subject matter of the insurance, *e.g.* the buildings or goods, if the concealment of that fact also conceals further facts stemming therefrom that are relevant under the test of materiality. Thus, it has been held, *obiter*, that where an insured is merely a tenant at will in premises which he insures, because a prudent insurer would wish to know that his option to reinstate the premises under the policy may be impossible to enforce, and such a clause normally appeared in such issued policies, the policy was vitiated.[85] The rule is that you must specify the subject matter of the insurance, not your interest in it,[86] so it will generally not matter if the insured does not disclose that he is a bailee[87] or mortgagee[88] of the subject matter.

3–69

Contractual modification of the duty and remedies

As mentioned above, the insurer can modify the duty owed by the proposer for insurance by, for example, confining the request for information to a specified period. Thus, only details of losses in the past five years might be sought. A contract of insurance could even exclude the duty of disclosure of an insured or his agent by an appropriate wording, and in the same way the contract could exclude the insurer's right to avoid liability

3–70

[81] See Chapter 20, below.
[82] *Thames & Mersey Marine Insurance Co. v. Gunford Ship Co.* [1911] A.C. 529, HL.
[83] (1885) 15 Q.B.D. 368, CA.
[84] See Chapter 20, below.
[85] *Anderson v. Commercial Union Assurance Co.* (1885) 1 T.L.R. 511; not commented on by the Court of Appeal (1885) 55 L.J.Q.B. 146, CA.
[86] *Mackenzie v. Whitworth* (1875) L.R. 10 Exch. 142 at 148, *per* Bramwell J.; *London & North Western Railway Co. v. Glyn* (1859) 1 E. and E. 652 at 664, *per* Crompton J.; *Crowley v. Cohen* (1832) 3 B. and Ad. 478 at 485, *per* Lord Tenterden C.J.
[87] *London & North Western Railway Co. v. Glyn,* (1859) 1 E. and E. 652.
[88] *Ogden v. Montreal Insurance Co.* (1853) 3 C.P. 497.

for breach of the duty of disclosure. However, the intention of the parties must be clear and unequivocal in the contract.[89] Such a provision was upheld in a professional indemnity insurance in *Kumar v. A.G.F. Insurance Ltd*,[90] where the non-avoidance clause was held to be fully effective to prevent the normal consequences of both breach of warranty as well as non-disclosure of a material fact at inception of the insurance. That clause had provided that the insurers would not seek to "avoid repudiate or rescind this insurance upon any ground whatsoever including in particular non-disclosure or misrepresentation". Such a provision can be drafted as to only assist innocent members of the insured, but not dishonest members of the insured, as in *Arab Bank plc v. Zurich Insurance Co.*[91]

7. AFFIRMATION BY THE INSURER

3–71   The law in the context of an insurer being alleged to have affirmed, or elected to continue with, the insurance contract has recently been reviewed by Mance J. (as he then was) in the fire insurance case of *Insurance Corporation of the Channel Islands v. The Royal Hotel Ltd*[92] His lordship's conclusions were that affirmation[93]:

(i)   involves an informed choice to treat the contract as continuing, made with knowledge of the facts giving rise to the right to avoid it;

(ii) actual knowledge is required, not any form of constructive knowledge, but a person who deliberately and for tactical reasons decided not to acquire definite knowledge of a matter which he believed it likely that he could confirm, must be treated as having knowledge of that matter[94];

(iii) for practical purposes, knowledge pre-supposes the truth of the matters known, and a firm belief in their truth, as well as sufficient justification for the belief in terms of experience, information and/or reasoning;

(iv) the insurer need not know all the facts provided he knows sufficient of the facts to know that he has the right to elect to treat the contract as discharged or continuing; and

(v)   the making of his choice must be communicated unequivocally to the insured before there can be a binding affirmation. The communication itself or the surrounding circumstances must demonstrate objectively or unequivocally that the insurer affirming is making an informed choice.

---

[89] *H.I.H. Casualty & General Insurance Ltd v. Chase Manhattan Bank & others* [2000] T.L.R. 668.
[90] [1999] 1 W.L.R. 1747.
[91] [1999] 1 Lloyd's Rep. 262.
[92] [1998] Lloyd's Rep. I.R. 151.
[93] *ibid.* at 161–162.
[94] *ibid.* at 172.

Expanding on this last aspect, Mance J. said[95]:

3–72

> "Whether conduct amounts to an unequivocal communication of a choice to affirm requires therefore, an objective assessment of the impact of the relevant conduct on a reasonable person in the position of the other party to the contract. A reasonable person in that position must, it seems to me, be treated as having a general understanding of the possibility of choice between affirmation and objection. In affirmation (as distinct from estoppel), the actual state of mind of the other party is not the test. Affirmation depends on the objective manifestation of choice."

The insurers were held[96] to have affirmed the fire insurance in this case because, despite being aware of the falsity of many of the invoices underlying the trading of the hotel, and thus their right to rescind the insurance for non-disclosure of this "moral hazard" aspect of the hotel risk proposed, they (through their solicitors) continued to defend the litigated claim on other grounds when any reasonable person in the shoes of the insured would realise the insurers knew of the false trading figures. Moreover, the insurers had then participated in a tri-partite arbitration upon quantum, again without taking any issue upon their liability under the insurance policy. Thereafter, the insurers had pursued trying to agree costs under the arbitrator's second interim award, which the judge concluded could only underline the view that the insurers, by their conduct, recognized unequivocally the validity of that award and the fire policy itself. The case is a salutary lesson for insurers trying to keep their remedy of rescission for known matters as an "ace" up their sleeve, whilst "stringing" the insured along in protracted litigation where rescission for non-disclosure or misrepresentation is not pleaded.

3–73

---

[95] *ibid.* at 162.
[96] *ibid.* at 171–175.

CHAPTER 4

THE DUTIES AND LIABILITIES OF INSURANCE BROKERS AND INTERMEDIARIES

1. THE ROLE OF INSURANCE BROKERS AND OTHER INTERMEDIARIES

Introduction

4–01   Although the regime is about to be altered by the repeal of this legislation by the Financial Services and Markets Act 2000, at the time of writing "Insurance broker" is a title that should only be used by those registered with the Insurance Brokers Registration Council pursuant to the Insurance Brokers (Registration) Act 1977.[1] It is an offence for an unregistered individual or an unenrolled body corporate to use the description "insurance broker", or any other description falsely implying registration or enrolment,[2] but there is no restriction on carrying out the functions of an insurance broker under any other title or description, which explains the growth of persons and companies using descriptions such as "insurance services", "insurance consultants", and "insurance agents" to avoid registration under the Act. Registered brokers are generally members of the British Insurance and Investment Brokers Association ("B.I.I.B.A."), a long-established association promoting education and training of insurance brokers and their staff. Formal training and examinations for all those within the insurance industry as a whole are provided by the Chartered Insurance Institute ("C.I.I."), the highest qualification being "Chartered Insurer". There is a new body that seeks to regulate the whole of the general insurance community in the United Kingdom, which is the General Insurance Standards Council ("G.I.S.C."). It is an independent, non-statutory organisation which was set up to regulate the sales, advisory and service standards of its membership, who are insurers, agents, brokers and other intermediaries. The G.I.S.C. aims to set standards above those presently existing under the 1977 Act and put in place by the Association of British Insurers ("A.B.I."), and its Commercial Code is reproduced in Appendix 15. These non-statutory Codes are helpful in determining a question of negligence as they represent the context in which a non-registered broker must operate, and also assists the court in not setting unrealistically high or perfectionist standards.[3]

Registration under the 1977 Act

4–02   To become an insurance broker under the 1977 Act, a person must satisfy the Council[4] that he holds an approved qualification together with

---

[1] The Act is reproduced in Appendix 11, below.

[2] The Insurance Brokers (Registration) Act, 1977, ss.22–24.

[3] *Harvest Trucking Co. Ltd v. P.B. Davis* [1991] 2 Lloyd's Rep. 638, at 644, *per* H.H.J. Diamond Q.C., sitting as a judge of the Commercial Court.

[4] *ibid.*, s.3.

a minimum of three years' full-time[5] experience of insurance broking or of acting as an agent for two or more insurance companies. If the approved qualification is not held, the minimum period of necessary full-time experience required is five years. The Council must also be satisfied as to the applicant's character and suitability to be a registered insurance broker, and that if he is carrying on business as an insurance broker at the time that the application is made, that he is complying with the Council's rules regarding capital and solvency margins.[6] A person who is authorised to sell investments under the Financial Services Act 1986 automatically meets the suitability requirement of the 1977 Act.[7] A Code of Conduct applies to all registered brokers, and this is reproduced in the Appendix. By section 12 of the Act all registered insurance brokers must maintain professional indemnity insurance for the protection of their clients.

Broker is agent of client, not the insurer

It is important to remember that the broker or other intermediary,   4-03
unless he is an employed or tied agent of an insurer, is, in law, the agent of the person seeking insurance and not the agent of the insurer.[8] This principle applies both when the insurance is being placed by the broker and thereafter, for instance, when a claim arises under the policy. It is therefore quite wrong for the broker to accept instructions from the insurer to obtain a loss adjuster's report for them upon a claim by the insured, and not to disclose that report to the insured. Megaw J. (as he then was) thoroughly criticised such a practice in *Anglo-African Merchants Ltd v. Bayley*[9] on the basis that, under established rules of agency, no agent who has accepted an employment from one principal can in law accept an engagement inconsistent with his duty to the first principal, unless he makes the fullest disclosure to each principal of his interest, and obtains the consent of each principal to the double employment.[10] Shortly afterwards, in *North and South Trust Co. v. Berkeley*,[11] Donaldson J. (as he then was) repeated the condemnation of this long-established practice by Lloyd's brokers,[12] and stated that the insured could claim damages if, and to the extent that, the partial dislodgement of the single agency agreement causes him loss or damage.[13] The fact that the broker is the insureds' agent is even now often not understood by insureds, who mistakenly regard the

[5] Part-time experience is not sufficient, *Pickles v. Insurance Brokers Registration Council* [1984] 1 W.L.R. 748.

[6] See the Insurance Brokers Registration Council (Accounts and Business Requirements) Rules Approval Order 1979 (S.I. 1979 No.489), as amended by S.I. 1981 No.1630, which are reproduced in the Appendix, below.

[7] Financial Services Act 1986, s.138.

[8] *Rozanes v. Bowen* (1928) 32 Ll. L. Rep. 98 at 101, *per* Scrutton L.J., CA; *Newsholme Bros. v. Road Transport & General Insurance Co. Ltd* [1929] 2 K.B. 356, CA; *Deeny v. Walker and others* [1996] L.R.L.R. 276 at 282, *per* Gatehouse J.

[9] *Anglo-African Merchants Ltd v. Bayley* [1970] 1 Q.B. 311.

[10] *Fulwood v. Hurley* [1928] 1 K.B. 498 at 502, *per* Scrutton L.J., CA.

[11] [1971] 1 W.L.R. 470.

[12] This practice is now prohibited by the Lloyd's Code of Practice for Lloyd's Brokers (1988) unless fully informed consent from both parties has been obtained.

[13] [1971] 1 W.L.R. 470 at 486.

broker as a representative of the insurer for receipt of information in regard to both the proposal or renewal, and claims.

Dual agency of broker

4-04   The precarious position in which brokers (wherever "broker" is used below in this Chapter, it should be understood to be a shorthand for "broker or other intermediary") place themselves when they allow themselves to be agents of both the insured and the insurer is illustrated by the case of *Woolcott v. Excess Insurance Co. Ltd (No.2)*.[14] Here, the brokers effectively arranged insurance for the claimant with themselves, in that they were authorised by the defendant insurers to bind insurances for their account, and initial documents of insurance and endorsements on their behalf. It was found as a fact that the brokers were aware of the serious criminal past of the claimant, but, without passing on that information to the insurance company, issued the claimant with contents insurance. Their principals for this purpose, the defendant insurance company, were therefore imputed with knowledge of the claimant insured's criminal past, and were thus unable to subsequently rescind the insurance policy for alleged non-disclosure of that criminal past. The broker, however, were held liable to indemnify the insurance company in respect of their liability to the claimant, for breach of their duty to convey those material facts to the insurance company in their role as agent of the insurer.

2. DUTIES TO CLIENTS

The duty is to exercise all reasonable care and skill

4-05   It has long been accepted that the broker/client relationship gives rise to an implied contractual duty that the broker will exercise all reasonable care and skill in the performance of his instructions. This term is also imposed by section 13 of the Supply of Goods and Services Act 1982, and, by section 16, can only be negated or varied if, and in so far as, the test of "reasonableness" under the Unfair Contract Terms Act 1977 is met. The broker will also owe a co-extensive duty of care in the common law tort of negligence arising from the broker's position of being a person professing to have special skill. The duty of an insurance broker or other intermediary is the same, and it is to exercise such a reasonable and ordinary degree of care and skill "as a person of average capacity and ordinary ability in his situation and profession might fairly be expected to exert".[15]

Limitation of actions against brokers

4-06   The normal time bars under the Limitation Act 1980 are six years from the date that the cause of action accrued in contract (date of breach of contract), or in tort (date of damage). This period may be extended in the

---

[14] [1979] 2 Lloyd's Rep. 210.
[15] *Harvest Trucking Co. Ltd v. P.B. Davis* [1991] 2 Lloyd's Rep. 638 at 643, *per* H.H.J. Diamond Q.C., sitting as a judge of the Commercial Court.

case of claims in tort only, where the period can be extended under section 14A of the Act (as amended by the Latent Damage Act 1986) to a period of three years from when the negligent act was or could reasonably have been discovered. There is, though, a long-stop period of 15 years from the date of the act complained of. In relation to claims against brokers by their clients, the date of the accrual of the cause of action in both contract and tort are likely to be the same, namely, the date on which the ineffective or voidable insurance is obtained by the broker for his client. The cause of action does not accrue only at the later date of an insured risk occurring, nor when the insurer exercises his election to rescind the policy, *e.g.* for non-disclosure of material facts. The Court of Appeal has determined this to be the correct position in *Knapp and Knapp v. Ecclesiastical Insurance Group plc and Smith*,[16] determining that the earlier first instance decisions in *Iron Trade Mutual Insurance Co. Ltd v. Buckenham*[17] and *Islander Trucking Co. Ltd v. Hogg Robinson*[18] were distinguishable from the present case, having been concerned with reinsurance and a form of direct insurance respectively. The second defendant broker had acted for the claimants for many years and was alleged to know the matters not disclosed to insurers which led to the insurers' right to rescind the policy *ab initio*. The broker had filled in the proposal form and was alleged not to have warned the claimants of the significance of the matters later complained of by the insurers, and not to have asked sufficient questions of the claimants to ensure that the claimants complied with their duty of disclosure upon renewal. The broker successfully applied to have the claim against him struck out on the grounds that the writ was issued more than six years after the cause of action arose. In the words of Hobhouse L.J.[19]:

> "The [claimants] in the present case had paid their renewal premium without getting in return a binding contract of indemnity from the insurance. They had acted to their detriment: they did not get that to which they were entitled. The fact that how serious the consequences of the negligence would be depended upon subsequent events and contingencies did not alter this; such considerations go to the quantification of the [claimants'] loss not to whether or not they have suffered loss. The risk of loss existed from the outset . . ."

Compliance with instructions

The exact scope of the broker's or other intermediary's authority to   **4–07**
effect a contract of insurance on behalf of his client is to be determined from the client's instructions to the broker. The broker is not under any obligation to advise the client upon what risks the client should seek to insure,[20] unless the client seeks such advice whereupon the broker is under a duty to use reasonable skill and care in so advising. Nor is the broker obliged, unless asked, to tell the client that the insurance being sought is

---

[16] [1998] Lloyd's Rep. I.R. 390, CA.
[17] [1990] 1 All E.R. 808.
[18] [1990] 1 All E.R. 826.
[19] [1998] Lloyd's Rep. I.R. 390 at 402, CA.
[20] *O'Brien v. Hughes-Gibb and Co. Ltd* [1995] L.R.L.R. 90.

unsuitable for the client's needs.[21] If the client does not specify which insurer is to be approached, then it is perfectly proper for the broker to exercise his bona fide discretion as between different insurers offering the requisite insurance.[22] Similarly, a broker is entitled to effect an insurance on terms which are strictly outside his instructions, but are as close to them as can be obtained,[23] unless the client instructed that no insurance was to be effected at all if the specified instructions could not be met.[24] This is because the broker is generally entitled to construe his instructions in a reasonable manner, especially if there was some ambiguity in those instructions.[25]

4-08   Should the broker depart from his instructions, and effect an insurance other than that which he was engaged to effect, the law will not permit him to excuse himself by merely stating that the client should have checked the insurance details[26]:

> "When a broker is engaged to effect an insurance, especially when the broker employed is a broker of repute and experience, the client is entitled to rely upon the broker to carry out his instructions, and is not bound to examine the documents drawn up in performance of those instructions and see whether his instructions have, in fact, been carried out by the broker. In many cases the principal (*i.e.* the client) would not understand the matter, and would not know whether the documentation did in fact carry out his instructions. Business could not be carried on if, when a person has been employed to use care and skill with regard to the matter, the employer is bound to use his own care and skill to see whether the person employed has done what he was employed to do. I think the principal is entitled to rely upon the reputation of the person whom he employs."

4-09   An example of the complete failure of the broker to carry out his instructions is the case of *Fraser v. B. N. Furman (Productions) Ltd*[27] where the defendant employers sued their brokers in third party proceedings. The defendant employers had been sued by their employee for damages following her accident at work in 1962, as a result of which accident she sustained serious injuries. The defendants had instructed the brokers to re-place their various insurances in 1959, including their employers' liability insurance. Upon investigation in 1962, it emerged that those brokers had failed to place any employers' liability insurance contrary to their instructions. Upon determining that such insurance, if effected, would have provided an indemnity to the defendant employers in respect of the employee's claim and costs, the Court of Appeal held the

[21] *Waterkyn v. Eagle Star & British Dominions Insurance Co. Ltd and Price, Forbes and Co. Ltd* (1920) 5 Ll. L. Rep. 42.

[22] *Moore v. Mourgue* (1776) 2 Cowp. 479.

[23] *Waterkyn v. Eagle Star & British Dominions Insurance Co. Ltd and Price, Forbes and Co. Ltd* (1920) 5 Ll. L. Rep. 42.

[24] *King v. Chambers & Newman (Insurance Brokers) Ltd* [1963] 2 Lloyd's Rep. 130.

[25] *Ireland v. Livingston* (1872) L.R. 5 H.L. 395; *James Vale and Co. v. Van Oppen and Co. Ltd* (1921) 37 T.L.R. 367; *Dixon v. Hovill* (1828) 4 Bing. 665.

[26] *Dickson and Co. v. Devitt* (1916) 86 L.J.K.B. 315, *per* Atkin J. (as he then was); *Strong & Pearl v. S. Allison and Co. Ltd* (1926) 25 Ll. L. Rep. 504; *Bollom and Co. Ltd v. Byas Mosley and Co. Ltd* [2000] Lloyd's Rep. I.R. 136.

[27] [1967] 1 W.L.R. 898, CA.

negligent brokers liable to the defendants to the same extent as that insurance indemnity. Again, in *United Marketing Co. v. Hasham Kara*[28] brokers were liable where they had failed to renew their client's fire insurance despite clear instructions so to do, and the client later sustained a loss by fire. In *Ackbar v. C.F. Green and Co. Ltd,*[29] the brokers failed to obtain passenger cover within motor insurance contrary to their instructions.

The second defendant broker would have been liable in *Victor Melik and Co. Ltd v. Norwich Union Fire Insurance Society Ltd and Kemp*[30] for his breach of duty in properly raising matters with the first defendant insurers, if the insurers had been able to rely on a breach of the alarm warranty in a burglary insurance. The claimant company had premises in London, which were used as a warehouse for treating leather skins. The premises were insured against, *inter alia*, theft arranged by the second defendant brokers, and that insurance contained an alarm condition which was stated to be a condition precedent to the insurers' liability. This required the alarm to be kept in efficient working order, to be kept in full operation at all times, and for the maintenance contract company to be informed immediately of any defect. After one burglary in October 1977, the insurers required improvements to security and this was completed on December 16, 1977. On December 20, 1977, at 9 p.m., the claimants were informed that there was a line fault on the alarm system that was connected to the control centre. The claimants inspected the premises and set the alarms to audible only having found that the telephones were not working. They then informed the alarm maintenance company and the G.P.O. of the defect, and the police were asked to make extra patrols of the premises. **4–10**

The claimants then contacted their broker at 10 p.m. to check that they were fully covered by their insurance. The broker confirmed that they were definitely covered. The next morning the G.P.O. informed the claimants that the telephone lines could not be repaired until the following day. The claimants conveyed this by telephone to the broker and specifically asked him to check with the insurers whether they were insured that night, or what alternative action could be taken. An hour or so later the broker rang back and confirmed that he had spoken to the insurers and the claimants were definitely covered by the insurance. That night the claimants' premises were again burgled. In fact, Woolf J. (as he then was) held that the broker had failed to convey to the insurers' representative either that the telephone link would not be repaired that day, or that he was seeking an authoritative decision on the continuing applicability of the insurance. That was a breach of the broker's duty to raise the matter much more clearly than he did with the insurers, and to get the clear and positive answer the claimant's director required. Instead, the broker had relied upon his own judgment, his own view, that the claimants were insured. **4–11**

Needless to say, if the broker incorrectly passes on information to the insurers given to him by his client he will be negligent. This occurred in **4–12**

---

[28] [1963] 1 W.L.R. 523, PC.
[29] [1975] Q.B. 582.
[30] [1980] 1 Lloyd's Rep. 523.

O. and R. Jewellers Ltd v. Terry and Jardine Insurance Brokers Ltd.[31] On renewal, the broker had very properly gone though the previous year's proposal form with his jeweller client, and it was clarified that the client insured had wrongly answered that each of his four safes had both an ordinary key and an early morning alarm (EMA) key. The client had also explained that the keys to three of the safes were locked overnight in safe 2. This was of importance, because there was a condition precedent in the jewellers block policy that all safe keys were removed from the premises overnight. Rather than inform insurers of this at this time, and without making notes about what his client told and showed him, the broker merely arranged for the underwriters to hold covered until a fully completed new proposal form was forwarded. More than two months passed before the broker sought to pass on the information about the keys to the underwriters when he sought removal of the relevant condition precedent. The broker negligently passed on information that one of the safe's keys were kept overnight in another safe.

Delay

4–13   It is not usually negligent for a broker to delay, for a matter of days, sending his client a copy of the insurance policy so that the client can verify that his instructions have been carried out.[32] A broker must carry out his instructions within a reasonable time of their receipt, and equally must promptly inform their client of the cancellation, or the threat of cancellation, of the insurance they have arranged.[33] Without express instructions to the contrary, though, the instructions need not be carried out immediately.[34] Circumstances may impose urgency, though, for example, where the broker knows that the insured believes that he has two insurances for the same risk and is going to cancel one, and the broker learns that the other insurance is cancelled by the insurer, a delay of a week or so to inform the insured is too long.[35] If the broker is, however, unable to procure the insurance he was instructed to obtain, it has been said that it is his duty to inform his client "at once" of his inability to do so.[36] Certainly, the broker is under a duty to report to the client upon their failure to procure the insurance, and, if necessary, seek further instructions.[37] If the effecting of the insurance is delayed through no fault of the broker he will not be liable to his client if a loss occurs in the interim, for instance, where there is a period before the risk is accepted whilst waiting for the insurers' surveyor to inspect the premises which are to be insured.[38]

---

[31] [1999] Lloyd's Rep. I.R. 436.
[32] *United Mills Agencies Ltd v. R.E. Harvey, Bray and Co.* [1952] 1 All E.R. 225n.
[33] *London Borough of Bromley v. R.A. Ellis & A. Luff and Sons* [1971] 1 Lloyd's Rep. 976, CA.
[34] *Cock, Russell and Co. v. Bray, Gibb and Co. Ltd* (1920) 2 Ll. L.Rep. 71.
[35] See *Cherry Ltd v. Allied Insurance Brokers Ltd* [1978] 1 Lloyd's Rep. 274, discussed below.
[36] *Hood v. West End Motor Packing Co.* [1917] 2 K.B. 38 at 47, *per* Scrutton L.J., CA.
[37] *Eagle Star Insurance Co. Ltd v. National Westminster Finance Australia Ltd* (1985) 58 A.L.R. 165, PC.
[38] *Avonale Blouse Co. Ltd v. Williamson and Geo. Town* (1948) 81 Ll. L. Rep. 492.

Choice of insurer

Particular care is to be expected from an insurance broker who advises   **4–14**
his client upon who to insure with. If, for instance, a client comes to his
broker and states that he feels that his present insurer is charging excessive
premiums, and instructs the broker to find another insurer offering lower
premiums, the broker must exercise reasonable care in recommending
another insurer. If the broker advises his client to remove his insurance to
the X Insurance Company, which offers lower premiums, but is under
much attack in the financial press with regards to their financial stability,
the broker will not be discharging his duty to his client with the necessary
appropriate degree of skill and care.[39] A broker is expected to keep watch
on the financial position of the insurers with whom he may place insurance.
Similarly, a broker will probably be negligent if he places the insurance
with an unauthorised insurer if the client is unable to enforce the
insurance.[40]

Moreover, if an insurance broker advises his client to insure with a   **4–15**
particular insurer, for whatever reason, in preference to others, then the
broker is expected to know the full details and exclusions of that policy he
recommends, so that the insurance will properly insure the client against
the risk he wishes to insure. A failure of the broker to ensure that all
features of the policy suit his client's needs may well render the broker
liable to his client if the client is subsequently unable to recover under the
insurance because of the non-compliance with a condition or exclusion of
which he had not been appraised by his broker. Thus, in *McNealy v.
Pennine Insurance Co. Ltd,*[41] the brokers were found liable for failing in
their duty to make as certain as they could that their client came within the
categories of persons acceptable to the insurer from whom insurance was
being sought for the client. The facts were that in June 1971, before leaving
for a six-week tour in Italy with a band in which he played the guitar as a
respite from his main occupation as a property repairer, Mr McNealy went
to offices of the second defendant brokers to insure his Triumph motor
car, which he was picking up on his return from Italy. He told the brokers
that he wanted to effect motor insurance ready for his return to England.
The brokers were in touch with several insurance companies, and recommended the first defendants because they offered very low rates to a
limited class of motorists. The brokers had in their office a leaflet headed
"Underwriting Instructions" issued by the first defendant insurers, and
this set out, amongst other things, a list of "Risks not acceptable".
Amongst those excluded were "bookmakers, jockeys and others connected
with racing", "whole or part-time musicians", "journalists and press
photographers", "students", "service personnel" and any person who had
not been resident in England for a period of 10 years.

The brokers knew all these exclusions but, nevertheless, when Mr   **4–16**
McNealy went in he was simply asked, "What is your occupation?" to

[39] *Osman v. J. Ralph Moss Ltd* [1970] 1 Lloyd's Rep. 313, CA.
[40] See *Bates v. Barrow Ltd* [1995] 1 Lloyd's Rep. 680.
[41] [1978] 2 Lloyd's Rep. 18, CA.

which Mr McNealy replied "property repairer". The proposal form asked for "Full details of occupation". On November 4, 1971, Mr McNealy had an accident and his passenger was injured, so he claimed under his motor insurance with the first defendants. They rescinded the policy for non-disclosure of the fact that he was a part-time musician. The Court of Appeal held that the brokers were liable to indemnify Mr McNealy in respect of his liability to his injured passenger even in the absence of any expert evidence on broking practice. Lord Denning M.R. said[42]:

> "It was clearly the duty of the broker to use all reasonable care to see that the assured, Mr. McNealy was properly covered. An obvious step in the course of doing his duty would have been to say to Mr. McNealy: The Pennine will not cover you if you are a full or part-time musician, a book-maker, a jockey, or anything to do with racing. He ought to have gone through the whole list with Mr McNealy and said: You are not going to be accepted if you are in one of these categories because, if you are, the insurance company can get out of it. I am afraid the broker did not do his duty. He did not go through that list with Mr McNealy at all. He simply asked him what was his occupation, and Mr. McNealy said 'property repairer'. The broker ought to have gone on and asked: 'Have you ever been or are you a full or part-time musician?', and the answer would certainly have been 'Yes'. On the answer being 'Yes', the broker should have said: It is no good trying to insure with the Pennine. You had better go to one of the companies who are ready to insure full or part-time musicians, but that will no doubt be at a higher premium. The broker did not do that at all. In other words, he did not do all that was reasonable to see that Mr. McNealy was properly covered."

4–17   Similarly, in *Mint Security Ltd v. Blair*,[43] it was held that a Lloyd's broker effecting insurance for the client of a non-Lloyd's broker, has a duty to send a copy of the insurance slip to their instructing non-Lloyd's broker. In that case, the Lloyd's broker did not inform the insured or their non-Lloyd's broker that a two-year-old proposal form was being incorporated into the policy. In the event, a material variation in the insured's procedures there represented led to the underwriter's ability to repudiate liability for a £20,000 claim that arose on this cash-in-transit insurance. The insured were held entitled to recover this sum from the Lloyd's brokers who had failed to inform them, or their brokers, in circumstances where the judge held that some arrangement on the vetting of staff procedures would otherwise have been achieved between the insured and the Lloyd's underwriters. On the other hand, the mere instruction by a non-Lloyd's broker to a Lloyd's broker to obtain a quotation and subsequently to effect insurance in accordance with the quotation, is not enough to infer the assumption of direct responsibility to the non-Lloyd's broker's principal (the insured) to, for example, explain a warranty.[44] The normal situation is that there is a contract between the producing broker and the placing broker at Lloyd's, but special factors will be needed to prove the exceptional

---

[42] *ibid.* at 20.
[43] [1982] 1 Lloyd's Rep. 188.
[44] *Pangood Ltd v. Barclay Brown and Co. Ltd* [1999] Lloyd's Rep. 405, CA.

case of a contract between the insured and the placing broker.[45] Such might occur where the placing broker replaces the producing broker by complete substitution of the role to place or procure the insurance itself.[46]

If the broker gives fair advice which the client understands, then there is **4–18** no breach of duty. Thus, if a company which manufactures electronic equipment wants product liability cover, and the broker manages to obtain such cover, but subject to an exclusion of loss caused "failure of any goods to perform their intended function", the broker is acting properly if he informs his client of the limitation and states that the premium was "exceedingly reasonable" for the cover offered.[47]

Cancellation of insurance

It is perhaps obvious that where the insurer requests further information **4–19** from the broker regarding an existing insurance and demands an answer within seven days, and states that a failure to answer the query will lead to the insurance being cancelled, and the broker does nothing, he will be liable to his client, the insured, if he then suffers a loss that he believed was properly insured.[48] Rather, the duty of the broker is to inform his client swiftly of a cancellation or threat of cancellation of the insurance.

A further example is provided by *Cherry Ltd v. Allied Insurance Brokers* **4–20** *Ltd*[49] The claimants were manufacturers of suede and leather garments, and had a considerable number of insurance policies to protect the business. One of those insurances covered loss of profit and other consequential losses caused by the destruction of, or damage to, their premises. This insurance was placed, through the agency of the defendant brokers, with General Accident, and renewal fell on December 19, in common with many of their various insurances. The course of dealing between the claimants and the brokers was that the brokers would effect renewal of the various policies on the due dates and paid the premiums to the insurers, and subsequently recovered those premiums paid from the claimants.

In about March 1974, the claimant's company secretary, Mr Kelly, **4–21** became greatly dissatisfied with the defendant broker's services and attracted to the services of a rival broker. In May, the rival broker was appointed to act for the claimant, and on June 8, 1974, Mr Kelly wrote to the defendant brokers and told them that with effect from June 19, 1974, they would cease to act on the claimant's behalf. He added that all policies that the defendants had placed on the claimant's behalf must be cancelled on that date. There was, in fact, no right given to the claimant to cancel its policies mid-term, and the defendant brokers pointed this out at a meeting with Mr Kelly on June 9, 1974, after they had received his letter. It was agreed that the broker would try and negotiate with the various insurance companies for the return of a proportional part of the premium to reflect

---

[45] *Prentis Donegan and Partners Ltd v. Leeds & Leeds Co. Inc.* [1998] 2 Lloyd's Rep. 326.
[46] *ibid.* at 332, *per* Rix J. (as he then was).
[47] *Nittan v. Solent Steel Fabrication Ltd* [1981] 1 Lloyd's Rep. 633.
[48] *London Borough of Bromley v R.A. Ellis & A. Luff and Sons* [1971] 1 Lloyd's Rep. 97, CA.
[49] [1978] 1 Lloyd's Rep. 274.

cancellation on June 19. This they did with varying degrees of success. A further meeting took place on August 13, 1974, when the defendant broker told Mr Kelly that some of the insurers refused to cancel their policies without just cause, and that included the General Accident in relation to the consequential loss policy, and the material damage insurers, Triumph. Mr Kelly was left with the impression that he should go to his new brokers and obtain cancellation of the new policies so that the policies with General Accident and Triumph could run their course until December 18, 1974. This he did with effect from August 15.

4–22   Therafter, on August 21, 1974, General Accident wrote to the defendant brokers saying that they had reconsidered the matter and now agreed to cancel the consequential loss policy and allow a *pro rata* return of premium from June 19. The defendant broker did nothing for a week. General Accident were asked to reverse the cancellation, but the claimant company were not informed of the cancellation. As luck would have it, on August 29, the day before the defendant broker decided to write to the claimant to explain what had happened, the claimant company suffered a disastrous fire at their premises. On that date, of course, they had no consequential loss insurance, so naturally sued the defendant brokers for breach of contractual duty of care and negligence. Not surprisingly, the claimant company was successful, Cantley J. holding that the defendant brokers were negligent in the advice they gave on August 13 that the claimant had double insurance.

Advising the insured of onerous terms or restrictions

4–23   The broker is under a duty to inform his client of onerous terms and restrictions in the policy of insurance that he obtains in execution of his instructions to effect an insurance.[50] Provided the broker properly informs his client in respect of those terms or restrictions, he has correctly carried out his obligations.[51] The broker's duty has been explained as follows[52]:

> "It is not normally an ordinary part of the broker's or intermediary's duty to construe or interpret the policy to his client, but this again is not a universal rule. If a broker or intermediary is asked to explain the terms of a policy to his client and does so, then he must exercise due care in giving an accurate explanation. Again if the only insurance which the intermediary is able to obtain contains unusual, limiting or exempting provisions which, if they are not brought to the notice of the assured, may result in the policy not conforming to the client's reasonable and known requirements, the duty falling on the agent, namely, to exercise reasonable care in the duties which he has undertaken, may in those circumstances entail that the intermediary should bring the existence of the limiting or exempting provisions to the express notice of the client, discuss the nature of the problem with him and take reasonable steps either to obtain alternative insurance, if any is available, or alternatively to advise the client as to the best way of acting so that his business procedures conform to any requirements laid down by the policy."

[50] *Youell v. Bland Welsh and Co. Ltd (No.2)* [1990] 2 Lloyd's Rep. 431.
[51] *King v. Chambers & Newman (Insurance Brokers) Ltd* [1963] 2 Lloyd's Rep. 130.
[52] *Harvest Trucking Co. Ltd v. P.B. Davis* [1991] 2 Lloyd's Rep. 638 at 643, *per* H.H.J. Diamond Q.C., sitting as a judge of the Commercial Court.

One situation where the broker may well come under a duty to explain **4–24** policy terms is where new terms are imposed by insurers upon a renewal, or upon a change of insurer, or upon the client insured seeking a change in the insurance — for example, to extend a transit insurance to more and larger vehicles. Where the client has given instructions for the renewal of the insurance on existing terms, it is not sufficient in such circumstances for the broker to merely forward his client a letter stating, without comment, the terms of a special endorsement, for instance, that no claim would be admitted for theft of or from any vehicle which is not individually attended. Such a stringent security requirement should alert a competent broker to its significance for his client in circumstances where the broker had sufficient knowledge of his client's business practices, and consequently knew his client could not arrange attendance on lorries 24 hours a day. The competent broker should report the requirement to his client and ascertain in some detail whether the clause met the client's insurance requirements, and, if not, to obtain further instructions.[53]

Where the client instructs his broker to obtain quotations for the insur- **4–25** ance against fire of his business premises, the broker is under a duty to advise his client about any special terms that the insurer wishes to include in the proposed insurance. Similarly, a broker was held responsible for not advising his client properly about a change in policy terms when the insurance was moved to a different insurer in *George Barkes (London) Ltd v. L.F.C. (1988) Ltd*[54] In early 1995, the claimant printers instructed the defendant brokers to renew the insurance on their premises and contents. The brokers obtained a quotation from the claimants' then insurers, C.U., but the claimants were dissatisfied with the premium quoted and instructed the brokers to attempt to obtain cover elsewhere. In February 1995 the brokers procured a substantially lower quotation from another insurer, R.I., which was acceptable to the claimants. The new quotation covered substantially similar risks, but unlike the C.U. policy excluded "extended theft" (*i.e.* theft other than that resulting from entry by forcible and violent means). The brokers sent a copy of R.I.'s proposal form to the claimant's for completion. The form stated that extended theft cover was not included, but the claimant's managing director did not appreciate the significance of this provision, and the brokers did not draw his attention to it. The claimants duly completed the proposal form and a policy was issued.

In November 1995, computer equipment worth some £19,000 was **4–26** stolen from the claimants by means which did not involve forcible or violent entry, so the claimants were unable to recover under the insurance. They therefore sued their brokers for failing to bring it to their attention. It was held that the instruction given by the claimants to their brokers was to seek to arrange effective insurance at a lower premium, but on the basis that any significant changes in cover would first be brought to their attention. Moreover, the judge accepted expert evidence to the effect that "it is the broker's role to ensure the client understands the choices". The limitation

[53] [1991] 2 Lloyd's Rep. 638. at 644–645.
[54] [2000] P.N.L.R. 21, Central London County Ct.

on the cover was not adequately presented by the brokers to the claimants. No attempt was made by the brokers to draw the claimants' managing director's particular attention to the proposal form where it mentioned extended theft as something which he should explicitly consider. Nor was any warning given that by entering into the R.I. policy the claimants might be giving up under the previous policy. As regards the question of whether this was a significant derogation of cover, if the brokers had raised the matter with the claimants they would have ascertained, contrary to their perceived understanding, that there was a real risk of walk-in theft from the claimants' premises. The mere statement on the compliment slip accompanying the R.I. proposal form that the proposed cover was "almost as good" was not sufficient to discharge the brokers' duty to provide the claimants with enough information for them to make an informed choice in accordance with their instructions.

Extent of explanation varies with client

4–27   Registered insurance brokers, under paragraph 2(11) of their statutory Code of Conduct:

> ". . . shall explain to the client the differences in, and the relative costs of, the principal types of insurance . . . which in the opinion of the insurance broker, would suit the client's needs. In doing so, insurance brokers may take into consideration the knowledge held by the client when deciding to what extent it is in the client's interest to have the terms and conditions of the policy . . . explained to him."

The G.I.S.C.'s non-statutory Commercial Code[55] deals with the matter rather more extensively:

> "**8.** *Members* will provide adequate information in a comprehensive and timely way to enable *Commercial Customers* to make an informed decision about the *General Insurance Products* or *General Insurance Activity*-related services being proposed.
> **9.** If they are acting on behalf of the *Commercial Customer*, *Members* will explain the differences in, and the relative costs of, the types of insurance, which in the opinion of the *Member*, would suit the *Commercial Customer's* needs. In so doing *Members* will take into consideration the knowledge held by their *Commercial Customers* when deciding to what extent it is appropriate for their *Commercial Customers* to have the terms and conditions of a particular insurance explained to them.
> **10.** *Members* will advise *Commercial Customers* of the key features of the insurance proposed, including the essential cover and benefits, any significant or unusual restrictions, exclusions, conditions or obligations, and the period of cover. In so doing, *Members* will take into consideration the knowledge held by their *Commercial Customers* when deciding to what extent it is appropriate for *Commercial Customers* to have the terms and conditions of a particular insurance explained to them.
> **11.** If *Members* are unable to match *Commercial Customers'* requirements they will explain the differences in the insurance proposed."

---

[55] Reproduced in Appendix 15.

The extent to which a broker is required to explain material terms of the   **4–28**
insurance effected was in question in *Gunns v. Par Insurance Brokers.*[56]
There was no reference to the Insurance Brokers' Code of Conduct, but
the judge was satisfied that the brokers had properly carried out their duty
to explain a change in policy terms when a new burglary insurance was
arranged covering the claimant jeweller's jewellery when at his home. The
claimant was accepted as being a little dyslexic, but the judge pointed out
that this had not prevented him becoming a successful businessman.
Accordingly, the brokers discharged their duty in circumstances where
they informed the claimant by letters that only one insurer would offer any
insurance, and they stated that that insurer excluded theft of valuables
other than by forcible and violent entry or exit.[57]

Where broker completes proposal form
Whilst Codes of Conduct may emphasise that the broker must place   **4–29**
responsibility for the contents of the proposal form answers firmly with
their client, the proposer, the commercial reality is that it is far from
uncommon for brokers to complete part or all of a proposal form as part
of their service to their client. For instance, the Insurance Brokers' Code
of Conduct at paragraph 2(20) states:

> "In completion of the proposal form, claim form, or any other material doc-
> ument, insurance brokers shall make it clear that all answers or statements
> are the client's own responsibility. The client should always be asked to
> check the details and told that the inclusion of incorrect information may
> result, *inter alia*, in a claim being repudiated. On request, a client shall be
> supplied with a copy of the proposal form or other relevant document at the
> time of completion."

The G.I.S.C. Commercial Code[58] deals more fully with the duty of   **4–30**
disclosure of material facts to insurers:

> "**18.** *Members* will explain to *Commercial Customers* their duty to disclose
> all circumstances material to the insurance and the consequences of any
> failure to make such disclosures, both before the insurance commences and
> during the policy.
> **19.** *Members* will make it clear to *Commercial Customers* that all answers
> or statements given on a proposal form, claim form, or any other material
> document, are the *Commercial Customer's* own responsibility. *Commercial
> Customers* should always be asked to check the accuracy of information
> provided.
> **20.** If *Members* believe that any disclosure of material facts by their
> *Commercial Customers* is not true, fair or complete, they will request their
> *Commercial Customers* to make the necessary true, fair or complete disclo-
> sure, and if this is not forthcoming must consider declining to continue
> acting on their *Commercial Customer's* behalf."

---

[56] [1997] 1 Lloyd's Rep. 173.
[57] See Chapter 12, below.
[58] The G.I.S.C. Commercial Code is reproduced in Appendix 15.

4–31   The broker will not be liable to his client if the client is given the final opportunity to check the accuracy of the proposal form answers. The Court of Appeal so held in *O'Connor v. B.D.B. Kirby and Co.*[59] where the broker had incorrectly completed a proposal form on behalf of his client, and had then passed the completed form to his client to check the answers and sign the form. The client did not notice the incorrect answer to one question inserted by his broker and signed the form. In the event, when a loss arose, the insurer rescinded the policy *ab initio* because of the erroneous answer given in the proposal form. The client, O'Connor, sued the defendant brokers for damages in the sum of monies rendered irrecoverable, but was unsuccessful. The Court of Appeal held, on previous authorities,[60] that it is the duty of the proposer for insurance to see and make sure that the information contained in the proposal form is accurate, it being no argument that he did not read it properly, or was not fully appraised of its contents. The broker is also not liable if the client confirms the accuracy of the proposal form answers by other means, *e.g.* a separate letter.[61] Special considerations, though, may impose a higher duty on the broker when proposal forms are filled in, in the case of "stupid, illiterate, senile people, and other such persons in similar categories".[62]

4–32   Brokers will incur liability to their clients where inaccurate information is passed on to the insurer in circumstances where final responsibility for proposal form answers has not been passed to the client in the manner. The responsibility becomes that of the broker, on behalf of his client, to disclose to the insurer all material facts concerning the risk, made known to him by his client, and the broker will be liable to his client for breach of that responsibility as a breach of his duty of care owed to his client. Indeed, section 19 of the Marine Insurance Act 1906 applies equally to non-marine insurance as well as marine insurance, and this states that the broker or other agent effecting an insurance, must disclose to the insurer every material circumstance in his knowledge, or which in the ordinary course of business ought to be known to him.[63] Thus, in *Dunbar v. A. and B. Painters Ltd*[64] the brokers were held liable in third party proceedings to their client, the defendants, in relation to an employers' liability insurance which had been rescinded by the insurers for non-disclosure of material facts. The brokers had filled in the proposal form for their clients and had incorrectly stated the claims' record to be two claims for £5,000 and £250, when they had been £20,000 and £10,000, and the brokers had dealt with those claims. On the other hand, where the client is aware that there is an omission in the presentation of material facts, *e.g.* claims history, he will

---

[59] [1972] 1 Q.B. 90, CA; followed *Kapur v. J.W. Francis and Co. (No.2)* [2000] Lloyd's Rep. I.R. 361, CA.

[60] *Biggar v. Rock Life Assurance Co.* [1902] 1 K.B. 516; *Newsholme Bros. v. Road Transport & General Insurance Co. Ltd* [1929] 2 K.B. 356, CA.

[61] *Commonwealth Insurance Co. v. Groupe Spinks SA* [1983] 1 Lloyd's Rep. 67 at 82, *per* Lloyd J. (as he then was).

[62] *Gunns v. Par Insurance Brokers* [1997] 1 Lloyd's Rep. 173, at 177, *per* Sir Michael Ogden Q.C., sitting as a High Court judge.

[63] *Simner v. New India Assurance Co. Ltd* [1995] L.R.L.R. 240.

[64] [1986] 2 Lloyd's Rep. 38, CA.

be entirely to blame for the ability of the insurer to rescind the policy for non-disclosure or misrepresentation of such facts, irrespective of whether his broker failed to point out the omission.[65]

Advising on answering the proposal form questions

If the broker knows that a key director of the insuring company, or its parent company, has serious convictions, the broker is under a duty to advise his client, the insuring company, to disclose those convictions to the insurer. This was the finding in *O. and R. Jewellers Ltd v. Terry and Jardine Insurance Brokers Ltd*,[66] but it was based on a concession by the second defendant brokers that if it was found that they knew that the individual concerned was connected with the parent company of the client company, they were under a duty to advise on disclosure. The concession seems to have been correctly made as the standards of care from insurance brokers rises, and such a duty to advise is recognised in the G.I.S.C. Commercial Code at clause 18 cited above.

4–33

Information outside the proposal form passed to the insurer

Similarly, the broker owes a duty to his client in respect of information outside the proposal form conveyed to the insurers. For instance, in *Warren v. Henry Sutton and Co.*[67] the insured driver, Mr Warren, wanted to extend his motor insurance to cover an additional driver, Mr Wright, so he instructed the defendant brokers to arrange this. The existing insurers, Legal and General, sought information about Mr Wright's driving record from the brokers who, without checking the position, stated that Mr. Wright had no accidents, convictions or disabilities. In fact, Mr Wright had a very bad driving record, including a conviction for dangerous driving, and the policy was rescinded for misrepresentation by Legal and General when they learned the true position after Mr Wright was involved in an accident when driving the insured car. Mr Warren was pursued by the Motor Insurers' Bureau to recoup its outlay in meeting third party claims arising from that accident, and he successfully sued for a declaration that he was entitled to an indemnity from the brokers in respect of that recoupment. As discussed earlier, the passing of incorrect information by the broker to the insurer also occurred in *O. and R. Jewellers Ltd v. Terry and Jardine Insurance Brokers Ltd.*[68]

4–34

Advising on points of law

When advice is sought by a client from his broker, the client is entitled to accept that the advice is correct, unless the broker informs him to the contrary. For instance, a client may seek his broker's advice on a question of law relevant to the risk that he wishes to have insured. Whilst the broker may not hold himself out to be a lawyer, he should do all he can to ascertain the correct answer to his client's query, otherwise he exposes

4–35

[65] *Kapur v. J.W. Francis and Co. (No.2)* [1999] Lloyd's Rep. P.N. 834, CA.
[66] [1999] Lloyd's Rep. I.R. 436.
[67] [1976] 2 Lloyd's Rep. 276, CA.
[68] [1999] Lloyd's Rep. I.R. 436.

himself to a possible claim for the negligent giving of advice. In *Sarginson Brothers v. Keith Moulton and Co. Ltd,*[69] Hallett J. said:

> "In my view, if people occupying a professional position take it upon themselves to give advice upon a matter directly connected with their own profession, then they are responsible for seeing that they are equipped with a reasonable degree of skill and a reasonable stock of information so as to render it reasonably safe for them to give that particular piece of advice . . . I do not for one moment say that they are bound to be acquainted with everything. I think it is open to them always to say: 'Well, this is a difficult matter; I shall have to make inquiries.' They can say, if they like: 'This is a matter for a solicitor, not for me'; and if they went to a solicitor he would very likely say: 'You had better consult Counsel.' No one is under obligation to give advice on those difficult matters. If they are going to give advice, they can always qualify their advice and make it plain that it is a matter which is doubtful or upon which further investigation is desirable; but if they take it upon themselves to express a definite and final opinion, knowing, as they must . . . that their clients would act upon that, then I do think they are responsible if they give that information without having taken reasonable care to furnish themselves with such information, of whatever kind it be, as will render it reasonably safe, in the view of a reasonably prudent man, to express that opinion."

4–36   In *Sarginson*, which related to events during the Second World War, the brokers had advised Sarginsons, who were timber merchants, that its stock of timber in Coventry could not be insured against damage by enemy action. That advice was wrong. The timber could actually have been insured under the statutory War Risks (Commodities) Scheme insurance. The broker had recently sought cover under that Scheme for the contents of a builder's yard and had been informed by an insurance company operating under the Scheme that such stock was uninsurable. Without making a specific further enquiry about the stock of timber, the broker had merely assumed, incorrectly, that the timber would also be uninsurable, but he had failed to look at section 11 of the War Risks Insurance Act 1939 and the statutory rules and orders made under it to determine the exceptions.

4–37   More recently, in *F.N.C.B. Ltd v. Barnet Devanney (Harrow) Ltd,*[70] the question for the Court of Appeal was whether the defendant brokers had been negligent, in 1989, in failing to procure a mortgagee protection clause in an insurance arranged for the claimant bank, which had lent money secured on a mortgage over the properties being insured, and the building owner. One of the issues was whether, in 1989, a reasonably competent broker would have known that the clause was unnecessary, because it was the law that a co-insured is not tainted by the wrongful acts of his co-insured under a composite insurance.[71] Morritt L.J. was in no doubt that a reasonable broker would not have known such a legal principle that, in the case of mortgages, was only firmly established some years later.[72] Thus, the broker had been negligent in not arranging for the inclusion of the

---

[69] (1943) 73 Ll. L. Rep. 104 at 107.
[70] [2000] P.N.L.R. 248, CA.
[71] See further Chapter 17, below.
[72] In *New Hampshire Insurance Co. v. M.G.N. Ltd* [1997] L.R.L.R. 24, CA.

mortgagee protection clause in the buildings insurance policy. As regards the giving of legal advice, Morritt L.J. stated[73]:

> ". . . it is not the function of an insurance broker to take a view on undetermined points of law. The protection to be afforded to the client should, if reasonably possible, be such that the client does not become involved in legal disputes at all. As in the case of a solicitor the insurance broker should protect his client from unnecessary risks including the risk of litigation . . ."

Producing broker responsible for placing broker's non-disclosure to insurer

Where a client instructs a broker to obtain a policy for him, and that producing broker has to instruct a placing broker, *e.g.* a Lloyd's broker, to effect the insurance, the producing broker will be liable to his client if the placing broker fails to pass on material information to the underwriters.[74] In these circumstances, there will generally be no contract between the client and the placing broker, and no duty in tort owed by the placing broker to the ultimate client in the absence of particular reliance by the client on the placing, rather then producing, broker and some assumption of responsibility by the placing broker.[75]   **4-38**

3. MEASURE OF DAMAGES FOR BREACH OF DUTY

Ineffective insurance arranged

Where the broker has caused his client to hold a worthless and ineffective insurance policy, the broker is liable in damages measured by the extent of the indemnity that would have been provided by a valid insurance policy. This follows from normal rules relating to the measure of recoverable damages for breach of contract (to put the client into the position he would have been if the contract with the broker had been properly performed), and tort (to put the client into the position he would have been in if there had been no negligence). The policy will therefore have to be scrutinised to ascertain what measure of indemnity would have been recoverable against the insurers in the particular material damage or liability policy concerned.   **4-39**

Measure where insured may not have recovered from insurers

The correct way of arriving at the assessment of damages where the broker argues in his defence to a negligence action that damages should be reduced, or measured at nil, because the insured, *i.e.* his client, was guilty of breaches of the policy's terms, is to be assessed as the loss of a chance of the insured having been able to have recovered under the policy. This has been considered by the Court of Appeal on two occasions. The first was *Fraser v. B.N. Furman (Productions) Ltd*[76] (discussed above) where   **4-40**

---

[73] [2000] P.N.L.R. 248 at 260, CA.

[74] *Coolee Ltd v. Wing Heath and Co.* (1930) 47 T.L.R. 78.

[75] *Pangood Ltd v. Barclay Brown and Co. Ltd* [1999] Lloyd's Rep. 405 at 408, *per* Beldam L.J., CA.

[76] [1967] 1 W.L.R. 898, CA.

brokers had failed, in breach of their duty, to obtain employers' liability insurance for their clients. An employee, Fraser, successfully sued the employers, and they in turn sought an indemnity against that claim from their brokers. It was agreed that, if the brokers had performed their duty, they would have obtained a policy from the Eagle Star Insurance Company and that policy would have contained a reasonable precautions condition.[77] The broker argued that their client had suffered no loss because, even if the policy had been obtained, the clients would have been in breach of this condition and thus not have recovered under the policy.

4-41   Whilst the Court of Appeal unanimously held that the clients would not have been in breach of such a condition, and that the clients were entitled to a full indemnity on an alternative ground, Diplock L.J. (as he then was) said[78]:

> "What damage they have suffered does not depend upon whether Eagle Star would have been entitled as a matter of law to repudiate under their standard policy, but whether as a matter of business they would have been likely to do so. What the employers have lost is the chance of recovering indemnity from the insurers. If Eagle Star would not have been entitled to repudiate liability in law, *cadit quaestio*; the damages recoverable would amount to a full indemnity. Even if they would have been entitled in law, however, to repudiate liability, it does not in my view follow that the employers would be entitled to *no* damages. The court must next consider in that event, what were the chances that an insurance company of the highest standing and reputation, such as Eagle Star, notwithstanding their strict legal rights, would, as a matter of business, have paid up under the policy."

4-42   Applying this test, Diplock L.J. had gone on to conclude that the employers were entitled to a full indemnity because of the "extreme unlikelihood" that Eagle Star would have taken the point on the breach of condition. That conclusion was reached for a number of reasons. First, no evidence had been called from a representative of Eagle Star by the brokers to state that Eagle Star would have taken the point. Secondly, the character of the breach of the reasonable conditions clause by an employer was a difficult issue, which would render its prospects of success as dubious, which a reputable insurer would bear in mind. This, the more so, given the absence of reported cases where insurers had argued such a breach, in none of which the argument for breach had succeeded.

4-43   The second case, *Dunbar v. A. and B. Painters Ltd*,[79] also concerned the brokering of employers' liability insurance. The facts are discussed briefly above, but the facts pertinent to the measure of damages were that the brokers argued that, even if the policy had been effected without their negligent misrepresentation of the claims history, the client employer could not have recovered because the accident had occurred at a height above 40 feet, and working above that height was expressly excluded from the policy. The Court of Appeal had again taken the approach that the proper

---

[77] See Chapter 2, above, for discussion of such provisions.
[78] [1967] 1 W.L.R. 898 at 904, CA.
[79] [1986] 1 Lloyd's Rep. 38, CA.

approach was for the court to assess the chances that the relevant insurers would have taken the height point, and, then to tailor the award of damages accordingly. In that case, the Court of Appeal upheld the judge of first instance's decision, having heard representatives of the insurers called by the employers, that the insurers would not have taken the point, *i.e.* the chances that the insurers would have taken the point were nil. The burden of proof is on the brokers who assert that the insurers would have taken a point depriving their client of an indemnity, to prove it on the balance of probabilities.[80]

Measure where client may not have been able to obtain insurance cover at all

Following those two decisions of the Court of Appeal, the deputy judge in *O. and R. Jewellers Ltd v. Terry and Jardine Insurance Brokers Ltd*[81] assessed the chances that the client jewellers would have been able to obtain insurance given the serious criminal convictions for burglary of a director of the parent company of the client company. Evidence was called from two underwriters and a broker, all men of long experience. The first underwriter said that he did not think convictions stopped people getting insurance somewhere, though the restrictions might be very severe and the premium very high. Probably it would be necessary to ensure that the person with the convictions had nothing to do with the running of the company seeking insurance. For his part, the broker thought it unlikely in the extreme that any insurance could have been placed. The second underwriter was firmly of the view that no cover could have been obtained at all so long as that person remained a director of the main board because the honesty of the people insured was so important in the jewellery business. **4-44**

The judge was satisfied that the relevant director with the convictions did have something to do with the management of the claimant company, and was in a position to play a greater part in it if he chose. On the insurance evidence, the judge was also satisfied that if his convictions and his position as a director of the parent company of the claimants had been disclosed to potential insurers, it would have been impossible to get insurance cover for the claimants. But it was important to go on and consider what would have then happened. The chairman of both companies had given evidence that the director with convictions would have had to go because he would not have allowed any of the parent company's subsidiaries to trade without insurance. The judge felt that beyond that it was very hard to go, and that he entered the field of "pure guess work or little more than guess work", as stated by Kerr J. in *Everett v. Hogg, Robinson and Gardner Mountain (Insurance) Ltd*.[82] The position was further complicated by the broker's further arguments that the claimant company was in breach of the condition precedent that keys for safes 1, 3 and 4 were locked overnight in safe 2, because the claimants in fact kept the keys for safe 4 secreted in the offices each night. The judge was not satisfied, **4-45**

[80] *Everett v. Hogg, Robinson & Gasrdner Mountain (Insurance) Ltd* [1973] 2 Lloyd's Rep. 217 at 223, *per* Kerr J. (as he then was).
[81] [1999] Lloyd's Rep. I.R. 436.
[82] [1973] 2 Lloyd's Rep. 217 at 224.

however, that the brokers had discharged the burden on them of establishing that the insurers would have taken that point because safe 4 was
only used at the time for the storage of company and personal papers.

4-46   In the final analysis, the judge had to weigh up the chance of the
claimant's having recovered the £850,000 maximum indemnity under the
relevant policy. He pointed out that this question covered all the uncertainties he had discussed: uncertainties whether, if there had been no
breach of duty, the claimants would have got insurance and on what
terms. If they had, uncertainties whether their claim would have been
compromised or fought to a finish with insurers. If compromised, for how
much? If fought to a finish, with what result? Rather than evaluate each of
these possibilities the judge thought that he had "to take into account all
the ifs and buts and come to a comprehensive estimate of the chance".
Doing that, he concluded that the claimants had lost a 30 per cent chance
of recovering the full claim of £850,000, which equated to damages of
£255,000.

Where the negligence was not operative

4-47   If the broker can establish that his negligence did not cause any loss,
then no substantial damages will be awarded, only nominal damages. The
brokers succeeded on such an argument in *George Barkes (London) Ltd v.
L.F.C. (1988) Ltd.*[83] The facts have been discussed above, but, briefly, the
broker had failed to point out to the client the slightly reduced cover on a
new policy, which had, as the client wanted, a much reduced annual
premium. The now uninsured event occurred — the walk-in theft of computer equipment from the insured premises, and the client sued the broker
for the value of the lost equipment which would have been covered by the
previous policy. The broker in the event was found negligent, but argued
that the client had suffered no real loss, because the client would not have
chosen to maintain the previous policy at the higher premium.

4-48   The judge found that the claimant client had entrusted the broker to
procure effective insurance in relation to the various categories of insurance held under the previous combined insurance policy, at the lowest possible premium. In other words, that the client instructed the broker to
obtain similar cover, but not identical cover. The judge implied this to be
the position on two grounds. First, that the client must have realised that
different insurers carry on business on different terms. Secondly, the client
could have responded to the broker's note by seeking clarification of the
financial losses exclusion mentioned in the note.[84] That said, it was also
implied that any significant changes in cover should have been brought to
the client's attention for specific approval. But as to the consequences of
the broker's negligence here, the judge rejected the client's managing director's evidence, given with the benefit of hindsight, that he would have
reverted to the previous insurers rather than save the £600 premium.

---

[83] [2000] P.N.L.R. 21, Central London County Ct.
[84] *ibid.* at 27.

Rather, the judge found that his overriding interest had been to achieve a reduction in the premium.[85]

Deductions from damages to be awarded

Three sums may need to be deducted from the value of the loss or dam- **4-49** age sustained[86]:

(a) any additional excess under the policy not taken out, as against the policy actually effected, relevant to the payment of an indemnity in respect of the loss or damage now uninsured;

(b) any saving of premium to the client that occurred by reason of the change to the insurance complained of;

(c) where there was no change of insurer, but problems with the insurance effected, any recovery obtained from the relevant insurer.[87]

There is to be no deduction, though, of recoveries by the client under separate secondary or contingency insurance that it had maintained to cover the event of irrecoverable sums under its principal insurance cover. This is because such insurance was effected for the client's own benefit, with its own money, and was therefore not to be for the benefit of negligent brokers whose services the client had used.[88]

Interest on damages

As identified by the judge in *George Barkes (London) Ltd v. L.F.C.* **4-50** *(1988) Ltd*, above, interest will not run from the date of the loss or damage, as in the case of suing the insurer, but from the date when the insured could otherwise expect to have been paid out by the insurers, if the claim had been covered.[89] This may be some weeks after the loss or damage was sustained, and in the ordinary case would not include a sum in respect of interest for the period between the loss or damage occurring and the date of payment out by the insurer. The usual rate of eight per cent *per annum* simple interest will generally be appropriate.

---

[85] *ibid.* at 30.

[86] *ibid.* at 31–32; *cf. Eagle Star Insurance Co. Ltd v. National Westminster Finance (Australia) Ltd* (1985) 58 A.L.R. 165, PC.

[87] *F.N.C.B. Ltd v. Barnet Devanney (Harrow) Ltd* [2000] P.N.L.R. 248 at 263, para. 32, *per* Morritt L.J., CA.

[88] *ibid.* at 263, paras 33–39, *per* Morritt L.J.; following *Parry v. Cleaver* [1970] A.C. 1, HL.

[89] [2000] P.N.L.R. 21 at 32, CA.

PART II

LIABILITY INSURANCES

CHAPTER 5

EMPLOYERS' LIABILITY INSURANCE

1. STATUTORY REQUIREMENTS OF COMPULSORY INSURANCE

The obligation to insure

Since January 1, 1972, the Employers' Liability (Compulsory Insurance)   **5–01**
Act 1969 has required every employer carrying on a business, trade or profession[1] in Great Britain[2] to take out and maintain insurance with an
authorised insurer[3] against liability for bodily injury or disease sustained
by his "employees", and arising out of and in the course of their employment (see below) in Great Britain in that business. Nationalised industries,
local and police authorities and various other government agencies are,
however, exempt from these requirements.[4]

Employees

The 1969 Act defines "employee" in section 2(1) as: **5–02**

> "an individual who has entered into or works under a contract of service or
> apprenticeship with an employer whether by way of manual labour, clerical
> work or otherwise, whether such contract is expressed or implied, oral or in
> writing."

But, in section 2(2) it is additionally provided that an employer is not
required to insure:

> "(a) in respect of an employee of whom the employer is the husband, wife,
> father, mother, grandfather, grandmother, step-father, step-mother,
> son, daughter, grandson, granddaughter, stepson, stepdaughter,
> brother, sister, half-brother, or half-sister; or
> (b) except as otherwise provided by regulations, in respect of employees
> not ordinarily resident in Great Britain."

Separate provisions have been made by regulation in respect of workers
on offshore installations.[5]

---

[1] Employers' Liability (Compulsory Insurance) Act 1969, s.1(3)(c).
[2] *ibid.,* s.1(1), but not Northern Ireland, s.7(2).
[3] *ibid.,* s.1(3)(b), authorised under the Insurance Companies Act 1982.
[4] *ibid.,* s.3(1) and (2), and also see Employers' Liability (Compulsory Insurance) Regulations
1998 (S.I. 1998 No. 2573), reg.9(1) and Sched.2.
[5] Offshore Installations (Application of the Employers' Liability (Compulsory Insurance)
Act 1969) Regulations 1975 (S.I. 1975 No. 1289), and the Employers' Liability (Compulsory
Insurance) (Offshore Installations) Regulations 1975 (S.I. 1975 No. 1443).

The Regulations

5–03   The current 1998 Regulations[6] provide that four types of conditions in approved policies are prohibited. An insurer cannot provide that he shall be under no liability, or that any such liability otherwise arising shall cease in the event of non-compliance with these prohibited types of condition. These prohibited types of conditions provide a considerable measure of protection to employees in respect of insured employers who might otherwise place themselves in breach of policy conditions, thereby depriving the injured employee from obtaining the fruits of their personal injuries litigation. It is important to note, though, that insurers are entitled to rely on such provisions in order to recoup from solvent insured employers, sums expended in satisfying employees' claims against the insured employer.[7] The four types of prohibited condition will be considered in turn, but there have not been any reported decisions upon them.

(1) In the event of some specified thing being done or omitted to be done after the happening of the event giving rise to a claim under the policy

5–04   This would seem to embrace all claims notification conditions as well as all policy terms seeking to prevent recovery in circumstances where, for instance:

    (a) all claims correspondence has not been forwarded to the insurer,
    (b) the insured employer is said not to have provided all assistance and/or information to the insurer,[8]
    (c) the insured employer admits liability, or
    (d) the insured employer makes a settlement without the insurer's prior written consent.

The aim is to overcome the pre-1969 Act position, as in *Farrell v. Federated Employers Insurance Association Ltd,*[9] where the Court of Appeal held that the insurers could escape liability under the policy by reliance on the insured employer's breach of a condition precedent providing that every claim, writ, etc., should be forwarded "immediately" to the insurers. A writ had been received by the insured employer on January 7, but was not forwarded to the insurers until March 3, after judgment in default had been entered against the employer. The fact that notification conditions are prohibited conditions when it comes to the insurer's primary liability to indemnify the insured employer, can still be overlooked, as occurred in *Taylor v. Builders Accident Insurance Ltd*[10] which concerned a claimant exercising his direct rights against employers' liability insurers under the

---

[6] Employers' Liability (Compulsory Insurance) General Regulations 1998 (S.I. 1998 No. 2573), reg.2(1).
[7] *ibid.,* reg.2(3).
[8] It is important to remember that this obligation to provide the information will only arise if and when the insurer requests such information, *Wilkinson v. Car & General Insurance Corp. Ltd* (1914) 110 L.T. 468 at 471–472, *per* Lord Reading C.J.
[9] [1970] 1 W.L.R. 1400, CA.
[10] [1997] P.I.Q.R. P247.

Third Parties (Rights Against Insurers) Act 1930 after the insolvency of the insured employer.

(2) Unless the policy holder takes reasonable care to protect his employees against the risk of bodily injury or disease in the course of their employment

This relates to the insured employer taking reasonable care to protect   **5–05** his employees against the risk of bodily injury or disease in the course of their employment with the insured employer. Again, there were pre-1969 Act cases, such as *Woolfall and Rimmer Ltd v. Moyle,*[11] *Fraser v. B.N. Furman (Productions) Ltd,*[12] and *London Crystal Window Cleaning Co. Ltd v. National Mutual Indemnity Insurance Co. Ltd*[13] where insurers fought their liability to indemnify the insured employers in respect of employees' personal injury claims, but insurers have now been deprived of this defence in employers' liability insurance claims.

(3) Unless the policy holder complies with the requirements of any enactment for the protection of employees against the risk of bodily injury or disease in the course of their employment

This is directed to the large body of health and safety legislation that   **5–06** imposes many strict liability offences where certain required safety measures are not put in place or operated by the employer. It would obviously be unsatisfactory if the insurer could escape liability under this compulsory insurance merely by establishing the employer's commission of a strict liability offence under such legislation.

(4) Unless the policy holder keeps specified records or provides the insurer with or makes available to him information therefrom

Such provisions are usually inserted for the purpose of premium adjust-   **5–07** ment at the end of a period of insurance, employers' liability insurance being rated partly on the annual wages and salaries paid by the employer during the period of insurance.

Minimum level of cover

The policy must provide a minimum of £5 million cover in the aggre-   **5–08** gate, including costs and expenses of any claims,[14] but policies now commonly provide £10 million cover.[15] Where the insured is a company with one or more subsidiaries, this requirement can be met by treating the company and its subsidiaries as a single employer.[16] Further, there must not be any policy excess or deductible (*i.e.* first amount of any claim or aggregation of claims) payable by the insured or any employee.[17]

---

[11] [1942] 1 K.B. 66, CA.
[12] [1967] 3 All E.R. 57, CA.
[13] [1952] 2 Lloyd's Rep. 360.
[14] Employers' Liability (Compulsory Insurance) General Regulations 1998 (S.I. 1998 No. 2573), reg.3(1).
[15] See Section 2A of the specimen combined policy at Appendix 1.
[16] Employers' Liability (Compulsory Insurance) General Regulations 1998, reg.3(2).
[17] *ibid.*, reg.2(2).

Issue and production of certificate of insurance

5–09   Every authorised insurer who enters into a contract of insurance with an employer in accordance with the 1969 Act must issue the insured employer with a Certificate of insurance in the specified form.[18] The Certificate must be issued within 30 days of the commencement or renewal of the insurance,[19] and the insured employer must display easily legible copies of it throughout the period of insurance at each place of business, with such copies being reasonably protected from being defaced or damaged.[20] The 1998 Regulations also introduced a fresh requirement to assist future employee claimants, employers and liquidators, as applicable, in tracing the relevant insurer at the time the injury was sustained by the claimant employee, namely, in requiring employers to retain each Certificate, or a copy of it, for a period of 40 years.[21] There are additionally new requirements regarding production of Certificates to,[22] and inspection thereof by,[23] inspectors appointed under the 1969 Act.[24] A flaw in the form of Certificate required to be issued is that it does not recite the exclusions and limitations to the policy, and merely gives the dates of commencement and termination of the insurance. To that extent the Certificate is misleading to employees because of these omissions, but judicial criticism[25] has not prompted any change in the form of the Certificate.

No civil liability for failure to insure

5–10   An individual employer who fails to take out compulsory employers' liability insurance, and any director, manager, secretary or other officer of a company who consents to or connives at such a failure to insure, or whose neglect facilitates that failure to insure, commits an offence.[26] Currently, the fine (level 4) can be up to £2,500 for each day that the employer is not insured. Whilst there is this criminal sanction, a majority of the Court of Appeal in *Richardson v. Pitt-Stanley*[27] has decided that company officers do not incur any civil liability to injured employees by reason of their failure to take out compulsory employers' liability insurance as required by the 1969 Act. The facts were that the claimant employee had suffered an accident in the course of his employment and sued his employing company for damages for personal injuries. He obtained a judgment in default against the company for damages to be assessed, but the company went into liquidation with no assets to satisfy

---

[18] *ibid.*, reg.4(1).

[19] *ibid.*, reg.4(2).

[20] *ibid.*, regs 5(1), (2) and (3).

[21] *ibid.*, regs 4(4) and (5).

[22] *ibid.*, reg.6.

[23] *ibid.*, reg.7.

[24] *ibid.*, regs 1 and 8, and s.4(2)(b) of the 1969 Act.

[25] *Dunbar v. A. & B. Painters Ltd* [1986] 2 Lloyd's Rep. 38 at 43 , *per* Balcombe L.J., CA.

[26] 1969 Act, s.5, as amended by the Criminal Law Act 1977, Sched. 6 and the Criminal Justice Act 1982, s.46.

[27] [1995] Q.B. 123, CA, applied *Martin v. Lancashire County Council* [2000] Lloyd's Rep. 665, CA.

the judgment. The company had failed to take out any employers' liability insurance as required by the 1969 Act, so the claimant obtained no transfer of rights against an insurer under the Third Parties (Rights Against Insurers) Act 1930.[28] The claimant therefore brought an action against the previous directors and secretary of the company claiming that they were liable in damages to him because of their commission of an offence under section 5 of the 1969 Act. The damages he claimed were for the economic loss he suffered by reason of the failure to insure, which equated to the sum that he would have received from an employers' liability insurer if a compulsory policy had been in place. The appeal concerned whether the statement of claim should be struck out as disclosing no reasonable cause of action. Both Russell and Stuart-Smith L.J. (Sir John Megaw dissenting) distinguished the wording in the 1969 Act (". . . every employer . . . shall insure . . ."), from that in section 35 of the Road Traffic Act 1930 ("it shall not be lawful for any person to use . . .") offence[29], which had been determined in *Monk v. Warbey*[30] to introduce a civil liability upon persons upon a failure to take out compulsory motor insurance. Their lordships pointed to the fact that the 1969 Act did not declare the doing of an act to be unlawful and then separately provide a criminal penalty for breach, but was confined to merely classifying the act of not taking out such insurance as a criminal offence.[31] In his dissenting judgment, Sir John Megaw relied on the first exception in statutory interpretation set out by Lord Diplock in *Longhop Ltd v. Shell Petroleum Co. Ltd(No.2)*,[32] which provides that a civil liability should be found to exist where the obligation imposed by the relevant statute "was imposed for the benefit or protection of a particular class of individuals". His lordship also pointed out that the consequence of holding that there was no civil liability led to the result that employees could not seek injunctive relief against an employer they knew had failed to take out employers' liability insurance.[33] There is much force in this dissenting view, but the point seems settled. All that is open to such employees would seem to be to make contact with the 1969 Act inspectors who could presumably threaten the employer with prosecution if the employer failed to remedy the situation and take out the necessary insurance.

[28] See Chapter 21, below.
[29] See, now, Road Traffic Act 1988, s.143(1)(a), which provides that "a person must not use a motor vehicle on a road unless there is in force in relation to the use of the vehicle by that person such a policy of insurance . . ."
[30] [1935] 1 K.B. 75.
[31] [1995] Q.B. 123 at 130 and 132, CA.
[32] [1982] A.C. 173 at 185, HL.
[33] [1995] Q.B. 123 at 135, CA, although it is submitted that the analysis of the circumstances cited by Sir John Megaw is flawed because his lordship postulated that an already injured employee might seek the injunctive relief, and ignores the fact the subsequent employers' liability insurance would not cover past injuries. The point is valid in respect of employees who might want to force their employer to take out employers' liability insurance as their protection against insolvency of the employer in respect of future accidents at work.

2. SUBJECT MATTER OF EMPLOYERS' LIABILITY INSURANCE

Liability of employer to employee

5–11   The essential subject matter of an employer's liability policy is the amount of damages that the employer may become liable to pay his employees in respect of accidental death or bodily injury (including disease) caused during the period of insurance and arising out of and in the course of employment with that employer in connection with his business. An example of employers' liability cover within a commercial combined insurance policy is at Appendix 1, Section 2, and within a Shop-keepers' Policy at Appendix 2, Section 8. An employers' liability insurance is not akin to personal accident insurance, because the employer may not be liable for the death or injury of his employees in law, and therefore there is no automatic payment on the employee suffering an accident.[34] It is, though, a long-recognised form of contract of indemnity.[35] Reference may be made to the specimen employers' liability sections of the combined liability policies contained in the Appendix. An important feature is that these policies are usually provided on an "occurrence" basis, *i.e.* liability is only covered for employees' claims where the injury or disease occurred in the period of insurance, irrespective of when the employee actually makes his claim against the employer.

5–12   An employer may be liable to his employees by reason of breach of his common law duty to take reasonable care to ensure the safety of his employees and/or breach of a statutory duty, *e.g.* to fence machinery.[36] Under this general duty not to be negligent, an employer does not guarantee the safety of his employees and an employer does not stand in the position of, for instance, a nurse and an imbecile child,[37] or schoolmaster and pupil.[38] Thus, an employer will not be liable for the juvenile behaviour of fellow employees, such as rushing to get to the canteen.[39] If clear instructions and proper equipment are provided by the employer, he will not be liable to an employee who disregards such instructions or the availability of the correct equipment,[40] or who manages to unforeseeably injure himself whilst performing a simple task.[41]

Foreseeability of accident

5–13   In assessing whether injury to the employee was foreseeable, the court will obviously have regard to the general state of knowledge at the time of

---

[34] *Lancashire Insurance Co. v. IRC* [1899] 1 Q.B. 353; *Fraser v. Furman (Productions) Ltd* [1967] 1 W.L.R. 687 at 904, CA; *Dunbar v. A & B Painters Ltd* [1986] 2 Lloyd's Rep. 38 at 42, CA.

[35] *British Cash & Parcel Conveyors Ltd v. Lamson Store Service Co. Ltd* [1908] 1 K.B. 1006 at 1012, *per* Cozens-Hardy M.R., CA.

[36] See, *e.g.* the Factories Act 1961 and the Offices, Shops and Railway Premises Act 1963.

[37] See *Smith v. Austin Lifts Ltd* [1959] 1 All E.R. 81 HL.

[38] See *Withers v. Perry Chain Co. Ltd* [1961] 1 W.L.R. 1314, CA.

[39] *Lazarus v. Firestone Tyre & Rubber Co., The Times*, May 2, 1963.

[40] *Paris v. Stepney Borough Council* [1951] A.C. 367, HL.

[41] *Vinnyey v. Star Paper Mills Ltd* [1965] 1 All E.R. 175.

the accident. Thus, an employer will not be expected to anticipate effects unknown by any ordinary prudent employer, *e.g.* deafness caused by a particular repetitive and noisy process. But an employer will be expected to react over time and take appropriate measures in the light of the advancing knowledge of industrial injuries and diseases to ensure the reasonable safety of his employees.[42]

In the course of employment

An employer is only responsible, however, while his employee is engaged   **5–14**
in his employment; but what he does in the course of his employment, while at his place of employment, and while entering and leaving it, for all that the employer is responsible.[43] In other words, the obligation of the employer extends to cover all such acts as are normally and reasonably incidental to a man's day's work.[44] Whilst, then, the employer's duty is general — to take all reasonable steps to avoid risk to his employees — for convenience it is often split up into different categories — such as safe tools, safe place of work, or safe system of work — but it always remains one general duty[45] at common law.

Common extensions to the indemnity relating to costs

In addition to the insurance policy providing for an indemnity in respect   **5–15**
of sums that the insured employer becomes legally liable to pay as damages to employees in respect of accidental death, bodily injury or illness or disease caused during the period of insurance, the indemnity will generally be expressed to include:

(a) the legal costs recoverable from the insured employer from the claimant employee;
(b) all the costs and expense incurred in connection with the conduct of the defence or settlement of the employee's claim against the insured employer — but with the proviso that the insurer must have given his written consent to those costs and expenses being incurred, and that consent will not apply unless the insurer has sole control over the conduct of the proceedings on the insured's behalf;
(c) all solicitor's (but not counsel's) fees for representation, with the written consent of the insurer, at either or both:

(i) any coroner's inquest or other fatal inquiry;
(ii) any proceedings in any court of summary jurisdiction (*e.g.* a magistrates' court) arising out of an alleged breach of duty which may be the subject of an indemnity under the policy.

---

[42] *Wright v. Dunlop Rubber Co Ltd Cassidy v. Dunlop Rubber Co. Ltd* (1972) 13 K.I.R. 255, CA; *Stokes v. Guest, Keen & Nettlefold (Bolts & Nuts) Ltd* [1968] 1 W.L.R. 1776.
[43] *Brydon v. Stewart* (1855) 2 Macq 30, *per* Lord Cranworth L.C, HL.
[44] *Davidson v. Haley Page Ltd* [1945] 1 All E.R. 235, C.A., at 237, *per* Lord Greene M.R.
[45] *Wilson v. Tyneside Window Cleaning Co.* [1958] 2 Q.B. 110 at 116, *per* Parker L.J., CA.

5–16   This indemnity will not extend to fines or any award of prosecution costs or witness expenses ordered against the insured (or director or other employee of the insured), nor to a successful conviction where there is a finding of a deliberate or intentional criminal act or omission of the insured (or his director or other employee prosecuted). The safety legislation concerned is the Health and Safety at Work Act 1974,[46] prosecutions being brought under section 36 or 37 thereof (as defined in section 38) for breach of statutory duty as set out in sections 2 to 8 of the Act. Insurers vary, but some may restrict this extension to prosecutions that are brought relating to claims by employees which form the subject of the main indemnity of the policy, *i.e.* employers' legal liability to pay damages to an injured employee.

Extended definition of the insured business

5–17   Most employers' liability policies give cover beyond that strictly required to be insured under the 1969 Act, and grant an indemnity in respect of the liability of the insured with an extended meaning being provided for "in connection with the business". Thus, this term will expressly include such matters as[47]:

(a) the provision and management of canteen, social sports and welfare organisations for the benefit of the insured's employees and fire and ambulance services;

(b) private work carried out with the consent of the Insured by employees for any director, partner or senior executive of the insured;

(c) the occupation, use and/or maintenance of premises of the business.

Territorial limits to cover

5–18   Thee policy will specify that the indemnity is only to operate whilst:

(a) an employee is employed in Great Britain, Northern Ireland, the Isle of Man or the Channel Islands (including offshore installations in territorial waters around Great Britain and its Continental Shelf); or

(b) an employee is temporarily employed anywhere else in the world provided the employee is normally resident in the area set out in (a) (an alternative wording may define this second category as being dependent upon whether the contract of service or apprenticeship was entered into within the area set out in (a)).

Inspection of premises

5–19   Insurers vary in their approach to the inspection of the insured's premises. Some provide, as an extra benefit under the policy, a service to

---

[46] And as applied to Northern Ireland under the Health and Safety at Work (Northern Ireland) Order 1978 (S.I. 1978 N.I. No.9); as amended by S.I. 1998 No. 2795 (N.I. 18).
[47] See the definition of "business" in Section 2 of the specimen combined policy at Appendix 1.

inspect the insured's premises whenever required and suggest changes or improvements with the aim of reducing the number of deaths, or the severity of injuries and diseases. This advice, however, is only given on the express condition that the insurer accepts no responsibility for that advice. As an alternative to this method, the insurer may merely provide a condition in the policy that he shall have, at all reasonable times, free access to inspect each place of business at which the insured employs persons covered by the policy.

Notifiable changes in activities

The insurer may include in his policy a provision entitling him to cancel **5–20** the policy where certain specified changes occur unless the full circumstances have been notified to the insurer and accepted in writing. The following may be specified as notifiable changes:

(a) the insured's business is wound up, carried on by a liquidator or receiver or permanently discontinued;

(b) the insured's interest in the business ceases other than by will or operation of law;

(c) there is any alteration in the system of work or any circumstance arises which increases the likelihood of the death of, or injury to, any employee of the insured.

Warranties relating to business activities

Alternatively, the answering of questions in the proposal form about the **5–21** nature of the business being proposed for insurance can give rise to continuing or future warranties that only those activities will be carried out. Changing the business activities will thereby entitle the insurer to repudiate the insurance from the date that warranty is breached by the insured employer. Accordingly, all employers when completing a proposal form for employers' liability insurance, must be careful to give correct details of the circumstances in which the workmen are to be employed. Moreover, during the currency of the insurance, they must be vigilant not to vary from that specified description of their work without the knowledge and consent of the insurer.

This is demonstrated by *Beauchamp v. National Mutual Indemnity* **5–22** *Insurance Co. Ltd*[48] where a builder, who had not previously undertaken any demolition work, took out a policy to cover the demolition of a mill. Not surprisingly, the insurers asked in the proposal form "are there any explosives used?" and the builder answered "no". At the foot of the proposal form he then signed a declaration that the policy was only to apply to his demolition of the one specified mill. Finlay J. held that on the general law,[49] questions and answers in proposal forms are capable of being converted into conditions of an insurance policy, which, if breached, entitle

---

[48] [1937] 3 All E.R. 19.
[49] *Provincial Insurance Co. Ltd v. Morgan* [1933] A.C. 240, HL; *Dawsons Ltd v. Bonnin* [1922] 2 A.C. 413, HL.

the insurer to repudiate the policy. This being so, his Lordship held, *inter alia*, that the insurers were entitled to repudiate the policy in this case where the accident had occurred when explosives were being used in this demolition work for two reasons, firstly the breach of the future (promissory) warranty regarding explosives, and secondly, that the use of explosives constituted a change of risk[50]:

> "It is necessary here to ascertain what was being insured and what was being referred to. The plaintiff, as I mentioned, was a builder. He was a person who was not doing any other demolition work. This insurance was solely in respect of the one isolated demolition job, so to speak, at this Alexandra Mill, at Oldham, and it seems to me, therefore, that the proposal form must inevitably have reference to the future, because though, in fact, the plaintiff was in business, he was not insuring anything with regard to his general business, but was insuring in respect only of this special job in the future. Accordingly, it seems to me that the whole of the proposal must be regarded as having reference to a future event, and when, in these circumstances, he is asked 'Are any acids, gases, chemicals, explosives, or any other dangerous preparations used in your business,' that does not, of course, mean his present business of a builder: it means the business on which he is going to embark, the business of demolition. Accordingly, it seems to me that it does have the nature of a warranty or a condition.
>
> I think that the true view to take is that he was insuring what I may conveniently call ... a non-explosive demolition ... It is, perhaps, significant that [the plaintiff] made it quite clear to me that, but for one circumstance, as to which he was clearly mistaken, he would have thought it right to inform the insurance company with reference to the use of explosives. That point was this. He seemed to think that it was not necessary so to do because the explosives were not being used by him, but by a gentleman whom he had employed for the purpose. Quite clearly, that could make no difference. I cannot resist the view that, in the first place, this was, as I think, a warranty. If it is necessary to go into the matter ... I should say that there was a change in the risk ..."

5–23   That case may be contrasted, however, with two others. In *Woolfall and Rimmer Ltd v. Moyle*,[51] a question and answer in a proposal form were held to relate only to existing facts, and thus did not constitute any promissory warranty that those facts would remain true and correct throughout the period of insurance. In answer to a question: "Are your machinery, plant and ways properly fenced and guarded and otherwise in good order and condition?" the employer had written "yes" in the proposal form. Lord Greene M.R. gave the opinion of the Court of Appeal in regard to the nature of the warranty given[52]:

> "It is said [by the insurers] that the question does not merely relate to the moment of time at which the proposer is answering it, but extends to the future condition of the machinery, plant and ways during the currency of the policy. In my opinion, there is not a particle of justification for reading into that perfectly simple question any element of futurity whatsoever ... The value of the question, as I construe it, to the underwriters is that it enables them to find out

[50] [1937] 3 All E.R. 19 at 22.
[51] [1942] 1 K.B. 66, CA.
[52] [1941] 3 All E.R. 304 at 306–307, CA.

what sort of person they are dealing with, *i.e.* whether he is the sort of person who keeps his machinery plant and ways properly fenced and guarded and otherwise in good order and condition . . . If the underwriters in fact intended that this question should carry the meaning which they now suggest, nothing would have been easier than to say so . . . In my judgment, the meaning of this question is perfectly clear, and there is no evidence on the facts of this case that the particular plank which was the cause of this accident was not in good order and condition at the time when the question was answered, or, indeed, that it was in the possession of the [employer] at all."

In the second case, the knowledge of the insurer's agent was imputed to the   **5–24** insurer, with the result that the insurers were unsuccessful in their effort to avoid the policy for breach of a "basis of the contract" clause[53] in a proposal form. The insured was inaccurately described as a "joiner", rather than a "joiner and builder", in the proposal form in *Holdsworth v. Lancashire and Yorkshire Insurance Co.*[54] The facts were special in that an agent of the insurers had filled in the proposal form for the employers' liability insurance and had placed therein the incomplete description of the insured's business. When the policy arrived, and prior to the insured paying any premium, the insured asked the agent to alter the description in the policy to "joiner and builder". The agent obtained the sanction of the chief clerk of the local branch office of the insurers, and then the first premium was paid. The head office of the insurers were never informed of this alteration of description of the insured, and when he subsequently made a claim for indemnity, the insurers pleaded that the description "joiner" was the "basis of the contract", this condition being breached therefore entitled them to avoid the policy. Bray J. was firmly of the view that the insurers were unable to avoid the policy, and were liable to indemnify the insured, upon the grounds that:

(a) by receiving the premiums, the insurers were precluded from denying the agent's authority to alter the contract;

(b) in those circumstances the knowledge of the agent was the knowledge of the insurance company; and

(c) even if the policy had not been altered, the company would have been liable, because the contract must be treated as having been negotiated by the agent with a joiner and builder, and the knowledge of the agent must be treated as the knowledge of the company.

3. INSURER'S RIGHT OF RECOVERY AGAINST INSURED EMPLOYER

Freedom to insert contractual right of recovery

As mentioned at the beginning of this chapter, regulations prohibit con-   **5–25** ditions of certain types in employers' liability policies.[55] Insurers, however,

---

[53] See Chapter 2 for general discussion of "basis of the contract" provisions.
[54] (1907) 23 T.L.R. 521.
[55] See text and see paras 5–03 to 5–07, above.

often include a right of recovery condition within the policy,[56] under the
provisions of which the insurer may seek to recover the indemnity paid
under the policy to the insured in circumstances where such a prohibited
clause is in the policy, *e.g.* that the insured employer shall take reasonable
care to protect the employees from injury (this is the precise risk, of course,
that the insured was obliged to insure). Such a "claw-back" provision is
not prohibited by the 1998 Regulations.[57] Such a clause may read:

> "The insured shall repay to the insurer all sums paid by the insurer which the
> insurer would not have been liable to pay but for the provisions of any law
> relating to compulsory insurance of liability to employees in Great Britain,
> Northern Ireland, the Isle of Man, or the Channel Islands (including
> offshore installations in territorial waters around Great Britain and its
> Continental Shelf)."

It is, therefore, still important to consider the meaning of such provisions
and some illustrations of the possible impact of these types of condition
are considered below.

Ignorance of policy terms

5–26   It seems, somewhat unjustly it is submitted, that the insured will be
bound by the provisions relating to, for instance, immediate notice of
claims, even if he does not know of the condition because, for example, the
accident occurs on day one of the insured's operations as an employer and
he has not yet received a copy of the policy terms. A majority decision of
the Court of Appeal in *Re Coleman's Repositories Ltd and Life and Health
Assurance Association*[58] is against this proposition, but was decided without reference to earlier authorities[59] now approved by the Court of Appeal
in *Rust v. Abbey Life Assurance Co. Ltd.*[60] It has to be said, however, that
this does contrast with the normal principles of contract law relating to
the need for prior notice of burdensome terms contained in the other contracting party's standard form of contract.

Provision 1

5–27   *Some specified thing being done or omitted to be done after the happening
of the event giving rise to a claim under the policy insurers will generally
specify the claims procedure to be followed by the insured concerning notification of the claim to the insurer, the forwarding of all claims correspondence, the assistance of the insured, and the non-admittance of liability or
settlement being made to the claimant employee without the insurer's written
consent.* Thus, where the notification provision read:

[56] See Section 2A of the specimen combined policy at Appendix 1.
[57] Employers' Liability (Compulsory Insurance) General Regulations 1998, reg.2(3).
[58] [1907] 2 K.B. 798 *per* Vaughan Williams L.J. and Buckley L.J. (Fletcher Moulton L.J.
dissenting), CA.
[59] *Adie & Sons v. Insurance Corp. Ltd* (1898) 14 T.L.R. 544; and *General Accident Insurance
Corp. v. Cronk* (1901) 17 T.L.R. 233, DC.
[60] [1979] 2 Lloyd's Rep. 334 at 339, *per* Brandon L.J., CA.

"Every claim, notice, letter, writ . . . or other document served on the employer shall be notified or forwarded to the [insurers] immediately on receipt."

The Court of Appeal held that nothing short of forwarding every specified document received by the insured employer immediately upon receipt will satisfy the condition's requirements. Whilst accepting that "immediately" means "with all reasonable speed considering the circumstances of the case",[61] Lord Denning M.R. rejected the insured's argument that the forwarding of a writ, received on January 7, to the insurers on March 3 (after judgment in default had been entered against the insured) came within that definition[62]:

"The writ was served here on January 7, 1966 and notice was given to the insurers on March 3, 1966, that is, some eight weeks later. This was, (the plaintiff says), all reasonable speed. I do not think so. I think that, in the circumstances of the case, the plaintiff's solicitors ought to have told the insurers about the writ soon after they received the letter of January 17, 1966 from the receiver (of the plaintiff company). 'With all reasonable speed' would mean by the end of January 1966 at latest . . . The plain fact is that the writ was not notified with all reasonable speed."

It can be added that correspondence to the insured from the insurer to the effect that writs should be served on the insured does not amount to a waiver of the requirements of such notification condition.[63]

The above clause is wider in effect than one which provides: **5–28**

"the insured should forward to the head office or any branch office of the insurers every written notice or information as to any verbal notice of claim arising through any accident or disease covered under the said policy as soon as possible after the receipt of such notice or information."

This is because reference is made only to notices of claim and, accordingly, an insured will not be in breach if other notices and other documents are sent to him relating to a claim but he does not forward them to the insurer.[64]

Where the insured is required to "give all such information and assis-   **5–29** tance to the insurer" to enable the insurer to settle or resist any claim by an employee of the insured, it is important to remember that the obligation only arises when the insurer requires, for example, information.[65] Furthermore, if the notification condition is not truly a condition precedent, the insurer may not be able to recover his outlay from the insured employer.

---

[61] *Re Coleman's Repositories Ltd & Life & Health Assurance Association* [1907] 2 K.B. 798 at 807 *per* Fletcher Moulton L.J., CA.

[62] *Farrell v. Federated Employers Insurance Association Ltd* [1970] 3 All E.R. 632 at 635 *per* Lord Denning M.R. and at 638, *per* Megaw L.J. concurred with that finding, CA.

[63] *ibid.* at 636, *per* Lord Denning M.R. and at 637, *per* Megaw L.J..

[64] *Wilkinson v. Car & General Insurance Corp. Ltd* (1914) 110 L.T. 468, CA.

[65] *ibid.* at 471–472, *per* Lord Reading C.J.

Provision 2

5–30   *Provision that the insured employer takes reasonable care to protect his employees against the risk of bodily injury or disease in the course of their employment.* This duty of care under the contract of insurance, owed by the insured employer to the insurer, is to be differentiated from the insured employer's duty of care to his employee (liability for breach of which constitutes the subject matter of employers' liability insurance). If the two duties were indistinguishable, it would obviously be rather futile for the employer to insure, for he would then merely be indemnified and always have to repay the indemnity to the insurer. Lord Greene M.R. explained this construction of the condition in *Woolfall and Rimmer Ltd v. Moyle*[66]:

> "In approaching the construction of that condition, it is important to remember the context in which it is found. A duty to take care is a duty which arises by virtue of the relationship between the person on whom such a duty lies and the person towards whom it is to be discharged. That relationship may arise by contract, or it may arise by mere operation of law, by reason of the fact that two persons are thrown into a particular relationship with one another. In the present case, the duty that this condition purports to impose is a contractual duty imposed on the insured towards the underwriters, who are indemnifying the insured against a variety of risks, a very important proportion of which arises in cases of negligence either by the insured himself or by persons for whose negligence he is vicariously responsible to his employees. Of course, in the many classes of risks which are covered, there are some, and no doubt very important ones, in respect of which a workman can recover from the employer without the necessity of establishing negligence. On the other hand, there are a multitude of risks covered in which the workman must establish negligence if he is to succeed.
>
> The argument which was presented to us with great skill and ingenuity by counsel for the appellants [the insurers] was based on the contention that the condition in question is imposing upon the insured a duty to take care co-terminus with, and similar in quality to, the obligation to take care which lies upon the employer vis-à-vis his workmen. In my judgment that is the wrong method of approach to this question. The effect of the argument of counsel for the appellants would be to exclude from the scope of the indemnity which the policy purports at the outset to give a very large and important class of case which in the body of the policy is expressed to fall within it."

5–31   What of the application of this separate duty of care owed to the insurer when a claim is made by an employee founded in negligence of the employer? Lord Greene M.R. continued[67]:

> "On the facts of the present case, it would appear that the insured, a limited company, employed a foreman who was obviously a competent and skilled man, and who was reasonably and rightly relied upon by his employers. They employed him, not merely to see that the company was provided with appropriate scaffolding material, but also to select from the stock in hand at any moment material which would be suitable for any particular job. It is conceded by counsel for the appellants — and quite rightly conceded in my view — that, in entrusting to this foreman the task of providing suitable and

---

[66] [1941] 3 All E.R. 304 at 307–309, CA; followed in *T.F. Maltby Ltd v. Pelton SS Co. Ltd* [1951] 2 All E.R. 954n.
[67] *ibid.* at 309.

safe material for scaffolding and selecting suitable material for a particular job, the employers were taking a reasonable precaution within the meaning of [the] condition 5. No doubt, *vis-à-vis* a workman injured through the negligence of the foreman, that would not be a sufficient answer to a claim. However, this seems to me to be irrelevant . . ."

Goddard L.J. concurred, and added some remarks on the general application of the policy condition[68]:

> "It is a condition which is put in for the protection of the underwriter, or perhaps one might say to limit the field of the underwriter's liability to the extent that he is saying:
>
>> 'I will insure you against the consequences of your negligence, but understand that I am insuring you on the footing that you are not to regard yourself because you are insured, as free to carry on your business in a reckless manner. You are to take those reasonable precautions to prevent accidents which ordinary business people take. That is to say, you are to run your business in the ordinary way, and not in a way which invites accidents.'
>
> If you found that an employer whose premises had dark entries, tunnels and what not provided no lights, or failed to provide lights where there were stairs which could not be seen in the dark, or failed to provide fencing along places where, if there were no fencing, it would be reasonable to suppose many people would fall over, or if in his business he used explosives about where any youth who was employed on the place could tamper with them and cause damage and destruction, I think it could be said that he was not taking reasonable precautions to prevent accidents."

5–32

In the subsequent case of *Fraser v. B. N. Furman (Productions) Ltd,*[69] the Court of Appeal again considered a "reasonable precautions" condition in an employers' liability policy, and Diplock L.J. (as he then was) identified three considerations to be borne in mind when construing this condition[70]:

5–33

(a) It is the insured personally who must take reasonable precautions. Failure by an employee to do so, although the employer might be liable vicariously for the employee's negligence or breach of statutory duty, would not be a breach of the condition;

(b) The obligation of the employer is to take precautions to prevent accidents, which means taking measures to avert dangers which are likely to cause bodily injury to employees;

(c) "Reasonable" does not mean reasonable as between the employer and employee, but as between the insured and the insurer having regard to the commercial purpose of the contract, which is *inter alia* to indemnify the insured against liability for his (the insured's) negligence.

---

[68] *ibid.* at 311.
[69] [1967] 3 All E.R. 57, CA.
[70] *ibid.* at 60.

5–34   Diplock L.J. (as he then was) further explained the meaning of "reasonable"[71]:

> "Obviously the condition cannot mean that the insured must take measures to avert dangers which he does not himself foresee, although the hypothetical reasonably careful employer would have foreseen them. That would be repugnant to the commercial purpose of the contract, for failure to foresee dangers is one of the commonest grounds of liability in negligence. What in my view is 'reasonable' as between the insured and the insurer, without being repugnant to the commercial object of the contract, is that the insured should not deliberately court a danger, the existence of which he has recognised, by refraining from taking any measures to avert it. Equally the condition cannot mean that, where the insured recognises that there is a danger, the measures which he takes to avert it must be such as the hypothetical reasonable employer, exercising due care and observing all the relevant provisions of the Factories Act, 1961, would have taken . . .
> In other words, it is not enough that the employer's omission to take any particular precautions to avoid accidents should be negligent; it must be at least reckless, *i.e.*, made with actual recognition by the insured himself that a danger exists, not caring whether or not it is averted. The purpose of the condition is to ensure that the insured will not refrain from taking precautions which he knows ought to be taken because he is covered against loss by the policy . . ."

5–35   The facts of the claim were that the claimant employee was injured when a welding machine, which operated like an ordinary press, came down on her hand. The machine had originally been provided by the manufacturers with two buttons. The operator needed both hands to press these to put the press in motion, thus providing a precaution against the danger of the operator putting his or her hand into the press when it was moving. Some 18 months prior to the accident, the machine had been changed, and changed to the design of the manager of the factory (which was a small one) with the knowledge and assistance of the managing director, the employers being in effect a one-man company. As a result of this change, the buttons which had hitherto operated as a precaution against danger to the operator were removed, and a table was placed in front of the machine which removed the operator further from the working parts. The trial judge of that action found that, in breach of statutory duty, the employer was liable for not securely fencing a dangerous part of machinery, for negligently altering the machine, and negligently failing to give sufficient instructions to the injured operator how to avoid danger.

5–36   In this action concerning the position of the insured employer and the insurers, the Court of Appeal considered the findings of the trial judge in the employee's action and dismissed the appeal by the insurers. To succeed, the insurers needed to show affirmatively that the failure to take precautions, or that the particular measure taken in altering this machine, was done recklessly, *i.e.* with actual recognition of the danger to employees which was in issue, and without care as to whether or not that danger was

[71] *ibid.* at 61.

averted. The trial judge had found nothing of the sort, and had actually stated that on the balance of probabilities neither the managing director nor any of the staff appreciated the danger which was involved. Accordingly, there was no breach of the reasonable precautions condition.[72]

Provision 3

Provision that the insured complies with the requirements of any enact- 5–37
ment for the protection of employees against the risk of bodily injury or disease in the course of their employment. The same principles apply to conditions to comply with all statutory obligations and regulations imposed on the insured as to conditions to take all reasonable precautions to prevent accidents (see Provision 2 above at paragraph 5–30).

Provision 4

Provision that the insured keeps specified records or provides the insurer 5–38
with or makes available to him information therefrom. This provision is often inserted for the purpose of premium adjustment, for premiums on employers' liability policies are rated on the amount of wages and salaries paid to employees. Such a condition may read:

> "The Insured shall within 30 days from the end of each period of insurance render to the Insurer such particulars and information as the Insurer may require. The premium for such period shall thereupon be adjusted and the difference paid by or allowed to the Insured as the case may be subject to the retention by the Insurer of the amount specified in the schedule as the minimum premium."

Such a provision entitles the insurer to ask the court to order the insured to render an account of wages, salaries, and other earnings (as appropriate) paid to employees and pay any adjustment premium after expiry of the policy.[73]

4. COMMON POLICY EXCLUSIONS

Exclusions concerning business activities

Obviously, insurers assess each risk brought to them in relation to the 5–39
sort of work undertaken by the employees and, indeed the type of workers employed (*e.g.* skilled or unskilled). In order to define the insured risk, the insurer is free to impose excluded types of work,[74] and the 1969 Act does not interfere with this freedom other than as detailed above. Some excluded risks may be insurable for an additional premium. Instances of common exclusions are:

---

[72] *ibid.* at 62, *per* Diplock L.J. (as he then was).

[73] *General Accident Assurance Corp. Ltd v. Day* (1904) 21 T.L.R. 88; *Re Bradley & Essex & Suffolk Accident Indemnity Society* [1912] 1 K.B. 415, CA; *Garthwaite v. Rowland* (1948) 81 Ll. L. Rep. 417.

[74] *Kearney v. General Accident Fire & Life Assurance Corp. Ltd* [1968] 2 Lloyd's Rep. 240.

(i) any work of demolition except demolition of

> (a) a building when such work forms part of a contract for erection of a structure being private dwellings, flats, shops or offices having a completed height of 2 (3,4,5, etc.) floors and roof space;
> (b) a structure not forming part of any building and not exceeding 3.5 metres in height.

(ii) pile driving, quarrying or the use of explosives;
(iii) the construction of roads or the laying of main sewers;
(iv) the handling of any part or unit exceeding 255kg in weight;
(v) work on roofs other than of private dwellings, flats, shops, offices, (including the ground floor and basement) and roof space[75];
(vi) work other than office work;
(viii) loading or discharging vessels.

5–40   Employers must appreciate that if work is undertaken which is in a list of specified excluded activities, then it will probably follow that the insurers will be fully entitled to defend any resulting claim for indemnity under the employers' liability policy, on the ground that the liability incurred to an injured employee was incurred outside the scope of the issued policy.[76] An instance of this occurred in *Kearney v. General Accident Fire and Life Assurance Corpn Ltd*[77] where the employer, who was liable to an employee who was killed when he fell while employed painting roof trusses of a building, sought to recover an indemnity under either or both of two employers' liability policies. Both actions failed, though, on the ground of exclusion policies as the building being painted came within the defined excluded works.

5–41   The first policy contained the following clause:

> "The Corporation shall not be liable by virtue of this policy if at any time the Employer undertakes any work other than painting private dwellings and/or shops consisting of not more than two floors (including the ground floor) and attic, and/or single storey buildings not exceeding 25ft in height."

Neild J. said in relation to that exclusion clause[78]:

> "It seems to me sufficient to say that the building here on which work was being done was not a private dwelling, it was not a shop, and although it was a single storey building it exceeded 25ft, the highest part of the roof being 59ft and the lowest 20ft. I am quite satisfied that that has no application and that the claimant cannot rely upon that policy."

[75] In *Dunbar v. A. & B. Painters Ltd* [1986] 2 Lloyd's Rep. 38, CA, there was a height restriction of 40 feet.
[76] But in *Dunbar v. A. & B. Painters Ltd* [1986] 2 Lloyd's Rep. 38, CA, which concerned a claim for professional negligence against insurance brokers in effecting an employers liability policy, the Court of Appeal accepted that the particular insurer concerned would not have relied on the height exclusion clause to escape liability.
[77] [1968] 2 Lloyd's Rep. 240.
[78] *ibid.* at 243.

The second policy included an endorsement which stated: **5–42**

> "It is hereby understood and agreed that any work in connection with:
>
> (a) Gasometers;
> (b) Towers;
> (c) Steeples;
> (d) Bridges;
> (e) Viaducts;
> (f) Blast Furnaces;
> (g) Colliery Overhead Winding Gear;
> (h) Hangars;
> (i) Roofs other than of Private Dwellings and/or Shops, consisting of not more than three floors (including the ground floor) and attic, is expressly excluded from the Indemnity granted under this Policy."

Neild J. felt that there were two quite separate points to consider. The   **5–43**
first was whether the building was a hangar, *i.e.* a building to house aero-
planes, or whether the change of user of the building, it now being used as
a factory, took it outside the exclusion (h). Whilst Neild J. could see the
force of such an argument where, *e.g.* stables, had by reconstruction or
conversion been turned into small houses, there had been no such alterations in the physical characteristics of the building in this case. Also, the
insurance company, by those exclusions, clearly had in mind the physical
characteristics of the building[79] because of the special hazards associated
therewith. Hazards of petrol may be more grave in an aeroplane hangar or
a big shed housing buses. Equally, the special hazard of height must be
behind the exclusions relating to gasometers, towers, steeples and hangars,
because of the danger of people falling from a height. Accordingly, the
claimant could not recover under this second policy either.

The second point was whether the work being undertaken was work "in   **5–44**
connection with" a roof or roofs and thus came within exclusion (i) of the
policy. Again, there seemed two facets of this argument, the first being
whether the part of the structure on which the deceased was working, *i.e.*
the roof trusses, was part of the roof of the building. Neild J. considered
that the struts and members which formed part of the span or the framework of the span must sensibly and realistically be regarded as a part or
section of the roof in question. Secondly, if it was wrong to consider it
part of the roof, was the work "in connection with" the roof. Applying the
test in *A. Hatrick and Co. Ltd v. R.*[80], "in connection with" meant "connected with, subserving and being ancillary to", that which was being
done here, the painting of trusses and the underside of the outer cover or
skin was certainly "connected with, subserving or ancillary to" the work in
connection with the roof or roof work.

Asbestosis and similar diseases

During the 1960s, before the introduction of the 1969 Act, insurers of   **5–45**
employers whose activities involved the use of, or contact with, asbestos,

[79] *ibid.* at 244.
[80] [1923] A.C. 213, PC.

sought to exclude related disease claims from employees. Due to the
delayed nature of asbestos-related disease, disputes upon the scope of
such exclusions can still emerge. Just such happened in *Cape plc v. The Iron
Trades Employers Insurance Association Ltd*.[81] Here, the claimant employers, who were asbestos makers, claimed a declaration that the defendant
insurers were not entitled to refuse to indemnify them against their liability
for claims against them in respect of pain, injury, loss and damage suffered
by reason of an ex-employee developing mesothelioma. The dispute was
upon the scope of an exclusion that was contained in their employers'
liability policies for the years 1966 to 1971 in respect of, namely, "claims
arising from pneumoconiosis or pneumoconiosis accompanied by tuber-
culosis". The question was whether the policy covered the claimant
employer's liability to employees in respect of injury or disease caused by
mesothelioma, or whether such claims were excluded on the basis that
"pneumoconiosis" was used as a catch-all word to embrace all asbestos
related disease caused by inhalation of asbestos dust, rather than used in
a strict medical sense as meaning fibrosis of the lungs caused by inhalation
of dust.[82] Rix J. (as he then was) held that the mesothelioma claims were
not caught by the terms of the exclusion for a number of reasons, including that there was no certainty as to the meaning of "pneumoconiosis"
beyond its medical and statutory definition,[83] and the exclusion was not
even expressed in terms of "asbestosis". The claimant obtained the
required declaration of entitlement to an indemnity, and the insurers'
counterclaim for rectification therefore failed.

RISKS INSURED

Liability to employees only

5-46   The first facet of the risk insured that requires examination is the determination of which persons are within by the definition of "employee" in
the policy. Earlier forms of policies were narrower in their terms in com-
parison with modern policies, which meet the needs of present conditions
more aptly. For instance, an old policy which referred to persons in the
"direct employment" of the insured was held not to extend to an unskilled
labourer supplied by a building firm to work for the insured, the insured
not being responsible for his wages.[84] The Employers' Liability (Compulsory Insurance) Act 1969[85] requires the employer to insure the risk of his
liability to any person employed by the employer under either a contract
of service or a contract of apprenticeship. It is therefore important to
examine the meaning of "contract of service", for whilst another, *e.g.*
temporary, employee may properly be adjudged in law to be a workman in

[81] [1999] L.T.L. April 21, Case No. C8600509.
[82] It was common ground that this was a different disease from that of mesothelioma.
[83] See the National Health Insurance (Industrial Injuries) Act 1946, s.57(3) and the Social
Security Act 1975, Sched.20.
[84] *Etchells, Congdon & Muir Ltd v. Eagle Star & British Dominions Insurance Co. Ltd* (1928)
72 Sol. Jo. 242.
[85] s.2(1) thereof.

respect of an injury he has suffered, that concept does not affect the contract of service itself. Being a personal contract, no contract of service can be transferred from one employer to another without the employee's consent, and this consent is not to be raised by operation of law, but only by the real consent in fact of the man, express or implied. The essential test is whether the employee himself was transferred, or, in contradistinction, only the use and benefit of his work.[86]

This principle has been stated by the House of Lords in *Nokes v.* **5-47** *Doncaster Amalgamated Collieries Ltd.*[87] where the question was whether an employee had his contract of service transferred to a new company formed by the amalgamation of his employing company with another company. It was held that this transfer could not occur without the consent of the employee (servant). When considering the proposition of automatic transfer of the contract of service to a newly constituted company, Lord Atkin said[88]:

> "My Lords, I confess it appears to me astonishing that apart from overriding questions of public welfare power should be given to a court or anyone else to transfer a man without his knowledge and possibly against his will from the service of one person to the service of another. I had fancied that ingrained in the personal status of a citizen under our laws was the right to choose for himself whom he would serve: and that this right of choice constituted the main difference between a servant and a serf."

In the subsequent case of *Denham v. Midland Employers Mutual Assurance* **5-48** *Ltd*[89] this principle was reiterated, and the transfer of employment deemed to take place in order to establish who was liable to an injured workman was differentiated by Denning L.J. (as he then was)[90]:

> "In none of the transfer cases which have been cited to us had the consent of the man been sought or obtained. The general employer has simply told him to go and do some particular work for the temporary employer and he has gone. The supposed transfer, when it takes place, is nothing more than a device — a very convenient and just device, mark you — to put liability on to the temporary employer; and even this device has in recent years been very much restricted in its operation."

The case concerned injury to a labourer employed by Eastwoods Ltd **5-49** who was directed to help Le Grand Sutcliffe and Gell Ltd, contractors who were engaged by Eastwoods to do some work on their land. The labourer had been killed in an accident which founded liability on Le

---

[86] *Moore v. Palmer* (1886) 2 T.L.R. 781 at 782, *per* Bowen L.J., CA.

[87] [1940] A.C. 1014, H.L.

[88] *ibid.* at 1026; see also the speech of Viscount Simon L.C. at 1024. To protect the continuity of employment of employees in circumstances where there is a relevant transfer of an undertaking from one person to another (by sale or other disposition, but not by changes of control brought about by a share purchase), the contracts of service of employees are automatically transferred, irrespective of the consent of the employees, under the Transfer of Undertakings (Protection of Employment) Regulations 1981 (S.I. 1981 No. 1794), effecting EEC Directive 77/187 ([1977] O.J. L161).

[89] [1955] 2 Q.B. 437, CA.

[90] *ibid.* at 443–444.

Grands as the labourer had worked under the specific directions of that company's foreman. Le Grands sought an indemnity under their employers' liability policy with the defendant insurers which covered liability to "any person under a contract of service . . . with the insured". The Court of Appeal rejected the claim on the ground that the labourer (one Clegg) had a contract of service with Eastwoods, not Le Grands. Denning L.J. (as he then was) explained[91]:

"His contract of service was with Eastwoods and Eastwoods alone. They selected him. They paid him. They alone could suspend or dismiss him. They kept his insurance cards and paid for his insurance stamps. He was never asked to consent to a transfer of the contract of service and he never did so. If he was not paid his wages, or if he was wrongfully dismissed from the work, he could sue Eastwoods for breach of contract and no one else. If he failed to turn up for work Eastwoods alone could sue him. I see no trace of a contract of service with Le Grands except the artificial transfer raised by the law so as to make Le Grands liable to others for his faults or liable to him for their own faults; and I do not think the artificial transfer so raised is 'a contract of service' within this policy of assurance. There was no contract of service between Clegg and Le Grands. Le Grands are, therefore, not entitled to recover against the Midland Employers Mutual Assurance Company under the employers' liability policy . . ."[92]

5–50   To overcome the confines of this wording, and to meet the demands of employers seeking this class of insurance, the following categories of persons will commonly be expressly deemed to be a person under a contract of service or apprenticeship with the insured employer whilst working for the insured in connection with his business (as defined):

(a) any labour masters and persons supplied by them;
(b) any person supplied to the insured;
(c) any person hired by the insured from another employer;
(d) any person borrowed by the insured from another employer;
(e) any labour-only sub-contractor;
(f) self-employed persons;
(g) voluntary helpers;
(h) Manpower Services Commission trainees; and
(i) persons under work experience schemes.

Labour only sub-contractor
5–51   The term "labour only sub-contractor" came to be considered in *Colder v. H. Kitson Vickers and Sons (Engineers) Ltd*[93] where the defendants' employers liability policy was extended to cover liability to labour only sub-contractors. The claimant had worked for the defendants for some years under various arrangements. In 1979 he was employed by them as a lorry driver and then to help break up a steelworks. In November 1979 he replaced one of the three-man team engaged in breaking up a

[91] *ibid.* at 444.
[92] But Le Grands were held to be entitled to recover under their public liability policy.
[93] [1988] I.C.R. 232, CA.

minesweeper, on the suggestion of a director of the defendants. The men were paid on a tonnage recovered basis, the defendants' yard manager calculated the amount of the tonnage removed by the three men and paid the plaintiff in cash. The claimant then shared the receipts with the others. No deduction for tax or National Insurance contributions was made, and the men used the equipment supplied by the defendants, and their dock manager and their safety officer kept a check on the standards maintained. That equipment included a dockside crane and its driver was employed by the defendants. If the three men could not work on the minesweeper because the crane was not working, they were given other work to do.

The insurers denied liability on the basis that the claimant did not come **5–52** within the terms of the words "labour only sub-contractor", *inter alia*, on the ground that as the defendants had no contract with anyone to break up the minesweeper, it followed that the claimant could not be a "subcontractor". The Court of Appeal firmly rejected this contention, and emphasised that they were construing a commercial document and industry used the term "sub-contractor" in a wide sense, therefore the policy should be construed in this wide way. The Court also approved the explanation of the reasons for which this extension to policies was made, as set out in the judgment of French J. in the Court below, where his Lordship had said it was made[94]:

> "to include within the cover the activities of persons such as workers in the building industry who were and are known colloquially as 'on the lump', that is persons who were, to all intents and purposes, employees but who were regarded as self-employed because they were paid without deductions for tax or National Insurance. The word 'sub-contractor' was a natural one to use because, in the vast majority of cases, there will be a contractor between the building owner and the workmen in question. However, to exclude from the ambit of the extended meaning workmen 'on the lump' who happen to be engaged by a building owner direct seems to me to be entirely restrictive and liable to lead to absurd results. Thus, in the instant case, if the defendants had started breaking the minesweeper as contractors and then had bought the minesweeper and continued to break the vessel as principals, cover that would otherwise avail the workman would cease from the moment the defendants purchased the vessel. I take 'labour only subcontractor' in this context to denote one who is paid only for his labour and who is paid without deduction of tax and National Insurance."

Arising out of and in the course of employment

The second aspect to be considered is how the injury arose. The insurer **5–53** will not, in the absence of an extension of cover, be liable under an employers' liability policy to indemnify the insured employer if the employee has been awarded damages from his employer for injury that was not "arising out of and in the course of employment" *e.g.* undertaking a purely private task for his employer, which was not in connection with the employer's business (as defined in the policy). In many situations, however,

---

[94] *ibid.* at 256.

the effect of the employee being injured other than "arising out of and in the course of employment" means that the employer is not liable to compensate him in any event, and no real question of policy indemnity arises.

5–54   If, for instance, an employee is ordered to travel to another place to perform his work, that journey will be within the course of employment,[95] but his travel from home to his place of work by transport will generally not be, even though it is supplied or arranged by the employer, for the employee is not obliged to travel by this means.[96] The general rule being that a workman is not usually employed until he reaches his place of business.[97]

5–55   In *Charles R. Davidson and Co. v. M'Robb*,[98] Lord Finlay contrasted the two questions as to an accident occurring in the course of a workman's employment and arising out of his employment, and said[99]:

> "The word 'employment' must mean the same thing when in apposition with 'in the course of' as it means when in apposition with 'out of'. 'Arising out of the employment' obviously means arising out of the work which the man is employed to do and what is incidental to it — in other words, out of his service. 'In the course of the employment' must mean, similarly, in the course of the work which the man is employed to do, and what is incident to it — in other words, in the course of his service. In the case of a domestic servant who sleeps and takes his meals in his master's house he is in the course of his service all the time — his service is interrupted if he goes out on his own business or pleasure. A workman who by the terms of his employment takes his meals on his employer's premises is in the course of his service in being there at meal-times."

5–56   On the other hand, an injury suffered by an employer who slipped on an oily surface when she was going to wash her tea-cup has been held to be reasonably incidental to the work she was employed to do,[1] and so has returning from the canteen.[2] An employee injured on the entry staircase of his employer's premises on coming to work is also within this definition,[3] for if in going to or coming from his work he has to use an access which is part of his employer's premises, or which he is only entitled to traverse because he is going to or coming from his work, he is held to be on his master's business while he is using that access.[4]

5–57   In recent times, the Court of Appeal[5] has held that the test of whether an employee is acting "in the course of his employment", is not the strict

---

[95] *Holmes v. Great Northern Railway. Co.* [1900] 2 Q.B. 409, CA.

[96] *St Helens Colliery Co. Ltd v. Hewitson* [1924] A.C. 59, HL.; *Ramsay v. Wimpey & Co. Ltd* [1951] S.C. 692; *Vandyke v. Fender* [1970] 2 Q.B. 292, CA; *cf. Weaver v. Tredegar Iron & Coal Co. Ltd* [1940] A.C. 955, HL.

[97] *Blee v. London & North Eastern Railway Co.* [1938] A.C. 126, HL.; but for exceptions see *Stitt v. Woolley* (1971) 115 Sol. Jo. 708, CA.; and *Paterson v. Costain & Press (Overseas) Ltd* [1979] 2 Lloyd's Rep. 204, CA.

[98] [1918] A.C. 304, HL.

[99] *ibid.* at 314.

[1] *Davidson v. Handley Page Ltd* [1945] 1 All E.R. 235, CA.

[2] *Armstrong, Whitworth & Co. Ltd v. Redford* [1920] A.C. 757, HL.

[3] *Bell v. Blackwood Morton & Sons Ltd* 1960 S.C. 11.

[4] *Northumbrian Shipping Co. Ltd v. McCullum* (1932) 48 T.L.R. 568 at 572, *per* Lord MacMillan, HL.

[5] *R. v. Commissioners Industrial Injuries, ex p. Amalgamated Engineering Union (No. 2)* [1966] 2 Q.B. 31, CA.

test of whether he is at the relevant time performing a duty for his employer. He may be "in the course of his employment" even when he acts casually, negligently, or even disobediently, so long as it is something reasonably incidental to his contract of employment. But an employee may interrupt the course of his employment if:

(a) he goes away from work for purposes of his own. Thus, if the guard of a train takes it on himself to drive the train and is injured while driving, he is then outside the course of his employment.[6]

(b) at his place of work he does something which has nothing to do with his employment. So, where a man is employed to hook goods on to a crane, but instead takes it on himself to drive a fork-lift truck.[7]

(c) if, being away from his place of work he does not return to it when he should, the question arises of whether in any particular case he has interrupted his employment. This is a question of fact and degree. An example is a worker overstaying his 10-minute tea-break by 5 minutes in order to finish smoking a cigarette.[8]

(d) in relation to recreational activities, an employee who is injured during such activities, may be within the course of his employment, or undertaking something incidental to it, or outside it, depending upon the facts. Being injured whilst playing darts in the canteen during a lunch break has been held to have occurred in the course of employment,[9] but playing in his employer's football team at his employer's pitch has not, although not to play would have caused the employer's displeasure.[10] An injury sustained during a physical training course organised by the employer with the object of fitting employees for anticipated strenuous duties might, however, be in the course of employment.[11]

6. COMMENTARY ON THE LIMITATIONS OF COMPULSORY EMPLOYERS' LIABILITY INSURANCE

Restricted business activities

Despite the fact that employers' liability insurance is a compulsory insurance and provides cover for the majority of employee's claims, the indemnity under the policy, as discussed above, can legitimately be restricted in scope by the insurer and thus arguably defeat the purposes of the 1969 Act. First, the cover will invariably be expressly limited to specified business activities of the insured employers. If the insured

5–58

---

[6] *Noble v. Southern Railway Co.* [1940] A.C. 583 at 596, *per* Lord Atkin, HL.

[7] *R v. Commissioners Industrial Injuries, ex p. Amalgamated Engineering Union (No. 2)* [1966] 2 Q.B. 31 at 48, *per* Lord Denning M.R., CA.

[8] *ibid.*

[9] *Knight v. Howard Wall Ltd* [1938] 4 All E.R. 667, CA.

[10] *R. v. National Insurance Commissioners, ex p. Michael* [1976] 1 All E.R. 566; affirmed [1977] 1 W.L.R. 109, CA.

[11] [1977] 1 W.L.R. 109 at 121, *per* Lawton L.J., CA.

employer has failed to accurately describe his business activities to the
insurer so that the policy does not include the activity in which an
employee sustains accidental injury, then the injured employee may find
that his employer's policy will not indemnify his employer, with potentially
disastrous consequences for the injured employee. Similarly, through no
fault of his own, and despite the regime of compulsory insurance, an
injured employee can find his employer uninsured in circumstances where
that employer has either changed or expanded the activities of the business
without getting an appropriate amendment to the policy's definition of the
insured business and the employee was injured in the course of those
changed or expanded — but uninsured — activities.[12]

Exclusion of activities

5–59   Secondly, insurers can legitimately exclude certain activities by suitable
policy wordings or endorsements, again leaving an employee injured during such activities, with redress only against his employer's assets, if any.
Just such happened in *Kearney v. General Accident Fire and Life Assurance
Corp. Ltd*,[13] where the employer was unable to recover an indemnity in
respect of his liability to an employee who fell while painting roof trusses of
a building, because painting at such a height breached a height exclusion
within the policy.

Insurer able to rescind policy

5–60   A third feature of this compulsory scheme of insurance under the 1969
Act is that there is no restriction placed on insurers rescinding the policy
ab initio on the ground of non-disclosure or misrepresentation of material
fact, repudiating the policy for breach of a warranty, or refusing a claim
for breach of a non-prohibited condition precedent to liability. There are,
therefore, many potential and actual situations where an injured employee
(and the employer) can or does find that there is no insurance cover in
respect of the employer's liability for an injury sustained in the course of
employment in the insured business, despite the statutory compulsory
insurance regime.

Identification of insurers of past employers

5–61   There are two further matters that require specific comment. The first is
that there is a real problem presented by long-tail disease claims, in that
often the employer will have ceased its business activities, and the injured
ex-employee consequently has no means of identifying which insurer provided employers' liability insurance to his previous employer during his
years of employment. In such circumstances, any prospective action by the
injured ex-employee against his erstwhile employer (assuming he can be
ascertained and found) is fraught with the risk of incurring considerable

---

[12] See, for instance, the case of *Beauchamp v. National Mutual Indemnity Insurance Co. Ltd*
[1937] 3 All E.R. 19, where a liability policy only covered demolition without the use of
explosives, but three employees were injured when the employer chose to use explosives to aid
demolition of a building.
[13] [1968] 2 Lloyd's Rep. 240.

legal fees to obtain a judgment, but without being able to obtain satisfaction of that judgment and the costs incurred from an insurer at the end of that litigation. Whilst the new 1998 Regulations, discussed above, have introduced a requirement for employers to keep readable copies of each Certificate of Insurance for a period of 40 years, there is no penalty for breach of this requirement. Realistically, therefore, it is submitted that officers of defunct businesses are hardly likely to bother complying with this requirement. The inability of many past employees, who wish to make personal injury claims against demised businesses, to obtain details of their employer's past insurers will accordingly remain and thwart those claims. It is submitted that only the introduction of a national register of employers' liability insurances would begin to meet this problem, and then only if it were historic, in the sense of requiring registration of all policies from, for example, 1980.

Lack of "safety net" scheme

The second major criticism of the present scheme of compulsory employers' liability insurance, is that there is no "safety net" to catch uninsured liabilities, unlike the compulsory motor insurance position where the insurance industry has to fund a "safety net" arrangement under the Motor Insurers Bureau Agreements to cover uninsured drivers.[14] An injured employee is not helped by the fact that an employer who fails to insure as required by the 1969 Act commits an offence, because there is no equivalent civil liability arising upon those who are responsible for that failure. Nor is an injured employee in any better position if the absence of effective insurance cover has come about because of a policy exclusion which the employer had unfortunately not appreciated. It is submitted that there is a need for a "safety net" of some sort in order to protect injured employees' rights in respect of accidents sustained at work.

5–62

7. TRANSFER OF UNDERTAKINGS

Nearly 20 years after the introduction of the Transfer of Undertakings (Protection of Employment) Regulations 1981,[15] the question of whether the "old" employer's liability insurance covers the "old" employer's liability to an employee sustaining injury in the course of his employment with the "old" employer has been resolved. These regulations had been introduced to give effect to the Acquired Rights Directive 1977[16] which sought to safeguard an employee's rights and obligations on transfer of an undertaking. In *Bernodone v. Pall Mall Services Group Ltd*,[17] the Court of Appeal upheld Blofeld J.'s ruling that the regulations were wide enough to affect the transferor employer's contract with a

5–63

[14] See Chapter 10, below.
[15] S.I. 1981 No. 1794.
[16] Council Directive 77/187 ([1977] O.J. L161).
[17] [2000] Lloyd's Rep. I.R. 665, CA.

third party, *i.e.* the insurer, and so t̲r̲a̲n̲s̲f̲e̲r̲ ̲t̲o̲ ̲t̲h̲e̲ new transferee employer all the transferor employer's r̲i̲g̲h̲t̲s̲ ̲u̲n̲d̲e̲r̲ an employer's liability policy taken out before the transfer.

5–64   Peter Gibson L.J. first considered the statutory duty of non-exempted employers to insure against liability for injury sustained by their employees arising out of and in the course of their employment under section 1 of the 1969 Act. Thus employees were protected while employed by an employer which later transferred its business within the 1977 Regulations. On transfer, a liability which was transferred ceased to be enforceable against the transferor,[18] but, his lordship recognised, the transferee would be very unlikely to have employer's liability insurance which covered a liability arising before the injured employee became the employee of the transferee business, and, moreover, the transferor could become insolvent. Accordingly, unless the employee had the same benefits and potential rights under the 1969 Act and the Third Parties (Rights Against Insurers) Act 1930[19] after the transfer as he did before, he could be seriously disadvantaged by the transfer.

5–65   The Directive's purpose was to protect the employee's rights. Regulation 5 had to be construed against that purpose and it was widely drawn in its terms:

> "(2) . . .on the completion of a relevant transfer. . .
>
> (a) all the transferor's rights, powers, duties and liabilities under or in connection with any such contract [of employment], shall be transferred by virtue of this Regulation to the transferee; and
> (b) anything done before the transfer is completed by or in relation to the transferor in respect of that contract or a person employed in that undertaking or part shall be deemed to have been done by or in relation to the transferee."

5–66   The transferor employer's relevant "right" in this case was its right to recover from the employer's liability insurers an indemnity under the policy in respect of the transferor's liability as employer to an employee injured in the course of his employment. That liability, be it arising in contract or in tort, was a liability which the transferor employer had been required to insure under the 1969 Act. In the Court of Appeal's view, the transferor's rights under the employer's liability insurance taken out by the transferor, must be regarded as a right within the scope of regulation 5(2)(a), *i.e.* as a right "in connection with" the injured employee's contract of employment with the transferor employer. The justice of this result, it is submitted, cannot be questioned, because, as both Blofeld J. and Peter Gibson L.J. said, the transferor's insurers (who had received a premium to cover that liability to the transferor's employees) would otherwise be able to keep that premium but escape liability under the issued insurance.

---

[18] *Allan v. Sterling District Council* [1995] I.C.R. 1082.
[19] See Chapter 21, below.

In the combined appeals of *Bernadone* and *Martin v. Lancashire County*   **5–67**
Council,[20] the Court of Appeal confirmed that an employer's liabilities in
tort to his employees which arise from and are in connection with the contract of employment, are transferred to a new employer. This was so in the
case of *Martin*, who had sued in negligence, and *Bernadone* where the
claimant had sued in negligence and breach of statutory duty under
section 2 of the Occupiers' Liability Act 1957. In all cases, though, the particular circumstances of the alleged liability must be examined to see
whether it did arise from, or was in connection with the claimant's
contract of employment.[21]

8. INSURERS' LIABILITY WHERE ONE OR MORE EMPLOYER LIABLE TO EMPLOYEE

Progressive injuries

Where a particular injury or disease was caused by a specific, identifi-   **5–68**
able incident in the course of the employee's employment, no problem
arises in terms of identifying which employer and insurer is liable to meet
any liability to the employee. On the other hand, where the injury or
disease is progressively made worse by prolonged exposure during work to,
e.g. noise, inducing deafness, each proven exposure to excessive noise will
give rise to a separate claim against each previous employer in relation to
each period of deleterious exposure.[22] The calculated hearing loss for each
period will enable the insurers of the different employers, or the various
insurers over time of the same employer, to know their liability arising
from the period they insured the employer. The position seems to be the
same in the case of vibration white finger claims.[23]

Where, however, the employee's claim relates to the suffering of a disease,   **5–69**
such as mesothelioma, after many years of exposure to a particular substance, the question arises of which past employer is liable, because such
diseases cannot be traced to any single incident of exposure. In such
circumstances, the law imposes joint and several liability on all previous
employers (and, consequently, on their insurers) who caused the employee
to be exposed to the injurious substance, *e.g.* asbestos dust. Thus, if only
one employer is sued, that employer and his insurers will have to meet the
entire claim even if it was not the sole cause, as long as that exposure materially contributed to the disease.[24] If judgment is obtained for the full value
of the claim, the claimant is debarred from subsequently commencing
fresh proceedings against a different employer in respect of the same
injury or disease.[25] If more than one employer is sued, and one or more

[20] [2000] Lloyd's Rep. I.R. 665, CA.
[21] *ibid.* at 674, para.39, *per* Peter Gibson L.J.
[22] *Thompson v. Smiths Shiprepairers (North Shields) Ltd* [1984] 1 All E.R. 881.
[23] *Armstrong v. British Coal Corp.*, unreported September 30, 1997; H.H.Judge Stephenson
sitting as a judge of the High Court at Newcastle-upon-Tyne.
[24] *Bonnington Castings Ltd v. Wardlaw* [1956] A.C. 613, HL.
[25] *Jameson v. Central Electricity Generating Board & Babcock Energy Ltd* [2000] 1 A.C. 455,
HL.

found liable for contributing to the disease, each will be liable to the claimant in full,[26] but when apportioning that liability as between defendant employers (and thus their insurers), the courts have adopted the approach that employers will contribute in proportion to the respective lengths of the claimant's exposure when in their employment.

Two different accidents and joinder of insurers

5–70   In *Myers v. Dortex International Ltd*,[27] the claimant had suffered two accidents at work. Both resulted in back injury whilst moving heavy materials. The dates of the accidents spanned two periods of insurance, each with a different insurer. The claimant claimed that the second accident was responsible for his major injury, leading to his inability to work in the future, and there was a large loss of future earnings claim. Lloyd's underwriters were the insurers for the second period of insurance, and were conducting the defence on behalf of the insured defendant employer. The defence disputed the facts and alleged that the second accident had happened because of the claimant's own negligence and bad practice on his part. The insurers for the first period of insurance were AXA, and shortly after the commencement of the proceedings, fearing that any loss might be attributed to the first rather than the second accident, applied to have the claim in relation to the first accident stayed, and an order that separate proceedings be issued in respect of the first accident. Those orders were refused by Astill J.

5–71   AXA, therefore, some time later,[28] applied to be joined into the present action, but Steele J. refused the application on the ground that natural justice did not require AXA to be joined. AXA appealed, contending that the discretion under the then RSC, O.15, r.15(6)(b)[29] had been wrongly exercised. The Court of Appeal dismissed the appeal, without citation of previous authorities.[30] Clearly, the lateness of the application for joinder was a very material consideration. It was made after the action was set down for trial on May 27, 1998, that is, after exchange between the claimant and the defendant of medical evidence, occupational therapy evidence, and evidence from consulting engineers. The application was made by summons returnable on June 15, 1998, and the trial was fixed for March 10, 1999. The Court of Appeal refused to go behind Steele J.'s thorough assessment of whether it would be just and convenient to determine the issue, which was between AXA and its own insured — the defendant, during the course of the trial of the claimant's action against the defendant.

5–72   Buxton L.J. went on to say that there was a more fundamental difficulty. This had two aspects, the first being that there was only one defendant in the case, whereas[31]:

---

[26] *Bryce v. Swan Hunter Group plc* [1988] 1 All E.R. 659.

[27] [2000] Lloyd's Rep. I.R. 529, CA.

[28] Having been wrongly advised by initial Counsel that there was no mechanism to apply for joinder. Joinder is discussed in Chapter 22, below.

[29] See now, CPR, r. 19.2(a).

[30] See Chapter 22.

[31] *ibid.* at 533.

"The dispute that AXA wishes to ventilate is, as they say, not against Mr Myers as such, it is against Dortex. The reason that they are issue with Dortex is that they have not succeeded in persuading Dortex to conduct the case in the way that AXA would wish it to be conducted; or, alternatively, have not been able to reach any compromise with the other insurers as to how liability, if any, should be apportioned between them. That is not in my judgment an appropriate, let alone convenient and just, issue to be ventilated in these proceedings. Further, the way in which it is sought to ventilate it is by AXA appearing at the trial and adducing evidence potentially different from that of [the existing medical experts] going to the causation of the injuries. The [claimant] will then be faced with two different cases. That is to be done to ensure that the trial judge makes a sufficient apportionment of liability between the two accidents for the insurance company to know how much it ought to pay out in compensation to its insured.

How the trial would progress is a mystery . . . The question of how these injuries occurred and what was responsible for them, is plainly in issue in the main action. I have every confidence that the trial judge trying a case of this importance to both parties will set out in his or her judgment a careful account of how the accident and the injuries occurred. That should be amply sufficient for insurers and insured, all of whom have existing contractual responsibilities to each other in this respect, to work out what their respective liabilities are for meeting whatever damages are awarded."

CHAPTER 6

PUBLIC LIABILITY INSURANCE

1. SUBJECT MATTER OF PUBLIC LIABILITY INSURANCE

Introduction

6–01   The purpose of a commercial concern taking out public liability insurance is to obtain an indemnity in respect of its liability to third parties in respect of injury or death, or loss or damage to their property. The public liability policy wording will make it clear that risks covered by other policies that are likely to be in existence regarding other specific risks, *e.g.* employers' liability[1] or product liability, are excluded from its scope. In other words, public liability insurance covers liability to the public at large arising out of the fact that the commercial concern is in existence and operating. Accordingly, the two broad fields of liability covered by a public liability policy are:

(a) risks arising from the ownership, occupation or management of the insured business premises; and

(b) risks arising from the activities of employees or agents to third parties, *i.e.* vicarious liability of the employing insured business.

Legal liability of the insured

6–02   Before discussing the general risks embraced by the indemnity wording under a public liability policy, there is one particular point to be made in relation to this indemnity. That is that the subject matter of the policy is the legal liability of the insured, which must arise out of some event during the period of insurance, even if the claim is made years later. The policy's operative insuring clause, may be similar[2] to the following:

> "The insurer will indemnify the Insured against all sums which the Insured shall become legally liable to pay as compensation for:
>
> (a) accidental death of or personal injury to or illness or disease contracted by any person;
>
> (b) accidental loss or damage to property happening in connection with the Business and occurring during the period of Insurance."

6–03   This means that the policy is a liability policy, and therefore the insured cannot recover anything under the main indemnity clause or make any claim against the underwriters until the insured have been found liable and so sustained a loss.[3] In other words, the insured's liability to a third party who

---

[1] See the definition of "legal liability" in Section 1 of the specimen policy at Appendix 1.

[2] See also Section 1 A(1) of the specimen combined policy at Appendix 1 (which actually includes products liability cover).

[3] *West Wake Price & Co. v. Ching* [1957] 1 W.L.R. 45 at 49, *per* Devlin J. (as he then was).

has suffered loss, damage or injury must be ascertained and determined to exist, either by judgment of the court or by an award in arbitration or by agreement.[4] The words of the insurance indemnity always need to be carefully considered in each particular case. For instance, where the insuring words refer to an indemnity against the insured's liability "at law" to third parties, giving those words their ordinary meaning means that this indemnity extends to contractual liability even where there is no liability at common law.[5] An indemnity against "all sums which the Insured shall become legally liable to pay" is likely to include liability for loss of profits in a claim brought against the insured,[6] and an indemnity in respect of "compensation" to be paid may include exemplary damages awarded against the insured.[7] An indemnity against liability for "damages" includes a sum awarded for pre-judgment interest.[8] Where the indemnity is in respect of the insured's "liability" to third parties, the insured can recover his owns costs incurred in remedying physical damage to third parties' properties rather than engaging others to execute the remedial work.[9]

There must be a true liability in law against the insured in order for an **6–04** indemnity to arise, however, and the court will examine the facts where the insurer disputes that a legal liability existed. Thus, in *Concrete Ltd v. Attenborough*[10] the insured could not recover an indemnity in respect of a claim for negligence and/or breach of statutory duty brought against them which they had settled of their own accord. Two firms of sub-contractors (one being the insured) were working on reconstruction work when an employee of the other sub-contractors fell through a hole in the floor which the insured sub-contractors had not protected or fenced. It was this claim by the workman that the insured had settled. Branson J., however, held that this workman had no valid claim in law against the insured for he was not an invitee to premises they occupied and therefore they owed him no duty of care in that respect. Accordingly, the insured had no legal liability to be indemnified under their public liability policy. Similarly, in *Jan de Nul (U.K.) Ltd v. N.V. Royale Belge*[11] the insurers challenged, unsuccessfully, their insured's liability in law to various persons who had made claims for loss and damage arising from the insured's dredging operations.

In the case of a liability policy covering sums which the insured became **6–05** liable to pay as damages to third parties "howsoever arising", the court will be more circumspect in determining the insured's right to recover sums paid to third parties in settlement of claims. In *P&O Steamship*

---

[4] *Post Office v. Norwich Union Fire Insurance Society Ltd* [1967] 2 W.L.R. 709 at 714 and 717, *per* Lord Denning M.R. and Salmon L.J., CA.

[5] *M/S Aswan Engineering Establishment Co. Ltd v. Iron Trades Mutual Insurance Co. Ltd* [1989] 1 Lloyd's Rep. 289.

[6] *A.S. Screenprint Ltd v. British Reserve Insurance Co. Ltd* [1999] Lloyd's Rep. I.R. 430, CA.

[7] See the rather special facts in *Lancashire C.C. v. Municipal Mutual Insurance Ltd* [1996] 3 W.L.R. 493, CA.

[8] *Cox v. Bankside Members Agency Ltd* [1995] 2 Lloyd's Rep. 437 at 461, *per* Sir Thomas Bingham, M.R., CA.

[9] *Jan de Nul (U.K.) Ltd v. N.V. Royale Belge* [2000] 2 Lloyd's Rep. 700.

[10] (1939) 65 Ll. L. Rep. 174.

[11] [2000] 2 Lloyd's Rep. 700.

Navigation Co. v. Youell,[12] the insured operators of luxury cruise ships suffered a series of mishaps in respect of three of their cruise ships in 1991–1992, leading to their receipt of a large number of complaints and passengers' claims. To avoid a multiplicity of separate claims and to preserve its good name, the insured quickly negotiated and agreed compensation packages with the complainants. These were agreed to be in full and final settlement of any passenger claims. The insurers defended the insured's claim for an indemnity under the policy in respect of all these payments, on the ground that, because the insured's standard terms and conditions excluded such claims by passengers, the insured could not show its legal liability to pay damages to the passengers.

6–06 The Court of Appeal first considered the validity of that defence, but concluded that a court would refuse to give effect to the exclusions of liability pursuant to the Unfair Contract Terms Act 1977. The passengers' claims for damages for disappointment and distress were therefore sustainable and, accordingly, the insured established the necessary liability in damages to those passengers. The Court of Appeal added that the nature of the compromise designed to avoid and/or satisfy claims in respect of liability to passengers should not be determinative of the question whether or not there was a valid claim under the policy. Whilst some of the claims which had been settled had been characterised by the claimants' solicitors as claims for return of monies paid for which there had been a total failure of consideration, the court felt it was appropriate for it to take a view "across the board" of all the claims in approaching the question of liability and compensation. In so doing, the court concluded that the claims were for damages for the insured's failure to provide an enjoyable and relaxing holiday.

Expenditure reasonably incurred to prevent or minimise further loss

6–07 There is no implied term in this type of insurance to the effect that the insured is entitled to be indemnified in respect of expenditure he reasonably incurs with the purpose of preventing, or minimising, further loss which might otherwise fall upon the insurer consequent on the occurrence or event. Nor will such expenditure fall within an extension of insurance cover to provide an indemnity in respect of "all other costs and expenses in relation to any matter which may form the subject of a claim for indemnity [against liability for damages in respect of accidental loss of or damage to material property]".

6–08 Those issues were determined by the Court of Appeal in *Yorkshire Water Services Ltd v. Sun Alliance and London Insurance plc.*[13] The insured water company sought to recover from its insurers some £4.6 million which the insured had spent on urgent flood alleviation works in order to avert further damage to the property of others, and to prevent, or reduce the possibility of, claims, following an escape of sewage sludge from its land into an adjacent river. This was apparently the first time that English

---

[12] [1997] 2 Lloyd's Rep. 136, CA.
[13] [1997] 2 Lloyd's Rep. 21, CA.

courts have been asked to consider whether an insured can recover monies expended to prevent or minimise loss which would, or might, fall to a liability insurer. The Court of Appeal rejected the argument that such costs could be covered by the extended indemnity, because liability policies were written in terms of being an indemnity in respect of sums which the insured had become legally liable to pay. In the words of Stuart-Smith L.J., such recoverable sums[14]:

> "must obviously involve payment to a third party claimant and not expenses incurred by the insured in carrying out works on his land or paying contractors to do so. And the liability must be to pay damages and compensation."

The Court of Appeal also rejected the insured's argument for an implied   **6–09** term that such expenditure should be recovered from the defendant insurers. First, the court considered that the suggested term was inconsistent with the express condition in the policy that the insured, at his own expense, was to take "reasonable precautions to prevent any circumstances or to cease any activity which may give rise to liability". Secondly, there was no need to imply the proposed term because the policies worked perfectly without the suggested implied term. Thirdly, the mere fact that an obligation was imposed for the benefit of another, was not sufficient for the implication that the latter would reimburse the expense of performing it. Fourthly, the insured was under a duty in tort not to cause injury to its neighbours. Fifthly, section 74 of the Marine Insurance Act 1906[15] prevented such an implied term in marine insurance, and, the principles of marine insurance being not significantly different from non-marine insurance, there was no reason why it should be implied in a non-marine policy. Finally, the proposed term was virtually unworkable, because it would not be possible to decide what expenditure of the insured was reasonable, short of expensive litigation.[16]

Risks insured

It can readily be imagined that there are an infinite variety of business   **6–10** concerns, and the premises risks and vicarious liability risks of each concern will be different. All that can be discussed here are the general areas of liability that may or may not be applicable as a risk of any particular business concern, and in each case it will have to be considered whether the liability incurred is within the scope of the specific operative insuring clause. The insured must establish not only that he has incurred a loss, but

[14] *ibid.* at 28, col. 2.

[15] "Where the assured has effected an insurance in express terms against any liability to a third party, the measure of indemnity, subject to any express provision in the policy, is the amount paid or payable by him to such third party in respect of such liability."

[16] The Court of Appeal was referred to many American authorities, but was not referred to the Australian decision in *Guardian Assurance Society Ltd v. Underwood Construction Pty. Ltd* (1974) 48 A.L.J.R. 307 at 309, where the Court of Appeal of Queensland said that "it may be" that costs reasonably incurred by an insured person pursuant to a contractual obligation, or in fulfillment of a duty to prevent or minimize liability to a third party, should be regarded as falling within a general indemnity against liability to others.

that the loss was proximately caused by the insured peril, and this is not to be determined simply by the way that the third party frames his claim against the insured.[17]

Accidental loss or damage

6–11   What may be properly considered to be "accidental" loss or damage was the subject of *Corbin v. Payne*.[18] The insured operated a car fragmentiser machine and held a public liability policy which indemnified him against "all sums . . . as the assured . . . shall become legally liable to pay in respect of claims made against the assured arising from . . . accidental loss of or damage to material property". In 1985, the insured's neighbour had issued proceedings against him for nuisance and sought an injunction relating to the noise, vibration and ejection of metal from the machine. The insured claimed an indemnity under the policy, but the insurers contended that it was outside the ambit of the policy. The action by the neighbour proceeded to trial, during the course of which the insured settled the neighbour's claim for £140,000.

6–12   The claim for an indemnity under the policy then proceeded to trial and the insurers then appealed against the first instance decision that they were liable to pay part of that sum to the insured. On the appeal, Mustill L.J. said that plainly the reason why the insured had agreed to settle the claim by his neighbour was that if the action had proceeded to judgment he would, as the judge had made clear during the hearing, have been pre-vented from using the fragmentiser. The payment was therefore a means of ensuring that in spite of the characteristics of the machine he could carry on with its profitable operation. To read the policy as entitling the insured to purchase at the insurers' expense the liberty to go on using a noisy and possibly dangerous machine which he had chosen to bring on to his land and install near to his neighbour's residence was far removed from the tenor and obvious intent of the policy. Although it could be envisaged that if the action had proceeded to judgment the insured might have had some claim under the policy, the sum that he paid under the settlement was well outside it. Accordingly, the insured was not entitled to any recovery against the insurers under the policy.

"In connection with" the business

6–13   This phrase, referring to the business as described to the insurer in any proposal form, has a wide meaning and has been construed as meaning "connected with, subserving and being ancillary to"[19] the business insured. The operative wording may well not refer to "the insured's business" in general, but to a rather more specific definition of the insured's business activities from which resulting liability is indemnified. This can occur where a more unusual risk is insured. Such was the case in *Captain Boynton's World's Water Show Syndicate Ltd v. Employers' Liability Assurance Corp.*

[17] *MDIS Ltd v. Swinbank & others* [1999] Lloyd's Rep. I.R. 516, CA.
[18] *The Times*, October 11, 1990, CA.
[19] *A. Hatrick & Co. Ltd v. R.* [1923] A.C. 213, PC.

Ltd,[20] where the insured were showmen who operated a large lake upon which boats and a water bicycle propelled by means of paddle wheels worked by the feet, as well as a water chute which flat-bottomed boats came down and were propelled across the lake. A person was using the water bicycle when he was struck by a boat which had come down the chute, and the insured sought an indemnity in respect of their liability for the injury. The policy provided an indemnity in respect of "personal injury caused to any person . . . by any accident to the boats and chutes", but the insurers contended that this accident was outside the scope of these words for there was no accident "to" the boats and chutes, but one to a water bicycle. The Court of Appeal rejected that defence and held that the insured could recover under this public liability policy, because there was an accident to a boat (when it collided with the water bicycle), and by reason of this accident a person had suffered personal injury.

The definition of the place of business

Pictorial Machinery Ltd v. Nicolls[21] provides an example of the inter-relationship between the operative insuring words referring to the insured's business, and the definitions of that business and the insured's premises set out in the policy schedule, where the indemnity referred to "accidents occurring in or about" the places described in the Schedule. The material part of the policy stated that the insurers would provide an indemnity in respect of the legal liability of the insured for: **6–14**

> "Bodily injury (fatal or non-fatal) to persons and/or damage to property resulting from any accidents occurring in or about the places described in the Schedule hereto during the period [of insurance] caused by the fault or negligence of the assured or any of their employees whilst engaged in the assured's business as specified in the schedule hereto and/or by any defect in the assured's premises ways works machinery or plant used in the said business in or about the said places . . ."

The relevant accident arose from the dropping of a glass container of acetone by a boy engaged by the insured to deliver the containers, which he was doing, at a customer's premises. The resulting conflagration badly damaged the premises of that customer and that of his neighbours. These premises were some three minutes' walk from the insured's premises in Hatton Garden, London. The Schedule gave the nature of the insured's business in respect of which the policy was issued as "Printer's engineers and suppliers", and the place at which that business was carried on was described as "47 Hatton Garden, EC1 . . . and/or elsewhere where assured's employees may be working". One line of defence to the insured's claim taken by the insurers was that the mere fact that the boy was on the premises of someone else, and on those premises in the course of his duties, did not justify the court in holding that he was "working" there and   **6–15**

---

[20] (1895) 11 T.L.R. 384, CA.
[21] (1940) 67 Ll. L. Rep. 461.

was therefore outside the scope of this policy. Humphreys J. swiftly dismissed that argument[22]:

> "I can only say in my view the boy was working, and working as the servant of his employers, in delivering those goods until the moment when he ceased to deliver them, just as much as if he had been manufacturing something on behalf of his employers. Delivery was the work on which he was engaged. In my view he was working on the premises of [the customer] in the interests of his employers just as much as I think my servant is working for me when I tell him to go and post a letter. Until he has posted that letter I do not think I could be heard to say that he was not on my premises and therefore he was not working at the place where he was employed; for 'the place where he was employed' is to be read as the place where he is working in my interest and on my behalf, and I think that point fails."

2. VICARIOUS LIABILITY OF THE INSURED BUSINESS

Vicarious liability of the insured business

6–16   Vicarious liability means that one person takes the place of another so far as liability is concerned[23] and, as regards a commercial concern or business, be it a limited company, partnership, or sole proprietor, relates to that business's liability to third parties for the acts or omissions of their:

(a) employees;
(b) agents;
(c) independent contractors.

These will be considered in turn.

Vicarious liability for employees

6–17   In terms of the vicarious liability of an insured for the negligent acts or omissions of persons working for his business causing injury, loss or damage to third parties or their property, "employee" has an extended meaning beyond simply meaning a person who is under a contract of service[24] with the insured. The insured will be liable if the insured had the right to control the way in which the act involving negligence, and injury, loss or damage to third parties or their property, was done.[25] Thus persons loaned from other employers to undertake a process or operation for the insured may be an employee for the purposes of vicarious liability of the insured for his acts or omissions.[26] In other words, when one person lends his employee to another for a particular employment, the employee, for anything done in that particular employment, must be dealt with as the employee of the man to whom he

[22] (1940) 45 Com. Cas. 334 at 341.
[23] *Launchbury v. Morgans* [1971] 2 Q.B. 245 at 253, *per* Lord Denning M.R., CA.
[24] See, *e.g. Ready Mixed Concrete (South East) Ltd v. Ministry of Pensions & National Insurance* [1968] 2 Q.B. 497, for a threefold test to be applied to determine whether a contract of service exists.
[25] *Mersey Docks & Harbour Board v. Coggins & Griffiths (Liverpool) Ltd & McFarlane* [1947] A.C. 1 at 12, *per* Viscount Simon, at 17, *per* Lord Porter, and at 23, *per* Lord Uthwatt, HL.
[26] See, *e.g. McArdle v. Andmac Roofing Co.* [1967] 1 W.L.R. 356, CA.

is lent, although he remains the general employee of the person who lent him.[27] This test of the right to control the way in which the person in question carried out his negligent act becomes difficult, however, where that person is hired by the insured from his general employer to undertake work involving use of a machine or the driving of a vehicle supplied by the general employer. If the hirer merely instructs the driver/operator where and when to go and do his work, this may generally be said to be insufficient for the hirer to become vicariously liable for the driver/operator's negligence.[28] Rather, the driver/operator needs to be under the general direction and control of the hirer either in fact,[29] or by right under the hire contract.[30]

Liability for agents

Agents are persons authorised to act on behalf of another (their principal) **6–18**
who will be liable for their negligence whilst they are carrying out duties within the scope of the authority conferred on them by their principal[31]; or the agent acts outside his authority but his principal adopts his act under the doctrine of ratification.[32] A simple example of the vicarious liability of a principal for the negligent act of his agent is provided by *Brooke v. Bool*[33] where the owner of a lockup shop lived next door to his shop and was told by his lodger that he smelt gas from his shop. The shop-owner and his lodger went to investigate and, unfortunately, the lodger, now acting as the agent of the shop-owner for this foray, carried a naked light into the shop. The owner was held liable to the tenant of his shop for the damage consequent upon the resulting gas explosion.

Liability for independent contractors

As a general proposition it can be said that if an independent contractor **6–19**
is employed to do a lawful act, and in the course of the work he or his servants (employees) or agents commit some casual act of wrong or negligence, the employer is not answerable.[34] On the other hand, where the independent contractor is effectively acting as the agent of his employer to perform a task or carry out a duty that is the employer's, the employer is liable for all the damage or loss caused to third parties in consequence of the performance of that work by the independent contractor.[35] As has been explained by Salmon J. (as he then was)[36]:

---

[27] *Rourke v. White Moss Colliery Co.* (1877) 2 C.P.D. 205 at 209, *per* Cockburn C.J.
[28] See, *e.g. Dewar v. Tasker & Sons Ltd.* (1907) 23 T.L.R. 259, CA; *Century Insurance Co Ltd v. Northern Ireland Road Transport Board* [1942] A.C. 509, HL.
[29] *G.W. Leggott & Son v. C.H. Normanton & Son* (1928) 98 L.J.K.B. 145.
[30] *Arthur White (Contractors) Ltd v. Tarmac Civil Engineering Ltd.* [1967] 1 W.L.R. 1508, HL, where a crane and driver were hired under the standard form of contract used in the plant hire industry.
[31] *Heatons Transport (St Helens) Ltd v. Transport & General Workers Union* [1973] A.C. 15 at 99 *per* Lord Wilberforce, HL.
[32] *Wilson v. Tumman* (1843) 6 Man & G. 236; 12 L.J.C.P. 306.
[33] [1928] 2 K.B. 578, DC.
[34] *Pickard v. Smith* (1861) 10 C.B.N.S. 470, *per* Williams J.
[35] The employer may be entitled to a contribution from the independent contractor; see, *e.g. Daniel v. Rickett, Cockerell & Co. Ltd & Raymond* [1938] 2 K.B. 322.
[36] *Green v. Fibreglass Ltd* [1958] 2 Q.B. 245 at 250.

"By virtue of a contract or by the operation of law, an obligation may be imposed on a man to do an act or to ensure that it is done and done carefully. In such cases the defendant cannot shelter behind any independent contractor he may have employed."

6–20   Such liability may arise against the employer for public nuisance,[37] private nuisance, trespass,[38] or negligence.[39] But the employer of an independent contractor is not responsible for the negligent performance of a task by the contractor (or his servants or agents) if such task is collateral to the non-delegable task being performed. Such act is outside the scope of the duty imposed on the employer (which is being performed by the contractors).[40]

3. PREMISES RISKS

Escape of dangerous things

6–21   Where an insured has brought something onto his land that can be a danger to others if it escapes, he will be liable under the rule in *Rylands v. Fletcher*[41] for loss, damage or injury caused to third parties by reason of the escape. Water in large quantities[42] is a dangerous thing, as well as the more obvious examples of loaded firearms, poison, explosives,[43] inflammable gases or liquids, and fire.[44] Where a person brings upon land of which he is in *de facto* possession for purposes of his business dangerous materials which would not naturally be upon the land, he is under an obligation to keep those materials under control, so as not to cause mischief to his neighbours.[45]

6–22   There is no liability under this rule, however, where non-dangerous items escape from business premises as is demonstrated by *British Celanese Ltd v. A.H. Hunt (Capacitors) Ltd*[46] The defendants manufactured electronic components and stored strips of metal foil on their premises. Three and a half years earlier some of these foil strips had blown off their premises and caused a power failure to the immediate locality when they blew onto a nearby electricity substation. Again some strips blew away and caused a temporary power failure to neighbouring factories. The plaintiff company sought to recover in respect of their loss and sued the defendants. It was held that the defendants would not be liable under the rule in *Rylands v. Fletcher* because neither the manufacturing of electrical or electronic components, nor the storing of metal foil on the premises,

---

[37] *Ellis v. Sheffield Gas Consumers Co.* (1853) 2 E. and B. 767; 23 L.J.Q.B. 42.
[38] *Upton v. Townend* (1855) 17 C.B. 30.
[39] See, *e.g. Penny v. Wimbledon UDC* (1899) 2 Q.B. 72; 68 L.J.Q.B. 704, CA.
[40] *Dalton v. Angus* (1881) 6 App. Cas. 740, HL.
[41] (1868) L.R. 3 H.L. 330, HL.
[42] *ibid.*; *Western Engraving Co. v. Film Laboratories Ltd* [1936] 1 All E.R. 106, CA.
[43] *Dominion Natural Gas Co. Ltd v. Collins & Perlins* [1909] A.C. 640 at 646, *per* Lord Dunedin, PC.
[44] *Black v. Christchurch Finance Co.* [1894] A.C. 48, PC.
[45] *Belvedere Fish Guano Co Ltd v. Rainham Chemical Works Ltd Feldman & Partridge* [1920] 2 K.B. 487, at 502, *per* Atkin L.J. (as he then was), CA.
[46] [1969] 1 W.L.R. 959.

could be regarded as a special use of the land bringing with it increased
danger to others within the meaning of the rule. (The defendants were
found liable, however, in both negligence and private nuisance.)

Fire

In respect of fire, however, the Fires Prevention (Metropolis) Act 1774,   **6–23**
which applies to the whole of England,[47] but not to Scotland,[48] modifies
the legal position if a fire starts on land accidentally.[49] The occupier of the
land will under section 86 be protected from liability for damage caused by
the spread of the fire unless continued by the occupier's negligence, *e.g.* by
failing to turn off the tap controlling inflammable liquid that has caught
fire.[50] The 1774 Act affords no protection, though, in the case of fires
which have been started intentionally or caused by negligence.[51]

Electricity

Electricity brought onto the business premises in the ordinary course of   **6–24**
events is not a "dangerous thing" and thus there is no liability upon the
occupier of business premises if an unknown defect in the wire causes a
fire which spreads without negligence to neighbouring properties.[52] The
occupier will be liable, however, if the wiring was in such a condition as to
constitute a nuisance, or had been negligently installed or maintained
(either by himself, his servants or his agents, including independent
contractors).[53]

Dangerous premises and lawful visitors

Under the Occupiers' Liability Act 1957, the occupier of premises owes   **6–25**
the "common duty of care" to his visitors, which is defined under section
2(2) as being:

> "A duty to take such care as in all the circumstances of the case is reason-
> able to see that the visitor will be reasonably safe in using the premises for
> the purposes for which he is invited or permitted by the occupier to be
> there."

This duty is cast on the occupier, rather than the owner, for he has the   **6–26**
immediate control and supervision of the premises, and it has two facets
— as regards the physical state of the premises, and as regards the dangerous use of the premises. By way of illustration, an occupier has been
held liable when a cleaner slipped on a highly polished floor,[54] but not

---

[47] *Filliter v. Phippard* (1847) 11 Q.B. 347.
[48] *Westminster Fire Office v. Glasgow Provident Investment Society* (1888) 13 App. Cas. 699,
HL.
[49] Construed as meaning "without negligence", *Mulholland & Tedd Ltd v. Baker* [1939] 3
All E.R. 253 at 255, *per* Asquith J.
[50] *Musgrove v. Pandelis* [1919] 2 K.B. 43, CA.
[51] See, *e.g. Vaughan v. Menlove* (1837) 3 Bing. N.C. 468; 6 L.J.C.P. 92; *Maclenan v. Segar*
[1917] 2 K.B. 325; *Mason v. Levy Auto Parts of England Ltd* [1967] 2 Q.B. 530.
[52] *Collingwood v. Home & Colonial Stores Ltd* [1936] 3 All E.R. 200, CA.
[53] *Spicer v. Smee* [1946] 1 All E.R. 489.
[54] *Adams v. S.J. Watson & Co. Ltd* (1967) 117 N.L.J. 130.

when a stevedore slipped on an oily patch on a ship's deck[55]; when a visitor fell when stepping over a fallen bag,[56] but not when a customer in a shop fell over some cartons[57]; when a customer in a public house fell down an unlit narrow staircase long after permitted hours,[58] but not when an elderly lady slipped on the stairs of a block of flats which were unlit because of faulty adjustment of the time-switch[59]; and when a plasterer came into contact with a live electric light wire which had carelessly been switched on by the occupier's maintenance electrician,[60] but not when a customer in a shop was injured by the fall of part of a ceiling which had recently been plastered.[61]

6–27   Under section 2(3) of the Act, the occupier must be prepared for children to be less careful than adults, and at common law permitting children to come onto premises or moveable structures can be deemed by failure to maintain a fence around the premises.[62] Whilst a pond,[63] a river,[64] a trench on land being developed[65] and a heap of paving slabs[66] have been held not to constitute allurements or traps to children, a lorry laden with sugar,[67] broken glass on wasteland where children were allowed to play,[68] a building in the course of demolition,[69] and a tree close to a footpath[70] have.

6–28   In determining whether the occupier of premises has discharged his common duty of care to visitors, section 2(4)(b) provides that the occupier is not liable for damage caused to a visitor owing to the faulty execution of any work of construction, maintenance or repair done by an independent contractor, if:

(a) he acted reasonably in entrusting the work to an independent contractor; and

(b) he had taken such steps (if any) as he reasonably ought to satisfy himself that the contractor was competent; and

(c) the work had been properly done.

6–29   The Defective Premises Act 1972 throws a duty upon developers, local authorities and others who arrange for builders, sub-contractors, and professional men (*e.g.* architects), and such builders, etc., who take on work for or in connection with the provision of a dwelling, to see that the work

[55] *Lowther v. H Hogarth & Sons Ltd* [1959] 1 Lloyd's Rep. 171.
[56] *Blackett v. British Railways Board, The Times*, December 1967.
[57] *Doherty v. London Co-operative Society Ltd* (1966) 110 Sol. Jo. 74.
[58] *Stone v. Taffe* [1974] 1 W.L.R. 1575, CA.
[59] *Irving v. L.C.C.* (1965) 193 Estates Gazette 539.
[60] *Fisher v. C.H.T. Ltd(No 2)* [1966] 2 Q.B. 475, CA.
[61] *O'Connor v. Swan & Edgar Ltd* (1963) 107 Sol. Jo. 215.
[62] *Cooke v. Midland Great Western Railway of Ireland* [1909] A.C. 329, HL.
[63] *Hastie v. Edinburgh Magistrates* (1907) S.C. 1102.
[64] *Stevenson v. Glasgow Corp.* (1908) S.C. 1034.
[65] *Phipps v. Rochester Corp.* [1955] 1 Q.B. 450.
[66] *Latham v. R. Johnson & Nephew Ltd* [1913] 1 K.B. 398, CA.
[67] *Culkin v. McFie & Sons Ltd* [1939] 3 All E.R. 613.
[68] *Williams v. Cardiff Corp.* [1950] 1 K.B. 514, CA.
[69] *Davis v. St Mary's Demolition & Excavation Co. Ltd.* [1954] 1 W.L.R. 592.
[70] *Buckland v. Guildford Gas Light & Coke Co.* [1949] 1 K.B. 410.

which is done is done in a workmanlike or, as the case may be, professional manner, with proper materials and so that as regards that work the dwelling will be fit for habitation when completed. Moreover, under section 4 of the 1972 Act, the landlord's duty of care where premises are let under a tenancy which puts him under an obligation to the tenant for their maintenance or repair, is "a duty to take such care as is reasonable in all the circumstances to see that they are reasonably safe from personal injury or from damage to their property caused by a relevant defect".

Dangerous premises and trespassers

A trespasser is one "who goes on the land without invitation of any sort **6–30** and whose presence is either unknown to the proprietor or, if known, is practically objected to".[71] An occupier of land is liable to a trespasser only if he breaches the duty under the Occupiers' Liability Act 1984,[72] which is "to take such care as is reasonable in all circumstances of the case to see that he does not suffer injury on the premises by reason of the danger concerned". This duty is concerned with any risk of trespassers (or other non-invitees) suffering injury on the premises by reason of any danger due to the state of the premises or to things done or omitted to be done on them, and, under section 1(3) arises in respect of such if:

(a) he (the occupier) is aware of the danger or has reasonable grounds to believe that it exists;
(b) he knows and has reasonable grounds to believe that the order is in the vicinity of the danger concerned or that he may come into the vicinity of the danger (in either case, whether the other has lawful authority for being in that vicinity or not); and
(c) the risk is one against which, in all the circumstances of the case, he may reasonably be expected to offer the other some protection.

An example of liability of the occupier of commercial premises is **6–31** afforded by *Pannett v. McGuiness and Co.*[73] when workmen of the defendant contractor lit a bonfire to burn their rubbish on a demolition site, having chased away children from the fire, then left it unattended. The contractors were held liable to a five-year-old boy who was burnt when he trespassed onto the site and went to the fire.

Liability to adjoining premises

An occupier of premises will be liable in negligence if he fails to take **6–32** reasonable care that his property does not get into such a state as to be dangerous to adjoining property or persons lawfully thereon.[74] This is a

---

[71] *Robert Addie & Sons (Collieries) Ltd v. Dumbreck* [1929] A.C. 358 at 371 *per* Lord Dunedin, HL.

[72] s. 1(4) Occupiers' Liability Act 1984, abolished the "humanity" test laid down in *British Railways Board v. Herrington* [1972] A.C. 877 at 939–940, HL.

[73] [1972] 2 Q.B. 599, CA.

[74] *Cunard v. Antifyre Ltd* [1933] 1 K.B. 551 at 557, *per* Talbot J.

personal duty that cannot be delegated, and thus, if independent contractors whilst rebuilding certain premises cause damage to neighbouring property by reason of their negligent interference with their right of support from the occupier's premises, the occupier himself will be liable.[75] Similarly, an occupier will be liable if his premises are being demolished or repaired, and the contractors cause damage to neighbouring property or injury to persons on adjoining land by, for example, falling masonry.[76]

Highways

6–33   Buildings, walls and fences adjoining the highway must be maintained in such condition as not to be dangerous to users of the highway, otherwise occupiers, and sometimes the owners, will be liable in nuisance to third parties who suffer personal injury (from an attachment to the building that is rotten and falls[77]) or damage to their property (*e.g.* by a wall collapsing[78]).

4. EXTENSIONS TO STANDARD COVER

Legal costs

6–34   Insurers will generally agree to indemnify the insured against legal costs,[79] both as regards those recoverable from the insured by the claimant, and as regards such costs and expenses incurred in connection with negotiations, actions or proceedings whilst the insurer retains the absolute conduct and control of such, and provided such costs have been incurred with the insurer's written consent. That consent must not be unreasonably withheld.[80] The wording of the indemnity must be carefully considered in every case, both in order to determine whether an indemnity is available in respect of legal costs, and the extent of any such indemnity.

Defence legal costs

6–35   There is no implied term in a liability policy that insurers are to be under an obligation to fund the insured's own defence costs if the insured is under no liability to the third party claimant.[81] Express words providing an indemnity in respect of costs incurred in defending claims are needed in the policy, otherwise there is a risk that a court will construe the insuring words restrictively and prevent the insured's recovery of them. For instance, in *Xenos v. Fox*[82] an insurance indemnity in respect of sums

---

[75] *Hughes v. Percival* (1883) 8 App. Cas. 443, HL.
[76] *Emblen v. Myers* (1860) 6 H. and N. 54; 30 L.J. Ex. 71.
[77] *Tarry v. Ashton* (1876) 1 Q.B.D. 314 at 260.
[78] *Wringe v. Cohen* [1940] 1 K.B. 229, CA.
[79] See Appendix 1, Section 1A(2).
[80] *Hulton & Co. Ltd v. Mountain* (1921) 8 LL. L. Rep. 605, HL; *Capel-Cure Myers Capital Management Ltd v. McCarthy* [1995] L.R.L.R. 498 at 504, *per* Potter J.; *cf. Thornton Springer v. National Employers Mutual Insurance Co. Ltd* [2000] 2 All E.R. 489 at 514–515, *per* Colman J.
[81] *Baker v. Black Sea & Baltic General Insurance Co. Ltd* [1998] 1 W.L.R. 974 at 979–982, *per* Lord Lloyd, HL.
[82] (1869) L.R. 4 C.P. 665.

which the insured "shall thereby become liable to pay damages" was held not to include the insured's own costs incurred in successfully defending a claim, because no claim under the policy arose, *i.e.* there was no liability established against the insured. An extension of cover in respect of "all costs and expenses incurred with [the insurers'] written consent in the defence or settlement of any claim made against the assured which falls to be dealt with under this [insurance]" does not provide an indemnity in the event of the insured's successful defence of claim brought against him. This is because the primary insuring provision requires a liability to be established to bring the main indemnity into operation.[83] Whether a particular item of legal costs is reasonably related to the defence or settlement of a claim covered by the policy indemnity will ultimately be a question of fact.[84] The insurers may become liable to indemnify the insured in respect of the costs of a successful defence of the third party claim, despite contrary policy provisions, if they make an agreement with the insured to that effect. Such an agreement requires an offer, an acceptance, and valuable consideration flowing from both the insured and the insurers. The insured's consideration will be sufficient if the insured makes an express, or implied, promise to forestall the commencement of proceedings against the insurer under the liability policy.[85] Further, the insurers might be unable to deny their liability for defence costs where the claim has been defended on the common assumption that the insurers would pay all, or a particular portion, of the defence costs sufficient to establish an estoppel by convention.[86]

Claimants' legal costs

Similarly, express words are required to cover an award of claimant's **6–36** costs if the primary insuring indemnity is expressed in terms of "damages", or "compensation". Without an extension to cover costs awarded against the insured, such an indemnity provision will not cover the insured's costs incurred in CPR, Pt 20 proceedings instigated by him,[87] nor the costs of unsuccessfully defending the claim brought against him.[88] Different considerations will come into play if the policy indemnity is expressed in wider terms, such as "loss arising from any claim or claims", when costs of defending or settling a claim may well be covered by those words.[89] Nor will a successful claimant's award of costs be covered by an insurance indemnity in respect of "all sums for which the Insured shall become

---

[83] See *Thornton Springer v. N.E.M. Insurance Co. Ltd* [2000] 2 All E.R. 489 (professional indemnity insurance).
[84] *New Zealand Forest Products Ltd v. New Zealand Insurance Co. Ltd* [1997] 1 W.L.R. 1237, PC; applied *Thornton Springer v. N.E.M. Insurance Co. Ltd* [2000] 2 All E.R. 489.
[85] As in *Thornton Springer v. National Employers Mutual Insurance Co. Ltd*, [2000] 2 All E.R. 489 at 515–516.
[86] *ibid.* at 516–518.
[87] See *Cross v. British Oak Insurance Co. Ltd* [1938] 2 K.B. 167.
[88] *G.I.O. (N.S.W.) v. Crowley* [1975] 2 N.S.W.L.R. 78; *Broadland's Properties Ltd v. Guardian Assurance Co. Ltd* (1984) 3 A.N.Z.I.C. 60.552; *Miltenburgh v. A.M.P. Fire & General Insurance Co. Ltd* (1981) 1 A.N.Z.I.C. 60.442; *Commercial & General Insurance Co. Ltd v. G.I.O. (N.S.W.)* (1973) 47 A.L.J.R. 612.
[89] See the professional indemnity insurance cases of *Forney v. Dominion Insurance Co. Ltd* [1969] 1 W.L.R. 928, and *J. Rothschild Assurance plc v. Collyear* [1999] Lloyd's Rep. I.R. 6.

legally liable to pay as compensation". This is because "compensation" refers to compensation by way of damages, and therefore does not include an award of costs.[90] The special circumstances in which a third party claimant may seek costs directly against the defendant insured's insurers is considered in Chapter 22, below.

6–37   The wording of the indemnity must be carefully considered in every case, therefore, both in order to determine whether an indemnity is available in respect of legal costs, and the extent of any such indemnity. If the policy's limit of indemnity is expressed as a monetary sum as regards "all damages costs and expenses payable by the Insured", then that monetary limit will apply only to damages and costs payable by the insured to the third party claimant, and sums incurred in respect of defence costs will be unlimited in value and will not fall to be brought into account in the monetary limit of indemnity. This is because the limit applies to costs "payable" by the insured, and an insurance policy so drafted must be construed against the industry background where the costs of defending a claim would, in the overwhelming majority of cases, be paid not by the insured, but by the insurers direct to the solicitors nominated by them to conduct the defence.[91] A further difficulty may arise where several claims are made against the insured, but some claims are not covered by the insurance indemnity. An apportionment of the costs between such claims, or between insured and uninsured defendants, may be necessary where the same solicitors and/or counsel are used to defend the claims. Where the insurers have consented to the incurring of such legal costs, then, in the absence of some specific agreement, there will be no apportionment of the legal costs incurred where those costs relate to the defence of both the insured and the uninsured claimant/defendant. There will only be an apportionment where there is separate and distinct work which, as a matter of fact, did not have a dual purpose.[92]

6–38   The policy indemnity may also be extended by some insurers to cover the costs incurred with the insurer's written consent of:

(a) representation at any coroner's inquest or fatal enquiry in respect of any death; or

(b) defending in any court of summary jurisdiction any proceedings in respect of any act or omission causing or relating to any event which may be the subject of an indemnity under the public liability policy.

Extension to scope of insured business

6–39   Insurers will also generally be prepared to extend the main indemnity to cover:

[90] *Aluminium Wire & Cable Co. Ltd v. Allstate Insurance Co. Ltd* [1985] 2 Lloyd's Rep. 280 at 288, col.1.
[91] *Citibank N.A. v. Excess Insurance Co. Ltd* [1999] Lloyd's Rep. I.R. 122 at 128 (professional indemnity insurance).
[92] *New Zealand Forest Products Ltd v. New Zealand Insurance Co. Ltd* [1997] 1 W.L.R. 1237, P.C.; followed in *Thornton Springer v. N.E.M. Insurance Co. Ltd* [2000] 2 All E.R. 489.

(a) private work carried out by the employees of the insured for any director or executive of the insured;

(b) non-manual work carried out during temporary visits anywhere in the world by directors or employees is generally covered if it is in connection with the insured's business;

(c) the insured's business will usually be expressly defined to include the occupation, use and/or maintenance of premises in connection with the business.

Compensation for court attendance

As very low rates of witness expenses are recoverable in court proceedings the insured business is generally offered by insurers a standard extension to more accurately represent actual costs of witnesses attending court as witnesses in relation to a relevant claim which falls for an indemnity under the insurance. For instance, an extension may provide:

6–40

> "In the event of any director partner or Employee of the Insured attending court as a witness at the request of the Insurer in connection with a claim in respect of which the Insured is entitled to indemnity under this Cover the Insurer will provide compensation to the Insured at the following rates for each day on which attendance is required:
>
> (a) any director or partner   £100 per day;
> (b) any Employee   £50 per day."

Cover for legal and contractual liability

Most public liability policies will include an exclusion of liability assumed by the insured under any contract,[93] but it is possible to obtain an extension of cover, usually for an additional premium, to include cover in respect of contractual liability. This is sometimes called Third Party (Legal and Contractual Liability) Insurance. Such an indemnity provision may read[94]:

6–41

> "The company subject to the terms exclusions and conditions herein contained will indemnify the insured up to the limits stated in the Schedule in respect of any one accident or occurrence or event irrespective of the number of claims occasioned hereby against all sums which the insured shall become liable at law to pay as damages and such sums for which liability in tort or under statute shall attach to some party or parties other than the insured but for which liability is assumed by the insured under indemnity clauses incorporated in contracts and/or agreements whilst engaged on the business described in the Schedule in respect of or in consequence of accidental death or injury or sickness to any person and/or accidental loss of or damage to property from whatsoever cause arising during the period of insurance."

Wrongful accusation of shoplifting

Shops and other retail outlets may wish to obtain an extension to cover claims for damages for, for example, false imprisonment, from suspected

6–42

---

[93] See *Dominion Bridge Co. Ltd v. Toronto General Insurance Co.* [1964] 1 Lloyd's Rep. 194, CA (British Columbia).

[94] This wording is adapted from that found in *Aswan M/S Engineering Establishment Co. Ltd v. Iron Trades Mutual Insurance Co. Ltd.* [1989] 1 Lloyd's Rep. 289.

thieves arrested by the insured's staff but who are subsequently acquitted by the criminal courts. Such an extension may provide[95]:

> "The definition of Injury shall extend to include liability for accidental damage and distress caused by wrongful accusation of shoplifting, false arrest and false imprisonment, or detention, provided that the liability of the Insurer shall not exceed £25,000 in any one period of insurance."

Legal costs (Consumer Protection Act 1987)

6–43   The insurer may extend the standard cover to indemnify the insured and, at the insured's request, any director partner or employee of the insured in respect of legal costs and expenses incurred with the insurer's written consent in connection with the defence of a prosecution including an appeal against any conviction resulting from proceedings brought under Part II of the Consumer Protection Act 1987 It is usually provided, though, that the extended cover does not apply:

(a) where indemnity is provided by any other insurance;

(b) in respect of fines or penalties of any kind; or

(c) where the prosecution is consequent upon any deliberate or intentional act or omission.

5. COMMON POLICY TERMS

Reasonable precautions against loss

6–44   This type of provision is discussed generally in Chapter 2 above, but there have been a number of cases reported specifically relating to public liability insurance, and these are considered here. The wording can be simple, such as:

> "The insured shall take all reasonable precautions to prevent loss or damage . . ."

Alternatively, it can be in a more detailed form along the following lines:

> "The insured shall take and cause to be taken all reasonable precautions to:
>
> (a) comply with all statutory obligations and regulations imposed by any authority;
>
> (b) prevent accidents; and
>
> (c) must exercise reasonable care in the selection of employees."

6–45   This more detailed type of provision was considered in *Pictorial Machinery Ltd v. Nicolls*[96] where condition 8, stated to be a condition precedent to the liability of the insurers, read:

---

[95] See also Appendix 2, Section 7B.
[96] (1940) 67 Ll. L. Rep. 461.

"The assured shall and will at all times exercise reasonable care in seeing that the ways implements plant machinery and appliances used in their business are substantial and sound and in proper order and fit for the purposes for which they are used and that all reasonable safe-guards and precautions against accidents are provided and used."

The insured were printers' engineers and suppliers who received an order for two glass containers of acetone from customers who were close by. The insured sent a boy to deliver these by hand, but when putting the bottles down on the customer's premises the boy negligently dropped one of them. The container broke and the acetone escaped and caused a serious fire which damaged the premises of the customers together with neighbouring premises belonging to other parties. The insured sought an indemnity under their public liability policy, but the insurers defended the claim, inter alia, on the ground of breach of this condition.

Humphreys J. referred[97] to the earlier judgment in *Concrete Ltd v.*   **6–46**
Attenborough,[98] the facts of which are discussed at the beginning of this Chapter, where Branson J. had said of the same clause:

"If he [the insured] has taken reasonable care to see that those things are substantial and sound, if it turns out that they are not substantial and sound, and accidents happen by reason of their unsoundness, he is entitled to compensation; but if he has not taken reasonable care to secure himself by seeing that they are sound he cannot turn round upon his underwriters and say: 'You must pay me for that lack of care'."

To put this condition in perspective, it is important to remember that this duty of care owed by the insured to the insurer under the contract of insurance is not the same as his duty to the world at large, otherwise the insured could never recover under a public liability policy for his liability to third parties sounding in negligence. Humphrey J. explained the purport of the clause from the insurer's point of view in this way[99]:

"We are indemnifying you against something we do not know much about; we do not know what the circumstances may be; but we are indemnifying you up to perhaps 'X' thousand of pounds for any negligence on the part of yourself in any direction or any of your employees. That being so we call upon you to do what every person according to the common law of this country is expected to do if he is going to ask for damages, and that is to behave like a reasonable person; and we ask you to take reasonable steps — not to guarantee — to see that your premises are in good order and that your machinery is safeguarded."

There will be a breach of a reasonable precautions condition, therefore,   **6–47**
when the insured himself recognises a danger, but deliberately courts it by taking measures which he himself knows are inadequate to avert that danger. In other words, negligence of the insured is insufficient, for that is

[97] (1940) 45 Com. Cas. 334 at 343–344.
[98] (1939) 65 Ll. L. Rep. 174.
[99] (1940) 45 Com. Cas. 334 at 344; see also *Aluminium Wire & Cable Co. Ltd v. Allstate Insurance Co. Ltd*. [1985] 2 Lloyd's Rep. 280.

the very risk being insured; rather, the omission to take any particular precautions to avoid either a specific accident, or accidents of a type, must be
made with actual recognition by the insured himself that a danger exists,
and not caring whether or not it is averted. This duty is a personal one
owed by the insured to the insurer, to be construed having regard to the
commercial purpose of the contract, and the mere fact that one of the
insured's employees fails to take reasonable precautions does not establish
a breach by the insured of this contractual duty owed to the insurer.[1]

6–48   The position is illustrated by *M/S Aswan Engineering Establishment Co.
Ltd v. Iron Trades Mutual Insurance Co. Ltd.*[2] When shipping goods by
separate consignments, the insured's managing director learned that the
method of packing of the first and second consignments sent by sea had
been found to be deficient, causing damage to the goods. He learned from
the manufacturers of the packing that this deficiency could be rectified by
modifying the method of the packing of the containers in which the goods
were shipped, but he deliberately refrained from having that modified
packing used in consignments shipped subsequently. The court held that
this placed the insured in breach of this condition, because the managing
director was reckless, and he was the *alter ego* of the insured company.[3] If,
however, the managing director had known nothing of the problem
because, *e.g.* an employee had failed to inform him, there might well have
been no breach of the condition, depending upon the precise facts.[4]

Non-admission of liability condition

6–49   Invariably, insurers place a condition in the policy to the effect that the
insured must not make any admission of liability, or seek to compromise
or settle any claim made against him without the specific consent of the
insurer, if he wishes to recover under his policy. An example of such a
condition is:

> "The insured shall not, except at his own cost, take any steps to compromise
> or settle any claim or admit liability without specific instructions in writing
> from the Insurers nor give any information or assistance to any person
> claiming against him."

6–50   Such provisions are valid and the insured must comply with them if he
is not to debar himself from recovery under the policy.[5] Thus, consent by
a liquidator of an insured company to judgment in a third party's claim
against the insured will constitute a breach of this type of condition precedent to liability of the insurers, without proof of prejudice to the insurers.[6]

---

[1] See the judgment of Diplock L.J. (as he then was) in *Fraser v. B.N. Furman (Productions)
Ltd*. [1967] 1 W.L.R. 898, CA, cited in the discussion of this topic in Chapter 5, above.
[2] [1989] 1 Lloyd's Rep. 289.
[3] *ibid.* at 295, col.1.
[4] See in this regard the commercial vehicle insurance case of *Conn v. Westminster Motor
Insurance Association Ltd* [1966] 1 Lloyd's Rep. 407, CA, discussed in Chapter 10, below.
[5] *Post Office v. Norwich Union Fire Insurance Society Ltd* [1967] 2 W.L.R. 709 at 714 *per*
Lord Denning M.R. and at 717, *per* Salmon L.J., CA.
[6] See *Total Graphics Ltd v. AGF Insurance Ltd* [1997] 1 Lloyd's Rep. 599 (professional
indemnity insurance).

This type of condition is not contrary to public policy on the ground of being prejudicial to the administration of justice, because there is a world of difference between giving a factual account of what happened, without giving any expression of opinion as to blame, and an admission of liability.[7] It has been said, *obiter*, in the High Court of Australia, that it would be beyond reason to read such a condition as being breached if, in answering forensic questions either by requests for further information or in the witness box, what the insured answered could be treated as an admission of liability.[8] In the same case, it was also said, *obiter,* that the insurer must not arbitrarily withhold his consent, for its power of restraining settlement by the insured must be exercised in good faith having regard to the interests of the insured as well as to its own interests, and in the exercise of its power to withhold consent the insurer must not have regard to considerations extraneous to the policy of indemnity.[9] Finally, as this is a condition as between the insured and the insurer, the condition will not be breached by an employee or agent of the insured making an admission of liability to a claimant without the insured's authority to make that admission.[10]

Limit of liability for "any one accident"

Quite different results follow where an insurer has placed a limit on his   **6–51** liability in relation to "any one accident" as against "any one accident or occurrence", considered in the next paragraph. In *South Staffordshire Tramways Co v. Sickness and Accident Assurance Association,*[11] the limit of indemnity in respect of "claims for personal injury and damage to property" was £250 in respect of "any one accident", a tram belonging to the insured overturned and in so doing caused injury to 40 passengers. The defendant insurers argued that only one accident had occurred and thus the limit of their indemnity was £250. The Court of Appeal rejected this contention after considering the clauses in full, which read:

> "So far as regards claims for personal injuries and damage to property made against the assured in respect of accidents caused by vehicles . . . and for which accidents shall be liable, the [insurers] shall pay the assured the sum of £250 in respect of any one accident."

Bowen L.J. explained that such person had suffered injury from a   **6–52** separate accident within the meaning of the policy[12]:

> "But on looking at the policy we see introduced the words 'in respect of accidents'. What do those words mean? Do they mean that that is to be treated as only one accident, which has happened to a great number of persons? I should not think that anyone would suppose, looking at the first part of the agreement, that the word 'accident' was used otherwise than in the sense of

---

[7] *Terry v. Trafalgar Insurance Co. Ltd* [1970] 1 Lloyd's Rep. 524 at 526 (motor insurance).
[8] *Distillers Co. Bio-Chemicals (Aust.) Pt. Ltd v. Ajax Insurance Co. Ltd* (1974) 130 C.L.R. 1 at 8 *per* Menzies J.
[9] *ibid.* at 26–27, *per* Stephen J.
[10] *Tustin v. Arnold & Sons* (1915) 84 L.J.K.B. 2214.
[11] [1891] 1 Q.B. 402, CA.
[12] *ibid.* at 407–408.

injury accidentally caused to the person. The difficulty here arises from the qualification introduced afterwards; but as, until that clause is reached, the document is clearly using the word 'accident' in that meaning, I think the word must receive the same construction in the phrase limiting the liability of the defendants . . . the word 'accident' is here used in the sense of mischief to an individual."

Limit of indemnity for all claims arising out of "any one accident or occurrence"

6–53   Where the word "occurrence" is used in the clause limiting the liability of the insurer, this is likely to be construed as referring to the matter from the insurer's point of view *vis-à-vis* the insured, and therefore to refer to the number of claims made by the insured under the policy.[13]

Thus, whilst there may be two or more accidents arising out of one incident, mishap or "occurrence", the policy indemnity will be restricted in the aggregate to the specified limit.[14] Reference can also be made to the cases on this topic in Chapter 16, below.

Notice of claims and assistance to insurer

6–54   Insurers will generally specify the claims procedure to be followed by the insured when he wishes to make a claim under the policy following receipt of a third party's claim upon him (the insured). If the requirement is limited to forwarding every written notice of claim received, the insured will not be in breach of this condition if he does not forward other notices or documents.[15] The usual requirement is to forward the documents either "forthwith" or "immediately". The latter term is to be construed as meaning "with all reasonable speed considering the circumstances of the case".[16] Thus, where the insured is required to give written notice to the insurers "of any accident or claim or proceedings immediately the same shall have come to the knowledge of the insured", and that requirement is a condition precedent to the liability of the insurers, the failure to forward a writ served on the insured will disentitle the insured to an indemnity, without proof of prejudice to the insurer.[17] If the insurer has failed to make such a requirement a condition precedent to liability, though, the insurer may only be entitled to make a cross-claim in damages in respect of the quantifiable prejudice he has suffered by reason of the insured's breach of the requirement. It seems that in a case where the insured is in serious breach of a claims notification condition, this may give rise to the insurer's right not to indemnify the insured in respect of the particular non-notified claim.[18]

[13] *Forney v. Dominion Insurance Co. Ltd* [1969] 1 W.L.R. 928 (professional indemnity insurance).

[14] *Allen v. London Guarantee & Accident Co. Ltd* (1912) 27 T.L.R. 254.

[15] *Wilkinson v. Car & General Insurance Corpn Ltd.* (1914) 110 L.T. 468, CA.

[16] *Re Coleman's Repositories Ltd & the Life & Health Assurance Association* [1907] 2 K.B. 798 at 807, *per* Fletcher Moulton L.J., CA.

[17] *Pioneer Concrete (U.K.) Ltd v. National Employers Mutual General Insurance Association Ltd* [1985] 1 Lloyd's Rep. 274; approved in *Motor & General Insurance Co. Ltd* [1994] 1 W.L.R. 462 at 469, PC.

[18] *Alfred McAlpine plc v. BAI (Run-off) Ltd* [2000] 1 Lloyd's Rep. 437. See further, Chapter 2, above.

There is also authority to the effect that an insurer cannot rely on a breach of a notice condition where that notice condition is contained in a policy which had not yet been delivered to the insured.[19]

A rather wider form of notification condition, requiring notification to   **6–55** the insurer of circumstances that may give rise to a claim, can often be found in modern policies. Such a provision had to be construed in *Berliner Motor Corp. and Steiers Lawn and Sports Inc. v. Sun Alliance and London Insurance Ltd.*[20] The condition read:

> "Upon the happening of any Event which may give rise to a claim . . . the Insured shall forthwith give written notice to the Company with full particulars."

In March 1972, proceedings were commenced against the insured company's United States subsidiary, and that claim came to the notice of the insured company not later than December 11, 1972, but the insurers were not advised until October 25, 1973, when the insured gave them notice of the claim. Bingham J. (as he then was) held that the insurers could successfully defend the claim under the policy for[21]:

> "There very plainly was a gross breach of its condition and as a result of the breach the insurers lost any opportunity to consider what line (the insured) should adopt in the proceedings and to act as *dominus litis*."

There was no breach of a requirement to notify insurers of an occurrence   **6–56** "likely" to give rise to a claim under the policy in *Layher Ltd v. Lowe.*[22] The insured had supplied components, including securing wedges, for the temporary scaffolding erected to enable repairs to a roof to be carried out. The insured had neither designed the scaffolding, nor the roof. In January 1990, a storm blew off the roof, killing two workmen and causing substantial damage. Two years later, the building owners commenced an action against the scaffolding contractors, and the insured was then joined into the proceedings. Lloyd's underwriters defended the insured's claim for an indemnity in respect of this claim made against them, on the ground of the alleged breach of this condition because the insured had not notified them of the incident in January 1990. The Court of Appeal held that "likely" in this condition meant, when viewed objectively, there was at least a 50 per cent chance of a claim being made, but that the defendant underwriters had failed to show that, in January 1990, the insured was "likely" to face a claim covered by the policy.

That decision was applied in *Jacobs v. Coster,*[23] where no breach of the   **6–57** condition was found to have committed by the insured. Here, the

---

[19] *Re Coleman's Depositories & Life & Health Assurance Association* [1907] K.B. 798, CA.
[20] [1983] 1 Lloyd's Rep. 320.
[21] *ibid.* at 325; see also *Pioneer Concrete (U.K.) Ltd v. National Employers Mutual General Insurance Association Ltd* [1985] 1 Lloyd's Rep. 274, where failure to pass on a served writ was a clear breach of such condition.
[22] [2000] Lloyd's Rep. I.R. 510, CA.
[23] [2000] Lloyd's Rep. I.R. 506, CA.

insured held public liability cover in respect of his petrol filling business, and a condition precedent required immediate notice to insurers of circumstances "likely" to give rise to a claim. On March 23, 1994, a customer of the insured fell on the forecourt, and she was carried into the petrol station kiosk and an ambulance was called. The insured had inspected the forecourt after the accident but did not notify the insurers of it. Over six months later, the injured customer wrote to the insured alleging that she had broken her leg after slipping on diesel fuel spilt on the forecourt, and she later brought an action against the insured claiming damages for personal injuries arising from the accident. Applying the objective test, the Court of Appeal held that there was no evidence that the defendant insured and his wife knew of anything wrong with the forecourt. Further, they had not been blamed by the claimant at the time of her accident. Laws L.J. specifically rejected the insurer's submission that that person had suffered a non-trivial injury requiring her removal to hospital by ambulance, itself demonstrated without more that there was at least a 50 per cent chance that in due course she would make a claim. Laws L.J. said he "should be loath to think that our society has reached such a sorry state".[24] Accordingly, the insured was not in breach of this condition precedent to liability and his claim for an indemnity failed. It would also seem to be appropriate to test the correctness of the giving of such notice against what actually happened in due course.[25]

6–58   Where there is a provision requiring the insured to render all such information and assistance to the insurer to enable the insurer to settle or resist any claim, its effect is that an obligation to assist only arises once the insurers have requested information or assistance.[26]

6. COMMON EXCLUSIONS

Pollution risks

6–59   In recent times, insurers have become very concerned about the cover they provide for pollution risks, and the Association of British Insurers have issued a model wording which seeks to exclude cover for all pollution risks that are not fortuitous and unintentional events, and are other than prolonged. Thus a long established leak in an industrial pipe which is discovered after many months or years will not be covered. The model wording[27] is as follows:

> "A. This policy excludes all liability in respect of Pollution or Contamination other than caused by a sudden identifiable unintended and unexpected incident which takes place in its entirety at a specific time and place during the Period of Indemnity.

---

[24] *ibid.* at [14].

[25] *J. Rothschild Assurance plc v. Collyear* [1999] Lloyd's Rep. I.R. 6 at 23.

[26] *Wilkinson v. Car & General Insurance Corp. Ltd* (1914) 110 L.T. 468 at 471–472, *per* Lord Reading C.J., CA.

[27] See Appendix 1, Section 1, Definition of "Gradual Pollution".

All Pollution or Contamination which arises out of one incident shall be deemed to have happened at the time such incident takes place.

    B. The liability of the Company for all compensation payable in respect of all Pollution or Contamination which is deemed to have happened during the Period of Indemnity shall not exceed £   in the aggregate.

    C. For the purposes of this Endorsement 'Pollution or Contamination' shall be deemed to mean:

      (i) all pollution or contamination of buildings or other structures or of water or land or the atmosphere; and

      (ii) all loss or damage or injury directly or indirectly caused by such pollution or contamination."

In *Jan de Nul (U.K.) Ltd v. N.V. Royal Belge*[28] there was an exclusion of   **6–60** "non-accidental pollution", where "pollution" was defined as:

"... impairment by alteration of the existing quality features of the air, the water [or] the earth by adding or withdrawing substances or energy"

and "accident" was defined as:

"... a sudden occurrence which is unintentional and unexpected for the policyholder."

The case concerned the insured's dredging operations in Southampton Water which caused, *inter alia*, the deposit of silt on nearby shellfish beds. Moore-Bick J. approached the question of whether the exclusion applied in the following way[29]:

"When asking what is meant by pollution . . . I think one must go first to the definition . . . The question therefore, is whether the deposit of silt of this kind on land forming part of the estuary can properly be classed as an alteration of the existing quality features of the water or earth. That depends to a considerable extent on the nature of the land on which it is deposited and the use to which that land was previously being put. In an area which is a natural habitat and breeding ground for shellfish the deposit of a layer of silt sufficient to cause the destruction of a significant part of the stock can in my judgment properly be described as an alteration of the existing quality features of the water or earth amounting to impairment of the environment and so constitute pollution for these purposes . . . [Counsel for the insurers] submitted that in this case the damage cannot be regarded as 'accidental' since it was not on any view the result of a sudden and unforeseen occurrence but of a particular method of working persisted in over a period of many weeks. I think that must be right and it follows, therefore, that the claim relating to the damage to the clam beds in Dibden Bay falls within the scope of this exclusion."

Contractual liabilities

Liability for any amount in respect of liquidated damages or penalties   **6–61** which attaches solely because of a contract or agreement, will be

---

[28] [2000] 2 Lloyd's Rep. 700.
[29] *ibid.* at 733.

excluded,[30] but special cover may be obtainable for the insured's business, discussed in "extensions to cover" above.

Professional negligence

6–62   Any liability arising from services rendered in a professional capacity whether or not any fee is charged will be excluded in standard form cover.[31] This risk is outside the scope of a public liability policy and separate insurance should be taken out in respect of it. It is beyond the scope of the present work to deal with professional indemnity insurance, which is also distinguished from other liability insurances in that it is of a "claims made" basis, rather than a "claims arising" basis.

Product liability risks

6–63   These risks are excluded from the standard public or third party liability policy cover, but may be covered by a special extension or in a section of a combined commercial liability insurance policy, examples of which are given in the Appendix. Product liability cover is considered in Chapter 7, below. An example[32] of a policy exclusion clause is:

> "Any liability arising from any commodities or goods sold, supplied, hired out, constructed, erected, installed, cleaned, repaired, serviced or processed by or on behalf of the insured but this exclusion will not apply to food and beverages sold or supplied by the insured for consumption on the insured's premises."

6–64   An exception of this type was considered in *Wayne Tank and Pump Co Ltd v. Employers' Liability Assurance Corpn Ltd*[33] where the public liability policy excluded liability in respect of:

> "death injury or damage caused by the nature or condition of any goods or the containers thereof sold or supplied by or on behalf of the insured."

The insured had installed certain electrically operated equipment under contract at X Ltd's factory, and this equipment was wholly unsuitable for its purpose and was a potential fire hazard. After installation, an employee of the insured switched it on even though it had not yet been tested, and left it unattended throughout the night. In consequence a fire broke out causing extensive damage to the factory. In an action for breach of contract X Ltd were awarded some £150,000 damages against the insured, it being found that the two causes of the fire were (1) the dangerous nature of the equipment, and (2) the conduct of the insured's employee in switching it on and leaving it unattended. The insured claimed indemnity from the insurers in respect of this liability, it being common ground that the fire was an "accident" within the terms of the policy.

---

[30] See, *e.g.* Appendix 1, Section 1, Exclusion A(f).
[31] *ibid.*, Exclusion A(b)(ii).
[32] See also Appendix 1, Section 1, Exclusions A(d) and (e).
[33] [1974] Q.B. 57, CA.

The Court of Appeal held that the insurers were entitled to deny liability **6–65**
by reason of the exception clause for the following reasons:

(a) Once the equipment had been installed in X Ltd's factory it constituted goods "supplied" by the insured within the exception
clause. It was not necessary to show that the contract with X Ltd
had been completed or that the property in the equipment had
passed to X Ltd in order to establish that the equipment had
been "supplied";

(b) The exception clause was applicable because:

(i) (*per* Lord Denning M.R. and Roskill L.J.) the damage had
been "caused" by the dangerous nature of the equipment
supplied since it had been the proximate cause of the fire. For
the purposes of insurance law, in cases where there were two
competing causes, the dominant or effective cause was to be
taken as the proximate cause even though it was more remote
in point of time. The dominant and effective cause of the fire
was the dangerous nature of the equipment rather than the
conduct of the insured's employee which had merely precipitated the fire[34];

(ii) in any event, in cases where there were two causes of a loss, one
within the general words of the policy and the other within an
exception clause in the policy, the insurers were entitled to rely
on the exception and were not liable for the loss.[35]

Aircraft, watercraft and other motor vehicle risks

Risks that should be insured under the provisions of Part VI of the **6–66**
Road Traffic Act 1988, that is in respect of third party insurance or other
security covering liability arising from the use of a motor vehicle on a public
road, are excluded.[36] Commercial motor vehicle insurance is considered in
Chapter 10, below. This exclusion is generally expressed as relating to any
liability arising from the ownership or possession or use by or on behalf of
the insured of any:

(a) aircraft aerospatial device or hovercraft;
(b) watercraft;
(c) mechanically propelled vehicle or mobile plant

(i) which is licensed for road use; or
(ii) or which compulsory insurance or security is required; or
(iii) which is more specifically insured.

However, such an exclusion may be expressed as not applying during the
act of loading or unloading motor vehicles, or the bringing to or taking

---

[34] Applying *Leyland Shipping Co. Ltd v. Norwich Union Fire Insurance Society Ltd* [1918]
A.C. 350, HL.
[35] See Chapter 17, below, for proximate cause of loss.
[36] See Appendix 1, Section 1, Exclusion A(b)(i).

away of a load from such vehicle, or the use of any mechanically propelled vehicle or mobile plant solely as a tool of trade (but the insurer will insert an excess in respect of any claim arising from damage to underground installations occurring whilst such vehicle or plant is being used as a tool of trade).

Injury to or death of employees

6–67   This risk of injury to or death of employees is the subject of compulsory employers' liability insurance, which is considered in chapter 5, above. Accordingly, a public liability policy, or a public liability section of a commercial combined liability policy, will exclude this risk.[37] Such an exclusion may be expressed as excluding "all liability arising from the death of or injury to or illness or disease contracted by any employee of the insured which arises out of and in the course of his employment by the insured."

6–68   This type of exclusion clause in a public liability policy was considered in *Denham v. Midland Employers Mutual Assurance Ltd*[38] where the particular clause read:

> **"Exclusions**
> This policy does not cover:
>
> 1. Liability for death of or bodily injury to any person under a contract of service or apprenticeship with [the insured] where such death or injury arises out of and in the course of his employment by [the insured]."

The facts were that a labourer had been lent to the insured to undertake unskilled work consisting of all sorts of rough work and odd jobs and included handling a rope in connection with the erection of a rig for the purpose of putting it on a drum. He was under the specific direction of the insured's foreman, but remained under the pay of his general employer who paid his National Insurance contributions, and was unfortunately killed whilst performing this work. The Court of Appeal[39] held that, although the insured would have been liable as a temporary employer for injury to a third person by the negligence of this labourer in the course of his work, and similarly the insured were liable to his widow in the present case, the labourer's contract of service was with his original employer alone. It was only the use and benefit of his services which had been transferred to the insured. Accordingly, as the insured could not recover under their employers' liability policy, they would recover under their public liability policy, which had excluded the employers' liability risk.

6–69   **The making good of faulty workmanship**
The insurer will only intend to cover the insured in respect of liability to third parties arising from the performance of the insured's business

---

[37] See Appendix 1, Section 1, definition of "Legal Liability".
[38] [1955] 2 Q.B. 437, CA.
[39] *Per* Denning, Birkett and Romer L.JJ.

activities, and not the risk that the insured has not performed that activity itself properly in circumstances where the insured is simply liable to his customer to put matters right.[40] The effect of this type of exclusion was illustrated in *Pioneer Concrete (UK) Ltd v. National Employers Mutual General Insurance Association Ltd*[41] where the insured dismantled and moved a batching plant for mixing concrete for the insured company. Several months later, a hopper forming part of that plant tipped forward and fell on its side carrying with it various conveyor belts and causing a good deal of damage to the hopper and associated machinery. The main reason for the collapse appeared to have been that the feet of the metal structure which supported the hopper were inadequately secured to the concrete foundations on which they stood. Bingham J. (as he then was) rejected the insurers' contention that all the damage was excluded by virtue of its being costs of "the making good of faulty workmanship", but did consider that a sum in respect of additional work to replace the holding down bolts for the cement silo to the foundations, the wrong bolts having been fitted by the insured, were properly excepted from the scope of the insured's public liability policy.

Data protection risks

This risk is not usually totally excluded from the policy indemnity, but will extend, by a suitable wording, to include liability for accidental damage and distress under sections 22 and 23 of the Data Protection Act 1984, provided that: **6–70**

(a) the liability arises from data for which the insured are registered under the Act;

(b) the insured are not in business as a Computer Bureau;

(c) the insured do not supply data for a fee other than to a data subject;

(d) in respect of such accidental damage and distress the liability of the insurer shall not exceed £50,000 during any period of insurance.

Risks relating to asbestos

Public liability cover will generally exclude liability arising in connection with the use or removal of asbestos.   **6–71**

---

[40] See Appendix 1, Section 1, Exclusion A(c)(iv).
[41] [1985] 1 Lloyd's Rep. 274.

CHAPTER 7

PRODUCTS LIABILITY INSURANCE

1. SUBJECT MATTER OF PRODUCTS LIABILITY INSURANCE

Legal liability

7–01   (The purpose of products liability insurance is to provide an indemnity to the insured in respect of his legal liability to the purchasers or users of products he sells or manufactures)(This legal liability can arise, in relation to purchasers, in contract under the implied conditions of sale imposed by the Sale of Goods Act 1979, or to purchasers and other users of the products under the Consumer Protection Act 1987 or the general law of the tort of negligence) These risks insured are considered below. The subject matter of products liability insurance is the legal liability of the insured to third parties, and it is a general principle of all liability insurances that the legal liability must arise before the insured becomes entitled to an indemnity under the insurance. This is because it is the legal liability of the insured which constitutes his loss to be indemnified under the main indemnity clause.[1] That is to say, the insured's liability to the injured person must be ascertained and determined to exist, either by judgment of the court or by an award in an arbitration or by agreement before the right to an indemnity arises.[2]

Caused by injury or physical damage

7–02   The subject matter of products liability insurance covers the insured's legal liability for death or bodily injury, and loss of or damage to material property. The indemnity therefore does not extend to the insured's legal liability to other persons for pure economic loss, *e.g.* loss of profits, without that being a consequence of actual injury or physical damage. The Court of Appeal has made clear in two cases that the legal liability must arise from some event involving physical damage. In the first case the indemnity only referred to "loss or damage", whilst in the second case it was far more detailed and required "loss of or physical damage to physical property".

7–03   In *A.S. Screenprint Ltd v. British Reserve Insurance Co. Ltd*[3] the insured were printers and had products liability cover with the defendant insurers as an extension to public liability cover in the following terms (subject to certain exceptions):

---

[1] *West Wake Price & Co v. Ching* [1956] 3 All E.R. 821 at 825, *per* Devlin J (as he then was). See further, the discussion in Chapter 6, above.

[2] *Post Office v. Norwich Union Fire Insurance Society Ltd* [1967] 2 Q.B. 363 at 373–374 and 377, *per* Lord Denning M.R. and Salmon L.J., CA; *Concrete Ltd v. Attenborough* (1939) 65 Ll. L. Rep. 174; *Berliner Motor Corp. & Steiers Lawn & Sports Inc. v. Sun Alliance & London Insurance Ltd.* [1983] 1 Lloyd's Rep. 320 at 324 *per* Bingham J.; *Thorman v. New Hampshire Insurance Co. (U.K.) Ltd* [1988] 1 Lloyd's Rep. 7 at 10, *per* Lord Donaldson, M.R., CA.

[3] [1999] Lloyd's Rep. I.R. 430, CA.

"Goods manufactured sold or supplied
Notwithstanding anything contained in the contrary in Exceptions 7 or 10 the Company will indemnify the Insured against all sums which the Insured shall become legally liable to pay in respect of death, bodily injury, illness, loss or damage happening anywhere in the World (excluding the United States of America and Canada) during the period of insurance and caused by goods (including containers) manufactured, sold, supplied, repaired, altered, serviced, installed or treated in the course of the Business from any premises within Great Britain, Northern Ireland, the Isle of Man or the Channel Islands . . ."

Whilst the policy was in force the insured received a print order from LMG Folding Cartons Ltd ("LMG"). This was an order for them to screenprint 52,000 units of Maltesers gift boxes in gold and varnish them. It was a term of the contract that they should ensure the use of "low odour" food quality inks and varnish. The insured carried out the order and redelivered the relevant boards to LMG, and LMG then supplied the boards to Mars, which manufactures and sells Maltesers, to be made up into boxes.

Shortly afterwards, Mars complained that the Maltesers packed in these boxes had been contaminated by the packaging and soon made a claim against LMG in the sum of £282,243.84. Having suffered this loss, LMG sought recourse against the insured printers. Three years later they issued a writ against the printers which alleged breach of contract and claimed two categories of loss, first, the sum of £282,243.84 which they had had to pay Mars, and secondly, the sum of £980,244 being assessed loss of profits for the four succeeding years on further orders from Mars, which orders were not forthcoming by reason of the contamination on this occasion. Faced with that claim, the insured sought to recover under their insurance policy. The defendant insurers accepted that the first claim, the £282,243.84 liability to LMG, would be covered by the products liability extension, but they disputed their liability in respect of any liability of their insured in respect of LMG's claim for consequential loss of profits. The insured sought a declaration as to their right to an indemnity in respect of their loss of profits. That claim failed before H.H. Judge Kershaw Q.C. in the Manchester Mercantile Court, on the basis that this loss was caused by Mars' reaction to LMG's breach of contract rather than by the goods supplied. The insured appealed to the Court of Appeal. This claim for a declaration was, it seems, unusual because it was prospective in that the insured had not yet agreed liability (the report is not clear on this), and the courts will generally refuse to entertain such hypothetical claims for declaratory relief.[4]   **7–04**

The Court of Appeal unanimously rejected the insured's appeal. Hobhouse L.J. gave the leading judgment and the presence of the necessary ingredients of a claim under product liability cover were explained in this way[5]:   **7–05**

---

[4] See *Meadows Indemnity Co. Ltd v. The Insurance Corp. of Ireland plc* [1989] 2 Lloyd's Rep. 298, CA.
[5] *ibid.* at 434.

". . . The indemnity is in respect of any sums which the insured shall become legally liable to pay. There is no problem about that because the declaration asked for assumes that there will be such a liability. If there is no such legal liability then of course there is no liability to indemnify. It goes on. 'Legally liable to pay' has to be 'in respect of' — I stress the words 'in respect of' — 'death, bodily injury, illness, loss or damage happening anywhere in the world (excluding the united States of America and Canada) during the period of insurance". The liability to pay has to be in respect of what, in its context, is clearly some physical event. It is something which can be said to have happened somewhere. It is an event which is happening during the period of insurance. The event can be death, bodily injury, illness or loss or damage. The words 'loss or damage' must, in my judgment, be construed in context as something that relates to a physical event. It goes on: 'And caused by goods (including physical containers) . . . supplied . . . or created in the course of the Business' of the assured. There is no difficulty about that last step provided it is understood what it relates to.

The [insured] in the present case did treat and/or supply printed material. They treated it for LMG or supplied it to them. That supply of those goods has caused further events. It has caused the contamination of the Maltesers. So the [insured] are able to progress from the third element to the second element, namely they can show the goods which they treated have caused damage — which is a physical event occurring somewhere and occurring during the period of insurance — to the packaging and the Maltesers. That is the limit of what they can prove as a matter of physical causation.

One then asks whether the legal liability to pay is in respect of that loss or damage. It is at this point that, in my judgment, the train of reasoning upon which the [insured's] argument has to be based breaks down.

They have to progress from legal liability in respect of the damage to the packaging and damage to the Maltesers to a loss of goodwill by LMG and loss of profits over a period in the future. The loss of profit in 1990, 1991 and 1992 are not events which are either directly or indirectly covered by this policy. They cannot be correctly described as loss or damage which has happened somewhere; nor have they happened at least partially during the period of insurance.

The conclusion at which I arrive is similar to that of the judge: the relevant head of loss is not caused by any defects in the packaging but is caused by Mars choosing not to place further orders with LMG. The same point can be demonstrated by appreciating that causation is, in the context of this cover, a physical concept: the loss or damage has to happen physically during the period of insurance. It is not possible to treat a liability to pay compensation in respect of an economic loss which arises from a loss of goodwill as being in respect of physical loss or damage physically caused. Loss of goodwill is not covered by this policy. The [insured] have failed to bring themselves within the relevant part of the cover. The declaration made by the judge was correct."

7–06   The second case is *Rodan International Ltd v. Commercial Union Assurance Co. plc* which this time concerned a successful appeal from the judgment of Judge Kershaw, Q.C., in the Manchester Mercantile Court, heard by a Court of Appeal where Hobhouse L.J. gave the leading, this time by a majority in part, judgment. The foundation of Rodan's claim under their product liability cover was as follows. In January and February 1992, Rodan had supplied a commercial customer, Newbrite, with

6 [1999] Lloyd's Rep. I.R. 495, CA.

about 100 tons of soap powder in one ton bags. It was delivered to a packaging company, Excelsior Packers, who broke down the bulk and packed the powder into 400 gramme and 800 gramme cardboard cartons. The cartons were printed for sale as a Newbrite branded product. Newbrite supplied the cartons of soap powder to the retail trade. After a while Newbrite began to receive complaints from customers, and quantities of cartons of powder were returned to Newbrite. The problem was that the cartons had become stained and the powder in the cartons had become caked.

Newbrite sued Rodan on the ground that the soap powder supplied was   **7–07** not of merchantable quality in that liquid constituents of the soap powder had migrated into the cardboard cartons, causing the cartons to stain. Further, as those constituents were hydroscopic, they attracted moisture from the atmosphere causing it to penetrate into the powder so that it became caked. Judgement was entered against Rodan for £144,000, including £26,148 interest, made up of:

- *Item 1* — £41,702: following the discovery of the defects, Newbrite had sold the powder at a reduced price, the sum representing the difference between the normal and actual prices and corresponding to the difference between the market value of sound and defective powder.
- *Item 2* — £1,025: this sum represented the additional expenditure which Newbrite had incurred in handling powder rejected by customers and unsold powder.
- *Item 3* — £18,514: this sum represented the cost of a further 300,000 cartons for which Newbrite had or was required to pay, into which would have been packed a further 214,000 tons of powder which Rodan had promised to deliver. Following the delivery of the original consignment of defective powder, Newbrite did not proceed with the further orders of powder from Rodan.
- *Item 4* — £57,611: this sum represented the loss of profits which Newbrite would have made from selling Rodan powder over the next 18 months. Newbrite claimed that the brand name "Newbrite" had been destroyed and that it would take 18 months to re-establish a similar brand using a different supplier.

Rodan were insured at the material time by a policy with the defendant   **7–08** insurers where the relevant which provided an indemnity to Rodan in respect of:

> "all sums which the Insured shall become liable to pay for compensation and claimants' costs and expenses in respect of any Occurrence to which this cover applies . . ."

And "Occurrences" were defined as employers' liability, public liability and product liability including:

"Loss of or physical damage to physical property not belonging to the
Insured or in the charge or under the control of the Insured . . ."

Judge Kershaw, Q.C. held that an exclusion in respect of liability for
replacing, etc., defective goods supplied operated to exclude Rodan recovery
in respect of Items 1 and 2 to Newbrite, and this is discussed below where
that type of exclusion is discussed. As regards Items 3 and 4, he held that
Rodan were entitled to recover an indemnity, and Commercial Union
appealed against that ruling. The Court of Appeal unanimously allowed
the insurers appeal on the ground that Items 3 and 4 related to the future
non-performance of the obligations of Rodan towards Newbrite, and did
not relate to any quantification of the loss which Newbrite suffered as a
result of the relevant physical Occurrence, which was the staining of the
cartons. By a majority (Pill L.J. dissenting), the Court also held that Items
1 and 2 would have been covered but for the exclusion.

7–09   Giving the leading judgment, Hobhouse L.J. stated that it was not
enough for the insured to establish an Occurrence, one had to go further
and identify the extent of that Occurrence. The Occurrence had to extend
beyond damage to the supplied product itself, it had to extend to physical
damage to something else. Thereafter, one had to analyse which Items of
damage were "in respect of" the Occurrence, in other words, did the relevant Item represent a liability to pay compensation in respect of the
Occurrence. This, Hobhouse L.J. said Judge Kershaw had not done[7]:

> "That is most clearly illustrated by his conclusion that Rodan were entitled
> to an indemnity in respect of their liability for future loss of profits and
> expenditure thrown away on the purchase of cartons to be used for future
> powder that it was intended should be supplied by Rodan to Newbrite but
> never was. These future losses of Newbrite related not to the supply of the
> 80 tons but to the non-supply or the non-acceptance of further powder.
> They certainly do not relate to any physical consequence of the damage to
> the cartons in which the 80 tons were packed by Newbrite's packers. The
> phrase 'in respect of' carries with it a requirement that the liability relate to
> the identified Occurrence. It is not sufficient that it should simply have had
> some connection with it.
>   The effect of the decision of the judge to treat the words 'in respect of the
> Occurrence' as meaning no more than 'in connection with the same causes
> of action as gave rise to the liability for the Occurrence' transforms this
> cover from a products liability cover to a policy covering general contractual
> liabilities. A products liability policy in which the cover provided is defined
> in words such as those used in the present policy is confined to liability for
> physical consequences caused by the commodity or article supplied. The lia-
> bility of the assured in damages will have to be expressed in terms of money
> but that liability must be in respect of the consequences of the physical loss
> or damage to physical property (or some personal — 'bodily' — injury). Pro-
> vided that the commodity or article supplied has caused the physical conse-
> quence, the compensation payable by the assured to the third party will
> include, and the liability of the insurer to indemnify the assured, will extend
> to the totality of the loss which the third party is entitled to recover from the
> assured by way of damages in respect of that physical consequence."

[7] [1999] Lloyd's Rep. I.R. 495 at 500.

Thus, the liability of the insured to a third party in respect of the actual   **7–10**
physical damage caused by the supplied product is covered, as is any compensation for the third party's future loss of earnings actually lost as a
consequence of the physical loss or injury, but Items 3 and 4 in the claim
of Newbrite were not of such a character. They did not relate to any quantification of the loss which Newbrite suffered as a result of the relevant
physical Occurrence, the staining of the cartons in which Newbrite packed
the first 80 tons delivered. Rodan were accordingly not entitled to an
indemnity for those Items under the insurance cover. Items 1 and 2 were
of such a character, but were caught by a specific exclusion of such liability
(see below).

2. RISKS INSURED

Liability in contract

Subject to the issues of causation by a physical event and specific exclu-   **7–11**
sions in a policy, the contractual liability of the insured to his customers
will be covered by a products liability insurance. Apart from any liability
in tort for negligence (see below), the vendor or manufacturer of goods
whose products cause loss or damage to other products, or death or injury
to the purchasers, because of defects, can be liable for breach of implied
terms under the Sale of Goods Act 1979 (as amended by the Sale of
Goods Act 1994) relating to the satisfactory quality of, and fitness for
purpose of, goods sold.

Implied term of satisfactory quality

Under section 14 of the 1979 Act, where goods are sold in the course of   **7–12**
a business, the seller, irrespective of whether he be the manufacturer,
wholesaler, retailer or dealer of the products in question, is deemed to have
sold those goods subject to an implied condition of satisfactory quality:

> "(2) Where the seller sells goods in the course of a business, there is an
> implied [condition][8] that the goods supplied under the contract are of satis-
> factory quality.
> (2A) For the purposes of this Act, goods are of satisfactory quality if they
> meet the standard that a reasonable person would regard as satisfactory,
> taking account of any description of the goods, the price (if relevant) and
> all other relevant circumstances.
> (2B) For the purposes of this Act, the quality of the goods includes their
> state and condition and the following (among others) are in appropriate
> cases aspects of the quality of goods —
>
> (a) fitness for all the purposes for which goods of the kind in question are
> commonly supplied,
> (b) appearance and finish,
> (c) freedom from minor defects,
> (d) safety, and
> (e) durability.

[8] Sale of Goods Act 1979 (as amended), s.14(6), for England, Wales and Northern Ireland.

(2C) The term implied by subsection (2) above does not extend to any matter making the quality of the goods unsatisfactory —

    (a) which is specifically drawn to the buyer's attention before the contract is made,

    (b) where the buyer examines the goods before the contract is made, which that examination ought to reveal, or

    (c) in the case of a contract for sale by sample, which would have been apparent on a reasonable examination of the sample."

Examples of unsatisfactory quality

7–13   It is virtually inconceivable that a court would not find any goods which caused death or personal injury to the purchaser, or loss of or damage to his property, as being anything other than of unsatisfactory quality and award appropriate damages against the seller. Incidentally, this implied term arises in all sales of goods in the course of business, irrespective of whether the goods are new goods or second-hand goods.[9] The following are some examples of defects in goods causing personal injury to the purchasers in breach of the condition of satisfactory quality (or the previous statutory implied term of merchantable quality):

- where a stone in a bun caused the purchaser to suffer the breaking of a tooth on contact[10];
- where beer was contaminated with arsenic causing illness to the purchaser[11];
- where a boy purchased a plastic catapult and when using it the catapult snapped and part of it ruptured the boy's eye.[12]

On the other hand, goods which are defective but would not cause injury if used properly, will not be adjudged as being in breach of the implied condition of merchantable quality. Thus, where pork sold was contaminated with trichinae and the purchaser became ill after eating it, but the court heard that the pork would not have been harmful if cooked properly, the pork was held to be of merchantable quality.[13]

Implied term as to fitness for purpose

7–14   Again, where goods are sold in the course of a business, there is an implied condition that the goods are fit for any particular purpose made known to the seller which gives the buyer a right of action for breach, provided he actually did rely on the skill and judgment of the seller in providing those goods for that purpose, and that such reliance was not unreasonable. Thus, under section 14(3):

"Where the seller sells goods in the course of a business and the buyer, expressly or by implication, makes known:

[9] *Bartlett v. Sidney Marcus Ltd* [1965] 1 W.L.R. 1013, CA.
[10] *Chaproniere v. Mason* (1905) 21 T.L.R. 633, CA.
[11] *Wren v. Holt* [1903] 1 K.B. 610, CA.
[12] *Godley v. Perry* [1960] 1 W.L.R. 9.
[13] *Heil v. Hedges* [1951] 1 T.L.R. 512.

(a) to the seller . . .

any particular purpose for which the goods are being bought, there is an implied [condition][14] that the goods supplied under the contract are reasonably fit for that purpose, whether or not that is a purpose for which such goods are commonly supplied, except where the circumstances show that the buyer does not rely, or that it is unreasonable for him to rely, on the skill or judgment of the seller . . ."

Whether goods are "reasonably" fit for their purpose is a matter for the court, for goods will not be impliedly guaranteed to be fit for any particular purpose, as Lord Pearce had discussed[15]: **7–15**

"I would expect a tribunal of fact to decide that a car sold in this country was reasonably fit for touring even though it was not well adapted for conditions in a heat-wave; but not, if it could not cope adequately with rain. If, however, it developed some lethal or dangerous trick in very hot weather, I would expect it to be found unfit. In deciding the question of fact the rarity of the unsuitability would be weighed against the gravity of its consequences. Again, if food was merely unpalatable or useless on rare occasions, it might well be reasonably suitable for food. But I should certainly not expect it to be held reasonably suitable if even on very rare occasions it killed the consumer. The question for the tribunal of fact is simply 'were these goods reasonably fit for the specified purposes?'"

Examples of defective products

Examples of defective products causing personal injury or damage to property are: **7–16**

- where a chemical that reacted explosively with water was sold in glass ampoules, and one container shattered when the label was being washed off, causing a violent explosion[16];
- where a milk dealer supplied milk contaminated with typhoid which caused the death of a customer[17];
- where a hot water bottle burst causing the purchaser to be scalded[18];
- where the bottle supplied containing lime juice and soda water exploded[19];
- where tinned salmon poisoned a buyer's wife[20];
- where coal supplied was placed on the fire and due to the presence of explosive matter the resulting explosion damaged the purchaser's house[21];

---

[14] Sale of Goods Act 1979 (as amended), s.14(6), for England, Wales and Northern Ireland.
[15] *Henry Kendall & Sons v. William Lillico & Sons Ltd* [1969] 2 A.C. 31 at 115, HL.
[16] *Vacwell Engineering Co Ltd v. B.D.H. Chemicals Ltd* [1971] 1 Q.B. 88.
[17] *Frost v. Aylesbury Dairy Co. Ltd* [1905] 1 K.B. 608, CA.
[18] *Preist v. Last* [1903] 2 K.B. 148, CA.
[19] *Geddling v. Marsh* [1920] 1 K.B. 668; *cf.* where a deposit is paid on a returnable bottle, for there is no contract of sale, merely a contract of hire; see *Beecham Foods Ltd v. North Supplies (Edmonton) Ltd* [1959] 1 W.L.R. 643.
[20] *Jackson v. Watson & Sons* [1909] 2 K.B. 193, CA.
[21] *Wilson v. Rickett, Cockerell & Co. Ltd* [1954] 1 Q.B. 598, CA, where the claim actually failed because the sale had been on brand-named coalite (though there was a breach of s.14(3)); *cf. Duke v. Jackson* (1921) S.C. 362.

- where fire extinguishers were operated at a fire at the purchaser's premises and, rather than extinguishing the fire, exploded causing even greater damage to the premises.[22]

On the other hand, a tweed jacket has been held as being reasonably fit for its purpose despite causing dermatitis to the wearer, because the wearer had not made known her particular susceptibility to dermatitis to the seller.[23] An illustration of where a purchaser does not rely on the seller's skill or judgment is where he asks for a particular branded article.[24] Further, it must be mentioned that the general principles relating to the remoteness of damage apply, thus where an obviously defective product is used the seller will not be liable because it is beyond his reasonable contemplation that the obviously defective product will be used by the purchaser.[25]

Hired goods

7–17   It is an implied term of a contract of hire that the article hired out is as fit for its contemplated purpose as reasonable care and skill can make it.[26]

The Consumer Protection Act 1987

7–18   In 1985 a new Directive of the European Community laid down a regime of liability for defective products[27] and Member States had to introduce this regime into their national laws. The United Kingdom gave effect to this Directive by the Consumer Protection Act 1987 which, by section 2(1), provides a right of action effectively to anyone who suffers personal injury or property damage caused by a defective product supplied after March 1, 1988. A wide range of persons are made liable:

(i) *Producers*: which includes manufacturers of a product or a component of the finished product, those who have won or abstracted a substance, and those who apply an industrial or other process to achieve the product.[28]

(ii) *Own branders*: defined as any person who, by putting his name on the product or using a trade mark or other distinguishing mark in relation to the product, has held himself out to be the producer of the product.[29]

(iii) *Importers*: defined as any person who has imported the product into a Member State from a place outside the Member State in order, in the course of any business of his, to supply it to another.[30]

---

[22] *Sir Robert McAlpine & Sons Ltd v. Minimax Ltd* [1970] 1 Lloyd's Rep. 397.
[23] *Griffiths v. Peter Conway Ltd* [1939] 1 All E.R. 685, CA.
[24] *Wren v. Holt* [1903] 1 K.B. 610, CA.
[25] *Lexmead (Basingstoke) Ltd v. Lewis* [1982] A.C. 225, HL.
[26] *Mowbray v. Merryweather* [1895] 2 Q.B. 640, CA; *Hadley v. Droitwich Construction Co. Ltd* [1968] 1 W.L.R. 37, CA.
[27] Directive 85/374.
[28] Consumer Protection Act 1987, s.1(2).
[29] *ibid.*, s.2(2)(b).
[30] *ibid.*, s.2(2)(c).

(iv) *Suppliers*: suppliers are liable essentially if they are by the injured party to identify any of the above persons but they fail so to do within a reasonable time of the request.[31]

Defects covered by the Act

"Defect" receives a wide definition under section 3(1) of the Act: **7–19**

> "there is a defect in a product for the purposes of this Part if the safety of the product is not such as persons generally are entitled to expect; and for those purposes 'safety', in relation to a product, shall include safety with respect to products comprised in that product and safety in the context of risks of damage to property, as well as in the context of risks of death or personal injury."

All circumstances must be taken into account by the court in determining what "persons generally are entitled to expect", including such matters as the manner in which, and purposes for which, the product has been marketed, its get-up, the use of any mark in relation to the product and any instructions for, or warnings with respect to, doing or refraining from doing anything with or in relation to the product; what might reasonably be expected to be done with or in relation to the product; and the time when the product was supplied by its producer to another.[32]

Strict liability

The principle of strict liability has replaced the common law principle   **7–20**
of fault, but the onus is still on the claimant to prove that the defect caused his injury or damage wholly or partly.[33] It is also important to mention that the Act does not apply to property damage where the property, at the time that it is lost or damaged:

> ". . . is not —
> (a) of a description of property ordinarily intended for private use, occupation or consumption; and
> (b) intended by the person suffering the loss or damage mainly for his own private use, occupation or consumption."[34]

The Act does not apply, though, where the value of the property damage does not exceed £275,[35] or to damage to the actual product itself,[36] or to claims for pure economic loss unconnected with physical damage.[37]

---

[31] *ibid.*, s.2(3).
[32] *ibid.*, s.3(2).
[33] *ibid.*, s.2(1).
[34] *ibid.*, s 5(3).
[35] *ibid.*, s.5(4).
[36] *ibid.*, s.5(2).
[37] *ibid.*

Defences

7–21   Apart from contributory negligence[38] and statutory limitation of three years rather than the normal six years in respect of property damage,[39] section 4(1) of the Act provides six special defences:

(i) where the defect is attributable to compliance with any requirement imposed by or under any enactment or with any Community obligation;

(ii) where the defendant did not at any time supply the product to another;

(iii) a supplier is not liable if:

(a) he only supplied the product otherwise in the course of business of his, and

(b) he is not a producer, own brander, or importer, or, if he is, that he is so by virtue of things done otherwise than with a view to profit;

(iv) where the defect did not exist at the time the defendant parted with it;

(v) if the product is a component, where the defect is a defect in the completed product and due solely to the design of that finished product;

(vi) that the state of scientific and technical knowledge at the relevant time was not such that a producer of products of the same description as the product in question might be expected to have discovered the defect if it had existed in his products while they were under his control.[40]

Manufacturer's duty of care in negligence

7–22   The manufacturer of products owes a duty to take reasonable care in their manufacture, so that the products may be used or consumed in the manner intended, without causing injury to persons or damage to property. This has been established since the renowned decision in *Donoghue v. Stevenson*[41] which abolished the rule that only a contractual relationship between the manufacturer and the injured party could found any liability on the manufacturer. The assumed facts were that a young lady had been bought a bottle of ginger beer to pour over her ice cream in a cafe. The bottle was opaque, and after she had drunk some, it was alleged that a snail in a state of decomposition had been poured out of the bottle with the remainder of the ginger beer. The young lady thereupon suffered shock and severe gastroenteritis, and subsequently sued the manufacturer of the ginger beer in negligence, and the matter was taken to the House of Lords where it was held that the pleadings

[38] *ibid.,* s.6(4).
[39] *ibid.,* s.6(6) and Sched. 1.
[40] *ibid.,* s.4(1)(e).
[41] [1932] A.C. 562, HL.

showed a good cause of action in law. Lord Atkin expounded the principle thus[42]:

> "My Lords, if your Lordships accept the view that this pleading discloses a relevant cause of action you will be affirming the proposition that by Scots and English law alike a manufacturer of products, which he sells in such a form as to show that he intends them to reach the ultimate consumer in the form in which they left him, with no reasonable possibility of intermediate examination, and with the knowledge that the absence of reasonable care in the preparation or putting up of the products will result in an injury to the consumer's life or property, owes a duty to the consumer to take that reasonable care.
>
> It is a proposition which I venture to say no one in Scotland or England who is not a lawyer would for one moment doubt.
>
> It will be an advantage to make it clear that the law in this matter, as in most others, is in accordance with sound common sense."

This statement of the manufacturer's duty of care has stood the test of   **7–23**
time over a period in excess of fifty years in all respects except one — the element of no reasonable possibility of intermediate examination. Rather, the duty of care is present so long as the product in question is intended to reach the ultimate consumer or user in the same condition or state as it left the manufacturer, as explained by Lord Wright in a subsequent case[43]:

> "The decision in *Donoghue*'s case did not depend on the bottle being stoppered and sealed: the essential point in this regard was that the article should reach the consumer or user subject to the same defect as it had when it left the manufacturer."

It matters not whether the manufacturer has sold the product or has   **7–24**
merely issued free samples.[44] The term "manufacturer" has also been given an extended meaning and is now understood to include:

- assemblers, *e.g.* of machinery[45];
- builders, *e.g.* of overhanging fixtures[46];
- erectors, *e.g.* of tombstones[47];
- installers, *e.g.* of electrical items[48];
- processors, *e.g.* of water for consumption[49]; and
- repairers, *e.g.* of mechanical parts or machines.[50]

---

[42] *ibid.* at 599.

[43] *Grant v. Australian Knitting Mills Ltd* [1936] A.C. 85 at 106–107, HL.

[44] *Hawkins v. Coulsdon & Purley U.D.C.* [1954] 1 Q.B. 319 at 333, *per* Denning J. (as he then was), CA.

[45] *Howard v. Furness Houlder Argentine Lines Ltd & A. & R. Brown Ltd* [1936] 2 All E.R. 781.

[46] *Sharpe v. E.T. Sweeting & Son Ltd* [1965] 1 W.L.R. 665.

[47] *Brown v. Cotterill* (1934) 51 T.L.R. 21.

[48] *Hartley v. Mayoh & Co.* [1953] 2 All E.R. 525; *Wayne Tank & Pump Co Ltd v. Employers' Liability Assurance Corp. Ltd* [1974] Q.B. 57, CA.

[49] *Barnes v. Irwell Valley Water Board* [1939] 1 K.B. 21, CA.; *Read v. Croydon Corp.* [1938] 4 All E.R. 631.

[50] *Stennett v. Hancock & Peters* [1939] 2 All E.R. 578; *Heseldine v. C.A. Daw & Son Ltd* [1941] 2 K.B. 343, CA.

7–25   Apart from the obvious examples of breach of the manufacturer's duty
of care which causes personal injury, *e.g.* by a sweet manufacturer failing
to prevent a piece of wire getting into his sweets,[51] or a tool manufacturer
producing a chisel with brittle metal liable to splinter,[52] reported cases can
be sub-divided to illustrate four facets of this manufacturer's duty of care:

   (i) The product must itself be capable of safe use or consumption.
       Obvious examples are foods and drinks that are fit for consump-
       tion,[53] and mechanical parts that are properly designed, con-
       structed and fitted.[54]

  (ii) Any container of a product must be reasonably safe, whether
       produced by the manufacturer, or bought in from another
       manufacturer.[55] Where the container is bought in by the product
       manufacturer, the duty requires him to take reasonable care to
       see that the container is fit for its purpose, *e.g.* that it will with-
       stand the ordinary risks of delivery.[56]

 (iii) Products must be labelled when a failure to do so correctly is
       likely to cause danger to person or property. Thus it was held
       negligent for a company marketing a chemical that reacted
       violently with water in an explosive manner to merely label the
       containers "harmful vapour".[57] Appropriate labelling should
       warn users of any dangerous characteristics of the product.[58]

  (iv) If the product, although not dangerous if used properly, is likely
       to become dangerous if proper methods or precautions are not
       followed, the manufacturer must give proper instructions for the
       product's use. Any such instructions must, of course, be accurate[59]
       and adequate.[60]

7–26   Thus, if a suitability test is advisable to prevent harmful results on full
use, such should be advised,[61] and if such instructions are provided the
manufacturer has fulfilled his duty.[62] Where a product may be put to a
wide variety of uses, and the manufacturer includes instructions that the
product "must be examined and tested by user before use", such instructions may amount to the exercising of reasonable care by the manufacturer,
and he will not be liable merely because a user fails to obey the instructions[63] or a retailer fails to pass on the instructions to a user.[64]

---

[51] *Barnett v. H. & J. Packer & Co. Ltd* [1940] 3 All E.R. 575.
[52] *Mason v. Williams & Williams Ltd & Thomas Turton & Sons Ltd* [1955] 1 W.L.R. 549;
Davie v. New Merton Board Mills Ltd [1959] A.C. 604, HL.
[53] *Donoghue v. Stevenson* [1932] A.C. 562, HL.
[54] *Malfroot v. Noxal Ltd* (1935) 51 T.L.R. 551; *Lambert v. Lewis* [1978] 1 Lloyd's Rep. 610.
[55] *Donoghue v. Stevenson* [1932] A.C. 562 at 595, *per* Lord Atkin, HL.
[56] *Marshall & Son v. Russian Oil Products Ltd* (1938) S.C. 773.
[57] *Vacwell Engineering Co. Ltd v. B.D.H. Chemicals Ltd* [1971] 1 Q.B. 88.
[58] *Devilez v. Boots Pure Drug Co. Ltd* (1962) 106 Sol. Jo. 552.
[59] *British Chartered Co. of South Africa v. Lemon Ltd* (1915) 113 L.T. 935, PC.
[60] *Angle-Celtic Shipping Co. Ltd v. Elliott & Jeffery* (1926) 42 T.L.R. 297.
[61] *Parker v. Oloxo Ltd & Senior* [1937] 3 All E.R. 524.
[62] *Holmes v. Ashford* [1950] 2 All E.R. 76, CA.
[63] *ibid.*
[64] *Kubach v. Hollands* [1937] 3 All E.R. 907.

The length of time between the manufacturer providing the product, and the injury or damage being caused by that product, will be a necessary consideration when determining whether the product is still in the condition in which the manufacturer provided it,[65] and, accordingly, the temporary or permanent nature of the product will also be a consideration in determining whether there has been a breach of the manufacturer's duty of care.[66] The fact that the product has passed into other hands before coming to the injured party is a further consideration that a court will bear in mind, for the product may be exposed to vicissitudes which may render it defective or noxious for which the manufacturer could not in any view be held to blame.[67]

Manufacturer's defences

The usual defences to an action in negligence of consent of the   **7–27**
claimant, contributory negligence, *novus actus interveniens*, and failure of claimant to examine the product where examination is contemplated before use,[68] are available to a manufacturer. Accordingly, in *Farr v. Butters Bros. and Co.*[69] the manufacturers of a crane negligently sent out a defective crane in pieces to be assembled by the buyers. During assembly and erection, the buyer's foreman noticed the defect, but nevertheless continued to construct it, and, indeed, used the crane before the defect was remedied. He was killed in a resulting accident and it was held that the manufacturers were not liable because the chain of causation had been broken.

Retailer's duty of care

The retailer's contractual liability to his customer for defective goods   **7–28**
has already been discussed, but the retailer also owes a duty in tort to warn persons to whom he supplies a product of any danger in that product known to him, or any known defect rendering the product unfit for its contemplated use. Thus, in *Clarke v. Army & Navy Co-operative Society*[70] the defendant retailers were held liable to a customer for injuries she sustained when opening a tin of disinfectant powder. The defendants had known of the danger because of previous complaints they had received, yet they had not warned their customer, the claimant, of the danger.

Supplying goods produced by a manufacturer about whom the defen-   **7–29**
dant retailers knew nothing, yet failed to make inquiry, when an inquiry would have revealed the inexperience and lack of qualification of the manufacturer, was held to amount to negligence and render the defendants liable for injury suffered by a customer when a cleaning fluid had exploded on use in *Fisher v. Harrods Ltd.*[71] Obviously, where the retailer

[65] *Paine v. Colne Valley Electricity Supply Co. Ltd & British Insulated Cables Ltd* [1938] 4 All E.R. 803.
[66] *Eccles v. Cross & M'Illwham* (1938) S.C. 697.
[67] *Donoghue v. Stevenson* [1932] A.C. 562 at 622, *per* Lord Macmillan, HL.
[68] *London Graving Dock Co Ltd v. Horton* [1951] A.C. 737 at 750, *per* Lord Porter, HL.
[69] [1932] 2 K.B. 606, CA.
[70] [1903] 1 K.B. 155, CA.
[71] [1966] 1 Lloyd's Rep. 500; see also *Watson v. Buckley Osborne Garrett & Co. Ltd & Wyrovoys Products Ltd* [1940] 1 All E.R. 174.

knows of the potentially dangerous or defective condition of products he sells, yet neither examines the goods himself nor warns the purchaser that they should be examined properly before use, that retailer is in breach of his duty of care. An illustration would be the seller of a second-hand car of some age.[72] On the other hand, that type of situation must be differentiated from one where the retailer neither knows of the defect in the product, nor could have learnt of it by either reasonable inspection or reasonable inquiry, *e.g.* a retailer cannot be expected to examine tinned goods which of their nature are to be opened only immediately before use.[73]

3. COMMON EXTENSIONS TO COVER

7–30   The insurer will generally provide an indemnity in respect of any legal costs recoverable by any claimant against the insured as well as the main indemnity in respect of compensation paid to the claimant. The insurer will also invariably extend the indemnity under the policy to include all the costs and expenses incurred with the insurer's written consent whilst exercising his right under the policy to have absolute conduct and control of all negotiations, actions or proceedings brought by any claimant against the insured (see Chapter 20, below). A third common extension is cover for solicitor's fees incurred with the insurers' written consent in relation to the following:

(i) any coroner's inquest or other fatal inquiry;
(ii) proceedings in any court of summary jurisdiction arising out of any alleged breach of statutory duty.

4. MISDESCRIPTION OF THE INSURED

7–31   If the insured is not accurately and precisely described in the policy schedule, the question may arise of whether the policy requires formal rectification, or whether the court can construe the description relying on extrinsic evidence without actually requiring rectification of the policy. This issue arose in *Nittan (U.K.) Ltd v. Solent Steel Fabrication Ltd, trading as Sargrove Automation and Cornhill Insurance Co. Ltd*[74] where the defendant insured sued their insurers in third party proceedings (now CPR, Pt 20 proceedings), as a result of the claimants' claim against them. One ground of defence of the insurers was that the insured could not recover under the products liability policy because the claim was based on an excluded risk. The insured contended that the exclusion did not apply because they, the insured, had been misdescribed in the exclusion clause.

---

[72] *Andrews v. Hopkinson* [1957] 1 Q.B. 229.
[73] *Gordon v. M'Hardy* (1903) 6 F. (Ct of Sess.) 210; *cf.* if the tin was evidently punctured before sale.
[74] [1981] 1 Lloyd's Rep. 633, CA.

The facts were that the defendant insured had an existing policy with   **7–32**
the insurers and in 1973 agreed to take over the assets, but not the liabilities,
of Sargrove Electronic Controls Ltd, a company which manufactured
electronic equipment. In February 1974, in relation to that class of business,
the insured began to trade under the business name of Sargrove Automation.
The insured's brokers communicated with the insurers in order to adjust
the existing policy to meet the requirements of the newly acquired
business. They wrote:

> "Details of 'Sargrove' requirements:
> This firm are a division of Ins'd and need not be mentioned in title."

The insurers required the insured to complete a proposal form for this
product liability extension, and, as the electronic equipment had a definite
control function, the insurers offered only limited product liability cover in
a letter dated March 25, 1974. This was agreed and cover was granted,
backdated to February 8, 1974 by an endorsement to the existing policy
stating:

> ". . . the Business of the Insured is:
> Metal Fabrications and Manufacture of Electronic Apparatus and not as
> previously stated.
> All other terms and conditions remain as heretofore."

The insured was named in the policy as "Solent Steel Fabrications Ltd",   **7–33**
but the exclusion clause dated May 30, 1974 at all points referred to the
insured as "Sargrove Electronic Controls Ltd". That company had, of
course, ceased to carry on business, having disposed of all its assets to the
insured, Solent Steel Fabrications Ltd The judge at first instance held that
the insurers could not rely on the exclusion clause in the absence of rectification of the endorsement, but that there was no case for rectification so
that the insurers had to suffer the consequences of their mistake in
describing the insured incorrectly. The Court of Appeal reversed this
decision, and held that the misdescription was merely a misnomer which
the court could ignore when construing the policy. Brightman L.J.
explained the matter thus[75]:

> "In my opinion, in construing a document, the Court is at liberty, as a matter
> of construction, to correct a misnomer. A misnomer is not, in my view,
> necessarily a mistake which requires the equitable remedy of rectification.
> The misnomer may be a mere clerical error. A simple example would be the
> use in a conveyance of the expression 'the vendor' where clearly 'the pur-
> chaser' was intended. It is not necessary to rectify the conveyance to enable it
> to be read and take effect as the parties plainly intended. The words "Sargrove
> Electronic Controls Limited' are used three times in the endorsement of May
> 30. The words mean 'Solent Steel trading as Sargrove Automation' — that is
> to say, carrying on the business of manufacturers of electronic apparatus as
> stated in the wording of the earlier endorsement."

[75] [1981] 1 Lloyd's Rep. 633 at 639.

5. COMMON EXCLUSIONS

Product guarantee risk

7–34　　The liability of the insured to their customers or ultimate consumers in relation to the replacement, repair or recall of any product supplied, manufactured or sold caused by defects in the supplied product will generally be excluded. Such liability needs to be separately insured under a product guarantee insurance.[76] Such an exclusion clause may read:

> "This cover shall not apply to liability in respect of recalling removing repairing replacing reinstating or the cost of or reduction in value of any commodity article or thing supplied installed or erected by the Insured if such liability arises from any defect therein or the harmful nature or unsuitability thereof."

7–35　　The scope of this exclusion was in issue in *Rodan International Ltd v. Commercial Union Assurance Co. plc*,[77] the facts of which have already been given above. The exclusion concerned Items 1 and 2 of Newbrite's claim against Rodan, who held products liability cover with the defendant insurers. These related to losses suffered by Newbrite (Rodan's customer) in selling the stocks of the defective soap powder, including additional handling costs arising. The Court of Appeal unanimously held that this exclusion, called Special Clause H in Commercial Union's policy, did exclude any liability of Rodan to Newbrite in respect of such costs. *Per* Hobhouse L.J.[78]:

> "Item 1 was a liability in respect of the reduction in value of the commodity supplied. Similarly, Item 2 related to the cost of recalling or removing the commodity supplied. The general intention of special clause H is apparent from its wording and is supported by the heading used 'Damage to Goods Supplied'. It makes it clear that the cover in the policy relates to physical consequences not mere financial consequences and relates to the liability for physical consequences of the supply of defective goods but not to breaches of contract as such.
>
> An argument was advanced on behalf of Rodan that the acts referred to in Special Clause H — recalling, removing, repairing, replacing, reinstating — refer to things done by the assured not by the third party. In my judgment that submission was clearly wrong. The subject matter of the cover and of Special Clause H is the liability of the assured to pay compensation to the third party. Thus it must be liability for expenditure incurred by the third party which is excluded by Special Clause H."

7–35　　A shorter form of exclusion was considered in *Nittan (U.K.) Ltd v. Solent Steel Fabrication Ltd, trading as Sargrove Automation & Cornhill Insurance Co. Ltd*[79]:

---

[76] This covers replacement or repair, and reinstallation, costs.
[77] [1999] Lloyd's Rep. I.R. 495, CA.
[78] *ibid.* at 500–501.
[79] [1981] 1 Lloyd's Rep. 633, CA.

"The insurers shall not be liable for injury loss or damage caused by or arising out of the failure of any such goods to perform their intended function."

One argument of the insured was that if this exclusion was given effect it would deprive the cover of any content at all. Although Wien J. accepted this contention at first instance, the Court of Appeal rejected this proposition. The claimants manufactured smoke detector units and obtained an electronic timer from the defendant insured. In May 1975, the timer was provided and installed in the claimants' premises by the defendants for use when subjecting their smoke detector units to heat and humidity treatment. Two months later, there was a serious malfunction of the equipment due to miswiring of a micro safety switch, as a result of which the smoke detectors being processed were subjected to incorrect process and were badly overheated and damaged. The malfunction was not due to a defect in design (which was excluded) but to the incorrect assembly by an employee of Solent Steel. The claimants sued the defendants, who in turn claimed an indemnity from the insurers. The insurers sought to rely on the above exclusion of liability.

Brightman L.J. explained the court's reasoning as to why the exclusion was effective in this case[80]:

7–37

"I have reached the firm conclusion that the exception applies. The intended function of the equipment was a control function - the control of the processing of the smoke detectors. That processing included the application of heat. Therefore the equipment failed to perform its intended function. Therefore the exception applies. Therefore [the insurer] is not liable for accidental bodily injury to any person or for accidental loss of or damage to any property caused by or arising out of the failure of the equipment to perform its intended function. Therefore the defence to the third party notice succeeds.

I do not think that this conclusion deprives the insurance cover of any content in relation to the electronics business of Solent Steel. It leaves the cover intact as an indemnity against liability to pay compensation for injury, loss or damage which is not caused by and does not arise out of the malfunction of equipment. The risk of any injury, loss or damage may not be great. If it were, no doubt this would be reflected in a high premium. Impossible examples of injury or damage were canvassed during the course of the argument in relation to the equipment supplied to Nittan, but I do not think that such an explanation is a fruitful exercise. For all we know, and for all [the insurer] knows, there may be a number of non-functional hazards inherent in other electronic apparatus now manufactured or hereafter to be manufactured by Solent Steel. I think that the exception must be given its plain meaning, and I do not think that we are entitled, although I was at one time tempted, to seek some means of narrowing the meaning of the exception in order to produce a policy content more readily identifiable."

Catastrophe risk

Because a small component in an aircraft, ship, watercraft, offshore installation, or nuclear installation can lead to a disaster of catastrophic

7–38

---

[80] *ibid.* at 640.

dimensions if the component is defective, insurers generally exclude this risk and will require an additional premium before the exclusion will be removed. Such an exclusion clause may read:

> "No indemnity is provided hereunder in respect of products knowingly sold, supplied or manufactured for use in or forming any part of any aircraft, ship, watercraft, offshore installation or nuclear installation."

Contractual liability

7–39   The insurer only intends to insure the insured manufacturer or retailer in relation to ascertainable risks, and will therefore exclude additional liability in respect of products voluntarily undertaken or accepted by an insured under contractual provision with purchasers. This is a well-known exception, and is intended to cover a situation in which the insured has assumed by agreement a liability which would not have attached had he not done so, and is not intended to exclude all liability for breach of contract.[81] An exclusion clause of this nature may be in the following terms:

> "No indemnity is provided hereunder in respect of any liability assumed by the Insured by any express term in any agreement or contract (other than liability arising out of a condition or warranty of goods implied by law) unless such liability would have attached in the absence of such agreement or contract."

Thus, if a manufacturer causes retailers to display promotional material provided by the manufacturer which contains a specific express statement or assurance regarding the quality or other property of the product, any liability founded on any collateral contract that might be held to exist between the manufacturer and the eventual customer,[82] would be excluded by such exclusion clause. An example of the finding of a collatreral contract is *Wells (Merstham) Ltd v. Buckland Sand & Silica Co. Ltd.*[83], where the claimant bought sand for growing chrysanthemums from a retail outlet having been given an express reliance from the manufacturer that it was suitable for this purpose, when it was not.

7–40   **Employer's liability risks**

The liability of an insured manufacturer or retailer in respect of death, bodily injury or illness or disease sustained by the insured's employee arising out of and in the course of his employment with the insured, will be excluded under the products liability insurance because this risk is covered by compulsory employers' liability insurance.[84] The latter and not the former insurance therefore covers the liability of an employer in respect of

---

[81] *A.S. Screenprint Ltd v. British Reserve Insurance Co. Ltd* [1999] Lloyd's Rep. 430 at 435, *per* Beldham L.J., CA.

[82] Following *Carlill v. Carbolic Smoke Ball Co.* [1893] 1 Q.B. 256, CA; but also see the comments of the Court of Appeal in this regard in *Lexmead (Basingstoke) Ltd v. Lewis* [1982] A.C. 225; revsrsed on different grounds [1982] A.C. 225, HL.

[83] [1965] 2 Q.B. 170.

[84] See Chapter 5, above, which includes consideration of who is an employee and what is the course of his employment.

personal injury suffered by his employee because of a defect in equipment provided by his employer for the purposes of business under the Employer's Liability (Defective Equipment) Act 1969.

Professional negligence risks

The insurer will exclude risks which, in the case of a particular insured, should more appropriately be the subject of professional negligence insurance. Where such a risk is excluded, the clause may read:

7–41

> "This policy does not cover liability arising out of advice, plan, design, formula or specification given for a fee in connection with any Product supplied (other than normal instructions for proper use or maintenance)."

Territorial exclusion

Most insurers will exclude all liability arising through or caused by any product which is directly or indirectly exported to the United States of America or Canada with, or even without, the insured's specific knowledge. This is because the insurers will not have rated the risk to reflect the vigorous product liability laws and high awards of damages in those countries. A territorial exclusion clause had to be construed in *Berliner Motor Corp. & Steiers Lawn & Sports Inc. v. Sun Alliance & London Insurance Ltd.*[85] The insured (NVL) were manufacturers of motorcycles, and their products liability policy granted an indemnity in respect of their liability at law for damages and claimant's costs and expenses in respect of accidental injury to any persons anywhere in the world arising from products supplied from the United Kingdom. This indemnity was subject to a number of exceptions and Exception 6 provided:

7–42

> "The company shall not be liable in respect of. . .
>
> (6) any action for damage arising in connection with products supplied brought against (NVL) in any territory outside Great Britain . . . in which (NVL) is represented by a branch or by any person domiciled in such territory."

In 1966, the National Traffic and Motor Vehicle Safety Act 1966 came into force in the United States. Its object was to impose federal control over vehicle design and manufacture in the interests of safety and section 1399(e) provided that:

7–43

> "It shall be the duty of every manufacturer offering a motor vehicle . . . for importation into the United States to designate in writing an agent upon whom service of all administrative and judicial processes . . . may be made for, and on behalf of said manufacturer and to file such designation with the Secretary . . ."

In accordance with this requirement, NVL in 1969 designated their Californian subsidiary as its agent, but that fact was not disclosed to the insurers. One day in 1971, the purchaser of an NVL motorcycle had an

---

[85] [1983] 1 Lloyd's Rep. 320.

accident which he attributed to a defect in the motorcycle, and, in 1972, commenced proceedings against, *inter alia*, the California subsidiary of NVL. Judgment was entered in due course for the purchaser of the motorcycle against the distributors, who in turn were granted judgment against NVL, in the Circuit Court of Cook County, Illinois. The distributors (Berliner) then sued on their judgment in the English High Court.

7–44   Bingham J. (as he then was) analysed the provisions of Exception 6 and concluded[86]:

(i) The expression "territory" was a vague term deliberately chosen to embrace both sovereign states and dependent territories. The contention that each state of the United States, and thus that NVL were represented in California but not Illinois was rejected for the court would not contemplate an enquiry of the constitutional standing of constituent states, regions, provinces or departments of countries.

(ii) The expression "represented" was not a precise term, but in context its intent was that an insured is represented in the foreign territory if it has a presence there either by one of its own branches or through a locally domiciled agent.

(iii) That NVL were not "represented" in the United States at the relevant time because the Californian subsidiary had no agency role save for the compulsory purposes of the 1966 Act.

(iv) The remaining point in this regard concerned whether the action involving NVL had been brought in Illinois or in England, in respect of which Bingham J. held[87]:

"Had there been no submission by NVL to the jurisdiction in Illinois NVL might have been able to resist the claim here on the ground that the Illinois Court had no jurisdiction, and thus it might have been said that NVL had no liability in law in respect of which they were entitled to indemnity. But as it was the Illinois Court undoubtedly did have jurisdiction and judgment against NVL was duly entered here. I need not consider the effect of an Illinois judgment based on an assumption of jurisdiction which would not be recognised here. These considerations lead me to conclude that the plaintiffs' claim against NVL did fall within the policy cover and not within the exception and thus NVL were prima facie entitled to indemnity."

6. COMMON CONDITIONS

7–45   The usual conditions precedent relating to the insured's obligation to notify the insurer of any claims[88]; the insurer's right of control of proceedings; to require the assistance of the insured in such proceedings; and the insured's obligation to take reasonable precautions, will be the same as

---

[86] *ibid.* at 324.
[87] *ibid.* at 325.
[88] See *Berliner Motor Corp. & Steiers Lawn & Sports Inc. v. Sun Alliance & London Insurance Ltd* [1983] 1 Lloyd's Rep. 320.; see also Chapter 18, below.

those found in public liability policies and reference should be made to the discussion of these conditions in Chapter 6, above.

Aggregate limit of indemnity

The term relating to the limit of indemnity will, however, be different to that in public liability policies, and will not apply to each and every occurrence in regard to which the insured makes a claim during the year of insurance. Rather it will apply to the aggregate sum of claims during the year of insurance. Thus if the limit of indemnity is £1m, one claim of £1m in the beginning of the period of insurance will leave the insured uninsured in respect of claims arising during the remaining period of insurance. Similarly, an aggregate limit of indemnity will be exhausted by ten claims of £100,000, or any other combination of claims by the insured, amounting to £1 million.

7–46

CHAPTER 8

DIRECTORS' AND OFFICERS' LIABILITY INSURANCE

1. SUBJECT MATTER OF DIRECTORS' AND OFFICERS' INSURANCE

Introduction

8–01   The purpose of this type of insurance is the provision of an indemnity against financial losses arising from claims against directors and officers of companies for actual or alleged breach of contract, mis-statement, breach of trust, breach of duty, act, neglect, error, omission, breach of warranty of authority, or wrongful trading. Reference may be made to the specimen policy contained in Appendix 8. It is not a policy to protect a director or officer against loss of earnings arising from being dismissed, or, for instance, being disqualified from being a director. From April 1, 1990, the Companies Act 1989, section 137(1) removed the restriction that section 310 of the Companies Act 1985 imposed, which had prevented companies from purchasing and maintaining for any director, or other officer or auditor, insurance against any liability of the sort falling within section 310(1). Those liabilities are specified as "in respect of any negligence, default, breach of duty or breach of trust . . . in relation to the company". There is, therefore, no longer any need for directors and officers to take out their own policies as was the case before the removal of that restriction on companies effecting such insurances for their benefit. It should be noted that the fact that a company has purchased or maintained such insurance must be stated in the company's annual report.[1]

The indemnity and the insured

8–02   Unlike all other policies considered in this book, directors' and officers' insurance is written on a "claims-made" basis. This means that the indemnity only attaches to claims made against the insured directors and officers during the period of insurance. Furthermore, the indemnity only applies to such claims duly notified to the insurer, provided notification is the subject of a suitable condition precedent to the insured's right of recovery under the policy.[2] The indemnity will be limited to losses, as defined in the policy, in respect of which the insured directors and officers have not been provided with an indemnity by their company. The practice and requirements of insurers vary as to the identification of the insured directors and officers. The policy schedule may refer to named directors and officers, or, alternatively, refer to the directors and officers of the company as duly notified to the insurers from time to time. The policy will usually expressly state that it is severable or composite policy, insuring each director and

[1] Companies Act 1989, s.137(2).
[2] See Chapter 18, below.

officer in respect of his own liability. Accordingly, non-disclosure or mis-representation by one of the insured directors or officers will not affect the recovery of an indemnity under the policy by any other innocent director or officer.[3]

2. COMPANY DIRECTORS AND OFFICERS

Directors

Whilst the Companies Act 1985 provides[4] that every public company **8–03** registered after 1929 must have at least two "directors", and every private company must have at least one "director", no statutory definition of the term director is provided other than it is stated that the term "includes any person occupying the position of director by whatever name called".[5] Various titles are encountered in practice, for example, those occupying the position of director may be called "governors", or the "committee of management". There will generally be little difficulty encountered in identifying the *de jure* directors of a company because the company's first directors are usually named in the Articles of Association and, thereafter, subsequent appointments will be governed by the Articles.

Each registered company must record the names of those persons per- **8–04** forming the functions of directors in certain ways. First, the company must keep at its registered office a register of its directors and secretaries, giving their full names and addresses, and other details, and must notify the Registrar of Companies within 14 days of any changes.[6] Secondly, every company registered since November 1916 must print the names of all directors, or none, on all letterheads on which the company name appears. Thirdly, the company must maintain a register of directors' interests and dealings in the company's shares.[7] Fourthly, every company must keep a copy of each of its directors' contracts at its registered office or at its principal place of business in England, Scotland or Wales (depending on where it is registered), or at the place where its register of members is kept.[8]

There may be, apart from validly appointed (*de jure*) directors, other **8–05** persons who are in a position to act as directors. Such *de facto,* or constructive directors[9] may be prevented from being *de jure* directors by a technical defect in their purported appointment or lack of appropriate share-qualification. In any event, they are in the same fiduciary position with their company as *de jure* directors.[10]

---

[3] This would be the case even in the absence of an express provision, *New Hampshire Insurance Co. v. M.G.N. Ltd* [1997] L.R.L.R. 24, CA.

[4] Companies Act 1985, s.282.

[5] *ibid.,* s.741.

[6] *ibid.,* s.288.

[7] *ibid.* ss.324 and 325.

[8] *ibid.,* s.318.

[9] *ibid.,* s.288(6).

[10] *Re Canadian Land Reclaiming & Colonizing Co., Coventry & Dixon's Case* (1880) 14 Ch. D. 660 at 670, CA.

Company officers

8–06   The determination of precisely who is an "officer" of the company may be a rather more difficult matter in any particular instance, because the legislation merely states that the term officer "includes a director, manager or secretary".[11] Again, the actual title of the position held by the person within the company structure may be of little or no assistance. Thus, although the statutory definition states that a "manager" will be a company's "office", it was held in *Gibson v. Barton*[12] that a company's local branch manager was not an "officer" of that company.

8–07   Lord Denning M.R. has stated that "the word "manager" means a person who is managing the affairs of the company as a whole".[13] Further, in *Re A Company*,[14] Shaw L.J. said:

> "The expression 'manager' should not be too narrowly construed. It is not to be equated with a managing or other director or general manager. As I see it, any person who in the affairs of the company exercises a supervisory control which reflects the general policy of the company for the time being or which is related to the general administration of the company is in the general sphere of management. He need not be a member of the board of directors. He need not be subject to specific instructions from the board. If he fulfils a function which touches the central administration of the company, that is sufficient in my view to constitute an 'officer' or 'manager' of the company."

8–08   Accordingly, the individual in question must have been entrusted with power to transact the whole affairs of the company in a particular regard. For instance, whilst duly appointed company liquidators[15] and auditors[16] have been held to be company officers, and, indeed, a solicitor employed part-time on a salary to perform particular duties,[17] persons engaged by the company to perform tasks in the normal pursuit of those persons' trade, business or profession, will not, in all probability, be considered by a court to be company officers. This principle is discernible from a line of cases where professional accountants performed a particular accounting task,[18] a solicitor who was engaged on the normal professional basis to conduct particular affairs of the company,[19] and management consultants appointed to investigate and report on the management of the company,[20] were all held not to be company officers.

---

[11] Companies Act 1985, s.744.
[12] (1875) L.R. 10 Q.B. 329.
[13] *Registrar of Restrictive Trading Agreements v. W.H. Smith & Son Ltd.* [1969] 1 W.L.R. 1460 at 1467, CA.
[14] [1980] 1 Ch. 138 at 144, CA.
[15] *Re Windsor Steam Coal Co. (1901) Ltd.* [1929] 1 Ch. 151, CA.
[16] *Re London & General Bank* [1895] 2 Ch. 166, CA.
[17] *Re Liberator Permanent Benefit Building Society* (1894) 71 L.T. 406; by analogy, other professionals engaged on a part-time basis, or a full-time basis, to perform specified company functions, may well be considered to be "officers".
[18] *Re Western Counties Steam Bakeries & Milling Co.* [1879] 1 Ch. 617, CA.
[19] *Re Kingston Cotton Mill Co.* [1896] 1 Ch. 6 at 14, CA.
[20] *Openshaw v. Fletcher* (1916) 32 T.L.R. 372, CA.

3. RISKS INSURED

Introduction

The risks insured under directors' and officers' liability insurance will be **8–09**
expressed as claims arising from the insured's commission of the alleged
culpable act or omission in his capacity as a director or officer of the stated
company or companies. This overriding proviso must, of course, always be
remembered when considering the applicability or otherwise of the insurance. The primary insuring words will refer to claims for actual or alleged
breach of contract, mis-statement, breach of trust, breach of duty, act,
neglect, error, omission, breach of warranty of authority, or wrongful
trading. The following matters are therefore, prima facie, within the scope
of a directors and officers' insurance policy.

Negligent performance of duties

The essence of the principle that a director or officer of a company can **8–10**
be liable for the negligent performance, *i.e.* the failure to exercise due care
and skill, of his duties is that they are the agents of their company and, as
such, owe the company a duty of care. As Cairns L.J. explained in
Ferguson v. Wilson[21]:

> "The company itself cannot act in its own person, for it has no person; it can
> only act through directors, and the case is, as regards those directors, merely
> the ordinary case of principal and agent. Wherever an agent is liable those
> directors would be liable . . ."

Although the view has been expressed that their position is more that of **8–11**
a managing partner than a mere agent,[22] a better description, if necessary,
is perhaps "managing agent".[23] A company suing its director for negligence will need to satisfy the court upon the precise duties allegedly not
performed by the director, and upon the fact that he has been negligent in
the exercise of his powers.[24] No precise code can be formulated to cater for
the multifarious situations that arise within companies and the exercise of
powers by directors as to the manner in which the work within a company
is to be distributed between the board of directors and the staff, and Lord
Macnaghten doubted that such a code would be sensible[25]:

> "I do not think it desirable for any tribunal to do that which Parliament has
> abstained from doing—that is, to formulate precise rules for the guidance or
> embarassment of businessmen in the conduct of business affairs. There
> never has been, and I think there never will be, much difficulty in dealing
> with any particular case on its own facts and circumstances; and, speaking
> for myself, I rather doubt the wisdom of attempting to do more."

[21] (1866) 2 Ch. App. 77 at 89.
[22] *Automatic Self-Cleansing Filter Syndicate Co. Ltd v. Cuninghame* [1906] 2 Ch. 34 at 45, *per* Cozens-Hardy L.J., CA.
[23] *Re Faure Electric Accumulator Co.* (1888) 40 Ch. D. 141 at 151, *per* Kay J.
[24] *Overend & Gurney Co. v. Gibb & Gibb* (1872) L.R. 5 H.L. 480 at 495, *per* Lord Hatherley L.C., HL.
[25] *Dovey v. Cory* [1901] A.C. 477 at 488, HL.

8-12   It is also worth noting that a managing director is in the same position as any other director in terms of considering his powers and duties — the court must look to the company's Articles and Memorandum of Association. Viscount Kilmuir L.C. in *Harold Holdsworth and Co. (Wakefield) Ltd v. Caddies*[26] firmly rejected the proposition that a managing director holds a specific office with identifiable powers which override provisions in the company's Articles as had been held to be the situation by Asquith J. (as he then was) in *Collier v. Sunday Referee Publishing Co. Ltd.*[27] The court will, however, consider certain matters to assist in their determination of the duties of particular directors, as explained by Romer J. in *Re City Equitable Fire Insurance Co. Ltd*[28]:

> "The position of a director of a company carrying on a small retail business is very different from that of a director of a railway company. The duties of a bank director may differ widely from those of an insurance director, and the duties of a director of one insurance company may differ from those of a director of another. In one company, for instance, matters may normally be attended to by the directors themselves. The larger the business carried on by the company the more numerous, and the more important, the matters that must of necessity be left to the managers, the accountants and the rest of the staff . . .
>   In order . . . to ascertain the duties that a person appointed to the board of an established company undertakes to perform, it is necessary to consider not only the nature of the company's business, but also the manner in which the work of the company is in fact distributed between the directors and the other officials of the company, provided always that this distribution is a reasonable one in the circumstances, and is not inconsistent with any express provisions of the articles of association."

8-13   In that particular case, it was held that the directors of this large insurance company could not personally supervise the safe custody of the company's securities, that task, of necessity, had to be left to officials of the company, such as the managers and accountants. A matter such as the raising of finance is one of management, within the responsibility of directors.[29] A director may rely on advice he received before carrying out a particular act for the company to defeat a claim that he was negligent. Thus, in *Dovey v. Cory*,[30] a director of a joint stock company which was engaged in banking, assented to payments of dividends out of capital and to advances on improper security, was held by the House of Lords not to have been negligent in the performance of his duties as a director. On the facts, their Lordships were satisfied that he had honestly relied on the judgment, information, and advice of the chairman and general manager of the bank, and was misled by their statements. He had no cause to suspect that

---

[26] [1955] 1 W.L.R. 352 at 356–358, HL.
[27] [1940] 2 K.B. 647 at 651.
[28] [1925] Ch. 407 at 427; affirmed by the Court of Appeal on different grounds [1925] Ch. 407 at 500.
[29] *Howard Smith Ltd v. Ampol Petroleum Ltd* [1974] A.C. 821 at 832, *per* Lord Wilberforce, PC.
[30] [1901] A.C. 477, HL.

these persons were otherwise than of great integrity, skill and competence, and he was therefore not negligent.

The speech of Lord Halsbury L.C. provides an insight into judicial **8–14** opinion upon charges of neglect aimed at directors of companies[31]:

> "The charge of neglect appears to rest on the assertion that Mr Cory, like the other directors, did not attend to any details of business not brought before them by the general manager or the chairman, and the argument raises a serious question as to the responsibility of all persons holding positions like that of directors, how far they are called upon to distrust and be on their guard against the possibility of fraud being committed by their subordinates of every degree. It is obvious if there is such a duty it must render anything like an intelligent devolution of labour impossible. Was Mr Cory to turn himself into an auditor, a managing director, a chairman, and find out whether auditors managing directors, and chairmen were all alike deceiving him? That the letters from the auditors were kept from him is clear. That he was assured that provision had been made for bad debts, and that he believed such assurances, is involved in the admission that he was guilty of no moral fraud; so that it comes to this, that he ought to have discovered a network of conspiracy and fraud by which he was surrounded, and found out that his own brother and the managing director (who have since been made criminally responsible for frauds connected with their respective offices) were inducing him to make representations as to the prospects of the concern and the dividends properly payable which have turned out to be improper and false. I cannot think that it can be expected of a director that he should be watching either the inferior officers of the [company] or verifying the calculations of the auditors himself. The business of life could not go on if people could not trust those who are put into a position of trust for the express purpose of attending to details of management. If Mr Cory was deceived by his own officers — and the theory of his being free from moral fraud assumes under the circumstances that he was — there appears to me to be no case against him at all."

Standard of care required of a director

It must be emphasised that there is no concept of the "reasonable director" **8–15** as such, rather, the test is whether the director called into question has shown ordinary care and diligence, as he would have done if, being a reasonable man, he was conducting his own affairs. Hoffmann L.J. (as he then was) in *Re D'Jan of London Ltd*[32] has stated that the duty of care owed by a director at common law is that duty now embodied in section 214(4) of the Insolvency Act 1986. It is the conduct of:

> "a reasonably diligent person having both –
>
> (a) the general knowledge, skill and experience that may reasonably be expected of a person carrying out the same functions as are carried out by that director in relation to the company, and
> (b) the general knowledge, skill and experience that that director has."

There are, thus, two aspects to the standard of care to be expected, one **8–16** objective, and the other subjective. In *D'Jan*, the liquidator sued the

---

[31] *ibid.* at 485–486.
[32] [1994] 1 B.C.L.C. 561, CA; following his own earlier decision as Hoffmann J. in *Norman v. Theodore Goddard* [1991] B.C.L.C. 1028.

former director, Mr D'Jan for negligence and breach of duty, brought under the summary procedure under section 212 of the Insolvency Act 1986. The case concerned Mr D'Jan's signing of a proposal form for a combined business insurances proposal to the Guardian Royal Exchange Assurance plc. One of the insured items was the company's stock which was to be insured against, *inter alia*, fire. Due to non-disclosure of a material fact, the insurers were able to rescind the policy *ab initio* when the company later made a claim for a loss of stock by fire to the value of £174,000. Hoffmann L.J. held that Mr D'Jan had signed the usual declaration at the end of the proposal form without checking the contents of the answers, which task he had left to the company's insurance broker. One question on the proposal form, though, had asked if any director had been director of any company which had gone into liquidation. The broker had answered "No", but, in fact, Mr D'Jan had been a director of a different company which had gone into liquidation in the previous year.

8–17   In finding Mr. D'Jan in breach of his duty of care, in accordance with that under section 214 of the Insolvency Act 1986, Hoffmann L.J. said[33]:

> ". . . in failing even to read the form, Mr D'Jan was negligent. [His Counsel] said that the standard of care which directors owe to their companies is not very exacting and signing forms without reading them is something which a busy director might reasonably do. I accept that in real life, this often happens. But that does not mean that this is not negligent. People often take risks in circumstances in which it was not necessary or reasonable to do so. If the risk materialises, they may have to pay a penalty. I do not say that a director must always read the whole of every document which he signs. If he signs an agreement running to 60 pages of turgid legal prose on the assurance of his solicitor that it accurately reflects the board's instructions, he may well be excused from reading it all himself. But this was an extremely simple document asking a few questions which Mr D'Jan was the best person to answer. By signing the form, he accepted that he was the person who should take responsibility for its contents . . . Both on the objective test and, having seen Mr D'Jan, on the subjective test, I think that he did not show reasonable diligence when he signed the form. He was therefore in breach of his duty to the company."

8–18   So it follows that a director, for example, of a life assurance company, does not guarantee that he has the skill of either an actuary or a physician.[34] On the other hand, if the director does possess a particular skill, or professes a particular calling or vocation, he will be expected to show an appropriate degree of care and diligence when such expertise may be used in discharging his duties.[35] The greater standard of care, with resulting increased liability, is well illustrated by *Bairstow v. Queens Moat Houses plc*[36] where four past directors were found liable for over £26 million. in respect of past dividends they authorised. Nelson J. held:

---

[33] *ibid.* at 563.
[34] *Re City Equitable Fire Insurance Co. Ltd* [1925] Ch. 407 at 428, *per* Romer J., CA.
[35] *Hart & Hodge v. Frame, Son & Co.* (1839) 6 Cl. and Fin. 193, HL.
[36] [2000] 1 B.C.L.C. 549.

(i) a director who authorised the payment of an unlawful dividend in breach of his duty as a quasi trustee would be liable to repay such dividends if he knew that the dividends were unlawful, whether or not that actual knowledge amounted to fraud; or

(ii) if he knew the facts that established the impropriety of the payments, even though he was unaware that such impropriety rendered the payment unlawful; or

(iii) if he must be taken in all the circumstances to have known all the facts which rendered the payments unlawful; or

(iv) if he ought to have known, as a reasonably competent and diligent director, that the payments were unlawful.

Dealing with finances

Directors will not be liable in negligence for merely making an investment that later fails. In *Overend and Gurney Co v. Gibb and Gibb*,[37] defendant directors decided that their company should buy a bill broking and money dealing business, in exercise of a power conferred on them by the Memorandum and Articles of Association. This purchase proved ruinous for their company, but it was held by the House of Lords that whilst it might be said the directors were imprudent, they were not personally liable without it being shown that the character of the business being bought was such as to have made it obviously apparent that it would fail.

8–19

Directors must not be lax in their authorisation of financial dealings of the company. This was illustrated in *Chapeleo v. Brunswick Permanent Building Society*.[38] Here, the claimants had made loans to the defendant building society through the secretary, who, in return, gave the claimants a receipt. After the society's limit of borrowing had been reached, the directors authorised the secretary to receive further sums from the claimants. Subsequently, the secretary absconded with these further sums and the directors, joined in the action as second defendants, were held liable to the claimants who had suffered the loss as a direct consequence of the directors' failure to limit advances to the society within its prescribed limits.

8–20

As regards the duties of directors in relation to the application of the company's funds, Romer J. in *Re City Equitable* enunciated what he considered to be four aspects of directors' duties[39]:

8–21

> "(a) A director who signs a cheque that appears to be drawn for a legitimate purpose is not responsible for seeing that the money is in fact required for that purpose, or that it is subsequently applied for that purpose, assuming, of course, that the cheque comes before him for signature in the regular way, having regard to the usual practice of the company. This is because the director must, of necessity, trust the officials of the company to perform properly and honestly the duties allocated to them.
>
> (b) Before any director signs a cheque, or parts with a cheque signed by him, he should satisfy himself that a resolution has been passed by the

[37] (1872) L.R. 5 H.L. 480.
[38] (1881) 6 Q.B.D. 696, CA.
[39] [1925] Ch. 407.

board, or committee of the board (as the case may be), authorising the signature of the cheque; and where a cheque has been signed between meetings, he should obtain the confirmation of the board subsequently to his signature. The authority given by the board should not be for the signing of numerous cheques to an aggregate amount, but a proper list of the individual cheques, mentioning the payee and the amount of each, should be read out at the board meeting or committee meeting, and subsequently transcribed into the minutes of the meeting.

(c) It is the duty of each director to see that the company's moneys are from time to time in a proper state of investment, except so far as the articles of association may justify him in delegating that duty to others.

(d) Before presenting their annual report and balance sheet to their shareholders, and before recommending a dividend, directors should have a complete and detailed list of the company's assets and investments prepared for their own use and information, and ought not to be satisfied as to the value of their company's assets merely on the assurance of their chairman, however apparently distinguished and honourable, nor with the expression of the belief of their auditors, however competent and trustworthy."

Non-executive directors' standard of care

8–22   Higher standards of care would appear to be owed by full-time directors as compared with part-time, or non-executive, directors, who, as stated by Jessel M.R., are simply required[40]:

"to use reasonable diligence having regard to their position . . . [a non-executive] director, who only attends at the board occasionally, cannot be expected to devote as much time and attention to the business as a sole managing partner of an ordinary partnership, but they are bound to use fair and reasonable diligence in the management of their company's affairs, and to act honestly."

8–23   An example of this lower standard for non-executive directors that has been applied in the past is illustrated by the *Re Cardiff Savings Bank, Marquis of Bute's Case.*[41] It is doubtful whether modern court would be as reluctant to find fault. Here the Marquis was appointed president of the Cardiff Savings Bank when he was six months old, in fact inheriting the office from his father. Despite the fact that the Marquis attended only one board meeting of the bank in the 38 years preceding the action, he was found not liable in respect of certain irregularities in the lending operations of the bank. Further, Romer J., again in the *Re City Equitable* case, supported this view that a non-executive director is not required to give continuous attention to the affairs of the company, where he said[42]:

"His duties are of an intermittent nature to be performed as periodical board meetings, and at meetings of any committee of the board upon which he happens to be placed. He is not, however, bound to attend all such meetings, though he ought to attend whenever, in the circumstances, it is reasonably to do so."

[40] *Re Forest of Dean Coal Mining Co.* (1878) 10 Ch. D. 450 at 452, CA.
[41] [1892] 2 Ch. 100.
[42] [1925] Ch. 407 at 429.

Non-executive directors who have special skills will still be expected to **8–24** owe a duty of care commensurate with those skills in the same way as executive directors, albeit to that lesser degree given the occasional nature of the duties to be performed. This can be seen in *Dorchester Finance Co. Ltd v. Stebbing*,[43] where the conduct of an executive director and two non-executive directors was called into question. The claimant was a money-lending company, and had three directors at all material times: the defendants S., P. and H. Only S. was involved in the company on a full-time basis, and P. and H. each made only infrequent visits to the company. Both S. and P. were qualified accountants, and H., although unqualified, had considerable accountancy experience. The fact was that S. had caused the claimant company to make loans to other persons and to companies with whom he had some connection or dealing. He achieved this, in part at least, because P. and H. signed cheques on the company's account in blank. These loans were subsequently not recovered by the company, because they did not comply with the Moneylenders Acts and adequate securities had not been taken, so the company sued these three directors for negligence and misappropriation of the company's property. Foster J. held that all three directors were liable in damages to their appointing company, the claimants, in these circumstances.

In regard to company officers generally, it can be said that non-director **8–25** company officers owe their companies a duty to exercise reasonable skill and care in performing their tasks as an implied term of their contracts of employment.[44]

No duty to investigate without cause

In each case where negligence is alleged against a director, or other **8–26** officers, it can only be emphasised that the court will search carefully, but if it fails to find anything that should have made the director realise that there is something suspicious or out of the ordinary then it will not find negligence proved. An illustration of this is the following case. In *Prefontaine v. Grenier*[45] the collapse of a bank was due to overdrafts which the cashier —who was the principal executive officer under the directors of the bank whose accounts had been duly audited by a board of auditors duly appointed and entirely independent of the directors, had irregularly and improperly allowed to certain of the bank's customers. The claimant was a director with unlimited liability who had been compelled to pay a large sum of money to the creditors and depositors of the bank, and he sued the defendant, who had been the president of the bank for damages for his neglect in exercising proper supervision of the company's officers. The main ground upon which the claimant relied was that the defendant had not exercised such a control over the details of the bank's business as to enable him to detect and put a stop to the irregular practices of the cashier.

---

[43] [1989] B.C.L.C. 498.
[44] *Lister v. Romford Ice & Cold Storage Co. Ltd* [1957] A.C. 555, HL.
[45] [1907] A.C. 101, PC.

8-27   The Privy Council dismissed this action against the defendant, and the reasoning of the court was given in the speech of Sir Arthur Wilson[46]:

"Before examining the question of [the defendant's] liability it may be well to notice that the cashier was the principal executive officer of the bank under the directors. There is nothing to show that either the defendant or his brother directors had any reason to suspect or distrust that officer. The accounts periodically submitted to the directors were prepared by him, or under his directions. They were duly audited by the board of auditors appointed . . . such auditors being thus entirely independent of the directors. In those accounts the total assets and liabilities of the bank were correctly stated according to the books, but the accounts were so framed as not to disclose the fact that the totals included unauthorised overdrafts. The contention on the part of the plaintiff was that it was the duty of the defendant to have exercised such control as to have detected the overdrafts which were, in fact, concealed from him and from his co-directors.

The alleged duty of the defendant was based, first upon the fact that he was the president of the bank, and, secondly, that he received a salary for acting in that capacity . . .

In this country questions as to the nature and extent of the duty and responsibility of directors and others, in respect of the affairs of companies, have been frequently under consideration. Attempts have repeatedly been made to render them personally liable, on the ground that they have trusted the regularly authorized officers of the company; that they have failed to detect, and been misled by, misrepresentation or concealment by such officers, when there was no reason for doubting their fidelity . . .

The fact that the defendant was remunerated for his services as president does not seem to their Lordships to strengthen the case against him. Indeed, the modest scale, of his remuneration is scarcely consistent with the idea that he, a man of considerable position, and with a business of his own, was ever expected to give his time and labour to the detailed control of the work of the bank. It is much more consistent with the idea that he was expected to do what he did, that is to say, to devote some two hours a day to the business of the bank, two hours largely taken up with official interviews . . .

A special charge of negligence was pressed against the defendant in the argument of the appeal, based on the evidence of a Mr Gagnon, who held the post of inspector under the bank.

There is nothing in the evidence to show the terms of his appointment, and no formal definition of the extent of his duties. The defendant said in his evidence that Gagnon's duties were limited to the inspection of branches and agencies outside [the head office]. On one occasion Gagnon was specially employed to examine into a matter in the head office. He says he was dissatisfied with what he found, and that he pressed upon the defendant that he, Gagnon, should be empowered to make a complete inspection. He says that his suggestion was not very well received, that the defendant rejected the idea that the inspector should be put to supervise the work of the head official of the bank.

It was contended that the omission to authorize the suggested inspection was an act of negligence on the part of the defendant, and that if the suggested inspection had been carried out the overdrafts which led to the fall of the bank would, or might have been, brought to light. Their Lordships are not prepared to say that there was negligence in omitting to sanction an inspection inconsistent with the ordinary method of conducting the affairs of the bank, nor has it been shown that there was any direct connection between the matters excepted to by Gagnon and the fatal overdrafts."

[46] *ibid.* at 109–111.

Liability for misfeasance   8–28

Once a company's liquidation has commenced, many categories of
persons may apply to the court to examine the conduct of current or past
directors, or other officers of the company, by the issue of a misfeasance
summons under section 212 of the Insolvency Act 1986. The grounds of
such an application by the liquidator, official receiver, creditor or other
contributor, is that such director or other officer "has misapplied or
retained or become liable or accountable for any money or property of the
company, or been guilty of any misfeasance or breach of trust in relation
to the company". This summons can be issued to seek investigation of
allegations of negligence.[47] The court may then order the director to
compensate the company for his misfeasance, but this is discretionary, and
the court also has a general power under the Companies Act 1985[48] to
relieve the director or officer of his liability to his company.[49] Thus, in *Re
Claridge's Patent Asphalte Co. Ltd*[50] a director was relieved from liability
for applying his company's money to an *ultra vires* purpose because he was
acting on counsel's opinion that the purpose was *intra vires* the company.
On the other hand, the court refused to grant relief to a director in *Re City
of London Insurance Co. Ltd*[51] who had permitted his co-director to hold
a very large amount of the company's money for several months without
inquiry, prior to that co-director's misappropriation of the money.

It has also been held to be misfeasance for a director to vote for pay-   8–29
ment of brokerage and commission included in a much larger item on the
annual balance sheets, that payment in fact being for a fraudulent operation to raise the price of the company's shares on the stock market. The
director was not showing reasonable care in not enquiring into this
payment.[52] As it has once been put[53]:

> "If directors apply money of the company for purposes so outside its powers
> that the company could not sanction such application, they may be made
> personally liable as for a breach of trust. On the other hand, if they apply
> the money of the company or exercise any of its powers in a manner which
> is not *ultra vires*, then a strong case and clear case of misfeasance must be
> made out to render them liable."

Directors successfully defended allegations under misfeasance sum-   8–30
monses in *Re Halt Garage (1964) Ltd.*[54] The liquidator of the company
alleged misfeasance by the husband and wife directors of this garage business, and failed as against the husband, and succeeded as against the wife.
The facts were that the couple had built up the business from 1964 and
were the sole directors and shareholders. In 1967, the wife became ill and

---

[47] *Re Westlowe Storage & Distribution Ltd* [2000] 2 B.C.L.C. 590.
[48] Companies Act 1985, s.727.
[49] But not to others, *Customs & Excise Commissioners v. Hedon Alpha Ltd* [1981] Q.B.
818, CA.
[50] [1921] 1 Ch. 543.
[51] (1925) 41 T.L.R. 521.
[52] *Re Railway & General Light Improvement Co., Marzetti's Case* (1880) 42 L.T. 206, CA.
[53] *Re Faure Electric Accumulator Co.* (1888) 40 Ch. D. 141 at 152, *per* Kay J.
[54] [1982] 3 All E.R. 1016.

in the December it became apparent that she would not be active in the business again. The husband continued to work virtually full-time in the business until 1971, when the company went into voluntary liquidation, the business having gone into decline from 1967–1968. Throughout the period from January 1968 to March 1971 the husband drew director's remuneration of some £2,500 per annum, rising to £3,500 per annum, and the wife drew director's remuneration of £1,500 per annum reducing to some £500 per annum even though during the period she took no active part in the business.

8–31   Throughout that period the drawings of remuneration were mainly out of capital because the company was suffering a trading loss. The liquidator had sought recovery of the whole or part of these drawings on the ground that they were guilty of misfeasance and breach of trust in making these drawings. Oliver J. held that where payments of remuneration to a director were made under the authority of the company acting in general meeting pursuant to an express power in its articles to award director's remuneration, and there was no question of fraud on the company's creditors or on minority share-holders, the competence of the company to award the remuneration depended on whether the payments were genuinely director's remuneration (as opposed to a disguised gift out of capital) and not on an abstract test of benefit to the company. As regards the husband's drawings, there was no evidence that they were patently excessive or unreasonable having regard to the company's turnover which exceeded £100,000 per annum, therefore the claim for misfeasance against him failed. In regard to the wife's drawings, although the company's articles included power to award remuneration for the mere assumption of the office of director even where the director was not active in the conduct of the company's business, that power predicated that a director would receive remuneration for services rendered or to be rendered, and the mere fact that the label of "director's remuneration" was attached to the drawings did not preclude the court from examining their true nature. Having regard to the wife's inactivity during the period in question, it could not be said that the whole of the amounts drawn by the wife in that period were genuine awards of remuneration to her for holding office as a director. That part of her drawings in excess of what would have been a reasonable award of remuneration for holding office as a director amounted to a dis-guised co-proprietorship of the business and was *ultra vires* the company, therefore, it was repayable to the liquidator.

Similarly, directors were held not liable in *Re Horsley and Weight Ltd*[55]

8–32   concerned an allegation of misfeasance against two directors who had pro-cured a pension policy for a retiring director, H., in the year prior to the company's being compulsorily wound up, and two directors, who were the only shareholders in the company. The facts were that the company had a number of objects in its Memorandum of Association, all expressed to be separate objects. One object was to "grant pensions to employees and ex-employees and directors and ex-directors". C. and F. were the main two directors of the company and its sole shareholders, with their respective

[55] [1982] Ch. 442, CA.

wives and H. making a complement of five directors. In 1975, shortly before H. was to retire, C. told him that in recognition of his service the company would grant him a retirement pension which would be secured by the company taking out a pension policy at a premium of £10,000. C. and F., without the authority of the board of directors, or of the company in general meeting, effected this policy and signed the cheques for the premium. It was accepted that C. and F. acted in good faith, after considering whether it was proper to take out the policy in the light of the company's financial state, and evidence did not establish that they ought to have appreciated that payment of the premium would cause loss to the company's creditors.

The Court of Appeal upheld the judge's dismissal of the allegation of **8–33** C. and F.'s misfeasance. Since the power to grant a pension was a substantive object, it was irrelevant whether the grant of a pension pursuant to that power would benefit or promote the commercial prosperity of the company, and was therefore *intra vires* the company. Further, this was not misfeasance by C. and F. who had acted in good faith, even though this was an unauthorised act, because, being the only shareholders of the company, C. and F.'s assent to this *intra vires* act had the effect of ratifying the transaction even though this was done informally.[56]

Liability for torts of the company

The mere fact that a person is a director of a limited liability company **8–34** does not by itself render him liable for torts committed by the company during the period of his directorship,[57] rather, to establish a prima facie case it must be shown that the director ordered or procured the acts to be done by the servants of the company.[58] In *British Thomson-Houston Co. Ltd v. Sterling Accessories Ltd,*[59] Tomlin J. rejected the argument advanced by the claimant company whose patent had been infringed by the defendant company, that the company should be regarded as having acted as the directors' agent merely because the directors were its sole directors and shareholders, and stated[60]:

> "I apprehend that, where it is sought to fix a defendant with liability for a tort, it must be established either that he is himself the tortfeasor, or that he is the employer or principal of the tortfeasor, in relation to the act complained of, or, at any rate, the person on whose instructions the tort has been committed."

C. Evans and Sons Ltd v. Spritebrand Ltd[61] concerned allegations of **8–35** infringement of copyright, and when delivering the judgment of the court, Slade L.J. said[62]:

---

[56] *Parker & Cooper Ltd v. Reading* [1926] Ch. 975.
[57] *Rainham Chemical Works Ltd v. Belvedere Fish Guano Co. Ltd* [1921] 2 AC 465 at 488, *per* Lord Parmoor, HL; *Prichard & Constance (Wholesale) Ltd v. Amata Ltd* (1924) 42 R.P.C. 63.
[58] *Performing Rights Society Ltd v. Ciryl Theatrical Syndicate Ltd* [1924] 1 KB 1 at 14, *per* Atkin L.J., CA; *Wah Tat Bank Ltd v. Chan Cheng Kum* [1975] A.C. 507 at 514–515, *per* Lord Salmon, PC.
[59] [1924] 2 Ch. 33.
[60] *ibid.* at 317.
[61] [1985] 1 W.L.R. 317, CA.
[62] *ibid.* at 329.

"The authorities . . . clearly show that a director of a company is not automatically to be identified with his company for the purpose of the law of tort, however small the company may be and however powerful his control over its affairs. Commercial enterprise and adventure is not to be discouraged by subjecting a director to such onerous potential liabilities. In every case where it is sought to make him liable for his company's torts, it is necessary to examine with care what part he played personally in regard to the act or acts complained of. Furthermore, I have considerable sympathy with judges, particularly when dealing with commercial matters, who may be anxious to avoid or discourage unnecessary multiplicity of parties by the joinder of directors of limited companies as additional defendants in inappropriate cases . . . the very fact of such joinder could in some cases operate to put unfair pressure on the defendants to settle. In some instances, where the joinder is demonstrably a mere technical move, a striking out application may well be justified.

Nevertheless, in my judgment, with great respect to Nourse J. (and to Whitford J. who has since followed him) in expressing a principle in the *White Horse*[63] case said to be applicable to all torts, he expressed it in terms which were not sufficiently qualified . . . In particular, I would accept that if the plaintiff has to prove a particular state of mind or knowledge on the part of the defendant as a necessary element of the particular tort alleged, the state of mind or knowledge of the director who authorised or directed it must be relevant if it is sought to impose personal liability on the director merely on account of such authorisation or procurement; the personal liability of the director in such circumstances cannot be more extensive than that of the individual who personally did the tortious act. If, however, the tort alleged is not one in respect of which it is incumbent on the plaintiff to prove a particular state of mind or knowledge (*e.g.* infringement of copyright) different considerations may well apply."

8–36   Slade L.J. continued, however, by remarking on the confines of his judgment, namely, that he dismissed the director's appeal against a refusal to strike out the writ on the basis that it is not the law of England that a director of a company who has authorised, directed and procured the commission by the company of a tort of the nature specified in section 1(2) of the Copyright Act 1956 can in no circumstances be personally liable to the injured party unless he directed or procured the acts of infringement in the knowledge that they were tortious or not. His lordship did not regard this striking out application as an appropriate occasion for the Court of Appeal to attempt a comprehensive definition of the circumstances in which a director of a company who has authorised, directed and procured a tortious act to be done will be held personally liable.

8–37   Consideration of a number of the reported cases may be of assistance. In *Wah Tat Bank Ltd v. Chan Cheng Kum*,[64] the respondent was a shipowner and chartered his ships to a shipping company of which he was managing director. He was sued by the appellant bank for conversion of a consignment of goods which the shipping company had delivered without authority from the bank, the bank having advanced money on those goods against the mate's receipts. The Privy Council held that on the evidence the respondent was a party to the conversion. After emphasising that each

---

[63] *White Horse Distillers Ltd v. Gregson Associates Ltd* [1984] R.P.C. 61 at 91–92.
[64] [1975] A.C. 507, PC.

case depends upon its own particular facts, Lord Salmon explained that in this case there was uncontradicted evidence that the respondent, as chairman and managing director of the shipping company, had agreed with the directors of the company, to whom the bank had advanced money, the terms upon which that company would continue wrongfully to convert goods consigned to the bank, just as they had done in the past. In those circumstances, there was no answer to the claimant bank's claim.[65]

A managing director of a company which owned a ship on which the claimant suffered personal injuries, was found liable in negligence to the claimant in *Yuille v. B. & B. Fisheries (Leigh) Ltd & Bates, The Radiant*.[66] The claimant's claim was based on a claim that the ship had defective equipment, namely a tow-rope which had coiled around him and amputated his feet, and it is important to note in this case that Bates, the defendant company's managing director, was accepted as being the alter ego of the company. The court found that the ⅜ inch trawl wire provided for towing emergencies was inadequate, and that there was insufficient lighting provided preventing the claimant from foreseeing the event, and that the claimant had an action against Bates personally, in addition to his action against the company. Members of the crew of a ship improperly sent to sea in an unseaworthy condition would be persons in a sufficiently close relationship with the responsible director of the company to create a legal duty on the part of the latter to exercise reasonable care, and Wilmer L.J. continued[67]:

8–38

> "In circumstances such as these, I believe that the plaintiff, if he can establish that he is within the appropriate relationship where duty is owed can have this remedy against the individual wrongdoer, if he can fix who that individual wrongdoer is . . . It is well-established now that, provided you can fix the responsibility on to a particular individual, a right of suit against that individual exists . . .
>
> So far as I know, that principle has never been doubted. I see no difficulty, therefore, in law, provided the facts warrant it, in coming to the conclusion that an officer of a company, whether he be a director or whether he be any other official in the service of the company, is in law capable of being a joint tortfeasor with the company itself, which, of course, would also be vicariously liable for his wrongful acts."

A director who had personally demonstrated a process, the subject of another's patent, to a representative of a potential investor in his company, and who had personally handled goods from a customer for the carrying out of such a process, and been present when such a process was carried out commercially by the company's workmen, was held to be personally liable to the patent-holder in *Reitzman v. Grahame-Chapman and Derustit Ltd*.[68] Harman J. found no difficulty in this case because of the active

8–39

[65] [1975] A.C. 507 at 515.
[66] [1958] 2 Lloyd's Rep. 596.
[67] *ibid.* at 619; referring to *Donoghue v. Stevenson* [1932] A.C. 562; *The Koursk* [1924] P. 140 at 155, *per* Scrutton LJ., CA.
[68] (1950) 67 R.P.C. 178; affirmed 68 R.P.C. 25, CA.

engagement of the director in directing the company's breach of the patent,[69] and applied *dicta* of Lord Buckmaster that[70]:

> "if, . . . those in control expressly direct that a wrongful thing be done, the individuals as well as the company are responsible for the consequences."

and of Atkin L.J. (as he then was)[71]:

> "If the directors themselves directed or produced the commission of the act they would be liable in whatever sense they did so, whether expressly or impliedly."

8–40   The House of Lords considered this area of law in *Williams v. Natural Life Health Foods*[72] where the director of a "one man company" was sued personally for negligent misstatement concerning certain information contained in his company's promotional literature. The company sold franchises, and made much of this director's personal expertise in relation to this. The House of Lords rejected the claims against the director, emphasising the absence of the director's personal assurance to the claimant that the statements were accurate. In the absence of such assumption of personal responsibility, no duty of care arose.

Liability under company contracts

8–41   In common with other agents who negotiate contracts on behalf of a principal, in this case their appointing company, directors and other officers will be personally liable upon contracts where they either do not adequately inform the other contracting party that they are merely acting as agents, or breach their warranty of authority to enter into and perform the contract. An example of the former incursion of personal liability is *Bridges and Salmon v. The Swan*[73] the defendant director was held personally liable on a contract with the claimants. The facts were that the defendant was the owner of a motor boat, which the claimants knew to belong to him, and he ordered certain repairs to be undertaken. He contended that he had been acting as agent of his company, which was to pay for the repairs, but the court accepted the evidence of the claimants that the defendant had not made it clear to them that he was ordering the repairs on behalf of the company, rather than himself. Accordingly, the defendant director was personally liable to meet the cost of the repairs ordered.

8–42   As regards breach of warranty of authority causing a director to incur personal liability, *Firbank's Executors v. Humphreys*[74] is illustrative, where the claimant had contracted with the defendant director's company to build a railway, and under that agreement he was entitled to be paid in cash, so the claimant agreed to accept the company's debenture stock in

---

[69] *ibid.* at 185.
[70] *Rainham Chemical Works Ltd v. Belvedere Fish Guano Ltd* [1921] 2 A.C. 465 at 476, HL.
[71] *Performing Rights Society Ltd v. Ciryl Theatrical Syndicate Ltd* [1924] 1 K.B. 1 at 14, CA.
[72] [1998] 1 W.L.R. 830, HL.
[73] [1968] 1 Lloyd's Rep. 5.
[74] (1886) 18 Q.B.D. 54, CA.

lieu of cash. The defendant directors therefore issued to the claimant certificates for the agreed amount of debenture stock, such certificates being signed by two of the defendants. Unknown to the defendant directors, all the debenture stock that the company was entitled to issue had been issued, with the effect that the certificate issued to the claimant was an over issue, and, consequently, valueless. Subsequently, the company went into liquidation, but its debenture stock retained its par value, and the claimant learned then that the stock was worthless, and so he sued the directors personnally.

The claimant's case was that the directors were agents of the company **8–43** and had authority to issue debenture stock binding on the company, provided the powers of issuing such stock had not been exhausted; but they had no authority to make any over issue so as to bind the company. By issuing those certificates the directors impliedly affirmed that they had authority to issue them, and that he, the claimant, accepted them, relying on that affirmation of authority. His resulting loss should therefore be recoverable from the directors personally. The Court of Appeal applied a line of authority[75] which provided that where a person, by asserting that he has the authority of the principal, induces another person to enter into any transaction that he would not have entered into but for that assertion, and the assertion turns out to be untrue, to the injury of the person to whom it is made, it must be taken that the person making it undertook that it was true, and he is liable personally for the damage that has occurred.[76] The defendant directors were therefore held personally liable to the claimant.

One of those earlier authorities was *Weeks v. Propert*[77] where the defen- **8–44** dants were the directors of a railway company and they issued a prospectus inviting persons to lend money to the company on the security of debentures. The claimant was a trustee of certain funds and he lent a sum of money to the company, obtaining a debenture. Unknown to him, the company had already exceeded its borrowing powers so that it was not liable on those debentures, since they were *ultra vires*. It was held that the claimant's action against the directors personally, succeeded for they were in breach of their warranty that the company had power to issue valid debentures against loans made, that warranty being implied from the prospectus. A statutory liability is now imposed on all persons who allow their name to be associated with a prospectus which induces persons to subscribe for securities by means of false statements.[78]

A public liability company cannot now commence trading or exercise **8–45** borrowing powers unless and until it has received a certificate from the Registrar of Companies. If it does so, the transactions are enforceable against the company, but if the company fails to meet its obligations within 21 days of being called upon to do so, the directors are jointly and

---

[75] *Collen v. Wright* (1857) 7 E. and B. 301; affirmed 8 E. and B. 647; *Dixon v. Renter's Telegram Co.* (1877) 3 C.P.D. 1, CA.
[76] (1886) 18 Q.B.D. 54 at 60, *per* Lord Esher M.R. and at 62, *per* Lindley L.J., CA.
[77] (1873) L.R. 8 C.P. 427.
[78] See the Companies Act 1985, s.67.

severally liable to indemnify a person who has suffered loss or damage by reason of the company's failure to meet its obligations.[79]

Liability on cheques, etc.

8–46   Directors and other company officers may also incur personal liability where they sign or authorise the signature, on behalf of their company, of any bill of exchange, promissory note, cheque, or order for money or goods where it is not duly paid by the company, and the name of the company is not mentioned thereon in full and in legible characters.[80] There are several reported examples of these claims. In *Penrose v. Martyr*,[81] a company secretary was held liable when he accepted a bill of exchange that was subsequently dishonoured by omitting the indication that the company was a limited liability company, he had written "Accepted. John Martyr, Secy to the sd Coy." More recently, in *British Airways Board v. Parish*,[82] the managing director of a company was held personally liable in the sum of nearly £24,000 in relation to the amount outstanding on cheque which did not bear his company's full name. As Megaw L.J. explained[83]:

> "The defect in the present case was the important one that the word 'Limited' was omitted . . . There is no doubt on the admitted facts that the cheque was not duty paid by the company, in the sense that it was not paid when it ought to have been paid by the company — that is, when it was first presented and payment was refused. At that moment the position in law was that the cheque had not been duly paid by the company . . . once the position arises . . . the personal liability of the officer of the company — in this case the defendant — comes into existence at that date."

8–47   It has been held, though, that "Ltd" is perfectly sufficient, the full word "Limited" is not necessary.[84] In *Hendon v. Adelman*[85] the directors of L. & R. Agencies Ltd were held liable on a cheque signed "L. R. Agencies Ltd" which was dishonoured. However, claimants will not succeed if they themselves have drawn up the deficient documents with the misdescription, as was found in *Durham Fancy Goods Ltd v. Michael Jackson (Fancy Goods) Ltd*[86] where the claimants had drawn up a bill of exchange and acceptance referring to "M Jackson (Fancy Goods) Ltd". That case was distinguished, though, by the Court of Appeal in *Maxform SpA v. Mariani and Goodville Ltd*[87] where the claimants had drawn up the bill of exchange in the trading name of the company, but the defendant director had accepted it without any addition to his signature and there was no mention of the company's correct registered name.

---

[79] *ibid.*, s.117.
[80] *ibid.*, s.349(4); but see *Bondina Ltd v. Rollaway Shower Blinds Ltd* [1986] 1 W.L.R. 517, CA.
[81] (1858) E.B. and E. 499.
[82] [1979] 2 Lloyd's Rep. 361, C.A.
[83] *ibid.* at 364.
[84] *F. Stacey A. Co. Ltd v. Wallis* (1912) 28 T.L.R. 209.
[85] (1973) 117 Sol. Jo. 631.
[86] [1968] 2 Q.B. 839; [1968] 2 Lloyd's Rep. 98.
[87] [1981] 2 Lloyd's Rep. 54, CA.

Independent duty of care

There may be occasions when a director or other company officer owes **8-48** an injured party a wholly separate duty of care from that owed by his company. One instance has already been discussed above, *Yuille v. B. & B. Fisheries (Leigh) Ltd & Bates, The Radiant*[88] where a managing director permitted a ship to go to sea in an unseaworthy condition in circumstances where he knew it was for him to ensure necessary repairs were done and proper equipment provided. Another instance was *Fairline Shipping Corp. v. Adamson*[89] where a company (G.M. Ltd) operated a cold store as part of its business of buying and reselling game and meat products. Only on very rare occasions did G.M. Ltd use the premises to store goods which did not belong to it. In September 1971, the defendant bought the freehold of the store, it being a term of the agreement that he would grant a lease of the store to G.M. Ltd. The defendant also acquired a 50 per cent holding in G.M. Ltd, which was in financial difficulties, and became its managing director. The business of buying and selling the company's products remained under the management of other directors, but by January 1972 it was clear that G.M. Ltd was in serious financial difficulty and probably could not be saved. From that time on the defendant was only concerned with the liquidation of the business, and thereafter, apart from the directors, the only person on its payroll was an assistant employed by the defendant to look after his interests.

The financial and secretarial side of the business was then conducted by **8-49** the defendant and his assistant, with the help of the defendant's secretary who did the necessary typing from other premises owned by the defendant, correspondence on behalf of G.M. Ltd being typed on that company's headed notepaper. At the beginning of March 1972, the claimants' agent contacted V., a director of G.M. Ltd, who arranged, on behalf of G.M. Ltd, for a consignment of meat, vegetable and fat products to be stored at the cold store. V. informed the defendant, who raised no objection to the arrangement, and the consignment was duly delivered into the store on March 14. The defendant then realised that there was nothing in writing to confirm the arrangement and on March 23 a letter was written to the claimants, reading:

> "I confirm the arrangement regarding the storage of goods in my premises ... My invoice for £61.00 being the first month's rental due will be sent to you on or around the April 14, 1972."

That letter was written on the defendant's personal notepaper, and was signed by his secretary "for" him. The claimants' agents received that letter and accepted it without querying why it had not come from G.M. Ltd, but they knew that the defendant was a businessman of substance. An invoice was sent to the claimants' agents by the defendant on April 14, again on the defendant's own notepaper, asking for the cheque to be sent to his other business address.

[88] [1958] 2 Lloyd's Rep. 596.
[89] [1975] Q.B. 180.

8–50   While the claimants' consignment was in the store, no steps were taken to check on the temperature of the chamber in which the goods were stored. During this time the defendant visited the store to show round prospective purchasers of the premises, and on these visits he heard the refrigeration machinery and assumed all was well. On April 16, it was discovered that one of the fans distributing cold air into the chamber had broken down and the contents of the chamber had thawed. The claimants' claim against the defendant on the ground of novation of the contract of bailment failed, but they succeeded in negligence. Kerr J. (as he then was) based his judgment on the ground that if an employer is liable to a claimant in tort on the basis of the doctrine of vicarious liability, the servant/employee can also be held personally liable, though, in practice, it is usually much more convenient and worthwhile to sue his employers. That being the law as regards servants, it could not be more favourable to company directors[90]:

> "I do not think that the refinements of the concepts of legal possession and bailment are or should be determinative of liability in the tort of negligence.
> The real answer to the question of his liability in negligence to the plaintiffs is not necessarily excluded as a matter of law on the ground that there was no contract with him and that he is also not to be regarded as a bailee with a right to the legal possession of the goods. Depending on the facts, he may nonetheless owe a duty of care to the plaintiffs and be liable in negligence for breach of that duty. The fact that he was a director of (G.M. Ltd) and that the company was the contracting party does not necessarily exclude his personal liability. The legal position in this connection can be conveniently illustrated by reference to two cases, but such examples could easily be multiplied. In *Adler v. Dickson*[91] the plaintiff's contract with the defendant's employers, although excluding all liability for negligence, nevertheless did not preclude her from recovering damages in negligence from the defendant, a servant of the company with which she had contracted, because he owed her a personal duty of care apart from his contractual obligations to his employers, and because he was held to be in breach of that duty. That was a case of personal injury, but I do not see why a case of damage to the plaintiff's property must be regarded differently in law. Take the facts of *Morris v. C.W. Martin and Sons Ltd*.[92] In that case the plaintiff's fur coat was stolen by a servant of the defendants, who were sub-contractors and sub-bailees of the coat without any contractual or other nexus existing between the plaintiff and the defendants. The plaintiff recovered damages against the defendants for the loss of her coat because they were held responsible for the act of their servant. It is however clear that if she had chosen to sue the servant personally in the tort of conversion[93] she would equally have succeeded, indeed with less difficulty. But would the position on this basis have been any different if instead of stealing the coat the servant had negligently caused or allowed it to be ruined in the process of cleaning it. If he had carelessly plunged it into a vat of green dye or left it in cleaning fluid for so long that it became destroyed by some foreseeable chemical action, could he not have been made liable in negligence as well as his employers? I do not see why it should follow as a matter of law that in such cases an action could only be

[90] [1975] Q.B. 180 at 190–191.
[91] [1955] 1 Q.B. 158, CA.
[92] [1966] 1 Q.B. 716, CA.
[93] See now the Torts (Interference with Goods) Act 1977.

maintained against his employers. A duty of care by somebody else's servant to the owner of goods, and a breach of that duty by a particular servant, may of course be much more difficult to establish than a wrongful conversion of the goods by such a servant. But this depends on the facts."

As at the relevant time, G.M. Ltd could only perform its duties in **8–51** relation to these goods through its human servants and agents, who were the directors, and the only one of these who concerned himself with these goods in any way after their delivery was the defendant, the defendant assumed and owed a duty of care to the claimants in respect of the storage of their goods in his premises. The letter of March 23 reflected that position, and as the defendant was in breach of that duty, he was personally liable to the claimants.

Wrongful trading

This[94] was first introduced in 1985[95] and is now defined in section 214 of **8–52** the Insolvency Act 1986. It has limited application, because only the liquidator of an insolvent company can invoke it, and it is limited to a duty on directors to take steps to mitigate the loss suffered by creditors of the company. Furthermore, the liquidator must identify a date on which the directors either knew, or ought to have known,[96] that the insolvent liquidation was inevitable. The directors will usually be expected to seek appropriate professional assistance in determining the steps that they should individually and collectively take. The standard of care placed upon the directors under section 214 of the Insolvency Act 1986 has already been mentioned above, and it has both an objective, and a subjective element. Simply to trade on in the hope that things will get better is not sufficient, even in the case of a company largely dependent on weather conditions in order to carry out its work, but the effects of the bad weather will be taken into account in determining the extent of the liability of the directors in terms of causation of the losses sustained by creditors.[97] Where matters are in complete disarray, and accounts have not been prepared properly so that the court cannot accurately determine the date on which inevitable insolvency should have been recognised, the court will still determine that start date as best it can.[98]

Proceedings for wrongful trading are not common. The normal conse- **8–53** quence of a finding of wrongful trading is an order that the defaulting director or directors make a financial contribution to the insolvent company, thereby increasing that company's assets available to distribute among its unsecured[99] creditors. Further ancillary orders are available under section

[94] See further Milman and Durrant, *Corporate Insolvency Law and Practice* (3rd ed. 1999, Sweet & Maxwell, London), Chap. 12.
[95] Insolvency Act 1985, s.15.
[96] For instance, if the company's accounts had been prepared timeously, *Re Produce Marketing Consortiun Ltd (No.2)* [1989] B.C.L.C. 520.
[97] *Re Brian D. Pierson Contractors Ltd* [1999] B.C.C. 26.
[98] *Re Purpoint Ltd* [1991] B.C.C. 121.
[99] *Re M.C. Bacon Ltd (No.2)* [1990] B.C.L.C. 607 at 612–613, *per* Millett J. (as he then was). *cf. Re Produce Marketing Consortium Ltd (No.2)* [1989] B.C.L.C. 520 at 554, *per* Knox J.

215 of the Act, such as an order that a debt owed to the contributor be reduced to deferred status, or the imposition of a charge on the matrimonial home of co-directors.[1]

4. EXCLUSIONS FROM COVER

Dishonesty, fraud and malicious conduct

8–54   The policy will not provide an indemnity in respect of claims arising from allegations concerning any dishonest or fraudulent act or omission by an insured director (but will indemnify other directors not concerned with those particular allegations) except in regard to the costs and expenses reasonably incurred by the director in his successful defence of such claims. Accordingly, the directors in *Prudential Assurance Co. Ltd v. Newman Industries Ltd (No.2)*,[2] who were sued for damages on the ground of their conspiracy to deceive the company's shareholders, would not be indemnified under a directors' and officers' liability policy. Nor would the blatant and dishonest misuse of directors' powers by dispensing, by way of gratuitous payment to one of the directors, moneys borrowed for the purpose of the company's business, as in *Re George Newman & Co.*[3] Similarly, a claim arising from certain directors engaging their company in a course of dishonest trading, (by passing off their company's goods as those of another company, in circumstances where those same directors had themselves inspected the finished product, and had discussed the marketing and naming of those goods at board meetings), as in *T. Oertli A.G. v. E.J. Bowman (London) Ltd*,[4] nor a claim based on deceit, as in *Walsham v. Stainton*,[5] would be included in the scope of a directors' and officers' liability policy.

Fraudulent trading

8–55   Claims arising out of allegations of fraudulent trading under section 213 of the Insolvency Act 1986 will also not be covered by reason of this exclusion. Proceedings may only be instigated by the liquidator of an insolvent company, and it must be shown that the director or officer was taking some positive steps in carrying on business in a fraudulent manner.[6] The collection of assets acquired in the course of business and the distribution of the proceeds of those assets in the discharge of business liabilities can constitute "carrying on business" where there is a continuous course of active conduct and not merely a passive suffering of undischarged liabilities.[7] If a company continues to carry on business and to incur debts at a time when there was to the knowledge of the directors, no reasonable prospect of the creditors ever receiving payment of those debts, it is, in

---

[1] *Re Fairmount Tours (Yorkshire) Ltd* (1989) 6 Insolvency Lawyer and Practice 184.
[2] [1982] Ch. 204, CA.
[3] [1895] 1 Ch. 674, CA.
[4] [1956] R.P.C. 282; on appeal [1957] R.P.C. 388, CA; affirmed [1959] R.P.C. 1, HL.
[5] (1863) 1 De G.J. and Sm. 678.
[6] *Re Maidstone Buildings Provisions Ltd* [1971] 1 W.L.R. 1085.
[7] *Re Sarflax Ltd* [1979] Ch. 592.

general, a proper inference that the company is carrying on business with intent to defraud.[8] The words "defraud" and "fraudulent purpose" are words which connote actual dishonesty involving, according to current notions of fair reading among commercial men, real moral blame.[9] Provided there is dishonesty, even a single transaction designed to cheat an individual creditor of the company will be sufficient to establish fraudulent trading.[10]

Criminal acts

Obviously, losses arising from criminal proceedings are excluded by this exception, e.g. for a failure to comply with building regulations by the director's company,[11] or market manipulation contrary to section 47 of the Financial Services Act 1986. An extension may, however, be obtained to cover legal defence costs incurred with the insurers' prior written consent, relating to investigations preparatory to criminal proceedings.   **8–56**

Obtaining any profit or advantage by breach of fiduciary duty

Liability of directors and officers relating to their obtaining of a bene-   **8–57** fit or profit will be expressly excluded from the cover provided by the insurance policy. This effectively excludes all claims for breach of fiduciary duty that might be brought against directors or officers by their company. A company has no physical existence, and its money and property are entrusted to the directors to manage and exercise the powers granted over their use by the Memorandum and Articles of Association. As a consequence, directors are in position of trust on equitable principles[12]:

> "Directors are clearly not trustees identical with trustees of a will or a marriage settlement. In particular, so far as at present relevant, they have business to conduct and business functions to perform in a business manner, which are not normally at any rate associated with trustees of a will or marriage settlement. All their duties, powers and functions qua directors are fiduciary for and on behalf of the company."

So property in their hands, or under their control, is theirs for the   **8–58** company, i.e. for the company's purposes in accordance with their duties, powers and functions may differ from the purposes of a strict settlement and the duties, powers and functions may differ from the purposes of a strict settlement and the duties, powers and functions of its trustees, the directors and such trustees have this indisputably in common — that the property in their hands or under their control must be applied for the specified purposes of the company or the settlement; and to apply it otherwise is to misapply it in breach of the obligation to apply it to those

---

[8] *Re William C. Leitch Bros. Ltd* [1932] 2 Ch. 71.
[9] *Re Patrick & Lyon Ltd* [1933] Ch. 786 at 790, *per* Maugham J.; see also *Re Gerald Cooper Chemicals Ltd.* [1978] Ch. 262.
[10] *R. v. Lockwood* [1986] Crim. Law Rev. 286, CA.
[11] *The Times*, April 18, 1984.
[12] *Selangor United Rubber Estates Ltd v. Cradock (a bankrupt) (No.3)* [1968] 1 W.L.R. 1555 at 1575.

purposes for the company or the settlement beneficiaries. So, even though the scope and operation of such obligation differs in the case of directors and strict settlement trustees, the nature of the obligation with regard to property in their hands or under their control is identical, namely, to apply it to specified purposes for others beneficially. This is to hold it on trust for the company or the settlement beneficiaries as the case may be. That is what holding on trust means.

8–59   The main aspect of this fiduciary duty is that the directors, and indeed company officers,[13] must not allow their personal interest to override their duty to act in the interests of the company[14] and to act *intra vires* the powers conferred on them.[15] Another aspect of the duty is that the director or other officer must not make any secret profit from his position — if he does, the company may seek an order that he account to them for that secret profit and such claims may well be excluded from the scope of a directors' and officers' liability policy, see below. Such an instance occurred in *Boston Deep Sea Fishing & Ice Co. v. Ansell*[16] where the promoter of the claimant company had agreed with the defendant that he should be employed as managing director of the intended company for five years at a yearly salary. By the Articles of Association it was provided that the defendant should be managing director for five years at the yearly salary mentioned in the agreement, payable quarterly. Afterwards the company contracted for the construction of certain fishing-smacks, and unknown to the company, took a commission from the shipbuilders on the contract. Several months afterwards the claimant company passed a resolution at an extraordinary meeting dismissing the defendant from his office on the ground of other alleged acts of misconduct, which they were unable to substantiate in these proceedings. At the time of dismissal, the claimants were unaware of the defendant's receipt of the commission from the shipbuilders.

8–60   The defendant was also a shareholder in two other companies — an ice company and a fish-carrying company, and both paid bonuses to shareholders who employed them to supply ice or carry fish. The defendant employed these companies in respect of the claimant company's business and received bonuses in this respect. The Court of Appeal ordered the defendant to account to the claimants for these secret profits. Speaking first about those bonuses, Cotton L.J. said[17]:

> "The question is not whether the company could directly have claimed this sum, but whether, when their agent has received this profit in respect of a contract which he had entered into on behalf of the company as their agent for goods supplied to the company, the company are not entitled as against their agent to claim that money. In my opinion they are. It is a profit arising from a contract which he, on the part of the company, entered into in

---

[13] *Re Morvah Consols Tin Mining Co, McKay's Case* (1875) 2 Ch. D. 1, CA.
[14] *Piercy v. S. Mills & Co. Ltd.* [1920] 1 Ch. 77.
[15] *Re Sharpe, Re Bennett, Masonic & General Life Assurance Co. v. Sharpe* [1892] 1 Ch. 154, CA.
[16] (1888) 39 Ch. D. 339, CA.
[17] *ibid.* at 355.

consequence of the supply to the company by his order of a particular quantity of ice. It was said that he was entitled under the articles to enter into contracts and business with the company. He was so, but that, in my opinion, did not justify him, when contracting on behalf of the company, to put into his own pocket a profit obtained simply and entirely in consequence of the goods being supplied under that order to the Plaintiff company . . . In my opinion, the Plaintiffs are entitled to that which they ask, and if they are not satisfied with the statement of the amount, on account as to the sums so received by him as bonuses from the Ice Company . . ."

Cotton L.J. then dealt with the commission from the shipbuilding company and stated a broader principle[18]:   **8–61**

"If a servant, or a managing director, or any person who is authorized to act, and is acting, for another in the matter of any contract, receives, as regards the contract, any sum, whether by way of percentage or otherwise, from the person with whom he is dealing on behalf of his principal, he is committing a breach of duty . . . Where an agent entering into a contract on behalf of his principal, and without the knowledge or asset of that principal, receives money from the person with whom he is dealing, he is doing a wrongful act, he is misconducting himself as regards his agency."

In *Regal (Hastings) Ltd v. Gulliver*,[19] a high point was perhaps reached where, to assist their company to buy out other rival companies in the area, the directors formed a new company to buy those other companies. After the rival companies had been bought the directors sold their shares in the new, acquiring company at £2.80 per share, having subscribed for them originally at £1 per share. The claimant company then sued them for the profit they had made, and the House of Lords upheld that claim[20]:   **8–62**

"The directors standing in a fiduciary relationship to [the claimant company] in regard to the exercise of their powers as directors and having obtained these shares by reason and only by reason of the fact that they were directors . . . are accountable for the profits which they have made out of them."

The lack of *mala fides* (bad faith) was emphasised as being irrelevant[21]:   **8–63**

"The rule of equity which insists on those, who by use of a fiduciary position make a profit, being able to account for that profit, in no way depends upon fraud or absence of bona fide, or upon such questions . . . as whether the profit would or should otherwise have gone to the plaintiff, or whether the profiteer was under a duty to obtain the source of the profit for the plaintiff, or whether he took a risk, or acted as he did for the benefit of the plaintiff, or whether the plaintiff has in fact been damaged or benefited by his action. The liability arises from the mere fact of the profit having been made . . . The profiteer, however honest and well intentioned, cannot escape the risk of being called to account."

---

[18] *ibid.* at 357.
[19] [1942] 2 A.C. 134n; [1942] 1 All E.R. 378, HL; see also *Boardman v. Phipps* [1967] 2 A.C. 46, HL.
[20] *ibid.* at 389, *per* Lord Russell.
[21] *ibid.* at 386, *per* Lord Russell.

8–64   Another example of the penalising of the lack of probity by directors occurred in *Industrial Development Consultants Ltd v. Cooley*.[22] Here, the defendant, who was a qualified architect of some distinction, was employed as managing director of the claimant company, which provided a construction consultancy service for gas boards. One regional gas board was offering a lucrative contract, and the defendant acted on behalf of the claimants in the negotiations. These proved unsuccessful largely on the basis that the gas board did not wish to appoint a consultancy company, but made it clear to the defendant that they would be willing to appoint him personally. The defendant therefore feigned ill health and the claimants allowed him to terminate his employment. On learning of the defendant's personal appointment, the plaintiffs brought an action for the recovery of the profit the defendant had made on his appointment. Roskill J. (as he then was) gave judgment to the claimants, essentially because the defendant would otherwise make a large profit from his having allowed his personal interests to override his fiduciary duty to his company. It thus did not matter that the claimants themselves had had little chance of obtaining the benefit of that contract themselves, otherwise the defendant would gain the benefit of a windfall, which could not be right.

8–65   *Regal (Hastings) Ltd v. Gulliver*[23] was applied recently in *Gencor A.C.P. Ltd v. Dalby*[24] where a director was found in breach of their fiduciary duties in dishonestly diverting company monies to himself or his Virgin Islands company, abetted by the company secretary, who was also sued. Rimer J. emphasised that it is no answer for the director or officer to his strict liability to account to the company for benefits or gains, that the company could not or would not have taken up the business opportunity that the director or officer took up fort his own benefit. Nor is it an answer that the director's own skill or property were also used in the course of making the profit. The only escape from potential accountability is the obtaining of prior approval of the company's shareholder's after full disclosure of all facts and circumstances.[25]

Claims for personal injury or material damage

8–66   The policy will exclude from its scope claims made for personal injuries or material damage to property. These risks should be covered by appropriate employers' liability insurance,[26] public liability insurance,[27] and, perhaps, product liability insurance.[28] Thus, the action in *Yuille v. B. and B. Fisheries (Leigh) Ltd and Bates, The Radiant*[29] discussed above, would be outside the scope of a directors' and officers' liability policy, as being for personal injuries, and so would the proceedings in *Fairline Shipping*

---

[22] [1972] 1 W.L.R. 443.
[23] [1942] 2 A.C. 134n.
[24] [2000] 2 B.C.L.C. 734.
[25] *ibid.*, at 741, para.17.
[26] See Chapter 5, above.
[27] See Chapter 6, above.
[28] See Chapter 7, above.
[29] [1958] 2 Lloyd's Rep. 596.

Corp. v. Adamson,[30] as being in respect of material damage to property, in that case, bailed goods.

National insurance and similar debts

Whilst the personal liability of directors under section 64 of the Social Security Act 1998 to pay National Insurance Contributions debts are often excluded, this exclusion may be deleted in many cases on request. **8–67**

Professional negligence

Any claim which arises from the breach of a professional duty to a client or customer of the company, or other third party who relies on the director's or officer's advice, design, specification or other professional services, will generally be excluded. These risks should be covered by appropriate professional negligence insurance policies. **8–68**

Liability under personal guarantees or warranties

Liability assumed by any director or officer by a guarantee, *e.g.* in respect of the company's overdraft, or contractual warranty (other than claims for breach of warranty of authority), *e.g.* on sale of shares, is excluded expressly from the scope of the policy. This risk needs to be insured under a suitable warranty and indemnity insurance.[31] **8–69**

Pollution

Any liability relating to pollution of any kind will be excluded, although some policies will provide legal costs cover, up to a specified limit, for the defence of criminal or regulatory proceedings relating to a pollution occurrence, or civil proceedings for alleged loss in share value, provided those proceedings arise from an alleged act otherwise covered by the policy. **8–70**

Losses covered by previous policies or undisclosed claims

Both to avoid any question of double insurance arising, and to provide protection against non-disclosure (short of rescission of the policy), policies will usually expressly exclude all claims which were or should have been notified under previous policies, and all liability relating to circumstances which the insured director or officer knew, at inception of the policy, might reasonably be expected to produce a claim.[32] **8–71**

Fines and penalties

The policy will expressly exclude any fines and penalties imposed on directors and officers in criminal and other proceedings. Such an indemnity would probably be contrary to public policy and thus unenforceable by the insured directors or officers themselves in any event.[33] **8–72**

[30] [1975] Q.B. 180.
[31] See Chapter 9, below.
[32] This will be a question of fact; see the professional indemnity insurance case of *Hamptons Residential Ltd v. Field* [1997] 1 Lloyd's Rep. 302.
[33] See Chapter 1, above.

WARRANTY AND INDEMNITY INSURANCE

1. INTRODUCTION

9–01   Purchasers of company shares have remedies against the company's directors in many respects. An action may lie against the directors as regards mispresentations regarding the company's profitability,[1] or other representations intended to attract investors[2] (although not in respect of a false report to the Stock Exchange upon which a share quote is obtained[3]). Retired directors, though, are not liable in respect of reports prepared subsequent to their retirement, even if the retired director knows his name appears on the report.[4] Such actions may be founded in common law, for instance, in deceit[5] or fraud,[6] or for negligent mis-statement.[7]

9–02   The Companies Act 1985[8] provides another avenue of liability through which directors and other persons[9] who are associated with the issue of a prospectus or any other document[10] by which the offer of shares or debentures to the public is made, may find themselves liable.[11] Subscribers of shares or debentures who suffer loss or damage by reason of any "untrue" statement included in the document upon which they have relied have a right to compensation, and a statement is "untrue" if it is misleading in the form and context in which it is included.[12]

9–03   This statutory remedy often has the advantage to the aggrieved purchaser in that the directors, etc., are liable once the statement is shown to be misleading, unless the directors, etc., prove that they are entitled to one of the statutory defences[13]:

> (i) that, having consented to become a director of the company, he withdrew his consent before the issue of the prospectus, and that it was issued without his authority or consent; or

---

[1] *Briess v. Woolley* [1954] A.C. 333, HL.

[2] *Scott v. Dixon* (1859) 29 L.J. Ex. 62n.

[3] *Peek v. Gumey* (1873) L.R. 6 H.L. 377 at 397, *per* Lord Chelmsford.

[4] *Re National Bank of Wales* [1901] 2 Ch. 629, CA.; affirmed *sub. nom. Dovey v. Cory* [1901] A.C. 477, HL.

[5] *Walsham v. Stainton* (1863) 1 De G.J. & Sm. 678.

[6] *Andrews v. Mockford* [1896] 1 Q.B. 372, C.; *Peek v. Gumey* (1873) L.R. 6 H.L. 377, HL; *Cullen v. Thomson's Trustees & Kerr* (1862) 4 Macq. 424, H.; *Barry v. Croskey* (1861) 2 John and H. 1; *Stainbank v. Fernley* (1839) 9 Sim. 556; *Levy v. Langridge* (1838) 4 M. and W. 337.

[7] *Esso Petroleum Co. Ltd v. Mardon* [1975] Q.B. 819; on appeal [1976] Q.B. 801, CA; see also Misrepresentation Act 1967, s.2(1).

[8] Companies Act 1985, s.67.

[9] Including any report or memorandum issued with it, *ibid.*, s.71(b).

[10] *ibid.*, ss.67(2) and (3), and 744.

[11] *ibid.*, s.58(1).

[12] *ibid.* s.71(a).

[13] *ibid.*, s 68(1) and (2).

(ii) that the prospectus was issued without his knowledge or consent, and that on becoming aware of its issue he forthwith gave reasonable public notice that it was issued without his knowledge or consent; or

(iii) that, after issue of the prospectus and before allotment under it he, on becoming aware of any untrue statement in it, withdrew his consent to its issue and gave reasonable public notice of the withdrawal and of the reason for it; or

(iv) as regards every untrue statement not purporting to be made on the authority of an expert[14] or of a public official document or statement:

(a) he had reasonable ground to believe, and did up to the time of the allotment of the shares or debentures (as the case may be) believe, that the statement was true; and

(b) as regards every untrue statement purporting to be a statement by an expert or contained in what purports to be a copy of or extract from a report or valuation, of an expert, it fairly represented the statement, or was a correct and fair copy, of or extract from the report or valuation, and he had reasonable ground to believe and did up to the time of issue of the prospectus believe that the person making the statement was competent to make it and that person had given the required[15] consent to the issue of the prospectus and had not withdrawn that consent before delivery of a copy of the prospectus for registration or, to the defendant's knowledge, before allotment under it; and

(c) as regards every untrue statement purporting to be made by an official person or contained in what purports to be a copy of or extract from a public official document, it was a correct and fair representation of the statement or copy of or extract from the document.

Notwithstanding these remedies, it is now the prevailing practice for those who take over or merge with a company, be it another company, or individuals), to extract warranties and indemnities from the vendors in relation to many matters under a sale agreement, and it is these contractual warranties and indemnities that are the subject matter of "Warranty and indemnity insurance". **9–04**

2. RISKS INSURED

The provision of warranty and indemnity insurance is a very specified field and only a few insurers will offer cover. Certainly, the insurer will wish to see a copy of the latest draft sale agreement containing the warranties and **9–05**

[14] See for meaning the Companies Act 1985, s. 62.
[15] *ibid.*, s.61.

indemnities, a copy of the disclosure letter, and a copy of the accounts used as the basis of the negotiations for the sale of the company, prior to agreeing to insure, and if so, at what premium, for these are of the substance of the insurance indemnity and are thus "material" in insurance law terms.[16] It must also be emphasised that particular policies may be modelled to suit the individual circumstances of each proposed sale put to the insurers, and, therefore, the policy wording may vary in the primary insuring clause especially.

9–06   Generally, the insurance policy issued will recite that the named insured have sold the whole (or otherwise) of the shares formerly held by them in the company trading (or, formerly trading, as the case may be) as (whatever), and the insured will be and the sale agreement/covenant will be identified in the schedule to the policy. The primary insuring clause may read:

> "The insurers hereby agree to indemnify the Insured in respect of their liabilities assumed under the terms of the Agreement/Covenant specified in the schedule hereto for damages compensation and claimants' costs and expenses arising from claims made during the Period of Insurance for breach of warranties or indemnity provisions contained in the Agreement/ Covenant by any one or more of the Insured."

9–07   In particular instances, the insurance may be extended to include claims for misrepresentations contained in other documents, *e.g.* in the absence of any directors' and officers' liability insurance[17] being applicable to indemnify the directors or other officers responsible for the issue of a prospectus, etc., for the sale of shares or debentures in the company. It is common for there to be a significant excess in respect of any claims, which will be measured in many thousands of pounds.

Profits warranty or indemnity

9–08   The wording adopted in this clause regarding the underlying basis of the agreement to purchase the company will, of course, vary depending upon the nature of the company sold, *e.g.* whether it is a trading or manufacturing company, or a holding company, and whether the indemnity is suitable, which will depend upon whether the purchase price was agreed on the basis of a multiple of the net profits earned by the company, as disclosed in the accounts proffered to the purchasers. With that rider, the following is a possible form of profit warranty or indemnity clause contained in the sale agreement. References to the vendors are to the selling shareholders who are contracting the sale of their shares as identified further in the sale agreement and are a party to it, and are expressly bound jointly and severally.[18] For example:

> "(1) In circumstances where the net profit of the Company for the next accounting year ending on   shall be less than £   , the Vendors

---

[16] And may well be made the "basis of the contract", see further Chapter 2 for the effect of this provision.

[17] See Chapter 8, above.

[18] For right to contribution, see the Civil Liability (Contribution) Act 1978.

shall, within (28) days of the issue of the hereunder provided joint certificate by Messrs   (named firms of accountants), pay to the Purchaser an amount representing (3) times the shortfall, and if a loss is so certified the Vendors shall, within (56) days, pay the Purchaser an amount representing (3) times the net profit earned in the accounting year ended.   (the accounting year disclosed and relied on in the sale agreement).

(2) The net profit or loss of the Company shall be jointly certified by Messrs   (named firms of accountants) whose certificate shall be deemed to act as experts and not as arbitrators[19] and any dispute or difference or question which may arise between them in connection with the said certification shall be referred to the decision of a single chartered accountant or firm of chartered accountants to be agreed upon between them or, in default of such agreement within a period of (10) days, to be selected at the instance of either firm by the President for the time being of the Institute of Chartered Accountants in England and Wales, who shall act as expert in connection with the giving of such decision which shall be binding.

(3) All costs and expenses incurred in relation to the certification of the net profit or loss of the Company by the said accountants shall be payable by the Purchaser in the event of there being no shortfall or net loss, in all other instances the said costs and expenses shall be borne by the Vendors and payable at the same time as any other sum hereunder is due to be paid to the Purchaser."

Other warranties

The vendors will also in the sale agreement expressly warrant to the **9–09** purchaser that many matters are as represented to the purchaser, and be required to place on deposit at a named bank to cover their liability for breach of any of the warranties. The liability for breach of the warranties may be expressly limited to a specified period, after which such remaining deposit moneys are returnable to the vendors. The "disclosure letter" will qualify these warranties, and be appended to the sale agreement. This disclosure letter will generally provide:

(i) a copy of the company's Memorandum and Articles of Association;

(ii) particulars of industrial property (*i.e.* patents, trade marks, registered designs, applications for any of the foregoing, trade or business names, and copyright);

(iii) a schedule of employees showing all remuneration payable and other benefits provided or which the company is bound to provide, including all profit-sharing, incentive and bonus schemes;

(iv) particulars of any pension scheme operated by the company;[20]

(v) a list of guarantees and other contingent liabilities entered into by the vendors to assist the company and from which the purchaser will undertake to use his best endeavours to secure the release of the vendors.

---

[19] See *Baber v. Kenwood Manufacturing Co. Ltd & Whinney Murray & Co.* [1978] 1 Lloyd's Rep. 175, CA.
[20] As defined by the Income and Corporation Taxes Act 1988, s. 612(1).

9–10   The general warranties relate to identification and specification of:

   (i) *Share capital*: the authorised share capital issued and unissued, both ordinary and preference, and the amount held by each of the vendors free from all liens, charges and encumbrances or interests in favour of any other person (or as specified);

  (ii) *Company resolutions*: any special resolutions of the company or any class of its members, made otherwise than at annual general meetings;

 (iii) *Options*: any future, existing, or contingent rights of persons to call for the issue of any share or loan capital of the company;

  (iv) *Returns:* that the company and its directors have complied with the provisions of the Companies Act 1985 and all returns, particulars, resolutions and other documents required to be delivered on behalf of the company to the Registrar of Companies or other authority;

   (v) *Accounts*: that the accounts have been prepared in accordance with the requirements of all relevant statutes and generally accepted accountancy principles and are true and accurate in all material respects and show a true and fair view of the assets and liabilities of the company as at the specified balance sheet date and the profits of the company for the year ended as specified;

  (vi) *Provision or liabilities*: that full provision has been made in the accounts for all liabilities and capital commitments of the company outstanding at the balance sheet date, whether contingent, quantified or disputed;

 (vii) *Stock valuation and accounting policies*: that for the purposes of the company's accounts the stock in trade and work in progress, as appropriate, have been valued on a basis consistent with the company's audited accounts for the preceding three years;

(viii) *Books*: that all proper and necessary books of account, minute books, registers and records have been maintained by and are in possession of the company;

  (ix) *Subsequent business*: that the company has carried on its business in its usual and ordinary course since the balance sheet date;

   (x) *Financial provision*: that there has been no adverse change to the company's position or future prospects since the balance sheet date to the vendors' best knowledge or belief;

  (xi) *Title to assets*: that the company has good title to all assets included in the accounts subject to (if applicable) named charges, liens or encumbrances;

 (xii) *Distributions*: that no distribution of capital or income has been declared since the balance sheet date;

(xiii) *Stock condition*: that the company's stock in trade is in good condition and can be sold for its usual price;

(xiv) *Debts*: that bad debt provision in the accounts is adequate and that no debts stated in the balance sheet have been released;

(xv) *Industrial property*: that the company is the sole beneficial owner of the industrial property rights stated in the disclosure letter;

(xvi) *Litigation*: that the company is not engaged in any litigation or arbitration proceedings except as notified to the Purchaser:

(xvii) *Insurances*: that the company's insurances are in the usual form and protect in full the assets of the company;

(xviii) *Contracts*: that the company is party only to the specified contracts, *e.g.* hire and rental agreements, joint venture agreements, or other special contracts outside the normal course of the company's business.

Tax warranties

Specific wordings will, of course, have to be formulated in each instance, **9–11** but the warranties covering the following areas may be included in the agreement for sale:-

(i) *Tax liability provision*: that the accounts contain full provision or reserve for all the company's tax liability in respect of income, profits or gains earned, accrued or received, and deferred taxation;

(ii) *Returns*: that the company has duly and punctually made all returns and provided all information required by the taxation authorities and specifying any present or likely dispute thereon;

(iii) *Payment*: that the company has punctually paid all taxes to which it has become liable to pay;

(iv) *PAYE*: that the company has correctly and properly operated the Pay As You Earn system and accounted to the Inland Revenue for the tax so deducted, including *ex-gratia* payments and compensation for loss of office,[21] benefits in kind[22] and vouchers[23];

(v) *Other deductions*: that the company has deducted and accounted to the Inland Revenue all amounts in respect of payments to non-residents to purchase United Kingdom patent rights[24]; payment of rent to non-residents[25]; annual interest[26]; any payments to sub-contractors in the construction industry[27] and agency workers[28];

(vi) *Close companies*: that clearance of the take-over has been obtained against an apportionment being made of its income for any year of the takeover (note, trading income is now exempt from shortfall apportionment)[29];

(vii) *Expenses*: that the company has not incurred any expense in connection with the provision of any benefit for a participator or

---

[21] Income and Corporation Taxes Act 1988, s.148.
[22] *ibid.*, ss.154–168.
[23] *ibid.*, ss.141–144.
[24] *ibid.*, s. 524.
[25] *ibid.*, s.43.
[26] *ibid.*, ss.349 and 350.
[27] *ibid.*, ss. 559–567.
[28] *ibid.*, s. 134.
[29] *ibid.*, s. 423.

his associate[30] or made a loan[31] to a director or his associate which may fall to be treated as a distribution;

(viii) *Transfer consent*: that the company has not without the prior consent of the Treasury entered into any agreement for the transfer of its trade or business to a non-resident;[32]

(ix) *Groups*: that the Disclosure Letter contains full particulars of all elections made by the company relating to group income[33] and that all such elections are in force and the company has not paid any dividend without advance corporation tax or appropriate deduction of income tax;

(x) *Disclosure Letter*: that the Disclosure Letter contains full particulars of all arrangements and agreements relating to group relief[34] to which the company is or has been a party and are all valid;

(xi) *Capital*: that any capital asset acquired by the company from another company in the same group is given at a base cost not lower than the figure at which they stand in the balance sheet;[35]

(xii) *Liability*: that no liability to corporation tax will arise as a result of the company being taken over on chargeable gains to other companies in the same group;[36]

(xiii) *Surrender of ACT*: that the Disclosure Letter contains full particulars of all arrangements and agreements to which the company is or has been a party relating to the surrender of advance corporation tax made or received by the company;[37]

(xiv) *Depreciatory transactions*: that the company will not be eliminated from claiming an allowable loss on the disposal of shares in another company[38] or on any expenditure on any share or security;[39]

(xv) *Roll-over relief*: that the company has made no claim for rolling over a capital gain[40] in connection with the replacement of business assets;

(xvi) *Tax losses and ACT carry forward*: that there has been no major change in the business of the company so that the company is precluded from carrying forward trading losses[41] or surplus advance corporation tax[42] beyond the change in ownership;

(xvii) *Straightline growth*: that no asset owned by the company is subject to a deemed disposal and reacquisition by the company.[43]

---

[30] *ibid.*, s. 418.
[31] *ibid.*, ss. 419–422.
[32] *ibid.*, ss.765–769.
[33] *ibid.*, s. 247.
[34] *ibid.*, ss. 402–413.
[35] Taxation of Chargeable Gains Act 1992, ss.171 and 176.
[36] Income and Corporation Taxes Act 1988, s.347.
[37] *ibid.*, s.240.
[38] Taxation of Chargeable Gains Act 1992, ss.176 and 177.
[39] *ibid.*, s.125.
[40] *ibid.*, ss.152 and 153.
[41] Income and Corporation Taxes Act 1988, s. 768.
[42] *ibid.*, s.245.
[43] Taxation of Chargeable Gains Act 1992, Sched. 2.

3. THE INDEMNITY

Costs and expenses

The policy will provide an indemnity to the insured in respect of costs   **9–12**
and expenses incurred arising from claims made upon the insured to
breach of the warranties and indemnities given in the specified sale agreement or other contract. Such costs and expenses indemnified will be
included in the limit of indemnity of the policy, and only those costs and
expenses incurred "with the consent of the insurer" will be recoverable.
This means that at every important stage of the proceedings involving
costs, the application for the consent of the underwriters should be made
by the insured, and express consent must be given, or implied consent by,
e.g. conduct, or the necessity for seeking consent has been waived.[44]

4. EXCLUSIONS FROM COVER

Fraud and dishonesty

Claims arising through the fraud or dishonesty of the insured are   **9–13**
excluded. Unless the policy states that the policy is not to operate as a policy
issued to the persons named as the insured as a group, a claim for fraud or
dishonesty against one insured will debar any of the insured from recovering
an indemnity under the policy. An express provision is required that the
policy is, for the purposes of this exception, to apply as if a separate policy
had been issued to each director or other share vendor referred to in the
schedule to the policy.

Promissory warranties

The policy is likely to exclude claims made by the purchaser of the com-   **9–14**
pany arising from any breach of undertakings entered into by the insured
or any one or more of them, relating to their future conduct. The purpose
of this exception is to exclude claims for breach, for example, of restrictive
covenants relating to the selling directors not being employed by other
companies involved in the same business or trade as the company that has
been sold, perhaps, for a specified period of time or limited location.

5. POLICY CONDITIONS

Observance of conditions

The policy will invariably state that the insured's compliance with   **9–15**
and observance of the policy conditions is a condition precedent to the
liability of the insurer under the policy, and this will be strictly applied by
the courts.[45]

---

[44] *E. Hulton & Co. Ltd v. Mountain* (1921) 8 Ll. L. Rep. 249 at 250, *per* Bankes L.J., *obiter*,
CA.
[45] See Chapter 2 above.

Notification

9–16   As discussed in Chapter 18, below, the insured will usually be required to give written notice to the insurer as soon as possible[46] (or "immediately",[47] or "forthwith"[48]) after receiving information of any claim or loss or any occurrence for which there may be liability under the policy with full particulars thereof. Further, every letter, claim, writ, summons and process relating to the claim shall be forwarded to the company on receipt.

Non-admission of liability and control of proceedings

9–17   As discussed in Chapter 18, below, the insured must make no admission, offer, promise, payment or indemnity to the claimant either by himself or his agent without the written consent of the insurer, who shall have the right to take over and conduct in the name of the insured the defence or settlement of any claim, and have full discretion upon defence or settlement of any claim or proceedings.

Assistance to insurer

9–18   The insured will be required to either do or permit to be done at the expense of the insurer, all such acts and things as may be reasonably required[49] by the insurer for the purpose of defending the claim or of enforcing any right, remedies, reliefs or indemnities from other parties.

---

[46] See *Verelst's Administratrix v. Motor Union Insurance Co. Ltd* [1925] 2 K.B. 137; *Farrell v. Federated Employers Insurance Association Ltd* [1970] 1 W.L.R. 1400, CA.

[47] *i.e.* with all reasonable speed considering the circumstances of the case, *Farrell v. Federated Employers Insurance Association Ltd* [1970] 1 W.L.R. 1400, CA. *Re Coleman's Depositories Ltd & the Life & Health Assurance Association* [1907] 2 K.B. 798 at 807, *per* Fletcher-Moulton L.J., CA.

[48] See *Berliner Motor Corp. & Steiners Lawn & Sports Inc. v. Sun Alliance & London Insurance Ltd* [1983] 1 Lloyd's Rep. 320 at 325, *per* Bingham J. (as he then was).

[49] *ibid.*

CHAPTER 10

COMMERCIAL VEHICLES INSURANCE

1. INTRODUCTION

Commercial vehicle insurances are not issued in the same form and scope **10–01** as comprehensive private car insurances. For instance, personal benefits relating to injury sustained personally by the person insured are not generally included, nor an indemnity in respect of loss or damage to personal effects, rugs and clothing from the insured vehicle. There is also no "driving other vehicles" extension generally granted in respect of commercial vehicles as most businesses operate a sufficient fleet of their own to cope with their needs, and each of those vehicles will be covered, no doubt, by the issued insurance. In common with private vehicle insurance, if the insured parts with the property in and possession of an insured vehicle, he is obviously no longer insured to use that vehicle unless there is an extension to cover the use of vehicles not belonging to him. Even this, however, is of no assistance if the insured has disposed of his sole insured vehicle, for his policy will immediately lapse on the disposal until such time as his insurers agree to insure any replacement vehicle.[1] Small businesses with only one insured vehicle should take particular note of this. Whilst a motor policy has been held to lapse on the death of the insured, e.g. a sole proprietor, in respect of the deceased's vehicle if it is not sold,[2] there need not necessarily be a lapsing of policy whilst an insured awaits a replacement vehicle after disposing of the insured vehicle.[3] As regards partnerships, it has been suggested that on a new partnership being formed, for damage to the insured's property, insurers will have a good defence to the policy, but not in respect of third party liability claims.[4] This Chapter deals first with the regime of compulsory motor insurance, and then with various aspects of the extent of cover afforded under commercial vehicle insurances.

2. COMPULSORY MOTOR VEHICLE INSURANCE

The statutory scheme

All persons[5] using, or causing or permitting any other person to use, a **10–02** motor vehicle on a road are required by law to have in force in relation to the use of that vehicle by himself or that other person, as the case may be,

---

[1] *Rogerson v. Scottish Automobile & General Insurance Co. Ltd* (1931) 41 Ll. L. Rep. 1, HL; *Tattersall v. Drysdale* [1935] 2 K.B. 174.
[2] *Kelly v. Cornhill Insurance Co. Ltd* [1964] 1 All E.R. 321, HL.
[3] *Dodson v. Peter H. Dodson Insurance Services, The Times*, January 24, 2001, CA.
[4] See *Jenkins v. Deane* (1933) 47 Ll. L. Rep. 342.
[5] Except those persons and bodies specified in the Road Traffic Act 1988, s.143, *e.g.* county councils, police authorities, tramcars operated under statutory powers.

a policy of insurance[6] (or a security[7]) in respect of third-party risks. From April 3, 2000, the obligation has been extended[8] to also cover use in a "public place", which is not defined, in order to comply with the E.C.'s Motor Insurance Directives. A body called the Motor Insurers Bureau ("M.I.B."), funded by the authorised insurers dealing in motor insurance in Great Britain, provides a "safety net" for satisfying judgments against either uninsured or untraced drivers. The terms of these two Agreements are set out in the Appendix. It should be noted that there are various pre-conditions to the M.I.B.'s liability, and they must be complied with. For instance, the requirement that notice must be given by the third party claimant to the M.I.B. within seven days of the commencement of proceedings, is not met by merely sending letters to the M.I.B. setting out his claim for damages and that legal aid had been granted to obtain a medical report.[9]

Motor vehicle

10–03   A "motor vehicle" means any mechanically propelled vehicle intended or adapted for use on roads.[10] The propulsion may be petrol-driven, oil-driven, steam-driven[11] or battery-driven,[12] and provided there is a reasonable prospect of the vehicle being made mobile again in the event of a breakdown, the vehicle remains a motor vehicle requiring insurance.[13] A diesel dumper suitable for being driven on a road in transit, or to carry material from one site to another, will require insurance[14]; but occasional, as against general, use of a dumper not otherwise suitable for road use, does not seem to require insurance cover.[15] An Euclid earth scraper, capable of travelling at 45 mph has been held as being intended for use on roads.[16]

Road

10–04   In terms of definitions, a "road" means any highway and any other road to which the public has access, including bridges over which a road passes.[17] Private roads[18] and forecourts[19] may fall within the term "road" under the test of public access, that being a matter of fact and degree,[20]

---

[6] See the Road Traffic Act 1988, s.145 for requirements in respect of policies of insurance.
[7] ibid., ss.144, 146 and 155. The minimum security is £500,000; see the Road Traffic Act 1991, s. 20.
[8] The Motor Vehicles (Compulsory Insurance) Regulations 2000 (S.I. 2000 No. 726).
[9] Stinton v. Stinton [1995] R.T.R. 167, CA.
[10] Road Traffic Act 1988, s.185(1). See also ss.186–188 and exemptions in ss.189 and 193; a Ford Transit Van has been held to be embraced by a policy covering the insured whilst driving any "motor car", Laurence v. Davies [1972] 2 Lloyd's Rep. 231.
[11] Waters v. Eddison Steam Rolling Co. Ltd [1914] 3 K.B. 818.
[12] Elieson v. Parker (1917) 81 J.P. 265.
[13] Binks v. Department of the Environment [1975] R.T.R. 318.
[14] See Daley v. Hargreaves [1961] 1 W.L.R. 487.
[15] Chalgray Ltd v. Aspley (1965) 109 Sol. Jo. 394.
[16] Childs v. Coghlan (1968) 112 Sol. Jo. 175.
[17] Road Traffic Act 1988, s.192(1).
[18] Adams v. Metropolitan Police Commissioners [1980] R.T.R. 289.
[19] Bugge v. Taylor [1941] 1 K.B. 198; Thomas v. Dando [1951] 2 K.B. 620.
[20] R. v. Shaw [1974] R.T.R. 225, CA.

gauging whether the general public has access to the road in question, and not merely a special class of the general public, and whether that access is at least by the tolerance of the owner or proprietor of the road in question.[21] The car parks in the combined appeals heard in *Clarke v. General Accident Fire and Life Assurance Corp. plc*[22] which were held not to be roads, because they were a destination in their own right rather than being a route to a destination, will now be covered by the new term of "public place".

Risks insured by compulsory motor insurance

The policy of insurance must[23]:   **10–05**

(i) insure such person, persons or classes of persons as may be specified in the policy in respect of any liability which may be incurred by him or them in respect of the death of or bodily injury to any person or damage to property caused by, or arising out of, the use of the vehicle on a road or other public place in Great Britain; and

(ii) in the case of a vehicle normally based in the territory of another member State, insure him or them in respect of any civil liability which may be incurred by him as a result of an event related to the use of the vehicle in Great Britain if according to the law of that home territory there would be a higher level of cover;

(iii) must, in the case of a vehicle normally based in Great Britain, insure him or them in respect of any liability which may be incurred by him or them in respect of the use of the vehicle and of any trailer, whether or not coupled, in the territory other than Great Britain and Gibraltar of each of the member States of the Communities according to the law on compulsory insurance against civil liability in respect of the use of vehicles of the State where the liability may be incurred, or to a higher level of cover if the insurance in Great Britain would be greater; and

(iv) must also insure him or them in respect of any liability which may be incurred by him or them under the provisions of this Part of the Act relating to the payment for emergency treatment.[24]

Risks not covered by compulsory motor insurance

There is no compulsory requirement for the vehicle insurance to cover[25]:   **10–06**

(i) liability in respect of the death, arising out of and in the course of his employment, of a person in the employment of a person insured by the policy or of bodily injury sustained by such a person arising out of and in the course of his employment[26] (this

[21] *Deacon v. A.T. (a minor)* [1976] R.T.R. 244.
[22] [1998] 1 W.L.R. 1647, HL.
[23] Road Traffic Act 1988, s.145(3) and (4). Cover must be for £250,000 in respect of property damage.
[24] *ibid.*, ss.157–159.
[25] *ibid.*, s.145(4).
[26] This risk must be insured, though, under the Employer's Liability (Compulsory Insurance) Act 1969. See Chapter 5, above.

phrase should receive the same interpretation in both motor insurances and employers' liability insurances[27] or

(ii) more than £250,000 in respect of damage to property caused by, or arising out of, any one accident involving the insured vehicle;

(iii) damage to the insured vehicle itself;

(iv) liability in respect of damage to goods carried for hire or reward in or on the insured vehicle, or in or on any trailer (whether or not coupled) drawn by the insured vehicle;

(v) liability in respect of damage to property in the custody or control of any insured person; or

(vi) any contractual liability.

Certificate of motor insurance

10–07   A policy of insurance is of no effect for the purposes of the Road Traffic Act 1988[28] unless and until there is delivered by the insurer to the person by whom the policy is effected a certificate of insurance in the form prescribed by regulations.[29] Delivery of the certificate of insurance has statutory benefits to the insured person(s), though, the purpose of the legislation is really to assist the injured third parties (see below).

Operation of compulsory insurance

10–08   If, after the delivery of the Certificate of Motor Insurance, any person insured by the terms and conditions of that policy who thereafter has judgment entered against him in respect of the matters in paragraph 10–04, above, the insurer must satisfy that judgment, including claimant's costs and any award of interest on the damages.[30] These statutory provisions are in addition to[31] the rights of successful third party claimants against the defendant insured's insurers under the Third Parties (Rights Against Insurers) Act 1930.[32] The insurer is free, however, to provide in the policy for his subsequent recovery from the insured of any sum paid out only because of this statutory duty to satisfy such judgments.[33]

Preconditions to statutory obligation on insurers to satisfy judgments

10–09   The statutory duty only comes into force if the following circumstances apply[34]:

(i) the insurer had notice of the bringing of the proceedings (see below) before or within seven days of their commencement; or

(ii) that execution of the judgment has not been stayed pending an appeal; or

[27] *Vandyke v. Fender* [1970] 2 Q.B. 292, CA.
[28] *Quaere*, but for the purposes of general insurance law is of effect?
[29] Road Traffic Act 1988, ss.147(1) and 161(2).
[30] *ibid.,* s.151(1).
[31] *ibid.,* s.153(1).
[32] See Chapter 21, below.
[33] Road Traffic Act 1988, s.145(6).
[34] *ibid.,* s.152(2) and (3).

(iii) that the insurance has not been cancelled before the happening of the insured event and either:

(a) the Certificate was surrendered to the insurer, or a statutory declaration made that it was lost or destroyed, prior to that occurrence; or

(b) that after the said occurrence, but within fourteen days from the taking of effect of the cancellation of the policy, the Certificate was surrendered or the statutory declaration made; or

(c) that either before or after the happening of the event, but within fourteen days from the effective policy cancellation, the insurer has commenced proceedings for recovery of the certificate; or

(iv) that the insurer has not obtained a declaration in proceedings, commenced within three months of the commencement of the injured party's proceedings against the person who obtained the insurance that he, the insurer, is entitled to avoid the policy for common law[35] misrepresentation or non-disclosure of a material fact.[36]

Notice of commencement of proceedings

References to "commencement of the proceedings" in the above provisos means commencement of legal proceedings[37]:

10–10

"Notification that a claim may be made is not the same as notification of the commencement of proceedings, and there is obviously good reason why the commencement of proceedings is the material time. Insurers may have repudiated liability as against their insured but they may have their own reasons for taking over control of any litigation there may be. It may well be that if the facts are gone into for example, a plaintiff may have no grounds of claim at all and unless the insurers have notice of the commencement of the proceedings, they are not in a position to intervene. It is important from the insurer's point of view too, that they have notice not later than seven days after the commencement of proceedings because of the danger of judgment in default of appearance being given against a defendant assured. All these considerations leave me in no doubt that 'proceedings' means legal proceedings."

Some degree of formality is required in the giving of such a notice, and the mere casual mention by the insured to an agent of the insurer during a friendly chat, that an action was being brought against him, has been held to be insufficient.[38] Indeed, an insurer can defend the third party

10–11

---

[35] See Chapter 3, above, for the general law.

[36] The insurer is restricted to the grounds specified in the notice he must himself serve on the person covered by the insurance if he is someone other than the person who effected the insurance, *Zurich General Accident & Liability Insurance Co. Ltd v. Morrison* [1942] 2 K.B. 53, CA.

[37] *McGoona v. Motor Insurers' Bureau & Marsh* [1969] 2 Lloyd's Rep. 34 at 46, *per* Lawton J. (as he then was), *obiter*.

[38] *Herbert v. Railway Passengers Assurance Co.* [1938] 1 All E.R. 650.

claimant's action on behalf of the insured driver all the way through to judgment, and only then raise lack of notice to escape the statutory duty to satisfy the judgment.[39] It seems that the notice need not necessarily be in writing, but the adequacy of the notice will always depend on the facts of the particular case.[40] A prudent solicitor acting for the claimant third party would be well advised to ensure that the insurer received written notice within seven days after the commencement of proceedings, in order to prevent any argument on the point.[41]

10–12   Written notice to the insurers from the claimant third party's solicitors within time, to the effect that if the claim set out is not settled by a certain date, then they are instructed to file action against the insured owner of the car, would seem to be sufficient notice.[42] On the other hand, it is probably insufficient for the claimant's solicitors of the insurer's repudiation of liability to the insured and adding "because you will appreciate, we shall have to take proceedings as against [the driver]". This is because there is a difference between saying that proceedings will be brought, and, saying proceedings will almost inevitably be brought.[43] Similarly, in *Harrington v. Pinkey*,[44] the Court of Appeal held that there was no proper notice of the bringing of proceedings, simply notice that the third party claimant's solicitors would advise their client to institute proceedings against the insured. Further, it has been held that where the insured person is sued, and he then joins by third-party notice (now CPR, Pt 20 proceedings) another party whom he blames for the accident, the requirement of seven days' notice of proceedings concerning the third party is measured, not from the date of the issue of the third-party notice, but from the date of any receipt by the insured of a counterclaim from the third party.[45] The reason for this is that the insured does not become liable to pay damages to the third party on the issue of a third-party notice, but will be at risk (and thus his insurer) once the third party makes a counterclaim.

Declaratory proceedings by insurer against insured
10–13   Any proceedings brought by the insurer under (iv) above must be notified to the third party claimant in the proceedings against the insured, and the insurer will be precluded from setting up any grounds not mentioned in his notice to that injured claimant.[46] It should further be appreciated that that notice has to be served within seven days of the insurer's commencement of proceedings for a declaration against the insured.[47] The third party claimant is then entitled[48] to be made a co-defendant with the

[39] *Wake v. Page, The Times*, February 9, 2001, CA.
[40] *Desouza v. Waterlow* [1999] R.T.R. 71.
[41] *ibid.*
[42] *Ceylon Motor Insurance Association v. Thambugula* [1953] A.C. 584, PC.
[43] *Weldrick v. Essex & Suffolk Equitable Insurance Society Ltd* (1950) 83 Ll. L. Rep. 91 at 102, *per* Birkett J.
[44] [1989] 2 Lloyd's Rep. 310, CA.
[45] *Cross v. British Oak Insurance Co. Ltd* [1938] 2 K.B. 167.
[46] *Zurich General Accident & Liability Insurance Co Ltd v. Morrison* [1942] 2 K.B. 53, CA.
[47] Road Traffic Act 1988, s.152(3).
[48] *ibid.*

insured in those proceedings,[49] where the insurer must prove not only that the non-disclosed or misrepresented fact was material,[50] but also that the insurer's own mind was so affected,[51] to show that the person effecting the insurance "obtained" it by the non-disclosure or misrepresentation of the material fact(s).

Non-avoidance of statutory duty to satisfy judgment

For the benefit of those suffering death or personal injury from the use   **10–14**
of motor vehicles on roads, insurers are prevented from escaping their statutory liability (above) to satisfy judgment against anyone[52] insured under their policy once a Certificate of Motor Insurance has been delivered, in relation to certain policy conditions or terms. However, as mentioned already, once having satisfied the judgment, the insurer becomes fully entitled to recover that sum, if he can, from the person he has so indemnified.[53] There are ten[54] categories of policy exceptions or conditions that the insurer is not entitled to rely upon as against the person insured in respect of death or personal injury caused to successful claimants who have sued the insured driver or owner to judgment. All other policy terms, conditions and exceptions of the policy apply and the insurer can rightfully refuse to indemnify the person covered by compulsory insurance if those terms, conditions, or exceptions so entitle the insurer to avoid the policy or liability thereunder:

(i) the age or physical or mental condition of persons driving the vehicle (this includes rendering of no effect an exclusion of liability in respect of a driver whilst under the influence of drugs or intoxicating liquor,[55] but for other purposes such exclusions are effective even where there is no causal connection between the driver's condition and the accident[56]);

(ii) the condition of the vehicle (see below for discussion of such policy terms);

(iii) the number of persons that the vehicle carries (an exception applying when the vehicle is "conveying any load in excess of that for which it is constructed" will not be interpreted as imposing a limit on the number of persons being carried on the vehicle[57]);

(iv) the weight or physical characteristics of the goods that the vehicle carries (an exception applying when the vehicle is "conveying any load in excess of that for which it is constructed" does not cover

---

[49] *Merchants' & Manufacturers' Insurance Co. Ltd v. Hunt* [1941] 1 K.B. 295, CA.
[50] Road Traffic Act 1988, s.151(9)(b).
[51] *Zurich General Accident & Liability Insurance Co. Ltd v. Morrison* (1942) 72 Ll. L. Rep. 167 at 172, *per* MacKinnon L.J., CA; see also Chapter 3, above.
[52] Road Traffic Act 1988, ss.148(7) and 151(2); *Tattersall v. Drysdale* [1935] 2 K.B. 174.
[53] *ibid.*, ss.148(2), 151(7) and 151(8).
[54] *ibid.*
[55] *Herbert v. Railway Passengers Assurance Co. Ltd* [1938] 1 All E.R. 650; *G.F.P. Units Ltd v. Monksfield* [1972] 2 Lloyd's Rep. 79.
[56] *Louden v. British Merchants Insurance Co. Ltd* [1961] 1 All E.R. 705.
[57] *Houghton v. Trafalgar Insurance Co. Ltd* [1954] 1 Q.B. 247, CA.

carrying an excessive number of passengers,[58] nor drawing a load in excess of that which may be conveyed on the vehicle[59]);

(v) the times at which or the areas within which the vehicle is used[60];

(vi) the horse power or cylinder capacity or value of the vehicle;

(vii) the carrying on the vehicle of any particular apparatus;

(viii) the carrying on the vehicle of any particular means of identification other than any means of identification required to be carried by or under the Vehicles (Excise) Act 1971;

(ix) the requirement to do specified things after the happening of the event (*e.g.* give notice of claim to the insurer). The notification provision is discussed further below;

(x) the limitation or exclusion of passenger liability.

Most important to note is that insurers can validly impose restrictions on the insurance cover with respect to the uses for which the insured vehicle is used, and not be obliged to satisfy any judgment relating to the vehicle's use in non-compliance with the restriction or exclusion.

3. OTHER RISKS COVERED

Loss or damage to the insured vehicle

10–15   A comprehensive commercial vehicle insurance will, apart from the compulsory insurance element, generally cover loss or damage to the insured vehicle.[61] For instance it may provide:

> "The Insurer will indemnify the Insured against loss or damage (including damage by frost) to any vehicle described in the Schedule and its accessories and spare parts while thereon.
>
> The Insurer may at its own option repair reinstate or replace such vehicle or any part thereof of its accessories or spare parts or may pay in cash the amount of the loss or damage. If to the knowledge of the Insurer the vehicle is the subject of a hire purchase agreement such payment shall be made to the owner described therein whose receipt shall be a full and final discharge to the Insurer in respect of such loss or damage. The Insured's estimate of value stated in the Schedule shall be the maximum amount payable by the Company in respect of any claim for loss or damage.
>
> If such vehicle is disabled by reason of loss or damage insured under this Policy the Insurer will bear the reasonable cost of protection and removal to the nearest repairers. The company will also pay the reasonable cost of delivery to the Insured after repair of such loss or damage not exceeding the reasonable cost of transport to the address of the Insured in Great Britain, the Republic of Ireland and Northern Ireland, the Isle of Man, or the Channel Islands, stated therein."

Exclusions to insured vehicle cover

10–16   The policy will usually expressly exclude the following:

---

[58] *ibid.*

[59] *Jenkins v. Deane* (1933) 47 Ll. L.Rep. 342.

[60] See *Palmer v. Cornhill Insurance Co. Ltd* (1935) 52 Ll. L. Rep. 78.

[61] See the specimen policies at Appendices 5 and 9 (excluding Sections H & I).

(i) the excess (*i.e.* the first £x of each claim);

(ii) loss of use, depreciation, wear and tear, mechanical or electrical breakdowns, failures or breakages;

(iii) damage to tyres caused by application of brakes or by road punctures, cuts or bursts;

(iv) loss or damage arising during (unless it be proved by the insured that the loss or damage was not occasioned thereby) or in consequence of earthquake, riot[62] or civil commotion.[63]

"Loss or damage"

There is a loss within the insurance indemnity where a vehicle is sold to another through an agent who is guilty of conversion of that vehicle, whether or not he was initially given possession of the vehicle by means of a fraudulent misrepresentation that he would legitimately sell the vehicle and hand the proceeds over to the insured.[64] That situation is to be differentiated, however, from a direct sale of the vehicle by the insured to another, whose cheque, which is accepted in payment for the vehicle, subsequently turns out to be worthless. Because of the concluded sale agreement and the resulting transfer of property in the vehicle, he has lost the purchase moneys.[65] However, in *Dobson v. General Accident Fire and Life Assurance Corp. plc*[66] the Court of Appeal held that in determining whether goods were the subject of a "theft" within the risks insured under the policy, the consent of the owner to the property being taken was irrelevant to that determination. Accordingly, if the insurance covers "loss or damage caused by theft", the sale of the insured goods for a worthless cheque will constitute a loss caused by theft covered by the insurance, and the insurers will be liable to indemnify their insured. The peril "theft" will be construed in accordance with its plain and ordinary meaning and thus include a loss of the insured vehicle by robbery.[67]

10–17

"To any vehicle"

Where a part of the vehicle is taken elsewhere for its repair, the policy still covers all component parts of that vehicle against loss or damage. This proposition follows from the judgment of Du Parcq J. in *Seaton v. London General Insurance Co. Ltd*[68] where the insurers contended that the

10–18

---

[62] This is to be understood in the criminal law sense. See *London & Lancashire Fire Insurance Co. v. Bolands Ltd* [1924] A.C. 836 at 847, *per* Lord Sumner, HL, which is defined in *Field v. Metropolitan Police Receiver* [1907] 2 K.B. 853. See *Crozier v. Thompson* (1922) 12 Ll. L. Rep. 291.

[63] See *Bolivian Republic v. Indemnity Mutual Marine Assurance Co. Ltd,* [1909] 1 K.B. 785, C.A.; *Levy v. Assicwazioni Generali* [1940] AC 791, PC; *Spinney's (1948) Ltd v. Royal Insurance Co. Ltd* [1980] 1 Lloyd's Rep. 406; *Cooper v. General Accident, Fire & Life Assurance Corp. Ltd* (1922) 13 Ll. L. Rep. 219, HL; *Boggan v. Motor Union Insurance Co.* (1923) 16 Ll. L. Rep. 64, HL.

[64] *Webster v. General Accident Fire & Life Assurance Corp. Ltd* [1953] 1 Q.B. 520.

[65] *Eisinger v. General Accident Fire & Life Assurance Corp. Ltd* [1955] 2 All E.R. 897.

[66] [1990] 1 Q.B. 274; approved in *R. v. Gomez* [1993] 1 All E.R. 1, HL.

[67] *Hayward v. Norwich Union Insurance Ltd, The Times,* March 8, 2001, CA.

[68] (1932) 43 Ll. L. Rep. 398 at 398–399.

removal of the engine from the vehicle meant that there was no longer a "vehicle" under the insurance:

> "The answer, is that one must look against what risks the company have insured him, and it seems to be almost beyond dispute that the mere fact that he has taken the engine out of the vehicle does not prevent the vehicle as a whole from being insured. I agree that, the moment you take a thing into two pieces, in one sense the risk is increased, but the mere fact that it may be possible for the assured under the policy to do things which mean that at one time the risks undertaken by the company are greater than at another time does not mean that if the assured does any of these things, he ceases to be insured. It may be that under the terms of the policy and with the latitude allowed the company at times would find themselves under a heavier liability at one time than another."

In that case the insured was thus held entitled to recover in respect of the engine, which was damaged by a fire in the repair workshop.

"Accessories and spare parts while thereon"

10–19   Provided the accessories and spare parts are on the insured vehicle at the time of their loss or damage, then they are within the scope of the policy cover. Thus, special meters, *e.g.* a tachograph or taximeter,[69] are protected by the insurance.

Articulated vehicles

10–20   The particular wording of the insurance needs to be considered in respect of the cover provided for a detached trailer of an articulated vehicle. Cover for liability incurred in respect of a detached trailer is only compulsory outside Great Britain and Gibraltar in member states of the European Community, if that state's laws render such insurance cover compulsory.[70] British insurers may either include or exclude trailer risks, and there is a tendency to exclude loss of the trailer itself whilst it is detached from the insured tractor unit.

4. LIABILITY TO THIRD PARTIES FOR MATERIAL DAMAGE TO PROPERTY

10–21   A comprehensive commercial vehicle insurance will provide an indemnity up to a specified limit (usually above the compulsory sum of £250,000) in respect of liability for material damage to property in addition to the compulsory cover for liability for death or personal injury suffered by third parties. The indemnity may read:

> "The Insurer will indemnify the Insured in the event of an accident caused by or through or in connection with any vehicle described in the Schedule or in connection with the loading or unloading of such vehicle against liability at law for damages and claimant's costs and expenses in respect of:

---

[69] *Rowan v. Universal Insurance Co. Ltd* (1939) 64 Ll. L. Rep. 288, CA.
[70] See s.145(3)(b) of the Road Traffic Act 1988.

(a) death of or bodily injury to any person;
(b) damage to property limited to £X in respect of any one claim or number of claims arising out of one cause.

The Insurer will pay all costs and expenses incurred with its written consent.[71]

The Insurer will pay the solicitor's fee for representation at any coroner's inquest or fatal inquiry in respect of any death which may be the subject of indemnity under this Section or for the defending in any Court of Summary Jurisdiction any proceedings in respect of any act causing or relating to any event which may be the subject of indemnity under this Section."

Applicable exclusions

The policy will usually expressly exclude: **10–22**

(i) death, injury or damage caused or arising beyond the limits of any carriageway or thoroughfare in connection with:

    (a) the bringing of the load to such vehicle for loading thereon; or
    (b) the taking of the load from such vehicle after unloading therefrom by any person other than the driver or attendant of such vehicle;

(ii) death of or bodily injury to any person in the employment of the person claiming to be indemnified arising out of and in the course of such employment[72];

(iii) damage to property belonging to the insured[73] or held in trust by or in the custody or control of the insured or being conveyed by such vehicle[74];

(iv) damage to any bridge, viaduct or weighbridge or to any road or anything beneath by vibration or by the weight of such vehicle or of the load carried by such vehicle.

5. GENERAL POLICY EXCEPTIONS AND CONDITIONS

The insured drivers

Not only the person who effects the insurance can be the insured under   **10–23**
a motor insurance policy, but statute allows any persons or classes of persons specified as being indemnified to validly have benefit of the insurance and a cause of action upon it against the insurer,[75] subject of course, to its conditions and any right of the insurer to avoid the policy.[76] The benefit

---

[71] Consent should be sought at every important stage in the proceedings, *E. Hulton & Co. Ltd v. Mountain* (1921) 8 Ll. L. Rep. 249 at 250, *per* Bankes L.J., *obiter*, CA.

[72] This risk is the subject of compulsory employers' liability insurance; see Chapter 5, above.

[73] This includes other insured vehicles of the insured.

[74] This risk can be covered by a carriers' insurance; see Chapter 13, below.

[75] Road Traffic Act 1988, s.148(7).

[76] *Guardian Assurance Co. Ltd v. Sutherland* [1939] 2 All E.R. 246.

will extend to any non-compulsory indemnity granted within a policy issued to cover the compulsory third party liability in respect of death or personal injury.[77] It is important to note that since 1987 the insurer is obliged to satisfy judgments against all drivers of the insured vehicle under the statutory scheme, even if they are not, for instance a named driver, if the risk otherwise meets the requirements of that obligation.[78]

10–24   Where the commercial vehicle insured is used for hire or reward, whether for the carriage of goods or passengers, it is usual for the drivers to be restricted to the insured personally (if an individual or partnership) and the insured's employees, this latter category being determined by the general of employment law.[79]

10–25   If the commercial vehicle is not used for hire or reward, but general business use, *e.g.* transporting the insured's own goods, the policy extends the indemnity to:

> "any person who is driving such vehicle on the Insured's order or with his permission provided such person holds a licence to drive such vehicle or has held and is not disqualified from holding or obtaining such a licence."

On the insured's order or with his permission

10–26   This wording was considered in *Browning v. Phoenix Assurance Co. Ltd*[80] and it is clear that it is a question of fact for the court to determine whether or not the driver was driving on the insured's order or with his permission. This case concerned a garage employee's driving of the insured vehicle having been given the insured's permission to drive it for the purpose of warming up the oil prior to draining. As Picher J. explained:

> "[The insured] gave the statement to the defendant's representative, which I have read, as early as 10 December and in that statement it will be remembered that he said he had authorised the plaintiff 'to drive the car at his convenience to get it thoroughly warm before draining off the oil.' He said nothing about authorising the plaintiff to drive it for any other purpose. I accordingly determine that the request made or the permission given by [the insured] on December 1 . . . was a request made or a permission given to drive the car for a longish run at his convenience, taking the family as passengers, for the sole purpose of getting the transmission oil warmed up before it was drained. It is now clear that the plaintiff was not driving the car for this purpose when he met with the accident and consequently was not driving it 'on the insured's order or with his permission' and that the car was therefore not at risk under the policy at the time of the accident."

---

[77] See *Austin v. Zurich General Accident & Liability Insurance Co. Ltd* [1944] 2 All E.R. 243, at 248, *per* Tucker J.; affirmed [1945] K.B. 250, CA; and *Barnet Group Hospital Management Committee v. Eagle Star Insurance Co. Ltd* [1960] 1 Q.B. 107.

[78] Road Traffic Act 1988, s.151(2)(b), introduced by the Motor Vehicles (Compulsory Insurance) Regulations 1987 (S.I. 1987 No. 2171).

[79] But see the special facts of *Burton v. Road Transport & General Insurance Co. Ltd* (1939) 63 Ll. L. Rep. 253, where the wording was "any person in the insured's employ" was held by Branson J. to have a very wide meaning, *cf.* "in the insured's employment" in *Lyons v. May* [1948] 2 All E.R. 1062.

[80] [1960] 2 Lloyd's Rep 360.

Obviously, if the insured gives permission for anyone to drive the **10–27** vehicle except "X", if "X" drives the car, that policy will not cover him;[81] but where general permission to drive is given to "Y" on a loose understanding that "Y" will obtain his own vehicle insurance as soon as possible, "Y" will be covered if he is unsuccessful in obtaining his own insurance by the time of the relevant accident.[82] Given that businesses are impossible to run without delegation of authority, and, of course, the fact that companies have no physical existence, in determining whether a particular driver has permission to drive the vehicle, the court will be cognisant of permission granted by an agent who is authorised to give such permission by the person who has effected the insurance.[83]

It has been held that drivers given appropriate permission to drive the **10–28** insured vehicle by the insured remain covered by the policy in the event of the insured's demise during the currency of the policy, it being irrelevant that the deceased insured, who effected the policy, is no longer in a position to revoke that permission.[84] If a driver is within the scope of the policy, it will be an irrelevant consideration for the purposes of the insurance indemnity, that the person injured by his driving of the vehicle is also among that class of persons insured under the policy, or even the very person who effected the insurance.[85]

Driving other vehicles with the consent of the owner

If there is an extension of the policy to provide the minimum Road **10–29** Traffic Act cover in respect of other vehicles being driven with "the consent of the owner thereof", there is similarly a question of fact to be determined as to whether there was such "consent". Further, even if there is consent for one purpose, there may be no consent for another purpose of use of the vehicle. Thus, in *Singh v. Rathour*,[86] where the defendant had borrowed a minibus from an association of which he was a member, ostensibly for purposes of that association, but later used the minibus for other purposes, the Court of Appeal held that the defendant did not have the necessary consent of the association so as to be entitled to claim an indemnity under his own policy of motor insurance. Similarly, where the owner of a vehicle had given his consent to a person taking and driving, subject to an express or implied limitation as to the purposes for which it was to be used, the Court considered that if that person, having taken the vehicle, drove it for purposes outwith that limitation, he did not have "the consent of the owner" to that driving within the meaning of that phrase in a policy of motor insurance.

[81] See *Paget v. Poland* (1947) 80 Ll. L. Rep. 283.
[82] See *Tattersall v. Drysdale* [1935] 2 K.B. 174.
[83] This principle was applied in *Pailor v. Co-operative Insurance Society Ltd* (1930) 38 Ll. L. Rep. 237, CA.
[84] *Kelly v. Cornhill Insurance Co. Ltd* [1964] 1 All E.R. 321, HL.
[85] *Digby v. General Accident Fire & Life Assurance Corp. Ltd* [1943] A.C. 121, HL.
[86] [1988] 1 W.L.R. 422, CA.

Holds a licence to drive such vehicle or has held . . . such a licence

10–30   There is county court authority that a person driving a vehicle for which
he holds a provisional licence is covered by this wording, if it is for the
appropriate class of vehicle, even if he is driving in breach of the terms of
that provisional licence.[87] However, any licence issued to a person who has
failed to give particulars of all orders of endorsement within the last four
years is of no effect[88] and presumably that person will not "hold" a driving
licence if he is in possession of a licence which comes into force on a subsequent date,[89] but a person does "hold" a licence that has been issued to
him by his concealment of his disqualification,[90] or by wrongful retention
of the licence when it should have been surrendered to the court upon disqualification, but will be excluded by the disqualification provision
(below). Merely applying for a licence is not equivalent to "holding" a
licence.[91]

Not disqualified for holding or obtaining such a licence

10–31   "Disqualified" means disqualified either by order of a court,[92] or by
statute by reason of age.[93] But a person who has held a licence but is
refused renewal because of his mental condition is not "disqualified",[94]
and a person who is disqualified until he passes a test[95] is not "disqualified" from holding or obtaining a provisional driving licence.[96]

The condition of the insured vehicle

10–32   A common condition precedent to the liability of the insurer inserted in
commercial vehicle insurances is one providing that:

> "The Insured shall take all reasonable steps to safeguard from loss or
> damage and maintain in efficient condition the vehicle or vehicles described
> in the Schedule."

As mentioned above, this type of condition precedent will not operate
as regards statutory indemnification of third party death or personal
injury or property damage in so far as the condition precedent is regarded
by the court as relating to the condition of the vehicle,[97] but will apply to
other policy indemnities and recovery from the insured of any sum paid
under that statutory indemnification. How far such conditions precedent
have been held to relate to the condition of the insured vehicle is discussed
below.

---

[87] *Rendlesham v. Dunne* [1964] 1 Lloyd's Rep. 192.
[88] Road Traffic Offenders Act 1988, s.45(3).
[89] *Kinsey v. Hertfordshire County Council* [1972] R.T.R. 498.
[90] *Adams v. Dunne* [1978] R.T.R. 281.
[91] *Lester Bros. (Coal Merchants) Ltd v. Avon Insurance Co. Ltd* (1942) 72 Ll. L. Rep. 109.
[92] *Edwards v. Griffiths* [1953] 2 All E.R. 874.
[93] *Mumford v. Hardy* [1956] 1 All E.R. 337; *R. v. Saddleworth Justices* [1968] 1 W.L.R. 556;
Road Traffic Act 1988, s.101.
[94] *Edwards v. Griffiths* [1953] 2 All E.R. 874.
[95] Under the Road Traffic Offenders Act 1988, s.36.
[96] *ibid.*, s.37(3).
[97] *ibid.*, s.148(2)(b), discussed above.

Maintain in efficient condition

The condition requires the insured to maintain the vehicle so as to   **10–33**
enable it to do what is normally and reasonably required of it[98] or, in other
words, maintain the vehicle in a roadworthy condition.[99] The running of
the insured vehicle with tyres that are known to have no tread,[1] or a foot-
brake that does not work,[2] are clear breaches of this condition precedent.
Such a condition imposes a personal duty on the insured requiring the
insured to have an adequate system of maintenance of vehicles, but this
personal obligation is not breached by casual negligence of an employee
engaged on maintenance duties,[3] or if the vehicles are maintained
regularly yet still are in an inefficient condition unknown to the insured[4]:

> "[The insurers] relied not only upon what they contended was the inefficient
> condition of the tyres, but also on the inefficient condition of the brakes.
> They took the view, not without reason, that the inefficient condition of the
> brakes might well (and probably did) have something to do with this
> accident. The plaintiff, however, was able to produce evidence which the
> learned [judge below] accepted (as he was fully entitled to do) that some nine
> days before the accident the plaintiff had had the brakes checked, recen-
> tralised, and adjusted . . . Moreover, the [judge] further accepted the plain-
> tiff's evidence, that, although it may be that as a rule the sort of defects
> which these brakes suffered would have been all too apparent to anyone
> driving the car, the plaintiff, in fact, did not appreciate that the car was
> suffering from any such defects and had no reason to do so. It, therefore,
> followed on those findings that, although the brakes were inefficient, it could
> not be said that the plaintiff had failed to take reasonable steps to maintain
> them. He had sent the vehicle in for examination nine days before the
> accident. He had no reason to suppose that the garage had not done its work
> properly for [the price], and the brakes appeared to be all right during the
> intervening period."

All reasonable steps to safeguard from loss or damage

There is county court authority that this part of the condition relates   **10–34**
solely to the physical state of the vehicle, being linked, as it is, to the
requirement to maintain the vehicle in efficient condition. It was therefore
held[5] that the insured was not in breach of the condition by permitting a
provisional licence-holder to drive the vehicle whilst unaccompanied by a
qualified driver. However, more recently the Court of Appeal clearly
regarded to general duty to protect the insured vehicle from loss as being
divisible from the obligation to maintain the vehicle where they both

---

[98] *McInnes v. National Motor & Accident Insurance Union Ltd* [1963] 2 Lloyd's Rep. 415 at
417.
[99] *Brown v. Zurich General Accident & Liability Insurance Co. Ltd* [1954] 2 Lloyd's Rep. 243
at 246, *per* Sellers J.
[1] *ibid.*; *Conn v. Westminster Motor Insurance Association Ltd* [1966] 1 Lloyd's Rep. 407, CA.
[2] *Jones & James v. Provincial Insurance Co. Ltd* (1929) 35 Ll. L. Rep. 135.
[3] *Liverpool Corp. v. T. & H.R. Roberts (a firm)* [1964] 3 All E.R. 56; applying *Woolfall &
Rimmer Ltd v. Moyle* [1942] 1 K.B. 66, CA.
[4] *Conn v. Westminster Motor Insurance Association Ltd* [1966] 1 Lloyd's Rep. 407 at 414,
per Salmon L.J., CA.
[5] *Rendlesham v. Dunne* [1964] 1 Lloyd's Rep. 192; followed in *Taylor v. National Insurance
& Guarantee Corp.* [1989] C.L.Y. 2059.

appear in the same condition. Thus, where the insured company's authorised employee left the keys in a company owned Ferrari motor car when he went across the road into the company's offices, this rendered the insured company in breach of its obligation to take reasonable care to protect the car from loss or damage thereby debarring its recovery of the value of the Ferrari when it was stolen.[6]

10–35   An alternative form of this type of condition precedent may read:

> "The underwriters shall not be liable if the policy holder shall fail to take every reasonable precaution to safeguard from loss or damage any insured car or accessories fitted thereto and to keep the same in proper state of repair. The underwriters will not be liable to indemnify the policy holder in respect of liability arising whilst any insured car is driven or used in an unsafe condition either before or after an accident."

In *Lefevre v. White*,[7] Popplewell J. followed the earlier decision of Cumming-Bruce J. (as he then was) in *Liverpool Corporation v. T. and H. R. Roberts (a firm)*[8] upon a similar provision, that the first sentence of the condition precedent imposes a duty to take due reasonable precautions so as to keep the vehicle in a good state of repair. The second sentence expresses the consequences in terms of contractual liability on a failure on the part of the insured to exercise the duty imposed by the first sentence of the condition precedent. The second sentence did not impose a separate and absolute obligation, independent of the obligation in the first sentence of the condition precedent.

10–36   Being an exception, the onus of proof will be on the insurer to prove the exception applies (unless the policy places the burden of proof on the insured), *i.e.* that the vehicle was in an "unsafe" or "unroadworthy" condition.[9] It is unclear, however, whether it must be shown to be in that condition when it sets out on its journey, or whether it was in that condition some little time before the accident, though, it is perhaps unarguable that the exception does not apply to a mishap causing the vehicle to go out of control and have the accident.[10]

Whilst the vehicle is being driven

10–37   This wording has been held as not requiring any knowledge on the part of the insured or other driver of the vehicle, and is therefore to be distinguished from the type of clause considered above which places an obligation on the insured to "take all reasonable steps, etc." Lord Alness in *Trickett v. Queensland Insurance Co. Ltd*[11] said that:

---

[6] *Devco Holder Ltd v. Legal & General Assurance Society Ltd* [1993] 2 Lloyd's Rep. 567, CA.

[7] [1990] 1 Lloyd's Rep. 569.

[8] [1965] 1 W.L.R. 938.

[9] *Barren v. London General Insurance Co. Ltd* [1935] 1 K.B. 238.

[10] *ibid.* at 101–102, *per* Goddard J. (as he then was); see also *Trickett v. Queensland Insurance Co. Ltd* (1936) 53 Ll. L. Rep. 225 at 228, *per* Lord Alness, PC; and *Clarke v. National Insurance & Guarantee Corp. Ltd* [1963] 2 Lloyd's Rep. 35 at 38, *per* Harman L.J., CA.

[11] *Trickett v. Queensland Insurance Co. Ltd,* (1936) 53 H.L. Rep. 225 at 228.

"Their Lordships cannot find any justification for supplementing the terms of the proviso by adding to it the words 'to the knowledge of the driver', as they are invited to do by the [assured], or for reforming the contract into which he entered. It is not immaterial to observe in this connection that, in certain of the other provisos which are adjacent to that with which the [Court] are concerned, the knowledge of the assured is set out *eo nomine*, where it is intended that knowledge should form a condition of the contract between the parties."

In direct conflict with that decision, though, Popplewell J. in *Lefevre v.*   **10–38** *White*,[12] without having been referred to the earlier decision, held that knowledge of the insured was necessarily required because there had to be a breach of the duty to take reasonable care by the insured. Thus, it was held to have been perfectly reasonable for the insured, with a car with a long M.O.T. test certificate and no obvious sign of difficulty with the brakes, to have run the car for a period of time without inspection by a garage. The insured, however, did breach the duty of reasonable care by having seen that one of the tyres was close to needing changing, and, indeed, had been to a garage to see if they could get a tyre for the following week, but continued to drive the car.[13] It is submitted that the reasoning in *Lefevre v. White* is the correct approach, so that it is a personal duty of the insured, and knowledge must be implicit for breach of such a duty.

Unsafe

Driving at night when the lights of the vehicle are not working amounts   **10–39** to driving whilst the vehicle is in an "unsafe" condition,[14] but the mere falling of a load from the vehicle does not, of itself, constitute the vehicle being "unsafe".[15] Obviously, "unsafe" refers to the vehicle itself and not to equipment upon it such as a tow-rope.[16]

Unroadworthy

Gross overloading of a vehicle, though not affecting the soundness of   **10–40** the vehicle itself, can render the vehicle "unroadworthy". This was the finding of the Court of Appeal in *Clarke v. National Insurance and Guarantee Corp. Ltd*[17] in a case concerning a Ford Anglia car which had an accident when it held nine persons including the driver, where Harman L.J. explained[18]:

"This car was grossly overloaded; that was agreed by everybody. That it could be driven safely the experts agreed . . . There are two views about this matter, and one of them is this. It was not . . . the condition of the car which caused the trouble, but the misuse of the car by [the insured], and that is not a matter which comes within the exception. On the other hand. Counsel for

---

[12] [1990] 1 Lloyd's Rep. 569.
[13] *ibid.* at 572.
[14] *ibid.*
[15] *A.P. Salmon Contractors Ltd v. Monksfield* [1970] 1 Lloyd's Rep. 387.
[16] *Jenkins v. Deane* (1933) 47 Ll. L. Rep. 342.
[17] [1964] 1 Q.B. 199, CA.
[18] *ibid.* at 377.

> the [insurance company] says that when looking at this car standing at the kerb loaded with nine persons just before it started, anybody would say that the car in that condition was unroadworthy, unsafe, and that. . . it was being driven in an unroadworthy condition . . . I think that, on the whole, this exception did apply."

Restrictions on the use of the insured vehicle

10–41   Insurers are perfectly free to exclude certain uses of the vehicle from the scope of the policy. Commercial vehicle insurances will generally provide either an exception relating to other uses, or a warranty that the vehicle(s) will only be used for "social, domestic and pleasure purposes, and use in connection with the insured's business excluding use for hire or reward". Such a wording is suitable for the insurance of vehicles only carrying the insured's own goods, but if commercial carriage is undertaken the last six words will be deleted by the insurer. Insurers will usually add that the carriage of passengers other than for hire or reward is permitted. In the final analysis, if the accident occurs whilst the vehicle could be said to have been used for more than one purpose, one permitted under the insurance and one not, to solution to the problem is best reached by determining the essential character of the journey in the course of which the accident occurred.[19]

Business use

10–42   It is vital that the business user is expressly covered, because the words "social, domestic and pleasure purposes" alone do not include business use of the vehicle.[20] If the business use is expressed as that connected with "the insured's business as stated in the Schedule", any use of the vehicle by the insured in connection with other business ventures not specified in the Schedule is excluded,[21] as is a joint use of the vehicle, *e.g.* for included and excluded businesses,[22] except, perhaps when a vehicle is being used jointly for permitted business and social uses when it has been suggested that cover may well be afforded[23]:

> "A case might arise where the person insured under the policy would extend a courtesy to a friend or acquaintance, or it might be a stranger, who was, in fact, carrying on some business and was assisted in carrying on that business by the facilities which were given to him by the insured. In such a case, if the facts found were that the insured, as a matter of kindness, courtesy or charity, gave a lift — to use a colloquial phrase — to someone who happened to be on business on his own, I have no doubt that the proper view to take would be that the car was, for the time being, being used for a social purpose, and it would not the less be used for a social purpose because the person benefiting by the courtesy was on business."

[19] *Seddon v. Binnions* [1978] 1 Lloyd's Rep. 381, CA.
[20] *Wood v. General Accident Fire & Life Assurance Corp. Ltd* (1948) 82 Ll. L. Rep. 77; *Seddon v. Binions (Zurich Insurance Co. Ltd, Third Party)* [1978] 1 Lloyd's Rep. 381, CA.
[21] *Jones v. Welsh Insurance Corp. Ltd* [1937] 4 All E.R. 149.
[22] *Passmore v. Vulcan Boiler & General Insurance Co. Ltd* (1935) 54 Ll. L. Rep. 92; see also *Seddon v. Binions,* [1978] 1 Lloyd's Rep. 381, CA.
[23] *ibid.* at 94, *per* du Parcq J., *obiter.*

In circumstances where the insured lends an insured vehicle to another **10–43** person, provided the policy covers such permitted drivers, the purpose of that use is, of course, crucial as to whether it will be included in the words "social, domestic and pleasure purposes and use for the business of the insured". Whilst the lending of a vehicle to an Urban District Council to ferry visiting foreign Council officials to the airport at the end of their visit for purposes of arranging the "twinning" of the two areas has been held to be a social purpose,[24] it was suggested by the judge that it would be otherwise if they were visiting merchants who had come to see their customers — that would be a business user.[25]

Whilst sharing of the costs of a journey between passengers can, in certain circumstances, result in the insurer being obliged to make a statutory indemnification to those insured in respect of third party liability for death or personal injury or property damage,[26] for all other purposes insurers are quite free to exclude use of the vehicle "for hire or reward", *i.e.* use for a money payment.[27] The courts have shown reluctance, though, to find that arrangements between friends to share costs to work[28] or elsewhere[29] are not pure "social, domestic or pleasure purposes", but are astute to find that lifts given to persons other than friends, where there is an expectation of monetary payment at the conclusion of the journey, is use "for hire or reward".[30]

Two further aspects require specific mention under this heading. The first **10–44** concerns the change-over of a business operation from that run by a sole-proprietor or partnership, to one owned by a limited company. If during the currency of the commercial vehicle policy the business is converted into a limited company, the issued policy will not cover any business use pursuant to the limited company's business[31] until amended to name the insured as ". . . . . Ltd". The second matter is that where the insured proposes for vehicle insurance to cover his business use, and yet is issued with a policy which recites that "use by the insured in connection with his business or profession" is excluded, that exclusion will have precedence over the primary insuring words. The result is that policies issued must be checked carefully by the insured, or his broker on his behalf, to ensure that the insured's business is not prima facie covered, but, in fact, excluded by a subsequent provision,[32] *e.g.* motor-trade use, or for hire or reward (in the case of a transport business).

Notification of claims

Any provision in a vehicle policy providing that no liability shall arise **10–45** under the policy, or that any liability so arising shall cease, in the event of

---

[24] *D.H.R. Moody (Chemists) Ltd v. Iron Trades Mutual Insurance Co. Ltd* [1971] 1 Lloyd's Rep. 386.
[25] *ibid.* at 388, *per* Wrangham J.
[26] Road Traffic Act 1988, s.150.
[27] See *Wyatt v. Guildhall Insurance Co. Ltd* (1937) 57 Ll. L. Rep. 90 at 93, *per* Branson J.
[28] *Bonham v. Zurich General Accident & Liability Insurance Co. Ltd* (1945) 78 Ll. L. Rep. 245 at 247, *per* MacKinnon L.J., CA.
[29] *McCarthy v. British Oak Insurance Co. Ltd* [1938] 3 All E.R. 1.
[30] See *Orr v. Trafalgar Insurance Co. Ltd.* (1948) 82 Ll. L. Rep. 1, CA.
[31] *Levinger v. Licenses & General Insurance Co. Ltd* (1936) 54 Ll. L. Rep. 68.
[32] See *Gray v. Blackmore* [1934] 1 K.B. 95.

some specified thing being done or omitted to be done after the happening of the event giving rise to a claim in respect of the death of or personal injury to a third party or their property, is of no effect in regard to statutory indemnification.[33] All claims requirements placed upon the insured by his insurer are ineffective, though, only as regards statutory indemnification and are otherwise perfectly valid as regards material damage claims in respect of the insured vehicle itself, or the insurer's right of reimbursement of any sum paid under the statutory indemnity.

Knowledge of the claim

10–46   If a time limit is provided for notice of claim to be made by the insured to the insurers it must be adhered to by the insured. The insurer need not show any prejudice suffered by reason of the non-compliance,[34] as must any time limit for commencement of proceedings against the insurer.[35] Obviously, where such a clause makes reference to "after it has come to the knowledge of the insured or the insured's representative for the time being", compliance or non-compliance is to be judged from a base date of the time of acquisition of knowledge of the loss or claim by the insured or his representative.[36]

10–47   Even in the absence of any words referring to "knowledge" of the insured company of the loss or damage, MacKinnon J. (as he then was), in the commercial vehicle insurance case of *Baltic Insurance Association of London Ltd v. Cambrian Coaching and Goods Transport Ltd*[37] held that the insured had to have knowledge of the event before any period for notification of the claim commenced. There the relevant provision was that the insured was the notify insurers "immediately on the occurrence of any accident or loss", and MacKinnon J. held that the obligation had to be considered in the light of business conditions. Here the insured was a company operating coaches and other commercial vehicles and MacKinnon J. stated[38]:

> "The question is whether the [insurance company], on whom I think the onus is, have established that there has been a breach by the [insured] of this undertaking that notice shall be given in writing to the [insurance company] immediately upon the occurrence of any accident or loss. I do not gather that [the insurance company] says that the fact the driver knew on November 29 would be sufficient knowledge of the [insured] to involve them in liability of handing on his knowledge, and even if it were so, it cannot avail the [insurance company] in this case, because it is apparent that the information sent in the letter of December 17 and accepted and received as being within a reasonable time, that it must have been to the knowledge of the driver on November 29 that an accident had happened. Does it make any difference that not only the driver knew but that he told another man in the [insured's] employ — a man named Watson — and that Watson did not for some days hand it on to the responsible person? . . .

---

[33] Road Traffic Act 1988, s.148(5).
[34] See Chapter 2, above.
[35] *Walker v. Pennine Insurance Co. Ltd* [1980] 2 Lloyd's Rep. 156, CA.
[36] *Verelst's Administratrix v. Motor Union Insurance Co. Ltd* [1925] 2 K.B. 137.
[37] (1926) 25 Ll. L. Rep. 195.
[38] *ibid.* at 197.

I am quite satisfied on the evidence that the [insured's] claims manager did not know anything about this matter. He did not receive any report from Watson or the driver until after the receipt of the letter of December 1 from [the claimant's insurance company]. If the driver's knowledge would not be sufficient knowledge of the [insured] so as to make it necessary immediately to inform the plaintiffs, I do not see why Watson's should. Watson was the man whose duty it was to collect any reports of the drivers and bring them round to the responsible officer. I will assume that the driver did say something to Watson on November 29 or 30, though I have no doubt the driver was telling us what he believes is accurate and honest, but I very much doubt after this lapse of time that he can be certain of it. But even assuming he did say something to Watson on November 29 or 30, I am not satisfied that thereupon there came upon the [insured] a duty under this condition of communicating that information to the insurance company when the responsible officials of the [insured] the people properly concerned with claims and with forwarding information under the insurance policy, knew nothing of it whatever. I do not see any difference between the knowledge of Watson or of the driver, and that the driver had knowledge of the accident about November 29 must have been apparent to the plaintiffs when they received the information contained in the letter of December 17 and accepted that as sufficient."

MacKinnon J.'s judgment, however, can be interpreted as treating the matter as essentially one of waiver, and it could thus still be open to argue that the duty or obligation is to give notice of the loss or claim arises when the accident occurs. To avoid these pitfalls, every business or commercial concern should ensure that it has an efficient internal accident reporting system and a rapid notification of claims to insurers system to prevent breach of notification conditions.

10–48

Waiver
Waiver of compliance with the notification provision was specifically pleaded and found in *Webster v. General Accident Fire and Life Assurance Corpn Ltd.*[39] A loss occurred on February 26, and the insured's solicitor did not go to see a branch claims manager of the insurers on May 19. That manager said that he would report it to head office. The policy required written notice to be given to the head office by the insured "as soon as possible" after the occurrence of any accident, loss or damage. It was held that the insurance company had thus led the insured to believe that no written notice was being required and, therefore, the insurance company could not rely on that breach of condition.

10–49

Erroneous details provided
There is no compliance with a notification provision in circumstances where the insured notifies the insurers of an accident within the required time period, but the accident he describes is entirely different to the actual accident. Thus, if the insured was driving a vehicle and collided with a stationary vehicle, but reports to the insurer that another person was driving

10–50

[39] [1953] 1 Q.B. 520.

the vehicle without permission, this was non-compliance with the condition precedent as to notification of the accident.[40]

Non-admission of liability

10–51   This type of condition is not contrary to public policy[41] and, if prejudice is necessary for the insurer to rely on a breach, sufficient prejudice is shown by the insurer being shut out from any negotiations which may have led to a reduction in his liability under the policy.[42] The better and accepted view now is that the insurer does not need to show any prejudice.

Notification of intended prosecution

10–52   If the insurers learn of the intended prosecution from another source, *e.g.* the police, and inform the insured that they wish to undertake his defence of those proceedings, that can constitute a waiver of the requirement of the insured to comply with a condition requiring him to inform them of any intended prosecution.[43]

Insurer's right to conduct proceedings

10–53   Lord Denning M.R. has expressed the view, *obiter*, that as regards any prosecution of an insured driver relating to an accident, an insurer's powers under the policy to take over and control proceedings involving the insured do not extend to prevent him from either conducting his own defence without legal representation, or refusing the solicitor suggested by his insurer and using a solicitor of his own choice.[44]

Double insurance[45]

10–54   Where the driver of a vehicle involved in an accident is covered, for instance, by the vehicle owner's commercial vehicle insurance and by his own vehicle insurance, then rateable proportion clauses in those policies will be given effect. This means that the insurers must contribute in proportion to their respective liabilities in the absence of double insurance.[46] Thus, if two motor insurers are under a statutory obligation to satisfy a judgment obtained by an injured third party claimant, both insurers must contribute equally to the amount due to be paid.[47]

Internal insurance industry agreements

10–55   An insured who is indemnified under his own vehicle insurance policy in respect of damage sustained in an accident caused by the negligence of the driver of another vehicle is at full liberty to sue that negligent driver for the full amount of the damage he has suffered. No internal insurance industry agreement, such as the previous "knock-for-knock" agreement

---

[40] *Cox v. Orion Insurance Co. Ltd* [1982] R.T.R. 1, CA.
[41] See Chapter 2, above.
[42] *Terry v. Trafalgar Insurance Co. Ltd* [1970] 1 Lloyd's Rep. 524.
[43] *Barrett Bros. (Taxis) Ltd v. Davies* [1966] 1 W.L.R. 1334, CA.
[44] *ibid.*
[45] See, generally, Chapter 20, below.
[46] *Legal & General Assurance Society Ltd v. Drake Insurance Co. Ltd* [1992] 1 Q.B. 887, CA.
[47] *Eagle Star Insurance Co. Ltd v. Provincial Insurance plc* [1994] 1 A.C. 130, PC.

applying between the two drivers' respective insurers, can affect this right.[48] If the innocent driver recovers against the negligent driver, he must reimburse to his insurers any sum that exceeds his uninsured "excess" and loss of "no claims" discount.

6. NON-DISCLOSURE AND MISREPRESENTATION OF MATERIAL FACT

Introduction

As seen in Chapter 3, above, insurers may rescind *ab initio* a policy obtained by a misrepresentation or non-disclosure of a material fact which induced them to enter into the contract of insurance. Even in the case of statutory indemnification, insurers may rescind the policy, if they have a common law right (as against contractual right) to, provided proper notification of the proceedings for a declaration against the insured is given to any third party claiming against the insured in respect of damages for death or personal injury.[49] In all other instances, the insurers may also rely on contractual provisions, *e.g.* a "basis of the contract" declaration,[50] to rescind the policy. The onus of proof is always on the insurers, who must prove the non-disclosure or misrepresentation of the material fact at the time it is made, and their inducement.[51]

10–56

Insured's personal details

Insurers have been held entitled to avoid a policy issued to a proposer who stated he was 21 years old when he was only 19, in circumstances where it was clear to the proposer that no insurance would be issued to anyone under 21 years of age.[52] If the proposer describes himself as being in one specified business or occupation, but is in fact in another, then this can amount to grounds for rescission for material non-disclosure or misrepresentation. Thus, where a bookmaker told the insurers he was a "dealer",[53] and where a property repairer was also a part-time musician, the latter fact being undisclosed,[54] their respective insurers were held entitled to rescind the policies. Insurers have failed to establish their right to rescission in respect of driving experience, where the proposer had answered the question: "Please state how long you have driven a motor car?" with "Several years", without disclosing that it was intermittent driving experience, and some of it without a driving licence.[55] Again, insurers failed where the proposer answered the question: "Have you driven cars regularly and continuously in the United Kingdom during the

10–57

---

[48] *Morley v. Moore* [1936] 2 K.B. 359, C.A.
[49] Road Traffic Act 1988, s.152(2); see above.
[50] See Chapter 2, above.
[51] *James v. British General Insurance Co. Ltd* [1927] 2 K.B. 311; *Whitwell v. Autocar Fire & Accident Co. Ltd* (1927) 27 Ll. L. Rep. 418; *Adams v. London General Insurance Co.* (1932) 42 Ll. L. Rep. 56.
[52] *Broad v. Waland* (1942) 73 Ll. L. Rep. 263, there was also breach of a "basis" clause.
[53] *Holmes v. Cornhill Insurance Co. Ltd* (1949) 82 Ll. L. Rep. 575.
[54] *McNealy v. Pennine Insurance Co. Ltd* [1978] 2 Lloyd's Rep. 18, CA.
[55] *Corcos v. De Rougemont* (1925) 23 Ll. L. Rep. 164.

past twelve months?" with "yes", without disclosing that the total period of his driving experience was eight months, with half of it being on private land rather than public roads,[56] and in a case where the proposer for an inexperienced driver's policy did not disclose that he had failed a driving test.[57]

Insurance and loss history

10–58   The courts are rather more disposed, it seems, to finding that facts concerning the insurance and loss record of the proposer are material facts. Thus, insurers successfully rescinded policies where the proposer did not disclose three "disappearances" of a previous car insured with other insurers[58] where the proposer answered the question: "What accidents have occurred in connection with your motor cars during the past two years including cost?" with "Damaged wings", when in fact, he had had seven accidents in the previous year, all involving damage to the car wings, and he had also knocked down a pedestrian[59]; where the proposer did not give the names of all his previous motor insurers despite a specific question in the proposal form[60]; where previous refusals to insure were not disclosed despite a specific question in the proposal form[61]; where the proposer did not disclose a previous cancellation of a policy for non-payment of premium[62]; or where the proposer did not disclose previous special terms of insurers despite a question in the proposal form.[63] The accident record of a person who will regularly be permitted to drive the insured vehicle has also been held to be material and should therefore be voluntarily disclosed to the insurer.[64]

Previous convictions

10–59   In the same way, previous convictions for matters concerning motor vehicles of the proposer or regular drivers,[65] may[66] or may not[67] be material, but where a "basis" clause is used, or the truth of answers and full disclosure is warranted, immateriality is no hurdle to the insurer.[68] If an insurer

---

[56] *Zurich General Accident & Liability Insurance Co. Ltd v. Morrison* [1942] 2 K.B. 53, CA.
[57] *ibid.*
[58] *Farra v. Hetherington* (1931) 40 Ll. L. Rep. 132.
[59] *Dent v. Blackmore* (1927) 29 Ll. L. Rep. 9.
[60] *ibid.*
[61] *Mundy's Trustee (a bankrupt) v. Blackmore* (1928) 32 Ll. L. Rep. 150; *Holt's Motors Ltd v. South East Lancashire Insurance Co. Ltd* (1930) 37 Ll. L. Rep. 1, CA; *Cornhill Insurance Co. Ltd v. Assenheim* (1937) 58 Ll. L. Rep. 27; *cf.* facts of *Broad & Montague Ltd v. South East Lancashire Insurance Co. Ltd* (1931) 40 Ll. L. Rep. 328; and *Whitwell v. Autocar Fire & Accident Co. Ltd* (1927) 27 Ll. L. Rep. 418.
[62] *Norman v. Gresham Fire & Accident Insurance Society Ltd* (1935) 52 Ll. L. Rep. 292 at 301, *per* Lewis J., *obiter.*
[63] *Dent v. Blackmore* (1927) 29 Ll. L. Rep. 9; *cf. MacKay v. London General Insurance Co. Ltd* (1935) 51 Ll. L. Rep. 201, where insurer had to rely on the "basis" clause.
[64] *Dunn v. Ocean Accident & Guarantee Corp. Ltd* (1933) 47 Ll. L. Rep. 129, CA.
[65] *Jester-Barnes v. Licences & General Insurance Co. Ltd* (1934) 49 Ll. L. Rep. 231; *Bond v. Commercial Union Assurance Co. Ltd* (1930) 36 Ll. L. Rep. 107.
[66] *Taylor v. Eagle Star Insurance Co. Ltd* (1940) 67 Ll. L. Rep. 136.
[67] *MacKay v. London General Insurance Co. Ltd* (1935) 51 Ll. L. Rep. 201.
[68] *Jester-Barnes v. Licences & General Insurance Co. Ltd* (1934) 49 H.L. Rep. 231; *Cleland v. London General Insurance Co. Ltd* (1935) 51 Ll. L. Rep. 156, CA.

chooses to use a question in a proposal form, though, it must always be borne in mind that the insurer may be taken to have waived further information on that matter. Thus, if the insurer asks: "Have you or your driver ever been convicted or had a motor licence endorsed?" this will be construed as only requiring disclosure of motoring convictions.[69] Or if the question is framed so as to refer to convictions related to "driving", the proposer need not disclose other motoring convictions, e.g. permitting a car to be used with no insurance, or no vehicle excise licence,[70] or a construction and use regulation offence,[71] unless there is a warranty that he is not witholding any material fact.[72] The provisions of the Rehabilitation of Offenders Act 1974 must now be borne in mind when considering whether a previous conviction can be material, i.e. it cannot be material if "spent" under the provisions of the Act.[73] An endorsement of a driving licence does not come within the scope of the Act, and cannot therefore be rehabilitated so as to excuse failing to disclose it in answer to proposal form questions.[74]

Particulars of the vehicle

It is a material misrepresentation for a proposer to state in obtaining the **10–60** insurance that he is the owner of the vehicle when he is not,[75] but it will be immaterial that the vehicle is not actually registered in his name.[76] The question of materiality of the cost of an insured vehicle and its age have only been considered in relation to the untruth of answers subject to a "basis" clause.[77] A question relating to the "cost price" of the insured vehicle has been held to mean the cash price paid by the insured plus the trade-in value of another vehicle exchanged.[78] The location at which the vehicle is garaged may not be material,[79] or even another use of the garage.[80]

7. BREACH OF WARRANTY

Strict compliance

Breach of a warranty contained in a contract of insurance gives the **10–61** insurer a right to repudiate the policy, and the materiality or immateriality of the information is irrelevant, as with a "basis of the contract" declaration or agreement. Thus, where a female proposer used her maiden name when she was in fact married, she was held to have breached a warranty

---

[69] Cleland v. London General Insurance Co. Ltd, (1935) 51 H.L. Rep. 156, CA.
[70] Taylor v. Eagle Star Insurance Co. Ltd (1940) 67 Ll. L. Rep. 136.
[71] Revell v. London General Insurance Co. Ltd (1934) 50 Ll. L. Rep. 114.
[72] As in Cleland v. London General Insurance Co. Ltd (1935) 51 H.L. Rep. 156, CA.
[73] See Chapter 3, above.
[74] Power v. Provincial Insurance plc [1998] R.T.R. 60, CA.
[75] Guardian Assurance Co. Ltd v. Sutherland [1939] 2 All E.R. 246.
[76] James v. British General Insurance Co. Ltd [1927] 2 K.B. 311.
[77] Santer v. Poland (1924) 19 Ll. L. Rep. 29; Alien v. Universal Automobile Insurance Co. Ltd (1933) 45 Ll. L. Rep. 55.
[78] Brewtnall v. Cornhill Insurance Co. Ltd (1931) 40 Ll. L. Rep. 166.
[79] Dawsons Ltd v. Bonnin [1922] 2 A.C. 413 at 420, per Viscount Haldane and at 429, per Viscount Finlay, CA.
[80] Johnson & Perrott Ltd v. Holmes (1925) 21 Ll. L. Rep. 330.

given as to the truth of her statements.[81] Similarly, giving an inaccurate statement as to where the insured vehicle will be garaged, being untrue, breaches such a warranty.[82] On the other hand, the terms of the warranty have to be carefully considered. If a business states that the vehicle will be used in the pursuit of its business, *e.g.* "for the delivery of coal", and the truth of that statement is warranted, it is not rendered untrue merely by the vehicle being occasionally used to carry other goods or materials in addition to coal.[83] Thus, where the question is framed in terms of "to your knowledge will . . .", an answer is not untrue and there is no breach of a warranty regarding the truth of answers, if it is honestly answered, even in relation to future events.[84]

10–62   The courts have also shown themselves reluctant to hold answers that really describe the intended user of the vehicle as amounting to warranties that they shall be used solely and exclusively for those identified purposes and no other occasional use. If a business states that the vehicle will be used in the pursuit of its business, *e.g.* "for the delivery of coal", and the truth of that statement is warranted, it is not rendered untrue merely by the vehicle being occasionally used to carry other goods or materials in addition to coal.[85] Again, in *Farr v. Motor Traders Mutual Insurance Society Ltd*,[86] the owner of a taxi business insured his two taxis, he stated on the proposal form that each taxi was to be driven in one shift each 24 hours. He declared that this was true, and the statements in the proposal were to be the "basis" of the contract of insurance. Later, one cab broke down so the other cab was driven two shifts each 24 hours for a short period. Some months later, during normal operation of both cabs, one cab was involved in an accident, and the insurers sought to rescind the insurance from when the one cab had been used twice a day. The Court of Appeal rejected that there was a warranty that the cabs would only be used once in each 24-hour period, and held that the statements and declaration actually amounted to a decription of the insured risk. The effect of this was that whilst a cab was being driven more than one shift in 24 hours, this was not in compliance with the described risk as insured, so there would be no cover operative, but cover would resume once the cab resumed use in one shift each 24 hours.

10–63   The use of the word "warranty" or "warranted" is, therefore, not conclusive upon the question of whether the term is truly a warranty with all its legal consequences. As was observed subsequently, *obiter*[87]:

> "In this class of policy when persons insert clauses, whether described as warranties or whether described as part of the description of the vehicle, indicating that the vehicle is to be used in some restricted way, my opinion

[81] *Dunn v. Ocean Accident & Guarantee Corp. Ltd* (1933) 47 Ll. L. Rep. 129, CA.
[82] *Dawsons Ltd v. Bonnin* [1922] 2 A.C. 413, HL.
[83] *Provincial Insurance Co. Ltd v. Morgan* [1933] A.C. 240, HL.
[84] *Kirkbride v. Banner* [1974] 1 Lloyd's Rep. 549.
[85] *Provincial Insurance Co. Ltd v. Morgan* [1933] A.C. 240, HL.
[86] [1920] 3 K.B. 669, CA.
[87] *Roberts v. Anglo-Saxon Insurance Association Ltd* (1927) 27 Ll. L. Rep. 313 *per* Bankes L.J., *obiter*, CA.

in that case . . . is and would be that the parties had used that language as words descriptive of the risk, and that, as a result, when the vehicle is not being used in accordance with the description it is not covered; but it does not follow at all that because it is used on some one occasion, or on more than one occasion, for other than the described use, the policy is avoided. It does not follow at all. If the proper construction, on its language, is a description of the limitation of the liability, then the effect would be that the vehicle would be off cover during the period which it was not being used for the warranted purpose, but that it would come again on the cover when the vehicle was again used for the warranted purpose. I am quite clear about that, and I have no difficulty in expressing my opinion in reference to that matter."

PART III

PROPERTY AND OTHER INSURANCES

CHAPTER 11

BUILDINGS INSURANCE

1. SUBJECT MATTER OF BUILDINGS INSURANCE

Introduction

The subject matter of buildings insurance is the property itself, but the **11–01** subject matter of any contract of insurance relating to such property was explained by Bowen L.J. in the leading case of *Castellain v. Preston*[1] as being:

> "not the bricks and materials used in building the house, but the interest of the insured in the subject matter of the insurance."

This, of course, is an expression of the fundamental principle of indemnity in insurance law that the insured must have an insurable interest in the subject matter of an insurance contract, so that the insured will suffer a financial loss should the property be damaged or destroyed, this loss being the measure of the insurance indemnity. The measure of the loss is discussed fully in Chapter 19, below, but the special case of the obligation on buildings insurers to expend insurance monies on the reinstatement of the insured building in certain circumstances, under the Fires Prevention (Metropolis) Act 1774, s. 83, should be noted. One particular example of the operation of that Act follows.

Loss of buildings subject to a contract of sale

The question of whether a landlord's insurers had to pay out under the **11–02** policy, where, at the time of the fire the landlord had entered into a contract of sale of the insured building, and thereafter received the full purchase monies upon completion of the sale, arose in *Lonsdale & Thompson Ltd v. Black Arrow Group plc.*[2] The tenant of the building sought a declaration that the policy monies should be expended on the reinstatement of the building pursuant to the 1774 Act. The insurers resisted the claim on the ground that their insured had suffered no loss personally, having received the purchase monies. Accordingly, the insurers argued, if they had no contractual liability to their insured they could have no statutory liability under the 1774 Act to expend the insurance monies on reinstating the building. The court rejected the insurers' contentions, and held that in determining whether the insured landlord would be getting more than an indemnity the court had to look at what his obligations were as to the use of the insurance proceeds. Under the lease the landlord was obliged to ensure all insurance monies received after a fire were expended on

[1] (1883) 11 Q.B.D. 380, at 397, CA.
[2] [1993] Ch. 361.

reinstating the building, and therefore the insurers were obliged to pay out the insurance monies for the reinstatement of the insured building.

2. DESCRIPTION OF THE INSURED BUILDINGS

Introduction

11–03   As with any other contract, a person suing upon a contract of insurance must be able to prove to the court a prima facie loss within the terms of that contract of insurance.[3] Therefore the insured must be able to demonstrate that the damaged or destroyed building is identified as being covered by the contract of insurance, and this necessarily involves showing that the building is sufficiently described in the proposal form (if any), and the schedule or other specification attached to the issued policy. If, for instance, the building at the date of the making of a contract of insurance does not accord with the physical description of it given to the insurers, *e.g.* in the number of storeys, this alone will be a bar to an action on that building under the issued policy.[4] This is also the case where the inaccurate description is written on an initialled Lloyd's slip.[5]

Express warranties

11–04   Express warranties are often introduced by insurers applying to the description of the insured buildings. For instance, the policy may state:

> "Unless otherwise stated the Buildings referred to in the schedule or in any endorsement hereon are constructed of brick, stone or concrete, and roofed with slated tiles, metal, concrete, asphalt or sheets or slabs composed entirely of incombustible mineral ingredients."

11–05   Each warranty must be examined carefully, though, and the court will consider the accuracy of the description at the time it was warranted, even if it is concerned with a continuing warranty. For instance, in *Hair v. Prudential Assurance Co. Ltd*[6] it was held:

(1) That there was no breach of warranty when the answer "yes" was given by the insured in answer to the question "are the buildings kept in a good state of repair", without the insured going into detail of the fact that the building had been the subject of a closing order eight years previously, but that various improvements had been carried out since then. The question was whether on the balance of probability, the building was kept in a good state of repair.[7]

---

[3] *Gorman v. Hand-in-Hand Insurance Co.* (1877) I.R. 11 C.L. 224, Ex. Ch.
[4] *Sillem v. Thorton* (1854) 3 E. and B. 868. at 882, *per* Lord Campbell C.J.; and *Dobson v. Sotheby* (1827) Mood. and M. 90 at 92, *per* Lord Tenterden C.J.
[5] *Grover & Graver Ltd v. Mathews* [1910] 2 K.B. 401.
[6] [1983] 2 Lloyd's Rep. 667.
[7] *ibid.* at 672, Woolf J. (as he then was) did not rule upon whether this was a continuing warranty.

(2) In relation to occupation of the buildings, the proper way to regard the questions and answers on occupation was to treat them as being an indication of the state of affairs which existed at the time the answers were given or was going to exist within the immediate future thereafter and was going to continue so far as the insured was concerned for the period of the policy, but they did not amount to a warranty that no change would occur.

If the insured, however, has been misled by the insurer or the insurer's   **11–06**
agent so that the insured has misdescribed the property, the insurer will not be able to rely on that incorrect description, even where the description has been expressly warranted as being correct.[8] Further, where the insurer, as is often the case, has the property surveyed, either by his own employee or an independent surveyor, for the purpose of describing the buildings to be the subject matter of the insurance, the insured will not be responsible for any misdescription thereby incorporated in the policy.[9]

Construing the description
When construing the words of description, the normal rules of con-   **11–07**
struction apply, e.g. words are to be given their normal meaning, and parol (oral) evidence is not generally admissible to show that the property damaged or destroyed was intended to be embraced by the chosen words but is not obvious on a perusal of the policy.[10] Parol evidence is admissible, though, in two instances to assist the court in interpreting the sense and meaning of the words of description used in the policy:

(a) If there is an ambiguity in meaning — but there must be a real[11] and latent[12] ambiguity that needs to be resolved; or
(b) where the words of description bearing some other meaning by reason of custom or usage of trade known to and intended by both the insured and insurer to be applicable to these words.[13]

Alteration in description and risk
Even in the absence of any express warranty governing the continued   **11–08**
accuracy of the description during the currency of the contract of insurance, the description in the policy amounts to a warranty that the insured will not voluntarily do anything to make the condition of the building vary from this description, so as thereby to increase the risk or liability of the insurer. In *Sillem v. Thornton*,[14] it was held that structurally increasing the

---

[8] *Newcastle Fire Insurance Co. v. Macmorran & Co.* (1815) 3 Dow. 255 at 263, *per* Lord Eldon L.C., HL.
[9] *Universal Non-Tariff Fire Insurance Co., Re Forbes & Co.'s Claim* (1875) L.R. 19 Eq. 485 at 498, *per* Sir R. Malins V.C.
[10] *Hare v. Barstow* (1844) 8 Jur. 928.
[11] *ibid.* at 929, *per* Lord Denman C.J.
[12] *Hordern v. Commercial Union Assurance Co.* (1887) 56 L.T. 240, PC.
[13] *Scott v. Bourdillion* (1806) 2 Bos. and P.N.R. 213.
[14] (1854) 3 E. and B. 868.

insured building from two storeys to three storeys after the commencement of the insurance did increase the risk and liability of the insurer, and
thus breach the implied warranty.[15]

11-09   On the other hand, an alteration which may increase the risk of fire, but
which does not affect the description, is not an alteration of the subject
matter of the insurance, because it does not make the original description
of the building in any way incorrect.[16] As Pollock C.B. said in *Baxendale
v. Harvey*[17]:

> "The society having had notice of the nature of the risk were not entitled to
> any notice by reason of an increase in danger. A person who insures may
> light as many candles as he please in his house, though each additional can-
> dle increases the danger of setting the house on fire."

11-10   If insurers wish to have the right to rescind the policy, or to repudiate
liability on the ground of breach of a condition precedent to liability,
where there is an alteration in any of the circumstances affecting the hazard,
rather than in the description of the subject matter, then the insurers must
do so in distinct terms.[18] Where such a distinct condition either prohibits
the introduction of specified items into the building,[19] or limits the
quantity,[20] or prohibits increase in the risk of destruction generally, such a
condition will apply even though such introduction or increase in risk did
not cause the actual fire loss.[21]

Express provision regarding increase in risk of loss

11-11   The effect of the following type of condition has been considered by the
courts on four occasions:

> "This policy shall be avoided with respect to any item thereof in regard to
> which there be any alteration after the commencement of this insurance . . .
> whereby the risk of destruction or damage is increased. . . unless such alter-
> ation be admitted by memorandum signed by or on behalf of the insurers."

11-12   In *Farnham v. Royal Insurance Co. Ltd*,[22] a specification attached to the
policy recorded the sum insured, the plan reference, and the descriptions of
the insured buildings (Item 1). At the date of the fire, the description was:

---

[15] *ibid.* at 888, *per* Lord Campbell C.J.; this decision was doubted by Wilkes J. in *Stokes
v. Cox* (1856) 1 H. and N. 533 at 536 and 538, but see *Simon Brooks Ltd v. Hepburn* [1961]
2 Lloyd's Rep. 43.

[16] *Pim v. Reid* (1843) 6 Man. and G. 1.

[17] (1859) 4 H. and N. 445 at 452; see also *Exchange Theatre Ltd v. Iron Trades Mutual
Insurance Co. Ltd* [1984] 1 Lloyd's Rep. 149 at 151 and 152, *per* Eveleigh L.J., CA.

[18] *Baxendale v. Harvey* (1859) 4 H. and N. 445 at 450, *per* Martin B., citing *Stokes v. Cox*
(1856) 1 H. and N. 533 (where a steam engine was introduced, the jury had found that this
did not breach a condition prohibiting an increase in the risk).

[19] *M'Ewan & Thompson v. Guthridge* (1860) 13 Moo. P.C.C. 304; see also *Hales v. Reliance
Fire & Accident Insurance Corp. Ltd* [1960] 2 Lloyd's Rep. 391.

[20] *Beacon Life & Fire Assurance Co. v. Gibb* (1862) 1 Moo. P.C.C.(n.s.) 73, PC.

[21] *Glen v. Lewis* (1853) 8 Exch. 607; *Beacon Life & Fire Assurance Co. v. Gibb* (1862) 1 Moo.
P.C.C.(n.s.) 73, PC.

[22] [1976] 2 Lloyd's Rep. 437.

". . . barn used for storage of Straw and Feeding Stuffs, Corrugated iron. Timber and small part brick built and roofed with corrugated asbestos and tiles."

Later correspondence, however, between insurer and insured varied the agreed use to that of storage of goods as part of the business of a general haulage depot.

The insured then permitted the barn to be used as a repair shop for large containers when some oxy-acetylene cutting of small plates and electric arc welding of broken fittings took place within the barn for some months prior to the fire. Was there an alteration in Item 1 whereby the risk of destructional damage was increased? Clearly there was, and the insured was unable to recover under the policy.

That case can be contrasted with *Exchange Theatre Ltd v. Iron Trades*   **11–13** *Mutual Insurance Co. Ltd*.[23] Item 1 under the policy were the buildings and landlord's fixtures and fittings, followed by the address of the buildings, and the words:

> "Said buildings are marked on a plan of the premises lodged with the company and are brick or store built and roofed with slates, tiles, concrete, timber and felt, or asbestos, lighted by electricity, heated by ducted warm air from two gas fired boilers and are occupied by the insureds for the purposes of their trade as dancing, restaurant, bingo, disco and function room proprietors."

The insured claimants subsequently introduced on to the premises a petrol-driven electric-generating machine, and for use in that machine they kept some petrol in a plastic container. A fire and explosion later occurred, attributed to petrol, which caused the destruction of the building, and the defendant insurers sought to avoid the policy for breach of the condition.

The Court of Appeal held that there was no breach of the condition.   **11–14** *Per* Eveleigh L.J.[24]:

> "What has to be asked is; does it constitute an alteration of the item; and the building is part of the description of the item . . . reading every word of it from 'The Buildings' down to 'disco and function room proprietors' I can find in respect of Item 1 no alteration whatsoever. What had happened was that something had been introduced into the building (with its attendant description of the subject matter of the insurance) which in fact had increased the danger of fire, and increased the risk — using the word 'risk' here in the sense of hazard — but it does not follow from that that that introduction is an alteration of the item. There are many cases where something has been done upon premises which has increased the danger against which the policy is intended to guard, but that does not of itself mean that the insurers are not on risk. It is not unusual to find a term in a policy specifically directed to limiting the kind of activity that may be carried on in the building and to find the prohibition of the storage of certain dangerous items or chemicals in a building. We are not concerned with any such, because they do not exist in this case. What Condition 2 is concerned with, as I see it, is alteration of the subject matter of the insurance."

---

[23] [1984] 1 Lloyd's Rep. 149, CA.
[24] [1984] 1 Lloyd's Rep. 149 at 151–152.

11-15   The Court of Appeal followed that reasoning in *Kausar v. Eagle Star Insurance Co. Ltd*[25] and held that such a condition does not mean that the policy lapses simply because the chance or risk of damage increases during the currency of the policy. What it means is the same as the common law position, that there will be no cover where the circumstances have so changed that it could properly be said by the insurers that the new situation wa something which, on the true construction of the policy, they had not agreed top cover. Insurer accept a premium and take upon themselves the risk of the insured peril occurring. They calculate the premium according to their assessment of the chances of the risk operating, and the fact that they may learn, with hindsight, that they got the assessment wrong does not begin to establish that what happened fell outside the cover they agreed to give.[26] Similarly, in *Hussain v. Brown*[27] a condition in a policy which requires the insured to give notice to the insurer of "any alteration likely to increase the risk of loss of or damage to the property insured", and to pay "such reasonable premium, if any, as may be required" by the insurers as a result, does not give rise to any right for the insurer to bring the insurance to an end if the insured fails to give the required notice. This is because the wording does not envisage the ending of the contract by the alteration, but only an adjustment of the premium payable.

Exclusion relating to storage of inflammable material

11-16   A condition excluding loss occurring whilst a specified inflammable material "is stored or kept in any building insured" will not be breached, however, where only a small quantity is introduced for a domestic or like purpose.[28] As Lord MacNaghten has said[29]:

> "What is the meaning of the words 'stored or kept' in collocation and in the connection in which they are found? They are common English words with no very precise or exact signification. They have a kindred meaning, and cover very much the same ground. The expression, as used in the statutory conditions, seems to point to the presence of a quantity not inconsiderable, or at any rate not trifling in amount, and to import a notion of warehousing or depositing for safe custody or keeping in stock for trading purposes. It is difficult, if not impossible, to give an accurate definition of the meaning, but if one takes a concrete case, it is not very difficult to say whether a particular thing is 'stored or kept' within the meaning of the condition. No one probably would say that a person who had a reasonable quantity of tea in his house for domestic use was 'storing or keeping' tea there, or (to take the instance of benzine, which is one of the prescribed articles) no one would say that a person who had a small bottle of benzine for removing grease spots or cleansing purposes of that sort was 'storing or keeping' benzine."

[25] [2000] Lloyd's Rep. I.R. 154, at 158, *per* Staughton L.J., CA.
[26] *ibid.* at 156–157, *per* Saville L.J.
[27] *Hussain v. Brown* [1996] 1 Lloyd's Rep. 627, CA.
[28] *Thompson v. Equity Fire Assurance Co.* [1910] A.C. 592, PC.
[29] *ibid.* at 596.

Express warranty regarding use, or non-use

Where a particular use or non-use is expressly warranted such will also   **11–17**
be construed with regard to habitual user or non-user, and not
occasional.[30] Thus, in *Dobson v. Sotheby*[31] a buildings insurance against
fire was effected on agricultural buildings described in the policy as "a
barn, situated in an open field, timber built and tile", and warranted
"where no fire is kept, and no hazardous goods are deposited". During the
currency of the policy the buildings required tarring, and a fire was
consequently lit inside, and a tar-barrel was brought into the building, for
the purpose of performing the necessary operations. In the absence and by
the negligence of the insured's employee, the tar boiled over, took fire, and the
premises were burnt down.

The defendant insurer contended that their actions breached the   **11–18**
warranty and rendered the policy void, but judgment was given to the
insured. As Lord Tenterden C.J. explained[32]:

> "If the Company intended to stipulate, not merely that no fire should
> habitually be kept on the premises, but that none should ever be introduced
> upon them, they might have expressed themselves to that effect; and the
> same remark applies to the case of hazardous goods also. In the absence of
> any such stipulation, I think that the condition must be understood as for-
> bidding only the habitual use of fire, or the ordinary deposit of hazardous
> goods, not their occasional introduction, as in this case, for a temporary
> purpose connected with the occupation of the premises."

3. INSURABLE INTERESTS IN BUILDINGS

Time of interest

The general principle of non-marine insurance law applies, namely, that   **11–19**
the interest in the building insured must exist both[33]:

(i) at the time of the effecting of the insurance contract; and
(ii) at the time of the loss.

There is one exception to this principle, and that is where there has been
a valid assignment of the policy.[34]

The nature of an insurable interest in buildings

The essence of insurable interest in buildings insurance is a proprietary   **11–20**
interest in the insured building, or a contractual right relating to the
insured building. This is because the insurance must indemnify the insured
against the loss of such a right upon some contingency affecting the possession or enjoyment of the insured.[35] A mere expectation of a proprietary

---

[30] *Shaw v. Robberds* (1837) 6 Ad. and El. 75.
[31] (1827) Mood. and M. 90.
[32] *ibid.* at 92.
[33] *Sadlers' Co v. Badcock* (1743) 2 Atk. 554 at 556, *per* Lord Hardwicke.
[34] For assignment, see Chapter 1, above.
[35] *Lucena v. Craufurd* (1806) 2 Bos. and Pul. 269 at 321, *per* Lord Eldon L.C.

interest or a contractual right in the building is insufficient.[36] The following categories of persons may have an insurable interest in buildings that can be insured.

Owners

11-21   An absolute owner of property is entitled to insure it,[37] as is a joint owner[38] (*e.g.* a partner regarding partnership property[39]) or a limited owner.[40] Property owned by a limited company is owned, of course, by the company, and not the shareholders or ordinary creditors of that company. Accordingly, neither of the latter two categories of person has an insurable interest in the buildings owned by the company, as explained by Lord Buckmaster in *Macaura v. Northern Assurance Co. Ltd*[41]:

> "the appellant . . . cannot establish his claim as creditor.
>
> Turning now to his position as a shareholder, this must be independent of the extent of his share interest. If he were entitled to insure holding all the shares in the company, each shareholder would be equally entitled, if the shares were in separate hands. Now, no shareholder has any right to any item of property owned by the company, for he has no legal or equitable interest therein. He is entitled to a share in the profits while the company continues to carry on business and a share in the distribution of the surplus assets when the company is wound up. If he were at liberty to effect an insurance against loss by fire of any item of the company's property, the extent of his insurable interest could only be measured by determining the extent to which his share in the ultimate distribution would be diminished by the loss of the asset - a calculation almost impossible to make. There is no means by which such an interest can be definitely measured and no standard which can be fixed of the loss against which the contract of insurance could be regarded as an indemnity.
>
> On the other hand, a creditor who has secured his debt over the company's buildings, has a legal interest in those buildings, and may insure."[42]

Partnership property

11-22   Where a partnership takes out an insurance on property, it has been suggested that where there is a change in the constitution of the partnership that effected the insurance, the "new" partnership cannot recover in respect of its losses of that property, because of the personal nature of

[36] *ibid.* at 325.

[37] *Hobbs v. Hannam* (1811) 3 Camp. 93; *Collingridge v. Royal Exchange Assurance Corp.* (1877) 3 Q.B.D. 173.

[38] *Page v. Fry* (1800) 2 Bos. and P. 240 at 243, *per* Heath J.

[39] *Reid v. Hollinshead* (1825) 4 B. and C. 867.

[40] *Warwicker v. Bretnall* (1882) 23 Ch. D. 188; *cf. Seymour v. Vernon* (1852) 21 L.J. Ch. 433; *Castellain v. Preston* (1883) 11 Q.B.D. 380 at 401, *per* Bowen L.J., CA; *Gaussen v. Whatman* (1905) 93 L.T. 101.

[41] [1925] A.C. 619 at 626-627, HL *cf. Paterson v. Harris* (1861) 1 B. and S. 336, where the point was not argued. Lord Buckmaster also approved *Moran, Galloway & Co. v. Uzielli* [1905] 2 K.B. 555 at 562, where Walton J. said:

"in so far as the plaintiff's claim depends upon the fact that they were ordinary unsecured creditors of the shipowners for an ordinary unsecured debt, I am satisfied that it must fail."

See also *Wilson v. Jones* (1867) L.R. 2 Exch. 139.

[42] See *Moran, Galloway & Co. v. Uzielli* [1905] 2 K.B. 555 at 562; *Briggs v. Merchant Traders' Ship Loan & Insurance Association* (1849) 13 Q.B. 167.

property insurances which renders the insurance void on the change of the constitution of the insured without the insurer's knowledge and consent.[43]

Mortgagees and mortgagors

Both a mortgagee, by virtue of his legal ownership,[44] and a mortgagor,   **11–23** by virtue of his equitable ownership,[45] have an insurable interest in the mortgaged property. Moreover, where the mortgage is made by deed, the mortgagee is generally entitled to insure, at the expense of the mortgagor, against loss or damage by fire any building being or forming part of the mortgaged property.[46] Equitable mortgagees over specific property may insure such property as is subject to their equitable interest.[47]

Tenants

Any tenant has an insurable interest in the building or buildings which   **11–24** he occupies,[48] except, perhaps, where a tenant remains in possession after expiry of a lease as a tenant at will before a newly contracted lease comes into effect.[49] The tenant probably has an insurable interest in the leased premises even if, by the terms of the lease, the tenant is relieved of the obligation to pay rent if the premises cannot be occupied consequent upon the occurrence of an insured peril.[50]

Vendors and purchasers

The vendor of a building has an insurable interest in that building   **11–25** because of legal ownership of the building, and also because the purchaser may not carry out the contract which would leave the vendor to suffer any loss or damage the building sustained after conclusion of the agreement to sell.[51] Even after completion of the conveyance, the vendor will retain an insurable interest so long as he (a) has a lien as unpaid seller,[52] or (b) has a contractual responsibility for the safety of the building.[53] The purchaser acquires an insurable interest upon the agreement to buy the building being concluded, even though he is not yet liable to pay for the building, for the risk now lies with him[54] and he should insure to the full value.

---

[43] *Jenkins v. Deane* (1933) 47 Ll. L. Rep. 342 at 347, col. 1, *per* Goddard J. (as he then was).
[44] *Castellain v. Preston* (1883) 11 Q.B.D. 380 at 398, *per* Bowen L.J., CA; *North British & Mercantile Insurance Co. v. London, Liverpool & Globe Insurance Co.* (1876) 5 Ch. D. 569 at 583, *per* Mellish L.J., CA.
[45] *Small v. United Kingdom Marine Insurance Association* [1897] 2 Q.B. 311 at 313, *per* Lord Esher M.R., CA.
[46] See Law of Property Act 1925, ss. 101, 108 and 109.
[47] *Westminster Fire Office v. Glasgow Provident Investment Society* (1888) 13 App. Cas. 699, HL.
[48] *Simpson v. Scottish Union Insurance Co.* (1863) 1 Hem. and M. 618; *Castellain v. Preston* (1883) 11 Q.B.D. 380, CA.
[49] *Callaway v. Ward* (1730) cited in 1 Ves. 318.
[50] See *Mark Rowlands Ltd v. Berni Inns Ltd* [1986] Q.B. 211, CA.
[51] *Castellain v. Preston* (1883) 11 Q.B.D. 380 at 385, *per* Brett L.J., CA; *Collingridge v. Royal Exchange Assurance Corp.* (1877) 3 Q.B.D. 173 at 177, per Lush J.
[52] *Castellain v. Preston* (1883) 11 Q.B.D. 380 at 401, *per* Bowen L.J., CA.
[53] *North British & Mercantile Insurance Co. v. Moffatt* (1871) L.R. 7 C.P. 25.
[54] *Paine v. Metier* (1801) 6 Ves. 349; *Poole v. Adams* (1864) 10 L.T. 287.

4. RISKS INSURED UNDER A "FIRE" POLICY

11–26   Buildings may be insured against additional special perils,[55] but the
basic form of insurance policy issued, although commonly known as a
"fire policy", will cover three risks:

    (a) fire;
    (b) lightning;
    (c) explosion.

The peril of fire
11–27   The word "fire", being contained in a commercial contract, must be
understood in its normal meaning and therefore has been construed as
meaning that there must have been an ignition — the concepts of "ignition"
and "burning" being synonymous.[56] Loss or damage caused by scorching
is thus not embraced by the word "fire", if there has been no ignition or
incandescence of the damaged property.[57] Similarly, if an insured building
is damaged by its windows and window frames being shattered, and its
structure weakened by reason of an explosion at nearby premises, this will
not be covered by the fire damage part of the insurance, for the damage
will have arisen by reason of the concussion of air, not through fire, even
though the explosion may have followed an ignition.[58]
11–28   To determine whether the loss or damage to the insured building has
been caused by the insured peril of fire, the true test is whether or not there
has been an ignition of the insured property which was not intended to be
ignited.[59] Or, put another way, has insured property been damaged otherwise than by burning as a direct consequence of the ignition of other
property not intended to be ignited? If that test is satisfied, all loss to the
insured building attributable to the fire is covered by the insurance, *e.g.*
cracking and scorching of the structure of the building, or damage to
fixtures and fittings caused by the heat or smoke.
11–29   Equally, damage caused to the insured building by the insured or other
persons in efforts to extinguish the fire or contain it will be covered
providing such efforts were bona fide and necessary.[60] This principle does
not extend, of course, to damage that is not truly caused by the fire —
which will be a matter of fact. For instance, a wall weakened by the fire
may collapse only a few days after the fire, but this damage may or may
not be covered depending upon the actual reason for the collapse, *e.g.* an
exceptionally high wind, rather than the weakening of the wall, may
amount to a *novus actus interveniens* breaking the chain of causation of

[55] See Section 3 of the specimen combined policy in Appendix 1.
[56] *Fleming v. Hislop* (1886) 11 App. Cas. 686 at 692, *per* Lord Selborne, HL.
[57] *Tempus Shipping Co. Ltd v. Louis Dreyfus & Co. Ltd* [1930] 1 K.B. 699 at 708, *per* Wright
J. (not affected by the appeal [1931] 1 K.B. 195, CA; affirmed [1931] A.C. 726, HL).
[58] *Everett v. London Assurance* (1865) 19 C.B.(n.s.) 126.
[59] *Harris v. Poland* [1941] 1 KB 462 at 468, *per* Atkinson J. (as he then was); following
Austin v. Drewe (1816) 2 Marsh. 130.
[60] *e.g.* blowing up part of the premises, *Stanley v. Western Insurance Co.* (1868) L.R. 3
Exch. 71 at 74, *per* Kelly C.B.

the damage. Alternatively, if the collapse was due to the inadequate shoring of the wall, the damage will be covered,[61] because the fire will still have been the proximate cause of the loss or damage. The issue of proximate causation of insured losses is addressed in detail in Chapter 17, below.

Common exceptions in "fire" policies

Unless the policy provides otherwise, the origin of the fire is immaterial **11–30** (unless the insured has conspired to commit arson[62]). Insurers accordingly usually expressly exclude loss or damage to buildings attributable to a fire arising from:

    (i) *Its undergoing any process involving the application of heat.*[63]
   (ii) *Earthquake.* If the fire at the insured premises was set in operation by an earthquake, and then spread by natural causes without the intervention of any other cause, that is, spread by the wind or by one thing catching fire from another, and so on and then spread without the intervention of any cause to the insured premises, then the damage will be within this exception.[64] Obviously, if the fire started before the earthquake, it is outside the exception.[65]
  (iii) *Subterranean fire.* For instance, a fire of volcanic origin, or a fire in a coal mine or oil well.
  (iv) *Riot.* This must be understood in its strict legal sense, rather than any extended popular meaning, therefore, the criminal law must be considered as providing the definition. According to *Field v. Metropolitan Police Receiver*,[66] there are five necessary elements to constitute a riot:

    (a) no fewer than three persons assembled;
    (b) with a common purpose;
    (c) the execution or inception of that common purpose;
    (d) an intent to help one another by force if necessary against any person who may oppose them in the execution of the common purpose; and
    (e) force or violence, not merely used in and about the common purpose, but displayed in such a manner as to alarm at least one person of reasonable firmness and courage.

---

[61] See *Reischer v. Berwick* [1894] 2 Q.B. 548, CA, where inadequate repairs were held not to amount to any intervening event breaking the chain of causation.

[62] See, below, allegation of arson by insurer.

[63] See the definition of "Insured Peril" in Section 3 of the specimen combined policy in Appendix 1.

[64] *Tootal Broadhurst Lee Co. Ltd v. London & Lancashire Fire Insurance Co., The Times,* May 21, 1908, PC.

[65] *Pawsey & Co. v. Scottish Union & National Insurance Co., The Times,* October 17, 1908, PC.

[66] [1907] 2 K.B. 853.

Where the riot exclusion operates, the insured may be able to recover compensation from the compensation authority under the Riot (Damages) Act 1886 (as amended by the Police Act 1964 and the Local Government Act 1972), but the Act requires both riot and tumultuous assembly.[67]

(v) *Civil commotion.* This term has no precise legal definition, but indicates a stage between a riot and a civil war,[68] where the element of turbulence or tumult is present,[69] the disturbances having a sufficient cohesion to prevent them from being the work of a mindless mob.[70] It is "an insurrection of the people for general purposes" which does not have to amount to rebellion against the government.[71]

(vi) *War, invasion, act of foreign enemy, hostilities (whether war be declared or not).*

(vii) *Civil war, rebellion, revolution, insurrection or military or usurped power.* In determining whether a civil war is in existence or not, a court would consider three questions[72]:

(a) Could it be said that the conflict was between two opposing "sides"?

(b) What were the objectives of the "sides", and how did they set about pursuing them? and

(c) What was the scale of the conflict, and its effect on public order and on the life of the inhabitants?

11–31   "Insurrection" and "rebellion" both suggest action against the government with a view to supplanting it,[73] as, indeed, does "revolution", each term perhaps suggesting varying degrees of organisation. "Usurped power" does not include a loss caused by a lawless mob.[74] "Military power" includes a foreign military power[75] as well as home government military power.[76]

The peril of lightning

11–32   It has been the practice of insurers for a substantial period to include lightning damage in fire policies, and this damage will thus be covered even though there is no ignition.

---

[67] *J.W. Dwyer Ltd v. Metropolitan Police District Receiver* [1967] 2 Q.B. 970.
[68] *Bolivia Republic v. Indemnity Mutual Marine Assurance Co. Ltd* [1909] 1 K.B. 785 at 800, *per* Farwell L.J., CA.
[69] *Levy v. Assicurazioni Generali* [1940] A.C. 791, PC.
[70] *Spinney's (1948) Ltd v. Royal Insurance Co. Ltd* [1980] 1 Lloyd's Rep. 406 at 438, *per* Mustill J.
[71] *Longdale v. Mason* (1780) 2 Marshall (2nd ed.) 791, *per* Lord Mansfield; approved in *London & Manchester Plate Glass Co. Ltd v. Heath* [1913] 3 K.B. 411, CA.
[72] *Spinney's (1948) Ltd v. Royal Insurance Co. Ltd* [1980] 1 Lloyd's Rep. 406 at 429–430, *per* Mustill J.
[73] *ibid.* at 436.
[74] *Drinkwater v. London Assurance Corp.* (1767) 2 Wits. 363.
[75] *Rogers v. Whittaker* [1917] 1 K.B. 942.
[76] *Curtis & Sons v. Mathews* [1919] 1 K.B. 425, CA.

The peril of explosion

In the absence of any mention of "explosion", a fire policy covers loss   **11–33**
or damage arising from an explosion caused by fire,[77] or, conversely, fire
damage following an explosion,[78] but not from an explosion independent
of fire.[79] In the first case all the loss and damage to the building will be
covered, both from concussion and fire, because the overriding, proximate
cause of the loss or damage was fire.[80] In the second instance, the insurance is against loss or damage caused by fire, and thus pure concussion
damage is outside the scope of the insurance, which is also the principle
behind the third instance. Where there is a fire in a building which causes
an explosion within that building, all the loss therein would be covered by
a fire insurance, but concussion damage to a neighbouring building would
not, as it would fall within the third case instanced above.[81]

In practice, modern fire policies will contain special provisions regarding   **11–34**
explosions. Insurance companies will usually insert a general condition
expressly including loss or damage caused by explosion. Where this is the
case, the explosion does not need to be caused by a fire, but explosions
caused by the excluded perils (ii) to (vii) above. "Explosion" in such policies
has been held to mean an event that is violent, noisy and caused by a very
rapid chemical or nuclear reaction or the bursting out of gas or vapour
under pressure.[82] Loss and damage to the insured building caused by
tephra emanating from volcanic explosions will also be covered.[83] The
insured peril of explosion will probably be limited to the explosion of the
following two categories, and the insurance against explosion of industrial
boilers and plant will need more specific boiler insurance.

Boilers used for domestic purposes only

Where this appears in a commercial buildings insurance, the cover   **11–35**
applies if the water is used for a purpose which is common to all ordinary
domestic establishments. A boiler is none the less used for domestic
purposes if its use is ancilliary to a trade, manufacture or business.[84]
In other words, the test is whether the user in its nature is domestic.[85]

---

[77] *Stanley v. Western Insurance Co.* (1868) L.R. 3 Exch. 71 at 74, *per* Kelly C.B.; *Curtis's A. Harvey (Canada) Ltd v. North British & Mercantile Insurance Co. Ltd* [1921] 1 A.C. 303, PC, approving *Hobbs v. Northern Assurance Co.* (1886) 12 S.C.R. 631.

[78] *Everett v. London Assurance* (1865) 19 C.B.(n.s.) 126 at 133, *per* Byles J. But not damage due only to concussion from the explosion, for this is not damage proximately caused by fire, see *Re Hooley Hill Rubber & Chemical Co. Ltd & Royal Insurance Co. Ltd* [1920] 1 K.B. 257 at 272, *per* Scrutton L.J., CA.

[79] *Re Hooley Hill Rubber & Chemical Co. Ltd & Royal Insurance Co. Ltd* [1920] 1 K.B. 257 at 274, *per* Duke L.J., CA.

[80] *Everett v. London Assurance* (1865) 19 C.B.(n.s.) 126.

[81] As in *Everett v. London Assurance* (1865) 19 C.B.(n. s.) 126, where a property was damaged when a neighbouring building's gunpowder magazine exploded.

[82] *Commonwealth Smelting Ltd v. Guardian Royal Exchange Assurance Ltd* [1984] 2 Lloyd's Rep. 608; affirmed [1986] 1 Lloyd's Rep. 121, CA.

[83] *Martini Investments v. McGuin* [2000] 2 Lloyd's Rep. 313.

[84] *Metropolitan Water Board v. Avery* [1913] 2 K.B. 257 at 265, *per* Bray J.; approved [1914] A.C. 118, HL.

[85] *Metropolitan Water Board v. Avery* [1914] 1 K.B. 221 at 239, *per* Buckley L.J., CA; approved [1914] A.C. 118, HL.

Accordingly, the explosion of a boiler (and this term may, on the facts of a particular case, be held to mean both a tank where water is heated and a larger transfer storage tank) used only for providing hot water to heat the insured building, is embraced by this wording.[86] It will be immaterial that workrooms and rooms used to store the goods of the business are heated by the system, for this does not prevent the boiler being "used for domestic purposes only".[87]

Explosion of gas

11–36   The insured peril may be explosion "in a building not being part of a gas works, of gas used for domestic purposes or used for lighting or heating the building". These words are clear enough in their meaning and need little explanation beyond stating that "domestic purposes" will be construed as in the preceding paragraph, and "gas", even in the absence of the remaining words, has been interpreted as meaning gas as normally supplied to premises and not gas created on the premises by a manufacturing process.[88]

Lloyd's "fire" policy

11–37   The Lloyd's fire policy commonly in use (Form C) deals with explosion in a different way. There are no exceptions as are found in insurance companies' policies, above, rather the policy is simply stated to cover the perils of fire and/or lightning and:

(i) fire consequent upon explosion, wherever the explosion occurs (this wording is apparently superfluous, because the absence of any general exception of explosion means that this peril is already covered by the peril of fire)[89];

(ii) explosion consequent upon the premises insured; (again, because of the absence of any general exclusion of explosion, these words are superfluous, the peril already being covered by the fire cover)[90];

(iii) explosion of domestic boilers and/or of gas used for domestic purposes or for heating and/or lighting (this cover therefore amounts to the same as that described in respect of the insurance companies' cover, above).

5. ADDITIONAL INSURABLE RISKS[91]

Perils from persons

11–38   Destruction or damage (by fire or otherwise, including explosion) of or to the insured premises which is directly caused by riot or civil commotion[92]

---

[86] *Willesden Borough Corp. v. Municipal Mutual Insurance Ltd* (1945) 78 Ll. L. Rep. 256, CA.
[87] *ibid.* at 259, *per* Mackinnon L.J., CA.
[88] *Stanley v. Western Insurance Co.* (1868) L.R. 3 Exch. 71 at 74, *per* Kelly C.B.
[89] *Everett v. London Assurance* (1865) 19 C.B.(n.s.) 126.
[90] *Stanley v. Western Insurance Co.* (1868) L.R. 3 Exch. 71, at 74, *per* Kelly C.B.; *Curtis's A. Harvey (Canada) Ltd v. North British & Mercantile Insurance Co. Ltd* [1921] 1 A.C. 303, PC.
[91] See the cover in Section 3 of the specimen policy in Appendix 1.
[92] See, above, common exceptions (iv) and (v) under "fire" cover, for interpretation of these words.

(excluded under the standard fire policy), strikers, locked-out workers or persons taking part in labour disturbances, will be covered, together with such caused by malicious persons, (often with the requirement that the malicious persons must have been acting on behalf of or in connection with a political organisation). This wording in its latter part obviously had reference to the Malicious Damage Act 1861, which has now been repealed and replaced by the Criminal Damage Act 1971, but insurers have not yet modified the wording.

Storm and tempest

These may be specifically insured. "Tempest" means no more than a severe storm.[93] "Storm" means something more prolonged and widespread than a gust of wind.[94] It connotes some sort of violent wind usually accompanied by rain or hail or snow. Storm does not mean persistent bad weather, nor does it normally mean heavy rain or persistent rain by itself.[95] In *Glasgow Training Group (Motor Trade) Ltd v. Lombard Continental plc*,[96] part of the roof of the insured building collapsed due to the additional loading imposed by a considerable quantity of snow which had landed on the roof. The claimants contended this had resulted from the insured peril of "storm". The court considered the definition in the Shorter Oxford Dictionary and concluded that a storm might involve an element of violence in the sense of rapid movement of air or liquid, it could also cover precipitation of an extreme or unusual intensity. In the particular case of snow, as opposed to rain or hail, the precipitation might be in itself of a less impetuous or rapid nature, but if the snow fell with a significant degree of intensity, the event was properly called a snow storm.

11–39

Whether a fall was or was not "heavy" was a question of fact and circumstance. There might be degrees of intensity of precipitation. In assessing the precipitation, the fallen snow might properly be considered. Duration was a relevant factor, but was a matter of degree and circumstance which did not admit of precise definition. As regards the word "violence" in the dictionary definition, the court was of the view that while violence was a matter of degree, the intensity of severity of an incident as well as its suddenness or the speed of impact involved in it, might be characterised as violence. In the present case, there had been significant falling of snow over a relatively short period and a degree of turbulence. Movement by car or on foot had become difficult or impossible. Accordingly, all presented a picture of conditions or of the effect of conditions to which the description "storm" was appropriate and the claimant insured were entitled to recover from the insurers.

11–40

---

[93] *ibid.* See also *Anderson v. Norwich Union Fire Insurance Society Ltd* [1977] 1 Lloyd's Rep. 253, CA.

[94] *S. & M. Hotels Ltd v. Legal & General Assurance Society Ltd* [1972] 1 Lloyd's Rep. 157 at 165, *per* Thesiger J.

[95] *Oddy v. Phoenix Assurance Co. Ltd* [1966] 1 Lloyd's Rep. 134 at 138, *per* Veale J.

[96] [1989] S.L.T. 375.

Flood

11–41   If "flood" appears by itself as a separate peril, seepage of water into a building may be included in the cover, but such seepage would not be included where the wording is "storm, tempest and flood" because, by analogy, something more abnormal than mere water seepage is intended. Rather, a flood is something large, sudden and temporary, not naturally there, such as a river overflowing its banks.[97] A "flood" should normally involve some natural phenomena or abnormal occurrence causing invasion of property by a large volume of water from an external source.[98] An accumulation of rainwater after a period of heavy rainfall causing an ingress of water some 3–4 inches deep was held by the Court of Appeal in *Rohan Investments Ltd v. Cunningham and others*[99] where the court also pointed out that the size and nature of the property, and the different circumstances which may give rise to flooding, prevents a rigid set of criteria being laid down.

Subsidence

11–42   Although insurers often regard this cover to only be in relation to collapse, or sinking in a vertical direction of the insured building, in *David Allen and Sons Billposting Ltd v. Drysdale*,[1] a policy issued against loss or damage caused by "subsidence and/or collapse" was held[2] capable of covering not only collapse and/or sinking of the building in a vertical direction, but also settlement, *i.e.* movement of the building structure in a lateral direction. Intentional demolition is not covered by such wording.[3] It is this risk that has caused buildings insurers most difficulty in the past few decades. Problems are encountered in practice as to the determination of the settlement of the building, and if the insurer can show that this is due to original poor foundations or poor workmanship, then the insurer will take advantage of the express exclusions of these causes that appear in modern policies.

11–43   Another problem is in relation to claims where the insurer is of the opinion that subsidence damage has resulted from a long-standing problem that has existed for longer than the particular insurer has been on risk for the insured building. Some insurers will consider making an *ex gratia* payment to their insured in these circumstances, this payment towards repairs being in proportion to the period on risk as against the total period the cause has operated on the property.

11–44   Many of the problems are highlighted in the domestic buildings insurance of *Kelly v. Norwich Union Fire Insurance Society Ltd*.[4] In 1971, the

---

[97] *Young v. Sun Alliance & London Insurance Co. Ltd* [1976] 3 All E.R. 561 at 563, *per* Shaw L.J., CA.

[98] *Computer & Systems Engineering plc v. John Lelliott (Ilford) Ltd* (1990) 54 B.L.R. 1, CA.

[99] [1999] Lloyd's Rep. I. R. 190, CA.

[1] [1939] 4 All E.R. 113.

[2] *ibid.* at 114, *per* Lewis J., where "collapse" was viewed in its primary meaning as denoting "falling or shrinking together or breaking down or giving way through external pressure or loss of rigidity or support."

[3] [1939] 4 All E.R. 113.

[4] [1989] 2 All E.R. 888, CA.

claimant bought the bungalow that he had been living in since 1961. The bungalow had been built on clay in the 1920s. From 1974 to 1976 there was a period of dry weather and an exceptionally hot summer in 1976, which led to the dessication of the site by the drying of the clay. In 1977, the plaintiff painted and decorated the bungalow and put in some new floor boards, and observed no cracks or trouble with the structure. The bungalow had no storage tank inside and the water supply was direct from the mains in the roadway. In 1977, there was a break in the pipe coming to the bungalow from the mains. That break was repaired some months later. The claimant then, in October 1977, commenced insurance of the buildings and contents with the defendant insurers. A second break in the water pipe occurred at the same point in 1978 and this was repaired immediately. There was a third escape of water in 1980 when the claimant insured noticed that water was tending to lie in the area where the repairs had been carried out at the stopcock.

In 1981, the insured found damage to his bungalow and claimed under **11–45** his policy for subsidence. The defendant insurers contended that they were not liable on the basis that the damage was caused by heave in that area lying under the ground between the stopcock and very close to the wall of the bungalow where there was a totally disconnected lead pipe. When the stopcock was turned on in its trench just inside the garden wall, the effect of it was to fill the little trench, either from a leak or for some other reason, and the water would then run from that trench through this lead pipe which acted as a kind of conduit from the stopcock trench, to just in front of the bungalow. This, they contended, must have been the means of producing quantities of additional water on to the clay sub-soil. This discharge occurred from early 1980. For his part, the plaintiff relied on the 1977 break and the 1980-onwards incursion of water from the lead pipe.

The insurance policy provided, *inter alia*, that the insurers would indem- **11–46** nify the insured for loss or damage caused by any of the insured perils, which included:

"(5) Bursting or overflowing of . . . water mains . . .
(10) Landslip or subsidence of the site on which the building stands . . ."

The Court of Appeal held that the insurers' liability was brought about by the happening of one of the insured perils, and the very description of the peril as being an insured peril meant that at the time when it became fact the insurance was already effective. Thus the insured risk must take place as an insured event during the period of insurance, which meant that the damage resulting from the insured risk must also arise during the period of insurance. Accordingly, the insured's claim under his buildings insurance failed, because he had failed to show that the specified peril occurred during the term of the insurance. The insured's problem was that the 1977 leakage admittedly began and ended before the term of the first policy began, and the wording of the policy did not support the view that the insurers had agreed to indemnify him against loss or damage suffered by his bungalow during the four years of the insurers being on risk, that damage resulting from the water leakage in 1977. No quantifiable loss or damage could be shown to have occurred by reason of the 1980 leakage alone.

Miscellaneous perils

11–47   The following perils may also be insurable:

> (i) *Impact.* Impact damage by any road vehicle, horses or cattle, not belonging to or under the control or custody of the insured's employees or any director of the business, is the usual form of cover.[5]
>
> (ii) *Aircraft.* Loss or damage of the insured building, by fire or otherwise, is usually covered if directly caused by aircraft and other aerial services or articles dropped therefrom, but excluding pressure wave damage caused by aircraft travelling at sonic or supersonic speeds.
>
> (iii) *Sprinkler leakage.* This cover is generally very limited, and the leakage must be accidental rather than caused by repairs or alterations, also, there may be a provision that the insured must take all reasonable steps to prevent frost and other damage to the sprinkler system.
>
> (iv) *Escape of water.* Damage to the insured building by reason of the bursting or overflowing of water tanks, apparatus or pipes — not necessarily in the insured premises — can be covered.

Special exclusion for terrorism in Northern Ireland

11–48   Since February 1, 1978, insurers have included an overriding exclusion which affects fire and special perils insurances on buildings in Northern Ireland, and which is designed to exclude all those instances where compensation can be claimed from the government.[6] This means loss or damage arising from:

> (a) civil commotion[7]; or
>
> (b) any unlawful, wanton or malicious act committed maliciously by a person or persons acting on behalf of or in connection with any unlawful association.

"Unlawful association" is expressly defined as meaning any organisation which is engaged in terrorism and includes an organisation which at any relevant time is a proscribed organisation within the meaning of the Northern Ireland (Emergency Provisions) Act 1973. "Terrorism"[8] is

---

[5] There is an internal industry agreement of June 1995 between members of the Association of British Insurers that where damage is covered both by this exptension, and theft cover, the theft insurer will pay the first £25,000 of the insured's claim.

[6] Under the Criminal Damage (Compensation) (Northern Ireland) Order 1977 (S.I. 1977 No. 1247) and the regulations (S.R.N.I. 1978/72) made thereunder.

[7] For definition, see common exception (v) under "Fire", above.

[8] Acts of members of such organisations in furtherance of the organisation's aims are not necessarily all "terrorist acts", see *Spinney's (1948) Ltd v. Royal Insurance Co. Ltd* [1980] 1 Lloyd's Rep. 406 at 439, *per* Mustill J.

expressly defined as the use of violence for political ends and includes any use of violence for the purpose of putting the public or any section of the public in fear.

Terrorism cover in remainder of the United Kingdom

For the rest of the United Kingdom, from January 1, 1993, insurers **11–49** have only provided limited cover of £100,000 for commercial buildings in respect of terrorist damage by explosions and the like under standard cover. Rating will be highest in the main U.K. cities with extra loadings for buildings adjacent to other buildings considered prime targets of terrorist activity. Higher sums insured are available by specific arrangement.

6. "REASONABLE PRECAUTIONS" CONDITION

Buildings insurance policies will normally include a condition precedent **11–50** that the insured shall exercise reasonable care to protect the property from loss or damage. To successfully rely on the insured's breach of such a condition precedent, the insurer must establish on the balance of probabilities that the insured was reckless, not merely negligent. The question of recklessness of a tenant who claimed to be entitled to the benefit of buildings insurance (which had not actually been arranged) arose in *Lambert v. Keymood Ltd*,[9] where the applicability of the recklessness test was specifically affirmed.[10] The facts were that quantities of combustible material were habitually stored or stacked by the defendant tenants outside and very near some 10,000 sq.ft. units they leased at a disused airfield in Herefordshire. The quantities of stored materials for recycling were very large, often consisting of six or seven trailers, and sometimes being up to 18 trailers. Those materials included a good deal of expanded polystyrene, plastic beer crates, and some rubberised polystyrene. The tenants also habitually lit bonfires three or four times a week. The bonfires were lit only in the morning and usually consisted of broken pallets and cardboard, occasionally with a small amount of rubberised polystyrene.

Laws J. found the following facts from the evidence of the tenants' **11–51** witness, Mr Partington:

   (i) tending the bonfire was generally his responsibility;
  (ii) the stack of burning material was generally four to six feet square and four feet high;
 (iii) others might light fires as well as himself;
 (iv) anyone might add material to the fire after it had been started;
  (v) he or fellow-employees would rake out the fire before going home at 6 p.m., but this was not usually done earlier in the day. The fire would generally be out within one and a half and two hours of being lit, but it was not regularly checked at that sort of time.

---

[9] [1999] Lloyd's Rep. I.R. 80.
[10] *ibid.* at 89; applying *Fraser v. B.N. Furman (Productions) Ltd* [1967] 1 W.L.R. 898, CA.

11–52   There had been a visit to the premises by the landlord's then insurers' surveyor only three months before the fire had occurred on May 4, 1994. Laws J. was satisfied on hearing from that surveyor, that he had told another employee of the tenants, a Mr Smith, that he considered that both the stored materials and the bonfire site should be moved a substantial distance further away from the buildings. The tenants had not been given a copy of the surveyor's letter to the landlord, embodying his recommendation that both the stored materials and all burning should take place at 20 metres away from the buildings. After the survey visit, the tenants had moved the bonfire site, but the evidence established that the movement had been minimal, about six feet. As regards the storage of flammable materials, the tenants' manager had arranged for materials to be moved away from one of the units, but, before too long, materials were again being stacked up with materials delivered to the tenants by that unit. No attempt had ever been made to remove materials from the other two units. Overall, Laws J. concluded that there was in reality no system to see that the fires were safe and did not spread. Adding the proximity of the bonfire site to one unit in particular, and the storage of large quantities of flammable materials close to the buildings, he considered that this was a situation of obvious danger. Given also the express warnings given by the insurance surveyor three months' earlier, and the tenants' "token and minimal response", the situation became one "of obvious danger which the defendants' recklessly ignored".[11]

7. CONCEALMENT OF MATERIAL FACTS

11–53   As discussed in detail in Chapter 3, above, insurers have the right to rescind *ab initio* contracts of insurance where they were induced to enter into the contract by the insured's concealment of material facts when proposing for the insurance. A "material fact" is any fact which a prudent insurer would wish to know in assessing the risk proposed.

Description of the insured buildings

11–54   The insurers' defence of material non-disclosure of matters relating to the description of the insured building failed in *Re Universal Non-Tariff Fire Insurance Co., Forbes and Co.'s Claim*[12] where all the insured factory buildings were described as being built of brick and roofed with slate. After a fire at the factory, it was discovered that one of the buildings was not roofed with slate but with tarred felt, and the insurers sought to treat the insurance as void for misdescription. Malins V.-C. rejected the insurers' evidence that they would have refused the risk if they had known of the felt roof. Moreover, he held that even if the misdescription had been material, this would not have availed the insurers here, because their agent had drawn up the policy description, the insured had not been responsible for it.

[11] *ibid.* at 91–92.
[12] (1875) L.R. 19 Eq. 485.

The insurer's defence of non-disclosure also failed in *Kausar v. Eagle*   **11–55**
Star Insurance Co. Ltd[13] where the insurers failed to establish that the
insured hairdressing salon was also being used as a Turkish social club.
The Court of Appeal held that the evidence only established that on one
occasion there were a number of men drinking coffee at some tables. The
insurers further failed to satisfy the court that the fact that the insured, at
the time of the policy's renewal, was conducting possession proceedings
against her tenant, which had become highly acrimonious, was a material
fact. The insured had honestly believed that she would obtain a possession
order against the tenant in a couple of weeks thereafter, when the troubles
with the tenant would be at an end. In these circumstances, and given the
evidence of the underwriter at trial that he thought (wrongly) that insurers
were protected by the express condition, the insurers failed to establish
that they were influenced by the non-disclosure into renewing the policy.

Those cases may be contrasted with *Dawsons Bank Ltd v. Vulcan Insurance*   **11–56**
Co. Ltd[14] where the insured buildings were described as being "constructed
of brick walls and cement flooring in the ground storey, timber walls and
flooring in the upper storey with shingled roof". The Privy Council
accepted that there was a material misdescription of the buildings. In
delivering judgment, Lord Atkin said[15]:

> "It appears to their Lordships, on the footing that those outside lateral walls
> were as to one-third of their length brick and as to two-thirds timber, quite
> impossible to resist the inference that that would be a material departure
> from the actual description, which was that all the ground floor walls were
> brick. There seems to be some controversy as to what the lateral divisions
> were which divided up the building. Whether they were of brick, as this
> witness stated, right through from back to front, in two cases, and made of
> corrugated iron in respect of the other two, it still leaves the description of
> the building inaccurate, and it is, as appears to their Lordships, inaccurately
> described in a manner which was material for insurance purposes."

Disclosure to insurer's agent

The insurers cannot rely on concealment of a material fact where full   **11–57**
disclosure has been made to their agent with authority to receive such
information. This is discussed in Chapter 3, above. Thus, in *Pimm v.*
Lewis[16] a condition of the policy stated that it should be void if the insured
should "omit to communicate any matter material to be made known to
the insurer" did not avail insurers. A corn-mill was insured under a fire
policy through the insurer's agent who lived in the locality and knew the
mill well, but the insured did not state on the insurance proposal that rice
chaff, which was more inflammable, was also ground at the mill. The court
held that the insured could recover, for the insured had not omitted to
communicate that fact as a matter to be made known to the insurer,
because the fact was already known to the insurer through his local agent.

[13] [2000] Lloyd's Rep. I.R. 154, CA.
[14] (1934) 50 Ll. L. Rep. 129, PC.
[15] *ibid.* at 131.
[16] (1862) 2 F. and F. 778.

Previous fires

11–58   A blatant example of non-disclosure of a previous fire occurred in *Bufe v. Turner*.[17] The insured had insured one of his buildings, a warehouse, on the day following a fire at his boatbuilder's shop which was next to the warehouse. The insured was held unable to recover, the policy was avoided by his failure to disclose the material fact of the fire in the neighbouring shop, and the fact that he knew there was a danger that a further fire might break out (as indeed had happened within two days, that fire spreading to the warehouse).

11–59   The duty of disclosure includes previous losses suffered by what was essentially the same business, albeit when it was a different legal entity. This is illustrated by *Arterial Caravans Ltd v. Yorkshire Insurance Co. Ltd*,[18] where S., a businessman, had in 1955 set up the insured company, which became dormant by 1957, to sell caravans manufactured by him. The manufacturing business was then incorporated in 1956 with this businessman as its sole director and traded until 1968. In 1965, the manufacturing premises of the company were severely damaged by fire, causing a move to other premises until cessation in 1968. The first company, which was formed in 1955, was then reactivated in 1968, and commenced trading from the old manufacturing premises with S. as the sole director. This was the insured company which had then sought fire insurance from the defendant insurers.

11–60   The insurers' representative and then their district manager interviewed him. The latter asked whether the business had had any experience of losses or claims in the past, but S., on behalf of the insured company, made no disclosure of the fire at the premises in 1965 when they were owned by the second company. The insurers sought to avoid the policy, for non-disclosure of a material fact when a fire claim was made in 1970. Chapman J. held that the business was essentially the same business throughout its history, manufacturing and selling caravans, being carried on from the same premises, but for the years 1965–1968. The failure to inform the insurer of the previous fire suffered by the insured company's predecessor in the business amounted to a material non-disclosure entitling the insurers to avoid the policy.

11–61   The insured company had also argued that because they had not answered a question in the proposal form about previous losses, that the insurers had waived such disclosure. That plea was rejected on the ground that, in all the circumstances, the defendant insurers were not debarred from this right to avoid the policy by having accepted a proposal form which remained blank in respect of questions about previous losses. The insurers could not be held to have waived the non-disclosure of a fact of which they had no knowledge whatever. Waiver could only be found where an insurer has been put on inquiry about a particular matter and does not go into it further.

---

[17] (1815) 6 Taunt. 338.
[18] [1973] 1 Lloyd's Rep. 169; see also *Locker A Woolf Ltd v. Western Australian Insurance Co. Ltd* (1936) 54 Ll. L. Rep. 211 at 214, *per* Slesser L.J., CA.

Previous fires suffered by the business must be disclosed even if they   **11–62**
occurred at different premises. Thus, in *Marene Knitting Mills Pty Ltd v.
Greater Pacific General Insurance Ltd,*[19] the claimant company suffered a
fire at their new premises in 1973, but had not disclosed to the defendant
insurers that their previous premises, at a quite different location, had
suffered four fires within the last fifteen years. The Privy Council held that
once it is clear that the fire or fires were suffered by the same business, they
are material and must be disclosed to the insurer. The court would not be
diverted from that finding for the insurers by other facts, *e.g.* that the
management and/or labour force had changed, or the geographical migration of the business since the fires.

Proposal form questions may make it perfectly clear that the insurer   **11–63**
wishes to know about all previous losses by fire suffered by the proposer, not
limited to fires affecting buildings. In these circumstances, partial disclosure
only of previous fires in buildings can also amount to non-disclosure
entitling the insurers to avoid the policy upon satisfactory evidence of
materiality and inducement. In *Condogianis v. Guardian Assurance Co.
Ltd,*[20] the insured in his proposal for fire insurance on business premises
faced this question:

> "Has the proponent ever been a claimant on a fire insurance company in
> respect of the property now proposed, or any other property? If so, state
> when and name of company."

The insured quite rightly revealed that he had made a fire claim in
respect of a motor vehicle a few years earlier, but did not disclose that he
had made another fire claim for a different vehicle five years before that.
The insurers were held entitled to rescind the policy of non-disclosure of
this material fact.

Previous insurance history

It is a prevalent practice for insurers to ask questions in the proposal   **11–64**
form about the insured's previous insurance history, extending beyond
information relating only to earlier fire losses. The wording of such
questions is, of course, vital in considering replies made by the insured. If
the question is:

> "Are you or have you been insured in this or any other office?"

That question has been construed as referring only to the particular
premises to be insured, unless other premises are distinctly referred to. Thus,
where an insured did not disclose that he had insurance on his own dwelling
house when he was seeking to insure his business premises, there was held to
be no misstatement, non-disclosure or breach of warranty by the insured
who had answered "No" to this question.[21] Alternatively, if the question is:

---

[19] [1976] 2 Lloyd's Rep. 631, PC.
[20] [1921] 2 A.C. 125, PC.
[21] *Golding v. Royal London Auxiliary Insurance Co. Ltd* (1914) 30 T.L.R. 350.

"Has any other office declined to accept or renew your insurance?"

This question will not be construed in addition to its ordinary interpretation as meaning "Has any other office declined to transfer to you an existing insurance in respect of other property you have acquired?"[22]

11-65   As with disclosure of previous fires (above), where the insured is a limited company, the question will be construed as referring to the business in whatever previous form. In *Locker and Woolf Ltd v. Western Australian Insurance Co. Ltd*,[23] one of the questions in the proposal form was:

> "Has this or any other insurance of yours been declined by any other company?"

The claimant company had only recently been formed by two persons who had previously carried on the business in partnership. Two years earlier that partnership's application for an insurance on a business vehicle had been declined by another insurer, but this fact was not disclosed to the defendant insurers. The Court of Appeal held that this question required that earlier decline to be disclosed as it clearly affected the "moral hazard" the defendant insurers faced when considering whether to accept the proposal.

11-66   Similarly, in *Arthrude Press Ltd v. Eagle Star and British Dominion Insurance Co. Ltd*,[24] the claimant company had just been formed by a man who, up to the time of incorporation, had carried on the string and paper merchant and printing business on his own account. He had been refused fire insurance by one insurer for the premises, but the plaintiff company subsequently sought fire insurance for the same premises from a second insurer, the defendants. One of the questions in the proposal form was:

> "Has your insurance ever been declined by any office?"

The answer was put in the negative. When a fire claim was made some time later, the defendant insurers, on learning the true position, avoided liability under the policy. The Court of Appeal held for the insurers, Banks L.J. saying[25]:

> "reading this proposal and asking oneself what this means: 'Has your insurance ever been declined by any office?', that is not referring to the individual who happens to put forward the policy. It is perfectly obvious the question was and ought to have been understood as meaning: 'Has this risk ever been declined by any office?'"

11-67   Even in the absence of specific questions put by the insurers concerning the insured's previous insurance history, the common law duty to disclose material facts to the insurer remains. For example, it has been said that an

---

[22] *ibid.*
[23] [1936] 1 K.B. 408, CA.
[24] (1924) 19 Ll. L. Rep. 373, CA.
[25] *ibid.* at 374.

insured should disclose the nature of his interest in some circumstances, *e.g.* that he is a tenant at will.[26] It has also been held an insured must also disclose the fact that a previous insurer has declined to renew an insurance on the same risk,[27] but there is no general duty of disclosure in respect of other risks. In *Ewer v. National Employers' Mutual General Insurance Association Ltd*,[28] the insured had carried on business in partnership with S., and although S. ceased to be a partner two years before the insured effected an insurance on the business premises, they remained joint owners of those premises, and S. occasionally lent the insured money to carry on the business. When a fire subsequently occurred, the defendant insurers unsuccessfully contended that the insured should have disclosed, when effecting and renewing the insurance, without any questions being asked:

(i) every claim which he had ever had upon any other insurance policy whatever the subject matter;

(ii) the fact that any other insurance company had declined to insure or to renew an insurance upon another subject matter; and

(iii) similar details of S's insurance history.

MacKinnon J. (as he then was) rejected all three of these contentions.

8. BREACH OF WARRANTY OR CONDITION

Proposal form answers

Insurers often wish to give themselves rights to reject claims under the **11–68** insurance relating to information given at the time the insurance was sought additional to their rights to rescind the insurance for material non-disclosure. Such terms may take the form of warranties (when materiality of the fact is effectively deemed) or a general condition, *e.g.* stating that the policy shall be void if the insured has made any misdescription, misstatement or omission regarding the description of the insured buildings, or some other matter. The most common form is the "basis of the contract" declaration in the proposal form which makes any inaccuracy in the proposal form answered a ground for the insurer to rescind the contract pursuant to that contractual, rather than common law, right. This is an extremely powerful weapon for the insurer to enable the insurer to retain the premium but escape liability for a claim by finding any immaterial inaccuracy in those answers given by the insured. Fortunately, many insurers now only require a declaration that the answers are correct to the best of the proposer's knowledge and belief, so insurers can only rely on this contractual right upon proving the proposer did not believe the answer was true and accurate, or knew it was untrue. However, even with this limitation, a declaration that adds that no material fact has been withheld or suppressed still requires full, and not partial, disclosure of all

---

[26] *Anderson v. Commercial Union Assurance Co.* (1885) 55 L.J.Q.B. 146, CA.
[27] *Re Yager & Guardian Assurance Co. Ltd* (1912) 108 L.T. 38.
[28] [1937] 2 All E.R. 193.

material facts known to the proposer, prevents the proposer from arguing waiver of material facts not the subject of proposal form questions.[29]

Security alarm

11–69   Where the proposer expressly warrants the truth of answers in the proposal form and agrees to them being the "basis of the contract" with the insurer, a question that often arises is whether the answer constitutes a continuing warranty that the answer will remain true throughout the period of insurance. This arose in the context of a security alarm in *Hussain v. Brown*[30] where the insured, when proposing for the insurance had warranted the truth of his answer to the following question:

> "Are the premises fitted with any system of intruder alarm? If YES give name of installing company. (Please provide a copy alarm specification if applicable.)"

The insured had answered "Yes" and "See specification", and he had forwarded a specification for a proposed security alarm. By the time that the risk was accepted by underwriters, the alarm had been fitted with modifications required by the underwriters. Some four months later there was a fire at the insured's premises in Bury, and he admitted that the alarm system was inoperative both before and at the time of the fire.

11–70   The underwriters contended that the answer amounted to a continuing warranty that the premises were fitted with an intruder alarm, that this alarm was operational and/or would be habitually set by the insured when the premises were unattended. The Court of Appeal rejected the underwriters' defence, and construed the answer as only referring to the time that the answer was given, because the question was in the present tense, and there was nothing to suggest that an undertaking was being given as to the future. As Saville L.J. pointed out, the importation of a continuing warranty was a draconian term and, therefore, if underwriters wanted such protection then it was up to them to stipulate for it in clear terms.[31]

Waiver of non-disclosure

11–71   Insurers can waive disclosure of certain facts, as discussed in Chapter 3, and can also waive their right to rescind the insurance contract *ab initio*. Waiver always requires a conscious decision to relinquish a right with full knowledge of the full facts and the unequivocal communication of that decision to the insured. The insured raised waiver in the recent case of *Callaghan v. Thompson*[32] where the insured contended that the underwriters knew of his undisclosed convictions for robbery and possession of a firearm prior to the payment of a £25,000 second interim payment on the relevant fire claim. That £25,000 had been paid to the insured by his own insurance brokers following the underwriters' loss adjusters' intimation to

---

[29] *Unipac (Scotland) Ltd v. Aegon Insurance Co. (U.K.) Ltd* [1999] Lloyd's Rep. I.R. 502.
[30] [1996] 1 Lloyd's Rep. 627, CA.
[31] *ibid.* at 630.
[32] [2000] Lloyd's Rep. I.R. 125.

the insured's loss assessors that the underwriters would deal with the claim under the terms of the policy. The plea failed, however, because the underwriters themselves had only remained silent about that second interim payment, and the insurance broker who had sent the insured's solicitor that second payment, whilst he had certain limited authority to grant cover on behalf of the underwriters, had no authority to forward any sum to the insured in respect of the claim.

9. FRAUDULENT CLAIMS

As seen in Chapter 1, if the insured makes a fraudulent claim, even in the absence of an express term, he loses all benefit under the insurance policy. Thus, if the insured sets fire to the insured buildings, or conspires with others that the buildings should be deliberately fired, the insurers are entitled to avoid the policy.[33] Generally, insurers will provide an express clause in the policy, e.g.: **11–72**

> "If the claim be in any respect fraudulent or if any fraudulent means or devices be used by the insured or anyone acting on his behalf to obtain any benefit under this policy or if any destruction or damage be occasioned by the wilful act or with the connivance of the insured all benefit under this policy shall be forfeited."

Further, if the insurer discovers the fraud after payment of the claim, the insurer may recover that payment. The insurer cannot recover, however, the costs of investigation of the claim, even as damages for breach of contract.[34] An assignee of the benefit of a fraudulent claimant or one who claims jointly with a fraudulent claimant, will also be unable to recover.[35] On the other hand, where separate and distinct interests are insured by different insureds under the same policy, e.g. landlord and tenant, or mortgagor and mortgagee, the innocent party may still recover in respect of his separate interest.[36] **11–73**

If the insured sues the insurer, once a prima facie case has been established of loss by fire, the onus shifts to the insurers to show that the fire was caused or connived at by the insured.[37] On the other hand, an insurer may choose to initiate proceedings and seek a declaration that he is entitled to rescind the policy on the ground of fraud by the insured, either in setting fire to the property, or in advancing his claim by fraudulent means. Being a civil action, the general standard of proof is the balance of probabilities, but modern cases have emphasised that where a criminal act or fraud is raised, a very high degree of probability within the general **11–74**

[33] *Herbert v. Poland* (1932) 44 Ll. L. Rep. 139.
[34] *London Assurance v. Clare* (1937) 57 Ll. L. Rep. 254, where Goddard J. (as he then was) suggested an action might lie in deceit, at 270.
[35] *Central Bank of India Ltd v. Guardian Assurance Co. Ltd & Rustomji* (1934) 54 Ll. L. Rep. 247, PC.
[36] *General Accident, Fire & Life Assurance Corp. Ltd v. Midland Bank Ltd* [1940] 2 K.B. 388, CA. See further, Chapter 17, paras 17–35 to 17–38, below.
[37] *Slattery v. Mance* [1962] 1 Q.B. 676.

standard of the balance of probability must be shown by the party alleging such behaviour on the part of the other party to the civil action. The more serious the allegation, the higher the degree of probability — but this will never be so high a degree as a criminal court.[38]

11–75   There are several reported modern cases where the insurers have proved, to the requisite high standard, that the claims were fraudulent. In *S. and M. Carpets (London) Ltd v. Cornhill Insurance Co. Ltd*,[39] Watkins J. (as he then was) concluded that he could not trust and believe the evidence of the insured's managing director in the light of his performance in the witness box and his evasive answers to the police when first questioned about the fire. This belief in the untruth of the managing director's account of his activities at the time the fire was started, together with the expert evidence that the fire was deliberately started with the aid of flammable liquid within the premises, and the poor trading position of the insured company, led to the conclusion that the managing director had set fire to the premises. Accordingly, the claim was fraudulent and failed.

11–76   Similarly, in *Watkins and Davies Ltd v. Legal and General Assurance Co. Ltd*[40] Neill J. emphasised[41] that the heavy onus on insurers to prove that a claim is fraudulent is not discharged merely by providing evidence of suspicious circumstances. Scientific evidence is also required to add weight to allegation of fraud. In the present case, the plaintiff company had a poor trading position and only seven weeks before the fire the cover on stock had been tripled. The expert evidence was that the fire was deliberately started using a flammable liquid in substantial quantity which was directly ignited, and that an intruder could not have gained access because the steel front doors had been securely locked. In the light of all this evidence, Neill J. was satisfied that the fire had been started deliberately by the insured's managing director, and gave judgment for the insurers.

11–77   Fraud was also proven in *Broughton Park Textiles (Salford) Ltd v. Commercial Union Assurance Co. Ltd*[42] where there was a substantial fire at the insured's premises in Manchester. The insured company was wholly owned by a Mr Hyman Cohen, and he was the last person to leave the premises on the day of the fire, sometime between 5.25 and 5.40 p.m. At 5.41 p.m. an automatic alarm had been triggered in the premises, which from the position of the sensor and the known seat of the fire, indicated that the fire had been burning for not less than ten minutes. At 5.49 p.m. the first fire tenders arrived and had to break into the premises as all external doors were secure. The experts on both sides agreed that there were only two explanations for the fire: either an electrical fault or arson by Mr Cohen.

---

[38] *Hornal v. Neuberger Products Ltd* [1957] 1 Q.B. 247 at 263–264 and 266, *per* Hodson and Morris L.JJ., CA; see further Chapter 1, above, and further cases on fraudulent claims in Chapter 12, below.

[39] [1981] 1 Lloyd's Rep. 667; affirmed [1982] 1 Lloyd's Rep. 423, CA.

[40] [1981] 1 Lloyd's Rep. 674.

[41] *ibid.* at 679.

[42] [1987] 1 Lloyd's Rep. 194.

Simon Brown J. determined that in order for the insured's claim to be a **11–78** true and honest one, the following four basic conditions had to be satisfied in the case[43]:

(i) that an electrical fault of an unclear nature and precipitated by an unknown cause, must have developed on the day in question so as to cause arcing within the hollow wall, such arcing itself causing smouldering of wood over an appreciable time;

(ii) that smouldering must have become translated into a flaming fire at almost the precise time that Mr Cohen left the premises, that is assuming in his favour that he left at 5.30 p.m. or just before and not, as he in fact told the Fire Officer, at 5.40 p.m.;

(iii) that (a) Mr Cohen and the assistants failed to detect the smoke or smell or smouldering wood before it finally ignited because it was being funnelled up the hollow wall and dissipated; and (b) Mr Cohen did not notice the outbreak of flame because he had by chance just left the premises beforehand;

(iv) that there was an innocent explanation for the various "troubling" aspects of Mr Cohen's evidence at the trial and its inconsistencies with previous statements.

In the result, his Lordship held that the insurers had discharged the requisite, heavy onus of proving that arson was the cause of the fire on the civil burden of proof.

A fourth case concerned a fire in insured factory premises in London, **11–79** *Polivitte Ltd v. Commercial Union Assurance Co. plc.*[44] The insured company were manufacturers of ladies' and children's clothing. The person responsible for running the plaintiffs was Mr Jaami, who was a director and held 50 of the 100 issued and fully-paid shares. The other director and shareholder was Mr Nadeem. Mr Jaami was effectively the manager assisted by his brother-in-law Mr Shah who became a director in 1983. The company also employed three other persons. Very little capital had been introduced into the company and, in practice, the company ran on bank overdraft and receipts and, apart from very modest fixed assets, the only other assets were stock and debtors. On November 29, 1983, a fire occurred at the insured premises and the insured company claimed under the policy.

The insurers denied liability contending that the plaintiffs either set fire **11–80** to the premises deliberately or if the fire in fact started accidentally, its existence was known to Mr Jaami or Mr Nadeem, or both of them, before they left the premises on the night of November 29. With regard to the company, the insurers alleged that it was manifestly in financial difficulty with an increasing debt; no prospect of repaying the bank; losing its established customers; its overdraft due for renewal or review and its directors deeply committed personally. As for the fire, the insurers alleged that all the evidence pointed to the fire being present at the onset of flame stage

---

[43] *ibid.* at 201.
[44] [1987] 1 Lloyd's Rep. 379.

when Mr Jaami, Mr Nadeem and two of the employees left the premises. If, however, the fire had started accidentally, it would at least have been at the heavy smouldering stage, giving off a considerable amount of smoke when they left. The insured denied these allegations, and argued that the fire was caused accidentally, probably by two unnamed and otherwise unidentified visitors disposing of burning cigarette ends in a waste bin outside the accounts office. Garland J. was satisfied on the evidence at trial that the fire must have been in being when Mr Jaami and the others left the premises, so the insurers had succeeded in showing that there was arson, or, alternatively, Mr Jaami left the premises well aware of the fire, if it had started accidentally.

11–81   Fraud, involving the faking of a burglary at the insured hotel, was also proved against the insured ailing business in *Grave v. G.A. Bonus plc*,[45] and also in *McGregor v. Prudential Insurance Co. Ltd*,[46] where it was emphasised that it was not sufficient to merely establish that arson by the insured was the most plausible possibility. Nor would insurers satisfy the test in circumstances of uncertainty of the identity of the arsonist being either the insured or someone else. Rather, the insurers must establish that the arsonist was the insured and that there was no other credible explanation.

11–82   Insurers were unable to prove fraud by the insured though, in *Exchange Theatre Ltd v. Iron Trades Mutual Insurance Co. Ltd (No. 2)*.[47] The Court of Appeal did, however, order a retrial because Lawson J. at first instance[48] had held that the alleged fire-raiser had gone to the vicinity of the petrol fire to put out that fire in the insured bingo hall, and such finding was unsupportable on the expert evidence adduced at the trial. That evidence was that the ignition of the petrol would have caused a spontaneous fire-ball due to the heavy petrol vapour pervading the area. The alleged fire-raiser had, indeed, been badly burnt to his front and a properly reasoned explanation of that fact could only fairly be obtained by a retrial upon all issues except one, that being that the alleged fire-raiser did not go to the relevant area of the hall in order to extinguish a petrol fire.

11–83   Insurers were also unsuccessful in proving that the claim was fraudulent in *McLean Enterprises Ltd v. Ecclesiastical Insurance Office plc.*[49] Staughton J. pointed out that the mere fact the insured company's owner had a motive for starting the fire, namely that the company was trading at a loss, the motive alone was not sufficient proof that the owner started the fire. The evidence as to time was not inconsistent with accidental fire. There was a conflict of expert evidence as to whether the fire had been started deliberately with an accelerant, or accidentally, by careless disposal of a cigarette by one of the many persons in the insured public house when the fire started. Faced with this evidence, Staughton J. concluded that the insurers did not meet the high burden of proof required.

---

[45] [1999] 2 Lloyd's Rep. 716.
[46] [1998] 1 Lloyd's Rep. 112.
[47] [1984] 2 Lloyd's Rep. 169, CA.
[48] [1983] 1 Lloyd's Rep. 674.
[49] [1986] 2 Lloyd's Rep. 416.

Waiver and estoppel

As stated above in respect of concealment of material facts, the insurer **11–84** can waive the fraudulent conduct of the insured, but such requires full knowledge of the insurer and a deliberate decision communicated to the insured to relinquish that right of rescission.[50] In the recent case of *Baghbadrani v. Commercial Union Assurance Co. plc,*[51] the insured failed to establish waiver where the insured had threatened proceedings unless the claim was resolved, to which the insurers had replied that it was not its intention to deny liability. That response was actually misleading, because the insurers wanted to find grounds to deny liability, but had not yet found such grounds. The response was incapable of constituting a waiver, though, because the insurers did not have actual knowledge of any right to rescind for fraud by the insured, and they were merely playing for time to investigate further. It was also pointed out that whilst estoppel could bind an insurer if a sufficient unequivocal representation was made, estoppel was in its nature an equitable remedy which would be refused to a party guilty of continuing misconduct.

---

[50] *Insurance Corp. of the Channel Islands v. McHugh & the Royal Hotel Ltd* [1997] L.R.L.R. 94.
[51] [2000] Lloyd's Rep. I.R. 94.

CHAPTER 12

CONTENTS INSURANCE

1. SUBJECT MATTER OF CONTENTS INSURANCE

Introduction

12–01   The interest of persons in goods and other contents of buildings may be insured by three methods. The first is by cover being provided as an extension under the buildings "fire policy" discussed in the preceding chapter, and the second is for the contents to be insured by a separate policy against "all risks". The extent of protection afforded to an insured is significantly different, because of the variation in perils embraced by the operative indemnifying words of these insurance policies. General contents, *e.g.* office furniture and machinery, are usually insured separately from stock in trade and work in progress, because different premium-rating and other underwriting considerations will apply. Often provision is made for a variable premium to be charges on stock or materials in trade and work in progress, according to quantities verified and declared to the insurer periodically. Thirdly, stock and work in progress are often insured under a "burglary" policy.

Extent of the indemnity

12–02   Contents insurance is a contract of indemnity, so that the insured can only recover the true value of the insured property which has been lost or damaged. In *Grimaldi Ltd v. Sullivan,*[1] where the insured was a dealer in classic watches who held an "all risks" policy in respect of his stock. He bought several Cartier watches which turned out to be fake, and the Police seized them. The insured applied for their return, but Cartier successfully opposed that application, so the insured sought recovery of the cost of those watches from the insurers. The Court of Appeal held that the insured could not recover an indemnity on that basis, and could only recover what the imitation Cartier watches were worth, not what he had mistakenly paid for them. The failure of the insurer to admit liability in respect of damage to insured machinery by an insured peril, however, only gives rise to the insured's right to recover an indemnity by action and interest on that sum, and not damages for consequential losses caused by the breach of the contract of insurance to reflect the delay in obtaining that indemnity.[2] Interest is discretionary, but should be awarded from the date of loss, unless other considerations come into play.[3]

[1] [1997] C.L.C. 64, CA.
[2] *Sprung v. Royal Insurance (U.K.) Ltd* [1999] Lloyd's Rep. I.R. 111, CA.
[3] See Chapter 19, para. 19–21, below.

2. CONTENTS OTHER THAN STOCK-IN-TRADE

The cover

There is no uniform wording adopted by insurers to describe the **12–03**
contents insured,[4] but will generally be along the following lines:

"Machinery, Plant and All Other Contents therein and thereon, the property
of the Insured or held by them in trust for which they are responsible excluding
Stock and Materials in Trade and property more specifically insured by
other insurances."

The policy may define "All Other Contents" as being:

"(a) Money, Securities and Stamps (other than National Insurance
Stamps) for an amount not exceeding £   .
(b) National Insurance Stamps (including any liability for destruction or
damage by fire and any other peril hereby insured against established
upon the Insured for such stamps affixed to cards unless more specifically insured.
(c) Documents, Manuscripts and Business Books but only for the value
of the materials as stationery together with the cost of clerical labour
expended in writing up and not for the value to the insured of the
information contained therein.[5]
(d) Computer Systems Records but only for the value of the materials
together with the cost of clerical labour and computer time expended
in reproducing such records (excluding any expense in connection
with the production of information to be recorded therein) and not
for the value to the Insured of the information contained therein for
an amount not exceeding £   .
(e) Patterns, Models, Moulds, Plans and Designs but only for the value of
the material together with the cost of labour in reinstatement.
(f) Pedal cycles, clothing, tools and other Personal Effects of Directors,
Executives, Employees, Visitors and Guests of the Insured for an
amount not exceeding £   . for any one person."

Property held "in trust"

The above wording with regard to property not belonging to the insured **12–04**
refers to property held "in trust" by the insured. This is not confined to the
equitable definition of trusteeship, but refers to what may be termed as
"commercial trusteeship" and will be discussed in the next section entitled
"Insurable interest in contents".

Property for which the insured is responsible

The words "for which they are responsible" are often omitted, but their **12–05**
inclusion in the indemnity wording actually has the effect of limiting the
cover. This is because if there is a fire which starts accidentally, then, for
example, the warehouseman in whose warehouse the fire started, is not

---

[4] See Section 4 of the specimen combined policy at Appendix 1, and Section 1 of the specimen shopkeeper's policy.
[5] See *Frewin v. Poland* [1968] 1 Lloyd's Rep. 100.

responsible to the owners of goods destroyed by the fire,[6] unless there is an element of negligence or nuisance[7] in its origin or spread, subject, of course, to any contractual liability to the owners assumed by the warehouseman, for example. With regard to all bailees, however, in an action by the owners, the onus is upon bailees to show that the fire was caused without negligence on their part[8] and that the origin of the fire was accidental.[9] Where the insured is accordingly not held responsible for the items damaged or destroyed by fire, as the wording requires, the insured cannot recover under his insurance for the benefit of the owners. If those vital words "for which they are responsible" are not included, the insurer cannot refuse liability on the ground that the insured bailee is not liable to the bailor in respect of the loss of the goods.

12–06   Thus, in *North British & Mercantile Insurance Co. v. Moffat*[10] the insured tea merchants were covered by insurance against loss of chests of tea in their warehouses which were their own or "in trust or on commission for which they are responsible". A fire occurred and destroyed a quantity of tea in chests which had been sold by the insured. Property in the goods and the risk of loss had therefore passed to the purchasers. The insured were not liable to the purchasers for this loss and therefore could not recover the value of those destroyed chests of tea, for the benefit of the purchasers, because the insured was not liable in law to the purchasers. In exactly the same way, in *Engel v. Lancashire and General Assurance Co. Ltd*[11] a furrier was insured against burglary in respect of both his own goods and those in his possession on trust or on commission for which he was "responsible". A burglary took place, and the insured lost both goods of his own and goods which were in his custody as bailee. As there had been no negligence on his part relating to the burglary, and "responsibility" in the policy had to be interpreted as referring to legal liability, the court held that the insured could only recover in respect of his own goods which were stolen. Those entrusted to him had been stolen without attaching any liability to the insured and were thus not goods for which he was "responsible".

3. STOCK-IN-TRADE

12–07   This should be specifically insured, and, again, the insuring words will usually refer to stock and materials in trade and work in progress, *e.g.* "the

---

[6] Fires Prevention (Metropolis) Act 1774, s.86. The Act, despite its title, is of general application throughout England and Wales; *Re Barker, ex p. Gorely* (1864) 4 De G.J. & Sm. 477; followed in *Re Quicke's Trust Poltimore v. Quicke* [1908] 1 Ch. 887; *Sinnott v. Bowden* [1912] 2 Ch. 414.

[7] See Rylands v. Fletcher (1868) L.R. 3 H.L. 330; *Mason v. Levy Auto Parts of England Ltd* [1967] 2 Q.B. 530; *Balfour v. Barty-King* [1957] 1 Q.B. 496, CA.

[8] This includes his servants, guests, independent contractors or anyone in the building with his leave or licence, *H. & N. Emannuel Ltd v. Greater London Council* [1971] 2 All E.R. 835, CA.

[9] *I.& J. Hyman (Sales) Ltd v. Benedyke & Co. Ltd* [1957] 2 Lloyd's Rep. 601.

[10] (1871) L.R. 7 C.P. 25.

[11] (1925) 21 Ll. L. Rep. 327.

property of the insured or held by them in trust or on commission for which they are responsible". The same comments are relevant to this wording as already considered above, but it can be added that the word "trade" will be construed as relating only to the stock and materials of the insured's business as identified to the insurer. That business or trade will normally be described in the insurance policy's schedule. Accordingly, an engineering company would not be able to recover in respect of a damaged stock of, for instance, retail household goods which had been acquired as a speculation without the knowledge of the insurers. Similarly, goods in a factory that were temporarily housed there during transit from another factory on a journey elsewhere, were held not to be within the term "stock-in-trade" of the factory where they were temporarily housed and accordingly not insured.[12]

4. INSURED'S INSURABLE INTEREST IN CONTENTS

Owners

An absolute owner[13] or a joint owner, *e.g.* a partner regarding partner-   **12–08**
ship property,[14] may insure it against fire and other risks. Company property is owned by the company, and therefore a shareholder of that company has no insurable interest in that same property.[15] An ordinary creditor also has no insurable interest in the debtor company's property.[16] Only a secured creditor who has secured his debt either by a fixed or floating charge over the relevant company property may insure that property.[17] If a partnership has insured the firm's property, and then the partnership changes its constitution, *i.e.* becomes a new entity, without the knowledge and consent of the insurer, it seems that on the dissolution of the insuring partnership, the insurance continues for the benefit of the continuing partners who retain an interest in the insured property.[18]

Vendors and purchasers

The vendor of goods has an insurable interest in those goods for two   **12–09**
reasons: firstly, because of his legal ownership of those goods, and, secondly, because he will have to suffer any loss or damage suffered by the goods from any mishap which occurs after the conclusion of the agreement to sell, in circumstances where the purchaser refuses to carry out the purchase.[19] His interest will continue so long as his lien for the purchase

---

[12] *Boag v. Economic Insurance Co. Ltd* [1954] 2 Lloyd's Rep. 581.

[13] *Inglis v. Stock* (1885) 10 App. Cas. 263 at 270, *per* Lord Blackburn, HL.

[14] *Reid v. Hollinshead* (1825) 4 B. & C. 867.

[15] *Macaura v. Northern Assurance Co. Ltd* [1925] A.C. 619 at 626–627, *per* Lord Buckmaster, HL; *Moran, Galloway & Co. v. Uzielli* [1905] 2 K.B. 555 at 562, *per* Walton J.

[16] *ibid.*

[17] *Moran, Galloway & Co. v. Uzielli* [1905] 2 K.B. 555; *Briggs v. Merchant Traders' Ship Loan and Insurance Association* (1849) 13 Q.B. 167.

[18] *Jenkins v. Deane* (1933) 47 Ll. L. Rep. 342 at 347, *per* Goddard J. (as he then was), discussed in Chapter 1, above.

[19] Following *Castellain v. Preston* (1883) 11 Q.B.D. 380 at 385, *per* Brett L.J., CA; *Collingridge v. Royal Exchange Assurance Corp.* (1877) 3 Q.B.D. 173 at 177, *per* Lush J.; *Reed v. Cole* (1764) 3 Burr. 1512.

money,[20] or his right to retrieve the goods in transit,[21] continues. The purchaser has an insurable interest in goods when either the property[22] or the risk[23] in the goods has passed to him, and it does not matter if the purchase is on an approval basis.[24] Obviously, the purchaser's interest in any goods he buys ceases in the event of his rejecting those goods, but continues for so long as he is responsible for their safe return to the vendor.[25]

Persons holding goods "in trust or on commission"

12–10   All bailees, be they carriers, factors, warehousemen or wharfingers, have been held to have an insurable interest in the goods entrusted to them. Their own interest is limited to the extent of their commission or other charges on the bailment, but it is clear that they can insure for the whole value of the goods, holding that balance over their own interest for the benefit of the owners of the goods, provided the policy shows that intention. Such policies are not prevented by statute because they are on goods, which are an expressly excluded class of insurance subject matter, otherwise the insured would be limited to recovering the extent of his own interest.[26]

12–11   Warehousemen successfully recovered the full value of goods "in trust or on commission" destroyed by fire in *Waters and Steel v. Monarch Fire and Life Assurance Co.*[27] irrespective of the fact that the owners were not aware of the insurance, nor had been charged for it. *Per* Lord Campbell C.J.[28]:

> "I have come to the conclusion that the plaintiffs are entitled to judgment, the first question is whether, upon the construction of the contract, those goods were intended to be covered by the policy. I think in either policy the description is such as to include them. What is meant in those policies by the words 'goods in trust'? I think that means goods with which the assured were entrusted; not goods held in trust in the strict technical sense, so held that there was only an equitable obligation in the assured enforceable by a subpoena in Chancery, but goods with which the assured were entrusted in the ordinary sense of the word. They were so entrusted with the goods deposited on their wharfs; I cannot doubt the policy was intended to protect such goods; and it would be very inconvenient if wharfingers could not protect such goods by a floating policy. Then, this being the meaning of the

---

[20] Sate of Goods Act 1979, s.41; *London and North Western Railway Co. v. Glyn* (1859) 1 E. & E. 652.

[21] Sale of Goods Act 1979, s.44; *Kendall v. Marshall, Stevens & Co.* (1883) 11 Q.B.D. 356, CA; *Clay v. Harrison* (1829) 10 B. & C. 99.

[22] *Sparkes v. Marshall* (1836) 2 Bing. N.C. 761; *Inglis v. Stock* (1885) 10 App. Cas. 263.

[23] *Neale v. Reid* (1823) 1 B. & C. 657; *Joyce v. Swann* (1864) 17 C.B.(n.s.) 84; *Castle v. Playford* (1872) L.R. 7 Exch. 98.

[24] *Bevington and Morris v. Dale & Co. Ltd* (1902) 7 Com. Cas. 112 at 113, *per* Kennedy J.

[25] See *Colonial Insurance Co. of New Zealand v. Adelaide Marine Insurance Co.* (1886) 12 App. Cas. 128, PC.

[26] Life Assurance Act 1774, s.4.

[27] (1856) 5 E. & B. 870.

[28] *ibid.* at 880–881; see also *Castellain v. Preston* (1883) 11 Q.B.D. 380 at 398, *per* Bowen L.J., CA; *Hepburn v. Tomlinson (Hauliers) Ltd* [1966] A.C. 451 at 467, *per* Lord Reid, HL; see also *John Rigby (Haulage) Ltd v. Reliance Marine Insurance Co. Ltd* [1956] 2 Q.B. 468, CA.

policy is there anything illegal in it? It cannot now be disputed that it would be legal at common law; and [the defendant] properly admits that it is not prohibited by the terms of any statute. And I think that a person entrusted with goods can insure them without orders from the owner, and even without informing him that there was such a policy. It would be most inconvenient in business if a wharfinger could not, at his own cost, keep up a floating policy for the benefit of all who might become his customers. The last point that arises is to what extent does the policy protect those goods. The defendants say that it was only the plaintiffs personal interest. But the policies are in terms contracts to make good 'all such damage and loss as may happen by fire to the property hereinbefore mentioned'. That is a valid contract, and, as the property is wholly destroyed, the value of the whole must be made good, not merely the particular interest of the plaintiffs. They will be entitled to apply so much to cover their own interest, and will be trustees for the owners as to the rest."

Similarly, a policy insuring goods being carried by the insured, against **12–12** "all risks of loss and damage however arising" has been held to extend to the full value of those goods lost or damaged by an insured peril.[29] The position where, however, the wording refers to goods "in trust or on commission for which the insured are responsible", and its effect of reducing the insurance cover , has been discussed above. The insurance cover does not include loss or damage of goods without fault or contractual liability of the bailee.[30]

5. RISKS INSURED

Under a "fire policy"
The insurance provisions relating to the three risks of "fire", "lightning" **12–13** and "explosion" are examined in detail in the previous chapter dealing with buildings insurance and the scope will be identical in respect of contents of the buildings, *e.g.* subject to the same exceptions and the same principles of proximate cause of the loss or damage. The previous chapter should also be referred to in regard to additional risks that contents may be insured against under an extension to the "fire policy".

Under an "all risks" policy
This insurance is expressed as being against loss or damage to the **12–14** insured contents from "all risks" that are not excluded on the face of the policy. Nevertheless, there are four implied limitations to the scope of "all risks" insurance[31]:

   (a) *Act of insured*: the loss or damage must not be caused by the
       deliberate act of the insured, for there must be some abnormal

[29] *Hepburn v. Tomlinson (Hauliers) Ltd.* [1966] A.C. 451, HL; see also *London and North Western Railway. Co. v. Glyn* (1859) 1 E. & E. 652.
[30] *North British and Mercantile Insurance Co. v. Moffatt* (1871) L.R. 7 C.P. 25; and see paras 12–05 to 12–07, above.
[31] *British and Foreign Marine Insurance Co. v. Gaunt* [1921] 2 A.C. 41 at 57–58, *per* Lord Sumner, HL.

circumstances, accidental and fortuitous, amounting to a casualty[32];

(b) *Fair wear and tear*: inevitabilities are not included, as an "all risks" insurance is only against events which may happen not those which will certainly happen[33];

(c) *Illegality*: where the insured has deliberately infringed the law to procure or keep the insured goods, public policy will prevent his recovery for their loss or damage under the policy, for otherwise the court would be assisting the insured to derive a profit from his illegal acts[34];

(d) *Inherent vice*: the insurance is presumed to only insure the goods from external perils and not from its own nature. Hence, putrefaction of meat over a period of time is not covered.[35]

12–15   To constitute a "loss" under an "all risks" policy, the insured must satisfy the court upon the requisite test of uncertainty of recovery,[36] that is, whether, after all reasonable steps to recover the goods have been taken by the insured, recovery is uncertain.[37] An unsuccessful search for the items may be sufficient to satisfy this test,[38] but goods that are temporarily irrecoverable, even for a considerable time, are not to be considered "lost" unless there is some evidence that they will not ultimately be returned.[39] The doctrine of constructive total loss in marine insurance law, applied where there is unlikelihood of recovery of the insured item, has no application to the sphere of non-marine insurances.[40] Further, a loss within the policy may be proved in circumstances where insured items are entrusted to the charge of a person who subsequently dishonestly disposes of them and absconds with the proceeds.[41] Such an instance must be distinguished, however, from a sale of insured items in consideration of a cheque that transpires to be worthless. In this latter case, the insured has not suffered a "loss" of his goods, he has simply been deprived of the proceeds of sale of those items.[42]

---

[32] *British and Foreign Marine Insurance Co. v. Gaunt* [1921] 2 A.C. 41 at 46–47, *per* Lord Birkenhead, HL; *London and Provincial Leather Processes Ltd v. Hudson* [1939] 2 K.B. 724.

[33] *ibid.* and *Wilson (Thomas), Sons & Co. v. Xantho (Cargo Owners)* (1887) 12 App. Cas. 503 at 509, *per* Lord Herschell, HL.

[34] *Geismar v. Sun Alliance and London Insurance Ltd* [1978] Q.B. 383, where the insured lost items which he had previously brought into this country in deliberate infringement of the Customs and Excise Act 1952. Contrast *Euro-Diam Ltd v. Bathurst* [1990] 1 Q.B. 1, CA, which concerned the export of diamonds with false invoices to enable the purchaser to evade German import tax law.

[35] *Taylor v. Dunbar* (1869) L.R. 4 C.P. 206.

[36] *Holmes v. Payne* [1930] 2 K.B. 301 at 310, *per* Roche J.

[37] See *Webster v. General Accident Fire and Life Assurance Corp. Ltd* [1953] 1 Q.B. 520 at 532, *per* Parker J.

[38] *Holmes v. Payne* [1930] 2 K.B. 301.

[39] *Mitsui v. Mumford* [1915] 2 K.B. 27; *Campbell & Phillipps Ltd v. Denman* (1915) 21 Com. Cas. 357; *Moore v. Evans* [1918] A.C. 185, HL; *London and Provincial Leather Processes Ltd v. Hudson* [1939] 2 K.B. 724.

[40] *Moore v. Evans* [1918] A.C. 185 at 193–197, *per* Lord Atkinson, HL.

[41] *Webster v. General Accident Fire and Life Assurance Corp. Ltd* [1953] 1 Q.B. 520; *Metal Scrap and By-Products Ltd v. Federated Conveyors Ltd* [1953] 1 Lloyd's Rep. 221.

[42] *Eisinger v. General Accident Fire and Life Assurance Corp. Ltd* [1955] 2 All E.R. 897.

Exclusions to "all risks" cover

There are certain exceptions which are commonly inserted in "all risks"   **12–16**
policies:

(i) *War, invasion, act of foreign enemy, hostilities (whether war be declared or not) civil war, rebellion, revolution, insurrection, military or usurped power.* For the meaning of these words, refer to the discussion in the previous Chapter.

(ii) *Loss, destruction or damage directly occasioned by pressure waves caused by aircraft or other aerial devices travelling at sonic or supersonic speed.*

(iii) *Loss or damage caused by malicious damage, riot or civil commotion outside Great Britain, the Channel Isles or the Isle of Man.* For the interpretation of "riot" and "civil commotion", reference should be made to their consideration in the preceding Chapter 11.

(iv) *Loss or damage from confiscation or detention by customs or government officials.* This refers to deliberate acts[43] by such officials.

(v) *Loss by disappearance or shortage if only revealed by stocktaking.* The extent of the indemnity afforded for theft under this type of exclusion wording in an "all risks" policy, can be contrasted, in combination with (vi) following, to the cover provided by a "burglary" policy, below. The insurance protection is not dissimilar in its essential features.

(vi) *Loss or damage arising through theft from any unattended unlocked vehicle.* "Unattended" must be construed having regard to the particular policy, but a vehicle has been held to be unattended when not under observation by its driver who had gone into a shop for some 15 minutes,[44] or whilst kept under observation by a driver urinating behind some bushes beside a lay-by.[45] A driver who is in the vehicle, but who is asleep, is not leaving the vehicle unattended[46] (see further, Chapter 13).

(vii) *Terrorist damage* exceeding £100,000.

"Forcible and violent entry" under a "burglary" policy

A variety of wordings may be encountered in practice, but the essential   **12–17**
quality of the majority is the requirement of breaking and entering of the
insured premises to constitute a valid loss within the policy terms, hence
the colloquial adage often ascribed to this type of insurance, *i.e.* burglary
insurance. A typical commercial theft/burglary policy will cover loss "by
theft following upon actual forcible and violent entry upon the premises".

---

[43] See *Curtis & Sons v. Mathews* [1919] 1 K.B. 425 at 430, *per* Bankes L.J., CA.

[44] *Ingleton of Ilford Ltd v. General Accident Fire and Life Assurance Corp. Ltd* [1967] 2 Lloyd's Rep. 179.

[45] *Starfire Diamond Rings Ltd v. Angel* [1962] 2 Lloyd's Rep. 217, CA.

[46] *Plaistow Transport Ltd v. Graham* [1966] 1 Lloyd's Rep. 639; for "unattended" buildings see *Roberts v. Eagle Star Insurance Co. Ltd* [1960] 1 Lloyd's Rep. 615; *Victor Melik & Co. Ltd v. Norwich Union Fire Insurance Society Ltd & Kemp* [1980] 1 Lloyd's Rep. 523.

This wording was contained in an insurance upon the stock in trade of a shop in *Re George and Goldsmith and General Burglary Insurance Association Ltd.*[47] The front door of the shop was shut, but not locked or bolted, in the early morning before business hours, when, during the temporary absence of the insured's employee, someone opened that door by turning the handle and entered the shop. A locked show case within the shop was broken into and various items of stock were then stolen. The Court of Appeal held that there has been no "forcible and violent entry upon the premises" and the claim under this policy failed.

12–18   That instance can be contrasted with the events in *Re Calf & Sun Insurance Office*[48] where a similarly worded policy was issued to the insured tailor in respect of his stock in trade. The premises were as follows: trimming room in the basement; shop on the ground floor; fitting room on the first floor (these three floors were defined as the insured premises); and upper floors were occupied by either the insured or his tenants as residences. During the currency of the policy a person entered the building in the normal way, in daytime, and concealed himself in a coal cellar in the basement. That night, after the shop and trimming room had been locked up, he left the coal cellar and entered the trimming room from the passage, having used an instrument to slide back the catch of the lock and so opened the door. This thief took a quantity of goods from the trimming room and went up the stairs to the shop with the goods, whereupon he broke open the door to the shop and left the building through the front door. The Court of Appeal determined that there were forcible and violent entries made to both the trimming room and the shop, these comprised part of the insured business premises and the insured was therefore entitled to be indemnified.

12–19   More recently, in *Dino Services Ltd v. Prudential Assurance Co. Ltd*[49] the Court of Appeal rejected the insured's contention that "forcible and violent" was to be equated with "forcible and unlawful" in relation to the means of entry. "Violent" was an ordinary word which had a different meaning from "unlawful", and whilst violence was often unlawful, it was not necessarily so. Mann L.J. did observe, however, that whilst these words had been in currency for nearly one hundred years, they ought to be the subject of scrutiny by insurers.[50] The facts were that the insured's premises where they maintained, rebuilt and repaired Ferrari motor cars were locked up by the owner one evening and he drove to a nearby public house. He left the keys to his premises in the glove compartment and later on made his way home leaving the car parked where it was. In the morning the car was gone and when he went to his premises he discovered that during the night they had been entered unlawfully by means of his own keys and valuable property had been taken. The insurers successfully resisted the insured's claim, for the Court of Appeal held that the ordinary meaning of the phrase "entry

[47] [1899] 1 Q.B. 595, CA.
[48] [1920] 2 K.B. 366, CA.
[49] [1989] 1 All E.R. 422, CA.
[50] *ibid.* at 432 and 387.

by forcible and violent means" could not be applied to the action of moving the lever of a lock into its open position by means of its proper key and then turning a knob or pushing the door open to go inside. That would be forcible, but there was nothing violent about it at all.

Interpretation of burglary and theft

"Burglary" or "theft" in the wording, in the absence of any contractual **12–20** definition in the policy, will be assigned the same meaning as that given to it by the criminal law. Accordingly, in the event of there being any uncertainty as to whether the facts constitute a loss by "theft" or "burglary", recourse must be had to the Theft Act 1968 and relevant case law. Thus, where an insurance covered a firm in respect of loss by theft whilst goods were on their premises, to prove such a loss the insured had to show that the person who stole the goods formed the intention to steal them whilst on the premises. As the thief in *Grundy (Teddington) Ltd v. Fulton*[51] was a lorry driver who had collected those goods within his normal duties, the Court of Appeal upheld the judge's finding that the insured had not proven that the goods were dishonestly appropriated, *i.e.* stolen, by the driver within their premises, rather than when he deviated from his proper route with those goods. Accordingly, the insured could not recover under the policy.

Recently, in *Dobson v. General Accident Fire and Life Assurance Corp.* **12–21** *plc*[52] the Court of Appeal held that there is a loss by theft, as defined under the criminal law, of goods which are sold to a rogue who intends to permanently deprive the owner of those goods and hands over a stolen or worthless cheque to the seller of insured goods. It was held irrelevant to the criminal law that the seller had willingly handed over possession of the goods in exchange for the cheque. This decision has now received approval in the House of Lords in *R. v. Gomez*.[53] Where the insured peril is "theft committed by persons present on the premises of the assured", this does not cover a theft of securities achieved by an unknowing and innocent agent who is given possession of the securities on the premises, whose principal has the dishonest intention of stealing them when they are given to him by that agent.[54]

Exclusions to "burglary" cover

There are several exceptions commonly found in burglary insurances: **12–22**

> (i) *War and kindred risks.* The precise exclusions will be along similar lines as those in "all risks" policies. An isolated case of burglary during an air raid was held not to amount to a loss falling within an exception relating to "loss occasioned by hostilities, or loot sack or pillage in connection therewith" in *Winicofsky v. Army*

---

[51] [1983] 1 Lloyd's Rep. 16, CA.
[52] [1990] 1 Q.B. 274.
[53] [1993] 1 All E.R. 1, HL.
[54] *Deutsche Genossenschaftsbank v. Burnhope* [1996] 1 Lloyd's Rep. 113.

and Navy General Assurance Association Ltd.[55] Where a burglary
policy was issued to a bakery and it excluded, *inter alia*, theft by
"riot" that exclusion was held by the House of Lords as not being
confined to cases of theft antecedent or simultaneous to a riot,
but included a case where the manner of the theft itself constituted a riot. As four armed men had entered the insured premises
and held up the insured's employees with revolvers and stole all
the money in the cashier's office, this conduct amounted to a riot
and the insured was unable to recover.[56] Problems with incidents
in Northern Ireland[57] has resulted in insurers inserting the special
exclusion relating to premises in the province detailed in the
preceding Chapter.

(ii) *Theft by insured's employees or customers.* Where there is an
exception relating to thefts by members of the insured's staff, the
exception will extend by natural implication to cases where an
employee assists thieves, *e.g.* by admitting them to the insured
premises, and then departs from the scene whilst the theft takes
place. His aiding and abetting will, in law, operate to render him
liable as a principal offender, *i.e.* a thief.[58] It is for the defendant
insurer to prove that the loss falls within the exception (unless, as
is often the case, the burden of proving that the loss is not within
an exception is placed expressly upon the insured). The insurer
may establish such a theft by evidence which possibly might not
be admitted or sufficient to convict in a criminal prosecution; and
evidence that the employee was seen in discussion with three
notorious thieves two days prior to the theft is admissible to prove
his complicity in the theft, but mere evidence of bad character is
not admissible.[59] If theft by customers of the insured is excepted,
a loss falls outside that exception if the goods were entrusted to
a person pretending to be an agent of potential customers who
dishonestly makes off with them, as the goods were not handed
over to a "customer" as such.[60]

6. THE INSURED PREMISES

12–23   It may first be said that the insured must always show a prima facie loss
within the terms of the issued policy.[61] Thus, if goods are insured "whilst
in warehouse anywhere in the United Kingdom", the insured will fail at
this first hurdle if the goods are lost whilst on a lorry parked in an open
space within a locked compound enclosed by a high bricked wall topped

[55] (1919) 88 L.J. K.B. 1111.
[56] *London and Lancashire Fire Insurance Co. Ltd v. Bolands Ltd* [1924] A.C. 836, HL.
[57] See also *Cooper v. General Accident. Fire and Life Assurance Corp. Ltd* (1923) 92 L.J.P.C.
168, HL; *Motor Union Insurance Co. Ltd v. Boggan* (1923) 130 L.T. 588, HL.
[58] *Saqui and Lawrence v. Steams* [1911] 1 K.B. 426, CA.
[59] *Hurst v. Evans* [1917] 1 K.B. 352.
[60] *Lake v. Simmons* [1927] A.C. 487, HL.
[61] *Regina Fur Co. Ltd v. Bossom* [1958] 2 Lloyd's Rep. 425, CA.

with barbed wire, because that compound will not be within the ordinary and popular meaning of the word "warehouse".[62]

The extent of the insured "premises" was in question in *John A. Pike* **12–24** *(Butchers) Ltd v. Independent Insurance Ltd*.[63] The insured were wholesale butchers with premises in north London, and they suffered a burglary one evening. The assumed facts were that the thieves forced open the gates at each side of the premises, enabling them to gain access to the building through a side door, and then proceeded to force internal doors which led to a workshop and thence to a cold store from which they stole some meat. The thieves then forced another gate so that they could drive away with the meat. The policy covered property:

> "Section C
>
> (a) the property . . . whilst contained within the Premises (which shall not include any garden yard or outbuilding) occupied by the Insured . . . shall be lost or damaged due to:-
>
> (i) theft (or any attempt thereat) involving entry to or exit from the Premises by forcible or violent means . . .
>
> Exclusions
>
> The company shall not be liable under this section for loss or damage
>
> (a) . . .
> (b) . . .
> (c) loss arising from fraud or dishonesty of the insured or any partner, director or employee . . .
>
> but this exclusion shall not apply to any theft involving actual forcible and violent entry or exit from any building."

The insurers resisted the insured's claim on the ground that neither entry **12–25** to, nor exit from, the premises (being the building and not the yard under the definition) had not been achieved by forcible and violent means, because the building's side door had either been opened by a duplicate key, or had already been open. The defence succeeded at first instance, but the insured succeeded on appeal. The Court of Appeal held that "the Premises" were those premises described in the policy's appendix and those premises included the yard. The restriction in Section C(a) was that property was only insured if it was not in the yard, but, properly construed, the reference to "the Premises" in sub-section (i) was thus a reference to the entire premises of the insured as referred to in the policy's appendix. Indeed, the fact that it was thought necessary to have an express exclusion of the yard in clause (a) supported the view that the insured premises were the entire premises described in the appendix. Thus, the second reference to "the Premises" in (i) was not qualified in the same way that the first reference was in (a).[64]

---

[62] *Leo Rapp Ltd v. McClure* [1955] 1 Lloyd's Rep. 292; see also *Barnett and Block v. National Parcels Insurance Co. Ltd* [1942] 2 All E.R. 55n, CA.
[63] [1998] Lloyd's Rep. I.R. 410, CA.
[64] *ibid.* at 417, *per* Evans L.J.

Furthermore, any description of insured premises in the policy must be considered to refer to the physical description at the time the insurance was concluded. If the insured premises are extended without the knowledge of the insurer, any loss from that extension to the insured premises, will not be recoverable.[65]

12–26   Where the insured premises are warranted to be always occupied, or occupied at night, an insured is not to be deprived of recovery by reason of his temporary absence from the premises either by reason of an emergency,[66] or even simply because the insured chose to go out for a few hours,[67] even if the loss occurred during such absence. On the other hand, where cover was to cease if the premises "became unoccupied" in *Marzouca v. Atlantic and British Commercial Insurance Co. Ltd*,[68] the attendance of a night watchman outside the premises who never entered the building was held by the Privy Council as not to amount to occupation. Lord Hodson explained[69]:

> "'became unoccupied' must relate to the absence of physical presence in the building as distinct from physical presence outside the building. This does not mean that mere temporary absence necessarily involves a cesser of occupation. In the nature of things one does not spend 24 hours under the same roof for 365 days a year. . . . The occupation to be effectual must, however, be actual not constructive. It must at least involve the regular daily presence of someone in the building."

7. BURGLAR ALARM PROVISIONS

12–27   It is very common to find requirements relating to burglar alarms in contents insurance policies. Such a provision may read as follows:

> "It is a condition precedent to all liability:
>
> (a) that the Burglar Alarm shall be put into full and proper operation whenever the premises are closed for business or left unattended; and
> (b) that such alarm be maintained under contract by the manufacturers."

The insurer may properly avoid liability under such a provision if the insured leaves the premises unattended, even for a period of two-and-a-half hours, without his putting the burglar alarm into full and proper operation.[70]

12–28   As ever, the wording of such provisions is of extreme importance, and the above wording can be contrasted with the ramifications of the following

---

[65] *Simon Brooks Ltd v. Hepburn* [1961] 2 Lloyd's Rep. 43; *Sillem v. Thornton* (1854) 3 E. and B. 868.

[66] *Winicofsky v. Army and Navy General Assurance Association Ltd* (1919) 88 L.J.K.B. 1111.

[67] *Simmonds v. Cockell* [1920] 1 K.B. 843; "Occupation includes possession as its primary element, but it also includes something more. Legal possession does not of itself, constitute an occupation" *per* Lush J. in *R. v. St. Pancras Assessment Committee* (1877) 2 Q.B.D. 581, at 588; applied in *Wolfe v. Surrey County Council Clerk* [1905] 1 K.B. 439.

[68] [1971] 1 Lloyd's Rep. 449, PC.

[69] *ibid.* at 453.

[70] *Roberts v. Eagle Star Insurance Co. Ltd* [1960] 1 Lloyd's Rep. 615.

condition found in *Victor Melik & Co. Ltd v. Norwich Union Fire Insurance Society Ltd and Kemp*[71]:

> "It is a condition precedent to liability that (a) the burglar alarm installed at the premises . . . is kept in efficient working order . . . (c) the maintenance contract company is immediately advised of any defect; (d) the burglar alarm is kept in full operation at all times when the premises are unattended."

The burglar alarm system fitted at the insured's premises was connected to a G.P.O. line which in turn connected with a control centre. If there was an intrusion upon the premises at a time when the alarm was operating, then a message would be sent along the G.P.O. line to a control centre which would in turn inform the key-holder of the insured that the alarm had been activated and would also inform the police at a police station two minutes away from the premises. On December 20 at 9 p.m. the insured was informed that there was a line fault on the alarm system that was connected to the control centre. The insured inspected the premises and discovered that the telephones were not working. The alarms were reset to audible only and both the maintenance contractors and the G.P.O. were informed of the defect and the police were asked to make extra patrols of the premises.

12–29 The following day, G.P.O. repair men attended the premises but discovered there was an external line fault and a different team of engineers would have to investigate this on another day. On the evening of December 21, therefore, the alarm was again set to audible only and the police were again asked to make extra patrols. That night thieves stole property from the insured premises. The insured, sought to recover under their policy, but the insurers defended the claim, *inter alia*, on the ground that the above condition had been breached. It was accepted that the thieves had cut all outgoing lines from the premises by taking the top off a manhole outside the premises and cutting the wires that led to the premises through the manhole. It was also accepted that the place where the line was cut outside the premises was an area which was not within the insured's responsibility.

12–30 In his consideration of clause (a) of the condition — that the burglar alarm was to be "kept in efficient working order" — Woolf J. (as he then was) said[72]:

> "the burglar alarm is not required to be in efficient working order; it is required to be kept in efficient working order. The insertion of the word 'kept', in my view, implies within it a requirement that before there can be a breach of that condition by an insured, he must be aware of the facts which give rise to the alarm not being in efficient working order, or if he is not aware of those facts he should at least be in a position where exercising common care, he should have known of those facts. Furthermore, in my view, he must be given (having been acquainted with those facts or being in a situation where he must be deemed to be aware of those facts) a sufficient opportunity to have the alarm installed once more restored to proper working order. Were the situation otherwise, the consequences would be as follows.

---

[71] [1980] 1 Lloyd's Rep. 523.
[72] *ibid.* at 530.

The burglar alarm is obviously only intended to be in operation when the premises are unattended. Yet the way the clause is drawn, even if the premises were attended so there would be no requirement for the burglar alarm to be in operation, because the burglar alarm was not in efficient working order, a person would have no right to recover. What is more, as I have indicated, the inefficiency of the burglar alarm could be through no fault of the insured, it could be through no fault of the maintenance company but through some sort of latent defect which nobody could protect themselves against. Yet, in such circumstances, because of the wording of this clause, were it to be construed other than I have indicated, an insured could find himself without any form of cover whatsoever . . .

However, in order to interpret this clause, it is necessary to gather the intent from the words used by the parties to the policy and I am satisfied that the Norwich Union could not have intended that the policy should have been interpreted in that way, and equally that the insured would not have intended it to be interpreted in this way. Therefore, the situation here is that the word 'kept' has the effect of treating this clause as being similar to a clause in a lease setting out an obligation of a landlord to keep the premises in repair. The obligation is one to repair promptly on notice, but not one which is absolute in terms . . . I should also indicate that, in my view, the burglar alarm installed at these premises was at all times in efficient working order. What was not in efficient working order was the line, the property of the Post Office which had been cut in the way I have described. That line was cut outside the premises of the insured. The cut prevented the alarm doing what was intended, but the alarm itself was operating efficiently and, therefore, if it had been necessary for me to do so, I would have also said there was no breach of sub-clause (a) on that ground."

12–31   Woolf J. then dealt with sub-clause (d), which concerned the question of the keeping of the alarm in full operation[73]:

"the fact that, as I have already indicated, the cutting of the telephone line did not interfere with the burglar alarm itself provides an answer to the contention that sub-clause (d) has been contravened.

The burglar alarm on the night in question was kept in full operation when [the insured] left the premises having put the alarm into operation. It in fact was an alarm which would not achieve its full object, but in my view, it was still an alarm which was in full operation. What was not in full operation was the link which led to the control centre. On that ground alone it would be enough to say that the Norwich Union had not made out its contention that sub-clause (d) was contravened. I would, however, also rely if necessary on my interpretation of the word 'kept' in sub-clause (d) as being the same as in sub-clause (a). Again, the alarm was kept in full operation at all times within the meaning of that clause because in fact the word 'kept' required the plaintiffs to do what they sought to do in this case, namely, to get the alarm back into full operation and it did not require them to have it in full operation at all times."

8. RESTRICTIONS ON USE OF THE INSURED PREMISES

12–32   The words of description or words of prohibition of user will have to be carefully construed in the light of the policy as a whole, and general

[73] *ibid.* at 531.

propositions are inadvisable, but examples follow. Where any description of fire-heat other than common place fires was prohibited by a fire policy, it was held in *Glen v. Lewis*[74] that the wording necessitated a stringent interpretation rendering the policy void, as expressly provided, where fire-heat was introduced into the premises, it being immaterial here that there was only a temporary introduction.

A standard question in many proposal forms for commercial   **12–33** contents will concern the risk of fire and will therefore ask, *e.g.* "Are any inflammable oils or goods used or kept on the premises?" The answer to that question has been held to bind the insured throughout the whole currency of the policy as the reply in the content of the question amounted to a continuing warranty, and thus the introduction of inflammable goods into the insured shop in *Hales v. Reliance Fire and Accident Insurance Corp. Ltd*[75] amounted to both a breach of that warranty, and a breach of the description of the premises which was the "basis" of the contract.[76]

9. DESCRIPTION AND ALTERATION OF INSURED CONTENTS

The insured should always ensure that he correctly describes the con-   **12–34** tents to be insured, otherwise the insured will not be able to prove the loss falls within the risk insured. An illustration of this essential fact is afforded by *A.F. Watkinson & Co. Ltd v. Hullett*[77] where the insured, having described themselves in their proposal for fire insurance as "paper-board manufacturers" sought and were issued cover in respect of their "contents" at their premises. The contents of those premises were later destroyed by fire and a claim lodged by the insured. In fact, the contents were between 400 and 500 tons of waste paper, the insured really being waste paper merchants rather than manufacturers of paper-board. Goddard J. (as he then was) stated[78]:

> "The stock which [the insurer] intended to underwrite, and did underwrite, was the stock of a paper board manufacturer and not a waste paper business at all. That is how they are described in the policy and that was all that was told to him. 'Contents situate in or about premises at Leigh's Nurseries, Ponders End' meant, as far as the underwriters were concerned, that they were underwriting the stock of a paper board manufacturer; they were not underwriting the stock of a waste paper merchant at all."

Another illustration is afforded by *Herman v. Phoenix Assurance Co.*   **12–35** *Ltd*[79] where the insured described the contents to be covered as "general merchandise" under a fire policy. In fact the majority of the goods were

[74] (1853) 8 Exch. 607.
[75] [1960] 2 Lloyd's Rep. 391.
[76] For "basis of the contract" conditions, see Chapter 2, above.
[77] (1938) 61 Ll. L. Rep. 145.
[78] *ibid.* at 148.
[79] (1924) 18 Ll. L. Rep. 371, CA.

valuable furs. Although the insured lost his claim because it was held to be fraudulent, Scrutton L.J. stated his view that[80]:

> "I am extremely doubtful whether, if you insure general merchandise, and the nature of the greater part of it is valuable furs, you are not guilty of concealment in not stating what you know of the nature of the goods."

12–36   Support for this approach is also found in *Anglo-African Merchants Ltd v. Bayley*[81] where the insured wished to insure his goods in a warehouse under an "all risks" cover, however, he described his consignment of 23-year-old, unused Army surplus leather jerkins as "new men's clothes in bales for export". Megaw J. (as he then was) held that the insured could not recover for he had not disclosed the facts that the goods were war surplus and that they were more than 20 years old, both being material facts. The insured's claim, therefore, fell on this ground.

12–37   An alteration in the contents described was considered in *Exchange Theatre Ltd v. Iron Trades Mutual Insurance Co. Ltd*[82] where building contents, *i.e.* machinery plant, trade and office furniture, fixtures, fittings and utensils, were insured under a fire policy which provided:

> "This policy shall be avoided with respect to any item thereof in regard to which there be any alteration . . . whereby the risk of destructional damage is increased."

The insured subsequently brought a petrol generator and a quantity of petrol into the insured premises, and the insurers repudiated liability when the contents were destroyed by fire and explosion on the ground of breach of this condition. Lawson J. held that the introduction of these items was an alteration to the contents of the building described in Item 2, whereby there was an increase in the risk of destructional damage to those contents. The insurers, accordingly, could rightly rely on the clause to avoid the policy in respect to the contents cover. The Court of Appeal upheld this view.[83]

10. REASONABLE PRECAUTIONS CONDITION

12–38   Virtually all insurances issued to cover commercial risks will contain a condition precedent to liability[84] that:

> "the insured shall take all reasonable precautions to prevent loss or damage."

This clause came to be considered in the content of the burglary insurance issued in *Victor Melik & Co. Ltd v. Norwich Union Fire Insurance Society*

[80] *ibid.* at 372.
[81] [1970] 1 Q.B. 311.
[82] [1983] 1 Lloyd's Rep. 674.
[83] [1984] 1 Lloyd's Rep. 149, CA.
[84] See Chapter 2, above.

Ltd and Kemp,[85] the facts of which have already been given above. Woolf J. (as he then was) dealt at length with the approach to be taken by the court when considering whether the condition was breached by the insured[86]:

> "an argument was put forward which was attractive and economical. It was contended that because [the insured] said in evidence that, if they had thought the premises were not insured they would not have left them unattended, they must have thought it reasonable to keep someone in attendance. Therefore, as there is no one in attendance, this is a case where all reasonable precautions to prevent loss or damage have not been taken. In relation to that contention, in my view, it has to be borne in mind that an obligation to take all reasonable precautions is not the same as an obligation to take every practicable precaution and in order to decide whether a precaution is a reasonable precaution, one has to look at all the circumstances.
>
> What are the relevant circumstances here? First of all, there is the fact (and this is important, in my view) that the premises on the night of December 21 were to all intents and purposes secure from a physical point of view. I emphasize that because after the burglary on October 30 a representative of the plaintiffs did stay on the premises all night, but then the premises were not secure as the burglary had left them in a condition where it was no longer possible to lock the doors.
>
> Secondly, it must be borne in mind that although the link to the control centre was not working, and this was known to the plaintiffs, the alarm was otherwise working and in operation. This is important because unless one was in a position (which the plaintiffs were not at the time) of knowing that the wire had in fact been cut by thieves as part of a campaign to break into the premises, the plaintiffs were in a position where they could reasonably assume that so far as the outside world was concerned, these were premises which looked as though they were fully protected by an alarm system.
>
> Thirdly, the plaintiffs if they had stayed at the premises, would not have been able to satisfactorily set the alarm, because the alarm was of a sort which was only designed to operate when the premises were vacated. The nature of the equipment used was such that whereas it would be conceivable for a person to be in the premises and stay in one room with the alarm in operation, it would not in the ordinary circumstances by practical or realistic for them to do so for the whole night. The plaintiffs were in the position that they would think if they stayed at the premises they would have had to leave the alarm off altogether and it is questionable as to whether or not the alarm would be more valuable than the presence of a representative of the plaintiffs in the event of a break in.
>
> Fourthly, the premises are not far from the local police station, five minutes' walk, 500 yards was referred to in evidence.
>
> Fifthly, the plaintiffs had arranged on the night in question that the police would, because of the defect in the alarm, make more regular visits to the premises than would otherwise be the case. On that basis it does seem to me that the bell could be of great value because it could lead to the police being alerted and with premises of this sort, bearing in mind the nature of the attack which would have to be launched against the premises, I could see that importance would be attached to leave the alarm *in situ* and in operation although it would not have the benefit of the link to the central control.
>
> Sixthly, there was a suggestion made . . . to the possibility of getting a security firm to attend the premises. They would have the advantage which

---

[85] [1980] 1 Lloyd's Rep. 523.
[86] *ibid.* at 531–532.

the plaintiff would not have of being able to communicate to the outside world by some form of radio. It has to be borne in mind that a representative of the plaintiffs would be staying in the premises without the benefit of a working telephone. The answer to this, in my view, is to be found in the evidence of Mr W . . ., a very experienced underwriter, who said that really from a practical point of view, bearing in mind the dates in relation to Christmas, you would never get a security firm to attend the premises. Although this might otherwise have been something which it would have been sensible to do, in my view it was not a reasonable precaution in the circumstances which then existed. After all, it would be during December 21 some time about 4 o'clock that the plaintiff would be aware that this line was not going to be repaired, and it was only at that late stage that they would have opportunity of trying to find a security firm to take the steps which would be needed if security was to be provided by an outside firm at these premises. In my view, there was no failure in that respect.

I consider that taking into account the nature of the premises and the protection which was provided by the alarm, the plaintiff in fact did take all reasonable precautions. I am supported in my view as to that, by the fact on the following night, after the . . . burglary, again nobody stayed at the premises and that was the position notwithstanding that the Norwich Union were fully aware of all the facts and had attended the premises with their assessor and notwithstanding the fact that the plaintiffs were also then being advised by a responsible assessor. Furthermore, the police had not previously advised the plaintiffs to have some one present and even after the burglary apparently did not advise them to have someone present."

12–40   A condition in a burglary policy issued to shop premises that the insured "is to take all precautions as regards securing all doors and win dows and other means of entrance or otherwise" has been construed as not requiring internal show case doors to be secured.[87]

11. CONDITION PRECEDENT REGARDING RECORD-KEEPING

12–41   Policies for shopkeepers and other retail risks will often have some warranty or condition precedent regarding the keeping of business records. *Bennett v. Yorkshire Insurance Co. Ltd*[88] concerned a shopkeeper's policy which contained a condition precedent that:

> "The insured shall keep proper books of account with a complete record of all purchases and sales and all such books shall be regularly entered up as soon as such purchases or sales have taken placed."

The insured made a claim for loss suffered by breaking and entering and theft of stock at his shop. The insurers did not admit the burglary nor the alleged theft of stock, and also contended that the insured's records were incomplete. The insured gave evidence that all invoices for stock he purchased were totalised periodically, and as regards sales, at the end of

---

[87] *Re George and Goldsmiths and General Burglary Insurance Association Ltd* [1899] 1 Q.B. 595 at 609 *per* A.L. Smith L.J., CA.
[88] [1962] 2 Lloyd's Rep. 270.

the day he would enter up into a little red exercise book the money in the till, which he said would be the whole of the day's takings from the shop. The insurers disputed that the purchases were all recorded, and disputed that all sales were recorded, that is, they disputed the completeness of the records rather than their lack of any detail. The insured's real problem was the total absence of any records as to wages paid. The insured's evidence was that he paid his own wages, and that of the two employees, out of cash from sales of other stock not entered up with the other purchase invoices. In the light of this evidence, the insured's counsel had been forced to argue that the judge should discount his client's evidence as to the wages as all lies. Thompson J. accepted that the insured had, indeed, told lies in evidence about only trading from one shop, but there was no way around the fact that the insured's evidence amounted to paying wages from unrecorded sales. The insurers therefore proved the breach of the condition precedent.

12. CONCEALMENT OF MATERIAL FACTS

When effecting an insurance on property, an insured must disclose his **12–42** criminal record,[89] and his commission of any criminal offence, even if acquitted at trial, for it is the underlying fact that he has committed a crime that must be disclosed.[90] Thus, an insured need not disclose allegations of offences made against him if he has not in fact, committed the alleged offence.[91] In each case, however, the defendant insurers will need to call evidence to prove the materiality of the non-disclosure and their inducement to make the underwriting decision.[92] Questions in the proposal form must, of course, be answered correctly by the proposer. Where a proposal asked: "Have you or your spouse been subject to any declaration of bankruptcy or conviction of arson, fraud, forgery, theft, robbery or handling of stolen goods?", the reference to "fraud" requires disclosure of any offence of which fraud was the critical element, because there is no offence of "fraud" itself. Therefore, an offence of obtaining property by deception contrary to section 15(1) of the Theft Act 1968 would need to be disclosed when answering that question.[93]

Moral hazard

An insurer may successfully prove that the moral hazard relating to key **12–43** personnel within an insured limited company are material.[94] In *Regina Fur*

---

[89] *Woolcott v. Sun Alliance and London Insurance Ltd* [1978] 1 All E.R. 1253 at 1257, *per* Caulfield J.; *Woolcott v. Excess Insurance Co. Ltd* [1978] 1 Lloyd's Rep. 633; retrial ordered without affecting that finding [1979] 1 Lloyd's Rep. 231, CA; reported *Woolcott v. Excess Insurance Co. Ltd* [1979] 2 Lloyd's Rep. 210.

[90] *Quaere*, very minor offences not resulting in prosecution and convictions, see *Roselodge Ltd v. Castle* [1966] 2 Lloyd's Rep. 113 at 133, *per* McNair J.

[91] *Reynolds and Anderson v. Phoenix Assurance Co. Ltd* [1978] 2 Lloyd's Rep. 440 at 460, *per* Forbes J.; *cf. March Cabaret Club and Casino Ltd v. London Assurance Ltd* [1975] 1 Lloyd's Rep. 169 at 177, *per* May J.

[92] See Chapter 3, above.

[93] *Golloway v. Guardian Royal Exchange (U.K.) Ltd* [1999] Lloyd's Rep. I.R. 209, CA.

[94] *Roselodge Ltd v. Castle* [1966] 2 Lloyd's Rep. 105, CA.

Co. Ltd v. Bossom,[95] Pearson J. (as he then was) was satisfied on the evidence that an isolated conviction more than 20 years old was a material fact that should have been disclosed, but in *Reynolds and Anderson v. Phoenix Assurance Co Ltd*,[96] Forbes J. was not satisfied that an 11–year-old conviction was material on the evidence presented. The key personnel in that company must also disclose their own business history where they have traded unsuccessfully on their own account or been declared bankrupt, and must disclose such history relating to moral hazard in all the names or guises they may have adopted over time.[97]

12–44   In *Roselodge Ltd v. Castle*,[98] the insured company held an "all risks" policy in respect of diamonds held in pursuit of their trade as jewellers. After a robbery when a large amount of diamonds were stolen, the insurers defended the claim on the ground of non-disclosure of material facts. The first fact relied on was the undisclosed conviction of the plaintiff company's principal director for bribing a police officer some 18 years earlier, when he received a fine of £75. This offence centred on a parking offence which the director had sought to avoid being reported by the officer. McNair J. concluded[99]:

> "I have come to the conclusion that it is not established to my satisfaction that Mr. Rosenberg's offence and conviction on a matter which has no direct relation to trading as a diamond merchant was a material fact which would have influenced a prudent underwriter."

The second fact relied on by the insurers was the undisclosed conviction of the plaintiff sales manager for smuggling diamonds into the United States some eight years earlier. That person had been employed for some six years by the plaintiff company since his return to this country upon his release, after serving part of his sentence of three years' imprisonment. McNair J. held on the evidence that this whole incident was a material fact which would have influenced the prudent underwriter.[1]

Previous losses

12–45   Previous losses from the insured risk must be disclosed by the insured, as is illustrated by *Krantz v. Allan and Faber*[2] where a question in the proposal asked: "Have you ever sustained a loss?" and the reply given was: "Yes, last March, £150". The insured did not disclose a £60 claim for a burglary loss a year before, nor the receipt of a £2 *ex gratia* payment from insurers for loss of a coat other than through burglary. Bray J.[3] held that the former, but not the latter, loss was a material fact that should have been disclosed even in the absence of any question in a proposal form.

---

[95] [1957] 2 Lloyd's Rep. 466; see also *Schoolman v. Hall* [1951] 1 Lloyd's Rep. 139, CA.
[96] [1978] 2 Lloyd's Rep. 440.
[97] *Gallé Gowns Ltd v. Licenses and General Insurance Co. Ltd* (1933) 47 Ll. L. Rep. 186.
[98] [1966] 2 Lloyd's Rep. 113.
[99] *ibid.* at 132.
[1] [1966] 2 Lloyd's Rep. 113 at 133.
[2] (1921) 9 Ll. L. Rep. 410; following *Condogianis v. Guardian Assurance Co.* [1921] 2 A.C. 125, PC.
[3] *ibid.* at 412.

This requirement extends to disclosing losses sustained but never **12–46** claimed under an insurance policy either out of choice, or because, there was no insurance[4] for it is the fact of the suffering of previous losses that is material, not that a claim was made against insurers.[5] Thus, if contents were stolen but subsequently returned by the police, that loss must still be disclosed to the insurer.[6] Claims upon other policies, however, in respect of a different subject-matter, are unlikely to be a material fact.[7] Previous losses suffered by key personnel of an insured limited company, *e.g.* the chairman, must also be disclosed apart from losses suffered by the insured company specifically.[8]

Previous insurance history
Whether any given circumstance concerning the insured's previous **12–47** insurance history are a material fact which should be disclosed, is a question of fact for the court to decide, and expert evidence may assist in that decision. Thus, in a given instance, the fact that a partner when previously trading on his own was refused a similar insurance can be determined to be a material fact, non-disclosure of which entitles the insurer to avoid the policy, *e.g.* where a partner had previously carried on the same business, at the same premises, on his sole account and had been refused a burglary insurance by another insurer.[9]

Similarly, the fact that key personnel of a limited company have previously been refused an insurance when trading on their own account may be material.[10]

But the fact that a different insurer has refused to issue or declined to renew,[11] an insurance on a different subject matter, is unlikely to be held to constitute a material fact,[12] unless a question in the proposal form specifically requests information in relation to any insurances.[13]

13. FRAUDULENT CLAIMS

As has been seen in Chapter 1, above, a dishonest claim under an insurance **12–48** policy constitutes a breach of the insured's continuing duty of good faith owed to the insurer. Whilst it is unnecessary,[14] most policies insert an express provision stating that the insured will lose all benefit under the

[4] *Becker v. Marshall* (1922) 12 Ll. L. Rep. 413, CA.
[5] *Rozanes v. Bowen* (1928) 32 Ll. L. Rep. 98, CA.; *Lyons v. J.W. Bentley Ltd* (1944) 77 Ll. L. Rep. 335; *Roberts v. Avon Insurance Co. Ltd* [1956] 2 Lloyd's Rep. 240.
[6] *Morser v. Eagle Star & British Dominions Insurance Co. Ltd* (1931) 40 Ll. L. Rep. 254.
[7] *Ewer v. National Employers' Mutual General Insurance Association Ltd* [1937] 2 All E.R. 193.
[8] *Gallé Gowns Ltd v. Licenses & General Insurance Co. Ltd* (1933) 47 Ll. L. Rep. 186.
[9] *Glicksman v. Lancashire & General Assurance Co. Ltd* [1927] A.C. 139, HL.
[10] See *Gallé Gowns Ltd v. Licenses & General Insurance Co. Ltd* (1933) 47 Ll. L. Rep. 186.
[11] *Ascott v. Cornhill Insurance Co. Ltd* (1937) 58 Ll. L. Rep. 41.
[12] *Ewer v. National Employers' Mutual General Insurance Association Ltd* [1937] 2 All E.R. 193.
[13] *Locker & Woolfe Ltd v. Western Australian Insurance Co. Ltd* [1936] 1 K.B. 408, CA, where a question in the proposal form was framed in wide terms: "Has this or any other insurance of yours been declined by any other company?"; see also *Condogianis v. Guardian Assurance Co.* [1921] 2 A.C. 125, PC.
[14] *Galloway v. Guardian Royal Exchange (U.K.) Ltd* [1999] Lloyd's Rep. I.R. 209, CA.

policy if a claim is in any respect fraudulent. If the claim is to any material, rather than immaterial, extent fraudulent, the whole claim is tainted with fraud.[15] Put another way, if, taken in isolation, the fraudulent part of the claim is sufficiently serious to justify stigmatising it as a breach of the insured's duty of good faith, the insurer's liability is discharged.[16] A claim is fraudulently inflated if the claim is made in an amount which the insured clearly knows he has not suffered.[17]

12–49   An extreme example of fraud in claims under a contents policy is provided by the case of *Nsubuga v. Commercial Union Assurance Co. plc.*[18] The insured was a businessman from Uganda who had come to the United Kingdom in 1990 and had commenced a shop business at the beginning of 1994. The shop in London was intended to be a general store specialising particularly in groceries and African goods. On August 4, 1994, he had signed a proposal form for insurance with the defendants covering, *inter alia*, the risk of fire. He was informed on August 15, 1994 that the defendants were holding covered for a total sum insured of £37,660 as follows:

Stock in trade	£20,000
Stock of tobacco cigars cigarettes	£ 1,500
Trade and office furniture fixtures fittings	£12,560
Landlord's fixtures fittings	£ 3,600

12–50   The premises caught fire at about 10.20 p.m. on August 20, 1994, and the insured made a claim under the policy. He claimed the full £20,000 in respect of stock in trade. Part of that claim, for just over £10,000, was accepted by the insurers as genuine, but the balance was resisted on the grounds it was fraudulent or fraudulently exaggerated. The first part of the balance was for £6,058.90 on the basis of purchase invoices in the months of July and August, making allowances on an estimated basis for the amounts sold. The remaining £4,000 was presented as a balancing item. The insured explained the lack of documentation to support these claims by saying that he had handed stock records and his purchase ledger to the insurer's loss adjusters. Having heard from the loss adjusters, Thomas J. rejected that explanation. The insured's other explanation was that the documents were in a drawer under the counter in the office and had been destroyed in the fire. The judge also rejected this explanation upon the evidence of the fire officer who attended the fire that a ledger book in that drawer would have been intact, or substantially intact. Indeed, the officer had found a book of loose papers in that drawer that were not burned.

12–51   There was a further ground for rejecting these second and third elements of the insured's stock claim. The insured had said in evidence that those sums represented a stock of fruit of fruit and vegetables, but this was in stark contrast to what he had said in an interview shortly after the fire, on

---

[15] *ibid.* at 213, *per* Lord Woolf M.R.
[16] *ibid.* at 214, *per* Millett L.J.
[17] *Orakpo v. Barclays Insurance Services* [1995] L.R.L.R. 443, CA.
[18] [1998] 2 Lloyd's Rep. 682.

September 24, 1994, the insured had said that at the time of the fire almost all the fruit and vegetables had been sold off, "but there were some green bananas, onions and the like". Further, his assistant had said in interview that the only stock of fruit and vegetables that he could recall at the close of business on the day of the fire were some green bananas. In addition, there was other evidence that the shop was sparsely stocked. Thomas J. was therefore "satisfied beyond any reasonable doubt" that there never was any quantity of fruit and vegetables amounting to £10,000 and that this claim was fraudulent.[19]

Mr Nsubuga had also claimed the full sum insured of £1,500 in respect **12–52** of his stock of tobacco, cigars and cigarettes. This was on the basis of the absence of purchase documents, and that there would be accurate within five per cent either way. Thomas J. considered that it was clear that this sum was put forward in the belief that there was going to be "horse trading" between the insured's loss assessors and the insurer's loss adjusters. The relevant question was, therefore, given the fact that the claim was formulated by the insured's loss assessor, could the court be sure or satisfied on the criminal standard of proof that the claim was fraudulent? Thomas J. concluded that, although he had doubts about the genuineness of the claim, he was not sure, even on a high balance of probabilities, that the claim was fraudulently made, or fraudulently exaggerated. The defendant insurer therefore failed to establish that allegation of fraud.[20]

A further ground relied on by the insurer was an allegation that the **12–53** insured was guilty of fraudulent conduct in the presentation of the claim. Thomas J. held that this ground was also made out to the requisite criminal standard of proof. The relevant matter was Mr. Nsubuga's failure to disclose to the insurer's loss adjusters when they were investigating the claim, that the local council had levied distress on his goods for non-payment of the rates for the shop, shortly before the fire. This was directly relevant in three respect. First, it was directly relevant to the general stock claim, because it would be material for the loss adjusters to know in examining the records that distress had recently been levied. Secondly, it was plainly relevant to the claim in respect of tobacco, because a quantity of cigarettes had been subject to the distress. Thirdly, it was relevant to the loss of profits claim under the business interruption cover of the insurance policy, being a very important pointer to the viability of the business. Given the fact that Mr. Nsubuga was an experienced businessman in Uganda and that he had then taken a course in business in the United Kingdom, Thomas J. was satisfied that he plainly knew that the levying of distress was a highly material fact to the way the insurer would approach the claim. Accordingly, Thomas J. was sure, on the criminal standard of proof, that Mr. Nsubuga knew it was material and had fraudulently decided the conceal it from the loss adjusters.[21]

---

[19] *ibid.* at 686–688.
[20] *ibid.* at 688.
[21] *ibid.* at 688–690.

12–54   Thomas J. also found that the insured's claim in respect of fixtures and
fittings was fraudulent. Part of the insured's claim was in respect of the
destroyed cold store which he claimed had been installed for the sum of
£6,900 and produced an invoice from the supplier for that sum. The
invoice had clearly had a "6" added before the "9" and had initially shown
the sum of £900. The supplier gave evidence that he had only charged
£900, as he only installed the plant and not the insulation, and was still
awaiting payment of the V.A.T. on that sum from the insured. Mr. Nsubuga,
however, said that he had paid £6,900 to the supplier which had been
recorded in a book destroyed in the fire. The insurer called evidence from
a refrigeration expert who said that a cold room would have cost between
£1,000 and £1,750 to install in 1994. The insured produced a quotation of
£7,000 for the installation of a cold store to support his £6,900 claim, but
did not call evidence at court to prove that quotation. Thomas J.
concluded that Mr. Nsubuga's account was wholly untrue and that he had
deliberately and fraudulently altered the invoice.[22]

12–55   Fraud was also found by a jury in the all risks insurance claim in *Haase
v. Evans*,[23] where the insured claimed in respect of stolen pictures and
objets d'art which had very recently been purchased by him for about
£6,000. In his claim form he had sought £18,706, and in his subsequent
writ the sum claimed was £22,794.

[22] *ibid.* at 690–691.
[23] (1934) 84 Ll. L. Rep. 131.

CHAPTER 13

CARRIERS' INSURANCE

1. SUBJECT MATTER OF CARRIERS' INSURANCE

Introduction

The first category of subject matter of carriers' insurance concerns the carrier's insurable interest in the goods entrusted to him for carriage, and is thus a form of property insurance. The second category is cover for the carrier's legal liability to the owners of the goods. This insurance cover is generally referred to as "goods in transit" insurance, and such policies will usually refer to specific insured goods, but more commonly will take the form of a "floating" annual policy on goods carried by the insured "in trust or on commission". Policies will generally be offered for transit within the United Kingdom only, or for international transit by vehicle where the carriage is subject to the Convention on the Contract for the International Carriage of Goods by Road (C.M.R.).

13–01

Carrier may insure for full value of goods

The principle that a carrier, as a bailee, may insure to the full value of those goods, has been established for well over a century, and emanated from the decision in *Waters and Steel v. Monarch Fire and Life Assurance Co.*[1] where wharfingers held an insurance against fire on, *inter alia*, "goods in trust or on commission" and were awarded judgment for the full value of those goods. Being an insurance on goods, the court held that the insured were not limited by statute[2] to recover only the value of their own interest in the goods lost in the fire, *i.e.* the value of their lien in respect of their charges, but could recover the full value of the goods. The insured in such circumstances are entitled to apply so much to cover their own interest, and will be trustees for the owners as to the rest.

13–02

This principle that a bailee may insure to the full value of goods entrusted to him, and where his recovery exceeds his interest he is liable to account to the bailor for the balance, remained unchallenged until the insurers argued the point in *Hepburn v. A. Tomlinson (Hauliers) Ltd*[3] before the House of Lords. Here, carriers had effected a goods in transit policy against "all risks" in respect of tobacco, the property of the Imperial Tobacco Company, whilst being carried by themselves, and claimed the full value of cigarettes when they were stolen. Lord Reid delivered the leading speech and said[4]:

13–03

---

[1] (1856) 5 E. and B. 870.

[2] The Life Assurance Act 1774, limiting an insured's recovery under a policy to his own interest at the time of the contract (*Dalby v. India & London Life Assurance Co.* (1854) 15 C.B. 365) does not apply to insurances on goods, ships and merchandises by section 4 thereof.

[3] [1966] A.C. 451, HL. Applied *D.G. Finance Ltd v. Scott & Eagle Star Insurance Co. Ltd* [1999] Lloyd's Rep. I.R. 387, CA.

[4] *ibid.* at 467–468.

"A bailee can if he chooses merely insure to cover his own loss . . . and if he does that of course he can recover no more under the policy than sufficient to make good his own personal loss . . . But equally he can if he chooses insure up to his full insurable interest—up to the full value of the goods entrusted to him. And if he does that he can recover the value of the goods though he has suffered no personal loss at all. But in that case the law will require him to account to the owner of the goods who has suffered the loss or, as Lord Campbell says, he will be trustee for the owners. I need not consider whether this is a trust in the strict sense or precisely on what ground the owner can sue the bailee for the money which he has recovered from the insurer . . . The fact that a bailee has an insurable interest beyond his own personal loss if the goods are destroyed has never been regarded as in any way inconsistent with the overriding principle that insurance of goods is a contract of indemnity. The question is whether the bailee has insured his whole interest—in effect has taken out a goods policy—or whether he has only insured against personal loss . . .

The answer to that question must depend on the true construction of the policy."

Legal liability of carrier at common law

13–04   This legal liability of the carrier to the owner of the goods he carries is the second category of subject matter of carriers' insurance. Where the carrier only wishes to insure his common law liability, the cover may be expressed as being:

"the legal liability of the insured for loss of or damage to general merchandise of every description belonging to the insured or held by the insured in trust for which the insured are themselves responsible . . ."

13–05   The vital words at the end of these insuring words define the scope of the indemnity afforded under this insurance contract, and thus if the carrier is not legally responsible for the loss, then there is no right under the policy for the carrier to recover the value of the goods and make payment of the same to the owners.[5] This has particular ramifications for a private carrier, who is responsible only if he has been negligent in the wide sense of the term,[6] as against a common carrier (one who trades as a carrier available to the public at large)[7] who is absolutely responsible[8] for the safety of the goods, subject to certain common law exceptions.[9] Where the

---

[5] See *North British & Mercantile Insurance Co. v. Moffatt* (1871) L.R. 7 C.P. 25; *Engel v. Lancashire & General Assurance Co. Ltd* (1925) 21 Ll. L. Rep. 327.

[6] As was the case in *A. Cohen & Co. Ltd v. Plaistow Transport Ltd* [1968] 2 Lloyd's Rep. 587.

[7] See *A. Siohn & Co. Ltd v. R.H. Hagland & Son (Transport) Ltd* [1976] 2 Lloyd's Rep. 428.

[8] *Coggs v. Bernard* (1703) 2 Ld. Raym. 909 at 918, *per* Holt C.J. The exceptions are:

    (i) an act of God;
    (ii) an act of the Queen's enemies;
    (iii) the fault of the consignor or owner of the goods;
    (iv) the inherent vice of the goods; or
    (v) by any cause where the consignor has been guilty of fraud.

The onus of proving that the damage to the goods was caused by one of these exceptions lies on the common carrier. See also *Forward v. Pittard* (1785) 1 Term Rep. 27 at 33, *per* Lord Mansfield C.J.

[9] Nor will carrier be responsible if the owner undertakes to insure, *Coupar Transport (London) Ltd v. Smith's Acton Ltd* [1959] 1 Lloyd's Rep. 369.

carrier is involved in international carriage by road,[10] the contract of carriage will be governed by the Carriage of Goods by Road Act 1965[11] and this contractual liability can be insured under a policy generally known as a Goods in Transit (C.M.R.) policy.

Goods "in trust"

Of course, it is of vital importance to determine the meaning of the phrase "in trust". In the *Waters* case, above, Lord Campbell C.J. said this[12]:   **13–06**

> "The first question is whether, upon the construction of the contract, those goods were intended to be covered by the policy. I think in either policy the description is such as to include them. What is meant by the words 'goods in trust'? I think that means goods with which the assured are entrusted; not goods held in trust in the strict technical sense, so held that there was only an equitable obligation on the assured enforceable by a subpoena in Chancery, but goods with which they were entrusted in the ordinary sense of the word. They were so entrusted with the goods deposited on their wharfs; I cannot doubt that the policy was intended to protect such goods; and it would be inconvenient if wharfingers could not protect such goods by a floating policy . . . and I think that a person entrusted with goods can insure them without orders from the owner, and even without informing him that there was such a policy. It would be most inconvenient in business if a wharfinger could not, at his own cost, keep up a floating policy for the benefit of all who might become his customers."

Policies issued in respect of a carrier's liability will, in common with the insurance of the goods themselves, often refer to goods held "in trust" by the carrier. Whether actual possession by the insured carrier was a necessary component for goods to be "in trust" fell to be considered in *John Rigby (Haulage) Ltd v. Reliance Marine Insurance Co. Ltd.*[13] A consignment of copper ingot bars lay in Liverpool docks, and the insured claimants had entered into an oral arrangement with the owner's shipping agents to carry consignments of copper for reward to consignees in Birmingham, whenever they had vehicles available. A certain X, driving a lorry, called at the Liverpool office of the insured and on his representations that he was employed by a transport company which was on the insured's list of subcontractors, and that the lorry belonged to that company and he wanted a load for the return journey to Birmingham, he was given a collection order for 440 of the copper ingot bars by the acting manager of the insured company. X duly presented the collection order to the shipping agents at the docks, the ingots were loaded on to his lorry, and he was given delivery   **13–07**

[10] Carriage by sea and air is outside the scope of this work.
[11] Applying the Geneva Convention of 1956.
[12] (1856) 5 E. and B. 870 at 880–881; *Castellain v. Preston* (1883) 11 Q.B.D. 380 at 398, *per* Bowen L.J., CA: "A person with a limited interest may insure either for himself and to cover his own interest only, or he may insure so as to cover not merely his own limited interest, but the interest of all others who are interested in the property."
[13] [1956] 2 Q.B. 468, CA.

and a note by the dock checker on presentation of which to the police at the dock gates, he was passed out. X was not a servant of, nor did the lorry belong to, the sub-contracting transport company, and neither he nor the copper ingots were seen again. The defendant insurers knew, in this case, that sub-contractors might be used. The insured carriers contended that in the circumstances they had no defence to a claim by the owners of the copper, and therefore claimed that they were entitled under the policy to be indemnified by the defendant insurer. The insurer denied liability on the ground, *inter alia*, that the ingots were at no time in the possession of the carriers and thus not held by them "in trust" as required in the policy.

13–08   The Court of Appeal held that, although the giving of the collection order was as between the insured carrier and X, an invalid authority to X to receive the goods, it was also an offer by the carriers to the owners for whom the goods were being carried to undertake their carriage to Birmingham. That offer having been accepted by the representatives of the owners, the carriers were entrusted with the goods under the contract thus concluded, and being liable for being loss, were entitled to be indemnified under the policy by the defendants. The court was strongly influenced by the decision, previously referred to of *Waters and Steel v. Monarch Fire and Life Assurance Co.*[14] and Singleton L.J. explained his reasoning in this way[15]:

> "The loss fell upon the [insured] because they sent a man and lorry to receive the goods and they gave him an authority to receive them on their behalf. The man was handed the goods on the authority of the [insured], and he signed for them on the delivery order to (the consignees). Thus the goods were entrusted to the one the [insured's] drivers sent in order that the [insured] could carry out their contract to convey. In other words, they were entrusted to the [insured]."

2. RISKS INSURED

13–09   **"All risks" cover**

The insurance cover will be expressed to be in relation to "all risks of loss or damage however arising", though policies often expressly state that the following risks are included:

   (i) *Strikes.*
   (ii) *Riots*: This means as defined by the criminal law, *i.e.* that no fewer than three persons are assembled with a common purpose which is executed or incepted by them, with an intention to help one another by force if necessary against any person who may oppose them. Moreover, the display of force or violence must alarm at least one person of reasonable firmness and courage.[16]

---

[14] (1856) 5 E. and B. 870.
[15] [1956] 2 Q.B. 468 at 482, CA; and see, *per* Jenkins L.J. at 484.
[16] *Field v. Metropolitan Police Receiver* [1907] 2 K.B. 853.

(iii) *Civil commotions*: This term connotes a stage between a riot and a civil war,[17] where the element of turbulence or tumult is present,[18] the disturbances having a sufficient cohesion to prevent them from being the work of a mindless mob.[19] In other words, it is "an insurrection of the people for general purposes" which does not amount to rebellion against the government.[20]

(iv) *Malicious damage*.

The wording of specific policies vary, and the construction of the ambit of the indemnity afforded by the insurance must always be interpreted upon the particular words in question. Thus, if the policy covers "transit by land", the insurance will not cover the goods if put in canal barges,[21] and transit "in and around London" does not include transit outside that area, *e.g.* Winchester.[22]   **13–10**

Common exclusions

The "all risks" nature of the cover does not mean that absolutely every risk will be covered by the goods in transit element of the cover. Typical exclusions will relate to: **13–11**

(a) deterioration through delay;

(b) loss of market[23];

(c) loss or damage which is in any way caused or facilitated by the dishonesty of any person in the service of or employed by the insured;

(d) loss or damage caused by explosives or goods of a dangerous nature carried on the vehicle[24];

(e) loss or damage caused by hooks or slings;

(f) loss or damage arising from war, invasion, act of foreign enemy, hostilities (whether war be declared or not), civil war, rebellion, revolution, insurrection, military or usurped power[25];

(g) Northern Ireland risks[26];

(h) loss or damage due to wear and tear, moth, vermin, insects, damp, rust, mildew, depreciation or gradual deterioration or spontaneous combustion.[27]

---

[17] *Bolivia Republic v. Indemnity Mutual Marine Assurance Co.* [1909] 1 K.B. 785 at 800, CA.

[18] *Levy v. Assicurazioni Generali* [1940] A.C. 791, PC.

[19] *Spinney's (1948) Ltd v. Royal Insurance Co. Ltd* [1980] 1 Lloyd's Rep. 406 at 438, *per* Mustill J.

[20] *ibid.* at 436.

[21] *Ewing & Co. v. Sicklemore* (1918) 35 T.L.R. 55, CA; in *Pennsylvania Co. for Insurances on Lives & Granting Annuities v. Mumford* [1920] 2 K.B. 537, CA, "transit between any houses or places" was held not to cover movement of the property between rooms of the same building.

[22] *Richardson v. Roylance* (1933) 47 Ll. L. Rep. 173.

[23] This would not be covered in any event, unless expressly included, *Emanuel Lewis & Son Ltd v. Hepburn* [1960] 1 Lloyd's Rep. 304.

[24] Unless specifically insured.

[25] For the extent of these perils, see Chapter 11.

[26] See Chapter 11, above.

[27] These excluded risks prevent the insurer being liable in respect of natural perils either affecting, or an inherent vice of, the subject matter of the insurance.

Common extensions of cover

13–12   A goods in transit policy may be extended beyond simply covering risks whilst the goods are "in transit" (discussed below). Cover can be extended to cover risks while the goods are stored in certain prescribed place, but, as ever, the precise words may lead to a dispute over whether a particular loss is covered by the insurance indemnity. In *Wulfson v. Switzerland General Insurance Co. Ltd*,[28] the policy had been extended to cover the goods whilst "in store" at a depository. It was held that the cover included storage of the goods on the depository premises whilst still in vans, and the insurer's contention that the goods had to stored in a covered building was rejected.

13–13   Where cover was extended to cover the goods "whilst in warehouse", it was decided in *Leo Rapp Ltd v. McClure*[29] that, in absence of any special meaning, "warehouse" must be given its ordinary and popular meaning and thus a locked compound, enclosed by a high brick wall topped with barbed wire, is not by its nature a "warehouse". In *Firmin and Collins Ltd v. Allied Shippers Ltd*,[30] the extension referred to the goods "whilst in a public warehouse". The court held that those words meant a warehouse operated as a business to the public and, accordingly, did not extend to cover a private arrangement between the insured and a friend for storage of goods under a railway archway.

13–14   In *London Tobacco Co. (Overseas) Ltd v. D.F.D.S Transport Ltd & others*,[31] the third defendant carrier's liability cover provided that the carrier would be indemnified if the property was "damaged" whilst being "loaded upon carried by or off-loaded from any vehicle described in the Schedule as being insured". "Damage" was defined as "physical loss, destruction, damage or misdelivery". The third defendant was a small firm of road hauliers and were the sub-contractors of the first and second claimants in respect of the carriage of a consignment of their cigarettes from their premises in Enfield by road via Ramsgate to Bucharest. In turn, the third defendant employed the fourth defendant, Mr Berwick, as their sub-contractor. Mr Berwick duly collected the box trailer containing the cigarettes with his own tractor unit, and at this time (it was assumed) had already decided with co-conspirators to steal those cigarettes. He therefore drove to a pre-arranged service station where his co-conspirators drove it away. The cigarettes were never recovered and were thus "lost" within the meaning of the policy.

13–15   The third defendant was sued by the claimants, the first defendant and the second defendant, but the insurers denied liability and were joined in the action. The insurers argued that the insured third defendant had declined an extension of cover in respect of theft by bogus sub-contractors, and therefore the policy did not cover this theft by Mr Berwick. The Court of Appeal rejected the insurers defence because Mr Berwick was not a

---

[28] [1940] 3 All E.R. 221.
[29] [1955] 1 Lloyd's Rep. 292.
[30] [1967] 1 Lloyd's Rep. 633.
[31] [1994] 1 Lloyd's Rep. 394, CA.

"bogus" sub-contractor, but was a valid sub-contractor as defined in the policy "... any person not being an employee to whom property is entrusted for reward by ... the insured and of whose services the insured makes use for the performance of the contract". To establish their defence, the insurers needed to have shown that Mr Berwick's engagement by the third defendant was "merely a sham", and it was not sufficient to show that the third defendant would have been entitled to avoid their contract with him on the grounds of his dishonest intent. Mr. Berwick was properly described as a sub-contractor even though he was dishonest and had no intention of performing the sub-contract.[32]

3. IN TRANSIT

Commencement of transit

The point in time that transit commences when concerned with a   **13–16**
carrie's insurance policy is to be determined from the aspect of the goods themselves, not the transporting vehicle. This was first considered in *Sadler Bros Co. v. Meredith*[33] by Roskill J. (as he then was). The claimants were cleaners of ship's interiors and had insured themselves against loss or damage to goods "in transit by Commercial Vehicles operated by the Assured" (*i.e.* themselves) "or whilst being loaded or unloaded, or whilst in garage, warehouse or depot, anywhere in the United Kingdom". The claimants had loaded some of their equipment onto their van outside their premises one morning with the purpose of transporting the equipment to a ship which they were to clean, and had then been requested by a policeman to move the van on some 70 yards due to the narrowness of the street. Two employees moved the van, locked it and returned to the claimants premises. On returning ten minutes later they found the van had been stolen. Although the van was subsequently recovered, the equipment was not.

The defendant insurers denied liability, contending, *inter alia*, that the   **13–17**
equipment was not "in transit". After considering the interpretation of the words "whilst in course of transit" given in two cases concerning the London Lighterage Clause,[34] Roskill J. said[35]:

> "what one is considering is the goods themselves being in course of transit and not the question of the means of conveyance in which that transit is taking place, be it ship transit, railway transit, bullock, or whatever it may be; it is being in motion. And I think that there one wants to bear in mind that transit has in its nature the element of carriage about it and the carriage starts not when the movement of the vehicle in which the carriage is taking place starts, but when the goods are placed on the vehicle ... and I think here 'transit' means the passage or carriage of goods from one place to another ..."

[32] *ibid.* at 397, *per* Hirst L.J.
[33] [1963] 2 Lloyd's Rep. 293.
[34] *William Soanes Ltd v. F.E. Walker Ltd* (1946) 79 Ll. L. Rep. 646; *Kilroy Thompson Ltd v. Perkins & Homer Ltd.* [1956] 2 Lloyd's Rep. 49.
[35] [1963] 2 Lloyd's Rep. 293 at 307.

His lordship also rejected the insurer's contention that there were two transits, the first from the street to its parking position, and the second, the intended one to the docks, considering such an argument was "an unreal view of the facts".[36]

13–18   As for the words "including loading or unloading" there is no doubt that this means what it says, and a loss of goods once they have arrived at their destination is covered if they have not yet been unloaded because the "transit" continues until unloading has been completed — see *Hepburn v. A. Tomlinson (Hauliers) Ltd*,[37] discussed below.

13–19   This approach of determining the issue from the point of view of the goods, was again adopted by the Court of Appeal in *Crows Transport Ltd v. Phoenix Assurance Co. Ltd*[38] where a rather wider cover had to be interpreted. This policy provided "all risks" cover on general merchandise "in the custody or control of the insured . . . whilst temporarily housed during the course of transit whether on or off the vehicles . . ." The insured claimants were road hauliers and a customer had delivered 17 cartons of gramophone records to their premises, whereupon their manager had placed them just outside his office door, down some steps. Seven cartons were stolen and the defendant insurers denied liability on the ground that the goods were not at the time of their loss in course of transit (it being otherwise accepted that the claimants had taken all reasonable steps to safeguard the goods). Lord Denning M.R. approached the problem in the following manner[39]:

> "It is quite clear that these goods were 'in the custody or control of the insured.' They were not being 'loaded upon carried by or unloaded from' any of the plaintiffs' vehicles. The question is whether they were 'temporarily housed during the course of transit whether on or off the vehicles.' The sole question is whether it was 'during the course of transit.'
>
> The county court judge held that these goods were not in the course of transit. He said:
>
>> '. . . the course of transit does not begin until some step has been taken by the hauliers towards loading the goods on to one of their own, or a sub-contractors', or other hauliers', vehicle.'
>
> I think that this is too narrow a construction. It seems to me that goods are 'temporarily housed during the course of transit' if they are housed as an incident of the transit, such as when they are temporarily housed for a few hours awaiting loading. Counsel for the defendants stressed that it has to be transit 'per the insured's vehicles.' I agree; but they are in transit per the insured's vehicles when they are awaiting loading in those vehicles. Instances were put in the course of argument. When you take a parcel to the post office or to a railway station and you hand it over and get a receipt, the goods are in transit from the moment when the post office or the railway take them. They are in transit by the post office or the railway's vehicles, as the case may be, because from that moment onwards everything that is done is incidental to that transit. So, here, it seems to me that, from the moment

[36] *ibid.* at 308.
[37] [1966] A.C. 451, HL.
[38] [1965] 1 All E.R. 596, CA.
[39] *ibid.* at 597.

that the plaintiffs accepted these goods from Decca and took them down the steps, they were there temporarily housed awaiting loading on the plaintiffs' own vehicles. It was an incident of the transit by those vehicles. That seems to me to be 'in transit per [the plaintiffs] vehicles'."

The test is not likely to now be contested. Thus, in *S.C.A. (Freight) Ltd* **13–20** *v. Gibson*,[40] counsel for the insured and the insurer both agreed that the above authorities established that the transit of a consignment of books had begun, at least when some of the books had been loaded onto one of two lorries sent to convey the consignment.[41]

Deviations and transit
Are goods no longer in transit if the transporting vehicle parks up **13–21** before the destination is reached? In *Sadler Bros. Co. v. Meredith*,[42] discussed above, Roskill J. (as he then was) stated that the goods were still being carried, and therefore were still in transit from the one place to the other even though the lorry in which they were being carried was temporarily parked.[43] But what is the situation where there is a prolonged period during which the vehicle is parked up? This fell to be considered in *Hepburn v. A. Tomlinson (Hauliers) Ltd*[44] where the goods, a quantity of cigarettes, were carried by the insured in lorries hired to the owners of the goods and to be employed for the owners' sole use, and were taken to the owners' warehouse in London, where they arrived after working hours and were consequently not immediately unloaded. On arrival the lorries and their contents were taken into the charge of the owners' night watchman. The lorries were to have been unloaded the following morning and their contents checked, but, without any negligence on the part of the insured carriers, the goods were stolen.

The policy covered the goods against all risks: **13–22**

> "whilst being carried and/or in transit anywhere in the United Kingdom including loading and unloading. Including risk during halts and/or whilst garaged and/ or elsewhere overnight".

The House of Lords held that the goods were still "in transit" when they were stolen, since the policy defined "in transit" as "including loading an unloading". *Per* Lord Reid[45]:

> "My Lords, the first point taken by the appellant [the insurer] is that this is a goods in transit policy and that the cigarettes were no longer on risk when they were stolen, because the transit had come to an end when the lorries were driven in to [the insurers'] warehouse and left there for the night. But the words in the policy are 'whilst being carried and/or in transit anywhere in the United Kingdom including loading or unloading.' So I need not

[40] [1974] 2 Lloyd's Rep. 533.
[41] *ibid.* at 534.
[42] [1963] 2 Lloyd's Rep. 293.
[43] *ibid.* at 307.
[44] [1966] A.C. 451, HL.
[45] *ibid.* at 466.

consider what the result would be if the word 'transit' stood alone. Here it is defined as including loading or unloading. Counsel attempted to argue that there were two separate periods of risk, the period of transit and the period of loading or unloading and that in this case the period of transit had come to an end and the period of unloading had not commenced when the theft took place. But in my opinion that is quite inconsistent with the wording of the policy which must mean that the period of transit during which the goods are on risk is extended so as to include unloading and only comes to an end when the unloading is completed. I am therefore clearly of opinion that the goods were still on risk when stolen."

13–23 Does the transit continue in circumstances where there can be said to be a break in the transit or a deviation from the planned route of transit? If, for instance, the driver of a loaded lorry decides to take it from its place of loading and use it to journey to a nearby city in order that he may go sight-seeing, if a mishap befalls the loaded goods whilst the driver is undertaking that journey, are the goods still "in transit" within the meaning of a goods in transit policy, or are the goods no longer covered by the insurance? Ackner J. (as he then was) in *S.C.A. (Freight) Ltd v. Gibson*[46] stated that goods cease to be in transit when they are on a journey which is not in reasonable furtherance of their carriage to their ultimate destination. Obviously, a detour which is reasonably necessary to enable a driver to obtain food, or rest, would be in furtherance of the safe and expeditious carriage of the goods to their ultimate destination. It would be an ordinary incident in the transit of goods by the carrier's vehicles.

13–24 It will always be a question of degree, though, in the particular facts of an individual case, as to whether what occurred was or was not in reasonable furtherance of the carriage of goods. A deviation which is wholly unrelated to the usual and ordinary method of pursuing the adventure would prevent the goods being "in transit" within the meaning of the policy. As regards the facts in *S.C.A. (Freight) Ltd v. Gibson*, this concerned a CMR goods in transit policy covering the carrier's liability. The insured agreed to carry a consignment of books from Rome to Manchester. The insured carrier sent two lorries to the consignor's premises in Ciampino, near Rome. When night came, one lorry had been fully loaded and the other partly loaded. The loading would have been completed the next day and the drivers would have set off for England. Instead, they decided to take the loaded vehicle on a trip to the centre of Rome where the lorry overturned, causing substantial damage to the books. Dismissing the carrier's claim under the insurance Ackner J. stated[47]:

"The journey was designed solely and wholly for the benefit of the drivers who, assuming that the trip was a short one, would hardly be likely to return to [the place of loading] to sleep much before midnight. The prospects of a safe and expeditious delivery of the goods were in no way advanced by this journey, for, on the bare facts, there is no basis for suggesting that the drivers' efficiency was either added to or even maintained by this expedition.

[46] [1974] 2 Lloyd's Rep. 533 at 535; and see the marine insurance case of *Pearson v. Commercial Union Assurance Co.* (1876) 1 App. Cas. 498 at 507–508, HL.
[47] *ibid.* at 535–536.

Clearly, as was dramatically demonstrated [by the accident], the goods themselves were put at a far greater risk than had they been left in the consignor's premises. In short, the journey was a joy ride and the goods were carried on expedition wholly unconnected with the furtherance of their carriage."

End of transit

In *Bartlett and Partners Ltd v. Meller*,[48] the insured merchants held a **13–25** policy covering their goods against "all risks" in transit, but excluding cover when the goods were at the insured's two premises. The insured claimed under the policy for 99 golf jackets and other goods that the insured contended had been lost during transit between its two premises. Sachs J. rejected the claim, *inter alia*, on the ground that the insured had failed to prove the goods had actually been lost in transit. *Obiter*, Sachs J. said that he considered that the "transit" covered by the policy ceased when the laden vehicle had arrived at such excluded premises and the unloaded goods given into the charge of the staff at those premises, even though the goods might not be physically within the excluded premises.[49] Such would not seem to be the case, however, where the transit is defined in the policy as "including loading and unloading", because the "transit" would continue until the unloading of the goods was completed.[50]

4. FINANCIAL LIMITS OF COVER

The insurer may limit his liability under the policy in respect of specified **13–26** goods, and this will be perfectly valid. For instance, a clause may read:

"Notwithstanding the terms of the Indemnity the maximum liability accepted by the company in respect of non-ferrous metals is limited to a maximum of £   "

Where there is such a provision, it may apply to liability in respect of the goods themselves, or the carrier's liability to the owners of the goods, or both.[51] Equally, the insurer can apply separate limits of liability for different circumstances of loss.[52] If the insurance premium is assessed on the basis of the insured's declaration as to the maximum value of goods to be carried at any one time, the insurer may provide for "average" to apply, *i.e.* the amount recoverable under the policy will only be payable in proportion to the value of the goods carried as against the declared maximum value of goods carried.[53]

---

[48] [1961] 1 Lloyd's Rep. 487.
[49] *ibid.* at 489.
[50] *Hepburn v. Tomlinson (Hauliers) Ltd.* [1966] A.C. 451 at 466, *per* Lord Reid, HL.
[51] *Avandero (U.K.) Ltd v. National Transit Insurance Co. Ltd* [1984] 2 Lloyd's Rep. 613.
[52] *Mint Security Ltd v. Blair* [1982] 1 Lloyd's Rep. 188.
[53] *Bartlett & Partners Ltd v. Meller* [1961] 1 Lloyd's Rep. 487. See Chapter 19, paras 19–37 to 19–43, below, for the conditions of average.

5. CONDITIONS, WARRANTIES AND EXCLUSIONS

Introduction

13–27   As seen in Chapter 2, insurers are entitled to require compliance with warranties or conditions upon which the contract of insurance is founded, and breach will enable the insurer to rescind the policy completely, or, in the case of an express provision that compliance will be a condition precedent to liability, repudiate liability in respect of a claim or claims under the policy. In each case, the status of the provision will need to be carefully considered to determine whether it is a warranty, a condition precedent, a mere condition, an exclusion, or a clause delimiting the risk, as discussed in Chapter 2.

Unattended vehicles

13–28   Insurers commonly insert a condition in goods in transit policies that provides that the insurance does not cover goods whilst in a vehicle which is unattended, unless the vehicle, for example, has been securely locked. First, the meaning of "unattended" has to be considered, and much will depend on the duration of the absence of the driver. The leading case on the interpretation of "unattended" vehicles is *Starfire Diamond Rings Ltd v. Angel*[54] which concerned the transit cover in a jeweller's block policy. The policy excluded theft or disappearance from vehicles "left unattended", and the exclusion was upheld as applying upon the facts, which appear from the following part of Lord Denning M.R.'s judgment[55]:

> "I do not think that the words 'left unattended' are capable of any precise definition. It is a mistake for a lawyer to attempt a definition of ordinary words and to substitute other words for them. The best way is to take the words in their ordinary sense and apply them to the facts. In this case, the meaning of 'left unattended' is, I think, best found by considering the converse. If a car is 'attended', what does it mean? I think it means that there must be someone able to keep it under observation, that is, in a position to observe any attempt by anyone to interfere with it, and who is so placed as to have a reasonable prospect of preventing any unauthorized interference with it. I must say that it seems to me that this car was 'left unattended'. What impresses me is the distance which [the driver] went away from the car — 37 yards. As he walked up the track, I cannot think that he could have had his head turned round looking over his shoulder all the time: for a good part of the time he must have been looking ahead. Then he moved round into the bushes [to urinate]. We have had photographs which were taken of what he could see from those bushes and we have the evidence. The finding of the Judge[56] that 'from the place where he was standing, it . . . was difficult to see anything more than the roof of the car.' At that distance and with those powers of observation, it is quite plain that a thief could come up to the car, crouch down under cover of the car, break the glass — as indeed the thief seems to have done — and extract the suitcase — as this thief did — without [the driver] seeing it or knowing about it at all. Then, as we know, this thief got so far away that he was not seen in suspicious circumstances

---

[54] [1962] 2 Lloyd's Rep. 217, CA.
[55] *ibid.* at 219.
[56] [1962] 1 Lloyd's Rep. 526 at 529.

until after he had passed the other car. It seems to me the distance that [the driver] went and the obscurity of his view was such that this car was 'left unattended'."

Starfire was applied in *Ingleton of Ilford Ltd v. General Accident Fire and Life Assurance Corpn Ltd.*[57] The driver of a van was delivering wines and spirits to a shop and was inside the shop for some 15 minutes. The van had been parked immediately outside the shop, under a street light at about 4 o'clock on a November afternoon, with the keys left in the ignition. The van and its contents were stolen and one of the grounds on which the insurers defended the claim was that the vehicle was not securely locked whilst "unattended". Phillimore J.[58] held that the van was unattended: **13–29**

"because I think it clear he was in [the shop] for a quarter of an hour, I have no doubt he was chatting during that time . . . and it seems very doubtful if he was really keeping much observation on his van in the light of the fact that it was removed and the engine presumably started without his ever observing that anything had taken place. The fact is that from where he was of course he could not see the far side of the van, he had no view of the driver's door, he could not see if anybody got into the driver's seat, he was not in a position to keep it under observation, that is to say in a position to observe any attempt by anyone to interfere with it or so placed as to have a reasonable prospect of preventing any unauthorized interference with it.

In my judgment this is a hopeless claim. This van on the facts was quite clearly unattended, and the best proof of that is that the whole thing was removed with all its contents without its attendant even being aware of what had happened."

The circumstances in that case can be contrasted with a number of others. In *Langford v. Legal and General Assurance Society Ltd,*[59] the insured, a market trader, packed her stock in two large suitcases and placed them behind the passenger seat of her Volvo Estate car. She drove home and parked alongside the kitchen window. She got out, locked the car doors, went into the house, with a view to returning immediately to take out the suitcases. She saw through the kitchen window a person standing by the car. On going outside she discovered the suitcases had been stolen and claimed against her insurers. The court held that the insurers had failed to prove that the car was unattended in any sensible and practical meaning of the words. Judge Hawser, Q.C. said[60]:   **13–30**

"I do not think that the fact that the car was not actually in her view for a period of somewhere around five seconds can be regarded as an action in which the vehicle was not attended by the insured or an employee. I think that one must take a practical, common-sense view of these matters . . . the question always is one of fact for the Court to determine in all the circumstances . . . and I am satisfied . . . that the vehicle was attended at this time in any sensible and practical meaning of those words."

[57] [1967] 2 Lloyd's Rep. 179.
[58] *ibid.* at 181–182.
[59] [1986] 2 Lloyd's Rep. 103.
[60] *ibid.* at 107.

13–31   Similarly, in *T. O'Donoghue Ltd v. Harding*[61] there was a jewellers' policy which excepted loss by theft or disappearance from a vehicle "when such vehicles are left unattended". The insured's salesman was travelling with a briefcase containing jewellery and needed some petrol. He drove into a petrol station and selected the pump nearest the kiosk. He locked the car, filled it with petrol and left the car locked while he went into the kiosk. From the cash point he had an excellent view of the car down to the top of the bonnet level and boot lid lever. He kept the car more or less under constant observation and was only distracted when he was signing his American Express slip and collecting the VAT receipt. He was away from the car for no more than two minutes, and only had his back to the car for two or three seconds. Bearing in mind that the filling up with petrol was a normal incident of his driving and employment as a salesman, and that the salesman had conducted himself so as to have a reasonable prospect of preventing an interference or of raising an alarm in the event of an interference, or taking some steps to lead to the apprehension of the thieves, Otton J. held that the insurers had failed to establish that the car was unattended at the time of the theft at the petrol station. The burden had, of course, been on the insurers to prove that an exception excluded the loss.

13–32   The *O'Donoghue* case was distinguished in *Sanger and Apter v. Beazley*,[62] where Longmore J. stated that attendance requires reasonable observation to be kept on the vehicle if the driver leaves the car for any reason.[63] The facts were that Mr Apter was travelling from Wigan to London in his car, with some insured jewellery in the course of the business. He felt unwell, so drove into the Sandbach Motorway Service Station, initially into the main service car park. In need of a drink, he decided to visit the shop at the services petrol station. He drove to the petrol area and parked between two petrol pumps, got out, locked the car and walked towards the shop. Seeing that the shop was crowded, he decided first to wash his hands. On the evidence, the judge rejected Mr Apter's evidence that he had washed his hands at an outside tap before purchasing a can of drink in the shop, instead determining that he had gone to wash them in the gentleman's lavatory. The insurers produced video evidence from the cameras located at the petrol service station. This showed that Mr Apter was out of the picture for 68 seconds from when he had headed to the kiosk shop and deciding to go elsewhere, and then returning to the picture to go to the kiosk. It was during this 68 seconds that the jewellery in the car had been stolen. In any event, on either version of where he washed his hands, the judge held that the exclusion relating to theft when a vehicle was unattended applied to debar the insured's claim in this case. This was because Mr Apter was clearly not in a position to observe any attempt to interfere with his car, nor was he so placed as to have a reasonable prospect of preventing such interference.

---

[61] [1988] 2 Lloyd's Rep. 281.
[62] [1999] Lloyd's Rep I.R. 424.
[63] *ibid.* at 429.

Mere presence near the vehicle may not, therefore, be sufficient to establish **13–33** that it was attended. A crucial element seems to be whether the person said to be in attendance was able to either observe, or prevent, unauthorised interference with the vehicle and its contents. Mere presence within the vehicle, however, seems sufficient. In *Plaistow Transport Ltd v. Graham*,[64] it was held by Neild J., apparently without citation of any authorities, that the fact that the lorry driver was asleep, indeed, so heavily asleep that he slept through the theft of his load, did not mean that his lorry was "unattended". The insurers therefore failed to establish breach of the applicable warranty to the effect that the lorry was never to be "unattended".

If it is common ground between the insurer and the insured that the **13–34** vehicle was unattended, or that is established, the further limiting provisions must be considered. For example, a provision in the policy may require attendance of the vehicle only between certain times:

"This policy does not cover liability or loss, destruction or damage in respect of or arising from or caused by thefts of or from vehicles left unattended between 6 p.m. and 6 a.m. unless:
(i) such vehicle is locked and garaged in a building which is securely closed and locked or
(ii) such vehicle is locked and parked in a yard which is fully enclosed and securely closed and locked."

Such provision must be complied with to prevent a claim being excluded under the policy. There might, however, as in *J. Lowenstein & Co. Ltd v. Poplar Motor Transport (Lymm) Ltd*,[65] not be a total exclusion of cover, but a provision that if the condition "cannot" be complied with, there is to be 20 per cent co-insurance by the insured. "Cannot" in these circumstances means that, despite the planning of journeys to ensure compliance with legislation controlling drivers' hours of work, unforeseen circumstances physically prevent compliance, such as the inability to find a secure lorry park despite reasonable efforts to find one, or other circumstances, for instance, late loading, prevented lawful compliance because of the driver's hours of working.

Warranty of night garaging

A goods in transit policy contained the following term in *A. Cohen &* **13–35** *Co. Ltd v. Plaistow Transport Ltd*[66]:

"Warranted vehicles garaged in locked garage at night, except when employed on night journeys, but then never left unattended."

A lorry and its load was taken from the defendant carrier's premises between 6 a.m. and 8 a.m., and the carrier sought an indemnity under his goods in transit policy. The claim failed because MacKenna J. was not

---

[64] [1966] 1 Lloyd's Rep. 639.
[65] [1968] 2 Lloyd's Rep. 233.
[66] [1968] 2 Lloyd's Rep. 587.

satisfied that the load was stolen (*i.e.* taken without the connivance of the defendant carrier), but, *obiter*, his Lordship stated that[67]:

> (a) the parking of the loaded lorry in the carrier's yard, albeit behind locked gates, was a breach of the warranty; and
> (b) "night" should be construed with reference to lighting-up time.

Violent entry to vehicle

13–36   Some policies will include liability in respect of goods on vehicles which are unattended, provided the vehicle was securely locked, but only in circumstances where the loss or damage follows upon forcible entry of the vehicle.[68] A form of such an exclusion of liability was called into question in *Princette Models Ltd v. Reliance Fire and Accident Insurance Corp. Ltd*,[69] which read:

> ". . . the Corporation will not accept liability hereunder for theft [of] property from unattended car(s) or other motor vehicles whether in the street, garage or elsewhere unless such cars or vehicles are of a fully enclosed type and unless all doors, windows, windscreens and other openings of the vehicle(s) are left closed, securely locked and properly fastened and unless any such door, window, windscreen, opening, lock or fastener has been smashed by violent forcible means wherever entry, access or theft has been effected."

Pearson J. held that it is the material entry or access for the theft that makes the breach of condition, and, on the facts of the case, the insured could not show any "smashing" of any lock on the cab doors to effect an entry which enabled the van to be driven away by the thief, and, therefore, the claim under the policy failed. A subsequent smashing of the locks on the back door of the van to facilitate the removal of the goods in the van was not sufficient to fulfil this condition.[70]

Reasonable precautions condition

13–37   Invariably, goods in transit policies will contain a provision that:

> "the Insured shall take all reasonable precautions for the protection and safeguarding of the goods and/or merchandise and use such protective appliances as may be specified in the Policy and all vehicles and protective devices shall be maintained in good order."

Insurers will often defend a claim on the basis of a breach of this provision, together with other grounds of defence available in the circumstances.[71]

---

[67] *ibid.* at 592.

[68] See, *e.g. Ingleton of Ilford Ltd v. General Accident Fire & Life Assurance Corp. Ltd* [1967] 2 Lloyd's Rep. 179; see also *Re Calf & Sun Insurance Office* [1920] 2 K.B. 366, CA; and *Dino Services Ltd v. Prudential Assurance Co. Ltd* [1989] 1 All E.R. 422, CA, for interpretation of "forcible and violent entry".

[69] [1960] 1 Lloyd's Rep. 49.

[70] *ibid.* at 57.

[71] See *J. Lowenstein & Co. Ltd v. Poplar Motor Transport (Lymm) Ltd* [1968] 2 Lloyd's Rep. 233; and *Ingleton of Ilford Ltd v. General Accident Fire & Life Assurance Corp. Ltd* [1967] 2 Lloyd's Rep. 179.

Failure to lock all locks on a vehicle when it is unattended, for instance, will show a failure to take all reasonable precautions[72] against loss.

This type of provision has been held to be limited in its scope, though, **13–38** to reasonable precautions in respect of what is mentioned in the clause, namely the need to protect the physical safety of the goods, or, alternatively, it requires recklessness on the part of the insured in respect of other matters. Thus in *W. & J. Lane v. Spratt,*[73] the insurers were unsuccessful in arguing that the condition had been breached, after the insured made one unsuccessful attempt to take up the reference offered by a driver seeking work, and had then gone ahead and employed him. The very next day that driver disappeared with one of the insured's lorries and a valuable load. Roskill J. emphasised that insurers should use express terms to extend the due diligence clause's effect to include the vetting of staff if that is what they wanted to provide for.[74] Moreover, Roskill J. held that this particular provision did not amount to a condition of the contract of insurance, breach of which would entitle the insurer to repudiate the policy. Breach, however, may permit the insurer to argue that he is not liable for a loss suffered by reason of the facts constituting the breach, on the basis that those facts were the proximate cause of the loss.[75]

Warranty as to records

Where the goods covered by a transit policy are money, a warranty may be **13–39** required that a complete record of the money in transit and on the premises shall be kept, and that such record shall be deposited in some place other than in the safe(s) containing the money, that warranty must be complied with to place a liability on the insurer in respect of a loss otherwise covered.[76]

Warranted procedures

Breach of procedures given in a continuing warranty will, of course, **13–40** entitle the insurers to repudiate the insurance. Equally, breach of a condition precedent to the insurer's liability will entitle the insurer to repudiate liability in respect of a related claim. An example of the latter is found in *Mint Security Ltd v. Blair*[77] which concerned a cash in transit policy, where compliance with the continuing warranty was made a condition precedent to liability of the insurer. The question was whether the condition precedent had been broken. The policy stated:

> "It is a condition precedent to recovery hereon that equipment/personnel/ procedures as described in the proposal forms and attachments thereto shall not be varied . . ."

---

[72] *Princette Models Ltd v. Reliance Fire & Accident Insurance Corp. Ltd* [1960] 1 Lloyd's Rep. 49 at 55, *per* Pearson J.

[73] [1970] 2 Q.B. 480.

[74] *ibid.* at 489.

[75] *ibid.* at 493–495; following *Yorkshire Dale S.S. Co. Ltd v. Minister of War Transport, "The Coxwold"* [1942] A.C. 691 at 702–703, HL.

[76] *Vaughan Motors & Sheldon Motor Services Ltd v. Scottish General Insurance Co. Ltd* [1960] 1 Lloyd's Rep. 479.

[77] [1982] 1 Lloyd's Rep. 188.

13–41   The insured, a security firm which transported cash to banks and post offices, had answered the following questions in the proposal form:

> "**14.** Do you undertake not to entrust cash or other valuables to a crew unless at least one member, driver or guard, has been in your employ for at least a year?
>   Answer: Yes
> **16.** State briefly the period of regular training required to produce a fully trained member and the minimum you require new staff to complete before using them on operations?
>   Answer: Fully trained two months. Minimum period one month.
> **20.** What will be the maximum value which will be at risk any one time outside an armoured vehicle, *i.e.* pavement risk?
>   Answer: £10,000.
> **30.** Do you undertake to obtain reference from previous employers of new staff?
>   Answer: Yes."

13–42   A sum of money was stolen during a delivery, and the insured sought to recover the loss under the policy, but the insurers defended the claim on the ground of breach of warranty. Staughton J. observed that this warranty would not be breached by "a casual non-observance of it by one of the plaintiff's minions", for that would not amount to a variation of a procedure.[78] In the instant case the facts were that:

(a) no member of the crew had been in the insured's employment for at least a year;

(b) at least one member of the crew had not been trained before embarking on operations;

(c) more than £10,000 was outside the vehicle at the time; and

(d) the crew's references had been inadequately checked.

The result was that Staughton J. held that the insured's claim failed, because[79]:

> "the action of the crew in taking more than £10,000 outside the vehicle at any one time was not a variation of procedures, merely non-observance by them of the plaintiffs rule. But in respect of the other breaches alleged . . . I find that there had been a variation of procedures; these were not casual breaches, but the result of decision at some level of management or administration. Indeed, it was the plaintiffs' case that with the change in the nature of the business, it was no longer practicable to comply with the old procedures. To some extent at least — in relation to the minimum employment period — this was proved. So a breach of warranty is made out."

13–43   A further example is that of *Richardson v. Roylance*[80] where a cash in transit policy covered money up to £20,000 whilst in transit to the insured builder's house and other "places of disbursement". The policy also covered cash whilst at such other premises subject to the following proviso:

---

[78] *ibid.* at 197.
[79] [1982] 1 Lloyd's Rep. 188 at 197.
[80] (1933) 47 Ll. L. Rep. 173.

"No claim shall attach to this policy in respect of ... any loss occurring when the premises are closed unless the cash or notes are in a locked safe or strong room."

The insured failed to recover in respect of a sum of money stolen or lost   **13–44** at one of those places of disbursement, because the money had been stored there stored in a padlocked wooden box, which did not meet the specified description of "a locked safe or strong room". In the words of Branson J.[81]:

> "I think that, whatever the definition of a locked safe or strong room, it cannot be stretched to include a wooden box knocked up by a builder's carpenter for the purpose of containing plans and documents, even though it is finished off with a padlock."

[81] *ibid.* at 174.

CHAPTER 14

THEFT BY EMPLOYEE (FIDELITY) AND RELATED INSURANCES

1. THEFT BY EMPLOYEE (FIDELITY) INSURANCE

Subject matter of fidelity insurance

Introduction

14–01   Jessel M.R. once described fidelity insurance from the insurer's point of view as being "a kind of insurance against fraud by persons employed by others in situations of trust".[1] Its purpose is to indemnify the employers of fraudulent persons in respect of loss suffered personally by the insured employer by reason of the fraudulent acts of persons placed by the insured in positions of trust. The particular scope of the issued policy, of course, varies according to the precise wording used, and some examples are discussed below,[2] but no policy is likely to be construed as insuring the employer against losses from crimes that are not the fault of an employee, *e.g.* for robbers without any fault or complicity on the part of the employee.[3]

Time of loss

14–02   One other matter with regard to the subject matter of fidelity insurance is that the defalcations of the persons in positions of trust must occur during the currency of the policy,[4] unless a contrary intention is found in the policy wording, although the policy may well not require that such loss need be discovered within the period of currency of the insured, *e.g.* a period of many months may be allowed after the expiry of the policy.[5] For Limitation Act 1980 purposes, though, an action becomes time-barred against the insurer six years after the occurrence of the loss, not its discovery.[6] Negligence of the employer in supervision of the dishonest employee is no defence to the insurer.[7] The policy is generally an annual policy.[8]

---

[1] *Re Norwich Provident Insurance Society, Bath's Case* (1878) 8 Ch. D., 334 at 341, CA.

[2] See also specimen policy at Appendix 7, and extension of cover in Section 6 of the specimen combined policy at Appendix 1.

[3] See *Walker v. British Guarantee Association* (1852) 21 L.J.Q.B. 257.

[4] *Allis-Chalmers Co. v. Maryland Fidelity and Deposit Co.* (1916) 114 L.T. 433, HL.

[5] 18 months, & 24 months, in *Universities Superannuation Scheme Ltd v. Royal Insurance (U.K.) Ltd.* [2000] Lloyd's Rep. I.R. 524.

[6] *ibid.*

[7] *Mansfield Union Guardians v. Wright* (1882) 9 Q.B.D. 683, CA.

[8] But see *Solvency Mutual Guarantee Co. v. Froane* (1861) 7 H. & N. 5; *Solvency Mutual Guarantee Co. v. Freeman* (1861) 7 H. & N. 17; and *Solvency Mutual Guarantee Co. v. York* (1858) 3 H. & N. 588.

Employees only

Policies will usually be restricted to breach of the duty of fidelity by **14-03** employees, and not other categories of persons. Where a fidelity policy referred to the indemnification of the insured in respect of the defalcations of "the employees of" the insured, and also included a limitation of that liability in respect of acts of "sales representatives" and "general agents" of the insured, it has been held that the latter did not extend the insurance cover to sales representatives and general agents who were not the "insured's employees".[9] During the course of the judgment, the following definitions were given[10]:

- *"sales representative"*: a natural person who is a representative or agent of another legal person (whether natural or not) to sell something on behalf of that person, whether employed by him or not.
- *"general agent"*: a legal person, natural or otherwise, usually but not invariably an independent contractor, engaged to sell or market the product of another legal person.

In the instant case, it was held that a limited company came within the **14-04** terms of a fidelity policy's cover by reason of there being an extended meaning to the definition of "employee", which covered employees of the insured's general agents.

An employer may insure in respect of unnamed employees under a floating policy on his workforce, or in respect of named employees. In the latter case, the policy will commonly add that the loss must have been incurred by the named employee acting "in the capacity stated in the Schedule". It is essential that the loss arises from an employee's capacity as notified to the insurer and as specified in the policy schedule, otherwise the loss will not be covered.[11] The specimen policy contained in Appendix 7, is an example of the latter type of policy. The floating policy will usually require the ascertainment of the particular defalcating individual in the event of a claim.

Change in employee's terms or duties

If the insurance policy, its schedule, or the incorporated proposal form **14-05** answers do not specify the employees terms of employment, then neither a change in the employees' terms of employment,[12] nor an increase in the burden of the employees' duties,[13] will prevent the insured recovering under the policy. However, where the policy recites the remuneration of

---

[9] *Excess Life Assurance Co. Ltd v. Fireman's Insurance Co. of Newark New Jersey* [1982] 2 Lloyd's Rep. 599 at 602, *per* Webster J.

[10] *ibid.* at 615.

[11] *Wembley U.D.C. v. Poor Law and Local Government Officers' Mutual Guarantee Association Ltd* (1901) 17 T.L.R. 516; *Cosford Union v. Poor Law and Local Government Officers' Mutual Guarantee Association Ltd* (1910) 103 L.T. 463.

[12] *Sanderson v. Aston* (1873) L.R. 8 Ex. 73.

[13] *Skillet v. Fletcher* (1867) L.R. 2 C.P. 469.

the employees, the fact that the employee is no longer paid by salary, but by commission, will constitute an alteration in the insured and prevent recovery under the insurance. In these instances, all changes in terms of employment and duties of employees should be referred to insurers throughout the period of insurance, and appropriate amendment of the insurance cover agreed to prevent avoidance of a future claim for a material alteration in the risk, particularly where such information has been requested in the original proposal.[14] A specific policy condition may also expressly state that alterations in the risk require the insurer's written consent.

Loss of money, securities and other property

14–06   The scope of the subject matter so described was considered in *New Hampshire Insurance Co. v. Philips Electrical North America Corp. (No.2)*.[15] The claimant insurers sought declarations that they were not liable to indemnify the defendant insured in respect of various losses assumed for the purposes of the litigation to have been caused by the fraudulent conduct of one Filson, a President of a division of PENAC. The insurers accepted that embezzlement of US$910,721 by Filson, where he and two colleagues had used a travel company to fraudulently over-charge PENAC in arranging travel, was covered by "loss of money, securities and other property". But the insurers disputed their liability to indemnify PENAC in relation to two other claims under the policy.

14–07   The first disputed claim was for US$24,935,260 in respect of Filson's deliberate supply to customers of PENAC's products, which he knew to be defective and would fail, causing PENAC to incur a liability to replace them. Clarke J. granted the insurers a declaration of non-liability as there had been no loss of relevant property. The defective products which Filson had sold to customers had not been lost, as they had been supplied to PENAC's customers and paid for. PENAC's alternative argument that the replacement products supplied to customers to replace the defective ones supplied earlier by Filson, was also rejected. This was because the policy provided what was essentially property cover, and PENAC's claim amounted to a claim to be indemnified against its liability to third parties, namely its customers, to either pay damages or replace the defective products.

14–08   The second disputed claim related to US$218,000 in bonuses that Filson had received from PENAC based on his sales of the defective products, and on alleged manipulation of the books to create fictional sales. PENAC succeeded on this claim, and the insurer's contention that only physical losses were insured was rejected. Clarke J. held that PENAC's argument that upon a correct construction of "money, securities and other property", loss of money held in PENAC's bank accounts by payment to Filson of

---

[14] See *North Western Railway Co. v. Whinray* (1854) 10 Exch. 77; *cf.* unspecified details of the employer's contract of employment, *e.g.* variation in period of notice required to dismiss the employee, *Sanderson v. Aston* (1873) L.R. 8 Exch. 73.

[15] [1999] Lloyd's Rep. I.R. 66.

bonuses fraudulently obtained was covered. This interpretation stemmed from the policy's definition of "securities" which included choses in action, namely, "all negotiable and non-negotiable instruments or contracts representing either money or property and includes revenue and other stamps in current use, tokens and tickets". Funds in a bank account were within that definition and, even if that were wrong, such funds were within the description "other property".[16]

Forgery, irregularity, fabrication or duplication of any securities

In *Courtaulds plc v. Lissenden*,[17] the defendant underwriters insured Courtaulds plc and any subsidiary company against: **14–09**

> ". . . any loss the Assured may sustain or liability the Assured may incur on account of any of the contingencies . . . discovered during the currency of this Policy and against all costs and expenses incurred in relation to such loss . . ."

One of the contingencies insured against was "forgery, irregularity, fabrication or duplication of any securities as defined in the schedule to the Policy". The policy in question ran from April 1981. The facts were that a Mr Vriens was, until 1981, employed by a subsidiary company as their accountancy and administration manager, and was one of two signatories to the Belgian bank account of the company. For some 10 years from January 1971, on average two or three times a month, he abstracted sums from this bank account by preparing and signing unauthorised bank transfers in favour of an account of his own and forging the necessary second signature on those transfers.

The fraud was discovered by the insured in June 1981, and it was   **14–10**
common ground that the bank transfers fell within the definition in the policy. The insured claimed, not merely the sums abstracted by Mr Vriens, but also other losses in the form of loss of use of such moneys, or of the extra bank overdraft interest paid in respect of those sums abstracted during the past ten years. The basis of their claim was that these were losses sustained on account of the forgery and fabrication of the bank transfers. Saville J. rejected their claim to be entitled to an indemnity in relation to those additional losses, on the ground that they were neither the direct nor indirect result of the unlawful abstractions from the bank account. Rather they resulted from the insured believing, or assuming, that previous payments had been or would be properly utilised and that further payments were properly required — beliefs or assumptions brought about, not by the forgery or fabrication of bank transfers, but doubtless to a very large extent by the passive and active concealment by Mr Vriens of what he was doing.

---

[16] *ibid.* at 71.
[17] [1986] 1 Lloyd's Rep. 368.

Risks covered

Embezzlement

14-11   This must be understood in the same way as a criminal charge for embezzlement, *i.e.* the employee must have made away with money that was really his employers' and converted it to his own use, so that he might have the benefit of it and might cheat his employers out of it. Moreover, it is essential that the employee did what he did fraudulently and dishonestly, because mere carelessness, mere puzzleheadedness, mere objection to discharge his routine business and keep accounts, or mere careless omissions would not of themselves constitute, or even evidence, the crime that must have been committed in order that the insured may recover.[18]

Theft

14-12   This must also be construed in relation to the criminal law, in particular the offence of theft under the Theft Act 1968, unless some different, express meaning is given to "theft" under the terms of the policy.[19]

Dishonest or fraudulent act

14-13   This wording was considered in *Excess Life Assurance Co. Ltd v. Firemen's Insurance Co. of Newark New Jersey*[20] where the general agent of the claimant insured company was held to be within the policy definition of "employee", but it had to be further ascertained whether that agent, the Lambert Group, had caused the loss to the insured by their dishonest or fraudulent act. Webster J. approached the problem thus[21]:

> "In order to decide this question I do not find it necessary to decide whether, as between Excess and the policyholders, the policies were valid, voidable or void. As between Excess and the Group, I am satisfied on the evidence that the policies were, so far as Mr Lambert was concerned, a sham to enable his Group to be paid commissions. I am satisfied that the premiums were paid not because of any legal obligation of the Group or of the 'policyholder' but because, unless they were paid regularly each month, no further commissions would be paid to the Group. It may very well be that Mr Lambert hoped to be able to continue to pay the premiums until he would either 'lapse' the policies or 'surrender' them, and it may very well be that if he had 'surrendered' them he would have used the proceeds to enable the borrowers from him to pay off their loans. If that was his intention, which it probably was, then it seems to me, for all practical purposes, and if there was any valid policy in effect at all, that it was he or his Group who was insuring the lives of the borrowers and not the borrowers insuring their own lives.
>
> If that is the proper analysis of the circumstances in which the commissions were paid, then in my judgment Excess lost the commissions immediately they paid them to the Lambert Group under the mistaken impression that they were paying them as commissions due on policies taken out by the

---

[18] *Debenhams Ltd v. Excess Insurance Co. Ltd* (1912) 28 T.L.R. 505, *per* Hamilton J.
[19] See *Grundy (Teddington) Ltd v. Fulton* [1983] 1 Lloyd's Rep. 16, CA, discussed in Chapter 12, above; *cf Algemeene Bankvereeniging v. Langton* (1935) 40 Com. Cas. 247 at 256 and 259, CA.
[20] [1982] 2 Lloyd's Rep. 599.
[21] *ibid.* at 625.

borrower, and I am satisfied that had they known that it was Mr Lambert or his Group, and not the borrowers, who were insuring their lives they would not have continued the relationship. In these circumstances it seems to me that they lost the commission immediately they paid it. It was no longer their money, and when they paid it they did not have in exchange or receive in return that which they thought they had, namely an expectation that premiums would be paid by the borrower on the policies in question for about seven years.

If Excess had to show that they had lost the 'commissions' in the same way as, for instance, if they had to show that they had lost a security or a motor car, then difficult questions might well arise as to whether they had passed the property in the commissions, security or motor car, and whether they had lost not the commissions but what they expected to receive in exchange, or whether they had been temporarily rather than permanently deprived of the commissions. But where, as in the present case, the bond covers simply the word 'loss', it seems to me that the question should be looked at broadly in the way I have approached it and that I should ask and answer two questions only: 'Have Excess suffered a loss?', to which the answer is that they have clearly 'lost' money, and 'Was that loss caused by the dishonest or fraudulent act of the Lambert Group?', to which in my judgment the answer is that it was.

In my judgment, therefore, the commissions paid, less the premiums received, constituted losses by the dishonest or fraudulent act of the Lambert Group."

A refinement of this wording was considered recently in *New Hampshire* **14–14** *Insurance Co. v. Philips Electronics North America Corp. (No.2).*[22] Here, the policy provided:

"Such fraudulent or dishonesty acts as insured under this Section shall mean only fraudulent or dishonest acts committed by an employee with the manifest intent:

(a) to cause the Insured to sustain such loss; and
(b) to obtain financial benefit for the Employee, or for any other person or organisation intended by the Employee to receive such benefit, other than salaries, commissions, fees, bonuses, promotions, awards, profit sharing, pensions or other employee benefits earned in the normal course of employment."

The questions arose as to whether provisos (a) and (b) had been met so as to entitle the insured, PENAC, to an indemnity, or, as the claimant insurers contended in the declarations they sought, that they were not liable to Philips.

The action proceeded on the basis that the contents of PENAC's Proof **14–15** of Loss were true. As mentioned above, this alleged fraudulent conduct in Illinois on the part of one Filson, the President of Advance, a division of PENAC. The loss as of December 31, 1994 was at least US$28,063,982 including:

(i) US$910,721 allegedly embezzled by Filson and two colleagues through a travel company which was given the benefit of arranging

---

[22] [1999] Lloyd's Rep. I.R. 66.

PENAC's travel arrangements and which fraudulently over-charged PENAC;

(ii) US$24,935,260 in respect of defective ballasts. It was alleged that Filson deliberately continued to supply ballasts (regulators for fluorescent lights) knowing that they were subject to a defect which would cause them to fail and impose an obligation on PENAC to replace them;

(iii) US$218,000 to bonuses paid to Filson which had not been earned in the ordinary course of business but which had been fraudulently obtained. The bonuses arose from sales of ballasts under (ii) above and also for an alleged manipulation of the books to create fictional sales.

14-16   The insurers accepted liability for item (i), and obtained a declaration of non-liability in respect of (ii) as there was no insured loss (see above). As regards item (iii), the remaining question was whether Mr Filson had the necessary "manifest intent" within the proviso. As the allegedly fraudulent acts of Mr Filson had taken place in Illinois, and because all the witnesses were there, it was common ground that the question of whether Mr Filson had the necessary "manifest intent" was a matter for determination by a jury in Illinois, because there was no sufficient statement of agreed facts to enable Clarke J. to determine that issue. It was common ground, or not seriously in dispute, however, that the jury would be properly directed on the question of "manifest intent" if they were told that they must be satisfied to the relevant standard of proof in Illinois that Mr Filson had the clear, obvious and apparent intent to cause PENAC to sustain the loss, that in considering that question they should consider all the circumstances of the case and that in doing so it was open to them to hold that Mr Filson had that intent if he believed that the loss was substantially certain. Accordingly, as Clarke J. could not determine that PENAC was bound to fail in its claim, he could not grant the insurers the declaration of non-liability that they sought.[23]

Fraud or dishonesty

14-17   In *Ravenscroft v. Provident Clerks' and General Guarantee Association*,[24] a fidelity policy issued to the plaintiff in respect of the "fraud or dishonesty" of Mr C. Mr C had first carried on his business as an excursion agent, and had been obliged to buy tickets from the different railway companies like any of the public, but subsequently he wished to obtain them on credit. The plaintiff had agreed to stand surety for C to the Alta Italian Railway Company against C's fraud or dishonesty, and insured his risk with the defendants.

Under his agreement with the Alta Italian Railway Company, C could have their tickets upon credit on condition that at the end of the first fortnight he was to send in an account and pay in gold the whole of the

---

[23] *ibid.* at 78.
[24] (1885) 5 T.L.R. 3.

moneys, less commission, which he had received during the preceding month from the sale of their tickets. This he had not only failed to do, but he had actually pledged tickets and was now substantially in arrear with the company. The plaintiff claimed under the policy and succeeded on a finding that C's acts amounted to fraud or dishonesty.

Common provisions

General

It is often provided that immediately following the discovery of an act **14–18** of fraud or dishonesty on the part of any employee, the indemnity shall be at an end so far as any further act of fraud or dishonesty on the part of such Employee is concerned.[25] As just mentioned above, it is usually provided that, unless the insurer consents in writing to any alteration in the risk, the insurer shall not be liable to make any payment if the nature of the business of the insured shall be changed, or the precautions and checks for securing accuracy of accounts and stocks stated in the proposal shall not be duly observed. Further, any sum of money which, but for the fraud or dishonesty of an employee, would have become payable to him, shall be deducted from the amount of the loss before a claim is made under the policy.

Notification to insurer of misconduct

If there is a condition in the policy that the insured must notify the **14–19** insurer of the discovery of dishonest conduct of an employee which is covered by the fidelity insurance, that condition is not breached if the insured does not notify the insurer of mere suspicions of such misconduct causing a loss, for the loss must be ascertained to constitute a breach of the condition. In *Ward v. Law Property Assurance and Trust Society,*[26] the issued fidelity policy contained a condition to the effect that when any liability was incurred under the policy, the party entitled to make a claim in respect of the amount, immediately upon discovering or receiving notice, that such liability had been incurred, should forward a written statement of all the particulars thereof, as far as he could, to the insurer; and that the policy was to become void from the beginning if such notice was not sent within six days.

The insured had employed W to solicit orders and receive payments **14–20** from customers daily, which he was to pay at once into the insured's bankers, unless the payments were made after banking hours, when they were to be paid in the next morning. On May 17, some two months after the lapse of the policy, the insured received a letter from W stating that he, W, had not banked all money received and would repay his deficiency as soon as he could. Upon receipt of this letter the insured made

---

[25] This may also be the common law position in any event, see *Sanderson v. Aston* (1873) L.R. 8 Exch. 73.

[26] (1856) 4 W.R. 605; see also *Byrne v. Muzio* (1881) 8 L.R. Ir. 396.

inquiries as to the deficiencies for which W had failed to account, and placed the matter in the hands of his solicitor on May 30. The insured and the solicitor stated that it took some time to ascertain whether any of the deficiencies had occurred during the continuance of the policy, and as soon as that was ascertained they notified the insurers on 6 June of those embezzlements.

14–21   The insurers claimed the policy was void for breach of this notification condition, but this contention was rejected by Erle J.[27]:

> "It is clear that if the policy had been in force down to May 17 he ought to have sent the information to the company at once, or he would have failed in fulfilling the condition referred to, because it confesses an embezzlement of £90 on a particular day; but is it a clear proof of an embezzlement before March 7, on which day the policy expired? He received large sums of money every week, and therefore upon this letter the plaintiff had no clear proof that the company was liable, since that depended upon whether the embezzlements were before or after March 7; consequently there was, until that was ascertained, no clear notice that any liability had been incurred, and the argument that the condition has not been performed fails. If indeed the policy had been on the condition that when the insurer received certain information which raised suspicion, and might turn out correct after investigating the proofs, he should give notice, then no doubt, where there was any ground of suspicion it ought to have been communicated to the company; but there is no such condition here — it is that when the insured knows of any liability having been incurred, he is to give notice to the company."

Prosecution of employee

14–22   In the past, but less likely now, is the inclusion by the insurer of a provision that the insured should prosecute the dishonest employee at the request of the insurer. Such a provision may be couched in such a manner as to amount to a condition precedent to the insured employer's recovery in respect of that employee's defalcations. This was found to be the case in *London Guarantee Co. v. Fearnley*[28] where there was this proviso:

> "Provided that the employer shall if, and when, required by the company (but at the expense of the company, if a conviction be obtained), use all diligence in prosecuting the employed to conviction for any fraud or dishonesty (as aforesaid) in consequence of which a claim shall have been made under this policy, and shall, at the company's expense, give all information and assistance to enable the company to sue for and obtain reimbursement, by the employed, or by his estate, of any money which the company shall have become liable to pay."

14–30   The House of Lords[29] held that this stipulation required two separate and divisible things, the former being a valid condition precedent to the liability of the insurer. As Lord Blackburn explained[30]:

[27] (1856) 4 W.R. 605 at 605.
[28] (1880) 5 App. Cas. 911, HL.
[29] Lord Selborne L.C. dissenting.
[30] (1880) 5 App. Cas. 911 at 916–917.

"The provision in question as to the employer, when required, using all diligence in prosecuting the employed to conviction is coupled with a stipulation that he shall give all assistance to enable the company to obtain reimbursement from the employed or his estate is different; that latter stipulation of the company to pay: the company cannot be entitled to reimbursement till it has, at least, become liable to pay. It seems to me unlikely that those who framed the policy stipulated for the prosecution by the employer, with a view to facilitate reimbursement, and I do not think the words such as to require us to put this construction on the instrument, a construction which seems to me unreasonable. I think that the two matters are separate and independent, and that the employer, who is not entitled to recover except for loss by embezzlement, shall, if required, subject his proof to the test of bringing it before a magistrate, and so subjecting it to the defence of the person accused of embezzlement, before (the company) are called on to say whether the proof is satisfactory. The stipulation thus understood is one not at all unreasonable, and is one the nature of which makes it necessary, for the protection of the company, that it should be made a condition precedent to an action for damages, for not doing this would give the company no redress."

Misrepresentation of material fact

Where the alleged misrepresentation concerns the insured's procedures, **14–24** of crucial importance is whether the proposal form questions and answers are properly regarded as dealing with procedures as at the date of the proposal, or are statements that those procedures will continue to apply for the future period of insurance. The insurers successfully avoided a fidelity policy for misrepresentation in *Towle v. National Guardian Assurance Society*,[31] where the defendant insurers had granted a policy to the Commissioners of Taxes in respect of a specified tax collector. The proposal form had asked the following questions and received the answers below:

"**1.** The duties and responsibilities which will devolve upon the applicant?
   Answer: to collect and account for the sums collected.
2. The largest sum at any one time to be held in his hands, and for how long a time?
   Answer: from £100 to £200, not longer than a week.
3. Whether any stock-in-trade will be entrusted to his custody for sale — if so, its probable value and description, and how often stock will be taken by the employer?
   Answer: (left blank)
4. The checks used to secure accuracy in his accounts, and at what periods the employer will balance and close his cash account?
   Answer: checked weekly by the Surveyor of Taxes.
5. Whether the balance agreed at every such period will be then paid over; or if the employment necessarily requires a balance to be carried from account to account, state as nearly as possible what maximum sum he will be authorised to retain in hand. Also, whether his capability of settling such balance will be occasionally tested by his employers?
   Answer: Yes."

---

[31] (1861) 30 L.J. Ch. 900; see also *Benham v. United Guarantee and Life Assurance Co.* (1852) 7 Exch. 744.

14-25   The truth of the answers was declared by the insured and the proposal form was incorporated into the policy by its recital. The named tax collector absconded with £654, and it was found that although it had been the practice prior to his appointment to check weekly the accounts of the collectors who preceded him, such practice was not continued after his appointment. A claim by the insured for the loss of the £654 by the collector's dishonest absconding was dismissed by the Court of Appeal, it being held that the policy was void from its outset by reason of misrepresentation. Knight Bruce L.J. explained[32]:

> "Upon the evidence, I am of opinion that the answers thus given to the questions . . . were, though not wholly, yet, to a material extent, incorrect, and, without or with whatever intention untrue. I mean with regard to the past. I think also that, as to the future, departed from. The answer to the second question was incorrect by many hundreds of pounds, and by many weeks. The answer to No 4 was simply untrue as to the past, and was disregarded otherwise. These departures from accuracy, so important as, in my judgment, they are, not having been waived by the insurers or communicated to them, had the effect, I think, of avoiding the [insurance]. Upon this ground, therefore . . . the suit, in my judgment, fails."

Warranted procedures

14-26   A distinction must be drawn from procedures that are warranted for the future by, for instances, proposal form questions and answers as to procedures during the period of insurances which are declared to be true and to form the basis of the insurance contract, and must be strictly performed, from mere statements as to the duties of the employees of the insured. This distinction is illustrated by the decision in *Hearts of Oak Building Society v. Law Union and Rock Insurance Co. Ltd*[33] where the insurers were unable to prove that the policy was rendered void by reason of nonperformance of the duties described to be that of the employee. The claimant building society had insured the fidelity risk of a number of their employees, including M, who received mortgage moneys and answered the questions in the proposal form as follows:

> "Under the heading 'With respect to the duties of the officers', please reply as fully as possible to the following questions.
>
> Q. How often are they [the named employees] required to send statements of cash received?
>
> Answer: Daily
>
> Q. How often do you require them to pay over to you and is he allowed to retain a balance in hand? If so, how much? And do you see that they have the amount in their possession?
>
> Answer: M should not retain and should pay over as received."

14-27   Condition 1 of the policy provided:

---

[32] (1861) 30 L.J. Ch. 900 at 911.
[33] [1936] 2 All E.R. 619.

"This policy is entered into . . . on the distinct understanding that the business of the employer shall continue to be conducted, and the remuneration (except by way of increase thereof) and the duties of the employed, the moneys to be entrusted to them, and the checks to be kept upon their accounts shall remain in every particular in accordance with the questions and replies referred to within, and if during the continuance of this policy any circumstances shall occur or change be made which shall have the effect of making the actual facts differ from the statements contained or implied in such questions and replies, or any of them, without notice thereof being given to the company, and the consent and approval in writing of the company being obtained, or if any suppression or misstatement of any fact affecting the risk of the company be made at any time, or if the employer continue any of the employed in his service after having discovered any act of fraud of dishonesty on his or their part, this policy shall be void . . ."

In fact, shortly before filling out the annual proposal form for renewal, **14–28** the insured building society were aware that M had on occasion, not passed on money as soon as he received it. The insurers therefore resisted a claim when it was discovered that M had defaulted with a large amount of the insured's money, on the grounds of misrepresentation in the proposal form answers, and breach of Condition 1. Goddard J. (as he then was) first rejected the defence that the answers in the proposal form amounted to promissory warranties that such duties would be performed by M, and then held that the condition was not breached in the circumstances[34]:

"In this case it seems to me that it is quite impossible, especially when one remembers that this is a fidelity guarantee policy, to construe these undertakings as a promise that during the currency of the policy M would faithfully carry out his duties, which is what the argument comes to, because that is the very thing against which insurance is being taken out, and it cannot be said that this is a promise that M would never retain and would always pay over the money as received and that he would always send statements of cash in daily, because, of course, if M always did that and the claimants could always say that he did that, there would be no point at all in insurance. I think these questions are merely directed to finding out what was the system in force in the respondents' office, so that the insurers could see whether the respondents' office system was such that they would accept the risk. So far as that part of the case is concerned, I have no doubt whatsoever.
. . . it was said that, the actual facts differed from the statements in the questions and answers, because M had not in fact been accounting daily, and had not in fact been handing over the money the day after it was received, and it was said: 'You knew he had not done it.'
In my judgment that is not the meaning of this condition at all as applied to this case. I think it means this: if a change occurs which shows that these answers are inaccurate (in other words, that there has been a change in the duties of M, so that it was no longer his duty to account daily or hand over the money the day after it was received, and that he had been told that, instead of doing that, he was to do it monthly, quarterly, or something of that sort) the company are to be informed, because it might well be that they would not be willing to write the risk any longer: they would say that that was not a satisfactory check . . . It also applies . . . to a suppression or misstatement . . . [but such argument was not raised in the pleadings in this case]."

[34] [1936] 2 All E.R. 619 at 624–626.

Composite insurance policies

14–29   The aftermath of the Maxwell group frauds in the early 1990's threw up the question of whether various fidelity insurance policies issued to the Maxwell group of companies over a number of years were joint policies, so that non-disclosure by any one company would entitle the insurers to rescind the whole insurance, or were composite policies so that non-disclosure by one more companies would not taint insured companies innocent of non-disclosure. The Court of Appeal's decision in *New Hampshire Insurance Co. v. M.G.N. Ltd & others*[35] was that the "insured" in an insurance contract was the person with whom the insured contracted. The party who was bound as such had to be a natural or legal person and something called a group could not be a party to a contract otherwise than as in circumstances where there was a contract with all the group's members. Further, the "insured" under an insurance was the person who was interested in the property or other event covered by the insurance and whose loss was to be made good. The Maxwell group had no joint interest, rather the companies that formed the group had their own separate interests in their own property to insure. The insurers must have known this because of the disparate business activities of the component companies of the group, and accordingly the intention of the parties and the effect of the policies was that all the contracts of insurance were composite in nature, with each company's interests being separately insured.[36] This led to two consequences, first, that if one company was deprived of money, securities or other property by an insured peril, an insured loss occurred even if the money, securities or property was received by another company within the group.[37] The second result was that the policy limits applied separately and non-cumulatively to each company in each policy year.[38]

2. SPECIAL POLICIES FOR FINANCIAL INSTITUTIONS

Introduction

14–30   Banks, other financial institutions, and those who deal in securities and the like, *e.g.* stockbrokers, require, and have long been able to obtain, a much wider form of fidelity insurance cover. The risks embraced and the dishonest persons covered are extended beyond dishonesty and trusted employees respectively, and this form of policy is worthy of separate discussion. The subject of these special policies, sometimes known as "All-in" or "In and out" policies, will be all or some of the following: bonds, debentures, stocks, scrip, shares, transfers, certificates, coupons, warrants or other securities, cash, cheques, bank notes, bills of exchange, promissory notes, title deeds of landed property, or any documents of value.

---

[35] [1997] L.R.L.R. 24, CA. See also paras 17–35 to 17–38, below.
[36] *ibid.* at 56–57, *per* Staughton L.J.
[37] *ibid.* at 58.
[38] *ibid.* at 62–63.

Risks covered

Very wide cover is generally given by these policies, and the risks will   **14–31**
embrace dishonesty by customers as well as the insured's employees, or
even other persons whosoever, and examples of wordings and their scope
are given below:

> "Lost, destroyed or otherwise made away with by robbery, theft, fire,
> embezzlement, burglary or abstractions or taken out of their possession or
> control by any fraudulent means, whether with or without violence, and
> whether from within or without and whether by the officers clerks and
> servants of the said assured or any other person or by the negligence or
> fraud of the said officers, clerks or servants."

In circumstances where an employee of an insured bank has abstracted   **14–32**
from the bank's custody a number of bonds and sold them through a broker
who paid the sale proceeds by way of a cheque drawn in favour of the
insured (his employer), and this cheque was entered in the insured bank's
book in the ordinary way, and almost immediately the employee withdrew
the moneys by getting the cashier, by means of fraudulent misstatement,
to draw a cheque, the proceeds of which he was able to deal with, that loss
was recoverable under the policy. The basis of the decision[39] is that the loss
which the bank claimed was directly attributable to, and the result of, the
abstraction of the bonds shortly before — the whole sequence really forming
one and the same transaction.

That instance can be distinguished, though, from a situation where   **14–33**
more than one transaction takes place. For instance, if a new customer
opens an account with the bank and presents a number of promissory
notes, on a representation that they were drawn by the customer's clients,
and the amount of those notes are credited, less discount, to the customers
account, the whole amount credited then being withdrawn from the
account by the customer, the loss suffered by the bank upon subsequent
discovery that the promissory notes are forgeries is not recoverable. This is
because the policy contemplates solely a loss or abstraction of physical
things taken away from the bank.[40]

The words following "lost, destroyed or otherwise made away with"   **14–34**
qualify how the insured event must occur for a recovery under the policy
to be obtained, it is not enough merely to show that, *e.g.* moneys, have
been lost or destroyed.[41] In a case where a bank manager fraudulently sold
a form of bond no longer used by the bank to customers, and received
sums in payment therefore and made away with those moneys, it was held
that this amounted to a making away with by theft of moneys in which the
insured bank (the manager's employers) were interested. Greer L.J.
explained the decision thus[42]:

---

[39] *Liberty National Bank of New York v. Bolton* (1925) 21 Ll. L. Rep. 3, CA.
[40] *Century Bank of City of New York v. Young* (1914) 84 L.J.K.B. 385 at 386, *per* Lord
Cozens-Hardy M.R., CA
[41] *Algemeene Bankvereeniging v. Langton* (1935) 40 Com. Cas. 247 at 253, *per* Greer L.J., CA
[42] *ibid.* at 254.

"at the time that the money was tendered by the customer to the bank the bank manager at Malines had full authority to receive moneys but no authority to issue a bond signed by himself alone; but when he received the moneys he received them as agent for the bank within his actual authority, although he ought not to have issued the bond in respect of the moneys so received without first writing to the head office and getting the bond; and I suppose the way that would happen would be that he would tell the customer: 'I will take your money, if you like to pay it to me, but I shall have to get the bond from the head office,' and the customer would have said: 'Under those circumstances I will wait until you get the bond,' or he might have said: 'I am dealing with people whom I know and who have always dealt honestly with me; you can have the moneys now and I will get the bond later.' But the moneys, once they were paid into the hands of the manager of the bank with the intention that he should receive them as manager of the bank, on behalf of the bank, and once they got on to the bank's premises, in my judgment were moneys within the policy which were lost to the bank by reason of the dishonesty of their branch manager."

14–35   The interpretation to be given to those words qualifying the loss (*i.e.* fire, burglary, theft, robbery), are dealt with elsewhere within this book and reference may be made thereto if necessary, suffice it to say that the latter three words should be understood in their technical meaning ascribed by the criminal law.[43]

14–36   The wide cover granted in such policies is also demonstrated by the case of *Pawle and Co. v. Bussell*[44] where a policy containing the above indemnity clause had been issued to a firm of stockbrokers. The facts were that a customer commenced dealing with the insured one September and he paid for the shares he bought partly by post-dated cheques. In December, he would deal with him only on a cash basis. On December 21, this customer bought further shares through the insured and on December 23 wished to take them up. The insured's managing clerk pointed out that he could only hand over the shares as against cash, but the customer said that he had seen the head of the firm, who had agreed to let this particular deal through on the old terms. The managing clerk accepted this statement and handed the shares over, and they were paid for by the customer partly in cash and partly by a post-dated cheque. A week later, that cheque was dishonoured and it was found that the shares had been disposed of by the customer.

14–37   The insured firm claimed on the policy for the value of the dishonoured cheque, on the ground that the customer's conduct amounted to a theft, or that the certificates had been taken out of their control by fraudulent means or by the negligence of their servants (*i.e.* the mistake of their managing clerk). The defendant insurers contended that the loss was not covered by the policy, since the certificates were voluntarily given to the customer by the managing clerk, and that the policy could not be extended to insure the firm against being cheated by a client. The court held that the customer, when he gave the insured firm the post-dated cheque, knew that

---

[43] *ibid.* at 259, *per* Maugham L.J., where a test of construction judged by the standard of "ordinary commercial men" construing the phrase was favoured.
[44] (1916) 85 L.J.K.B. 1191.

it would be dishonoured and that he therefore got the certificates by fraudulent means. The transaction amounted to a "theft" of the shares and a "taking of them out of the possession and control of the insured by fraudulent means" within the meaning of the policy. Bailhaiche J. said[45]:

> "The strongest way of putting the case for the defendants is that this is not a policy to secure the plaintiffs from being cheated by their customers. But I think that is putting it on too broad lines."

A very similar wording was also considered in *Wasserman v. Blackburn*[46] **14–38** where the insured had been induced to discount certain bills of exchange by false representations from one Harrison that the bills were genuine bills, which had been drawn in respect of instalments of the purchase price of motor cars payable by the purchasers under hire-purchase agreements. The bills were dishonoured, and the insured sought to recover those amounts discounted on the ground that they suffered loss through the fraud or dishonesty of Harrison, and that the bills were forged negotiable instruments. Roche J. did not consider that the circumstances fell within those words of the policy for the loss was occasioned by false pretences or fraud which were not mentioned,[47] but the loss was embraced by additional wording contained within the particular policy:

> "or shall sustain . . . any other loss whatsoever through the theft, fraud, larcency, embezzlement, or other dishonesty of a forgery by any . . . person".

Insured occurrence to be "on the premises of the insured"
The Lloyds bankers policy issued by the defendant underwriter to the **14–39** claimant bank in *Deutsche Genossenschaftsbank v. Burnhope*[48] covered the bank against direct financial losses suffered by it in a variety of circumstances, including:

> "*On premises*
> By reason of property lost through:
>
> A. (a) burglary, robbery or hold-up; or
>   (b) theft, larceny or false pretences, committed by persons present on the premises of the assured or on the premises where the property is located; or
>   (c) mysterious unexplainable disappearance; or
>   (d) being damaged, destroyed or misplaced howsoever or by whomsoever caused, whilst such property is in or upon any premises wherever situated.
>
> B. Property being lost through any of the perils specified in A above, while in the possession of a customer or any representative of such

---

[45] *ibid.* at 1193.
[46] (1926) 43 T.L.R. 95.
[47] But it does not seem from the report that the attention of Roche J. was directed to *Liberty National Bank of New York v. Bolton* (1925) 21 Ll. L. Rep. 3, CA; *Century Bank of the City of New York v. Young* (1914) 84 L.J.K.B. 385, CA; and *Pawle & Co. v. Bussell* (1916) 85 L.J.K.B. 1191, so that this part of the judgment may be doubted.
[48] [1995] 1 W.L.R. 1580, HL.

> customer, when on the premises of the assured, whether or not the assured is legally liable for such loss . . . and excluding in any event loss caused by such customer or representative."

14-40   The relevant facts were that in April 1991 a company called Wallace Smith Trust C. Ltd ("the company") was customer of the bank at its Aldersgate branch and had a credit line of up to £9 million secured by treasury bills and bank certificates of deposit of approximately that value. On April 22, 1991, Mr Smith, the chairman of the company, asked the bank to agree to a variation of the credit terms, whereby the bank would allow the company to take possession of the securities held by it until close of business on any day in exchange for a letter of undertaking by the company that the latter would produce specified securities acceptable to the bank by the close of business on that day. The bank did so agree. On April 26, 1991, Mr Towers, a junior employee of the company telephoned the bank and stated that the company wished to withdraw the securities held by the bank in exchange for a letter undertaking that the company would deliver certain alternative securities, namely a Credit Lyonnais certificate of deposit for £5 million and a Morgan Guaranty Trust Co. certificate for £4 million. The alternative securities were acceptable to the bank.

14-41   Later that day Mr Towers attended at Aldersgate and handed over a letter signed by Mr Smith on behalf of the company, undertaking to deliver to the bank that day, as soon as received by the company, the specified alternative securities. The bank employee who received the letter asked Mr Towers when she could expect delivery of the alternative securities, and Mr Towers replied that it would be by the close of business on the same day. The original securities were then handed over to Mr Towers. The alternative securities were, in fact, never delivered to the bank. On April 29, 1991, the activities of the company were suspended on the orders of the Bank of England and Mr Smith was arrested. On the next day the Bank of England presented a petition to wind up the company, and Mr Smith was charged with fraudulent trading under section 458 of the Companies Act 1985. The company's credit line loan, amounting to £9,012,452, fell due for repayment on that day and the bank made a written demand for repayment. No repayment of any part of the sum had then ever been made.

14-42   In these circumstances the bank claimed against the underwriters under the policy, claiming £9 million under the above clause on the basis that the loss suffered by it through the securities in question having been stolen from it by the company on April 26, 1991, or, alternatively, through its having been induced to hand over the securities by false pretences on the part of the company. The underwriters refused to pay, so the bank raised an action for payment, and applied for summary judgment by summons in the Commercial Court. Hobhouse J. (as he then was) directed a trial of the preliminary issue of law as to whether the facts alleged in the bank's points of claim disclosed a good cause of action under the policy. Later, Hobhouse J. determined that preliminary issue against the bank. There was no dispute that the bank suffered the loss, nor that the securities were the subject of a theft within the definition of section 1 of the Theft Act

1968, but Hobhouse J. held that there was no theft "committed by persons present on the premises of the assured". This was because the only person present on the premises of the bank had been Mr Towers, and there was no suggestion that he had been dishonest in any way or had committed any criminal offence. Rather, the criminal offence of theft had been committed by Mr Smith and, through him, by the company. The bank appealed to the Court of Appeal and, by a majority, the appeal had been allowed on the basis that the company had been present in the bank's premises through its representative, Mr Towers. The underwriters obtained leave to appeal to the House of Lords.

By a majority of four to one,[49] the House of Lords allowed the appeal **14–43** on the ground that Mr Smith, who was the directing mind of the company and of the theft itself, was not on the premises to facilitate the theft so no insured event occurred. Lord Keith gave the leading speech[50]:

> "The reason why the company was guilty of theft in the circumstances of this case was that its directing mind and will, Mr Smith, was himself guilty of theft. It was he who formed the dishonest intention of permanently depriving the bank of the securities, and who arranged for the innocent Mr Towers to deliver to the bank his letter containing false representations and to uplift the securities against it. If there had been no company involved and if it had been Mr Smith as an individual to whom the bank had granted the loan and who had deposited his own securities with the bank, so that the theft was committed by Mr Smith alone, then it could not be said, consistently with the ordinary use of language, that Mr Smith was present in the bank when the securities were uplifted by Mr Towers. Section 61 of the Law of Property Act 1925 provides that in all contracts and other instruments 'person' included a corporation unless the context otherwise requires. No doubt if Mr Smith had, in this case, taken delivery of the securities in the premises of the bank, the company, as well as Mr Smith himself, would have been criminally liable for the theft, and it could be said that the company had been present in the premises of the bank within the meaning of clause 2. That is because Mr Smith was the directing mind and will of the company. But the company's liability would be irrelevant, since theft would in any event have been committed by a real live person on those premises, in the shape of Mr Smith. In the situation where Mr Smith could not be said to be present on the bank's premises then neither could that be said of the company.
>
> It is apparent that the purpose of clause 2A(a) was to limit in some way the liability of the insurers for theft from the bank . . . what was in contemplation was a theft by a real live person in the bank."

Operation of peril determined by English law

Where cover is granted by insurers beyond English jurisdiction, for **14–44** instance to international companies, but subject to the laws of England, there seems to be a conflict between authorities upon whether the law of the place where the loss occurred, or that of England, will be applied to determine if an insured peril has occurred. Thus, in *Equitable Trust Co. of New York v. Henderson*[51] the relevant policy covered losses:

---

[49] Lords Keith, Lloyd, Nicholls & Hoffmann (Lord Steyn dissenting).
[50] [1995] 1 W.L.R. 1580 at 1584.
[51] (1930) 47 T.L.R. 90.

> "Taken, received, transferred, delivered, or acted upon any transfers, powers of attorney, bonds, scrip, or other securities or documents whatsoever . . . which may prove (a) to have been forged or invalid, (b) to have been stolen, (c) to have other want of or defect of title."

It was held that "forged" in this wording has been construed as meaning an existing state of fact and was not a term of art to be construed according to the criminal law of the place where the loss happened. Accordingly, as the loss occurred in New York by means of the insured being induced to lend money to a firm on presentation of a false statement of the firm's assets and liabilities, the loss incurred could not be brought within the policy, which was subject to the law of England, by the argument that such false statement constituted "forgery" in the State of New York.[52] This seems to be the correct approach for a policy issued subject to the laws of England, but in *New Hampshire Insurance Co. v. Philips Electronics North America Corp. (No.2)*,[53] discussed above, the parties were content for a court in Illinois to determine whether the culprit had the "manifest intent" required by the policy, but it may simply be that pragmatic reasons of practicality prevailed on that occasion, where all the witnesses lived in Illinois.

"and any other loss whatsoever"

14–45   The House of Lords had to interpret whether the claimed loss of drafts by fraud was covered in *Lazard Bros and Co. Ltd v. Brooks*[54] where the indemnity was extended to cover securities, etc.

> "Lost mislaid or accidentally destroyed and whether from within or without and whether by officers, clerks, or servants of the insured . . . and any other loss whatsoever through the theft, fraud, larceny, embezzlement or other dishonesty of or forgery by any such officer, clerk, servant, person or persons."

The facts were that the insured merchant bankers allowed one Mr Hirsch-Faber credit facilities in respect of a shipment of hides and skins, so that in due course the purchase price would be available to the insured in respect of their acceptances. In truth, there was no genuine sale and Mr Hirsch-Faber put forward the shippers' draft accompanied by a fictitious invoice and a false letter of indebtedness from a firm pretending to be the buyers. The insured, believing that they were dealing with genuine transactions and trusting Mr Hirsch-Faber, accepted the drafts, which were then discounted with various banks and financial houses who took them in good faith, who thus became holders for value, and in due course the drafts were paid by the insured.

14–46   Before any of the drafts matured, Mr Hirsch-Faber died insolvent, and those who gave letters of indebtedness and were probably parties in the fraud and shared in the spoils, were also insolvent. The insured sought to

---

[52] *Equitable Trust Co. of New York v. Henderson* (1930) 47 T.L.R. 90.
[53] [1999] Lloyd's Rep. I.R. 66.
[54] (1932) 43 Ll. L. Rep. 372, HL.

recover the moneys they lost under their policy within the words "any other loss whatsoever", but the insurers defended the claim, *inter alia*, on the ground that these words were not wide enough to cover the pecuniary loss which the insured had sustained in this case where, in fact, the insured had neither lost nor were deprived of any document or security mentioned in the preamble to the policy. The House of Lords upheld the insured's claim because the words "any other loss whatsoever" could not bear any other meaning that that which they expressed, *viz*. any loss of the kind about to be described which was not covered by the previous clause. Secondly, the words "person or persons" were not limited to persons *ejusdem generis* with officers, clerks, or servants of the insured. The real and effective cause of the loss was the fraudulent obtaining of the acceptance.

Limit for "each and every loss"

The policy may only provide an indemnity for the first part of the ulti- **14–47** mate net loss "by each and every loss or occurrence". It may therefore, on occasion, be necessary to determine whether a particular fraud effected upon the insured constitutes one loss or occurrence, or many.[55] Where the insured agrees to make advances to a customer upon the security of that customer's promissory notes and invoices in respect of goods sold by the customer in his business, and daily, even for years, the amount of the note and invoices is debited to the customer's loan account and credited to his current account, each day's loan is a separate loss or occurrence. Should they prove to be fraudulent the insured can only recover to the extent that each day's loan exceeds the specified uninsured amount.[56]

3. CREDIT INSURANCE

Subject matter of credit insurance

Introduction

Businesses may be able to obtain credit insurance on either their whole **14–48** turnover (non-facultative policies), or in respect of one or more named creditors (facultative policies). In the former instance, the insurers will wish to be informed of details of the proposing business' trading pattern for several years, estimates for future turnover, the credit control system that the proposer operates, the history of debtors, and the proposer's standard terms and conditions (if any) upon which it seeks to carry on its business. In the case of facultative insurance, the insurers will wish to know the previous and predicted trading pattern of the specified debtor businesses who are customers of the proposer's business, the credit control system, any history of non-payment, and the standard terms and conditions upon which business is governed between them.

[55] "Occurrence" is looked at from the point of view of the insured, *Forney v. Dominion Insurance Co. Ltd* [1969] 1 W.L.R. 928 at 934, *per* Donaldson J. (as he then was).
[56] *Philadelphia National Bank v. Price* [1938] 2 All E.R. 199, CA.

Adjustment of premium

14–49   Credit insurance is often rated according to the value of goods despatched or services invoiced under contracts by the insured to which the policy applies. The due observance of the requirement to supply monthly declarations to the insurer may well be made a condition precedent to the insurer's liability under the policy. Other policy conditions may conflict with this, though, as in *Kazakstan Wool Processors (Europe) Ltd v. Nederlandsche Credietverzekering Maatschappij N. V.*[57] where another condition stated:

> "In the event of any breach of any condition precedent we also have the right to retain any premium paid and give written notice terminating the policy and all liability under it."

The insured ceased trading in May 1998, and thereafter failed to submit nil declarations as required, and also failed to pay some small sums in respect of premium and credit limit charges. The insured had made a claim before May 1998, and that was paid out in June 1998, and then the insured made further claims in August 1998, just before expiry of the policy. The Court of Appeal[58] upheld Toulson J.'s decision that the above condition did not permit the insurer to recover the earlier settlement made before it terminated the policy in September 1998. To "terminate the policy and all liability under it" could not be reasonably construed as including any liability which had already crystallised, even if not yet paid. The provision was effective, though, to terminate all future and contingent liabilities, including those August 1998 claims which had not yet crystallised, because the requisite six month default period had not run before the right of termination was exercised by the insurers.

Alteration in the risk

14–50   In each case it will be necessary to see whether there is an express term restricting or excluding[59] cover in the case of alterations in the risk, such as an alteration in the contractual rights between the insured creditor and the debtors or debtors not in contemplation of the insured and insurer at the time they entered into the insurance.[60] Equally, the significant reduction of instalment payments by the debtor will be a material alteration in the risk insured, even in the absence of an express term.[61] It will also be necessary to consider whether the operation of the credit control system, and the incorporation of standard terms of trading, are the subject of future warranties which must be complied with throughout the period of insurance in order to be able to recover an indemnity under the policy.

---

[57] [2000] Lloyd's Rep. I.R. 371, CA.
[58] Waller L.J. dissenting.
[59] *Finlay v. Mexican Investment Corp.* [1897] 1 Q.B. 517.
[60] *Law Guarantee Trust and Accident Society Ltd v. Munich Reinsurance Co.* [1912] 1 Ch. 138 at 154, *per* Warrington J.
[61] *Hadenfayre v. British National Insurance Society Ltd* [1984] 2 Lloyd's Rep. 393.

Risks insured

Insolvency or bankruptcy of debtors

The usual peril insured against is the insolvency or bankruptcy of the **14–51** insured's general debtors (non-facultative policies) or the particular debtors specified in the insurance policy (facultative policies). Alternatively, the peril may be the non-payment of the debt within the due period agreed between the insured creditor, or within a specified time after default. On occasion, the description of the insured peril will be far more narrow as in *Waterkyn v. Eagle Star & British Dominions Insurance Co. Ltd*,[62] where the insured peril was the bankruptcy or insolvency of specified Russian banks "directly due to damage or destruction of the premises and contents of the said banks through riots, civil commotions, wars, civil war, revolutions, rebellions, military or usurped power". The insured therefore had to prove three matters, namely (i) insolvency of those banks, (ii) damage or destruction of the banks' premises and their contents, and (iii) that the specified perils had caused that damage or destruction. What had happened was that the Bolshevists had abolished private banks and confiscated all their assets. Accordingly, the insured was unable to recover under the insurance because there had been no physical "damage or destruction" of those banks, the destruction of their business by confiscation not being within the scope of the policy.

Exclusion of fraud

The risk being insured is insolvency of the debtors, not losses arising **14–52** from dishonesty. One form of the exclusion of other risks provides that the insurers shall not be liable for:

> "Any claim or claims arising directly or indirectly out or caused directly or indirectly by fraud, attempted fraud, misdescription or deception by any person, firm, organisation or company."

This exclusion is widely drawn, and will embrace where the debtor companies default on repayment because their owner dishonestly absconds with the loan monies.[63]

Concealment of material facts

The question of non-disclosure of material facts arose in *Svenska* **14–53** *Handelsbanken v. Sun Alliance and London Insurance plc*[64] in the context of two commnercial mortgage indemnity (CMI) insurance policies issued to Svenka by Sun Alliance. Under a CMI policy, the insurer covers a lender of an advance secured on the mortgage of commercial property against the risk that, following a default by the borrower, the security will not repay the principal of the advance, interest and associated costs. Such

---

[62] (1920) 5 Ll. L.Rep. 42.
[63] Conceded by the insured banks in *Banque Financière de la Cité SA v. Westgate Insurance Co. Ltd* [1991] 2 A.C. 249, HL.
[64] [1996] 1 Lloyd's Rep. 519.

cover typically insures the insured for up to 70 per cent ("bottom-slice") of the agreed value of the property. CMI insurance is available for the excess of that up to 90 per cent ("top slice"). Svenka had advanced £39.5 million to Tervale Ltd, the owner of a portfolio of five office buildings in Euston, Harrow and Aberdeen on a loan to value ratio of 90 per cent. The rental incomes were insufficient to cover even the interest due under this loan, so £2.6 million of the advance was placed in a blocked deposit account as additional security available to Svenka in the event of default. They also took an unsecured £10 million guarantee from Mr Waldman, the beneficial owner of Tervale Ltd Subsequently, Sun Alliance sought to rescind the CMI policies on a number of grounds.

14–54　　Rix J. (as he then was) was satisfied that Sun Alliance had established that it had been induced to enter into the insurance by reason of Svenka's misrepresentation that the blocked deposit monies (£2.6 million) were sufficient to cover the annual interest accruing under the loan (£3.7 million).[65] Alleged misrepresentations concerning Svenka's ability to control the rental income, and the purpose of the loan to Tervale, were dismissed,[66] but further concealments were established[67]:

> (i) that Svenka had wrongly asserted that the reason for the lack of available accounts for Tervale Ltd was its recent establishment;
> (ii) that Svenka had exaggerated their previous dealings with Mr Waldman;
> (iii) that Svenka, contrary to its implied assertion, had not carried out a reasonable investigation into Mr Waldman; and
> (iv) that Svenka had failed to disclose that it would not have made the loan without the 100 per cent CMI insurance that it obtained.

14–55　　In addition, Rix J. held that the above misrepresentations , although not actually contained within a proposal form, they were part of the "proposal" as defined in the policy, namely, "any information supplied by or on behalf of the Insured in addition [to a signed proposal form and declaration] or in substitution therefore". Accordingly, they placed Svenka in breach of the condition precedent in clause 4 of each of the policies,[68] which provided:

> "The following shall be conditions precedent to any liability of the Company . . .
>
> (b) the truth of the Proposal in all material respects."

14–56　　Insurers failed to establish either non-disclosure or misrepresentation, however, in *Bank Leumi Le Israel B.M. v. British National Insurance Co. Ltd*.[69] The claimant bank had insured the risk of non-repayment of a

---

[65] *ibid.* at 562.
[66] *ibid.* at 563.
[67] *ibid.* at 564–566.
[68] *ibid.* at 567.
[69] [1988] 1 Lloyd's Rep. 71.

US$5.5 million. loan to Sagittarius Films Ltd with the defendant and other insurers. The loan was to enable Sagittarius to make a film. When the loan was not repaid, the insurers contended that the bank ought to have disclosed that the film was no longer going to be produced by Sagittarius, and that Sagittarius had divested itself of various rights. The first defence failed on the ground that it had not been represented that Sagittarius were to produce the film themselves, rather, the draft agreement shown to underwriters was more consistent with Sagittarius intending to make the necessary arrangements than intending themselves to be the exclusive producers. The second defence also failed, because there was no evidence to support the contention that Sagittarius once owned, but ceased to own the worldwide copyright before the insurance had been effected.

CHAPTER 15

BUSINESS INTERRUPTION INSURANCE

1. SUBJECT MATTER OF BUSINESS INTERRUPTION INSURANCE

Introduction

15–01   The insurance of losses flowing from damage to insured business premises is known under a variety of terms, *e.g.* "business interruption insurance", "consequential loss insurance", "business interruption insurance", "loss of profits insurance", "use and occupation insurance". The purpose of this insurance is to indemnify the insured business, within the limits specified in the policy, in respect of particularised items, such as loss of profits that could have been earned but for the interruption caused by the insured perils[1]; or, alternatively, the "fixed" or "overhead" costs that the business has to continue paying despite any interruption or cessation of work (*e.g.* wages, standing charges); or the increased costs incurred by the insured business whilst work is continued.

Underlying policy needed

15–02   An essential feature of the standard forms of business interruption policy is that they will only operate as a follow-on insurance in the sense that the peril causing the business interruption must already be an insured peril covered by an underlying material damage insurance (*e.g.* buildings, contents or engineering[2]). See, for example, Section 5 of the specimen combined insurance policy at Appendix 1. Thus, if a fire occurs at the insured business premises and the fire insurers admit liability in respect of lost or destroyed property, the business interruption insurers follow that lead and will indemnify the insured. On the other hand, should the insurers of the material damage risk avoid their policy with the insured, or repudiate liability under their policy for, for example, breach of a condition precedent to liability, the insured will not be able to recover from the business interruption insurer either.[3] Provided that the material damage insurer has paid or admitted liability, the insured can recover. The business interruption insurer cannot defend the insured's claim on the ground that the material damage insurer has recouped his outlay in a subrogated claim against a tortfeasor.[4] This operation of the business interruption policy "following

---

[1] The loss must occur during the currency of the policy, *Sexton v. Mountain* (1919) 1 Ll. L. Rep. 507.

[2] *Burls & Harvey Ltd and Alchemy Ltd v. Vulcan Boiler and General Insurance Co. Ltd* [1966] 1 Lloyd's Rep. 161.

[3] *Beauchamp v. Faber* (1898) 3 Com. Cas. 308.

[4] *Bailliere, Tindall & Cox v. Drysdale* (1949) 82 Ll. L. Rep. 736 at 744, *per* Morris J.

on" from the material damage insurance stems from the following provision contained in all standard form business interruption policies:

> "Provided that at the time of the happening of the damage there shall be in force an insurance covering the interest of the Insured in the property at the premises used for the purposes of the business[5] against such damage and that payment shall have been made or liability admitted therefor under such insurance."

Admission or payment by material damage insurer

In *Shanly v. The Allied Traders' Insurance Co. Ltd*[6] the insurers defended **15–03** a business interruption claim, *inter alia*, on the ground that this provision had not been met. The circumstances were that the insured's cinema was burned to the ground. The insured took his claims against the buildings and contents material damage insurers to arbitration when they disputed liability. The arbitration did not progress to a hearing, instead those two insurers submitted to arbitrator's awards for sums amounting to about half of the insured's claims against them, and paid those sums. The defendant business interruption insurers, however, contended that such did not satisfy their policy's requirement that the material damage insurers "shall have paid for or admitted liability in respect of such damage". It was submitted that those insurers had compromised those arbitrations for reasons best known to themselves because there were allegedly clear grounds for the policies to have been avoided for concealment of material fact. McCardie J. firmly rejected that defence saying:

> "If that be not an admission of liability, I know not what admission could be made or received in the Courts".[7]

Indemnity taxable

Amounts recovered by the insured under business interruption insur- **15–04** ances are receipts inseparably connected with the ownership and conduct of the insured business, which are not windfalls, although perhaps an unusual mode of deriving gain from the business. Accordingly, such amounts are an ordinary receipt of the insured's business, in the sense that in the case of a business prudently conducted such amounts will ordinarily be received so often as the risk insured against materialises, and are thus taxable.[8]

---

[5] In the case of a property development company, the unissued drawings of its independent consultants in a temporary office on a redevelopment site are embraced by these words, *Glengate-KG Properties Ltd v. Norwich Union Fire Insurance Society Ltd* [1996] 1 Lloyd's Rep. 614 at 619–620, *per* Neill L.J., CA.

[6] (1925) 21 Ll. L. Rep. 195.

[7] *ibid.* at 197.

[8] *IRC v. Newcastle Breweries Ltd* (1927) 96 L.J.K.B. 735, HL; *J. Gliksten & Son Ltd v. Green (Inspector of Taxes)* [1929] A.C. 381, HL; *R. v. British Columbia Fir and Cedar Lumber Co. Ltd* [1932] A.C. 441, PC; *London and Thames Haven Oil Wharves Ltd v. Attwooll (Inspector of Taxes)* [1967] Ch. 772, CA.

2. THE INDEMNITY

Valued loss of profits

15–05   One method that can be adopted is for the insurance to provide that a fixed sum, *e.g.* £1,000, is paid in respect of each working day that work is wholly stopped because of an insured peril, *e.g.* fire damage, and that a proportionate part of that sum shall be paid in respect of each working day that is not wholly stopped (and a method of calculating the correct proportion is provided). This type of valued policy is known as a time loss insurance. If such a valued policy is issued, the insured daily sum must be paid by the insurer for each interrupted working day, subject only to proportionate reduction for partial interruption, unless there is a further proviso, *e.g.*:

> "if the standing charges shall be reduced or cease to be paid, the amount of loss hereunder shall be reduced accordingly."

Where the policy contains this provision, the daily sum provisionally valued at, *e.g.* £1,000, is reduced in accordance with this provision.[9] The standing charges may well be specified in a definitions clause in the policy.

15–06   Another means of quantifying or valuing the loss of profits to be paid under a business interruption policy is to provide that the loss of profits shall be valued at the inception of the insurance, *e.g.* £150,000, and, in the event of the business being interrupted by an insured peril, the insurers will pay the same proportion of that sum as the material damage insurers pay on that insurance.[10] Thus if the business premises and contents are insured against fire to the value of £250,000 and a fire occurs resulting in £50,000 being paid by the buildings and contents insurer (*i.e.* one-fifth of the limit of indemnity), the consequential loss insurers will pay one-fifth of £150,000, *i.e.* £30,000. This calculation of indemnity in respect of loss of profits may, however, be complicated by the following provisions to the benefit of the insurer:

> "(i) in the event of the amount insured exceeding the probable annual profits of the business to be determined by an assessor the loss under the policy shall be reduced accordingly;
> (ii) if the standing charges shall be reduced or cease to be paid during the period of the loss the amount of the indemnity shall be reduced."

15–07   Where such provisions occur, the insured is only entitled to recover under the policy the proportionate amount (*i.e.* £30,000 in the example above) subject to any reduction necessary under the supplementary provisions.[11]

A third method is for the loss of profits to be valued at a specified percentage of whatever amount is recovered under the material damage policy.[12] For instance, the specified percentage may be 80 per cent of the

---

[9] *City Taylors Ltd v. Evans* (1921) 91 L.J.K.B. 379, CA.
[10] *Beauchamp v. Faber* (1898) 3 Com. Cas. 308.
[11] *Brunton v. Marshall* (1922) 10 Ll. L. Rep. 689.
[12] *Bailliere, Tinsdall & Cox v. Drysdale* (1948) 82 Ll. L. Rep. 736.

amount recovered under the material damage insurance, and if £10,000 is recovered for fire damage to the insured's business premises, a sum of £80,000 will therefore be recoverable from his business interruption insurer under this method. It will, incidentally, be irrelevant to the calculation that the material damage insurers, exercising their rights of subrogation, have recovered the indemnity paid to the insured from another person who was responsible for the peril occurring[13] (*e.g.* where a neighbouring business permitted sparks to drift over to the insured's business premises so causing the fire damage).

Unvalued loss of profits

A further way in which the indemnity may be expressed in the policy is **15–08** by means of an agreed percentage on the amount by which the turnover in each month after the insured peril occurs and disrupts the business shall, in consequence of the peril occurring, be less than the turnover for the corresponding month of the preceding year. Such an indemnity was provided in *Recher & Co. v. North British and Mercantile Insurance Co.*,[14] where the policy further provided that the amount of all losses under the policy were to be assessed by the insured's auditors. That latter proviso means that the audtor's assessment will be conclusive against the insurers, unless the insurers can establish that the auditor has misdirected himself in point of law, or had omitted to take into consideration some material fact. But there can be no challenge on the ground that the audior's assessments were factually erroneous.

An alternative form of unvalued indemnity is similar to that in paragraph **15–09** 15–08 above, and will require calculation, but provides for the whole period of interruption to be considered as against the estimated results for that period, and limits the loss of profits recoverable for that period to a percentage ascertained in respect of loss of estimated turnover, *e.g.* if turnover falls ten per cent from the estimated turnover predicted for the interrupted period, then the loss of profits are also limited to 10 per cent of the loss of profits earned as against estimated. Such a clause may read as follows[15]:

> "Loss of profits sustained during the periods of indemnity in consequence of the within-mentioned interruption or interference, but not exceeding the ascertained percentage of the sum by which the turnover of such period shall, in consequence of such interruption or interference, fall short of the estimated turnover. Provided that if any of the specified standing charges shall be reduced or cease to be paid or payable the amount of the loss shall be reduced accordingly."

Standing charges

Just as a reduction in turnover caused by business interruption or inter- **15–10** ference will tend to reduce the profits of the business, it will also create a situation where standing charges (overheads) become a greater proportion

---

[13] *ibid.*
[14] [1915] 3 K.B. 277.
[15] *Polikoff Ltd v. North British and Mercantile Insurance Co. Ltd* (1936) 55 Ll. L. Rep. 279.

of operating costs. Many businesses therefore wish to protect themselves from this effect of the increasing ratio of fixed charges to turnover by insurance, just as they insure their loss of profits. The standing charges covered by the insurance will usually be specified in a Schedule to the policy,[16] and may comprise the following:

(i) interest on loans, bank overdrafts, debentures and mortgages;
(ii) rent, rates and taxes: but the insured is not entitled to claim under the policy for income tax or corporation tax that it had estimated it would pay without the interruption, but is no longer payable because of the reduced profits caused by the interruption or interference with its business[17];
(iii) directors' and auditor's fees;
(iv) salaries and commission to directors and permanent staff: wages are not salaries, nor are they commissions[18];
(v) wages to skilled employees: it will be a matter of fact whether employees remunerated by a weekly wage are skilled or unskilled employees[19];
(vi) insurance premiums: This term "insurance premiums" must be construed in its ordinary meaning, and thus does not include contributions paid by a business concern in respect of its employees' National Insurance contributions[20];
(vii) legal, advertising and travelling expenses;
(viii) printing, stationery and stamps;
(ix) telephones, electric lighting and heating, gas and water charges;
(x) repairs to premises, depreciation of such buildings, plant and machinery that was not, *e.g.* destroyed by the fire or other insured peril: indeed, any reduction in depreciation in respect of any damaged building, plant or machinery of the insured, must be brought into account when assessing the insured's claim under this head[21];
(xi) general expenses: the insurer will generally provide that a maximum payment under this head is to be a certain percentage of the total specified standing charges, *e.g.* five per cent. This is a heading under which an expense which is not an abnormal one or otherwise special to a particular period, may be included. The

---

[16] But see *Mount Royal Assurance Co. v. Cameron Lumber Co. Ltd* [1934] A.C. 313, PC, where they were unidentified, the indemnity being in respect of fixed charges and expenses of the business "to the extent only that such fixed charges and expenses would have been earned had no fire occurred".

[17] *Polikoff Ltd v. North British and Mercantile Insurance Co. Ltd* (1936) 55 Ll. L. Rep. 279, at 289.

[18] *ibid.* at 285, *per* Branson J.: "The distinction between salary and commission on the one hand and wages on the other hand is quite well understood in every business concern, and I cannot think that it is possible that anybody would have thought that the weekly wage paid to a packer, or the weekly wage paid to a driver, could ever be considered as coming under the definition of 'salaries and commission to directors and permanent staff'."

[19] *ibid.* at 285.

[20] *ibid.* at 288.

[21] *ibid.* at 289.

test of whether the expense in question was a general expense or not would appear to be whether that expense was entered in the insured's accounts as a general expense or under a separate account, *e.g.* machinery maintenance, packing materials.[22]

Increased cost of working

The increased cost of working as a result of the business interruption or   **15–11**
interference to the business premises or stock as appropriately insured, may be insured. Such a clause may read:

> "Increase in the cost of working necessarily incurred by the insured in consequence of such interruption or interference to maintain during the period of indemnity a turnover not exceeding the estimated turnover; provided that if the total sum insured shall be less than the sum of the net profit which would have been earned and all standing charges (insured and otherwise) of the business which would have been incurred during the annual currency of the policy had the business not been interrupted or interfered with the amount payable shall be proportionately reduced."

This separate item covers any increased costs incurred by the insured in order to continue in business such as the rental costs of alternative premises during reinstatement of the damaged or destroyed insured business premises, or the additional costs incurred by having to purchase partly manufactured goods rather than raw materials which cannot be converted into the finished goods during the interruption or interference.[23]

The insured must have in fact had to pay more money in respect of any   **15–12**
item claimed in order to be able to recover. The mere fact that, *e.g.* wages, form a greater percentage element of the business expenses during the interruption or interference does not constitute a claim under this head of increased cost of working.[24]

3. INSURANCE OF GROSS PROFIT ON THE "DIFFERENCE" BASIS

For many years in the UK the major insurance companies and Lloyd's   **15–13**
have adopted a standard approach and wording, and this will insure two items. Firstly, loss of Gross Profit and, secondly, increased costs of working, both resulting from the insured peril and paid for the period of indemnity (usually one year maximum from the insured event, *e.g.* fire). An example of the wording can be seen in the specimen commercial combined policy in the Appendix. The loss of Gross Profit is calculated by ascertaining the proportion which turnover less variable charges represents of the turnover of the business, and this proportion is then applied to the reduction in turnover caused by the insured event.

---

[22] *ibid.* at 288.
[23] *Henry Booth & Sons v. Commercial Union Assurance Co. Ltd* (1923) 14 Ll. L. Rep. 114.
[24] *Polikoff Ltd v. North British and Mercantile Insurance Co. Ltd* (1936) 55 Ll. L. Rep. 279 at 289–290.

15–14   Here is an illustration of the calculation of the indemnity.

- *Before fire*
  Turnover is £1,000,000
  Variable charges are £700,000
  Therefore, the "Remainder" as it is known is £300,000,
  comprised, say, of Standing Charges of £200,000 and Net Profit
  of £100,000.
  The Rate of Gross Profit of the business is calculated as:

$$\frac{\text{Remainder}}{\text{Turnover}} \times \frac{100}{1} = \frac{300,000}{1,000,000} \times \frac{100}{1} = 30\%$$

- *After Fire*
  Turnover is £400,000
  Therefore, the indemnity is the Rate of Gross Profit ×
  Reduction in Turnover, *i.e.*

$$30\% \times (£1,000,000 - £400,000) = 30\% \times £600,000 = £180,000$$

The position of the insured business after the fire becomes:

Turnover	£400,000
Less Variable charges (now reduced)	£280,000
	£120,000
Plus Insurance indemnity	£180,000
	£300,000
Less Standing charges	£200,000
Net Profit (as before fire)	£100,000

15–15   The increase in cost of the working element of the indemnity compensates the insured business in respect of "the additional expenditure necessarily and reasonably incurred for the sole purpose of avoiding or diminishing the reduction in turnover" which would otherwise have taken place. Such payments can be made for very varied expenditure and are commonly paid in regard to additional overtime wages for either the insured's employees, trying to make good the loss of production, or to builder's or other tradesmen's workers to speed up the restoration of the damaged property and plant.

Provision for savings

15–16   A "savings" clause applies to both of the above insured items, though, providing for a deduction of "any sum saved during the Indemnity Period in respect of those charges and expenses of the Business payable out of Gross Profit which cease or are reduced because of the loss or damage".

Provision for trading adjustments

15–17   Additionally, an adjustment will be provided for Annual Turnover, Rate of Gross Profit and Standard Turnover as defined "to provide for variations in or other circumstances affecting the business so that the adjusted figures represent as far as possible the results which but for the loss or damage would have been obtained during the Indemnity Period". This is inserted for the obvious reason that national and international trading conditions vary constantly, and can be influenced by such matters as credit restrictions, economic recession or inflation, industrial disputes, or even an expanding market for the company's products arising from new outlets or an advertising campaign. This type of clause appeared in the policy considered in *Polikoff Ltd v. North British and Mercantile Insurance Co. Ltd*[25] and the court upheld the arbitrator's findings that the insured's estimated turnover was abnormally increased owing to the intensive advertising campaign which the insured had embarked upon. The provisions of this clause were therefore held to operate and thus reduced the percentage of the increase in turnover taken into the calculation of the recoverable loss.

Where gross profit is defined as being net profit plus certain specified   **15–18**
insured standing charges, the apportionments clause below is inserted:

> "If any standing charges of the business be not insured by this policy then in computing the amount recoverable hereunder as increase in cost of working that proportion only of the additional expenditure shall be brought into account which the sum of the net profit and the insured standing charges bears to the sum of the net profit and all the standing charges."

Where gross profit is defined as turnover less variable standing charges, there is no need for such an apportionment clause because all the standing charges are automatically included in the insurance by the definition of gross profit.

Common conditions

It is common for policies to provide for the automatic termination of   **15–19**
business interruption cover as follows:

> "This Policy shall become void if:
>
> (a) the business be wound up or carried on by a liquidator or receiver or permanently discontinued, or
> (b) the Insured's interest cease otherwise than by death, or
> (c) any alteration be made either in the business or in the premises or property therein whereby the risk of damage is increased
>
> at any time after the commencement of this insurance unless its continuance be admitted by memorandum signed by or on behalf of the Insurer."

Increase in risk[26]

To determine whether there is a breach of a provision prohibiting an   **15–20**
increase in the risk of loss or damage after the insurance has been effected, McCardie J. in *Shanly v. The Allied Traders' Insurance Co. Ltd*[27] pointed out that this depends on what was the general position as known to the insurers at the time they accepted the risk. There, the insurers provided

---

[25] (1936) 55 Ll. L. Rep. 279.
[26] See Chapter 11, above, for further cases concerning the meaning of this provision.
[27] (1925) 21 Ll. L. Rep. 195.

business interruption insurance for the insured's business as a cinema proprietor of a converted theatre in Limerick. The theatre stage remained, as did the drop stage at the back, the side wings, the footlights, and the normal features of a theatre. The insurers knew all this. There was no warranty against theatrical performances, music hall entertainment, variety turns, or the employment of scenic effects. The insurers defended the claim, *inter alia*, on the ground of the insured's breach of this provision by the introduction of theatrical or scenic performances in addition to the activities of the cinema which thereby increased the risk of fire.

15–21   It was true that after inception of the insurance, the insured decided to introduce, as was common in England and Ireland at that time (1921), a couple of variety turns, for the purpose of breaking the monotony of the cinema performance and the interval whilst changing the film. One was a singer, who simply sang in front of the cinema screen for 10–12 minutes. In a different week, the act was two men dancing and singing for 15 minutes with a single cloth as scenery. In another week there was a 10 minute double act by two men sat in chairs in front of the screen, with one singing and one playing the banjo. Finally, in one week there was a singer and, separately, a harpist who was also a ventriloquist, with no scenery at all. McCardie rejected the insurers' contention that there was any fact concerning any of these variety turns that could be regarded as an increase in the risk within the meaning of the policy.

Profits from alternative premises after insured event

15–22   Because of the Court of Appeal's decision in *City Tailors Ltd v. Evans*[28] to the effect that the insured did not have to bring into account profits earned by the business at new premises opened after the destruction of the insured premises, insurers now include an express clause specifying that sales or services from premises elsewhere than the insured premises shall be taken into account in calculating the turnover during the indemnity period.

4. RISKS INSURED

15–23   As already mentioned, business interruption insurance envisages that the business carried on by the insured at the premises identified to the insurers shall be interrupted or interfered with in consequence of the occurrence of a specified peril. Although newer forms of policy will provide an "all risks" business interruption cover, possibly without the need for a material damage insurance to be in operation to cover "all risks", the standard form of UK policy will name the perils in like fashion to the "fire" policy on the business premises and contents, *i.e.*:

> (i) Fire (whether resulting from explosion or otherwise) not occasioned by or happening through:

[28] (1921) 126 L.T. 439, CA.

(a) its own spontaneous fermentation or heating or its under-going any process involving the application of heat

(b) earthquake, subterranean fire, riot, civil commotion, war, invasion, act of foreign enemy, hostilities (whether war be declared or not), civil war, rebellion, revolution, insurrection or military or usurped power.

(ii) Lightning.

(iii) Explosion, not occasioned by or happening through any of the perils specified in (i)a above:

(a) of boilers used for domestic purposes only;

(b) of any other boilers or economisers on the premises;

(c) in a building not being part of any gas works, of gas used for domestic purposes or used for lighting or heating the building.

The interpretation and scope of this wording is fully discussed in Chapter 11, above, and reference should be made thereto if a question arises upon the construction to be applied. Business interruption cover can also be obtained in relation to other "special perils", *e.g.* flood, subsidence, where the insured already possesses such cover under a material damage insurance. Again, reference should be made to Chapter 11 for consideration of those "special perils" which can be insured, and their coverage.

Common extensions

For an additional premium, a business may have its consequential loss   **15–24**
policy extended to insure itself against loss resulting from a reduction in turnover due to interruption or interference with the business of, *e.g.*:

(a) associated companies;

(b) suppliers;

(c) processors;

(d) sub-contractors;

(e) customers;

(f) supplies of electricity, gas, water or steam;

(g) prevention or denial of access because of damage at neighbouring premises.

5. BUSINESS INTERRUPTION UNDER MACHINERY BREAKDOWN INSURANCE

Risk covered and exclusions

Machinery breakdown insurance can be extended to provide business   **15–25**
interruption cover. The insured business' machinery and plant permanently situated at the premises may be insured against "sudden and accidental damage by any fortuitous cause", other than those specifically excluded. The exclusions will generally be against loss and damage arising from:

(i) fire, lightning, explosion, earthquake, storm and tempest;
(ii) aircraft and/or articles dropped therefrom;
(iii) water discharged or leaking from any automatic sprinkler installation at the premises;
(iv) wear and tear, corrosion, erosion, failure of any part or parts
the nature or functions of which necessitate their regular
replacement;
(v) operation of safety devices other than from causes which but for
such operation would have damaged the machinery or plant to
which such safety devices are connected.

Exclusion for wear and tear, etc.

15–26   This exclusion was at the centre of the dispute between the insured and
the insurer in *Burts & Harvey Ltd v. Vulcan Boiler and General Insurance
Co. Ltd*.[29] The case shows the distinction between the excluded peril causing the loss or damage, when it operates, and situations where matters
within the insured peril only arise as a consequence of an insured peril,
when it is inoperative to debar recovery. The insured operated a chemical
plant for the production of maleic anhydride which was insured with the
defendants in respect of business interruption breakdown insurance of the
type described above. It was a new plant and production had commenced
on May 19, 1961, but after nine hours it broke down. The cause was outside the insurance cover on that occasion. Production was started again on
May 27, but on June 4, 1961 the plant had to be shut down again due to
the build up of high pressures within it. Production re-commenced on
August 6, and the insured claimed for its losses on the basis that the high
pressures were caused by a crack in a tube in the heat exchanger. This
crack had allowed water to mix with gaseous maleic anhydride and to
form very corrosive maleic acid which then caused the damage. The insurers
denied liability contending, *inter alia*, that the loss was due to the excluded
causes of corrosion and/or was occasioned by the excluded peril of a
gradually developing flaw or defect (see exclusion (iv), above).

15–27   The expert evidence produced to the court was in agreement that during
the construction of the honeycombed heat exchanger, which consisted of
280 mild steel tubes surrounded by a water jacket, the expansion process
by which a watertight joint was created at each end of these tubes to the
steel end plate (called drifting), had gone wrong. Splits had developed near
the bottom plate of the honeycomb, whereby steam had escaped into the
gaseous maleic anhydride. Later, water escaped through those splits and
produced, in the end, maleic acid. That acid had the disastrous eroding
effect of washing away the steel of a dozen tubes at the bottom end of the
heat exchanger. Lawton J. (as he then was) determined that the steam had
begun to escape about four hours before the rising pressure was first
noticed on June 4, a further four hours passing before the plant had been
shut down. There could not have been any splits outside the end plates
before then, otherwise trouble would have been encountered before then.

[29] [1966] 1 Lloyd's Rep. 161.

Lawton J. held that the dominant or proximate cause[30] of this accident   **15–28**
was the splitting of one or more tubes in the heat exchanger, that event
leading to the formation of the maleic acid and then the corrosion and
erosion of the tubes of the heat exchanger. The insurer's defences therefore
failed, because the corrosion was a consequence of sudden and accidental
damage by a fortuitous cause which event was the insured peril. Construing
the exclusion as applied to this case, Lawton J. held that it related to the
effect of gaseous maleic anhydride upon the tubes through which it would
pass in the ordinary process of production, and did not operate to exclude
any corrosion or erosion which was consequential upon any breakdown of
the plant due to the failure of a component.[31]

6. CONCEALMENT OF MATERIAL FACTS

The defence of concealment of material facts failed in *Shanly v. The*   **15–29**
Allied Traders' Insurance Co. Ltd,[32] the facts of which are given above,
there was an express provision requiring disclosure of material facts after
inception of the insurance. Upon the evidence that the insurance industry
was well aware of the practice of cinemas at that time to employ variety
turns in this manner, McCardie J. held that the insurers had failed to prove
that any of the variety turns employed by the insured cinema owner
constituted circumstances that a prudent insurer would have regarded as
material.

7. FRAUDULENT CLAIM

One of the several defences of the insurers in *Nsubuga v. Commercial*   **15–30**
Union Assurance Co. plc,[33] the facts of which are dealt with in Chapter 12,
above, was that the insured had advanced his business interruption claim
by fraudulent means. The insured had produced a notebook to his loss
assessor, telling him that this was his sales book, and the loss assessor
calculated the insured's claim on this basis. Thomas J., however, accepted
forensic evidence called by the insurers that the entries in that notebook
were not entered daily as stated by the insured, but in blocks, and that the
March 1994 entries were clearly written before the alleged January 1994
figures. There was also forensic accountancy evidence accepted by the
court, that the purported entries in the notebook did not coincide with the
pattern of trading of the insured's business. The insured's claim was
accordingly rejected, Thomas J. being satisfied, on the criminal standard
of proof, that the insured had created those entries, and such activities
were plainly a fraudulent means of advancing his claim disentitling him to
any benefit under the policy.

---

[30] This is discussed in Chapter 17, below.
[31] [1966] 1 Lloyd's Rep. 161 at 170.
[32] (1925) 21 Ll. L. Rep. 195.
[33] [1998] 2 Lloyd's Rep. 682.

15–31   Similarly, in *Insurance Corp. of the Channel Islands Ltd v. McHugh and Royal Hotel Ltd*,[34] Mance J. (as he then was) held that Mr McHugh, the hotel's company secretary and a director, acted on behalf of the Royal Hotel Ltd, had used fraudulent means or devices to promote the hotel's trading position and to obtain benefits under the business interruption insurance. Mr McHugh had instructed an accounts clerk in the hotel's parent company to create false invoices to show accommodation at the hotel being let to the parent company, prior to renewal of the insurance. The purpose was to create a more favourable turnover and occupancy rate, by some 35 per cent, for the hotel to present to its bankers. More false invoices were created in the same manner in the three months prior to the fire in June 1992. The presentation of those false turnover and accommodation rate results resulted in the loss of all benefit under the business interruption policy.

15–32   *Baghbadrani v. Commercial Union Assurance Co. Ltd*[35] is a further example of the insurers being able to satisfy the high burden of proof upon them. The insured had made a business interruption claim under his insurance following a fire at the insured private school during refurbishment works. The school catered for foreign students from Iran, and the claim was made on the basis that some 60 students would have been present after the refurbishment works, but for the fire. The court concluded, though, that the photocopy documents advanced by the insured, allegedly from the Iranian Government, were known to be forgeries. Further, that the conduct of the claim after the commencement of proceedings was fraudulent, and so disentitled the insured from recovering.[36]

---

[34] [1997] L.R.L.R. 94.
[35] [2000] Lloyd's Rep. I.R. 94.
[36] *ibid.* at 111–118.

CHAPTER 16

CONTRACTORS' INSURANCE

1. SUBJECT MATTER OF CONTRACTORS' INSURANCE

The subject matter that can be insured under policies commonly known **16–01**
as "contractors 'all risks' insurance" ("C.A.R.") is twofold. First loss or
damage to property (*e.g.* buildings, machinery, plant) or the particular
building site can be insured, and, secondly, the liability of the contractor
during the course of the building work can be covered. These separate
subject matters can be insured under distinct policies, or more usually
under one comprehensive form of policy covering material damage,
employers' and public liability. A contract works policy will cover material
damage only to the contract works themselves, and a specimen policy is at
Appendix 3. Examples of C.A.R. policies are at Appendix 4 and 6.
Various extensions are possible, *e.g.* in respect of latent defects and defective or faulty material, workmanship or design. Material damage cover
applies to the permanent works (*i.e.* that being constructed) and temporary
works (*i.e.* temporary shoring, framework or formwork necessary to
achieve construction of the permanent works), together with machinery,
plant and materials brought on site and property elsewhere designated for
that contract (*e.g.* a staircase being made at a factory).

2. JOINT AND COMPOSITE INSURANCE

Introduction
The policies generally provide that the contractor and the employer are the **16–02**
insured and that the insurance will operate as regards their respective rights
and interests. If both are named as "joint insured", the interests of the contractor and employer being different, the court will construe such a policy as
a composite, rather than joint, policy insuring each named insured for the
whole contract works.[1] The convenience of including further persons within
the definition of "the insured" in contractors' insurance, such as sub-
contractors of the main contractor, has been recognised by insurers and
contractors alike, and the practice has grown widespread in the past twenty
years. This convenience has been recognised by Lloyd J. (as he then was)[2]:

---

[1] *Petrofina (U.K.) Ltd v. Magnaload Ltd* [1984] Q.B. 127; *General Accident Fire and Life
Assurance Corp. Ltd v. Midland Bank Ltd.* [1940] 2 K.B. 388, CA. For examples of the scope
of provisions in the building contract as to the contractor insuring, see *Gold v. Patman &
Fotheringham Ltd* [1958] 2 All E.R. 497, CA, and *James Archdale & Co. Ltd v. Comservices
Ltd* [1954] 1 W.L.R. 459, CA.
[2] *Petrofina (U.K.) Ltd v. Magnaload Ltd* [1984] Q.B. 127 at 136, *per* Lloyd J. (as he then
was); applying *Commonwealth Construction Co. Ltd v. Imperial Oil Ltd* (1976) 69 D.L.R.(3rd)
558, Supreme Ct of Canada; *Waters and Steel v. Monarch Fire and Life Assurance Co.* (1856)
5 E. & B. 870; and *Hepburn v. A. Tomlinson (Hauliers) Ltd* [1966] A.C. 451, HL considered.

"In the case of a building or engineering contract, where numerous sub-contractors may be engaged, there can be no doubt about the convenience from everybody's point of view, including, I would think, the insurers, of allowing the head contractor to take out a single policy covering the whole risk, that is to say covering all contractors and sub-contractors in respect of loss of or damage to the entire contract works. Otherwise each sub-contractor would be compelled to take out his own separate policy. This would mean, at the very least, extra paperwork; at worst it could lead to overlapping claims and cross-claims in the event of an accident. Furthermore, as (the insurance witness) pointed out in the course of his evidence, the cost of insuring his liability might, in the case of a small sub-contractor, be uneconomic. The premium might be out of all proportion to the value of the sub-contract. If the sub-contractor had to insure his liability in respect of the entire works, he might well have to decline the contract. For all these reasons I would hold that a head contractor ought to be able to insure the entire contract works in his own name and the name of all his sub-contractors, just like a bailee or mortgagee, and that a sub-contractor ought to be able to recover the whole of the loss insured, holding the excess over his own interest in trust for the others."

16–03　　　　But the full ramifications of this practice are still being worked out. There have been problems of privity of contract, the non-naming of the various sub-contractors, and issues of agency of the insuring party and the then unknown sub-contractors. Colman J. considered in *National Oilwell (U.K.) Ltd v. Davy Offshore Ltd*[3] that these problems could be overcome by the doctrines of undisclosed principal and ratification, even where ratification was after loss.[4] As later pointed out in *Hopewell Project Management Ltd v. Ewbank Preece Ltd*,[5] there must have been an intention on the part of the person arranging the composite insurance to make insurance arrangements on behalf of the party contending he is covered, before that other party can, in law, ratify the arranging person's act of insuring on his behalf. Fortunately, the Contracts (Rights of Third Parties) Act 1999, in force on May 11, 2000, now removes the problem of privity of contract and agency provided the specific contract does not exclude the Act's provisions. Section 1 of the Act allows the third party to directly enforce the benefit conferred on him by a contract if the term of the relevant contract purports to confer a benefit on him, unless, on a proper construction of the contract, it appears that the parties did not intend the term to be enforceable by the third party. The definition of third parties is extensive, covering named persons, members of a specified class, or a person answering a description, even if the person (*e.g.* a company not yet incorporated) is not in existence when the contract is entered into.

Sub-contractors

16–04　　　　In *Petrofina (U.K.) Ltd v. Magnaload Ltd*,[6] Lloyd J. (as he then was) held that a policy that insured certain named parties such as the employer

---

[3] [1993] 2 Lloyd's Rep. 582.
[4] Refusing to follow *Grover & Grover Ltd v. Mathews* [1910] 2 K.B. 401.
[5] [1998] 1 Lloyd's Rep. 448.
[6] [1984] Q.B. 127. See also *Stone Vickers v. Appledore Ferguson Shipbuilders Ltd* [1991] 2 Lloyd's Rep. 288; reversed. [1992] 2 Lloyd's Rep. 578, CA.

and the main contractor and "sub-contractors" in the project, also insured sub-sub-contractors because[7]:

> "Strictly speaking Magnaload were not sub-contractors but sub-sub-contractors. But I would hold that they were nevertheless sub-contractors within the word 'sub-contractors' as contained in the policy. To my mind the word 'subcontractors' in the context of the policy, must include sub-sub-contractors."

But in *Hopewell Project Management Services Ltd v. Ewbank Preece*   **16–05**
Ltd.[8] Mr Recorder Jackson, Q.C. (as he then was), had to determine whether the defendant firm of consulting engineers, which provided certain engineering services to the claimant project managers, was covered by the claimant's C.A.R. policy. That policy provided, *inter alia*:

> "Name of insured: Hopewell Project Management Ltd and/or Hopewell Energy (Philipines) Corporation . . . and/or Slipform Engineering and/or subcontractors. Insured Contract: Dismantling the gas turbine units . . . and the re-erection and refurbishment including testing and commissioning . . . at Novotas . . ."

Some six months later, an endorsement to the policy amended the name of the insured to include, *inter alia*, "and/or all contractors and subcontractors". The defendant firm had been engaged by the claimants prior to their taking out the initial C.A.R. policy, and provided three engineers during the works. Two gas turbines were damaged during commissioning, which the claimants contended was due to the defendant engineers' negligence. On the facts, the learned judge considered that those three engineers had been useful, but it could not be said that they were "an integral and necessary part of the construction process itself".[9] Nor was it envisaged under the original terms of the defendants' retainer that they would be such. The learned judge therefore held that the defendant firm was not embraced by the description of the insured in the policy[10]:

> "In my view, the phrase 'contractors and subcontractors' in the definition of the insured . . . refers to persons, firms or companies whose activities involved, or at least included, physical construction work. In my judgment, having regard to the services which the defendants were intended to perform and did perform, the defendants did not fall within the definition of 'insured'."

Consequence of co-insurance
It would be nonsensical if those parties if those parties who were   **16–06**
co-insured under the C.A.R. policy could make claims against one another in respect of damage to the works.[11] The Court of Appeal have

---

[7] [1984] Q.B. 127 at 133.
[8] [1998] 1 Lloyd's Rep. 448.
[9] *ibid.* at 456, applying *Canadian Pacific Ltd v. Base-Fort Security Services* [1991] 77 D.L.R. (4th) 178 at 185, (British Columbia CA).
[10] *ibid.*
[11] *ibid.* at 458.

now confirmed in *Co-operative Retail Services Ltd v. Taylor Young Partnership Ltd & others*[12] that where the claimant, in this case the building owner, and the defendants, in this case subcontractors, were co-insured under a joint names C.A.R. policy, those subcontractors could not be liable to the building owners, or their insurers exercising rights of subrogation. The answer was said to rely on the provisions of the contract between the co-insured, and not on any suggested principle of circuity of action. Applying this test Brooke L.J. said[13]:

> "To put it simply, they [the main contractor and the electrical subcontractor], like CRS, had entered into contractual arrangements which meant that if a fire occurred, they should look to the joint insurance policy to provide the fund for the cost of restoring the fire damage (and for paying any consequential professional fees) and that they would bear other losses themselves (or cover them by their own separate insurance) rather than indulge in litigation with each other . . .
>
> In other words . . . (the cost of the reinstatement work and the professional fees attendant on that work) are completely provided for under this contractual scheme, and there can be no question of Wimpey being liable to CRS for anything once this contractual scheme has worked itself out even if otherwise allegations of negligence might have been sustained against them . . ."

Further, the Court held that the electrical subcontractor did not owe a duty of care in tort to CRS in respect of damage by fire in the present circumstances where they were expressly insured under the joint names policy provided for, and given that the insurers under that policy waived any rights of subrogation against them.

3. DURATION OF THE INSURANCE

16–07   The cover will generally be expressed to be during construction only, ceasing on handover of the buildings, unless the buildings are being built by the insured for sale or lease, in which case cover will be extended for six months on private houses, or three months on other buildings. The insurance can be arranged by the contractor either on an annual basis or, alternatively, for the duration of a particular building contract at a specific site or sites, *e.g.* the erection of a housing estate or construction of a motorway. Thus, in *Paul Tudor Jones II and Marsh & McLennan Inc. v. Crowley Collosso Ltd*[14] there was a C.A.R. policy which did not cover the property damaged after a certificate of substantial completion had been issued in respect of the works, where the policy provided:

> "The Insurer shall not be liable for:
> J) loss of or damage to any part of the permanent works
>   (i) after such part has been taken into use by the owner . . . or
>   (ii) for which a certificate of completion has been issued . . ."

[12] [2000] B.L.R. 461, CA.
[13] *ibid.* at 475–476.
[14] [1996] 2 Lloyd's Rep. 619.

The premium for material damage and public liability cover will be **16–08** based on the insured's turnover or the contract price in the case of particular contract cover. The employers' liability cover will, as is normal for such cover, be based on wages paid during the period of cover. Where a specific contract is to be covered, plus a suitable maintenance period, it may be found that, because of construction delays, the period of insurance needs to be extended. In the normal absence of any express term in the policy obligating the insurer to extend the duration of the policy, any extension in the period of insurance will necessarily have to be by mutual agreement, as is demonstrated by *Jones Construction Co v. Alliance Assurance Co. Ltd*.[15] The policy stated the period of insurance to be from January 8, 1956 to September 30, 1959, plus 12 months' maintenance, and provided:

> "The Insurers . . . will indemnify the Insured . . . for loss arising during the period stated in the Schedule or any subsequent period in respect of which the Insured shall have paid and the Insurers accepted the premium required for this extension of the terms of this Policy."

Condition 2 provided:

> "If there shall occur any change involving a material alteration in the facts set out in this Policy and forming the basis of this insurance the Insured shall, as soon as possible, give notice in writing to the Insurers and the premium shall if necessary be adjusted by agreement."

By agreement, in January 1958, another policy was issued in exactly the **16–09** same terms, except that the contract period and the duration of the policy was extended by five months to 50 months, plus 12 months' maintenance. During 1959, the building contract was further extended by 11 months, and the insured contractors requested a corresponding extension of the period of insurance covered by the policies, subject to an appropriate adjustment of premium. The defendant insurers refused to extend that period, and the contractors sought a declaration that the defendants were obliged to extend the period of insurance under the terms of the policies. Pearson J. refused this declaration[16] and the contractors appealed, but the Court of Appeal likewise refused the declaration. Danckwerts L.J. delivered the judgment of the court as follows[17]:

> "Before us the matter was put . . . that regard must be had to the main purpose of the policy, that is to say that it was plain in the circumstances that the main object of the policy was to provide cover for the contractors over the whole period of the contract, however long it might be, and that therefore the period during which the risk of the insurers existed must be coincident with the period during which the contract remained in force . . .[18] In other words, the principle relied upon as applying in this case was, as I understand

---

[15] [1961] 1 Lloyd's Rep. 121, CA.
[16] [1960] 1 Lloyd's Rep. 264.
[17] [1961] 1 Lloyd's Rep. 121 at 129–131.
[18] Reliance for this proposition was placed on the cases of *Glynn v. Margetson & Co.* [1893] A.C. 351, HL, and *Soufracht V/O v. Temple S.S. Co. Ltd* (1945) 173 L.T. 373, HL.

it, this, that where you find there is inconsistency in the terms of a written document — a printed document — or ambiguity, regard must be had to the plain object of the contract in question, and it is permissible, and, indeed, I think it was said, compulsory, to modify or even to reject, the portions of the written provisions of the contract so as to give effect to what is really the object of the whole transaction. But, as was pointed out by Lord Justice Jenkins in the case of *G.H. Renton & Co. Ltd v. Palmyra Trading Corp. of Panama*[19] . . . and his observations, I may say, were approved in the House of Lords by Viscount Kilmuir L.C.[20] . . . it is not open to the parties to create difficulties and ambiguities and to invoke that principle if they do not exist already. Nevertheless, it is said that if there are provisions in this policy which are inconsistent with the provision of cover for the whole of the liability period of the contracting party, then those provisions in this policy must be rejected.

. . . It seems to me that on the words of the opening provisions of the policy, . . . or any subsequent period in respect of which the Insured shall have paid and the Insurers accepted the premium required for this extension of the terms of this Policy. . .

it is impossible to come to any other conclusion than that the insurers were only accepting the risk, subject to their volition, for the period which was expressly mentioned, and it seems to me it would be a very strong step to take to force further risks upon the insurers, unless they had plainly, by the terms of their contract, agreed to extend the period of their risk, without further consultation with their own interests and considerations."

16–10   The express dates of cover in an "all risks" policy were, however, held not to express all the terms as to the period of cover by Webster J. in *Linden Alimak Ltd v. British Engine Insurance Ltd*[21] where contemporary documents showed a mutual intention of the insured and the insurers that the insurance was to continue until a specified event, namely, the successful load testing of the insured crane, rather than the particular date expressed in the issued policy.

4. MATERIAL DAMAGE COVER

16–11   The building owner will have an insurable interest in the contract works up to their full value, but so will all contractors, subcontractors and professionals involved in the construction because any of them might incur legal liability for negligently causing damage to the contract works.[22] A typical policy wording will cover loss or damage from "all risks" (unless expressly excluded)[23]:

"On the works temporary or permanent including Plant, Materials, Buildings completed or in the course of erection, and all property brought on to the site including motor vehicles (except those licensed for general road use), the

[19] [1956] 1 Q.B. 462 at 502, CA.
[20] [1957] A.C. 149 at 164, HL.
[21] [1984] 1 Lloyd's Rep. 416 at 421.
[22] *Petrofina (U.K.) Ltd v. Magnaload Ltd* [1984] 1 Q.B. 127; *National Oilwell (U.K.) Ltd v. Davy Offshore Ltd* [1993] 2 Lloyd's Rep. 582; *Hopewell Project Management Ltd v. Ewbank Preece Ltd* [1998] 1 Lloyd's Rep. 448.
[23] See also the specimen policies at Appendix 4 and 6.

property of the Insured or for which they are responsible, all whilst on site and whilst in transit from . . . to . . ."

For which they are responsible

This means property for which they are legally responsible, not morally   **16–12**
responsible, and without such legal responsibility there is no right of the insured to recover in respect of loss or damage of the, *e.g.* plant or machinery, and make payment to the owner of that property.[24] It is unlikely, however, that one of the insured under the policy is not either the owner or legally responsible for property brought on to the site.

In transit

By analogy with the authorities concerning carriers' insurance,[25] where   **16–13**
transit cover is provided in the policy (for it may not be) it covers "the passage or carriage of goods from one place to another",[26] and transit begins from the moment of physical acceptance[27] of the goods, *e.g.* plant or machinery, from the owner or carrier, and ceases when the goods are given into the charge of staff at the destined premises even though not physically unloaded.[28]

Works temporary or permanent

Obviously, this phrase must be construed by having regard to what the   **16–14**
insured contractor was actually going to do under the contract.[29] Permanent works means the construction works to be permanently achieved under the building contract, *i.e.* the final product, for example, a three storey building. But such must be achieved by building or rebuilding, and where a retaining wall which the contractor was required to "maintain repair and renew" this has been held as not to form part of the permanent works.[30] In contra-distinction, temporary works are those works which do not form part of the finished building, but have to be carried out to enable construction of the building to take place. Shoring or temporary sheet piling, used to support the sides of excavations during construction of a basement, would fall into this latter category, as would formwork provided to cast concrete sections of the eventual building. Thus, if a particular existing structure on the construction site is not going to be rebuilt, but merely have its appearance improved, that structure will not constitute part of the works; or, similarly, where a contractor is building a new wing on a mansion, the existing mansion-house is not part of the works, even if the contractor had agreed to give that mansion-house a coat of paint.[31]

---

[24] *North British and Mercantile Insurance Co. v. Moffatt* (1871) L.R. 7 C.P. 25; *Engel v. Lancashire and General Assurance Co. Ltd* (1925) 21 Ll. L. Rep. 327.

[25] See Chapter 13, above.

[26] *Sadler Bros. Co. v. Meredith* [1963] 2 Lloyd's Rep. 293 at 307, *per* Roskill J. (as he then was).

[27] *Crows Transport Ltd v. Phoenix Assurance Co. Ltd* [1965] 1 All E.R. 596, at 597, *per* Lord Denning M.R., CA; see also *S.C.A. (Freight) Ltd v. Gibson* [1974] 2 Lloyd's Rep. 533.

[28] *Barlett & Partners Ltd v. Meller* [1961] 1 Lloyd's Rep. 487 at 489, *per* Sachs J.

[29] *Rowlinson Construction Ltd v. Insurance Co. of North America (U.K.) Ltd* [1981] 1 Lloyd's Rep. 332 at 336, *per* Lloyd J. (as he then was).

[30] *ibid.* at 336.

[31] *ibid.*

5. LIABILITY COVER

Introduction

16–15   The particular contract conditions affecting the liability of the contractor for loss or damage that may arise are of great concern, obviously, to the insurer when deciding whether to accept the contractual liabilities assumed by the contractor, and, if so, what premium to charge. Accordingly, contractual liability of the insured contractor may be either included or excluded from the insurance cover provided. Subject to certain exceptions, contractual liability is now usually offered as standard. Further, the indemnity may be limited to the amount of damages that the contractor is legally liable to pay a third party for accidental damage occurring during construction, usually extending to include the costs and expenses[32] of defending any legal action claiming damages from the contractor for accidental loss or damage, again occurring during the specified works. Many contracts are performed under one of the standard forms of conditions mentioned below.

16–16   A standard form of indemnity wording in relation to third party liability of the contractor is:

> "Against all sums for which the insured shall become liable to pay as damages consequent upon:
> (a) accidental bodily injury to or illness or disease of any person;
> (b) accidental loss of or damage to property occurring as a result of and solely due to the performance of the insured contract happening on or in the immediate vicinity of the contract site;
> (c) accidental obstruction, nuisance or trespass."

Many construction contracts are performed under one of the standard forms of conditions mentioned below, the more important liability provisions of which are mentioned below. It must be said, however, that unless there is an express provision within the policy that the contractor shall only undertake work on these standard conditions, the insurance cover will still apply even though many of the provisions of the policy which are designed for ordinary building contracts cannot be made to apply to it. This is because, neither as a matter of construction or common sense, should the policy be construed as being limited to such standard contracts.[33]

16–17   **Exclusion of liability assumed under contract**

Where a policy excluded "liability assumed under any contract" the Supreme Court of Canada[34] has held that this wording means that any liability that would be the contractor's under ordinary legal provisions, if repeated as a liability of the contractor in the building contract, comes within the excluded liability of the insurer because the liability is now a joint liability, in that case, in both contract and in tort. It is uncertain

---

[32] *Howard Farrow Ltd v. Ocean Accident and Guarantee Corp. Ltd* (1940) 67 Ll. L. Rep. 27.
[33] *Rowlinson Construction Ltd v. Insurance Co. of North America (U.K.) Ltd* [1981] 1 Lloyd's Rep. 332 at 336, *per* Lloyd J.
[34] *Dominion Bridge Co. Ltd v. Toronto General Insurance Co.* [1964] 1 Lloyd's Rep. 194.

whether an English court would follow this reasoning, although Devlin J. (as he then was) has held that a claim framed in both negligence and fraud (which was an excluded risk) was not covered by a professional negligence policy — but this was because, despite the forms of the statement of claim, the claims were primarily based on the alleged fraud of the insured's agent.[35]

Extension for contingent charges

If cover is also provided for "contingent charges" relating to the contractor's liability, this term does not include the fee of an expert appointed by the contractor to assess whether he is liable for a particular loss upon the building contract, unless engaged to assist both the contractor and the insurer in the matter.[36]   **16–18**

6. INSURING PROVISIONS OF STANDARD FORMS OF CONSTRUCTION CONTRACTS

Building works

Many building contracts are subject to the conditions laid down by the Joint Contracts Tribunal ("JCT"). This is a body comprised of the Royal Institute of British Architects, the National Federation of Building Trades Employers, the Royal Institution of Chartered Surveyors, the Association of County Councils, the Association of Metropolitan Authorities, the Association of District Councils, the Greater London Council, the Committee of Associations of Specialist Engineering Contractors, the Federation of Associations of Specialists and Sub-contractors, the Association of Consulting Engineers and the Scottish Building Contract Committee. The JCT form of contract is published in six versions, *e.g.* for lump-sum contracts with private and local authority employers, and for re-measurement contracts. Substantial revisions were made over time to the 1980 Form, and the latest is the 1998 Form.   **16–19**

Relevant provisions of the lump-sum versions are: **16–20**

Clause 2

This provides that the contractor's obligation is to carry out and complete the works shown on the contract drawings and other contract documents, but states that the contractor has no liability for the efficacy of the design.

Clause 17.3

This provides a Defects Liability Period (usually six months) after Practical Completion, and the contractor must put right, without charge, any defects appearing within that period.

---

[35] *West Wake Price & Co. v. Ching* [1957] 1 W.L.R. 45.
[36] *Mitchell Conveyor and Transporter Co. Ltd v. Pulbrook* (1933) 45 Ll. L. Rep. 239 at 242, *per* Roche J.

Clause 20

(a) Under this clause the contractor assumes liability for any injury or death of any person arising out of or in the course of or caused by the carrying out of the contract works, unless caused by the employer (the building owner) or a person for whom the employer is responsible;

(b) in respect of damage to or loss of any personal or real property other than the works and site materials arising out of or in the course of the works and due to negligence, omission or default of the contractor or persons for whom he is responsible.

Clause 21

This is the insuring clause obliging the contractor to take out and maintain appropriate insurances, to cover his liabilities under clause 20. This must include compulsory employers' liability insurance. Additionally, and at the employers' option, the contractor may be asked to insure in joint names damage to any property other than the works caused by collapse, subsidence, heave, vibration, weakening or removal of support or lowering of ground water.

Clause 22

The appropriate sub-clause will vary depending upon whether the works are the erection of a new building, or alteration to an existing building, when the contractor is required to insure against loss or damage by fire, lightning, explosion, etc., or is required to bear the risk in respect of loss or damage by fire, etc., or if existing buildings are being extended or altered, then the contractor must bear the risk of fire, etc., damaging the existing building and/or unfixed materials and goods owned by him or for which he is responsible. Under the terms of some Forms, *e.g.* the 1980 local authorities edition, the insurance is only taken out for the employer, the contractor and nominated sub-contractors, thus domestic subcontractors are not one of the co-insured under the joint names policy.[37]

When central government is the employer, the form of contract is often the government's own form, known as GC/Works/1, edition 3 which was substantially revised in April 1990.

Civil engineering works

16–21   Works of this nature are commonly carried out under the General Conditions of Contract known as the ICE (Institution of Civil Engineers and Federation of Civil Engineering Contractors) Form. The following are the relevant provisions of the 6th edition, 1991:

---

[37] *British Telecommunications plc v. James Thomson and Sons (Engineers) Ltd* [1999] Lloyd's Rep. 105, HL (Sc.)

Condition 20(1)
The contractor accepts total responsibility for the care of the works, temporary and permanent, and in the event of any loss or damage must repair and make good the same at his own expense, unless caused by the excepted risks as defined in Condition 20(2).

Condition 20(2)
The excepted risks are riot (insofar as it is uninsurable), war, invasion, act of foreign enemy, hostilities (whether war be declared or not) civil war, rebellion, revolution, insurrection or military or usurped power[38] or a cause solely due to use or occupation by the employer of any portion of the works in respect of which a certificate of completion has been issued, or a cause solely due to the engineer's design of the works.

Condition 21
The contractor must insure in the names of the employer and his own name against loss or damage from all risks (other than the excepted perils above) for which he is responsible under the terms of the contract for the duration of the period of construction and the maintenance period:
(a) the works and temporary works to the full value of such works;
(b) the materials, plant and other equipment for incorporation in the works for the full replacement cost plus an additional 10 per cent.

Electrical and mechanical engineering contracts
Works involving the erection and installation of electrical and mech-   **16–22**
anical plant are normally carried out under the General Conditions of Contract issued jointly by the Institution of Mechanical Engineers ("I. Mech. E."), the Institution of Electrical Engineers ("I.E.E.") and the Association of Consulting Engineers, under Model Form MF/1 (1988 edition).

7. HOUSING GRANTS, CONSTRUCTION AND REGENERATION ACT 1996

From May 1, 1998, all future construction contracts, unless specifically   **16–23**
exempted by the Act, will be deemed to contain a compulsory adjudication scheme in accordance with the Act. The decision of the appointed adjudicator will be enforceable[39] unless and until that decision is challenged by one or other of the parties to the relevant construction contract. Such challenge will have to be by arbitration if the contract contains an arbitration clause, unless both parties agree to use litigation, or by proceedings in the courts. Consequently, C.A.R. insurers now generally require very

---

[38] See Chapter 11, above.
[39] *Macob Civil Engineering Ltd v. Morrison Construction Ltd* [1999] B.L.R. 93.

prompt notification of receipt of an adjudication notice under the Act, and the conduct of proceedings condition will apply to the adjudication so that insurers will have control of the process. It should be noted that the adjudication process is usually to be completed within 28 days and is inquisitorial. It may therefore not fully investigate all the legal and factual issues in the desired detail.

8. WARRANTY COVER AND APPLICATION OF POLICY EXCESS

16–24   In circumstances where a contractor undertakes construction work upon which he provides a guarantee or warranty as to its quality, under which any deficiency will be put right by the contractor, that risk under the guarantee or warranty may also be insured under a contractors' all risks policy, subject to an additional premium being paid. Where such extension of cover is granted, however, the insurer will usually insist on the insured contractor paying the first £x of each and every claim. It therefore becomes important to consider this "excess" which must be borne by the insured.

16–25   In *Trollope & Colls Ltd v. Haydon*[40] the insured contractors entered into a contract with a town development corporation for the erection of dwellings with garages and issued their deed of warranty which provided, *inter alia*:

> "**1.** The Contractor . . . HEREBY UNDERTAKES to form construct and build the dwellings and garages. . . with such care and skill as to ensure that the dwellings and garages . . . will be weathertight for a period of at least five years and the Contractor HEREBY WARRANTS that the . . . dwellings and garages will be and remain watertight . . .
> **2.** . . . the Contractor undertakes that if at any time or times any failure or defect shall occur . . . which . . . renders the dwellings and garages or any of them no longer watertight . . . the Contractor will carry out . . . such works . . . to rectify the failure or defect . . . at the Contractors' own expense."

16–26   The defendant insurer agreed to indemnify the plaintiffs against claims arising from the deed of warranty in these terms:

> "**1.** . . . it is understood and agreed that this policy extends to cover all claims and expenses and the like incurred by [the contractors] by reason of signing and arising from the warranty . . . in respect of contract for the erection of [dwellings and garages] . . .
> **2.** It being further understood and agreed that in respect of this Contract only, Underwriters will be liable for all claims up to £100,000 in the aggregate but warranted the contractors shall bear the first £25 of each and every claim."

---

[40] [1977] 1 Lloyd's Rep. 244, CA.

Some two to three years after construction, because of defects in the building, the weather penetrated many dwellings and garages, and the contractors sought to recover under the policy.

The Court of Appeal held that the costs of repairing and correcting the   **16–27** defects were recoverable under the policy, but that each repair to each garage or dwelling was a separate claim upon the contractors and therefore each repair was subject to the £25 excess. The word "claims" in the policy cover did not mean claims on the insurer since the subject matter of the insurance was not only claims by the development corporation, but also "expenses and the like incurred by the Contractors". Accordingly, the true construction and effect of the policy terms was that all costs and expenses incurred by the contractors pursuant to their obligation to the development corporation arising under the deed of warranty in carrying out the work to render watertight any dwelling or garage which had ceased to be weathertight, constituted one separate claim and that the contractors had to bear the first £25 of each such claim.

9. DEFECTIVE OR FAULTY MATERIALS, WORKMANSHIP OR DESIGN

Inclusion of cover

In *Mitchell Conveyor and Transporter Co. Ltd, v. Pulbrook*,[41] the risk was   **16–28** included in the insurance cover by this clause:

> "including any loss for the cost of replacing any defective and/or faulty material or workmanship and/or design or imperfections in the original or substituted construction of the [power station] insured . . ."

The insured claimants were contractors who had undertaken to design and construct a power station and had insured under a contractors' all risks policy. Problems were encountered when granolithic (a mixture of granite chippings and concrete) was laid on top of a covering of dry concrete, the result being some cracking and other areas not adhering to the underlying layer of concrete. Under the building contract the contractor was liable to put these matters right, but the contractor settled this liability for a sum of money rather than put the flooring right. It was this sum that the contractor sought to recover under this clause in the policy. The defendant insurer refused to meet the claim, *inter alia*, on the ground that the defectiveness of the granolithic flooring was due to the nature of the two-to-one mix used (a three-to-one mix was accepted as being more suitable), and such a defect was not embraced by the terms of the clause. Roche J., however, considered that this defence failed because the contractor had agreed that design or plan of work with the richer mixture of granolithic recommended by the employees engineer, and so far as that was the cause of the problem, it was part of the designing or planning of

---

[41] (1933) 45 Ll. L. Rep. 239.

the work which was part of the insured contractor's contract with their employer.[42]

16–29   On occasion, the cover may be extended to include the costs of repairing or replacing the defective parts. The question arose in *Shell (U.K.) Ltd v. C.L.M. Engineering Ltd*[43] as to whether such an extension covered pure economic loss suffered by the insured in repairing defective parts in the carrier pipes containing the flowline bundles of their construction project in the North Sea. The contract between Shell and the defendant contractors specified certain minimum well-fluid arrival temperatures at the Gannet A production platform. In order to ensure that the minimum well-fluid temperatures were achieved, the cavity of the carrier pipes were filled with an insulation medium. The medium chosen was a gel comprising monoethylene glycol, a polysaccharide known commercially as biozan and a stabiliser, EDTA. The carrier pipes containing the flowline bundles were laid between June 30, 1991 and mid-August 1991. The gel was inserted into the flowline bundles in August 1991. A certificate of completion in respect of this work was issued by Shell to the defendants giving a completion date of January 15, 1992, and the first oil was produced in October 1992. In November 1993, Shell began to monitor the arrival temperature of the oil and gas from the flowline bundles, and found that the arrival temperatures were lower than those required by the operating parameters. Shell contended that the insulating gel broke down into hard gel and liquid monoethylene glycol by reason of a fault in the design of the gel by the contractors, or by faulty construction or workmanship.

16–30   Shell's policy of insurance covered physical loss or damage to the insured project works, including that arising from error in design and/or defective construction or workmanship, for the period up to 24 months from September 1992. The relevant further extension provided:

> "This insurance also covers the cost(s) of repairing or replacing any defective part or parts of the property insured arising from fault or error in design or from faulty and/or defective construction or workmanship or materials which occurs during the period of this insurance or manifests itself or is discovered and reported no later than 24 months from September 1993 . . .
>
>   It is understood and agreed with respect to pipelines and flowlines that deformation of any kind shall be covered hereunder whether or not caused by or contributed to by fault or error in design or by faulty and/or defective construction, workmanship or materials . . ."

16–31   Shell's case was that the above extension provided insurance cover for the costs incurred by Shell if it has to repair or replace any part of the property insured which was defective by reason of faulty design, construction or materials irrespective of whether physical loss or damage had been sustained by the insured property. In contrast, the underwriters contended that there was only an indemnity against the cost of repair or replacement of the defective part if the insured property had suffered

---

[42] *ibid.* at 243.
[43] [2000] 1 All E.R. (Comm.) 940.

physical loss or damage as a result of the defect. Shell placed particular emphasis on the use of the word "also" in the further extension of cover, together with the absence of a reference back to the first extension or express limitation to (or even mention of) the need for physical loss or damage. The underwriters', however, placed emphasis on the outcome of Shell's interpretation which they said rendered the policy no less than a guarantee of the contractors' performance.

David Steel J. considered that Shell's construction of the extension of   **16–32** cover involved some considerable straining of the language, for example, the concept of defective materials "which occurs" during the period of the insurance was not easy to grasp. Just as importantly, Shell's analysis gave rise to some surprising results in terms of coverage:

    (i) if the fault occurred during the currency of the policy, the under-writers must provide an indemnity for the cost of replacement regardless of when the fault was discovered, perhaps decades later;

   (ii) if the fault (and in this case not just of design but also of construction or materials) occurred before the inception of the policy, the underwriters must provide an indemnity if, but only if, the fault was discovered prior to September 1995.

On the other hand, the implication of the words "giving rise to physi-   **16–33** cal loss of and/or physical damage" (as in the first part of the extension of cover) before the words "which occurs" in the further extension of cover, gave the remainder of the paragraph its ordinary and natural meaning. It seemed commercially absurd for there to be a disparity of cover between the first extension and the second extension, dependent on whether the fault or defect occurred before or after the inception of the cover. It would also mean that the second extension covered inherent vice and latent defects which were impliedly excluded by section 55 of the Marine Insurance Act 1906, and contrary to an express incorporated exclusion of "loss damage or expenses caused by inherent vice or nature of the subject matter insured." Accordingly, David Steel J. held that the further extension of cover did not embrace pure economic suffered by the insured, Shell, but only losses arising from physical loss or damage to the insured works.

Exclusion of the risk

This risk may be excluded by a term such as: **16–34**

    "This insurance shall not apply to or include:

       (i) cost of making good faulty workmanship or construction;
      (ii) loss or damage arising from faulty design and liabilities resulting therefrom."

That exclusion clause was considered by the High Court of Australia in *Queensland Government Railways and Electric Power Transmission Pty Ltd*

v. Manufacturers' Mutual Insurance Ltd[44] where the claimants had engaged
a contractor to replace a railway bridge built in 1897 which had been swept
away by flood waters. Prismatic piers (similar to the original piers, but
strengthened) were being erected when they were overturned by flood
waters after exceptionally heavy rains. Both the railway authority and the
contractor were named as the insured under a contractors' all risks policy,
and they sought to recover in respect of this loss under the policy, but the
insurers denied liability, contending that the loss was due to the faulty
design of the new piers in that the piers were subjected to greater trans-
verse forces during the flood than had been realised. It was held that the
loss was due to faulty design, for that term was not confined to a personal
failure or non-compliance with standards which would be expected of
designing engineers. The court held[45] that the exclusion was not against
loss from "negligent designing", but against loss from "faulty design", the
latter being more comprehensive than the former.

16–35   A different form of exclusion wording was considered by the Court of
Appeal of British Columbia in *Pentagon Construction (1969) Co. Ltd v.
United States Fidelity and Guaranty Co.*,[46] where the policy provided:

> "Exclusions:
> 7. This insurance does not cover:
>
> (a) loss or damage caused by:
>   (i) faulty or improper material, or
>   (ii) faulty or improper workmanship, or
>   (iii) faulty or improper design."

The insured contractors had agreed to build a sewage treatment plant
for a local authority, and one of the components was a concrete tank. The
plans called for a number of steel struts to be laid across the top of the
tank with each of them welded to a plate let into the concrete wall beneath
it. Before the ends of the struts were welded to the plates, and before any
backfilling had been done, the plaintiffs tested the tank by pouring water
into it. When the level reached 12-and-a-quarter feet, one of the sides of the
tank bulged, and so the tank was ruined. The plaintiff sought to recover the
cost of repairing this damage, but the defendant insurers argued that this
damage was within the exclusion clause provisions (ii) or (iii).

16–36   The court first considered whether the exclusion relating to faulty or
improper design applied, on the common ground that the tank would not
have failed if it had not been tested in the way it was until after the ends
of the struts had been welded in place. The court held that there was no
faulty or improper design. Robertson J. said[47]:

> "My view is that the word 'design' as it is used in the policy expresses a concept
> of the finished product of the work to be done by Pentagon under the contract
> and that that concept finds its expression in the plans and specifications;

---

[44] [1969] 1 Lloyd's Rep. 214.
[45] *ibid.* at 217.
[46] [1978] 1 Lloyd's Rep. 93.
[47] [1978] 1 Lloyd's Rep. 93 at 97.

those plans and specifications themselves are not, however, the design. It follows that detailed instructions of how the work of construction is to be carried out are not part of the design of the tank. Consequently, the lack of instructions as to the order in which the welding and the testing were to be done cannot be faulty or improper design."

If what occurred was not from faulty or improper design, was it excluded as being faulty or improper workmanship? The court held that this exclusion did operate, as explained by Robertson J.[48]:   **16–37**

"There was argument directed in essence to establishing whether or not there was on the part of an employee of Pentagon negligence that caused the failure of the tank. This appeared to be predicated by Pentagon on the idea that 'loss or damage' caused by 'faulty or improper workmanship' had in mind only specific acts that could be characterized as faulty workmanship or improper workmanship, such as manual operations of the artisan . . .

In my view, this was not all that was intended to be comprehended by the words. The workmanship referred to comprehended as well the combination, or conglomeration, of all the skills that were directed to the building of the tank.

What the insurer intended to protect itself by clause 7(a)(ii) was having to compensate the insured for 'loss or damage caused by faulty or improper workmanship' in those simple terms. If there was faulty or improper workmanship by any one person at one or more times, or by any several persons at one or more times, or by a combination of persons at one time or at several times, or otherwise howsoever, and that workmanship caused the loss or damage, the insurance was not to cover the loss or damage. Once it is established that loss or damage in respect of which Pentagon makes a claim to be indemnified was caused by faulty or improper workmanship, it is neither necessary nor proper to inquire further. There it is. The claim is not covered.

The achievement of the result called for by the contract required a number of steps to be taken in a particular sequence; failure to take them in that sequence could constitute faulty or improper workmanship; all too obviously it did so here. It is of no consequence why the proper sequence was not observed, or what individual was to blame for the failure to observe it, or whether he was employed by Pentagon, or that one cannot fix the blame on any particular person. Whatever the reason for it may have been, there was improper workmanship and it caused the damage to the tank."

In *Kier Construction Ltd v. Royal Insurance (U.K.) Ltd*[49] the single site insurance policy excluded the cost of repairing, rectifying or replacing temporary works which were "defective in material or workmanship". The insured had contracted with C.E.G.B. to provide cooling water works for the Sizewell B powerstation. Part of insured contractor's temporary works was the construction of two cofferdams using sheet steel piles. During the course of the works these piles were found to have been damaged and, in consequence, the walls of the cofferdams were not watertight, as they should have been. The damage to the piles was caused by the nature of the soil into which the piles were driven, and it was accordingly held that the   **16–38**

[48] *ibid.* at 98.
[49] (1993) 30 Con. L.R. 45.

loss was not excluded as there was nothing objectively "defective" about the piles or the workmanship.

Exclusion of increased costs due to re-designing property which is defectively designed

16–39   This type of provision has arisen in three cases, although the second case was only concerned with the application of the appropriate deductible to each and every loss. In *Hitchens (Hatfield) Ltd v. Prudential Assurance Co. Ltd,*[50] the Court of Appeal had to consider an exclusion within an inclusion clause. The inclusion clause of the Contractors' Combined Insurance provided that:

> "The Insurer will indemnify the Insured in respect of All Risks of loss and/or damage of whatsoever nature to . . . the Works . . .
> The insurance provided by . . . this Policy includes:
>
> 3. Loss, destruction or damage to the property insured or any part thereof arising out of any defect error or omission in design plan specification material or workmanship subject to the following provisos:
>   (iv) no amount shall be admitted in respect of any increased costs due to redesigning the property insured or any part thereof which is defectively designed."

16–40   During September 1984, the insured claimants were working on the development of a site for residential housing at Filsham Valley, St Leonards-on-Sea. The development was on a sloping site of some nine degrees and in order to build the houses the plaintiffs terraced the site so as to provide four levels of benches increasing the slope between them to 22 degrees. When some of the houses had been built, after heavy rain, there was a series of minor and one large landslip. The houses were not damaged but the benches where further houses were to be built needed to be reinstated. A preliminary point of law was raised upon whether the insurers had to prove that increased costs due to re-designing the benches (which now included drainage and piling to prevent a repeat of slippage) was due to the design of the works being negligent or arrived at with some element of personal failure or non-compliance by the plaintiffs, or whether such costs were automatically excluded by sub-clause (iv) above. Argument centred on whether "defectively designed" in sub-clause (iv) must be construed as referring to negligently designed. The insurers argued that the words merely referred back to the body of the clause where the words "defect in design" were neutral, and meant defective in fact, not negligently defective.

16–41   Both the insured's counsel and the insurers' counsel relied on the decision of the High Court of Australia in *Queensland Government Railway and Electric Transmission Pty Ltd v. Manufacturers Mutual Insurance Ltd,*[51] discussed above, where the wording was "faulty design". The insurers

[50] [1991] 2 Lloyd's Rep. 580, CA.
[51] [1969] 1 Lloyd's Rep. 214.

relied on the decision itself, the insured relied on the difference in the wording and the dicta of Windeyer J. in his judgment. In delivering the Court of Appeal's judgment in favour of the insured's contention, Parker L.J. said that the difference between "faulty design" and "negligent designing" was considered at length in the judgment of Windeyer J. and the entire judgment merited attention, but he found it sufficient to approve two passages from the judgment where Windeyer J. said:

> "Here we are not concerned with the word 'fault' or 'faulty' as an attribute, importing blame, or a person, or a personified thing. We are concerned with the word 'faulty' as descriptive of an inanimate thing. The words 'fault' and 'faulty' then have a different sense. They, again according to their derivation, connote a falling short; but not now a falling short in conduct or behaviour. They designate an objective quality of a thing. It is 'faulty' because it has defects, flaws or deficiencies. This use of the word 'faulty' in relation to a thing is old and quite common. Dr Johnson defined 'faulty' in this sense as meaning:
>
>> 'defective, bad in any respect, not fit for the use intended. The word can be applied not only to concrete things, but also to plans or designs to be used to produce intended results . . .'
>
> It seems to me that into the question of whether they were of faulty design there has been intruded unnecessarily a consideration of whether the faults of the design were the result of fault in the designer. In other words, fault in the sense of shortcoming in the static quality and character of a thing has become involved with fault in the sense of shortcomings in conduct and action.
>
> The case for the respondents was not, I think, advanced by comparison of 'faulty design' and 'faulty workmanship', also used in the policy. I do not think that either phrase can be used to expand or contract the effect of the other. Indeed I think rather that, properly construed, they illustrate the very distinction to which I have referred. Faulty workmanship I take to be a reference to the manner in which something was done, to fault on the part of a workman or workmen. A faulty design, on the other hand, is a reference to a thing. If the words were 'faulty designing' the two phrases might perhaps be comparable: but the words are 'faulty design'. I think that, reading those words in their ordinary meaning, the collapse of the piers was the result of their design being faulty."

Parker L.J. considered proviso (iv) was directed to costs due to "redesigning" what had been "defectively designed", and the use of the word "re-designing" appeared to him to point to personal activity or conduct, and he could see no reason to hold that the following words in proviso (iv), namely "defectively designed", should be construed differently. Both "designing" and "designed" were parts of a verb referring to the designer's activity rather than the inanimate product of his work.[52] Moreover, Parker L.J. considered that the plain purpose of the all risks cover, as demonstrated by the opening words of the relevant sections (*e.g.* clause 3, above), was that the insurers should be liable for the full costs of reinstatement of loss, etc., due to fault, error, etc., in design, plan, etc. He could see no reason in the light of the changed wording of proviso (iv),   **16–42**

[52] [1991] 2 Lloyd's Rep. 580 at 585.

which referred to the activity of design, to conclude that the intention was to exclude any increased costs due to re-designing even where the original fault in design was not negligent and at least some reason to conclude that the insurers' intention was to exclude such costs where the original fault in design was negligent.[53]

16-43   In the second case, *Mitsubishi Electric (U.K.) Ltd v. Royal London Insurance (U.K.) Ltd & others,*[54] the dispute was not about whether the works of repair comprised additional costs of improvement to the specification (which were excepted from the exclusion), but about how the deductible of £250,000 was to be applied. The insured were engaged to carry out the design, manufacture and installation of 94 essentially identical toilet modules required for a new building. They carried out the work, but after about a year, the wall tiles and floor coverings started coming away from the installed modules. The fault was traced to the cementitious board to which they were attached, this board being unable to withstand the changes of temperature and moisture to which it was exposed. All 94 toilet modules required expensive remedial work by the insured. The question was whether the deductible had to be applied only once to the total sum of the remedial works, or applied 94 times so that the insurers were under no liability.

16-44   The C.A.R. policy excluded:

> "c) the costs necessary to replace or rectify any defect in design plan specification materials or workmanship but should damage result from such defect this exception shall be limited to the additional costs of improvement to the design plan or specification . . .
> f) the Deductibles as expressed in the Schedule."

The deductible provision provided, *inter alia*:

> "(1) The first £250,000 of each and every loss in respect of any component part which is defective in design plan specification materials or workmanship . . ."

The Court of Appeal held that "loss" in the deductible provision must refer to an insured loss because the deductible could not apply to an uninsured loss. Further, that the words "any component part which is defective in design plan specification materials or workmanship" could only apply to the cementitious board, not to the toilet modules, and the insurers' counsel actually conceded this upon reflection. Finally, that the ordinary meaning of the deductible clause would identify the cementitious board as the defective component or "component part" in this case, and "it must on a common sense view be regarded as one defective component or component part, not 94".[55]

16-45   The third case is *Cementation Piling and Foundations Ltd v. Aegon Insurance Co. Ltd and Commercial Union Insurance Co. plc.*[56] The first

---

[53] *ibid.* at 586.
[54] [1994] 2 Lloyd's Rep. 249, CA.
[55] *ibid.* at 253, *per* Hirst L.J.
[56] [1995] 1 Lloyd's Rep. 97, CA.

defendant insurers provided a guarantee policy to various parties involved in a project, and were liable to pay if the insured could not recover under a separate policy with the second defendant insurers (C.U.). The C.U. policy was called "Project All Risks. Public Liability. Non Negligent Indemnity Insurance", and Section 1 covered "physical loss of or damage to the property insured howsoever caused" during the period of insurance. Exception 2 to this Section provided:

> "The Insurers shall not be liable in respect of the cost of replacing or recti-fying defects in design, materials or workmanship unless the property insured suffers actual loss, destruction or damage as a result of such defect. However additional costs of introducing improvements, betterments or corrections in the rectification of the design, material or workmanship caus-ing such loss or damage shall always be excluded."

The insured subcontractors were contracted to carry out, complete and maintain bored, piling and continuous diaphragm walls forming part of a series of quays to be constructed within the existing docks at Barrow-in-Furness. The whole project included the filling and reclaiming of a redun-dant part of one of the docks. This area was reclaimed from the sea by depositing pumped sand dredged from Morecambe Bay to form a land area or berm some seven hectares in area protruding 2.5 metres above the sea.

The diaphragm walls were constructed by excavating cavities in the sand **16–46** in the precise shape of the concrete sections which would form the diaphragm walls of the dock. As the excavations were carried out, the cavities were continuously filled with liquid bentonite, which maintained the integrity of the cavity. Steel reinforcement cages were lowered into the cavity, which was then filled with liquid concrete through a "tremi" pipe at the foot of the cavity. At the joints between the sections one metre side panels were cast in such a shape as to enable the next panel to abut and provide a tight fit behind the diaphragm wall in the finished dock. Upon completion of the sections, the sand in the centre was dredged out to a depth of 19 metres and removed, allowing seawater to enter and take its place. It was then found that quantities of sand fill, which had previously been placed in the area retained by the walls, had escaped into the newly constructed docks. It was discovered that, in a number of places, there were gaps and voids between adjacent panels, which had permitted sand to escape. There were also places where the steel reinforcement for the panels were exposed, or where the reinforcement was inadequately covered by concrete.

The subcontractors were obliged to carry out works to remedy these **16–47** matters. It was accepted by the parties that the need for these works arose from defects in design, materials and workmanship. The losses suffered by the subcontractors were of three types

(1) rectification of the gaps and/or voids in the diaphragm walls;
(2) removal of the sand fill and the dock bed; and
(3) grouting and filling behind the diaphragm walls of the voids from which the sand fill had escaped.

The issue for decision was whether the costs of (1), amounting to £442,000, were covered by the policy. C.U. admitted that the costs of (2) and (3) were covered. Upon C.U.'s appeal, the Court of Appeal, despite finding it a "perplexing document",[57] upheld the first instance decision[58] that the berm was part of the insured property and it had been damaged by the escape of the sand fill. Further, that it was impossible to say that the berm had been repaired when the spaces left by the escaping sand had been filled, since that sand was bound to escape through the holes in the wall which had not been filled. Accordingly, the cost of remedying the defects in the wall was part of the indemnity due from the insurers in respect of "physical damage to the property".

10. NON-DISCLOSURE OF MATERIAL FACT

16–48   There is judicial support for the view that an insurer cannot complain of non-disclosure of the full terms of the construction contract, even if it contains unusual provisions, because it is evident from the nature of the policy sought by the contractor that there is a contract, and, having been put on notice, the insurer should ask to see the contract if he is concerned as to its terms and conditions.[59] Where an annual policy is issued, it may well expressly provide that particular types of contract must be disclosed and the agreement of the underwriter obtained before that contract risk will be covered. If the insurer seeks to avoid liability subsequently on the ground of non-compliance with this provision, the insurer will have to prove, of course, that the particular contract came within the exclusion clause.

16–49   In *Rowlinson Construction Ltd v. Insurance Co. of North America (U.K.) Ltd*,[60] the annual policy provided:

> "9. Special Category Contracts: Unless the estimated value of the Contract is below £10,000 the Insured shall provide the Company with full details in advance of the commencement of operations under any contract involving:
>
> (1) Bridges or other work in or over water or tidal or coastal areas;. . . and shall pay such additional premium and bear any amended Excess as the Company may require, if the risk in connection with the Contract is to be insured hereunder."

16–50   The insured claimant had not given notice as required under this provision and sought approval of a contract where land was to be developed, and the site boundary's existing retaining wall on a river bank was to be repaired and renewed. The wall collapsed during the contract period and the insured sought to recover the cost of repairing the wall, but the defendant

---

[57] *ibid.* at 102, *per* Sir Ralph Gibson.
[58] [1993] 1 Lloyd's Rep. 526.
[59] *Mitchell Conveyor and Transporter Co. Ltd v. Pullbrook* (1933) 45 Ll. L. Rep. 239 at 244, *per* Roche J.
[60] [1981] 1 Lloyd's Rep. 332.

insurers contended, *inter alia*, that the building contract had fallen within the Special Category Contracts provisions, had not been approved, and that they were therefore not liable for this loss. This defence failed on the ground that the notice provision did not apply to the works because they were not within the defined "Special Category Contracts". *Per* Lloyd J.[61]:

> "The question of construction is whether this contract involved 'bridges or other work in or over water or tidal or coastal areas.' To my mind it is plain that it did not. True, there was a river along one boundary, washing the retaining wall on its southern side. Though it is called a river, it was . . . Little more than a muddy brook. But even if it had been a substantial river, no part of the wall was built in or over the river. It was beside the river, not in it or over it. So . . . I would hold that this contract did not involve work in or over water."

An insurer can, however, complain of non-disclosure of facts where a **16–51** specific, detailed proposal for insurance of building works has been made, and, before issue of the policy, the proposers decide to change of construction of the foundations given in the proposal. Thus, in *St Paul Fire and Marine Insurance Co. (U.K.) Ltd v. McConnell Dowell Constructors Ltd*[62] the insurers successfully rescinded a C.A.R. policy. The defendants had proposed for the insurance relating to the construction of new parliament buildings in the Marshall Islands, New Zealand. Various schematic drawings and plans for the project, showing the projected buildings had piled foundations, were forwarded to the insurers on January 9, 1990, together with a quotation slip which, *inter alia*, referred to the floor slab being supported "on approximately 50 piles 450 mm & 350 mm in diameter". The lead insurer initialled the slip on January 15, 1990, with cover to commence on February 16, 1990, for 22 months. In fact, on November 13, 1989, the defendants had decided that piled foundations were not needed and that they would proceed with spread foundations, but this was never communicated to the insurers. On December 21, 1990, the it was discovered that the partially completed buidings were affected by subsidence. The insurers sought a declaration that they were entitled to rescind the policy *ab initio* on the ground of non-disclosure of the material fact of the change in foundation design.

The Court of Appeal upheld the decision of Potter J.[63] that the evidence **16–52** given by the actual underwriters established beyond doubt that if they had been informed not merely that the project included piled foundations, but that the ground conditions were questionable, notwithstanding that spread foundations were proposed to be used, on no view would they have underwritten the insurance at the same premium on terms which included the subsidence risk. The ground conditions were such as to make it questionable whether shallow/spread foundations, without additional safeguards, were an acceptable alternative to deep foundations. These facts were

[61] [1981] 1 Lloyd's Rep. 332 at 335.
[62] [1996] 1 All E.R. 96, CA.
[63] (1993) 37 Con. L.R. 96.

matters which would certainly have affected the prudent insurer's estimate
or appreciation of the risk proposed, and were therefore material facts
which had not been disclosed, or, alternatively, misrepresented facts.

11. INCREASE IN RISK

16–53   An insurer cannot avoid liability under a contractors' all risks policy by
pleading that the risk of the contractor incurring liability has been
increased after the policy was issued by variations being made, *e.g.* in floor
covering mixes. As has been explained by Roche J., the nature of this type
of policy foresees that variations may be made[64]:

> "I am unable to assent to the proposition that the mere fact that the risk
> increased after the policy was effected covering that risk, avoids the policy
> or frees the underwriter from liability. If authority were needed for quite
> such a universal proposition, the case of *Pim v. Reid*,[65] is sufficient authority.
> Of course, it depends what is the subject matter of the insurance and what
> are the conditions of the insurance; . . . if there was an insurance here that
> the underwriter would insure the work to be done by the plaintiff company
> under the contract, whether by express words or necessary implication, in
> terms that the works were to be done in a certain way and no other, then the
> variations in the works might either avoid the policy or render the loss from
> the increased risk irrecoverable. But so far from that being the case, there is,
> as might be expected in a construction contract of this magnitude, express
> provision for all sorts of variations; and accordingly I do not find, either by
> express words or by implication, any provision that the variation of the
> works, although it may increase the risk attaching to the work, will avoid the
> policy."

---

[64] *Mitchell Conveyor and Transport Co. Ltd v. Pullbrook* (1933) 45 Ll. L. Rep. 239 at 245.
[65] (1843) 6 Man. & G. 1.

PART IV

CLAIMS

CHAPTER 17

THE LOSS

1. LOSS

Introduction

It has been said that[1]:   17–01

> "Mere temporary deprivation would not under ordinary circumstances constitute a loss. On the other hand complete deprivation amounting to a certainty that the goods could never be recovered is not necessary to constitute a loss. It is between these two extremes that the difficult cases lie, and no assistance can be derived from putting cases which are clearly on the one side or the other of the dividing line between the two. If assistance is to be obtained at all from considering a hypothetical case it can only be done by taking one which raises somewhat similar considerations to the case which [the court has] to decide."

Webster J. referred to this *dictum* in *Webster v. General Accident Fire and*   17–02
Life Assurance Corp. Ltd[2] which concerned a claim for the loss of a car under a motor policy. A fraudster had obtained possession of the insured car from the insured upon representing that he had a buyer for it. Having driven it away the fraudster promptly sold it at auction and kept the proceeds. The insured had approached the police, who had told him that any attempt to recover the car would be unavailing. The insurers took the point that even if there was a prima facie loss within the policy, there was, on the facts, no loss proved because the insured at all times knew where the car was and that he had not shown that it was irrecoverable. Parker J. rejected the insurer's contention, holding that it was never necessary for a claimant to prove that in all circumstances the chattel is irrecoverable. Every case would depend on its own facts, but that an insured was not entitled to sit by and do nothing. Equally, though, he was not bound to launch into legal proceedings or if necessary carry them to the House of Lords. The correct test is whether, after all reasonable steps to recover the insured property have been taken by the insured, recovery is uncertain.

The test of the recovery of the insured property being uncertain was   17–03
also applied in *Holmes v. Payne*[3] when a pearl necklace was held to have been lost within the meaning of the policy, when the insured had diligently searched for it but could not find it.

There is no loss of insured property under a theft policy, though, if the property has been confiscated because the insured has failed to pay the requisite import duty.[4] Nor is there a loss under an "all risks" policy where

---

[1] *Moore v. Evans* [1917] 1 K.B. 458 at 471, *per* Banks L.J.; affirmed [1918] A.C. 185, HL., CA.
[2] [1953] 1 Q.B. 520.
[3] [1930] 2 K.B. 301.
[4] *Geismar v. Sun Alliance & London Insurance Ltd* [1978] 1 Q.B. 383.

goods were sent abroad and seized there, but kept in safe custody, and
there was no reason to suppose that they would be irrecoverable once war
between the two countries concerned ceased.[5] On the other if goods,
insured against "all risks", are consigned abroad and are wrongfully seized
by persons in that other country, as judged by the law of that country,
there will be a loss within the policy, for there will have been a "fortuitous
occurrence" or an "accidental loss".[6]

2. PROXIMATE CAUSE OF LOSS

17–04   An insurer usually only contracts to indemnify the insured against loss
or damage caused by the perils specified in the policy, and it is therefore
essential that the loss is shown to have been brought about by an insured
peril. In other words, "the insurer promises to pay in a certain event and
in no other, namely, in case of loss caused in a certain way, and the question is whether the loss was caused in that way, and whether the event
occurred".[7]

17–05   The "cause" of a loss is that which is the effective or dominant cause of
the occurrence,[8] to be decided on common sense principles.[9] This principle
is of great antiquity, as was admirably explained by Lord Shaw in the leading marine insurance case[10]:

> "The doctrine of cause has been since the time of Aristotle, and the famous
> category of material, formal, efficient and final causes, one involving the
> subtlest of distinctions. The doctrine applied in these to existences rather
> than occurrences. But the idea of the cause of an occurrence or the produc-
> tion of an event or the bringing about of a result is an idea perfectly famil-
> iar to the mind and to the law, and it is in connection with that that the
> notion of *proxima causa* is introduced. Of this, I will venture to remark that
> one must be careful not to lay the accent upon the word 'proximate' in such
> a sense as to lose sight of or destroy altogether the idea of cause itself. The
> true and overruling principle is to look at a contract as a whole, and to ascer-
> tain what the parties to it really meant. What was it which brought about the
> loss, the event, the calamity, the accident? And this not in an artificial sense,
> but in that real sense which parties to a contract must have had in their
> minds when they spoke of cause at all. To treat *proxima causa* as the cause
> which is nearest in time is out of the question. Causes are spoken of as if
> they were as distinct from one another as beads in a row or links in a chain,
> but — if this metaphysical topic has to be referred to — it is not wholly so.
> The chain of causation is a handy expression, but the figure is inadequate.
> Causation is not a chain but a net. At each point influences, forces, events,
> precedent and simultaneous, meet, and the radiation from each point

---

[5] *Moore v. Evans* [1918] A.C. 185, HL.

[6] *London and Provincial Leather Processes Ltd v. Hudson* [1939] 2 K.B. 724.

[7] *Becker, Gray & Co. v. London Assurance Corp.* [1918] A.C. 101 at 113, *per* Lord Sumner, HL.

[8] *Wayne Tank and Pump Co. Ltd v. Employers' Liability Assurance Corp. Ltd* [1974] Q.B.
57 at 66, *per* Lord Denning M.R., CA.

[9] *ibid.*; *Boiler Inspection and Insurance Co. of Canada v. Sherwin-Williams Co. of Canada
Ltd* [1951] A.C. 319, PC.; *J.J. Lloyd Instruments Ltd v. Northern Star Insurance Co. Ltd* [1987]
1 Lloyd's Rep. 32 at 37, col.2, *per* Lawton L.J., CA.

[10] *Leyland Shipping Co. Ltd v. Norwich Union Fire Insurance Society Ltd* [1918] A.C. 350 at
368–371, HL.

extends infinitely. At the point where these various influences meet it is for the judgment as upon a matter of fact to declare which of the causes thus joined at the point of effect was the proximate and which was the remote cause. What does 'proximate' here mean? To treat proximate cause as if it was the cause which is proximate in time is, as I have said, out of the question. The cause which is truly proximate is that which is proximate in efficiency. That efficiency may have been preserved although other causes may meantime have sprung up, which have yet not destroyed it, or truly impaired it, and it may culminate in a result of which it still remains the real efficient cause to which the event can be ascribed . . .

In my opinion, accordingly, proximate cause is an expression referring to the efficiency as an operating factor upon the result. Where various factors or causes are concurrent, and one has to be selected, the matter is determined as one of fact, and the choice falls upon the one to which may be variously ascribed the qualities of reality, predominance, efficiency. Fortunately, this much would appear to be in accordance with the principles of a plain business transaction and it is not at all foreign to the law.

. . . The true efficient cause never loses its hold. The result is produced, a result attributable in common language to the casualty as a cause, and this result, proximate as well as continuous in its efficiency, properly meets . . . the language of the expression 'proximately caused'."

The "proximate cause" rule seeks to do no more than to carry into effect **17–06** the intention of the two parties — insurer and insured — to the insurance contract, impliedly if necessary[11]:

"It must be admitted that the terminology of causation in English Law is by no means ideal. It would be better for a little plain English. I think 'direct cause' would be a better expression than *causa proxima*. Logically, the antithesis of proximate cause is not real cause but remote cause. There is no mystery about it. Cause and effect are the same for underwriters as for other people. Proximate cause is not a device to avoid the trouble of discovering the real cause or the 'common sense cause', and, though it has been and always should be rigorously applied in insurance cases, it helps one side no oftener than it helps the other. I believe it to be nothing more or less than the real meaning of the parties to a contract of insurance . . . I daresay few assured have any distinct view of their own on this point, and might not even see it if it were explained to them: but what they intend individually does not depend upon what they understand individually. If it is implied in the nature of the bargain, then they intend it in law; just as much as if they said it in words. I think that it is so implied. Indemnity involves it apart from decisions. In effect it is the act of the parties."

Exclusion of the normal rule

Being a rule derived from the presumed intention of the parties to the **17–07** insurance contract, it is open to the parties to adopt express language in that contract to oust the "proximate cause" rule and thus alter the scope of the indemnity provided by the insurer. The courts have considered wording in policies where exclusion related to claims "directly or indirectly" caused by specified factors. Thus, in *Coxe v. Employers' Liability Assurance Corpn Ltd*[12] a personal accident policy excluded death "directly

---

[11] *Becker, Gray & Co. v. London Assurance Corp.* [1918] A.C. 101 at 112, *per* Lord Sumner.
[12] [1916] 2 K.B. 629.

or indirectly caused by . . . war". The insured was killed by a train when walking along a railway line in wartime. He was an army officer and was on duty at this time, on his way to speak to guards along the track, and the court refused to upset the arbitrator's finding that his death was indirectly caused by war, and held that the proximate cause rule was excluded by use of this wording[13]:

> ". . . I find it impossible to reconcile those words with the maxim *causa proxima non remota spectatur*. If you are to say that the proximate cause, whether direct or indirect, is to be looked at, it does not appear to me that you are making a consistent and intelligent result. I do not understand what is the indirect cause, and the only effect one can give to these words is to say that the maxim *causa proxima non remota spectatur* is excluded, and you may go further back in the chain of causation than the proximate and immediate cause."

Exclusions

17–08   Similarly, an exclusion may be of very wide effect. Where a burglary and theft policy covered business premises in Dublin, subject to a proviso that "this insurance does not cover loss directly or indirectly caused by or happening through or in consequence of . . . riots", it was held in *London and Lancashire Fire Insurance Co. Ltd v. Bolands Ltd*[14] by the House of Lords that this proviso was not confined to a case where the theft was facilitated by an antecedent or simultaneous riot, but included a case where the theft itself, in the manner in which it was conducted, constituted a riot at law.

17–09   Again, in *Oei v. Foster (Formerly Crawford) and Eagle Star Insurance Co.*,[15] the policy gave an indemnity to the insured persons in respect of damage to property caused by accident through their negligence. An exclusion, however, stated that the indemnity did not apply to damage arising "directly or indirectly from ownership or occupation of land". In Oei's absence, Foster was sleeping in Oei's property and ate some meals there. One day, a fire broke out in the kitchen caused by fat being ignited when the cooker was left switched on, and Oei sued Foster for the damage. Foster brought his insurers into the action, but the insurers defended the claim on the basis of the exclusion. Glidewell J. (as he was) held that the exclusion applied[16]:

> "that occupation was of itself a cause, albeit an indirect cause, of the damage. I take the view that it was an indirect cause on that state of the facts. I do so for this reason, that in my view cooking meals is a necessary, indeed, inevitable incident of the (F's) occupation of the house and thus, in my view, it can properly be said that if the damage was caused by (F) leaving the cooker turned on when she went out of the house then that damage did arise indirectly from her, and indeed her husband's occupation of the Oei's house. I am seeking to emphasize that there could well be circumstances in which,

[13] *ibid.* at 631, *per* Scrutton J. (as he then was).
[14] [1924] A.C. 836, HL.
[15] [1982] 2 Lloyd's Rep. 170.
[16] *ibid.* at 174.

on the facts, the damage would not arise merely from the occupation by other persons of the house; there might be no sufficiently clear cause or connection between the occupation and the damage and then it would be purely a matter of history. But on the facts of this case I take the view that such a connection, albeit indirect, is made out."

3. TWO PROXIMATE CAUSES OF LOSS

Liability insurances

Porter J., in the professional indemnity insurance case of *Davies v.* **17–10**
Hosken[17] considered that it would be "much too subtle" to say that the insured's right to recover under the policy depended upon what form of action the clients chose to take when they sued him, for he felt that English law is not "so narrow as that". The insured's clerk had set out to make a positive act of stealing clents' money, so Porter J. held that this positive act did not come within the insuring words of "neglect, omission or error" and was therefore outside the scope of the policy indemnity.

Shortly after, in *Goddard and Smith v. Frew*,[18] another case concerning professional indemnity insurance, the insured's agent had not accounted for rent monies by him on behalf of the insured. The Court of Appeal took the view that whether or not the claim was covered was to be determined by the Court determining the "real" or "proximate" cause of the liability to the insured's clients. Here, the Court was in no doubt that that was embezzlement by the insured's agent, and such dishonesty was not insured under the policy's terms, which referred to "any act" or "omission" by the insured or his agent.

Subsequently, Devlin J. (as he then was) distinguished the Court of **17–11**
Appeal's decision in *Goddard and Smith v. Frew* (above) on the ground that the Court of Appeal had not there "had to distinguish between two suggested causes" of the loss. What is confusing about Devlin J.'s judgment is that he concluded that the Court of Appeal in *Goddard and Smith v. Frew* would have distinguished between those two causes "by ascertaining which of the two causes was the proximate cause",[19] but Devlin J. did not undertake such an exercise himself. Instead, Devlin J. let the form of the claim against the insured prevail, and, because the claimants raised three causes of action in their pleadings — negligence, monies had and received, and conversion — he held that this was a "mixed" claim which was not covered by the professional indemnity policy[20]:

". . . I have reached the conclusion that there is in fact a simpler and more effective test which is the correct one. It depends simply on the true construction of the policy. Businessmen often want to write into a document words which they think will amplify its meaning, but which lawyers reject as superfluous; nevertheless, the writing in of superfluities sometimes helps to clarify questions of construction. If a layman wanted a phrase such as

[17] [1937] 3 All E.R. 192 at 194.
[18] [1939] 4 All E.R. 358, CA.
[19] *ibid.* at 58.
[20] *ibid.*

'claims in respect of negligence' to be altered to read 'claims in respect of negligence only' or 'claims in respect of negligence but not in respect of fraud,' a lawyer would tell him that these additions were superfluous, since negligence meant negligence and nothing else and did not include fraud. That is plainly enough the effect of the decision in *Goddard and Smith v. Frew*.[21] But if words such as these were there, they would serve to show that a claim in respect of negligence and in respect of fraud is excluded from the description in the policy. To come within the policy the character of the claim must be unmixed. It must be negligence alone. Applying this test, which I think is the right one, the claim in this case is outside the policy."

17–12   The need for the court to analyse a claimant's claim against the insured to determine whether the liability policy covers that claim, was accepted by Mustill J. (as he then was) in *Rigby v. Sun Alliance & London Insurance Ltd*,[22] rejecting that the court could do this "simply by taking the pleadings in the action at their face value. Similarly, Bingham J. (as he then was) in *Johns v. Kelly*,[23] considered that an insured's right to recover under his professional indemnity policy was not governed or limited "by the natureof the claims made against them". The test was rather whether an insured liability was the "direct, effective and proximate" cause of the claimant's loss, even if there were other causes of that loss.

In *Total Graphics Ltd v. A.G.F. Insurance Ltd*,[24] Mance J. (as he then was) does not appear to have been referred to the above decisions except for *West Wake Price & Co. v. Ching*, but still concluded that he had to determine the "dominant, real or effective cause" of the claims against the insured.[25] The dominance of the view that the substance, not the form, of the claimant's claim against the insured has now been confirmed by the Court of Appeal in the public liability policy case of *P&O Steam Navigation Co. v. Youell*,[26] the facts of which are discussed, in Chapter 6, above.

Excluded causes in liability insurances
17–13   There will be few problems in practice relating to the proximate cause of a liability incurred by the insured because the insurance indemnity is granted with reference to such sums as the insured is legally liable to pay another party by reason of a peril, *e.g.* negligence, included within the scope of the policy issued to him by the insurer, then, prima facie, the insured is entitled to an indemnity. Difficulties will tend to be encountered, though, in respect of the operation of exclusion clauses in the policy, *i.e.* although the insured has incurred a legal liability, that liability was incurred in a manner excluded from the scope of the policy. The test is whether the excluded peril was, or was not, the dominant and effective cause of the insured incurring liability to a third party. This is demonstrated by the Court of Appeal's decision in *Wayne Tank and Pump Co.*

[21] [1939] 4 All E.R. 358, CA.
[22] [1980] 1 Lloyd's Rep. 359 at 362.
[23] [1986] 1 Lloyd's Rep. 468.
[24] [1997] 1 Lloyd's Rep. 599
[25] *ibid.* at 606.
[26] [1997] 2 Lloyd's Rep. 136, CA.

Ltd v. Employers Liability Association Corp. Ltd,[27] where the insured claimants were liable to customers of theirs to whom they had supplied certain electrical equipment which caught fire. The fire had broken out after one of the insured's employees had switched on the equipment and left it unattended all night, despite the fact that it had not yet been tested. The insured claimed under their public liability insurance in respect of their liability to the insured, but the defendant insurers relied on an exclusion of liability incurred by the insured consequent on "damage caused by the nature or condition of any goods . . . supplied by" them. The Court of Appeal held that this exclusion clause operated because the dominant and effective cause of the loss was the nature of the goods supplied (*i.e.* the electrical equipment), rather than the negligence of the employee leaving the equipment switched on overnight without having tested it.

Lord Denning M.R. pointed out that the dominant and effective cause **17–14** is to be determined "by common sense" — it is not necessarily the cause which is latest in time.[28] Roskill L.J. said[29]:

> "In some cases no doubt the event which 'triggers off' the untoward consequences of the defective state of the apparatus . . . may be so far removed, either in time or in nature or for some other reason as to break the chain of causation. But in the present case I think this apparatus was so defective that what happened thereafter, though aggravating the defects and precipitating the ultimate result, never prevented the defective nature of the apparatus from being the effective cause of the loss."

Property insurances

On very few occasions will the commonsense test of causation produce **17–15** a combined direct cause of loss of or damage to property, but should this test provide such a conclusion, "for the purposes of a contract of insurance, it is sufficient if an insured event is, in this sense, a co-operating cause of the loss".[30] Although no reported case has found such co-incident causes of a loss or damage to property, this proposition is founded on the judgment of Lindley L.J. in a marine insurance case concerning the sinking of a ship when temporary repairs to damage below the water-line proved ineffective and the Court of Appeal held that this loss of the ship was covered by the policy[31]:

> "The sinking of this ship was proximately caused by the internal injuries produced by the collision, and by water reaching and getting through the injured parts whilst she was being towed to a place of repair. The sinking was due as much to one of these causes as to the other; each was as much a proximate cause of her sinking as the other, and it would, in my opinion, be contrary to good sense to hold that the damage by the sinking was not

[27] [1974] Q.B. 57, CA.
[28] *ibid.* at 66. See also *J.J. Lloyd Instruments Ltd v. Northern Star Insurance Co. Ltd* [1987] 1 Lloyd's Rep. 32 at 39, col.2, *per* Slade L.J., CA.
[29] *ibid.* at 74.
[30] *Heskell v. Continental Express Ltd.* [1950] 1 All E.R. 1033 at 1048, *per* Devlin J. (as he then was).
[31] *Reischer v. Berwick* [1894] 2 Q.B. 548 at 551, CA. See also *Lloyd (J.J.) Instruments Ltd v. Northern Star Insurance Co. Ltd* [1987] 1 Lloyd's Rep. 32, CA.

covered by this policy . . . I feel the difficulty in expressing in precise language the distinction between causes which co-operate in producing a given result. When they succeed each other at intervals which can be observed it is comparatively easy to distinguish them and to trace their respective effects; but under other circumstances it may be impossible to do so."

17–16   Damage to a plate glass window effected by a mob attracted to a fire in a neighbouring property is not damage proximately caused by fire,[32] nor is damage caused to insured premises by atmospheric concussion resulting from a fire and explosion in neighbouring premises.[33] On the other hand damage caused by walls of a burning building collapsing,[34] or by water being used to extinguish the fire,[35] or by other measures necessarily and reasonably taken to check the spread of the fire,[36] is damage proximately caused by fire, as may be loss by theft of goods being salved from a fire.[37] A civil commotion in the neighbourhood may entitle a court to find by inference that a loss by, apparently, theft, was actually caused by reason of that civil commotion.[38]

17–17   The difference between one circumstance being a cause of the loss, and another being merely a circumstance facilitating that cause's effect is illustrated by *Winicofsky v. Army and Navy General Assurance Association Ltd*[39] where the insured claimed for the theft of goods, stolen whilst he was sheltering in a shelter during a wartime air-raid, under a burglary policy covering his shop. Bray J. held that the insurers could not rely on an exclusion clause providing that they would not be liable for "loss or damage occasioned by hostilities, riots or civil commotion, or for loot, sack, or pillage in connection therewith". The burglary was not a loss caused by hostilities, though no doubt an air-raid, which was an act of hostilities, produced a state of affairs which made things easier for the burglars. Moreover, nor did Bray J. consider that the burglary could properly be regarded as "loot, sack, or pillage" in connection with hostilities, not least because these descriptive words referred to something much more than one isolated case of burglary.

Excluded causes in property insurances

17–18   As with liability insurances, if the court can determine that an excluded cause is the dominant and effective cause of loss or damage, although

---

[32] *Marsden v. City and County Assurance Co.* (1865) L.R. 1 C.P. 232.

[33] *Everett v. London Assurance* (1865) 19 C.B.(n.s.) 126.

[34] *Re Hooley Hill Rubber and Chemical Co. Ltd and Royal Insurance Co. Ltd* [1920] 1 K.B. 257 at 271, *per* Scrutton L.J., CA; *Johnston v. West of Scotland Insurance Co.* 1828 7 Sh. (Ct of Sess.) 52.

[35] *Ahmedbhoy Habbibhoy v. Bombay Fire and Marine Insurance Co.* (1912) 107 L.T. 668, PC.

[36] *Stanley v. Weston Insurance Co.* (1868) L.R. 3 Exch. 71; approved *Symington & Co. v. Union Insurance Society of Canton* (1928) 97 L.J.K.B. 646, CA; and *Curtis's and Harvey (Canada) Ltd v. North British and Mercantile Insurance Co.* [1921] 1 A.C. 303, PC.

[37] *McGibbon v. Queen Insurance Co.* (1866) 10 L.C.J. 227; *Harris v. London and Lancashire Fire Insurance Co.* (1866) 10 L.C.J. 268.

[38] *Cooper v. General Accident Fire and Life Assurance Corp. Ltd* (1923) 13 Ll. L. Rep. 219, HL; *Motor Union Insurance Co. Ltd v. Boggan* (1923) 130 L.T. 588, HL.

[39] (1919) 88 L.J.K.B. 1111.

there are other insured causes contributing to the occurrence of loss and damage, the whole loss or damage is excluded. Conversely, if the insured peril is the dominant and effective cause of the loss or damage, the insured is entitled to recover under the policy.[40] Different considerations apply, though, to circumstances where a property loss or material damage occurring to insured property is truly the product of two causes, joint and simultaneous, one of which is expressly excluded by the policy. In this situation, the insurers will have the benefit of the exclusion and the loss is not apportioned, but excluded in whole.[41] Thus, where a burglary policy excluded claims "for loss by theft, robbery, or misappropriation by members of the assured's . . . staff", and jewellery was stolen from the assured's shop by thieves admitted by H, a member of the assured's staff, the Court of Appeal held that the whole loss was excluded and the Court would take no account of the fact that the thieves physically removed the jewellery and not H. As Cozens-Hardy M.R. explained[42]:

"I think that this is a case in which H was actually guilty of theft, and that the loss has been occasioned by theft by H, one of the plaintiff's staff. Then it was said that you must in some way apportion the loss; that it was not all due to H; but that it was, in fact, more due to the other men who came in with their tools and carried off the jewels in sacks or other receptables. I entirely decline to follow that. I do not think that the doctrine of asportation[43] ought to be applied in a case of this kind. H was a thief, the loss was owing to his theft; the case falls within the proviso, and the underwriters are not liable."

4. DELIBERATE ACTS OF THE INSURED

Insurance is against fortuitous events only, and a wilful or deliberate act **17–19** by the insured (as against negligence) means that the insured has not merely exposed the insured property to the chance of injury, or himself to a liability to a third party, he has caused the loss himself[44] and may not recover under the policy. Lord Atkin has stated that this is on the principle of public policy, as well as on ordinary principles of insurance law that an insured cannot by his own deliberate act cause the event upon which the insurance money is payable, for the insurers will be taken not to have agreed to pay on that happening.[45]

A more obvious example of the insured being debarred from recovering an indemnity under an insurance is the insured burning down his own

[40] *Martini Investments v. McGuin* [2000] 2 Lloyd's Rep. 313 at 314, col.2, *per* Timothy Walker J.
[41] *Board of Trade v. Hain S.S. Co. Ltd* [1929] A.C. 534 at 541, *per* Lord Sumner, and, at 544, *per* Lord Atkin, HL; see also *Leyland Shipping Co. Ltd v. Norwich Union Fire Insurance Society Ltd* [1918] A.C. 350 at 371, *per* Lord Shaw, HL.
[42] *Saqui and Lawrence v. Steams* [1911] 1 K.B. 426 at 434–435, CA; *cf. Greaves v. Drysdale* [1936] 2 All E.R. 470, CA, where inadequate proof of employee's complicity.
[43] The doctrine of "carrying away" in the former offence of larceny.
[44] *British and Foreign Marine Insurance Co. v. Gaunt* [1921] 2 A.C. 41, H.L., at 57, *per* Lord Summer.
[45] *Beresford v. Royal Insurance Co. Ltd* [1938] A.C. 586 at 595, HL.

insured premises and then seeking to recover under his fire policy.[46] However, where insurers allege that the insured caused the peril which was the proximate cause of the loss, e.g. fire, the onus of proof falls on the insurers to prove on the balance of probabilities that the insured deliberately caused the loss, and the more serious the allegation, the higher the standard of proof required within that test of the balance of probabilities.[47] Suspicious circumstances are insufficient and scientific evidence may be required.[48] The insured will also be unable to recover in respect of acts of wilful misconduct which are committed by other persons with his connivance,[49] etc., which are proved by the insurer.[50] The deliberate act in itself, of course, takes the cause of the loss or damage outside the prima facie scope of the primary insuring words, for instance, the deliberate demolition of a building is not embraced by the insured peril of "collapse".[51]

Public policy and criminal acts of the insured

17–20   Where a policy is perfectly legal, but the insured's enforcement of it is tainted with illegality, dishonesty, or the like, the courts may well not enforce the insured's right of recovery against the insurer on the ground of public policy. This is because it is a basic principle of insurance law that the insured cannot recover an indemnity in respect of the direct foreseen consequences of his own intentional acts.[52] This principle arises as a matter of construction in non-life insurances, that they are contracts made to cover the consequences of fortuitous events only, unless there are clear words in the insurance policy covering such a contingency.[53] For instance, where an insured has brought items of jewellery into this country without declaring them to the customs authorities, the court refused to enforce his contents policy upon a subsequent theft of that jewellery from his house.[54] The insured must, however, be aware of his evasion of legal requirements or prohibitions.[55]

17–21   This public policy principle, sometimes referred to by its Latin maxim *ex turpi causa non oritur action,* does not render the policy void, but acts to prevent a criminal or his accomplices enforcing a policy otherwise cov-

---

[46] *Upjohn v. Hitchens* [1918] 2 KB 48 at 58, *per* Scrutton L.J., CA; and *City Taylors Ltd v. Evans* (1921) 38 T.L.R. 230 at 233–234, CA.

[47] *Slattery v. Mance* [1962] 1 Q.B. 676; *Grunther Industrial Developments Ltd and GID Ltd v. Federated Employers Insurance Association Ltd* [1976] 2 Lloyd's Rep 259, CA; *S. & M. Carpets (London) Ltd v. Cornhill Insurance Co. Ltd* [1981] 1 Lloyd's Rep. 667; *Watkins & Davis Ltd v. Legal and General Assurance Co. Ltd* [1981] 1 Lloyd's Rep. 674; see also *Exchange Theatre Ltd v. Iron Trades Mutual Insurance Co Ltd (No.2)* [1984] 2 Lloyd's Rep. 169, CA.

[48] *Watkins & Davis Ltd v. Legal and General Assurance Co. Ltd* [1981] 1 Lloyd's Rep. 674 at 679, *per* Neill J.

[49] *Midland Insurance Co. v. Smith* (1881) 6 Q.B.D. 561; *P. Samuel & Co. Ltd v. Dumas* [1924] A.C. 431, HL.

[50] *Shaw v. Robberds* (1837) 6 Ad. & El. 75 at 84, *per* Denman L.C.J.; *Lind v. Mitchell* (1928) 45 T.L.R. 54 at 56, *per* Scrutton L.J.

[51] *David Allen & Sons Billposting Ltd v. Drysdale* [1939] 4 All E.R. 113.

[52] *Britton v. Royal Insurance Co.* (1866) 4 F. & F. 905.

[53] *Beresford v. Royal Insurance Co.* [1938] A.C. 586 at 595, *per* Lord MacMillan, HL.

[54] *Geismar v. Sun Alliance and London Insurance Ltd* [1977] Q.B. 383.

[55] *Parkin v. Dick* (1809) 11 East. 502; *Cunard v. Hyde* (1859) 2 E. & E. 1; *Wilson v. Rankin* (1865) L.R. 1 Q.B. 162; *Dudgeon v. Pembroke* (1877) 2 App. Cas. 284, HL.

ering the loss or damage. If a insured, like any other litigant, cannot maintain his cause of action without showing, as part of such a cause of action, that he has been guilty of illegality, then the courts will not assist him in his cause of action.[56] Before the turn of the nineteenth century, the public policy bar had been expressed even more widely, as barring recovery in the case of civil wrongs in addition to criminal acts,[57] but this seems to state the principle too widely. The principle applies to both property[58] and liability[59] insurances. The principle was stated by Lord Atkin in *Beresford v. Royal Insurance Co.*[60] as follows:

"I think that the principle is that a man is not to be allowed to have recourse to a Court of Justice to claim a benefit from his crime whether under a contract or a gift. No doubt the rule pays regard to the fact that to hold otherwise would in some cases offer an inducement to crime or remove a restraint to crime, and its effect is to act as a deterrent to crime. But apart from these considerations the absolute rule is that the Courts will not recognise a benefit accruing to a criminal from his crime."

As regards liability insurances (*e.g.*, motor and employers' liability poli-   **17–22** cies), competing public policy considerations come into play, in that the insured "benefits" from the policy only to the extent that the judgment awarded against him is satisfied. To deprive the insured of his indemnity insurance may often merely result in the third party being unable to be compensated for his loss or damage because of the insured's insufficient funds. These competing public considerations may apply either to permit an insured to recover despite his criminal act,[61] or prevent him recovering,[62] and judicial opinion will vary upon the exercise of the public policy bar on recovery.

The matter has been considered in many motor insurance cases, the first of   **17–23** which was *Tinline v. White Cross Insurance Association*,[63] where Bailhache J. allowed the insured driver to recover an indemnity under his insurance even though the admitted negligent driving amounted to manslaughter. He rejected the insurer's defence of public policy in this way[64]:

"The fact that one of the three persons [struck] was killed is, as I have said, really immaterial for the purposes of this case; it was the incident of the accident, or the accident of the accident, an accident due, it is true, to gross negligence, but the policy is an insurance against negligence whether slight or great, and it seems to me to cover this case. It must of course be clearly understood that if this occurrence had been due to the intentional act on the

---

[56] *Scott v. Brown, Doering, McNab & Co.* [1892] 2 Q.B. 724 at 734, *per* A.L. Smith L.J., CA; *Holman v. Johnson* (1775) 1 Cowp. 341 at 343, *per* Lord Mansfield C.J.

[57] *Burrows v. Rhodes and Jameson* [1899] 1 Q.B. 816 at 828–829, *per* Kennedy J.

[58] *Geismar v. Sun Alliance and London Insurance Ltd* [1978] Q.B. 383.

[59] *Gray v. Barr* [1971] 2 Q.B. 554, CA.

[60] [1938] A.C. 586 at 595, HL.

[61] *Tinline v. White Cross Insurance Association Ltd* [1921] 3 K.B. 327; *James v. British General Insurance Co.* [1927] 2 K.B. 311; *Gardner v. Moore* [1984] A.C. 548, H.L.

[62] *Gray v. Barr* [1971] 2 Q.B. 554, CA; *Hardy v. Motor Insurers' Bureau* [1964] 2 Q.B. 745, CA; *Meah v. McCreamer (No.2)* [1986] 1 All E.R. 943.

[63] [1921] 3 K.B. 327.

[64] *ibid.* at 332.

part of the plaintiff, the policy would not protect him. If a man driving a motor-car at excessive speed intentionally runs into and kills a man, the result is not manslaughter but murder. Manslaughter is the result of an accident and murder is not, and it is against accident and accident only that this policy insures."

17–24   Shortly afterwards, in *James v. British General Insurance Co. Ltd*,[65] Roche J. was presented with a very similar case. Again the insured driver had become inebriated before deciding to drive his car, and a death occurred in the ensuing accident. This resulted in the insured being convicted of manslaughter. The insured sought an indemnity in respect of his liabilities arising from the accident. Being satisfied that the insured's driving of his car whilst drunk arose "by reason of folly and not premeditation", Roche J. followed Bailhache J.'s decision in *Tinline,* above, for he considered the facts indistinguishable and "the decision was right in principle".[66] He would only exclude recovery for "the wilful and advertent doing of the act" that led to the insured's liability to a third party.[67]

17–25   Both *Tinline* and *James* were considered by the Court of Appeal in *Haseldine v. Hosken*,[68] but neither approved nor disapproved. The case concerned a solicitor's professional indemnity policy. The insured solicitor had entered into an agreement with his client regarding costs, whereby the solicitor agreed not to charge his client if the litigation was unsuccessful, but if it was successful he would be entitled to both charge fees and a 40 per cent share of any moneys awarded at trial, or paid under any settlement or compromise. The action was lost, and the successful third party sued Haseldine directly claiming damages for champerty and/or maintenance. The Court of Appeal held that Haseldine had entered into a champertous agreement which (at that time) was a crime from its outset and thus illegal from the start. The fact that Haseldine had not appreciated either the illegality or the criminality of the agreement, did not enable him to recover under his indemnity insurance. The *ratio* thus fits in with the debarring of recovery where the insured deliberately, in the sense of intentionally, does something which amounts, in law, to a crime, and that led directly to the loss in respect of which the insured seeks to recover an indemnity under a policy of insurance.

17–26   Another 30 years passed by before the courts again considered this principle of public policy. This was in another motor insurance case, that of *Hardy v. Motor Insurers Bureau*.[69] It was concerned with the extent of the 1946 Motor Insurers Bureau Agreement in respect of uninsured drivers, rather than a claim between an insured driver and his motor insurer, and also related to the consequences of a criminal act of the insured upon a third party's recovery of damages. The facts were that the third party claimant was a security guard at a large metal works. He sought to question the driver of a van bearing a stolen road fund licence by stopping the

---

[65] [1927] 2 K.B. 311.
[66] *ibid.* at 325.
[67] *ibid.* at 323.
[68] [1933] 1 K.B. 822 at 835, *per Scrutton L.J.* and at 838, *per* Greer L.J., CA.
[69] [1965] 2 Q.B. 745, CA; affirmed in *Gardner v. Moore* [1984] A.C. 548, HL.

van in the road and asking the driver, who was a worker at the factory, to pull in. While the claimant was holding on to the open door of the van with his head inside, the driver drove off at high speed, dragging the claimant along the road for some distance and causing him bodily injury. The driver was convicted of maliciously inflicting grievous bodily harm on the claimant.

The driver was uninsured, so he claimant sought to recover the judg-   **17–27** ment damages that he obtained by consent against the driver from the Motor Insurers Bureau, pursuant to that body's Agreement with the Minister of Transport dated June 17, 1946, which covered "any liability which id required to be covered by a policy of insurance . . . under the Road Traffic Act 1930", which Act had first introduced compulsory motor insurance. The Bureau argued that it did not have to meet this liability, because it was a liability that was not required to be insured pursuant to the Act. This, it was argued, was because this was a liability arising from the driver's wilful and deliberate criminal act. The Court of Appeal disagreed. In considering whether the driver could have recovered if he had in fact held motor insurance, Lord Denning M.R. postulated[70]:

> ". . . could he have claimed indemnity under the policy? Clearly not, for the good and sufficient reason that no person can claim reparation or indemnity for the consequences of a criminal offence where his own wicked and deliberate intent is an essential ingredient in it: *Beresford v. Royal Insurance Co. Ltd*.[71] This rule is not rested on an implied exception in the policy of insurance. It is based on the broad rule of public policy that no person can claim indemnity or reparation for his own wilful and culpable crime. He is under a disability precluding him from imposing a claim."

The other members of the Court expressed the principle in their own   **17–28** words. Pearson L.J. said[72]:

> "There is a principle of public policy that an insured person cannot recover an indemnity from his insurers in respect of the consequences of the insured person's own intentional criminal act. If he were allowed to do so, he would be reaping the fruits of his own crime and profiting by his own wrong, and that is contrary to public policy."

Finally, Diplock L.J. (as he then was) put forward a rather different and apparently less restrictive resumé of the public policy rule as applied to contracts of insurance[73]:

> "All that the rule means is that the courts will not enforce a right which would otherwise be enforceable if the right arises out of an act committed by the person asserting the right (or someone who is regarded in law as his

---

[70] *ibid.* at 760.
[71] [1938] A.C. 586, HL, where it was held that the insured took his own life whilst sane, which at the time was a crime, so that the insured's personal representatives could not recover under the insured's life policy.
[72] [1964] 2 Q.B. 745 at 762, CA.
[73] *ibid.* at 767.

successor) which is regarded by the court as sufficiently anti-social to justify the court's refusing to enforce that right."

17–29   The matter was not considered again until the Court of Appeal upheld the insurers' defence of public policy in *Gray v. Barr*[74] where the defendant insured sought an indemnity under the liability section of his "Hearth and Home" policy. This covered him in respect of all sums which he became legally liable to pay as damages in respect of bodily injury to any person caused by accidents. One night in June 1967, the insured, Barr, went to the claimant's farm in search of his wife who had been committing adultery with the claimant. Barr went equipped with a loaded shotgun. When he entered the claimant's farmhouse the claimant, Gray, was standing at the top of the stairs. Barr asked if his wife was there and Gray (correctly) told him that she was not. Barr proceeded up the stairs, holding the gun at the port, saying that he wanted to see for himself. Gray barred his way, and told Barr to get out. Barr then deliberately fired a shot into the ceiling, the two then grappled and Barr fell backwards down the stairs, and in his fall the gun went off, killing Gray.

17–30   Lord Denning M.R. held that as the killing arose out of Barr's own "wilful and culpable" (following *Hardy,* above) conduct of proceeding up the stairs with the loaded gun after having been told to leave, and, accordingly, Barr was not entitled to recover an indemnity under the insurance in respect of his liability.[75] Salmon L.J. pointed out that whilst "public policy is rightly regarded as an unruly steed which should be cautiously ridden", he was "confident that public policy undoubtedly requires that no one who threatens unlawful violence with a loaded gun should be allowed to enforce a claim for indemnity against any liability he may incur as a result of having so acted".[76] Salmon L.J., though, was emphatic that he was neither intending to lay down any wider proposition, nor was he determining that a person who committed manslaughter could never, under any circumstances, recover an indemnity.

17–31   Finally, Phillimore L.J. agreed that recovery was barred on the ground of public policy and that the sequence of events that night had to considered as a whole. Bearing this in mind, and recalling that on ordinary principles of insurance law an insured cannot by his own deliberate act cause the event upon which the insurance money is payable, he went on to hold that public policy prevented recovery in this particular case.[77] It is submitted that Phillimore L.J. alone was correct to consider not just the criminality of the act, but also whether the consequences of that act were directly caused by that criminal act, or merely an unintended and indirect result.

17–32   More recently, the courts have approached the question of this public policy bar to enforcement of contractual or other rights by applying the so-called public conscience test. This was first propounded by Hutchison

---

[74] [1971] 2 Q.B. 554, CA.
[75] *ibid.* at 568.
[76] *ibid.* at 581.
[77] *ibid.* at 585–587.

J. in a claim for conversion of a cheque which was said to be part of a fraudulent financing scheme. Hutchison J. said that there was a two fold test, first, whether there had been illegality of which the court should take notice and, second, "whether in all the circumstances it would be an affront to the public conscience if by affording him the relief sought the court was seen to be indirectly assisting or encouraging the [claimant] in his criminal act".[78] The Court of Appeal applied this public conscience test in the subsequent property insurance case of *Euro-Diam Ltd v. Bathurst*.[79] This concerned a claim in respect of a consignment of precious stones exported to West Germany which was stolen from a German company's warehouse. The insured claimant's invoice had understated the value of the stones in order to evade German customs duty, but the Court of Appeal allowed the claim to succeed because the false invoice had nothing to do with the insured deriving any benefit, as it only assisted the consignee in Germany. The English contract of insurance was not tainted with illegality because the correct value had been declared to the insurers.

17–33 This public conscience test has been rejected in property rights cases by a bare majority in the House of Lords in *Tinsley v. Milligan*,[80] in favour of a test of requiring a claimant to establish his legal or equitable property interest without relying on his own illegality. As regards an action for negligence, the Court of Appeal in *Clunis v. Camden and Islington Health Authority*[81] applied the illegality test, but added a rider of circumstances where it could be said that the claimant did not know the nature and quality of his act or that what he doing was wrong. Australia has followed[82] the "sufficiently anti-social test" of Diplock L.J. in *Hardy v. Motor Insurance Bureau*,[83] and the High of Australia has specifically rejected the test propounded in *Tinsley v. Milligan*[84] on the basis that discouraging unlawful acts is not the only relevant policy consideration. There is also the consideration of preventing injustice and the enrichment of one party at the expense of another.[85]

17–34 For the present time, therefore, the applicable principle in relation to insurance law can be no better summarised than by stating that a person cannot recover an indemnity under an insurance against a liability which arises from a crime committed by the insured himself, whether of deliberate violence or otherwise, except:

(i) in the exceptional circumstance of where compulsory insurance is required, when the law considers that public policy is better served by permitting a recovery from an insurer which will not truly benefit the insured, but will actually be paid to the third

---

[78] *Thackwell v. Barclays Bank plc* [1986] 1 All E.R. 676 at 687.
[79] [1990] 1 Q.B. 1 at 35, *per* Kerr L.J., CA.
[80] [1994] 1 A.C. 340, HL.
[81] [1998] Q.B. 978, CA.
[82] *Fire & All Risks Insurance Co. Ltd v. Powell* [1966] V.R. 513 (F.C.); *S. & Y. Investments (No.2) Pty Ltd v. Commercial Union Assurance Co. of Australia Ltd* (1986) 82 F.L.R. 130.
[83] [1965] 2 Q.B. 745, CA.
[84] [1994] 1 A.C. 340, HL.
[85] *Nelson v. Nelson* (1995) 70 A.L.J.R. 47 at 70, *per* Toohey J.

party who sustained injury or damage from the criminal act of the insured, which liability is required by statute to be insured,[86] or

(ii) the crime involved mere inadvertence or negligence, or, at least, no moral culpability or turpitude.

5. JOINT AND COMPOSITE INSURANCES

17–35   Where an insurance is held in the names of the joint owners of the property insured, or in respect of potential joint liability, the wilful misconduct of one insured will prevent the other joint owner recovering under that joint policy, because otherwise the joint owner who was guilty of misconduct would obtain a benefit from the insurance. That situation of joint insurance is very different, though, from the situation where a composite policy is arranged in the names of several insured for their respective rights and interests in, *e.g.* insured property. In this latter situation, an innocent insured will be able to recover where their interests in the insured property are not inseparable from that of the particular insured who is guilty of wilful misconduct, non-disclosure, or breach of warranty.

17–36   This distinction was first established in *General Accident, Fire and Life Assurance Corp. Ltd v. Midland Bank Ltd,*[87] which was an action for recovery of policy moneys paid jointly to all the named insured upon discovery of the fraud of one of their number. A fire policy had been taken out to cover the plant and stock of Plant Bros Ltd, and the buildings containing the stock and plant, in favour of the company, the Midland Bank Ltd, and Scoffin & Willmott Ltd, for their respective rights and interests. Under Condition 5 of the policy, all benefits under the policy were to be forfeited if a claim was in any respect fraudulent. A fire subsequently occurred on the premises and claims were put in by Plant Bros. Ltd in respect of the stock and plant and certain of the buildings and were met by the insurers, the cheque being payable in the name of the three insured. That cheque was endorsed so that Plant Bros. Ltd could have the benefit of it. The stock and plant belonged only to Plant Bros. Ltd, but the buildings affected by fire belonged to Scoffin & Willmott Ltd, as freeholders, Plant Bros. Ltd being only tenants at will. The Midland Bank Ltd held debentures of Plant Bros. Ltd to secure an overdraft in respect of which they had a floating charge over that company's assets, and Scoffin & Willmott Ltd were guarantors of Plant Bros. Ltd's overdraft.

17–37   The Court of Appeal held that the insurance moneys were not recoverable from either Midland Bank Ltd or Scoffin & Willmott Ltd as the insurance was not a joint insurance, but a composite insurance and those untainted by the fraudulent misconduct of another insured, were fully entitled to be fully indemnified under the insurance to the extent of their

---

[86] See *Lancashire County Council v. Municipal Mutual Insurance Ltd* [1997] Q.B. 897 at 907, *per* Simon Brown L.J., CA.
[87] [1940] 2 K.B. 388, CA.

respective interests in the various property insured. Greene M.R. explained the difference between joint and composite insurances[88]:

> "How then can there be a joint insurance in any true sense of that phrase of the interest of a freeholder in freehold premises and the interest of a debenture holder holding a floating charge on that mass of property, including, among other things, these premises? There is no joint risk; there is no joint interest; the measure of the loss suffered by these two parties will be different, calling for a different measure of indemnity, and, accordingly, it seems to me that there is no joint element about the thing at all.
>
> Such a policy, in my judgment may be more accurately described as a composite policy, because it comprises, for reasons of obvious convenience, in one piece of paper, the interests of a number of persons whose connection with the subject matter of the insurance makes it natural and reasonable that the whole matter should be dealt with in one policy."

This decision was followed in *Woolcott v. Sun Alliance and London Insurance Ltd*[89] where the insurers were held entitled to avoid a fire policy to the extent that it applied to a mortgagor who had not disclosed a previous conviction which was a material fact, but not in so far as the policy related to the mortgagee building society which was also named as an insured under the policy. Again, this was on the ground that the insurance was a composite, and not joint, insurance. There have been many decisions concerning composite insurances, including the ramifications for the insurer's exercise of subrogation rights against co-insured parties, in respect of contractors' insurances. These are discussed in Chapter 16, above.   **17–38**

6. PROOF OF LOSS

Insured to prove loss prima facie within policy

The onus of proving that a loss has occurred by an insured peril, and that the claim is therefore prima facie within the scope of the insurance contract, lies firmly with the insured. Insurers are fully entitled to put the insured to strict proof both as to the fact of the loss and of the cause of that loss. This principle and how it is to be applied in practice was expounded by Lord Evershed M.R. in *Regina Fur Co. Ltd v. Bossom*[90] a case concerning an alleged loss by theft of furs: **17–39**

> "I think that a defendant — whether he is an underwriter or any other kind of defendant — is entitled to say, by way of defence, 'I require this case to be strictly proved, and admit nothing.' Where such is the defence, the onus remains throughout upon the plaintiffs to establish the case they are alleging. Where such is the form of pleading, it is not only obligatory upon the defendants but it is not even permissible for them to proceed to put forward some affirmative case which they have not pleaded or alleged; and it is not, therefore, right that they should, by cross-examination of the plaintiffs or

---

[88] [1940] 2 K.B. 388 at 405, CA.
[89] [1978] 1 W.L.R. 493. See also *New Hampshire Insurance Co. v. M.G.N. Ltd* [1997] I.R.L.R. 24, CA, at para. 14–29, above.
[90] [1958] 2 Lloyd's Rep 425 at 428, CA.

otherwise, suggest such an affirmative case. The defendants are acting correctly if they follow the course adopted in this case that is, so to challenge, at each point, and by proper evidence, where it is advisable, and by cross-examination, the case which the plaintiffs seek to make good."

17-40   In other words, once it is shown that the loss has been caused by the insured peril, the claimant insured has made out a prima facie case, and the onus is then upon the defendant insurer to show, on a balance of probabilities, that the peril or loss was caused or connived at by the insured.[91] There are several examples of the insured failing to make out that the loss is prima facie covered by the insurance. In *Richardson v. Roylance*,[92] the insured was unable to show that a loss in Winchester was covered by a cash in transit policy providing an indemnity where the loss occurred "in and around London". In *Anderson v. Norwich Union Fire Insurance Society Ltd*,[93] the insured could not satisfy the court that heavy rainfall amounted to a "storm". In *Young v. Sun Alliance and London Insurance Ltd*,[94] the insured could not show that ingress of water from an underground stream amounted to a "flood"; and in *Re George and Goldsmiths and General Burglary Insurance Association Ltd*,[95] the insured could not establish that the theft of jewellery from a showcase broken open by thieves fell within the peril of "theft following upon actual forcible and violent entry upon the premises".

Loss within an exception
17-41   The position depends on whether the exception forms part of the primary insuring words, and so defines the primary scope of the insurance indemnity, or whether the exception is contained in a separate clause and may therefore be regarded as a special case limiting the prima facie general scope of the policy. The distinction is not always easy to establish. For instance, in *Hurst v. Evans*[96] an "all risks" jewellery policy provided an indemnity in respect of "loss or damage arising from any cause whatever on land or water save and except . . . loss by theft or dishonesty committed by any servant . . . of the assured". The evidence at trial established a loss by theft and tended to implicate in the theft a servant in the exclusive employment of the insured. Lush J. held that it was incumbent on the claimant insured to prove a theft by some person other than a servant in his exclusive employment and, as the claimant had failed to do this, he could not recover under the policy. His Lordship went on to hold, though, that where insurers, as in the present case, had not put the insured to strict proof, but had alleged that the servant had assisted in

[91] *Slattery v. Mance* [1962] 1 Lloyd's Rep. 60 at 62, *per* Salmon J.; *Gorman v. Hand-in-Hand Insurance Co.* (1877) I.R 11 C.L. 224; *Marsden v. City and County Assurance Co.* (1866) L.R. 1 C.P. 232; *Everett v. London Assurance* (1865) 19 C.B.(n.s.) 126; *Austin v. Drewe* (1816) 6 Taunt. 436.
[92] (1933) 47 Ll. L. Rep. 173.
[93] [1977] 1 Lloyd's Rep. 253, CA.
[94] [1976] 3 All E.R. 561, CA.
[95] [1899] 1 Q.B. 595, CA.
[96] [1917] 1 K.B. 352; see also *Firestone Rubber Tyre Co. v. Vokins & Co. Ltd* [1951] 1 Lloyd's Rep. 32.

the theft, the insurers might establish — for the burden was on them to prove that positive allegation — such complicity by evidence which possibly might not be admitted or sufficient to convict in a criminal prosecution. Thus, evidence that two days before the theft the servant was seen in conference with three notorious thieves was admissible to prove his complicity, but evidence of the servant's bad character was not admissible.[97]

On the other hand, where a clear exception is inserted in a separate clause, the insurers bear the burden of proof to show that a loss that is prima facie within the policy's primary insuring words, is included within the provisions of the exceptions clause.[98] The principles applicable for determining the burden of proof were laid down by Bailhache J. in *Munro, Brice & Co. v. War Risks Association Ltd*[99]: **17–42**

(a) The claimant must prove such facts as bring him prima facie within the terms of the promise;

(b) When the promise is qualified by exceptions, the question whether the claimant need prove facts which negative their application does not depend upon whether the exceptions are to be found in a separate clause or not. The question depends upon an entirely different consideration, namely, whether the exception is as wide as the promise, and thus qualifies the whole of the promise, or whether it merely excludes from the operation of the promise particular classes of cases which, but for the exception, would fall within it, leaving some part of the general scope of the promise unqualified. If so, it is sufficient for the plaintiff to bring himself prima facie within the terms of the promise, leaving the defendant to prove that, although prima facie within its terms, the claimant's case is in fact within the excluded exceptional class;

(c) When a promise is qualified by an exception which covers the whole scope of the promise, a claimant cannot make out a prima facie case unless he bring himself within the promise as qualified;

(d) Whether a promise is a promise with exceptions or whether it is a qualified promise is in every case a question of construction of the instrument as a whole;

(e) In construing a contract with exceptions it must be borne in mind that a promise with exceptions can generally be turned by an alteration of phraseology into a qualified promise. The form in which the contract is expressed is therefore material.

Contractual modification of the burden of proof

As a matter of agreement between parties, the onus of proof of any particular fact, or of its non-existence, may be placed on either party in **17–43**

---

[97] See also *Samuels v. Tompson* (1910), *The Times*, November 12, 1910.
[98] *Motor Union Insurance Co. Ltd v. Boggan* (1923) 130 L.T. 588, HL; *Greaves v. Drysdale* (1935) 53 Ll. L. Rep. 16 (reversed on facts (1936) 55 Ll. L. Rep. 95, CA).
[99] [1918] 2 K.B. 78 at 88 (reversed on facts *Munro, Brice & Co v. Marten* [1920] 3 K.B. 94, CA).

accordance with the agreement made between them.[1] Such a clause may provide[2]:

> "In any action, suit or other proceedings, where the company alleges that by reason of the provisions of this (exceptions) condition any loss or damage is not covered by this insurance, the burden of proving that such loss or damage is co\vered shall be upon the insured."

---

[1] *Levy v. Assicurazioni Generali* [1940] A.C. 791, PC; *Re Hooley Hill Rubber and Chemical Co. Ltd and Royal Insurance Co. Ltd* [1920] 1 K.B. 257 at 273, *per* Scrutton L.J., CA; *Pawsey & Co. v. Scottish Union and National Insurance Co., The Times*, October 17, 1908, PC; *Winnipeg Electric Co. v. Geel* [1932] A.C. 690, PC; *Grell-Taurel Ltd v. Carribean Home Insurance Co. Ltd* [2000] Lloyd's Rep. I.R. 614, High Court of Justice Trinidad and Tobago.
[2] *Levy v. Assicurazioni Generali*, [1940] A.C. 791, PC.

CHAPTER 18

NOTIFICATION OF CLAIM OR LOSS

1. TIME OF NOTIFICATION

Requirement of notification to insurers

The procedure of the insured's notification of claims to his insurer is   **18–01**
dealt with expressly in each policy as a matter of invariable course. Whilst
property insurances will be limited to requiring the insured to notify the
insurer of losses, or damage claims, liability insurances generally provide
that the insured must notify the insurer of both (a) claims received by the
insured from third parties, and (b) occurrences that may give rise to future
claims from third parties.

Property insurance

Insurers vary on whether they require claims to be notified within a   **18–02**
specified number of days, or adopt more general words. Being concerned
with ascertainable material damage to property, the date of the loss or
damage will be a certain and determinable fact and compliance or breach
of a notification provision will be not be problematic. For instance, in *T.
H. Adamson & Sons v. Liverpool and London and Globe Insurance Co. Ltd,*[1]
a cash in transit policy specified that the defendant company "shall be
under no liability hereunder in respect of any loss which has not been
notified to the company within 15 days of its occurrence". Thus cash
losses which were not notified within 15 days of the actual occurrence of
the loss were held not to be included, even though not discovered until
subsequently.

Liability insurance provisions

For liability insurances, however, time will usually expressly run from   **18–03**
the date of the receipt by the insured of a notification of a claim from a
third party,[2] *e.g.* "the insured must notify the insurer within 14 days of the
receipt of any writ or written notification of claim being made against
him". Less specific provisions, however, such as "as soon as possible",[3]
have to be interpreted in all the circumstances of the case and the particular
wording adopted in the provision. Obviously, if the wording identifies time
as running from the date of knowledge of the insured or his representative, time does not run from the date the insured event actually occurred,

---

[1] [1953] 2 Lloyd's Rep. 355; see also *Cassel v. Lancashire and Yorkshire Accident Insurance
Co. Ltd* (1885) 1 T.L.R. 495.

[2] *The Vainqueur José* [1979] 1 Lloyd's Rep. 557; *cf. Ward v. Law Property Assurance and
Trust Society* (1856) 27 L.T.(o.s.) 155.

[3] *Verelst's Administratrix v. Motor Union Insurance Co. Ltd* [1925] 2 K.B. 137; and five
months delay is not "as soon as possible", *Farrell v. Federated Employers Insurance
Association Ltd.* [1970] 1 W.L.R. 1400, CA.

but the date of knowledge.[4] In *Berliner Motor Corp. and Steiers Lawn and Sports Inc. v. Sun Alliance and London Insurance Ltd*[5] a public liability policy provided:

> "Upon the happening of any Event which may give rise to a claim . . . the Insured shall forthwith give written notice to the Company with full particulars."

Proceedings were commenced against the insured company's United States subsidiary in March 1972, and came to the notice of the insured company not later than December 11, 1972, but the insurers were not advised until October 25, 1973, when the insured gave notice of the claim. Bingham J. considered this constituted a "gross breach" of the policy provision.[6]

18–04　　Under an employers' liability policy requiring "immediate" notice of any accident causing injury to a workman, a delay of notification from October 10, the date of the accident, to December 4 was held not to meet the provision's requirements.[7] "Immediately" has been held to mean "with all reasonable speed considering the circumstances of the case",[8] and Lord Denning M.R. accepted that definition in the later case of *Farrell v. Federated Employers Insurance Association Ltd*[9] where the notification provision read:

> "Every claim, writ, notice, letter, writ or other document served on the employer shall be notified or forwarded to the company immediately on receipt."

Per Lord Denning M.R.[10]:

> ". . . the writ was served here on January 7, 1966 and notice was given to the insurers on March 3, 1966, that is, some eight weeks later. This was, [the plaintiff says], all reasonable speed. I do not think so, I think that, in the circumstances of the case, the plaintiffs solicitors ought to have told the insurers about the writ soon after they received the letter of January 17, 1966 from the receiver [of the plaintiff company]. 'With all reasonable speed' would mean by the end of January at the latest . . . The plain fact is that the writ was not notified with all reasonable speed."

18–05　　The particular wording must be carefully examined in each instance. For example, the insured will not be in breach of the notification provision where he does not forward other notices or documents sent to him relating to a claim to the insurers, if it reads[11]:

---

[4] *ibid.*

[5] [1983] 1 Lloyd's Rep. 320.

[6] *ibid.* at 325.

[7] *Re Williams and Lancashire and Yorkshire Accident Insurance Co.'s Arbitration* (1902) 51 W.R. 222.

[8] *Re Coleman's Repositories Ltd and Life and Health Assurance Association* [1907] 2 K.B. 798 at 807 *per* Fletcher-Moulton L.J., CA.

[9] [1970] 1 W.L.R. 1400, CA.

[10] *ibid.* at 1406.

[11] *Wilkinson v. Car and General Insurance Corp. Ltd* (1914) 110 L.T. 468, CA.

> "the insured should forward to the head office or any branch office of the
> insurers every written notice or information as to any verbal notice of claim
> arising through any accident or disease covered under said policy as soon as
> possible after the receipt of such notice or information."

Knowledge of notification provision

It is submitted that the insured will not be bound by the insurer's usual   **18–06**
provisions relating to, *e.g.* notification of claims, if he is unaware of them,
for instance, because he has not yet received the policy. A majority decision
of the Court of Appeal[12] is supports this proposition, but was made without reference to earlier authorities[13] which have received approval in the
Court of Appeal.[14] This topic is considered further in Chapter 2, above.

Mode of compliance

As a rule, policies will require notice of claims to be made in writing, but   **18–07**
in the absence of that specification, oral notice to the insurer will suffice.[15]
Whilst the notification clause may provide that the insured shall give the
notice required, this will not be breached if the insured's duly authorised
agent, *e.g.* insurance broker, gives the notice to the insurer.[16] It is uncertain
whether any person can give the notice, irrespective of authority from the
insured so to do, even if he has an interest in the insurers learning of the
claim (*e.g.* he is the claimant where the insured holds a relevant liability
insurance), but certainly insurers in such circumstances may waive the
insured's compliance with the notification provisions.[17] Obviously, where
the insured is a partnership, notice by one partner is quite sufficient[18] on
behalf of the firm.

2. WHAT CONSTITUTES A "CLAIM" FOR LIABILITY INSURANCE PURPOSES

In liability insurances, the indemnity is in respect of the insured's liability to   **18–08**
third parties in relation to claims made by those third parties successfully
against the insured. The insurers therefore wish to be involved in the conduct of the defence or settlement of any claims by third parties against
their insured from the outset, hence the requirement for prompt notification by their insured to them of such claims. But the question arises as to
what constitutes a "claim" against an insured so as to oblige the insured to

---

[12] *Re Coleman's Repositories Ltd and Life and Health Assurance Association* [1907] 2 K.B. 798, CA.
[13] *Adie & Sons v. Insurance Corp. Ltd* (1898) 14 T.L.R. 544; *General Accident Insurance Corp. v. Cronk* (1901) 17 T.L.R. 233.
[14] *Rust v. Abbey Life Assurance Co. Ltd* [1979] 2 Lloyd's Rep. 334, at 339, *per* Brandon L.J., CA.
[15] *Re Solvency Mutual Guarantee Society, Hawthorne's Case* (1862) 31 L.J. Ch. 625.
[16] *Patton v. Employers' Liability Assurance Corp.* (1887) 20 L.R. Ir. 93; *The Vainqueur Jose* [1979] 1 Lloyd's Rep. 557.
[17] *Barrett Bros. (Taxis) Ltd v. Davies* [1966] 1 W.L.R. 1334 at 1339, *per* Lord Denning M.R., CA.
[18] *Davies v. National Fire and Marine Insurance Co. of New Zealand* [1891] A.C. 485, PC.

notify the insurers of it pursuant to the notification of claims condition in liability policies? The first definition was provided by Devlin J. (as he then was) in *West Wake Price & Co. v. Ching*[19] which concerned an accountants professional indemnity policy:

> "I think that the primary meaning of the word 'claim' — whether used in a popular sense or in a strict legal sense — is such as to attach it to the object that is claimed; and it is not the same thing as the cause of action by which the claim may be supported or as the grounds on which it may be based."

18–09   Devlin J. expanded upon this brief observation a little later in his judgment[20]:

> "If the word is to be used with any precision, it must be defined in relation to the object claimed. The grounds for the claim or the causes of action which support it can give it colour and character, but cannot give it its entity . . .
>
> In particular, if a claim is identified as something that has to be paid . . . it must be something that is capable of separate payment: one cannot pay a cause of action. It follows, I think, that if there is only one object claimed by one person, then there is only one claim, however many may be the grounds or the causes of action which can be raised in support of it: likewise, where several claims are each dependent on the same cause of action (as, for example, where one cause of action leads to alternative claims for an injunction, damages or an account or other different forms of relief), there remains only one cause of action, however many claims it may give rise to."

18–10   Some time later, in *Soole v. Royal Insurance Co. Ltd*[21] Shaw J. (as he then was) had to consider whether a claim had been made by a third party against the insured under a policy that indemnified the insured "in the event of any person or persons at any time within a period of thirty years after the date shown above as commencing date claiming to be entitled to enforce such hereinbefore recited restrictive covenants". So, again, the court was not actually concerned with any issue of breach of a notification condition, but rather the consideration of what constituted a claim with relevance to the primary insuring words of the insurance policy, but such must logically have a direct bearing upon what claims must be notified.

18–11   The facts were that a developer bought a piece of land and intended to demolish the one existing property and build six houses on the plot. A restrictive covenant upon the plot provided that only one building could be built on it. In September 1964, a neighbour, through his solicitors, wrote to the vendor of the plot referring to the restrictive covenant and intimating that he was not prepared to modify or waive the restriction, and would take action to see that the restriction was not broken. That letter was sent on to the then purchaser, Mr Soole's company, and correspondence was entered into for some months between the respective

---

[19] [1957] 1 W.L.R. 45 at 55.
[20] *ibid.* at 57.
[21] [1971] 2 Lloyd's Rep. 332.

solicitors without any conclusion. In May 1965, Mr Soole arranged the insurance policy to cover him against subsequent claims to enforce the restrictive covenant, without mentioning to the insurers that there had been this correspondence between his and the neighbour's solicitors where action had been threatened. Days after inception of the policy, that neighbour joined with two other neighbours and issued proceedings claiming that they were entitled to the benefit of the restrictive covenant. Mr. Soole claimed under the policy but the insurers refused to indemnify him, *inter alia*, on the ground that this claim against him had been intimated prior to the commencement of the insurance and was therefore outside its ambit.

Shaw J. rejected this defence on the basis that the policy provided an **18–12** indemnity against the consequences of a valid claim, although there was provision for an indemnity in respect of defence costs incurred with the written consent of the insurers, and the "claim" must therefore be one that is pursued and established:

> "As I see the matter, the reason or motive for insuring is, of course, the possibility or threat of loss, but unless and until the possibility becomes an actuality or the threat becomes effective, the indemnity provided under a policy is inoperative. It is only the incidence of the risk insured against that gives rise to a liability in the insured. In the instant case the bare assertion of a purported claim to enforce the restrictive covenant might create a temporary concern, but nothing more. Only if it was pursued and established and put into effect so as to give rise to loss or damage or expense to the insured of a character falling within one or other of the five categories set out in the indemnity clause would the liability of the insurer arise at all.
>
> There is perhaps one qualification which calls for a passing mention. By sub-clause (iv) of the indemnity, cover is provided in respect of any costs and expense incurred by the insured in defending proceedings brought to enforce the restrictive covenant. This would apply in a case where such proceedings ended in the favour of the insured, as well as any other proceedings. It is, however, to be observed that the indemnity in these circumstances is conditional on the insurer having consented in writing to the incurring of those costs or expenses. It is not difficult to envisage cases (the present one was thought to be such) where it might be doubtful that the restrictive covenant still survived or was enforceable at the suit of the particular claimant. Where there is at least a prospect of defeating or perhaps discouraging such a claim appearing, as it does, to fall within the policy, it is in the interests of the insurer to support the insured in resisting it. If in the event it is shown to be groundless, this incidental liability will have been assumed ad hoc by the insurers really for their own protection. They are only contingently liable in those circumstances where there could have been no loss to the insured because the claim to enforce the covenant turned out to be without substance. This does not, therefore, detract from the proposition which seems to me to decide the question of construction, namely, that 'claiming' as used in the indemnity clause must involve in addition to the assertion of a right against the assured the enforcement of the right resulting in detriment of the nature covered by the indemnity. A claim intimated and abandoned, or litigated and rejected, is not a claim that calls for any cover and is not the subject-matter of the policy."[22]

_____

[22] *ibid.* at 337.

Occurrences likely to give rise to a claim

18–13   On the above reasoning, it would seem that an insured would not need
to notify his insurers of, *e.g.* threats to sue, unless (as is usual) the notification clause is widely drafted and requires notification of "the occurrence
of any event likely to give rise to a claim" as well as written notice of "any
claim". This wider provision was considered in *Thorman v. New Hampshire
Insurance Co. (U.K.) Ltd*[23] where the Court of Appeal held, unsurpris-
ingly, that the insured architects had correctly notified their insurers of the
issue of a writ against them, though not yet served, for it constituted an
"occurrence which may be likely to give rise to a claim" under the professional indemnity policy. In the *Thorman* case, the Court of Appeal also
considered what constituted a "claim" for the purposes of the policy, and,
it is submitted, this must mean for all purposes under the policy including
the notification of claims provisions. The Court was not referred to the
Soole judgment discussed above, but was referred to the passages in the
judgment of Devlin J. (as he then was) in *West Wake Price & Co. v. Ching*[24]
quoted above, and Stocker L.J. in the leading judgment expressly approved
those passages[25]:

> "For my part, these appear to me to be definitions which can be accepted
> without further refinement. They do not, however, solve the question since
> the application of the definition may vary according to the circumstances in
> which it falls to be construed. For a 'claim' to be substantiated against a
> defendant, whether expressed in a contract or in tort, it obviously must be
> proved in every case (1) that a duty was owed, (2) that there was a breach of
> that duty and (3) damage resulted from that breach. As a matter of formal
> procedure they can be pleaded as an assertion of a general duty, an allega-
> tion of its breach and causative proof of damage for that breach. In a case
> where substantial building works are concerned there may be a variety of
> heads of damage, and a variety of breaches of duty arising out of different
> aspects of the general duty owed. Thus, for example, in one claim there may
> be allegations of a breach of the duty to design, with defects and damage
> resulting from that breach; a breach of the duty to supervise, with different
> and distinct resultant damage; and a breach of the duty to specify, again
> with its own separate consequential damage. These may all be brought in
> one action, particularised by the various distinct breaches of duty and
> consequential damage. They may, however, be brought as separate actions
> provided neither the breaches of duty nor the damage claimed in the first
> action embrace the breaches and damage claimed in the second . . .
>   Thus, in such a context the word 'claim' is apt to embrace both the general
> claim, subsequently particularized as a series of temperate breaches and
> damage, or can apply to each of series of separate and distinct claims, all
> arising from the negligence of the architect in the course of performing a
> single contract. In the former case there would, in my view, be only one
> 'claim', in the latter, several claims. Which is appropriate will depend upon
> the facts of each case and the circumstances in which the word 'claim' falls
> to be considered and construed . . . Plainly a claim can only be enforced by
> legal proceedings where the appropriate cause of action is pleaded and
> proved, but the cause of action is not, itself, a claim but the necessary vehicle

---

[23] [1988] 1 Lloyd's Rep. 7, CA.
[24] [1957] 1 W.L.R. 45.
[25] [1988] 1 Lloyd's Rep. 7 at 15–16.

for its legal enforcement and the contrary has not been contended in argument in this case . . .

It seems to me, therefore, that the question whether there is one claim or a series of separate claims depends upon the facts of each case and the context in which the question falls to be decided. The context, in my view, is whether all the defects [are] embraced in a general claim, or only those relating [to certain defects], were notified as a claim during the relevant period of insurance."

3. ASSISTANCE TO INSURER AND PARTICULARS OF LOSS

Generally, insurers will also specify that the insured shall render all such information and assistance to them in relation to the conduct of the defence of a liability claim, or, in the case of material damage or financial loss insurances, in relation to details of how the loss of or damage to property occurred. This has been the position for hundreds of years, and the courts have recognised that their purpose is to protect insurers from fraud by the insured by allowing the insurers to investigate the claim timeously and effectively.[26] It is important to remember that the obligation to assist only arises when the insurer requests such information or assistance,[27] and, moreover, the insurer cannot insist on the insured giving assistance that is not within his power to give. Thus, if an insured diplomat commits an act rendering him legally liable to a third party, and is ordered by his superior to waive his diplomatic immunity from suit, there is no breach of this type of condition even though such waiver was made against the wishes of the insurer.[28]   **18-14**

On the other hand, the insurer may provide in the policy that the insured must furnish "full particulars" of their claim. This has been held to mean "the best particulars the insured can reasonably give which will enable the insurers to form a judgment as to whether the insured has sustained an insured loss.[29] The furnishing of details of losses in a material damage claim within the time period required by the policy does not, however, prevent the insured subsequently supplementing that information with further estimates and the like as they become available. This is because no new claim is being made about some other insured incident, even if the new repair estimate includes some items and excludes others that were in the earlier estimate.[30]   **18-15**

Where the insured was required to provide a detailed account of their loss "as the nature and circumstances of the case will admit" and they did not do so as fully and completely as they could have done, this was held to be a breach of the requirement in *Hiddle v. National Fire and Marine*   **18-16**

---

[26] *Worsley v. Wood* (1796) 6 Term Rep. 710 at 718, *per* Lord Kenyon; *Gamble v. Accident Assurance Co.* (1869) I.R. 4 C.L. 204 at 214, *per* Pigot C.B.

[27] *Wilkinson v. Car and General Insurance Corp. Ltd* (1914) 110 L.T. 468 at 471–472, *per* Lord Reading C.J., CA.

[28] *Dickinson v. Del Solar* [1930] 1 K.B. 376.

[29] *Mason v. Harvey* (1853) 8 Exch. 819 at 820–821, *per* Pollock C.B.

[30] *Northern Suburban Property and Real Estates Co. Ltd v. British Law Fire Insurance Co. Ltd* (1919) 1 Ll. L. Rep. 403.

Insurance Co. of New Zealand.[31] A fire had taken place on January 10 at the premises of the insured, who traded as general store keepers. Virtually all the insured's stock was destroyed in the fire, as were the insured's stock-sheets and stock-book. The cash-book and the customers' ledger survived the fire, having been stored in the safe. The insured submitted a simple schedule of its losses by five generalised categories of stock, giving a figure for the value of each category at the time of the fire and a figure for the amount claimed in respect of each category. The Privy Council upheld the insurers' defence to the claim that this was not sufficient compliance with the condition because:

> "at the time of forwarding their statement they had in their possession mate-rials which enabled them to give a much fuller, more detailed, and better account for the purpose of enabling the insurance company to test the real-ity and extent of the loss."[32]

18–17   Similarly, in *Welch v. Royal Exchange Assurance*[33] the Court of Appeal held that a provision in a fire policy that the insured should "give to the corporation all such proofs and information with respect to the claim as may reasonably be required", was breached by the insured who refused to comply with repeated requests from the insurers for details of bank accounts, used and controlled for the purposes of his insured business, standing in the name of his mother. It is significant that the later produc-tion of the bank accounts when the claim was referred to arbitration did not save the insured from his breach of this condition precedent, as MacKinnon L.J. explained[34]:

> "I have said that I arrive at that conclusion with some regret. The insur-ance company failed to establish any of their numerous charges of fraud. The arbitrator has found that the assured ought to have produced these account, but that, when produced, they contained, in fact, nothing which justified, or tended to justify, a refusal to pay his claim. This means that the [assured] has an honest claim for a large amount, but by reason of his stupid obstinacy over an immaterial matter he has enabled the [insurers] to refuse to pay anything. To lose any sum, however large, may be the proper penalty of dishonesty. To lose some £20,000 as the result of stupidity does seem excessive, even if it be true that the claimant has only himself to blame for that result."

Certificates relating to confirmation of loss

18–18   It used to be commonly provided in fire insurance policies that it was a condition precedent to the liability of the insurers to make a payment under the policy that the insured was to produce a proper certificate of loss to accompany the particulars of loss. Where the insured was required to procure a certificate of "the minister, churchwardens and some reputable householders of the parish importing that they knew the character, etc. of

---

[31] [1896] A.C. 372, PC.
[32] *ibid.* at 375, *per* Lord Davey.
[33] [1939] 1 K.B. 294, CA.
[34] *ibid.* at 314.

the assured, and believe that he really sustained the loss and without fraud", this was held to require strict compliance. Accordingly, a certificate signed only by four reputable householders of the parish, but not the minister and the churchwardens, did not meet the requirements of the condition precedent. The non-co-operation or refusal of those other persons did not prevent breach of the provision.[35] This type of provision is unlikely to be found in modern policies of insurance, presumably because insurers now utilise the professional services of loss adjusters and solicitors to investigate claims on their behalf.

4. NON-ADMISSION OF LIABILITY CONDITION

Invariably, insurers insert a condition in liability policies that the insured **18-19** shall not make any admission of liability to the third party making the claim against him, unless the insurer gives permission for such an admission. This obligation is placed on the insured, and therefore covers admissions that the insured authorises others to make on his behalf, but such a condition will not be breached by the admission of liability by the insured's employee or agent who makes that admission without the insured's authority.[36] It has also been suggested that this type of condition will not be breached by the insured answering forensic questions in the course of the claimant's proceedings against him, either by requests for further information under CPR, Pt 18, or in the witness box.[37]

There is county court authority that such non-admission of liability **18-20** conditions are not contrary to public policy.[38] It had been contended that such conditions were prejudicial to the administration of justice, tending to cause the insured person to lie about what had happened, or at least conceal the truth, but that was considered a fanciful argument, for these conditions do not require the insured to lie, but to merely refrain from admissions of liability. It was also contended that the insurer had to show that he had been prejudiced by any admission by the insured[39] in order to claim a right to enforce this condition precedent to the insurer's liability, but it was held that if prejudice was required, an admission of full liability on the day of the accident coupled with a later contention to his own insurer by the insured that he was not fully to blame, amounted to sufficient prejudice.

---

[35] *Worsley v. Wood* (1796) 6 Term Rep. 710; *Mason v. Harvey* (1853) 21 L.T.(o.s.) 158.

[36] *Tustin v. Arnold & Sons* (1915) 84 L.J.K.B. 2214; see also *Burr v. Ware R.D.C.* [1939] 2 All E.R. 688, CA, where it was held that admissions of negligence by an employee is not evidence against his employer in the absence of proof that the employee was an agent of the employer to make such admissions; *Roberts v. Morris* [1965] Crim. L.R. 46.

[37] *Distillers Co. Bio-Chemicals (Aust.) Pty Ltd v. Ajax Insurance Co. Ltd* (1974) 130 C.L.R. 1 at 8, *per* Menzies J., High Ct of Australia.

[38] *Terry v. Trafalgar Insurance Co. Ltd* [1970] 1 Lloyd's Rep. 524, Mayor's and City of London Ct.

[39] Reliance was placed on *Barratt Bros. (Taxis) Ltd v. Davies* [1966] 1 W.L.R. 1334, CA, heard prior to the Court of Appeal's decision in *Farrell v. Federated Employers Insurance Association Ltd.* [1970] 1 W.L.R. 1400, CA.

5. CONSEQUENCES OF BREACH

18–21 The consequences of breach of a policy provision requiring notice of loss, and the like, will depend upon the proper construction of the insurance contract. The provision may amount to a condition precedent to the payment of the claim, or the insured's right of recovery. The question of construction of conditions in policies is addressed more fully in Chapter 2, but a few examples are provided here. Where there was a specified time period for delivery of an account provided and no claim was payable until such account was given, it was held that the word "until" had the effect of making compliance with the time period non-imperative and an account could be rendered at any time whereupon the insurer was liable to pay under the policy.[40] The same is not true where the provision uses the word "unless", and the provision is more likely to be a condition precedent to the insured's right of recovery, so that he loses all benefit of the insurance for the claim in respect of which he has not complied with the requirements. This was the finding of the Court of Appeal in *Welch v. Royal Exchange Assurance*[41] where it was provided that "unless" the insured should "give to the corporation all such proofs and information with respect to the claim as may reasonably be required", no claim under the policy would be payable. The insured breached this condition, and it was held to be a condition precedent which, in the face of non-compliance, debarred the insured from pursuing the claim further and released the insurers from liability in respect of that claim.

Imperative words

18–22 Where the words are clearly imperative, *e.g.* "the insured shall. . .", it seems that the courts will more readily infer that compliance is a condition precedent to the right of recovery itself, rather than to actual payment of the claim.[42] Thus, in *Farrell v. Federated Employers Insurance Association Ltd*[43] it was a condition of an employers' liability policy that "Every. . . writ. . . served on the employers shall be notified or forwarded to [the insurers] immediately on receipt". This was held by the Court of Appeal to be a condition precedent to the insured's right of recovery under the policy. The insured had been served with the writ on about January 7 but did not notify the insurers about the proceedings until March 3, this was not "immediately" and the insurers were therefore entitled to rely on the breach of the condition to relieve themselves of liability. *Per* Lord Denning M.R.[44]:

> "The plain fact is that the writ was not notified with all reasonable speed. The condition was not fulfilled. The insurers are entitled to rely on it."

---

[40] *Weir v. Northern Counties Insurance Co.* (1879) 4 L.R. Ir. 689.
[41] [1939] 1 K.B. 294, CA; see also *Whyte v. Western Assurance Co.* (1875) 22 L.C.J. 215, PC.
[42] See *Mason v. Harvey* (1853) 8 Exch. 819; *Ralston v. Bignold* (1853) 22 L.T.(o.s.) 106.
[43] [1970] 1 W.L.R. 1400, CA.
[44] *ibid.* at 1406.

Prejudice to insurers not required upon breach of condition precedent

One argument raised in the *Farrell* case was whether the insurers had to   **18–23**
show that they were prejudiced by reason of the condition being broken.[45]
In fact, judgment in default of appearance to the writ had been entered by
the plaintiff against the insured employer prior to their notifying the
insurers of the proceedings. It was argued that the insurers had suffered no
prejudice because they could easily apply to have that judgment set aside.
Lord Denning M.R. did not see why they should be put to that trouble in
order to rely on the breach of condition precedent.[46] Megaw L.J. considered
what would be the position in the case even if the proposition regarding
prejudice were accepted; it was of no avail in the present case because there
was undoubtedly prejudice to the insurers by reason of the breach of the
condition.[47]

In a subsequent case, Mocatta J. remained doubtful that prejudice had   **18–24**
to be shown by the insurer in order that he may rely on the insured's
breach of condition precedent, but concluded that if prejudice is necessary
to sustain such a defence, relatively little prejudice has to be shown by the
insurer in order for him to escape liability.[48] Most recently, in the public
liability insurance case of *Pioneer Concrete (U.K.) Ltd v. National
Employers Mutual General Insurance Association Ltd,* [49] Bingham J. (as he
then was) has specifically rejected the contention that prejudice needs to be
shown on general principles of contract law. This must be right.

6. WAIVER AND ESTOPPEL ON THE PART OF THE INSURER

A breach of a condition may be circumvented by the insured by showing   **18–25**
either that the insurer elected to waive the condition regarding notification,
or that the insurer led him to believe by words or conduct that the insurer
was not relying on the breach of the condition, and he was thereby
induced to alter his position.

Waiver by insurer of compliance with notice provision

Waiver requires a conscious act of election by the insurer with either full   **18–26**
personal knowledge of the breach, or with knowledge of his agent
imputed to him.[50] Thus, in *Yorkshire Insurance Co. v. Craine*[51] the respondent had insured goods in his premises against fire with the appellant
insurance company. The policy stipulated that the insured was to give
notice of any loss or damage under the policy "forthwith", and a specified
time was given for the delivery to the insurer of detailed particulars of the

---

[45] *Barratt Bros. (Taxis) Ltd v. Davies* [1966] 1 W.L.R. 1334, CA.
[46] *Farrell v. Federated Employers Insurance Association Ltd*, [1970] 1 W.L.R. 1400 at 1406.
[47] *ibid.* at 1409.
[48] *The Vainqueur José* [1979] 1 Lloyd's Rep. 557 at 566.
[49] *Pioneer Concrete (U.K.) Ltd v. National Employers Mutual General Insurance
Association Ltd* [1985] 2 All E.R. 395 at 403.
[50] See, *e.g. Wing v. Harvey* (1854) 5 De G.M. & G. 265.
[51] [1922] 2 A.C. 541, PC; see also *Macaura v. Northern Assurance Co. Ltd* [1925] A.C. 619,
HL.

claim. It was stated, also, that failure on the part of the insured to observe this condition would preclude the insured from recovering under the policy. Additionally, there was a salvage provision, under which the insurers might take possession of the premises and of any goods thereon at the date of the fire, and had power to sell those goods. Whilst the insured gave notice forthwith to the insurers of a claim following a fire at his premises, he failed to meet the time requirement for delivery of the full particulars of the claim, and the insurers in due course defended the claim on the basis of this breach of condition. The insurers, however, before expiry of that time limit, had taken possession of the premises under the policy's provisions, and remained in possession for four months without selling any of the goods. The Privy Council held that this amounted to a waiver of the insurer from requiring the insured to comply with the time period for delivery of full particulars of the claim, for their actions could only be justified (*i.e.* the continued possession) upon the footing that the policy was still in existence.

18–27   Waiver was also established in *Webster v. General Accident Fire and Life Assurance Corp. Ltd*[52] where the court upheld an arbitrator's finding that the insurers had waived their right to rely on a condition requiring receipt of written notice of claim, in circumstances where the insured's solicitor had given oral notice of claim to the insurer's branch claims manager, who had said that he would report it to head office. In contrast, where a notice provision requires notice to be given to the insurers' head office, a mere local agent does not bind the insurers if he purports to accept late notification, for he has no apparent authority to waive policy conditions on behalf of his principals, the insurers.[53]

18–28   If the insurer deals with a claim, despite non-compliance with policy requirements regarding notification of claims by a specified manner, this conduct will amount to a waiver. Accordingly, in *Barratt Bros. (Taxis) Ltd v. Davies*,[54] the insurers had learned, from a source other than the insured, of proceedings against the insured, those proceedings being covered by the liability policy issued to him. With this knowledge, they wrote to the insured expressing a wish to undertake the defence of those proceedings. The Court of Appeal held that they had waived their right to rely on the insured's breach of condition to notify. Equally, a condition requiring certification by an independent person of a loss may be waived by the insurers sending their own representative or agent and informing the insured that evidence verifying the claim from that representative or agent will suffice, and the insurers may not subsequently then seek to rely on the condition requiring independent certification.[55]

18–29   Waiver was unsuccessfully raised in *Farrell v. Federated Employers Insurance Association Ltd*[56] under an employers' liability policy. The facts were that Farrell had been injured on November 10, 1962 whilst working

---

[52] [1953] 1 Q.B. 520.
[53] *Brook v. Trafalgar Insurance Co.* (1946) 79 Ll L. Rep. 365, CA.
[54] [1966] 1 W.L.R. 1334, CA.
[55] *Burridge & Son v. F.H. Homes & Sons Ltd* (1918) 87 L.J.K.B. 641.
[56] [1970] 1 W.L.R. 1400, CA.

for the insured employers, who did not notify the defendant insurers until April 1, 1963. On August 16, 1963, Farrell consulted solicitors who wrote to his employers claiming damages and asking them to forward the letter to their insurance company. The employers sent it to the defendant insurers, who wrote to Farrell's solicitors saying that no liability was admitted but arranging for a medical examination. Several letters passed, and the insurers also wrote to the insured employers that their chief officer had instructed that the matter be dealt with without prejudice to their liability under the policy. This letter was sent on April 8, 1964. On July 28, 1964, Farrell's solicitors wrote to the insurers asking "who is to accept service of proceedings on [the employers'] behalf". On August 4, 1964, the insurers replied: "should you wish to issue proceedings, we have no objection to them being issued on [the employers]", the usual practice being for the insurers to offer to accept service. It was argued before the Court of Appeal that by the letter of August 4, 1964 the insurers had waived compliance with the condition in the policy requiring the insured employers to notify or forward immediately on receipt, *inter alia*, every writ concerning any claim. Lord Denning M.R.[57] rejected that contention, considering that the mere invitation to serve the writ on the insured employers did not relieve the insured employers' of their duty to notify the insurers when they received it, and could not therefore constitute a waiver of reliance by the insurers on that condition.

Where a number of things must be done by the insured within a time **18–30** period which are all performed, and the insurer subsequently requests compliance with a further thing to be done, which the insurer should have requested within that same time period, this can amount to a waiver of compliance with the original requirements. Such conduct amounts to a waiver because, again, the insurers have not sought to rely on the breach and regard themselves as not liable. This was the reasoning of the Court of Appeal in *Toronto Railway Co. v. National British and Irish Millers Insurances Co. Ltd*[58] where a fire policy contained a condition precedent to payment of the claim (as against liability) that the claim would not be payable until after notice, ascertainment, estimate and satisfactory proof of the loss had been received by the insurers. It was also provided, though, that the insurers could require, further to those proofs and particulars, a magistrate or notary public to certify that he had examined the circumstances and believed the insured had honestly sustained the loss as appraised. After compliance with the other requirements and no request for such certification, a long correspondence ensued at the end of which the insurer asked to be supplied with a certificate of a magistrate or a notary public, and, further, said that if that certificate, in their opinion, was insufficient, they would require the loss to be ascertained by disinterested appraisers. It was held that the insurers had waived their right to rely on the condition precedent to payment and judgment was given to the insured.

---

[57] *ibid.* at 1406.
[58] (1914) 111 L.T. 555, CA.

Insurer entitled to reasonable time

18–31   Where an insured has filed a late notification of claim under the policy, mere lapse of time between that late notification and the actual decision of the insurers to rely on the breach is not enough to establish a waiver. This is because the insurer is entitled to have a reasonable time in which to make up his mind about a claim.[59] In *Allen v. Robles*,[60] the Court of Appeal held that for the insurers to lose their right to rely on the late notification by lapse of time, there has to have been some prejudice suffered by the insured, or third party rights had intervened, or there was a delay that was so long as to evidence that the insurers had accepted liability. Sensible insurers will either take rapid decisions on late notification to prevent the insured raising the issue of waiver, or write to the insured in express terms that they will continue to deal with a claim "without prejudice" to their right to raise non-notification after further deliberation. The latter course should be sufficient to preserve their rights in respect of the breach. Unlike the United Kingdom, in North America and Canada, liability insurers are obliged to conduct the defence of claims against their insureds, and so the latter course is adopted far more often, usually being recorded in formal non-waiver agreements. The topic of the insurers' exercise of their contractual right to take over and control proceedings, and the related question of waiver in this respect, is considered below in Chapter 20.

Estoppel

18–32   Estoppel can be raised by the insured in appropriate circumstances where the insurer has unequivocally done some act, or made some representation, that is inconsistent with the insurer's right to decline a claim, or rescind an insurance policy, on the ground of the insured's breach of the notification condition in the policy. If the insured has relied on the conduct or representation to alter his position, the insurer is unable to revoke the representation by reasonable notice which might otherwise be the case.[61] Megaw L.J. in the *Farrell's* case,[62] treated the argument of counsel as amounting to a plea of estoppel, rather than waiver, against the insurers. The insurers' letter to Farrell's solicitors had read:

> "We have received your letter dated July 28, and we would state that we have not concluded our enquiries into this matter, and should you wish to issue proceedings, we have no objection to them being issued on [the employers]."

[59] *McCormack v. National Motor and Accident Insurance Union* (1930) 40 Comm. Cas. 76; *Liberian Insurance Agency Inc. v. Mosse* [1977] 2 Lloyd's Rep. 560 at 565.

[60] [1969] 1 W.L.R. 1193; followed in *Forsikringsaktieselskapet Vesta v. Butcher* [1986] 2 All E.R. 488.

[61] *Ajayi v. Briscoe (Nigeria) Ltd* [1964] 1 W.L.R. 1326 at 1330, *per* Lord Hodson, PC; *Finagrain SA v. Kruse* [1976] 2 Lloyd's Rep. 508 at 545, *per* Brown L.J., CA; *The Kanchenjunga* [1990] 1 Lloyd's Rep. 391 at 399, *per* Lord Goff, HL.

[62] [1970] 1 W.L.R 1400, CA.

Per Megaw L.J.[63]:

> "It is said that that in effect constitutes an estoppel: that the plaintiffs' solic-
> itors were entitled to treat that as being a representation or a statement
> which meant that the insurers were not concerned to be told about the issue
> of any writ or other proceedings thereafter. In my judgment, the letter,
> accompanied by the evidence which was given in relation to it, is quite inca-
> pable of bearing such a meaning or producing such an effect."

Of course, his lordship was no doubt bearing in mind that here was a   **18–33**
third party, exercising rights under the 1930 Act, directly against insurers
of the employer against whom the third party had obtained judgment. The
parties to the policy were the employers and the insurers, and it therefore
was an attempt to say that a representation or statement made to a third
party to that contract could amount to an estoppel by the insurers as
between them and the employers (in whose shoes the third party subsequently stood). That argument therefore seemed misconceived on behalf
of the third party.

---

[63] *ibid.* at 1408, C.A. See also para. 11–84, above.

CHAPTER 19

THE INSURANCE INDEMNITY

1. THE PRINCIPLE OF INDEMNITY

19–01 Contracts of insurance have the underlying purpose of providing the insured with an indemnity against his loss, be it a liability incurred to a third party in the case of liability insurances, or loss of his own property or the property of others in his care in the case of property and financial insurances, and this purpose is enforced by the law. Accordingly, this fundamental rule of indemnity — that the insured shall recover no more than his loss — is a rule of universal application throughout the law of insurance. There will be a limit specified in the schedule to the insurance policy, though, which defines the limit of the recovery under the policy (the "sum insured"). In the case of old and used property, the sum payable will, unless the policy provides for settlement "new for old" (which is common for private household insurances, but rare for commercial insurance policies) be reduced to reflect the used nature of the destroyed or damaged insured property. This deduction is known as a reduction for "betterment". The recovery under the policy is usually further limited in that the insured will have to bear the first specified sum of each and every loss or claim, and this is known as the "excess" or "deductible". Finally, the extent of the indemnity recoverable in respect of any claim under the insurance may be further restricted by "averaging" of the claim, which is the proportional reduction of the sum payable by the insurers to reflect under-insurance by the insured, if there is a suitable condition of average within the policy's terms and conditions.

19–02 Long ago, the legal principle that the insured can recover no more than his loss was put in the following way[1]:

> "It has been truly stated that a policy of insurance is a contract indemnity, and that while the insured may name any sum he likes as the sum for which he will pay the premium, he does not, by so proposing that sum, nor does the company by accepting the risk, conclude themselves as to the amount which the plaintiff is to recover in consequence of each loss—because, although the plaintiff cannot recover beyond the sum insured upon each particular item . . . he cannot recover even that sum unless he proves that he has sustained damage, and then he will recover a sum commensurate to the loss which he has sustained; and therefore [the question] is, what is the actual damage sustained by the plaintiff on the subjects of insurance in consequence of the [insured peril]."

19–03 The overwhelming importance of the basic legal principle of indemnity was subsequently enunciated by Brett L.J. in *Castellain v. Preston* in the following manner[2]:

---

[1] *Vance v. Forster* (1841) Ir. Cir. Rep. 47 at 50, *per* Pennefather B.
[2] (1883) 11 Q.B.D. 380 at 386, CA.

"In order to give my opinion upon this case, I feel obliged to revert to the very foundation of every rule which has been promulgated and acted on by the courts with regard to insurance law. The very foundation, in my opinion, of every rule which has been applied to insurance law is this, namely, that the contract of insurance contained in a marine or fire policy is a contract of indemnity, and of indemnity only, and that this contract means that the assured, in case of a loss against which the policy has been made, shall be fully indemnified, but shall never be more than fully indemnified. That is the fundamental principle of insurance, and if ever a proposition is brought forward which is at variance with it, that is to say, which either will prevent the assured from obtaining a full indemnity, or which will give to the assured more than a full indemnity, that proposition must certainly be wrong."

Liability insurances

Problems of the extent of the indemnity do not generally arise in practice upon liability policies, because the loss is the extent of the liability incurred at law to the third party claimant, and, usually, both the third party's and the insured's legal costs and expenses relating to that action (incurred with the insurer's consent), are covered by the insurance indemnity wording. The problems that may arise relating to the extent of the indemnity afforded by the wording of liability insurances is considered in Chapter 6, above, save for the application of excesses, or deductibles, which are considered below.

19–04

Other insurances

Problems more often occur in relation to other policies. A number of aspects have to be considered in turn, namely, valued or unvalued policies, reinstatement or repair, salvage, betterment and application of the average clause. The amount payable to an insured in respect of a loss covered by more than one insurance, may give rise to the insurers having the right to claim contribution from the other insurers towards the indemnification of the insured, and this is discussed in Chapter 20, below.

19–05

2. CALCULATION OF THE INDEMNITY

Valued policies

Although popular in marine insurance practice, insurers rarely agree to ascribe pre-loss agreed values to property the subject of non-marine commercial insurances within the United Kingdom. This valuation of the subject matter of the policy between insurer and insured, when it occurs, will be conclusive as the measure of the indemnity under that insurance,[3] in the absence of fraud or mistake, where that subject matter is totally destroyed by an insured peril. Where the property forming the subject matter of the insurance is not totally destroyed, but merely damaged by the insured peril, any agreed value attaching to the damaged property still has application. This is the effect of the decision in *Elcock v. Thomson*,[4]

19–06

---

[3] *Bousfield v. Barnes* (1815) 4 Camp. 228; *Maurice v. Goldsborough Mort A. Co. Ltd* [1939] A.C. 452, PC.
[4] [1949] 2 K.B. 755.

where a mansion and its outbuildings had an agreed value of £106,850 under a fire policy. A fire occurred and damaged part of the mansion and the court had to consider the calculation of the indemnity payable under this valued fire policy, in circumstances where the mansion and outbuildings were really only worth £18,000 prior to the fire, and £12,600 afterwards. Morris J. considered that the insured was entitled to recover the true percentage depreciation based upon the agreed value rather than the true value, *i.e.*:

$$\text{indemnity} = \frac{(18,000 - 12,600 = 5,400) \times 106,850}{18,000} = £32,055$$

19–07   Morris J.'s reasoning was as follows[5]:

> "In my judgment, on the facts of the present case, the assured are entitled to be indemnified in respect of the depreciation which was caused by the fire, and, in quantifying such depreciation, the insurable value of the mansion as agreed by the parties cannot be set aside and disregarded. I observe that, at the end of the schedule to the policy, in the words by which such agreement as to value is expressed, it is stipulated that in the event of loss the property would be assumed to be of the value recorded and would be assessed accordingly. In the body of the policy the words used are 'to insure from loss or damage.' I have considered whether any significance is to be attached to the fact of the use only of the word 'loss' at the end of the schedule, and whether it could be argued that the agreement as to value was only to apply in the event of the destruction or loss of an item as opposed to damage occurring to it. No such point was, however, taken or argued, and I cannot imagine that any significance attaches to the use only of the word 'loss'.
>
> It would be strange and unnatural if an agreed value were to apply only in the event of complete destruction and not in the event of partial destruction. The respective words 'loss' and 'damage', as used in the policy, seem to be synonymous. It would not seem to be the case that the word 'loss' is only referable to complete destruction. Apart from this, however, the opening words of the provision, *viz.* the words 'The sum set opposite each item in this specification has been accepted by the underwriters and the assured as being the true value of the property insured', appear to contain agreement as to value irrespective of the meaning of the word 'loss' which is later used."

19–08   The calculation of the indemnity payable for partial loss of property given an agreed value under a policy of insurance is therefore:

$$\frac{\text{(true value } \textit{less} \text{ true value after damage)}}{\text{true value preceding damage}} \times \text{agreed value}$$

19–09   Insurers often provide for agreed values in consequential loss insurance policies, where an agreed value for loss of profits is given at the inception of the policy, but the calculation for loss of profits from interruption of the business may be complicated by the fact that it may be provided that the insured will only recover the same proportion of the agreed loss of profits as the material damage insurer has paid on his policy.[6] Thus, if the material damage insurer pays half of the limit of indemnity on the material

[5] *ibid.* at 763–764.
[6] *Beauchamp v. Faber* (1898) 3 Com. Cas. 308.

damage policy, then the consequential loss insurer will only pay half the agreed value of loss of profits. Moreover, insurers may provide that they receive the benefit of any reduction in loss of profits, *e.g.* by reduction in standing charges.[7] Consequential loss insurance is discussed in Chapter 15, above.

Unvalued policies

The specifying of a "sum insured" in the insurance policy, without more, does not indicate an agreed value on the property insured so as to render the policy a valued policy, but merely indicates a ceiling on recovery by the insured.[8] Where the policy contains no agreed values to be attributed to the insured property, the following rules apply: **19–10**

  (i) *Total loss*: the amount payable to the insured is the value of the property at the place[9] and time[10] it was destroyed.
  (ii) *Partial loss*: the amount payable to the insured is the difference in value of the property before and after it was damaged.[11]

In each case, therefore, the value of the property before the loss or damage is to be that property's market value immediately prior to the loss or damage, unless the loss or damage can only be made good by the reinstatement of the property when the value will be the cost of reinstatement.

This test of the measure of indemnity for unvalued policies was laid   **19–11** down relatively recently by the Court of Appeal in *Leppard v. Excess Insurance Co. Ltd.*[12] The facts were that the insured purchased a cottage from his father-in-law, who had previously only received one offer, of £1,500 from a local farmer whose land surrounded the cottage, on the basis that he would share the eventual profit. He insured the cottage for £10,000 in 1974, and increased the sum insured to £12,000 the following year. He tried selling the cottage for £12,000, but the farmer hindered any sale by challenging the right of way to the cottage over his land and would not allow a water-main to be run over his land. The insured admitted that, in these circumstances, he would have accepted £4,500 for the sale of the cottage. The cottage was then destroyed by fire, and the insured claimed £8,694 for the cost of its reinstatement after making an allowance for betterment. The policy wording was standard in that it provided that the insurers:

"at [their] option by payment reinstatement or repair indemnify the insured in respect of a loss or damage caused by . . . [the perils]."

---

[7] *Brunton v. Marshall* (1922) 10 Ll. L. Rep. 689.

[8] *Kyzuna Investments Ltd v. Ocean Marine Mutual Insurance Association (Europe)* [2000] 1 All E.R. (Comm.) 557.

[9] *Rice v. Baxendale* (1861) 7 H. & N. 96 at 101, *per* Bramwell B.

[10] *Chapman v. Pole* (1870) 22 L.T. 306 at 309, *per* Cockburn L.J.; *Westminster Fire Office v. Glasgow Provident Investment Society* (1888) 13 App. Cas. 699, at 711, *per* Lord Selborne, HL.

[11] *Westminster Fire Office v. Glasgow Provident Investment Society*, (1888) 13 App. Ca. 699, HL.

[12] [1979] 2 All E.R. 668, CA.

19–12   The defendant insurers contended that the insured was entitled to recover only his actual loss, which was the market value of the cottage at the time of the fire, agreed at £4,500, less the agreed site value of £1,500, and the Court of Appeal upheld this principle that an insured can only recover his actual loss, even where the policy expressly stated that the full value of the property is to be deemed to be the reinstatement cost. Megaw L.J. (as he then was) explained[13]:

> "What the insurers have agreed to do is to indemnify the insured in respect of loss or damage caused by fire. The 'full value' is the cost of replacement. That defines the maximum amount recoverable under the policy. The amount recoverable cannot exceed the cost of replacement. But it does not say that that maximum is recoverable if it exceeds the actual loss. There is nothing in the wording of the policy, including the declaration [of full value] which is incorporated therein, which expressly or by any legitimate inference provides that the loss which is to be indemnified is agreed to be, or is to be deemed to be, the cost of reinstatement, the 'full value', even though the cost of reinstatement is greater than the actual loss. The plaintiff is entitled to recover his real loss, his actual loss, not exceeding the cost of replacement.
>   There remains the second question. Was the plaintiffs actual loss the cost of the reinstatement of the cottage? Or was it, as the defendants contend, the market value of the property as it was at the time of the fire? The defendants do not rely upon any general principle in support of their submission. They say, rightly in my judgment, that this is a question of fact, and that one must look at all the relevant facts of the particular case to ascertain the actual value of the loss at the relevant date. Of course, one is entitled to look to the future so as to bring in relevant factors which would have been foreseen at the relevant date as being likely to affect the value of the thing insured in one way or the other, if the loss of it had not occurred on that date, but on the evidence in this case . . . the plaintiff . . . at the relevant date, wished to sell the house, and was ready and willing to sell it for £4,500 — indeed, on his own evidence, for less. [The plaintiff] submits that he was not bound to sell it. Of course not. He might thereafter, if the loss had not occurred, have changed his mind. The value of the property might have increased or it might have decreased. But there is no getting away from the reality of the case: 'It was' (I am quoting again from the judgment) 'an empty cottage that he had for the purpose of sale' . . . If the plaintiff himself was ready and willing, as he plainly was, to sell the property for £4,500, or less, on October 25, 1978, just before the fire, how can it be said that that was not its actual value at that time: unless, indeed, some reason could be shown why the plaintiff himself should have made a mistake about, or under-estimated, its real value. No basis is shown for any such suggestion. The amount of the loss here, in my judgment, is shown by the facts to have been the figure agreed, hypothetically, on this basis, as £3,000."

19–13   Lane L.J. (as he then was) concurred[14]:

> "It is clear, with great respect to the [trial] judge, that by awarding the [reinstatement] sum that he did to the plaintiff, the plaintiff is undoubtedly £5,000 or so better off than if he had succeeded in achieving his ambition of selling this cottage for £4,500 or £4,000. That means, in short, that he has received more than an indemnity against his loss. He has had a bonus. This

---

[13] *ibid.* at 674.
[14] *ibid.* at 676.

is an indemnity policy: it entitles him to the amount of his loss, and no more. Accordingly, it seems to me that the amount to which he is entitled in respect of this fire is the £3,000 which is the agreed value of the cottage as it was immediately before the fire. That is all he is entitled to recover."

The calculation of the indemnity recoverable under the policy is, therefore, the actual or real loss to the insured, measured at the time of the loss and immediately after, taking all relevant matters in consideration, and "market value" may express this loss.[15] Increases in value of the insured building or insured goods,[16] arising after inception of the policy in question, are thus accounted for, as is any reduction in value. Where a claim is made for loss of insured stock, but the insured's stock records are shown to be unreliable, the court will still seek to quantify the loss as best it can on the material before it.[17]

The situation of the market value being lower than the cost of rein-   **19–14**
statement also led to a dispute between the insured and the insurer as to which is the proper measure to be applied, in *Reynolds and Anderson v. Phoenix Assurance Co. Ltd*,[18] where the insurers also put forward the argument that a further alternative measure was the cost of modern replacement property. The insured bought some old mailings in Suffolk for the storage and milling of grain and insured them for £18,000 in 1969. In 1973, the insured increased the sum insured to £550,000, to represent rebuilding costs, and in November of that year, a fire destroyed some 70 per cent of the makings. The insurers offered about £55,000 as indemnity, that sum representing the cost of buying a modern replacement building of steel and asbestos construction and land upon which to build it. The insured rejected this offer, and argued that he was entitled to the cost of reinstating the makings, *i.e.* some £247,000.

Forbes J. held that the insured was entitled to judgment representing the   **19–15**
cost of reinstatement, less a sum of £10,000 on the facts, for the element of betterment to the insured. The insured was held to be entitled to this sum on the basis that he genuinely intended to reinstate the buildings, and could, therefore, only be properly indemnified by such sum being paid, and that this intention was not a mere eccentricity. Forbes J. rejected the objective test being applied of whether a sensible commercial concern would choose reinstatement or a replacement modern structure, and criticised the "market value" test when applied to buildings, emphasising that each case had to be considered on its own facts[19]:

"you are not to enrich or impoverish: the difficulty lies in deciding whether the award of a particular sum amounts to enrichment or impoverishment. This question cannot depend in my view on an automatic or inevitable assumption that the market value is the appropriate measure of the loss.

---

[15] *McLean Enterprises Ltd v. Ecclesiastical Insurance Office plc* [1986] 2 Lloyd's Rep. 416.
[16] See *J. Gliksten & Son Ltd v. Green* [1929] A.C. 381; *Re Wilson and Scottish Insurance Corp. Ltd* [1920] 2 Ch 28.
[17] As in *Atlantic Metal Co. Ltd v. Hepburn* [1960] 2 Lloyd's Rep. 42.
[18] [1978] 2 Lloyd's Rep. 440.
[19] *ibid.* at 452–453.

Indeed in many, perhaps most cases, market value seems singularly inept, as its choice subsumes the proposition that the assured can be forced to go into the market (if there is one) and buy a replacement. But buildings are not like tons of coffee or bales of cloth or other commodities unless perhaps the owner is one who deals in real property. To force an owner who is not a property dealer to accept market value if he has no desire to go to market seems to me a conclusion to which one should not easily arrive. There must be many circumstances in which an assured should be entitled to say that he does not wish to go elsewhere and hence that his indemnity is not complete unless he is paid the reasonable cost of rebuilding the premises *in situ*. At the same time the cost of reinstatement cannot be taken as inevitably the proper measure of indemnity . . . The question of the proper measure of indemnity thus becomes a matter of fact and degree to be decided in the circumstances of each case."

19–16   It follows that where there is no market value that can fairly be attributed to the lost or damaged goods or buildings, one value that can be attached is the cost of reinstatement. Accordingly, in *Pleasurama Ltd v. Sun Alliance & London Insurance Ltd*,[20] where an established bingo hall was nearly totally destroyed, Parker J. held that the cost of reinstating the building was the only measure of indemnity available because there was insufficient evidence of the market value for established bingo halls to enable any kind of reliable estimate of market value to be made.[21]

19–17   However, the mere taking of the cost of replacement or reinstatement as the measure of indemnity for whole or partial losses of goods which have no available market for replacement was criticised by Winn J. in *Richard Aubrey Film Productions Ltd v. Graham*.[22] The claimant insured held an "all risks" insurance to indemnify him against the loss or damage to all the raw stock of a motion picture to be filmed. The insured limit was £18,000, although at the time of the loss by theft of part of the film, the claimant held the right to exploit the film for £20,000. Winn J. considered that the measure of indemnity was not simply the cost of re-shooting the film lost, but, rather, upon the facts, the measure of indemnity was £15,300. No reasoning was given, though, for this figure for the estimated market value, other than his Lordship assessed there would be difficulties in re-shooting because the starring children were now older, and that the editing and final completion of the film would cost £3,000.

Cost of insured items, not resale value

19–18   Stock-in-trade will generally have an available market from which a market value can be gauged of the destroyed or damaged goods, and the insured is also entitled to the costs of transporting replacement goods to the place at which they were lost.[23] This market value is not the price for which those goods would have been sold on to customers (unless the policy expressly provides otherwise), but the price of obtaining other similar goods. This is illustrated by *Atlantic Metal Co. Ltd v. Hepburn*[24]

---

[20] [1979] 1 Lloyd's Rep. 389.
[21] *ibid.* at 393.
[22] [1960] 2 Lloyd's Rep. 101 at 105.
[23] *Rice v. Baxendale* (1861) 7 H. & N. 96 at 102, *per* Bramwell B.
[24] [1960] 2 Lloyd's Rep. 42.

where some metal was stolen from the insured's warehouse, and a claim was made based on the selling price of the metal of £250 per ton, but Pearson J. held that the insured was only entitled to recover the £234 per ton replacement cost.

No right to betterment

The "market value" test can be imagined to be equally as inappropriate in the case of machinery, and other goods not forming the business' stock-in-trade. If production machinery is destroyed, nothing short of the physical replacement of the machinery will truly indemnify the insured for his loss. Where equivalent replacement second-hand machinery is available from somewhere no problem arises, but where there is no ready used replacement available, new machinery will be the only option for the insured, but he has no right to demand new machinery from the insurer.[25] Unless the insurer has elected to reinstate, the insurer will seek to pay a monetary indemnity that reflects the fact that the insured is now getting the latest technically improved machinery which will improve the insured's manufacturing process, and thus profitability, and it will be new machinery. A deduction is then made on the cost of the new machinery by the insurer, usually in a sum agreed between the insurer and the insured, this deduction being called an allowance for "betterment".[26] The insured will be entitled to the costs of transporting replacement second-hand machinery to his premises, and, where appropriate, for putting the machinery up and replacing it in status quo.[27]

19–19

Successive losses

Unless a provision in the insurance policy alters the position, the marine insurance principle[28] applies and the insured is entitled to recover a full indemnity, up to the sum insured, in respect of each insured loss that occurs during the period of insurance.[29] Insurers may insert to types of provision to alter the position. The first is to provide an "aggregate" limit to all claims made within the period of insurance. The second way is to introduce an "automatic reinstatement" condition that requires the insured to pay an additional premium after the happening of a loss in order for the policy sums insured to be reinstated to the full value.

19–20

Payment of interest

The insured is not entitled to the payment of interest in respect of the monetary settlement made by the insurer, even if the insurer has taken months, or even years, to arrive at its decision to pay an indemnity and

19–21

---

[25] Ewer v. National Employers' Mutual General Insurance Association Ltd [1937] 2 All E.R. 193 at 203, per MacKinnon J.

[26] Vance v. Forster (1841) Ir. Cir. Rep. 47 at 50, per Pennefather B.

[27] ibid.

[28] Marine Insurance Act 1906, s.77.

[29] Joyce v. Kenard (1871) L.R. 7 Q.B. 78 at 83, per Lush J.; Prosser v. Lancashire and Yorkshire Accident Insurance Co. Ltd (1890) 6 T.L.R. 285, at 286, per Lord Esher M.R., CA; Re Law Car and General Insurance Corp. [1913] 2 Ch. 103, at 118, per Cozens-Hardy M.R., CA.

determine how that indemnity should be. The insured will only be able to seek payment of interest where he has commenced proceedings against the insurer for recovery of an indemnity under the policy, or damages in the same sum[30] for breach of contract. Such an award of interest is a discretionary amount as determined by, either the county court under section 69 of the County Courts Act 1984, or the High Court under section 35A of the Supreme Court Act 1981. Courts have previously erred towards the payment of interest from the date that sum an indemnity should have been paid, that is after a reasonable period of time being allowed for the insurer to investigate the claim.[31] Very recently, however, Langley J. has said that interest should be payable from the date the cause of action accrued for the relevant payment arose, and there is no special exception relating to insurance cases.[32] Non-payment of interest to the insured will amount to a windfall to the insurer, unless other factors come into play, such as the insured's unco-operative behaviour or attempts to exaggerate the losses.[33] Indeed, if the insured has misled the insurer, or concealed information, this would be a reason to refuse interest.[34] The period from which the interest will commence will not usually be the date of the loss, but from a date after a reasonable period of time during which the insurer is entitled to investigate the claim.[35]

3. REINSTATEMENT AND REPAIR

General principles

19–22   Insurers are obliged to pay in money an indemnity in respect of insured property destroyed or damaged by an insured peril, unless the terms of the insurance contract provide that they may alternatively reinstate or repair the property themselves.[36] Such a provision is now usually inserted, making the choice that of the insurer by election, but, as can be seen from *Leppard v. Excess Insurance Co. Ltd*,[37] discussed above, this does not entitle the insurers to do anything other than select the form of the indemnity. Most building insurances will contain a clause along the following lines:

> "If the Insurers elect or become bound to reinstate or replace any property the Insured shall at his own expense produce and give to the Company all such plans, documents, books and information as the Insurers may reasonably

---

[30] See further Chapter 22, below.

[31] See, *e.g. Atlantic Metal Co. Ltd v. Hepburn* [1960] 2 Lloyd's Rep. 42.

[32] *Kuwait Airways Corp. v. Kuwait Insurance Co. SAK & others (No.3)* [2000] Lloyd's Rep. I.R. 678; see also *Baillerie, Tindall & Cox v. Drysdale* (1949) 82 Ll. L. Rep. 736, where Morris J. (as he then was) awarded interest on a business interruption insurance claim from the date that the insured's claim was properly made, that is once the material damage insurer had admitted liability.

[33] See *Adcock v. Co-operative Insurance Society Ltd* [2000] T.L.R. 338, CA.

[34] *Rhesa Shipping Co. SA v. Edmunds* [1984] Lloyd's Rep. 555 at 559, *per* Sir John Donaldson M.R., CA; reversed. on a different point [1985] 1 W.L.R. 948, HL.

[35] *ibid.*; see also *McClean Enterprises Ltd v. Ecclesiastical Insurance Office plc* [1986] 2 Lloyd's Rep. 416 at 727–428.

[36] *Rayner v. Preston* (1881) 18 Ch. D. 1, at 10, *per* Brett L.J., CA.

[37] [1979] 2 All E.R. 668, CA.

require. The Insurers shall not be bound to reinstate exactly or completely but only as circumstances permit and in reasonably sufficient manner and shall not in any case be bound to expend in respect of any of the items insured more than the sum insured thereon."

This provision for the insurer's election to reinstate or repair, does not **19–23** alter the insured's contractual right under the insurance to a full indemnity in respect of his loss or damage, within the confines of the other terms of the policy, *e.g.* limit of indemnity. Where the insurer can elect to pay or reinstate, such election must be made within a reasonable time.[38] If the insurer elects to reinstate, he must restore the property to its original condition[39] (subject to any provision in the insurance contract to the contrary, *e.g.* "as circumstances permit and in reasonably sufficient manner"), otherwise the insured will have a remedy in damages to complete the work of reinstatement.[40] Equally, in circumstances where the insurer has elected to reinstate, but is later prevented from reinstating the property by a supervening event outside his control, the insured is entitled to a monetary indemnity.[41] The final part is important, for in its absence an insurer would seem to be liable to complete reinstatement whatever the cost, the limit of indemnity contained in the policy schedule, of course, being restricted to application to a monetary indemnity.

Statutory reinstatement of buildings

In England and Wales,[42] but not Scotland or Ireland,[43] certain persons **19–24** have the right to demand that the insurance company (but not a Lloyd's underwriter[44]), shall expend the insurance money payable to their insured upon the physical reinstatement of a building damaged or destroyed by fire. The Act applies, incidentally, not merely to buildings, but also to permanent, as against temporary or trade, fixtures and fittings that would normally pass under a conveyance of real property.[45] This right is given by section 83 of the Fires Prevention (Metropolis) Act 1774, which defines those persons so entitled as "any person or persons interested in or entitled unto any house or houses or other buildings which may hereafter be burnt down, demolished or damaged by fire". The Act was passed with the purpose of deterring insured persons from setting fire to their own buildings, and it has therefore been held that the insured himself has no such right conferred by the Act.[46]

---

[38] *Sutherland v. Sun Fire Office* (1852) 14 D. (Ct of Sess.) 775; *Scottish Amicable Heritable Securities Association v. Northern Assurance Co.* (1883) 11 R. (Ct. of Sess.) 287.

[39] *Alchorne v. Favill* (1825) 4 L.J.(o.s.)Ch. 47.

[40] *Home District Mutual Insurance Co. v. Thompson* (1847) 1 E. & A. 247.

[41] *Brown v. Royal Insurance Co.* (1859) 1 E. & E. 853; *Anderson v. Commercial Union Assurance Co.* (1885) 55 L.J.Q.B. 146, CA.

[42] *Re Barker, ex p. Gorely* (1864) 4 De G.J. & S.M. 477; *Re Quicke's Trusts* [1908] 1 Ch. 887.

[43] *Westminster Fire Office v. Glasgow Provident Investment Society* (1888) 13 App. Cas. 699, HL; *Andrews v. Patriotic Assurance Co. (No. 2)* (1886) 18 L.R. Ir. 355 at 366, *per* Palles C.B.

[44] *Portavon Cinema Co. Ltd v. Price and Century Insurance Co. Ltd* [1939] 4 All E.R. 601.

[45] *Re Barker, ex p. Gorely* (1864) 4 De G.J. & S.M. 477; *Re Quicke's Trusts, Poltimore v. Quicke* [1908] 1 Ch. 887.

[46] *Reynolds and Anderson v. Phoenix Assurance Co. Ltd* [1978] 2 Lloyd's Rep. 440 at 462, *per* Forbes J.

19-25   The question of what persons are embraced by the words "interested in or entitled unto" any building, has come before the courts on several occasions. A person who has a legal charge, *e.g.* a mortgage, upon the building damaged or destroyed by fire has the statutory right, irrespective of the amount of that charge and irrespective of any lack of entitlement to the policy moneys, in respect of the mortgagor's insurance.[47]

Mortgagees of buildings also have an additional right under the Law of Property Act 1925[48] to compel a mortgagor who has received insurance moneys upon the mortgaged building, to expend it on reinstatement of the building. So also will a tenant have the statutory right upon his landlord's insurance of the building,[49] or, conversely, the landlord upon the tenant's insurance.[50]

Pending sale of building

19-26   A tenant can also enforce the expenditure of the insurance moneys from the landlords' insurance on reinstatement of the insured building where, at the time of the fire, the landlord has entered into a contract for the sale of the building, it being no answer for the insurers to contend that as their insured received the full purchase moneys after the fire they had therefore personally suffered no loss. This was the decision in *Lonsdale & Thompson Ltd v. Black Arrow Group plc.*[51] The facts were that by a lease dated December 4, 1978, the defendant landlords let a warehouse to the claimant tenants for 25 years. The landlords covenanted that they would cause the premises to be insured in a sum not less than the full reinstatement value against specified risks including fire. Clauses 1 and 2(2) of the lease provided that the tenant should pay by way of additional rent a sum corresponding to the premium. By clause 3(2), it was the duty of the landlord "in case of destruction or damage to the demised premises by any insured risk . . . to ensure . . . that all moneys payable . . . shall with all convenient speed . . . be laid out and applied in building, repairing or otherwise reinstating the premises."

19-27   Clause 13 of Section A of the landlords' insurance provided that "in the event of the property insured being destroyed or damaged the basis upon which the amount payable under . . . the policy is to be calculated shall be the reinstatement of the property destroyed or damaged". On December 21, 1989, the landlords contracted to sell the freehold, subject to the lease in favour of the claimants. Completion occurred on March 22, 1990. Between these two dates, on February 8, 1990, the warehouse was destroyed by fire. However, completion proceeded and the price of the freehold was paid in accordance with the terms of the contract without regard to the fire damage. Under section 83 of the Fires Protection

---

[47] See the judgment of Parker J. in *Sinnott v. Bowden* [1912] 2 Ch. 414; applied *Halifax Building Society v. Keighley* [1931] 2 K.B. 248.
[48] Law of Property Act 1925, s.108(2).
[49] *Wimbledon Park Golf Club Ltd v. Imperial Insurance Co. Ltd* (1902) 18 T.L.R. 815.
[50] *Vernon v. Smith* (1821) 5 B. & Ald. 1; *Matthey v. Curling* [1922] 2 A.C. 180, HL; *Re Barker, ex p. Goreley* (1864) 4 De G.J. & S.M. 477.
[51] [1993] 11 L.S. Gaz. R. 46.

(Metropolis) Act 1774 the claimants, as tenants, were entitled to require the insurers to discharge such liability as they might have to their insured under the policy by reinstating the premises. The claimants had duly served the requisite notice on the insurers pursuant to the Act.

The insurers had declined to comply with that notice on the ground that **19–28** they did not have any contractual liability to their insured and could not, therefore, have any statutory liability to the claimant tenants. They said they were not obliged to do more than indemnify the insured in respect of injury to its freehold interest, because it was only in respect of that interest that it could have suffered any loss. The result of the contract of sale was that at the time of the fire the insured had parted with its entire beneficial interest in the property, retaining no other interest than its vendor's lien for the price. When, upon completion, the insured received the price in full without any abatement on account of the fire, it was completely indemnified for its loss. As for their insured's liability to lay out the insurance proceeds in reinstatement, that arose only if and when they were received. It followed, the insurers argued, that nothing was payable by them. The court did not agree with the insurers' contentions and held that the question of whether the measure of the insurers' liability was limited to the injury done to the landlords' reversion, depended on the terms of the policy. Insurances on property were prima facie to be construed as contracts of indemnity. Subject to the express terms of the policy, the measure of the indemnity was the diminution in value of the thing insured as a result of the operation of the insured peril. The parties might agree that the damage suffered by the thing insured would be assessed on some agreed basis. There might, for example, be an agreed undamaged value. There might be a provision, such as the one found in this case, that the cost of reinstatement, which would otherwise be no more than evidence of the diminution in value of the property, should be the measure of the insurers' liability. But such provisions did not prevent the contract of insurance from being one of indemnity. They merely required the value of the indemnity to be calculated on conventional facts. It remained necessary to look at the particular position of the insured to see whether in the circumstances they would, by recovering the contractual measure, obtain more than an indemnity.

If the insured only had a limited interest in the property, being, for example, **19–29** a tenant or reversioner, a trustee, a mortgagee or a bailee, the value of his own interest might have diminished by much less than the value of the property or the cost of its reinstatement. But it did not necessarily follow that if the insured recovered the whole diminution in the value of the property or the whole cost of reinstatement, he would be getting more than an indemnity. That depended on what his legal obligations were as to the use of his insurance proceeds. If he was accountable for the proceeds to the owner of the other interests, then he would not be receiving more than an indemnity, if the insurers paid the full amount for which the property was insured. That would be so, whether the insured was accountable to the owners of the other interests as a trustee of the proceeds of the insurance, or simply on the basis that he owed them a contractual obligation to pay those proceeds over to them, or to employ them in reinstatement. None of that meant that a party with a limited interest who insured the entire interest in the property was insuring on behalf of the others as well as for himself. All that it meant was that his obligations as to the use of the insurance moneys, once they had been paid, were relevant in determining whether he would recover more than an indemnity by getting the measure of loss provided for in the policy. Accordingly, the insurers were liable to the landlord for the full reinstatement value and the landlords were bound to reinstate the premises on the tenants' behalf.

Right of purchaser of real property

19–30   A purchaser of real property may also have the statutory right against the vendor's insurers should a fire occur between exchange of contracts and completion of the conveyance.[52]

Mode of enforcement of statutory reinstatement

19–31   To enforce this statutory right to compel the insurer to spend the insurance moneys on reinstatement of the building, interested persons must make their "request" in terms — to merely ask the insurance company not to pay anything to the insured will be insufficient.[53] If the insurance company is unwilling to comply with such a request, the interested party may apply to the court for a mandamus to compel the insurance company to lay out the insurance moneys on reinstatement,[54] or may seek an injunction restraining payment of the insurance moneys to the insured.[55] Of course, if the relevant interested party has contractually recognised the insured's right to the insurance moneys, the insured can seek an injunction to restrain the interested party from requesting the insurance company to lay out those moneys on reinstatement.[56]

Suspicion of fraud or arson

19–32   Section 83 of the 1774 Act also provides that the insurance company are authorised and required to lay out the insurance moneys, so far as they will go, on reinstating any buildings damaged or destroyed by fire where the company has grounds for suspicion that the insured has been guilty of fraud or of wilfully setting fire to such buildings. Both limbs of section 83 (*i.e.* suspicion or request) do not apply if:

(a) the insured, within 60 days of the claim being adjusted, gives a sufficient security to such company that the insurance moneys will be so laid out, or

(b) the said insurance moneys are in that time settled and disposed of to and amongst all the contending parties, to the satisfaction and approbation of the governors or directors of the insurance company.

[52] *Rayner v. Preston* (1881) 18 Ch. D. 1 at 15, *per* James L.J. (*obiter*), CA.
[53] *Simpson v. Scottish Union Insurance Co.* (1863) 1 Hem. & M. 618.
[54] *ibid.*; considered *Sun Insurance Office v. Galinsky* [1914] 2 K.B. 545; *cf. Wimbledon Park Golf Club Ltd v. Imperial Insurance Co. Ltd* (1902) 18 T.L.R. 815.
[55] *Wimbledon Park Golf Club Ltd v. Imperial Insurance Co. Ltd* (1902) 18 T.L.R. 815.
[56] *Reynard v. Arnold* (1875) 10 Ch. App. 386.

4. SALVAGE

Where property of any description is damaged or destroyed by an
insured peril for which the insurer either makes payment to the insured, or
reinstates or repairs that property, the debris vests in the insurer to obtain
what he can for it as salvage.[57] Similarly, where goods are damaged to such
an extent that the insurer replaces them, either an actual total loss, or a
constructive total loss, be it machinery or whatever, the damaged goods
vest in the insurer upon such replacement or monetary payment under the
policy. If it were otherwise the insured would be more than indemnified[58]
in respect of the loss or damage suffered. This salvage is transferred on the
principle of equity expressed by Lord Hardwicke in *Randal v. Cockran*[59]
that the person who originally sustained the loss was the owner, but after
satisfaction is made to him, the insurer becomes the owner.[60]

19–33

It seems that this transfer of rights in salvage-matter need not necessarily
occur, rather it is at the option of the insurer, who may prefer not to take
over the salvage, for instance, if by so doing liabilities may be incurred to
third parties.[61] In practice, many insurers prefer that the insured be encouraged to dispose of salvaged materials himself, his claim being adjusted by
an allowance for a reasonable sum for salvage value. For instance, retail
goods may be placed in a salvage sale, although such a sale may be less
acceptable in the case of wholesale goods or manufacturer's raw materials.

19–34

Most material damage policies will contain the following type of condition relevant to the salvaging of property by the insurer[62]:

19–35

"On the happening of any destruction or damage in respect of which a claim
is or may be made under this Policy, the Insurer, and every person authorised
by the Insurer, may, without thereby incurring any liability and without
diminishing the right of the Insurer to rely on any conditions of this Policy,
enter, take or keep possession of the building or premises where the destruction or damage has happened, and may take possession of or require to be
delivered to them any of the property hereby Insured and may keep possession of and deal with such property for all reasonable manner. This
Condition shall be evidence of the leave and licence of the insured to the
Insurer so to do. If the Insured or anyone acting on his behalf shall not comply with the requirements of the Insurer or shall hinder or obstruct the
Insurer in doing any of the above mentioned acts, then all benefit under this
policy shall be forfeited. The Insured shall not in any case be entitled to
abandon any property to the Insurer whether taken possession of by the
Insurer or not."

[57] *Skipper v. Grant* (1861) 10 C.B.(n.s.) 237 at 245, *per* Williams J.
[58] *Dane v. Mortgage Insurance Corp. Ltd* [1894] 1 Q.B. 54 at 61, *per* Lord Esher M.R., CA;
Re Law Guarantee Trust and Accident Society Ltd (1913) 108 L.T. 830 at 832, *per* Neville J.
[59] (1748) 1 Ves. Sen. 98.
[60] *Rankin v. Potter* (1873) L.R. 6 H.L. 83 at 118, *per* Blackburn J.; see also *Skipper v. Grant*
(1861) 10 C.B.(n.s.) 237; *Oldfield v. Price (Secretary of General Fire Assurance Co.)* (1860) 2
F. & F. 80; *Kaltenbach v. Mackenzie* (1878) 3 C.P.D. 467 at 470–471, *per* Brett L.J., CA.
[61] *Allgemeine Versicherungs-Gesellschaft Helvetia v. German Property Administrator* [1931]
1 K.B. 672 at 688, *per* Scrutton L.J., CA.
[62] *Ahmedbhoy Habibhoy v. Bombay Fire and Marine Insurance Co.* (1912) 107 L.T. 668,
PC.

London salvage corps

19–36   Certain insurers insuring property in Greater London against fire risks
have established salvage corps or associations, and it is the duty of the
London Fire Brigade, subject to regulations made by the Greater London
Council, to afford all necessary assistance to such salvage corps or associations which attend fires to save insured property. Further, the fire brigade
must hand over property saved from the fire to the custody of an officer of
such corps or association, upon his application.[63]

5. APPLICATION OF AVERAGE FOR UNDER-INSURANCE OF PROPERTY

19–37   It is now the practice for insurers to include two clauses in nearly all
types of commercial policies upon property, the purport of these clauses
being to provide that the insured only recovers the proportion that his loss
bears to the risk known to the insurer, and upon which the insurer assessed
the premium. Additionally, fire policies generally provide for the importation
of "average" provisions, as they are known, where two or more policies are
held covering the same risk (see further, Chapter 20). In the absence of an
"average" clause, the insured may recover the full sum insured (assuming
such under-insurance does not amount to a non-disclosure of a material
fact).[64]

Common average clauses

19–38   The first of the two conditions of "average" usually to be found will be
in a form dependent upon whether the policy is a floating policy (*e.g.* upon
goods stored in a warehouse, or in-transit) based upon a maximum value
of the goods declared to the insurer, or a policy where the insured simply
specifies a maximum sum insured for all property covered by the insurance. In the first case, to adjust the claim in proportion to the value
declared in the policy, the clause may read:

> "If after the occurrence of any loss or damage it is found that the amount
> of the last declaration previous to the loss or damage is less than the
> amount that ought to have been declared then the amount recoverable hereunder . . . shall be reduced in the same proportion as the amount of the last
> declaration bears to the amount that ought to have been declared."

The declared value should be the total value of the insured property and
is not the sum insured which is the limit of the insurer's liability under the
policy. The premium for policies which contain a declared value clause is
assessed on this declared value. The clause operates, therefore, where the
declared value has understated the value of the insured property (in the
absence of the insurer repudiating the policy for material non-disclosure),
and reducing the indemnity in proportion to the understatement of

[63] Metropolitan Fire Brigade Act 1865, s. 29.
[64] *Hair v. Prudential Assurance Co. Ltd* [1983] 2 Lloyd's Rep. 667; *cf. Carreras v. Canard S.S. Co.* [1918] 1 K.B. 118.

declared value. Thus, the calculation of the indemnity payable by the insurer is:

$$\frac{\text{Declared value of insured property}}{\text{Actual value at time of loss/damage}} \times \text{loss} = \text{indemnity}$$

If, therefore, the contents of a building owned by a warehouseman are insured under a "floating" fire policy where the declared value of the contents at any one time is given by the insured as £250,000, but, due to a temporary increase in business the insured warehouseman has goods to the value of £300,000 stored in the building at the time of the fire, and £60,000 worth of goods are damaged, the amount recoverable under the fire policy with this average clause will be: **19–39**

$$\frac{£250,000}{£300,000} \times £60,000 = £50,000$$

In the second case, the condition of "average" is the "Pro Rata Condition of Average" (otherwise called the "First Condition of Average" or the "Condition of Average"). It is inserted in virtually all non-floating policies on property, and will be in this type of form: **19–40**

> "Whenever a sum insured is declared to be subject to Average, if the property covered thereby shall at the breaking out of any fire or at the commencement of any destruction of or damage to such property by any other peril hereby insured against be collectively of greater value than such sum insured, then the insured shall be considered as being his own insurer for the difference and shall bear a rateable share of the loss accordingly."

When there is under-insurance, upon a loss occurring the clause operates to reduce the indemnity payable under the policy in direct proportion to the amount that the insured is underinsured. The calculation is: **19–41**

$$\frac{\text{sum for which the property is insured}}{\text{value of property at time of loss/damage}} \times \text{loss} = \text{indemnity}$$

Thus, if a building and contents are insured under a fire policy as, respectively, Item I and Item II in the sums of £300,000 and £200,000, and a fire occurs causing damage to the contents only of £50,000 when the true value of the contents is £250,000, the indemnity payable will be:

$$\frac{£300,000 + £200,000}{£300,000 + £250,000} \times £50,000 = £45,455$$

Second condition of average

The second "condition of average" usually found in property insurances is not truly an average clause, but rather a clause excluding property already insured under another policy of lesser scope than the instant policy (*i.e.* the rules of contribution do not apply). It thus regulates the payment to be made by the several insurers of the lost or damaged property. Such a clause may read: **19–42**

"But if any of the property included in such average shall at the breaking out of any fire, or at the commencement of any destruction of or damage to such property by any other peril hereby insured against, be also covered by any other more specific insurance, *i.e.* by an insurance which at the time of such fire or at the commencement of such destruction or damage applies to part only of the property actually at risk and protected by this insurance and to no other property whatsoever, then this policy shall not insure the same except only as regards any excess of value beyond the amount of such more specific insurance, or insurances, which said excess is declared to be under the protection of this policy and subject to average as aforesaid."

19–43   Thus, when this clause is inserted in, for instance, a policy covering the buildings and all the stock-in-trade of the insured, and the insured also holds another policy upon a particular portion of that stock-in-trade, the wider, former, policy will only operate upon the buildings and that portion of the stock-in-trade not insured under the latter, and more restricted, policy. The wider policy also applies "average" to such losses as occur and are covered by it.

Taking the same example worked through in discussion of the "Pro Rata Average Condition" above, with the further fact that £30,000 of cover in respect of the contents is provided under a contents-only insurance, the calculation for the indemnity recoverable under the main policy is:

$$\frac{\text{sum insured}}{\text{value at time of loss}} \times (\text{loss } \textit{less} \text{ loss insured elsewhere})$$

$$= \frac{£500,000}{£550,000} \times (£50,000 - £30,000)$$

$$= \frac{£500,000}{£550,000} \times £20,000 = £18,182$$

6. EXCESS AND FRANCHISE CLAUSES

Excess or deductible

19–44   In many forms of commercial insurance, the insurer will provide that the insured shall bear "the first £x" of each and every claim under the policy, and the courts will uphold the effect of such a provision, for it represents the bargain struck between the parties to the insurance contract and defines the scope of the indemnity granted under the policy.[65] The question of how to apply such provisions in individual cases has been determined in three reported decisions.[66]

19–45   In *Australia & New Zealand Bank Ltd v. Colonial & Eagle Wharves Ltd*,[67] the defendant wharfingers held an all risks policy on goods at their warehouses which provided for an excess of £100 each and every claim. Over a period of a year, the wharfingers misdelivered the claimant bank's

---

[65] *Bartlett & Partners Ltd v. Meller* [1961] 1 Lloyd's Rep. 487.
[66] A different approach is necessary in the case of "claims-made" professional indemnity policies, *Haydon v. Lo & Lo* [1997] 1 W.L.R. 198, PC.
[67] [1960] 2 Lloyd's Rep. 241.

goods on some thirty occasions. The bank claimed against the wharfingers and they claimed an indemnity for loss of the goods under the policy held with the third party insurers. The bank's claim was settled by the defendants with the consent of the insurers for £17,000, but the insurers contended that there were thirty "claims" to which the excess applied. The wharfingers for their part argued that, on the facts of the case, there was only one claim. McNair J. considered[68] this question involved a short point on construction which was largely one of first impression. The word "claim" was a word of common occurrence in the field of insurance, and it seemed to him, both in the language of insurance and in common parlance that "claim" meant either the right to make a claim or an assertion of a right. In the instant case of insurance which provided the wharfingers with a qualified indemnity against claims made against them by their customers, it might mean either a claim against the wharfingers by the bank in either of those two senses, or a claim by the wharfingers on the insurers in either of those two senses. His Lordship considered it to be plain to him that the object of the clause was to exempt underwriters from the liability to pay small claims, which the wharfingers had to bear themselves in consideration of a reduced premium, and he concluded that, in this clause, "claim" meant the occurrence of a state of facts which justifies a claim on underwriters and did not mean the assertion of a claim on the underwriters. What was relevant was the facts which gave rise to the claim or claims and not the particular form in which the claim was put forward, either against the wharfingers or the underwriters. In this case, there was a right in the bank to claim in respect of each misdelivery and therefore his Lordship held that thirty excesses were to be deducted from the overall liability of the insurers for £17,000, i.e. £3,000.

In the subsequent case of *Trollope and Colls Ltd v. Haydon*,[69] contrac- **19–46** tors took out a policy to cover both their liability to third parties and their own expenses incurred, arising upon the warranty they gave as to watertightness of the houses and garages on a development they had built. The policy provided that "the contractors shall bear the first £25 of each and every claim". Over the next two years the contractors agreed to carry out extensive remedial works to many of the houses because of defects giving rise to water penetration into the houses and garages. A preliminary issue laid before the Court of Appeal was whether there was only one excess of £25 to be applied, or £25 in respect of each defect or failure occurring in any house or garage, or some other formula. The Court of Appeal held that it meant £25 was to be deducted from the repair costs of each house or garage which was not watertight. This was because the undertaking given by the contractors was to carry out such work as was necessary to render watertight any house or garage that proved not to be watertight, within a period of five years from completion. Thus the expenses incurred by the insured contractors in making watertight any dwelling or garage,

---

[68] *ibid.* at 255.
[69] [1977] 1 Lloyd's Rep. 244, CA.

which had by reason of failures or defects ceased to be weathertight, would give rise to one claim against the insurers.

19–47   Most recently, the question of the application of a deductible of £250,000 in a building works policy in respect of each and every loss arising from "any component part which is defective in design plan specification materials or workmanship" was considered by the Court of Appeal in *Mitsubishi Electric U.K. Ltd v. Royal London Insurance (U.K.) Ltd*[70] The claimant insured was engaged under a sub-contract to carry out the design, manufacture and installation into a building development in London, 94 essentially identical toilet modules. These toilet modules were self-contained toilet modules containing lavatory cubicles, hand basins and the usual wash-room accessories. Instead of being constructed on-site within the shell of the uncompleted building, the toilet modules were prefabricated off the site and lowered by crane into the building as it rose floor by floor. The modules were then integrated into the building.

19–48   Each of the modules had tiles on its internal walls and a floor covering. The tiles and the floor covering were fixed with adhesive to an underlying material or substrate (the cementitious board). The claimants completed their installation of the 94 modules in May 1990. In mid-1991, the walls of the modules were found to be bowing and the tiles cracking. This was caused, it was said, by a defect in the cementitious board which was unable to withstand the changes of temperature and moisture to which it was exposed. The claimant insured incurred losses in carrying out remedial works to the toilet modules and they claimed under their building works insurance on the basis that their claim arose from one defective component part (*i.e.* the cementitious board). Alternatively, it was claimed that there was a single loss (relating to all the damaged toilet modules. Thus it was claimed that the deductible of £250,000 was to be applied once only. The insurer contended that there were 94 claims, to each of which the deductible was applicable. The Court of Appeal held that the common sense view[71] had to be that there was only one defective component or component part, namely the cementitious board used throughout. Accordingly, the deductible was only to be applied once to the total claim for the repairs to all 94 toilet modules.

19–49   It should be noted that where the insurer bona fide exercises his right under the policy to conduct the defence and settle claims made against the insured, any settlement of such claims will bind the insured irrespective of the fact that the insured has to bear the first £x of such claims.[72] The expression "deductible" tends to be used by insurers in relation to large excesses, *e.g.* £5,000. It should also be noted that the excess or deductible may be expressed to apply to the claim after adjustment pursuant to any "average" condition.

---

[70] [1994] 2 Lloyd's Rep. 249, CA.
[71] *ibid.* at 253, *per* Sir Thomas Bingham M.R. (as he then was).
[72] *Beacon Insurance Co. Ltd v. Langdale* [1939] 4 All E.R. 204, CA.

Excess of loss provision

An insurer will sometimes insert an "excess of loss" provision rather **19–50** than a simple excess or deductible provision, but this measure is usually only adopted on reinsurance of the insurer's risk. The basic principle is that the insurer only becomes liable on his policy when the relevant loss under a primary or first layer insurance has exceeded that primary insurance's sum insured. For example, a primary insurance may insure contents up to the value of £50,000, and a second "excess of loss" insurance may cover that layer of contents' value in excess of £50,000.

Franchise clause

A franchise clause as it is called provides that claims under a certain **19–51** amount, or a certain proportion of the sum insured, will not be covered by the insurance. Where the loss suffered does exceed such a franchise amount, however, the insured will be indemnified in full in respect of the loss, and not merely for the loss exceeding the franchise amount.[73]

The provision will be worded so that the insured is unable to accumulate over a period of time a number of losses incurred on different occasions in order to exceed this franchise provision.[74]

7. LOSS ADJUSTERS AND LOSS ASSESSORS

Loss adjusters

Most loss adjusters are trained and examined by the independent **19–52** Chartered Institute of Loss Adjusters, and will act for the insurer to assess the loss and adjust the amount recoverable under the terms and conditions of the policy of insurance under which the claim falls to be considered. They will report to the insurer's claims managers, and report any suspicious circumstances relating either to the loss itself, or the amount claimed in respect of the loss. It will be the adjusters who conduct meetings with the insured, and correspond with the insured, on behalf of the insurer in accordance with their instructions. Any terms of settlement reached with the insured will be reduced to writing and will be expressed as not binding until accepted by the insurer principal. Once a bona fide settlement of a claim under the insurance is concluded, the insured cannot seek any additional payment for a loss which he missed by either ignorance or carelessness,[75] and a subsequent action commenced by the insured may be stayed on application of the insurer,[76] or, presumably, be summarily struck out under CPR, Pt 24 on the ground of accord and satisfaction. Being a person professing some special skill, a loss adjuster must act with appropriate skill and care in performing the tasks for which he has been engaged, otherwise he will be liable for his insurer principal's consequent loss.

---

[73] *Paterson v. Harris* (1861) 1 B. & S. 336.
[74] *Stewart & Co. v. Merchants' Marine Insurance Co.* (1885) 16 Q.B.D. 619, CA.
[75] *Elliott v. Royal Exchange Assurance Co.* (1867) L.R. 2 Exch. 237 at 247, *per* Pigott B.
[76] *Adams v. Saunders* (1829) 4 C. & P. 25 (marine insurance).

Disclosure of loss adjuster's reports in proceedings between insured and insurer

19–53   An adjuster's report obtained by the insurer is not a document privileged from discovery and inspection to a claimant insured unless the dominant purpose of its procurement is the obtaining of legal advice. If obtained for the dual purposes of legal advice and of enabling the insurers to be informed of all the facts in order to come to a decision upon whether they are entitled to repudiate the policy for breach of a condition, the report must be disclosed.[77] If, though, the insurers procure a non-routine report (perhaps after the routine report has been obtained) specifically for submission to its legal advisers for advice on whether the claim should be paid or resisted, e.g. because fraud is suspected,[78] then that document is privileged from disclosure to the insured.

Involvement of insured's broker

19–54   If the insured's broker, unknown to the insured, is also acting for the insurer for the purpose of obtaining an adjuster's report on a claim for the insurer, despite this breach of duty to the insured, the broker cannot be forced to, and should not, disclose that report to the insured.[79] The practice of insurers seeking an adjuster's report through the insured's insurance broker who has placed the insurance has been strongly criticised, it being suggested that the insurer should obtain the report through another medium. However, disclosure of such a report to the broker, in whole or in part, can be made if it would be helpful in arriving at a fair and proper settlement of a claim — but, in the absence of the express consent of the insured, such a disclosure should not be made subject to a condition that the broker should withhold relevant information from the insured.[80]

Loss assessors

19–55   On the other hand, loss assessor is the term given to those who act for insured claimants to negotiate with the insurer's appointed loss adjusters. A few firms may hold themselves out as able to act either as adjusters or assessors. If, unknown to the insured who has engaged him, the assessor/adjuster is also acting for the relevant insurer, any settlement between the insured and insurer may be set aside by the insured rescinding the settlement arrived at by reason of the secret commission received by the assessor/adjuster from the insurer.[81] In such a circumstance, the insured is under no liability to pay the assessor/adjuster's fee and can even recover a fee paid

---

[77] *Victor Melik & Co. Ltd v. Norwich Union Fire Insurance Society Ltd and Kemp* [1980] 1 Lloyd's Rep. 523 at 524; applying *Waugh v. British Railways Board* [1980] A.C. 521, HL.

[78] *Re Highgrade Traders Ltd* [1984] B.C.L.C. 151, CA.

[79] *North and South Trust Co. v. Berkeley* [1971] 1 All E.R. 980.

[80] *Anglo-African Merchants Ltd v. Bayley* [1969] 1 Lloyd's Rep. 268 at 280, *per* Megaw J. (as he then was).

[81] *Taylor v. Walker* [1958] 1 Lloyd's Rep. 490; *cf.* if the commission from the insurers was disclosed, *Leete v. Wallace* (1888) 58 L.T. 577. Secret commissions are not permitted by the Code of Conduct of the Chartered Institute of Loss Adjusters.

in advance.[82] To avoid possibly expensive litigation[83] upon the amount of the fee to which the assessor/adjuster is entitled, it is probably best to agree the percentage fee prior to the engagement of the assessor/adjuster. In the normal course, an assessor must act with appropriate skill and care in the discharge of his duties on behalf of the insured. If he breaches this professional duty he will be liable for his client's consequent loss, *e.g.* by not entering a claim on behalf of his client insured within 30 days as required by the policy conditions in circumstances where the insurer would not otherwise have avoided the policy.[84]

Binding determination of amount of indemnity

Occasionally, an insurance policy will provide that an assessor, adjuster **19–56** or other person, *e.g.* accountant, shall be appointed, whose conclusions on the quantification of the loss are made binding on both the insured and insurer. Although occupying an analogous position, the assessor/adjuster will not be acting as an arbitrator, and many difficulties can arise: for example, is the assessor to occupy a quasi-judicial position in which he is bound to disclose to the insured any information given to him by the insurers? At what stage do his findings bind the parties? It may be that the investigation at first fully supports the insured's claim and the adjuster reports accordingly, but that later he obtains further information which throws a different light upon the matter. Are the insurers bound by the first report?[85] Indeed, when the assessor's or adjuster's decision is challenged, the assessor or adjuster may be called as a witness and cross-examined in order to ascertain whether he made his quantification in accordance with the policy's terms and conditions.[86] However, the adjuster's assessment will be conclusive as to the amount recoverable by the insured unless it is shown that the adjuster has misdirected himself in point of law, or has omitted to take into consideration some material fact.[87]

---

[82] *ibid.*

[83] As in *Hugh Allen & Co. Ltd v. Holmes Ltd* [1969] 1 Lloyd's Rep. 348, CA.

[84] As alleged in *March Cabaret Club & Casino Ltd v. Thompson & Bryan* [1975] 1 Lloyd's Rep. 169.

[85] *Frewin v. Poland* [1968] 1 Lloyd's Rep. 100 at 103, *per* Donaldson J. (as he then was).

[86] *Recher & Co. v. North British and Mercantile Insurance Co.* [1915] 3 K.B. 277.

[87] *ibid.*

CHAPTER 20

RIGHTS OF THE INSURER

1. DOUBLE INSURANCE AND CONTRIBUTION

20–01   Where double insurance exists, the insured, at common law, may pursue one or more of the insurers until he is indemnified in respect of that loss,[1] but may recover nothing more than an indemnity, *i.e.* the full amount of the loss which he has suffered.[2] Indeed, by virtue of the Life Assurance Act 1774, in the case on insurances of buildings[3] (but not goods or merchandises which are excluded from the Act), the insured is additionally prevented by statute from recovering more than the extent of his insurable interest, *i.e.* the loss suffered.

20–02   As regards the insurer, once he has made payment to the insured under his policy in circumstances of double insurance, that insurer becomes entitled to seek contribution from the co-insurers in his own name,[4] unless such payment was purely voluntary.[5] To save on the necessity of instituting a fresh action, the modern practice is for insurers to insert a clause in the policy limiting their liability to a rateable proportion of all insurers' liability to the insured (sometimes called the importation of average clause) discussed below. In order for there to be a situation of double insurance, and the right to contribution to arise, or for such clauses to operate, four matters need to be shown to establish that there is double insurance.

Same subject matter

20–03   The insurances must have the same subject matter,[6] otherwise there is no double insurance and no right to contribution. Two cases concerning the insurance of goods illustrate this requirement. First, *North British & Mercantile Insurance Co. v. London, Liverpool and Globe Insurance Co.*[7] shows that not only must the same subject matter be covered by two or more insurances, but also the same interest in that subject matter. The subject matter of the insurances was, effectively, a quantity of grain stored in the bailee wharfingers premises which they had insured under a floating policy upon their own goods for which they were responsible, which the owner bailors had also insured under a property insurance. The grain was damaged by fire in circumstances that the bailee wharfingers were liable in law for its

---

[1] *Godin v. London Assurance Co.* (1758) 1 Burr. 489.

[2] *North British and Mercantile Insurance Co. v. London, Liverpool and Globe Insurance Co.* (1877) 5 Ch. D. 569, CA; *Scottish Amicable Heritable Securities Association v. Northern Assurance Co.* 1883 11 R. (Ct of Sess.) 287 at 303, *per* Lord Moncrieff.

[3] Section 3; *Hebdon v. West* (1863) 3 B. & S. 579.

[4] *Austin v. Zurich General Accident and Liability Insurance Co. Ltd* [1945] K.B. 250 at 258, *per* MacKinnon L.J., CA.

[5] *Legal and General Assurance Society Ltd v. Drake Insurance Co. Ltd* [1992] 1 Q.B. 887, CA.

[6] *Godin v. London Assurance Co.* (1758) 1 Burr. 489 at 492, *per* Lord Mansfield C.J.

[7] (1877) 5 Ch. D. 569, CA.; followed *Darrell v. Tibbitts* (1880) 5 Q.B.D. 560.

loss, and the Court of Appeal held that there was no double insurance under the bailor's policy, for the bailee's insurers were in law the only liable insurer.

Secondly, in *Boag v. Economic Insurance Co. Ltd*[8] the insured held two **20–04** policies of insurance. One was a policy covering the stock-in-trade of two factories owned by the insured, the other was a goods-in-transit policy. Cigarettes were transferred from one factory to another by lorry and there destroyed by fire. It was held that there was no double insurance because these cigarettes formed the stock-in-trade of the factory from which they were moved, and never formed part of the stock-in-trade of the second factory as they were only temporarily housed there. Thus the subject matter of the insurance covering the respective stock-in-trade of the factories was not destroyed in the appropriate factory and the insurers had no liability under that insurance — only the goods-in-transit insurers were liable.

The various policies may, it seems, cover other subject matters not **20–05** common between them without affecting the right to contribution for the relevant loss provided that there is double insurance in all other respects with regard to the loss that occurred.[9]

Same risk

The second requirement is that the several policies must all cover the **20–06** same peril or risk that has caused the loss.[10] Thus, in *American Surety Co. of New York v. Wrightson*,[11] where the risk of dishonesty of the bank's employees was covered by a fidelity insurance, and by a much wider and more varied policy covering dishonesty of any person, as well as losses from fire, burglary, and transit risks, double insurance existed. Hamilton J., *obiter*, however, expressed the view that the principle will not apply where policies are widely different in their scope.[12]

Same interest

When two persons interested in the same subject matter insure that **20–07** property independently without specifying their interest, both may recover in full from their respective insurers for there is no double insurance without the insurances covering the same interest. This is the case where a landlord and a tenant insure the same building, the tenant being under an obligation to repair, but not to insure.[13] The same result occurs where the mortgagor and mortgagee insure their own interests alone by separate insurances,[14] or where bailor and bailee insure their separate interests.[15]

[8] [1954] 2 Lloyd's Rep. 581.
[9] This was conceded as being the position in *American Surety Co. of New York v. Wrightson* (1910) 16 Com. Cas. 37.
[10] *North British and Mercantile Insurance Co. v. London, Liverpool and Globe Insurance Co.* (1877) 5 Ch. D. 569 at 581, *per* James L.J., CA
[11] (1910) 16 Com. Cas. 37.
[12] *ibid.* at 56.
[13] *Andrews v. Patriotic Assurance Co. (No. 2)* (1886) 18 L.R. Ir. 355; *Portavon Cinema Co. Ltd v. Price and Century Insurance Co. Ltd* [1939] 4 All E.R. 601.
[14] *Scottish Amicable Heritable Securities Association v. Northern Assurance Co.* (1883) 11 R. (Ct of Sess.) 287.
[15] *North British and Mercantile Insurance Co. v. London. Liverpool and Globe Insurance Co.* (1877) 5 Ch. D. 569 at 584, *per* Mellish L.J., CA.

20–08   There will be double insurance where one party takes out one insurance, and another interested party takes out another insurance, both insurances covering their interests[16] in the same subject matter, provided, of course, that the loss concerns their common interest, *e.g.* a loss by flood. Thus, if one insuring party is wholly responsible to the other party for the loss there is no common loss, only loss to one, the interest of which is recoverable under the responsible party's insurance, and that insurer has no right to contribution from the other insurer.[17]

Valid and enforceable policies
20–09   Each insurance must be valid and enforceable so that the insured may call upon each separate insurer to indemnify him for the loss to enable the principle of double insurance to apply. Thus, there is no double insurance, and therefore no entitlement to contribution, where one insurer has avoided the policy or repudiated liability in respect of the loss by reason of breach of a warranty or condition,[18] and, indeed, an insurer may raise such entitlement to avoid or repudiate as against another insurer seeking contribution.[19] Nor is there double insurance where the other policy has lapsed, or has not yet come into force,[20] or is legally unenforceable for any other reason.[21]

Mutual exception clauses in policies
20–10   Pertinent to consideration of whether each policy is valid and enforceable in respect of the loss suffered is the question of the effect of an exclusion clause in each policy excepting an indemnity where another insurance indemnifies the insured. In the motor insurance case of *Weddell v. Road Transport and General Insurance Co. Ltd,* [22] Rowlatt J. held that mutual exception clauses in several insurances, otherwise being valid and enforceable and creating a situation of double insurance, will cancel each other out and be of no effect.

Exception clause in one policy only
20–11   Where only one policy seeks to exclude cover in respect of risks indemnified under other insurances, this may be a valid exclusion depending upon the form of wording used in the exclusion condition.[23] One of the issues that arose for decision in the construction insurance case of *Petrofina (U.K.) Ltd v. Magnaload Ltd*[24] was whether the contractors all risks insurers

---

[16] *Nichols & Co. v. Scottish Union and National Insurance Co.* 1885 14 R. (Ct. of Sess.) 1094.
[17] *North British and Mercantile Insurance Co. v. London, Liverpool and Globe Insurance Co.* (1877) 5 CR. D. 569, CA.
[18] *Austin v. Zurich General Accident and Liability Insurance Co. Ltd* [1945] 1 K.B. 250; *Monksfield v. Vehicle and General Insurance Co. Ltd* [1971] 1 Lloyd's Rep. 139.
[19] *Monksfield v. Vehicle and General Insurance Co. Ltd* [1971] 1 Lloyd's Rep. 139.
[20] *Sickness and Accident Assurance Association v. General Accident Assurance Corp.* (1892) 19 R. (Ct of Sess.) 977.
[21] *Woods v. Co-operative Insurance Society* (1924) S.C. 692.
[22] [1932] 2 K.B. 563.
[23] *Niger Co. Ltd v. Guardian Assurance Co. Ltd* (1922) 13 Ll. L. Rep. 75, HL; *National Employers Mutual General Insurance Association Ltd v. Haydon* [1980] 2 Lloyd's Rep. 149, CA.
[24] [1984] Q.B. 127.

could benefit from such an exclusion clause to escape liability when damage was sustained to work in progress at an oil refinery. This damage was caused by the defendant sub-sub-contractors' negligence, and they held liability insurances with several other insurers. Section 1 of the contractors all risks policy indemnified the claimant insured and his sub-contractors "against loss or damage to the insured property whilst at the contract site". Section 2 covered the contractual liability of the contractors to maintain the contract works during the maintenance period, and Section 3 covered third party liability (excluding liability in respect of the contract works). The policy also contained a general exception in the following terms:

> "The insurer shall not be liable in respect of loss, damage or liability which ... is insured by or would but for the existence of this policy be insured by any other policy or policies except in respect of any excess."

Lloyd J. (as he then was) agreed with the defendants' submissions that **20–12** the exception, properly construed, was only intended to take effect in the case of true double insurance. There cannot be double insurance unless the same insured is covered in respect of the same property against the same risks. Thus if in the present case there were another policy on the contract works, covering the same risks, then that would be a true case of double insurance, but here the other policies held by the defendants were not policies on property, but liability policies. There was therefore no double insurance in the present case and the exception did not apply.

In the subsequent case of *Wimpey Construction U.K. Ltd v. D.V. Poole*,[25] **20–13** which also happened to be concerned with damage to contract works, there was the a proviso in the extension of cover in the defendant Lloyd's underwriter's professional indemnity policy covering design work issued to the claimant contractors. This extension of cover provided a negligent design indemnity to Wimpeys where they acted in more than capacity in a same project, namely (1) builders or project owners and contractors and designers, (2) contractors and designers, or (3) building or project owners and designers. If Wimpeys incurred loss or damage in any of those capacities, Wimpeys were entitled to recover as if a claim had been made against them. A proviso to this extension stated that an indemnity would only be provided where:

> "such loss, damage, or expense is not insured by any other policy."

A quay wall had been constructed as part of an extension to the fitting **20–14** out facilities at a shipyard in Southampton. After construction this wall moved out because the anchor wall tying back to the quay wall as originally designed by Wimpeys was situated too close to the quay wall. This liability was accepted by the defendant to be covered by the professional

---

[25] [1984] 2 Lloyd's Rep. 499.

indemnity policy, but the defendant denied liability under the extension for works of repair to a warehouse wall, which had moved, and the mono-tower crane base, which had settled. One line of defence was reliance on the above proviso, on the ground that Wimpeys had two other policies, a public liability policy and a contractor's all risks policy, both of which were in force at all material times. The cost of repairing the warehouse was, in principle, recoverable under the public liability policy, and the cost of repairing and making good the crane foundations might have been recoverable under the contractors all risks policy. Following Lloyd J.'s decision in *Petrofina*,[26] Webster J. held that the exception only applied where there was true double insurance. Webster J. further held that there was no such double insurance in the present case because, whilst a claim under the main part of the professional indemnity policy would constitute double insurance with the separate public liability policy, this extension of cover, properly construed, was "in no sense insurance against liability: it is insurance against Wimpeys' own financial loss, without liability to a third party for that loss."[27] There was also no double insurance with the property section of the contractors all risks policy, because the insured risks were different.

Quantification of contribution between insurers

20–15   Where double insurance applies, insurers will be liable to contribute in proportion to their respective liabilities in the absence of double insurance. In *American Surety Co. of New York v. Wrightson*,[28] already mentioned above, a loss of US$2,680 occurred which was covered by one policy with a limit of indemnity of US$2,500, and a second policy with a limit of indemnity of US$40,000. Hamilton J. held that the insurers would share this loss in the proportion of 2,500:2,680.

20–16   In *Commercial Union Assurance Co. Ltd v. Hayden*,[29] the Court of Appeal held that this principle of assessment still applies where the loss falls below both limits of indemnity of the respective policies. Two public liability insurances were in existence, the claimant insurer's policy having a limit of indemnity of £100,000, and the defendant insurer's policy having a limit of indemnity of £10,000. The relevant loss was £4,425, and the defendant insurer argued that he should only be liable for one eleventh of that loss to represent their respective maximum liabilities. The Court of Appeal rejected that argument, however, and firmly endorsed and applied the independent liability test. Therefore, in the instant case, the loss being within both limits of indemnity, the insurers would contribute in the proportion of 4,425:4,425, *i.e.* one half each. Of course, when applying this independent liability test to determine contribution, all relevant conditions of each policy must be considered, *e.g.* the application of average in the case of under-insurance.

[26] *Petrofina (U.K.) Ltd v. Magnaload Ltd* [1984] Q.B. 127.
[27] [1984] 2 Lloyd's Rep. 499 at 516.
[28] (1910) 16 Com. Cas. 37.
[29] [1977] Q.B. 804, CA.

Rateable proportion clause

In the motor insurance case of *Gale v. Motor Union Insurance Co.*,[30]   **20–17**
Roche J. held that where both applicable policies (in this case, that of the
driver and that of the car owner) have clauses that provide that each
insurer is only liable for his rateable proportion of the insured loss, those
mutual clauses will be effective, and each insurer will be liable rateably.

Over-payment by insurer in ignorance of double insurance

An insurer who pays out the insured in full in ignorance of there being   **20–18**
any double insurance, cannot recover a contribution from the other
insurer in respect of that sum paid which he did not have to pay. This was
the finding of the Court of Appeal in *Legal and General Assurance Society
Ltd v. Drake Insurance Co. Ltd*[31] where two motor policies contained a
rateable proportion clause in the following similar terms:

> "If at the time any claim arises under the policy there is any other insurance
> covering the same loss, damage or liability the company will not pay or
> contribute more than its rateable proportion if the person claiming to be
> indemnified is the policy holder, nor make any payment or contribution if
> the person claiming to be indemnified is not the policy holder."

The facts were that the claimant insurers insured the relevant driver for   **20–19**
12 months from August 1975. In June 1976, the driver injured a third party
and proceedings brought by the third party were settled by the claimants.
The claimants then discovered that the defendants had also insured the
driver at the time of the accident and brought an action against them,
claiming a 50 per cent contribution from them as co-insurers. By a majority
decision, the Court of Appeal held that where an insured had effected
double insurance to cover the same loss, the right of one insurer to a contribution from the second insurer in meeting the claim accrued at the time
of loss. Therefore, even if the insured lost his contractual right to an
indemnity from the second insurer by reason of breach of a notification
condition, the right of the first insurer to contribution was not extin-
guished. The Court of Appeal went on to hold, unanimously, that as the
claimant insurers had not been compelled to pay out in full in respect of
the insured driver's liability to the third party, it amounted to a voluntary
payment of the excess over their actual 50 per cent liability. Being voluntary,
the equitable principle of contribution did not arise in this case and the
defendant insurers were not liable to make a contribution to the claimant
insurers.

Notification of double insurance

Buildings and contents insurances, in particular, often contain a prom-   **20–20**
issory condition to the effect that the insured must inform the insurer if he
effects double insurance during the currency of the insurance. Breach of
such a condition can lead to the insurer being entitled to either rescind the

---

[30] [1928] 1 K.B. 359.
[31] [1992] 1 Q.B. 887.

policy, or repudiate liability. The effect of this type of condition was considered in *Australian Agricultural Co. v. Saunders*[32] where the claimants
first effected a fire policy upon wool with the defendant "in any shed, or
store, or station, or in transit to Sydney by land only, or in any shed or
store, or on any wharf in Sydney until placed on board ship". The policy
limit was £3,000 and it contained a provision as follows:

> "No claim shall be recoverable if the property insured be previously or
> subsequently insured elsewhere, unless the particulars of such insurance be
> notified to the company in writing."

20–21   The claimant, during the currency of this policy, also effected an insurance with a marine insurance company for cover of £16,500 upon wool,
the risk being described as "at and from the River H to Sydney per ships
and steamers, and thence per ship or ships to London, including the risk
of craft from the time that the wools are first waterborne and of transhipment or landing and reshipment at Sydney". The frequent practice at
Sydney port was that wool arriving there for shipment was not delivered
direct to the ship for which it was intended, but was conveyed to the stores
belonging to the persons who were acting as the stevedores of the ship,
and was there pressed for the purpose of reducing its bulk. By the practice
and course of business, the stevedore's receipt was regarded as between the
ship and the shippers as equivalent to the mate's receipt, and bills of lading
were given in exchange for it. Certain wool belonging to the plaintiffs was
forwarded by several consignments by several steamers from the river to
Sydney, where the claimants' agent had the wool conveyed to his own
stores, and entered into a contract for its conveyance to London on board
a ship.

20–22   The wool was then transported from his warehouses, to the stores of the
stevedores of the ship, who gave the usual receipts for the same. While in
the stevedores' warehouses, a portion of the wool was destroyed by fire,
and the claimants sought to recover in respect of this loss under the policy
effected with the defendant. This claim was resisted on the ground that the
marine policy came within the condition's scope and therefore ought to
have been communicated to the company in writing. The court held that
the claimants could recover under the fire policy because:

    (i) the second policy did not apply to the keeping of the wool on
        land (*i.e.* in the stevedores' warehouses), but only to marine risks.
        There was thus no double insurance, and the wool was not
        "insured elsewhere";
    (ii) by "insured elsewhere" was meant a specific insurance of the
        same risks, and the words of the condition were not satisfied in
        the case of different policies upon different risks by the mere
        possibility of one overlapping the other under some possible
        circumstances.

[32] (1875) L.R. 10 C.P. 668.

As explained by Bramwell B.[33]:

> "It is true that there was a subsequent insurance of the goods, but the words must be read with some limitation, or the result would be absurd. The insurance elsewhere must, to be within the clause, be an insurance as to a portion of the risks covered by the policy sued on. If that is so, it seems to me this is not a case of double insurance such as was intended, inasmuch as the plaintiffs could not have recovered this loss on the marine policy. It was argued on the defendant's behalf that a possibility that the same risk might be covered by both policies was sufficient under [the relevant clause] to defeat the fire policy. I doubt very much whether that is so. I doubt whether a mere possibility that some portion of the risk covered by both policies might accidentally coincide constitutes such a double insurance as was meant."

Thus, such a condition will not render the policy containing it void, if   **20–23** there is either no overlapping of insurances (*i.e.* double insurance), or merely an accidental, possible overlap of insurances. Of course, if the subsequent insurance never attaches, the condition is not breached as there is no double insurance, as was found to be the case in *Equitable Fire and Accident Office Ltd v. Ching Wo Hong*[34] where the respondent had insured his shop's goods and stock-in-trade under a fire policy effected with the appellants containing the following condition:

> "On effecting any insurance or insurances during the currency of this policy elsewhere on the property hereby insured . . . the insured must . . . give notice to the company thereof . . . and unless such notice be given, the insured will not be entitled to any benefit under this policy . . . The giving of such [notice] shall be a condition precedent to the recovery of any claim under this policy."

The respondent subsequently arranged another insurance on the same goods and stock-in-trade, but never paid the premium on this later insurance and the Privy Council held, on the facts, that this second policy never became effective by reason of non-payment of the premium. Accordingly, there was no breach of the condition in the appellants' policy for the respondent had not "effected" another insurance, and he was therefore entitled to recover in respect of a fire loss under the appellants' policy.

If the condition requires notification to the insurer of all other policies   **20–24** upon the insured property, and this has been complied with, there is no breach of such condition by the insured if those other insurances are substituted or replaced by others with the same, or even a larger amount of cover, if the condition does not require notification of the names of the other insurers.[35] It might be otherwise, however, if the notified insurances were endorsed on the policy in accordance with a condition, but were then allowed to lapse or were surrendered, rather than being merely "transferred" to another insurer.[36]

---

[33] (1875) L.R. 10 C.P. 668 at 674.
[34] [1907] A.C. 96, PC.
[35] *National Protector Fire Insurance Co. Ltd v. Nivert* [1913] A.C. 507, PC.
[36] *ibid.* at 513, *per* Lord Atkinson.

2. INDEMNIFICATION *ALIUNDE*

20–25   As Lord Blackburn said[37]:

> "The general rule of law is that where there is a contract of indemnity . . . and a loss happens, anything which reduces or diminishes that loss reduces or diminishes the amount which the indemnifier is bound to pay; and if the indemnifier has already paid it, then, if anything which diminishes the loss comes into the hands of the person to whom he has paid it, it becomes an equity that the person who has already paid the full indemnity is entitled to be recouped by having the amount back."

20–26   The following year, in *Castellain v. Preston*,[38] a case concerning a fire insurance, Cotton L.J. explained the nature of indemnification:

> "I think that the question turns on the consideration of what a policy of insurance against fire is, and on that the right of the plaintiff depends. The policy is really a contract to indemnify the person insured for the loss which he has sustained in consequence of the peril insured against which has happened, and from that it follows, of course, that as it is only a contract of indemnity, it is only to pay that loss which the assured may have sustained by reason of the fire which has occurred. In order to ascertain what that loss is, everything must be taken into account which is received by and comes to the hand of the assured and which diminishes that loss. It is only the amount of the loss, when it is considered as a contract of indemnity, which is to be paid after taking into account and estimating those benefits or sums of money which the assured may have received in diminution of the loss . . ."

20–27   Cotton L.J. continued by stating that the insurers are entitled to have indemnification *aliunde* (by another) brought into account when measuring the insured's right to recover under the insurance against them[39]:

> "If the proposition is stated in that manner, it is clear that the office [insurer] would be entitled to the benefit of anything received by the assured before the time when the policy is paid, and it is established by the case of *Darrell v. Tibbitts*[40] that the insurance company is entitled to that benefit, whether or not before they pay the money they insist upon a calculation being made of what can be recovered in diminution of the loss by the assured; if they do not insist upon that calculation being made, and if it afterwards turns out that in consequence of something which ought to have been taken into account in estimating the loss, a sum of money or even a benefit, not being a sum of money is received, then the office, notwithstanding the payment made, is entitled to say that the assured is to hold that for its benefit, and although it was not taken into account in ascertaining the sum which was paid, yet when it has been received it must be brought into account, and if it is not a sum of money, but a benefit that has been received, its value must be estimated in money."

---

[37] *Burnand v. Rodocanachi, Sons & Co.* (1882) 7 App. Cas. 333 at 339; see also *Randal v. Cockran* (1748) 1 Ves. Sen. 98.
[38] (1883) 11 Q.B.D. 380, CA.
[39] *ibid.* at 393–394, but see *Naumann v. Ford* (1985) 275 Estates Gazette 542.
[40] (1880) 5 Q.B.D. 560, CA.

Full indemnity prior to receipt of other monies

An insurer cannot resist a claim for a full indemnity on the ground that **20–28** the insured is entitled to an indemnity *aliunde*, which he has not yet received[41] (*e.g.* an insured landlord having the benefit to call upon his tenants to reinstate or repair premises under a covenant in the lease), unless the insurance contract expressly calls, *e.g.* for money owing, to be brought into account when assessing the loss payable under the insurance.[42]

Liability to insurer for sums later received

The insured, after indemnification by the insurer, must then account to **20–29** the insurer for any sums he subsequently recovers in whole or partial extinguishment of the relevant insured loss,[43] but only to the extent that such indemnification *aliunde* compensates for the insured's actual loss and thus amounts to a double indemnity, as against accounting pound for pound of the insurance moneys received. Accordingly, no right to account arises where the indemnity *aliunde* only compensates the insured in respect of an amount of the actual loss not recovered under the insurance.[44] A simple example of this would be where an insured suffered an actual loss of £1,000 but only received £500 under his insurance (for whatever reason), and received £400 from another non-insurance source (otherwise the insurer may seek contribution). As the insured has still only received £900 in regard to a £1,000 loss, he has not reached the point of being doubly indemnified and the insurer has no right to call for an account of any moneys recovered. Obviously, the insured need only account to the insurer in respect of sums otherwise received that are in respect of the insured loss,[45] as against a loss not covered by the insurance,[46] and the insured is entitled to an allowance in respect of costs incurred in securing such partial or whole indemnification from another party.[47] But see "voluntary gifts", below.

Subsequent recovery of insured goods

If insured goods are, for example, stolen, and the insurers make a full **20–30** indemnity of the insured's loss by either monetary payment or replacement, upon any subsequent recovery of the insured goods, the insured may either return the moneys or replacement goods, or surrender the recovered goods to the insurer as salvage. This was established in *Holmes v. Payne*[48] where an insured necklace was believed to have been lost and the

---

[41] *ibid.* at 561, *per* Brett L.J., following *North British and Mercantile Insurance Co. v. London, Liverpool and Globe Insurance Co.* (1877) 5 Ch. D. 569, CA; *Collingridge v. Royal Exchange Assurance Corp.* (1877) 3 Q.B.D. 173.

[42] See, *e.g. Fifth Liverpool Starr-Bowkett Building Society v. Travellers Accident Insurance Co. Ltd* (1893) 9 T.L.R. 221.

[43] *Re Miller Gibb & Co. Ltd* [1957] 2 All E.R. 266.

[44] *Tunno v. Edwards* (1810) 12 East. 488.

[45] *Thames and Mersey Marine Insurance Co. v. British and Chilian SS Co.* [1916] 1 K.B. 30, CA; *Law Fire Assurance Co. v. Oakley* (1888) 4 T.L.R. 309.

[46] *Sea Insurance Co. v. Hadden* (1884) 13 Q.B.D. 706, C.A.

[47] *Hatch Mansfield & Co. v. Weingott* [1907] 2 K.B. 814.

[48] [1930] 2 K.B. 301.

insurers agreed to provide a replacement. The original necklace was then found some months later in the lining of the insured's cloak. Because the necklace had been "lost", the replacement agreement was held to be valid, but the court held that both necklaces could not be kept, either the replacement or the original had to be handed back to the insurers.

Interest on sums recovered

20–31   Any award of interest on damages awarded to an insured against a third party in respect of the insured loss, where the insured has received a full indemnity from his insurer, must be accounted for to the insurer. For the position to be otherwise would lead to the insured being over-compensated, contrary to the basic principle of indemnification, and the insurer under-compensated. Thus, interest awarded in respect of a period before settlement was received from the insurer, will belong to the insured, and interest accruing after that settlement date, will belong to the insurer.[49] In practice, however, the insured's entitlement to the pre-settlement interest is often ignored by the insured and insurer, or, where there has been a delay in settlement, the settlement agreement will formally assign all the insured's rights, and thus the right to interest, to the insurer who can then sue the wrongdoer in his own name rather than the insured's name. Such an assignment is only complete when notice has been given to the proposed defendant in accordance with section 136 of the Law of Property Act 1925.

Voluntary gifts

20–32   Voluntary gifts to an insured from a third party which either diminish or extinguish the insured loss can cause difficulty. The test is the intention of the third party, and if the gift was bestowed with an intention to benefit the insured alone in respect of his loss, it belongs to the insured, and to hold otherwise would be to divert the gift from its intended object to a different person,[50] *i.e.* the insurer. But if the gift was made only with the intention of reducing or extinguishing the relevant loss, this must be accounted for to the insurers.[51] The insured is not liable to pay interest to the insurer on sums he subsequently has to account for to the insurer.[52]

3. SUBROGATION

Introduction

2—33   As a natural consequence of the fundamental principle of indemnity applied to all indemnity insurances, the insurer, once he has admitted the insured's claim and has paid the sum payable under the policy,[53] becomes

---

[49] *H. Cousins & Co. Ltd v. D. & C. Carriers Ltd* [1971] 2 Q.B. 230, CA.

[50] *Castellain v. Preston* (1883) 11 Q.B.D. 380 at 395, *per* Cotton L.J. and at 404, *per* Bowen L.J., CA.

[51] *Steams v. Village Main Reef Gold Mining Co.* (1905) 10 Com. Cas. 89, CA.

[52] *ibid.*

[53] *Mason v. Sainsbury* (1782) 3 Doug. K.B. 61; but see facts of *Scottish Union and National Insurance Co. v. Davis* [1970] 1 Lloyd's Rep. 1, CA, where it was held no indemnity had been paid.

entitled to be subrogated (substituted) to the position of the insured in respect of the loss. This restitutionary remedy arises from either equity,[54] or, perhaps more probably, from an implied term of the indemnity contract (which can be varied or excluded by express terms) by operation of law.[55]

Whatever its origin, the doctrine of subrogation operates so that[56]:

20–34

> "As between the underwriter and the assured the underwriter is entitled to the advantage of every right of the assured, whether such right consists in contract, fulfilled or unfulfilled, or in remedy for tort capable of being insisted on or already insisted on, or in any other right, whether by way of condition or otherwise, legal or equitable, which can be, or has been exercised or has accrued, and whether such right could or could not be enforced by the insurer in the name of the insured by the exercise or acquiring of which right or condition the loss against which the assured is insured, can be, or has been diminished."

It is unsettled, however, whether the doctrine of subrogation comes into operation when the insurer has made full indemnity under the terms of the policy, or only when the insured has been fully indemnified in respect of his actual loss — dicta are ambiguous on this point, *e.g.* the insurer "cannot be subrogated into a right of action until he has paid the sum insured and made good the loss"[57]; and "The underwriter [has] no right to subrogation unless and until he [has] fully indemnified the insured under the policy".[58]

Express term

Most practical problems will, though, be solved by express wording in the policy. A typical express condition that will be found in many policies, which gives the insurer effective subrogation rights prior to actual payment of an indemnity to the insured, is:

20–35

> "The company shall be entitled to undertake in the name of, and on behalf of, the Insured the absolute conduct, control and settlement of any proceedings, and at any time to take proceedings at its own expense and for its own benefit, but in the name of the Insured, to recover compensation or secure indemnity from the Third Party in respect of anything covered by this policy."

It is implicit in such a condition that the insurer has authority to settle a claim on behalf of the insured against a third party, not merely once proceedings have been commenced against that third party, but also if an

[54] *Burnand v. Rodocanachi, Sons & Co.* (1882) 7 App. Cas. 333 at 339, *per* Lord Blackburn, HL; *M. H. Smith (Plant Hire) Ltd v. Mainwaring* [1986] 2 Lloyd's Rep. 244, CA.
[55] *Mason v. Sainsbury* (1782) 3 Doug. K.B. 61; *Clark v. Inhabitants of Blything* (1823) 2 B. & C. 254; *Yorkshire Insurance Co. Ltd v. Nisbet Shipping Co. Ltd* [1962] 2 Q.B. 330 at 339–340, *per* Diplock J. (as he then was); *Hobbs v. Marlowe* [1977] 2 All E.R. 241 at 253–254, *per* Lord Diplock, HL.
[56] *Castellain v. Preston* (1883) 11 Q.B.D. 380 at 387, *per* Brett L.J., CA
[57] *ibid.* at 389, *per* Brett L.J.
[58] *Page v. Scottish Insurance Corp.* (1929) 98 L.J.K.B. 308 at 311, *per* Scrutton L.J., CA.

offer of settlement is made prior to and without the necessity of commencing proceedings.[59]

Recovery of interest against wrongdoer

20-36 It has also been held that if insurers have to borrow at a commercial rate or apply their own funds and so lose their investment value to meet a claim by their insured, then recovery of that amount against a wrongdoer in an action by subrogation should carry interest at the commercial rate, *e.g.* one per cent above base rate,[60] (but in recent years this has actually equated to slightly less than the usual interest rate awarded of 8 per cent per annum).

Exercise of the right of subrogation

20-37 Being subrogated to the insured's rights does not entitle the insurer to be in any better position to exercise those rights against third parties than the insured himself,[61] and, therefore, it must be borne in mind that terms and conditions in contracts with third parties may limit or exclude those rights.[62] Such terms and conditions with third parties may be a material fact that should be disclosed to the insurer,[63] which should be remembered.

Binding earlier settlement

20-38 The insurer may find himself prevented from pursuing further claims against an allegedly negligent third party by reason of the wording of an earlier settlement of a claim arising from the same incident. This happened in *Kitchen Design and Advice Ltd v. Lea Valley Water Co.*[64] The insured claimants suffered damage to their stock, fixtures and fittings at their premises caused by a burst in the defendants' water main. The claimants claimed on their property insurance and this claim was settled by their insurers (QBE Insurance (U.K.) Ltd). QBE exercised their subrogation rights and claimed in respect of this property damage, in the claimants' name, against the defendants.

The defendants' insurers (Commercial Union) negotiated a settlement of this claim and sent QBE a form of discharge as follows:

> "We, the QBE Insurance Ltd, hereby agree to accept the sum of £15,000 in full satisfaction, liquidation and discharge of all claims we have or may have against Lea Valley Water Company in connection with a burst water main in High Road, Finchley, London N12 on February 1, 1984. We understand and appreciate that the offer of settlement is made entirely without prejudice and without admission of legal liability."

20-39 QBE signed the discharge form on July 2, 1984. In November 1984, the claimants advanced for the first time to QBE a claim for insured loss of profits in consequence of the business interruption. QBE settled this claim

[59] *Kitchen Design and Advice Ltd v. Lea Valley Water Co.* [1989] 2 Lloyd's Rep. 221.
[60] *Metal Box Ltd v. Currys Ltd* [1988] 1 W.L.R. 175.
[61] *Simpson v. Thomson* (1877) 3 App. Cas. 279, HL.
[62] *Thomas & Co. v. Brown* (1899) 4 Com. Cas. 186.
[63] *Tate v. Hyslop* (1885) 15 Q.B.D. 368, CA.
[64] [1989] 2 Lloyd's Rep. 221.

and then sought, again by subrogation, to recover this amount from the defendants. They failed in this attempt. Phillips J. held that the natural meaning and effect of the form of discharge QBE had signed was that the defendants were to be discharged of all liability in respect of claims by QBE's insured to which QBE were or might become subrogated. The risk of further claims was one of the very matters which the discharge was intended to protect the defendants and their insurers from, and there was no doctrine of mistake that the claimants could invoke which avoided the effect of the form of discharge.

On the other hand, if it is the insured who has taken it upon himself to compromise any claim against a wrongdoer which would otherwise have reduced the claim under the insurance policy, the insured will be liable to the insurer in damages for the value of any right wrongfully renounced,[65] or any claim wrongly settled.[66] The calculation of such prejudice might well be a rather problematic amount for the insurer to establish in practice, though. The insurer is more likely to, instead, rely on the insured's breach of the usual "control of proceedings" condition precedent, discussed below, to repudiate liability rather than embark on costly litigation trying to establish the extent of the prejudice that the release or settlement caused him.

An example of this situation is afforded by *West of England Fire Insurance Co. v. Isaacs*[67] where the defendant, a sub-tenant of premises, was insured under a fire policy with the plaintiffs. A fire occurred and the insured recovered an indemnity from the plaintiffs. The tenant had covenanted with the defendant sub-tenant, and the landlord, to insure the premises but had not properly performed that undertaking. For some reason, the defendant paid over the insurance moneys to the tenant, and moreover, released him from any liability for breach of the covenant. The Court of Appeal upheld the plaintiff insurers' action against their insured for return of the insurance moneys because the insured had prejudiced the insurers' right under subrogation to pursue the tenant for that amount by reason of the tenant's breach of covenant. **20–40**

Tenant paying towards landlord's property insurance

The position between a buildings insurer claiming subrogation through the landlord's rights against his tenant, who has contributed to the insurance premiums as required by the lease, was considered in *Mark Rowlands Ltd v. Berni Inns Ltd*[68] In this case the basement tenants were obliged to pay the landlord an insurance rent equal to the amount spent by the landlord in insuring the basement, being a fair proportion of the premiums paid by the landlord to insure the whole building against loss or damage **20–41**

---

[65] *West of England Fire Insurance Co. v. Issacs* [1897] 1 Q.B. 227; *Phoenix Assurance Co. v. Spooner* [1905] 2 K.B. 753; *Horse, Carriage and General Insurance Co. Ltd v. Petch* (1917) 33 T.L.R. 131.
[66] *Boag v. Standard Marine Insurance Co. Ltd* [1937] 2 K.B. 113, at 128, *per* Scott L.J.; *Phoenix Assurance Co. v. Spooner* [1905] 2 K.B. 753.
[67] [1897] 1 Q.B. 226, CA.
[68] [1986] Q.B. 211, CA.

by, *inter alia*, fire. For his part, the landlord covenanted, *inter alia*, to keep the whole building so insured and to lay out any moneys received under the insurance in rebuilding or reinstating the basement leased to the tenant. The lease further provided that the tenant would be relieved of his obligation to repair and to pay rent in the event of damage to the basement by an insured peril. The whole building was in fact then destroyed by a fire caused by the tenant's negligence. The insurer paid the landlord the moneys due under the policy and then brought an action against the tenant seeking to recover as damages the sum paid out to the landlord. The claim failed.

20–42   The Court of Appeal considered that the landlord's leasehold covenant to insure against, *inter alia*, fire, which necessarily covered fire caused either by accident or by negligence, indicated that it had been the intention of the landlord and the tenant that in the event of the damage to the building by fire — whether due to accident or negligence — the landlord's loss was to be recouped from the insurance moneys and that in that event they were to have no further claim against the tenant for damages in negligence. Another way of coming to the same conclusion, the court held, was that in situations such as the present, the tenant is entitled to say that the landlord has been fully indemnified in the manner envisaged by the provisions of the lease and that he cannot therefore recover damages from the tenant in addition, so as to provide himself with what would in effect be a double indemnity. The decision appears to leave the way open for a landlord to recover damages from a negligent tenant where similar covenants apply, but where, for some reason, insurance moneys are not recovered under the insurance.

The proceedings by the insurer

20–43   The insurer must bring the action against the third party in the insured's name,[69] and not his own, unless (i) the insured has made a formal assignment of his rights to the insurer mentioned above with notice to the third party,[70] or (ii) statute confers a right of action directly upon the insurers.[71] It is well understood in insurance law that an insured is bound to allow insurers who have made an indemnity to sue third parties responsible for that loss in the insured's own name,[72] and will be compelled so to do by the court provided the insurers give an indemnity relating to the costs to be incurred in the action against the responsible third party.[73] Of course, technically being the claimant on the record, the insured himself will have to comply with all court procedures relating to the action, *e.g.* discovery of documents in his possession[74] (the insurer, not technically being a party to

---

[69] *Mason v. Sainsbury* (1782) 3 Doug. K.B. 61.

[70] *King v. Victoria Insurance Co. Ltd* [1896] A.C. 250, PC; *Compania Colombiana de Seguros v. Pacific Steam Navigation Co.* [1964] 1 All E.R. 216 at 230; Law of Property Act 1925, s. 136.

[71] See, *e.g.* Riot (Damages) Act 1886, s.4(1).

[72] *Dane v. Mortgage Insurance Corp.* [1894] 1 Q.B. 54 at 61, *per* Lord Esher M.R., CA.

[73] *King v. Victoria Insurance Co.* [1896] A.C. 250, PC; *Duus, Brown & Co. v. Binning* (1906) 11 Com. Cas. 190; *England and England v. Guardian Insurance Ltd* [2000] Lloyd's Rep. I.R. 404.

[74] *Wilson v. Raffalovich* (1881) 7 Q.B.D. 553.

the action will not have to, *e.g.* disclose documents in his possession),[75] and if the insured abandons an appeal, the insurers cannot seek to pursue that appeal.[76] Similarly, an insurer cannot sue in their insured's name if the insured no longer exists. Thus in *M. H. Smith (Plant Hire) Ltd v. Mainwaring*[77] an insurers subrogation action against the party allegedly responsible for the loss was struck out because the insured limited company had already been wound-up prior to the commencement of the proceedings brought in its name by the insurer.

Alternatively, the insurer could himself institute proceedings against the responsible third party and join the insured as a second defendant, and ask the court to order that the first defendant pay damages to the second defendant, combined with a declaration that the second defendant holds those damages in trust for the claimant insurer.[78]   **20–44**

No subrogation against a co-insured

If the responsible party is also an insured under a policy naming several insureds, or categories of insureds, *e.g.* "contractors", then the insurer cannot, unless the policy provides otherwise, exercise his rights of subrogation against the responsible party, because that party is also his insured and an insurer cannot sue one co-insured in the name of the other.[79] The determination of who is a co-insured for these purposes is discussed in Chapter 16, above, and in Chapter 17, under "Joint and composite insurances", above.   **20–45**

Express waiver of subrogation rights

Many policies will provide that the insurer will not seek to exercise subrogation rights against specified third parties. Such an express waiver of subrogation rights invariably occurs in employers' liability policies in relation to employees who cause a loss which is covered by the policy. This practice followed the finding in *Lister v. Romford Ice and Cold Storage Co. Ltd*[80] that a right of subrogation exists in these circumstances. Whilst it has been suggested that the court may find a reason in equity for not permitting an insurer to exercise his subrogation rights,[81] an internal insurance industry agreement to which the third party is not privy, is insufficient at common law to enable a third party to seek enforcement of it for his benefit.[82] A third party may well now be able to enforce the express   **20–46**

---

[75] *James Nelson & Sons Ltd v. Nelson Line (Liverpool) Ltd* [1906] 2 K.B. 217, CA; see also *Page v. Scottish Insurance Corp.* (1929) 140 L.T. 571 at 576.

[76] *The Millwall* [1905] P. 155, CA.

[77] [1986] 2 Lloyd's Rep. 244.

[78] *King v. Victoria Insurance Co.*[1896] A.C. 250 at 255–256; *John Edwards & Co. v. Motor Union Insurance Co. Ltd* [1922] 2 K.B. 249 at 254, *per* McCardie J.; *Re Miller, Gibb & Co. Ltd* [1957] 1 W.L.R. 703 at 707.

[79] *Petrofina (U.K.) Ltd v. Magnaload* [1984] Q.B. 127; *Co-operative Retail Services Ltd v. Taylor Young Partnership* [2000] B.L.R. 460, CA.

[80] [1957] A.C. 555, HL.

[81] See *Morris v. Ford Motor Co. Ltd* [1973] Q.B. 792 at 801, *per* Lord Denning M.R., CA; *The Surf City* [1995] 2 Lloyd's Rep. 242.

[82] *Hobbs v. Marlowe* [1978] A.C. 16, HL; *Stone Vickers Ltd v. Appledore Ferguson Shipbuilders Ltd* [1992] 2 Lloyd's Rep. 578, CA.

waiver of subrogation rights against him, contained in the insurance policy, pursuant to his rights under the Contracts (Rights of Third Parties) Act 1999.

Legal position of the insured

20–47   It seems that the insured is free to proceed against the third party responsible for his insured loss himself, even where the insurers wish to conduct that action themselves. The insurers will be unable to prevent the insured taking this action, irrespective of whether they have[83] or have not yet[84] indemnified the insured in respect of this loss. The insurers will have a lien over any identifiable moneys recovered by the insured, and this proprietorial right takes precedence over any rights of a trustee in bankruptcy, and any other calls on an insured's normal cash flow, including a charge to the Legal Aid Board in respect of costs.[85] Further, the insured must prosecute that action so as to bona fide protect the insurers' interests, otherwise he risks being liable in damages to the insurers for the amount they have lost.[86] Thus the insured will be liable to the insurers for the return of the insurance moneys if he settles an action with the third party by accepting a sum being the balance of the claim exceeding the insurance moneys received.[87] As discussed above, any release or compromise by the insured of a third party's liability to him in respect of a loss which is covered by an insurance indemnity, is unwise, whether done before or after the indemnity is paid by the insurer.

Defences valid against subrogating insurer

20–48   The third party pursued by insurers exercising their right of subrogation may, of course, raise all defences available to him against the insured, because the action is strictly that of the insured.[88] It is no defence that the insured, in whose name the action is brought, has suffered no loss because he has been fully indemnified by his insurers, for this would give the benefit of the insurance to the third party who has not paid a premium for that benefit, or, in any event, seems unconscionable.[89] The third party may also refer to the policy under which the insurers are exercising the subrogation and rely, for example, on an express waiver of subrogation against themselves on the basis that the contract of insurance itself limits the right to subrogation.[90] The third party may also point to the fact that the insurance itself is illegal and, therefore, unenforceable so that it cannot give rise to

---

[83] *Morley v. Moore* [1936] 2 K.B. 359, CA; *Bourne v. Stanbridge* [1965] 1 W.L.R. 189, CA; *cf. Law Fire Assurance Co. v. Oakley* (1888) 4 T.L.R. 309, *per* Mathew J.
[84] *Commercial Union Assurance Co. v. Lister* (1874) 9 Ch. App. 483; *Page v. Scottish Insurance Corp.* (1929) 140 L.T. 571, CA.
[85] *England and England v. Guardian Insurance Ltd* [2000] Lloyd's Rep. I.R. 404, applying *Lord Napier and Ettrick v. Hunter* [1993] A.C. 713, HL.
[86] *West of England Fire Insurance Co. v. Isaacs* [1897] 1 Q.B. 226, CA.
[87] *Phoenix Assurance Co. v. Spooner* [1905] 2 K.B. 753.
[88] See, *e.g. Simpson v. Thomson* (1877) 3 App. Cas. 279, HL.
[89] *Caledonia North Sea Ltd v. London Bridge Engineering Ltd* [2000] Lloyd's Rep. I.R. 249, Ct of Sess. (Inner House); applying *Bradburn v. Great Western Railway Co.* (1874) L.R. 10 Ex. 1, and *Quebec Fire Insurance Co. v. St. Louis* (1851) 7 Moo P.C. 286.
[90] *Thomas & Co. v. Brown* (1899) 4 Com. Cas. 186 at 192, *per* Mathew J.

any right of subrogation.[91] This right of the third party sued to refer to the policy does not extend, however, to argue the technical merits of the insurers' decision to make an indemnity under the terms of the policy provided the insurers made the indemnity honestly.[92]

4. CONTROL OF PROCEEDINGS BY INSURER

Under modern practice, insurers invariably insert conditions in policies **20–49** that give them full powers to control all proceedings involving the insured, both in respect of the claim in respect of which the insured is seeking an indemnity under a liability policy, and in respect of potential rights exercisable against third parties who may be responsible for the loss covered by the insurance. In the latter regard, the insurers are given effective rights of subrogation, not under the common law and equity as discussed above, but contractually under the policy. Thus, there will be no requirement for the insurers to have actually made an indemnity to the insured under the policy in order to give rise to their subrogation rights. Such a condition may read:

> "The Insurer shall be entitled to take over and have the absolute control and conduct of any claim or proceeding using where necessary for its own benefit the name of the Insured."

This type of condition was first considered shortly after the introduction **20–50** of compulsory motor insurance under the Road Traffic Act 1930 in *Groom v. Crocker*.[93] It was established by the Court of Appeal in this case that there are limits to the insurers' rights when exercising their right of control under such a provision. Specifically, on the facts of this case, the court held that they insurers were abusing their power by instructing the solicitor appointed by them to conduct the defence, to admit the injured third party's claim, without first having consulted their insured, the defendant. The insurers' motive was simply to enable them to come to an agreement with the insurers of the other party concerning another action, in which the present insured was in no way involved. The duty to consult arose, even though the insurer was going to meet the full cost of meeting the third party's claim. The insured accordingly succeeded in obtaining an award of damages for libel against the appointed solicitors, as well as nominal damages for their breach of contractual duty towards him.

Duties of the appointed solicitor

In *Groom v. Crocker*, Sir Wilfred Greene M.R. held that whilst the con- **20–51** dition did not, in terms, refer to the position of solicitors, the condition clearly entitled the insurers to nominate a solicitor to act in the conduct of

---

[91] *The Palm Branch* [1916] P. 230.
[92] *King v. Victoria Insurance Co.* [1896] A.C. 250, PC.
[93] [1938] 1 K.B. 194, CA.

the proceedings to which the condition related.[94] As for the practical working of this arrangement where the insurers appoint a solicitor, and yet the insured is clearly a client of those solicitors and owed a professional duty in that regard, his lordship put is in this way[95]:

> "The right given to the insurers is to have control of proceedings in which they and the assured have a common interest — the assured because he is the defendant and the insurers because they are contractually bound to indemnify him. Each is interested in seeing that any judgment to be recovered against the assured shall be for as small a sum as possible . . . The effect of the provisions in question is, I think, to give the insurers the right to decide upon the proper tactics to pursue in the conduct of the action, provided that they do so in what they bona fide consider to be the common interest of themselves and their assured."

20–52   The normal consequence of this is that the insured becomes liable to pay the solicitor's costs, even if the insurers are also liable to pay for those costs.[96] In each case it will be advisable to give careful consideration to the precise terms upon which those solicitors were instructed.[97] If insurers fund defence costs of an insured which fall within an applicable policy excess, the insured will be under an obligation to reimburse the insurers.[98]

MacKinnon L.J. agreed that tactical decisions were the province of the insurers under such a condition, but said that if the appointed solicitor had reason to discern a conflict, or possible conflict, of interest between the insurers and the insured, it is the duty of the solicitor to inform the insured of the matter. If the insured then insists on a course of which the insurers disapprove, the insurers can refuse to conduct or control the proceedings any longer, and leave the insured to do so at his own cost, and at the risk, if the insurers are right in their view, of being unable to recover that cost under his policy.[99]

20–53   In a later case where this type of condition was being considered, Lord Denning M.R. expressed the view that:

> "A man who is accused is entitled to have a solicitor of his own choice or to defend himself if he likes. The insurers cannot compel him to have their own solicitor."[1]

The reason being that to hold otherwise would be contrary to public policy. Without the voluntary resolution of that issue, presumably the insured's only course of action would be to fund his defence with the lawyer of his choice, and later sue his insurers. If the insurers could not then justify their objection to the solicitor which the insured chose to

[94] *ibid.* at 202.
[95] *ibid.* at 203.
[96] *Adams v. London Improved Motor Coach Builders Ltd* [1921] 1 K.B. 495, at 501 and 504.
[97] *Cox v. Bankside Members Agency Ltd* [1995] 2 Lloyd's Rep. 437 at 451, *per* Sir Thomas Bingham M.R., CA.
[98] *ibid.*
[99] *Groom v. Crocker*, at 207–208, [1938] 1 K.B. 194, CA.
[1] *Barrett Bros (Taxis) Ltd v. Davies* [1966] 1 W.L.R. 1334 at 1336, CA.

appoint, their resistance to the appointment of that solicitor would presumably constitute a breach of the bona fide exercise of their powers under the condition entitling the insured to recover the reasonable costs incurred by him to that appointed solicitor.

In contrast to the above rather roundabout attack on the insurers and **20–54** their exercise of their powers under a "control of proceedings" condition in an action against the appointed solicitors, the subsequent case of *Beacon Insurance Co. Ltd v. Langdale*[2] involved action brought by an insured directly against his insurers. Here, the motor insurers decided to settle a motor accident claim against the insured with a denial of liability, and wrote to the insured explaining that they regarded the settlement of £45 as amounting only to the injured third party's out-of-pocket expenses, whilst his injuries were severe having particular regard to his age. The insurers then sought to recover the £5 policy excess under the motor policy from the insured. The insured defended that action, contending that (i) the insurers were not entitled to settle the claim without notice to him, and that (ii) they had not acted reasonably in the exercise of their authority under the condition. The Court of Appeal upheld the judgment against the insured for the recovery of the £5 excess in this settled claim and rejected those defences on the facts of the case as explained by Slesser L.J.[3]:

> "In my opinion, the facts of this case are entirely different from those in *Groom v. Crocker*. In that case, the solicitors for a certain society delivered a defence on behalf of the [insured] admitting negligence, and the [insured], who was in the position of the appellant here, was not notified of the delivery of the defence, and did not learn of it until after judgment had been given against him in his brother's action. In my opinion, this case, so far from being a case like *Groom v. Crocker*, appears to have been one in which the insurance company behaved at all times with complete propriety. They drew the attention of the assured, on the claim form itself, to the terms of the contract. They made what they believed to be, in his interest and theirs, an advantageous settlement, and they were at pains to show that the settlement should be made with a denial of liability, so that no one could say that they had admitted any culpability whatever on his behalf."

That case illustrates that the vast majority of settlements made by **20–55** liability insurers in the ordinary course of their business, pursuant to their power to control the proceedings under this type of condition, will be unchallengeable. Provided liability insurers meet the requirement of the bona fide exercise of those powers, with due regard to the insured's interests as well as their own, no specific discussion necessarily need take place with the insured regarding a proposed settlement, where that settlement involves a denial of liability. On the other hand, the specific consent of the insured would seem to be required before any settlement involving any admission of liability is concluded with the third party claimant.

---

[2] [1939] 4 All E.R. 204, CA.
[3] *ibid.* at 206.

Exercise of control of proceedings and waiver and estoppel in respect of the insured's right to an indemnity

20–56   Exercising their power to control and conduct proceedings can operate to prevent the insurer later arguing that the claim is not covered by the policy. *Evans v. Employers' Mutual Insurance Association Ltd*[4] is clear Court of Appeal authority that where insurers know of a breach of condition or warranty, or concealment of material facts by the insured, but undertake or continue to undertake the defence of a third party claim against their insured, that conduct is capable of constituting a waiver of their right to refuse an indemnity to their insured under the policy in respect of those known grounds. In this case, the insured driver faced claims from several persons who had been injured in a collision. During the investigation of his motor insurance claim within the defendant insurers' offices, the claims superintendent who was authorised to deal with such matters, in accordance with the practice of the office, passed the claim form, and the original proposal form, on to a clerk for the purpose of checking the statements they contained and noting any discrepancies therein. The clerk noticed a discrepancy, namely that the insured had declared on the proposal form that he had been driving for five years, but on the claim form stated he had only been driving for six weeks. The clerk did not consider it important and did not call the claims superintendent's attention to this discrepancy. Thereafter, the defendant insurers paid the insured's own claim in respect of his own car, and took over the negotiation of the personal injury claims by the third parties. After a while, but before settlement, the claims superintendent became aware of the discrepancy between the statements in the proposal form and those in the claim form, whereupon the insurers had repudiated their liability under the policy.

20–57   The Court of Appeal upheld an arbitrator's decision that the knowledge of the clerk had to be imputed to his employers, the defendant insurers, because that knowledge was gained by the clerk in the ordinary course of the duties entrusted to him. Accordingly, the insurers must be treated as having received the information contained in those two documents and, by their conduct in taking over control of the conduct of settlement discussions, had affirmed the policy, thereby waiving their right to repudiate liability under the policy.

On the other hand, without such specific knowledge of their right to rescind the insurance policy, or rely on a breach of warranty or condition precedent to liability, it has been said *obiter* that the mere act of undertaking or continuing the defence of a claim does not found an estoppel.[5] This is on two bases, first that such conduct is an equivocal, not an unequivocal, act which does not amount to a representation that they are liable to indemnify the insured. Second, that in any event such a represen-

---

[4] [1936] 1 K.B. 505, CA.
[5] But see *T.S.B. Bank plc v. Robert Irving and Burns* [1999] Lloyd's Rep. I.R. 528.

tation would not be one of fact, but one of law, which cannot found an estoppel.[6]

Undue influence in dealings between insurer and the third party claimant

When dealing with third party claimants, liability insurers must be careful not to give such a claimant grounds to permit his subsequent challenge to any settlement agreement reached with him on the ground of undue influence. Such a challenge arose in *Horry v. Tate & Lyle Refineries Ltd*[7] where the claimant brought an employers' liability claim against the defendant employers following an accident in 1979. In exercise of their power to conduct settlement discussions, the defendant employers' liability insurers corresponded directly with the claimant. The claimant told them that he did not have a solicitor and asked them whether they thought he should. The insurers replied that they did not think that would be necessary, and asked the claimant to produce a medical report, which he did. The insurers then asked him to undergo a medical examination by their own consultant, adding that when that report was to hand, they would be in a position to "quantify your claim" (rather than "make an offer"). The claimant replied that he would await their quantification of his claim before consulting his Union's lawyers. In evidence, the insurers' claims inspector, who had dealt throughout with the claimant, freely accepted that the claimant was looking to and relying on the insurers to tell him the "right figure" for his claim. After that medical report was obtained the claimant returned to work. One day sometime later, the claims inspector turned up to see the claimant without prearrangement, and the claim was discussed between them and settled at £1,000.

20–58

The claimant employee thereafter commenced an action against his employers in respect of the injury, and the employers' insurers raised the defence of the settlement of the claim. In reply, the claimant contended that the settlement could not be relied on because, *inter alia*, it had been induced by the undue influence of the insurers through their claims inspector. Peter Pain J. held that a fiduciary relationship arose between the insurers and the unrepresented claimant in these circumstances, and that the insurers had failed to discharge that duty because they had permitted their own interest in settling the claim at the lower end of the applicable bracket for hernia claims. His lordship considered that the insurers could have discharged that duty by advising the claimant employee to get some independent advice about their offer before settling. Alternatively, that not having been done, it was incumbent on the insurers to have offered a figure which was considerably higher and towards the upper part of the bracket

20–59

---

[6] *Soole v. Royal Insurance Co. Ltd* [1971] 2 Lloyd's Rep. 332. Compare the position in Australia where the claim under the policy is treated as a contingent liability before the liability of the insured to a third party is established, so that the insurer's insistence on taking over the conduct of the defence is regarded as an unequivocal representation that estops the insurer from later contesting his liability to the insured under the policy, *Club Motor Insurance Agency Ltd v. Swann* [1954] V.L.R. 754; *Borthern Assurance Co. Ltd v. Cooper* [1968] Qd. R. 46; *Hansen v. Marco Engineering (Aust.) Pty. Ltd* [1948] V.L.R. 198.

[7] [1982] 2 Lloyd's Rep. 416.

appropriate to hernia claims, in view of the severity of the claimant's hernia in this case. Secondly, his lordship felt that it was the insurers' duty to specify what reduction they were making in respect of contributory negligence which was inherent in their offer, either by way of percentage or by way of figures. Thirdly, they should have provided the claimant with a copy of the medical report provided by his own doctor. Fourthly, they should have made sure that the claimant employee understood that this settlement would be "the end of the road" if he entered into it, and no further claim could be made in respect of the accident, particularly as there was a 15 per cent chance of recurrence of the hernia. Finally, the insurers should have advised the claimant to think the matter over and to delay until he had had an opportunity of both testing himself back at work and fully considering the offer.

20–60   The *Horry* case may properly be considered an example of the flagrant breach of the fiduciary duty that can arise where the insurers know that the claimant is not obtaining legal advice, and is relying on them to make a fair and proper quantification of his claim. The decision went further than the earlier decision of Paull J. in *Saunders v. Ford Motor Co. Ltd*[8] where the failure of the insurers' claims manager to make it clear to the unrepresented claimant employee, who was seeking compensation from his employers in respect of an eye injury, that he could receive no more money, led to the finding that the settlement had not been in full and final settlement. Therefore, the claimant was held not to be barred from pursuing further damages in a subsequent action against his employers. *Obiter* Paull J. emphasised that insurers' representatives must take great care when settling such claims directly with claimants. Three necessary elements of a satisfactory system were suggested by Paull J.:

(i) the insurers' representative must get to know all the material facts medically and otherwise before he settles;

(ii) where he knows that there is no possibility of a defence, he should tell the claimant so, making sure on the settlement receipt that there is no denial of liability which may be brought up against the claimant later; and

(iii) he must make sure that he starts negotiations with a reasonable sum, not a very low sum.

Insurer cannot rely on unjust and inequitable settlement with third party or judgment

20–61   Where a third party claimant initially sues only for the uninsured excess in respect of a loss caused by the defendant, and that action is stayed by reason of the acceptance of the defendant's payment into court, a second action arising from the same cause of action is not permissible to recover further losses. The claimant, or his insurers exercising subrogation rights, may, however, apply for a removal of the stay on the first action to enable enlargement of that action to embrace the insured losses, and such may be

---

[8] [1970] 1 Lloyd's Rep. 379.

permitted on repayment of the sum paid into court to the defendant.[9] A defendant, or his insurers, cannot therefore, raise any absolute bar to the enlargement of claims by a claimant after his acceptance of a payment into court made by the defendant, or insurers exercising their right of control of the defence.

Matters were taken further by the Court of Appeal in *Hayler v. D.G. Chapman*[10] where the Court stated that it had the power to set aside a judgment given after a contested hearing, even after payment of the judgment monies by the defendant's insurers. To do so, though, the court would need evidence as to the conduct of the parties showing that it was unjust and inequitable for the judgment to stand and act as a bar to any additional claim. Such evidence might be that the defendant's insurers deliberately exploited misunderstandings between the claimant and his insurers so as to contest at trial the claimant's own claim for uninsured losses which had been made without his insurer's knowledge, with the purpose of then raising the fact of the trial judgment as a bar to a later action by the claimant's insurer (exercising rights of subrogation) in respect of the larger insured losses.[11]

20–62

5. INSURER'S RIGHT TO REPAYMENT OF THE INDEMNITY FOR FRAUD AND MISTAKE

Apart from the insurer's right to reimbursement of his outlay, or part of it, in the case of the insurer's successful pursuit of a subrogated claim, or the insured's own successful action against a wrongdoer responsible for the loss which was covered by the insurance, discussed above, the insurer is entitled to recover his outlay in two circumstances. The first is in the case of the discovery of the insured's fraud upon him, where the insurer can rescind the insurance contract and recover back what he paid out,[12] or, it has been suggested, recover the amount paid out as damages for fraud in the tort of deceit.[13] The second, is in the case of payment by the insurer under the mistake of fact that he was liable to make payment under the policy.

20–63

A contract is liable to be set aside in equity, but not at common law,[14] if the parties were under a common misapprehension either as to facts or as to their respective rights, provided that the misapprehension was fundamental and that the party seeking to set it aside was not himself at fault.[15] The authority in the field of insurance is the decision of Lord Denning

20–64

---

[9] *Derrick v. Williams* [1939] 2 All E.R. 559, CA; *Lambert v. Mainland Market Deliveries Ltd* [1977] 1 W.L.R. 825, CA; *Buckland v. Palmer* [1984] 3 All E.R. 554, CA.

[10] [1989] 1 Lloyd's Rep. 490, CA.

[11] *ibid.* at 492, *per* Taylor L.J.(as he then was).

[12] *Clough v. L.N.W.R.* (1871) L.R. 7 Ex. 26.

[13] *London Assurance v. Clare* (1937) 57 Ll. L. R. 254.

[14] *Bell v. Lever Bros.* [1932] A.C. 161, HL. The earlier decision in *Kelly v. Solari* (1841) 11 L.J. Ex. 10 where recovery of insurance settlement monies paid under a mistake of fact as to the validity of the policy where the insurer had known the true facts, but had forgotten them at the time of payment, must now be regarded as wrongly decided.

[15] *Solle v. Butcher* [1950] 1 K.B. 671 at 693, *per* Denning L.J. (as he then was), CA.

M.R. applying this principle, invented by himself, in *Magee v. Pennine Insurance Co. Ltd.*[16] In 1961, the claimant, who was then aged 58 and could not drive, bought a car on hire-purchase terms through a garage. He wanted the car for his son of 18 to drive. The claimant signed an insurance proposal form, the details of which were written in by the proprietor of the garage. This proposal wrongly stated that the claimant was the holder of a provisional licence and that he himself and his elder son of 35, who had an annual licence, would drive the car in addition to his younger son. The declaration signed by the claimant said that the answers in the proposal were true and it was to be the basis of the contract of insurance with the defendant insurance company. The policy was issued and renewed each year, the car being replaced by another covered under the policy of 1964. On April 25, 1965, the car was involved in an accident when being driven by the younger son. The car skidded into a shop window and was a complete wreck. The claimant claimed £600 under the policy as the value of the car. On May 12, 1965, insurance brokers wrote to the claimant telling him that the insurers were prepared to offer him £385 in settlement of his claim. The claimant accepted the offer. The insurers then interviewed the claimant and realised that they could rescind the policy because of the inaccuracies in the proposal form, and the claimant sued for the £385 due under the compromise agreement. The insurance company defended the action on the ground of mistake as to the validity of the policy.

20–65   A majority of the Court of Appeal held that the oral compromise agreement was voidable by the insurance company on the ground of mistake. While Fenton Atkinson L.J. held that it was "right and equitable" that the compromise was voidable on the ground of mutual mistake in a fundamental and vital matter, Lord Denning M.R. held that it was voidable in equity[17]:

> ". . . it is clear that, when the insurance company and Mr. Magee made this agreement to pay £385, they were both under a common mistake, which was fundamental to the whole agreement. Both thought that Mr. Magee was entitled to claim under the policy of insurance, whereas he was not so entitled. The common mistake does not make the agreement to pay £385 a nullity, but it makes it liable to be set aside in equity.
>
> This brings me to a question which has caused me much difficulty. Is this a case in which we ought to set the agreement aside in equity? I have hesitated on this point, but I cannot shut my eyes to the fact that Mr. Magee has no valid claim on the insurance policy: and, if he had no claim on the policy, it is not equitable that he should have a good claim on the agreement to pay £385, seeing that it was made under a fundamental mistake. It is not fair to hold the insurance company to an agreement which they would not have dreamt of making if they had not been under a mistake. I would, therefore, uphold the appeal and give judgment for the insurance company."

---

[16] [1969] 2 Q.B. 507, CA. See also the marine insurance case of *Norwich Union Fire Insurance Society Ltd v. Price Ltd* [1934] A.C. 455, PC, where subsequent investigation showed that the fruit, the subject of the insurance, was sold because it was ripening and not as a result of a peril of the sea.

[17] [1934] A.C. 455 at 514–515.

It is to be noted that an essential element was the insurance company's **20–66** ignorance of the true situation, and it is therefore to be distinquished from cases such as *Evans v. Employers' Mutual Insurance Association Ltd*,[18] discussed above, where the claims handler did examine the facts of the case but simply failed to realise the significance of facts which would have entitled his employers, the insurers, to rescind the policy. A further important point is that *Magee* was concerned with an oral compromise agreement, whereas written agreements of compromise can only be set aside on the well established principle of *non est factum*, which requires the signatory to be fundamentally mistaken about the contents of the document signed,[19] and will therefore be most unlikely to have any application in the present context. Further, the decision in Magee has no application to situations where the insurer weighs up the merits of compromising an insured's claim, fully conscious that further investigation might subsequently give them grounds to rescind the policy or repudiate the claim for breach of a condition precedent or a warranty. One final comment on the question of the possible recovery of settlement monies paid by insurers where both parties are mistaken as to the validity of the claim is that the developing area of equitable restitutionary in the case of unjust enrichment, which can apply in circumstances of mistake of fact or law,[20] may have some application in this area.

---

[18] [1936] 1 K.B. 505, CA.
[19] *Gallie v. Lee* [1971] A.C. 1004, HL.
[20] *Kleinwort Benson Ltd v. Lincoln City Council & others* [1999] 2 A.C. 349, HL.

CHAPTER 21

THIRD PARTY RIGHTS AGAINST LIABILITY INSURERS

1. INTRODUCTION

21–01 As the insurer only has an obligation to indemnify an insured under a liability policy to the extent that the insured is legally liable to a third party, and this obligation is based solely on the insurance contract to which the third party is not privy, it cannot be said that the insurer owes any obligation or debt to a third party who has obtained judgment against the insured.[1] Parliament has therefore remedied this legal position whereby a third party who had suffered injury or loss for which the insured was legally responsible could not obtain satisfaction of his judgment by reason, for instance, of the insured's insolvency, primarily by the Third Parties (Rights Against Insurers) Act 1930, and, in respect solely of employers' liability policies, by the Employers' Liability (Compulsory Insurance) Act 1969.

21–02 Even in a situation where the insured obtained an indemnity from the insurer in satisfaction of the third party's claim, but on receipt of the insurance moneys the insured went bankrupt,[2] or into liquidation,[3] those insurance moneys merely formed part of the insured's assets to be divided amongst all the creditors of the insured. As Atkin L.J. explained[4]:

> "The position in law seems to me clearly to be that a third party in a case like the present has no claim in law or in equity of any sort against the insurance company, or against the money paid by the insurance company, nor has he any claim against the person who injures him, the assured, to direct the assured to pay over the sum of money received under the insurance policy to him. The amount that the assured, in fact, received is part of his general assets. As a general rule the expediency of that, I think, cannot be disputed . . . I find it impossible to see how a special right, arising out of circumstances which ordinarily occur in cases of solvency, could come into existence merely because the assured happened to be in difficulties or financial weakness, or to become bankrupt, or, if a company, to have a winding-up order made against it."

2. RIGHTS OF THIRD PARTIES AGAINST INSURERS ON BANKRUPTCY, ETC. OF THE INSURED

21–03 The Third Parties (Rights Against Insurers) Act 1930 is confined to protect third parties where the insured wrongdoer becomes bankrupt or

---

[1] *Israelson v. Dawson, Port of Manchester Insurance Co. Garnishees* [1933] 1 K.B. 301, CA; *France v. Piddington (Co-operative Insurance Society Ltd, Garnishees)* (1932) 43 Ll. L. Rep. 491; *Loftus v. Port of Manchester Insurance Co. Ltd* (1933) 45 Ll. L. Rep. 252; *Jabbour v. Custodian of Israeli Absentee's Property of State of Israel* [1954] 1 All E.R. 145.
[2] *Hood's Trustees v. Southern Union General Insurance Co. of Australasia* [1928] Ch. 793, CA.
[3] *Re Harrington Motor Co. Ltd, ex p. Chaplin* [1928] Ch. 105, CA.
[4] *ibid.* at 110.

insolvent, either before or after the liability of the insured wrongdoer to the third part is established. The Act provides by section 1(1)(a) and (b):

> "(1) Where under any contract of insurance a person (hereinafter referred to as the insured) is insured against liabilities to third parties which he may incur, then —
>
> (a) in the event of the insured becoming bankrupt or making a composition or arrangement with his creditors; or
> (b) in the case of the insured being a company, in the event of a winding-up order [or administration order][5] being made, or a resolution for a voluntary winding-up being passed, with respect to the company, or of a receiver or manager of the company's business or undertaking being duly appointed or of possession being taken, by or on behalf of the holders of any debentures secured by a floating charge, of any property comprised in or subject to the charge [or upon approval of a voluntary arrangement for the purposes of Part 1 of the Insolvency Act][6];
>
> if, either before or after that event, any such liability as aforesaid is incurred by the insured, his rights against the insurer under the contract in respect of the liability shall, notwithstanding anything in any Act or rule of law to the contrary, be transferred to and vest in the third party to whom the liability was so incurred."

This transfer of the insured's right under the 1930 Act, is also applied to the situation of a deceased debtor (the insured) having an order being made under section 130 of the Bankruptcy Act 1914 for the administration of the deceased's estate, where the rights under the deceased's liability insurances will vest in a third party who proves in bankruptcy the liability of the deceased to him.[7] Where such a statutory transfer of rights under a liability insurance occurs, the third party so vested with the insured's rights may also recover to the same extent as the insured was entitled to, and is thus liable to any uninsured excess, *i.e.* the first £X of any claim, specified in the policy.[8]   **21–04**

3. RESTRICTED CIRCUMSTANCES OF THE ACT'S APPLICABILITY

The transfer of an insured's rights under a liability insurance to third parties only operates in the circumstances enumerated in section 1(1)(a) and (b) above, as was pointed out by Scrutton L.J. in a case concerning motor insurance[9]:   **21–05**

> "I think there is no doubt why the . . . Statute of 1930 was passed. There had been a series of cases dealing partly with collision insurance and partly with

---

[5] Inserted by the Insolvency Act 1986, s.235(1), Sched.8, para. 7(2).
[6] *ibid.,* s.439(2), Sched. 14.
[7] Third Parties (Rights Against Insurers) Act 1930, s.1(2).
[8] *ibid.,* s.1(4).
[9] *McCormick v. National Motor and Accident Insurance Union Ltd.* (1934) 49 Ll. L. Rep. 361 at 363, CA.

other forms of insurance, in which this happened: a person had claimed indemnity against another person who was insured. He had got a judgment entitling him to £1000, let us say. The defendant then went bankrupt, and the plaintiff who had got that judgment for £1000 wrote to the trustees in bankruptcy and said: 'Pay me the £1000.' 'No', said the trustees in bankruptcy, 'This £1000 is the property of the bankruptcy; it is a question for the general body of creditors and not for you. You can prove in respect of the debt for £1000 and you may get £500, or £100, or nothing, or you may get the £1000, according to the number of other people who prove against the property of the Bankrupt.'

There are several cases in regard to that. Of course, that proposition looked wrong, that a man should have a judgment against a bankrupt for £1000 before the bankruptcy and that the judgment should give him no right over the property of the bankrupt except merely as one of the general body of creditors of the bankrupt. So I think that this Act of 1930 was passed to deal with the difficulty, and it gave a third party who was injured by [the insured] certain rights against the defendant against whom he got a judgment if he went bankrupt but not otherwise."

21–06   The Act's provisions do not apply in circumstances where the insured, being a company, is wound up voluntarily merely for the purposes of reconstruction or of amalgamation with another company.[10] Moreover, the dissolution of a company resulting from it being struck off the register as a defunct company under section 652 of the Companies Act 1985, is a circumstance that is outside the scope of the provisions of the 1930 Act,[11] as is the mere factual insolvency of the insured company.[12]

Requirement of contract of insurance
21–07   Whilst a fully workable definition of a contract of insurance is an evasive thing to evolve, and is discussed in Chapter 1, it can be said that there are three essential elements to a contract of insurance[13]:

(a) the contract must provide that the insured will become entitled to something on the occurrence of some event;
(b) the event must be one which involves some element of uncertainty (outside the control of the insurer)[14]; and
(c) the insured must have an insurable interest in the subject matter of the contract.

Indemnity must not be discretionary
21–08   Where a contract of insurance is held to exist[15] between the insured and insurer, this will not entitle the third party to obtain a benefit that is at the discretion of the insurer, as Mocatta J. explained in a marine insurance

---

[10] Third Parties (Rights Against Insurers) Act 1930, s.1(6)(a).
[11] *Re Harvest Lane Motor Bodies Ltd* [1969] 1 Ch. 457.
[12] *Re Allobrogia S.S. Corp.* [1978] 3 All E.R. 423, at 433 *per* Slade J.
[13] *Medical Defence Union Co. Ltd v. Department of Trade* [1980] Ch. 82 at 89–90, *per* Megarry V.-C.; see also discussion in Chapter 1, above.
[14] *Department of Trade and Industry v. St Christopher Motorists Association Ltd* [1974] 1 W.L.R. 99, at 106, *per* Templeman J. (as he then was), this rider was again left undecided.
[15] This was specifically considered in *Re Allobrogia S.S. Corp.* [1978] 3 All E.R. 423 at 427–428.

case where an indemnity in respect of liability for forwarding expenses was at the sole discretion of the committee of the mutual indemnity society under its rule 7(h)[16]:

> "The next point arising is whether this is a claim falling within the ambit of section 1 of the 1930 Act. [The indemnity society] submitted that the provisions of rule 7(h) made it clear that there was no insurance of a claim in relation to forwarding expenses, but merely the possibility of what one might regard as an *ex gratia* payment in respect of them. Section 1(1) of the Act deals and deals only with the position where a person is insured against liabilities to third parties which he may incur and provides that in such a case if the insured is wound up and before that event any such liability as aforesaid — *i.e.* to third parties — is incurred, his rights against the insurer under the contract in respect of the liabilities shall be transferred to and vest in the third party. If the member is not insured in respect of forwarding expenses, no rights relating thereto are transferred under the Act of the third party. I think this argument is well founded and I do not consider the fact that this provision about forwarding expenses is contained within a contract of insurance results in the member being insured in respect of forwarding expenses."

Incurring of an insured liability

Section 1(1) of the 1930 Act makes it clear a third party liability **21–09** incurred, either before or after the insured becomes bankrupt or is wound up, is covered by the Act's provisions. A liability, as defined by the indemnifying provisions of the relevant contract of insurance, must, however, be "incurred". Thus, where the insurance provides, as it usually does in liability insurances, that the insurers "will indemnify the insured against all sums which the insured shall become legally liable to pay as compensation in respect of loss of or damage to property", then it follows that the liability to the third party is only "incurred" within the meaning of the Act, when the insured's liability to the injured third party is ascertained and determined to exist at law, either by judgment of the court, or by an award in an arbitration, or by agreement[17] (a settlement or compromise).

This has the ramification that a third party can have no rights trans- **21–10** ferred to him under the 1930 Act, if the insured's liability to him has not been established prior to the commencement of the proceedings against the insurer. If the third party is unable to establish the insured's liability to him, *e.g.* by reason that the insured being a company that has been dissolved and cannot be resurrected for the purpose of establishing that liability, the third party simply has no remedy.[18] The correct procedure, therefore, is for the third party to sue the insured, even if the third party knows that the insured is already bankrupt (or, if a company, is in liquidation), and only once judgment has been obtained against the now insolvent insured, should the third party seek to invoke his rights under the 1930 Act. There is now a 20-year period during

---

[16] *The Vainqueur José* [1979] 1 Lloyd's Rep. 557 at 580.
[17] *Post Office v. Norwich Union Fire Insurance Society Ltd* [1967] 2 Q.B. 363 at 373–374, *per* Lord Denning M.R., CA.
[18] *Bradley v. Eagle Star Insurance Co. Ltd* [1989] A.C. 957, HL.

which a limited company that has been dissolved may now be resurrected for the purpose of a third part's claim for damages in respect of personal injury or death.[19]

Companies wound up by, or provisional liquidator appointed by, court order

21–11   No permission of the court is required by the third party to sue a limited company that is in voluntary liquidation, but permission of the winding-up court is required to commence or continue proceedings against a company that is being compulsorily wound up by the court, or a company that has had a provisional liquidator appointed by the court.[20] The Court of Appeal in *Post Office v. Norwich Union Fire Insurance Society Ltd*[21] anticipated that such discretionary leave would automatically be given, but the failure to obtain such permission may render the proceedings a nullity, which cannot be cured by a retrospective application. There are conflicting decisions on this point.[22] Further, Slade J. (as he then was) has pointed out in *Re Thompson & Riches Ltd*[23] that there may be difficulties to be resolved in resurrecting a company that has been struck off by the Registrar of Companies, where that company has subsequently been dissolved by order of the court in ignorance of the striking off of that company. That said, an analysis of over 1,000 applications to restore dissolved companies under sections 651 and 653 of the Companies Act 1985 has revealed that every application was successful, but only 169 concerned applications relating to the 1930 Act (60 per cent of which related to employers' liability insurance).[24]

21–12   Presumably, if the liability insurer of a "struck off" or insolvent company learns of an application to either restore the company, or to pursue proceedings against an insolvent company, could seek leave to be joined to such an application for the purpose of resisting that application on the ground that it was fruitless. Although there is no case law on such a step being taken by an insurer, in principle such an application is permissible.[25] If joined, it must be assumed that to successfully resist such an application, the insurer would have to show a very clear case indeed that he was not liable to indemnify the company in respect of the liability that the third party is seeking to establish against the "struck off" or insolvent company. If there was any real argument upon the applicability of the insurance policy to the potential liability, the court would probably be inclined to the view that any insurance cover issue should be left to run its course in the ensuing litigation.

---

[19] Companies Act 1989, s.141.
[20] Insolvency Act 1986, s.130(2).
[21] [1967] 2 Q.B. 367 at 375, 377 and 378.
[22] *Re National Employers Mutual General Insurance Association* [1995] B.C.C. 774; *cf. D. M. Stevenson & Co. v. Radford & Bright Ltd* (1902) 10 S.L.T. 82.
[23] [1981] 1 W.L.R. 682.
[24] Law Commission Consultation Paper No. 152, pp.205–206.
[25] *Stanhope Pension Trust Ltd v. Registrar of Companies* [1994] 1 B.C.L.C. 628, CA.

The transfer of rights under the insurance

Under section 1(1) of the 1930 Act, the injured third party "steps into   **21–13**
the shoes of the wrongdoer".[26] Thus, it can be said that under section 1 of
the Act of 1930 the injured person cannot sue the insurance company
except in such circumstances as the insured himself could have sued the
insurance company.[27] The third party acquiring the insured's rights
"cannot pick out one bit — pick out the plums and leave the duff
behind"[28]; he will be in no better a position than the insured was under the
insurance contract. As discussed below, the insurers can avail themselves,
as against the third party vested with rights under the 1930 Act, of all the
defences which would have been available to them as against the insured,[29]
e.g. breach of condition.[30] The insurers are not entitled, though, to raise in
defence against the third party obtaining the rights of the insured, any liability of the insured to them, e.g. in respect of unpaid premiums under
adjustment of premiums provisions. Where insurers did attempt to set off
such premiums unpaid by the insured against the third party's claim,
Cumming-Bruce J. in *Murray v. Legal and General Assurance Society Ltd*[31]
held they could not:

> "In my view, in the words used to create the statutory subrogation, the
> draftsman did carefully limit the subrogation to the rights under the con-
> tract in respect of the liability incurred by the insured to the third party.
> Rights which are not referable to the particular liability of the insurer to the
> particular third party are not transferred. Thus all conditions in the policy
> which modify or control the obligations of the insurers to cover a given
> liability to a third party are the subject of transfer . . . The right to recovery
> of the premiums in this case was not a term of the policy which arose in
> respect of the liability of the insured to the third party. The defendants are
> in my view left in regard thereto with the same rights as the general body of
> creditors, namely, to prove in the bankruptcy. It follows that the plaintiff
> [third party] is entitled to judgment in this case."

Litigation by the third party

The case law produces a situation where the third party might have to   **21–14**
bring three sets of proceedings:

(i) for restoration of a dissolved company, or for continuance of
proceedings against an insolvent company;

---

[26] *Post Office v. Norwich Union Fire Insurance Society Ltd* [1967] 2 Q.B. 363 at 373, *per*
Lord Denning M.R., CA.

[27] *ibid.* at 374.

[28] *ibid.* at 376, *per* Harman L.J.; followed *Re Allobrogia S.S. Corp.* [1978] 3 All E.R. 423 at
431, *per* Slade J.

[29] *Farrell v. Federated Employers Insurance Association Ltd* [1970] 1 W.L.R. 1400 at 1402,
per Lord Denning M.R., CA; *Austin v. Zurich General Accident and Liability Insurance Co.
Ltd* [1945] K.B. 250, CA.

[30] For example, condition as to roadworthiness of the insured vehicle, *Lefevre v. White*
[1990] 1 Lloyd's Rep. 569; or to "take reasonable precautions to prevent accidents" in a public
liability policy, *Aswan M/S Engineering Establishment Co. Ltd v. Iron Trades Mutual
Insurance Co. Ltd* [1989] 1 Lloyd's Rep. 289.

[31] *Murray v. Legal and General Assurance Society Ltd* [1969] 3 All E.R. 794 at 799–800.

    (ii) an action against the insured company or individual to establish liability;

   (iii) thereafter, an action against the insurer for an indemnity under the terms of the liability insurance.

The Court of Appeal in *Carpenter v. Ebblewhite*[32] has made it clear that the courts will not permit a third party claimant to circumvent matters by directly joining the defendant's insurers as a second defendant to his action and seek a declaration as to that insurer's liability to satisfy his claim against the first defendant (the insured). The Court of Appeal has also ruled that a third party claimant has no *locus standi* to seek a declaration against an insurer to the effect that the insurer is obliged to indemnify their insured against that third party's claim.[33]

21–15   It is indeed unfortunate that the procedure should be so complicated and, in consequence, so expensive, for an injured third party where the statutory transfer of the insured's rights under the 1930 Act was doubtless intended to assist third parties to recover against the insurers of insolvent wrongdoers. If the third party does succeed in establishing the insolvent insured defendant's liability to him, provided the insurance applies to this liability and extends to cover a claimant's legal costs,[34] then he will be reimbursed for his assessed legal costs of the action. But the recoverable costs may be reduced in proportion to the policy limit where the judgment sum exceeds that policy limit.[35] Where the insured wrongdoer is already bankrupt or insolvent there is, in practice, no likelihood of the joinder of the insurer as a CPR, Pt 20 to the injured third party's main action, because trustees in bankruptcy and company liquidators will not be inclined to expend other creditor's money on such proceedings which can only assist a single, and at that time contingent, creditor.

21–16   The real injustice occurs in situations where the injured party only learns of his potential claim against an insured party, *e.g.* an ex-employer, much later in time, *e.g.* in the case of disease claims such as asbestosis or mesothelioma, at which time the insured employer has long disappeared, or, in the case of a limited company, has been dissolved many years earlier. In such circumstances, there may not be much point in the injured claimant going to the trouble of restoring the company to the register of companies in order to establish liability, because the identity of the employers' liability insurer will be unknown to him in the absence of a national register of such compulsory insurances, let alone voluntary insurances. Occasionally, past directors or old company documents can be traced to assist claimants to identify the relevant insurer, but this cannot be regarded as satisfactory. The problems facing an injured claimant, *e.g.* an ex-employee, in these circumstances are very real indeed — yet somewhere there will be an insurer, who has received a premium to cover the

---

[32] [1939] 1 K.B. 347, CA.

[33] *D. G. Finance v. Scott and Eagle Star Insurance Co. Ltd* [1999] Lloyd's Rep. I.R. 387, CA.

[34] The extent of the insurance indemnity is discussed in Chapter 2, above.

[35] *Aluminium Wire and Cable Co. Ltd v. Allstate Insurance Co. Ltd* [1985] 2 Lloyd's Rep. 280.

employer's liability risk. Yet there is no legal requirement upon insurers to assist third party claimants by searching their records and thus assist the claimants to obtain proper redress that the 1930 Act intended. As discussed below, the present disclosure obligations are limited in both scope and applicability.

Insurer may apply to be joined as second defendant

Strangely, whilst the third party claimant cannot join the insurer as a second defendant for a declaration that he is liable to indemnify the insured first defendant, the law takes the totally contrary view in the case of the insurer himself applying to be joined into the main action as a second defendant. This is discussed in Chapter 22, below.
21–17

4. INSURER'S DEFENCES

Limitation

The third party gains the transfer of the insured defendant's rights against his liability insurer on the date he obtained judgment against the insured. He must therefore commence hid action against the insurer within the normal time period of six years from that date. Thus, in *Lefevre v. White*[36] a road accident had occurred on July 22, 1972, and the injured Mr Lefevre was a passenger in the insured's vehicle. Mr Lefevre commenced proceedings against the insured driver on December 7, 1977, by which time he knew that the insurers were in dispute with their insured as to their liability to indemnify him in respect of this accident. On December 16, 1981, Mr Lefevre obtained a judgment against the insured driver for £275,000. On December 9, 1987, the insured driver was made bankrupt on Mr Lefevre's petition based on this judgment. Thereafter, on June 3, 1988, Mr Lefevre commenced proceedings against the insurers pursuant to the 1930 Act. Upon the bankruptcy of the insured driver, Popplewell J. considered the nature of the rights transferred to Mr Lefevre to be that he had his own cause of action direct against the insurers. That cause of action was to exercise his right to claim all the benefits which attached to the insured driver. Accordingly, being a liability policy under which the insured driver had a right to sue the insurers upon liability being established against the judgment on December 16, 1981, Mr Lefevre, as a third party, could only exercise the rights to claim which previously existed in the insured driver. His action against the insurers was therefore time-barred as it had been commenced more than six years after the judgment on December 16, 1981.
21–18

No public policy defence available against third party

Mance J. (as he then was) in *Total Graphics Ltd v. A.G.F. Insurance Ltd*[37] held that as public policy only creates a personal disability to recover
21–19

---

[36] [1990] 1 Lloyd's Rep. 569.
[37] [1997] 1 Lloyd's Rep. 599 at 606, applying *Hardy v. Motor Insurance Bureau.* [1964] 2 Q.B. 745, CA.

against the insurer in respect of a liability otherwise covered by the liability insurance, and thus a party exercising rights transferred under the 1930 Act was not affected by any such personal disability.

Breach of notice of claim and control of proceedings conditions

21–20   The 1930 Act does not seem to achieve its aim to work justice in the case of the careless insured, or worse, a contriving insured, who does not give due notification of the third party's claim to his liability insurer. Except in the case of compulsory employers' liability insurance,[38] where such a condition is properly construed as a condition precedent to the insurer's liability,[39] the giving of late notice, or the total failure to give notice, will debar the third party judgment creditor's enforcement of the insurance indemnity in respect of that judgment. There are several reported cases where the insurer's defence on these grounds has been upheld as against a blameless third party seeking to exercise his transfer of rights under the 1930 Act.

21–21   In *Hassett v. Legal and General Assurance Society Ltd,*[40] a public liability policy issued by the defendant insurers to the insured contained the following conditions:

> "**4.** Any communication whatever relating to the accident must be forwarded to the Society immediately.
> **5.** On receiving from the insured notice of any claim the Society may take upon themselves the settlement of the same . . . The Society shall if and so long as they desire have the absolute conduct and control in the name and on behalf of the insured of the defence to any proceedings that may be taken to enforce any claim covered by this policy."

21–22   The insured had failed to notify the defendant insurers at all of service of the plaintiffs writ, nor, indeed, of judgment being entered against them in default of appearance. Atkinson J. held that the defendant insurers were fully entitled to rely on the breach of these conditions to successfully defend the claim against them under the 1930 Act[41]:

> "If there is one thing which is perfectly clear to my mind, it is that the moment any proceedings were started there was an obligation imposed upon the insured by these conditions to bring it to the notice of the insurance company, so that the insurance company would be in a position to exercise the rights which these conditions give them. Really, to argue, as has been argued, that these conditions do not impose such an obligation on the insured, seems to me to be almost arguing the impossible. At any rate, I am quite satisfied that the writ was 'a communication relating to an accident,' and it is implicit in every word of Condition 5 that if proceedings are started, the insurance company must be told about them and be put into a position to exercise their rights. If it were not so, scope would be given for the exaggerated claims going through without any inquiry or testing, and

---

[38] See Chapter 5, above.

[39] *cf. Alfred McAlpine plc v. B.A.I.(Run Off) Ltd* [2000] 1 Lloyd's Rep. 437, CA; see Chapter 2, above.

[40] (1939) 63 Ll. L. Rep. 278.

[41] *ibid.* at 281.

insurance companies would be swindled in all directions. That condition, the performance of which was an essential condition, and as it seems to me a condition precedent to the insurance company's liability, was never performed."

Similarly, in *Farrell v. Federated Employers Insurance Association Ltd*[42]   **21–23**
the Court of Appeal rejected the third party's claim under the 1930 Act because the insured had breached a notice of claims provision that:

> "Every claim, notice, letter, writ . . . or other document served on the [insured] shall be notified or forwarded to the [insurers] immediately on receipt."

The third party claimant's writ had been served on the insured on January 7, but was not notified to the insurers until March 3, which was clearly not "immediately", and the insured's defence succeeded.

Further, in *Berliner Motor Corp. and Steiers Lawn and Sports Inc. v. Sun*   **21–24**
Alliance and London Insurance Ltd[43] a combined products and public liability policy contained a condition that:

> "Upon the happening of any event which may give rise to a claim . . . the Insured shall forthwith give written notice to the [Insurers] with full particulars . . ."

The insured had notice of the third party claimant's claim on December 11, but did not advise the insurers until the following October 25, which "very plainly was a gross breach of this condition and as a result the insurers lost any opportunity to consider what line [the insured] should adopt in the proceedings and to act as *dominus litis*".[44] Accordingly, the claim under the 1930 Act was barred by reason of this breach by the insured.

Again, in *Pioneer Concrete (U.K.) Ltd v. National Employers Mutual*   **21–25**
General Insurance Association Ltd[45] the insured contractor's policy had required "immediate" notice of "any accident or claim or proceedings", which was stated to be a condition precedent to the insurer's liability to make any payment under the policy. The relevant incident had occurred on September 4, 1978, and writ was served on the company and the liquidator on April 11, 1979, Bingham J. (as he then was) held that the insurers had satisfied the burden of proof upon them to show that they had not received any notice of the service of the writ, and, accordingly, were entitled to rely on the breach by the insured to escape the claim under the 1930 Act.

In the majority of instances, the insurers will be able to rely on a breach   **21–26**
of a notification condition, even if they have somehow learnt of the third party claimant's claim against the insured, provided the insured himself has failed to comply with the precise terms of the condition. This is because such conditions usually require that the insured personally must

---

[42] [1970] 3 All E.R. 632, CA.
[43] [1983] 1 Lloyd's Rep. 320.
[44] *ibid.* at 325, *per* Bingham J. (as he then was).
[45] [1985] 1 Lloyd's Rep. 274.

give a notification of the claim, as in *The Vainqueur José*[46] where there was the following notification condition:

> "Every claim shall be notified as soon as possible but in no case later than twelve months after the [insured] has received notice that the claim is or may be made against him . . . if such notice . . . is not given or if a claim or liability is contested . . . without or contrary to any such direction . . . [the insurer] shall have power to reject the claim or to reduce the sum payable . . ."

21-27   Mocatta J. rejected the plaintiffs argument that relevant notice can be given by third parties and in particular by anyone who has an interest to do so (*e.g.* a third party claimant), for the wording clearly required the insured himself to give the notification, although notification by a duly authorised agent would be sufficient (*e.g.* his insurance broker or solicitor). Although there was an authority to the effect that an insurer could only rely on a notification condition if he shows prejudice by reason of the insured's breach,[47] the need to get a judgment entered in default of appearance set aside and the attendant expense and trouble of doing so, is to be regarded as sufficient prejudice, if any prejudice were required.[48] Thus, Mocatta J. considered[49]:

> ". . . if prejudice is necessary to sustain a defence by an insurer against a claim against him by his assured or by someone standing in the shoes of his assured under the 1930 Act like the plaintiffs here when the assured has not given timeous notice of his claim as provided for in his policy or cover, relatively little prejudice has to be shown by the insurer in order for him to escape liability under the time clause."

Non-disclosure or misrepresentation of material facts
21-28   A claim under the 1930 Act will be defeated by the insurer's raising the defence of non-disclosure of material facts by the insured which entitles them to rescind the policy.[50] Where insurers learn of facts which, if true, disclose that the insured has made a material non-disclosure, or misrepresentation, the insurers are entitled to make inquiries to satisfy themselves on the truth or otherwise of that information before deciding whether or not to avoid the policy for non-disclosure, and no estoppel arises against them until they have had that opportunity.[51]

Arbitration condition
21-29   An arbitration condition in the policy issued to the insured by the insurer must be complied with by a third party acquiring the insured's

---

[46] [1979] 1 Lloyd's Rep. 557 at 565, *per* Mocatta J.; although not referred to, *Hassett v. Legal and General Assurance Society Ltd* (1939) 63 Ll. L. Rep. 278, would also seem to support this reasoning.

[47] *Barratt Bros (Taxis) Ltd v. Davies* [1966] 1 W.L.R. 1334, CA.

[48] *Farrell v. Federated Employers Insurance Association Ltd* [1970] 1 W.L.R. 1400 at 1406, *per* Megaw L.J. and at 1403, *per* Lord Denning M.R., CA.

[49] *The Vainqueur José*, [1979] 1 Lloyd's Rep. 557 at 566.

[50] *Cleland v. London General Insurance Co. Ltd* (1935) 51 Ll. L. Rep. 156, CA.

[51] *McCormick v. National Motor and Accident Insurance Union Ltd* (1934) 49 Ll. L. Rep. 361, CA.

rights under the policy by virtue of the 1930 Act. This was the decision of the Court of Appeal in *Freshwater v. Western Australian Assurance Co. Ltd*[52] where a liability policy contained the following wide arbitration clause:

> "If any difference or dispute of any kind whatsoever shall arise between the insured . . . and the company in respect of this policy or in respect of any claim or of any matter or thing or any liability arising or alleged to have arisen hereunder or otherwise connected herewith directly or indirectly the same shall be referred to the final determination and award of, a single arbitrator to be agreed upon by both parties . . .
>
> It shall not be competent to prosecute any action against the company in a court of law for sums due or alleged to be due under this policy except for the amount of the award and the obtaining of the said award shall be a condition precedent to the liability of the company to make any payment under this policy."

The Court of Appeal held that, on the facts of the case, the insurers had not repudiated the policy as a whole, but relied on this third, contractual provision to refuse liability on the claim in question because of untrue answers given in the proposal form.[53] There would thus be an order staying court proceedings until the arbitration proceedings had been taken.

This decision has been followed,[54] and it has also been held that the **21–30** poverty of a third party acquiring rights under the 1930 Act is not a sufficient ground for insisting that arbitration proceedings must be taken.[55] Modern policies will only provide for arbitration of the amount due under the policy, and not questions of liability under the policy, so the effect of these decisions is now more limited. The Arbitration Act 1996, however, has taken away the court's discretion over whether to grant a stay or not which prevailed in the earlier Arbitration Acts.

Excluded risk

The insurer is entitled to raise in defence to a third party's claim under **21–31** the 1930 Act that the insured's liability to the third party arises by reason of a risk excluded from the insurance's indemnity provisions. Thus, in *Kearney v. General Accident, Fire and Life Assurance Corpn Ltd*[56] the insurers successfully defended the third party's claim under the 1930 Act against them under two employers' liability policies, because the plaintiff had been injured whilst working in a roof space at a height exceeding the 25 foot permitted by one policy, and because the building was a hangar, work in such premises being excluded from the second policy.

---

[52] [1933] 1 K.B. 515, CA.

[53] Following *Woodall v. Pearl Assurance Co.* [1919] 1 K.B. 593, CA; and *Golding v. London and Edinburgh Insurance Co. Ltd* (1932) 43 Ll. L. Rep. 487, CA; which distinguished the situation of a complete repudiation of the policy and all its terms as in *Jureidini v. National British and Irish Millers Insurance Co. Ltd* [1915] A.C. 499, HL.

[54] *Dennehy v. Bellamy* [1938] 2 All E.R. 262, CA.

[55] *Smith v. Pearl Assurance Co. Ltd* [1939] 1 All E.R. 95, CA.

[56] [1968] 2 Lloyd's Rep. 240.

Special case of employers' liability insurance

21–32   As discussed in Chapter 5, above, special statutory provisions apply in the case of compulsory employers' liability insurance which operate to restrict the insurer's ability to escape or reduce their liability to provide an indemnity. Thus, when a third party acquires the rights of an insured under an employers' liability policy, it should be remembered that the insurer will not be able to raise as a defence[57] to such action any breach of any condition seeking to provide, in whatever terms, that no liability (either generally or in respect of a particular claim) shall arise under the policy, or that any such liability so arising shall cease:

  (a) in the event of some specified thing being done or omitted to be done after the happening of the event giving rise to a claim under the policy (*e.g.* notification condition, or assistance to insurer condition);
  (b) unless the policy-holder takes reasonable care to protect his employees against the risk of bodily injury or disease in the course of their employment;
  (c) unless the policy-holder complies with the requirements of any enactment for the protection of employees against the risk of bodily injury or disease in the course of their employment; and
  (d) unless the policy-holder keeps specified records (*e.g.* of wages) or provides the insurer with or makes available to him information therefrom.

5. PROHIBITION OF VARIATION OF RIGHTS UPON BANKRUPTCY

21–33   Section 1(3) of the 1930 Act renders of no effect any policy provision which, directly or indirectly, purports to "avoid the contract or alter the rights of the parties thereunder" upon the bankruptcy, insolvency, etc. of the insured. The manifest purpose of this provision is to make certain that, upon the occurrence of any of the events in section 1(1) of the Act, the third party shall be able to take the full benefit of the rights of the insured against the insurer (such as they may be at that time), unaltered and undiminished.

21–34   The use of the phrase "directly or indirectly" in section 1(3) shows that a provision in a relevant contract can fall foul of section 1(3), even though it does not expressly and in terms purport to avoid the contract or alter the rights of the parties on the happening to the insured of any of the relevant events. The effect of the inclusion of the word "indirectly" is that any provision in such a contract which has the substantial effect of avoiding a contract, or altering the rights of the parties, on the happening to the insured of any such events is invalidated, even though the contract does not in terms so provide. The test to be applied, therefore, is[58]:

---

[57] Employers' Liability (Compulsory Insurance) General Regulations 1998 (S.I. 1998 No. 2573), reg. 2; made under the Employers' Liability (Compulsory Insurance) Act 1969.
[58] *Re Allobrogia S.S. Corp.* [1978] 3 All E.R. 423 at 432, *per* Slade J.

"Does the proviso in question have the substantial effect of avoiding the contract between the insured and the insurer, or of altering the rights of the parties on the happening to the insured of any of the events mentioned in section 1(1) of the 1930 Act?"

Thus, a proviso that the insured must have first paid any liability costs and expenses to the third party as a condition precedent to the right of recovery under the insurance, will be invalid as against a third party claiming under the 1930 Act.[59] So, also, will the more obvious cancellation condition of the following type, often found in employers' liability, public liability and product liability insurances, clearly be invalid under the 1930 Act: **21–35**

"The Insurer shall be entitled to cancel this Policy in the following circumstances unless such change has been notified and agreed by the Insurer in writing the business is wound up, carried on by a liquidator or receiver."

6. DUTY TO GIVE INFORMATION TO THIRD PARTIES

The duty

Obviously, the third party needs assistance to find out which insurer has issued a liability policy covering the relevant risk of the insured which caused the third party loss or injury. Section 2 of the 1930 Act therefore provides a statutory duty upon all persons in possession of the insured's property on the bankruptcy (or winding-up, etc. if the insured is a company),[60] and insurers,[61] to give the third party such information as may reasonably be required by him for the purpose of ascertaining whether any rights have been transferred to and vested in him by the 1930 Act, and for the purpose of enforcing such rights. The duty to give information includes a duty to allow all contracts of insurance, receipts for premiums, and other relevant documents in the possession or the power of the person on whom the duty is so imposed to be inspected and copies thereof to be taken.[62]   **21–36**

Who is under the duty

The following are therefore under this statutory duty: **21–37**

(a) a bankrupt;
(b) a debtor making a composition or arrangement with his creditors;
(c) a personal representative of a deceased debtor;
(d) a company when a winding-up order has been made;
(e) a company when a resolution for a voluntary winding-up has been passed;

[59] *ibid.* at 433.
[60] Third Parties (Rights Against Insurers) Act 1930, s. 2(1).
[61] *ibid.*, s. 2(2).
[62] *ibid.*, s. 2(3).

   (f) a receiver or manager of the company's business or undertaking who has been duly appointed;

   (g) persons in possession of property being taken by or on behalf of the holders of any debentures secured by a floating charge of such property; and

   (h) insurers.

When the duty arises

21-38   The practical use of this duty to provide information is rather limited, because the duty does not arise until after the third party has established the liability of the bankrupt or insolvent insured by judgment or settlement. This is rather later than the time when that information would really be useful, namely, when the third party claimant is deliberating upon whether to embark on possibly expensive litigation against a defendant who is either already bankrupt or insolvent, or who the claimant strongly suspects may soon be so. This requirement to establish liability first was confirmed in *Nigel Upchurch Associates v. The Aldridge Estates Investment Co. Ltd*[63] where the claimant was an architect who sued the defendant for fees, damages and a *quantum meruit*. His claim was included as a trade debt in an individual voluntary arrangement for the benefit of his creditors. The defendants denied liability and also counterclaimed damages which greatly exceeded the claimant architect's claim. Obviously, the defendants were anxious to ascertain whether the claimant had appropriate professional indemnity insurance cover, and, if so, what the limits of cover were. The defendants therefore sought an order under section 2 of the 1930 Act for information of the claimant's insurance from both the claimant himself and from the supervisor of his voluntary arrangement. The applications failed because it is the transfer of rights which triggers the duty to provide information.

21-39   There is no requirement on the insured defendant to make disclosure of documents relating to his insurance cover during the substantive action in which the third party claimant is seeking to establish the liability of the defendant to pay him damages. An application for specific disclosure of such documents was refused by the Court of Appeal in *Cox v. Bankside Members Agency Ltd*[64] on the basis that the information did not relate to matters in question in the proceedings, because the law does not regard doubt as to the opposing side's ability to pay as being a good reason for the discovery of assets.[65]

7. SUBSEQUENT SETTLEMENT BETWEEN INSURERS AND INSURED PERSONS

21-40   Section 3 of the 1930 Act also protects the transfer and vesting of the successful third party's rights upon establishing the liability of the insured

---

[63] [1993] 1 Lloyd's Rep. 535.
[64] [1995] 2 Lloyd's Rep. 437, CA.
[65] Following *Bekhor v. Bilton* [1981] Q.B. 923, CA.

defendant to him, by rendering ineffective against him any waiver, assignment, or other disposition made by, or payment made to, the insured after the third party has become vested with the insured's rights pursuant to the Act. Before such time as the rights are transferred to the third party claimant, certainly in cases where the defendant is under no statutory or professional duty to take out the relevant insurance, nor under any contractual duty to the claimant to insure, the court will not grant an injunction restraining the insured from compromising his insurance claim with his insurers.[66] Such an action is misconceived because it seeks to prevent the insured defendant dealing with his own assets in any way he chooses, even if the settlement sum will be inadequate to allow the claimant to recover the entire judgment sum, assuming he was to be fully successful.

8. DISTRIBUTION OF INSURANCE MONIES TO MULTIPLE CLAIMANTS

The Lloyd's litigation threw up a huge number of actions and previously **21–41** unconsidered legal issues. One of these was whether third party claimants pursuing the insolvent insured Names at Lloyd's would share the insurance indemnity in some manner, or whether the distribution would be made according to who had established their cases first in time. This was, indeed, a very unusual situation to find an insured defendant facing a very large number of claims from a great many different defendants. Suffice it to say that the Court of Appeal in *Cox v. Bankside Members Agency Ltd*[67] determined that the "first past the post" system would prevail, and that successful third party claimants would take their applicable "slices" out of the available pool of insurance monies, until it was exhausted, in strict accordance with the date of transfer of rights to them under the 1930 Act.

9. FOREIGN COMPANIES

An English court has jurisdiction to grant a winding-up order of a foreign **21–42** corporation if the company has some asset or assets within the jurisdiction and there are one or more persons concerned in the proper distribution of the assets over whom the jurisdiction is exercisable. This was the finding of Megarry V.-C. in *Re Compania Merabello San Nicholas SA*[68] where a third party petitioned the court for a winding-up order in the capacity as a creditor of the foreign company, having obtained a judgment against the company for a sum in excess of £12,000 for damage to their goods. Megarry V.-C. held that it was not necessary for the court to establish either that the company had a place of business within the jurisdiction, or

---

[66] *Normid Housing Association Ltd v. Ralphs* [1989] 1 Lloyd's Rep. 265 at 272–273, CA; referred to but neither approved nor disapproved in *Cox v. Bankside Members Agency Ltd* [1995] 2 Lloyd's Rep. 437 at 464–465, *per* Sir Thomas Bingham, M.R., CA.
[67] [1995] 2 Lloyd's Rep. 437, CA.
[68] [1973] Ch. 75.

that it had ever carried on business here, unless the winding-up petition was based on the circumstance that the company had ceased to carry on business or was carrying on business only to wind up its affairs.

21–43   The asset or assets do not have to be of a commercial nature, nor assets which indicate that the company has formerly carried on business within the jurisdiction. They can be of any nature, and are not required to be assets which would be distributable to creditors by the liquidator in the winding-up; it is sufficient if by the making of the winding-up order they would be of benefit to a creditor or creditors in some other way. In the instant case, the asset of the foreign company within the jurisdiction was a claim on its liability insurance, and the winding-up order was granted because the company was unable to pay its debt to the petitioning creditor (the third party who now stood to obtain the insured company's rights against the insurer by reason of the 1930 Act), and it was just and equitable to make the order because there was no real reason not so to do.

Where the asset of the foreign company consists only of a right of action, the court need not be satisfied that such right of action was certain to succeed — it is sufficient if the court can be satisfied that the action has a reasonable possibility of success. Where, then, the right of action is against an insurer, the court hearing the petition for the winding-up order will hear submissions upon the insurer's rights, if any, to avoid the claim under the insurance.[69]

10. REFORM OF THE 1930 ACT

21–44   In its Consultation Paper No.152, published in January, 1998, the Law Commission set out its provisional views. At the time of writing, the Law Commission's more definite proposals in response to that consultation process are still awaited. It is not appropriate to speculate in this book about those possible reforms, but reference can be made to the author's critique of the proposed reforms elsewhere.[70]

---

[69] *Re Allobrogia S.S. Corp.* [1978] 3 All E.R. 423.
[70] D. Jess, "Reform of direct rights of action by third parties against non-motor liability insurers" in [2000] L.M.C.L.Q. 192.

CHAPTER 22

LITIGATION AND PRACTICE

1. INTRODUCTION

The aim of this Chapter is to deal with some practical aspects of litigation **22–01**
between the insured and the insurer that have not been dealt with elsewhere in this book. The topics covered are:

   (i) limitation of actions;
  (ii) the nature of the insured's cause of action and remedies against
      the insurer;
 (iii) compliance with policy terms after rescission *ab initio* by insurer;
 (iv) compliance with policy terms after insurer's repudiation of a
      claim;
  (v) consequences of insurer putting the insured to proof;
 (vi) liability insurers and their costs liability to third party claimants;
 (vii) unauthorised insurance;
(viii) disclosure of documents in litigation;
 (ix) the Courts;
  (x) joinder of liability insurers into proceedings;
 (xi) jurisdictional issues.

2. LIMITATION OF ACTIONS

Material damage insurance

It is only recently that the question of when the insured's cause of action **22–02**
arises, and thus the six-year period of limitation under section 5 of the
Limitation Act 1980 commences, has been properly considered by the
courts. The decision of Pearson J. in *F. & K. Jabbour v. Custodian of Israeli
Absentee Property*[1] had left the point open as to whether the accrual of the
insured's cause of action was delayed by policy conditions requiring the
notification of a claim and such further details as the insurer might
require. In the subsequent marine insurance case of *Castle Insurance Co.
Ltd v. Hong Kong Shipping Co. Ltd,*[2] Lord Diplock said that the cause of
action accrues "at the time that the events occur which give rise to the
liability to pay" the insured, and not at the later time that the quantum of
the loss is ascertained.[3] That principle was accepted at first instance by
Hirst J. (as he then was) in another marine insurance case, *Bank of America*

---

[1] [1954] 1 W.L.R. 139.
[2] [1984] 1 A.C. 226 at 237, PC.
[3] See also *Chandris v. Argo Insurance Co. Ltd* [1963] 2 Lloyd's Rep. 65 at 74, *per* Megaw J.
(as he then was).

National Trust and Savings Association v. Chrismas.[4] Hirst J. again held that the insured's cause of action against the insurer arose when the loss, against which he is insured, occurs, and not at some later time when the insured demands payment, unless there are clear words in the policy which have the contrary effect.[5] Hirst J. declined to follow the only authority to the contrary, that of *Transthene Packaging Co. Ltd v. Royal Insurance (U.K.) Ltd.*[6]

22–03   The matter was thoroughly reviewed by Sir Peter Webster in *Callaghan v. Dominion Insurance Co. Ltd,*[7] a non-marine fire insurance case. The dominant view was followed by the judge, that time runs from the date of the loss, and not from the date on which the insurer rescinded the policy for non-disclosure. The fire had occurred at the insured premises on September 20, 1989. The policy was rescinded on May 16, 1990, and the proceedings were not commenced against the defendant insurers until May 16, 1996. It was held that the action should be struck out as it was time-barred, the proceedings not having been commenced within six years of the date of the loss occurring.

22–04   The argument that the insurer had a right to elect to indemnify the insured by various methods under the fire policy in question, and thereby the accrual of the cause of action was delayed by the terms of the policy, was rejected as merely going to the quantification of the primary liability of the insurer, not to that liability itself.[8] Those methods were payment of the loss in value of the property, payment of the amount of such damage, or reinstatement or replacement directly by the insurer. An argument that there was a postponement of the accrual of the insurer's primary liability, because the insured had to comply with certain specified conditions precedent "to the right of the insured to recover" under the policy, was also rejected. This was on the basis that those provisions related to the insured's secondary right to claim and recover in some particular amount, rather than to the insured's primary right to indemnify the insured in principle.[9] Langley J. followed *Callaghan* in *Universities Superannuation Scheme Ltd v. Royal Insurance (U.K.) Ltd*[10] and the point now seems firmly settled.

Liability insurance

22–05   The question of the date of the accrual of the insured's cause of action under a liability insurance policy was first considered *obiter* in the solicitors' professional indemnity insurance case of *West Wake Price & Co. v. Ching,*[11] where Devlin J. (as he then was) had stated that the insured "cannot recover anything undere the main indemnity clause or make any claim against the underwriters until they [the insured] have been found liable and

[4] [1993] 1 Lloyd's Rep. 137 at 151.
[5] *ibid.* at 544, col.2.
[6] [1996] L.R.L.R. 32.
[7] [1997] 2 Lloyd's Rep. 541.
[8] *ibid.* at 545, col.1.
[9] *ibid.* at 545, col.2.
[10] [2000] Lloyd's Rep. 524.
[11] [1957] 1 W.L.R. 45 at 49.

so sustained a loss". The Court of Appeal came to the same view in *Post Office v. Norwich Union Fire Insurance Society Ltd*,[12] which related to whether there had been a transfer of an insured's rights under the Third Parties (Rights Against Insurers) Act 1930[13] in respect of a public liability policy. Lord Denning M.R. said[14]:

> "The policy says that 'the company will indemnify the insured against all sums which the insured shall become legally liable to pay as compensation in respect of loss of or damage to property.' It seems to me that the insured only acquires a right to sue for the money when his liability to the injured person has been established so as to give rise to a right of indemnity. His liability to the injured person must be ascertained and determined to exist, either by judgment of the court or by an award in arbitration or by agreement. Until that is done, the right to indemnity does not arise . . .
>
> The insured could only have sued for an indemnity when his liability to the third person was established and the amount of the loss ascertained. In some circumstances the insured might sue earlier for a declaration, for example, if the insur[ance] company were repudiating the policy for some reason. But when the policy is admittedly good, the insured cannot sue for an indemnity until his own liability to the third person is ascertained."

The *obiter dicta* of Devlin J. in *West Wake Price & Co. v. Ching*,[15] and **22–06** the passage of Lord Denning M.R. in the *Post Office* case,[16] were both approved by a four to one majority of the House of Lords in *Bradley v. Eagle Star Insurance Co. Ltd*.[17] In his speech giving the majority decision, Lord Brandon said that the principle that the insured cannot sue for an indemnity from his insurers unless and until both the existence *and* the amount of his liability to a third party has been established by action, arbitration or agreement, is "unassailably correct".[18] The position is, therefore, that whereas time runs from the date of loss under a material damage insurance, irrespective of when that loss is quantified, for liability insurances time does not run until both liability and the extent of that liability have been established. Given the real possibility that liability alone may be dealt with at split trial, this has the effect — to the advantage of the insured — to delay the period of commencement of limitation for, quite possibly, many months or even considerably longer.

Inconsistent approach

With respect, it is not logical to have this difference in approach and **22–07** principle between material damage and liability insurances. Not only does it not actually sit squarely with Lord Denning M.R.'s view that declaratory relief, presumably in respect of the insurer's obligation to indemnify, could be sought before quantification of the ascertained liability, it is also directly contrary to Sir Peter Webster's identification in *Callaghan v.*

---

[12] [1967] 2 Q.B. 363, CA.
[13] See Chapter 21, above.
[14] [1967] 2 Q.B. 363, at 373–374, CA.
[15] [1957] 1 W.L.R. 45.
[16] [1967] 2 Q.B. 363, CA.
[17] [1989] 1 A.C. 957, HL.
[18] *ibid.* at 966.

Dominion Insurance Co. Ltd,[19] that there is a primary liability to indemnify once the insured loss arises, and a secondary liability to pay the amount of that indemnity in a particular sum. A further objection is that it is arguably contrary to the House of Lords' previous decision in the marine liability insurance case of *Firma C-Trade SA v. Newcastle Protection and Indemnity Association*.[20] There, Lord Goff said[21]:

> "I accept that, at common law, a contract of indemnity gives rise to an action for unliquidated damages, arising from the failure of the indemnifier to prevent the indemnified person from suffering damage, for example, by having to pay a third party. I also accept that, at common law, the cause of action [against an indemnifier] does not (unless the contract provides otherwise) arise until the indemnified person can show actual loss: see *Collinge v. Heywood*.[22] This is, as I understand it, because the promise of indemnity is simply a promise to hold the indemnified person harmless against a specified loss or expense. On this basis no debt can arise before the loss is suffered or the expenses incurred; however, once the loss is suffered or the expense incurred, the indemnifier is in breach of contract for having failed to hold the indemnified person harmless against the relevant loss or expense."

22–08   In *Callaghan*, Sir Peter Webster cited Lord Goff's speech and considered the reference to "by having to pay a third party" as appropriate in a case of liability insurance, because that is the moment that the loss occurs.[23] As it can be accurately said that as soon as liability is established against an insured defendant he is going to have to pay the third party, it matters not that the precise sum that he has to pay has not been established. Being an action for unliquidated damages, the principle, as utilised for material damage insurance, that the loss occurs without the amount of the loss being known, must, it is submitted apply in the same way to liability insurances. Both forms of insurance are indemnity insurances and there should accordingly be consistency in approach that the primary obligation to indemnify occurs upon the occurrence of the insured event — either material damage or the incurring of a legal liability to a third party. Thereafter, the secondary obligation arises which is usually to pay a monetary sum once it is ascertained by the court, by arbitration or by agreement. These issues were certainly never canvassed before the House of Lords in *Bradley v. Eagle Star Insurance Co. Ltd*,[24] and it is therefore hoped that the dichotomy in approach will be resolved in some later case.

3. THE INSURED'S CAUSE OF ACTION AGAINST THE INSURER

22–09   The insured's cause of action against his insurer is a claim for unliquidated damages for the breach of the contractual promise to indemnify him

---

[19] [1997] 2 Lloyd's Rep. 541.
[20] [1991] 2 A.C. 1, HL.
[21] *ibid.* at 35.
[22] [1839] Ad. & E. 634.
[23] [1997] 2 Lloyd's Rep. 541 at 543, col.2.
[24] [1989] 1 A.C. 957, HL.

against loss or damage arising from an insured event, subject to the limitations and conditions set out in the policy of insurance. This has been established, initially as regards marine insurance,[25] and also in respect of non-marine insurance. In *F. & K. Jabbour v. Custodian of Israeli Absentee Property*,[26] Pearson J. said:

> "The explanation of the use of the expression 'unliquidated damages' to describe a claim for indemnity under an insurance policy may be wholly or partly afforded by the old form of pleading in assumpsit, alleging a breach by non-payment . . . But as the only wrong admitted by the insurer is his failure to pay a sum due under contract, the amount of which has to be ascertained, he seems to be in much the same position as the person who owes and has failed to pay a reasonable price for goods sold and delivered or a reasonable remuneration for work done or services rendered. The claim is for unliquidated damages, but the word 'damages' is used in a somewhat unusual sense."

Donaldson J. (as he then was) applied *Jabbour* to a professional indemnity liability policy in *Forney v. Dominion Insurance Co. Ltd*,[27] and said: **22–10**

> "All actions against insurers under indemnity policies sound in unliquidated damages rather than debt."

More recently, this statement of the nature of the insured's cause of action has been reaffirmed by the House of Lords in the marine insurance case of *Firma C-Trade SA v. Newcastle Protection and Indemnity Association*,[28] and by the Court of Appeal in the non-marine material damage insurance case of *Sprung v. Royal Insurance (U.K.) Ltd*[29]

The insured's remedies
The insured is accordingly entitled to an indemnity within the terms of   **22–11**
the policy, and interest if he has had to commence proceedings.[30] But the insured is not entitled to further damages in respect of consequential losses that he may have sustained by reason of the insurer's refusal or failure to accept liability or meet his claim timeously or at all.[31] Hirst J. (as he then was) rejected the claim by the insured for special or general damages in respect of loss of income which would have been earned by a replacement vessel if the insurers had promptly met the insured's claim for indemnity in the marine insurance case of *The Italia Express (No.2)*.[32] This was on the ground that, *inter alia*, such a claim amounted to a claim for damages for the late payment of damages, and Lord Brandon had stated that "there

---

[25] *Pellas v. Neptune Marine Insurance Co.* (1879) 5 C.P.D. 34; *William Pickersgill & Sons Ltd v. London & Provincial Marine and General Insurance Co. Ltd* [1912] 3 K.B. 614.
[26] [1954] 1 W.L.R. 139 at 143.
[27] [1969] 1 W.L.R. 928 at 936.
[28] [1991] 2 A.C. 1, HL.
[29] [1999] 1 Lloyd's Rep. I.R. 111 at 115, *per* Evans L.J.
[30] See this topic in Chapter 19, above.
[31] *Grant v. Co-Operative Insurance Society Ltd* (1984) 134 N.L.J. 81 must now be regarded as having been wrongly decided.
[32] [1992] 2 Lloyd's Rep. 281.

is no such thing as a cause of action in damages for late payment of damages".[33] Hirst J.'s decision and treatment of Lord Brandon's dictum as being a statement of general principle was approved and followed by the Court of Appeal in *Sprung v. Royal Insurance (U.K.) Ltd*,[34] albeit with the *caveat* that the Court had not heard full or detailed argument on the point, Mr Sprung being a litigant in person.

22–12   The facts in *Sprung* were that the insured claimant held a policy with the defendant insurers covering material damage to the insured's business machinery. That machinery was vandalised on April 6, 1986, but the insurers rejected the claim for unclear reasons. Proceedings were issued in 1988, but it was not until March 1990 that the claimant obtained an interim payment for the value of the damaged machinery plus interest. The insured had simply not been able to afford to replace the damaged machinery and, therefore, had claimed consequential losses arising from his inability to operate part of his business due to the lack of the replacement machinery. It was this head of claim that was rejected by the Court of Appeal.

Although both of these decisions related to claims for consequential financial loss arising from non-payment, within a reasonable time, of indemnities under material damage insurances, there seems no reason for the same principle to apply to exclude claims for financial loss arising from the late payment by insurers under a liability insurance. In practical terms, however, such a claim is far less likely to ever arise because a defendant insured will usually have brought a CPR, Pt 20 claim against his liability insurer for an indemnity, so that the issues of the insured's liability to the claimant third party will be determined at the same time as the issue of the insurer's liability to make indemnity under the insurance.

22–13   *Sprung* was applied by Jonathan Parker J. in *Pride Valley Foods Ltd v. Independent Insurance Co. Ltd*,[35] where he struck out a claim for consequential damages alleged to have been suffered by reason of late payment of an indemnity under a business interruption policy. Whilst the Court of Appeal subsequently gave leave to appeal the strike out to enable further argument upon the correctness of the decision in *Sprung*, no such appeal was pursued. *Sprung* has also been followed in *England and England v. Guardian Insurance Ltd*.[36] For the present time, therefore, no such claims for consequential damages for late payment of the indemnity can be considered viable.[37]

Costs

22–14   Whilst the insured will normally obtain an order for costs on the "standard basis" if he is successful in an action against his insurer, it is within the court's discretion under CPR, Pt 44 to order the insurer to pay costs on the "indemnity basis". Under the standard basis of assessment, the court will only allow costs which are proportionate to the matters in

---

[33] *President of India v. Lips Maritime Corp.* [1988] A.C. 395, at 414, HL.
[34] [1999] Lloyd's Rep. I.R. 111, at 115–116, *per* Evans L.J., CA.
[35] Unreported, October 28, 1996.
[36] [2000] Lloyd's Rep. I.R. 404.

issue, and resolve any doubt which it may have as to whether costs were reasonably incurred, or reasonable and proportionate in amount, in favour of the paying party.[38] Where, on the other hand, there is an assessment on the "indemnity basis", the court will resolve any doubt which it may have as to whether costs were reasonably incurred, or were reasonable in amount, in favour of the receiving party.[39] The exercise of this discretion to make an order for indemnity costs must be carried out on judicial principles. In *The Griparian*,[40] which was not an insurance case, Rix J. (as he then was) ordered indemnity costs against a defendant who had persisted in an unsustainable allegation of fraud against the claimant. It will not be appropriate to order the losing party to pay indemnity costs where both parties to the litigation have lied to the court.[41] Those judicial principles were reviewed by Newman J. in the permanent health insurance case of *Wailes v. Stapleton Construction and Commercial Services Ltd and UNUM Ltd*.[42] He summarised the position to be as follows:

"the position appears to be that, where there are circumstances of a party behaving in litigation in a way which can be properly categorized as disgraceful, or deserving of moral condemnation, in such cases an order for indemnity costs may be appropriate.

There may be cases otherwise, falling short of such behaviour in which the Court considers it appropriate to order indemnity costs. The threshold of qualification which a party would appear to have to establish is that there has been, on the party to be impugned by such an order, some conduct which can properly be categorized as unreasonable, and I would add to that in a way which the Court is satisfied constitutes unreasonableness of such a high degree that it can be categorized as exceptional. There are varying ways in which [in] the course of litigation, parties to it could be categorized as having behaved unreasonably, but one would not, simply as a result of that, decide that they should pay costs on an indemnity basis."

4. COMPLIANCE WITH POLICY TERMS AFTER RESCISSION *AB INITIO* OR INSURER ALLEGING FRAUD

There is no final settled determination of whether an insurer who **22-15** rescinds the insurance policy *ab initio* may also seek to rely on breaches of policy conditions as an alternative to the main defence to the claim for indemnity or rescission of the insurance contract. In *Jureidini v. National British and Irish Millers Insurance Co. Ltd*,[43] the House of Lords asserted the principle that an insurer's repudiation of a claim *in toto* on a ground going to the root of the insurance contract precluded that insurer from

[37] This is not the position in Australia where consequential losses are recoverable where the insurer has wrongly brought the insurance contract to an end: *Edwards v. Insurance Office of Australia Ltd* (1933) 34 S.R. (N.S.W.) 88; *McCormack v. Hardboards Australia Ltd* (1984) 3 A.N.Z.I.C. 60.563.
[38] CPR, Pt 44, r.4(2).
[39] CPR, Pt 44, r.4(3).
[40] [1994] 1 Lloyd's Rep. 533.
[41] [1986] 3 All E.R. 163.
[42] [1997] 2 Lloyd's Rep. 112 at 117, col.1.
[43] [1915] A.C. 499, HL.

relying on a condition precedent to liability within the policy. The facts were that a fire policy contained an express condition precedent to "any right of action or suit upon this policy" that any difference in respect of the amount of the loss or damage be referred to arbitration and an award by such arbitrator be first obtained. The insured sustained a fire, and the insurers thereafter defended an action by the insured by alleging that the claim was fraudulent in that the insured had either set fire to the premises, or had connived at their being set on fire. In addition, the insurers raised the defence that any right of action only accrued once the insured had obtained an award from an arbitrator regarding the amount of the loss or damage.

22–16   Darling J. and a jury found that the insured had not set fire to the premises, nor had connived to set fire to them. The insurers appealed on the ground, *inter alia*, that the action could not be maintained because there had been no arbitration to assess the amount of the damage. The House of Lords unanimously rejected the appeal. Viscount Haldane V.-C. said that as Condition 12 provided that all benefit was to be forfeited in the event of a claim being in any way fraudulent, this amounted to a defence of the claim "which, if made out, went to the very root of the matter"[44] and, "when there is a repudiation which goes to the substance of the whole contract I do not see how the person setting up the repudiation can be entitled to insist on a subordinate term of the contract still being enforced".[45] In this case there had been a repudiation of the claim to an indemnity based on an express contractual term, and therefore the contract did not come to an end, but the insured became relieved of his obligation to further perform the contract and entitled to his right of action for damages "under" the contract. This distinction from a situation where the insurer rescinds the insurance at common law, and so treats the contract as though it never existed, was recognised by the Privy Council in *Heyman v. Darwins*.[46] It is submitted that the correct analysis should be that where the claim is rejected by the insurer on the basis that the contract never subsisted, *i.e.* there is a plea of rescission at common law for non-disclosure or misrepresentation, it cannot be right that the insurer can also maintain defences that if he is wrong about that then he can rely on defences relating to breaches of the terms of the insurance contract which he denies exists. However, there is at present only *obiter* support for this view in the Australian case of *Distillers Co. Bio-Chemicals (Australia) Pty Ltd v. Ajax Insurance Co. Ltd*.[47]

22–17   This issue recently came before Mance J. (as he then was) in *Total Graphics Ltd v. A.G.F. Insurance Ltd*,[48] but it does not appear that *Jureidini* was cited to the court. The case concerned an insurance broker's professional indemnity policy. The broker was alleged to have been negligent in the placing of insurance with a Lloyd's syndicate rather than with the Sun

---

[44] *ibid.* at 504.
[45] *ibid.* at 505.
[46] [1942] A.C. 356 at 373, *per* Viscount Simon L.C.; at 384, *per* Lord Wright; and at 398, *per* Lord Porter.
[47] (1973) 130 C.L.R. 1 at 10, *per* Menzies J. and at 13, *per* Gibbs J.
[48] [1997] 1 Lloyd's Rep. 599.

Alliance as instructed by the client. The Lloyd's syndicate had avoided the policy *ab initio* on the ground of non-disclosure of material facts by the broker, but compromised the client insured's claim for £1 million in the sum of £50,000. The client sued the broker and the broker was put into liquidation. Thereafter, the liquidator consented to judgment, and, a year later, also consented to damages and interest of over £1.5 million. The claimant client, in exercise of the transfer of rights from the insured brokers under the Third Parties (Rights Against Insurers) Act 1930, then commenced proceedings directly against the professional indemnity insurers. One of their defences was that the liquidator's consent to the judgment and the assessment of damages was in breach of an express condition precedent which provided that the insured broker "shall not admit liability for any claim or incur any costs or expenses in connection therewith without the written consent of the Insurers".

One of the claimant's answers to this was the argument that the policy was at an end, because the professional indemnity insurers had purported to avoid the policy and had tendered a return premium, which had been accepted by the liquidator. This, it was argued, amounted to the consensual ending of the contract, or the acceptance of the insurers' repudiatory breach of the contract which put the contract at an end. Mance J. held that the insurers' rescission of the insurance had been lawful, but dealt *obiter* with whether the breach of policy condition could have been relied on if there had been no lawful rescission. He concluded the breach could not have been relied on[49]:

22–18

> "The precise route by which this occurred is probably not critical. In addition to the possibilities of mutual agreement (which could only be set aside if entered into under some sort of mistake) and accepted repudiation, there may be a further possibility, that it was simply because the defendants and the liquidator acted on a common assumption that the insurance cover was at an end, from which neither could resile at least without giving notice."

5. COMPLIANCE WITH POLICY TERMS AFTER REPUDIATION OF CLAIM

In contradistinction with the above situations where the insurance contract has been rescinded *ab initio*, and, perhaps, where the insurer alleges fraud by the insured, in all other circumstances where the insurer disputes his liability *under* the contract of insurance, the insured must comply with the policy terms because he is suing for an indemnity *under* the contract. This is consistent with the general principles of contract law.[50] However, the insured will be able to rely on an express or implied waiver by the insurer, or any representation by the insurer in words or conduct such as to found an estoppel, to relieve him of this requirement of future compliance when pursuing the claim thereafter.

22–19

---

[49] *ibid.* at 608, col.2.
[50] *Fercometal SARL v. Mediterranean Shipping Co. SA* [1989] 1 A.C. 788, HL.

22-20   An example is *Toronto Railway Co. v. National British and Irish Millers Insurance Co. Ltd*,[51] where the defendant insurers undertook an adjustment of the loss claimed under the insurance, and then entered into a long correspondence with the insured about the claim. Only then did the insurers demand, pursuant to a condition precedent in the policy, a certificate by a magistrate or notary public certifying belief that the loss had been sustained. The Court of Appeal had no difficulty in finding that the insurers' conduct on the adjustment was inconsistent with the later insistence upon the conditions of proof and ascertainment of loss. Accordingly, it was held that the insurers had waived compliance with that condition precedent and could not defend the action on breach of that condition precedent. Another example is provided, albeit *obiter*, in the Court of Appeal's decision in *Sprung v. Royal Insurance (U.K.) Ltd*.[52] The insured had a material damage policy with the defendant insurers that provided, *inter alia*, that non-minor repairs could only be carried out with the insurers' consent, together with the usual provision that the insurers could choose to reinstate or replace the damaged insured plant or pay the amount of the damage. On April 5, 1986, the claimant insured's plant was damaged by vandals. It was discovered on April 7 and immediately notified to the insurers. During the next five weeks or so, representatives of the insurers visited the premises on at least two occasions and carried out some inspection there. A claim in respect of a weighbridge was paid promptly in May, but only a cursory inspection was made of the more extensive damage to other plant. The insurers' representatives simply denied liability for the latter damage on a ground which appears to have been to the effect that the insurers were not liable for what was called "wilful damage".

22-21   Two visits were made. The first was on April 14 when the insurers' representative said: "You are not covered for blatant vandalism". A second visit was by a different representative who simply said: "Sorry, you're not covered". Thus, at that stage, the insurers simply declined liability on a ground that they had not sought to justify under the terms of either the burglary or engineering policies that they had with the insured. No express reference was made by the insurers to the policy conditions which required the insurers' consent before any major repairs were carried out. Correspondence followed and there were discussions, but the insurers remained reluctant to pay. There was never any suggestion that the claim was anything other than honest and made in good faith throughout. A notice of claim was submitted on June 30.

22-23   In August 1986, there was some suggestion that the insurers might entertain a claim, so time estimates were prepared by engineering and electrical contractors who would be able to carry out the repairs. Those figures formed the basis of a claim which was later submitted on October 3 in the sum of £58,000. But that was too late to save the business even if that payment had been made. Correspondence continued, but no payment was forthcoming, so the insured issued a writ on October 26, 1988. A

---

[51] (1914) 111 L.T. 555, CA.
[52] [1999] 1 Lloyd's Rep. 111, CA.

defence was served on December 19, 1988, which raised no substantive defence except by reference to the policy condition requiring formal notice of the claim. The insured later obtained, by consent, an interim payment for the damage in the sum of some £30,000 in March 1990, but lost his claim for consequential losses at first instance and on appeal (see above). *Obiter*, the court dealt with the position that arose in April and May 1986, when the insured was effectively asking for the insurers' consent to the effecting of major repairs, but was met with the insurers' representative's refusal to go into any detail about getting the plant back into working order. Evans L.J.,[53] with whom Beldam L.J. expressly agreed,[54] said:

> "In my judgment the position which arose when the defendants dealt with this matter in the way they did (that is to say, by denying liability, even on a ground which subsequently they have not sought to uphold) placed the [insured] in a position where he was entitled and, indeed, bound to proceed as if he was uninsured. In other words, he could proceed to reinstate or repair the damaged property if he was so advised. If he decided to do so and then subsequently claimed against the defendants under the policy, it seems to me that the defendants would not be in a position to allege by way of defence that there had been breach of Condition (6); in other words, they would have disqualified themselves from saying that, the repairs having been carried out without their consent, the [insured] was not entitled to recover the promised indemnity under the policy."

6. CONSEQUENCES OF THE INSURERS PUTTING THE INSURED TO PROOF OF HIS CLAIM

The burden of proof on insurers who allege fraud on the part of the insured has been dealt with in Chapter 1, above. If the insurers do not go that far, they can "not admit" that an insured event has occurred and/or the extent of the loss, they are fully entitled to put the insured to proof of either or both matters by not admitting them in their defence to an action. The onus on the insured is not discharged by merely establishing a prima facie case, nor does the onus of proof somehow shift to the insurer to establish an affirmative answer to that prima facie case. The correct position is that the onus remains throughout upon the insured to establish the case they are alleging, as to the occurrence of the insured peril, or the extent of the loss arising, or both of those. This was the clear view of the Court of Appeal in *Regina Fur Co. Ltd v. Bossom*.[55] If the insured is unable to establish the case he alleges, for instance that a particular burglary took place in the circumstances and at the time alleged by the insured, upon the normal test of the balance of probabilities, his action will be dismissed.[56] The court does not need to go further and make an adverse finding against the insured, such as that the insured himself committed the burglary.[57] If,

22–23

---

[53] *ibid.* at 118, col.1.
[54] *ibid.* at 119, col.2.
[55] [1958] 2 Lloyd's Rep. 425 at 428, col.2, *per* Lord Evershed M.R., CA.
[56] *ibid.* at 434, *per* Sellers L.J.
[57] *ibid.* at 430, col.1, *per* Lord Evershed M.R.

on the other hand, the insurer alleges fraud or that the loss arose from the insured's own wilful misconduct, the burden is on the insurer to prove that allegation.[58]

22–24   The other side to this matter is that there are restrictions on the way that an insurer who simply does not admit the claim can defend the action at trial. The insurers may challenge, at each point, and by proper evidence, where it is admissible, and by cross-examination, the case which the claimant insured seeks to make good. But it is not permissible for the insurers to proceed to put forward some affirmative case which they have not pleaded or alleged. As a consequence, the insurers cannot, by cross-examination of the insured or otherwise, suggest any such affirmative case.[59] Questions solely directed to the credit of the insured, rather than the relevant issues in the case, are not admissible, even if the case depends, inevitably, on the view that the judge forms of the insured and his witnesses.[60] Applying this restriction in *Roselodge Ltd v. Castle*,[61] McNair J. did permit the insurers to run their defence on the basis that the insured's story was a false and fabricated one, and not that the insured was merely mistaken. It is clear that McNair J. had some doubts about the matter, because he said[62]:

> "The difference between putting up an affirmative case of fraud and seeking to establish by cross-examination that the [insured's] chief witness is putting forward a false story with perjured evidence is I feel rather fine."

22–25   In determining whether or not an insured has made out his case, it may well be a significant factor that no witness is called who saw or heard anything consistent with, for example, an alleged burglary.[63] Similarly, the fact that the insured business was in serious financial difficulties will be a factor to weigh up in the matter. Similarly, if the insured business is in a healthy financial state and there is accordingly no earthly reason why the insured should put forward anything but a perfectly bona fide claim, that will also be a matter to be weighed up by the judge.[64] Obviously, further matters to be weighed up will be whether the insured or his witnesses have answered questions in an evasive manner,[65] or given evidence that could not be right.[66]

[58] *Slattery v. Mance* [1962] 1 Q.B. 676.
[59] *ibid.* at 428, col.2, *per* Lord Evershed M.R.
[60] *ibid.* at 429, col.1, *per* Lord Evershed M.R.
[61] [1966] 2 Lloyd's Rep. 113.
[62] *ibid.* at 120, col.1.
[63] [1958] 2 Lloyd's Rep. 425 at 430, col.2, *per* Lord Evershed M.R., CA.
[64] *ibid.* at 431, col.2, *per* Lord Evershed M.R.
[65] *ibid.*
[66] *ibid.* at 432, col.1, *per* Lord Evershed M.R.

7. LIABILITY INSURERS AND THEIR COSTS LIABILITY TO THIRD PARTY CLAIMANTS OUTSIDE THE INSURANCE CONTRACT

Court may order any person to pay costs

In recent years the power of the court, under section 51 of the Supreme   **22–26**
Court Act 1981,[67] to order any person[68] to pay the costs of an action has
been invoked by third party claimants against the defendant's liability
insurers. This initiative followed the House of Lords' decision in *Aiden
Shipping Co. Ltd v. Interbulk Ltd, The Vimeira*,[69] that there was no justification for implying a limitation in the wide discretion as to costs given to
the court, to the effect that costs can only be awarded against the immediate
parties to the action. The court has full power to determine by whom the
costs are to be paid, although in the vast majority of cases it would be
unjust to make an order against a non-party. The making of such an order
is therefore always exceptional, and the court should treat an application
for an order with considerable caution.[70]

Position of insurers

It was recognised by Philips L.J. in *Murphy v. Young & Co. Brewery*[71] that   **22–27**
the position of insurers is more complex where the defendant's costs have
been funded by insurers at risk under a policy under which their liability is
limited to a sum which is insufficient to cover both liability and costs. Philips
L.J. also sat on the case of *T.G.A. Chapman Ltd v. Christopher.*[72] There the
successful claimants made the application where the settlement agreed
exhausted the defendant's £1 million limit of indemnity under his liability
insurance in respect of "all damages and claimants' costs". The claimants
were anxious to obtain the order against the liability insurers themselves,
because the defendant was simply unable to meet the full costs' liability himself due to impecuniosity. The Court of Appeal held that an insurer who
decides to take over the conduct of its insured's defence of, *e.g.* a negligence
action, cannot rely on any policy limit referring either to the costs awarded to
a successful third party claimant, or to an overall policy indemnity limit in
the defendant's insurance policy. The insurers' argument that it would be
unjust and undesirable on public policy grounds that they should be exposed
to greater overall liability in relation to damages and costs than the £1m. limit
of indemnity, was rejected. The Court of Appeal preferred the principle that
any party who maintained litigation should be liable for the costs of a
successful adverse party. Moreover, the court was of the view that the mere
fact that the third party claim was itself a subrogated action, did not mean
that the discretion should not be exercised in favour of the successful party.

---

[67] As substituted by s.4 of the Courts and Legal Services Act 1990.
[68] Even if domiciled outside the jurisdiction, *National Justice Compania Naviera SA v.
Prudential Assurance Co. Ltd, The Ikarian Reefer (No.2)* [2000] Lloyd's Rep. I.R. 230, CA.
[69] [1986] A.C. 965, HL.
[70] *Symphony Group plc v. Hodgson* [1994] Q.B. 179.
[71] [1997] 1 W.L.R. 1591 at 1601, CA.
[72] [1998] 1 W.L.R. 12, CA.

22–28   Philips L.J. set out five factors which, together, justified the making of the order[73]:

> (i) the insurers determined that the claim would be fought;
> (ii) the insurers funded the defence of the claim;
> (iii) the insurers had the conduct of the litigation;
> (iv) the insurers fought the claim exclusively to defend their own interests;
> (v) the defence failed in its entirety.

Philips L.J. then continued:

> "In the context of the insurance industry, the features may not be extra-ordinary. But that is not the test. The test is whether they are extraordinary in the context of the entire range of litigation that comes to the courts. I have no doubt that they are. It must be rare for litigation to be funded, con-trolled and directed by a third party motivated entirely by its own interests."

22–29   In *Pendennis Shipyard Ltd v. Magrathea (Pendennis) Ltd*,[74] an order was granted in respect of the entire costs of the action, notwithstanding that the insurer had ceased to conduct the insured's defence prior to trial, because it had been the insurer's denial of both liability and quantum that had led to a full trial. A partial order for costs was made in *Citibank N.A. v. Excess Insurance Co. Ltd v. Excess Insurance Co. Ltd*.[75] Costs were not ordered directly against the insurers in respect of the trial as to liability, on the ground that the defence was conducted not only in the insurer's interest, but also in the interest of the insured to protect the insured's reputation. But once liability had been established, the outstanding question of quantum was then conducted exclusively in the interests of the insurers, so they were ordered to pay the costs after the liability of the defendant insured had been established. It was also pointed out that such applications should generally be made immediately after the conclusion of the trial.[76]

Procedure
22–30   CPR, Pt 48, r.2(1) now provides that where the court is considering making a costs order under section 51 against a non-party, that party must be added as a party to the proceedings for the purposes of costs only, and he must be given a reasonable opportunity to attend a hearing at which the court will consider the matter further. Lightman J. has also summarised the established guidelines regarding the procedure to be adopted in *Bristol and West plc v. Bhadresa*.[77] Those guidelines are six fold, subject to the con-sideration that the court must ensure that the exercise of this jurisdiction does not give rise to a new and costly form of satellite litigation:

---

[73] *ibid.* at 20.
[74] [1998] 1 Lloyd's Rep. 315.
[75] [1999] Lloyd's Rep. I.R. 122.
[76] *ibid.* at 129, col.1, following *Bahai v. Rashidean* [1985] 1 W.L.R. 1337.
[77] [1999] Lloyd's Rep. I.R. 138 at 142.

(i) an application is appropriate only in plain and straightforward cases where the hearing can be measured in hours not days;

(ii) the application should normally be before the trial judge who is best equipped (and best informed) to determine the application summarily;

(iii) elaborate pleadings should be avoided;

(iv) the formal process of discovery and interrogatories are inappropriate;

(v) the ordinary rules of evidence will apply unless a departure from them will occasion no injustice and cross-examination on affidavits should generally not be permitted;

(vi) the court may be persuaded to depart from these principles in an exceptional case where justice requires a more extensive investigation into contested facts and, *e.g.* to order limited discovery or cross-examination if there is an impelling need for them.[78]

In the instant case, Lightman J. refused an application to conduct what would have been a week long mini-trial to investigate the insurers' decision to withdraw funding of the defendant solicitor's defence under the professional indemnity insurance.

Guidelines on exercise of discretion

Lightman J. in the *Bristol and West* case, above, also provided a   **22–31** summary of the Court of Appeal's guidelines in relation to the exercise of discretion upon these applications[79]:

(i) only in exceptional circumstances is the making of an order reasonable and just;

(ii) the court may be expected to be receptive to an application where the non-party has wantonly and officiously, without excuse or justification, intermeddled in a dispute between others where he has no interest whatever. This guideline does not apply to liability insurers because they have an interest in the outcome, irrespective of whether the insurer has yet determined whether the defendant is entitled to cover;

(iii) where there is no relevant limit to cover against liability, it may well be appropriate to order the non-party to pay those costs directly to the successful party. The same applies if the non-party has made a representation to the successful party that it is under an obligation to indemnify the unsuccessful party and the successful party relied on this representation;

(iv) where the defendant's costs have been funded by insurers under a policy under which their liability is limited to a sum insufficient to cover both liability and costs, there is no general rule that the

---

[78] See *Bailey v. I.B.C. Vehicles* [1998] 3 All E.R. 570 at 573a-c and 575a-b.
[79] [1999] Lloyd's Rep. I.R. 138 at 143–144.

insurers should, or should not, be held liable: the outcome turns on the facts of the particular case;

(v) in the case where an insurer has funded litigation by the insured, it is not sufficient to justify an order for costs against the insurer that the insurer has funded the litigation under a commercial agreement. Further exceptional features are called for, *e.g.* where insurers fund a defendant who has no assets and sole control over the litigation[80];

(vi) it is relevant whether the insurance is or is not limited to the one piece of litigation, and whether it is in the public interest that the insurance cover in question is being provided (as in the case of compulsory insurances).

22–32   In the instant case, Lightman J. refused the application for costs against the solicitors' indemnity fund. He considered that delay by an insurer in determining whether it is entitled or bound to refuse cover was not an exceptional circumstance justifying the making of an order for costs, particularly when the applicant was at all times alert to the question concerning dishonesty of the defendant solicitor. A further militating factor against the making of the order was that the insurer would have been required to waive privilege or indeed confidences before the issues raised could be fairly determined.[81] An order was also refused against consulting engineers' professional indemnity insurers in *Gloucester Health Authority v. M.A. Torpy and Partners Ltd*[82] because the defence had been run sensibly and reasonably for the benefit of both the insurers and the insured professionals, who co-operated fully in vigorously defending the claim, and there was no indication that the defence would have been conducted any differently if the action had been defended by solicitors instructed solely by the defendants themselves.

22–33   Circumstances not dissimilar to those in *Citibank*,[83] led to a costs order against professional indemnity insurers in *Monkton Court Ltd v. Perry Prowse (Insurance Services) Ltd.*[84] Again, the insurers had determined that the claim should be defended and the brokers were only at risk themselves for a £2,500 excess. The insured then ceased trading, but liability was not conceded until the following year. Thereafter, the insurers terminated the insurance and the solicitors' retainer, and, about a year later the trial took place at which the insured were not represented. Judgment was entered for £292,000 plus costs of £80,000, which was considerably more than the limit of indemnity under the insured's terminated liability insurance. The judge considered, though, that the defence had been conducted almost exclusively for the insurers' benefit, because liability had been an almost foregone conclusion, and because the insured's reputation did not need protection as it soon ceased to trade. The judge also dismissed the argu-

---

[80] As in *Chapman*, above.
[81] [1999] Lloyd's Rep. I.R. 138 at 145.
[82] [1999] Lloyd's Rep. 203.
[83] [1999] Lloyd's Rep. I.R. 122.
[84] [2000] 1 All E.R (Comm.) 566.

ment that the insurer, being a mutual insurer, was to be considered as acting solely in the interests of its members — of whom the present insured was one.

On the other hand, a costs order against professional indemnity insurers **22–34** was refused by the Court of Appeal in *Cormack and Cormack v. Excess Insurance Co. Ltd*.[85] The court re-emphasised that exceptional circumstances were needed to obtain a costs order against an insurer. It was not enough that the likely award to the third party claimant exceeded the limit of indemnity available under the policy, it still needed the key factor of the control being exercised over the proceedings solely, or very largely, in the insurers' interests. In the present case, although the insured surveyor had taken a very passive role in the defence of the claim, and, indeed, had ceased to practise, he had always known that the insurance indemnity might be inadequate and had never even asked the insurers to settle the claim rather than defend it. In these circumstances, the court was satisfied that the insurers acted at all times with due regard to the defendant insured's interests as well as their own interests, so that the key requirement of self-interest was not made out. This was so, even though the insurers had instigated an unsuccessful appeal against the judgment obtained at trial against the insured in circumstances where the judgment sum and costs exhausted the indemnity policy limit. Further, the court determined that liability insurers are not under any duty to third party claimants to inform them of any applicable limit of indemnity under the defendant insured's insurance policy. There being no duty, any failure to inform third party claimants that the policy limits would not cover an unsuccessful appeal by the defendant, could not amount to an exceptional circumstance justifying punishment in the form of a costs order.

8. UNAUTHORISED INSURANCE

Unauthorised insurer cannot enforce the contract

By section 132(1) of the Financial Services Act 1986, which has retrospec-   **22–35** tive effect,[86] an insurance contract entered into by an insurer who is not an insurer authorised to carry on insurance business under section 2 of the Insurance Companies Act 1982, is unenforceable by the insurer. This provision was introduced to overcome the Court of Appeal's decision in *Phoenix General Insurance Co. of Greece SA v. Halvanon Insurance Co. Ltd*[87] that such contracts were wholly unenforceable by either the insurer or the insured.

Insured can elect consequence

The insured, however, can now elect to treat the insurance contract as   **22–36** invalid and recover any money or other property paid or transferred by

---

[85] [2000] C.L.C. 1039, CA.
[86] *Group Josi Re v. Walbrook Insurance Co. Ltd* [1996] 1 W.L.R. 1152, CA; *Bates v. Barrow Ltd* [1995] 1 Lloyd's Rep. 680; overruling *D.R. Insurance Co. v. Seguros America Bernamex* [1993] 1 Lloyd's Rep. 120.
[87] [1988] Q.B. 216, CA.

him under the contract, together with compensation for any loss sustained by him as a result of having parted with it.[88] If such property has been transferred to a third party, the insured is entitled to recover its value.[89] Obviously, if this course is chosen, the insured is not entitled to recover any of the benefits under the insurance contract.[90] Alternatively, pro-vided[91] the insured reasonably believed that his entering into the contract did not constitute a contravention of section 2 of the 1982 Act, the insured may seek to enforce the insurance contract (always supposing the unau-thorised insurer has some assets). The court has a discretion to determine if it is just and equitable for the contract to be enforced.[92] There is as yet no reported decision on the exercise of this discretion.

Winding up of unauthorised insurer

22–37   If an unauthorised insurer refuses to cease its insurance business or seek authorisation, the Secretary of State can petition for the winding up of the unauthorised insurance company on the just and equitable ground under section 124A of the Insolvency Act 1986. Such an application was successful in *Re Sentinal Securities plc.*[93]

Authorised insurer issuing insurance beyond permitted category

22–38   It is unresolved whether an insurance written by an authorised insurer in a category of insurance business for which it is not authorised is void. Section 16(1) of the Insurance Companies Act 1982 prohibits an insurance company carrying on any activities, in the Ununted Kingdom or elsewhere, "otherwise than in connection with or for the purposes of its insurance business". The argument is that if insurances are issued in unauthorised categories, being prohibited by section 16(1), they are illegal and therefore void. *Obiter* views were expressed in the Court of Appeal in *Fuji Finance Inc. v. Aetna Life Insurance Co. Ltd.*[94] Morritt L.J. expressed the view that section 16 did not invalidate such insurance contracts,[95] whilst Sir Ralph Gibson was of the opposite view,[96] and Hobhouse L.J. declined to give a view.[97]

9. DISCLOSURE OF DOCUMENTS IN LITIGATION

Pre-action disclosure

22–39   With effect from April 26, 1999, the court has power to make an order for disclosure of specific documents, prior to the commencement of proceedings, against a likely party to subsequent litigation.[98]

---

[88] Financial Services Act 1986, s.132(1).
[89] *ibid.*, s.132(5).
[90] *ibid.*, s.132(4).
[91] *ibid.*, s.132(3)(a).
[92] *ibid.*, s.132(3)(b).
[93] [1996] 1 W.L.R. 316.
[94] [1997] Ch. 173, CA.
[95] *ibid.* at 194.
[96] *ibid.* at 196.
[97] *ibid.* at 199–200.
[98] CPR, Pt 31, r.16, and s.33(2) of the Supreme Court Act 1981 (as amended).

Disclosure against a non-party

Also from April 26, 1999, provided the documents sought are likely to **22–40** support an applying party's case in existing litigation, and disclosure is necessary to fairly dispose of the claim, or to save costs, the court may order a non-party to disclose or produce documents.[99]

The duty of disclosure of documents

Except in small track cases involving disputes under £5,000, parties must **22–41** disclose the existence of relevant documents that are, or have been, in the party's or his agent's control.[1] Accordingly, an insured must disclose the placing file of his broker or other intermediary, and all documents relating to quantum, including those of any loss assessor he has appointed, when in litigation with his insurer. For their part, the insurers will have to disclose their underwriting file and their loss adjuster's file regarding the claim. This duty of disclosure embraces all documents that are damaging to a party's case as well as all those that assist that party's case. The duty is that of the litigant, but his solicitor must ensure that his client understands his duty of disclosure and of preservation of all relevant documents.[2] The duty of disclosure continues until the proceedings are concluded.[3]

Standard disclosure

The duty is to provide what is called "standard" disclosure, which means **22–42** documents which a reasonable search has revealed, and a party's disclosure statement must set out the extent of the party's search to locate the documents he is required to disclose, and certify that he understands the duty and has carried out that duty.[4] An insurer, or the Motor Insurer's Bureau, may sign a disclosure statement on behalf of a party where the insurer, or the Motor Insurance Bureau has a financial interest in the result of proceedings brought wholly or partly by or against that party.[5] The reasonableness of the search includes such factors as the nature and complexity of the proceedings, the significance of any documents likely to be located, and the ease and expense of retrieval.[6] A dishonest disclosure statement renders the signatory to contempt of court proceedings.[7] Not only paper documents are caught by this duty, be they copies or originals, but "anything in which information of any description is recorded".[8] Accordingly, all computerised records and e-mails, photographs, video and sound recordings must be disclosed. A party may blank out sections of relevant documents that are either irrelevant or are the subject of a valid claim to privilege (see below).[9]

---

[99] CPR, Pt 31, r.17, and s.34(2) of the Supreme Court Act 1981.
[1] CPR, Pt 31r.8.
[2] CPR, Pt PD31, r.4(4).
[3] CPR, Pt 31, r.11(1).
[4] CPR, Pt 31, r.10(5) and (6), and Pt PD31, r.4(2).
[5] CPR, Pt PD31, r.4(7).
[6] CPR, Pt 31, r.7(2); and, Pt PD31.2.
[7] CPR, Pt 31, r.23.
[8] CPR, Pt 31, r.4.
[9] CPR, Pt 31, r.19(3).

Specific disclosure

22–43   Subject always to the overriding objective of the Civil Procedure Rules,[10] the court may, upon application, order a party to make specific disclosure of particular documents or classes of documents, or to carry out a search for specific documents or categories of documents and disclose any documents located as a result of that search.[11]

Inspection of documents

22–44   One party to litigation is entitled, subject to a valid objection, to inspect and take copies[12] of all documents:

    (i) disclosed by another party to the litigation; or
    (ii) referred to[13] in the other party's:

        (a) statement of case (pleading);
        (b) witness statement;
        (c) expert report[14];
        (d) affidavit.

A party must permit inspection within seven days of receipt of a notice to inspect, and in default that party will not be able to rely on the document unless the court gives permission.[15] Where a claim for privilege is set up against a claim for production of documents by the opposite party, as below, the party claiming privilege may apply to the court for an order permitting him to withhold inspection of a document or part of a document.[16] In determining such an application, the court may itself inspect such document, and invite representations from the other party, or other persons.[17]

Legal advice privilege

22–45   Letters and other communications made by a party to his solicitor on a confidential basis for the purpose of obtaining legal advice, and his solicitor's professional responses, are privileged from production. This exceptional rule has been justified on the basis that a party should be able to place "unrestricted and unbounded confidence in" his solicitor,[18] and that there "must be the freest possible communication between solicitor and client".[19] The privilege has long been extended to the obtaining of all legal

---

[10] CPR, Pt 1, r.1.
[11] CPR, Pt 31, r.12(2).
[12] CPR, Pt 31, r.14.
[13] *ibid.*
[14] Except the instructions to the expert, unless the court is satisfied that there are reasonable grounds for considering that those instructions are inaccurate or incomplete, see CPR, Pt 35. r.10(4).
[15] CPR, Pt 31, r.21.
[16] CPR, Pt 31, r.19(3); and, Pt 31PD4, r.5.
[17] CPR, Pt 31, r.19(6).
[18] *Anderson v. Bank of British Columbia* (1876) 2 Ch. 644 at 649, *per* Jessel M.R., CA.
[19] *Southwark and Vauxhall Water Co. v. Quick* (1878) 3 Q.B.D. 315 at 322, *per* Cotton L.J., CA.

advice, whether or not actual litigation is in being or pending. This privilege also extends to documents created by a third party for the purpose of the party claiming privilege obtaining legal advice, and to information obtained by the solicitor from others within his firm for the purpose of giving legal advice.[20] Advice given by in-house lawyers is embraced provided always that such communications concern legal, not administrative matters.[21] Instructions and briefs to counsel for advice are privileged, as are counsel's advices, opinions and settled draft documents.[22] In the insurance context, the issue of privilege is unaffected by the fact that the documents sought relate to an underlying claim by a third party in respect of which the claimant insured is indemnified by the defendant insurer. Thus the insurer cannot obtain an order for the inspection of the insured's correspondence with his solicitor and papers laid before counsel that relate to the insured's obtaining of legal advice upon the third party's claim against him.[23] As regards the situation where the solicitors and counsel are jointly instructed by the insured and the liability insurers, see below.

Litigation privilege

Once litigation is either contemplated or actually commenced, a wider privilege from inspection by the opposing party arises. All documents which then come into existence for the purpose of obtaining or giving advice in regard to that litigation, or for the purpose of the collection of evidence to be used in that litigation, are privileged.[24] This includes, therefore, draft witness statements and draft expert reports, and all other documents obtained by a solicitor with a view to enabling him to render advice on such litigation to his client,[25] but not documents which come into existence for some other purpose. In *Westminster Airways Ltd v. Kuwait Oil Co. Ltd*,[26] the Court of Appeal held that communications passing between an insured and his insurance brokers and his liability insurers, with respect to an accident which gave rise to the claim in the action, are covered by privilege. This is because such communications would be directed to the question of whether the third party's claim should be disputed or admitted, and if it was to be disputed, how best to conduct the defence.[27]

22–46

The all important test, though, is whether the dominant purpose of the author of the document, or the person under whose direction the document was produced, was to use the document or its contents to obtain legal advice, or to conduct or aid in the conduct of litigation either commenced or in reasonable contemplation.[28] Run of the mill loss adjusters' reports on

22–47

[20] *Anderson v. Bank of British Columbia* (1876) 2 CR. 644, CA.
[21] *Alfred Crompton Amusement Machines Ltd v. Commissioners. for Customs and Excise (No.2)* [1974] A.C. 405, HL.
[22] *Mostyn v. West Mostyn Coal and Iron Co.* (1876) 34 L.T. 531.
[23] *Daily Express (1908) Ltd v. Mountain* (1916) 32 T.L.R. 592, CA.
[24] *Anderson v. Bank of British Columbia* (1876) 2 CR. 644, CA.
[25] *Learoyd v. Halifax Banking Co.* [1893] 1 Ch. 686 at 690, *per* Stirling J.
[26] [1951] 1 K.B. 134, CA.
[27] *ibid.* at 146, *per* Jenkins L.J.
[28] *Waugh v. British Railways Board* [1980] A.C. 521, HL.

claims are not privileged unless and until the litigation is contemplated.[29] Also, accident report forms are compulsory so they are not protected by privilege even though one of their purposes is to obtain legal advice in respect of the accident.[30] On the other hand, a document procured by insurers which has the dominant purpose of being submitted for legal advice on whether the insured's claim should be paid or resisted, either on the grounds of the suspicion of fraud,[31] or because it involves a substantial claim in a complicated area of indemnity,[32] the document will be privileged.

22–48   A litigant will not be allowed to make use in evidence of another party's privileged document where it has been obtained by stealth or a trick, or by otherwise acting improperly, on the ground of public policy.[33] Equally, a litigant and his solicitors will be restrained by an injunction from making use of privileged documents accidentally handed over by a party entitled to privilege.[34]

Waiver of legal advice or litigation privilege

22–49   Privilege is not waived by the mere fact that the document is referred to in either a statement of case,[35] nor in an affidavit,[36] but if even part of a document is put in evidence, or read to the court, privilege will be waived for the whole document, unless the remainder deals with an entirely different subject-matter.[37] The judge will determine that issue by reading the whole document or transcript of a conversation, or hearing the tape recording of a conversation in full.[38] That waiver does not extend beyond that document so used, though, to other privileged documents relating to the matters referred to in that used document.[39] Further, the waiver of legal advice privilege does not involve a waiver of litigation privilege, so documents in the latter category remain privileged, *i.e.* once litigation was in reasonable contemplation.[40] For the implied waiver of privilege between an insured and his liability insurer where the solicitors are jointly appointed, see below.

Privilege against self-incrimination

22–50   A party will not be compelled by the court to give disclosure of documents,[41] or answer questions in cross-examination,[42] provided there is a

---

[29] *Seabrook v. British Transport Commission* [1959] 1 W.L.R. 509.

[30] *Lask v. Gloucester Health Authority* [1991] 2 Med. L.R. 379, CA.

[31] *Re Highgrade Traders Ltd* [1984] B.C.L.C. 151, CA.

[32] *Guiness Peat Properties Ltd v. Fitzroy Robinson Partnership* [1987] 1 W.L.R. 1027, CA.

[33] *I.T.C. Film Distributors Ltd v. Video Exchange Ltd* [1982] Ch. 431.

[34] *English and American Insurance Co. Ltd v. Herbert Smith* [1988] F.S.R. 232; *Webster v. James Chapman & Co.* [1989] 3 All E.R. 939; *Derby & Co. Ltd v. Weldon (No.8)* [1991] 1 W.L.R. 73, CA.

[35] *Roberts v. Oppenheim* (1884) 26 Ch. D. 724, CA.

[36] *Infields Ltd v. Rosen & Son* [1938] 3 All E.R. 591, CA.

[37] *Great Atlantic Insurance Co. v. Home Insurance Co.* [1981] 1 W.L.R. 529, CA.

[38] *Leif Hoegh & Co. A/S v. Petrolsea Inc. (The World Era)(No.2)* [1993] 1 Lloyd's Rep. 363.

[39] *General Accident Fire & Life Assurance Corp. Ltd v. Tanter, The Zephyr* [1984] 1 W.L.R. 100.

[40] *George Doland Ltd v. Blackburn Robson Coates & Co.* [1972] 1 W.L.R. 1338.

[41] Civil Evidence Act 1968, s.14.

[42] *Den Norske Bank A.S.A. v. Antonatos* [1999] Q.B. 271, CA.

real[43] risk that is apparent to the court[44] that the disclosure might tend to incriminate him or risk exposure to criminal prosecution. If there is no real danger that the prosecution would be able to make use of disclosed material, disclosure will be ordered by the court notwithstanding the claim of privilege.[45] This right is now embodied in Article 6 of the European Convention on Human Rights, which is incorporated into English law from October 2, 2000, under the Human Rights Act 1998.

"Without prejudice" communications

This is a rule relating to admissibility of evidence rather than whether   **22–51**
such documents need to be disclosed. It prevents a party using evidence of any negotiations, either oral or in writing, in the prosecution or defence of any civil claim. The rule is founded on the public policy consideration that litigants should be encouraged to settle their differences, and should thus be protected from being later embarrassed by an admission made solely for the purpose of attempting to reach a compromise.[46] All communications are protected, whether or not they are expressly referred to as being "without prejudice", provided that they relate to a genuine effort to resolve the dispute between them,[47] including discussion of the strengths and weaknesses of each other's cases.[48] The court will examine disputed documents to determine their true nature.[49]

But the rule is not absolute. First, if an issue arises upon whether the   **22–52**
dispute has been compromised by the parties, then evidence of the "without prejudice" communications that are alleged to have concluded the compromise are admissible on the determination of that issue.[50] Secondly, the justice of the case may require admission of "without prejudice" communications. This occurred in *Gnitrow Ltd v. Cape plc*[51] where the claimant company sought an indemnity or contribution from a third employer of employees who had sustained asbestosis-related personal injury during exposure whilst employed with all three employers. The insurers of the claimant had already come to a settlement with the second employer, and the third employer sought disclosure of the terms of that settlement. The Court of Appeal ordered inspection on a number of grounds, including the overriding objective of the Civil Procedure Rules, given that the extent of the third company's contribution could not be determined without that information, and that the privilege should not extend to the concluded agreement following "without prejudice" discussions. Similarly, in *Somatra Ltd v. Sinclair Roche & Temperley*[52] the Court of Appeal held that in the circumstances of a professional negligence

---

[43] *Renworth v. Stephanson* [1996] 3 All E.R. 244, CA.
[44] See, *e.g. National Association of Operative Plasterers v. Smithies* [1906] A.C. 434, HL.
[45] *A.T. & T. Istel Ltd v. Tully* [1993] A.C. 45, HL.
[46] *Cutts v. Head* [1984] Ch. 290, CA.
[47] *Chocoladefabriken Lindt & Sprungli A.G. v. Nestlé Co. Ltd* [1978] R.P.C. 287.
[48] *Unilever v. Procter & Gamble* [2000] 1 W.L.R. 2436, CA.
[49] *South Shropshire District Council v. Amos* [1986] 1 W.L.R. 1271, CA.
[50] *Walker v. Wilsher* (1889) 23 Q.B.D. 335.
[51] [2000] 1 W.L.R. 2327, CA.
[52] [2000] Lloyd's Rep. 673, CA.

claim against solicitors, who counterclaimed for fees owing, where the defendant solicitors deliberately chose to refer to "without prejudice" material in its application for a freezing order against their ex-client, then the ex-client would be able to refer to the full "without prejudice" material — both in evidence challenging the freezing order, and in evidence at the main trial.

Privilege between insured and insurer where solicitor appointed by liability insurer

22–53   Where the retainer of solicitors to defend a third party's claim against a defendant insured is joint,[53] on behalf of both liability insurers and the insured, but the insured and his insurer later enter into hostile litigation, it is well established that neither the insured nor the insurer can claim legal professional privilege in relation to documents which came into existence in relation to the earlier litigation against the insured.[54] The question of the point in time when that implied waiver ceases was addressed by the Court of Appeal in *T.S.B. Bank plc v. Robert Irving and Burns*.[55] The facts briefly were that solicitors were appointed jointly by the defendant surveyors and their professional indemnity insurers to defendant the claimant's claim for professional negligence. Insurers considered whether they could decline cover, but were advised by counsel that it had no grounds to justify denial of an indemnity to the insured. The action continued to be jointly defended, but then counsel and the appointed solicitor had a conference with one of the insured surveyors, during which he, and the solicitor, were cross-examined by counsel. Trusting, and having confidence in his solicitor and counsel, and being given no warning of the peril in which he had ben placed, the surveyor gave unguarded answers to counsel. Counsel then advised the insurers that, from those answers, they had grounds to repudiate liability, which they did shortly thereafter. The insured joined the insurers into the action claiming an indemnity against any liability to the claimant. The insurers served a defence pleading the matters revealed in that unguarded conference, and in response the insured surveyors applied to strike out those matters and sought an injunction preventing the insurers relying on the answers given at the conference.

22–54   The Court upheld the granting of both applications. The Court held that the waiver of privilege implicit in the joint retainers extends to[56]:

> (i) all communications made by the insured to the solicitors down to such time as an actual[57] conflict of interest between the insured and the insurer arose; and

---

[53] See further Chapter 20, above, about insurer's right to conduct the defence and the duties of the appointed solicitor.

[54] *C.I.A. Barca de Panama SA v. George Wimpey & Co. Ltd* [1980] 1 Lloyd's Rep. 598 at 615, *per* Bridge L.J. (as he then was), CA; cited with approval in *Brown v. Guardian Royal Exchange Assurance plc* [1994] 2 Lloyd's Rep. 325 at 329, *per* Neill L.J., CA; and in *T.S.B. Bank plc v. Robert Irving and Burns* [1999] Lloyd's Rep. I.R. 528 at 538, para.11, *per* Morritt L.J., CA.

[55] [1999] Lloyd's Rep. I.R. 528, CA.

[56] *ibid.* at 540, para.17, *per* Morritt L.J.

[57] But not merely possible conflict, *ibid.* at 540–541, *per* Tuckey L.J.

(ii) to all communications made by the insured to those solicitors after the notification by the solicitors to the insured of such conflict and the lapse of such further time as the insured reasonably requires to decide whether to instruct separate solicitors.

The court was in no doubt that there was an actual conflict of interests at the time the solicitor drafted the instructions to counsel for the conference and "to consider again on behalf of underwriters their liability to indemnify" the insured. Thus the waiver of privilege did not extend to the communications made by the surveyor to the solicitor and counsel at the subsequent conference.[58]

10. THE COURTS

Introduction

Insurance litigation may be litigated in any County Court, the Royal Courts of Justice in London, or any District Registry of the Queen's Bench or Chancery Division of the High Court, but it can also be litigated in one of the more specialist courts of England and Wales. A key distinction of the specialist courts is that a specialist judge hears all interlocutory applications as well as the eventual trial, whereas a District Judge will hear interlocutory applications in the County Court and the High Court District Registries (or Masters in the Royal Courts of Justice, London).   **22–55**

The Commercial Court

In London only, there is a Commercial Court within the Queen's Bench Division,[59] and insurance cases are specifically within this court's specialist remit of "commercial claims".[60] The Civil Procedure Rules ("CPR") apply to Commercial Court proceedings subject to the provisions of the relevant practice direction and the detailed Commercial Court Guide.[61] There are usually twelve judges available to sit in the Commercial Court. This Court tends to deal with the largest insurance disputes, particularly those which involve international parties.   **22–56**

Mercantile Courts and the London County Court Business List

On the regional level, and comparatively recently, Mercantile Courts have been established in Manchester, Liverpool, Birmingham, Bristol, Leeds, Newcastle upon Tyne, and Cardiff. The appointed Mercantile judges are Circuit Judges, but they sit permanently as judges of the High Court. In addition, in London, there is a Business List in the Central London County Court. These specialist courts have insurance claims specifically within their remit, and again are subject to the CPR subject to   **22–57**

---

[58] *ibid.* at 540, para.19, *per* Morritt L.J.
[59] Supreme Court Act 1981, s.6(1)(b).
[60] Practice Direction — Commercial Court, para.1.2(1)(v), supplementing CPR, Pt 49.
[61] *ibid.*, para.1.4.

the provisions of the relevant practice direction.[62] A *Mercantile Courts Guide*, and a *Guide to Practice in the Central London Court Business List*, have been issued.

11. JOINDER OF LIABILITY INSURER INTO PROCEEDINGS

22–58   Until April 26, 1999, the previous Order 15, rule 6(2)(b) of the Rules of the Supreme Court ("RSC") allowed the court to order the joinder of any person who "ought" to have been joined, or whose presence before the court was "necessary to ensure that all matters in dispute in the cause or matter may be effectually and completely determined and adjudicated upon", or between whom there "may exist a question or issue arising out of or relating to or connected with any relief or remedy claimed in the cause or matter". The application to the joinder of liability insurers was approved by the Court of Appeal in *Gurtner v. Circuit*[63] where the Motor Insurers Bureau was allowed to be joined as a defendant to an injured motorcyclist's action against a defendant driver who could not be located. The Bureau, under its Agreement with the Minister of Transport,[64] would become liable to satisfy any judgment against the untraced defendant driver whose insurer could not be identified. The Court of Appeal, upon the Bureau's undertaking to discharge any judgment against the defendant driver, permitted the Bureau to be joined as a second defendant under this rule, and to defend the action and to exercise all the rights of the first defendant in the action. Lord Denning M.R. considered that where the determination of a dispute between two parties by a court of law would directly affect a third person in his legal rights, or in his pocket, then the court in its discretion under this rule might allow him to be added as a party on such terms as it thought fit. By so doing, his lordship felt that the court achieved the object of the rule by enabling all matters in dispute to be "effectually and completely determined and adjudicated upon" between all those directly concerned in the outcome. It would be "most unjust" if the Bureau were bound to "stand idly by watching the [claimant] get judgment against the defendant without saying a word when they are the people who have to foot the bill".[65]

22–59   The Court of Appeal went further in *Wood v. Perfection Travel Ltd*[66] which was a case involving the Third Parties (Rights Against Insurers) 1930 Act. The defendant insured was a dissolved company that had been restored to the register for the purpose of enabling the third party claimant to establish liability and so acquire a transfer of the insured company's rights against the insurers. The reality was, of course, that the restored company had no funds to mount any defence whatsoever to the

---

[62] Practice Direction — Mercantile Courts and Business Lists, para.1.3, supplementing CPR, Pt 49.
[63] [1968] 2 Q.B. 587, CA.
[64] See Appendix 13, below, for the current Agreements.
[65] [1968] 2 Q.B. 587 at 332, CA.
[66] [1996] L.R.L.R. 233, CA.

third party's claim. The Court of Appeal therefore allowed the insurers to be joined in the action as a second defendant and conduct the first defendant's defence, as well as to challenge their liability to indemnify the insured company under the terms of the insurance. Even more recently, an employers' liability insurer's application to set aside a default judgment obtained against the insured employer only failed because the applicant insurers failed to set out, as required in any such application, the basis of any arguable defence of the insured to the claimant's claim for damages.[67]

There are limits to the liability insurer's ability to have his liability to **22–60** indemnify the insured determined. The insurer will not be able to pre-empt the injured third party's claim against the insured by seeking a declaration that the insured is not liable to that third party in an action between himself and the insured alleged wrongdoer. The Court of Appeal struck out such an attempt in *Meadows Indemnity Co. Ltd v. The Insurance Corp. of Ireland plc*[68] where a reinsurer attempted to seek a declaration that the primary layer insurer was not liable to indemnify the insured. The court followed the speech of Lord Diplock in *Gouriet v. Union of Post Office Workers*[69] where his lordship had said:

> "the jurisdiction of the court is not to declare the law generally or to give advisory opinions; it is confined to declaring contested legal rights, subsisting or future, of the parties represented in the litigation before it and not those of anyone else."

On the other hand, where an insured sought a declaration against its **22–61** product liability insurers as to the recoverability of certain elements of a claim made against him, neither the lower court, nor the Court of Appeal considered that there was any difficulty about dealing with the issue. Indeed, Hobhouse L.J. (as he then was) said[70]:

> "There is no problem about that because the declaration asked for assumes that there will be such a liability."

The new procedural rule under Part 19 of the Civil Procedure Rules **22–62** provides:

> "19.—1(2) The Court may order a person to be added as a new party if—
>
> (a) it is desirable to add the new party so that the Court can resolve all matters in dispute in the proceedings; or
> (b) there is an issue involving the new party and an existing party which is connected to the matters in dispute in the proceedings, and it is desirable to add the new party so that the Court can resolve that issue."

---

[67] *Rees & Rees v. Mabco Ltd and Eagle Star Insurance Co. Ltd* [1998] T.L.R. 806, CA.
[68] [1989] 2 Lloyd's Rep. 298, CA.
[69] [1978] A.C. 435, at 501, HL.
[70] *A.S. Screenprint Ltd v. British Reserve Insurance Co. Ltd* [1999] Lloyd's Rep. I.R. 430 at 434, CA.

The application of all the new Civil Procedure Rules is to be determined uncluttered by earlier authorities on the previous Rules of the Supreme Court 1981, and it seems that the only issue will be whether the interests of justice demand that the insurer should be allowed to defend.[71] Liability insurers are not necessarily going to be eager to apply for joinder in every circumstance, though, for they will be wary that they might subsequently be determined to be estopped from denying an indemnity to the defendant insured, as postulated by Diplock L.J. (as he then was) in *Fraser v. B. N. Furman (Productions) Ltd*[72] because they have conducted the insured's defence. They will equally wish to avoid later arguments of waiver along the lines briefly discussed by the Court of Appeal in *Barratt Bros. (Taxis) Ltd v. Davies*.[73] This issue is discussed in Chapter 20, above.

12. JURISDICTIONAL ISSUES

The proper law of an insurance contract relating to commercial risks situated outside the E.C.

22–63   With regard to risks situated outside the E. C., an express choice of law clauses will be effective under Article 3 of the Rome Convention.[74] If there is no express provision in the insurance policy, then, in general, the insurance contract will be governed by the law of the country with which it is most closely connected under Article 4(1) of the Rome Convention. That is presumed under Article 4(2) to be, in most cases, the country in which the insurer will perform the contract, *i.e.* where the insurer has its principal place of business, or in the country of another office where performance will be effected.

Proper law of insurance contracts within the E.C.

22–64   Different rules apply to insurance contracts covering risks situated in the United Kingdom or another Member State of the E. C. The current applicable E.C. Directives are the Second Non-Life Directive of June 1988[75] and the amending Third Non-Life Directive of June 1992.[76] These rules are now embodied in sections 94B and 96A, and Schedule 3A, Part I of the Insurance Companies Act 1982, which are reproduced in Appendix 11, below, to which reference should be made. The rules govern insurance contracts relating to the following commercial risks dealt with in this book:

   (i)   the insurance of land vehicles, including motor vehicles;
   (ii) goods in transit;
   (iii) insurance against loss or damage arising out of fire and natural forces;
   (iv) damage to property;

---

[71] *Rees & Rees v. Mabco Ltd and Eagle Star Insurance Co. Ltd* [1998] T.L.R. 806, CA.
[72] [1967] 1 W.L.R. 898 at 909, CA.
[73] [1966] 1 W.L.R. 1334, CA.
[74] Rome Convention (Contracts) (Applicable Law) Act 1990, Sched. 1.
[75] [1988] O.J. L172/1.
[76] [1992] O.J. L228/1.

    (v) use of motor vehicles, including third party risks and carrier's liability;

    (vi) general third party liability insurance;

    (vii) credit insurance;

    (viii) miscellaneous financial loss insurance, *e.g.* business interruption insurance.

The law applicable to the above contracts is set out in Schedule 3A of the 1982 Act, and depends upon where the risk is situated, although the parties to a goods in transit insurance contract may choose any law.[77] The situation of the risk is governed by section 96A of the 1982 Act. Where the insurance relates to buildings, or both buildings and contents, the risk is situated in the Member State in which the property is situated.[78] In respect of vehicle insurance, the risk is situated in the Member State of registration of the vehicle.[79] For all other relevant insurances, the situation of the risk is determined by the habitual residence of the policyholder if it is an individual,[80] or, if a company, by the Member State in which the company has its head office or branch or agency[81] to which the policy relates.[82]   **22–65**

Where the policyholder has his habitual residence or central administration within the same Member State as where the risk is situated, the law applicable to the contract is either the law of that Member State, or the law chosen by the parties if the law of that Member State allows.[83] Otherwise, the parties may choose to apply the law of the Member State where either the risk is situated, or where the policyholder has his habitual residence or central administration.[84] Where the insurance covers two or more risks relating to the business of the policyholder in more than one Member State, the choice of applicable law is extended to that of any such Member State, or the Member State where the policyholder has his habitual residence or central administration.[85] Where the above provisions allow the parties to exercise a choice of law, but they fail to do this with reasonable certainty in the terms of the insurance contract, or no choice is made, then the contract will be governed by the law of the Member State with which it is most closely connected.[86]   **22–66**

Jurisdiction of the English courts

In respect of civil and commercial matters,[87] this is now governed by the 1968 Brussels Convention, which was incorporated into English law from January 1, 1987, under the Civil Jurisdiction and Judgments Act 1982. It is beyond the scope of this work to provide anything other than a synopsis   **22–67**

---

[77] Insurance Companies Act 1982, Sched. 3A(1)(6).

[78] *ibid.*, s.96A(3)(a).

[79] *ibid.*, s.96A(3)(b).

[80] *ibid.*, s.96A(3)(d)(i).

[81] *ibid.*, s.96A(2).

[82] *ibid.*, s.96A(3)(d)(ii).

[83] *ibid.*, Sched. 3A 1(1); English law does so allow.

[84] *ibid.*, Sched. 3A 1(2).

[85] *ibid.*, Sched. 3A 1(3).

[86] *ibid.*, Sched. 3A 2(2).

[87] Brussels Convention 1968, Art. 1.

of the law in this area. It should be noted that the court is deprived of its common law jurisdiction to stay proceedings on the ground of *forum non conveniens* in respect of any action within the scope of the Civil Jurisdiction and Judgments Acts 1982 and 1991.[88] All Member States of the E.C. are contracting States under the Brussels Convention, and EFTA States may join the Brussels Convention regime under the Lugano Convention.[89] The general rule is that persons domiciled in a Contracting State may be sued either in the courts of that State, or, under the Convention, in the courts of another State. Where the English court is given specific jurisdiction to determine an insurance contract dispute under the Brussels and Lugano Conventions, proceedings may be commenced in England or Wales against a defendant outside England or Wales who is domiciled in a Contracting State. Permission of the Court to serve outside England or Wales is not needed provided there are no existing proceedings between the parties in Scotland, Northern Ireland, or another Contracting State.[90] A Scottish company which carries on business in England or Wales can be served at its principal place of business in England or Wales provided a copy of the claim form is sent to its registered office in Scotland.[91] Also, a company not registered in Great Britain, but with a branch in Great Britain, may be served within the jurisdiction in respect of the business of that branch,[92] or any matter,[93] by service on that branch. Such a company with a place of business[94] within the jurisdiction can be served within the jurisdiction at that place of business in respect of any matter.[95]

Special jurisdiction

22–68   The courts of England and Wales have jurisdiction under the Conventions to determine a claim in the following cases where the defendant insurer is not domiciled[96] within the jurisdiction:

(i) a counterclaim arising out of the same contract if the insurer has commenced proceedings in England or Wales[97];

(ii) if the dispute arises out of the operations of an insurer's branch, agency or other establishment[98] which is situated in England or Wales[99];

---

[88] *S. & W. Bersiford plc v. New Hampshire Insurance Co.* [1990] 2 Q.B. 631; *Arkwright Mutual Insurance Co. Ltd v. Bryanston Insurance Co. Ltd* [1990] 2 Q.B. 649.

[89] Effected by the Civil Jurisdiction and Judgments Act 1991.

[90] CPR, Pt 6, r.19(1).

[91] Companies Act 1985, s.725(2) and (3).

[92] *ibid.*, s.694A.

[93] CPR, Pt 6, r.2(2); *Sea Assets Ltd v. PT Garuda Indonesia* [2000] 4 All E.R. 371.

[94] See *Re Oriel* [1986] 1 W.L.R. 180; *Cleveland Museum of Art v. Capricorn International SA* [1990] 2 Lloyd's Rep. 166.

[95] Companies Act 1985, s.695.

[96] A company or association is domiciled in the State where it was incorporated and has its registered office, or from which its central management and control is exercised; Art. 53 and s.42 of the Conventions and Civil Jurisdiction and Judgments Act 1982.

[97] *ibid.*, Arts 6(3) and 11.

[98] An organ or business presence which is itself an extension or emanation of the insurer's own business and subject to its general control, *New Hampshire Insurance Co. v. Strabag Bau* [1990] 2 Lloyd's Rep. 61 at 69, *per* Potter J.

[99] Conventions and Civil Jurisdiction and Judgments Act 1982, Arts. 5(5), 7 and 8.

(iii) if the claimant policyholder is domiciled in England or Wales[1];

(iv) where proceedings are brought in England or Wales against a leading insurer, against a co-insurer[2];

(v) if the harmful event giving rise to a claim under a liability insurance, or an insurance on immoveable property, occurred in England and Wales[3];

(vi) if the insured is sued in England or Wales by an injured party, the liability insurer can be joined in C.P.R. Part 20 proceedings[4]; and

(vii) if jurisdiction is conferred on the courts of England and Wales in the body of the insurance contract.[5]

---

[1] *ibid.*, Art. 8(2).
[2] *ibid.*, Art. 8(3).
[3] *ibid.*, Art. 9.
[4] *ibid.*, Art 10.
[5] *ibid.*, Arts 12(2) and 17.

APPENDIX 1

THE CO-OPERATIVE INSURANCE SOCIETY ("CIS") COMMERCIAL COMBINED POLICY

Note: Words or expressions shown in italics are defined in the Definition of Terms at the end of this Section.

SECTION ONE

PUBLIC LIABILITY

What IS Insured

A. Legal Liability

1. *Legal Liability* arising in connection with the *Business*. **A1–01**
   The insurance extends to include *Legal Liability* arising in connection with the *Business*

   (i) from an event occurring outside the Geographical Limits, caused by

       (a) you or your directors, partners or *Employees* while temporarily outside the *Geographical Limits*
       (b) *Products* supplied from within the *Geographical Limits*

   (ii) under Section 3 of the Defective Premises Act 1972 or Article 5 of the Defective Premises (Northern Ireland) Order 1975 in connection with any premises disposed of by you which were prior to disposal owned by you, provided that the liability is not insured under another policy

   (iii) from loss of or damage to

       (a) any building, including its contents, temporarily in your custody or control or that of your directors, partners or Employees (but not owned, hired, let or rented by you) for the purposes of carrying out work
       (b) any building (including landlord's fixtures and fittings therein) hired, let or rented to you
       (c) directors' or *Employees'* property
       (d) customers' or visitors' property while temporarily on your premises (except property for alteration, cleaning, inspection, repair, servicing or storage).

We will not pay more than £2,000,000 in respect of all events

    (a)   arising from any one cause or
    (b)   occurring in any one Period of Insurance attributable to

        (i)   *Products*
       (ii)   *Pollution or Contamination*

2.   Costs and expenses incurred with our consent, including the cost of representation at any Coroner's Court, Fatal Accident Inquiry or Court of Summary Jurisdiction.

B. Additional Costs

A1–02 Costs and expenses incurred with our consent by you or your directors, partners of *Employees* in defending *Actions* arising in connection with the *Business* under

       (i)   the Health and Safety at Work etc. Act 1974, the Health and Safety Inquiries (Procedure) Regulations 1975 and the Health and Safety at Work (Northern Ireland) Order 1978
      (ii)   Part II of the Consumer Protection Act 1987
    (iii)   the Food Safety Act 1990 and the Food Safety (Northern Ireland) Order 1991

    provided that you give written notice to us immediately you have knowledge of an impending *Action* or any circumstances which might give rise to an *Action*.
    We will not pay more than £250,000 in respect of all Actions arising under the same Act in any one Period of Insurance

What IS NOT Insured

A.

A1–03   (a)   *Excluded Events.*
    (b)   Liability arising from

       (i)   the use by you or on your behalf of any aircraft, hovercraft, train, watercraft or *Road Vehicle*
      (ii)   advice, design, specification or treatment provided for a fee by or through you or your directors, partners or *Employees*
    (iii)   the direct export of any *Products* to the United States of America or Canada
    (iv)   *Gradual Pollution.*

    (c)   Liability arising from loss of or damage to

       (i)   material property owned by you
      (ii)   material property in your custody or control or that of your directors, partners or *Employees*, other than as insured under 1 (iii)
    (iii)   *Contract Works*
    (iv)   that part of any material property on which you or anyone acting on your behalf is or has been working if the loss or damage results directly from such work.

    (d)   Any claim in respect of

       (i)   loss of or damage to *Products*
      (ii)   the cost of recalling, altering, repairing, replacing or making any refund in respect of *Products* or *Contract Works*.

(e) Liability which arises only because of an agreement relating to

    (i) the sale or supply of *Products*

    (ii) a building hired, let or rent to you.

(f) Liquidated, punitive or exemplary damages, fines or penalties.

(g) Any claim which arises from an action brought in a court of law in the United States of America or Canada or in a country which operates under the laws of the United States of America or Canada, or from any proceedings to enforce a judgement in such an action.

B.

(a) Fines or penalties.   A1–04

(b) Any claim which arises from a deliberate act or omission by you or your directors, partners or *Employees*.

(c) Any claim where the *Action* is solely in connection with the health and safety of any *Employee*.

Additional Parties

If more than one party is named as Policyholder in the Schedule the insurance pro-   A1–05
vided by this Section will apply separately to each party.

At your request this insurance will also apply to

    (i) your directors, partners or *Employees* against any liability for which you would have been entitled to indemnity under this Section had the claim been made against you

    (ii) any officer or member of your canteen, social, sports, educational or welfare organisations or first aid, fire and ambulance services against any liability arising in their respective capacities

    (iii) any principal for whom you are carrying out a contract for the performance of work but only to the extent required by the contract

    (iv) the owner of plant hired-in by you but only to the extent of the conditions of hire.

We will not pay in total to all parties indemnified under this Section more than the monetary limits specified in the Section.

Endorsements

Operative only when the endorsement number is shown in the Specification under the heading "Endorsements Operative".

PL.1—Fire Precautions

This section does not insure liability arising from the use by you or your directors,   A1–06
partners or *Employees*, away from your premises, of any trade process or equipment involving the generation or application of heat unless

    (a) suitable portable fire extinguishers in full working order and complying with British Standard 5423 are made available at each area of work

    (b) all reasonable precautions are taken to prevent the outbreak of fire.

PL.2—Builders and Allied Trades

This Section does not insure liability arising from   A1–07

    (a)   demolition except demolition by you or under your supervision of

       (i)   buildings or parts of buildings, not more than 10 metres in height, where the work forms part of a contract for reconstruction, alteration or repair by you

      (ii)   other structures not more than 4 metres in height and not forming part of any building

    (b)   the construction, alteration, maintenance or repair of blast furnaces, bridges, chimney shafts, colliery overhead winding gear, cranes, dams, docks, gasholders, hangars, reservoirs, steeples, towers and viaducts

    (c)   piling, tunnelling, mining, work in tunnels or mines or the making of any excavations exceeding in any part a depth of 5 metres.

    (d)   the use of explosives.

PL.3—Hot Bitumen

A1–08   This Section does not insure liability arising from the use of hot bitumen, tar or asphalt.

PL.4—Member to Member Liability

A1–09   At your request the insurance provided by subsection A of this Section will apply separately to each member of your organisation provided that the member is not insured under another policy.

    We will not pay in total to all parties indemnified under the subsection more than the monetary limits specified in the subsection.

PL.5—Motor Traders

A1–10   This Section does not insure liability arising from

    (a)   the repair, servicing, inspection, maintenance, alteration or renovation of a customer's trailer or motor vehicle

    (b)   the sale, storage or supply of any trailer or motor vehicle or fuel for a trailer or motor vehicle.

PL.6—Treatment

A1–11   Subsection A 1) of this Section extends to include *Legal Liability* arising in connection with the *Business* from advice or treatment in respect of hairdressing, manicure, pedicure, facial and body massage, eyebrow plucking and shaping, ear piercing, transion slimming, the removal of hair by electrolysis, the use of make-up, oils and waxes, the use of sunbeds or the use of exercise equipment, subject to any relevant monetary limit specified in the subsection.

    This extension does not insure liability

    (a)   specifically excluded from subsection A of this Section (except as amended by this extension)

    (b)   arising from

       (i)   treatment carried out by any trainee unless working under the direct supervision of an experienced person

      (ii)   preparations supplied or used by you which are manufactured or made-up by you or to your order or from any formula supplied by you.

PL.7—Installations

A1–12   This Section does not insure any claim which arises from the failure of any intruder alarm, fire alarm or sprinkler or other security or protection system correctly to perform its intended function.

Claims Settlement Provisions

General

We will not be liable to make a payment under more than one Section or subsec-   **A1–13**
tion of this Policy in respect of loss of or damage to the same property caused by
the same event.

Legal Liability

We will settle a claim for damages by payment on the basis of the liability incurred,   **A1–14**
subject to any relevant monetary limit specified in this Section.

For the purpose of any claim settlement we may at any time at our option pay
you the maximum amount specified in this Section (less any sums already paid) or
any smaller amount for which the claim or claims may be settled. We will then be
under no further liability in respect of the claim or claims except for costs and
expenses incurred prior to the payment.

Definition of Terms

Each of the following words and expressions is given a specific meaning which   **A1–15**
applies wherever it appears in *italics* in this Section or in CAPITAL LETTERS in
the specification or any typed Endorsements for this Section.

Action(s): means legal proceedings (including appeal arising out of any prosecution, inquiry, emergency control order, forfeiture, improvement notice, order
to warn, prohibition notice, prohibition order or suspension notice.

Business: means the Business specified in the Schedule including

  (i) the ownership, occupation, repair, maintenance and decoration of your
       property in connection with the Business
 (ii) the provision and management of canteens, social, sports, education
       and welfare organisations for the benefit of your *Employees* and first
       aid, fire and ambulance services in connection with the Business
(iii) private work undertaken by an *Employee*, with your consent, for you or
       for your directors or partners.

Contract Works: means

  (i) works executed or in the course of execution, including materials and
       plant, in connection with contracts undertaken by you
 (ii) property which you are required to insure under clause 21.2.1 of the
       JCT Standard Form of Building Contract (1980 Edition), or any clause
       of similar intent in an equivalent contract.

Employee(s): means

  (i) anyone under a contract of service or apprenticeship with you
 (ii) anyone hired or borrowed by you
(iii) anyone engaged under a recognised work experience training scheme
 (iv) any labour master or labour-only sub-contractor or person supplied by
       them, or self-employed person (for labour only)

while working for you in connection with the *Business*.

Excluded Events: means

(i) the manufacture, repair, supply or distribution of aircraft or ships, or, with your specific knowledge, of machinery or components with aviation or marine applications

(ii) the manufacture, making-up, dispensing, supply or distribution of drugs, medicines or pharmaceuticals other than the dispensing, supply or distribution of proprietary preparations in unopened containers as supplied by the manufacturers

(iii) the manufacture, supply or distribution of asbestos or asbestos products, chemicals or petrochemicals of an explosive, toxic or noxious nature, or munitions.

Geographical Limits: means Great Britain, Northern Ireland, the Isle of Man and the Channel Islands.

Gradual Pollution: means *Pollution or Contamination* other than caused by a sudden identifiable unintended and unexpected incident which takes place in its entirety at a specific time and place during the Period of Insurance.

All such pollution or contamination which arises out of one incident will be deemed to have occurred at the time the incident takes place.

Injury: means bodily injury and includes illness, disease and death.

Legal Liability: means your legal liability for damages and claimants' costs and expenses in respect of

(i) accidental *Injury* to any person, not being an *Employee*

(ii) accidental loss of or damage to material property

(iii) accidental obstruction, trespass or nuisance.

Pollution or Contamination: means

(i) all pollution or contamination of buildings or other structures or of water or land or the atmosphere, and

(ii) all *Injury*, loss or damage directly or indirectly caused by such pollution or contamination.

Products: means goods (including their containers) sold, supplied, repaired, serviced, altered, renovated, processed or tested by you in the course of the *Business*.

Road Vehicle: means a mechanically propelled vehicle or any trailer attached to it, used in circumstances to which the Road Traffic Acts apply or for which you insure liability under a more specific policy.

SECTION TWO

EMPLOYERS' LIABILITY

What IS Insured

A. Legal Liability to Employees
1.   Legal Liability to Employees.   **A1–16**
     The insurance extends to include *Legal Liability to Employees* while tem-
porarily outside the *Geographical Limits*.
     We will not pay more than £10,000,000 in respect of all events arising from
any one cause.
     Compulsory Employers' Liability Insurance Laws:
     This insurance complies with the law relating to compulsory insurance of
liability to employees in Great Britain, Northern Ireland, the Isle of Man and
the Channel Islands. If we are obliged to make a payment which we would not
have been liable to make but for such law we will require you to refund the
amount paid.

2.   Costs and expenses incurred with our consent, including the cost of representation at any Coroner's Court, Fatal Accident Inquiry or Court of Summary
Jurisdiction.

B. Health and Safety at Work
Costs and expenses incurred with our consent by you or your directors, partners   **A1–17**
or *Employees* in defending *Actions* arising in connection with the *Business* under
the Health and Safety at Work etc. Act 1974, the Health and Safety Inquiries
(Procedure) Regulations 1975 and the Health and Safety at Work (Northern
Ireland) Order 1978, provided that you give written notice to us immediately you
have knowledge of an impending *Action* or any circumstances which might give
rise to an *Action*.
     We will not pay more than £250,000 in respect of all *Actions* arising in any one
Period of Insurance.

What IS NOT Insured

A.
Any claim which arises from   **A1–18**

     (a)   *Injury* to any *Employee* while working *Offshore*
     (b)   an event in respect of which liability is required to be insured under the
           compulsory motor insurance provisions of the Road Traffic Acts.

B.
     (a)   Fines or penalties.   **A1–19**
     (b)   Any claim which arises from

           (i)   a deliberate act or omission by you or your directors, partners or
                 Employees
           (ii) *Injury* to any *Employee* while working *Offshore*

(iii) an event in respect of which liability is required to be insured under the compulsory motor insurance provisions of the Road Traffic Acts.

(c) Any claim where the *Action* is solely in connection with the health and safety or anyone not an *Employee*.

Additional Parties

A1–20   If more than one party is named as Policyholder in the Schedule the insurance provided under this Section will apply separately to each party.

At your request this insurance will also apply to

(i) your directors, partners or *Employees* against any liability for which you would have been entitled to indemnity under this Section had the claim been made against you

(ii) any officer or member of your canteen, social, sports, educational or welfare organisations or first aid, fire and ambulance services against any liability arising in their respective capacities

(iii) any principal for whom you are carrying out a contract for the performance of work but only to the extent required by the contract

(iv) the owner of plant hired-in by you but only to the extent of the conditions of hire.

We will not pay in total to all parties indemnified under this Section more than the monetary limits specified in the Section.

Endorsements

Operative only when the endoresement number is shown in the Specification under the heading "Endorsements Operative".

CL.1—Woodworking Machinery

A1–21   This Section does not insure liability arising from the use by *Employees* of nonportable powered woodworking machinery.

CL.2—Builders and Allied Trades

A1–22   This Section does not insure liability arising from

(a) demolition except demolition by you or under your supervision of

(i) work forms part of a contract for reconstruction, alteration or repair by you

(ii) other structures not more than 4 metres in height and not forming part of any building

(b) the construction, alteration, maintenance or repair of blast furnaces, bridges, chimney shafts, colliery overhead winding gear, cranes, dams, docks, gasholders, hangars, reservoirs, steeples, towers and viaducts

(c) piling, tunnelling, mining, work in tunnels or mines or the making of any excavations exceeding in any part a depth of 5 metres.

(d) the use of explosives.

Claims Settlement Provisions

We will settle a claim for damages by payment on the basis of the liability **A1–23**
incurred, subject to any relevant monetary limit specified in this Section.

For the purposes of any claim settlement we may at any time at our option pay
you the maximum amount specified in this Section (less any sums already paid) or
any smaller amount for which the claim or claims may be settled. We will then be
under no further liability in respect of the claim or claims except for costs and
expenses incurred prior to the payment.

Definition of Terms

Each of the following words and expressions is given a specific meaning which **A1–24**
applies wherever it appears in *italics* in this Section in the specification or any typed
Endorsements for this Section.

Action(s): means legal proceedings (including appeal) arising out of any prosecution, inquiry.

Business: means the Business specified in the Schedule including

(i)   the ownership, occupation, repair, maintenance and decoration of your
      property in connection with the Business
(ii) the provision and management of canteens, social, sports, education
      and welfare organisations for the benefit of your *Employees* and first
      aid, fire and ambulance services in connection with the Business
(iii) private work undertaken by an *Employee*, with your consent, for you or
      for your directors or partners.

Employee(s): means

(i)   anyone under a contract of service or apprenticeship with you
(ii) anyone hired or borrowed by you
(iii) anyone engaged under a recognised work experience training scheme
(iv) any labour master or labour-only sub-contractor or person supplied by
      them, or self-employed person (for labour only)

while working for you in connection with the *Business*.

Geographical Limits: means Great Britain, Northern Ireland, the Isle of Man and
the Channel Islands.

Injury: means bodily injury and includes illness, disease and death.

Legal Liability to Employees: means your legal liability for damages and claimants'
costs and expenses in respect of *Injury* to any *Employee*.

Offshore: means from the time when the *Employee* embarks onto a conveyance at
the point of final departure to an offshore rig or offshore platform until such time
as the *Employee* disembarks from a conveyance onto land upon the *Employee's*
final return from the offshore rig or offshore platform.

SECTION THREE

FIRE AND SPECIAL PERILS

What IS Insured

A. Property: Insured Perils

A1–25   Loss of or damage to Property described in the Specification, caused by an *Insured Peril*.

We will not pay more than the relevant Sum Insured shown against each Item in the Specification in respect of any one event less the *Excess*, if applicable, specified in the Claims Settlement Provisions.

B. Loss of Rent

A1–26   Loss of *Rent* incurred during any period in which the *Buildings* are made unfit for occupation by any of the events insured under subsection A of this Section.

We will not pay more than the Sum Insured shown in the Specification in respect of any one event.

C. Contents Temporarily Removed

A1–27   Loss of or damage to machinery, fixtures, and fittings while temporarily removed from the *Premises* for the purpose of cleaning, repair or renovation, caused by an *Insured Peril*.

We will not pay more than 15% of the Sum Insured shown against *Other Contents* in the Specification in respect of any one event, less the *Excess*, if applicable, specified in the Claims Settlement Provisions.

D. Deeds

A1–28   Loss of or damage to *Deeds* caused by an *Insured Peril*, but only for their value as materials and the cost of labour expended in reproducing them.

We will not pay more than £2,500 in respect of any one event, less the *Excess*, if applicable, specified in the Claims Settlement Provisions.

E. Personal Effects

A1–29   Loss of or damage to *Personal Effects* caused by an *Insured Peril*.

We will not pay more than £500 in respect of any one person or more than £2,500 in respect of any one event, less the *Excess*, if applicable, specified in the Claims Settlement Provisions.

F. Underground Services

A1–30   Accidental damage to underground pipes, drains, ducts and cables (including their inspection covers) serving the *Buildings*, for which you are legally responsible.

We will not pay more than £10,000 in respect of any one event, less the *Excess*, if applicable, specified in the Claims Settlement Provisions.

G. Tenant's Liability

A1–31   If you are the tenant of the *Premises* and not the owner, damage to the *Premises* caused by an *Insured Peril* provided that you are legally responsible for the damage under the tenancy agreement, hire agreement or lease.

We will not pay more than

    (a)   the aggregate of the Sums Insured shown against *Stock* and *Other Contents* in the Specification or

    (b)   £10,000

whichever is the less, in respect of any one event,less the *Excess*, if applicable, specified in the Claims Settlement Provisions.

What IS NOT Insured

A.

    (a)   *Pollution or Contamination*   A1–32
    (b)   Loss of or damage to *Money*.
    (c)   Loss of or damage to motor vehicles and their accessories.
    (d)   Loss of or damage to dynamos, motors or any portion of the electrical apparatus, directly caused by its own overrunning, excessive pressure, short circuiting or self heating.

C.

    (a)   *Pollution or Contamination*   A1–33
    (b)   Loss of or damage to motor vehicles and their accessories
    (c)   Loss of or damage to dynamos, motors or any portion of the electrical apparatus, directly caused by its own overrunning, excessive pressure, short circuiting or self heating.

D.
Pollution or Contamination   A1–34

E.

    (a)   *Pollution or Contamination*   A1–35
    (b)   Loss of or damage to *Money*
    (c)   Loss of or damage to motor vehicles and their accessories.

F.
Pollution or Contamination   A1–36

G.

    (a)   *Pollution or Contamination*   A1–37
    (b)   Loss of or damage to dynamos, motors or any portion of the electrical apparatus, directly caused by its own overrunning, excessive pressure, short circuiting or self heating.

Indemnity to Contracting Purchaser
When you have agreed to sell your interest in the *Buildings*, the buyer will have the   A1–38
benefit of this insurance until completion of the sale unless the buyer is insured
under another policy.

Endorsements

A1–39   Operative only when the endoresement number is shown in the Specification under
the heading "Endoresements Operative".

FT.1—Storm, Flood and Escape of Water
A1–40   The definition of the term Insured Peril extends to include
8.   Storm or flood, Excluding

   (a)   loss or damage

      (i)   caused by frost, subsidence, heave or landslip
      (ii)   attributable solely to change in the water table level

   (b)   loss of or damage to movable property in the open, fences and gates.

9.   Escape of water from any automatic sprinkler installation or other fixed water
or heating system (but not loss of or damage to the system itself), excluding
loss or damage occurring while the *Buildings* are empty or not in use.

FT.2—Office Machines
A1–41   This Section extends to include accidental damage, other than caused by an
Insured Peril, to Office Machines in the Premises.
   We will not pay more than £5,000 in respect of any one event, Less the Excess
specified in the Claims Settlement Provisions.
   This extension does not insure

   (a)   loss of or damage to dynamos, motors or any portion of the electrical
         apparatus, directly caused by its own overrunning, excessive pressure,
         short circuiting or self heating
   (b)   damage caused by

      (i)   storm, flood, escape of water from any sprinkler installation or
            other fixed water or heating system, theft or attempted theft
      (ii)   wear and tear, depreciation, fungus, insects, vermin, atmospheric
            or climatic conditions, the action of light or any gradually operat-
            ing cause
      (iii)   any process of cleaning, altering, repairing, restoring, erecting,
            testing, servicing, maintaining or dismantling

   (c)   mechanical or electrical failure
   (d)   breakage of electrical bulbs or tubes unless the apparatus of which they
         form part is damaged at the same time
   (e)   loss of or damage to audio, video or computer tapes, cassettes, records
         or discs.

FT.3—Refrigerated Stock
A1–42   This Section extends to include loss of or damage to Stock in refrigerated cabinets,
freezers or cold rooms in the Premises caused by deterioration, contamination or
putrefaction resulting from

   (a)   rise or fall in temperature due to

      (i)   breakdown of or unforeseen damage to the equipment (including
            non-operation of any thermostatic or automatic controlling device
            forming part of the equipment or its installation) other than
            cuased by an *Insured Peril*

(ii) accidental failure of the public electricity or gas supply not occasioned by the deliberate act of the supply authority

(b) accidental escape of refrigerant or refrigerant fumes.

We will not pay more than £2,500 in respect of any one event, less the *Excess* specified in the Claims Settlement Provisions.

We will not pay any claim under this extension unless the equipment containing the *Stock* which is the subject of the claim is maintained in good working order.

Claims Settlement Provisions

General

(i) We will not be liable to make a payment under more than one Section or subsection of this Policy in respect of loss of or damage to the same property caused by the same event. **A1–43**

(ii) Excess: An *Excess* of £100 will apply to each claim for loss of or damage to property which is not a claim for loss or damage caused by *Insured Peril* 1, 2, 3 or 4.

If a claim is made under more than one Section or subsection of this Policy for loss or damage caused at the same time by the same event only one *Excess* will apply.

(iii) Subject to Average: If at the time of loss or damage the Sum Insured on any Item stated to be Subject to Average is less than the value of the Property or *Rent* insured under the Item you will be considered to be your own insurer for the difference and will bear a rateable proportion of the loss or damage.

Property

We will settle a claim for loss of or damage to property on the following basis by payment or, at our option, by replacement, reinstatement or repair, subject to any relevant monetary limit specified in this Section. **A1–44**

(i) Buildings

(a) If repair or replacement is carried out, the cost, including *Fees*, necessarily incurred in repairing or replacing that part of the *Buildings* which is destroyed or damaged. A deduction will be made for any depreciation and wear and tear if

(i) the *Buildings* do not have walls constructed wholly or brick, stone or concrete

(ii) that part of the *Buildings* which is the subject of the claim is not in a good state of repair at the time of the destruction or damage

(b) If repair or replacement is not carried out, what it would cost to settle a claim in the terms of (i)(a) above but with a deduction for any depreciation and wear and tear.

(ii) Fixed Glass: The cost (including alarm foil, lettering, painting, embossing, silvering and other ornamental work on the glass) of replacing the broken glass with glass of similar quality.

(iii) Other Property: The cost of repair of or replacement as new at current prices if an item is totally lost or destroyed. A deduction will be made for any depreciation and wear and tear

(a) in respect of *Stock*

    (b)   if that part of the property which is the subject of the claim is not maintained in good condition at the time of the loss or damage

    (c)   if repair or replacement is not carried out.

For the purpose of any claim settlement replacement, reinstatement or repair as near as is reasonably practicable will be sufficient even though the former appearance or condition of the property may not be precisely restored.

We will not be liable for the replacement of or work on any undamaged items or remaining parts solely because they form part of a set, suite, group or collection of articles of a similar nature, colour, pattern or design.

Rent

A1–45   We will settle a claim for loss of *Rent* by payment on the basis of the loss of *Rent* for those parts of the *Buildings* unfit for occupation. We will not pay more than that proportion of the Sum Insured on *Rent* shown in the Specification which the period necessary for the reinstatement of the *Buildings* bears to the period shown in the Specification.

Definition of Terms

A1–46   Each of the following words and expressions is given a specific meaning which applies wherever it appears in *italics* in this Section, in the Specification for this Section or in any Endorsement to this Section.

Buildings: means the principal building and its outbuildings, including landlord's fixtures and fittings therein and walls, gates and fences, at the Risk Address specified in the Schedule.

Business: means the Business specified in the Schedule.

Deeds: means deeds, documents, manuscripts, business books, computer system records, patterns, models, moulds, plans, drawings and designs, owned by you or for which you are legally responsible, in the *Premises*.

Employee(s): means

    (i)   anyone under a contract of service or apprenticeship with you

    (ii) anyone hired or borrowed by you

    (iii) anyone engaged under a recognised work experience training scheme

while working for you in connection with the *Business*.

Excess: means the amount of the claim which is to be borne by you. We will deduct that amount from the amount payable in respect of the claim after the application of any relevant monetary limits specified in this Section.

Fees: means

    (i)   reasonable architects', surveyors' and legal fees but not fees incurred in preparing any claim

    (ii) costs incurred with our consent in removing debris, dismantling, demolishing, shoring-up or propping of the destroyed or damaged portion or portions of the property insured but not costs or expenses

        (a)   incurred in removing debris except from the site of such property destroyed or damaged and the area immediately adjacent to the site

      (b)   arising from pollution or contamination of property not insured by this Section

  (iii)   the additional cost of reinstating the damaged parts of the *Buildings* incurred solely to comply with any statutory requirement, European Community legislation or local authority bye-law ut not the cost of compliance with any notice served on you before the damage occurred or for which there is an existing requirement which has to be implemented within a given period. We will not pay under this extension more than 15% of the Sum Insured on *Buildings* or in total under any item of this Section more than its sum insured.

Insured Peril: means

1.   Fire, excluding loss of or damage to property undergoing any process involving the application of heat.
2.   Lightning.
3.   Explosion, excluding loss or damage resulting from the bursting of any apparatus (other than boilers used for domestic purposes only), owned by you or under your control, in which internal pressure is due to steam only.
4.   Earthquake, subterranean fire or volcanic eruption.
5.   (i)   Aircraft or other aerial devices or articles dropped from them.
      (ii) Impact with the *Buidlings* by trains, road vehicles or animals.
6.   Riot, civil commotion, labour and political disturbances, excluding loss or damage in Northern Ireland.
7.   Malicious persons, excluding
      (a)   loss of or damage to glass
      (b)   loss or damage caused by theft
      (c)   loss or damage occuring while the *Premises* are empty or not in use
      (d)   loss or damage in Northern Ireland.

Money: means cash, bank notes, cheques, girocheques, postal orders, current postage stamps, National Insurance stamps, holidays-with-pay stamps, trading stamps, National Savings certificates and stamps, premium bonds, luncheon vouchers, gift tokens, consumer redemption vouchers, credit card sales vouchers and V.A.T. purchase invoices.

Office Machines: means calculators, cash registers, computers, facsimile and telex machines, franking machines, internal public address, radio and telephone systems, photocopiers, tape and video recorders, televisions, typewriters and word processors, other than *Stock*, owned by you or for which you are legally responsible and used by you in connection with the *Business*.

Other Contents: means

  (i)   machinery (including *Office Machines*), furniture, fixtures, fittings, internal decorations and all other contents in the *Premises*, but not landlord's fixtures and fittings, *Stock*, *Deeds* and *Personal Effects*
  (ii) shop fronts and other tenant's improvements to the *Premises*
 (iii) outdoor blinds, signs, aerials and satellite dishes, attached to the *Premises*.

Personal Effects: means the personal effects of your directors, *Employees*, customers and visitors, while on the *Premises*, but not property insured under another policy.

Pollution or Contamination: means loss or damage caused by pollution or contamination except loss of or damage to the property insured (unless otherwise excluded) caused by

(a)   pollution or contamination which itself results from an *Insured Peril*
(b)   an *Insured Peril* which itself results from pollution or contamination.

Premises: means those parts of the *Buildings* occupied by you in connection with the *Business*.

Rent: means rent receivable in respect of the *Buildings*.

Stock: means stock and materials in trade and goods in trust.

SECTION FOUR

THEFT

What IS Insured

A. Property: Theft
A1–47   Loss of or damage to Property described in the Specification, caused by *Theft*.
We will not pay more than the relevant Sum Insured shown against each item in the Specification in respect of any one event, less the *Excess* specified in the Claims Settlement Provisions.

B. Deeds
A1–48   Loss of or damage to *Deeds* caused by *Theft*, but only for their value as materials and the cost of labour expended in reproducing them.
We will not pay more than £2,500 in respect of any one event, less the *Excess* specified in the Claims Settlement Provisions.

C. Personal Effects
A1–49   Loss of or damage to *Personal Effects* caused by *Theft*.
We will not pay more than £500 in respect of any one person or more than £2,500 in respect of any one event, less the *Excess* specified in the Claims Settlement Provisions.

D. Buildings
A1–50   Damage to *Buildings* caused by *Theft*, provided that

(i)   the damage is not insured under another policy and
(ii)   if you are the tenant of the *Premises* and not the owner, you are legally responsible for the damage under the tenancy agreement, hire agreement or lease.

We will not pay ore than £10,000 in respect of any one event, less the *Excess* specified in the Claims Settlement Provisions.

E. Theft of Keys
The cost necessarily incurred in replacing and installing locks in the *Premises*   **A1–51**
(including the operating mechanism of any key-operated intruder alarm system) if
the keys to the locks are taken from the *Premises* by *Theft* or stolen from the
home(s) of their authorised holder(s).

We will not pay more than £500 in respect of any one event, less the *Excess* specified in the Claims Settlement Provisions.

What IS NOT Insured

A.
(a) *Excluded Events.*   **A1–52**
(b) Loss of or damage to *Money.*
(c) Loss of or damage to motor vehicles and their accessories.
(d) Loss of or damage to movable property in the open.

B.
Excluded Events.   **A1–53**

C.
(a) *Excluded Events.*   **A1–54**
(b) Loss of or damage to *Money.*
(c) Loss of or damage to motor vehicles and their accessories.
(d) Loss of or damage to movable property in the open.

D.
Excluded Events.   **A1–55**

E.
Costs incurred following   **A1–56**

(a) Excluded Events
(b) the theft from the *Premises* outside *Business Hours*, of keys to any
     intruder alarm, safe or strongroom.

Endorsements

Operative only when the endorsement number is shown in the Specification under   **A1–57**
the heading "Endorsements Operative".

B.1 (Rev)—Intruder Alarm
This Section does not insure loss or damage following entry or attempted entry to   **A1–58**
or exit from the *Premises* by forcible and violent means unless

(a) the *Premises* are protected by an *Intruder Alarm System* installed as
     agreed with us
(b) the *Intruder Alarm System* is maintained in full and efficient working
     order under a *Maintenance Contract*
(c) our written agreement is obtained for alteration to or substitution of
     any part of the *Intruder Alarm System* or the *Maintenance Contract*

(d) our agreement is obtained before the *Alarmed Premises* are left without at least one *Responsible Person* in attendance

    (i) except where the *Intruder Alarm System* is set in its entirety with the means of communication used to transmit signals in full operation

    (ii) if the police authority have withdrawn their response to alarm calls

(e) all keys to the *Intruder Alarm System* are removed from the *Premises* when they are left unattended

(f) you maintain secrecy of codes for the operation of the *Intruder Alarm System* and no details of these are left on the *Premises*

(g) you appoint at least two *Keyholders* and lodge written details (which must be kept up to date) with the alarm company and police authorities

(h) if the *Intruder Alarm System* is activated or the means of communication is interrupted during any period that the *Intruder Alarm System* is set, a *Keyholder* attends the *Premises* as soon as reasonably possible and does not leave them until the provisions set out in (d) above have been complied with, except where specifically agreed by us in writing

(i) you notify us as soon as possible and in any event not later than 10 a.m. on our next working day if you receive any notification

    (i) from the police authority that response to alarm signals or calls from the *Intruder Alarm System* may be restricted or withdrawn

    (ii) from a local authority or magistrate imposing any requirement for abatement of a nuisance

    (iii) that the *Intruder Alarm System* cannot be returned to, or maintained in, full working order and you comply with any subsequent requirements stipulated by us.

B.2—Entry to or Exit from the Buildings

A1–59 The definition of the term *Theft* is amended to mean theft or attempted theft, involving

    (i) violent and forcible entry to or exit from the buildings in which the *Premises* are situated or

    (ii) assault or violence or threat of assault or violence to

        (a) you or your directors, partners or *Employees*

        (b) any member of your family or a director's, partner's or *Employee's* family

        (c) any customer while on the *Premises*.

Claims Settlement Provisions

General

A1–60 (i) We will not be liable to make a payment under more than one Section or subsection of this Policy in respect of loss of or damage to the same property caused by the same event.

(ii) *Excess*: An *Excess* of £100 will apply to each claim.

    If a claim is made under more than one Section or subsection of this Policy for loss or damage caused at the same time by the same event only one *Excess* will apply.

(iii) *Subject to Average*: If at the time of loss or damage the Sum Insured on any Item stated to be Subject to Average is less than the value of the Property Insured under the Item you will be considered to be your own insurer for the difference and will bear a rateable proportion of the loss or damage.

Property

We will settle a claim for loss of or damage to property on the following basis by payment or, at our option, by replacement, reinstatement or repair, subject to any relevant monetary limit specified in this Section.

A1–61

   (i) *Buildings*: The cost, including *Fees*, necessarily incurred in repairing or replacing that part of the *Buildings* which is destroyed or damaged.

   (ii) *Fixed Glass*: The cost (including alarm foil, lettering, painting, embossing, silvering and other ornamental work on the glass) of replacing the broken glass with glass of similar quality.

   (iii) *Other Property*: The cost of repair or of replacement as new at current prices if an item is totally lost or destroyed. A deduction will be made for any depreciation and wear and tear

     (a) in respect of *Stock*
     (b) if that part of the property which is the subject of the claim is not maintained in good condition at the time of the loss or damage
     (c) if repair or replacement is not carried out.

For the purpose of any claim settlement replacement, reinstatement or repair as near as is reasonably practicable will be sufficient even though the former appearance or condition of the property may not be precisely restored.

We will not be liable for the replacement of or work on any undamaged items or remaining parts solely because they form part of a set, suite, group or collection of articles of a similar nature, colour, pattern or design.

Definition of Terms

Each of the following words and expressions is given a specific meaning which applies wherever it appears in *italics* in this Section, in the Specification for this Section or in any Endorsement to this Section.

A1–62

Alarmed Premises: means the *Premises* or those portions of the *Premises* protected by the *Intruder Alarm System*.

Buildings: means the principal building and its outbuildings, including landlord's fixtures and fittings therein and walls, gates and fences, at the Risk Address specified in the Schedule.

Business: means the Business specified in the Schedule.

Business Hours: menas the period during which you or your directors, partners or *Employees* are in or on the *Premises* in connection with the *Business*.

Deeds: means deeds, documents, manuscripts, business books, computer system records, patterns, models, moulds, plans, drawings and designs, owned by you or for which you are legally responsible, in the *Premises*.

Employee(s): means

     (i) anyone under a contract of service or apprenticeship with you
     (ii) anyone hired or borrowed by you
     (iii) anyone engaged under a recognised work experience training scheme

while working for you in connection with the *Business*.

Excess: means the amount of the claim which is to be borne by you. We will deduct that amount from the amount payable in respect of the claim after the application of any relevant monetary limits specified in this Section.

Excluded Events: means loss or damage

- (i) caused by theft or attempted theft by, or in collusion with, any of your directors, partners, *Employees* or members of your household
- (ii) occurring while the *Premises* are empty or not in use.

Fees: means

- (i) reasonable architects', surveyors' and legal fees but not fees incurred in preparing any claim
- (ii) costs incurred with our consent in removing debris.

Intruder Alarm System: means an intruder alarm system, comprising all component parts including the means of communication used to transmit signals.

Keyholder(s): means you or any person or keyholding company authorised by you who is available at all times to accept notification of faults or alarm signals relating to the *Intruder Alarm System*, attend, and allow access to the *Premises*.

Maintenance Contract: means a contract to provide both corrective and preventive maintenance with the installing company, as agreed with us.

Money: means cash, bank notes, cheques, girocheques, postal orders, current postage stamps, National Insurance stamps, holidays-with-pay stamps, trading stamps, National Savings certificates and stamps, premium bonds, luncheon vouchers, gift tokens, consumer redemption vouchers, credit card sales vouchers and V.A.T. purchase invoices.

Other Contents: means

- (i) machinery (including office machines), furniture, fixtures, fittings, internal decorations and all other contents in the *Premises*, but not landlord's fixtures and fittings, *Stock*, *Deeds* and *Personal Effects*
- (ii) shop fronts and other tenant's improvements to the *Premises*
- (iii) outdoor blinds, signs, aerials and satellite dishes, attached to the *Premises*

Personal Effects: means the personal effects of your directors, *Employees*, customers and visitors, while on the *Premises*, but not property insured under another policy.

Premises: means those parts of the *Buildings* occupied by you in connection with the *Business*.

Responsible Person: means you or any person authorised by you to be responsible for the security of the *Premises*.

Stock: means stock and materials in trade and goods in trust.

Theft: means theft or attempted theft, involving

- (i) violent and forcible entry to or exit from the *Premises* or
- (ii) assault or violence or threat of assault or violence to

(a) you or your directors, partners or *Employees*
(b) any member of your family or a director's, partner's or *Employee's* family
(c) any customer while on the *Premises*.

SECTION FIVE

BUSINESS INTERRUPTION

What IS Insured

A. Loss of Gross Profit

1. Loss of *Gross Profit* resulting from the *Business* at the *Premises* being inter-   **A1–63**
ferred with in consequence of loss or damage, caused by an *Insured Peril*, of or to

(i) *Property at the Premises*, provided that payment has been made or lia-bility admitted for the loss or damage under either Section Three or Section Four of this Policy

(ii) *Neighbouring Property* (whether the *Premises* or their contents are damaged or not), provided that liability would have been admitted for the loss or damage under either Section Three or Section Four of this Policy, had the loss or damage occurred to *Property at the Premises*.

2. Reasonable charges payable by you to your professional accountants for pro-ducing and certifying the exact amount of loss in connection with a claim under this Section.

We will not pay more than the Sum Insured showed in the Specification in respect of any one event.

What IS NOT Insured

A.
Loss resulting from   **A1–64**

(a) pollution or contamination other than loss resulting from loss of or damage to *Property at the Premises* or *Neighbouring Property* (not otherwise excluded), caused by

(i) pollution or contamination which itself result from an *Insured Peril*

(ii) an *Insured Peril* which itself results from pollution or contamination

(b) deliberate erasure, loss, distortion or corruption of information on computer systems or other records, programs or software

(c) loss of or damage to the property of any supply undertaking from which you obtain electricity, gas, telecommunications or water services, which prevents or hinders the supply of such services to the *Premises*.

Cessation of Interest

A1–65   This Section will be made void immediately if

    (a)   the *Business* is wound up, carried on by a liquidator or receiver, or permanently discontinued or

    (b)   your interest ceases other than by death unless we give our written consent to the contrary.

Claims Settlement Provisions

A1–66   We will settle a claim for loss of *Gross Profit* by payment on the basis of reduction in *Turnover* and increase in cost of working, subject to any relevant monetary limit specified in this Section. We will pay

    (i)   in respect of reduction in *Turnover*, the sum produced by applying the *Rate of Gross Profit* to the amount by which the *Turnover* during the *Indemnity Period* falls short of the *Standard Turnover* because of the loss or damage

    (ii)   in respect of increase in cost of working, reasonable and necessary additional expenditure incurred for the sole purpose of avoiding or diminishing the reduction in *Turnover* which otherwise would have taken place because of the loss or damage, up to the sum produced by applying the *Rate of Gross Profit* to the amount of the reduction so avoided

less any sum saved during the *Indemnity Period* in respect of those charges and expenses of the *Business* payable out of *Gross Profit* which cease or are reduced because of the loss or damage.

If during the *Indemnity Period* goods or services are supplied elsewhere than at the *Premises* for the benefit of the *Business* either by you or by others on your behalf the money paid or payable for them will be brought into account in arriving at the *Turnover* during the *Indemnity Period*.

If the Sum Insured shown in the Specification is less than the sum produced by applying the *Rate of Gross Profit* to the *Annual Turnover*, appropriately adjusted where the *Indemnity Period* exceeds 12 months, you will be considered to be your own insurer for the difference and will bear a rateable proportion of the claim.

Annual Turnover, *Rate of Gross Profit* and *Standard Turnover* will be adjusted as may be necessary to provide for variations in or other circumstances affecting the *Business* so that the adjusted figures represents as far as possible the results which but for the loss or damage would have been obtained during the *Indemnity Period*.

Definition of Terms

A1–67   Each of the following words and expressions is given a specific meaning which applies wherever it appears in italics in this Section, in the Specification for this Section or in any Endorsement to this Section.

Annual Turnover: means *Turnover* during the 12 months immediately before the date of the loss or damage.

Buildings: means the principal building and its outbuildings, including landlord's fixtures and fittings therein and walls, gates and fences, at the Risk Address specified in the Schedule.

Business: means the Business specified in the Schedule.

Gross Profit: means the *Turnover* less the cost price of goods sold or used, exclusive of Value Added Tax to the extent that you are accountable for it to the tax authorities.

Indemnity Period: means the period, beginning with the occurrence of the loss or damage and extending no longer than the Maximum Indemnity Period shown in the Specification, during which the results of the *Business* at the *Premises* are affected because of the loss or damage.

Insured Peril: means any peril for which, at the time of the loss or damage, there is in force insurance under either Section Three or Section Four of this Policy.

Neighbouring Property: means property in the vicinity of the *Premises*, the loss of or damage to which will prevent or hinder the use of or access to the *Premises*.

Premises: means those parts of the *Buildings* occupied by you in connection with the *Business*.

Property at the Premises: means property used by you at the *Premises* for the purpose of the *Business*.

Rate of Gross Profit: means the rate of *Gross Profit* earned on the *Turnover* during the financial year immediately before the date of the loss or damage.

Standard Turnover: means the *Turnover* during that period in the 12 months immediately before the date of the loss or damage which corresponds with the *Indemnity Period*, appropriately adjusted where the *Indemnity Period* exceeds 12 months.

Turnover: means the money paid or payable to you for goods and services supplied in the course of the *Business* at the *Premises*, exclusive of Value Added Tax to the extent that you are accountable for it to the tax authorities.

SECTION SIX

MONEY

What IS Insured

A. Non-negotiable Money
Loss of crossed cheques, crossed girocheques, crossed postal orders, stamped   **A1–68**
National Insurance cards, National Savings certificates, premium bonds, credit card sales vouchers and V.A.T. purchase invoices, owned by you or for which you are legally responsible in connection with the Business.
    We will not pay more than £100,000 in respect of any one event, less the *Excess* specified in the Claims Settlement Provisions.

B. Other Money
Loss of *Money*   **A1–69**

    1.   in the *Premises* during any period in which there is at least one *Responsible Person* in attendance.
        We will not pay more than

(a) £500 for loss from any room left unattended and unlocked unless the *Money* is contained in a locked cupboard, drawer, safe or strongroom and the key is removed from the room

(b) £5,000 in all

in respect of any one event, less the *Excess* specified in the Claims Settlement Provisions.

2. in the *Premises* during any period in which no *Responsible Person* is in attendance.

We will not pay more than

(a) £2,500 in all for loss from locked safes or strongrooms

(b) £500 for any other loss

in respect of any one event, less the *Excess* specified in the Claims Settlement Provisions.

3. in transit or in a bank night safe.

We will not pay more than £5,000 in respect of any one event, less the *Excess* specified in the Claims Settlement Provisions.

4. in your home or in the home of a director, partner or authorised *Employee* of your *Business*.

We will not pay more than £500 in respect of any one event, less the *Excess* specified in the Claims Settlement Provisions.

C. Fraud and Dishonesty: Employees

A1–70

1. Loss of money or goods owned by you or for which you are legally responsible in connection with the *Business*, directly caused by an act of fraud or dishonesty by an *Employee* and committed in the course of the *Employee's* employment by you during the uninterrupted currency of this Section.

We will not pay more than £500 for each *Employee* or £2,500 in all, in respect of all losses discovered in any one Period of Insurance (including any periods allowed for discovery after the termination of this Section), less the *Excess* specified in the Claims Settlement Provisions.

2. Reasonable charges payable by you to your professional accountants for producing and certifying the exact amount of loss in connection with a claim under this subsection.

D. Personal Accident: Assault

A1–71
Benefit, as set out below.

If you or any of your directors, partners or *Employees*, in the course of the *Business*, suffer accidental bodily injury as a direct result of assault with intent to steal *Money* we will pay to the injured person

(i) £5,000 if the injury is, within 12 months of its occurrence, the sole cause of

(a) death or

(b) complete and permanent loss of the sight of an eye or

(c) complete and permanent loss of the use of a hand or foot or

(d) permanent total disablement from attending to business or occupation of any kind.

If the person is under 16 years of age at the time of death we will pay £500 only

(ii) £25 per week for a period of up to 104 weeks from the date of injury during which that injury alone causes temporary total disablement from attending to the person's usual business or occupation.

We will not pay this Benefit in respect of any person who is under 16 years of age at the time of the injury.

We will not pay more than £5,000 for each person in respect of all injuries arising out of any one accident.
   We will also pay

   (iii) up to a total of £250 for related medical expenses which are reasonably and necessarily incurred by the injured person
   (iv) £10 for each 24 hours in hospital, up to a total of £250, if the injury results in the injured person's admission to hospital as an in-patient.

E. Clothing and Personal Effects: Assault
Loss of or damage to clothing and personal effects (including security bags, boxes   **A1–72**
and waistcoats) belonging to you or your directors, partners or authorised *Employees*, as a direct result of assault, in the course of the *Business*, with intent to steal *Money*.
   We will not pay more than £500 for each person in respect of any one event.

What IS NOT Insured

A.
   (a) Loss resulting from a business transaction.   **A1–73**
   (b) Consequential loss, shortage due to errors or omissions, or depreciation in value.
   (c) Loss arising from the fraud or dishonesty of your directors, partners or *Employees* or any member of your household.
   (d) Loss following the use of a combination code, key or duplicate key unless the combination code, key or duplicate key was obtained by violence or threat of violence to its authorised holder or to a member of the holder's family.
   (e) Loss from an unattended vehicle.

B.
Loss specifically included in or excluded from the insurance under subsection A of   **A1–74**
this Section.

C.
   1) (a) Loss arising from any act of fraud or dishonesty by an *Employee*,   **A1–75**
            committed subsequent to the discovery or suspicion of an act of fraud or dishonesty by the same Employee which is the subject of a claim under this subsection.
       (b) Loss discovered more than 18 months after the ending of the *Employee's* employment or of the termination of this Section, whichever occurs first.

Endorsements

Operative only when the endorsement number is shown in the Specification under   **A1–76**
the heading "Endorsements Operative".

CT.1(Rev)—Intruder Alarm:

A1–77   This Section does not insure loss or damage following entry or attempted entry to or exit from the *Premises* by forcible and violent means unless

(a)   the *Premises* are protected by an *Intruder Alarm System* installed as agreed with us

(b)   the *Intruder Alarm System* is maintained in full and efficient working order under a *Maintenance Contract*

(c)   our written agreement is obtained for alteration to or substitution of any part of the *Intruder Alarm System* or the *Maintenance Contract*

(d)   our agreement is obtained before the *Alarmed Premises* are left without at least one *Responsible Person* in attendance

   (i)   except where the *Intruder Alarm System* is set in its entirety with the means of communication used to transmit signals in full operation

   (ii)   if the police authority have withdrawn their response to alarm calls

(e)   all keys to the *Intruder Alarm System* are removed from the *Premises* when they are left untattended

(f)   you maintain secrecy of codes for the operation of the *Intruder Alarm System* and no details of these are left on the *Premises*

(g)   you appoint at least two *Keyholders* and lodge written details (which must be kept up to date) with the alarm company and police authorities

(h)   if the *Intruder Alarm System* is activated or the means of communication is interrupted during any period that the *Intruder Alarm System* is set, a *Keyholder* attends the *Premises* as soon as reasonably possible and does not leave them until the provisions set out in (d) above have been complied with, except where specifically agreed by us in writing

(i)   you notify us as soon as possible and in any event not later than 10 a.m. on our next working day if you receive any notification

   (i)   from the police authority that response to alarm signals or calls from the *Intruder Alarm System* may be restricted or withdrawn

   (ii)   from a local authority or magistrate imposing any requirement for abatement of a nuisance

   (iii)   that the *Intruder Alarm System* cannot be returned to, or maintained in, full working order and you comply with any subsequent requirements stipulated by us.

Claims Settlement Provisions

General

A1–78   (i)   We will not be liable to make a payment under more than one Section or subsection of this Policy in respect of loss of or damage to the same property caused by the same event.

(ii)   Excess: An *Excess* of £100 will apply to each claim for loss of *Money*. If a claim is made under more than one Section or subsection of this Policy for loss or damage caused at the same time by the same event only one *Excess* will apply.

Property

A1–79   We will settle a claim for loss of or damage to property on the following basis by payment or, at our option, by replacement, reinstatement or repair, subject to any relevant monetary limit specified in this Section.

(i)   Money: Payment of the amount of *Money* lost.
(ii) Other Property: The cost of repair or of replacement as new at current prices if an item is totally lost or destroyed, less a deduction for any depreciation and wear and tear.

For the purpose of any claim settlement replacement, reinstatement or repair as near as is reasonably practicable will be sufficient even though the former appearance or condition of the property may not be precisely restored.

Personal Accident: Assault
We will settle a claim for Benefit by payment of the relevant amounts specified in this Section. We will pay weekly Benefit only when the total amount payable for the claim has been agreed.

A1–80

Definition of Terms

Each of the following words and expressions is given a specific meaning which applies wherever it appears in *italics* in this Section, in the Specification for this Section or in any Endorsement to this Section.

A1–81

Alarmed Premises: means the *Premises* or those portions of the *Premises* protected by the *Intruder Alarm System*.

Buildings: means the principal building and its outbuildings, including landlord's fixtures and fittings therein and walls, gates and fences, at the Risk Address specified in the Schedule.

Business: means the Business specified in the Schedule.

Employee(s) means

(i)   anyone under a contract of service or apprenticeship with you
(ii)   anyone hired or borrowed by you
(iii) anyone engaged under a recognised work experience training scheme

while working for you in connection with the *Business*.

Excess: means the amount of the claim which is to be borne by you. We will deduct that amount from the amount payable in respect of the claim after the application of any relevant monetary limits specified in this Section.

Intruder Alarm System: means an intruder alarm system, comprising all component parts including the means of communication used to transmit signals.

Keyholder(s): means you or any person or keyholding company authorised by you who is available at all times to accept notification of faults or alarm signals relating to the *Intruder Alarm System*, attend, and allow access to the *Premises*.

Maintenance Contract: means a contract to provide both corrective and preventive maintenance with the installing company, as agreed with us.

Money: means cash, bank notes, cheques, girocheques, postal orders, current postage stamps, National Insurance stamps, holidays-with-pay stamps, trading stamps, National Savings certificates and stamps, premium bonds, luncheon vouchers, gift tokens, consumer redemption vouchers, credit card sales vouchers and V.A.T. purchase invoices.

Premises: means those parts of the *Buildings* occupied by you in connection with the *Business*.

Responsible Person: means you or any person authorised by you to be responsible for the security of the *Premises*.

SECTION SEVEN

GLASS

What IS Insured

A. Fixed Glass

A1–82 Accidental breakage of fixed glass, owned by you or for which you are legally responsible, in the *Buildings*.
The insurance extends to include

    (i) damage, caused by the breakage, to

        (a) frames and framework
        (b) alarm foil, lettering, painting, embossing, silvering and other ornamental work on the glass
        (c) the contents of display windows

    (ii) the reasonable cost of any necessary boarding up.

We will not pay more than £5,000 in respect of any one event, less the Excess specified in the Claims Settlement Provisions.

What IS NOT Insured

A.

A1–83 Any claim resulting from

    (a) the dilapidation of frames or framework
    (b) repairs or alterations to the Buildings
    (c) breakage occurring while the *Premises* are empty or not in use.

Claims Settlement Provisions

General

A1–84   (i) We will not be liable to make a payment under more than one Section or subsection of this Policy in respect of loss of or damage to the same property caused by the same event.

    (ii) Excess: An *Excess* of £100 will apply to each claim for loss of *Money*. If a claim is made under more than one Section or subsection of this

Policy for loss or damage caused at the same time by the same event only one *Excess* will apply.

Fixed Glass

We will settle a claim for loss of or damage to fixed glass by payment or, at our option, by replacement, reinstatement or repair, on the basis of the cost (including alarm foil, lettering, painting, embossing, silvering and other ornamental work on the glass) of replacing the broken glass with glass of similar quality, subject to any relevant monetary limit specified in this Section.

A1–85

For the purpose of any claim settlement replacement, reinstatement or repair as near as is reasonably practicable will be sufficient even though the former appearance or condition of the property may not be precisely restored.

We will not be liable for the replacement of or work on any undamaged items or remaining parts solely because they form part of a set, suite, group or collection of articles of a similar nature, colour, pattern or design.

Definition of Terms

Each of the following words and expressions is given a specific meaning which applies wherever it appears in *italics* in this Section, in the Specification for this Section or in any Endorsement to this Section.

A1–86

Buildings: means the principal building and its outbuildings, including landlord's fixtures and fittings therein and walls, gates and fences, at the Risk Address specified in the Schedule.

Business: means the Business specified in the Schedule.

Excess: means the amount of the claim which is to be borne by you. We will deduct that amount from the amount payable in respect of the claim after the application of any relevant monetary limits specified in this Section.

Premises: means those parts of the *Buildings* occupied by you in connection with the *Business*.

GENERAL EXCLUSIONS

1. Geographical Limits: This Policy does not insure any loss, damage, liability or injury arising outside Great Britain, Northern Ireland, the Isle of Man and the Channel Islands except as specifically set out in the Policy.

A1–87

2. Sonic Bangs: This Policy does not insure loss or damage occasioned by pressure waves caused by aircraft or other aerial devices travelling at sonic or supersonic speeds.

3. War Risks: This Policy does not insure any consequence whether direct or indirect of war, invasion, act of foreign enemy, hostilities (whether war be declared or not), civil war, rebellion, revolution, insurrection or military or usurped power.

4. Nuclear Risks: This Policy does not insure

(a) loss or destruction of or damage to any property whatsoever or any loss or expense whatsoever resulting or arising therefrom or any consequential loss

(b) any legal liability of whatsoever nature

directly or indirectly caused by or contributed to by or arising from the radioactive, toxic, explosive or other hazardous properties of any explosive nuclear assembly or nuclear component thereof or ionising radiations or contamination by radioactivity from any nuclear fuel or from any nuclear waste from the combustion of nuclear fuel.

5. Terrorism and Civil Commotion: Sections Three, Five, Six and Seven of this Policy do not insure loss or damage or consequential loss

    (a)   in England and Wales and Scotland but not the territorial seas adjacent thereto as defined in the Territorial Sea Act 1987, by fire or explosion occasioned by or happening through or in consequence directly or indirectly of terrorism, except to the extent stated in the Special Provision—Terrorism set out below

    (b)   in Northern Ireland occasioned by or happening through or in consequence directly or indirectly of

        (i)   civil commotion
        (ii) terrorism.

For the purposes of this Policy terrorism means any act of any person acting on behalf of or in connection with any organisation with activities directed towards the overthrowing or influencing of any government de jure or de facto by force or violence.

    In any action, suit or other proceedings where we allege that by reason of this definition any loss or damage is not covered by this Policy (or is covered only up to a specific limit of liability) the burden of proving that such loss or damage is covered (or is covered beyond that limit of liability) will be upon you.

Special Provision—Terrorism

Subject otherwise to the terms, definitions, exclusions, provisions and conditions of the Policy this insurance includes loss of or damage to insured property and consequential loss (where insured) in England and Wales and Scotland but not the territorial seas adjacent thereto as defined in the Territorial Sea Act 1987, by fire or explosion occasioned by or happening through or in consequence of terrorism as defined above, provided that our liability for all losses resulting from loss of or damage to insured property will not exceed

    (a)   £100,000 for buildings
        £100,000 for contents
        £100,000 for loss as a result of business interruption
        or
    (b)   any limit of liability or sum insured stated in the Policy whichever is the lower.

Any provision in this Policy which provides for any sum insured or limit of liability to be automatically reinstated following a loss will not apply to losses covered under this Special Provision.

6. Data Recognition: This Policy does not insure

    (a)   under Section One and any applicable endorsements, any legal liability of whatsoever nature directly or indirectly caused by or contributed to by or arising from the failure of any computer or other equipment or system for processing, storing or retrieving data, whether the property is owned by you or not, and whether occurring before, during or after the year 2000
        and
    (b)   under Section Three and Section Five and any applicable endorsements, loss or damage or loss of *Gross Profit* (as defined in Section Five),

directly or indirectly caused by or consisting of or arising from the failure of any computer, data processing equipment or media, microchip, integrated circuit or similar device or any computer software, whether the property is owned by you or not, and whether occurring before, during or after the year 2000
and

(c) under subsections A, B and C of Section Six and any applicable endorsements, loss directly or indirectly caused by or consisting of or arising from the failure of any computer, data processing equipment or media, microchip, integrated circuit or similar device or any computer software, whether the property is owned by you or not, and whether occurring before, during or after the year 2000

   (i) correctly to recognise any date as its true calendar date

   (ii) to capture save or retain, and/or correctly to manipulate, interpret or process any data or information or command or instruction as a result of treating any date otherwise than as its true calendar date

   (iii) to capture save retain or correctly to process any data as a result of the operation of any command which has been programmed into any computer software, being a command which causes the loss of data or the inability to capture save retain or correctly to process such data on or after any date

but under Section Three and Section Five this will not exclude subsequent loss or damage or loss of *Gross Profit* (as defined in Section Five) not otherwise excluded, which itself results from an *Insured Peril* (as defined in Section Three and Section Five).

CONDITIONS

1. **Observance of Terms**: Anyone claiming indemnity or Benefit under this Policy must comply with its terms as far as they can apply.   **A1–88**

2. **Precautions**: You must take all reasonable precautions to reduce or remove the risk of loss, damage, liability or injury.

3. **Alteration of Risk**: You must obtain our written consent before any alteration is made which increases the risk of loss, damage, liability or injury.

4. **Notification**: You must report any loss or damage to us in writing as soon as reasonably possible and notify the police immediately of any loss of money or any loss or damage caused by theft, attempted theft, riot or malicious persons. You must send any claim by a third party or notice of any proceedings to us immediately. No expense in making good damage may be incurred without our written consent except for emergency repairs to prevent further loss or damage.

5. **Conduct of Claim**: You must give us any help which we may reasonably ask for in connection with the claim. No property may be abandoned to us. We will be entitled to the full conduct and control of the defence or settlement of any claim from a third party, and no admission of liability may be made without our written consent.

6. Other insurance: If any other insurance covers the same loss, damage, liability or injury we will pay only our rateable proportion of any claim.

7. Cancellation: We may cancel this Policy or any of its Sections by sending at least 7 days' notice to your last known address. You will then be entitled to a proportionate return of premium. You too may cancel the Policy or any of its Sections. Any refund of premium will be calculated from the date we receive your written notice of cancellation and will be the full premium at our short period rates for the period each relevant Section has been in force.

THE CO-OPERATIVE INSURANCE SOCIETY ("CIS") SHOPKEEPER'S POLICY

SCHEDULE

Policyholder	Policy Number **A2–01**
Address	Agency Number
	Renewable on
Period of Insurance from to	

Risk Address
(if different from above)

Business

Item	Property (all owned by you or for which you are legally responsible)	Sum Insured (Subject to Average)
1	**Stock in Trade and Goods in Trust**, comprising	
	(a) Wines and spirits _____	£
	(b) Cigarettes, cigars, tobacco _____	£
	(c) Radio, television and other audio and video equipment; computers and associated equipment _____	£
	(d) All other stock in trade and goods in trust _____	£
2	**Trade Furniture** _____	£
	Total Sum Insured on Trade Contents	£
3	**Buildings** _____	£

Endorsements Operative	Policy Form Number	Cancelled Policy No.	Net First Premium

DEFINITION OF TERMS

Each of the following words and expressions is given a specific meaning which **A2–02** applies wherever it appears in italics in this Policy or in any Endorsement to this Policy.

Action(s): means legal proceedings (including appeal) arising out of any prosecution, inquiry, emergency control order, forfeiture, improvement notice, order to warn, prohibition notice, prohibition order or suspension notice.

Buildings: means the principal building and its outbuildings, built of brick, stone or concrete and roofed with slates, tiles, metal, concrete, asphalt or asbestos, landlord's fixtures and fittings therein, and walls, gates and fences, at the Risk Address shwon in the Schedule.

Business: means the Business specified in the Schedule and, for the purposes of Section Seven and Section Eight only, includes

(i)   the occupation, repair, maintenance and decoration of the *Premises*
(ii) the ownership of the *Buildings*, if the *Buildings* are insured under Section One of this Policy.

Business Hours: means the period during which you or your directors, partners or *Employees* are in or on the *Premises* in connection with the *Business*.

Business Machines: means calculators, cash registers, computers, facsimile and telex machines, franking machines, internal public address, radio and telephone systems, photocopiers, tape and video recorders, televisions, typewriters, word processors, scales, food slicers, mincers, coffee grinding machines tea and coffee making (but not vending) machines, rotisseries, dishwashing and glass washing machines, microwave ovens, toasters and hairdressing equipment, other than Stock in Trade or Goods in Trust, owned by you and for which you are legally responsible and used by you in connection with the *Business*.

Employee(s): means

(i)   anyone under a contract of service or apprenticeship with you
(ii)   anyone hired or borrowed by you
(iii) anyone engaged under a recognised work experience training scheme and for the purposes of Sections Seven and Eight only
(iv) any labour master or labour-only sub-contractor or person supplied by them, or self-employed person (for labour only)

while working for you in connection with the *Business*.

Excess: means the amount of the claim which is to be borne by you. We will deduct that amount from the amount payable in respect of the claim after the application of any relevant monetary limits specified in this Policy.

Excluded Events: means loss or damage caused by pollution or contamination except loss of or damage to the property insured (unless otherwise excluded) caused by

(i)   pollution or contamination which itself results from an *Insured Peril*.
(ii) an *Insured Peril* which itself results from pollution or contamination.

Fees: means

(i)   reasonable architects', surveyors' and legal fees but not fees incurred in preparing any claim
(ii) costs incurred with our consent in removing debris, dismantling, demolishing, shoring-up or propping of the destroyed or damaged portion or portions of the property insured but not costs or expenses

(a) incurred in removing debris except from the site of such property destroyed or damaged and the area immediately adjacent to the site
(b) arising from pollution or contamination of property not insured by this Policy

(iii) the additional cost of reinstating the damaged parts of the *Buildings* incurred solely to comply with any statutory requirement, European Community legislation or local authority bye-law but not the cost of compliance with any notice served on you before the damage occurred or for which there is an existing requirement which has to be implemented within a given period. We will not pay under this extension more than 15% of the Sum Insured on *Buildings* or in total under any item of the Policy more than its sum insured.

Indemnity Period: means the period, beginning with the occurrence of the loss or damage and ending not more than 18 months later, during which the results of the Business are affected because of the loss or damage.

Injury: means bodily injury and includes illness, disease and death.

Insured Peril: means

1. Fire, lightning, explosion, earthquake or volcanic eruption.
2. Riot, civil commotion, labour and political disturbances, excluding loss or damage in Northern Ireland.
3. Malicious persons, excluding

    (a) loss of or damage to glass
    (b) loss or damage occurring while the *Buildings* are empty or not in use
    (c) loss or damage in Northern Ireland.

4. Storm or flood, excluding

    (a) loss or damage
             (i) caused by frost, subsidence, heave or landslip
             (ii) attributable solely to change in the water table level
    (b) loss of or damage to movable property in the open, fences and gates.

5. Escape of water from any automatic sprinkler installation or other fixed water or heating system and, if the *Buildings* are insured under Section One of this Policy, the freezing of the system itself, excluding loss or damage

    (a) to the system itself
    (b) caused by subsidence, heave or landslip
    (c) occurring while the *Buildings* are empty or not in use.

6. Leakage of oil from any fixed oil-fired heating installation.
7. Falling trees or branches.
8. Theft or attempted theft involving

    (i) violent and forcible entry to or exit from the *Buildings*, excluding loss or damage occurring while the *Buildings* are empty or not in use or
    (ii) assault or violence or threat of assault or violence to

          (a) you or your directors, partners or *Employees*
          (b) any member of your family or a director's, partner's or *Employee's* family
          (c) any customer while on the *Premises*.

9. (i) Aircraft or other aerial devices or articles dropped from them.
    (ii) Impact with the *Buildings* by trains, road vehicles or animals.
10. Breakage of aerials, their fixtures or masts.

Money: means cash, bank notes, cheques, girocheques, postal orders, current postage stamps, National Insurance stamps, holidays-with-pay stamps, trading stamps, National Savings certificates and stamps, premium bonds, luncheon vouchers, gift tokens, consumer redemption vouchers, credit card sales vouchers and V.A.T. purchase invoices.

Neighbouring Property: means property in the vicinity of the *Premises*, the loss of or damage to which will prevent or hinder the use of or access to the *Premises*.

Offshire: means from the time when the *Employee* embarks onto a conveyance at the point of final departure to an offshore rig or offshore platform until such time as the *Employee* disembarks from a conveyance onto land upon the *Employee's* final return from the offshore rig or offshore platform.

Pollution or Contamination: means

    (i)   all pollution or contamination of buildings or other structures or of water or land or the atmosphere, and

    (ii)   all *Injury*, loss or damage directly or indirectly caused by such pollution or contamination.

Premises: means those parts of the *Buildings* occupied by you in connection with the *Business*.

Products: means goods (including their containers) sold, supplied, repaired, serviced, altered, renovated, processed or tested by you in the course of the *Business*.

Property at the Premises: means property used by you at the *Premises* for the purpose of the *Business*.

Standard Trading Profit: means the *Trading Profit* during that period in the 12 months immediately before the date of the loss or damage which corresponds with the *Indemnity Period*, appropriately adjusted where the *Indemnity Period* exceeds 12 months.

Subject to Average: means that if at the time of loss or damage the Sum Insured on any Item is less than the value of the Property insured under the Item you will be considered to be your own insurer for the difference and will bear a rateable proportion of the loss or damage.

Trade Furniture: means trade furniture and utensils (including *Business Machines*), safes, fixtures and fittings, interior decorations, the shop front and outdoor blinds, signs, aerials and satellite dishes attached to the *Premises*, but not landlord's fixtures and fittings.

Trading Profit: means money paid or payable to you for goods sold and delivered and for work carried out in the course of the *Business* at the *Premises* less the cost of related purchases, exclusive of Value Added Tax to the extent that you are accountable for it to the tax authorities.

CLAIMS SETTLEMENT PROVISIONS

General

(i)   We will not be liable to make a payment under more than one Section   **A2–03**
      or subsection of this Policy in respect of loss of or damage to the same
      property caused by the same event.

(ii) An *Excess* of £50 will apply to each claim under Section One for loss or
      damage to property which is not a claim for loss or damage caused by
      Insured Peril 1.

(iii) An *Excess* of £50 will apply to each claim under Section Two, Section
      Three and Section Five for loss of or damage to property.

(iv) If a claim is made under more than one Section or subsection of this
      Policy for loss or damage caused at the same time by the same event
      only one *Excess* will apply.

Property

We will settle a claim for loss of or damage to property on the following basis   **A2–04**
by payment or, at our option, by replacement, reinstatement or repair, subject to
any relevant monetary limit specified in this Policy.

(i)   Buildings:

      (a) If repair or replacement is carried out, the cost, including *Fees*,
           necessarily incurred in repairing or replacing that part of the
           Buildings which is destroyed or damaged. A deduction will be
           made for any depreciation and wear and tear if that part of the
           Buildings which is the subject of the claim is not in a good state of
           repair at the time of the destruction or damage.

      (b) If repair or replacement is not carried out, what it would cost to
           settle a claim in the terms of (i)(a) above but with a deduction for
           any depreciation and wear and tear.

(ii) Stock in Trade and Goods in Trust: The cost of repair or of replace-
      ment as new at current prices if an item is totally lost or destroyed, less
      a deduction for any depreciation and wear and tear.

(iii) Trade Furniture: The cost of repair of or replacement as new at current
      prices if an item is totally lost or destroyed. A deduction will be made
      for any depreciation and wear and tear if that part of the property
      which is the subject of the claim is not maintained in good condition at
      the time of the loss or damage.

(iv) Money: Payment of the amount of *Money* lost.

(v)   Glass: The cost (including alarm foil and lettering) of replacing the bro-
      ken glass with glass of similar quality.

For the purpose of any claim settlement replacement, reinstatement or repair as
near as is reasonably practicable will be sufficient even though the former appearance or condition of the property may not be precisely restored.

We will not be liable for the replacement of or work on any undamaged items or
remaining parts solely because they form part of a set, suite, group or collection of
articles of a similar nature, colour, pattern or design.

Personal Accident: Assault

A2–05   We will settle a claim for Benefit by payment of the relevant amounts specified in Section Four. We will pay weekly Benefit only when the total amount payable for the claim has been agreed.

Business Interruption

A2–06   We will settle a claim for loss of *Trading Profit* by payment, subject to any relevant monetary limit specified in Section Six, of

  (i)   the amount by which the *Trading Profit* during the *Indemnity Period* falls short of the *Standard Trading Profit* adjusted as may be necessary to provide for variations in or other circumstances affecting the *Business* so that the adjusted figure represents as far as possible the *Trading Profit* which but for the loss or damage would have been obtained during the *Indemnity Period*

  (ii) any additional expenditure, reasonably and necessarily incurred for the sole purpose of avoiding or diminishing the reduction in *Trading Profit* which otherwise would have taken place because of the loss or damage, up to the amount of the reduction so avoided

less any sum saved during the *Indemnity Period* in respect of charges and expenses of the *Business* which cease or are reduced because of the loss or damage.

If during the *Indemnity Period* goods or services are supplied elsewhere than at the *Premises* for the benefit of the *Business* either by you or by others on your behalf the money paid or payable for them will be brought into account in arriving at the *Trading Profit* during the *Indemnity Period*.

Legal Liability

We will settle a claim for damages by payment on the basis of the liability incurred, subject to any relevant monetary limit specified in this Section.

For the purpose of any claim settlement we may at any time at our option pay you the maximum amount specified in this Section (less any sums already paid) or any smaller amount for which the claim or claims may be settled. We will then be under no further liability in respect of the claim or claims except for costs and expenses incurred prior to the payment.

SECTION ONE

TRADE CONTENTS AND BUILDINGS

What IS Insured

A. Stock in Trade

A2–07   Loss of or damage to Stock in Trade and Goods in Trust in the *Premises*, caused by an *Insured Peril*.

We will not pay more than the relevant Sum(s) Insured shown against Item 1 in the Schedule, increased by up to 50% if the value of the Stock in Trade exceeds the

Sum(s) Insured by virtue only of seasonal increases in such stock, less the *Excess*, if applicable, specified in the Claims Settlement Provisions.

B. Trade Furniture

Loss of or damage to *Trade Furniture* caused by an *Insured Peril*.   A2–08

We will not pay more than the Sum Insured shown against Item 2 in the Schedule in respect of any one event, less the *Excess*, if applicable, specified in the Claims Settlement Provisions.

C. Trade Furniture Temporarily Removed

Loss of or damage to *Trade Furniture* while temporarily removed from the   A2–09
Premises for the purpose of cleaning, repair or renovation, caused by

  (i)   an *Insured Peril*
  (ii) theft or attempted theft involving violent and forcible entry to or exit
        from any building, not being part of the *Buildings*, to which the *Trade
        Furniture* is removed.

We will not pay more than 15% of the Sum Insured shown against Item 2 in the Schedule in respect of any one event, less the *Excess*, if applicable, specified in the Claims Settlement Provisions.

D. Freezer

Loss of or damage to frozen foods in a freezer or frozen food cabinet in the   A2–10
Premises caused by deterioration, contamination or putrefaction resulting from

  (a)   rise or fall in temperature due to

        (i)   breakdown of or unforeseen damage to the freezer or frozen food
              cabinet, (including non-operation of any thermostatic or auto-
              matic controlling device forming part of the installation) other
              than caused by an *Insured Peril*
        (ii) accidental failure of the public electricity or gas supply

  (b)   accidental escape of refrigerant or refrigerant fumes.

We will not pay more than £2,000 in respect of any one freezer or cabinet, less the *Excess* specified in the Claims Settlement Provisions.

E. Deeds

Loss of or damage to deeds, documents, manuscripts, business books, computer   A2–11
systems records, patterns, models, moulds, plans, drawings and designs, owned by
you or for which you are legally responsible, in the *Premises*, caused by an *Insured
Peril*, but only for their value as materials and the cost of labour expended in
reproducing them.

We will not pay more than £1,000 in respect of any one event, less the *Excess*, if applicable, specified in the Claims Settlement Provisions.

F. Personal Effects

Loss of or damage to the personal effects of your directors, *Employees*, cus-   A2–12
tomers and visitors, while on the *Premises*, but not property insured under another
policy, caused by an *Insured Peril*.

We will not pay more than £250 in respect of any one person or more than £1,000 in respect of any one event, less the *Excess*, if applicable, specified in the Claims Settlement Provisions.

G. Business Machines

A2–13   Accidental damage to *Business Machines* in the *Premises*.

We will not pay more than £5,000 in any one Period of Insurance, less the *Excess* specified in the Claims Settlement Provisions.

H. Underground Services

A2–14   Accidental damage to underground pipes, drains, ducts and cables (including their inspection covers) serving the *Buildings*, for which you are legally responsible.

We will not pay more than £10,000 in respect of any one event, less the *Excess* specified in the Claims Settlement Provision.

A2–15

I. Sanitary Fixtures

Accidental breakage of sanitary fixtures and fittings in the *Buildings*, owned by you or for which you are legally responsible.

We will not pay more than £10,000 in respect of any one event, less the *Excess*, if applicable, specified in the Claims Settlement Provisions.

A2–16

J. Tenant's Liability

If you are the tenant of the *Premises* and not the owner, damage to the *Premises* caused by an *Insured Peril* provided that you are legally responsible for the damage under the tenancy agreement, hire agreement or lease.

We will not pay more than 15% of the Total Sum Insured on Trade Contents in respect of any one event, less the *Excess*, if applicable, specified in the Claims Settlement Provisions.

A2–17

K. Theft of Keys

The cost necessarily incurred in replacing and installing locks in the *Premises* (including the operating mechanism of any key-operated intruder alam system) if the keys to the locks are taken from the *Premises* by theft as described in *Insured Peril* 8 or stolen from the home(s) of their authorised holder(s).

We will not pay more than £500 in respect of any one event, less the *Excess*, if applicable, specified in the Claims Settlement Provisions.

A2–18

L. Damage to the Buildings

Loss of or damage to the *Buildings* owned by you or for which you are legally responsible caused by an *Insured Peril*.

We will not pay more than the Sum Insured shown against Item 3 in the Schedule in respect of any one event, less the *Excess*, if applicable, specified in the Claims Settlement Provisions.

A2–19

M. Loss of Rent

Loss of rent, payable or receivable, in respect of that part of the *Buildings* not occupied for the purposes of the *Business* incurred during any period in which the *Buildings* are made unfit for occupation by and of the events insured under subsection L of this Section, but only for the period necessary for reinstatement.

We will not pay more than 15% of the Sum Insured shown against Item 3 in the Schedule in respect of any one event.

What IS NOT Insured

A2–20

A.
    (a) *Excluded Events.*
    (b) Loss or damage caused by theft or attempted theft by, or in collusion with, any of your directors, partners, *Employees* or members of your household.

(c) Loss of or damage to *Money*, motor vehicles and their accessories, furs, works of art and rare books.

B.

(a) *Excluded Events.*   A2–21
(b) Loss or damage caused by theft or attempted theft by, or in collusion with, any of your directors, partners, *Employees* or members of your household.
(c) Loss of or damage to *Money*, motor vehicles and their accessories, furs, works of art and rare books.

C.

(a) *Excluded Events*   A2–22
(b) Loss or damage in transit caused by theft.
(c) Loss or damage caused by theft or attempted theft by, or in collusion with, any of your directors, partners, *Employees* or members of your household.
(d) Loss of or damage to *Money*, motor vehicles and their accessories, furs, works of art and rare books.

D.

(a) *Excluded Events*   A2–23
(b) Loss or damage occasioned by the deliberate act of the supply authority.
(c) Loss of or damage to frozen foods in any freezer or frozen food cabinet unless the equipment which is the subject of the claim is maintained in good working order.

E.

(a) *Excluded Events.*   A2–24
(b) Loss or damage caused by theft or attempted theft by, or in collusion with, any of your directors, partners, *Employees* or members of your household.
(c) Loss of or damage to *Money*, motor vehicles and their accessories, furs, works of art and rare books.

F.

(a) *Excluded Events.*   A2–25
(b) Loss or damage caused by theft or attempted theft by, or in collusion with, any of your directors, partners, *Employees* or members of your household.
(c) Loss of or damage to *Money*, motor vehicles and their accessories, furs, works of art and rare books.

G.

(a) *Excluded Events*   A2–26
(b) Loss or damaged caused by any *Insured Peril* or any risk excluded under any *Insured Peril*.
(c) Loss of or damage to dynamos, motors or any portion of the electrical apparatus, directly caused by its own overrunning, excessive pressure, short circuiting or self heating.
(d) Damage caused by

   (i)   wear and tear, depreciation, fungus, insects, vermin, atmospheric or climatic conditions, the action of light or any gradually operating cause
   (ii) any process of cleaning, altering, repairing, restoring, erecting, testing, servicing, maintaining or dismantling.

(e) Mechanical or electrical failure.
(f) Breakage of electrical bulbs or tubes unless the apparatus of which they form part is damaged at the same time.
(g) Loss of or damage to audio, video, or computer tapes, cassettes, records or discs.

H.

A2–27 *Excluded Events.*

I.

A2–28 *Excluded Events.*

J.

A2–29 *Excluded Events.*

K.

A2–30 (a) *Excluded Events.*
(b) Costs incurred following

(i) loss or damage caused by theft or attempted theft by, or in collusion with, any of your directors, partners, *Employees* or members of your household.
(ii) the theft from the *Premises* outside *Business Hours*, of keys to any intruder alarm, safe or strongroom.

L.

A2–31 *Excluded Events.*

Indemnity to Contracting Purchaser

A2–32 When you have agreed to sell your interest in the *Buildings*, the buyer will have the benefit of this insurance until completion of the sale unless the buyer is insured under another policy.

SECTION TWO

MONEY

What IS Insured

A. Non-negotiable Money

A2–33 Loss of crossed cheques, crossed girocheques, crossed postal orders, stamped National Insurance cards, National Savings certificates, premium bonds, credit card sales vouchers and V.A.T. purchase invoices, owned by you or for which you are legally responsible in connection with the *Business*.

We will not pay more than £100,000 in respect of any one event, less the *Excess* specified in the Claims Settlement Provisions.

B. Other Money

A2–34 Loss of *Money* owned by you or for which you are legally responsible in connection with the *Business*

1. in the *Premises* during *Business Hours*.
   We will not pay more than

   (a) £250 for loss from any room left unattended and unlocked unless the *Money* is contained in a locked cupboard, drawer, safe or strongroom and the key is removed from the room

(b)   £3,000 in all

in respect of any one event, less the *Excess* specified in the Claims Settlement Provisions.

2.   in the *Premises* during any period in which no *Responsible Person* is in attendance.

We will not pay more than

(a)   £2,500 in all for loss from locked safes or strongrooms
(b)   £250 for any other loss

in respect of any one event, less the *Excess* specified in the Claims Settlement Provisions.

3.   in transit or in a bank night safe.

We will not pay more than £3,000 in respect of any one event, less the *Excess* specified in the Claims Settlement Provisions.

4.   in your home or in the home of a director, partner or authorised *Employee* of your *Business*.

We will not pay more than £250 in respect of any one event, less the *Excess* specified in the Claims Settlement Provisions.

What IS NOT Insured

A.

(a)   Loss resulting from a business transaction.

A2–35

(b)   Consequential loss, shortage due to errors or omissions, or depreciation in value.
(c)   Loss arising from the fraud or dishonesty of your directors, partners, or *Employees* or any member of your household.
(d)   Loss following the use of a combination code, key or duplicate key unless the combination code, key or duplicate key was obtained by violence or threat of violence to its authorised holder or to a member of the holder's family.
(e)   Loss from an unattended vehicle.

B.

Loss specifically included in or excluded from the insurance under subsection A   A2–36
of this Section.

SECTION THREE

FIDELITY GUARANTEE

What IS Insured

1.   Loss of money or goods owned by you or for which you are legally   A2–37
responsible in connection with the *Business*, directly caused by an act of fraud or dishonesty by an *Employee* and committed in the course of the *Employee's* employment by you during the uninterrupted currency of this Policy.

We will not pay more than £500 for each *Employee* or £2,500 in all, in respect of all losses discovered in any one Period of Insurance (including any periods allowed for discovery after the termination of this Policy), less the *Excess* specified in the Claims Settlement Provisions.

2. Reasonable charges payable by you to your professional accountants for producing and certifying the exact amount of loss in connection with a claim under this subsection.

What IS NOT Insured

A2–38

(a) Loss arising from any act of fraud or dishonesty by an *Employee*, committed subsequent to the discovery or suspicion of an act of fraud or dishonesty by the same *Employee* which is the subject of a claim under this Section.

(b) Loss discovered more than 18 months after the ending of the *Employee's* employment or of the termination of this Policy, whichever occurs first.

SECTION FOUR

PERSONAL ACCIDENT (ASSAULT)

What IS Insured

A. Personal Accident: Assault

A2–39   Benefit, as set out below.

If your or any of your directors, partners or *Employees*, in the course of the *Business*, suffer accidental bodily injury as a direct result of assault with intent to steal Stock in Trade, *Trade Furniture*, *Business Machines* or *Money* we will pay to the injured person

(i)   £5,000 if the injury is, within 12 months of its occurrence, the sole cause of

(a) death or
(b) complete and permanent loss of the sight of an eye or
(c) complete and permanent loss of the use of a hand or foot or
(d) permanent total disablement from attending to business or occupation of any kind.

If the person is aged under 16 years at the time of death we will pay £500 only

(ii) £25 per week for a period of up to 104 weeks from the date of injury during which that injury alone causes temporary total disablement from attending to the person's usual business or occupation.

We will not pay this Benefit in respect of any person who is aged under 16 years at the time of the injury.

We will not pay more than £5,000 for each person in respect of all injuries arising out of any one accident.

We will also pay

(iii) up to a total of £250 for related medical expenses which are reasonably and necessarily incurred by the injured person

(iv) £10 for each 24 hours in hospital, up to a total of £250, if the injury results in the injured person's admission to hospital as an in-patient.

B. Clothing and Personal Effects: Assault

Loss of or damage to clothing and personal effects (including security bags, boxes and waistcoats) belonging to you or your directors, partners or authorised *Employees*, as a direct result of assault, in the course of the *Business*, with intent to steal Stock in Trade, *Trade Furniture*, *Business Machines* or *Money*.

We will not pay more than £250 for each person in respect of any one event.

A2–40

SECTION FIVE

GLASS

What IS Insured

Accidental breakage of fixed glass, owned by you or for which you are legally responsible, in the *Premises*.

A2–41

The Insurance extends to include

   (i)   damage, caused by the breakage, to
      (a)   frames and framework
      (b)   alarm foil and lettering
      (c)   the contents of display windows
  (ii)   the reasonable cost of any necessary boarding-up
 (iii)   accidental breakage of mirrors

We will not pay more than £5,000 in respect of any one event, less the *Excess* specified in the Claims Settlement Provisions.

What IS NOT Insured

Any claim resulting from

A2–42

  (a)   breakage of armoured, bandit, bent, antique, decorated, embossed, ornamental or stained glass and neon and illuminated signs
  (b)   the dilapidation of frames or framework
  (c)   repairs or alterations to the *Buildings*
  (d)   breakage occurring while the *Premises* are empty or not in use.

Business Interruption

What IS Insured

A. Loss of Trading Profit

A2–43   **1.** Loss of *Trading Profit* resulting from the *Business* at the *Premises* being interrupted or interfered with in consequence of loss or damage to

(i) *Property at the Premises*, caused by an event insured under Section One or Section Five of this Policy, provided that payment has been made or liability admitted for the loss or damage under either of those Section

(ii) *Neighbouring Property* (whether the *Premises* or the Trade Contents are damaged or not) caused by an *Insured Peril* or accidental breakage of glass, provided that liability would have been admitted for the loss or damage under either Section One or Section Five of this Policy, had the loss or damage occurred to *Property at the Premises*.

2. Reasonable charges payable by you to your professional accountants for producing and certifying the exact amount of loss in connection with a claim under this Section.

We will not pay more than three times the Total Sum Insured on Trade Contents in respect of any one *Indemnity Period*.

What IS NOT Insured

A.

A2–44   Loss resulting from

(a) pollution or contamination other than loss resulting from loss of or damage to *Property at the Premises* or *Neighbouring Property* (not otherwise excluded), caused by

(i) pollution or contamination which itself results from an *Insured Peril*
(ii) an *Insured Peril* which itself results from pollution or contamination

(b) deliberate erasure, loss, distortion or corruption of information on computer software systems or other records, programs or software
(c) loss of or damage to the property of any supply undertaking from which you obtain electricity, gas, telecommunications or water services, which prevents or hinders the supply of such services to the *Premises*.

Cessation of Interest

A2–45   This Section will be made void immediately if

(a) the *Business* is wound up, carried on by a liquidator or receiver, or permanently discontinued or
(b) your interest ceases other than by death

unless we give our written consent to the contrary.

SECTION SEVEN

PUBLIC LIABILITY

What IS Insured

A. Legal Liability

1. Your legal liability for damages and claimants' costs and expenses in respect of accidental *Injury* to any person (not being an *Employee*), accidental loss of or damage to material property or accidental obstruction, trespass or nuisance arising   **A2–46**

    (i) in connection with the *Business* in or about the *Premises* or in the course of deliveries to or collections from customers by you or your directors, partners or *Employees*
    (ii) under Section 3 of the Defective Premises Act 1972 or Article 5 of the Defective Premises (Northern Ireland) Order 1975 in connection with any premises disposed of by you which were prior to disposal owned by you in connection with the *Business*, provided that the liability is not insured under another policy
    (iii) from *Products*
    (iv) from loss of or damage to

       (a) directors' or *Employees*' property
       (b) customers' or visitors' property while temporarily on your *Premises* (except property for alteration, cleaning, inspection, repair, servicing or storage).

    We will not pay more than £2,000,000 in respect of all events
    (a) arising from any one cause or
    (b) occurring in any one Period of Insurance attributable to

       (i) *Products*
       (ii) *Pollution or Contamination.*

2. Costs and expenses incurred with our consent, including the cost of representation at any Coroner's Court, Fatal Accident Inquiry or Court of Summary Jurisdiction.

B. Wrongful Arrest

Your legal liability for damages and claimants' costs and expenses in respect of wrongful arrest, false imprisonment, malicious prosecution or defamation of, or assault on, any person (other than an *Employee*) arising out of any allegation of theft on the *Premises*.   **A2–47**

We will not pay more than £25,000 (in addition to costs and expenses incurred with our consent) in any one Period of Insurance.

C. Additional Costs

Costs and expenses incurred with our consent by you or your directors, partners or *Employees* in defending *Actions* arising in connection with the *Business* under   **A2–48**

   (i) the Health and Safety at Work etc. Act 1974, the Health and Safety Inquiries (Procedure) Regulations 1975 and the Health and Safety at Work (Northern Ireland) Order 1978
   (ii) Part II of the Consumer Protection Act 1987
   (iii) the Food Safety Act 1990 and the Food Safety (Northern Ireland) Order 1991

provided that you give written notice to us immediately you have knowledge of an impending *Action* or any circumstances which might give rise to an *Action*.

We will not pay more than £250,000 in respect of all *Actions* arising under the Same Act in any one Period of Insurance.

What IS NOT Insured

A.

A2–49

(a) Liability arising from

    (i) the use by you or on your behalf of any aircraft, hovercraft, train, watercraft, or any mechanically propelled vehicle (other than domestic gardening equipment) or any trailer attached to it

    (ii) the making-up, dispensing, sale, supply or distribution of drugs, medicines or pharmaceuticals, or animal feedstuffs, other than proprietary preparations in unopened containers as supplied by the manufacturers

    (iii) advice, design, specification or treatment provided for a fee by or through you or your directors, partners of *Employees*.

(b) Liability arising from loss of or damage to

    (i) material property owned by you

    (ii) material property in your custody or control or that of your directors, partners or *Employees*, other than as insured under (1)(iv)

    (iii) that part of any material property on which you or anyone acting on your behalf is or has been working if the loss or damage results directly from such work.

(c) Any claim in respect of

    (i) loss of or damage to *Products*

    (ii) the cost of recalling, altering, repairing, replacing or making any refund in respect of *Products*.

(d) Liability which arises only because of an agreement relating to the sale or supply of *Products*.

(e) *Pollution or Contamination* other than cuased by a sudden identifiable unintended and unexpected incident which takes place in its entirety at a specific time and place during the Period of Insurance.

    All *Pollution or Contamination* which arises out of one incident will be deemed to have occurred at the time such incident takes place.

(f) Liquidated, punitive or exemplary damages, fines or penalties

(g) The direct export of any *Products* to the United States of America or Canada.

(h) Any claim which arises from an action brought in a court of law in the United States of America or Canada or in a country which operates under the laws of the United States of America or Canada, or from any proceedings to enforce a judgement in such an action.

C.

A2–50

(a) Fines or penalties.

(b) Any claim which arises from a deliberate act or omission by you or your directors, partners or *Employees*.

(c) Any claim where the Action is solely in connection with the health and safety of any *Employee*.

Additional Parties

If more than one party is named as Policyholder in the Schedule the insurance provided under this Section will apply separately to each party.

At your request this insurance will also apply to your directors, partners or *Employees* against any liability for which you would have been entitled to indemnity under this Section had the claim been made against you.

We will not pay in total to all parties indemnified under this Section more than the monetary limits specified in the Section.

A2–51

SECTION EIGHT

EMPLOYERS' LIABILITY

What IS Insured

A. Legal Liability

1. Your legal liability for damages and claimants' costs and expenses in respect of *Injury* to any *Employee*.

    We will not pay more than £10,000,000 in respect of all events arising from any one cause.

    Compulsory Employers' Liability Insurance Laws: This insurance complies with the law relating to compulsory insurance of liability to employees in Great Britain, Northern Ireland, the Isle of Man and the Channel Islands. If we are obliged to make a payment which we would not have been liable to make but for such law we will require you to refund the amount paid.

2. Costs and expenses incurred with our consent, including the cost of representation at any Coroner's Court, Fatal Accident Inquiry or Court of Summary Jurisdiction.

A2–52

B. Health and Safety at Work

Costs and expenses incurred with our consent by you or your directors, partners or *Employees* in defending *Actions* arising in connection with the *Business* under the Health and Safety at Work etc. Act 1974, the Health and Safety Inquiries (Procedure) Regulations 1975 and the Health and Safety at Work (Northern Ireland) Order 1978, provided that you give written notice to us immediately you have knowledge of an impending *Action* or any circumstances which might give rise to an *Action*.

We will not pay more than £250,000 in respect of all *Actions* arising in any one Period of Insurance.

A2–53

What IS NOT Insured

A.

Any claim which arises from

(a) *Injury* to any *Employee* while working *Offshore*

(b) an event in respect of which liability is required to be insured under the compulsory motor insurance provisions of the Road Traffic Acts.

A2–54

B.

    (a) Fines or penalties.

    (b) Any claim which arises from

        (i) a deliberate act or omission by you or your directors, partners or *Employees*

        (ii) *Injury* to any *Employee* while working *Offshore*

        (iii) an event in respect of which liability is required to be insured under the compulsory motor insurance provisions of the Road Traffic Acts.

    (c) Any claim where the *Action* is solely in connection with the health and safety of anyone not an *Employee*.

Additional Parties

A2–56   If more than one party is named as Policyholder in the Schedule the insurance provided under this Section will apply separately to each party.

At your request this insurance will also apply to your directors, partners or *Employees* against any liability for which you would have been entitled to indemnity under this Section had the claim been made against you.

We will not pay in total to all parties indemnified under this Section more than the monetary limits specified in the Section.

ENDORSEMENTS

A2–57   Operative only when the endorsement number is shown in the Schedule under the heading "Endorsements Operative".

SP.1—Hairdressing Treatment Risks

A2–58   Subsection A of Section Seven of this Policy extends to include legal liability for *Injury* or damage to material property arising in connection with the *Business* from advice or treatment in respect of hairdressing, manicure, pedicure, facial and body massage, eyebrow plucking and shaping or the use of make-up, oils and waxes.

This extension does not insure liability

    (a) specifically excluded from subsection A of Section Seven of this Policy (except as amended by this extension)

    (b) arising from

        (i) treatment carried out by any trainee unless working under the direct supervision of an experienced person

        (ii) preparations supplied or used by you which are manufactured or made-up by you or to your order or from any formula supplied by you

        (iii) any treatment necessitating the puncturing or cutting of skin.

SP.3—Baking

This Policy does not insure any loss, damage, liability or injury arising from baking carried out on the *Premises*.

SP.4—Slaughtering

This Policy does not insure any loss, damage, liability or injury arising from slaughtering carried out on the *Premises*.

SP.5—Oriental Carpets

This Policy does not insure loss of or damage to oriental carpets.

SP.6—Woodworking Machinery

This Policy does not insure any loss, damage, liability or injury arising from woodworking machinery used in connection with the *Business* at the *Premises*.

SP.7—Clothing

This Policy does not insure loss of or damage to clothing.

SP.8—Cooking

This Policy does not insure any loss, damage, liability or injury arising from cooking or the heating of food carried out in connection with the *Business* at the *Premises*.

SP.9—Photographic Equipment for Sale

This Policy does not insure loss, damage, or liability arising in connection with photographic equipment stocked for sale.

SP.10—Dyers and Cleaners

This Policy does not insure loss, damage, or liability or injury arising from dyeing or cleaning carried out on the *Premises*.

SP.11—No Fitting

This Policy does not insure loss, damage, or liability or injury arising from repair or fitting.

SP.12—Flood Exclusion

This Policy does not insure loss or damage caused by flood, *i.e.* the escape of water from the normal confines of any natural or artificial watercourse (other than water tanks, apparatus or pipes), lake, reservoir, canal or dam, or inundation from the sea, whether resulting from storm or otherwise.

SP.13—Intruder Alarm

This Policy does not insure loss or damage occurring at the *Premises* if caused by *Insured Peril* 8 unless

(a) the intruder alarm system in the *Premises* is

  (i) tested and put into operation outside *Business Hours* and on each occasion when the *Premises* are closed for business
  (ii) maintained in operation during *Business Hours* or on a 24-hour basis, where it, or any part of it, is designed to be so operated
  (iii) inspected and maintained under the terms of an agreement approved by us

(b) you notify us immediately

  (i) if warning, written or otherwise, is received from the police of withdrawal or limitation of their response to calls from the intruder alarm system
  (ii) of any circumstances or difficulties in connection with the system which might lead to such withdrawal or limitation.

GENERAL EXCLUSIONS

1. Geographical Limits: This Policy does not insure any loss, damage, liability or injury arising outside Great Britain, Northern Ireland, the Isle of Man and the Channel Islands except as specifically set out in the Policy.

A2–59

2. Sonic Bangs: This Policy does not insure loss or damage occasioned by pressure waves caused by aircraft or other aerial devices travelling at sonic or supersonic speeds.

3. War Risks: This Policy does not insure any consequence whether direct or indirect of war, invasion, act of foreign enemy, hostilities (whether war be declared or not), civil war, rebellion, revolution, insurrection or military or usurped power.

4. Nuclear Risks: This Policy does not insure

(a)   loss or destruction of or damage to any property whatsoever or any loss or expense whatsoever resulting or arising therefrom or any consequential loss

(b)   any legal liability of whatsoever nature

directly or indirectly caused by or contributed to by or arising from the radioactive, toxic, explosive or other hazardous properties of any explosive nuclear assembly or nuclear component thereof or ionising radiations or contamination by radioactivity from any nuclear fuel or from any nuclear waste from the combustion of nuclear fuel.

5. Terrorism and Civil Commotion: Sections Three, Five, Six and Seven of this Policy do not insure loss or damage or consequential loss

(a)   in England and Wales and Scotland but not the territorial seas adjacent thereto as defined in the Territorial Sea Act 1987, by fire or explosion occasioned by or happening through or in consequence directly or indirectly of terrorism, except to the extent stated in the Special Provision — Terrorism set out below

(b)   in Northern Ireland occasioned by or happening through or in consequence directly or indirectly of

(i)   civil commotion
(ii) terrorism.

For the purposes of this Policy terrorism means any act of any person acting on behalf of or in connection with any organisation with activities directed towards the overthrowing or influencing of any government de jure or de facto by force or violence.

In any action, suit or other proceedings where we allege that by reason of this definition any loss or damage is not covered by this Policy (or is covered only up to a specific limit of liability) the burden of proving that such loss or damage is covered (or is covered beyond that limit of liability) will be upon you.

Special Provision—Terrorism

Subject otherwise to the terms, definitions, exclusions, provisions and conditions of the Policy this insurance includes loss of or damage to insured property and consequential loss (where insured) in England and Wales and Scotland but not the territorial seas adjacent thereto as defined in the Territorial Sea Act 1987, by fire or explosion occasioned by or happening through or in consequence of terrorism as defined above, provided that our liability for all losses resulting from loss of or damage to insured property will not exceed

(a)   (i)   £100,000 for buildings
(ii) £100,000 for contents
(iii) £100,000 for loss as a result of business interruption

or

(b)   any limit of liability or sum insured stated in the Policy whichever is the lower.

Any provision in this Policy which provides for any sum insured or limit of liability to be automatically reinstated following a loss will not apply to losses covered under this Special Provision.

CONDITIONS

1. Observance of Terms: Anyone claiming indemnity or Benefit under this Policy must comply with its terms as far as they can apply.   **A2–60**

2. Precautions: You must take all reasonable precautions to reduce or remove the risk of loss, damage, liability or injury.

3. Alteration of Risk: You must obtain our written consent before any alteration is made which increases the risk of loss, damage, liability or injury.

4. Notification: You must report any loss or damage to us in writing as soon as reasonably possible and notify the police immediately of any loss of money or any loss or damage caused by theft, attempted theft, riot or malicious persons. You must send any claim by a third party or notice of any proceedings to us immediately. No expense in making good damage may be incurred without our written consent except for emergency repairs to prevent further loss or damage.

5. Conduct of Claim: You must give us any help which we may reasonably ask for in connection with the claim. No property may be abandoned to us. We will be entitled to the full conduct and control of the defence or settlement of any claim from a third party, and no admission of liability may be made without our written consent.

6. Other insurance: If any other insurance covers the same loss, damage, liability or injury we will pay only our rateable proportion of any claim.

7. Cancellation: We may cancel this Policy or any of its Sections by sending at least 7 days' notice to your last known address. You will then be entitled to a proportionate return of premium. You too may cancel the Policy or any of its Sections. Any refund of premium will be calculated from the date we receive your written notice of cancellation and will be the full premium at our short period rates for the period each relevant Section has been in force.

THE CO-OPERATIVE INSURANCE SOCIETY ("CIS") CONTRACT WORKS POLICY

Each of the following words and expressions is given a specific meaning which applies wherever it appears in *italics* in this Policy.   **A3–01**

Completion Date: means the date of issue of the certificate of practical completion of the *Contract Works* or the date of determination of the employment of the Contractor whichever is the earlier.

Contract Works: means works described in the contract and contract drawings and includes *Site Materials* and *Fees*.

Excess: means the amount of the claim which is to be borne by you. We will deduct that amount from the amount payable in respect of the claim after the application of any relevant monetary limits specified in this Policy.

Fees: means
  (i) reasonable architects', surveyors', consulting engineers' and legal fees but not fees incurred in preparing any claim
  (ii) costs incurred with our consent in removing debris, dismantling, demolishing, shoring up or propping of the destroyed or damaged portion or portions of the property insured by this Policy but not costs or expenses

  (a) incurred in removing debris except from the site of such property destroyed or damaged and the area immediately adjacent to the site
  (b) arising from pollution or contamination of property not insured by this Policy.

Site Materials: means all unfixed materials and goods delivered to, placed on or adjacent to the *Contract Works* and intended for incorporation therein

Specified Peril: means

  1. Fire, lightning, explosion or earthquake.
  2. Riot, civil commotion and labour and political disturbances.
  3. Storm, flood or the escape of water from any fixed water or heating system but not loss or damaged caused by frost, subsidence, heave or landslip.
  4. Aircraft and other aerial devices or articles dropped therefrom.

CLAIMS SETTLEMENT PROVISIONS

A3–02   Subject to the terms of, and the limits specified in, this Policy we will settle a claim by payment or, at our option, by replacement, reinstatement or repair, on the basis of the incurred cost of reinstatement or repair of the *Contract Works*.

For the purpose of any claim settlement, repair or replacement as near as is reasonably practicable will be sufficient even though the former appearance or condition of the property may not be precisely restored.

SECTION A

SPECIFIED PERILS

A3–03   **Section A is operative only if specified as operative in the Schedule**
Loss of or damage to the Contract Works caused by a *Specified Peril*.

We will not pay more than the Sum Insured specified in the Schedule in respect of any one event.

This Section does not insure an *Excess* of £250 in respect of each claim which is not a claim for loss or damage caused by fire, lightning, explosion or earthquake.

SECTION B

"ALL RISKS"

A3–04   **Section B is operative only if specified as operative in the Schedule**
Accidental loss of or damage to the *Contract Works*.

We will not pay more than the Sum Insured specified in the Schedule in respect of any one event.

This Section does not insure

(a)   (i)   an *Excess* of £1,000 in respect of each claim for loss or damage caused by frost, collapse, subsidence, heave or landslip
(ii)   an *Excess* of £250 in respect of each other claim which is not a claim for loss or damage caused by fire, lightning, explosion or earthquake

(b)   loss or damage caused by

(i)   wear and tear, depreciation, insects, vermin, atmospheric or climatic conditions or any gradually operating cause
(ii)   confiscation, destruction or requisition by order of the Government or any public authority

(c)   loss of or damage to any insured property which is in a defective condition due to a defect in design, plan, specification, materials or workmanship or which relies for its support or stability on any of the remainder of the insured property which is itself in such defective condition

(d)   loss of property by disappearance or shortage which is revealed only when an inventory is made or is not traceable to a specific event

(e)   the cost of

(i)   repairing, replacing or rectifying property which is defective in material or workmanship
(ii)   normal maintenance.

GENERAL EXCLUSIONS

1. Excluded Property: This Policy does not insure   A3–05

    (a)   loss of or damage to any part of the *Contract Works*

        (i)   after the part has been completed and delivered up to or taken into use by its owner, tenant or occupier or

        (ii) following the issue of a relevant certificate of practical completion

    (b)   loss of or damage to

        (i)   property which is or was part of any structure prior to the commencement of the *Contract Works*

        (ii) mechanically propelled vehicles and their accessories and trailers

        (iii) constructional plant, tools and equipment

        (iv) temporary buildings.

2. Excluded Events: This Policy does not insure

    (a)   loss of or damage to dynamos, motors or any part of the electrical apparatus directly caused by abnormal currents or self-heating

    (b)   loss or damage

        (i)   caused by pollution or contamination except (unless otherwise not insured by this Policy) loss of or damage to the property insured caused by

            (a)   pollution or contamination which itself results from

                (i)   a *Specified Peril*

                (ii) malicious persons other than thieves

                (iii) impact by any road vehicle or animal

            (b)   any peril listed in 2 (b)(i)(a) above which itself results from pollution or contamination

        (ii) which is attributable solely to change in the water table level.

3. Terrorism and Civil Commotion: Sections Three, Five, Six and Seven of this Policy do not insure loss or damage or consequential loss

    (a)   in England and Wales and Scotland but not the territorial seas adjacent thereto as defined in the Territorial Sea Act 1987, by fire or explosion occasioned by or happening through or in consequence directly or indirectly of terrorism, except to the extent stated in the Special Provision—Terrorism set out below

    (b)   in Northern Ireland occasioned by or happening through or in consequence directly or indirectly of

        (i)   civil commotion

        (ii) terrorism.

For the purposes of this Policy terrorism means any act of any person acting on behalf of or in connection with any organisation with activities directed towards the overthrowing or influencing of any government de jure or de facto by force or violence.

In any action, suit or other proceedings where we allege that by reason of this definition any loss or damage is not covered by this Policy (or is covered only up to a specific limit of liability) the burden of proving that such loss or damage is covered (or is covered beyond that limit of liability) will be upon you.

Special Provision—Terrorism

Subject otherwise to the terms, definitions, exclusions, provisions and conditions of the Policy this insurance includes loss of or damage to insured property and consequential loss (where insured) in England and Wales and Scotland but not the territorial seas adjacent thereto as defined in the Territorial Sea Act 1987, by fire or explosion occasioned by or happening through or in consequence of terrorism as defined above, provided that our liability for all losses resulting from loss of or damage to insured property will not exceed

(a)   £100,000 for buildings
      £100,000 for contents
      £100,000 for loss as a result of business interruption
      or
(b)   any limit of liability or sum insured stated in the Policy
      whichever is the lower.

Any provision in this Policy which provides for any sum insured or limit of liability to be automatically reinstated following a loss will not apply to losses covered under this Special Provision.

4. Consequential Loss: This Policy does not insure any consequential loss or damage or penalties under contract for delay or non-completion.

5. Geographical Limits: This Policy does not insure any loss, damage, liability or injury arising outside Great Britain, Northern Ireland, the Isle of Man and the Channel Islands except as specifically set out in the Policy.

6. Sonic Bangs: This Policy does not insure loss or damage occasioned by pressure waves caused by aircraft or other aerial devices travelling at sonic or supersonic speeds.

7. War Risks: This Policy does not insure any consequence whether direct or indirect of war, invasion, act of foreign enemy, hostilities (whether war be declared or not), civil war, rebellion, revolution, insurrection or military or usurped power.

8. Nuclear Risks: This Policy does not insure loss or damage to any property whatsoever or any loss or expense whatsoever resulting or arising therefrom or any consequential loss directly or indirectly caused by or contributed to by or arising from the radioactive, toxic, explosive or other hazardous properties of any explosive nuclear assembly or nuclear component thereof or ionising radiations or contamination by radioactivity from any nuclear fuel or from any nuclear waste from the combustion of nuclear fuel.

9. Data Recognition: Section B of this Policy and any applicable endoresements, does not insure loss or damage, directly or indirectly caused by or consisting of or arising from the failure of any computer, data processing equipment or media, microchip, integrated circuit or similar device or any computer software, whether the property is owned by you or not, and whether occurring before, during or after the year 2000

(i)   correctly to recognise any date as its true calendar date
(ii)   to capture save or retain, and/or correctly to manipulate, interpret or process any data or information or command or instruction as a result of treating any date otherwise than as its true calendar date
(iii) to capture save retain or correctly to process any data as a result of the operation of any command which has been programmed into any computer software, being a command which causes the loss of data or the inability to capture save retain or correctly to process such data on or after any date

but this will not exclude subsequent loss or damage not otherwise excluded, which itself results from a *Defined Peril*.

For the purpose of this exclusion:

Defined Peril: means to the extent that these are insured by this Section fire, lightning, explosion, aircraft or other aerial devices or articles dropped therefrom, riot, civil commotion, strikers, locked-out workers, persons taking part in labour disturbances, malicious persons, earthquake, storm, flood, escape of water from any tank apparatus or pipe, impact by any road vehicle or animal, theft or attempted theft, subsidence, ground heave or landslip.

10. Third Party Rights: A person, or company, who is not a party to this Policy has no right under the Contracts (Rights of Third Parties) Act 1999 to enforce any term of this Policy but this does not affect any right or remedy of a third party which exists or is available apart from that Act.

SCHEDULE

Policyholder(s):   **A3–06**

| Policy Number | CF |
| Agency Number | |

1. Employer _____

    Address _____

    _____

2. Contractor _____

    Address _____

    _____

Contract Works:

(i) Address _____

     _____

(ii) Description _____

     _____

Period of Insurance from _____ to _____
                                        or prior *Completion Date*

Section Operative _____ Sum Insured on *Contract Works* £ _____

Date of issue _____ Premium £ _____ Issued by _____

Any premium shown or any amount shown as payable takes account, where applicable, of Insurance Premium Tax.

CONDITIONS

1. Observance of Terms: You must comply with the terms of this Policy as far as   **A3–07**
they can apply.

2. Precautions: You must take all reasonable precautions to reduce or remove the risk of loss or damage.

3. Alteration of Risk: You must obtain our written consent before any alteration is made which increases the risk of loss or damage.

4. Notification: You must report any loss or damage to us in writing as soon as reasonably possible and notify the police immediately of any loss or damage caused by theft, attempted theft, riot or malicious persons. No expense in making good damage may be incurred without our written consent except for emergency repairs to prevent further loss or damage.

5. Conduct of Claim: You must give us any help which we may reasonably ask for in connection with the claim. No property may be abandoned to us.

6. Waiver of Subrogation (Sub-Contractors): We will not pursue a claim against any sub-contractor for loss or damage caused by a *Specified Peril* if the loss or damage occurred on or before the date of issue of the certificate of practical completion of the relevant sub-contractor, or any document issued in its place.

7. Other Insurance: If any other insurance covers the same loss or damage we will pay only our rateable proportion of any claim.

8. Cancellation: We may cancel this Policy by sending at least 7 days' notice to your last known address. You will then be entitled to a proportionate return of premium. You too may cancel the Policy. Any refund of premium will be calculated from the date we receive your written notice of cancellation and will be the full premium less premium at our short period rates for the period the Policy has been in force.

APPENDIX 4

THE CO-OPERATIVE INSURANCE SOCIETY ("CIS") CONTRACTORS' "ALL RISKS" POLICY

SCHEDULE

Policyholder   Policy Number

Address   Agency Number

Period of Insurance   from   to   Renewable on

Business   Turnover £

Contract Site(s)

Item	Insured Property	Sum Insured
1	*Works* and *Site Materials* – in respect of each *Contract* _____	the final contract price but not exceeding 125% of the original *Estimated Contract Price*
2	*Temporary Buildings* excluding hired-in property _____	£
3	*Plant* excluding hired-in property (limit any one item £) _____	£
4	Hired-in *Temporary Buildings* and *Plant* (limit any one item £) _____	£
5	Employees' personal effects and tools whilst on the *Contract Site(s)* (limit any one employee £) _____	£

Maximum Original Contract Period   months (exclusive of any maintenance or defects liability period)

Maximum Original Estimated Contract Price £

Important: If you undertake any contract outside the above maximum limits a separate policy may be required.
Endoresements Operative   Policy Form Number   Cancelled Policy No.   Net First Premium

DEFINITION OF TERMS

Each of the following words and expressions is given a specific meaning which applies wherever it appears in *italics* in this Policy.

Contract: means any contract undertaken by you in the course of the Business at the *Contract Site(s)*.

Contract Site(s): means the site(s) specified in the Schedule on which the *Works* are undertaken.

Estimated Contract Price: means the sum agreed between you and your principal or employer as payment for completion of the works or, where there is no principal or employer, the value of the works to be completed at a single site.

Excess: means the amount of the claim which is to be borne by you. We will deduct that amount from the amount payable in respect of the claim after the application of any relevant monetary limits specified in this Policy.

Insured Property: means the property described in the Schedule belonging to you or for which you are legally responsible.

Nuclear Materials: means

    (i)   nuclear fuel other than natural or depleted uranium capable of producing energy by a self-sustaining chain process of nuclear fission outside a nuclear reactor either alone or in combination with some other material and

    (ii) radioactive products or waste produced in, or any material made radioactive by, exposure to the radiation incidental to the production or use of nuclear fuel not including fabricated radioisotopes.

Plant: means constructional plant, tools and equipment for use in connection with the *Contract* but not *Works*, *Site Materials*, *Temporary Buildings*, employees' personal effects and tools or property on sites of contracts not insued by this Policy.

Production or Use of Nuclear Materials: means the production, manufacture, enrichment, conditioning, processing, reprocessing, use, storage, handling or disposal of *Nuclear Material*.

Site Materials: means the materials for incorporation in the *Works*, including any free issue materials (provided that their value is included within the relevant sum insured), while on *Contract Site(s)* or in transit by road, rail or inland waterway.

Speculative Development: means property built for sale or letting by you other than under a contract for a principal.

Substantial Completion: means the work remaining relates only to the prospective purchaser's or tenant's choice of decorations, fixtures and fittings.

Temporary Buildings: means temporary buildings, including fixtures and fittings therein, for use in connection with the *Contract*.

Works: means the permanent works and the temporary works executed in performance of the *Contract*.

CLAIMS SETTLEMENT PROVISIONS

A4–03   Subject to the terms of, and the limits specified in, this Policy claims are settled by payment or, at our option, by replacement, reinstatement or repair, on the basis of the cost of repair or of replacement as new at current prices if an item is totally lost or destroyed, less an allowance for any depreciation and wear and tear.

If we opt or become bound to replace, reinstate or repair any property, replacement, reinstatement or repair as nearly as reasonably practicable is to be deemed sufficient, although the former appearance or condition of the property may not be precisely restored.

Serious Losses Memorandum

Where loss of or damage to the *Insured Property* on any one *Contract Site* arises **A4–04** during any one period of 72 consecutive hours caused by storm, flood or earthquake it will be deemed to be a single event and therefore consistutes one loss and only one *Excess* will apply.

INSURED EVENTS

Physical loss of or physical damage to the *Insured Property*.   **A4–05** The indemnity extends to include

(i) *Professional Fees*: reasonable architects', surveyors' and consulting engineers' fees incurred as a result of loss of or damage to *Insured Property*, but not fees incurred in preparing any claim.

(ii) Debris Removal: costs and expenses necessarily incurred by you with our consent following loss or damage to *Insured Property* in

(a) removing and disposing of debris, dismantling, demolishing, shoring up or propping of the destroyed or damaged portion or portions of the *Insured Property* but not costs or expenses arising from pollution or contamination of property not insured by this Policy

(b) cleaning and/or repairing drains and service mains on the *Contract Site(s)*.

(iii) Public Authorities Requirements: the additional cost of reinstatement of the *Insured Property* incurred with our consent to comply with Building Regulations or local authority or other statutory requirements first imposed upon you following the loss or damage provided that the reinstatement is completed within 12 months of the occurrence of the loss or damage or within such further time as we may in writing allow.
We will not be liable for the cost of

(a) requirements relating to undamaged property or undamaged portions of property other than foundations (unless foundations are specially excluded from the insurance)

(b) any rate, tax, duty or development or other charge or assessment which may arise out of capital appreciation as a result of complying with any of the regulations or requirements referred to.

(iv) Speculative Development: loss of or damage to
(a) *Works* in respect of buildings constructed by you as a *Speculative Development* for a period of up to 90 days beyond the date of *Substantial Completion* of the last building on the *Contract Site(s)* pending transfer of ownership or letting

(b) contents of showhouses, showflats or show offices and the like on the *Contract Site(s)* until sold provided that cover will cease no later than 90 days beyond the date of *Substantial Completion* of the last building on the *Contract Site(s)*.
We will not be liable for loss or damage

(i) occurring during the period from 1st December to 1st March unless an efficient heating system is left on at all times throughout the period or the water system is drained

(ii) due to theft or malicious damage unless following forcible and violent entry or exit.
We will not pay more than £25,000 in respect of any one unit.

(v)   Principals Clause: liability arising from the action of your employers or principals, but only to the extent required by the *Contract* between you and the relevant employer and principal.

(vi)   Offsite Storage: loss of or damage to *Site Materials* whilst temporarily held in store away from the *Contract Site(s)* but not whilst being worked on in order to prepare them for incorporation in the Works.

We will not pay in respect of any one event in any one location more than

   (a)   15% of the Sum Insured on *Works* and *Site Materials* specified in the Schedule or £25,000 whichever is the less and

   (b)   any amount in addition which you must pay in order to comply with clauses 16 and 30.3 of the JCT Conditions of Contract or clause 54(3) of the ICE Form of Contract or any equivalent contract.

(vii)   Immobilised *Plant*: the cost of recovery or withdrawal of Plant (including hired-in *Temporary Buildings* or *Plant*) insured under this Policy which is unintentionally immobilised provided that such recovery or withdrawal is not made necessary solely by electrical or mechanical breakdown or derangement.

We will not pay more than the relevant Sum Insured shown against each Item in the Schedule in respect of any one event.

(viii)   Continuing Hiring Fees: continuing hiring fees for which you are responsible in connection with loss of or damage to hired-in *Temporary Buildings* or *Plant* insured under this Policy (including loss or damage which would have been insured but for the application of any *Excess*) in respect of the period, not exceeding 3 months from the date of the loss or damage, during which the property cannot be used solely as a result of the loss or damage.

We will not pay in respect of any one event more than £10,000

We will not be liable for

   (a)   hire charges for which you would not have been responsible if the Model Conditions of the Construction Plant Hire Association or Scottish Plant Owners Association had applied

   (b)   the first £250 of each claim or the first 2 days' hire charges whichever is the greater.

(ix)   Plans and Documents: clerical costs and expenses necessarily incurred in re-writing, redrawing or reproducing plans, drawings or other contract documents following their loss or damage by an event insured under this Policy.

We will not pay more than £50,000 in respect of any one event.

(x)   Expediting Expenses: the additional costs and expenses of overtime, weekend and shift working, plant hire charges, express delivery (including air freight) necessarily and reasonably incurred in expediting repair, reinstatement or replacement of loss or damage insured under this Policy.

We will not pay more than £50,000 in respect of any one event.

(xi)   Other Interests: the interest in the *Insured Property* of any party entering into an agreement with you (or any principal of yours) is noted in this insurance to the extent required by the agreement.

We will not be liable for

(a)   an *Excess* of

   (i)   £100 in respect of loss of or damage to employees' personal effects and tools

   (ii)   £500 in respect of other loss of or damage to *Insured Property*, caused by theft or malicious persons

   (iii)   £250 in respect of all other loss of or damage to *Insured Property*

(b) any *Contract* which involves

   (i) an original *Estimated Contract Price* in excess of the Maximum Original Estimated Contract Price specified in the Schedule

   (ii) an original contract period (excluding the maintenance period) in excess of the Maximum Original Contract Period specified in the Schedule

   (iii) work in, over or adjacent to water

   (iv) work on bridges, viaducts, subways, tunnels, motorways, dams, nuclear installations and the like

   (v) a depth of excavation exceeding 5 metres

(c) loss or damage for which you are relieved of responsibility under any contractual agreement

(d) loss of or damage to

   (i) deeds, bonds, bills of exchange, promissory notes, cash, bank notes, cheques or securities for money or stamps

   (ii) any vessel or craft or thing made or intended to be water-borne or air-borne, or any *Insured Property* in or on it other than *Site Materials* in transit by inland waterway

   (iii) any mechanically propelled vehicle or plant for which a Certificate of Motor Insurance or security is required by law other than a vehicle or item of plant which is not otherwise insured and which at the *Contract Site(s)* as a tool of trade or being carried to or from such site(s)

   (iv) any item of machinery, plant, tools or equipment caused by its own breakdown or its own explosion

   (v) any property (including that being altered or repaired) existing at the time of the commencement of the *Contract* other than materials supplied and delivered for incorporation in the *Works*

   (vi) *Temporary Buildings* or *Plant* (including hired-in *Temporary Buildings* or *Plant*) whilst away from the *Contract Site(s)* unless

     (a) at your permanent premises or

     (b) stored in your other locked premises, compound or garage or

     (c) in transit

   (vii) *Nuclear Material*

   (viii) any contractual work including decommissioning in or of any building, plant, equipment or other property which has been used, is used, or is designated to be used, for the *Production or Use of Nuclear Materials* without our prior agreement

(e) loss of or damage to the *Works* or any part thereof in respect of which a certificate of completion has been issued by or to you or which has been completed and handed over or taken into use with your permission for a purpose other than for the performance of the *Contract* except

   (i) in respect of any contract for which you are acting as the main contractor where a certificate of completion issued in respect of sub-contract work or works transfers responsibility for such work or works to you or

   (ii) during

     (a) any maintenance or defects liability period, not exceeding 12 months' duration, specified in the conditions of the Contract but only in respect of loss or damage for which you are liable arising from a cause occurring prior to the commencement of the maintenance or defects liability period

    (b) a period of 14 days after the engineer has issued a certificate of completion in accordance with your obligations under clause 21 of the ICE Form of Contract if applicable or any equivalent contract or for damage to work actually being undertaken during such maintenance or defects liability period solely in connection with your obligation under the *Contract* to remedy a defect or complete any snagging list and any *Plant* insured under Items 2, 3, 4 and 5 for use in connection therewith

  (f) the cost of

    (i) repairing, replacing or rectifying any property which is defective

      (a) in design, plan, specification, materials or workmanship or relies for its support or stability on such property which is defective, except for loss of or damage to the remainder of the property which is free of such defect but is accidentally damaged as a consequence of the defect

      (b) by reason of wear and tear, rust, mildew or other gradual deterioration

    (ii) normal upkeep or normal making good

  (g) penalities under contract for delay, non-completion or consequential loss of any nature except as specifically provided for by this Policy

  (h) loss of property by disappearance or by shortage if revealed only when an inventory is made or not traceable to an identifiable event.

GENERAL EXCLUSIONS

A4–06   **1. Geographical Limits**: This Policy does not insure any loss, damage, liability or injury arising outside Great Britain, Northern Ireland, the Isle of Man and the Channel Islands.

    2. Sonic Bangs: This Policy does not insure loss or damage occasioned by pressure waves caused by aircraft or other aerial devices travelling at sonic or supersonic speeds.

    3. War Risks: This Policy does not insure any consequence whether direct or indirect of war, invasion, act of foreign enemy, hostilities (whether war be declared or not), civil war, rebellion, revolution, insurrection or military or usurped power, confiscation, commandeering, nationalisation or requisition, or loss of or damage to any property by or under the order of any government de jure or de facto or public, municipal or local authority.

    4. Nuclear Risks: This Policy does not insure loss or damage to any property whatsoever or any loss or expense whatsoever resulting or arising therefrom or any consequential loss directly or indirectly caused by or contributed to by or arising from the radioactive, toxic, explosive or other hazardous properties of any explosive nuclear assembly or nuclear component thereof or ionising radiations or contamination by radioactivity from any nuclear fuel or from any nuclear waste from the combustion of nuclear fuel.

    5. Terrorism and Civil Commotion: This Policy do not insure loss or damage

    (a) in England and Wales and Scotland but not the territorial seas adjacent thereto as defined in the Territorial Sea Act 1987, by fire or explosion occasioned by or happening through or in consequence directly or indirectly of terrorism, except to the extent stated in the Special Provision — Terrorism set out below

(b) in Northern Ireland occasioned by or happening through or in consequence directly or indirectly of

   (i)   civil commotion
   (ii) terrorism.

For the purposes of this Policy terrorism means any act of any person acting on behalf of or in connection with any organisation with
activities directed towards the overthrowing or influencing of any government de jure or de facto by force or violence.

In any action, suit or other proceedings where we allege that by reason of this definition any loss or damage is not covered by this Policy
(or is covered only up to a specific limit of liability) the burden of proving that such loss or damage is covered (or is covered beyond that limit
of liability) will be upon you.

Special Provision — Terrorism

Subject otherwise to the terms, definitions, exclusions, provisions and conditions
of the Policy this insurance includes loss of or damage to insured property and
consequential loss (where insured) in England and Wales and Scotland but not the
territorial seas adjacent thereto as defined in the Territorial Sea Act 1987, by fire
or explosion occasioned by or happening through or in consequence of terrorism
as defined above, provided that our liability for all losses resulting from loss of or
damage to insured property will not exceed

  (a)   £100,000 for buildings
  (b)   any limit of liability or sum insured stated in the Policy

whichever is the lower

Any provision in this Policy which provides for any sum insured or limit of liability to be automatically reinstated following a loss will not apply to losses covered under this Special Provision.

6. Data Recognition: This Policy does not insure loss or damage, directly or indirectly caused by any Failure of a System resulting in loss or damage (whether
direct or indirect) to any such System or to any other Insured Property unless the
loss or damage results from a Defined Peril.

For the purposes of this Exclusion:

Failure of a System: means the failure or inability of a System (whether owned by
you or not)

   (i)   correctly to recognise or utilise any data concerning a date (whether a
date in the year 2000 or any other date) as being such calendar date as
the data is intended to represent
   (ii) to operate as a result of any command programmed into the System
utilising any date (whether a date in the year 2000 or any other date)

System: includes computers other computing and electronic and mechanical
equipment linked to a computer hardware software programs data electronic
data processing equipment Microchips and anything which relies on a
Microchip for any part of its operation

Microchip(s): includes integrated circuits and microcontrollers

Defined Peril: means to the extent that these are insured by this Policy fire, lightning, explosion, aircraft or other aerial devices or articles dropped therefrom,
riot, civil commotion, strikers, locked-out workers, persons taking part in
labour disturbances, malicious persons, storm, flood, escape of water from
any tank apparatus or pipe, impact by any road vehicle or animal, theft or

attempted theft, accidental escape of water from any automatic sprinkler installation, subsidence, ground heave or landslip.

Subject otherwise to the terms, exclusions and conditions of this Policy.

CONDITIONS

A4–07   **1. Observance of Terms**: Anyone claiming indemnity under this Policy must comply with its terms as far as they can apply.
2. Precautions: You must

    (i)   take all reasonable precautions to reduce or remove the risk of loss or damage
    (ii) maintain all buildings, furnishings, ways, works, machinery, plant and vehicles in sound condition and
    (iii) have any plant or equipment requiring statutory inspection so inspected.

3. Access: You must permit any person authorised by us access to the *Insured Property* at any reasonable time.
4. Alteration of Risk: You must obtain our prior written consent before any alteration is made which increases the risk of loss or damage.
5. Cessation of Work: If from any cause work ceases on the Contract Site for a continuous period in excess of 90 days immediate notice in writing must be given to us with the details of work completed and outstanding and on receipt of such notice we may, at our discretion, agree continuation of this insurance at special terms to be agreed.
6. Notification: You must report any loss or damage to us in writing as soon as reasonably possible and notify the police immediately of any loss or damage by theft, attempted theft, riot or malicious persons. No expense in making good damage may be incurred without our written consent except for emergency repairs to prevent further loss or damage.
7. Conduct of Claim: You must give us any help which we may reasonably ask for in connection with the claim. No property may be abandoned to us.
8. Other Insurance: If any other insurance covers the same loss or damage (or would have so covered but for the existence of this Policy) we will pay only any amount beyond that which would have been payable under such insurance had this Policy not been effected.
9. Cancellation: We may cancel this Policy by sending at least 7 days' notice to your last known address. You will then be entitled to a proportionate return of premium. You too may cancel the Policy. Any refund of premium will be calculated from the date we receive your written notice of cancellation and will be the full premium at our short period rates for the period the Policy has been in force.
10. Fraud: If any claim is in any respect fraudulent or if any fraudulent means or devices are used by you or anyone acting on your behalf to obtain any benefit under this Policy all your rights under it will be forfeited.
11. Arbitration: If any difference arises as to the amount to be paid under this Policy (liability being otherwise admitted) the difference will be referred to an arbitrator to be appointed in accordance with the statutory provisions in that behalf for the time being in force. Where any difference is by this condition to be referred to arbitration the making of an award will be a condition precedent to any right of action against us.

THE CO-OPERATIVE INSURANCE SOCIETY ("CIS") MOTOR VEHICLE POLICY

SCHEDULE

Policyholder   Policy Number   **A5–01**

Address   Agency Number

Period of Insurance   Insured Vehicle   Registration   Year of
from   to Midnight   Mark or Chassis   Registration
                                                or Engine Number

Policy Sections   Excess   Endorsements   Net First Premium or
Operative   Operative   Return (RTN) Premium

Note: Each of the Sections A to I is operative only if specified as operative in the Schedule.

SECTION A

THIRD PARTY LIABILITY

We will indemnify   **A5–02**

1. you
2. anyone driving with your permission who is allowed to do so by your current Certificate
3. anyone (other than the driver) using the Insured Vehicle with your permission for social, domestic or pleasure purposes
4. any passenger
5. the employer of anyone indemnified under this Section against legal liability for death, injury or damage to property arising from any accident involving the Insured Vehicle (or any trailer attached to it).

We will also pay costs and expenses incurred with our consent including the cost of

(i)   representation at any Coroner's Court, Fatal Accident Inquiry or Court of Summary Jurisdiction
(ii) defending proceedings arising from any death

in respect of any event which may be the subject of indemnity under this Section.

If this Policy is issued in the name of an individual this Section will operate whilst you are personally driving any motor vehicle which your current Certificate allows you to drive provided that there is no other insurance which indemnifies you.

This Section does not insure legal liability for

(a)   death of or injury to an employee arising out of and in the course of employment by anyone indemnified under this Section except as necessary to comply with the Road Traffic Acts
(b)   loss or damage to the Insured Vehicle or any property owned by or in the care of anyone indemnified under this Section
(c)   *Policies with prefix letters CM (Commercial Vehicle), MT (Agricultural and Forestry Vehicle) or MPH (Private Hire Car)* – damage to property exceeding £5,000,000 in respect of any one claim or number of claims arising from one accident. If indemnities to ore than one person are involved the insurance will apply to the aggregate amount and in priority to you.

Note: Compulsory Motor Insurance Laws

We will provide the compulsory minimum insurance for motor vehicles required in any country which is a member of the European Community or which has satisfied the Commission of the E.C. that its arrangements meet the requirements of Article 7(2) of E.C. Directive 72/166.

If the law of any country obliges us to make a payment for which, because of a breach of any of the terms or conditions of this Policy, we would not otherwise have been liable we will require you to refund the amount paid.

SECTION B

INSURED VEHICLE — LOSS OR DAMAGE

A5–03   We will indemnify you against loss of or damage to the Insured Vehicle (and/or its accessories) by, at our option, either paying the cost of repair or making a payment in settlement of not more than the market value.

For the purpose of any claim settlement repair as near as is reasonably practicable will be sufficient even though the former appearance or condition of the Insured Vehicle (and/or its accessories) may not be precisely restored.

If the Insured Vehicle is the subject of a hire purchase or leasing agreement any payment in settlement will be made to the legal owner.

We will also pay the reasonable cost of removing the Insured Vehicle to the nearest repairer and returning it after repair to your address as noted in our records.

Policies with prefix letters PM or FM (Motor Car)—New Vehicle Replacement

If, within 12 months of its registration as new in your name, the Insured Vehicle is stolen and not recovered or suffers damage insured by this Section and we agree that the cost of the repair will exceed 60% of the manufacturer's United Kingdom list price (including taxes) current at the time of the damage we will replace it with a new vehicle of the same make, model and specification, subject to availability. If a similar vehicle is not available we will replace it with the nearest equivalent model. Replacement will be made only at your request and with the consent of any other interested parties known to us. The Insured Vehicle will then become our property.

This Section does not insure

(a) loss or damage as set out in Section C

(b) loss of use, depreciation (including diminution in value as a consequence of repair), wear and tear or mechanical, electrical, electronic or computer failure or breakdown

(c) damage to tyres by punctures, cuts or bursts

(d) loss or damage resulting from riot or civil commotion outside Great Britain, the Isle of Man and the Channel Islands

(e) (i)   the first £50 of each claim for loss or damage and, in addition,

(ii) the amount shown in the Schedule under the heading "Excess" or such other amount as may be specified in any subsequent endorsements and, in addition,

(iii) *Policies with prefix letters PM or FM (Motor Car), CM (Commercial Vehicle), MPH (Private Hire Car)*—the amount specified below whilst the Insured Vehicle is being driven by or is in the care of anyone who is aged under 25 years.

Aged under 21 years   £200
Aged 21–24 years   £100

The amount specified in (i) above does not apply where a damaged windscreen or window is repaired and not replaced.

The amounts specified in (ii) and (iii) above do not apply where the claim is for damage to the windscreen or windows only and any resultant scratched bodywork.

SECTION C

INSURED VEHICLE—FIRE OR THEFT

We will indemnify you against loss of or damage to the Insured Vehicle (and/or **A5–04** its accessories) resulting from

1. fire, explosion or lightning or

2. theft (to include taking without lawful authority) or attempted theft

by, at our option, either paying the cost of repair or making a payment in settlement of not more than the market value.

For the purpose of any claim settlement repair as near as is reasonably practicable will be sufficient even though the former appearance or condition of the Insured Vehicle (and/or its accessories) may not be precisely restored.

If the Insured Vehicle is the subject of a hire purchase or leasing agreement any payment in settlement will be made to the legal owner. We will also pay the reasonable cost of removing the Insured Vehicle to the nearest repairer and returning it after repair to your address as noted in our records.

Policies with prefix letters PM or FM (Motor Car)—New Vehicle Replacement

If, within 12 months of its registration as new in your name, the Insured Vehicle is stolen and not recovered or suffers damage insured by this Section and we agree that the cost of the repair will exceed 60% of the manufacturer's United Kingdom list price (including taxes) current at the time of the damage we will replace it with a new vehicle of the same make, model and specification, subject to availability. If a similar vehicle is not available we will replace it with the nearest equivalent model. Replacement will be made only at your request and with the consent of any other interested parties known to us. The Insured Vehicle will then become our property.

This Section does not insure

(a) loss of use, depreciation (including diminution in value as a consequence of repair), wear and tear or mechanical, electrical, electronic or computer failure or breakdown

(b) loss or damage resulting from riot or civil commotion outside Great Britain, the Isle of Man and the Channel Islands.

Section D

Personal Accident Benefits

A5–05   If this Policy is in the name of an individual and you or your spouse suffer accidental bodily injury in connection with the Insured Vehicle or whilst in any other motor car we will pay to the injured person £5,000 if within 12 months that injury alone causes

(i)   death or

(ii)   complete and permanent loss of the sight of an eye or

(iii) complete and permanent loss of the use of a hand or foot or

(iv)   permanent total disablement from attending to any business or occupation.

We will not pay more than £5,000 for injury to any one person and we will not pay for injury to any one person more than one motor insurance policy.

Section E

Personal Effects

A5–06   We will pay up to a total of £250 for personal effects (other than money) lost or damaged whilst in or on the Insured Vehicle.

Section F

Medical Expenses

A5–07   We will pay up to £250 for medical expenses incurred by each person who is accidentally injured whilst in the Insured Vehicle.

SECTION G

TRAILERS

In Section B or C, where operative, the term "Insured Vehicle" includes a trailer   **A5–08**
(but not a caravan trailer) attached to the Insured Vehicle.

SECTION H

UNINSURED LOSS RECOVERY AND LEGAL HELPLINE

For the purposes of this Section   **A5–09**

1. "We", "us" and "our" means DAS Legal Expenses Insurance Company
   Limited, who administer this insurance on behalf of CIS.
2. "Insured Person" means you and, with your agreement,

   (i) anyone driving who is allowed to do so by your current Certificate
   (ii) any passenger

   whilst in or on the Insured Vehicle.

If an accident occurs which results in

1. loss of or damage to the Insured Vehicle or personal effects in or on the
   Insured Vehicle or
2. death of or injury to an Insured Person and we accept that there is
   reasonable prospect of a successful recovery against a negligent party
   we will, at your request,

   (i) negotiate to recover the Insured Person's uninsured losses and
        costs
   (ii) pay costs and expenses incurred with our consent together with
        third party costs for which the Insured Person is responsible.

In addition, where

1. the Insured Vehicle cannot be driven as a result of the damage and
2. the accident was entirely the fault of an identified driver of another
   motor vehicle on which there is valid motor insurance,

we will pay the cost of a temporary replacement vehicle supplied by us or hired
with our prior consent in Great Britain, Norther Ireland, the Isle of Man or the
Channel Islands.
Where we undertake to pay for a replacement hire vehicle you must

1. allow us to choose the vehicle hire company, the vehicle to be hired and
   the period of hire
2. comply with any conditions of hire
3. agree to our recovering any vehicle hire costs in your name and refund
   to us any costs recovered.

We will not

(a) negotiate in respect of claims relating to a contract involving the Insured Vehicle

(b) pay more than £50,000 in respect of all claims under this Section, including the legal costs of an appeal or of defending an appeal, arising from any one accident.

If claims from more than one Insured Person are involved the insurance will apply to the aggregate amount and in priority to you.

Note

1. We will be entitled to the full conduct and control of any claim or legal proceedings.

2. We will be entitled to appoint a legal representative where we regard it as necessary. An Insured Person may choose an alternative legal representative only where

    (i) we decide to commence legal proceedings or
    (ii) there is a conflict of interest.

    Any dispute as to the choice of legal representative or the handling of a claim will be referred to an independent arbitrator who will normally be the President of the Law Society.

3. An Insured Person must not settle a claim without our agreement.

EuroLaw Personal Motor Legal Advice Service

We will give you confidential advice by telephone on any personal motoring-related legal problem under the laws of the member countries of the European Union, the Isle of Man, the Channel Islands, Norway or Switzerland.

For the telephone numbers for a temporary replacement vehicle or legal advice, see "How to Make a Claim", below.

Section I

Road Rescue Plus

A5–10   For the purposes of this Section

1. any trailer or caravan trailer attached to the Insured Vehicle is insured

2. "Immobilised" means unable to be driven or made unroadworthy as a result of a road accident, breakdown, act of vandalism, fire, theft or attempted theft causing breakage or failure of any part essential to the Insured Vehicle's mobility

3. "Your Home" means your address as noted in our records.

We will provide assistance as set out below.

1. *Assistance and Recovery* — where the Insured Vehicle is Immobilised at home or at the roadside in Great Britain, Northern Ireland, the Isle of Man or the Channel Islands.

    (i) We will arrange and pay for a vehicle rescue operator to attend the scene of the incident for up to one hour to try to restore the Insured Vehicle's mobility.

    (ii) If the Insured Vehicle cannot be made roadworthy at the scene of the incident we will arrange and pay for it to be taken, together with the driver and up to six passengers, to a suitable garage, normally within 15 miles, to be repaired at your cost.

(iii) If the Insured Vehicle cannot be repaired the same day at a suitable garage we will arrange and pay for

(a) the Insured Vehicle, together with the driver and up to six passengers, to be taken to Your Home or the intended destination and, at your request, the Insured Vehicle will be taken to a garage of your choice within 15 miles of Your Home or the intended destination during one complete journey

or

(b) one night's hotel accommodation (bed and breakfast only) for the driver and up to six passengers

or

(c) a hire vehicle of up to 1100cc for a period not exceeding 24 hours. You will be responsible for the return of the hire vehicle and the collection of the Insured Vehicle after repair.

We will not pay more than £40 per person for hotel accommodation.

2. *Foreign Use* — for a journey planned between Your Home and a destination in any country outside Great Britain, Northern Ireland, the Isle of Man and the Channel Islands.

A. *Continental Roadside Assistance and Recovery*
If the Insured Vehcile is Immobilised we will arrange and pay for

(i) a vehicle rescue operator to attend the scene of the incident to try to restore the Insured Vehicle's mobility. If the Insured Vehicle cannot be made roadworthy at the scene of the incident it will be taken, together with the driver and up to six passengers, to a suitable garage for it to be repaired at your cost.
We will not pay more than £250 per journey for the cost of labour at the roadside and any necessary recovery

(ii) repairs necessary to secure the Insured Vehicle following theft or attempted theft of the vehicle or its contents.
We will not pay more than £100 per journey for the cost of labour

(iii) the location and despatch of any parts necessary to repair the Insured Vehicle.

B. *Completion of Journey*
If the Insured Vehicle is

(i) Immobilised for more than 8 hours and cannot be repaired locally,

or

(ii) stolen and not recovered

we will arrange and pay for

(i) (a) the transportation of the driver and up to six passengers and their personal effects to the intended destination and the return of the driver to the repairer's premises to collect the repaired vehicle

or

(b) reasonable hotel accommodation (bed and breakfast only) for the driver and up to six passengers for the period necessary for completion of repairs to the Insured Vehicle, provided your planned accommodation has been pre-paid and the costs cannot be recovered.

We will not pay more than £50 per person per day for accommodation expenses, up to a total of 6 days.

Where we have agreed that the appropriate means of transportation is an alternative hire vehicle for the period necessary for completion of repairs to the Insured Vehicle we will not pay more than £80 per day, up to a total amount of £800

(ii) delivery of the Insured Vehicle, if you are unable to collect it, to the intended destination after repair

(iii) a replacement hire vehicle in the United Kingdom pending the return of the Insured Vehicle to the United Kingdom if, following a breakdown or accident, the Insured Vehicle is repatriated more than 24 hours after the date of your return to Your Home.
We will not pay more than a total of £150.

C. *Repatriation of the Insured Vehcile*
  1. If, whilst it is outside Great Britain, Northern Ireland, the Isle of Man and the Channel Islands, the Insured Vehicle is

  (i) Immobilised and cannot be repaired locally before your intended return to Your Home, or
  (ii) stolen, and not recovered until after you return to Your Home,

  we will arrange and pay for
  (i) (a) the return of the Insured Vehicle to Your Home or to a garage of your choice in the United Kingdom
          or
      (b) a single ticket by rail and/or sea, or by air if travel by train and/or boat exceeds 12 hours, for you or your nominated driver to travel from the United Kingdom to collect the Insured Vehicle
  (ii) if applicable, storage of the Insured Vehicle pending its repair, repatriation or legal abandonment.
       We will not pay more than £100 for storage.

  Where the estimated repatriation cost exceeds the United Kingdom market value of the Insured Vehicle we will not pay more than the cost of legal abandonment and any customs duty imposed.
  2. If, at the time of your intended return to Your Home, the Insured Vehicle

  (i) is still Immobilised or
  (ii) has not been recovered after having been stolen we will pay for the return of the driver and up to six passengers to Your Home.

  3. *Emergency Driver*
       If during a journey, the sole driver in the party suffers accidental bodily injury or illness and as a result is unable to drive we will provide and pay for a driver to complete the journey or return the Insured Vehicle and up to six passengers to Your Home.

This Section does not insure
  (a) the cost of fuel or any spare parts required to restore the mobility of the Insured Vehicle
  (b) damage or costs incurred as a direct result of gaining access to the Insured Vehicle following your request for assistance
  (c) the costs incurred in obtaining a spare wheel or for roadside repair where you are unable to provide a serviceable spare wheel
  (d) recovery or assistance if the Insured Vehicle is partly or completely buried in snow, mud, sand or flood

(e) any amount under "2. Foreign Use" where spare parts can be obtained locally or any amount if spare parts are unavailable because

  (i)   they are no longer manufactured
  (ii) they cannot be obtained from a wholesaler or agent
  (iii) they cannot be exported to the country where the Insured Vehicle is located.

Note

1. If we arrange for temporary roadside repairs to be carried out following damage to the Insured Vehicle, or provide recovery to the destination, we shall not be liable to provide further assistance in respect of the same incident or insured event.
2. No recovery or assistance will be provided unless you contact the Emergency Helpline number shown in "How to Make a Claim" on page 7. You should not contact any agent or repairer direct.
3. You must attend the Insured Vehicle at the time we have informed you that assistance may be expected.
4. We will not arrange for assistance where the Insured Vehicle is considered to be dangerous or illegal to repair or transport.
5. We will not be liable for more than two claims arising from a common identified fault made under this Section during any period of insurance.
6. If we agree to provide assistance in Great Britain, Northern Ireland, the Isle of Man or the Channel Islands and our nominated agent is unable to attend the Insured Vehicle within one hour of your call to us, we will pay £10 as compensation, provided that

  (i)   the delay was not caused by circumstances beyond our control and
  (ii) you submit a written claim to us for the compensation.

For details of other RoadRescue services, and the telephone numbers to call for assistance, see "How to Make a Claim", below.

GENERAL EXCLUSIONS

1. Driving and Use: This Policy does not insure any damage, loss, injury, liability or assistance where to your knowledge or that of the person seeking indemnity any motor vehicle in respect of which this Policy provides indemnity is   **A5–11**

  (i)   being driven by anyone who is not allowed to drive by your current Certificate or
  (ii) being used outside the Limitations as to Use in your current Certificate except that
    (a)   the provision regarding a licence to drive will not operate when a licence is not required by law
    (b)   any indemnity provided under Section B will operate whilst the Insured Vehicle is in the care of a member of the motor trade for maintenance or repair or of a hotel, restaurant or commercial undertaking for parking.

2. Geographical Limits: This Policy does not insure any damage, loss, injury or liability arising outside Great Britain, Northern Ireland, the Republic of Ireland, the Isle of Man, the Channel Islands, Austria, Belgium, Croatia, Czech Repubic, Denmark, Finaldn, France, Germany, Gibraltar, Greece, Hungary, Iceland, Italy, Luxembourg, Netherlands, Norway, Portugal, Slovak Republic, Slovenia, Spain, Sweden and Switzerland.

3. Contractual Liability: This Policy does not insure any liability which arises only because of an agreement.

4. War Risks: This Policy does not insure any consequence whether direct or indirect of war, invasion, act of foreign enemy, hostilities (whether war be declared or not), civil war, rebellion, revolution, insurrection or military or usurped power.

5. Nuclear Risks: This Policy does not insure

(a) loss or destruction of or damage to any property whatsoever or any loss or expense whatsoever resulting or arising therefrom or any consequential loss

(b) any legal liability of whatsoever nature

directly or indirectly cuased by or contributed to by or arising from the radioactive, toxic, explosive or other hazardous properties of any explosive nuclear assembly or nuclear component thereof or ionising radiations or contamination by radioactivity from any irradiated nuclear fuel or from any nuclear waste from the combustion of nuclear fuel.

6. Third Party Rights: A person, or company, who is not a party to this Policy has no right under the Contracts (Rights of Third Parties) Act 1999 to enforce any term of this Policy but this does not affect any right or remedy of a third party which exists or is available apart from that Act.

CONDITIONS

A5–12 **1. Observance of Terms:** Anyone claiming indemnity or benefit under this Policy must comply with its terms as far as they can apply.

2. Precautions: You must take all reasonable precautions to keep the Insured Vehicle in a proper state of repair and to reduce or remove the risk of damage, loss or injury.

3. Notification: You must report any accident or loss to us as soon as reasonably possible. You must send any claim by a third party or notice of any proceedings to us immediately. If this Policy indemnifies you against damage to the Insured Vehicle (and/or its accessories) you may give instructions for the repair to be started provided that you notify us on the same day.

4. Conduct of Claim: Anyone claiming indemnity or benefit must give us any help which we may reasonably ask for in connection with the claim. We will be entitled to the full conduct and control of the defence or settlement of any claim from a third party and no admission of liability may be made without our consent.

5. Other Insurance: If any other insurance covers the same damage, loss or liability we will pay only our rateable proportion of any claim.

6. Cancellation: We may cancel this Policy by sending at least 7 days' notice to your last known address. You will then be entitled to a proportionate return of premium. You may cancel this Policy by returning your Certificate. Any refund of premium will be calculated from the date we receive your Certificate and will be the full premium less premium at our short period rates for the period the Policy has been in force.

ENDORSEMENTS

A5–13 *Each of the following Endorsements is operative only when the Endorsement number is shown in the Schedule under the heading "Endorsements Operative".*

M.561—Detached Trailer
The term "Insured Vehicle" includes any trailer of which we have been given details.   **A5–14**

M.655—Vehicle out of Use
The insurance provided by this Policy operates only whilst the Insured Vehicle is   **A5–15**
garaged and out of use.
The Scale of Discounts does not apply to this insurance.

M.630/M.631—Young Drivers' Memorandum
You have declared that one or more persons aged under 25 years, other than   **A5–16**
yourself, will drive the Insured Vehicle.

M.664—Protected Discount Memorandum
A 67% Discount (70% where you are aged 50 years or over) from the basic pre-   **A5–17**
mium is guaranteed, irrespective of claims, at the renewal date of this Policy following any Period of Insurance in respect of which we have accepted an extra
premium to provide such a guarantee.

FOR YOUR INFORMATION

The following notes will help you get the most from your Policy.   **A5–18**

How to contact us
Call your CIS representative
or
Call the CIS Sales and Service Centre 08000 282929
*Please note that telephone calls to the CIS Sales and Service Centre may be
recorded.*

Changes to the Policy or Certificate of Motor Insurance

Please contact us if   **A5–19**

   (i)   any of the information contained in the Schedule or Certificate is incor-
        rect when you receive it
  (ii)   you change your name, address or vehicle
 (iii)   you wish to amend the cover provided by your policy (*e.g.* increase of
        cover from third party fire and theft to comprehensive, change in driv-
        ing restrictions or the amount of voluntary excess).

If you change your vehicle you must obtain a new Certificate before you use the
replacement vehicle.
You should keep with your Policy any Endorsements issued to you.

Scale of Discounts

We operate a Scale of Discounts from basic premiums. After each claim-free   **A5–20**
policy year you will move one step up the Scale until you reach the maximum Discount. Should a claim (other than a claim for assistance under Section H or I) be
made or arise any Discount may be wholly or partially lost at the next renewal date
(except where the Protected Discount Scheme applies).

The current Scale of Discounts is published in our prospectus, which is available on request.

Foreign Use

This policy operates in

A5–21

(i) Great Britain, Northern Ireland, the Republic of Ireland, the Isle of Man and the Channel Islands

(ii) any member country of the European Union (currently Austria, Belgium, Denmark, Finland, France, Germany, Greece, Italy, Luxembourg, Netherlands, Portugal, Spain and Sweden)

(iii) any associated country (currently Croatia, Czech Republic, Gibraltar, Hungary, Iceland, Norway, Slovak Republic, Slovenia and Switzerland).

The policy will not normally be extended to operate in any other country but if you wish us to consider an application it should be made at least 28 days before commencement of the journey.

An International Motor Insurance Card (Green Card) is not required by law for the vehicle to be used in the above countries although we will normally supply one if you request it. We also publish Foreign Use Booklet which has further information on motoring abroad and advice on what to do in the event of an accident abroad.

Please contact us if you require a Green Card or a Foreign Use Booklet.

Car Sharing

A5–22 The receipt of contributions as part of a car sharing arrangement for social or other similar purposes in respect of the carriage of passengers on a journey in a vehicle insured under a motor car policy (*i.e.* a policy with prefix letters PM or FM) will not be regarded as constituting the carriage of passengers for hire (or the use of the vehicle for hiring) provided that

(i) the vehicle is not constructed or adapted to carry more than 8 passengers (excluding the Driver)

(ii) the passengers are not being carried in the course of a business of carrying passengers

(iii) the total contributions received for the journey concerned do not involve an element of profit.

This does not apply in the Isle of Man or the Channel Islands.

If you are in any doubt whether a car sharing arrangement is covered by the terms of a motor car policy an enquiry should be made to us.

HOW TO MAKE A CLAIM

A5–23 If the Insured Vehicle is lost or damaged or you have an accident causing injury to, or the death of, another person or damage to somebody else's property, you should contact your CIS representative or any CIS office as soon as possible.

Uninsured Loss Recovery and Legal Helpline (where Section H is operative)

Claims for uninsured loss recovery will be dealt with by the Motor Claims   **A5–24**
Centre, DAS Legal Expenses Insurance Company Limited, DAS House, Greenway
Court, Bedwas, Newport CF83 8DW.
For a temporary replacement vehicle under the terms of Section H telephone
0845 3003367.
The Eurolaw Personal Motor Legal Advice Service is available 24 hours a day, 7
days a week during the period of insurance – telephone 0845 3003366.

*CIS RoadRescue – policies with prefix letters PM or FM (Motor Car) or MC
(Motor Cycle)*

To assist you in the event of a breakdown or accident various 24-hour emer-   **A5–25**
gency services are available to you, dependent upon your policy cover. To take
advantage of the RoadRescue services *you must call the appropriate Emergency
Helpline number shown below at the time of the incident*. If you make your own
arrangements you cannot subsequently claim the benefits provided.
If we have agreed to provide assistance which you decide is no longer required
you must call to tell us; otherwise a charge may be payable.

Emergency Helpline Telephone Numbers
United Kingdom   08000 929069
Outside the United Kingdom   0044 161 930 8808
Please note that telephone calls to any number mentioned above may be recorded

- **Accident Recover Service**
  If the Insured Vehicle is immobile or unroadworthy following an accident tele-   **A5–26**
  phone the Emergency Helpline. We will arrange for the recovery of the vehicle to
  a suitable repairer (usually one of our appointed repairers near to your home or
  the destination) or to your home. If the repairer cannot accept the vehicle at the
  time of recovery, it will be stored free of charge for up to 48 hours. The driver and
  up to six passengers will be taken to your home or to the destination. Alternatively,
  we will arrange and pay for

  (i)   one night's accommodation (bed and breakfast only) subject to a
        maximum of £40 per person, or
  (ii)   a temporary hire vehicle up to 1100cc for a maximum of 24 hours.

- **Breakdown Assistance**
  If the Insured Vehicle breaks down assistance is available through the Emer-   **A5–27**
  gency Helpline. We will arrange for one of our approved repairers or recovery
  agents to attend the vehicle. Unless an additional premium has been paid for
  RoadRescue Plus and Section I is operative, this service is available only in the
  United Kingdom and the driver wil be required to pay call-out fee and the cost of
  any towing, labour or spare parts.

- **RoadRescue Plus (where Section I is operative)**
  If the Insured Vehicle is Immobilised the driver can telephone the Emergency   **A5–28**
  Helpline for prompt assistance. We will arrange for one of our approved repairers
  or recovery agents to attend the vehicle. Some or all of the costs, and the provision
  of specified ancillary services, will be insured – see policy Section I for details.

● Windscreen or Window Damage

A5–29   Emergency assistance is available where a windscreen or window is damaged; simply call the Emergency Helpline. The driver will be required to pay for any replacement or repair but where Section B is operative a United Kingdom repairer will normally submit the bill direct to us.

ROYAL & SUN ALLIANCE INSURANCE PLC ("RSA") CONTRACTORS' "ALL RISKS"— ANNUAL INSURANCE

The Company will indemnify the Insured by payment for the amount of or at the Company's option by repair reinstatement or replacement of Damage (meaning physical loss physical destruction or physical damage) to the Property Insured arising during the Period of Insurance from any cause whatsoever which is not specified in the Exclusions
Provided that: **A6–01**

1. such Property Insured belongs to or is the responsibility of the Insured
2. the Insured's Contribution (meaning the amount or amounts specified in any memorandum which the Insured agrees to pay) will be payable before the Company shall become liable to make any payment
3. the measure of indemnity shall be the cost of repair reinstatement or replacement by similar property less an appropriate deduction for wear and tear
4. the liability of the Company will not exceed

    (a) in respect of Item 1 the Estimated Contract Price or the Sum Insured shown in the Schedule whichever is the less
    (b) the Sum Insured applicable to each Item (excluding Item 1)
    (c) the Sum Insured where more than one Item is included but no individual Sums Insured are shown

    inclusive of any payment or payments under Extensions 4, 5, 6, 10 and 13 to this insurance relating to Damage to the Property Insured under such Item

DEFINITIONS APPLICABLE TO CONTRACTORS' "ALL RISKS" INSURANCE

Estimated Contract Price

The sum agreed between the Insured and his principal or employer as payment for completion of the works or where there is no principal or employer the value of the works to be completed at a single site **A6–02**

Contracts

A6–03   All constructional work undertaken by the Insured in the course of the Business but excluding any work which involves

(a) an original Estimated Contract Price or Contract Period (excluding the maintenance period) in excess of the Maxima shown in the Schedule
(b) work in over or adjacent to water
(c) bridges viaducts subways tunnels motorways dams and the like
(d) a depth of excavation exceeding 5 metres

Property Insured

A6–04   *Item 1*   *Permanent and Temporary Works*
The permanent works and temporary works executed in performance of the Contracts and materials for incorporation therein while on the sites of the Contracts or in transit by road rail or inland waterway within the Territorial Limits

Item 2   *Temporary Buildings*
Temporary buildings including fixtures and fittings therein for use in connection with the Contracts (but excluding hired-in property) anywhere within the Territorial Limits other than on sites of Contracts not insured by this Policy

Item 3   *Constructional Plant Tools and Equipment*
Constructional plant tools and equipment for use in connection with the Contracts (but excluding hired-in property and property described in Items 1, 2 and 5 herein) anywhere within the Territorial Limits other than on sites of Contracts not insured by this Policy

Item 4   *Hired-in Property*
Hired-in property as otherwise described in Items 2 and 3

Item 5   *Employees' Personal Effects*
Employees' personal tools and effects while on the sites of the Contracts within the Territorial Limits

Territorial Limits

A6–05   Great Britain Northern Ireland the Isle of Man or the Channel Islands

Speculative Development

A6–06   Property built for sale or letting by the Insured other than under a contract for a principal

Substantial Completion

A6–07   A building shall be deemed to be substantially complete when the work remaining relates only to the prospective purchaser's or tenant's choice of decoration fixtures and fittings

EXCLUSIONS TO CONTRACTORS' "ALL RISKS" INSURANCE

The indemnity will not apply to: A6–08

1. Damage for which the Insured is relieved of responsibility under any contractual agreement
2. Damage to
    (a) deeds bonds bills of exchange promissory notes cash bank notes cheques securities for money or stamps
    (b) any vessel or craft or thing made or intended to be water-borne or air-borne or any properth therein or thereon
    (c) any mechanically propelled vehicle or plant for which a Certificate of Insurance or security is required in accordance with the applicable Road Traffic Act but this Exclusion shall not apply to any such vehicle or item of plant which is not otherwise insured and which at the time of the Damage is being used at the site of the Contract as a tool of trade or while it is being carried to or from such site
    (d) any item of machinery plant tools or equipment caused by its own breakdown or its own explosion
    (e) any property (including that being altered or repaired) existing at the time of the commencement of the Contract other than materials supplied and delivered for incorporation in the works
    (f) the permanent works or any part thereof
        1. in respect of which a Certificate of Completion has been issued by or to the Insured or
        2. which has been completed and handed over or
        3. which has been taken into use with the permission of the Insured for a purpose other than for the performance of the Contract or
        4. which on a Speculative Development arises after Substantial Completion
        except as provided by Extensions 2, 3 and 8
    (g) any property insured by Items 2, 3 and 4 while such property is away from the site of any Contract unless it is temporarily
        1. at permanent premises of the Insured or
        2. stored in a locked premises compound or garage or
        3. in transit
3. the cost of
    (a) repairing replacing or rectifying any property which is defective
        1. in design plan specification materials or workmanship or which relies for its support or stability on such property which is defective
           This exclusion shall not apply to the remainder of the property which is free of such defect but is unintentionally damaged as a consequence of such defect
        2. by reason of wear tear rust mildew or other gradual deterioration
    (b) normal upkeep or normal making good
4. penalties under contract for delay or non-completion or consequential loss of any nature whatsoever except as otherwise specifically provided by this Policy
5. loss of property either by disappearance or by shortage if such disappearance or shortage is only revealed when an inventory is made or is not traceable to an identifiable event

6. (a) any consequence of war invasion act of foreign enemy hostilities (whether war be declared or not) civil war rebellion revolution insurrection military or usurped power confiscation commandeering nationalisation or requisition or Damage to any property by or under the order of any government de jure or de facto or public municipal or local authority

(b) Damage to any property whatsoever or any loss or expense whatsoever resulting or arising therefrom or any consequential loss directly or indirectly caused by or contributed to by or arising from

1. ionising radiations or contamination by radioactivity from any nuclear fuel or from any nuclear waste from the combustion of nuclear fuel
2. the radioactive toxic explosive or other hazardous properties of any explosive nuclear assembly or nuclear component thereof

7. Damage

(a) directly occasioned by pressure waves caused by aircraft or other aerial devices travelling at sonic or supersonic speeds

(b) 1. Elsewhere than in Northern Ireland Channel Islands and Isle of Man by fire or explosion occasioned by or happening through or in consequence directly or indirectly of Terrorism except to the extent stated in the "Special Provision — Terrorism", below

2. In Northern Ireland occasioned by or happening through or in consequence directly or indirectly of

(i) civil commotion
(ii) Terrorism

For the purposes of this policy Terrorism shall mean an act of any person acting on behalf of or in connection with any organisation with activities directed towards the overthrowing or influencing of any government de jure or de facto by force or violence

In any action suit or other proceedings where the Company alleges that by reason of this definition any Damage is not covered by this policy (or is covered only up to a specified limit of liability) the burden of proving that such Damage is covered (or is covered beyond that limit of liability) shall be upon the insured

Special Provision — Terrorism

Subject otherwise to the terms definitions exclusions provisions and conditions of the policy this insurance includes Damages elsewhere than in Northern Ireland Channel Islands and Isle of Man by fire or explosion occasioned by or happening through or in consequence of Terrorism as defined in Exclusion 7(b)

provided that the liability of the Company in respect of such Damage shall not exceed in respect of all losses arising out of any one occurrence

(a) £100,000 in total

or

(b) any limit of liability or sum insured stated in the policy as applying to that contract site or premises (including transit thereto or therefrom)

whichever is the lower

Any provision in this policy which provides for any sum insured or limit of liability to be automatically reinstated following a loss shall not apply to losses covered under this Special Provision

8. Damage to

    (a) Nuclear Material

    (b) Any constructional work including decommissioning in or of any building plant equipment or other property which has been used is used or is designated to be used for the Production or Use of Nuclear Material without the prior agreement of the Company

Definitions

Nuclear Material —

    (i) nuclear fuel other than natural or depleted uranium capable of producing energy by a self-sustaining chain process of nuclear fission outside a nuclear reactor either alone or in combination with some other material and

    (ii) radioactive products or waste produced in or any material made radioactive by exposure to the radiation incidental to the production or use of nuclear fuel not including fabricated radio isotopes

Production or Use of Nuclear Material —

The production manufacture enrichment conditioning processing reprocessing use storage handling or disposal of Nuclear Material

EXTENSIONS TO CONTRACTORS' "ALL RISKS" INSURANCE

Note: each of which is subject otherwise to the terms of this Policy.   A6–09

1. Automatic reinstatement following claim

The Sums Insured will not be reduced by the amount of any claim   A6–10
In consideration of this Extension the Insured shall pay an additional premium at a rate to be agreed on the amount of each claim for the period from the date of the incident to the date of the expiry of the Period of Insurance and any such additional premium will be disregarded for the purpose of any adjustment of premium under General Condition 5

2. Sub-contract works

In respect of any Contract for which the Insured is acting as the main contractor the reference under Exclusion 2F) herein to a Certificate of Completion will   A6–11
be deemed not to apply to a Certificate of Completion issued in respect of sub-contract work or works where such a Certificate is issued inter alia to transfer responsibility for such work or works to the Insured

3. Maintenance or Defects Liability period and I.C.E. Standard Conditions of Contract

A6–12   Notwithstanding the provisions of Exclusion 2F) the Company will indemnify the Insured for Damage to the permanent works or any part thereof occurring during

    (a)   any maintenance or defects liability period not exceeding 12 months duration or as specified in the Schedule but only in respect of Damage for which the Insured is liable arising from a cause occurring prior to the commencement of the maintenance period

    (b)   a period of 14 days after the Engineer shall have issued a Certificate of Completion where required under Clause 21 of the Institute of Civil Engineers' Contract Conditions (Fifth Edition) if applicable (or any subsequent revision or substitution thereof)

or for Damage to work actually being undertaken during such maintenance period solely in connection with the Insured's obligations under the Contract to remedy a defect or complete any snagging list and any constructional plant insured under Items 2, 3, 4 and 5 for use in connection therewith

4. Professional fees

A6–13   The Company will indemnify the Insured for architects' surveyors' and consulting engineers' fees necessarily incurred in the repair reinstatement or replacement of the Property Insured consequent upon Damage thereto for which Indemnity is provided by this Policy (but not for preparing any claim) The amount payable for such fees shall not exceed that authorised under the scales of the various institutes and bodies regulating such charges

5. Debris removal

A6–14   The Company will indemnify the Insured for costs and expenses necessarily incurred by the Insured with the consent of the Company in respect of

    (a)   debris removal and disposal

    (b)   dismantling and/or demolition   } of the portion or portions of the

    (c)   shoring up or propping   } Property Insured subject to Damage

    (d)   cleaning and/or repairing drains and service mains on site

resulting from any Damage for which indemnity is provided by this Policy but excluding any costs or expenses arising from pollution or contamination of property not insured by this Policy

6. Public Authorities requirements

A6–15   The Company will indemnify the Insured for such additional cost of reinstatement of the property as may be incurred with the Company's consent in complying with Building Regulations or local authority or other statutory requirements first imposed upon the Insured following the Damage provided that

the reinstatement is completed within twelve months of the occurrence of the Damage or within such further time as the Company may in writing allow
Provided that the Company shall not be liable in respect of costs for

— requirements relating to undamaged property or undamaged portions of property other than foundations (unless foundations are specifically excluded from the insurance)
— any rate tax duty development or other charge or assessment which may arise out of capital appreciation as a result of complying with any of the regulations or requirements referred to

7. Principals clause

This insurance extends to indemnify any employer or principal of the Insured   **A6–17**
but only to the extent required by the contract between the Insured and the said employer or principal Provided that the employer or principal shall observe and be subject to the terms exceptions and conditions of the insurance in so far as they can apply

8. Speculative Development (applicable to Item 1 only)

Notwithstanding Exclusion 2F)4) if the Contract involves Speculative Develop-   **A6–18**
ment the insurance under this Item) shall continue for a period of up to 90 days beyond the date of Substantial Completion of the last building on the site of the Contract pending transfer of ownership or letting
Damage to the contents of any building used as a showhouse showflat show office and the like is subject to the terms of Extension 9
Nothing in this Extension shall be deemed to extend cover beyond the date of expiration or non-renewal of the Policy

9. Showhouse contents

This insurance is extended to include damage to the contents of showhouses or   **A6–19**
showflats or show offices and the like on the site of the contract(s) until sold provided that

(a) cover shall cease no later than 90 days from the date that the last building on the site is substantially complete
(b) the liability of the Company shall not exceed £25,000 in respect of any one unit
(c) during the period from 1st December to 1st March an efficient heating system shall be left on at all times or the water system drained
(d) damage due to theft or malicious damage is restricted to that following forcible and violent entry or exit

10. Offsite storage (applicable to Item 1 only)

The insurance under this Item in respect of materials or goods designated for   **A6–20**
incorporation in the contract works is extended to apply while such materials or

goods are temporarily held in store away from the site of the Contract but not while such materials or goods are being worked upon in order to complete the same up to the point of their incorporation in the works

The Company's liability under this Extension shall be limited to 15 per cent of the Sum Insured by Item 1 or £25,000 (whichever is less) at any one location but this limitation shall not apply where and in so far as it is necessary for the Insured to comply with Clauses 16 and 30.3 of the JCT Conditions of Contract or Clause 54(3) of the ICE Form of Contract or any equivalent thereof

11. *Contract price increase* (applicable to Item 1 only)

A6–21   If the final price of the Contract exceeds the Sum Insured by Item 1 then the Sum Insured by this Item shall be increased proportionately to a figure not exceeding 125 per cent of the Sum Insured

12. *Immobilised plant* (applicable to Items 3 and 4 only)

A6–22   The insurance under these Items is extended to include the cost of recovery or withdrawal of constructional plant or equipment which is unintentionally immobilised provided that such recovery or withdrawal is not necessitated solely by reason of electrical or mechanical breakdown or derangement

13. *Other interests*

A6–23   The interest in the Property Insured of any party entering into an agreement with the Insured (or any principal of the Insured) is noted in this insurance to the extent that the agreement entered into with the Insured (or any principal of the Insured) requires such interest to be noted and is in respect of that part of the Property Insured to which the agreement relates

14. *Free issue materials* (applicable to Item 1)

A6–24   Reference to materials under this Item is deemed to include free issue materials provided that the value of such materials is included within both the Sum Insured and declaration of value in accordance with General Condition 5 of this insurance

15. *Plans and documents*

A6–25   The Company will indemnify the Insured for clerical costs necessarily incurred in re-writing redrawing or reproducing plans drawings or other Contract documents damaged within the Territorial Limits provided that the liability of the Company shall not exceed £50,000 in respect of any one occurrence of Damage

16. Expediting expenses

In the event of Damage to the Property Insured the cost of repair reinstatement or replacement admitted under this insurance shall subject to the consent of the Company include the additional costs of overtime weekend and shift working plant hire charges express delivery (including air freight) necessarily and reasonably incurred in expediting repair reinstatement or replacement of such Damage provided that the liability of the Company shall not exceed £50,000 in respect of any one occurrence of Damage

A6–26

17. Series losses

Where Damage of or to the property insured on any one contract site arises during any one period of 72 consecutive hours caused by storm tempest flood or earthquake it shall be deemed to be a single event and therefore constitute one loss with regard to the application of the Insured's contribution

A6–27

CONDITIONS APPLICABLE TO CONTRACTORS' "ALL RISKS" INSURANCE

1. Cessation of Work

A6–28

If from any cause work ceases on the site of the Contract for a continuous period in excess of 90 days immediate notice in writing must be given to the Company with the details of work completed and outstanding and the Company on receipt of such notice may at its discretion agree continuation of this insurance at special terms to be agreed

2. The Insured shall ensure that all plant and equipment requiring inspection under any Statute or Order is so inspected

3. The Insured shall give to the Company and every person authorised by the Company access to the Property Insured at all reasonable times

4. On the happening of any Damage the Insured shall

(a) notify the Company in writing immediately

(b) inform the Police immediately if the Damage is caused by thieves or malicious persons

(c) provide the Company with full details of Damage by riot civil commotion strikers locked-out workers or persons taking part in labour disturbances within seven days of its happening

(d) send to the Company a written claim not later than thirty days or such further time as the Company may in writing allow after the Damage has happened providing at the Insured's own expense all the detailed particulars and evidence regarding the cause and amount of the claim as the Company may reasonably require together with (if demanded) a statutory declaration of the truth of the claim and of any matters connected therewith

(e) do with due diligence and concur in doing and permit to be done all things which may be reasonably practicable to avoid or diminish the Damage and to prevent repetition

5. (a) The Company shall be entitled without incurring any liability under the Policy to

1. enter any building or premises where Damage has happened and take and keep possession of the property

2. deal with salvage in any reasonable way

but no property may be abandoned to the Company

    (b)   If the Company elects or becomes bound to reinstate or replace any property the Insured shall at his own expense produce and give to the Company all such plans documents books and information as the Company may reasonably require The Company shall not be bound to reinstate exactly or completely but only as circumstances permit and in reasonably sufficient manner and shall not in any case be bound to expend in respect of any one of the Items insured more than the Sum Insured thereon

    (c)   This Policy shall be proof that the Insured has given the Company the licence and authority that it may need to exercise its rights under this Condition

6. If any claim be in any respect fraudulent or if any fraudulent means or devices be used by the Insured or anyone acting on their behalf to obtain any benefit under this Policy all benefits hereunder shall be forfeited

7. If any difference shall arise as to the amount to be paid under this Policy (liability being otherwise admitted) such difference shall be referred to an Arbitrator to be appointed by the parties in accordance with the Statutory provisions in that behalf for the time being in force Where any difference is by this Condition to be referred to arbitration the making of an award shall be a Condition precedent to any right against the Company

8. Any claimant under this Policy shall at the request and at the expense of the Company take and permit to be taken all necessary steps in the name of the Insured for enforcing rights against any other party before or after any payment is made by the Company

The Company will not pursue any rights

    (a)   against any Company being Parent of or Subsidiary to the Insured or any Company which is a Subsidiary of a Parent Company of which the Insured is also Subsidiary in each case within the meaning of Sections 736 and 744 of the Companies Act 1985 or Articles 2 and 4 of the Companies (Norther Ireland) Order 1986

    (b)   against any sub-contractor engaged by the Insured if the contract is being performed under the JCT Standard Forms of Building Contract incorporating the 1986 Amendments to the Insurance and Related Liability Provisions (or the equivalent thereof)

        but this shall only apply to the extent that such waiver of subrogation is required in the above mentioned Amendments and only in so far as such a waiver is required by the sub-contract

9. Any information provided to the Company in accordance with General Condition 5 relating to turnover or final contract values shall include

    1.   the value of any materials and equipment provided by the employer or principal for incorporation in the Contract

    2.   professional fees incurred in the design and construction of the Contract

    3.   Value Added Tax which is irrecoverable by the Insured

APPENDIX 7

ROYAL & SUN ALLIANCE INSURANCE PLC ("RSA") FIDELITY POLICY

These sections are operative only if the letter set against them appears in the Schedule

SECTION A

FIDELITY

The Company will indemnify the Insured up to the Limits of Indemnity in respect of **A7–01**

1. loss of Property as a direct result of a Fraudulent Act committed during the Period of Insurance
2. auditor's fees necessarily incurred with the Company's written consent to substantiate the amount of any loss covered by this Section
3. the reasonable cost of rewriting or amending the software programs or systems where such rewriting or amending is necessary to correct the programs or amend the security codes following the fraudulent use of computer hardware or software programs or computer systems the subject of a claim for which liability is admitted under this Section

SECTION B

THIRD PARTY COMPUTER AND FUNDS TRANSFER FRAUD

The Company will indemnify the Insured up to the Limits of Indemnity in respect of **A7–02**

1. loss of Property as a direct result of Third Party Computer or Funds Transfer Fraud committed by a Third Party during the Period of Insurance
2. auditor's fees necessarily incurred with the Company's written consent to substantiate the amount of any loss covered by this Section
3. the reasonable cost of rewriting or amending the software programs or systems where such rewriting or amending is necessary to correct the programs or amend the security codes following the fraudulent use of computer hardware or software programs or computer systems the subject of a claim for which liability is admitted under this Section

Special Conditions

Application of the Limits of Indemnity

A7–03   The Company's liability for loss resulting from a Fraudulent Act or Third Party Computer or Funds Transfer Fraud will not exceed the amounts stated in the Schedule in respect of

1. Any One Claim
2. The Aggregate for all claims under the Policy

The Limit of Indemnity in respect of Any One Claim shall be the amount stated in the Schedule at the time of the occurrence of the Fraudulent Act or Third Party Computer or Funds Transfer Fraud (or if a series of related acts then the last act in the series)

Where different limits of indemnity are stated in the Schedule to apply to different Employees the Limit of Indemnity Any One Claim where two or more Employees are Acting in Collusion shall be the higher or highest of the limits of indemnity applicable to those Employees as stated in the Schedule

Irrespective of the number of premiums which shall be paid or payable and the number of years cover shall continue in force under this Policy (or any other insurance substituted by or issued in substitution for this Policy) the liability of the Company in respect of Any One Claim and in the Aggregate shall not be cumulative whether from one Period of Insurance to another Period of Insurance or otherwise

To the extent that the Aggregate Limit of Indemnity for any one Period of Insurance is not exhausted the unused element of the limit will not be available for any other Period of Insurance

Previous Insurance

A7–04   If this insurance immediately supersedes a Fidelity Insurance affected by the Insured (the "Superseded Insurance") the Company will indemnify the Insured in respect of any Fraudulent Act Discovered during the continuation of this insurance but committed during the continuation of the Superseded Insurance if the loss is not recoverable thereunder solely because the period allowed for Discovery has expired

Provided that

1. such insurance had been continuously in force from the time of the loss until inception of this insurance
2. the loss would have been insured by this insurance had it been in force at the time of the loss
3. the liability of the Company shall not exceed whichever is the lesser of

    (a) the amount recoverable under the insurance in force at the time of the loss or
    (b) the Limits of Indemnity under this insurance

    In any event the total liability of the Company in respect of Any One Claim continuing through both the term of the Superseded Insurance and the continuation of this insurance shall not exceed the Limit of Indemnity for Any One Claim stated in the Schedule

One Contract of Insurance

For all purposes including but not limited to the application of the Limits of   **A7–05**
Indemnity and consideration of when and how the Policy will respond all parties
included in the definition of the Insured in the Schedule shall constitute one
Insured and there shall be only one contract of insurance between that Insured and
the Company during the Period of Insurance

Conditions Precedent

It shall be a condition precedent of any liability of the Company under this Pol-   **A7–06**
icy that the Insured shall ensure compliance in full with each of the following:

1. Termination of Employment

Upon the termination of service of any Employee the Employer shall take all   **A7–07**
reasonable precautions to prevent a Fraudulent Act by that Employee
   For these purposes the Employer shall mean any party included within the definition of the Insured

2. References

The Insured shall ensure that satisfactory written or verbal references are   **A7–08**
obtained to confirm the honesty of each Employee who will be responsible for
Property computer operations or computer programming engaged after commencement of this Policy
   Such references shall be obtained directly from former employers for the three
years immediately preceding engagement and before the Employee is entrusted
without supervision
   References need ot be obtained in respect of Employees who have satisfactorily
and continuously served the Insured for at least one year in another capacity
before being entrusted with the duties referred to above
   In respect of Employees joining directly from school or government sponsored
youth training schemes one character reference shall be obtained
   A written record of any verbal reference shall be made at the time it is obtained
and the original copy of each written reference and the record of any verbal reference shall be retained by the Insured and shall be made available for inspection by
the Company

3. Minimum Standards of Control

The Insured shall ensure that the Minimum Standards of Control are operated   **A7–09**
or brought in to force and shall not make any change to the Minimum Standards
of Control unless the Company are advised and their written approval obtained
   The Minimum Standards of Control stated in the Schedule shall be maintained
in full operation throughout the currency of this Policy unless the Company are
advised and their written approval obtained

All Employees shall be instruced as to their duties or responsibilities in respect of the Minimum Standards of Control and be expected to comply

CLAIMS CONDITIONS

1. Reimbursement

A7–10   The Company shall be entitled if they so wish to take over and conduct in the name of the Insured all claims and rights of action of the Insured in respect of any act giving rise to a claim under this Policy
The Insured shall give all assistance as the Company may require

2. Other Insurances

A7–11   If at the time any claim arises under this Policy there be any other insurance fund indemnity or guarantee covering the same loss the Company shall not be liable except to the extent of any excess beyond the amount payable under such other insurance guarantee or indemnity had this Policy not been effected

3. Deduction from Loss

A7–12   All monies belonging to or the entitlement of the Employee in respect of whom a claim is made in the hands of the Insured shall insofar as legally permissible be deducted from the amount of the loss before a claim is made under this Policy

4. Recoveries

A7–13   Any recoveries made by either the Insured or the Company on account of such loss shall be applied in the following order

(a)   to reimburse the Insured in full for that part (if any) of the loss which exceeds the Limits of Indemnity (disregarding the amount of any Excess applicable)
(b)   to reimburse the Company if payment has already been made or if not to reduce that part of the loss for which the Company is responsible under this insurance
(c)   finally to reduce that part of the loss for which the Insured is responsible by virtue of any Excess under this Policy or for which other insurers under any other policy of insurance of which this Policy is in excess

5. Arbitration

A7–14   If any difference shall arise as to the amount to be paid under this Policy (liability being otherwise admitted) such difference shall be referred to an arbitrator to be appointed by the parties in accordance with the statutory provisions in that behalf for the time being in force

Where any difference is by this condition referred to arbitration the making of an award shall be a condition precedent to any right of action against the Company

6. Valuation

In the case of Securities the Company shall not be liable for more than the actual cash value of the Securities at the close of business on the business day immediately preceding the day on which the loss was Discovered or for more than the actual cost of replacing the Securities whichever is the less   **A7–15**

EXCLUSIONS

The Company shall not be liable for   **A7–16**

1. loss of interest penalities fines or consequential loss of any kind
2. the amont of the Excess
3. any loss caused by any Fraudulent Act of any Employee committed prior to the Commencement Date applicable to that Employee
4. any loss Discovered more than 24 months after

    (a) the termination of the Policy or
    (b) such loss was caused or commenced to be caused or
    (c) the resignation dismissal retirement or death of any Employee whose Fraudulent Act gave rise to a claim

    whichever occurs first
5. any loss where proof of the existence of Property or the amount of the loss is dependant solely upon an inventory computation or a profit and loss computation
6. any loss where the Fraudulent Act is committed by an Employee not resident within the Geographical Limits stated in the Schedule
7. any further Fraudulent Act committed by an Employee subsequent to the date of Discovery of a Fraudulent Act for which cover is provided under this Policy
8. under SECTION B for any loss or losses caused by any Employee insured under SECTION A of this Policy
9. under SECTIONS A and B for any loss or losses caused by fraudulent use of the telephone or other telecommunication system operated by the Insured

DEFINITIONS

Acting in Collusion shall mean all circumstances where two or more Employees are concerned or implicated together or materially assist each other in committing a Fraudulent Act   **A7–17**

Aggregate shall mean the maximum aggregate amount (howsoever arising) for which the Company shal be liable in respect of insurance available under the Policy in relation to the applicable Period of Insurance

Any One Claim shall mean all loss or losses caused by any Fraudulent Act or Third Party Computer and Funds Transfer either resulting from a single act or any number of related acts committed throughout the continuation of this insurance (or any insurance issued in substitution thereof or for which this insurance is substituted) irrespective of whether such acts are committed or caused prior to the inception of the Policy or during the Period of Insurance stated in the Schedule or during any subsequent Period of Insurance

Nothing in this definition will make the Company liable for acts committed prior to the Commencement Date or after the termination date except to the extent that cover is provided under the Previous Insurance section

Commencement Date shall mean the date from which insurance in respect of any Employee commenced

Discovery or *Discovered* shall mean when a director partner department director senior manager trustee or officer of the Insured becomes aware of acts which would cause a reasonable person to assume that a loss covered by this Policy has been or will be incurred even through the exact amount or details of such loss may not then be known

Employee shall mean any person who is

(a)   under contract of service or apprenticeship with the Employer or being trained under a Government approved training scheme under the control of the Employer

(b)   a director employed by the Employer under a contract of service and who controls no more than 5% of the issued share capital of the Employer

(c)   retired from full time employement with the Employer who is working for the Employer as a consultant under the control and direction of the Employer

in connection with the Business of the Employer whilst in the service of the Employer

Whilst in the service of the Employer shall include the period of 30 days immediately following the termination of service

The term *Employee* shall include: any person supplied by a staff employment agency who by arrangement with such agency is working for the Employer on a temporary or part-time basis in connection with the business to perform the functions and duties of an employee under the control or direction of the Employer but not including persons employed as drivers or in connection with warehouse duties or with computer operations or computer programming unless specifically stated as insured herein

Provided that any Condition relating to the obtaining by the Employer of references shall not apply to the temporary agency staff described above

For these purposes the term Employer shall mean any party included within the definition of the Insured

Excess shall mean the first part of Any One Claim borne by the Insured as specified in the Scheule at the time of the occurrence of the Fraudulent Act or Third Party Computer or Funds Transfer Fraud (or if a series of related acts the last act in the series) or as otherwise provided for by this Policy

Fraudulent Act shall mean any act of fraud or dishonesty committed by any Employee alone or Acting in Collusion with others committed with the clear intent of obtaining an improper personal financial gain (which shall not include salaries fees commission and other earnings in the normal course of employment) for themselves or for any other person or organisation intended by such Employee to receive such gain

Minimum Standards of Control shall mean the minimum standards of supervision accounting procedures and for checking the security of Property agreed between the Insurers and the Insured from time to time as set out in the latest Schedule

Money shall mean currency coins bank note and bullion

Property shall mean Money Securities or goods belonging to the Insured or for which they are legally responsible

Securities shall mean:

1. share certificates allotment letters bonds or debentures
2. promissory notes except
   (a) those issued or purporting to have been issued for use as currency
   (b) those secured or purporting to be secured directly or indirectly by assigned accounts or what purports to be assigned accounts
3. deeds of trust mortgages upon real property and upon interests in real property and assignments of such mortgages
4. letters of credit

Third Party Computer and Funds Transfer Fraud shall mean any act of fraud or dishonesty committed by a Third Party with the intent of obtaining an improper personal financial gain involving

(a) the manipulation of the Insured's computer hardware or software programs or systems
(b) fraudulent electronic instructions which purport to have been transmitted by the Insured

Third Party shall mean any person other than an Employee partner or director of the Insured

APPENDIX 8

ROYAL & SUN ALLIANCE INSURANCE PLC ("RSA") DIRECTORS' AND OFFICERS' INSURANCE POLICY

Note: This is a "claims made" policy which only covers Claims made against the Insured Persons and notified to the Insurer during the Period of Insurance and any Extended Reporting Periods; the terms and conditions on which cover is offered are as set out in the policy wording, set out below.

INSURING CLAUSE

1.1   The Insurer will pay on behalf of the Insured Persons Loss and Defence Costs for which the Company has not provided indemnity.   **A8–01**
1.2   The Insurer will pay on behalf of the Company Loss and Defence Costs but only when, and to the extent that, the Company is required or permitted to indemnify the Insured Persons for such Loss or Defence Costs.
1.3   The Insurer will pay on behalf of the Company costs and expenses incurred by a shareholder in pursuing a Claim against a Director or Officer and which the Company is liable to pay pursuant to an order of a court.

OTHER PROVISIONS

Severability

2.1   No fact relating to, or knowledge of, any Insured Person shall be imputed to any other Insured Person for the purpose of determining the availability of insurance for any Insured Person.   **A8–02**
2.2   The Proposal shall be construed as a separate application for cover by each of the Insured Persons with respect to the declarations and statements contained in the Proposal. No statement or knowledge possessed by any Insured Person shall be imputed to any other Insured Person for the purpose of determining the availability of insurance.
2.3   For the purposes of determining the Limit of Indemnity, the Policy will be construed as a joint policy with an aggregate limit available to all Insured Persons and to the Company collectively.

Liquidation of the Company

A8–03   **3.1**   In the event of the liquidation of the Company named in the Schedule (excluding for this purpose its Subsidiaries), this Policy shall remain in force until the expiry of the then current Period of Insurance unless cancellation is requested by all of the Insured Persons.

Acquisitions and Disposals

A8–04   **4.1**   If the Company creates or acquires during the Period of Insurance a new Subsidiary, either directly or indirectly through any existing Subsidiary, and the new Subsidiary so created or acquired:

    (a)   is registered outside the USA, its territories and possessions, or Canada; and

    (b)   does not have any of its Securities listed on any North American exchange;

the Company shall not have to provide the Insurer with full particulars of the new Subsidiary so created or acquired during the Period of Insurance and the new Subsidiary shall be covered under this Policy from the date of its creation or acquisition.

4.2   If the Company acquires or creates a Subsidiary that falls outside the parameters specified in Clause 4.1 (a) and (b) above, such new Subsidiary shall not be automatically covered under this Policy. If the Company specifically requests the cover provided under this Policy to be extended to include such new Subsidiary, then full particulars of the new Subsidiary must be supplied to the Insurer to allow the inclusion of such new Subsidiary to be considered. Should the Insurer agree to include such new Subsidiary within the scope of cover provided by this Policy, the Insurer will advise the Company of any laterations in the terms of this Policy and any additional premium payable. Upon acceptance of any notified alterations and the payment of any additional premium required by the Insurer, the Insurer will include such new Subsidiary within the scope of cover provided under this Policy by way of Endorsement, with effect from the date of acquisition or creation.

4.3   The provision of cover to newly created or acquired subsidiaries shall apply only to Wrongful Acts committed after the date the new Subsidiary was created or acquired by the Company. The Insurer will consider the provision of retroactive cover for any new Subsidiary in respect of Wrongful Acts committed, or alleged to have been committed, prior to the date of any acquisition or creation of such Subsidiary, upon specific request. If the Insurer agrees to provide such cover, it will be recorded by way of Endorsement.

4.4   If the Company named in the Schedule (excluding for this purpose its Subsidiaries) effects a sale of its controlling interest in a Subsidiary or a dissolution of a Subsidiary, cover under this Policy shall continue to apply during the Period of Insurance and any Extended Reporting Period in respect of persons who were Insured Persons of that Subsidiary prior to the sale or dissolution, for Claims relating to Wrongful Acts committed or alleged to have been committed prior to the date of sale or dissolution.

Extended Reporting Periods

5.1 If the Insurer declines to offer any terms for renewal of this Policy or the   **A8–05**
Insured refuses to renew this Policy, the Insured Persons shall be entitled to the
Extended Reporting Periods set out at 5.2 and 5.3, below. The offer of renewal
terms and conditions or premiums different from those in effect prior to renewal
shall not constitute refusal to renew.

5.2 Extended Reporting Period on Expiry of the Policy

(i) 12 months for no additional premium;

(ii) 24 months in return for payment of 25% of the Ful Annual Premium;

Provided that the application to the Insurer to exercise the right to these
Extended Reporting Periods is made within 15 days of the expiry of the Period of
Insurance and payment of the premium, if applicable, is made within 30 days (such
premium being non-refundable);

5.3 Extended Reporting Period for Former Directors and Officers

In the event that any Insured Person ceases to be a Director or Officer
during any Period of Insurance, such Insured Person shall be entitled to an
Extended Reporting Period for a period of 180 days after the expiry of the
Period of Insurance.

5.4 During any Extended Reporting Period the Insured Persons may continue
to notify Claims to the Insurer but only in respect of Wrongful Acts committed
prior to the expiry of the Period of Insurance.

Employment Practices

6.1 The Insurer will pay on behalf of the Insured Persons Loss and Defence   **A8–06**
Costs resulting from Employment Practice Claims against the Insured Persons,
whether directly or indirectly by a class action, or by the Equal Opportunity Commission or by any other country, European Union State or federal government
authority regulating employment practices, or by any other person or entity.

6.2 Notwithstanding the generality of Clause 6.1 above, the Insurer shall not
be liable for Loss and/or Defence Costs arising out of any Employment Practice
Claim made against the Insured Persons or the Company within the USA, its territories or possessions, or in Canada, or which is instituted or pursued before an
arbitrator or tribunal or in courts within the USA, its territories, possessions, or in
Canada (whether for enforecemtn of judgements or otherwise) or in which it is
contended that the laws of the USA or Canada should apply.

6.3 For the purposes of Clause 6 the Exclusion in Clause 10.5 shall be
amended by the deletion of the words "mental anguish".

Pollution

7.1 The Insurer will pay on behalf of the Insured Persons Defence Costs,   **A8–07**
subject to the aggregate limit specified in Sublimit (a) of the Schedule (such limit
being part of and not in addition to the Limit of Indemnity under this Policy)
incurred in defending themselves against criminal or regulatory proceedings in
respect of seepage, pollution or contamination of any kind which results from a
Wrongful Act.

7.2 The Insurer will pay on behalf of the Insured Persons Defence Costs, subject to the aggregate limit specified in Sublimit (b) of the Schedule (such limit being

part of and not in addition to the Limit of Indemnity under this Policy) in respect of civil proceedings by any shareholder and/or bondholder of the Company, either directly or derivatively, alleging loss in the value of the share capital of the Company by reason of seepage, pollution or contamination of any kind which results from a Wrongful Act.

7.3 This clause shall not apply to proceedings of any kind instigated or pursued outside of the European Union.

Outside Directorships

A8–08   **8.1** The Insurer will pay Loss and Defence Costs on behalf of the Insured Persons and any employees of the Company, who at the specific written request of the Company were, or now are, or may become a director or officer or occupy a position of equivalent status, of any Outside Directorship Company, for Claims against them in respect of an actual or alleged breach of trust, breach of duty, neglect, error, mis-statement, misleading statement, libel, slander, breach of contract, omission, breach of warranty of authority, Wrongful Trading or other act wrongfully committed or attempted by the Insured Persons in their respective capacities as directors (including de facto or shadow directors) or officers of such Outside Directorship Company provided that:

(i)   such cover shall only operate in excess of any other insurance in force in respect of such Outside Directorship Company and in excess of any indemnification provided to the Insured Persons by such Outside Directorship Company;

(ii) Such cover shall not apply in respect of any Claim:

(a)   by any director or officer of any Outside Directorship Company other than an Employment Practice Claim or Claims brought by such directors or officers for a contribution or indemnity in respect of a claim made against them;

(b)   by any Outside Directorship Company itself, other than shareholder and/or bondholder claims brought in the name of the Outside Directorship Company without the participation, solicitation or assistance of a director or officer of the Outside Directorship Company;

(c)   directly or indirectly caused by or arising out of the Failure of a System, taking or failure to take any corrective or other action in connection with the actual or possible Failure of a System, or a Wrongful Act in any way concerning any actual or possible Failure of a System.

8.2 In the event that the other insurance under sub-paragraph 8.1(i) above is provided by the Insurer, the total liability of the Insurer in respect of any Claim shall not exceed the greater of the Limit of Indemnity provided by this Policy or the limit of indemnity available under such other insurance.

Excess Reimbursement

A8–09   **9.1** Any Excess borne by the Company and/or the Insured Persons in respect of any Claim shall be reimbursed by the Insurer if final judgement or adjudication is given in favour of the Insured Persons by a court or tribunal of competent jurisdiction. For the purposes of this clause, final judgement or adjudication shall only be adjudged to have been given when all rights of appeal to higher tribunals have been foregone or exhausted.

EXCLUSIONS

The Insurer shall not be liable for: **A8–10**

10.1   Loss directly or indirectly relating to, arising from, or in any way connected with:

(a)   any dishonesty, fraud or malicious conduct found by way of final adjudication to have been committed by an Insured Person;

(b)   an Insured Person found by way of final adjudication to have gained any profit or advantage or to have received any remuneration to which he or she was not legally entitled.

10.2   fines, penalties and/or any other form of Loss which is uninsurable at law in the country to whose laws the Claim is subject.

10.3   Loss and/or Defence Costs directly or indirectly relating to, arising from, or in any way connected with any Claim brought against any Insured Person or the Company acting in the capacity of trustee or administrator of any occupational pension scheme or employment benefit programme.

10.4   Loss and/or Defence Costs directly or indirectly relating to, arising from, or in any way connected with any actual or alleged violation of any responsibility, obligation or duty imposed by the Employee Retirement Income Security Act of 1974 or any amendment, consolidation or re-enactment, or any similar provisions of state, statutory law or common law enacted in any other jurisdiction in which the Company operates.

10.5   Loss and/or Defence Costs resulting directly from the death, disease, mental anguish or illness of or bodily injury to any person, or loss of or material damage to property, including loss of use thereof, save that Insurers shall provide cover in respect of Defence Costs incurred in respect of any criminal proceedings, including those for corporate manslaughter (or any similar offence in any jurisdiction in which the Company operates) resulting from a Wrongful Act or Investigation.

10.6   Loss and/or Defence Costs directly or indirectly relating to, arising from, or in any way connected with seepage, pollution or contamination of any kind, save insofar as Defence Costs are covered pursuant to Clause 7 "Pollution", above.

10.7   Loss and/or Defence Costs directly or indirectly relating to, arising from, or in any way connected with:

(a)   ionising radiations or contamination by radioactivity, from any nuclear fuel, from any nuclear waste, or from the combustion of nuclear fuel;

(b)   the radioactive, toxic, explosive or other hazardous properties of any explosive nuclear assembly or nuclear component thereof.

10.8   Loss and/or Defence Costs incurred as a consequence of any circumstance:

(a)   notified or which should have been notified under any insurance which was in force prior to the Original Inception Date of this Policy; or

(b)   which was known to any of the Insured Persons at the Original Inception Date of this Policy and which might reasonably be expected to produce a Claim.

10.9   For the purposes of these Exclusions, Loss and Defence Costs shall include any costs and expenses otherwise covered under Clause 1.3.

GENERAL CONDITIONS

11.1 *Policy Voidable*

A8–11   In the event of the Insurer being entitled to avoid this Policy from inception, or from the time of any variation in the Insurance provided, the Insurer may at its discretion maintain this Policy in full force but exclude the consequences of any non-disclosure, misrepresentation, or other action giving rise to the right to avoid the Policy.

11.2 *Due Diligence*

A8–12   The Insured shall use due diligence and use all reasonable endeavours to do, and concur in doing, all such things as are reasonably practical to diminish any Loss or Defence Costs, and to assist with the defence and/or settlement of any Claim.

11.3 *Limit of Indemnity*

A8–13   The total aggregate liability of the Insurer in respect of all Loss and/or Defence Costs shall in no circumstances exceed the Limit of Indemnity described in the Schedule irrespective of how many Insured Persons may claim under this Policy during the Period of Insurance and any Extended Reporting Period, and irrespective of the number of Claims. For the avoidance of doubt, Insured Persons and the Company shall together be treated as one for the purposes of calculating the Limit of Indemnity.

11.4 *Series of Claims*

A8–14   Any Claim or series of Claims which have as their originating or source the same Wrongful Act(s), or which are otherwise causally connected, shall constitute a single Claim for the purposes of this Policy.

11.5 *Excess*

A8–15   Any Excess under this Policy shall be borne by the Company or the Insured Persons, as applicable.

11.6 *Change of Control*

A8–16   If an offer is made for the whole or controlling interest of the issued share capital of the Company named in the Schedule (excluding for this purpose its Subsidiaries), and that offer is declared or becomes unconditional in accordance with its terms, or in the case of a private limited company there is a change in ownership of the controlling interest of the share capital of the Company named in the Schedule (excluding for this purpose its Subsidiaries), the cover provided under this Policy shall be amended to apply only to Claims made during the Period of Insurance in respect of Wrongful Acts which were alleged to have taken place prior to the date that such offer is declared or becomes unconditional, or the change in ownership became effective.

CLAIMS CONDITIONS

12.1 Claims Notification

Notification of Claims must be sent to the Insurer at Royal and SunAlliance UK   **A8–17**
Commercial Claims, Stane Court, Albion Way, Horsham, Sussex RH12 1FB, for the attention of the D & O Claims Manager. The Insured shall notify the Insurer as soon as practicable in writing, but in any event, no later than 30 days after a Claim is first notified to the Company. The notification shall provide full details of the Claim, (including any Writ, Summons or other legal document, which must be forwarded to the Insurer immediately following receipt by the Insured) and the Insured shall provide Insurers with such further information and documentation as they shall reasonably require.

12.2 Notification of Circumstances

The Insured may give notice in writing of any fact, circumstance or event which   **A8–18**
could reasonably be anticipated to be likely to give rise to a Claim or Investigation against them. The notification shall provide full particulars of the fact, circumstances or event that could result in a Claim (including without limitation the identity of the potential claimant, the nature of the potential Claim, the likely quantum of the Claim and the Insured's preliminary views (if any) on the merits of any such potential Claim), and the Insured shall provide Insurers with such further information and documentation as they shall reasonably require. Any Claim arising from any such notification in a period of up to six years from the date of the notification shall be deemed to have been made in the Period of Insurance (including any activated Extended Reporting Period in which such notification has been given).

12.3 Claims Handling Procedure

Upon receipt of written notice in accordance with Clauses 12.1 and/or 12.2,   **A8–19**
Insurers shall be entitled to appoint a representative to investigate the Claim on their behalf. The Insured shall co-operate fully with Insurers' representative in the conduct of its enquiries, including but not limited to making available to it all necessary information and documentation as it may require together with facilities for the interviewing of all the Insured's personnel whom it may consider to be relevant to its enquiries.

12.4 Defence of Claim

The Insurer may at any time appoint lawyers of its choice and take over and con-   **A8–20**
duct in the name of the Insured the defence and settlement of any Claim. The Insured shall provide all reasonable information and assistance required by the

Insurer and its lawyers. The Insured shall not admit liabiity for or enter into any settlement or compromise in relation to any Claim against them, nor shall they incur any Defence Costs without the prior written consent of the Insurer.

12.5 *Subrogation*

A8–21   The Insurer shall be entitled to pursue or prosecute in the name of the Insured for the Insurer's benefit any associated recovery or third party proceedings. The Insured shall provide all reasonable information and assistance required by the Insurer, including doing all such things as are reasonably necessary to enable the Insurer to bring a claim in the name of the Insured.

12.6 *Disputes as to Contesting Legal Proceedings*

A8–22   In the event of a disagreement arising between the Insurer and the Insured as to whether or not to contest legal proceedings, the issue shall be remitted to a Queen's Counsel (whose identity shall be agreed by the parties and in default of such agreement shall be chosen by the Chairman for the time being of the Bar Council) whose decision on the probability of successfully defending the Claim shall be final.

12.7 *Disputes as to Policy Construction*

A8–23   In the event of a disagreement arising between the Insurer and the Insured concerning the construction of this Policy, either party shall be entitled to refer to arbitration any such matter which has not been resolved to its reasonable satisfaction. Any such matter shall be referred to a single arbitrator, who shall be either a solicitor or a barrister, as agreed upon by the parties, or failing such agreement, one who is nominated by the President for the time being of the Law Society. The arbitration will be carried out according to the terms of the Arbitration Act 1996 and the decision of the arbitrator shall be final and binding on the Insured and the Insurer. All costs of the arbitration shall be met in full by the party against whom the decision is made. If the decision is not clearly made against either party, the arbitrator shall have the power to apportion costs.

12.8 *Advancement of Defence Costs*

A8–24   The Insurer shall advance Defence Costs on behalf of the Insured prior to the resolution of a Claim, provided that such advance payments shall be repayable by the Insured to the Insurer in the event that it is determined that the Claim was not covered under the terms of this Policy.

12.9 *Non-Indemnification by the Company*

A8–25   If the Company is permitted or required to indemnify the Insured Persons in respect of any Loss and Defence Costs suffered by them but fails to do so, the Insurer shall pay such Loss and Defence Costs direct to the Insured Persons on behalf of the Company, provided that the Company shall be liable to pay any Excess due.

12.10 *Contribution*

Save as provided in Clause 8.2, if the Insured Persons are or would but for the **A8–26** existence of this Policy be entitled to cover under any other policy or policies in respect of any Claim or Investigation during the Period of Insurance or Extended Reporting Period if applicable, the Insurer shall not be liable for any Loss or Defence Costs or costs and expenses incurred in respect of any such Claim or Investigation save in respect of any amount in excess of that which is or would be payable in respect of such other policy or policies.

12.11 *Allocation*

If an Insured incurs both Loss and/or Defence Costs covered by this policy and **A8–27** losses and/or defence costs not covered by this policy, either because a Claim is made against both an Insured Person and the Company or because a Claim or Investigation includes both Loss and/or Defence Costs which are covered and those which are not, the Insurer shall:

    (a)   pay 100% of Defence Costs and
    (b)   in respect of Loss shall agree to negotiate in good faith with the Insured to seek to determine a fair and equitable allocation of the loss incurred taking into account the relative legal exposures of the parties.

If the Insured and the Insurer cannot agree on an allocation in respect of Loss, the Insured and the Insurer agree to remit the issue of allocation to a Queen's Counsel (whose identity shall be agreed between the parties and in default of agreement shall be chosen by the chairman for the time being of the Bar Council) whose decision shall be binding. All costs of the Arbitration shall be apportioned by the Queen's Counsel.

Any allocation or payment of Defence Costs shall not create any presumption as to the allocation of other Loss.

12.12 *Policy Law*

The policy shall be interpreted under, governed by and construed in accordance **A8–28** with the Laws of England and Wales. Save as provided in respect of Clauses 12.7 and 12.11, the Insurer and Insured agree to submit to the exclusive jurisdiction of the Courts of England and Wales.

INTERPRETATIONS

Claim: shall mean: **A8–29**

    (a)   any writ, suit or other proceedings served upon one or more Insured Persons in respect of a Wrongful Act or in relation to an Outside Directorship Company as provided in Clause 8.1;

(b) any written communication received by one or more Insured Persons
threatening commencement against them of proceedings in respect of a
Wrongful Act or in relation to an Outside Directorship Company as
provided in Clause 8.1;

(c) any criminal prosecution of an Insured Person resulting from a Wrongful Act or in relation to an Outside Directorship Company as provided
in Clause 8.1;

provided that it is first made against the Insured Persons during the Period of
Insurance or Extended Reporting Period if applicable.

Company: shall mean the Company named in the Schedule and any Subsidiary.

Defence Costs: shall mean:
legal costs, charges and expenses incurred by the Insured Persons with the
Insurer's prior written consent:

(a) in the defence of any Claim;
(b) in respect of an Investigation into the affairs of the Company or the
affairs of an Outside Directorship Company as provided in Clause 8.1;
(c) in resepct of any Investigation involving a Wrongful Act said to have
been committed by one or more Insured Persons or in respect of which
one or more Insured Persons are required to attend and/or give evidence by reason of their capacities as Directors or Officers;

provided that all such Defence Costs are in respect of a Claim and/or an Investigation first made against the Insured during the Period of the Insurance or
Extended Reporting Period if applicable and provided they are subject to the Limit
of Indemnity.

Director: shall mean any natural person who was, or is, or may be hereafter:

(a) a director of the Company including a de facto or shadow director (as
defined under section 741(2) of the Companies Act 1985 or any equivalent provision in the jurisdiction in which the Company is domiciled);
(b) a shadow director of any company directly as a result of his or her activities as a Director or Officer of the Company.

Employment Practice Claim: shall mean any claim brought by a past, present, or
prospective employee of the Company for or arising out of, any actual, or
alleged:

(a) wrongful and/or unfair dismissal or termination of employment (either
actual or constructive), wrongful failure to promote, negligent employment-related evaluation, wrongful deprivation of career opportunity,
wrongful disciplinary action or negligent employee evaluation, sexual or
workplace harassment of any kind (including the alleged creation of a
workplace environment conducive to harassment), wrongful failure or
refusal to grant tenure, employment-related defamation or unlawful discrimination whether direct, indirect or arising out of failure to provide
adequate employee policies and procedures;
(b) breach of any undertaking which has been transferred to the Company
by virtue of the Transfer of Undertakings (Protection of Employment)
Regulations and or the EC Acquired Rights Directive.

European Union: means the member states of the European Union, and shall be
extended to include the Channel Islands and the Isle of Man.

Excess: shall mean the amount for which the Insured is responsible for paying in respect of each and every Claim, as specified in the Schedule.

Extended Reporting Period: shall mean the period following the expiry of the Period of Insurance during which the Insured Persons may continue to notify Claims in accordance with the provisions of Clause 5.

Failure of a System: shall mean the failure of any System (whether or not owned by the Insured):

(a)   correctly to recognise or utilise any data concerning a date (whether a date in the year 2000 or any other date) as being such calendar date as the data is intended to represent;
and/or
(b)   to operate as a result of any command programmed in to the System utilising any date (whether a date in the year 2000 or any other date).

Financial Institution: shall mean any company that is predominantly or wholly engaged in providing financial services, including but not limited to those involved in the business of bank, a building society, insurance, assurance, an insurance intermediary, stockbroking, moneybroking, arbitrating, investment advice, venture capital, unit trusts, investment trusts, fund management or any similar form of activity.

Full Annual Premium: shall mean the annual premium payable by the Insured, including Insurance Premium Tax as applicable, relating to the Period of Insurance in question, including any additional premium which becomes payable subsequent to renewal pursuant to the provisions of this Policy.

Insured Persons: shall mean:

(a)   any natural person who was, or is, or may hereafter be, a Director of an Officer;
(b)   the legal representatives, estate or heirs of such Directors or Officers in the event of their bankruptcy, incapacity or death; or
(c)   the spouse of a Director or Officer in respect of any claim made against him or her (including a claim seeking the recovery of marital property transferred from a Director or Officer to his or her spouse) which arises directly from an actual or alleged Wrongful Act on the part of such Director or Officer and which is itself the subject of a Claim.

Insured: shall mean the Insured Persons and the Company.

Insurer: shall mean Royal & Sun Alliance Insurance plc.

Investigation: shall mean any formal or official investigation, examination or other proceedings made or commenced during the Period of Insurance, including any such proceedings initiated by the Department of Trade and Industry, the International Stock Exchange, the Bank of England, the Panel on Take-overs and Mergers, the Securities and Investments Board, the Financial Services Authority, the Health and Safety Executive, the Commission for Racial Equality or any other officially recognised regulatory, professional or trade body, or any similar body and any criminal investigations.

Limit of Indemnity: shall mean the limit specified in the Schedule.

Loss: shall mean:

(a) damages, compensation, contributions, judgements or settlements con-
     cluded with the Insurers' prior written consent;
(b) claimant's costs and expenses;
(c) punitive, exemplary and aggravated damages to the extent awarded by a
     court in any Member State of the European Union, and save insofar as
     uninsurable under the law of the country to which the Claim is subject,
     and in any event not including the multiple portion of any multiplied
     damages;
(d) all other costs and expenses ordered by a court or other legally autho-
     rised tribunal, or incurred with the Insurer's prior written consent, other
     than Defence Costs;

in respect of a Claim arising from a Wrongful Act made against the Insured Persons, jointly or severally, subject always to the Limit of Indemnity.

Microchip: shall include integrated circuits and microcontrollers.

Officer: shall mean:

(a) any natural person who was, or is, or may become an officer of the
     Company, other than its external auditor, liquidator, administrator,
     receiver or solicitor;
(b) any employee of the Company whilst acting in a managerial or supervi-
     sory capacity, including any employee of the Company who at the spe-
     cific written request of the Company is appointed to a managerial or
     supervisory position within any entity established for the sole purpose
     of any profit sharing, share option, sporting, social or welfare purpose
     and which exists predominantly for the benefit of any or all of the
     Insured Persons and employees of the Company and their families and
     dependants;
(c) any employee of the Company when such employee is named as a co-
     defendant in respect of a Claim made against a Director or Officer
     (which shall bear the meaning as defined in parts (a) and (b) of this def-
     inition only);
(d) any employee of the Company in respect of any Employment Practice
     Claim.

Original Inception Date: shall mean the date at which this insurance was origi-
     nally effected with the Insurer, whether under this policy or any preceding pol-
     icy. Provided that the insurance afforded by this Policy and any preceding
     policy effected with the Insurer has been continuous and without a break in
     time.

Outside Directorship Company: shall mean any company or non-profit organisa-
     tion which is not a Subsidiary, but shall not mean any company that:

(a) is a Financial Institution; or
(b) is registered in the USA, its territories and possessions, or in Canada; or
(c) has any of its Securities listed on any North American exchange.

Period of Insurance: shall mean the period specified in the current Schedule.

Policy: shall mean this policy of insurance, including the Proposal.

Proposal: shall mean the signed proposal form and declaration forwarded in con-
     nection with this Policy and any information supplied by or on behalf of the
     Insured in addition thereto or in substitution therefor.

Securities: shall mean shares, stock, bearer instruments, derivatives, bonds, warrants, debentures, rights under a depository receipt or other securities (or interests therein) of whatever nature.

Subsidiary: shall mean any company in which the Company:

    (a)   holds directly or indirectly more than 50% of the voting rights; or

    (b)   has the right to appoint or remove a majority of the board of directors;

provided always that cover shall only be provided in respect of Wrongful Acts committed during the period of time that such company falls within this definition.

System: shall include computers, other computing and electronic and mechanical equipment linked to a computer, hardware, software programs, data, electronic data processing equipment, Microchips and anything which relies on a Microchip for any part of its operation.

Wrongful Act: shall mean any actual or alleged breach of trust, breach of duty, neglect, error, mis-statement, misleading statement, libel, slander, breach of contract, omission, breach of warranty of authority, Wrongful Trading or other act wrongfully committed or attempted by the Insured Persons in their capacities as Directors or Officers or any matter claimed against the Insured Persons solely by reason of their acting as a Director or Officer.

Wrongful Trading: shall bear the meaning set out in section 214 of the Insolvency Act 1986 or any subsequent amendment or re-enactment thereof.

ROYAL & SUN ALLIANCE INSURANCE PLC ("RSA") COMMERCIAL VEHICLE POLICY

The Insurers will provide insurance in the terms of this Policy and Schedule in **A9–01** respect of accidental injury loss or damage happening during the Period of Insurance in Great Britain, Northern Ireland, the Republic of Ireland, the Isle of Man, the Channel Islands or during transit by sea between any of these territories.

The Period of Insurance includes any subsequent period for which the Insurers may accept payment for the renewal of this Policy.

The proposal and declaration and any premium payment agreement made by the Policyholder are the basis of and form part of this Policy.

Please read this Policy and the Certificate of Motor Insurance to ensure that they are in accordance with your requirements.

It is possible to choose the Law applicable to a contract of insurance covering a risk situated in the U.K. We have chosen Scottish Law to apply if you live in Scotland and English Law to apply if you live elsewhere in the U.K.

Payment of Your premium is evidence of acceptance of Our choice. If any other law is to apply it must be agreed by both parties and evidenced in writing.

SECTION 1

LOSS OR DAMAGE TO THE MOTOR VEHICLE

A. Cover

Comprehensive cover
If the Motor Vehicle (or its accessories or spare parts on it) is lost or damaged the **A9–02** Insurers will indemnify the Policyholder by at their own option repairing or replacing the Motor Vehicle or paying the amount of the loss or damage The Insurers' liability in respect of the Motor Vehicle including accessories or spare parts but excluding any trailer attached to it shall not exceed whichever is the lesser of

    (a)   the market value of the Motor Vehicle including its accessories and spare parts on it

    (b)   £20,000 unless any higher amount is shown in the Schedule for that Motor Vehicle

Cover for Fire and Theft only
If the Policy Cover is stated in the Schedule to be *"Third Party Fire and Theft"* **A9–03** the Insurers shall be liable under this Section only for loss or damage caused by fire lightning explosion theft attempted theft or the taking away of the Motor Vehicle without the consent of the Policyholder

B. Extensions

Motor Trade

A9–04   While the Motor Vehicle is in the custody of a member of the Motor Trade for maintenance or repair the following shall be inoperative

    (a)   Exception 1 below
    (b)   General Exception B1(a) and (c) of Section 6
    (c)   Endorsement 2 if applicable

Recovery and Redelivery

A9–05   Following loss or damage insured by this Policy the Insurers will pay the reasonable cost of

    (a)   protection and removal of the Motor Vehicle (if disabled) to the nearest competent repairers
    (b)   delivery after repair or after recovery of the Motor Vehicle to the Policyholder's address in the British Isles

Hiring or other Agreements

A9–06   If the Insurers know that the Motor Vehicle is hired leased or loaned to the Policyholder under a hire purchase agreement vehicle leasing agreement or other agreement any payment shall be made to the owner whose receipt shall be a discharge of any claim under this Section

Authority to Repair the Motor Vehicle

A9–07   Following damage insured by this Policy to the Motor Vehicle the Policyholder may authorise the repair of the Motor Vehicle provided that the Insurers are notified immediately

C. Exceptions

Exceptions to Section 1

In respect of each and every occurrence the Insurers *shall not be liable* for

A9–10   1.   the first amount stated below of any claim for loss or damage while the Motor Vehicle is being driven by or is in the charge of any person who

    (a) is under 21 years of age   £300
    (b) (i)   is under 25 but not under 21 years of age or
          (ii) holds a provisional licence to drive or has held a full licence to drive a vehicle of the same class as the Motor Vehicle for less than twelve months or
          (iii) does not hold a licence to drive but is driving in circumstances where a licence is not required by law   £150

This Exception shall not apply to loss or damage

    (a)   resulting from fire lightning explosion theft or attempted theft or the taking away of a Motor Vehicle without the consent of the Policyholder
    (b)   to the windscreen and/or windows where this is the only damage to the Motor Vehicle other than scratching of bodywork resulting from the glass breakage

    2. (a)   diminution in value following repair

(b) loss of use depreciation wear and tear or mechanical electrical electronic or computer failures breakdowns or breakages

3. damage to tyres by application of brakes or by punctures cuts or bursts
4. loss or damage directly occasioned by pressure waves caused by aircraft and other aerial devices travelling at sonic or supersonic speeds
5. loss of the Motor Vehicle resulting from deception by a purported purchaser or his agent
6. the first £50 of any claim solely for the replacement (but not repair) of glass in the windscreen and/or windows of the Motor Vehicle and any repairs to the bodywork resulting from the glass breakage
7. the first £100 of any claim for loss or damage caused by theft attempted theft or the Motor Vehicle being taken away without the consent of the Policyholder

This exception shall not apply to loss or damage

(a) to the windscreen and/or windows where this is the only damage to the Motor Vehicle other than scratching of bodywork resulting from the glass breakage
(b) occurring within or as a result of the Motor Vehicle being taken from a private locked garage

SECTION 2

LIABILITY TO THIRD PARTIES

A. Cover

Sub-Section 1—Indemnity to Policyholder

The Insurers will indemnify the Policyholder in respect of legal liability incurred   **A9–11**
for damages and claimant's costs and expenses in respect of accidental

(a) death of or bodily injury to any person (including passengers)
(b) loss of or damage to material property up to a limit of £1,000,000 any one claim or number of claims arising out of one cause
(c) stoppage of or interference with pedestrian vehicular rail air or waterborne traffic or escape or discharge of any substance or gas up to a limit of £1,000,000 any one claim or number of claims arising out of one cause

in connection with the use of the Motor Vehicle (including loading and unloading)

The Insurers will in addition pay in respect of any event which may be the subject of indemnity under this Sub-Section

(i) solicitors' fees for representation at any coroner's inquest or fatal inquiry or court of summary jursidiction
(ii) costs and expenses incurred with their written consent
(iii) the costs of defence against a charge of manslaughter or causing death by dangerous driving

Sub-Section 2—Indemnity to other Persons

The Insurers will also indemnify in the terms of Sub-Section 1   **A9–12**

(a) any person permitted to drive the Motor Vehicle under the terms of the Certificate of Motor Insurance

(b)   any passenger in the Motor Vehicle other than the driver
(c)   (i)   any Principal with whom the Policyholder has an agreement
      (ii) any Hirer of the Motor Vehicle other than under a hire purchase
            agreement
      provided that the Insurers shall not be liable in respect of liability
      arising from the act default or neglect of the Principal/Hirer his servant
      or agent
(d)   the legal personal representatives of any person entitled to indemnity
      under this Section in respect of liability incurred by that person

Sub-Section 3—Foreign Use Extension

A9–13   Notwithstanding any financial limitation in this Policy the Insurers will provide
indemnity in its terms while any vehicle insured by this Policy is in any country which
is a member of the European Union and any other country in respect of which the
Commission of the European Union is satisfied that arrangements have been made
to meet the requirements of Article 7(2) of the EEC Directive on insurance of civil
liabilities arising from the use of Motor Vehicles No. 72/166 but only to the extent
that any road traffic legislation requires insurance or security in the country concerned including costs and expenses incurred with the Insurers' consent

Sub-Section 4—Contingency Cover for Employees' Vehicles

A9–14   The Insurers will indemnify the Policyholder and no other person in the terms
of Sub-Section 1 while any Motor Vehicle not the property of or provided by the
Policyholder is being used in connection with the Policyholder's Business by any
person in the Policyholder's employ but the Insurers shall not be liable

(a)   if there is any other insurance covering the same liability
(b)   for loss or damage to such Motor Vehicle

B. Extensions

Towing

A9–15   This Policy shall operate while the Motor Vehicle is being used for the purpose
of towing

1.   one disabled mechanically-propelled vehicle
2.   any trailer providing that the Motor Vehicle towing the trailer is a
     Goods Carrying Vehicle and has a gross vehicle weight not exceeding
     3.5 tonnes
     Provided always that

(a)   the vehicle is not towed for reward
(b)   the Insurers shall not be liable by reason of this paragraph

     (i)   in respect of damage to the towed vehicle or trailer or prop-
           erty being conveyed by such vehicle or trailer
     (ii) if the Motor Vehicle to which any trailer is attached is draw-
           ing a greater number of trailers than is permitted by law

C. Exception

Exceptions to Section 2

A9–16   The Insurers *shall not be liable*

(a) for liability arising from the loading or unloading beyond the limits of any carriageway or thoroughfare by any person other than the driver or attendant of the Motor Vehicle

(b) for death or bodily injury arising out of and in the course of the injured person's employment by the person claiming indemnity under this Section except as is required by any road traffic legislation

(c) to indemnify any person driving unless that person holds a licence to drive the Motor Vehicle or has held and is not disqualified for holding or obtaining such a licence

(d) to indemnify any person not driving but claiming indemnity if to his knowledge the person driving does not hold a licence to drive the Motor Vehicle unless he has held and is not disqualified for holding or obtaining such a licence

(e) to indemnify any person other than the Policyholder if that person is entitled to indemnity under any other policy

(f) for damage to property owned by or in the custody or control of

    (i) the Policyholder or any person claiming indemnity or

    (ii) any person in the service of the Policyholder or any person claiming indemnity where the property is in the custody or control of that person by virtue of that service

(g) for damage to property being conveyed by the Motor Vehicle

(h) for any legal liabiity of whatsoever nature directly caused by or contributed to by or arising from the Motor Vehicle whle in or on that part of any commercial or military airport or airfield provided for

    (i) the take-off or landing of aircraft or the movement of aircraft on the ground

    (ii) aircraft parking, including any associated service roads, refuelling areas, ground equipment parking areas, aprons, maintenance areas and hangars

except as is required by any road traffic legislation

(i) for injury loss or damage directly or indirectly caused by *pollution* or *contamination* unless caused by a sudden identifiable unintended and unexpected incident which occurs in its entirety at a specific time and place during the Period of Insurance

(j) for the purpose of this exception *pollution* or *contamination* shall mean actual alleged or threatened release discharge escape or dispersal of any solid liquid gaseous or thermal irritant or contaminant including smoke vapour soot fumes acids alkalis chemical or waste (including materials to be recycled reconditioned or reclaimed)

but Exceptions c and d shall not apply when a licence is not required by law

D. Conditions

Right of Recovery

The Policyholder shall repay to the Insurers all sums paid by them under this Section because of the requirements of any law if the Insurers would not have been liable for those payments by the terms of this Policy   **A9–17**

Application of Limits of Liability

In the event of any accident involving indemnity to more than one person any limitation in this Policy of the amount of that indemnity shall apply to the aggregate amount and such indemnity shall apply in priority to the Policyholder   **A9–18**

SECTION 3

TRAILERS

A. Cover

A9–19   A trailer shall be insured in the terms of this Policy as though it were a Motor Vehicle if either

(a)   it is specified in the Schedule
or
(b)   it is not specified but

(i)   it is attached to
or
(ii)   it has been attached to and while away from the Policyholder's premises is temporarily detached from (but remains in the vicinity of)

a Motor Vehicle for which the Schedule shows that unspecified trailers are covered

B. Conditions

A9–20   Provided that

1.   while any such trailer is attached to a towing vehicle or power unit they shall together be regarded as one vehicle
2.   any plant permanently attached to a trailer shall be regarded as part of that trailer
3.   the Insurer's liability under Section 1 of this Policy—Loss or Damage to the Motor Vehicle—in respect of any trailer shall not exceed the amount shown in the Schedule

C. Exceptions

A9–21   The Insurers *shall not be liable*

1.   under paragraph b for trailers with plant permanently attached while the trailer is detached from the towing vehicle
2.   if the Motor Vehicle to which an insured trailer is attached is drawing a greater number of trailers than is permitted by law
3.   except so far as is necessary to meet the requirements of the Road Traffic Acts in connection with the operation as a tool of any trailer insured by this Policy unless the trailer is one specified in the Schedule

SECTION 4

OTHER CLAUSES

Rallies Competitions and Trials

While any Motor Vehicle insured by this Policy is used in a competition or rally   **A9–22**
or trial the insurance shall be restricted to those liabilities for which insurance is
compulsory by the Road Traffic Acts

This limitation shall not apply in respect of any event organised for the purpose
of encouraging road safety in which the route shall not exceed 100 miles and no
merit is attached to a competitor's performance on the public highway except in
relation to good road behaviour and compliance with the Highway Code If such
event includes driving tests the driving area shall not exceed 100 yards square and
no test shall be timed

Emergency Treatment

The Insurers will indemnify any person using the Motor Vehicle in respect of lia-   **A9–23**
bility under the Road Traffic Acts to pay for Emergency Treatment fees

No Claim Discount

If no incident resulting in a claim under this policy has occurred during the   **A9–24**
following Periods of Insurance the next renewal premium will be reduced by the
discount shown in the following scale

One year	20%
Two consecutive years	30%
Three consecutive years	40%
Four consecutive years	50%
Five consecutive years	60%

A claim arising from a single incident which occurs after a 60% discount has
been earned will reduce the discount at renewal to 40% and a 50% discount will
in the same circumstances be reduced to 30% and a 40% discount will be reduced
to 20%

Payments for the following will not affect the discount

(a) payment for Emergency Treatment
(b) payment under Section 1 in respect of breakage of the windscreen or
windows where this is the only damage to the Motor Vehicle other than
scratching of the bodywork resulting from the glass breakage
(c) payment under Sub-Section 4 of Section 2

If this Policy applies to more than one Motor Vehicle the No Claim Discount
shall apply as if a separate policy had been issued in respect of each Motor Vehicle

Cross liabilities

If the Policyholder comprises more than one party (which in the case of a part-   **A9–25**
nership includes each individual partner) the Insurers will indemnify each in the
terms of this Policy against liability incurred to the other as if such other was not
included as a Policyholder

SECTION 5

CONDITIONS

Condition 1—Compliance with Policy Terms

A9–26   The liability of the Insurers will be conditional on the Policyholder complying and as appropriate any other person entitled to indemnity complying as though he were the Policyholder with the terms of this Policy

Condition 2—Reasonable Precautions

A9–27   The Policyholder shall take and cause to be taken all reasonable precautions to prevent injury loss or damage and shall maintain the Motor Vehicle in a road-worthy condition The Insurers shall have free access to examine the Motor Vehicle at all reasonable times

Condition 3—Claims Procedure and Requirements

A9–28
    (a)   The Policyholder must report all accidents claims and civil or criminal proceedings to the Insurers in writing as soon as possible

    (b)   Every letter claim writ or other document relating to any accident claim or civil proceedings must be sent to the Insurers immediately and unacknowledged

    (c)   No admission of liability or promise of payment may be made without the Insurers' written consent

    (d)   The Policyholder will give all information and assistance as required

Condition 4—Insurers' Rights

A9–29
    (a)   The Insurers are entitled to take over and conduct the defence or settlement of any claim at their discretion

    (b)   The Insurers may at any time pay the limit of liabiity referred to in Sub Section 1 of Section 2 after deduction of any sum or sums already paid or any less amount for which any claim or claims can be settled and shall then relinquish the conduct and control thereof and be under no further liability in respect thereof except for the payment of costs and expenses incurred prior to the date of such payment

Condition 5—Non-Contribution

A9–30   If the damage or liability which is the subject of a claim under this Policy is or would but for the existence of this Policy be insured under any other insurance the Insurers shall not be liable under this Policy except to the extent of any excess beyond the amount payable under such other insurance had this Policy not been effected.

Condition 6—Cancellation

A9–31   This Policy may be cancelled

    (a)   by the Insurers sending thirty days notice by letter to the last known address of the Policyholder (and in the case of Northern Ireland to the Department of the Environment for Norther Ireland) The Policyholder shall be entitled to a pro rata return of premium calculated from the date of cancellation or if a Certificate of Motor Insurance has been issued from the date of return to the Insurers of such Certificate

    (b)   by the Policyholder who shall be entitled to a return of premium after deduction of premium at the Insurers' short period rates for the period the Policy has been in force calculated from the date of receipt by the Insurers of notice of cancellation or if a Certificate of Motore Insurance has been issued from the date of receipt by the Insurers of such Certificate

Condition 7—Cancellation Monthly Premiums

If this Policy is issued or renewed on the basis of monthly premiums the liability of the Insurers will cease in the event of non-payment of any monthly premium on its due date but before cancellation takes effect the Insurers will send seven days notice by letter to the last known address of the Policyholder   **A9–32**

SECTION 6

GENERAL EXCEPTIONS

Exception A—Change of Vehicle

If the Description of Vehicles in the Certificate of Motor Insurance refers to "Any Goods Carrying Vehicle" or other specified class of vehicle the property of the Policyholder or hired to him under a hire purchase agreement or leased to him under a vehicle leasing agreement the Insurers shall not be liable in respect of any vehicle except where particulars are already in their possession unless details are notified to the Insurers within seven days of the date of acquisition and are accepted by them   **A9–33**

Until the Insurers are notified of the acquisition of such vehicle the Policy Cover operative for that vehicle shall be the widest form described in the Schedule

Exception B—Use and Driving

The Insurers *shall not be liable* in respect of   **A9–34**

1. death injury loss or damage occurring or liability arising while the Motor Vehicle is being

   (a) used with the consent of the Policyholder or his representative otherwise than in accordance with the limitations as to use in the Certificate of Motor Insurance

   (b) driven by the Policyholder unless he holds a licence to drive the vehicle or has held and is not disqualified for holding or obtaining such a licence

   (c) driven with the consent of the Policyholder or his representative by any person

       (i) who is not specified in the Certificate of Motore Insurance

       (ii) who the Policyholder or his representative knows does not hold a licence to drive the vehicle unless he has held and is not disqualified for holding or obtaining such a licence

   but Exceptions (b) and (c) shall not apply when a licence is not required by law

Contractual Liability

2. any liability which attaches because of an agreement but which would not have attached in the absence of that agreement   **A9–35**

Radioactive Contamination

3. (a) loss or destruction of or damage to any property whatsoever or any loss or expense whatsoever resulting or arising therefrom or any consequential loss
   (b) any legal liability of whatsoever nature
       directly or indirectly caused by or contributed to by or arising from
       (i) ionising radiations or contamination by radioactivity from any irradiated nuclear fuel or from any nuclear waste from the combustion of nuclear fuel
       (ii) the radioactive toxic explosive or other hazardous properties of any explosive nuclear assembly or nuclear component thereof

War

A9–36
4. any consequence of war invasion act of foreign enemy hostilities (whether war be declared or not) civil war rebellion revolution insurrection or military or usurped power except so far as is necessary to meet the requirements of the Road Traffic Acts

Riot and Civil Commotion

A9–37
5. any consequence of riot or civil commotion occurring in Northern Ireland (this Exception does not apply to Section 2—Liability to Third Parties)

SECTION 7

ENDORSEMENTS

Note: These endorsements are operative only if the number set against them appears in the Schedule and are each subject otherwise to the terms exceptions and conditions of this Policy

Endorsement 1—Own Damage Excess
A9–38
In respect of each and every occurrence the Insurers shall not be liable for the first amount shown in the Schedule of any claim under Section 1—Loss or Damage to the Motor Vehicle This amount shall be in addition to any other amount for which the Insurers are not liable by reason of Exception 1 to Section 1 provided that

(a) if the name of any person or description of any class of persons is shown against this amount this Endorsement shall apply only while the Motor Vehicle is being driven by or is for the purpose of being driven in the charge of one of those persons
(b) this Endorsement shall not apply in respect of loss of or damage to the Motor Vehicle caused by fire lightning explosion theft or attempted theft or by the breakage of the windscreen or windows where this is the only damage to the Motor Vehicle other than scratching of bodywork resulting from the glass breakage

Endorsements 2—Exclusion of Damage Cover for Unnamed Drivers under 25

The Insurers shall be under no liability under Section 1—Loss or Damage to the Motor Vehicle—while the Motor Vehicle is being driven by or is for the purpose of being driven in the charge of any person under 25 years of age other than the person(s) specified in the Schedule except for loss or damage caused by fire lightning explosion theft or attempted theft or by the breakage of the windscreen or windows where this is the only damage to the Motor Vehicle other than scratching of bodywork resulting from the glass breakage   **A9–39**

Endorsement 3—Exclusion of Loss or Damage caused by Malicious Damage Theft or Frost

The Insurers shall not be liable under Section 1—Loss or Damage to the Motor Vehicle—for loss or damage caused by   **A9–40**

    (a)   malicious act
    (b)   theft or any attempted theft or the Motor Vehicle being taken away without the consent of the Policyholder
    (c)   frost

Endorsement 4—Third Party Working Risk

Except as is required by the Road Traffic Acts the Insurers shall not be liable under Section 2—Liability to Third Parties—in respect of liability arising out of   **A9–41**

    (a)   subsidence flooding or water pollution
    (b)   vibration or the removal or weakening of support of any property land or building
    (c)   the explosion of any vessel under pressure being part of plant attached to or forming part of the Motor Vehicle
    (d)   damage to pipes or cables

while the Motor Vehicle or attached plant is being operated as a tool

Endorsement 5—Excluding Third Party Working Risk

Except as is required by the Road Traffic Acts the Insurers shall not be liable under Section 2—Liability to Third Parties—in respect of liability arising out of the operation as a tool of the Motor Vehicle or attached plant   **A9–42**

Endorsement 6—Indemnity to Hirer including negligence of Hirer

Notwithstanding any restriction contained in paragraph c of Sub-Section 2 of Section 2—Liability to Third Parties—the Insurers will indemnify the Hirer of the Motor Vehicle in respect of any loss damage or liability covered by this Policy arising while such vehicle is let on hire other than under a hire purchase agreement provided that he is not entitled to indemnity under any other policy   **A9–43**

Endorsement 7—Cancelling No Claim Discount—Fleet Rated Policy

The No Claim Discount Clause in Section 4—Other Causes—of this Policy is cancelled   **A9–44**

Endorsement 8—Blanket Certificates Fleet Rated Policy

The No Claim Discount Clause in Section 4—Other Clauses—of this Policy is cancelled and Exception A of Section 6—General Exceptions—is amended to read: **A9–45**

The Insurers shall not be liable in respect of any Motor Vehicles (except where particulars are already in their possession) unless details are notified to the Insurers within thirty days of the end of each period of three months in the terms required by the Insurers.

Appendix 10

ROYAL & SUN ALLIANCE INSURANCE PLC ("RSA") PREMIER TRANSIT—HAULAGE

General Definitions

The following expressions shall have the meanings set out below wherever they appear in this Policy:

A10–01

British Isles: Great Britain, Northern Ireland, the Channel Islands, the Isle of Man, the off-shore islands and the Republic of Ireland

CMR: The Convention on the Contract for the International Carriage of Goods by Road (CMR)

Container: Any container, tanktainer, demountable body, flat or similar unit (including ancillary equipment whilst attached to any such unit)

Damage: Physical loss or damage, destruction or misdelivery

Employee:

    (a)   any person under a contract of service with you or
    (b)   any self employed individual providing you with labour only or
    (c)   any individual hired to or borrowed by you

Event: Any one occurrence or all occurrences of a series consequent upon or attributable to one original source or cause

Event Limit: The maximum amount we will pay for all claims arising out of any one event

Excess: The amount for which you are responsible in respect of each and every claim arising out of any one event (as ascertained after the application of any provisions relating to underinsurance)

Location Limit: The maximum amount we will pay if property housed in one or any number of buildings at any one site sustains damage as a result of any one event

Mainland Europe: Andorra, Austria, Belgium, the Czech Republic, Denmark, Estonia, Finland, France, Germany, Gibraltar, Hungary, Italy, Latvia, Liechtenstein, Lithuania, Luxembourg, Monaco, Netherlands, Norway, Poland, Portugal, San Marino, the Slovak Republic, Spain, Sweden and Switzerland

Property: Goods and/or merchandise carried, and/or handled and/or warehoused for reward other than:

(a)   containers
(b)   goods and/or merchandise owned or hired by or leased or loaned to you

Subcontractor: Any person (other than an employee) to whom property and/or
transportation equipment is entrusted for reward by you or on your behalf for
the performance of the whole or part of the contract

Terms: All terms, conditions, endorsements, exceptions, exclusions, memoranda,
notices, limits of liability, provisions and extensions contained in or added to
this Policy

Thief Attractive Property:

- Audio and/or visual and/or audio-visual equipment and/or accessories;
- Bottled perfumery;
- Bottled spirits;
- Clothing and/or footwear;
- Computer equipment and/or accessories;
- Jewellery and/or watches;
- Mobile telephones;
- Non-ferrous metals in sheet, bar, tube, ingot, coil, scrap or similar form;
- Photographic equipment and/or accessories
- Precious metals and/or articles made of or containing precious metals
  (other than bullion);
- Precious stones;
- Processed tobacco and/or tobacco products

Total Sum Insured: The maximum amount we will pay for any claim or series of
claims arising out of any one event

Trailer: Any trailer or semi-trailer

Transportation Equipment: Trailers, containers, load securing and stowage equipment and any ancillary and similar equipment for which cover is provided by
this Policy but excluding motor vehicles and self propelled equipment

Unattended: Where neither you nor any employee are in a position to keep the
vehicle and/or property under constant surveillance and at the same time have
a reasonable prospect of preventing any unauthorised interference with the
vehicle and/or property

Vehicle: Any motor vehicle (other than motor cycles) or trailer used for the carriage of property

Vehicle Limit: The maximum amount we will pay for all property in or on any
one motor vehicle, trailer or motor vehicle and trailer combination at any one
time

We: Royal & Sun Alliance Insurance plc

Western Europe: Andorra, Austria, Belgium, Denmark, France, Germany,
Gibraltar, Italy, Liechtenstein, Luxembourg, Monaco, Netherlands, Norway,
Portugal, San Marino, Spain, Sweden and Switzerland

You: The person or company or firm named in the Schedule as "The Insured".

GENERAL CONDITIONS APPLYING TO THE WHOLE POLICY

1. Variation of contract conditions

You must not agree to: **A10–02**

    (a)   vary the contract conditions shown as "insured" in the Schedule nor
    (b)   accept any special declaration of value nor
    (c)   accept any declaration of special interest in delivery

without our prior consent.

2. Reasonable precautions

You must at your own expense take all reasonable precautions to prevent or   **A10–03**
diminish any liability, damage or other loss which may give rise to a claim under
this Policy.

3. Subcontractors

    (a)   You must not entrust property and/or transportation equipment to any   **A10–04**
           subcontractor unless prior to acceptance they have agreed in writing:

           1.   to accept no less liability than you have and
           2.   to fully indemnify you for all loss and damage.

        This condition does not apply to property or transportation equip-
        ment entrusted by you to any subcontractor acting in the capacity of a
        shipping line, airline, port or railway operator.
    (b)   Under no circumstances whatsoever shall the benefit of this Policy pass
           to any subcontractor or the insurers of any subcontractor.

4. Cancellation

    (a)   We may cancel the Policy at any time giving 15 (fifteen) days notice to   **A10–05**
           that effect in writing by pre-paid letter post to either your insurance
           adviser or your last known address, in which case we will refund either:

           1.   the difference (if any) between the adjusted premium for the
               period during which insurance was in force in accordance with any
               premium adjustment clause shown in the Schedule and the pre-
               mium actually paid or
           2.   a pro rata portion of the premium paid for the unexpired Period
               of Insurance if no premium adjustment clause applies.

    (b)   We may cancel this Policy without notice if you:

           1.   cancel any credit agreement relating to this Policy and then fail to
               pay to us immediately the full amount of the premium or
           2.   fail to take the action specified in any default notice issued by us
               before the date shown in it or
           3.   fail to pay a first instalment of premium.

5. Thief attractive property event limit

A10–06   The event limit shall not exceed £40,000 for theft of thief attractive property left unattended whilst in your custody and control. This event limit will only apply if you or any employee are aware that thief attractive property is being carried, handled or warehoused.

6. Policy limits

A10–07   Irrespective of the number of parties claiming under this Policy the total amount payable by us in respect of all claims arising out of any one event shall not exceed any applicable limit of liability or maximum amount payable specified in the Policy or in the whole the Total Sum Insured.

7. Parties insured by this Policy

A10–08   Where "The Insured" named in the Schedule comprises more than one party, all such parties shall be treated as one party or legal entity so that there will be only two parties to the contract of insurance namely Royal & Sun Alliance Insurance plc and the parties named in the Schedule being jointly insured.

8. Other insurance

A10–09   If at the time of any claim there is (or but for the existence of this Policy there would be) any other insurance covering your interest in or liability for the property, transportation equipment and/or goods the indemnity will only apply in respect of any amount beyond that which would have been payable under such other insurance had this Policy not been in force.

9. Non-disclosure/misrepresentation

A10–10   This Policy shall be voidable by us if you have failed to disclose or have misrepresented or misdescribed any material information.

10. Law applicable to this contract

A10–11   The law applicable to this Policy and for disputes arising under or in connection with it shall be English law and the English Courts shall have jurisdiction.

11. Premium Adjustment

A10–12   This conditions applies only if a premium adjustment clause is included within the Schedule. The deposit premium shown in the premium adjustment clause is adjustable. You must keep an accurate record of all charges received or due during each Period of Insurance for each category shown in the premium adjustment clause. Within 3 (three) months of the expiry of each Period of Insurance you must declare to us the gross charges (including ferry charges and payments to subcontractors and other third parties but not duty and VAT) received or due for each such category. We will then adjust the deposit premium retrospectively at the rates shown subject to our retaining the amount specified as our minimum retention.

If requested by us declarations of charges must be certified by your accountants.

CLAIMS CONDITIONS APPLYING TO THE WHOLE POLICY

1. On the discovery of any circumstances or event which might give rise to a claim under this Policy irrespective of your views as to the validity of the claim and of the amount of the excess applicable you must:

(a) immediately notify the claims bureau specified below

(b) give immediate notice to the police in respect of damage caused by malicious persons or thieves.

(c) provide to the specified claims bureau within 10 (ten) working days (or such further time as we may have agreed) a detailed claim in writing and supply such further particulars as may be reasonably be required.

(d) immediately upon receipt provide to the specified claims bureau every letter, claim, writ, summons and/or other process.

2. You must not admit liability nor make any offer, promise or payment nor give indemnity without our written consent.

3. You must (at our expense) before or after we indemnify you give full co-operation and allow us to act as necessary for the purposes of enforcing any rights and remedies and obtaining relief or indemnity from other parties.

4. We shall be entitled to take over and conduct in your name the defence or settlement of any claim or to institute or prosecute in your name for our benefit any claim for indemnity or damages or otherwise and shall have full discretion in the conduct of any proceedings or in the settlement of any claim.

5. All benefit paid or which would otherwise be payable under this Policy shall be forfeited if any claim is in any respect fraudulent or any fraudulent means be used by you or anyone acting on your behalf to obtain any benefit under this Policy or any damage is occasioned by your wilful act or with the connivance of you or any relative of yours.

Specified Claims Bureau
The specified claims bureau is:

Homeline Claims Bureau Limited	24 hour Telephone number	01342 313711
Greenstede House	Facsimilie Number	01342 410024
Station Road		
East Grinstead		
West Sussex RH19 1DJ		

Premium Transit—Homeline Claims Service
Homeline is the UK's leading independent Goods in Transit claims handling, settlement and recovery service

The complexity of insurance, liability and procedural issues associated with moving goods nationally and internationally, requires experience with a high level of technical expertise. Homeline combine both with an understanding of customs and practices within the transport industry

The provision of Homeline's specialist claims service is unique to Royal & SunAlliance

GENERAL EXCLUSIONS APPLYING TO THE WHOLE POLICY

A10–14 We will not pay claims for:
1. damage to or your liability for:

  (a) documents, money, securities for money, negotiable instruments, bullion, unused postage stamps, credit cards, debit cards, charge cards and similar property.
  (b) trailers other than whilst being carried on a vehicle for reward.
  (c) property being towed other than on a trailer.
  (d) property in the course of a household, office, factory or similar removal.
  (e) property stored at a rental or under a contract for storage and distribution or otherwise upon request except as provided for under the Static Risks Section of this Policy (if shown in the Schedule as "included").
  (f) damage or injury to or death, disease or illness of any person or living creature.

2. the following unless caused by fire, theft, attempted theft or as a direct result of the collision or overturning of the conveying vehicle:

  (a) deterioration of perishable property or
  (b) damage to property caused by or arising from any change in temperature when carried or stored in a temperature controlled environment or
  (c) hardening of tarmac, concrete or similar property.

3. loss of market, loss of profits, delay or any consequential loss of any nature whatsoever and howsoever arising except as provided for in General Extension 4 (Consequential loss)
4. damage or liability caused by or arising from:

  (a) war, invasion, act of foreign enemy, hostilities (whether war be declared or not), military or usurped power, civil commotion, revolution, rebellion, insurrection or civil war.
  (b) confiscation, requisition or damage by order of any government or other officials or authorities.
  (c) ionising radiation or contamination by radioactivity from any nuclear fuel or from any nuclear waste from the combustion of nuclear fuel.
  (d) the radioactive, toxic, explosive or other hazardous properties of any explosive nuclear assembly or nuclear component thereof.

5. damage or liability caused by or arising from faulty packing or process where you have contracted to pack or to undertake any such process.
6. liability caused by or arising from the exercise by you of a lien whether contractual or otherwise.
7. theft of property by deception by any person purporting to be a subcontractor.
8. damage, liability, loss or expense of whatsoever nature directly or indirectly caused by or arising from:

  (a) the failure of a system
  (b) the taking of or failure to take any corrective or other action in connection with the actual or possible failure of a system

For the purposes of this Exclusion the expression:

  1. *"failure of a system"* means the failure or inability of any system to:

    (a) correctly recognise or utilise any data concerning a date as being such calendar date as the data is intended to represent

(b) operate as a result of any command programmed in to the system utilising any date.

2. "*system*" includes computers and/or other computing and electronic and mechanical equipment linked to a computer, hardware, software, programs, data, electronic data processing equipment, microchips and anything which relies on a microchip for any part of its operation.
3. "*microchip*" includes integrated circuits and microcontrollers.

ROAD HAULAGE SECTION

Indemnity

We will indemnify you for your liability for damage to property occurring within the territorial limits during any Period of Insurance whilst the property is being: **A10–15**

(a) loaded upon, carried by or unloaded from any vehicle shown as "insured" in the Road Haulage Section of the Schedule or
(b) temporarily stored in the course of transit (whether on or off a vehicle).

The indemnity will be to the extent of your liability for such damage:

1. under the contract conditions shown as "insured" in the Road Haulage Section of the Schedule
2. at common law if such contract conditions have been incorporated into the contract with your customer but cannot be enforced
3. if you do not use contract conditions or do not wish to restrict your liability for damage to property by application of contract conditions or common law and Item 3 (Full Responsibility) of the Road Haulage Section of the Schedule is shown as "insured".

Additional Exclusion

In addition to the General Exclusions we will not indemnify you under Item 3 (Full Responsibility) of the Road Haulage Section of the Schedule beyond your liability under any applicable International Convention.   **A10–16**

Additional Conditions

In addition to the General Conditions: **A10–17**

1. you must obtain and retain two satisfactory references from reliable sources for all drivers engaged after the inception of this Policy and prior to entrusting them with any property, transportation equipment or goods. Verbal references must be recorded in writing at the time they are taken. All such references must be produced to us promptly on demand. This condition does ot apply to drivers hired to you by any employment agency.
2. you must ot at any time own or operate a greater number of vehicles than the number specified in the Road Haulage Section of the Schedule.

Limits of Liability

A10–18   We will not pay more than the respective limits of liability specified in the Road Haulage Section of the Schedule or elsewhere in this Policy. Our maximum liability under this Policy will not exceed the Total Sum Insured.

If at the time of any damage your liability under Item 3 (Full Responsibility) of the Road Haulage Section of the Schedule for property:

> (a)   contained in or on any vehicle exceeds the vehicle limit or
> (b)   exceeds the event limit

then you will be considered as being your own insurer for the difference and shall bear a proportionate share of the claim accordingly.

EXTENSION APPLICABLE TO THE ROAD HAULAGE SECTION

A10–19   The following Extension (which is subject otherwise to the terms of this Policy) applies if the Road Haulage Section is shown as "included" in the Schedule.

Own Goods

A10–20   We will by payment (or at our option by repair, reinstatement or replacement) indemnify you for damage to goods occurring within the territorial limits during any Period of Insurance whilst being loaded upon, carried by or unloaded from any vehicle owned or operated by you and shown as "insured" in the Road Haulage Section of the Schedule provided that:

1.   for the purposes of this extension "goods" shall mean goods, equipment and/or merchandise belonging to you or hired, leased or loaned to you and appertaining to your business as Road Hauliers or Warehousekeepers provided that the corresponding Road Haulage Section or Static Risks Section is shown as "included" in the Schedule.
2.   the vehicle limit under this extension is £10,000.
3.   if at the time of any damage the value of goods contained in or on any vehicle exceeds the vehicle limit under this extension you will be considered as being your own insurer for the difference and shall bear a proportionate share of the claim accordingly.
4.   in addition to the General Exclusions we will not pay claims for:

> (a)   damage arising as a result of packing which was inadequate to withstand normal handling during transit.
> (b)   damage caused by or arising from inherent vice.
> (c)   wear and tear.
> (d)   mechanical, electrical or electronic breakdown, failure or derangement.
> (e)   damage to mobile telephones and/or trailers and/or containers.
> (f)   goods carried for reward.

OPTIONAL EXTENSIONS APPLICABLE TO THE ROAD HAULAGE SECTION

The following Optional Extensions (which are subject otherwise to the terms of   **A10–21**
this Policy) apply to this Section only if shown as "included" in the Road Haulage
Section of the Schedule.

1. Non-incorporation of contract conditions

We will indemnify you to the extent to which you have a liability at common law   **A10–22**
if you have failed to incorporate the contract conditions shown as "insured" in the
Road Haulage Section of the Schedule into the contract with your customer provided that:

(a) you intended to trade under such contract conditions and took reason-
     able steps to notify customers of their application and
(b) the failure to notify the customer of such contract conditions was due to
     an error and you can provie to our satisfaction that you had established
     procedures for such notification to be given to customers and that all
     employees had been instructed in writing to follow such procedures.

2. Commercial consideration

We will at your request indemnify you in those circumstances where you have   **A10–23**
incorporated the contract conditions shown as "insured" in the Road Haulage Section of the Schedule into the contract with your customer but for commerical reasons you wish to accept a wider liability for damage to property provided that:

(a) the maximum amount we will pay for all claims arising during any one
     Period of Insurance is the amount specified in the Schedule for this
     extension.
(b) you have not agreed prior to the event giving rise to the claim to accept
     such wider liability for damge to property.
(c) we will not indemnify you beyond your liability under any applicable
     International Convention.

3. Deterioration

General Exclusions 2a) and 2b) do not apply to property whilst being carried in   **A10–24**
a temperature controlled vehicle or container.

4. Trailers

We will indemnify you for damage to trailers belonging to you or for which you   **A10–25**
are responsible provided that:

(a) we will not pay claims for:

     1.   wear and tear, gradual deterioration, scratching, bruising or
          denting.

    2.   mechanical, electrical or electronic breakdown, failure or derangement.

    3.   damage to tyres by punctures, cuts, bursts or the application of brakes.

(b) we will not pay more for any one trailer than the amount specified in the Schedule for this extension.

(c) if at the time of any damage:

    1.   the value of any one trailer or

    2.   the total value of all trailers

belonging to you or for which you are responsible exceeds the respective amounts specified in the Schedule for this extension then you will be considered as being your own insurer for the difference and shall bear a proportionate share of the claim accordingly.

5. Bogus subcontractors

A10–26   General Exclusion 7 is deleted.

6. Drivers' personal effects

A10–27   We will at your request indemnify the driver of any vehicle owned or operated by you and shown as "insured" in the Road Haulage Section of the Schedule for damage to clothing and personal effects incurred whilst such driver is engaged in business on your behalf provided that:

(a) the event limit applicable to this extension is £500.

(b) we will not pay claims for damage caused by or arising from wear and tear.

(c) the excess applicable to this extension is £100.

STATIC RISKS SECTION

Indemnity

A10–28   We will indemnify you for your liability for damage to property occurring whilst warehoused in a building at any location address shown in the Static Risks Section of the Schedule during any Period of Insurance.

The indemnity will be to the extent of your liability for such damage:

    1.   under the contract conditions shown as "insured" in the Static Risks Section of the Schedule

    2.   at common law if such contract conditions have been incorporated into the contract with your customer but cannot be enforced.

Additional Exclusions

In addition to the General Exclusions we will not pay claims for: **A10–29**

1. unexplained discrepancies between your records and those of your customer or
2. unexplained shortage discovered during stocktaking or inventory check.

Limits of liability

We will not pay more than the respective limits of liability specified in the Static   **A10–30**
Risks Section of the Schedule or elsewhere in this Policy. Our maximum liability
under this Policy will not exceed the Total Sum Insured.

OPTIONAL EXTENSION APPLICABLE TO THE STATIC RISKS SECTION

The following Optional Extension (which is subject otherwise to the terms of   **A10–31**
this Policy) applies to this Section only if shown as "included" in the Static Risks
Section of the Schedule

Non-incorporation of contract conditions

We will indemnify you to the extent to which you have a liability at common law   **A10–32**
if you have failed to incorporate the contract conditions shown as "insured" in the
Static Risks Section of the Schedule into the contract with your customer provided
that:

(a) you intended to trade under such contract conditions and took reasonable steps to nofiy customers of their application and
(b) the failure to notify the customer of such contract conditions was due to an error and you can prove to our satisfaction that you had established procedures for such notification to be given to customers and that all employees had been instructed in writing to follow such procedures.

GENERAL EXTENSIONS

The following General Extensions (which are subject otherwise to the terms of   **A10–33**
this Policy) apply only to those Sections of the Policy shown as "included" in the
Schedule.

1. Transhipment and other costs

We will indemnify you for reasonable costs or liability incurred by you for: **A10–34**

(a) transhipment, recovery or removal of debris following damage to property, transportation equipment or goods or an accident to the conveying vehicle and/or

(b)   transhipment, recovery or other charges incurred to mitigate damage or prevent any claim provided that in each case:

   1.   your liability for damage to the property, transportation equipment or goods involved is insured elsewhere under this Policy.
   2.   the event limit applicable to this extension is £10,000.

2. Containers

A10–35   We will indemnify you for your liability for damage to containers for which you are responsible provided that we will not pay claims for:

(a)   more than £50,000 for any one container.
(b)   wear and tear, gradual deterioration, scratching, bruising or denting.
(c)   mechanical, electrical or electronic breakdown, failure or derangement.
(d)   containers owned by, hired by, leased or loaned to you or stored at a rental or under a contract for storage and distribution or otherwise on request.

3. General Average and Salvage Charges

A10–36   We will indemnify you for your liability for General Average and Salvage charges payable according to foreign statement or to York Antwerp Rules if in accordance with the contract of affreightment.

4. Consequential loss

A10–37   We will indemnify you for your liability for financial loss consequent upon:

(a)   damage to property (provided that your liability for such damage has been established and admitted as insured under this Policy)
(b)   accidental delay in delivering or releasing property (other than failure to meet a specific delivery or release date or time agreed by you)

provided that:

1.   the event limit applicable to this extension is £100,000
2.   we will not pay claims under this extension:

   (a)   unless you contracted in terms which:
      1.   excluded liability for such financial loss or
      2.   limited liability for such financial loss to an amount not exceeding twice the charges received by or due to you for the carriage, handling or warehousing of the damaged property.
   (b)   for financial loss consequent upon damage to goods and/or merchandise not being carried, handled or warehoused by you.

APPENDIX 11

STATUTES

FIRES PREVENTION (METROPOLIS) ACT 1774

(No. 14 GEORGE III, c.78)

[1774]

Money insured on houses burnt how to be applied

83.   And in order to deter and hinder ill-minded persons from wilfully setting **A11–01** their house or houses, or other buildings on fire, with a view of gaining to themselves the insurance money, whereby the lives and fortunes of many families may be lost or endangered; it shall and may be lawful to and for the respective governors or directors of the several insurance offices for insuring houses or other buildings against loss by fire, and they are hereby authorised and required, upon the request of any person or persons interested in or intitled unto any house or houses, or other buildings which may hereafter be burnt down, demolished or damaged by fire, or upon any grounds of suspicion that the owner or owners, occupier or occupiers, or other person or persons who shall have insured such house or houses or other buildings have been guilty of fraud, or of wilfully setting their house or houses or other buildings on fire, to cause the insurance money to be laid out and expended, as far as the same will go, towards rebuilding, reinstating or repairing, such house or houses or other buildings so burnt down, demolished or damaged by fire, unless the party or parties claiming such insurance money shall, within sixty days next after his, her, or their claim is adjusted, give a sufficient security to the governors or directors of the insurance office where such house or houses or other buildings are insured, that the same insurance money shall be laid out and expended as aforesaid, or unless the said insurance money shall be in that time settled and disposed of to and amongst all the contending parties, to the satisfaction and approbation of such governors or directors of such insurance office respectively.

[Note: Act excuded by Local Government Act 1972 (c. 70), s.140c(3) (as inserted by Local Government (Miscellaneous Provisions) Act 1982 (c.30), s.39(2)).]

MARINE INSURANCE ACT 1906

(6 Edw. 7, c.41)

[21st December 1906]

INSURABLE INTEREST

When Interest must Attach

A11–02   **6.**—(1) The assured must be interested in the subject-matter insured at the time of the loss though he need not be interested when the insurance is effected:

Provided that where the subject-matter is insured "lost or not lost," the assured may recover although he may not have acquired his interest until after the loss, unless at the time of effecting the contract of insurance the assured was aware of the loss, and the insurer was not.

(2) Where the assured has no interest at the time of the loss, he cannot acquire interest by any act or election after he is aware of the loss.

DISCLOSURE AND REPRESENTATION

Insurance is uberrimae fidei

A11–03   **17.** A contract of marine insurance is a contract based upon the utmost good faith, and, if the utmost good faith be not observed by either party, the contract may be avoided by the other party.

Disclosure by assured

A11–04   **18.**—(1) Subject to the provisions of this section, the assured must disclose to the insurer, before the contract is concluded, every material circumstance which is known to the assured, and the assured is deemed to know every circumstance which, in the ordinary course of business, ought to be known by him. If the assured fails to make such disclosure, the insurer may avoid the contract.

(2) Every circumstance is material which would influence the judgment of a prudent insurer in fixing the premium, or determining whether he will take the risk.

(3) In the absence of inquiry the following circumstances need not be disclosed, namely:—

(a) Any circumstance which diminishes the risk;

(b) Any circumstance which is known or presumed to be known to the insurer. The insurer is presumed to know matters of common notoriety or knowledge, and matters which an insurer in the ordinary course of his business, as such, ought to know;

(c) Any circumstance as to which information is waived by the insurer;

(d) Any circumstance which it is superfluous to disclose by reason of any express or implied warranty.

(4) Whether any particular circumstance, which is not disclosed, be material or not is, in each case, a question of fact.

(5) The term "circumstance" includes any communication made to, or information received by, the assured.

Disclosure by agent affecting insurance

19. Subject to the provisions of the preceding section as to circumstances which   **A11–05**
need not be disclosed, where an insurance is effected for the assured by an agent,
the agent must disclose to the insurer—

(a) Every material circumstance which is known to himself, and an agent to
insure is deemed to know every circumstance which in the ordinary
course of business ought to be known by, or to have been communicated to, him; and

(b) Every material circumstance which the assured is bound to disclose,
unless it come to his knowledge too late to communicate it to the agent.

Representations pending negotiation of contract

20.—(1) Every material representation made by the assured or his agent to the   **A11–06**
insurer during the negotiations for the contract, and before the contract is concluded, must be true. If it be untrue the insurer may avoid the contract.

(2) A representation is material which would influence the judgment of a prudent insurer in fixing the premium, or determining whether he will take the risk.

(3) A representation may be either a representation as to a matter of fact, or as
to a matter of expectation or belief.

(4) A representation as to a matter of fact is true, if it be substantially correct,
that is to say, if the difference between what is represented and what is actually
correct would not be considered material by a prudent insurer.

(5) A representation as to a matter of expectation or belief is true if it be made
in good faith.

(6) A representation may be withdrawn or corrected before the contract is
concluded.

(7) Whether a particular representation be material or not is, in each case, a
question of fact.

Valued policy

27.—(1) A policy may be either valued or unvalued.   **A11–07**

(2) A valued policy is a policy which specifies the agreed value of the subject-
matter insured.

(3) Subject to the provisions of this Act, and in the absence of fraud, the
value fixed by the policy is, as between the insurer and assured, conclusive of
the insurable value of the subject intended to be insured, whether the loss be
total or partial.

(4) Unless the policy otherwise provides, the value fixed by the policy is not conclusive for the purpose of determining whether there has been a constructive total
loss.

Unvalued policy

28. An unvalued policy is a policy which does not specify the value of the sub-   **A11–08**
ject-matter insured, but, subject to the limit of the sum insured, leaves the insurable value to be subsequently ascertained, in the manner herein-before specified.

WARRANTIES, ETC.

Nature of warranty

33.—(1) A warranty, in the following sections relating to warranties, means a   **A11–09**
promissory warranty, that is to say, a warranty by which the assured undertakes
that some particular thing shall or shall not be done, or that some condition shall
be fulfilled, or whereby he affirms or negatives the existence of a particular state of
facts.

(2) A warranty may be express or implied.

(3) A warranty, as above defined, is a condition which must be exactly complied with, whether it be material to the risk or not. If it be not so complied with, then, subject to any express provision in the policy, the insurer is discharged from liability as from the date of the breach of warranty, but without prejudice to any liability incurred by him before that date.

When breach of warranty excused

A11–10   **34.**—(1) Non-compliance with a warranty is excused when, by reason of a change of circumstances, the warranty ceases to be applicable to the circumstances of the contract, or when compliance with the warranty is rendered unlawful by any subsequent law.

(2) Where a warranty is broken, the assured cannot avail himself of the defence that the breach has been remedied, and the warranty complied with, before loss.

(3) A breach of warranty may be waived by the insurer.

Express warranties

A11–11   **35.**—(1) An express warranty may be in any form of words from which the intention to warrant is to be inferred.

(2) An express warranty must be included in, or written upon, the policy, or must be contained in some document incorporated by reference into the policy.

(3) An express warranty does not exclude an implied warranty, unless it be inconsistent therewith.

THE PREMIUM

When premium payable

A11–12   **52.** Unless otherwise agreed, the duty of the assured or his agent to pay the premium, and the duty of the insurer to issue the policy to the assured or his agent, are concurrent conditions, and the insurer is not bound to issue the policy until payment or tender of the premium.

Policy effected through broker

A11–13   **53.**—(1) Unless otherwise agreed, where a marine policy is effected on behalf of the assured by a broker, the broker is directly responsible to the insurer for the premium, and the insurer is directly responsible to the assured for the amount which may be payable in respect of losses, or in respect of returnable premium.

(2) Unless otherwise agreed, the broker has, as against the assured, a lien upon the policy for the amount of the premium and his charges in respect of effecting the policy; and, where he has dealt with the person who employs him as a principal, he has also a lien on the policy in respect of any balance on any insurance account which may be due to him from such person, unless when the debt was incurred he had reason to believe that such person was only an agent.

LOSS AND ABANDONMENT

Included and excluded losses

A11–14   **55.**—(1) Subject to the provisions of this Act, and unless the policy otherwise provides, the insurer is liable for any loss proximately caused by a peril insured against, but, subject as aforesaid, he is not liable for any loss which is not proximately caused by a peril insured against.

(2) In particular,—

   (a)   The insurer is not liable for any loss attributable to the wilful misconduct of the assured, but, unless the policy otherwise provides, he is liable for any loss proximately caused by a peril insured against, even though the loss would not have happened but for the misconduct or negligence of the master or crew;

   (b)   Unless the policy otherwise provides, the insurer on ship or goods is not liable for any loss proximately caused by delay, although the delay be caused by a peril insured against;

   (c)   Unless the policy otherwise provides, the insurer is not liable for ordinary wear and tear, ordinary leakage and breakage, inherent vice or nature of the subject-matter insured, or for any loss proximately caused by rats or vermin, or for any injury to machinery not proximately caused by maritime perils.

Partial and total loss

56.—(1) A loss may be either total or partial. Any loss other than a total loss, as hereinafter defined, is a partial loss.   **A11–15**

(2) A total loss may be either an actual total loss, or a constructive total loss.

(3) Unless a different intention appears from the terms of the policy, an insurance against total loss includes a constructive, as well as an actual, total loss.

(4) Where the assured brings an action for a total loss and the evidence proves only a partial loss, he may, unless the policy otherwise provides, recover for a partial loss.

(5) Where goods reach their destination in specie, but by reason of obliteration of marks, or otherwise, they are incapable of identification, the loss, if any, is partial, and not total.

Actual total loss

57.—(1) Where the subject-matter insured is destroyed, or so damaged as to cease to be a thing of the kind insured, or where the assured is irretrievably deprived thereof, there is an actual total loss.   **A11–16**

(2) In the case of an actual total loss no notice of abandonment need be given.

MEASURE OF INDEMNITY

Extent of liability of insurer for loss

67.—(1) The sum which the assured can recover in respect of a loss on a policy by which he is insured, in the case of an unvalued policy to the full extent of the insurable value, or, in the case of a valued policy to the full extent of the value fixed by the policy, is called the measure of indemnity.   **A11–17**

(2) Where there is a loss recoverable under the policy, the insurer, or each insurer if there be more than one, is liable for such proportion of the measure of indemnity as the amount of his subscription bears to the value fixed by the policy in the case of a valued policy, or to the insurable value in the case of an unvalued policy.

Total loss

68. Subject to the provisions of this Act and to any express provision in the policy, where there is a total loss of the subject-matter insured,—   **A11–18**

   (1)   If the policy be a valued policy, the measure of indemnity is the sum fixed by the policy:

   (2)   If the policy be an unvalued policy, the measure of indemnity is the insurable value of the subject-matter insured.

Partial loss of ship

A11–19   **69.** Where a ship is damaged, but is not totally lost, the measure of indemnity, subject to any express provision in the policy, is as follows:—

    (1) Where the ship has been repaired, the assured is entitled to the reasonable cost of the repairs, less the customary deductions, but not exceeding the sum insured in respect of any one casualty;

    (2) Where the ship has been only partially repaired, the assured is entitled to the reasonable cost of such repairs, computed as above, and also to be indemnified for the reasonable depreciation, if any, arising from the unrepaired damage, provided that the aggregate amount shall not exceed the cost of repairing the whole damage, computed as above;

    (3) Where the ship has not been repaired, and has not been sold in her damaged state during the risk, the assured is entitled to be indemnified for the reasonable depreciation arising from the unrepaired damage, but not exceeding the reasonable cost of repairing such damage, computed as above.

Partial loss of freight

A11–20   **70.** Subject to any express provision in the policy, where there is a partial loss of freight, the measure of indemnity is such proportion of the sum fixed by the policy in the case of a valued policy, or of the insurable value in the case of an unvalued policy, as the proportion of freight lost by the assured bears to the whole freight at the risk of the assured under the policy.

Partial loss of goods, merchandise, etc.

A11–21   **71.** Where there is a partial loss of goods, merchandise, or other moveables, the measure of indemnity, subject to any express provision in the policy, is as follows:—

    (1) Where part of the goods, merchandise or other moveables insured by a valued policy is totally lost, the measure of indemnity is such proportion of the sum fixed by the policy as the insurable value of the part lost bears to the insurable value of the whole, ascertained as in the case of an unvalued policy:

    (2) Where part of the goods, merchandise, or other moveables insured by an unvalued policy is totally lost, the measure of indemnity is the insurable value of the part lost, ascertained as in case of total loss:

    (3) Where the whole or any part of the goods or merchandise insured has been delivered damaged at its destination, the measure of indemnity is such proportion of the sum fixed by the policy in the case of a valued policy, or of the insurable value in the case of an unvalued policy, as the difference between the gross sound and damaged values at the place of arrival bears to the gross sound value:

    (4) "Gross value" means the wholesale price or, if there be no such price, the estimated value, with, in either case, freight, landing charges, and duty paid beforehand; provided that, in the case of goods or merchandise customarily sold in bond, the bonded price is deemed to be the gross value. "Gross proceeds" means the actual price obtained at a sale where all charges on sale are paid by the sellers.

Apportionment of valuation

A11–22   **72.**—(1) Where different species of property are insured under a single valuation, the valuation must be apportioned over the different species in proportion to their respective insurable values, as in the case of an unvalued policy. The insured value of any part of a species is such proportion of the total insured value of the same as the insurable value of the part bears to the insurable value of the whole, ascertained in both cases as provided by this Act.

(2) Where a valuation has to be apportioned, and particulars of the prime cost of each separate species, quality, or description of goods cannot be ascertained, the division of the valuation may be made over the net arrived sound values of the different species, qualities, or descriptions of goods.

Liabilities to third parties
74. Where the assured has effected an insurance in express terms against any lia-   **A11–23**
bility to a third party, the measure of indemnity, subject to any express provision in the policy, is the amount paid or payable by him to such third party in respect of such liability.

General provisions as to measure of indemnity
75.—(1) Where there has been a loss in respect of any subject-matter not   **A11–24**
expressly provided for in the foregoing provisions of this Act, the measure of indemnity shall be ascertained, as nearly as may be, in accordance with those pro-visions, in so far as applicable to the particular case.
(2) Nothing in the provisions of this Act relating to the measure of indemnity shall affect the rules relating to double insurance, or prohibit the insurer from dis-proving interest wholly or in part, or from showing that at the time of the loss the whole or any part of the subject-matter insured was not at risk under the policy.

Successive losses
77.—(1) Unless the policy otherwise provides, and subject to the provisions of   **A11–25**
this Act, the insurer is liable for successive losses, even though the total amount of such losses may exceed the sum insured.
(2) Where, under the same policy, a partial loss, which has not been repaired or otherwise made good, is followed by a total loss, the assured can only recover in respect of the total loss:
Provided that nothing in this section shall affect the liability of the insurer under the suing and labouring clause.

RIGHTS OF INSURER ON PAYMENT

Right of subrogation
79.—(1) Where the insurer pays for a total loss, either of the whole, or in the   **A11–26**
case of goods of any apportionable part, of the subject-matter insured, he there-upon becomes entitled to take over the interest of the assured in whatever may remain of the subject-matter so paid for, and he is thereby subrogated to all the rights and remedies of the assured in and in respect of that subject-matter as from the time of the casualty causing the loss.
(2) Subject to the foregoing provisions, where the insurer pays for a partial loss, he acquires no title to the subject-matter insured, or such part of it as may remain, but he is thereupon subrogated to all rights and remedies of the assured in and in respect of the subject-matter insured as from the time of the casualty causing the loss, in so far as the assured has been indemnified, according to this Act, by such payment for the loss.

Right of contribution
80.—(1) Where the assured is over-insured by double insurance, each insurer is   **A11–27**
bound, as between himself and the other insurers, to contribute rateably to the loss in proportion to the amount for which he is liable under his contract.
(2) If any insurer pays more than his proportion of the loss, he is entitled to maintain an action for contribution against the other insurers, and is entitled to the like remedies as a surety who has paid more than his proportion of the debt.

Effect of under insurance

A11–28   **81.** Where the assured is insured for an amount less than the insurable value or, in the case of a valued policy, for an amount less that the policy valuation, he is deemed to be his own insurer in respect of the uninsured balance.

RETURN OF PREMIUM

Return for failure of consideration

A11–29   **84.**—(1) Where the consideration for the payment of the premium totally fails, and there has been no fraud or illegality on the part of the assured or his agents, the premium is thereupon returnable to the assured.

(2) Where the consideration for the payment of the premium is apportionable and there is a total failure of any apportionable part of the consideration, a proportionate part of the premium is, under the like conditions, thereupon returnable to the assured.

(3) In particular—

(a) Where the policy is void, or is avoided by the insurer as from the commencement of the risk, the premium is returnable, provided that there has been no fraud or illegality on the part of the assured; but if the risk is not apportionable, and has once attached, the premium is not returnable;

(b) Where the subject-matter insured, or part thereof, has never been imperilled, the premium, or, as the case may be, a proportionate part thereof, is returnable:

   Provided that where the subject-matter has been insured "lost or not lost" and has arrived in safety at the time when the contract is concluded, the premium is not returnable unless, at such time, the insurer knew of the safe arrival;

(c) Where the assured has no insurable interest throughout the currency of the risk, the premium is returnable, provided that this rule does not apply to a policy effected by way of gaming or wagering;

(d) Where the assured has a defeasible interest which is terminated during the currency of the risk, the premium is not returnable;

(e) Where the assured has over-insured under an unvalued policy, a proportionate part of the premium is returnable;

(f) Subject to the foregoing provisions, where the assured has over-insured by double insurance, a proportionate part of the several premiums is returnable:

   Provided that, if the policies are effected at different times, and any earlier policy has at any time borne the entire risk, or if a claim has been paid on the policy in respect of the full sum insured thereby, no premium is returnable in respect of that policy, and when the double insurance is effected knowingly by the assured no premium is returnable.

Third Parties (Rights Against Insurers) Act 1930

(20 & 21 Geo. 5, c.25)

[10th July 1930]

An Act to confer on third parties rights against insurers of third-party risks in the event of the insured becoming insolvent, and in certain other events.

Be it enacted by the King's most Excellent Majesty, by and with the advice and consent of the Lords Spiritual and Temporal, and Commons, in this present Parliament assembled, and by the authority of the same, as follows:—

Rights of third parties against

1.—(1) Where under any contract of insurance a person (hereinafter referred to as the insured) is insured against liabilities to third parties which he may incur, then—   **A11–30**

    (a)   in the event of the insured becoming bankrupt or making a composition or arrangement with his creditors; or

    (b)   in the case of the insured being a company, in the event of a winding-up order [or an administration order][1] being made, or a resolution for a voluntary winding-up being passed, with respect to the company, or of a receiver or manager of the company's business or undertaking being duly appointed, or of possession being taken, by or on behalf of the holders of any debentures secured by a floating charge, of any property comprised in or subject to the charge [or of][2] [a voluntary arrangement proposed for the purposes of Part I of the Insolvency Act 1986 being approved under that Part;][3];

if either before or after that event, any such liability as aforesaid is incurred by the insured, his rights against the insurer under the contract in respect of the liability shall, notwithstanding anything in any Act or rule of law to the contrary, be transferred to and vest in the third party to whom the liability was so incurred.

(2) Where [the estate of any person falls to be administered in accordance with an order under]4 [section 421 of the Insolvency Act 1986],[5] then, if any debt provable in bankruptcy [(in Scotland, and claim accepted in the sequestration)][6] is owing by the deceased in respect of a liability against which he was insured under a contract of insurance as being a liability to a third party, the deceased debtor's rights against the insurer under the contract in respect of that liability shall, notwithstanding anything [any such order][7], be transferred to and vest in the person to whom the debt is owing.

(3) In so far as any contract of insurance made after the commencement of this Act in respect of any liability of the insured to third parties purports, whether directly or indirectly, to avoid the contract or to alter the rights of the parties thereunder upon the happening to the insured of any of the events specified in paragraph (a) or paragraph (b) of subsection (1) of this section or upon the [estate of any person falling to be administered in accordance with an order [section 421 of the Insolvency Act 1986][8]][9] making of an order under section 130 of the Bankruptcy Act 1914, in respect of his estate, the contract shall be of no effect.

---

[1] Words added by Insolvency Act 1985, s.235(1), Sched.8, para.7(2)(a).
[2] Words substituted by Insolvency Act 1985, s.235(1), Sched.8, para.7(2)(a).
[3] Words substituted by Insolvency Act 1986, s.439(2), Sched.14.
[4] Words substituted by Insolvency Act 1985, s.235(1), Sched.8, para.7(2)(a).
[5] Words substituted by Insolvency Act 1986, s.439(2), Sched.14
[6] Words inserted (S.) by Bankruptcy (Scotland) Act 1985, s.75(1) Sched.7, para.6(1).
[7] Words substituted by Insolvency Act 1985, s.235(1), Sched.8, para.7(2)(b).
[8] Words substituted by Insolvency Act 1986, s.439(2), Sched.14.
[9] Words substituted by Insolvency Act 1985, s.235(1), Sched.8, para.7(2)(c).

(4) Upon a transfer under subsection (1) or subsection (2) of this section, the insurer shall, subject to the provisions of section 3 of this Act, be under the same liability to the third party as he would have been under to the insured, but—

    (a) if the liability of the insurer to the insured exceeds the liability of the insured to the third party, nothing in this Act shall affect the rights of the insured against the insurer in respect of the excess; and

    (b) if the liability of the insurer to the insured is less than the liability of the insured to the third party, nothing in this Act shall affect the rights of the third party against the insured in respect of the balance.

(5) For the purposes of this Act, the expression "liabilities to third parties," in relation to a person insured under any contract of insurance, shall not include any liability of that person in the capacity of insurer under some other contract of insurance.

(6) This Act shall not apply—

    (a) where a company is wound up voluntarily merely for the purposes of reconstruction or of amalgamation with another company; or

    (b) to any case to which subsections (1) and (2) of section 7 of the Workmen's Compensation Act 1925, applies.

Duty to give necessary information to third parties

A11–31   **2.**—(1) In the event of any person becoming bankrupt or making a composition or arrangement with his creditors, or in the event of [the estate of any person falling to be administered in accordance with an order under][1][section 421 of the Insolvency Act 1986][2], or in the event of a winding-up order [or an administration order][3] being made, or a resolution for a voluntary winding-up being passed, with respect to any company or of a receiver or manager of the company's business or undertaking being duly appointed or of possession being taken by or on behalf of the holders of any debentures secured by a floating charge of any property comprised in or subject to the charge it shall be the duty of the bankrupt, debtor, personal representative of the deceased debtor or company, and, as the case may be, of the trustee in bankruptcy, trustee, liquidator, [administrator,][4] receiver, or manager, or person in possession of the property to give at the request of any person claiming that the bankrupt, debtor, deceased debtor, or company is under a liability to him such information as may reasonably be required by him for the purpose of ascertaining whether any rights have been transferred to and vested in him by this Act and for the purpose of enforcing such rights, if any, and any contract of insurance, in so far as it purports, whether directly or indirectly, to avoid the contract or to alter the rights of the parties thereunder upon the giving of any such information in the events aforesaid or otherwise to prohibit or prevent the giving thereof in the said events shall be of no effect.

[(1A) The reference in subsection (1) of this section to a trustee includes a reference to the supervisor of a [voluntary arrangement proposed for the purposes of, and approved under, Part I or Part VIII of the Insolvency Act 1986[...][5]][6][7]

(2) If the information given to any person in pursuance of subsection (1) of this section discloses reasonable ground for supposing that there have or may have been transferred to him under this Act rights against any particular insurer, that insurer

---

[1] Words added by Insolvency Act 1985, s.235(1), Sched.8, para.7(3)(a).
[2] Words substituted by Insolvency Act 1986, s.439(2), Sched.14.
[3] Words added by Insolvency Act 1985, s.235(1), Sched.8, para.7(3)(a).
[4] Word added by Insolvency Act 1985, s.235(1), Sched.8, para.7(3)(a).
[5] Words substituted by Insolvency Act 1986, s.439(2), Sched.14.
[6] Words added by Insolvency Act 1985, s.235(1), Sched.8, para.7(3)(b).
[7] S. 2(1A) added by Insolvency Act (c. 65), s. 235(1), Sched.8, para.7(3)(b).

shall be subject to the same duty as is imposed by the said subsection on the persons therein mentioned.

(3) The duty to give information imposed by this section shall include a duty to allow all contracts of insurance, receipts for premiums, and other relevant documents in the possession or power of the person on whom the duty is so imposed to be inspected and copies thereof to be taken.

Settlement between insurers and insured persons

3. Where the insured has become bankrupt or where in the case of the insured being a company, a winding-up order [or an administration order][1] has been made or a resolution for a voluntary winding-up has been passed, with respect to the company, no agreement made between the insurer and the insured after liability has been incurred to a third party and after the commencement of the bankruptcy or winding-up [or the day of the making of the administration order][2], as the case may be, nor any waiver, assignment, or other disposition made by, or payment made to the insured after the commencement [or day][3] aforesaid shall be effective to defeat or affect the rights transferred to the third party under this Act, but those rights shall be the same as if no such agreement, waiver, assignment, disposition or payment had been made.

A11–32

[Application to limited liability partnership

3A. —(1) This Act applies to limited liability partnerships as it applies to companies.

(2) In its application to limited liability partnerships, references to a resolution for a voluntary winding-up being passed are references to a determination for a voluntary winding-up being made.][4]

Application to Scotland

4. In the application of this Act to Scotland—

A11–33

    (a)   [...][5]

    (b)   any reference to [an estate falling to be administered in accordance with an order under][6] [section 421 of the Insolvency Act 1986][7], shall be deemed to include a reference to an award of sequestration of the estate of a deceased debtor, and a reference to an appointment of a judicial factor, under [section 11A of the Judicial Factors (Scotland) Act 1889][8], on the insolvent estate of a deceased person.

Short title

5. This Act may be cited as the Third Parties (Rights against Insurers) Act 1930.

A11–34

---

[1] Words added by Insolvency Act 1985, s.235(1), Sched.8, para.7(4).
[2] Words added by Insolvency Act 1985, s.235(1), Sched.8, para.7(4).
[3] Words added by Insolvency Act, s.235(1), Sched.8, para.7(4).
[4] Added by S.I. 2001 No.1090 (Limited Liability Partnerships Regulations 2001, Sched.5, para.2.
[5] Repealed (S.) by Bankrupcy (Scotland) Act 1985, s.75(1)(2), Sched.7, para.6(2)(a), Sched.8.
[6] Words added by Insolvency Act 1985, s.235(1), Sched.8, para.7(5).
[7] Words added by Insolvency Act, 1986, s.439(2), Sched.14.
[4] Words substituted (S.) by Bankrupcy (Scotland) Act 1985, s.75(1), Sched.7, para.6(2)(b).

Employers' Liability (Compulsory Insurance) Act 1969

(1969, c. 57)

[22nd OCTOBER 1969]

Be it enacted by the Queen's most Excellent Majesty, by and with the advice and consent of the Lords Spiritual and Temporal, and Commons, in this present Parliament assembled, and by the authority of the same, as follows:—

Insurance against liability for employees

A11–35   **1.**—(1) Except as otherwise provided by this Act, every employer shall insure, and maintain insurance, under one or more approved policies with an authorised insurer or insurers against liability for bodily injury or disease sustained by those of his relevant employees who are employed by him for work on or from an offshore installation, or on or from an associated structure in the course of an activity undertaken on or in connection with an offshore installation, and arising out of and in the course of their employment for that work.

(2) Regulations may provide that the amount for which an employer is required by this Act to insure and maintain insurance shall, either generally or in such cases or classes of case as may be prescribed by the regulations, be limited in such manner as may be so prescribed.

(3) For the purposes of this Act—

(a)   "approved policy" means a policy of insurance not subject to any conditions or exceptions prohibited for those purposes by regulations;

(b)   "authorised insurer" means a person or body of persons lawfully carrying on in the United Kingdom insurance business of a class specified in Schedule 1 or 2 to the Insurance Companies Act 1982, or, being an insurance company the head office of which is in a Member State, lawfully carrying on in a Member State other than the United Kingdom insurance business of a corresponding class and issuing the policy or policies in the course thereof;

(c)   "business" includes a trade or profession, and includes any activity carried on by a body of persons, whether corporate or unincorporate;

(d)   except as otherwise provided by regulations, an employer not having a place of business in Great Britain shall be deemed not to carry on business there.

[(e)   any expression to which a meaning is given by the Offshore Installations and Pipeline Works (Management and Administration) Regulations 1995, and to which a meaning is not given in this Act, shall have the same meaning in this Act.][1]

Employees to be covered

A11–36   **2.**—(1) For the purposes of this Act the term "employee" means an individual who has entered into or works under a contract of service or apprenticeship with an employer whether by way of manual labour, clerical work or otherwise, whether such contract is expressed or implied, oral or in writing.

(2) This Act shall not require an employer to insure—

(a)   in respect of an employee of whom the employer is the husband, wife, father, mother, grandfather, grandmother, step-father, step-mother, son, daughter, grandson, granddaughter, stepson, stepdaughter, brother, sister, half-brother or half-sister; or

(b)   [2]

[1] Added by S.I. 1995 No.738 (Offshore Installations and Pipeline Works (Management and Administration) Regulations, reg.21(2)(b).

[2] Repealed by S.I. 1995 No.738 (Offshore Installations and Pipeline Works (Management and Administration) Regulations, reg.21(3).

Employers exempted from insurance

3.—(1) This Act shall not require any insurance to be effected by—

(a) any such authority as is mentioned in subsection (2) below; or

(b) any body corporate established by or under any enactment for the carrying on of any industry or part of an industry, or of any undertaking, under national ownership or control; or

(c) in relation to any such cases as may be specified in the regulations, any employer exempted by regulations.

(2) The authorities referred to in subsection (1)(a) above

(a) a health service body, as defined in section 60(7) of the National Heath Service and Community Care Act 1990, and a National Service trust established under Part I of that Act or the National Health Service (Scotland) Act 1978 and a Primary Care Trust established under section 16A of the National Health Service Act 1977;

(b) are the Common Council of the City of London, the Council of a London Borough, the council of a county or county borough in Wales, the Broads Authority, a council constituted under section 2 of the Local Government, etc. (Scotland) Act 1994 in England and Wales or joint committee in Scotland which is so constituted as to include among its members representatives of any such council, the Strathclyde Passenger Transport Authority, any joint authority established by Part IV of the Local Government Act 1985, [the London Fire and Emergency Planning Authority][1], any police authority, the Service Authority for the National Criminal Intelligence Service and the Service Authority for the National Crime Squad.

Certificates of insurance

4.—(1) Provision may be made by regulations for securing that certificates of insurance in such form and containing such particulars as may be prescribed by the regulations, are issued by insurers to employers entering into contracts of insurance in accordance with the requirements of this Act and for the surrender in such circumstances as may be so prescribed of certificates so issued.

(2) Where a certificate of insurance is required to be issued to an employer in accordance with regulations under subsection (1) above, the employer (subject to any provision made by the regulations as to the surrender of the certificate) shall during the currency of the insurance and such further period (if any) as may be provided by regulations—

(a) comply with any regulations requiring him to display copies of the certificate of insurance [or make arrangements to secure the maintenance of such copies on offshore installations or associated structures][2] for the information of his employees;

(b) produce the certificate of insurance or a copy thereof on demand to any inspector duly authorised by the Secretary of State for the purposes of this Act and produce or send the certificate or a copy thereof to such other persons, at such place and in such circumstances as may be prescribed by regulations;

(c) permit the policy of insurance or a copy thereof to be inspected by such persons and in such circumstances as may be so prescribed.

[1] Words added by Greater London Authority Act (1999 c.29), Sched.29, Sched. Pt I, para. 12.
[2] Words inserted by S.I. 1995 No.738 (Offshore Installations and Pipeline Works (Management and Administration) Regulations, reg.21(4).

(3) A person who fails to comply with a requirement imposed by or under this section shall be liable on summary conviction to a fine not exceeding level 3 on the standard scale.

Penalty for failure to insure

A11–39   5. An employer who on any day is not insured in accordance with this Act when required to be so shall be guilty of an offence and shall be liable on summary conviction to a fine not exceeding [level 4 on the standard scale][1]; and where an offence under this section committed by a corporation has been committed with the consent or connivance of, or facilitated by any neglect on the part of, any director, manager, secretary or other officer of the corporation, he, as well as the corporation shall be deemed to be guilty of that offence and shall be liable to be proceeded against and punished accordingly.

[5A.—(1) In respect of any offshore installation, it shall be the duty of the owner of the installation to ensure that the requirements imposed by or under this Act are complied with and where, in respect of that installation—

    (a)   any employer is on any day not insured in accordance with this Act, the owner of the installation shall be guilty of an offence and liable on summary conviction to a fine not exceeding level 3 on the standard scale; or

    (b)   any person fails to comply with a requirement imposed by or under section 4 of this Act, the owner of the installation shall be guilty of an offence and liable on summary conviction to a fine not exceeding level 2 on the standard scale.

(2) In proceedings against the owner of an installation for an offence under this section it shall be a defence for the accused to prove—

    (a)   that he has used all due diligence to prevent the commision of the offence; and

    (b)   that any relevant contravention was committed without his consent, connivance or wilful default.

(3) Section 37 of the Health and Safety at Work, etc. Act 1974 shall apply in relation to an offence under this section as if it were an offence under that Act.

(4) In proceedings for an offence under this section an averment in any process of the fact that anything was done or situated within relevant waters shall, until the contrary is proved, be sufficient evidence of that fact as stated in the averment.

(5) Proceedings for any offence under this section may be taken, and the offence may for all incidental purposes be treated as having been committed, in any place in Great Britain.

(6) References in this section to "the owner", in relation to an offshore installation, are to the person who controls the operation of the installation.][2]

[5B. No proceedings shall be instituted in England and Wales for any offence under this Act in respect of an offshore installation except by the Secretary of State or by a person authorised in that behalf by the Secretary of State".][3]

---

[1] Words substituted by Criminal Justice Act 1982 (c.48), s.46 and Criminal Procedure (Scotland) Act 1975 (c.21), s.289G.

[2] Added by S.I. 1995 No.738 (Offshore Installations and Pipeline Works (Management and Administration) Regulations, reg.21(5).

[3] Added by S.I. 1995 No.738 (Offshore Installations and Pipeline Works (Management and Administration) Regulations, reg.21(5).

Regulations

6.—(1) The Secretary of State may by statutory instrument make regulations for   **A11–40**
any purpose for which regulations are authorised to be made by this Act, but any
such statutory instrument shall be subject to annulment in pursuance of a resolution of either House of Parliament.

(2) Any regulation under this Act may make different provision for different
cases or classes of case, and may contain such incidental and supplementary provisions as appear to the Secretary of State to be necessary or expedient for the purposes of the regulations.

Short title, extent and commencement

7.—(1) This Act may be cited as the Employers' Liability (Compulsory Insur-   **A11–41**
ance) Act 1969.

(2) This Act shall not extend to Northern Ireland.

(3) This Act shall come into force for any purpose on such date as the Secretary
of State may by order contained in a statutory instrument appoint, and the purposes for which this Act is to come into force at any time may be defined by reference to the nature of an employer's business, or to that of an employee's work, or
in any other way.

Insurance Brokers (Registration) Act 1977

(1977, c. 46)

[29th JULY 1977]

An act to provide for the registration of insurance brokers and for the regulation of their professional standards; and for purposes connected therewith.

Be it enacted by the Queen's most Excellent Majesty, by and with the advice and consent of the Lords Spiritual and Temporal, and Commons, in this present Parliament assembled, and by the authority of the same, as follows:—

THE INSURANCE BROKERS REGISTRATION COUNCIL

Establishment of Insurance Brokers Registration Council

A11–42   **1.**—(1) There shall be established a body to be called the Insurance Brokers Registration Council (hereinafter referred to as "the Council") which shall be a body corporate with perpetual succession and a common seal and shall have the general function of carrying out the powers and duties conferred on them by this Act.

(2) The Council shall be constituted in accordance with the Schedule to this Act and the supplementary provisions contained in that Schedule shall have effect with respect to the Council.

REGISTRATION AND TRAINING OF INSURANCE BROKERS

The insurance brokers register

A11–43   **2.** The Council shall establish and maintain a register of insurance brokers (hereinafter referred to as "the register") containing the names, addresses and qualifications, and such other particulars as may be prescribed, of all persons who are entitled under the provisions of this Act to be registered therein and apply in the prescribed manner to be so registered.

Qualifications for registration

A11–44   **3.**—(1) Subject to subsection (2) below and to section 16 of this Act, a person shall be entitled to be registered in the register if he satisfies the Council—

  (a) that he holds a qualification approved by the Council under section 6 of this Act, being a qualification granted to him after receiving instruction from an institution so approved; or

  (b) that he holds a qualification recognised by the Council for the purposes of this paragraph, being a qualification granted outside the United Kingdom; or

  (c) that he has carried on business as an insurance broker, or as a whole-time agent acting for two or more insurance companies in relation to insurance business, for a period of not less than five years; or

  (d) that he holds a qualification recognised by the Council for the purpses of this paragraph and has carried on business as mentioned in paragraph (c) above for a period of not less than three years; or

  (e) that he has been employed by a person carrying on business as mentioned in paragraph (c) above, or by an insurance company, for a period of not less than five years; or

  (f) hat he holds a qualification recognised by the Council for the purposes of this paragraph and has been employed by a person carrying on business as mentioned in paragraph (c) above, or by an insurance company, for a period of not less than three years; or

(g) that he has knowledge and practical experience of insurance business which is comparable to that of a person who has carried on business as an insurance broker for a period of five years; or

(h) that he holds a qualification recognised by the Council for the purposes of this paragraph and has knowledge and practical experience of insurance business which is comparable to that of a person who has carried on business as an insurance broker for a period of three years.

(2) A person shall not be entitled to be registered in the register by virtue of subsection (1) above uless he also satisfies the Council—

(a) as to his character and suitability to be a registered insurance broker; and

(b) in a case falling within paragraph (a), (b), (e) or (f) of subsection (1) above, that he has had adequate practical experience in the work of an insurance broker; and

(c) if he is carryhing on business as an insurance broker at the time when the application is made, that he is complying with the requirements of rules under section 11(1) of this Act.

(3) Subject to section 16 of this Act, a person shall be entitled to be registered in the register if he satisfies the Council that he or a partnership of which he is a member is accepted as a Lloyd's broker by the Committee of Lloyd's.

(4) The Secretary of State may, after consulting the Council, by order provide that any of the paragraphs in subsection (1) or (2) above shall be omitted or shall have effect subject to such amendments as may be specified in the order.

List of bodies corporate carrying on business as insurance brokers

4.—(1) The Council shall establish and maintain a list of bodies corporate carrying on business as insurance brokers (hereinafter referred to as "the list") containing the names, principal places of business and such other particulars as may be prescribed of all bodies corporate which are entitled under this section to be enrolled therein and apply in the prescribed manner tobe so enrolled. **A11–45**

(2) Subject to subsection (3) below and to section 16 of this Act, a body corporate shall be entitled to be enrolled in the list if it satisfies the Council—

(a) that a majority of its directors are registered insurance brokers; or

(b) in the case of a body corporate having only one director, that he is a registered insurance broker; or

(c) in the case of a body corporate having only two directors, that one of them is a registered insurance broker and that the business is carried on under the management of that director.

(3) A body corporate shall not be entitled to be enrolled in the list by virtue of subsection (1) above unless it also satisfies the Council that it is complying with the requirements of rules under section 11(1) of this Act.

(4) Subject to section 16 of this Act, a body corporate shall be entitled to be enrolled in the list if it satisfies the Council that it is accepted as a Lloyd's broker by the Committee of Lloyd's.

Appeals against refusal to register or enrol

5.—(1) Before refusing an application for registration under section 3 of this Act or an application for enrolment under section 4 of this Act, the Council shall give the person by whom or the body corporate by which the application was made an opportunity of appearing before and being heard by a committee of the Council. **A11–46**

(2) Where the Council refuse any such application, the Council shall, if so required by the person by whom or the body corporate by which the application was made within seven days from notification of the decision, serve on that person or body a statement of the reasons therefor.

(3) A person or bdoy corporate whose application is so refused may within twenty-eight days from—

    (a)   notification of the decision, or

    (b)   if a statement of reasons has been required under subsection (2) above, service of the statement,
          appeal against the refusal to the Court.

(4) The Council may appear as respondent on any such appeal and for the purpose of enabling directions to be given as to the costs of any such appeal the Council shall be deemed to be a party thereto, whether they appear on the hearing of the appeal or not.

(5) On the hearing of any such appeal the Court may make such order as it thinks fit and its order shall be final.

Approval of educational institutions and qualifications

A11–47   **6.**—(1) The Council may approve for the purposes of this Act any institution (hereinafter referred to as "an approved educational institution") where the instruction given to persons being educated as insurance brokers appears to the Council to be such as to secure to them adequate knowledge and skill for the practice of their profession.

(2) The Council may approve for the purposes of this Act any qualification (hereinafter referred to as "an approved qualification") which appears to the Council to be granted to candidates who reach such a standard of proficiency at a qualifying examination as to secure to them adequate knowledge and skill for the practice of their profession.

(3) Where the Council have refused to approve an institution or qualification under this section as suitable for any purpose, the Secretary of State, on representations being made to him within one month of the refusal, may, if he thinks fit, after considering the representations and after consulting the Council, order the Council to approve the institution or qualification as suitable for that purpose.

(4) The Council shall publish before the day appointed for the coming into operation of section 3(1)(a) of this Act, and from time to time thereafter, a list of approved educational institutions and approved qualifications.

Supervision of educational institutions and qualifying examinations

     7.—(1) It shall be the duty of the Council to keep themselves informed of the nature of the instruction given by any approved educational institution to persons being educated as insurance brokers and of the examinations on the results of which approved qualifications are granted.

(2) For the purposes of their duty under subsection (1) above the Council may appoint persons to visit approved educational institutions and to attend at the examinations held by the bodies which grant approved qualifications.

(3) It shall be the duty of visitors appointed under subsection (2) above to report to the Council as to the sufficiency of the instruction given by the institutions visited by them, or of the examinations attended by them, and as to any other matters relating thereto which may be specified by the Council either generally or in any particular case, but no visitor shall interfere with the giving of any instruction or the holding of any examination.

(4) Where it appears to the Council (as a result of a report under subsection (3) above or otherwise),—

    (a)   that the instruction given by any approved educational institution to persons being educated as insurance brokers or the examinations taken by such persons are not such as to secure the psosession by them of adequate knowledge and skill for the practice of their profession; and

(b) that by reason thereof the approval of the institution or qualification in question should be withdrawn,

the Council shall give notice in writing to the institution or body of their opinion, sending therewith a copy of any report on which their opinion is based.

(5) On the receipt of the notice the institution or body may, within such period (not being less than one month) as the Council may have specified in the notice, make to the Council observations on the notice and any report sent therewith or objections to the notice and report.

(6) As soon as may be after the expiration of the period specified in the notice under subsection (4) above the Council shall determine whether or not to withdraw their approval of the institution or qualification, as the case may be, taking into account any observations or objections duly made under subsection (5) above.

(7) The Council shall give notice in writing of any decision under this section to withdraw approval of an institution or qualification to the institution or body concerned and the decision shall not take effect until the expiration of one month from the date of the giving of the notice or, if during that time the institution or body makes representations with respect to the decision to the Secretary of State, until the representations are finally dealth with.

(8) Where the Council have decided to withdraw approval of an institution or qualification, the Secretary of State, on representations being made to him within one month from the giving of notice of the decision, may, if he thinks fit, after considering the representations and after consulting the Council order the Council to annul the withdrawal of approval.

(9) The Council may pay to visitors appointed under this section such fees and such travelling and subsistence allowances as the Council may determine.

Supplementary provisions as to the register and list

8.—(1) The register and list shall be kept by the registrar of the Council who **A11–49** shall be appointed by the Council.

(2) The Council may make rules with respect to the form and keeping of the register and list and the making of entries and alterations therein and, in particular—

(a) regulating the making of applications for registration or enrolment and providing for the evidence to be produced in support of any such applications;

(b) providing for the notification to the registrar of any change in the particulars required to be entered in the register or list;

(c) prescribing a fee to be charged on the entry of a name in, or the restoration of a name to, the register or list;

(d) prescribing a fee to be charged in respect of the retention in the register or list of any name in any year subsequent to the year in which that name was first entered in the register or list;

(e) providing for the entry in the register of qualifications (whether approved qualifications or not) possessed by persons whose names are registered therein and for the removal of such qualifications from the register, and prescribing a fee to be charged in respect of the entry;

(f) authorising the registrar to refuse to enter a name in, or restore it to, the register or list until a fee prescribed for the entry or restoration has been paid and to erase from the register or list the name of a person who or body corporate which, after the prescribed notices and warnings, fails to pay the fee prescribed in respect of the retention of that name in the register or list;

(g) authorising the registrar to erase from the register or list the name of a person who or body corporate which, after the prescribed notices and warnings, fails to supply information required by the registrar with a view to ensuring that the particulars entered in the register or list are correct;

(h) prescribing anything required or authorised to be prescribed by the provisions of this Act relating to the register or list.

(3) Rules under this section which provide for the erasure of a name from the register or list on failure to pay a fee shall provide for its restoration thereto on the making of the prescribed application in that behalf and on payment of that fee and any additional fee prescribed in respect of the restoration.

(4) Rules under this section prescribing fees may provide for the charging of different fees in different classes of cases and for the making of arrangements for the collection of fees with such body or bodies as may be prescribed.

Publication of register and list

A11–50   9.—(1) The Council shall cause the register and list to be printed and published within one year of the establishment of the Council and as often thereafter as they think fit.

(2) Where the register or list is not published in any year after the first publication thereof, the Council shall cause any alterations in the entries in the register or list which have been made since the last publication thereof to be printed and published within that year.

(3) A copy fo the register or list purporting to be printed and published by the Council, shall, as altered by any alterations purporting to be printed and published by the Council, be evidence in all proceedings that the individuals specified in the register are registered therein or, as the case may be, that the bodies corporate specified in the list are enrolled therein; and the absence of the name of any individual or body corporate from any such copy of the register or list shall be evidence, until the contrary is shown, that he is not registered or, as the case may be, that it is not enrolled therein.

(4) In the case of an individual whose name or a body corporate the name of which does not appear in any such copy of the register or list as altered as aforesaid, a certified copy, under the hand of the registrar, of the entry relating to that individual or body corporate in the register or list shall be evidence of the entry.

REGULATION OF CONDUCT

Code of conduct

A11–51   10.—(1) The Council shall draw up and may from time to time revise a statement of the acts and omissions which, if done or made by registered insurance brokers or enrolled bodies corporate, or by registered insurance brokers or enrolled bodies corporate in particular circumstances, constitute in the opinion of the Council unprofessional conduct.

(2) The statement shall serve as a guide to registered insurance brokers and enrolled bodies corporate and persons concerned with the conduct of registered insurance brokers and enrolled bodies corporate, but the mention or lack of mention in it of a particular act or omission shall not be taken as conclusive of any question of professional conduct.

Requirements for carrying on business

A11–52   11.—(1) The Council shall make rules requiring registered insurance brokers who are carrying on business as insurance brokers (hereinafter referred to as "practising insurance brokers") and enrolled bodies corporate to ensure—

(a) that their business have working capital of not less than such amount as may be prescribed;

(b)   that the value of the assets of their businesses exceeds the amount of the liabilities of their businesses by not less than such amount as may be prescribed; and

(c)   that the number of insurance companies with which they place insurance business, and the amount of insurance business which they place with each insurance company, is such as to prevent their businesses from becoming unduly dependent on any particular insurance company.

(2) The Council shall also make rules requiring practising insurance brokers and enrolled bodies corporate—

(a)   to open and keep accounts at banks for money received by them from persons with whom they do business;

(b)   to hold money so received in such manner as may be prescribed;

(c)   to keep such accounting records showing and explaining the transactions of their businesses as may be prescribed; and

(d)   to prepare and submit to the Council at such intervals as may be prescribed balance sheets and profit and loss accounts containing such information as may be prescribed for the purpose of giving a true and fair view of the state of their businesses.

(3) Without prejudice to the generality of subsections (1) and (2) above, rules under this section may empower the Council—

(a)   to require practising insurance brokers and enrolled bodies corporate to deliver at such intervals as may be prescribed reports given by qualified accountants and containing such information as may be prescribed for the purpose of ascertaining whether or not the rules have been complied with;

(b)   to require practising insurance brokers and enrolled bodies corporate to deliver at such intervals as may be prescribed statements made by them and containing such information as may be prescribed for the purpose of ascertaining whether or not the rules are being complied with; and

(c)   to take such other steps as they consider necessary or expedient for the purpose of ascertaining whether or not the rules are being complied with.

(4) Subject to subsections (5) and (6) below, an accountant is qualified to give reports for the purposes of the rules if he is a member of a recognised body of accountants or is for the time being authorised by the Secretary of State under section 161(1)(b) of the Companies Act 1948 (c. 58) or, in Northern Ireland, by the Department of Commerce for Northern Ireland under section 155(1)(b) of the Companies Act (Northern Ireland) 1960 (c. 22).

(5) An accountant shall not be qualified to give such reports—

(a)   in relation to a practising insurance broker, if he is an employee or partner of, or an employee of a partner of, the practising insurance broker;

(b)   in relation to an enrolled body corporate, if he is not qualified for appointment as auditor of the enrolled body corporate.

(6) A Scottish firm of accountants shall be qualified to give such reports if, but only if, all the partners are so qualified.

(7) Rules under this section may make different provision for different circumstances, and may specify circumstances in which persons are exempt from any of the requirements of the rules.

Professional indemnity, etc.

A11–53   12.—(1) The Council shall make rules for indemnifying—

(a) practising insurance brokers and former practising insurance brokers, and
(b) enrolled bodies corporate and former enrolled bodies corporate,

against losses arising from claims in respect of any description of civil liability incurred by them, or by employees or former employees of theirs, in connection with their businesses.

(2) The Council shall also make rules for the making of grants or other payments for the purpose of relieving or mitigating losses suffered by persons in consequence of—

(a) negligence or fraud or other dishonesty on the part of practising insurance brokers or enrolled bodies corporate, or of employees of theirs, in connection with their businesses; or
(b) failure on the part of practising insurance brokers or enrolled bodies corporate to account for money received by them in connection with their businesses.

(3) For the purpose of providing such indemnity and of enabling such grants or other payments to be made, rules under this section—

(a) may authorise or require the Council to establish and maintain a fund or funds;
(b) may authorise or require the Council to take out and maintain insurance with authorised insurers;
(c) may require practising insurance brokers or enrolled bodies corporate or any specified description of practising insurance brokers or enrolled bodies corporate to take out and maintain insurance with authorised insurers.

(4) Without prejudice to the generality of the preceding subsections, rules under this section—

(a) may specify the terms and conditions on which indemnity or a grant or other payment is to be available, and any circumstances in which the right to it is to be excluded or modified;
(b) may provide for the management, administration and protection of any fund maintained by virtue of subsection (3)(a) above and require practising insurance brokers or enrolled bodies corporate or any description of practising insurance brokers or enrolled bodies corporate to make payments to any such fund;
(c) may require practising insurance brokers or enrolled bodies corporate or any description of practising insurance brokers or enrolled bodies corporate to make payments by way of premium on any insurance policy maintained by the Council by virtue of subsection (3)(b) above;
(d) may prescribe the conditions which an insurance policy must satisfy for the purposes of subsection (3)(c) above;
(e) may authorise the Council to determine the amount on any payments required by the rules, subject to such limits, or in accordance with such provisions, as may be prescribed;
(f) may specify circumstances in which, where a registered insurance broker or enrolled body corporate for whom indemnity is provided has failed to comply with the rules, the Council or insurers may take proceedings against him or it in respect of sums paid by way of indemnity

in connection with a matter in relation to which there has been a failure to comply with the rules;

(g)   may specify circumstances in which, where a grant or other payment is made in consequence of the act or omission of a practising insurance broker or enrolled body corporate, the Council or insurers may take proceedings against him or it in respect of the sum so paid;

(h)   may make different provision for different circumstances, and may specify circumstances in which practising insurance brokers or enrolled bodies corporate are exempt from any of the rules;

(i)   may empower the Council to take such steps as they consider necessary or expedient to ascertain whether or not the rules are being complied with; and

(j)   may contain incidental, procedural or supplementary provisions.

DISCIPLINARY PROCEEDINGS

Preliminary investigation of disciplinary cases

13.—(1) The Council shall set up a committee, to be known as the Investigating Committee, for the preliminary investigation of cases in which—   **A11–54**

(a)   it is alleged that a registered insurance broker or enrolled body corporate is liable to have his or its name erased from the register or list on any ground specified in section 15 of this Act; or

(b)   a complain is made to the Council by or on behalf of a member of the public about a registered insurance broker or enrolled body corporate.

Any such case is hereinafter referred to as "a disciplinary case".

(2) A disciplinary case shall be referred to the Investigating Committee who shall carry out a preliminary investigation of it and, unless they are satisfied that there is insufficient evidence to support a finding that the registered insurance broker or enrolled body corporate is liable to have hsi or its name erased from the register or list, the Committee shall refer the case, with the results of their investigation, to the Disciplinary Committee set up under th next following section.

(3) The Council shall make rules as to the constitution of the Investigating Committee.

The Disciplinary Committee

14.—(1) The Council shall set up a committee, to be known as the Disciplinary Committee, for the consideration and determination of disciplinary cases referred to them under the last foregoing section and of any other cases of which they have cognizance under the following provisions of this Act.   **A11–55**

(2) The Council shall make rules as to the constitution of the Disciplinary Committee, the times and places of the meetings of the Committee, the quorum and the mode of summoning the members thereof.

(3) Rules under this section shall secure that a person, other than the Chairman of the Council, who has acted in relation to any disciplinary case as a member of the Investigating Committee does not act in relation to that case as a member of the Disciplinary Committee.

Erasure from the register and list for crime, unprofessional conduct, etc.

15.—(1) If a registered insurance broker or enrolled body corporate—   **A11–56**

(a)   is convicted by any court in the United Kingdom of any criminal offence, not being an offence which, owing to its trivial nature or the circumstances under which it was committed, does not render him or it unfit to have his or its name on the register or list, or

(b)   is judged by the Disciplinary Committee to have been guilty of unpro-
       fessional conduct,

The Disciplinary Committee may, if they think fit, direct that the name of the
insurance broker or body corporate shall be erased from the register or list.

(2) If it appears to the Disciplinary Committee that a registered insurance broker or an enrolled body corporate has contravened or failed to comply with any
rules made under section 11 or section 12 of this Act and that the contravention
or failure is such as to render the insurance broker unfit to have his name on the
register or the body corporate unit to have its name on the list, the Disciplinary
Committee may, if they think fit, direct that the name of the insurance broker or
body corporate shall be erased from the register or list.

(3) Where—

(a)   the name of a director of an enrolled body corporate is erased from the
       register under subsection (1) above, or
(b)   a director of any such body corporate is convicted of an offence under
       this Act, or
(c)   the name of a registered insurance broker employed by any such body
       corporate is erased from the register under subsection (1) above and the
       act or omission constituting the ground on which it was erased was
       instigated or connived at by a director of the body corporate, or, if the
       act or omission was a continuing act or omission, a director of the body
       corporate had or reasonable ought to have had knowledge of the con-
       tinuance thereof,

the Disciplinary Committee may, if they think fit, direct that the name of the
body corporate shall be erased from the list:

Provided that the Disciplinary Committee shall not take a case into consideration during any period within which proceedings by way of appeal may be brought
which may result in this subsection being rendered inapplicable in that case of
while any such proceedings are pending.

(4) If the Disciplinary Committee are of opinion as respects an enrolled body
corporate that the conditions for enrolment in section 4 of this Act are no longer
satisfied, the Disciplinary Committee may, if they think fit, direct that the name of
the body corporate shall be erased from the list.

(5) Where a registered insurance broker dies while he is a director of an enrolled
body corporate, he shall be deemed for the purposes of subsection (4) above to
have continued to be a director of that body until the expiration of a period of six
months beginning with the date of his death or until a director is appointed in his
place, whichever first occurs.

(6) When the Disciplinary Committee direct that the name of an individual or
body corporate shall be erased from the register or list, the registrar shall serve on
that individual or body a notification of the direction and a statement of the Committee's reasons therefor.

Restoration of names erased as result of disciplinary cases, etc.

A11–57   16.—(1) Where the name of an individual or body corporate has been erased
from the register or list in pursuance of a direction under the last foregoing section, the name of that individual or body corporate shall not again be entered in
the register or list unless the Disciplinary Committee on application made to them
in that behalf otherwise direct.

(2) An application under subsection (1) above for the restoration of a name to
the register or list shall not be made to the Disciplinary Committee—

(a)   within ten months of the date of erasure; or
(b)   within ten months of a previous application thereunder.

Erasure from register and list on grounds of fraud or error

17.—(1) If it is proved to the satisfaction of the Disciplinary Committee that   **A11–58**
any entry in the register or list has been fraudulently or incorrectly made, the Disciplinary Committee may, if they think fit, direct that the entry shall be erased
from the register or list.

(2) An individual may be registered or a body corporate enrolled in pursuance
of this Act notwithstanding that his or its name has been erased under this section,
but if it was so erased on the ground of fraud, that individual or body corporate
shall not be registered or enrolled except on an application in that behalf to the
Disciplinary Committee; and on any such application the Disciplinary Committee
may, if they think fit, direct that the individual or body corporate shall not be registered or enrolled, or shall not be registered or enrolled until the expiration of
such period as may be specified in the direction.

(3) Where the Disciplinary Committee direct that the name of an individual or
body corporate shall be erased from the register or list under this section, the registrar shall serve on that individual or body a notification of the direction and a
statement of the Committee's reasons therefor.

Appeals in disciplinary and other cases

18.—(1) At any time within twenty-eight days from the service of a notification   **A11–59**
that the Disciplinary Committee have under section 15 or 17 of this Act directed
that the name of an individual or a body corporate be erased from the register or
list that individual or body corporate may appeal to the Court.

(2) The Council may appear as respondent on any such appeal and for the purpose of enabling directions to be given as to the costs of any such appeal the Council shall be deemed to be a party thereto, whether they appear on the hearing of the
appeal or not.

(3) Where no appeal is brought against a direction under section 15 or section
17 of this Act or where such an appeal is brought but withdrawn or struck out for
want of prosecution, the direction shall take effect on the expiration of the time for
appealing or, as the case may be, on the withdrawal or striking out of the appeal.

(4) Subject as aforesaid, where an appeal is brought against a direction under
either of those sections, the direction shall take effect if and when the appeal is dismissed and not otherwise.

Procedure of Disciplinary Committee

19.—(1) For the purpose of any proceedings before the Disciplinary Committee   **A11–60**
in England or Wales or Norther Ireland the Disciplinary Committee may administer oaths, and any party to the proceedings may sue out writs of subpoena ad tes-
tificandum and duces tecum, but no person shall be compelled under any such writ
to produce any document which he could not be compelled to produce on the trial
of an action.

(2) The provisions of section 49 of the Supreme Court of Judicature (Consolidation) Act 1925 (c. 49) or of the Attendance of Witnesses Act 1854 (c. 34) (which   **A11–61**
provide a special procedure for the issue of such writs so as to be in force throughout the United Kingdom) shall apply in relation to any proceedings before the Disciplinary Committee in England or Wales or, as the case may be, in Northern
Ireland as they apply in relation to causes or matters in the High Court or actions
or suits pending in the High Court of Justice in Northern Ireland.

(3) For the purpose of any proceedings before the Disciplinary Committee in
Scotland, the Disciplinary Committee may administer oaths and the Court of Session shall on the application of any party to the proceedings have the like power as
in any action in that Court—

(a) to grant warrant for the citation of witnesses and havers to give evidence or to produce documents before the Disciplinary Committee, and for the issue of letters of second diligence against any witness or haer failing to appear after due citation,

(b) to grant warrant for the recovery of documents, and

(c) to grant commissions to persons to take the evidence of witnesses or to examine havers and receive their exhibits and productions.

(4) The Council shall make rules as to the procedure to be followed and the rules of evidence to be observed in proceedings before the Disciplinary Committee; and in particular—

(a) for securing that notice that the proceedings are to be brought shall be given, at such time and in such manner as may be specified in the rules, to the individual or body corporate alleged to be liable to have his or its name erased from the register or list;

(b) for securing that any party to the proceedings shall, if he so requires, be entitled to be heard by the Disciplinary Committee;

(c) for enabling any party to the proceedings to be represented by counsel or solicitor or (if the rules so provide and the party so elects) by a person of such other description as may be specified in the rules;

(d) for requiring proceedings before the Disciplinary Committee to be held in public except in so far as may be provided by the rules;

(e) for requiring, in cases where it is alleged that a registered insurance broker or enrolled body corporate has been guilty of unprofessional conduct, that where the Disciplinary Committee judge that the allegation has not been proved they shall record a finding that the insurance broker or body corporate is not guilty of such conduct in respect of the matters to whcih the allegation relates;

(f) for requiring, in cases where it is alleged that a registered insurance broker or enrolled body corporate is liable to have his or its name erased from the register or list under section 15(2) of this Act, that where the Disciplinary Committee judge that the allegation has not been proved they shall record a finding that the insurance broker or body corporate is not guilty of the matters alleged.

(5) Before making rules under this section the Council shall consult such organisations representing the interests of insurance brokers and bodies corporate carrying on business as insurance brokers as appear to the Council requisite to be consulted.

(6) In this section and in section 20 of this Act "proceedings" means proceedings under this Act, whether relating to disciplinary cases or otherwise.

Assessors to Disciplinary Committee

A11–62   **20.**—(1) For the purpose of advising the Disciplinary Committee on questions of law arising in proceedings before them there shall in all such proceedings be an assessor to the Disciplinary Committee who shall be a barrister, advocate or solicitor of not less than ten years' standing.

(2) The power of appointing assessors under this section shall be exercisable by the Council, but if no assessor appointed by them is available to act at any particular proceedings the Disciplinary Committee may appoint an assessor under this section to act at those proceedings.

(3) The Lord Chancellor or, in Scotland, the Lord Advocate may make rules as to the function of assessors appointed under this section, and, in particular, rules under this subsection may contain such provisions for securing—

(a) that where an assessor advises the Disciplinary Committee on any question of law as to evidence, procedure or any other matters specified in the rules, he shall do so in the presence of every party, or person representing a party, to the proceedings who appears thereat or, if the advice is tendered after the Disciplinary Committee have begun to deliberate as to their findings, that every such party or person as aforesaid shall be informed what advice the assessor has tendered;

(b) that every such party or person as aforesaid shall be informed if in any case the Disciplinary Committee do not accept the advice of the assessor on any such question as aforesaid,

and such incidental and supplementary provisions, as appear to the Lord Chancellor or the Lord Advocate expedient.

(4) Subject to the provisions of this section, an assessor under this section may be appointed either generally or for any particular proceedings or class of proceedings, and shall hold and vacate office in accordance with the terms of the instrument under which he is appointed.

(5) Any remuneration paid by the Council to persons appointed to act as assessors shall be at such rates as the Council may determine.

(6) The power to make rules conferred by this section shall be exercisable by statutory instrument.

COMMITTEES OF THE COUNCIL

General power to appoint committees

21.—(1) The Council may set up a committee for any purpose (other than a purpose for which the Council are required to set up a committee under this Act) and may delegate to a committee set up under this section, with or without restrictions or conditions, as they think fit, any functions exercisable by them except the following— **A11–62**

(a) the power to make rules under this Act,

(b) any functions expressly conferred by this Act on any committee set up under any of the foregoing provisions of this Act, and

(c) subject to any express provision for delegation in the rules, any functions expressly conferred on the Council by rules under this Act.

(2) The number of members of a committee set up under this section and their term of office shall be fixed by the Council.

(3) A committee set up under this Act may include persons who are not members of the Council, but at least two-thirds of the members of every such committee shall be members of the Council.

(4) Every member of a committee set up under this Act who at the time of his appointment was a member of the Council shall, upon ceasing to be a member of the Council, also cease to be a member of the committee:

Provided that for the purpose of this subsection a member of the Council shall not be deemed to have ceased by reason of retirement to be a member thereof if he has again been nominated or elected a member thereof not later than the day of his retirement.

RESTRICTION ON USE OF TITLES AND DESCRIPTIONS

Penalty for pretending to be registered, etc.

A11–63   22.—(1) Any individual who wilfully—

(a) takes or uses any style, title or description which consists of or includes the expression "insurance broker" when he is not registered in the register, or

(b) takes or uses any name, title, addition or description falsely implying, or otherwise pretends, that he is registered in the register,

shall be liable on summary conviction to a fine not exceeding £400, or on conviction on indictment to a fine.

(2) Any body corporate which wilfully—

(a) takes or uses any style, title or description which consists of or includes the expression "insurance broker" when it is not enrolled in the list, or

(b) takes or uses any name, title, addition or description falsely implying, or otherwise pretends, that it is enrolled in the list,

shall be liable on summary conviction to a fine not exceeding £400, or on conviction on indictment to a fine.

(3) References in this section to the expression "insurance broker" include references to the following related expressions, that is to say "assurance broker", "reinsurance broker" and "reassurance broker".

Excemptions from section 22

A11–64   23.—(1) Where a practising insurance broker dies, then, during the period of three months beginning with his death or such longer period as the Council may in any particular case allow, the last foregoing section shall not operate to prevent his personal representatives, his surviving spouse or any of his children or trustees on behalf of his surviving spouse or any of his children from taking or using in relation to his business, but in conjunction with the name in which he carried it on, any title which he was entitled to take or use immediately before his death.

(2) Where a practising insurance broker becomes bankrupt, then, during the period of three months beginning with the bankruptcy or such longer period as the Council may in any particular case allow, the last foregoing section shall not operate to prevent his trustee in bankruptcy or, in Northern Ireland, the assignee in bankruptcy, from taking or using in relation to his business, but in conjunction with the name in which he carried it on, any title which he was entitled to take or use immediately before the bankruptcy.

Offences by bodies corporate

A11–65   24. Where an offence under this Act which has been committed by a body corporate is proved to have been committed with the consent or connivance of, or to be attributable to any neglect on the part of, any director, manager, secretary or other similar officer of the body corporate, or any person purporting to act in any such capacity, he as well as the body corporate shall be guilty of that offence and shall be liable to be proceeded against and punished accordingly.

Miscellaneous

Accounts of Council

25.—(1) The Council shall keep proper accounts of all sums received or paid by them and proper records in relation to those accounts.

A11–66

(2) The Council shall appoint auditors to the Council who shall be members of a recognised body of accountants.

(3) The Council shall cause their accounts to be audited annually by the auditors to the Council and as soon as is practicable after the accounts for any period have been audited the Council shall cause them to be published and shall send a copy of them to the Secretary of State together with a copy of any report of the auditors thereon.

Service of documents

26. Any notice or other document authorised or required to be given under this Act may, without prejudice to any other method of service but subject to any provision to the contrary in rules under this Act, be served by post; and for the purpose of the application to this section of section 26 of the Interpretation Act 1889 (c. 63) (which relates to service by post) the proper address of a person or body corporate to whose registration or enrolment such a document relates shall be his or its address in the register or list.

A11–67

Rules, etc., made by Council

27.—(1) Rules made by the Council under sections 8, 11, 12, 13, 14 or 19 of this Act, the statement drawn up by the Council under section 10 of this Act or any revision of that statement made by the Council under that section shall not come into operation until approved by order of the Secretary of State.

A11–68

(2) The Secretary of State may approve rules made under section 19 of this Act either as submitted to him or subject to such modifications as he thinks fit; but where the Secretary of State proposes to approve any such rules subject to modifications he shall notify the modifications to the Council and consider any observations of the Council thereon.

(3) The Secretary of State may, after consulting the Council, by order vary or revoke any rules made under sections 8, 11 or 12 of this Act or revise the statement under section 10 of this Act.

Orders

28.—(1) The power to make orders under this Act shall be exercisable by statutory instrument; and any order made under this Act may be varied or revoked by a subsequent order so made.

A11–69

(2) Any statutory instrument by which that power is exercised, except one containing an order under section 30(3) of this Act or any such order as is mentioned in subsection (3) below, shall be subject to annulment in pursuance of a resolution of either House of Parliament.

(3) An order under section 3(4) or section 27(3) of this Act, an order under paragraph 2 of the Schedule to this Act approving a scheme subject to modifications or an order under paragraph 10 of that Schedule shall not be made unless a draft of the order has been approved by resolution of each House of Parliament.

Interpretation

29.—(1) In this Act, unless the context otherwise requires—

A11–70

"approved qualification" and "approved educational institution" have the meanings respectively assigned to them by section 6 of this Act;

"authorised insurers" means a person permitted under the Insurance Companies Act 1974 (c. 49) or the Insurance Companies (Northern Ireland) Order 1976 (No. S.I. 1976 (N.I. 3)) to carry on liability insurance business or pecuniary loss insurance business;

"the Council" means the Insurance Brokers Registration Council established pursuant to section 1 of this Act;

"the Court" means the High Court or, in relation to Scotland, the Court of Session or, in relation to Northern Ireland, a judge of the High Court of Justice in Northern Ireland;

"disciplinary case" has the meaning assigned to it by section 13 of this Act;

"employee", in relation to a body corporate, includes a director of the body corporate and "employed" shall be construed accordingly;

"enrolled" means enrolled in the list and "enrolment" shall be construed accordingly;

"functions" includes powers and duties;

"insurance business" means insurance business of any class relevant for the purposes of Part I of the Insurance Companies Act 1974, or Part II of the Insurance Companies (Northern Ireland) Order 1976, other than industrial assurance business, and "insurance broker" shall be construed accordingly;

"insurance company" means a person or body of persos (whether incorporated or not) carrying on insurance business;

"list" means the list of bodies corporate carrying on business as insurance brokers;

"practising insurance broker" means a registered insurance broker who is carrying on business as an insurance broker;

"prescribed" means prescribed by rules under this Act;

"recognised body of accountants" means any one of the following, namely—
the Institute of Chartered Accountants in England and Wales;
the Institute of Chartered Accountants of Scotland;
the Association of Certified Accountants;
the Institute of Chartered Accountants in Ireland;
any other body of accountants established in the United Kingdom and for the time being recognised for the purposes of section 161(1)(a) of the Companies Act 1948 (c. 58) by the Secretary of State;

"register" means the register of insurance brokers and "registered" and "registration" shall be construed accordingly;

"registered insurance broker" means a person who is registered in the register;

"the registrar" means the registrar of the Council appointed under section 8(1) of this Act.

(2) References in this Act to any other enactment (including an enactment of the Parliament of Northern Ireland and an Order in Council under the Northern Ireland Act 1974 (c. 28)) shall be construed as references thereto, as amended, and as including references thereto as extended, by or under any subsequent enactment.

Short title, extent and commencement

    30.—(1) This Act may be cited as the Insurance Brokers (Registration) Act 1977.   **A11–71**

    (2) This Act extends to Northern Ireland.

    (3) Subject to subsection (4) below, this Act shall come into operation on such date as the Secretary of State may by order appoint and different dates may be appointed for different provisions and for different purposes.

    (4) The day appointed for the coming into operation of section 22 of this Act shall not be earlier than the expiration of a period of two years beginning with the day appointed for the coming into operation of section 1 of this Act.

SCHEDULE

Constitution, etc., of Insurance Brokers Registration Council

    1. The Council shall consist of—   **A11–72**

    (a)   twelve persons chosen to represent registered insurance brokers of whom one shall be Chairman of the Council;

    (b)   five persons nominated by the Secretary of State of whom one shall be a barrister, advocate or solicitor, another shall be a member of a recognised body of accountants and a third shall be a person appearing to the Secretary of State to represent the interests of persons who are or may become policyholders of insurance companies.

    2.—(1) The persons chosen to represent registered insurance brokers in the first instance shall be nominated by the British Insurance Brokers' Association.

    (2) The persons chosen to represent registered insurance brokers after the retirement of those nominated under sub-paragraph (1) above shall be elected by registered insurance brokers in accordance with a scheme which—

    (a)   shall be made by the Council;

    (b)   shall not come into operation until approved by order of the Secretary of State; and

    (c)   may be varied or revoked by a subsequent scheme so made and so approved.

    (3) The Secretary of State may approve a scheme either as submitted to him or subject to such modifications as he thinks fit; but where the Secretary of State proposes to approve a scheme subject to modifications he shall notify the modifications to the Council and consider any observations of the Council thereon.

    (4) The Council shall submit a scheme to the Secretary of State for approval before the expiration of a period of two years beginning with the day appointed for the coming into operation of section 1 of this Act.

    (5) In the exercise of any functions under this paragraph due regard shall be had to the desirability of securing that the Council includes persons representative of all parts of the United Kingdom.

    3. Nominations of the first members of the Council shall so far as practicable be made before the day appointed for the establishment of the Council in time to enable the persons nominated to assume membership on its establishment.

    4.—(1) The term of office of—

    (a)   members nominated by the British Insurance Brokers' Association shall be such period, not exceeding four years, as may be fixed by the scheme;

    (b)   members elected by registered insurance brokers shall be such period as may be fixed by the scheme;

    (c)   members nominated by the Secretary of State shall be such period, not exceeding three years, as may be fixed by the Secretary of State.

    (2) In this paragraph "the scheme" means the scheme or schemes under paragraph 2 above which are for the time being in operation.

5. A member of the Council may at any time, by notice in writing addressed to the registrar, resign his office.

6.—(1) A person nominated or elected to fill a casual vacancy among the members of the Council shall hold office during the remainder of the term of office of the person whose vacancy he has filled.

(2) Any vacancy other than a casual vacancy in the membership of the Council shall be filled before the date on which the vacancy occurs.

7. A person ceasing to be a member of the Council shall be eligible to be again nominated or elected a member.

8.—(1) The Council shall have power to do anything which in their opinion is calculated to facilitate the proper discharge of their functions.

(2) The Council shall, in particular, have power—

    (a)   to appoint, in addition to a registrar, such officers and servants as the Council may determine;

    (b)   to pay to the members of the Council or their committees such fees for attendance at meetings of the Council or their committees and such travelling and subsistence allowances while attending such meetings or while on any other business of the Council as the Council may determine;

    (c)   to pay to their officers and servants such remuneration as the Council may determine;

    (d)   as regards any officers or servants in those case they may determine to do so, to pay to, or in respect of them, such pensions and gratuities, or provide and maintain for them such superannuation schemes (whether contributory or not), as the Council may determine;

    (e)   subject to the provisions of section 1 of the Borrowing (Control and Guarantees) Act 1946 (c. 58) or, in Northern Ireland, of section 2 of the Loans Guarantee and Borrowing Regulation Act (Northern Ireland) 1946 (c. 18) and of any order under those provisions for the time being in force, to borrow such sums as the Council may from time to time require for performing any of their functions under this Act.

(3) The powers of the Council and any of its committees may be exercised notwithstanding any vacancy, and no proceedings of the Council or of any of its committees shall be invalidated by any defect in the nomination or election of a member.

9. The Council may make standing orders for regulating the proceedings (including quorum) of the Council and of any committee thereof:

Provided that orders shall not be made under this paragraph with respect to the proceedings of the Disciplinary Committee.

10. The Secretary of State may, after consulting the Council, by order so amend the provisions of this Schedule as to vary the number of members and the manner in which they are chosed or appointed.

Insurance Companies Act 1982

(30 ELIZ. 2, C. 50)

[1982]

Law applicable to certain contracts of insurance

94B.—(1) The law applicable to a contract of insurance the effecting of which **A11–73** constitutes general business, and which covers risks situated in the United Kingdom or another Member State, shall be determined in accordance with the provisions of Part I of Schedule 3A to this Act.

[(1A) The law applicable to a contract of insurance to which Article 1 of the first long term insurance Directive applies shall be determined in accordance with the provisions of Part II of Schedule 3A to this Act if—

(a) where the policy holder is an individual, he is habitually resident in a Member State; or

(b) where the policy holder is not an individual, the establishment of the policy holder to which the contract relates is situated in a Member State.

(2) Subsections (1) and (1A) above do not apply in relation to a contract of reinsurance.][1]

Interpretation of expressions derived from insurance Directives

96A.—(1) In this Act—   **A11–74**

(a) "the first general insurance Directive" means Council Directive 73/239/EEC of 24 July 1973 on the co-ordination of laws, regulations and administrative provisions relating to the taking-up and pursuit of the business of direct insurance other than life assurance;

(b) "the second general insurance Directive" means Council Directive 88/357/EEC of 22 June 1988 on the co-ordination of laws, regulations and administrative provisions relating to direct insurance other than life assurance and laying down provisions to facilitate the effective exercise of freedom to provide services and amending Directive 73/239/EEC;

(c) "the third general insurance Directive" means Council Directive 92/49/EEC of 18 June 1992[2] on the co-ordination of laws, regulations and administrative provisions relating to direct insurance other than life assurance and amending Directives 73/239/EEC[3] and 88/357/EEC[4];

and "the general insurance Directives" means those Directives as amended and such other Directives as make provision with respect to the business of direct insurance other than life assurance.

(1A) The Directives amending the general insurance Directives referred to in subsection (1) above include Council Directive 90/618/EEC amending, particularly as regards motor vehicle liability insurance, Directive 73/239/EEC and Directive 88/357/EEC.

[1] Subsections 1A and 2 substituted for subsection 2 by S.I. 1993 No.174 (Insurance Companies (Amendment) Regulations, reg.5(3).
[2] O.J. L228, 11.8.92, page 1.
[3] O.J. L228, 16.8.73, page 3.
[4] O.J. L172, 4.7.88, page 1.

(1B) In this Act—

> (a) "the first long term insurance Directive" means Council Directive 79/267/EEC of 5 March 1979 on the co-ordination of laws, regulations and administrative provisions relating to the taking up and pursuit of the business of direct life assurance;
>
> (b) "the second long term insurance Directive" means Council Directive 90/619/EEC of 8 November 1990 on the co-ordination of laws, regulations and administrative provisions relating to direct life assurance, laying down provisions to facilitate the effective exercise of freedom to provide services and amending Directive 79/267/EEC;
>
> (c) "the third long term insurance Directive" means Council Directive 92/96/EEC of 10 November 1992[1] on the co-ordination of laws, regulations and administrative provisions relating to direct life assurance and amending Directives 79/267 EEC[2] and 90/619/EEC[3];.

and "the long term insurance Directives" means those Directives.

[(1C) Any reference in this Act to the first or third general insurance Directive, or to the first or third long term insurance Directive, is a reference to that Directive as amended by the Prudential Supervision Directive (within the meaning of the Financial Institutions (Prudential Supervision) Regulations 1996).][4]

(2) In this Act, in relation to an insurance company, "establishment" means the head office or a branch of the company; and references to a company being established in a State mean that the company has its head office or a branch there.

Any permanent presence of an insurance company in a State other than that in which it has its head office shall be regarded as a single branch, whether that presence consists of a single office which, or two or more offices each of which—

> (a)   is managed by the company's own staff;
> (b)   is an agency of the company; or
> (c)   is managed by a person who is independent but has permanent authority to act for the company in the same way as an agency.

(3) References in this Act to the Member State where the risk is situated are—

> (a)   where the insurance relates to buildings or to buildings and their contents (in so far as the contents are covered by the same policy), to the Member State in which the property is situated;[5]

---

[1] O.J. L360, 9.12.92, page 1.
[2] O.J. L63, 13.3.79, page 1.
[3] O.J. L330, 29.11.90, page 50.
[4] Added by S.I. 1996 No.1669 (Financial Institutions (Prudential Supervision) Regulations, Sched.5, para.8.
[5] S.96A(3) shall apply to determine whether a risk is situated in the United Kingdom for the purposes of Sched.7A, para.8 to the Finance Act 1994 as it applies to determine that question for the purposes of that Act, but as if for para.(a) of this section there were substituted:
   (3) References in this Act to the Member State where the risk is situated are—
     (a) where the insurance relates to building its contents or both (whether or not the contents are covered by the same policy), to the Member State in which the building is situated;
     (b) where the insurance relates to vehicles of any type, to the member State of registration;
     (c) in the case of policies of a duration of four months or less covering travel or holiday risks (whatever the class concerned), to the member State where the policy holder took out the policy;
     (d) in a case not covered by paragraphs (a) to (c)—
       (i) where the policy holder is an individual, to the Member State where he has his habitual residence;
       (ii) otherwise, to the Member State where the establishment of the policy holder to which the policy relates is situated.

    (b)   where the insurance relates to vehicles of any type, to the Member State of registration;

    (c)   in the case of policies of a duration of four months or less covering travel or holiday risks (whatever the class concerned), to the Member State where the policy holder took out the policy;

    (d)   in a case not covered by paragraphs (a) to (c)—

        (i)   where the policy holder is an individual, to the Member State where he has his habitual residence at the date when the contract is entered into;

        (ii)   otherwise, to the Member State where the establishment of the policy holder to which the policy relates is situated at that date.

(3A) In this Act references to the provision of insurance in the United Kingdom or any other EEA State are references to either or both of the following—

    (a)   the covering (otherwise than by way of reinsurance) of a risk situated there through an establishment in another EEA State ("the provision of general insurance"); and

    (b)   the covering (otherwise than by way of reinsurance) of a commitment situated there through an establishment in another EEA State ("the provision of long term insurance").

(4) In this Act the "ECU" means the unit of account of that name defined in Council Regulation (EEC) No.3180/78 as amended.

    The exchange rates as between the ECU and the currencies of the Member States to be applied for each year beginning on 31st December shall be the rates applicable on the last day of the preceding October for which rates for the currencies of all the Member States were published in the Official Journal of the Communities.

SCHEDULE 3A

Law Applicable to Certain Contracts of Insurance

General Rules as to Applicable Law

1.—(1) Where the policy holder has his habitual residence or central administration within the territory of the Member State where the risk is situated, the law applicable to the contract is the law of that Member State.

    However, where the law of that Member State so allows, the parties may choose the law of another country.

    (2) Where the policy holder does not have his habitual residence or central administration within the territory of the Member State where the risk is situated, the parties to the contract may choose to apply either—

    (a)   the law of the Member State where the risk is situated, or

    (b)   the law of the country in which the policy holder has his habitual residence or central administration.

    (3) Where the policy holder carries on a business and the contract covers two or more risks relating to his business which are situated in different Member States, the freedom of choice of the law applicable to the contract extends to the laws of those member States and of the country in which he has his habitual residence or central administration.

    In this sub-paragraph "business" includes a trade or profession.

A11–75

(4) Where the Member States referred to in sub-paragraph (2) or (3) grant greater freedom of choice of the law applicable to the contract, the parties may take advantage of that freedom.

(5) Notwithstanding sub-paragraphs (1) to (3), when the risks covered by the contract are limited to events occurring in a Member State other than the Member State where the risk is situated, the parties may always choose the law of the former State.

[(6) Where the risk—

    (a)   is situated in an EFTA state and falls within class 4, 5, 6, 7, 11 or 12 of Part I of Schedule 2 to this Act; or

    (b)   is situated in a Member State and is a large risk,

the parties to the contract may choose any law.

(7) Where the risk is situated in a Member State which has implemented the transitional provisions in Article 27 of the second general insurance Directive, the meaning of "large risk" for the purposes of sub-paragraph (6) above shall be determined in accordance with the law applicable in that State.][1]

Applicable Law in the Absence of Choice

A11–76   [**2.**—(1) The choice referred to in paragraph 1 must be expressed or demonstrated with reasonable certainty by the terms of the contract or the circumstances of the case.

(2) If that is not so, or if no choice has been made, the contract shall be governed by the law of the country (from amongst those considered in the relevant sub-paragraphs) with which it is most closely connected.

(3) Nevertheless, a severable part of the contract which has a closer connection with another country (from amongst those considered in the relevant sub-paragraphs) may by way of exception be governed by the law of that other country.

(4) A contract is rebuttably presumed to be most closely connected with the Member State where the risk is situated.][2]

Mandatory Rules

A11–77   **3.**—(1) The fact that in the cases referred to in paragraph 1 the parties have chosen a law does not, where all the other elements relevant to the situation at the time of the choice are connected with one Member State only, prejudice the application of the mandatory rules of the law of that Member State, which means the rules from which the law of that Member State allows no derogation by means of a contract.

(2) Nothing in [this Part of this Schedule][3] restricts the application of the rules of a part of the United Kingdom in a situation where they are mandatory, irrespective of the law otherwise applicable to the contract.

Supplementary provisions

A11–78   **4.**— (1) Where a Member State includes several territorial units, each of which has its own rules of law concerning contractual obligations, each unit shall be considered as a country for the purposes of identifying the applicable law.

---

[1] Para.(6) substituted for paras (6) and (7) by S.I. 1994 No.1696 (Insurance Companies (Third Insurance Directives) Regulations, Pt II, subpart VI, reg.49.

[2] Beware, this Schedule is not repealed. Sched.3A renumbered as Sched.3A, Pt I to allow for insertion of Sched.3A, Pt II by S.I. 1993 No.174, reg.5(5) by S.I.1993 No.174 (Insurance Companies (Amendment) Regulations, reg.5(4).

[3] Words substituted by S.I. 1993 No.174 (Insurance Companies (Amendment) Regulations, reg.5(4)(a).

(2) The provisions of [this Part of this Schedule][1] apply to conflicts between the laws of the different parts of the United Kingdom.

5.—(1) Subject to the preceding provisions of this Part of this Schedule, a court in a part of the United Kingdom shall act in accordance with the provisions of the Contracts (Applicable Law) Act 1990.

(2) In particular, reference shall be made to [those provisions][2]—

(a) to ascertain for the purposes of paragraph 1(1) and (4) what freedom of choice the parties have under the law of a part of the United Kingdom; and

(b) to determine whether the mandatory rules of another Member State should be applied in accordance with paragraph 3(1) where the law otherwise applicable is the law of a part of the United Kingdom.

[1] Words substituted by S.I. 1993 No.174 (Insurance Companies (Amendment) Regulations, reg.5(4)(a).

[2] Words substituted by S.I. 1993 No.174 (Insurance Companies (Amendment) Regulations, reg.5(4)(c).

Road Traffic Act 1988

(36 ELIZ. 2, C. 52)

[1988]

PART VI

THIRD-PARTY LIABILITIES

Compulsory insurance or security against third-party risks

Users of motor vehicles to be insured or secured against third-party risks
A11–79   **143.**—(1) Subject to the provisions of this Part of this Act—

   (a)   a person must not use a motor vehicle on a road or other public place
         unless there is in force in relation to the use of the vehicle by that per-
         son such a policy of insurance or such a security in respect of third
         party risks as complies with the requirements of this Part of this Act,
         and
   (b)   a person must not cause or permit any other person to use a motor
         vehicle on a road [or other public place]¹ unless there is in force in rela-
         tion to the use of the vehicle by that other person such a policy of insur-
         ance or such a security in respect of third party risks as complies with
         the requirements of this Part of this Act.

   (2) If a person acts in contravention of subsection (1) above he is guilty of an
offence.
   (3) A person charged with using a motor vehicle in contravention of this section
shall not be convicted if he proves—

   (a)   that the vehicle did not belong to him and was not in his possession
         under a contract of hiring or of loan,
   (b)   that he was using the vehicle in the course of his employment, and
   (c)   that he neither knew nor had reason to believe that there was not in
         force in relation to the vehicle such a policy of insurance or security as
         is mentioned in subsection (1) above.

   (4) This Part of this Act does not apply to invalid carriages.

Exceptions from requirements of third-party insurance or security
A11–80   **144.**—(1) Section 143 of this Act does not apply to a vehicle owned by a person
who has deposited and keeps deposited with the Accountant General of the
Supreme Court the sum of £500,000, at a time when the vehicle is being driven
under the owner's control.
   (1A) The Secretary of State may by order made by statutory instrument substitute a greater sum for the sum for the time being specified in subsection (1) above.
   (1B) No order shall be made under subsection (1A) above unless a draft of it has
been laid before and approved by resolution of each House of Parliament.
   (2) Section 143 does not apply—

─────────────
   ¹ Words inserted by S.I. 2000 No.726 (The Motor Vehicles (Compulsory Insurance)
Regulations 2000, reg.2(2)(b).

(a) to a vehicle owned—

    (i) by the council of a county or county district in England and Wales the Broads Authority, the Common Council of the City of London, the council of a London borough, a National Park authority, the Inner London Education Authority, the London Fire and Emergency Planning Authority or a joint authority (other than a police authority) established by Part IV of the Local Government Act 1985,

    (ii) by a council constituted under section 2 of the Local Government, etc. (Scotland) Act 1994, or

    (iii) by a joint board or committee in England or Wales, or joint committee in Scotland, which is so constituted as to include among its members representatives of any such council,

at a time when the vehicle is being driven under the owner's control,

(b) to a vehicle owned by a police authority [...][1], at a time when it is being driven under the owner's control, or to a vehicle at a time when it is being driven for police purposes by or under the direction of a constable, or by a person employed by a police authority [...][2] or

(ba) to a vehicle owned by the Service Authority for the National Criminal Intelligence Service or the Service Authority for the National Crime Squad, at a time when it is being driven under the owner's control, or to a vehicle at a time when it is being driven for the purposes of the body maintained by such an Authority by or under the Direction of a constable, or by a person employed by such an Authority;

(c) to a vehicle at a time when it is being driven on a journey to or from any place undertaken for salvage purposes pursuant to Part IX of the Merchant Shipping Act 1995,

(d) to the use of a vehicle for the purpose of its being proved in pursuance of a direction under section 166(2)(b) of the Army Act 1955 or under the corresponding provision of the Air Force Act 1955,

(da) to a vehicle owned by a health service body, as defined in section 60(7) of the National Health Service and Community Care Act 1990 by a Primary Care Trust established under section 16A of the National Health Service Act 1977[3], at a time when the vehicle is being driven under the owner's control.

(db) to an ambulance owned by a National Health Service trust established under Part I of the National Health Service and Community Care Act 1990 or the National Health Service (Scotland) Act 1978, at a time when a vehicle is being driven under the owner's control

(e) to a vehicle which is made available by the Secretary of State to any person, body or local authority in pursuance of section 23 or 26 of the National Health Service Act 1977 at a time when it is being used in accordance with the terms on which it is so made available,

(f) to a vehicle which is made available by the Secretary of State to any

---

[1] Words repealed by Greater London Authority Act (1999 c.29), Sched.27, para.61(a).
[2] Words repealed by Greater London Authority Act (1999 c.29), Sched.27, para.61(a).
[3] In relation to England and Wales:
    (da) to a vehicle owned by a health service body, as defined in section 60(7) of the National Health Service and Community Care Act 1990 or by the Commission for Health Improvement, at a time when the vehicle is being driven under the owner's control.

local authority, education authority or voluntary organisation in Scotland in pursuance of section 15 or 16 of the National Health Service (Scotland) Act 1978 at a time when it is being used in accordance with the terms on which it is so made available.

Requirements in respect of policies of insurance

A11–81   **145.**—(1) In order to comply with the requirements of this Part of this Act, a policy of insurance must satisfy the following conditions.

(2) The policy must be issued by an authorised insurer.

(3) Subject to subsection (4) below, the policy—

> (a) must insure such person, persons or classes of persons as may be specified in the policy in respect of any liability which may be incurred by him or them in respect of the death of or bodily injury to any person or damage to property caused by, or arising out of, the use of the vehicle on a road [or other public place][1] in Great Britain, and

> (aa) must, in the case of a vehicle normally based in the territory of another member State, insure him or them in respect of any civil liability which may be incurred by him or them as a result of an event related to the use of the vehicle in Great Britain if,-

>> (i) according to the law of that territory, he or they would be required to be insured in respect of a civil liability which would arise under that law as a result of that event if the place where the vehicle was used when the event occurred were in that territory, and
>> (ii) the cover required by that law would be higher than that required by paragraph (a) above, and

> (b) must, in the case of a vehicle normally based in Great Britain, insure him or them in respect of any liability which may be incurred by him or them in respect of the use of the vehicle and of any trailer, whether or not coupled, in the territory other than Great Britain and Gibraltar of each of the member States of the Communities according to

>> (i) the law on compulsory insurance against civil liability in respect of the use of vehicles of the State in whose territory the event giving rise to the liability occurred; or
>> (ii) if it would give higher cover, the law which would be applicable under this Part of this Act if the place where the vehicle was used when that event occurred were in Great Britain; and

> (c) must also insure him or them in respect of any liability which may be incurred by him or them under the provisions of this Part of this Act relating to payment for emergency treatment.

(4) The policy shall not, by virtue of subsection (3)(a) above, be required—

> (a) to cover liability in respect of the death, airising out of and in the course of his employment, of a person in the employment of a person insured by the policy or of bodily injury sustained by such a person arising out of and in the course of his employment, or
> (b) to provide insurance of more than £250,000 in respect of all such liabilities as may be incurred in respect of damage to property caused by, or arising out of, any one accident involving the vehicle, or
> (c) to cover liability in respect of damage to the vehicle, or

---

[1] Words inserted by S.I. 2000 No.726 (The Motor Vehicles (Compulsory Insurance) Regulations 2000, reg.2(3)).

(d) to cover liability in respect of damage to goods carried for hire or reward in or on the vehicle or in or on any trailer (whether or not coupled) drawn by the vehicle, or

(e) to cover any liability of a person in respect of damage to property in his custody or under his control, or

(f) to cover any contractual liability.

(4A) In the case of a person—

(a) carried in or upon a vehicle, or

(b) entering or getting on to, or alighting from, a vehicle,

the provisions of paragraph (a) of subsection (4) above do not apply unless cover in respect of the liability referred to in that paragraph is in fact provided pursuant to a requirement of the Employers' Liability (Compulsory Insurance) Act 1969.[1]

(5) In this Part of this Act "authorised insurer" means a person or body of persons carrying on insurance business within Group 2 in Part II of Schedule 2 to the Insurance Companies Act 1982 and being a member of the Motor Insurers' Bureau (a company limited by guarantee and incorporated under the Companies Act 1929 on June 14, 1946).

(6) If any person or body of persons ceases to be a member of the Motor Insurers' Bureau, that person or body shall not by virtue of that cease to be treated as an authorised insurer for the purposes of this Part of this Act or the Road Traffic (NHS Charges) Act 1999—

(a) in relation to any policy issued by the insurer before ceasing to be such a member, or

(b) in relation to any obligation (whether arising before or after the insurer ceased to be such a member) which the insurer may be called upon to meet under or in consequence of any such policy or under section 157 of this Act or section 1 of the Act of 1999 by virtue of making a payment in pursuance of such an obligation.

Requirements in respect of securities

146.—(1) In order to comply with the requirements of this Part of this Act, a   **A11–82**
security must satisfy the following conditions.

(2) The security must be given either by an authorised insurer or by some body of persons which carries on in the United Kingdom the business of giving securities of a like kind and has deposited and keeps deposited with the Accountant General of the Supreme Court the sum of £15,000 in respect of that business.

(3) Subject to subsection (4) below, the security must consist of an undertaking by the giver of the security to make good, subject to any conditions specified in it, any failure by the owner of the vehicle or such other persons or classes of persons as may be specified in the security duly to discharge any liabiity which may be incurred by him or them, being a liability required under section 145 of this Act to be covered by a policy of insurance.

(4) In the case of liabilities arising out of the use of a motor vehicle on a road [or other public place][2] in Great Britain the amount secured need not exceed—

(a) in the case of an undertaking relating to the use of public service vehicles (within the meaning of the Public Passenger Vehicles Act 1981, £25,000,

(b) in any other case, £5,000.

---

[1] 1969 c.57.

[2] Words inserted by S.I. 2000 No.726 (The Motor Vehicles (Compulsory Insurance) Regulations 2000, reg.2(4)).

Issue and surrender of certificates of insurance and of security

A11–83   147.—(1) A policy of insurance shall be of no effect for the purposes of this Part of this Act unless and until there is delivered by the insurer to the person by whom the policy is effected a certificate (in this Part of this Act referred to as a "certificate of insurance") in the prescribed form and containing such particulars of any conditions subject to which the policy is issued and of any other matters as may be prescribed.

(2) A security shall be of no effect for the purposes of this Part of this Act unless and until there is delivered by the person giving the security to the person to whom it is given a certificate (in this Part of this Act referred to as a "certificate of security") in the prescribed form and containing such particulars of any conditions subject to which the security is issued and of any other matters as may be prescribed.

(3) Different forms and different particulars may be prescribed for the purposes of subsection (1) or (2) above in relation to different cases or circumstances.

(4) Where a certificate has been delivered under this section and the policy or security to which it relates is cancelled by mutual consent or by virtue of any provision in the policy or security, the person to whom the certificate was delivered must, within seven days from the taking effect of the cancellation—

(a)   surrender the certificate to the person by whom the policy was issued or the security was given, or

(b)   if the certificate has been lost or destroyed, make a statutory declaration to that effect.

(5) A person who fails to comply with subsection (4) above is guilty of an offence.

Avoidance of certain exceptions to policies or securities

A11–84   148.—(1) Where a certificate of insurance or certificate of security has been delivered under section 147 of this Act to the person by whom a policy has been effected or to whom a security has been given, so much of the policy or security as purports to restrict—

(a)   the insurance of the persons insured by the policy, or

(b)   the operation of the security,

(as the case may be) by reference to any of the matters mentioned in subsection (2) below shall, as respects such liabilities as are required to be covered by a policy under section 145 of this Act, be of no effect.

(2) Those matters are—

(a)   the age or physical or mental condition of persons driving the vehicle,

(b)   the condition of the vehicle,

(c)   the number of persons that the vehicle carries,

(d)   the weight or physical characteristics of the goods that the vehicle carries,

(e)   the time at which or the areas within which the vehicle is used,

(f)   the horsepower or cylinder capacity or value of the vehicle,

(g)   the carrying on the vehicle of any particular apparatus, or

(h)   the carrying on the vehicle of any particular means of identification other than any means of identification required to be carried by or under the [Vehicles Excise and Registration Act 1994][1].

---

[1] Words substituted by Vehicle Excise and Registration Act (1994, c.22), Sched 3, para.24(1).

(3) Nothing in subsection (1) above requires an insurer or the giver of a security to pay any sum in respect of the liability of any person otherwise than in or towards the discharge of that liability.

(4) Any sum paid by an insurer or the giver of a security in or towards the discharge of any liability of any person which is covered by the policy or security by virtue only of subsection (1) above is recoverable by the insurer or giver of the security from that person.

(5) A condition in a policy or security issued or given for the purposes of this Part of this Act providing—

(a) that no liability shall arise under the policy or security, or

(b) that any liability so arising shall cease,

in the event of some specified thing being done or omitted to be done after the happening of the event giving rise to a claim under the policy or security, shall be of no effect in connection with such liabilities as are required to be covered by a policy under section 145 of this Act.

(6) Nothing in subsection (5) above shall be taken to render void any provision in a policy or security requiring the person insured or secured to pay to the insurer or the giver of the security any sums which the latter may have become liable to pay under the policy or security and which have been applied to the satisfaction of the claims of third parties.

(7) Notwithstanding anything in any enactment, a person issuing a policy of insurance under section 145 of this Act shall be liable to indemnify the persons or classes of persons specified in the policy in respect of any liability which the policy purports to cover in the case of those persons or classes of persons.

Avoidance of certain agreements as to liability towards passengers

149.—(1) This section applies where a person uses a motor vehicle in circumstances such that under section 143 of this Act there is required to be in force in relation to his use of it such a policy of insurance or such a security in respect of third-party risks as complies with the requirements of this Part of this Act.

A11–85

(2) If any other person is carried in or upon the vehicle while the user is so using it, any antecedent agreement or understanding between them (whether intended to be legally binding or not) shall be of no effect so far as it purports or might be held—

(a) to negative or restrict any such liability of the user in respect of persons carried in or upon the vehicle as is required by section 145 of this Act to be covered by a policy of insurance, or

(b) to impose any conditions with respect to the enforcement of any such liability of the user.

(3) The fact that a person so carried has willingly accepted as his the risk of negligence on the part of the user shall not be treated as negativing any such liability of the user.

(4) For the purposes of this section—

(a) references to a person being carried in or upon a vehicle include references to a person entering or getting on to, or alighting from, the vehicle, and

(b) the reference to an antecedent agreement is to one made at any time before the liability arose.

Insurance or security in respect of private use of vehicle to cover use under car-sharing arrangements

A11–86   **150.**—(1) To the extent that a policy or security issued or given for the purposes of this Part of this Act—

  (a)   restricts the insurance of the persons insured by the policy or the operation of the security (as the case may be) to the use of the vehicle for specified purposes (for example, social, domestic and pleasure purposes) of a non-commercial character, or

  (b)   excludes from that insurance or the operation of the security (as the case may be)—

   (i) use of the vehicle for hire or reward, or
   (ii) business or commercial use of the vehicle, or
   (iii) use of the vehicle for specified purposes of a business or commercial character,

    then, for the purposes of that policy or security so far as it relates to such liabilities as are required to be covered by a policy under section 145 of this Act, the use of a vehicle on a journey in the course of which one or more passengers are carried at separate fares shall, if the conditions specified in subsection (2) below are satisfied, be treated as falling within that restriction or as not falling within that exclusion (as the case may be).

 (2) The conditions referred to in subsection (1) above are—

  (a)   the vehicle is not adapted to carry more than eight passengers and is not a motor cycle,

  (b)   the fare or aggregate of the fares paid in respect of the journey does not exceed the amount of the running costs of the vehicle for the journey (which for the purposes of this paragraph shall be taken to include an appropriate amount in respect of depreciation and general wear), and

  (c)   the arrangements for the payment of fares by the passenger or passengers carried at separate fares were made before the journey began.

 (3) Subsections (1) and (2) above apply however the restrictions or exclusions described in subsection (1) are framed or worded.

 (4) In subsections (1) and (2) above "fare" and "separate fares" have the same meaning as in section 1(4) of the Public Passenger Vehicles Act 1981.

Duty of insurers or persons giving security to satisfy judgment against persons insured or secured against third-party risks

A11–87   **151.**—(1) This section applies where, after a certificate of insurance or certificate of security has been delivered under section 147 of this Act to the person by whom a policy has been offered or to whom a security has been given, a judgment to which this subsection applies is obtained.

 (2) Subsection (1) above applies to judgments relating to a liability with respect to any matter where liability with respect to that matter is required to be covered by a policy of insurance under section 145 of this Act and either—

  (a)   it is a liability covered by the terms of the policy or security to which the certificate relates, and the judgment is obtained against any person who is insured by the policy or whose liability is covered by the security, as the case may be, or

  (b)   it is a liability, other than an excluded liability, which would be so covered if the policy insured all persons or, as the case may be, the security covered the liability of all persons, and the judgment is obtained against the person other than one who is insured by the policy or, as the case may be, whose liabiity is covered by the security.

(3) In deciding for the purposes of subsection (2) above whether a liability is or would be covered by the terms of a policy or security, so much of the policy or security as purports to restrict, as the case may be, the insurance of the persons insured by the policy or the operation of the security by reference to the holding by the driver of the vehicle of a licence authorising him to drive it shall be treated as of no effect.

(4) In subsection (2)(b) above "excluded liability" means a liability in respect of the death of, or bodily injury to, or damage to the property of any person who, at the time of the use which gave rise to the liability, was allowing himself to be carried in or upon the vehicle and knew or had reason to believe that the vehicle had been stolen or unlawfully taken, not being a person who—

(a) did not know and had no reason to believe that the vehicle had been stolen or unlawfully taken until after the commencement of his journey, and

(b) could not reasonably have been expected to have alighted from the vehicle.

In this subsection the reference to a person being carried in or upon a vehicle includes a reference to a person entering or getting on to, or alighting from, the vehicle.

(5) Notwithstanding that the insurer may be entitled to avoid or cancel, or may have avoided or cancelled, the policy or security, he must, subject to the provisions of this section, pay to the persons entitled to the benefit of the judgment—

(a) as regards liability in respect of death or bodily injury, any sum payable under the judgment in respect of the liabiity, together with any sum which, by virtue of any enactment relating to interest on judgments, is payable in respect of interest on that sum,

(b) as regards liability in respect of damage to property, any sum required to be paid under subsection (6) below, and

(c) any amount payable in respect of costs.

(6) This subsection requires—

(a) where the total of any amounts paid, payable or likely to be payable under the policy or security in respect of damage to property caused by, or arising out of, the accident in question does not exceed £250,000, the payment of any sum payable under the judgment in respect of the liability, together with any sum which, by virtue of any enactment relating to interest on judgments, is payable in respect of interest on that sum,

(b) where that total exceeds £250,000, the payment of either—

(i) such proportion of any sum payable under the judgment in respect of the liability as £250,000 bears to that total, together with the same proportion of any sum which, by virtue of any enactment relating to interest on judgments, is payable in respect of interest on that sum or

(ii) the difference between the total of any amounts already paid under the policy or security in respect of such damage and £250,000, together with such proportion of any sum which, by virtue of any enactment relating to interest on judgments, is payable in respect of interest on any sum payable under the judgment in respect of the liability as the difference bears to that sum,

whichever is the less, unless not less than £250,000 has already been paid under the policy or security in respect of such damage (in which case nothing is payable).

(7) Where an insurer becomes liable under this section to pay an amount in respect of a liability of a person who is insured by a policy or whose liability is covered by a security, he is entitled to recover from that person—

    (a)   that amount, in a case where be became liable to pay it by virtue only of subsection (3) above, or

    (b)   in a case where that amount exceeds the amount for which he would, apart from the provisions of this section, be liable under the policy or security in respect of that liability, the excess.

(8) Where an insurer becomes liable under this section to pay an amount in respect of a liability of a person who is not insured by a policy or whose liability is not covered by a security, he is entitled to recover the amount from that person or from any person who—

    (a)   is insured by the policy, or whose liability is covered by the security, by the terms of which the liability would be covered if the policy insured all persons or, as the case may be, the security covered the liability of all persons, and

    (b)   caused or permitted the use of the vehicle which gave rise to the liability.

(9) In this section—

    (a)   "insurer" includes a person giving a security,

    (b)   [...][1]

    (c)   "liability covered by the terms of the policy or security" means a liability which is covered by the policy or security or which would be so covered but for the fact that the insurer is entitled to avoid or cancel, or has avoided or cancelled, the policy or security.

(10) In the application of this section to Scotland, the words "by virtue of any enactment relating to interest on judgments" in subsections (5) and (6) (in each place where they appear) shall be omitted.

Exceptions to section 151

A11–88   **152.**—(1) No sum is payable by an insurer under section 151 of this Act—

    (a)   in respect of any judgment unless, before or within seven days after the commencement of the proceedings in which the judgment was given, the insurer had notice of the bringing of the proceedings, or

    (b)   in respect of any judgment so long as execution on the judgment is stayed pending an appeal, or

    (c)   in connection with any liability if, before the happening of the event which was the cause of the death or bodily injury or damage to property giving rise to the liability, the policy or security was cancelled by mutual consent or by virtue of any provision contained in it, and also—

        (i)   before the happening of that event the certificate was surrendered to the insurer, or the person to whom the certificate was delivered made a statutory declaration stating that the certificate had been lost or destroyed, or

---

[1] Repealed by Road Traffic Act (1991, c.40), Sched.8.

(ii)   after the happening of that event, but before the expiration of a period of fourteen days from the taking effect of the cancellation of the policy or security, the certificate was surrendered to the insurer, or the person to whom it was delivered made a statutory declaration stating that the certificate had been lost or destroyed, or

(iii) either before or after the happening of that event, but within that period of fourteen days, the insurer has commenced proceedings under this Act in respect of the failure to surrender the certificate.

(2) Subject to subsection (3) below, no sum is payable by an insurer under section 151 of this Act if, in an action commenced before, or within three months after, the commencement of the proceedings in which the judgment was given, he has obtained a declaration—

(a)   that, apart from any provision contained in the policy or security, he is entitled to avoid it on the ground that it was obtained—

(i)   by the non-disclosure of a material fact, or

(ii)   by a representation of fact which was false in some material particular, or

(b)   if he has avoided the policy or security on that ground, that he was entitled so to do apart from any provision contained in it

[and, for the purposes of this section, "material" means of such a nature as to influence the judgment of a prudent insurer in determining whether he will take the risk and, if so, at what premium and on what conditions.]

(3) An insurer who has obtained such a declaration as is mentioned in subsection (2) above in an action does not by reason of that become entitled to the benefit of that subsection as respects any judgment obtained in proceedings commenced before the commencement of that action unless before, or within seven days after, the commencement of that action he has given notice of it to the person who is the plaintiff (or in Scotland pursuer) in those proceedings specifying the non-disclosure or false representation on which he proposes to rely.

(4) A person to whom notice of such an action is so given is entitled, if he thinks fit, to be made a party to it.

Bankruptcy, etc., of insured or secured persons not to affect claims by third parties   **A11–89**

153.—(1) Where, after a certificate of insurance or certificate of security has been delivered under section 147 of this Act to the person by whom a policy has been effected or to whom a security has been given, any of the events mentioned in subsection (2) below happens, the happening of that event shall, notwithstanding anything in the Third Parties (Rights Against Insurers) Act 1930, not affect any such liability of that person as is required to be covered by a policy of insurance under section 145 of this Act.

(2) In the case of the person by whom the policy was effected or to whom the security was given, the events referred to in subsection (1) above are—

(a)   that he becomes bankrupt or makes a composition or arrangement with his creditors or that his estate is sequestrated or he grants a trust deed for his creditors,

(b)   that he dies and—

(i)   his estate falls to be administered in accordance with an order under section 421 of the Insolvency Act 1986,

(ii)   an award of sequestration of his estate is made, or

(iii) a judicial factor is appointed to administer his estate under section 11A of the Judicial Factors (Scotland) Act 1889,

(c)   that if that person is a company—

>   (i) a winding-up order or an adminstration order is made with respect to the company,
>   (ii) a resolution for a voluntary winding-up is passed with respect to the company,
>   (iii) a receiver or manager of the company's business or undertaking is duly appointed, or
>   (iv) possession is taken, by or on behalf of the holders of any debentures secured by a floating charge, of any property comprised in or subject to the charge.

(3) Nothing in subsection (1) above affects any rights conferred by the Third Parties (Rights Against Insurers) Act 1930 on the person to whom the liability was incurred, being rights so conferred against the person by whom the policy was issued or the security was given.

Duty to give information as to insurance or security where claim made

A11–90   **154.**—(1) A person against whom a claim is made in respect of any such liability as is required to be covered by a policy of insurance under section 145 of this Act must, on demand by or on behalf of the person making the claim—

(a)   state whether or not, in respect of that liability—

>   (i) he was insured by a policy having effect for the purposes of this Part of this Act or had in force a security having effect for those purposes, or
>   (ii) he would have been so insured or would have had in force such a security if the insurer or, as the case may be, the giver of the security had not avoided or cancelled the policy or security, and

(b)   if he was or would have been so insured, or had or would have had in force such a security—

>   (i) give such particulars with respect to that policy or security as were specified in any certificate of insurance or security delivered in respect of that policy or security, as the case may be, under section 147 of this Act, or
>   (ii) where no such certificate was delivered under that section, give the following particulars, that is to say, the registration mark or other identifying particulars of the vehicle concerned, the number of other identifying particulars of the insurance policy issued in respect of the vehicle, the name of the insurer and the period of the insurance cover.

(2) If without reasonable excuse, a person fails to comply with the provisions of subsection (1) above, or wilfully makes a false statement in reply to any such demand as is referred to in that subsection, he is guilty of an offence.

Payments for Treatment of Traffic Casualties

Payment for hospital treatment of traffic casualties

A11–91   **157.**—(1) Subject to subsection (2) below, where—

(a)   a payment, other than a payment under section 158 of this Act, is made (whether or not with an admission of liability) in respect of the death of, or bodily injury to, any person arising out of the use of a motor vehicle on a road or in a place to which the public have a right of access, and

(b) the payment is made—

    (i) by an authorised insurer, the payment being made under or in consequence of a policy issued under section 145 of this Act, or

    (ii) by the owner of a vehicle in relation to the use of which a security under this Part of this Act is in force, or

    (iii) by the owner of a vehicle who has made a deposit under this Part of this Act, and

(c) the person who has so died or been bodily injured has to the knowledge of the insurer or owner, as the case may be, received treatment at a hospital, whether as an in-patient or as an out-patient, in respect of the injury so arising,

the insurer or owner must pay the expenses reasonably incurred by the hospital in affording the treatment, after deducting from the expenses any moneys actually received in payment of a specific charge for the treatment, not being moneys received under any contributory scheme.

(2) The amount to be paid shall not exceed [£2,949.00][1] for each person treated as an in-patient or [£295.00][2] for each person treated as an out-patient.

(3) For the purposes of this section "expenses reasonably incurred" means—

(a) in relation to a person who receives treatment at a hospital as an in-patient, an amount for each day he is maintained in the hospital representing the average daily cost, for each in-patient, of the maintenance of the hospital and the staff of the hospital and the maintenance and treatment of the in-patients in the hospital, and

(b) in relation to a person who receives treatment at a hospital as an out-patient, reasonable expenses actually incurred.

Payment for emergency treatment of traffic casualties

158.—(1) Subsection (2) below applies where—   **A11–92**

(a) medical or surgical treatment or examination is immediately required as a result of bodily injury (including fatal injury) to a person caused by, or arising out of, the use of a motor vehicle on a road, and

(b) the treatment or examination so required (in this Part of this Act referred to as "emergency treatment") is effected by a legally qualified medical practitioner.

(2) The person who was using the vehicle at the time of the event out of which the bodily injury arose must, on a claim being made in accordance with the provisions of section 159 of this Act, pay to the practitioner (or, where emergency treatment is effected by more than one practitioner, to the practitioner by whom it is first effected)—

(a) a fee of [£21.30][3] in respect of each person in whose case the emergency treatment is effected by him, and

(b) a sum, in respect of any distance in excess of two miles which he must cover in order—

---

[1] Figures substituted by S.I. 1995 No.889 (Road Traffic Accidents (Payment for Treatment) Order, art.2).

[2] Figures substituted by S.I. 1995 No.889 (Road Traffic Accidents (Payment for Treatment) Order, art.2).

[3] Figures substituted by S.I. 1995 No.889 (Road Traffic Accidents (Payment for Treatment) Order, art.3).

(i)   to proceed from the place from which he is summoned to the place
      where the emergency treatment is carried out by him, and
(ii) to return to the first mentioned place,

     equal to [41 pence][1] for every complete mile and additional part of a
mile of that distance.

(3) Where emergency treatment is first effected in a hospital, the provisions of
subsections (1) and (2) above with respect to payment of a fee shall, so far as applicable, but subject (as regards the recipient of a payment) to the provisions of section 159 of this Act, have effect with the substitution of references to the hospital
for references to a legally qualified medical practitioner.

(4) Liability incurred under this section by the person using a vehicle shall,
where the event out of which it arose was caused by the wrongful act of another
person, be treated for the purposes of any claim to recover damage by reason of
that wrongful act as damage sustained by the person using the vehicle.

Supplementary provisions as to payments for treatment

A11–93   **159.**—(1) A payment falling to be made under section 157 or 158 of this Act in
respect of treatment in a hospital must be made to the hospital.

(2) A claim for a payment under section 158 of this Act may be made at the time
when the emergency treatment is effected, by oral request to the person who was
using the vehicle, and if not so made must be made by request in writing served on
him within seven days from the day on which the emergency treatment was
effected.

(3) Any such request in writing—

(a)   must be signed by the claimant or, in the case of a hospital, by an exec-
      utive officer of [the hospital claiming the payment][2],
(b)   must state the name and address of the claimant, the circumstances in
      which the emergency treatment was effected, and that it was first
      effected by the claimant or, in the case of a hospital, in the hospital, and
(c)   may be served by delivering it to the person who was using the vehicle
      or by sending it in a prepaid registered letter, or the recorded delivery
      service, addressed to him at his usual or last known address.

(4) A payment made under section 158 of this Act shall operate as a discharge,
to the extent of the amount paid, of any liability of the person who was using the
vehicle, or of any other person, to pay any sum in respect of the expenses or remuneration of the practitioner or hospital concerned of or for effecting the emergency
treatment.

(5) A chief officer of police must, if so requested by a person who alleges that
he is entitled to a claim payment under section 158 of this Act, provide that person with any information at the disposal of the chief officer—

(a)   as to the identification marks of any motor vehicle which that person
      alleges to be a vehicle out of the use of which the bodily injury arose,
      and
(b)   as to the identity and address of the person who was using the vehicle
      at the time of the event out of which it arose.

---

[1] Figures substituted by S.I. 1995 No.889 (Road Traffic Accidents (Payment for
Treatment) Order, art.3).
[2] Words substituted by Road Traffic (NHS Charges) Act (1999, c.3), s.18(2)(b).

General

Regulations

160.—(1) The Secretary of State may make regulations for any purpose for **A11–94** which regulations may be made under this Part of this Act and for prescribing anything which may be prescribed under this Part of this Act and generally for the purpose of carrying this Part of this Act into effect.

In this Part of this Act "regulations" means regulations under this section and "prescribed" means prescribed by regulations.

(2) In particular, but without prejudice to the generality of subsection (1) above, the regulations may make provision—

(a)   as to forms to be used for the purposes of this Part of this Act,

(b)   as to applications for and the issue of certificates of insurance and certificate of security and any other documents which may be prescribed, and as to the keeping of records of documents and the providing of particulars of them or the giving of information with respect to them to the Secretary of State or a chief officer of police,

(c)   as to the issue of copies of any such certificates or other documents which are lost or destroyed,

(d)   as to the custody, production, cancellation and surrender of any such certificates or other documents, and

(e)   for providing that any provisions of this Part of this Act shall, in relation to vehicles brought into Great Britain by persons making only a temporary stay in Great Britain, have effect subject to such modifications and adaptations as may be prescribed.

Interpretation

161.—(1) In this Part of this Act—   **A11–95**

["hospital" means any institution which provides medical or surgical treatment for in-patents, other than—

(a)   a health service hospital within the meaning of the National Health Service Act 1977 or the National Health Service (Scotland) Act 1978,

(b)   one which is a military hospital for the purposes of section 15 of the Road Traffic (NHS Charges) Act 1999, or

(c)   any institution carried on for profit,][1]

"policy of insurance" includes a covering note,

"salvage" means the preservation of a vessel which is wrecked, stranded or in distress, or the lives of persons belonging to, or the cargo or apparel of, such a vessel, and

"under the owner's control" means, in relation to a vehicle, that it is being driven by the owner or by a servant of the owner in the course of his employment or is otherwise subject to the control of the owner.

(2) In any provision of this Part of this Act relating to the surrender, or the loss or destruction, of a certificate of insurance or certificate of security, references to such a certificate—

[1] Substituted by Road Traffic (NHS Charges) Act (1999, c.3), s.18(3).

(a) shall, in relation to policies or securities under which more than one certificate is issued, be construed as references to all certificates, and

(b) shall, where any copy has been issued of any certificate, be construed as including a reference to that copy.

(3) In this Part of this Act, any reference to an accident includes a reference to two or more causally related accidents.

Index to Part VI

A11–96   **162.** The expressions listed in the left-hand column below are respectively defined or (as the case may be) fall to be construed in accordance with the provisions of this Part of this Act listed in the right-hand colum in relation to those expressions.

Expression	Relevant provision
Accident	Section 161(3)
Authorised insurer	Section 145(2)
Certificate of insurance	Sections 147(1) and 161(2)
Certificate of security	Sections 147(2) and 161(2)
Hospital	Section 161(1)
Policy of insurance	Section 161(1)
Prescribed	Section 160(1)
Regulations	Section 160(1)
Salvage	Section 161(1)
Under the owner's control	Section 161(1)

Short title, commencement and extent

A11–97   **197.**—(1) This Act may be cited as the Road Traffic Act 1988.

(2) This Act shall come into force, subject to the transitory provisions in Schedule 5 to the Road Traffic (Consequential Provisions) Act 1988, at the end of the period of six months beginning with the day on which it is passed.

(3) This Act, except section 80 and except as provided by section 184, does not extend to Northern Ireland.

Contracts (Rights of Third Parties) Act 1999

(47 ELIZ. 2, C. 31)

[11ᵗʰ NOVEMBER, 1999]

An act to make provision for the enforcement of contractual terms by third parties

Be it enacted by the Queen's most Excellent Majesty, by and with the advice and consent of the Lords Spiritual and Temporal, and Commons, in this present Parliament assembled, and by the authority of the same, as follows:

Right of third party to enforce contractual term

1.—(1) Subject to the provisions of this Act, a person who is not a party to a contract (a "third party") may in his own right enforce a term of the contract if—   **A11–98**

    (a) the contract expressly provides that he may, or
    (b) subject to subsection (2), the term purports to confer a benefit on him.

(2) Subsection (1)(b) does not apply if on a proper construction of the contract it appears that the parties did not intend the term to be enforceable by the third party.

(3) The third party must be expressly identified in the contract by name, as a member of a class or as answering a particular description but need not be in existence when the contract is entered into.

(4) This section does not confer a right on a third party to enforce a term of a contract otherwise than subject to and in accordance with any other relevant terms of the contract.

(5) For the purpose of exercising his right to enforce a term of the contract, there shall be available to the third party any remedy that would have been available to him in an action for breach of contract if he had been a party to the contract (and the rules relating to damages, injunctions, specific performance and other relief shall apply accordingly).

(6) Where a term of a contract excludes or limits liability in relation to any matter references in this Act to the third party enforcing the term shall be construed as references to his availing himself of the exclusion or limitation.

(7) In this Act, in relation to a term of a contract which is enforceable by a third party—

"the promisor" means the party to the contract against whom the term is enforceable by the third party, and

"the promisee" means the party to the contract by whom the term is enforceable against the promisor.

Variation and rescission of contract

2.—(1) Subject to the provisions of this section, where a third party has a right under section 1 to enforce a term of the contract, the parties to the contract may not, by agreement, rescind the contract, or vary it in such a way as to extinguish or alter his entitlement under that right, without his consent if—   **A11–99**

    (a) the third party has communicated his assent to the term to the promisor,
    (b) the promisor is aware that the third party has relied on the term, or
    (c) the promisor can reasonably be expected to have foreseen that the third party would rely on the term and the third party has in fact relied on it.

(2) The assent referred to in subsection (1)(a)—

(a)   may be by words or conduct, and

(b)   if sent to the promisor by post or other means, shall not be regarded as communicated to the promisor until received by him.

(3) Subsection (1) is subject to any express term of the contract under which—

(a)   the parties to the contract may by agreement rescind or vary the contract without the consent of the third party, or

(b)   the consent of the third party is required in circumstances specified in the contract instead of those set out in subsection (1)(a) to (c).

(4) Where the consent of a third party is required under subsection (1) or (3), the court or arbitral tribunal may, on the application of the parties to the contract, dispense with his consent if satisfied—

(a)   that his consent cannot be obtained because his whereabouts cannot reasonably be ascertained, or

(b)   that he is mentally incapable of giving his consent.

(5) The court or arbitral tribunal may, on the application of the parties to a contract, dispense with any consent that may be required under subsection (1)(c) if satisfied that it cannot reasonably be ascertained whether or not the third party has in fact relied on the term.

(6) If the court or arbitral tribunal dispenses with a third party's consent, it may impose such conditions as it thinks fit, including a condition requiring the payment of compensation to the third party.

(7) The jurisdiction conferred on the court by subsections (4) to (6) is exercisable by both the High Court and a county court.

Defences, etc. available to promisor

A11–100   **3.**—(1) Subsections (2) to (5) apply where, in reliance on section 1, proceedings for the enforcement of a term of a contract are brought by a third party.

(2) The promisor shall have available to him by way of defence or set-off any matter that—

(a)   arises from or in connection with the contract and is relevant to the term, and

(b)   would have been available to him by way of defence or set-off if the proceedings had been brought by the promisee.

(3) The promisor shall also have available to him by way of defence or set-off any matter if—

(a)   an express term of the contract provides for it to be available to him in proceedings brought by the third party, and

(b)   it would have been available to him by way of defence or set-off if the proceedings had been brought by the promisee.

(4) The promisor shall also have available to him—

(a)   by way of defence or set-off any matter, and

(b)   by way of counterclaim any matter not arising from the contract,

that would have been available to him by way of defence or set-off or, as the case may be, by way of counterclaim against the third party if the third party had been a party to the contract.

(5) Subsections (2) and (4) are subject to any express term of the contract as to

the matters that are not to be available to the promisor by way of defence, set-off or counterclaim.

(6) Where in any proceedings brought against him a third party seeks in reliance on section 1 to enforce a term of a contract (including, in particular, a term purporting to exclude or limit liability), he may not do so if he could not have done so (whether by reason of any particular circumstances relating to him or otherwise) had be been a party to the contract.

Enforcement of contract by promisee

4. Section 1 does not affect any right of the promisee to enforce any term of the contract.   **A11–101**

Protection of promisor from double liability

5. Where under Section 1 a term of a contract is enforceable by a third party, and the promisee has recovered from the promisor a sum in respect of—   **A11–102**

    (a)   the third party's loss in respect of the term, or
    (b)   the expense to the promisee of making good to the third party the default of the promisor,

then, in any proceedings brought in reliance on that section by the third party, the court or arbitral tribunal shall reduce any award to the third party to such extent as it thinks appropriate to take account of the sum recovered by the promisee.

Exceptions

6.—(1) Section 1 confers no rights on a third party in the case of a contract on a bill of exchange, promissory note or other negotiable instrument.   **A11–103**

(2) Section 1 confers no rights on a third party in the case of any contract binding on a company and its members under section 14 of the Companies Act 1985.[1]

[(2A) Section 1 confers no rights on a third party in the case of any incorporation document of a limited liability partnership or any limited liability partnership agreement as defined in the Limited Liability Partnerships Regulations 2001 (S.I. 2001 No.1090).][2]

(3) Section 1 confers no right on a third party to enforce—

    (a)   any term of a contract of employment against an employee,
    (b)   any term of a worker's contract against a worker (including a home worker), or
    (c)   any term of a relevant contract against an agency worker.

(4) In Subsection (3)—

    (a)   "contract of employment", "employee", "worker's contract", and "worker" have the meaning given by section 54 of the National Minimum Wage Act 1998,
    (b)   "home worker" has the meaning given by section 35(2) of that Act,
    (c)   "agency worker" has the same meaning as in section 34(1) of that Act, and

---

[1] In its application to Northern Ireland:
    (2) Section 1 confers no rights on a third party in the case of any contract binding on a company and its members under Article 25 of the Companies (Northern Ireland) Order 1986
[2] Added by S.I. 2001 No.1090 (Limited Liability Partnerships Regulations 2001, Sched.5, para.20.

(d)   "relevant contract" means a contract entered into, in a case where section 34 of that Act applies, by the agency worker as respects work falling within subsection (1)(a) of that section.

(5) Section 1 confers no rights on a third party in the case of—

(a)   a contract for the carriage of goods by sea, or
(b)   a contract for the carriage of goods by rail or road, or for the carriage of cargo by air, which is subject to the rules of the appropriate international transport convention,

except that a third party may in reliance on that section avail himself of an exclusion or limitation of liability in such a contract.

(6) In subsection (5) "contract for the carriage of goods by sea" means a contract of carriage—

(a)   contained in or evidenced by a bill of lading, sea waybill or a corresponding electronic transaction, or
(b)   under or for the purposes of which there is given an undertaking which is contained in a ship's delivery order or a corresponding electronic transaction.

(7) For the purposes of subsection (6)—

(a)   "bill of lading", "sea waybill" and "ship's delivery order" have the same meaning as in the Carriage of Goods by Sea Act 1992, and
(b)   a corresponding electronic transaction in a transaction within section 1(5) of that Act which corresponds to the issue, indorsement, delivery or transfer of a bill of lading, sea waybill or ship's delivery order.

(8) In subsection (5) "the appropriate international transport convention" means—

(a)   in relation to a contract for the carriage of goods by rail, the Convention which has the force of law in the United Kingdom under section 1 of the International Transport Conventions Act 1983,
(b)   in relation to a contract for the carriage of goods by road, the Convention which has the force of law in the United Kingdom under section 1 of the Carriage of Goods by Road Act 1965, and
(c)   in relation to a contract for the carriage of cargo by air—

(i)   the Convention which has the force of law in the United Kingdom under section 1 of the Carriage by Air Act 1961, or
(ii) the Convention which has the force of law under section 1 of the Carriage by Air (Supplementary Provisions) Act 1962, or
(iii) either of the amended Conventions set out in Part B of Schedule 2 or 3 to the Carriage by Air Acts (Application of Provisions) Order 1967.

Supplementary provisions relating to third party

A11–104   7. —(1) Section 1 does not affect any right or remedy of a third party that exists or is available apart from this Act.

(2) Section 2(2) of the Unfair Contract Terms Act 1977 (restriction on exclusion etc. of liability for negligence) shall not apply where the negligence consists of the breach of an obligation arising from a term of a contract and the person seeking to enforce it is a third party acting in reliance on section 1.

(3) In sections 5 and 8 of the Limitation Act 1980 the references to an action founded on a simple contract and an action upon a specialty shall respectively include references to an action brought in reliance on section 1 relating to a sim-

ple contract and an action brought in reliance on that section relating to a specialty.[1][2]

(4) A third party shall not, by virtue of section 1(5) or 3(4) or (6), be treated as a party to the contract for the purposes of any other Act (or any instrument made under any other Act).

Arbitration provisions

8.—(1) Where—

(a) a right under section 1 to enforce a term ("the substantive term") is subject to a term providing for the submission of disputes to arbitration ("the arbitration agreement"), and

(b) the arbitration agreement is an agreement in writing for the purposes of Part I of the Arbitration Act 1996,

the third party shall be treated for the purposes of that Act as a party to the arbitration agreement as regards disputes between himself and the promisor relating to the enforcement of the substantive term by the third party.

(2) Where—

(a) a third party has a right under section 1 to enforce a term providing for one or more descriptions of dispute between the third party and the promisor to be submitted to arbitration ("the arbitration agreement"),

(b) the arbitration agreement is an agreement in writing for the purposes of Part I of the Arbitration Act 1996, and

(c) the third party does not fall to be treated under subsection (1) as a party to the arbitration agreement,

the third party shall, if he exercises the right, be treated for the purposes of that Act as a party to the arbitration agreement in relation to the matter with respect to which the right is exercised, and be treated as having been so immediately before the exercise of the right.

Northern Ireland

9.—(1) In its application to Northern Ireland, this Act has effect with the modifications specified in subsections (2) and (3).

(2) In section 6(2), for "section 14 of the Companies Act 1985" there is substituted "Article 25 of the Companies (Northern Ireland) Order 1986".

(3) In section 7, for subsection (3) there is substituted—

"(3) In Articles 4(a) and 15 of the Limitation (Northern Ireland) Order 1989, the references to an action founded on a simple contract and an action upon an instrument seal shall respectively include references to an action brought in reliance on section 1 relating to a simple contract and an action brought in reliance on that section relating to a contract under seal."

(4) In the Law Reform (Husband and Wife) (Northern Ireland) Act 1964, the following provisions are hereby repealed—

(a) section 5, and

---

[1] In its application to Northern Ireland:
(3) In Articles 4(a) and 15 of the Limitation (Northern Ireland) Order 1989, the references to an action founded on a simple contract and an action upon an instrument under seal shall respectively include references to an action brought in reliance on section 1 relating to a simple contract and an action brought in reliance on that section relating to a contract under seal.

[2] CONDITIONAL; in its application to Northern Ireland by Contracts (Rights of Third Parties) Act (1999, c.31), s.9(3).

(b)   in section 6, in subsection (1)(a), the words "in the case of section 4" and "and in the case of section 5 the contracting party" and, in subsection (3), the words "or section 5".

Short title, commencement and extent

A11–107   **10.**—(1) This Act may be cited as the Contracts (Rights of Third Parties) Act 1999.

(2) This Act comes into force on the day on which it is passed but, subject to subsection (3), does not apply in relation to a contract entered into before the end of the period of six months beginning with that day.

(3) The restriction in subsection (2) does not apply in relation to a contract which—

(a)   is entered into on or after the day on which this Act is passed, and
(b)   expressly provides for the application of this Act.

(4) This Act extends as follows—

(a)   section 9 extends to Northern Ireland only;
(b)   the remaining provisions extend to England and Wales and Northern Ireland only.

Appendix 12

STATUTORY INSTRUMENTS

The Employers' Liability (Compulsory Insurance) Regulations 1998

(1998 No. 2573)

Made	*October 13, 1998*
Laid before Parliament	*October 27, 1998*
Coming into force	*January 1, 1999*

The Secretary of State, in exercise of his powers under sections 1(2), 1(3)(a), 2(2), 3(1)(c), 4(1), (2) and 6 of the Employers' Liability (Compulsory Insurance) Act 1969 (including those provisions as applied with any relevant modifications and extensions by the Offshore Installations and Pipeline Works (Management and Administration) Regulations 1995), and of all other powers enabling him in that behalf, hereby makes the following Regulations:

Citation, commencement and interpretation

1.—(1) These Regulations may be cited as the Employers' Liability (Compulsory Insurance) Regulations 1998 and shall come into force on January 1, 1999.   **A12–01**

(2) In these Regulations—

"the 1969 Act" means the Employers' Liability (Compulsory Insurance) Act 1969;

"associated structure" means, in relatin to an offshore installation, a vessel, aircraft or hovercraft attendant on the installation or any floating structure used in connection with the installation;

"company" has the same meaning as in section 735 of the Companies Act 1985;

"inspector" means an inspector duly authorised by the Secretary of State under section 4(2)(b) of the 1969 Act;

"offshore installation" has the same meaning as in the Offshore Installations and Pipeline Works (Management and Administration) Regulations 1995;

"relevant employee" means an employee—

(a) who is ordinarily resident in the United Kingdom; or
(b) who, though not ordinarily resident in the United Kingdom, has been employed on or from an offshore installation or associated structure for a continuous period of not less than 7 days; or
(c) who, though not ordinarily resident in Great Britain, is present in Great Britain in the course of employment for a continuous period of not less than 14 days; and

"subsidiary" has the same meaning as in section 736 of the Companies Act 1985.

Prohibition of certain conditions in policies of insurance

A12–02   **2.**—(1) For the purposes of the 1969 Act, there is prohibited in any contract of insurance any condition which provides (in whatever terms) that no liability (either generally or in respect of a particular claim) shall arise under the policy, or that any such liability so arising shall cease, if—

(a)   some specified thing is done or omitted to be done after the happening of the event giving rise to a claim under the policy;

(b)   the policy holder does not take reasonable care to protect his employees against the risk of bodily injury or disease in the course of their employment;

(c)   the policy holder fails to comply with the requirements of any enactment for the protection of employees against the risk of bodily injury or disease in the course of their employment; or

(d)   the policy holder does not keep specified records or fails to provide the insurer with or make available to him information from such records.

(2) For the purposes of the 1969 Act there is also prohibited in a policy of insurance any condition which requires—

(a)   a relevant employee to pay; or

(b)   an insured employer to pay the relevant employee,

the first amount of any claim or any aggregation of claims.

(3) Paragraphs (1) and (2) above do not prohibit for the purposes of the 1969 Act a condition in a policy of insurance which requires the employer to pay or contribute any sum to the insurer in respect of the satisfaction of any claim made under the contract of insurance by a relevant employee or any costs and expenses incurred in relation to any such claim.

Limit of amount of compulsory insurance

A12–03   **3.**—(1) Subject to paragraph (2) below, the amount for which an employer is required by the 1969 Act to insure and maintain insurance in respect of relevant employees under one or more policies of insurance shall be, or shall in aggregate be not less than £5 million in respect of—

(a)   a claim relating to any one or more of those employees arising out of any one occurrence; and

(b)   any costs and expenses incurred in relation to any such claim.

(2) Where an employer is a company with one or more subsidiaries, the requirements of paragraph (1) above shall be taken to apply to that company with any subsidiaries together, as if they were a single employer.

Issue of certificates of insurance

A12–04   **4.**—(1) Every authorised insurer who enters into a contract of insurance with an employer in accordance with the 1969 Act shall issue the employer with a certificate of insurance in the form, and containing the particulars, set out in Schedule 1 to these Regulations.

(2) The certificate shall be issued by the insurer not later than thirty days after the date on which the insurance commences or is renewed.

(3) Where a contract of insurance for the purposes of the 1969 Act is entered into together with one or more other contracts of insurance which jointly provide insurance cover of no less than £5 million, the certificate shall specify both—

(a)   the amount in excess of which insurance ccover is provided by the policy; and

(b)   the maximum amount of that cover.

(4) An employer shall retain each certificate issued to him under this regulation, or a copy of each such certificate, for a period of 40 years beginning on the date on which the insurance to which it relates commences or is renewed.

(5) Where the employer is a company, retaining in any eye readable form a copy of a certificate in any one of the ways authorised by sections 722 and 723 of the Companies Act 1985 shall count as keeping a copy of it for the purposes of paragraph (4) above.

(6) In any case where it is intended that a contract of insurance for the purposes of the 1969 Act is to be effective, not only in Great Britain, but also—

(a)   in Northern Ireland, the Isle of Man, the Island of Guernsey, the Island of Jersey or the Island of Alderney;

(b)   in any waters outside the United Kingdom to which the 1969 Act may have been applied by any enactment,

the form set out in Schedule 1 to these Regulations may be modified by a reference to the relevant law which is applicable and a statement that the policy to which it relates satisfies the requirements of that law.

Display and production of copies of certificates of insurance

5.—(1) Subject to paragraph (4) below, an employer who has been issued with a certificate in accordance with regulation 4 above shall display one or more copies of it, in accordance with paragraphs (2) and (3) below, at each place of business at which he employs any relevant employee of the class or description to which such certificate relates.

(2) Any relevant certificate which is required to be displayed in accordance with paragraph (1) above, shall be displayed in such number and in such positions and be of such size and legibility that they may be easily seen and read by any relevant employees, and shall be reasonably protected from being defaced or damaged.

(3) Copies of a certificate which are reuqired to be displayed in accordance with paragraph (1) above shall be kept on display until the date of expiry or earlier termination of the approved policy mentioned in the certificate.

(4) The requirements of paragraphs (1), (2) and (3) above do not apply where an employer employs a relevant employee on or from an offshore installation or associated structure, but in such a case the employer shall produce, at the request of that employee and within the period of ten days from such request, a copy of the certificate which relates to that employee.

A12–05

Production of certificates of insurance to an Inspector

6. An employer who is required by a written notice issued by an inspector to do so shall produce or send to any person specified in the notice, at the address and within the time specified in the notice—

(a)   either the original or a copy of every certificate issued to him under regulation 4 above which relates to a period of insurance current at the date of issue of the notice;

(b)   either the original or a copy of every certificate issued to him under regulation 4 above and retained by him in accordance with regulation 4(4) above.

A12–06

Inspection of policies of insurance

7. Where a certificate is required to be issued to an employer in accordance with regulation 4 above, the employer shall during the currency of the insurance permit the policy of insurance or a copy of it to be inspected by an inspector—

A12–07

(a) at such reasonable time as the inspector may require;

(b) at such place of business of the employer (which, in the case of an employer who is a company, may include its registered office) as the inspector may require.

Production by inspectors of evidence of authority

A12–08   **8.** Any inspector shall, if so required when visiting any premises for the purposes of the 1969 Act, produce to an employer or his agent some duly authenticated document showing that he is authorised by the Secretary of State under section 4(2)(b) of the 1969 Act.

Employers exempted from insurance

A12–09   **9.**—(1) The employers specified in Schedule 2 to these Regulations are exempted from the requirement of the 1969 Act to insure and maintain insurance.

(2) The exemption applies to all cases to which that requirement would otherwise apply, except that for the employers specified in paragraphs 1, 12, 13 and 14 it applies only so far as is mentioned in those paragraphs.

Revocations and transitional

A12–10   **10.**—(1) Subject to paragraphs (2) and (3) below, the instruments specified in column 1 of Schedule 3 to these Regulations are hereby revoked to the extent specified in column 3 of that Schedule.

(2) Subject to paragraphs (4) and (5) below, in the case of an insurance policy commenced before, and current at January 1, 1999, regulations 2 to 6 of, and the Schedule to, the 1971 Regulations shall continue to apply, instead of regulations 2 to 6 of, and Schedule 1 to, these Regulations, until the expiry or renewal of the policy or until 1st January 2000, whichever is the earlier.

(3) The certificate required to be issued by regulation 4(1) of these Regulations in respect of insurance commenced or renewed on or after 1st January 1999 but before April 1, 1999 may, instead of being in the prescribed form, be in the form and contain the particulars specified in the Schedule to the 1971 Regulations.

(4) Every authorised insurer who has issued a certificate in the form, and containing the particulars, specified in the Schedule to the 1971 Regulations in respect of insurance current at April 1, 2000 shall replace it by that date with a certificate in the prescribed form and the replacement shall then be the relevant certificate for the purposes of regulation 5 of these Regulations.

(5) The certificates to which regulation 4(4) of these Regulations applies include any certificate of which a copy is required to be displayed or maintained by regulation 6(1) of the 1971 Regulations immediately before January 1, 1999, and any such certificate shall be treated for the purposes of regulation 6 of these Regulations as having been issued under regulation 4 of these Regulations.

(6) Regulation 7 of these Regulations applies where a certificate is required, in accordance with paragraph (2) above, to be issued in accordance with the 1971 Regulations as it applies where a certificate is required to be issued in accordance with regulation 4 of these Regulations.

(7) In this regulation—

"in the prescribed form" means in the form, and containing the particulars, required by regulation 4(1) and (3) of, and Schedule 1 to, these Regulations;

"the 1971 Regulations" means the Employers' Liability (Compulsory Insurance) General Regulations 1971 as in force on December 31, 1998, including those Regulations as applied by the Employers' Liability (Compulsory Insurance) (Offshore Installations) Regulations 1975.

Signed by authority of the Secretary of State

Alan Meale
Parliamentary Under Secretary of State, Department of the Environment, Transport and the Regions

SCHEDULES

SCHEDULE 1

REGULATION 4

CERTIFICATE OF EMPLOYERS' LIABILITY INSURANCE
(Where required by regulation 5 of the Employers' Liability (Compulsory Insurance) Reg-   **A12–11**
ulations 1998 (the Regulations), one or more copies of this certificate must be displayed at
each place of business at which the policy holder employs persons covered by the policy.)
Policy No.

1. Name of policy holder
2. Date of commencement of insurance policy.
3. Date of expiry of insurance policy.

We hereby certify that subject to paragraph 2:

1. the policy to which this certificate relates satisfies the requirements of the relevant
law applicable in [Great Britain]; and
2. (a) the minimum amount of cover provided by this policy is no less than £5 million; or
   (b) the cover provided under this policy relates to claims in excess of [£] but not
exceeding [£].

Signed on behalf of . . . ; (Authorised Insurer)

Signature

Notes:
Where the employer is a company to which regulation 3(2) of the Regulations applies, the
certificate shall state in a prominent place, either that the policy covers the holding company
and all its subsidiaries, or that the policy covers the holding company and all its subsidiaries
except any specifically excluded by name, or that the policy covers the holding company and
only the named subsidiaries.
Specify applicable law as provided for in regulation 4(6) of the Regulations.
See regulation 3(1) of the Regulations and delete whichever of paragraphs 2(a) or 2(b)
does not apply. Where 2(b) is applicable, specify the amount of cover provided by the relevant policy.

SCHEDULE 2

REGULATION 9

EMPLOYERS EXEMPTED FROM INSURANCE
1. A person who for the time being holds a current certificate issued by a government   **A12–12**
department stating that claims established against that person in respect of any liability to
such employees of the kind mentioned in section 1(1) of the 1969 Act as are mentioned in
the certificate will, to any extent to which they are incapable of being satisfied by that person,
be satisfied out of money provided by Parliament; but only in respect of employees covered
by the certificate.
2. The Government of any foreign state or Commonwealth country.
3. Any inter-governmental organisation which by virtue of any enactment is to be treated
as a body corporate.
4. Any subsidiary of any such body as is mentioned in section 3(1)(b) of the 1969 Act
(which exempts any body corporate established by or under any enactment for the carrying
on of any industry or part of an industry, or of any undertaking, under national ownership
or control) and any company of which two or more such bodies are members and which
would, if those bodies were a single corporate body, be a subsidiary of that body corporate.

5. Any Passenger Transport Executive and any subsidiary thereof.

6. London Regional Transport, and any of its subsidiaries or joint subsidiaries within the meaning of section 51(5) of the Transport Act 1968.

7. The Commission for the New Towns.

8. The Qualifications and Curriculum Authority

9. Any voluntary management committee of an approved bail or approved probation hostel within the meaning of the Probation Service Act 1993.

10. Any magistrates' courts committee established under the Justices of the Peace Act 1997.

11. Any probation committee established under the Probation Service Act 1993.

12. Any employer who is a member of a mutual insurance association of shipowners or of shipowners and others, in respect of any liabiity to an employee of the kind mentioned in section 1(1) of the 1969 Act against which the employer is insured for the time being with that association for an amount not less than that required by the 1969 Act and regulations under it, being an employer who holds a certificate issued by that association to the effect that he is so insured in relation to that employee.

13. Any licensee within the meaning of the Nuclear Installations Act 1965, in respect of any liability to pay compensation under that Act to any of his employees in respect of a breach of duty imposed on him by virtue of section 7 of that Act.

14. Any employer to the extent he is required to insure and maintain insurance by subsection (1) of section 1 of the 1969 Act against liability for bodily injury sustained by his employee when the employee is—

    (i)   carried in or upon a vehicle; or

    (ii) entering or getting on to, or alighting from, a vehicle, in the circumstances specified in that subsection and where that bodily injury is caused by or, arises out of, the use by the employer of a vehicle on a road; and the expression "road", "use" and "vehicle" have the same meanings as in Part VI of the Road Traffice Act 1988.

SCHEDULE 3

REGULATION 10

REVOCATIONS OF INSTRUMENTS

Reference	Title	Extent of revocation
S.I. 1971 No. 1117	The Employers' Liability (Compulsory Insurance) General Regulations 1971	The whole Regulations
S.I. 1971 No. 1933	The Employers' Liability (Compulsory Insurance) Exemption Regulations 1971	The whole Regulations
S.I. 1974 No. 208	The Employers' Liability (Compulsory Insurance) (Amendment) Regulations 1974	The whole Regulations
S.I. 1975 No. 194	The Employers' Liability (Compulsory Insurance) (Amendment) Regulations 1975	The whole Regulations
S.I. 1975 No. 1443	The Employers' Liability (Compulsory Insurance) (Offshore Installations) Regulations 1975	The whole Regulations
S.I. 1981 No. 1489	The Employers' Liability (Compulsory Insurance) (Amendment) Regulations 1981	The whole Regulations
S.I. 1992 No. 3172	The Employers' Liability (Compulsory Insurance) Exemption (Amendment) Regulations 1992	The whole Regulations
S.I. 1994 No. 520	The Employers' Liability (Compulsory Insurance) Exemption (Amendment) Regulations 1994	The whole Regulations
S.I. 1994 No. 3301	The Employers' Liability (Compulsory Insurance) General (Amendment) Regulations 1994	The whole Regulations

The Motor Vehicles (Third Party Risks) Regulations 1972

(1972 No. 1217)

Made	*August 1, 1972*
Laid before Parliament	*August 15, 1972*
Coming into Operation	*November 1, 1972*

The Secretary of State for the Environment in exercise of his powers under sections 147, 157 and 162 of the Road Traffic Act 1972 (c. 20), and under section 37 of the Vehicles (Excise) Act 1971 (c. 10), as extended by section 153 of the Road Traffic Act 1972, and of all other enabling powers, and after consultation with representative organisations in accordance with the provisions of section 199(2) of the Road Traffic Act 1972, hereby makes the following Regulations:

Commencement and citation

1. These Regulations shall come into operation on 1st November 1972 and may **A12–14** be cited as the Motor Vehicles (Third Party Risks) Regulations 1972.

2. The Motor Vehicles (Third Party Risks) Regulations 1961 (S.I. 1961 No. **A12–15** 1465) and the Motor Vehicles (Third Party Risks) (Amendment) Regulations 1969 (S.I. 1969 No. 1733) are hereby revoked.

Temporary use of existing forms

3. Nothing in these Regulations shall affect the validity of any certificate which **A12–16** has been issued before these Regulations came into force in a form prescribed by the Motor Vehicles (Third Party Risks) Regulations 1961, as amended by the Motor Vehicles (Third Party Risks) (Amendment) Regulations 1969, as in force immediately before the coming into operation of these Regulations, and any certificate in such a form may continue to be issued until the expiration of three years from the coming into force of these Regulations.

Interpretation

4.—(1) In these Regulations, unless the context otherwise requires, the follow- **A12–17** ing expressions have the meanings hereby respectively assigned to them:

"the Act" means the Road Traffic Act 1972;

"company" means an authorised insurer within the meaning of Part VI of the Act or a body of persons by whom a security may be given in pursuance of the said Part VI;

"motor vehicle" has the meaning assigned to it by sections 190, 192 and 193 of the Act, but excludes any invalid carriage, tramcar or trolley vehicle to which Part IV of the Act does not apply;

"policy" means a policy of insurance in respect of third party risks arising out of the use of motor vehicles which complies with the requirements of Part VI of the Act and includes a covering note;

"security" means a security in respect of third party risks arising out of the use of motor vehicles which complies with the requirements of Part VI of the Act;

"specified body" means—

    (a) any of the local authorities referred to in paragraph (a) of section 144(2) of the Act; or

    (b) a Passenger Transport Executive established under an order made under section 9 of the Transport Act 1968 (c. 73), or a subsidiary of that Executive, being an Executive or subsidiary to whose vehicles section 144(2)(a) of the Act has been applied; or

    (c) the London Transport Executive or a wholly-owned subsidiary of that Executive referred to in paragraph (e) of section 144(2) of the Act.

(2) Any reference in these Regulations to a certificate in Form A, B, C, D, E or F shall be construed as a reference to a certificate in the form so headed and set out in Part 1 of the Schedule to these Regulations which has been duly made and completed subject to and in accordance with the provisions set out in Part 2 of the said Schedule.

(3) Any reference in these Regulations to any enactment shall be construed as a reference to that enactment as amended by any subsequent enactment.

(4) The Interpretation Act 1889 (c. 63) shall apply for the interpretation of these Regulations as it applies for the interpretation of an Act of Parliament, and as if for the purposes of section 38 of that Act these Regulations were an Act of Parliament and the Regulations revoked by Regulation 2 of these Regulations were Acts of Parliament thereby repealed.

Issue of certificates of insurance or security

5.—(1) A company shall issue to every holder of a security or of a policy other than a covering note issued by the company:

    (a) in the case of a policy or security relating to one or more specified vehicles a certificate of insurance in Form A or a certificate of security in Form D in respect of each such vehicle;

    (b) in the case of a policy or security relating to vehicles other than specified vehicles such number of certificates in Form B or Form D as may be necessary for the purpose of complying with the requirements of section 162(1) of the Act and of these Regulations as to the production of evidence that a motor vehicle is not being driven in contravention of section 143 of the Act.

        Provided that where a security is intended to cover the use of more than ten motor vehicles at one time the company by whom it was issued may, subject to the consent of the Secretary of State, issue one certificate only, and where such consent has been given the holder of the security may issue duplicate copies of such certificate duly authenticated by him up to such number and subject to such conditions as the Secretary of State may determine.

(2) Notwithstanding the foregoing provisions of this Regulation, where as respects third party risks a policy or security relating to a specified vehicle extends also to the driving by the holder of other motor vehicles, not being specified vehicles, the certificate may be in Form A or Form D, as the case may be, containing a statement in either case that the policy or security extends to such driving or other motor vehicles. Where such a certificate is issued by a company they may, and shall in accordance with a demand made to them by the holder, issue to him a further such certificate or a certificate in Form B.

(3) Every policy in the form of a covering note issued by a company shall have printed thereon or on the back thereof a certificate of insurance in Form C.

A12–19   6. Every certificate of insurance or certificate of security shall be issued not later than four days after the date on which the policy or security to which it relates is issued or renewed.

Production of evidence as alternatives to certificates

A12–20   7. The following evidence that a motor vehicle is not or was not being driven in contravention of section 143 of the Act may be produced in pursuance of section

162 of the Act as an alternative to the production of a certificate of insurance or a certificate of security:

(1)   a duplicate copy of a certificate of security issued in accordance with the proviso to sub-paragraph (b) of paragraph (1) of Regulation 5 of these Regulations;

(2)   in the case of a motor vehicle of which the owner has for the time being deposited with the Accountant-General of the Supreme Court the sum of fifteen thousand pounds in accordance with the provisions of section 144(1) of the Act, a certificate in Form E signed by the owner of the motor vehicle or by some person authorised by him in that behalf that such sum is on deposit;

(3)   in the case of a motor vehicle owned by a specified body, a police authority or the Receiver for the metropolitan police district, a certificate in Form F signed by some person authorised in that behalf by such specified body, police authority or Receiver as the case may be that the said motor vehicle is owned by the said specified body, police authority or Receiver.

8. Any certification issued in accordance with paragraph (2) or (3) of the preceding Regulation shall be destroyed by the owner of the vehicle to which it relates before the motor vehicle is sold or otherwise disposed of.

Production of evidence of insurance or security on application of excise licences

9.—(1) Any person applying for a vehicle licence under the Vehicles (Excise) Act 1971 shall, except as hereinafter provided and subject to the provisions of Regulation 8 of the Motor Vehicles (International Motor Insurance Card) Regulations 1971 (S.I. 1971 No. 792), produce to the Secretary of State either: **A12–22**

(a)   a certificate of insurance, certificate of security or duplicate copy of a certificate of security issued in accordance with these Regulations indicating that on the date when the licence comes into operation there will be in force the necessary policy or the necessary security in relation to the user of the motor vehicle by the applicant or byother persons on his order or with his permission and such further evidence as may be necessary to establish that the certificate relates to such user; or

(b)   in the case where the motor vehicle is one of more than ten motor vehicles owned by the same person in respect of which a policy or policies of insurance have been obtained by him from the same authorised insurer, a statement duly authenticated by the authorised insurer to the effect that on the date when the licence becomes operative an insurance policy which complies with Part VI of the Act will be in force in relation to the user of the motor vehicle; or

(c)   evidence that section 143 of the Act does not apply to the motor vehicle at a time when it is being driven under the owner's control, in accordance with the following provisions—

(i)   in the case of a motor vehicle of which the owner has for the time being deposited with the Accountant-General of the Supreme Court the sum of fifteen thousand pounds in accordance with the provisions of section 144(1) of the Act, a certificate in Form E signed by the owner of the motor vehicle or by some person authorised by him in that behalf that such sum is on deposit;

(ii)   in the case of a motor vehicle owned by a specified body, a police authority or by the Receiver for the metropolitan police district, a certificate in Form F signed by some person authorised in that behalf by such specified body, police authority or Receiver as the case may be that the vehicle in respect of which the application for a licence is made is owned by the said specified body, police authority or Receiver.

(2) A person engaged in the business of letting motor vehicles on hire shall not, when applying for a licence under the Vehicles (Excise) Act 1971, be required to comply with the provisions of paragraph (1) of this Regulation if the motor vehicle in respect of which the licence is applied for is intended to be used solely for the purpose of being let on hire and driven by the person by whom the motor vehicle is hired or by persons under his control.

Keeping of records by companies

A12–23   10.—(1) Every company by whom a policy or a security is issued shall keep a record of the following particulars relative thereto and of any certificates issued in connection therewith:

(a) the full name and address of the person to whom the policy, security or certificate is issued;

(b) in the case of a policy relating to one or more specified motor vehicles the registration mark of each such motor vehicle;

(c) the date on which the policy or security comes into force and the date on which it expires;

(d) in the case of a policy the conditions subject to which the persons or classes of persons specified in the policy will be indemnified;

(e) in the case of a security the conditions subject to which the undertaking given by the company under the security will be implemented;

and every such record shall be preserved for one year from the date of expiry of the policy or security.

(2) Every specified body shall keep a record of the motor vehicles owned by them in respect of which a policy or a security has not been obtained, and of any certificates issued by them under these Regulations in respect of such motor vehicles, and of the withdrawal or destruction of any such certificates.

(3) Any person who has deposited and keeps deposited with the Accountant-General of the Supreme Court the sum of fifteen thousand pounds in accordance with the provisions of section 144(1) of the Act shall keep a record of the motor vehicles owned by him and of any certificates issued by him or on his behalf under these Regulations in respect of such motor vehicles and of the withdrawal or destruction of any such certificates.

(4) Any company, specified body or other person by whom records of documents are required by these Regulations to be kept shall without charge furnish to the Secretary of State or to any chief officer of police on request any particulars thereof.

Notification to the Secretary of State of ineffective policies or securities

A12–24   11. Where to the knowledge of a company a policy or security issued by them ceases to be effective without the consent of the person to whom it was issued, otherwise than by effluxion of time or by reason of his death, the company shall forthwith notify the Secretary of State of the date on which the policy or security ceased to be effective.

Provided that such noficiation need not be made if the certificate relating to the policy or security has been received by the company from the person to whom the certificate was issued on or before the date on which the policy or security ceased to be effective.

Return of certificates to issuing company

A12–25   12.—(1) The following provisions shall apply in relation to the transfer of a policy or security with the consent of the holder to any other person:

(a) the holder shall, before the policy or security is transferred, return any relative certificates issued for the purposes of these Regulations to the company by whom they were issued; and

(b) the policy or security shall not be transferred to any other person unless and until the certificates have been so returned or the company are satisfied that the certificates have been lost or destroyed.

(2) In any case where the consent of the person to whom it was issued a policy or security is suspended or ceases to be effective, otherwise than by effluxion of time, in circumstances in which the provisions of section 147(4) of the Act (relating to the surrender of certificates) do not apply, the holder of the policy or security shall within seven days from the date when it is suspended or ceased to be effective return any relative certificates issued for the purposes of these Regulations to the company by whom they were issued and the company shall not issue a new policy or security to the said holder in respect of the motor vehicle or vehicles to which the said first mentioned policy or security related unless and until the certificates have been returned to the company or the company are satisfied that they have been lost or destroyed.

(3) Where a policy or security is cancelled by mutual consent or by virtue of any provision in the policy or security, any statutory declaration that a certificate has been lost or destroyed made in pursuance of section 147(4) (which requires any such declaration to be made within a period of seven days from the taking effect of the cancellation) shall be delivered forthwith after it has been made to the company by whom the policy was issued or the security given.

(4) The provisions of the last preceding paragraph shall be withour prejudice to the provisions of paragraph (c) of subsection (2) of section 149 of the Act as to the effect for the purposes of that subsection of the making of a statutory declaration within the periods therein stated.

Issue of fresh certificates

13. Where any company by whom a certificate of insurance or a certificate of security has been issued are satisfied that the certificate has become defaced or has been lost or destroyed they shall, if they are requested to do so by the person to whom the certificate was issued, issue to him a fresh certificate. In the case of a defaced certificate the company shall not issue a fresh certificate unless the defaced certificate is returned to the company.   **A12–26**

Signed by authority of the Secretary of State.

John Peyton
Minister for Transport Industries,
Department of the Environment.

THE SCHEDULE

PART 1—FORMS OF CERTIFICATES

FORM A—CERTIFICATE OF MOTOR INSURANCE

Certificate No..................................... Policy No................................. (Optional)   **A12–27**

1. Registration mark of vehicle.
2. Name of policy holder.
3. Effective date of the commencement of insurance for the purposes of the relevant law.

4. Date of expiry of insurance.
5. Persons or classes of persons entitled to drive.
6. Limitations as to use.

I/We hereby certify that the policy to which this certificate relates satisfies the requirements of the relevant law applicable in Great Britain.

....
Authorised Insurers

Note: For full details of the insurance cover
reference should be made to the policy.

FORM B—Certificate of Motor Insurance

A12–28 Certificate No...................................... Policy No.................................(Optional)

1. Description of vehicles.
2. Name of policy holder.
3. Effective date of the commencement of insurance for the purposes of the relevant law.
4. Date of expiry of insurance.
5. Persons or classes of persons entitled to drive.
6. Limitations as to use.

I/We hereby certify that the policy to which this certificate relates satisfies the requirements of the relevant law applicable in Great Britain.

....
Authorised Insurers

Note: For full details of the insurance cover reference should be made to the policy.

FORM C—Certificate of Motor Insurance

A12–29 I/We hereby certify that this covering note satisfies the requirements of the relevant law applicable in Great Britain.

....
Authorised Insurers

FORM D—Certificate of Security

A12–30 Certificate No..................................... Security No.................................(Optional)

1. Name of holder of security
2. Effective date of the commencement of insurance for the purposes of the relevant law.
3. Date of expiry of insurance.
4. Conditions to which security is subject.

I/We hereby certify that the security to which this certificate relates satisfies the requirements of the relevant law applicable in Great Britain.

....
Persons giving security

Note: For full details of the cover
reference should be made to the security.

FORM E—Certificate of Deposit

I/We hereby certify that I am/we are the owner(s) of the vehicle of which the registration mark is .... and that in pursuance of the relevant law applicable in Great Britain I/we have on deposit with the Accountant-General of the Supreme Court the sum of fifteen thousand pounds.

A12–31

Signed ....
on behalf of............................

FORM F—Certificate of Ownership

We hereby certify that the vehicle of which the registration mark is .... is owned by...

A12–32

Signed ....
on behalf of............................

PART 2—Provisions relating to the forms and completion of certificates

1. Every certificate shall be printed and completed in black on white paper or similar material. This provision shall not apply to any reproduction of a seal or monogram or similar device referred to in paragraph 2 of this Part of this Schedule.

A12–33

2. No certificate shall contain any advertising matter, either on the face or on the back thereof:

Provided that the name and address of the company by whom a certificate is issued or a reproduction of the seal of the company or any monogram or similar device of the company, or the name and address of an insurance broker shall not be deemed to be advertising matter for the purposes of this paragraph if it is printed or stamped at the foot or on the back of such certificate.

3. The whole of each form as set out in Part 1 of this Schedule shall in each case appear on the face of the form, the items being in the order so set out and the certification being set out at the end of the form.

4. The particulars to be inserted on the said forms shall so far as possible appear on the face of the form, but where in the case of any of the numbered headings in Forms A, B, or D, this cannot conveniently be done, any part of such particulars may be inserted on the back of the form, provided that their presence on the back is clearly indicated under the relevant heading.

5. The particulars to be inserted on any of the said forms shall not include particulars relating to any exceptions purporting to restrict the insurance under the relevant policy or the operation of the relevant security which are by subsection (1) of section 148 of the Act rendered of no effect as respect the third party liabilities required by sections 145 and 146 of the Act to be covered by a policy or security.

6.—(1) In any case where it is intended that a certificate of insurance, certificate of security or a covering note shall be effective not only in Great Britain, but also in any of the following territories, that is to say Northern Ireland, the Isle of Man, the Island of Guernsey, the Island of Jersey or the Island of Alderney, Forms A, B, C and D may be modified by the addition thereto, where necessary, of a reference to the relevant legal provisions of such of those territories as may be appropriate.

(2) A certificate of insurance or a certificate of security may contain either on the face or on the back of the certificate a statement as to whether or not the policy or security to which it relates satisfies the requirements of the relevant law in any of the territories referred to in this paragraph.

7. Every certificate of insurance of certificate of security shall be duly authenticated by or on behalf of the company by whom it is issued.

8. A certificate in Form F issued by a subsidiary of a Passenger Transport Executive or by a wholly-owned subsidiary of the London Transport Executive shall indicate under the signature that the issuing body is such a subsidiary of an Executive, which shall there be specified.

The Motor Vehicles (Compulsory Insurance) (No. 2) Regulations 1973

(1973 No. 2143)

Made	*December 18, 1973*
Laid before Parliament	*December 21, 1973*
Coming into Operation	*January 1, 1974*

The Secretary of State for the Environment, being a Minister designated for the purposes of section 2(2) of the European Communities Act 1972 (c. 68) in relation to compulsory insurance in respect of, and other means of providing for, civil liability in relation to motor vehicles and trailers, in the exercise powers conferred by that section, hereby makes the following Regulations:

A12–34   **1.**—(1) These Regulations shall come into operation on 1st January 1974 and may be cited as the Motor Vehicles (Compulsory Insurance) (No. 2) Regulations 1973.

(2) The Motor Vehicles (Compulsory Insurance) Regulations 1973 (S.I. 1973 No. 1820) are hereby revoked.

A12–35   **2.**—(1) In these Regulations "vehicle" means any motor vehicle intended for travel on land and propelled by mechanical power, but not running on rails, and any trailer, whether or not coupled.

(2) For the purposes of these Regulations the territory in which a vehicle is normally based is—

(a)   the territory of the state in which the vehicle is registered, or

(b)   in cases where no registration is required for the type of vehicle, but the vehicle bears an insurance plate or distinguishing sign analogous to a registration plate, the territory of the state in which the insurance plate or the sign is issued, or

(c)   in cases where neither registration plate nor insurance plate nor distinguishing sign is required for the type of vehicle, the territory of the state in which the keeper of the vehicle is permanently resident.

(3) The Interpretation Act 1889 (c. 63) shall apply for the interpretation of these Regulations as it applies for the interpretation of an Act of Parliament.

A12–36   **3.** Section 145(3) of the Road Traffic Act 1972 (c. 20) (requirements in respect of policies of insurance) shall have effect as if:

(a)   in paragraph (a) after the words "on a road" there were inserted the words "in Great Britain";

(b)   after paragraph (a) there were added the following paragraph:

"(aa)   must insure him or them in respect of any liability which may be incurred by him or them in respect of the use of the vehicle and of any trailer, whether or not coupled, in the territory other than Great Britain and Gibraltar of each of the member states of the Communities according to the law on compulsory insurance against civil liability in respect of the use of vehicles of the state where the liability may be incurred; and".

A12–37   **4.** Section 146(3) of the Road Traffic Act 1972 (requirements in respect of securities) shall have effect as if the words "and up to the amount" and paragraphs (a) and (b) were omitted and there were added at the end of the following proviso:

"Provided that in the case of liabilities arising out of the use of a motor vehicle on a road in Great Britain the amount secured need not exceed—

    (a) in the case of an undertaking relating to the use of public service vehicles (within the meaning of Part III of the Road Traffic Act 1960), £25,000;

    (b) in any other case, £5,000."

5.—(1) It shall be an offence for a person to use a specified motor vehicle registered in Great Britain, or any trailer kept by a person permanently resident in Great Britain, whether or not coupled, in the territory other than Great Britain and Gibraltar of any of the member states of the Communities, unless a policy of insurance is in force in relation to the person using that vehicle which insures him in respect of any liability which may be incurred by him in respect of the use of the vehicle in such territory according to the law on compulsory insurance against civil liability in respect of the use of vehicles of the state where the liability may be incurred.   **A12–38**

(2) In this Regulation "specified motor vehicle" means a motor vehicle which is exempted from the provisions of sectin 143 of the Road Traffic Act 1972 (users of motor vehicles to be insured or secured against third-party risks) by virtue of section 144 of that Act.

(3) A person guilty of an offence under this Regulation shall be liable on summary conviction to a fine not exceeding £50 or to imprisonment for a term not exceeding three months, or to both such fine and such imprisonment.

(4) Proceedings for an offence under this Regulation may be taken, and the offence may for all incidental purposes be treated as having been committed in any place in Great Britain.

(5) Sections 180 (time within which summary proceedings for certain offences must be commenced) and 181 (evidence by certificate) of the Road Traffic Act 1972 shall apply for the purposes of an offence under this Regulation as if such an offence were an offence under that Act to which those sections had been applied by column 7 of Part I of Schedule 4 to that Act.

6.—(1) Any person appointed by the Secretary of State for the purpose (in this Regulation referred to as an "appointed person") may require a person having custody of any vehicle, being a vehicle which is normally based in the territory of a state which is not a member of the Communities or in the non-European territory of a member state or in Gibraltar, when entering Great Britain to produce evidence that any loss or injury which may be caused by such a vehicle is covered throughout the territory in which the treaty establishing the European Economic Community is in force, in accordance with the requirements of the lawws of the various member states on compulsory insurance against civil liability in respect of the use of vehicles.   **A12–39**

(2) An appointed person may, if no such evidence is produced or if he is not satisfied by such evidence, prohibit the use of the vehicle in Great Britain.

(3) Where an appointed person prohibits the use of a vehicle under this Regulation, he may also direct the driver to remove the vehicle to such place and subject to such conditions as are specified in the direction; and the prohibition shall not apply to the removal of the vehicle in accordance with the direction.

(4) Any person who—

    (a) uses a vehicle or causes or permits a vehicle to be used in contravention of a prohibition imposed under paragraph (2) of this Regulation, or

    (b) refuses, neglects or otherwise fails to comply in a reasonable time with a direction given under paragraph (3) of this Regulation,

shall be guilty of an offence and shall be liable on summary conviction to a fine not exceeding £50.

(5) Section 181 of the Road Traffic Act 1972 shall apply for the purposes of an offence under this Regulation as if such an offence were an offence under that Act to which that section had been applied by column 7 of Part 1 of Schedule 4 to that Act.

(6) A prohibition under paragraph (2) of this Regulation may be removed by an appointed person if he is satisfied that appropriate action has been taken to remove or remedy the circumstances in consequence of which the prohibition was imposed.

A12–40   7.—(1) Where a constable in uniform has reasonable cause to suspect the driver of a vehicle of having committed an offence under the preceding Regulation, the constable may detain the vehicle, and for that purpose may give a direction, specifying an appropriate person and directing the vehicle to be removed by that person to such place and subject to such conditions as are specified in the direction; and the prohibition shall not apply to the removal of the vehicle in accordance with that direction.

(2) Where under paragraph (1) of this Regulation a constable—

    (a)   detains a motor vehicle drawing a trailer, or
    (b)   detains a trailer drawn by a motor vehicle,

then, for the purpose of securing the removal of the trailer, he may also (in a case falling within sub-paragraph (a) above) detain the trailer or (in a case falling within sub-paragraph (b) above) detain the motor vehicle; and a direction under paragraph (1) of this Regulation may require both the motor vehicle and the trailer to be removed to the place specified in the direction.

(3) A vehicle which, in accordance with a direction given under paragraph (1) of this Regulation, is removed to a place specified in the direction shall be detained in that place, or in any other place to which it is removed in accordance with a further direction given under that paragraph, until a constable (or, if that place is in the occupation of the Secretary of State, the Secretary of State) authorises the vehicle to be released on being satisfied—

    (a)   that the prohibition (if any) imposed in respect of the vehicle under the preceding Regulation has been removed, or that no such prohibition was imposed, or
    (b)   that appropriate arrangements have been made for removing or remedying the circumstances in consequence of which such prohibition was imposed, or
    (c)   that the vehicle will be taken forthwith to a place from which it will be taken out of Great Britain to a place not in the European territory other than Gibraltar of a member state of the Communities.

(4) Any person who—

    (a)   drives a vehicle in accordance with a direction given under this Regulation, or
    (b)   is in charge of a place at which a vehicle is detained under this Regulation,

shall not be liable for any damage to, or loss in respect of, the vehicle or its load unless it is shown that he did not take reasonable care of the vehicle while driving it or, as the case may be, did not, while the vehicle was detained in that place, take reasonable care of the vehicle or (if the vehicle was detained there with its load) did not take reasonable care of its load.

(5) In this Regulation "appropriate person"—

    (a)   in relation to a direction to remove a motor vehicle, other than a motor vehicle drawing a trailer, means a person licensed to drive vehicles of the class to which the vehicle belongs, and

(b) in relation to a direction to remove a trailer, or to remove a motor vehicle drawing a trailer, means a person licensed to drive vehicles of a class which, when the direction is complied with, will include the motor vehicle drawing the trailer in accordance with that direction.

8. Nothing in section 145(2) (policies to be issued by authorised insurers) and section 147(1) (policies to be of no effect unless certificates issued) of the Road Traffic Act 1972 shall apply in the case of an insurance policy which is issued elsewhere than in the United Kingdom in respect of a vehicle normally based in the territory of a Member State of the Communities other than the United Kingdom and Gibraltar.   **A12–41**

9.—(1) Section 151(1) of the Road Traffic Act 1972 (duly to give information as to insurance or security where claim made) shall have effect as if in paragraph (b) for the words "the certificate" to the end there were substituted the words "any certificate of insurance or security delivered in respect of that policy or security, as the case may be, under section 147 of this Act, or where no such certificate was delivered under the said section the following particulars, that is to say, the registration mark or other identifying particulars of the vehicle concerned, the number or other identifying particulars of the insurance policy issued in respect of the vehicle, the name of the insurer and the period of the insurance cover.   **A12–42**

(2) Section 169(2) of the Road Traffic Act 1972 (forgery of certain documents) shall have effect as if after paragraph (g) there were inserted the following paragraph:

"(gg) any document produced as evidence of insurance in pursuance of Regulation 6 of the Motor Vehicles (Compulsory Insurance) (No. 2) Regulations 1973;".

Signed by authority of the Secretary of State

John Peyton,
Minister for Transport Industries,
Department of the Environment.

The Motor Vehicles (Compulsory Insurance) Regulations 1992

(1992 No. 3036)

Made	*2nd December 1992*
Laid before Parliament	*9th December 1992*
Coming into force	*31st December 1992*

The Secretary of State for Transport, being a Minister designated for the purpose of section 2(2) of the European Communities Act 1972 in relation to compulsory motor insurance in respect of, and other means of providing for, civil liability in relation to motor vehicles and trailers, in exercise of the powers conferred by that section, hereby makes the following Regulations:

A12–43   **1.** These Regulations may be cited as the Motor Vehicles (Compulsory Insurance) Regulations 1992 and shall come into force on December 31, 1992.

2.—(1) In section 145 of the Road Traffic Act 1988 (requirements in respect of policies of insurance) in subsection (3) after paragraph (a) there shall be inserted the following paragraph—

> (aa)   "must, in the case of a vehicle normally based in the territory of another member State, insure him or them in respect of any civil liability which may be incurred by him or them as a result of an event related to the use of the vehicle in Great Britain if,—
>
>> (i)   according to the law of that territory, he or they would be required to be insured in respect of a civil liability which would arise under that law as a result of that event if the place where the vehicle was used when the event occurred were in that territory, and
>> (ii)   the cover required by that law would be higher than that required by paragraph (a) above, and".

(2) In paragraph (b) of subsection (3) of that section (which requires a policy to provide insurance in respect of certain liabilities in accordance with the law on compulsory motor insurance of the State where the liability may be incurred) after the word "must" there shall be inserted", in the case of a vehicle normally based in Great Britain," and for the words from "the law" to the end of the paragraph there shall be substituted—

> "(i)   the law on compulsory insurance against civil liability in respect of the use of vehicles of the State in whose territory the event giving rise to the liability occurred; or
> (ii)   if it would give higher cover, the law which would be applicable under this Part of this Act if the place where the vehicle was used when that event occurred were in Great Britain; and".

(3) After subsection (4) of that section there shall be inserted the following subsection—

> "(4A) In the case of a person—
>
> (a) carried in or upon a vehicle, or
> (b) entering or getting on to, or alighting from, a vehicle, the provisions of paragraph (a) of subsection (4) above do not apply unless cover in respect of the liability referred to in that paragraph is in fact provided pursuant to a requirement of the Employers' Liability (Compulsory Insurance) Act 1969."

Signed by authority of the Secretary of State for Transport

Kenneth Carlisle
Parliamentary Under Secretary of State, Department of Transport

The Motor Vehicles (Compulsory Insurance) Regulations 2000

(2000 No. 726)

Made	*March 10, 2000*
Laid before Parliament	*March 13, 2000*
Coming into force	*April 3, 2000*

The Secretary of State for the Environment, Transport and the Regions, being a Minister designated for the purposes of section 2(2) of the European Communities Act 1972 in relation to compulsory insurance in respect of, and other means of providing for, civil liability in relation to motor vehicles and trailers, in exercise of the powers conferred by that section, hereby makes the following Regulations:

Citation, commencement and interpretation
1. These Regulations may be cited as the Motor Vehicles (Compulsory Insurance) Regulations 2000 and shall come into force on April 3, 2000.   **A12–44**

Amendment of the Road Traffic Act 1988 in respect of motor insurance requirements
2.—(1) The Road Traffic Act 1988 is amended in accordance with paragraphs (2) to (6) below.   **A12–45**
(2) In section 143 (users of motor vehicles to be insured or secured against third party risks)—

(a) in subsection (1)(a), after "road" there shall be inserted "or other public place";
(b) in subsection (1)(b), after "road" there shall be inserted "or other public place".

(3) In section 145(3)(a) (requirements in respect of policies of insurance), after "road" there shall be inserted "or other public place".
(4) In section 146(4) (requirements in respect of securities), after "road" there shall be inserted "or other public place".
(5) In section 165(1)(b) (obligation to provide name and address and produce documents to constable), after "road" there shall be inserted "or other public place".
(6) In section 170 (duty to stop and report accident)—

(a) in subsection (1), after "road" there shall be inserted "or other public place",
(b) in subsection (1)(b)(iii), after "road" there shall be inserted "or other public place".

Signed by authority of the Secretary of State for the Environment, Transport and the Regions

Larry Whitty
Parliamentary Under Secretary of State, Department of the Environment, Transport and the Regions

**The Insurance Brokers Registration Council (Code of Conduct) Approval
Order 1994**

(1994 No. 2569)

Made	*October 1, 1994*
Laid before Parliament	*October 6, 1994*
Coming into force	*November 21, 1994*

The Secretary of State, in exercise of the powers conferred by sections 27(1) and 28(1) of the Insurance Brokers (Registration) Act 1977 and of all other powers enabling him in that behalf, hereby makes the following Order:

A12–46   **1.** This Order may be cited as the Insurance Brokers Registration Council (Code of Conduct) Approval Order 1994 and shall come into force on November 21, 1994.

A12–47   **2.** The Code of Conduct drawn up by the Insurance Brokers Registration Council pursuant to section 10 of the Insurance Brokers (Registration) Act 1977 as set out in the Schedule to this Order is hereby approved.

A12–48   **3.** The Insurance Brokers Registration Council (Code of Conduct) Approval Order 1978 is hereby revoked.

Neil Hamilton

Parliamentary Under-Secretary of State,
Department of Trade and Industry

Appendix 13

DEPARTMENT OF TRANSPORT MOTOR INSURERS' BUREAU—THE UNTRACED DRIVERS' AGREEMENT (COMPENSATION OF VICTIMS OF UNTRACED DRIVERS)

Text of an agreement dated the 14 June 1996 between the Secretary of State for Transport and Motor Insurers' Bureau together with some ntoes on its scope and purpose

The Agreement

Recitals

1. On April 21, 1969 the Minister of Transport and Motor Insurers' Bureau entered into an Agreement ("the First Agreement") to secure compensation for Third party victims of road accidents when the driver responsible for the accident could not be traced.   **A13–01**

2. The First Agreement was replaced by a new Agreement ("the Second Agreement") which operated in respect of accidents occurring on or after December 1, 1972.   **A13–02**

3. The Second Agreement was added to by a Supplemental Agreement dated December 7, 1977 ("the Third Agreement") which operated in respect of accidents occurring on or after January 3, 1978.   **A13–03**

4. The Second Agreement and the Third Agreement have now been replaced by a new Agreement ("this Agreement:) which operates in respect of accidents occurring on or after July 1, 1996.   **A13–04**

5. The text of this Agreement is as follows: **A13–05**

Text of the Agreement

An agreement made the Fourteenth day of June 1996 betwen the Secretary of State for Transport ("the Secretary of State") and the Motor Insurers' Bureau, whose registered office is at 152 Silbury Boulevard, Milton Keynes, MK9 1NB ("the M.I.B.").   **A13–06**

It is hereby agreed as follows:

1.—(1) Subject to paragraph (2) of this clause, this Agreement applies to any case in which an Application is made to the M.I.B. for a payment in respect of the death of or bodily injury to any person caused by or arising out of the use of a motor vehicle on a road in Great Britain and the case is one in which the following conditions are fulfilled, that is to say—   **A13–07**

(a) the event giving rise to the death of injury occurred on or after July 1, 1996;

(b) the applicant for the payment either:

    (i) is unable to trace any person responsible for the death or injury, or

    (ii) in a case to which Clause 5 applies where more than one person was responsible, is unable to trace one of those persons.

(Any person so untraced is referred to as "the untraced person");

(c) the death or injury was caused in such circumstances that on the balance of probabilities the untraced person would be liable to pay damages to the applicant in respect of the death or injury;

(d) the liability of the untraced person to pay damages to the applicant is one which is required to be covered by insurance or security under Part VI of the Road Traffic Act 1988 ("the 1988 Act"), it being assumed for this purpose, in the absence of evidence to the contrary, that the vehicle was being used in circumstances in which the user was required by the 1988 Act to be insured or secured against third party risks;

(e) the death or injury was not caused by the use of the vehicle by the untraced person in any deliberate attempt to cause the death or injury of the person in respect of which an application is made; and

(f) the application is made in writing within three years from the date of the event giving rise to the death or injury.

(g) the incident was reported to the police within fourteen days or as soon as the applicant reasonably could and the applicant co-operated with the police.

(2) This Agreement does not apply to a case in which—

(a) the death or bodily injury in respect of which any such application is made was caused by or arose out of the use of a motor vehicle which at the time of the event giving rise to the death or bodily injury was owned by or in the possession of the Crown, unless the case is one in which some other person has undertaken responsibility for the existence of a contract of insurance under the 1988 Act.

(b) at the time of the accident the person suffering death or bodily injury in respect of which the application is made was allowing himself to be carried in a vehicle and either before or after the commencement of his journey in the vehicle, if he could reasonably be expected to have alighted from the vehicle, he knew or had reason to believe that the vehicle:

    (i) had been stolen or unlawfully taken; or

    (ii) was being used without there being in force in relation to its use a contract of insurance which complied with the 1988 Act; or

    (iii) was being used in the course of furtherance of crime; or

    (iv) was being used as a means of escape from or avoidance of lawful apprehension.

(3) For the purpose of paragraph (2) of this Clause—

(a) a vehicle which has been unlawfully removed from the possession of the Crown shall be taken to continue in that possession whilst it is kept so removed;

(b) references to a person being carried in a vehicle include references to his being carried in or upon, or entering or getting on to or alighting from the vehicle;

(c) "owner" in relation to a vehicle which is the subject of a hiring agreement or a hire purchase agreement means the person in possession of the vehicle under that agreement.

2.—(1) An application to the MIB for a payment in respect of the death or bodily injury to any person may be made: **A13–08**

- (a) by the person for whose benefit that payment is to be made ("the applicant"); or
- (b) by any solicitor acting for the applicant; or
- (c) by any other person whom the MIB may be prepared to accept as acting for the applicant.

(2) Any decision made, or award or payment given or made or other thing done in accordance with this Agreement to or by a person acting under paragraph 1(b) and (1)(c) of this Clause on behalf of the applicant, or in relation to an application made by such a person, shall, whatever may be the age, or the circumstances affecting the capacity, of the applicant, be treated as having the same effect as if it had been done to or by, or in relation to an application made by, an applicant of full age and capacity.

3. Subject to the following provisions of this Agreement, the MIB shall, on any   **A13–09**
application made to it in a case to which this Agreement applies, award to the applicant in respect of the death or injury for which the application is made a payment of an amount which shall be assessed in like manner as a court, applying English law in a case where the event giving rise to the death or injury occurred in England or Wales or applying the law of Scotland in a case where that event occurred in Scotland, would assess the damages which the applicant would have been entitled to recover from the untraced person in respect of that death or injury if the applicant had brought successful proceedings to enforce a claim for such damages against the untraced person.

4. In assessing the level of an award in accordance with Clause 3, the MIB shall   **A13–10**
be under no obligation to include in such award any sum in respect of loss of earnings suffered by the applicant where and in so far as the applicant has in fact been paid wages or salary or any sum in lieu of the same, whether or not such payments were made subject to an undertaking on the part of the applicant to repay the same in the event of the applicant recovering damages.

5.—(1) This Clause applies to any case: **A13–11**

- (a) to which this Agreement applies; and
- (b) the death or bodily injury in respect of which an application has been made to the MIB under this Agreement ("the relevant death or injury") was caused:

  - (i) partly by the untraced person and partly by an identified person, or by identified persons; or
  - (ii) partly by the untraced person and partly by some other untraced person or persons whose master or principal can be identified; and

- (c) in circumstances making the identified person or persons or any master or principal ("the identified person") liable to the applicant in respect of the relevant death or injury.

(2) If in a case to which this Clause applies one or other of the conditions in paragraph (3) of this Clause is satisfied, the amount of the award to be paid by the MIB to the applicant in respect of the relevant death or injury shall be determined in accordance with paragraph (4) of this Clause and its liability to the applicant shall be subject to paragraph (7) of this Clause and Clause 6 of this Agreement.

(3) The conditions referred to in paragraph (2) of this Clause are:

- (a) that the applicant has obtained a judgment in respect of the relevant death or injury against the identified person ("the original judgment") which has not been satisfied in full within three months from the date on which the applicant became entitled to enforce it ("the three month period"); or

(b) that the applicant—

  (i) has not obtained and has not been required by the MIB to obtain a judgment in respect of the relevant death or injury against the identified person, and
  (ii) has not received any payment by way of compensation from the identified person or persons.

(4) The amount to be awarded by the MIB to the applicant in a case to which this Clause applies shall be determined as follows—

(a) if the condition in paragraph (3)(a) of this Clause is satisfied and the original judgment is wholly unsatisfied within the three month period, the amount to be awarded shall be an amount equal to that proportion of a full award attributable to the untraced person;

(b) if the condition in paragraph (3)(a) of this Clause is satisfied but the original judgment is satisfied in part only within the three month period, the amount to be awarded—

  (i) if the unsatisfied part of the original judgment is less than the proportion of a full award attributable to the untraced person, shall be an amount equal to that unsatisfied part, or
  (ii) if the unsatisfied part of the original judgment is equal to or greater than the proportion of a full award attributable to the untraced person, shall be an amount equal to the untraced person's proportion;

(c) if the condition in paragraph (3)(b) of this Clause is satisfied the amount to be awarded shall be an amount equal to the proportion of a full award attributable to the untraced person.

(5) The following provisions of this paragraph shall have effect in any case in which an appeal from or any proceeding to set aside the original judgment is commenced within a period of three months beginning on the date on which the applicant became entitled to enforce the original judgment—

(a) until the said appeal or proceeding is disposed of the provisions of this Clause shall have effect as if for the three month period there were substituted a period expiring on the date when the said appeal or proceeding is disposed of;

(b) if as a result of the appeal or proceeding the applicant ceases to be entitled to receive any payment in respect of the relevant death or injury from any person or persons against whom he has obtained the original judgment the provisions of this Clause shall have effect as if he had neither obtained nor been required by the MIB to obtain a judgment against any person or persons;

(c) if as a result of the appeal or proceeding, the applicant becomes entitled to recover an amount which differs from that which he was entitled to recover under the original judgment, the provisions of this Clause shall have effect as if for the reference in paragraph (3)(a) to the original judgment there were substituted a reference to the judgment under which the applicant became entitled to the said different amount;

(d) if as a result of the said appeal or proceeding the applicant remains entitled to enforce the original judgment the provisions of this Clause shall have effect as if for the three month period there were substituted a period of three months beginning on the date on which the appeal or other proceeding was disposed of.

The provisions of this paragraph shall apply also in any case where any judgment given upon any such appeal or proceeding is itself the subject of a further appeal or similar proceeding and shall apply in such a case in relation to that further appeal or proceeding in the same manner as they apply in relation to the first mentioned appeal or proceeding.

(6) In this Clause—

(a) "full award" means the amount which would have fallen to be awarded to the applicant under Clause 3 in respect of the relevant death or injury if the untraced person had been adjudged by a court to be wholly responsible for that death or injury; and

(b) "the proportion of a full award attributable to the untraced person" means that proportion of a full award which on the balance of probabilities would have been apportioned by a court in proceedings between the untraced person and any other person liable in respect of the same event as the share to be borne by the untraced person in the responsibility for the event giving rise to the reevant death or injury.

(7) The MIB shall not be under any liability in respect of the relevant death or injury if the applicant is entitled to receive compensation from the MIB in respect of that death or injury under any Agreement providing for the compensation of victims of uninsured drivers entered into between the Secretary of State and the MIB.

6.—(1) Any liability falling upon the MIB upon an application made to it under **A13–12** this Agreement in respect of any death or injury, shall be subject to the following conditions:

(a) the applicant shall give all such assistance as may reasonably be required by or on behalf of the MIB to enable any investigation to be carried out under this Agreement, including, in particular, the provision of statements and information either in writing, or, if so required, orally at an interview or interviews between the applicant and any person acting on behalf of the MIB;

(b) at any time before the MIB has communicated its decision upon the application to the applicant, the applicant shall, subject to the following provisions of this Clause, take all such steps as in the circumstances it is reasonable for the MIB to require him to take to obtain judgment against any person or persons in respect of their liability to the applicant for the death or injury as having caused or contributed to that death or injury or as being the master or principal of any person who has caused or contributed to that death or injury; and

(c) if required by the MIB the applicant shall assign to the MIB or to its nominee any judgment obtained by him (whether or not obtained in accordance with a requirement under subparagraph (b) of this paragraph) in respect of the death or injury to which his application to the MIB relates upon such terms as will secure that the MIB or its nominee shall be accountable to the applicant for any amount by which the aggregate of all sums recoved by the MIB or its nominee under the judgment (after deducting all reasonable expenses incurred in effecting such recovery) exceeds the amount payable by the MIB to the applicant under this Agreement in respect of that death or injury.

(2) If the MIB requires the applicant to bring proceedings against any specified person or persons—

(a) the MIB shall indemnify the applicant against all costs reasonably incurred by him in complying with that requirement unless the result of those proceedings materially contributes to establishing that the untraced person did not cause or contribute to the relevant death or injury; and

(b) the applicant shall, if required by the MIB and at its expense, provide the MIB with a transcript of any official shorthand note taken in those proceedings of any evidence given or judgment delivered therein.

(3) In the event of a dispute arising between the applicant and the MIB as to the reasonableness of any requirement by the MIB under paragraph (1)(b) of this Clause or as to whether any such costs as are referred to in paragraph (2)(a) of this Clause were reasonably incurred, that dispute shall be referred to the Secretary of State whose decision shall be final:

Provided that any dispute arising between the applicant and the MIB as to whether the MIB are required to indemnify him under paragraph (2)(a) of this Clause shall, in so far as it depends on the question whether the result of any proceedings which the MIB has required the applicant to bring against any specified person or persons has or has ot materially contributed to establish that the untraced person did not cause or contribute to the relevant death or injury, be referred to the arbitrator in accordance with the following provisions of this Agreement, whose decision on that question shall be final.

A13–13   7. The MIB shall cause any application made to it for a payment under this Agreement to be investigated and, unless it decides that the application should be rejected because of a preliminary investigation has disclosed that the case is not one to which this Agreement applies, it shall cause a report to be made on the application and on the basis of that report it shall decide whether to make an award and, if so, the amount of the award which shall be calculated in accordance with the provisions of this Agreement.

A13–14   8. The MIB may before coming to a decision on any application made to it under this Agreement request the applicant to provide it with a statutory declaration to be made by the applicant, setting out to the best of his knowledge, information and belief the facts and circumstances upon which his claim to an award under this Agreement are based, or facts and circumstances as may be specified by it.

A13–15   9.—(1) The MIB shall notify its decision to the applicant and when so doing shall—

(a) if the application is rejected because a preliminary investigation has disclosed that it it not one made in a case to which this Agreement applies, give its reasons for the rejection; or

(b) if the application has been fully investigated provide him with a statement setting out:

(i) the circumstances in which the death or injury occurred and the relevant evidence,

(ii) the circumstances relevant to the assessment of the amount to be awarded to the applicant under this Agreement and the relevant evidence, and

(iii) if it refuses to make an award, its reasons for that refusal; and

(c) in a case to which Clause 5 of this Agreement applies specify the way in which the amount of that award has been computed and its relation to those provisions of Clause 5 which are relevant to its computation.

(2) Where the MIB has decided that it will not indemnify the applicant against the costs of any proceedings which it has under Clause 6(1)(b) required him to bring against any specified person or persons on the ground that those proceedings have materially contributed to establish that the untraced person did not cause or contribute to the relevant death or injury, it shall give otice to the applicant with a copy of any transcript of any evidence given or judgment delivered in those proceedings as is mentioned in Clause 6(2)(b) hereof which it regards as relevant to that decision.

10.—(1) Subject to the provisions of this Agreement, where the MIB has decided to make an award to the applicant, it shall pay the applicant the amount of that award if: **A13–16**

    (a) it has been notified by the applicant that the award is accepted; or

    (b) at the expiration of the period during which the applicant may give notice of an appeal under Clause 11 the applicant has not given the MIB either any such notification of the acceptance of it's award or a notice of an appeal under Clause 11.

(2) Such payment as is made under paragraph (1) of this Clause shall discharge the MIB from all liability under this Agreement in respect of the death or injury for which that award has been made.

11.—(1) The applicant shall have a right of appeal to an arbitrator against any decision notified to him by the MIB under Clause 9 if: **A13–17**

    (a) he gives notice to the MIB, that he wishes to appeal against its decision ("the otice of appeal");

    (b) he gives the MIB the notice of appeal within 6 weeks from the date when he was given notice of the decision against which he wishes to appeal; and

    (c) he has not previously notified the MIB that he has accepted its decision.

(2) The grounds of appeal are as follows:

    (a) where the application has not been the subject of a full investigation:

        (i) that the case is one to which this Agreement applies, and

        (ii) that the applicant's application should be fully investigated by the MIB with a view to its deciding whether or not to make an award to him and, if so, the amount of that award; or

    (b) where the application has been fully investigated:

        (i) that the MIB was wrong in refusing to make an award, or

        (ii) that the amount it has awarded to the applicant is insufficient; or

    (c) in a case where a decision not to indemnify the applicant against the costs of any proceedings has been notified to the applicant by the MIB under Clause 9(2), that the decision was wrong.

12. A notice of appeal under Clause 11 shall state the grounds of the appeal and shall be accompanied by an undertaking given by the applicant or by the person acting on his behalf under Clause 2(1)(b) and 2(1)(c), that— **A13–18**

    (a) the applicant will accept the decision of the arbitrator; and

    (b) the arbitrator's fee shall be paid to the MIB by the applicant or by the person who has given the undertaking in any case where the MIB is entitled to reimbursement of that fee under the provisions of Clause 22.

A13–19   **13.**—(1) When giving notice of his appeal or at any time before doing so, the applicant may:

>   (a)   make comments to the MIB on its decision; and
>   (b)   supply it with such particulars as he thinks fit of any further evidence not contained in the written statement supplied to him by the MIB which he considers is relevant to the application.

(2) The MIB may, before submitting the applicant's appeal to the arbitrator;

>   (a)   cause an investigation to be made into the further evidence supplied by the applicant under paragraph (1)(b) of this Clause; and
>   (b)   report to the applicant the result of that investigation and of any change in its decision which may result from it.

(3) The applicant may, within six weeks from the date on which the report referred to in paragraph (2)(b) of this Clause was sent to him, unless he withdraws his appeal, make such comments on the report as he may desire to have submitted to the arbitrator.

A13–20   **14.**—(1) In a case where the MIB receives from the applicant a notice of appeal in which the only ground of appeal which is stated is that the amount awarded to the applicant is insufficient, before submitting that appeal to the arbitrator the MIB may:

>   (a)   give notice to the applicant that if the appeal proceeds it will request the arbitrator to decide whether the case is one in which the MIB should make an award at all; and
>   (b)   at the same time as complying with paragraph (1)(a) of this Clause provide the applicant with a statement setting out such comments as it may consider relevant to the decision which the arbitrator should come to on that question.

(2) Where the MIB gives the applicant notice under paragraph (1)(a) of this Clause, the applicant may, within six weeks from the date on which that notice is given:

>   (a)   make such comments to the MIB and supply it with particulars of other evidence not contained in any written statement provided to him by the MIB as he may consider relevant to the question which the arbitrator is by that notice requested to decide; and
>   (b)   Clause 13 shall apply in relation to any comments made or particulars supplied by the applicant under paragraph (2)(a) of this Clause.

A13–21   **15.**—(1) Subject to paragraph (2) of this Clause, where the MIB receives a notice of appeal from the applicant under the provisions of this Agreement, unless the appeal is previously withdrawn, it shall:

>   (a)   submit that appeal to an arbitrator for a decision; and
>   (b)   send to the arbitrator for the purpose of obtaining his decision:
>
>>   (i) the application made by the applicant;
>>   (ii) a copy of its decision as notified to the applicant; and
>>   (iii) copies of all statements, declarations, notices, undertakings, comments, transcripts, particulars of reports provided, given or sent to the MIB under this Agreement either by the applicant or any person acting for him under Clause 2(1)(b) or 2(1)(c) by the MIB.

(2) In a case where the MIB causes an investigation to be made under Clause 13, the MIB shall not comply with paragraph (1) of this Clause until:

(a) the expiration of six weeks from the date on which it sent the applicant a report as to the result of that investigation; or

(b) the expiration of six weeks from the date on which it gave the applicant notice under Clause 14(1); or

(c) the expiration of six weeks from the date on which it sent the applicant a report as to the result of that investigation, if it has caused an investigation to be made into any evidence supplied under Clause 14(2).

16. On an appeal made by the applicant in accordance with this Agreement: **A13–22**

(a) if the appeal is against a decision by the MIB rejecting an application because a preliminary investigation has disclosed that the case is not one to which this Agreement applies, the arbitrator shall decide whether the case is or is not one to which this Agreement applies and, if he decides that it is such a case, shall remit the application to the MIB for full investigation and a decision in accordance with the provisions of this Agreement;

(b) if the appeal is against a decision by the MIB given after an application has been fully investigated by it (whether before the appeal or in consequence of its being remitted for such investigation under paragraph (a) of this Clause) the arbitrator shall decide, as may be appropriate, having regard to the grounds stated in the otice of appeal and to any notice given by the MIB to the applicant under Clause 14, whether the MIB should make an award under this Agreement to the applicant and, if so, the amount which it should award to the applicant under the provisions of this Agreement.

(c) if the appeal relates to a dispute which has arisen between the applicant and the MIB which is required by the proviso to Clause 6(3) to be referred to the arbitrator, the arbitrator shall also give his decision on that dispute.

Provided that where the arbitrator has allowed an appeal under paragraph (a) of this Clause all the provisions of this Agreement shall apply as if the case were an application to which this Agreement applies upon which the MIB had not communicated a decision.

17.—(1) Subject to paragraph (2) of this Clause, the arbitrator shall decide the **A13–23** appeal on the documents submitted to him under Clause 15(1)(b) and no further evidence shall be produced to him:

(2) The following shall apply where documents have been submitted to the arbitrator under Clause 15(1)(b):

(a) the arbitrator shall be entitled to ask the MIB to make any further investigation which he considers desirable and to submit a written report of its findings to him for his consideration; and

(b) the MIB shall send a copy of that report to the applicant who shall be entitled to submit written comments on it to the MIB within four weeks of the date on which that copy is sent to him; and

(c) the MIB shall transmit those comments to the arbitrator for his consideration.

18. The arbitrator by whom an appeal made by an applicant in accordance with **A13–24** the provisions of this Agreement shall be considered shall be an arbitrator to be selected by the Secretary of State from two panels of Queen's Counsel appointed respectively by the Lord Chancellor and the Lord Advocate for the purpose of determining appeals under this Agreement, the arbitrator to be selected from the panel appointed by the Lord Chancellor in cases where the event giving rise to the death or injury occurred in England or Wales and from the panel appointed by the Lord Advocate where that event occurred in Scotland.

A13–25   **19.** The arbitrator shall notify his decision on any appeal under this Agreement to the MIB and the MIB shall forthwith send a copy of the Arbitrator's decision to the applicant.

A13–26   **20.** Subject to the provisions of this Agreement, the MIB shall pay the applicant any amount which the arbitrator has decided shall be awarded to hi, and that payment shall discharge the MIB from all liability under this Agreement in respect of the death or injury in respect of which that decision has been given.

A13–27   **21.** Each party to the appeal will bear their own costs.

A13–28   **22.** The MIB shall pay the arbitrator a fee approved by the Lord Chancellor or the Lord Advocate, as the case may be, after consultation with the MIB.

Provided that, in any case where it appears to the arbitrator that there were no reasonable grounds for the appeal, the arbitrator may in his discretion decide:

    (a)   that his fee ought to be paid by the applicant; and

    (b)   that the person giving the undertaking required by Clause 12 shall be liable to reimburse the MIB the amount of the fee paid by it to the arbitrator, except in so far as that amount is deducted by the MIB from any amount which it is liable to pay to the applicant in consequence of the decision of the arbitrator.

A13–29   **23.** If in any case it appears to the MIB that by reason of the applicant being under the age of majority or of any other circumstances affecting his capacity to manage his affairs it would be in the applicant's interest that all or some part of the amount which would otherwise be payable to him under an award made under this Agreement should be administered for him by the Family Welfare Association or by some other body or person under a trust or by the Court of Protection (or in Scotland by the appointment of a Judicial Factor) the MIB may establish for that purpose a trust of the whole or part of the amount to take effect for a period and under provisions as may appear to it to be appropriate in the circumstances of the case or may initiate or cause any other person to initiate process in that Court and otherwise cause any amount payable under the award to be paid to and administered thereby.

A13–30   **24.** In any case in which an application has been made to the MIB under Clause 2(1) and in which a preliminary investigation under Clause 7 has disclosed that the case is one to which the Agreement, save for Clause 5, applies, the MIB may, instead of causing a report to be made on the application as provided by Clause 7, make, or cause to be made, to the applicant an offer to settle his application in a specified sum, assessed in accordance with Clause 3.

A13–31   **25.** Where an offer is made under Clause 24, there shall be provided to the applicant (at the same time) in writing particulars of:

    (a)   the circumstances in which the death or injury occurred and the relevant evidence, and

    (b)   the circumstances relevant to the assessment of the amount to be awarded to the applicant and the relevant evidence.

A13–32   **26.**—(1) On receipt by the MIB or its agent of an acceptance of the offer referred to in Clause 24:

    (a)   this acceptance shall have effect in relation to the application as if in Clause 7 the words "and, unless the MIB decide" to the end of that Clause, and Clauses 9 to 22 inclusive were omitted; and

    (b)   the MIB shall pay to the applicant the amount specified in the offer.

(2) The payment made by the MIB under paragraph (1)(b) of this Clause shall discharge it from all liability under this Agreement in respect of the death or injury for which the payment has been made.

27. This Agreement may be determined at any time by the Secretary of State or by the MIB by either of them giving to the other not less than twelve months previous notice in writing.

Provided that this Agreement shall continue to have effect in any case where the event giving rise to the death or injury occurred before the date on which this Agreement terminates in accordance with any notice so given.

A13–33

28. From June 14, 1996 the following periods of operation shall apply:

A13–34

    (a) this Agreement shall come into operation on July 1, 1996 in relation to accidents occurring on or after that date;

    (b) the Second Agreement shall cease and determine except in relation to applications arising out of accidents which occurred on or after December 1, 1972 and before the January 3, 1978; and

    (c) the Third Agreement shall cease and determine except in relation to accidents occurring on or after January 3, 1978 and before the July 1, 1996.

In witness whereof the Secretary of State for Transport has caused his Corporate Seal to be hereto affixed and the Motor Insurers' Bureau has caused its Common Seal to be hereto affixed the day and year first above written.

A13–35

THE CORPORATE SEAL of
the Secretary of State for Transport
hereunto affixed is authenticated by:

THE COMMON SEAL of
The Motor Insurers' Bureau
was hereunto affixed in the
presence of

....

....

Directors of the Board of Management

Secretary

NOTES

The following Notes are for the guidance of those who may wish to make application to the Motor Insurers' Bureau for payment under the Agreement, and for the guidance of their legal advisers, but they must not be taken as making unnecessary a careful study of the Agreement itself. Communications connected with the Agreement should be addressed to the Motor Insurers' Bureau ("the MIB"), whose address in 152 Silbury Boulevard, Central Milton Keynes, MK9 1NB

A13–36

1. This Agreement replaces a previous one dated November 22, 1972 and a Supplemental Agreement dated December 7, 1977 and continues the arrangements which have existed since 1946 under which the MIB has made ex gratia payments in respect of death or personal injuries resulting from the use of the road of a motor vehicle the owner or driver of which cannot be traced. Provision is made for an appeal against the MIB's decision in such cases.

A13–37

2. The Agreement dated November 22, 1972 applies to a death or bodily injury arising out of an accident occurring on a road in Great Britain on or after December 1, 1972 and before January 3, 1978. The Agreement dated November 22, 1972 as supplemented by the Supplemental Agreement dated January 7, 1977 applies in relation to accidents occurring on or after January 3, 1978 and before July 1, 1996. This Agreement applies in relation to accidents occurring on or after July 1, 1996.

A13–38

3. Subject to the terms of the Agreement, the MIB will accept applications for a payment in respect of the death of, or bodily injury to any person resulting from the use of a motor vehicle on a road in Great Britain in any cases in which—

A13–39

    (a) the applicant for the payment cannot trace any person responsible for the death or injury (or, in certain circumstances, a person partly responsible) (Clause 1(1)(b)); and

    (b)   the death or injury was caused in such circumstances that the untraced person would be liable to pay damages to the applicant in respect of the death or injury (Clause 1(1)(c)); and

    (c)   the untraced person's liability to the applicant is one which at the time the accident occurred, was required to be covered by insurance or security (Clause 1(1)(d)).

The MIB will not deal with the following:

    (a)   deliberate "running down" cases (Clause 1(1)(e));
    (b)   certain other cases relating to Crown vehicles; and
    (c)   certain categories of "voluntary" passenger (Clause 1(2)–(4)).

A13–40   **4.** Applications for a payment under the Agreement must be made in writing to the MIB within 3 years of the date of the accident giving rise to the death or injury (Clause 1(1)(f)).

A13–41   **5.** Under Clause 3, the amount which the MIB will award will (except for the exclusin of those elements of damages mentioned in Clause 4) be assessed in the same way as a Court would have assessed the amount of damages payable by the untraced person had the applicant been able to bring a successful claim for damages against him.

A13–42   **6.** Clause 5 relates to cases where an untraced person and an identified person are each partly responsible for a death or injury, and defines the conditions under which the MIB will in such cases make a contribution in respect of the responsibility of the untraced person.

A13–43   **7.** Under Clause 6(1)(b), the MIB may require the applicant to bring proceedings against any identified person who may be responsible for the death or injury, subject to indemnifying the applicant as to his costs as provided in Clause 6(2) and (3).

A13–44   **8.** On receipt of an application, the MIB will, if satisfied that the application comes within the terms of the Agreement, investigate the circumstances and, when this has been done, decide whether to make a payment and, if so, how much (Clause 7).

A13–45   **9.** The MIB may request the applicant to make a statutory declaration setting out all, or some, of the facts on which his application is based (Clause 8).

A13–46   **10.** The MIB may notify the applicant of its decision, setting out the circumstances of the case and the evidence on which it bases its decision and, if it refuses to make a payment, the reasons for the refusal (Clause 9).

A13–47   **11.** If the applicant wishes to appeal against the decision on the grounds specified in Clause 11(2), he must notify the MIB within six weeks of being notified of the decision, and he or any person acting on his behalf shall give the undertakings set out in Clause 12.

A13–48   **12.** The MIB may, as a result of the comments made and further evidence submitted by the applicant on its decision, investigate the further evidence, and if so it will communicate with the applicant again. In such a case the applicant will have six weeks from the date of that further communication in which to decide whether or not to go on with the appeal (Clause 13).

A13–49   **13.** Where the applicant appeals only on the grounds that the amount awarded to him is too low, the MIB may give him notice that if the matter proceeds to appeal, it will ask the arbitrator to decide also the issue of the MIB's liability to make any payment. The applicant will have six weeks from the date of any such notice in which to comment to the MIB on this intention (Clause 14.).

A13–50   **14.** Appeals will be decided by an arbitrator who will be a Queen's Counsel selected by the Secretary of State for Transport from one of two panels to be appointed by the Lord Chancellor and the Lord Advocate respectively (Clause 18).

A13–51   **15.** All appeals will be decided by the arbitrator on the basis of the relevant documents (as set out in Clause 15) which will be sent to him by the MIB. If the arbitrator asks the MIB to make a further investigation, the applicant will have an opportunity to comment on the result of that investigation (Clause 17).

16. The arbitrator may, at his descretion, award the cost of this fee against the applicant if he considers the appeal unreasonable; otherwise, each party to the appeal will bear their own costs, the MIB paying the arbitrator's fee (Clause 21 and 22).   **A13–52**

17. In certain circumstances, the MIB may establish a trust for the benefit of an applicant of the whole or part of any award (Clause 23).   **A13–53**

18. Clauses 24 to 26 provide for the use of a shorter form of procedure than that stipulated in Clause 7 with the object of securing speedier disposal of certain applications to the MIB. The MIB may, at its discretion, make an offer of an award in a specified sum providing the applicant at the same time with particulars of the circumstances of the case and of the evidence on which the offer is based. If the applicant is prepared to accept the offer, thus undertaking, on payment by the MIB, to forego any right of appeal to an arbitrator, the MIB will pay the sum offered forthwith. If the offer is not acceptable the application will thereafter be dealt with in accordance with the full procedure set out in the Agreement.   **A13–54**

The shorter form of procedure does not apply in a case where both an untraced person and an identified person may each partly be responsible for injuries giving rise to an application to the MIB.

MOTOR INSURERS' BUREAU—
COMPENSATION OF VICTIMS OF
UNINSURED DRIVERS

A13–55   Text of an Agreement dated August 13, 1999 between the Secretary of State for
the Environment, Transport and the REgions and Motor Insurers' Bureau
together with some notes on its scope and purpose.
       This agreement is made the thirteenth day of August 1999 between the Secretary
of State for the Secretary of State for the Environment, Transport and the Regions
(hereinafter referred to as "the Secretary of State") and the Motor Insurers'
Bureau, whose registered office is at 152 Silbury Boulevard, Milton Keynes MK9
1NB (hereinafter referred to as "MIB") and is supplemental to an Agreement
(hereinafter called "the Principal Agreement") made the 31st Day of December
1945 between the Minister of War Transport and the insurers transacting compulsory motor insurance business in Great Britain by or on behalf of whom the
said Agreement was signed and in pursuance of paragraph 1 of which MIB was
incorporated.

IT IS HEREBY AGREED AS FOLLOWS

Interpretation

General definitions

A13–56   1. In this Agreement, unless the context otherwise requires, the following
expressions have the following meanings—

"1988 Act" means the Road Traffic Act 1988;

"1988 Agreement" means the Agreement made on 21 December 1988 between the
       Secretary of State for Transport and MIB;

"bank holiday" means a day which is, or is to be observed as, a bank holiday under
       the Banking and Financial Dealings Act 1971;

"claimant" means a person who has commenced or who proposes to commence
       relevant proceedings and has made an application under this Agreement in
       respect thereof;

"contract of insurance" means a policy of insurance or a security covering a rele-
       vant liability;

"insurer" includes the giver of a security;

"MIB's obligation" means the obligation contained in clause 5;

"property" means any property whether real, heritable or personal;

"relevant liability" means a liability in respect of which a contract of insurance must be in force to comply with Part VI of the 1988 Act;

"relevant proceedings" means proceedings in respect of a relevant liability (and "commencement", in relation to such proceedings means, in England and Wales, the date on which a Claim Form or other originating process is issued by a Court or, in Scotland, the date on which the originating process is served on the Defender);

"relevant sum" means a sum payable or remaining payable under an unsatisfied judgment, including—

 (a) an amount payable or remaining payable in respect of interest on that sum, and

 (b) either the whole of the costs (whether taxed or not) awarded by the Court as part of that judgment or, where the judgment includes an award in respect of a liability which is not a relevant liability, such proportion of those costs as the relevant liability bears to the total sum awarded under the judgment;

"specified excess" means £300 or such other sum as may from time to time be agreed in writing between the Secretary of State and MIB;

"unsatisfied judgment" means a judgment or order (by whatever name called) in respect of a relevant liability which has not been satisfied in full within seven days from the date upon which the claimant became entitled to enforce it.

Meaning of references

2.—(1) Save as otherwise herein provided, the Interpretation Act 1978 shall apply for the interpretation of this Agreement as it applies for the interpretation of an Act of Parliament. **A13–57**

(2) Where, under this Agreement, something is required to be done—

 (a) within a specified period after or from the happening of a particular event, the period begins on the day after the happening of that event;

 (b) within or not less than a specified period before a particular event, the period ends on the day immediately before the happening of that event.

(3) Where, apart from this paragraph, the period in question, being a period of seven days or less, would include a Saturday, Sunday or bank holiday or Christmas Day or Good Friday, that day shall be excluded.

(4) Save where expressly otherwise provided, a reference in this Agreement to a numbered clause is a reference to the clause bearing that number in this Agreement and a reference to a numbered paragraph is a reference to a paragraph bearing that number in the clause in which the reference occurs.

(5) In this Agreement

 (a) a reference (however framed) to the doing of any act or thing by or the happening of any event in relation to the claimant includes a reference to the doing of that act or thing by or the happening of that even In relation to a Solicitor or other person acting on his behalf, and

 (b) a requirement to give notice to, or to serve documents upon, MIB or an insurer mentioned in clause 9(1)(a) shall be satisfied by the giving of the notice to, or the service of the documents upon, a Solicitor acting on its behalf in the manner provided for.

Claimants not of full age or capacity

A13–58   3. Where, under and in accordance with this Agreement—

    (a)   any act or thing is done to or by a Solicitor or other person acting on behalf of a claimant,

    (b)   any decision is made by or in respect of a Solicitor or other person acting on behalf of a claimant, or

    (c)   any sum is paid to a Solicitor or other person acting on behalf of a claimant, then, whatever may be the age or other circumstances affecting the capacity of the claimant, that act, thing, decision or sum shall be treated as if it had been done to or by, or made in respect of or paid to a claimant of full age and capacity.

Principal Terms

Duration of Agreement

A13–59   4.—(1) This Agreement shall come into force on October 1, 1999 in relation to accidents occurring on or after that date and, save as provided by clause 23, the 1988 Agreement shall cease and determine immediately before that date.

(2) This Agreement may be determined by the Secretary of State or by MIB giving to the other not less than twelve months' notice in writing but without prejudice to its continued operation in respect of accidents occurring before the date of termination.

MIB's obligation to satisfy compensation claims

A13–60   5.—(1) Subject to clauses 6 to 17, if a claimant has obtained against any person in a Court in Great Britain a judgment which is an unsatisfied judgment then MIB will pay the relevant sum to, or to the satisfaction of, the claimant or will cause the same to be so paid.

(2) Paragraph (1) applies whether or not the person liable to satisfy the judgment is in fact covered by a contract of insurance and whatever may be the cause of his failure to satisfy the judgment.

Exceptions to Agreement

A13–61   6.—(1) Clause 5 does not apply in the case of an application made in respect of a claim of any of the following descriptions (and, where part only of a claim satisfies such a description, clause 5 does not apply to that part)

    (a)   a claim arising out of a relevant liability incurred by the user of a vehicle owned by or in the possession of the Crown, unless—

       (i)   responsibility for the existence of a contract of insurance under Part VI of the 1988 Act in relation to that vehicle had been undertaken by some other person (whether or not the person liable was in fact covered by a contract of insurance), or

      (ii)   the relevant liability was in fact covered by a contract of insurance;

    (b)   a claim arising out of the use of a vehicle which is not required to be covered by a contract of insurance by virtue of section 144 of the 1988 Act, unless the use is in fact covered by such a contract;

    (c)   a claim by, or for the benefit of, a person ("the beneficiary") other than the person suffering death, injury or other damage which is made either—

    (i)   in respect of a cause of action or a judgment which has been assigned to the beneficiary, or

    (ii) pursuant to a right of subrogation or contractual or other right belonging to the beneficiary;

(d) a claim in respect of damage to a motor vehice or losses arising there from where, at the time when the damage to it was sustained—

    (i)   there was not in force in relation to the use of that vehicle such a contract of insurance as is required by Part VI of the 1988 Act, and

    (ii) the claimant either knew or ought to have known that that was the case;

(e) a claim which is made in respect of a relevant liability described in paragraph (2) by a claimant who, at the time of the use giving rise to the relevant liability was voluntarily allowing himself to be carried in the vehicle and, either before the commencement of his journey in the vehicle or after such commencement if he could reasonably be expected to have alighted from it, knew or ought to have known that—

    (i)   the vehicle had been stolen or unlawfully taken

    (ii) the vehicle was being used without there being in force in relation to its use such a contract of insurance as would comply with Part VI of the 1988 Act,

    (iii) the vehicle was being used in the course of furtherance of a crime, or

    (iv) the vehicle was being used as a means of escape from, or avoidance of, lawful apprehension.

(2) The relevant liability referred to in paragraph (1)(e) is a liability incurred by the owner or registered keeper or a person using the vehicle in which the claimant was being carried.

(3) The burden of proving that the claimant knew or ought to have known of any matter set out in paragraph (1)(e) shall be on MIB but, in the absence of evidence to the contrary, proof by MIB of any of the following matters shall be taken as proof of the claimant's knowledge of the matter set out in paragraph (1)(e)(ii)—

(a) that the claimant was the owner or registered keeper of the vehicle or had caused or permitted its use;

(b) that the claimant knew the vehicle was being used by a person who was below the minimum age at which he could be granted a licence authorising the driving of a vehicle of that class;

(c) that the claimant knew that the person driving the vehicle was disqualified for holding or obtaining a driving licence;

(d) that the claimant knew that the user of the vehicle was neither its owner nor registered keeper nor an employee of the owner or registered keeper nor the owner or registered keeper of any other vehicle.

(4) Knowledge which the claimant has or ought to have for the purposes of paragraph (1)(e) includes knowledge of matters which he could reasonably be expected to have been aware of had he not been under the self-induced influence of drink or drugs.

(5) For the purposes of this clause—

(a) a vehicle which has been unlawfully removed from the possession of the Crown shall be taken to continue in that possession whilst it is kept so removed,

(b) references to a person being carried in a vehicle include references to his being carried upon, entering, getting on to and alighting from the vehicle, and

(c)   "owner", in relation to a vehicle which is the subject of a hiring agreement or a hire-purchase agreement, means the person in possession of the vehicle under that agreement.

Conditions Precedent to MIB's Obligation

Form of application

A13–62   7.—(1) MIB shall incur no liability under MIB's obligation unless an application is made to the person specified in clause 9(1)—

(a)   in such form,
(b)   giving such information about the relevant proceedings and other matters relevant to this Agreement, and
(c)   accompanied by such documents as MIB may reasonably require.

(2) Where an application is signed by a person who is neither the claimant nor a Solicitor acting on his behalf MIB may refuse to accept the application (and shall incur no liability under MIB's obligation) until it is reasonably satisfied that, having regard to the status of the signatory and his relationship to the claimant, the claimant is fully aware of the contents and effect of the application but subject thereto MIB shall not refuse to accept such an application by reason only that it is signed by a person other than the claimant or his Solicitor.

Service of notices, etc.

A13–63   8. Any notice required to be given or documents to be supplied to MIB pursuant to clauses 9 to 12 of this Agreement shall be sufficiently given or supplied only if sent by facsimile transmission or by Registered or Recorded Delivery post to MIB's registered office for the time being and delivery shall be proved by the production of a facsimilie transmission report produced by the sender's facsimile machine or an appropriate postal receipt.

Notice of relevant proceedings

A13–64   9.—(1) MIB shall incur no liability under MIB's obligation unless proper notice of the bringing of the relevant proceedings has been given by the claimant not later than fourteen days after the commencement of those proceedings—

(a)   in the case of proceedings in respect of a relevant liability which is covered by a contract of insurance with an insurer whose identity can be ascertained, to that insurer;
(b)   in any other case, to MIB.

(2) In this clause "proper notice" means, except in so far as any part of such information or any copy document or other thing has already been supplied under clause 7—

(a)   notice in writing that proceedings have been commenced by Claim Form, Writ, or other means,
(b)   a copy of the sealed Claim Form, Writ or other official document providing evidence of the commencement of the proceedings and, in Scotland, a statement of the means of service,
(c)   a copy or details of any insurance policy providing benefits in the case of the death, bodily injury or damage to property to which the proceedings relate where the claimant is the insured party and the benefits are available to him,

(d)   copies of all correspondence in the possession of the claimant or (as the case may be) his Solicitor or agent to or from the Defendant or the Defender or (as the case may be) his Solicitor, insurers or agent which is relevant to—

     (i)   the death, bodily injury or damage for which the Defendant or Defender is alleged to be responsible, or

     (ii) any contract of insurance which covers, or which may or has been alleged to cover, liability for such death, injury or damage the benefit of which is, or is claimed to be, available to Defendant or Defender,

(e)   subject to paragraph (3), a copy of the Particulars of Claim whether or not indorsed on the Claim Form, Writ or other originating process, and whether or not served (in England and Wales) on any Defendant or (in Scotland) on any Defender, and

(f)   a copy of all other documents which are required under the appropriate rules of procedure to be served on a Defendant or Defender with the Claim Form, Writ or other originating process or with the Particulars of Claim,

(g)   such other information about the relevant proceedings as MIB may reasonably specify.

(3) If, in the case of proceedings commenced in England or Wales, the Particulars of Claim (including any document required to be served therewith) has not yet been served with the Claim Form or other originating process paragraph (2)(e) shall be sufficiently complied with if a copy thereof is served on MIB not later than seven days after it is served on the Defendant.

Notice of service of proceedings

10.—(1) This clause applies where the relevant proceedings are commenced in England or Wales.   **A13–65**

(2) MIB shall incur no liability under MIB's obligation unless the claimant has, not later than the appropriate date, given notice in writing to the person specified in clause 9(1) of the date of service of the Claim Form or other originating process in the relevant proceedings.

(3) In this clause, "the appropriate date" means the day falling—

(a)   seven days after—

     (i)   the date when the claimant receives notification from the Court that service of the Claim Form or other originating process has occurred,

     (ii) the date when the claimant receives notification from the Defendant that service of the Claim Form or other originating process has occurred, or

     (iii) the date of personal service, or

(b)   fourteen days after the date when service is deemed to have occurred in accordance with the Civil Procedure Rules, whichever of those days occurs first.

Further information

11.—(1) MIB shall incur no liability under MIB's obligation unless the claimant has, not later than seven days after the occurrence of any of the following events, namely—   **A13–66**

(a)   the filing of a defence in the relevant proceedings,

(b)   any amendment to the Particulars of Claim or any amendment of or addition to any schedule or other document required to be served therewith, and

(c) either—

    (i) the setting down of the case for trial, or

    (ii) where the court gives notice to the claimant of the trial date, the date when that notice is received, given notice in writing of the date of that event to the person specified in clause 9(1) and has, in the case of the filing of a defence or an amendment of the Particulars of Claim or any amendment of or addition to any schedule or other document required to be served therwith, supplied a copy thereof to that person.

(2) MIB shall incur no liability under MIB's obligation unless the claimant furnishes to the person specified in clause 9(1) within a reasonable time after being required to do so such further information and documents in support of his claim as MIB may reasonably require notwithstanding that the claimant may have complied with clause 7(1).

Notice of intention to apply for judgment

A13–67   **12.**—(1) MIB shall incur no liability under MIB's obligation unless the claimant has, after commencement of the relevant proceedings and not less than thirty-five days before the appropriate date, given notice in writing to the person specified in clause 9(1) of his intention to apply for or to sign judgment in the relevant proceedings.

(2) In this clause, "the appropriate date" means the date when the application for judgment is made or, as the case may be, the signing of judgment occurs.

Section 154 of the 1988 Act

A13–68   **13.** MIB shall incur no liability under MIB's obligation unless the claimant has as soon as reasonably practicable—

(a) demanded the information and, where appropriate, the particulars specified in section 154(1) of the 1988 Act, and

(b) if the person of whom the demand is made fails to comply with the provisions of that subsection—

    (i) made a formal complaint to a police officer in respect of such failure, and

    (ii) used all reasonable endeavours to obtain the name and address of the registered keeper of the vehicle or, if so required by MIB, has authorised MIB to take such steps on his behalf.

Prosecution of proceedings

A13–69   **14.** MIB shall incur no liability under MIB's obligation—

(a) unless the claimant has, if so required by MIB and having been granted a full indemnity by MIB as to costs, taken all reasonable steps to obtain judgment against every person who may be liable (including any person who may be vicariously liable) in respect of the injury or death or damage to property, or

(b) if the claimant, upon being requested to do so by MIB, refuses to consent to MIB being joined as a party to the relevant proceedings.

Assignment of judgment and undertakings

A13–70   **15.** MIB shall incur no liability under MIB's obligation unless the claimant has—

(a) assigned to MIB or its nominee the unsatisfied judgment, whether or not that judgment includes an amount in respect of a liability other than a relevant liability, and any order for costs made in the relevant proceedings, and

(b) undertaken to repay to MIB any sum paid to him—

    (i) by MIB in discharge of MIB's obligation if the judgment is subsequently set aside either as a whole or in respect of the part of the relevant liability to which that sum relates;

    (ii) by any other person by way of compensation or benefit for the death, bodily injury or other damage to which the relevant proceedings relate, including a sum which would have been deductible under the provisions of clause 17 if it had been received before MIB was obliged to satisfy MIB's obligation.

Limitations on MIB's Liability

Compensation for damage to property

16.—(1) Where a claim under this Agreement includes a claim in respect of   **A13–71**
damage to property, MIB's obligation in respect of that part of the relevant sum which is awarded for such damage and any losses arising therefrom (referred to in this clause as "the property damage compensation") is limited in accordance with the following paragraphs.

(2) Where the property damage compensation does not exceed the specified excess, MIB shall incur no liability.

(3) Where the property damage compensation in respect of any one accident exceeds the specified excess but does not exceed £250,000, MIB shall incur liability less the specified excess.

(4) Where the property damage compensation in respect of any one accident exceeds £250,000, MIB shall incur liability only in respect of the sum of £250,000 less the specified excess.

Compensation received from other sources

17. Where a claimant has received compensation from—   **A13–72**

(a) the Policyholders Protection Board under the Policyholders Protection Act 1975, or

(b) an insurer under an insurance agreement or arrangement, or

(c) any other source,

in respect of the death, bodily injury or other damage to which the relevant proceedings relate and such compensation has not been taken into account in the calculation of the relevant sum MIB may deduct from the relevant sum, in addition to any sum deductible under clause 16, an amount equal to that compensation.

Miscellaneous

Notification of decisions by MIB

18. Where a claimant—   **A13–73**

(a) has made an application in accordance with clause 7, and

(b) has given to the person specified in clause 9(1) proper notice of the relevant proceedings in accordance with clause 9(2),

MIB shall—

    (i) give a reasoned reply to any request made by the claimant relating to the payment of compensation in pursuance of MIB's obligation, and

(ii)   as soon as reasonably practicable notify the claimant in writing of its decision regarding the payment of the relevant sum, together with the reasons for that decision.

Reference of disputes to the Secretary of State

A13–74   **19.**—(1) In the event of any dispute as to the reasonableness of a requirement made by MIB for the supply of information or documentation or for the taking of any step by the claimant, it may be referred by the claimant or MIB to the Secretary of State whose decision shall be final.

(2) Where a dispute is referred to the Secretary of State—

(a)   MIB shall supply the Secretary of State and, if it has not already done so, the claimant with notice in writing of the requirement from which the dispute arises, together with the reasons for that requirement and such further information as MIB considers relevant, and

(b)   where the dispute is referred by the claimant, the claimant shall supply the Secretary of State and, if he has not already done so, MIB with notice in writing of the grounds on which he disputes the reasonableness of the requirement.

Recoveries

A13–75   **20.** Nothing in this Agreement shall prevent an insurer from providing by conditions in a contract of insurance that all sums paid by the insurer or by MIB by virtue of the Principal Agreement or this Agreement in or towards the discharge of the liability of the insured shall be recoverable by them or by the MIB from the insured or from any other person.

Apportionment of damages, etc.

A13–76   **21.**—(1) Where an unsatisfied judgment which includes an amount in respect of a liability other than a relevant liability has been assigned to MIB or its nominee in pursuance of clause 15 MIB shall—

(a)   apportion any sum it receives in satisfaction or partial satisfaction of the judgment according to the proportion which the damages awarded in respect of the relevant liability bear to the damages awarded in respect of the other liability, and

(b)   account to the claimant in respect of the moneys received properly apportionable to the other liability.

(2) Where the sum received includes an amount in respect of interest or an amount awarded under an order for costs, the interest or the amount received in pursuance of the order shall be dealt with in the manner provided in paragraph (1).

Agents

A13–77   **22.** MIB may perform any of its obligations under this agreement by agents.

Transitional provisions

A13–78   **23.**—(1) The 1988 Agreement shall continue in force in relation to claims arising out of accidents occurring before October 1, 1999 with the modifications contained in paragraph (2).

(2) In relation to any claim made under the 1988 Agreement after this Agreement has come into force, the 1988 Agreement shall apply as if there were inserted after clause 6 thereof

"6A. Where any person in whose favour a judgment In respect of a relevant liability has been made has—

(a) made a claim under this Agreement, and

(b) satisfied the requirements specified in clause 5 hereof,

MIB shall, if requested to do so, give him a reasoned reply regarding the satisfaction of that claim".

In witness whereof the Secretary of State has caused his Corporate Seal to be hereunto affixed and the Motor Insurers' Bureau has caused its Common Seal to be hereunto affixed the day and year first above written.

THE CORPORATE SEAL of the SECRETARY OF STATE FOR THE ENVIRONMENT TRANSPORT AND THE REGIONS hereunto affixed is authenticated by:

Authorised by the Secretary of State

THE COMMON SEAL of the MOTOR INSURERS' Bureau was hereunto affixed in the presence of:

Directors of the Board of Management
Secretary

Notes for the Guidance of Victims of Road Traffic Accidents

The following notes are for the guidance of anyone who may have a claim on the Motor Insurers' Bureau under this Agreement and their legal advisers. They are not part of the Agreement, their purpose being to deal in ordinary language with the situations which most readily occur. They are not in any way a substitute for reading and applying the terms of this or any other relevant Agreement, nor are they intended to control or influence the legal interpretation of the Agreement. These notes vary from the original as they have been updated to reflect recent developments. Any enquiries, requests for application forms and general correspondence In connection with the Agreement should be addressed to:

A13–79

Motor Insurers Bureau
152 Silbury Boulevard
Central Milton Keynes
Milton Keynes
MK9 1NB
Tel: 01908 830001
Fax: 01908 671681
DX: 84753 Milton Keynes 3

1. Introduction—MIB's role and application of the Agreement

1.1 The role of MIB under this Agreement is to provide a safety net for innocent victims of drivers who have been identified but are uninsured. MIB's funds for this purpose are obtained from levies charged upon insurers and so come from the premiums which are charged by those insurers to members of the public.

1.2 MIB has entered into a series of Agreements with the Secretary of State and his predecessors in office. Under each Agreement MIB undertakes obligations to pay defined compensation in specific circumstances. There are two sets of Agreements, one relating to victims of uninsured drivers (the "Uninsured Drivers" Agreements) and the other concerned with victims of hit and run or otherwise untraceable drivers (the "Untraced Drivers" Agreements). These Notes are addressed specifically to the procedures required to take advantage of the rights granted by the Uninsured Drivers Agreements. However, it is not always certain

A13–80

which of the Agreements applies. For guidance in such cases please see the note on Untraced Drivers at paragraph 11 below.

1.3 In order to determine which of the Uninsured Drivers Agreements is applicable to a particular victim's claim, regard must be had to the date of the relevant accident. This Agreement only applies in respect of claims arising on or after October 1, 1999. Claims arising earlier than that are covered by the following Agreements:—

    1.3.1   Claims arising in respect of an accident occurring between July 1, 1946 and February 28, 1971 are governed by the Agreement between the Minister of Transport and the Bureau dated June 17, 1946.

    1.3.2   Claims arising in respect of an incident occurring between March 1, 1971 and November 30, 1972 are governed by the Agreement between the Secretary of State for the Environment and the Bureau dated February 1, 1971.

    1.3.3   Claims arising in respect of an incident occurring between December 1, 1972 and December 30, 1988 are governed by the Agreement between the Secretary of State and the Bureau dated November 22, 1972.

    1.3.4   Claims arising in respect of an incident occurring between December 31, 1988 and September 30, 1999 are governed by the Agreement between the Secretary of State and the Bureau dated December 21, 1988.

2. MIB's obligation

A13–81   **2.1** MIB's basic obligation (see clause 5) is to satisfy judgments which fall within the terms of this Agreement and which, because the Defendant to the proceedings is not insured, are not satisfied.

2.2 This obligation is, however, not absolute. It is subject to certain exceptions where MIB has no liability (see clause 6), there are a number of pre-conditions which the claimant must comply with (see clauses 7 to 15) and there are some limitations on MIB's liability (see clauses 16 and 17).

2.3 MIB does not have to wait for a judgment to be given; it can become party to the proceedings or negotiate and settle the claim if it wishes to do so.

3. Claims which MIB is not obliged to satisfy

A13–82   MIB is not liable under the Agreement in the case of the following types of claim.

3.1 A claim made in respect of an unsatisfied judgment which does not concern a liability against which Part VI of the Road Traffic Act 1988 requires a vehicle user to insure (see section 145 of the Act). An example would be a case where the accident did not occur in a place specified in the Act. See the definitions of "unsatisfied judgment" and "relevant liability" in clause 1.

3.2 A claim in respect of loss or damage caused by the use of a vehicle owned by or in the possession of the Crown (that is the Civil Service, the armed forces and so on) to which Part VI does not apply. If the responsibility for motor insurance has been undertaken by someone else or the vehicle is in fact insured, this exception does not apply. See clause 6(1)(a).

3.3 A claim made against any person who is not required to insure by virtue of section 144 of the Road Traffic Act 1988. See clause 6(1)(b).

3.4 A claim (commonly called subrogated) made in the name of a person suffering damage or injury but which is in fact wholly or partly for the benefit or another who has indemnified, or is liable to indemnify that person. See clause 6(1)(c).

3.5 A claim in respect of damage to a motor vehicle or losses arising from such damage where the use of the damaged vehicle was itself not covered by a contract of insurance as required by law. See clause 6(1)(d).

3.6 A claim made by a passenger in a vehicle where the loss or damage has been caused by the user of that vehicle if:—

> 3.6.1   the use of the vehicle was not covered by a contract of insurance; and
>
> 3.6.2   the claimant knew or could be taken to have known that the vehicle was being used without insurance, had been stolen or unlawfully taken or was being used in connection with crime.

See clause 6(1)(e), (2), (3) and (4).

3.7 A claim in respect of property damage amounting to £300 or less, £300 being the "specified excess". See clause 16(2).

3.8 Where the claim is for property damage, the first £300 of the loss and so much of it as exceeds £250,000. See clause 16(3) and (4).

4. Procedure after the accident and before proceedings

4.1 The claimant must take reasonable steps to establish whether there is in fact   **A13–83**
any insurance covering the use of the vehicle which caused the injury or damage. First, a claimant has statutory rights under section 154 of the Road Traffic Act 1988 to obtain relevant particulars which he must take steps to exercise even if that involves incurring expense and MIB will insist that he does so. See clause 13(a).

4.2 Other steps will include the following:

> **4.2.1**   The exchange of names, addresses and insurance particulars between those involved either at the scene of the accident or afterwards.
>
> **4.2.2**   Correspoding with the owner or driver of the vehicle or his representatives. He will be obliged under the terms of his motor policy to inform his insurers and a letter of claim addressed to him will commonly be passed to the insurers who may reply on his behalf. See clause 9(2)(d).
>
> **4.2.3**   Where only the vehicle's number is known, enquiry of the Driver and Vehicle Licensing Agency at Swansea 5A99 1BP as to the registered keeper of the vehicle is desirable so that through him the identity of the owner or driver can be established or confirmed.
>
> **4.2.4**   Enquiries of the police (see clause 13(b)).

4.3 If enquiries show that there is an insurer who is obliged to accept and does accept the obligation to handle the claim against the user of the vehicle concerned, even though the relevant liability may not be covered by the policy in question, then the claim should be pursued with such insurer.

4.4 If, however, enquiries disclose that there is no insurance covering the use of the vehicle concerned or if the insurer cannot be identified or the insurer asserts that it is under no obligation to handle the claim or if for any other reason it is clear that the insurer will not satisfy any judgment, the claim should be directed to MIB itself.

5. When proceedings are commenced or contemplated

5.1 As explained above, MIB does not have to wait for a judgment to be   **A13–84**
obtained before intervening. Claimants may apply to MIB before the commencement of proceedings. MIB will respond to any claim which complies with clause 7 and must give a reasoned reply to any request for compensation in respect of the claim (see clause 18) although normally a request for compensation will not be met until MIB is satisfied that it is properly based. Interim compensation payments are dealt with at paragraph 8 below.

5.2 It is important that wherever possible claims should be made using MIB's application form, fully completed and accompanied by documents supporting the claim, as soon as possible to avoid unnecessary delays. See clause 7(1). Copies of the form can be obtained by downloading from this website or on request made by post, telephone, fax or the DX or on personal application to MIB's offices.

5.3 Where a claim is submitted to MIB, MIB with the claimant's agreement, deal with the claim on the basis of the pre-action Protocol set out in the Appendix. When it is decided to commence legal proceedings, contact should be made with MIB to ascertain if the case is one where it is appropriate for MIB to be joined as a defendant from the outset. In most cases this course will be beneficial, as it will simplify the task of notifying MIB of many of the legal processes as set out in Clauses 9 to 12, since once MIB is a defendant, the Court will advise the relevant events direct. However, this course can only be achieved with MIB's specific consent, using the form of words set out below in the pleadings and MIB will specify, in writing for the individual case, precisely what steps should be taken and which Clauses of the Agreement will waived. Any Clause which is not waived must be complied with.

MIB Joinder Pleadings

A13–85

1. The Second Defendant is a company limited by guarantee under the Companies Act. Pursuant to an Agreement with the Secretary of State dated (December 22, 1988 or August 13, 1999) (hereafter "the Agreement") the Second Defendant provides compensation in certain circumstances to persons suffering injury or damage as a result of the negligence of uninsured motorists.

2. The Claimant has used all reasonable endeavours to ascertain the liability of an insurer for the first defendant and at the time of commencement of these proceedings verily believes that the first Defendant is not insured.

3. The Claimant accepts that only if a final judgement is obtained against the First Defendant (which judgement is not satisfied in full within seven days from the date upon which the Claimant became entitled to enforce it) can the Second Defendant be required to satisfy the judgement and then only if the terms and conditions set out in the Agreement are satisfied. Until that time, any liability of the Second Defendant is only contingent.

4. To avoid the Second Defendant having later to apply separately to join itself in this action (which the Claimant must consent to in any event pursuant to Clause 14(b) of the Agreement*) the Claimant seeks to include the Second Defendant from the outset recognising fully the Second Defendant's position as reflected at 3 above and the rights of the Second Defendant fully to participate in the action to protect its position as a separate party to the action.

5. With the above in mind, the Claimant seeks a Declaration of the Second Defendant's contingent liability for damages to the Claimant in this action.

* This phrase is only relevant to the 1999 Agreement.

5.4 Unless MIB is joined to the action from the outset, the claimant must give MIB notice *in writing* that he has commenced legal proceedings. The notice, the completed application form (if appropriate) and all necessary documents must be received by MIB no later than 14 days after the date of commencement of proceedings. See clause 9(1) and (2)(a). The date of commencement is determined in accordance with the definitions of "relevant proceedings" and "commencement" given in clause 1.

5.5 This notice *must* have with it the following:

5.5.1 a copy of the document originating the proceedings, usually in England and Wales a Claim Form and in Scotland a Sheriff Court Writ or Court of Session Summons (see clause 9(2)(b));

5.5.2 normally the Particulars of Claim endorsed on or served with the Claim Form or Writ (see clause 9(2)(e), although this document may be served later in accordance with clause 9(3) if that applies);

5.5.3 in any case the documents required by the relevant rules of procedure (see clause 9(2)(f).

5.6 In addition, other items as mentioned in clause 9(2), *e.g.* correspondence with the Defendant (or Defender) or his representatives, need to be supplied where appropriate.

5.7 It is for the claimant to satisfy himself that the notice has in fact been received by MIB. Clause 8 applies to service of documents by post and fax. MIB prefer service by fax as it is almost instantaneous and can be confirmed quickly. However, whilst Clause 8 is specific as to the method of giving notice MIB will not automatically reject notice given by other means, provided the otice comples with the Agreement in all other respects. Nonetheless, claimants would be wise to comply with Clause 8, as doing so provides certainty that the appropriate notice has been received.

5.8 It should be noted that when MIB has been given notice of a claim, it may elect to require the claimant to bring proceedings and attempt to secure a judgment against the party whom MIB alleges to be wholly or partly responsible for the loss or damage or who may be contracted to indemnify the claimant. In such a case MIB must indemnify the claimant against the costs of such proceedings. Subject to that, however, MIB's obligation to satisfy the judgment in the action will only arise if the claimant commences the proceedings and takes all reasonable steps to obtain a judgment. See clause 14(a).

6. Service of proceedings

6.1 If proceedings are commenced in England or Wales the claimant must inform MIB of the date of service (see clause 10(1) and (2)).   **A13–86**

6.2 If service of the Claim Form is effected by the Court, notice must be given within 7 days from the earliest of the dates listed in clause 10(3)(a)(i) or (ii) or within 14 days from the date mentioned in clause 10(3)(b) (the date of deemed service under the court's rules of procedure). Claimants are advised to take steps to ensure that the court or the defendant's legal representatives inform them of the date of service as soon as possible. Although a longer period is allowed than in other cases, service may be deemed to have occurred without a Claimant knowing of it until some time afterwards.

6.3 Where proceedings are served personally, notice must be given 7 days from the date of personal service (see clause 10(3)(a)(iii)).

6.4 In Scotland, proceedings are commenced at the date of service (see clause 1) so notice should already have been given under clause 9 and clause 10 does not apply there.

7. After service and before judgment

7.1 Clauses 11 and 12 set out further notice requirements. However, the need to comply with these Clauses can be avoided by joining MIB to the legal action from the outset as a Defendant as explained above (Note 5.3). Where this is done, MIB will specifically waive reliance on these clauses, in writing. If these clauses are not waived in the individual case, they must be complied with.   **A13–87**

7.2 Notice of the filing of a defence, of an amendment to the Statement or Particulars of Claim, and the setting down of the case for trial must be given not later than 7 days after the occurrence of such events and a copy of the document must be supplied (see clause 11(1)).

7.3 MIB may request further information and documents to support the claim where it is not satisfied that the documents supplied with the application form are sufficient to enable it to assess its liability under the Agreement (see clause 11(2)).

7.4 If the claimant intends to sign or apply for judgment he must give MIB notice of the fact before doing so. This notice must be given at least 35 days before the application is to be made or the date when judgment is to be signed (see clause 12).

7.5 At no time must the claimant oppose MIB if it wishes to be joined as a party to proceedings and he must if requested consent to any application by MIB to be joined. Conflicts may arise between a Defendant and MIB which require MIB to become a Defendant or, in Scotland, a party Minuter if a defence is to be filed on its behalf (see clause 14(b)).

8. Interim payments

A13–88   In substantial cases, the claimant may wish to apply for an interim payment. MIB will consider such applications on a voluntary basis but otherwise the claimant has the right to apply to the court for an interim payment order which, if granted, will be met by MIB.

9. After judgment

A13–89   **9.1** MIB's basic obligation normally arises if a judgment is not satisfied within 7 days after the claimant has become entitled to enforce it (see clause 1). However, that judgment may in certain circumstances be set aside and with it MIB's obligation to satisfy it. Sometimes MIB wishes to apply to set aside a judgment either wholly or partially. If MIB decides not to satisfy a judgment it will notify the claimant as soon as possible. Where a judgment is subsequently set aside, MIB will require the claimant to repay any sum previously paid by MIB to discharge its obligation under the Agreement (see clause 15(b)).

9.2 MIB is not obliged to satisfy a judgment unless the claimant has in return assigned the benefit to MIB or its nominee (see clause 15(a)). If such assignment is effected and if the subject matter of the judgment includes claims in respect of which MIB is not obliged to meet any judgment and if MIB effects any recovery on the judgment, the sum recovered will be divided between MIB and the claimant in proportion to the liabilities which were and which were not covered by MIB's obligation (see clause 21).

10. Permissible deductions from payments by MIB

A13–90   **10.1** Claims for loss and damage for which the claimant has been compensated or indemnified, *e.g.* under a contract of insurance or under the Policyholders Protection Act 1975, and which has not been taken into account in the judgment, may be deducted from the sum paid in settlement of MIB's obligation (see clause 17).

10.2 If there is a likelihood that the claimant will receive payment from such a source after the judgment has been satisfied by MIB, MIB will require him to undertake to repay any sum which duplicates the compensation assessed by the court (see clause 15(b)).

11. Untraced drivers

A13–91   **11.1** Where the owner or driver of a vehicle cannot be identified application may be made to MIB under the relevant Untraced Drivers Agreement. This provides, subject to specified conditions, for the payment of compensation for personal injury. It does not provide for compensation in respect of damage to property.

A13–92   **11.2** In those cases where it is unclear whether the owner or driver of a vehicle has been correctly identified it is sensible for the claimant to register a claim under both this Agreement and the Untraced Drivers Agreement following which MIB will advise which Agreement will, in its view, apply in the circumstances of the particular case.

APPENDIX 14

DEPARTMENT OF THE ENVIRONMENT, TRANSPORT AND THE REGIONS—CODE OF PRACTICE FOR TRACING EMPLOYERS' LIABILITY INSURANCE POLICIES

PART 1

DETR GUIDANCE NOTES

A. Introduction

Background

In law, an employer may be liable to pay compensation to an employee who suf-   **A14–01**
fers injury or disease sustained during their employment.[1]

Employers are required by law to insure against this potential liability. The current relevant legislation is the Employers' Liability (Compulsory Insurance) Act 1969—which came into force on January 1, 1972—and associated Regulations.[2] The aim of the 1969 Act is to ensure that funds are available to pay any compensation for which an employer is liable. The Act does not guarantee an employee compensation for injury or disease sustained during their employment— they would need to prove the employer's liability. But it is intended to protect employees.

An employee claiming damages from their employer, will normally need to trace the insurance policy their employer held at the relevant time. A recent review of the Act showed that this can be a problem, particularly for employees suffering from industrial diseases which have taken a long time to develop. The greatest difficulties are experienced where the relevant employer is no longer in business. (The employee may need to trace a policy for a period before 1972; many employers had such insurance in earlier decades.) There are also instances where relevant insurance records have been lost, or have not been retained, by an employer who is still trading.[3] In all of these cases, the only surviving information about a policy may be that held by the insurer.

An employee who cannot identify their employer's insurance policy, may be

---

[1] The employee would need to show that the employer had been negligent, or in breach of their statutory duty of care.

[2] The Employers' Liability (Compulsory Insurance) Regulations 1998 (S.I. 1998/2573), which came into force on January 1, 1999.

[3] An employer who is required by law to be insured, is now required to retain for 40 years any certificate of insurance issued to him on/after January 1, 1999; also the certificate for any previous policy which was current on December 31, 1998 or January 1999.

unable to seek compensation.[4] The Government is concerned about this unsatis-factory situation. It wants insurers to do everything practicable to help employees to trace policies.

The press release accompanying the new Employers' Liability (Compulsory Insurance) Regulations announced on October 27, 1998, that this Department would work with the insurance industry to draw up a Code of Practice to help in tracing employers' liability policies. This Code has been developed by DETR and the industry in consultation with each other; its evolution was greatly assisted by the comments received on a draft version, which was distributed during spring 1999 to those with an interest—employees' and employers' organisations, the legal profession and the different parts of the insurance industry.

Purpose of the Code

A14–02   Its purpose is two-fold: to help employees needing to trace insurance policies taken out by employers in the past; and to ensure that insurers keep future records in ways which will make tracing such policies much easier. The Code should help employees and their representatives—normally it is the employee's solicitor who will try to identify the employer's insurance policy.

Legal status

A14–03   This is a voluntary Code entered into by insurance companies and Syndicates at Lloyd's. It does not provide potential claimants, or employers, with any rights which do not already exist in law. **This is not a statutory code**.

Content

A14–04   This Code sets out the procedures insurers will follow, and the standards they will meet, if they are asked to help trace an employer's insurance policy. It also contains commitments on record keeping.

Two Parts to the Code

A14–05   An employer may buy employers' liability insurance from:

      i)   an insurance company, or
      ii) an underwriting Syndicate at Lloyd's.

Because these two types of organisation operate in different ways, there are two parts to this Code: the ABI Code, and the NMA Code. But each has the same pur-pose, approach and standards.

Most insurance companies in the United Kingdom belong to the Association of British Insurers (the ABI), a trade association. The ABI's Code for its members is Part 2 of this document.

Lloyd's is a marketplace in which many Syndicates transact various kinds of business; some Syndicates underwrite the insurance of employers' liability risks.[5] Most Syndicates belong to the Non-Marine Association (the NMA), a trade asso-ciation. The NMA's Code for its members is Part 3 of this document.[6]

Scope

A14–06   The purpose of the Code is to improve the tracing of employers' insurance policies.

---

[4] Inability to trace an insurance policy can also be a problem for an employer. If they can-not establish their right to be indemnified, claims will have to be met from their own resources.

[5] Lloyd's itself is not an insurer.

[6] Neither the ABI nor the NMA are insurers.

Whether a particular employer was liable for an injury or disease suffered by an employee, is a separate issue—which should be pursued in the normal way. There is no provision under the Code for accepting claims for compensation, or for evaluating or negotiating such claims.[7]

Compulsory policies and voluntary policies

Employers who are not obliged by law to have employers' liability insurance, may nevertheless choose to buy this type of cover—for instance, some public sector employers do so. Insurers will follow the Code in dealing with enquiries about voluntary employers' liability policies, in the same way as for they would for policies taken out in order to comply with the law.   **A14–07**

Effective date

This Code was launched in November 1999.   **A14–08**

B. Making an Enquiry

Do you need to ask an insurer for information?

Before putting forward an enquiry under this Code, you should make every effort to trace your employer and submit a claim to them. The Code is really intended to help those who cannot obtain information about a relevant insurance policy from their employer or former employer.   **A14–09**

Questions which insurers may ask

You may conclude that you need to put an enquiry to an insurer. Under the Code, insurers undertake to search their records when given a minimum amount of information. This minimum is described in paragraph 2(ii) of each Code.[8]   **A14–10**

You may be asked to provide more information than this—an insurer may ask you to complete an enquiry form like the one at the end of this document. You are not obliged to provide this information. But if you do, the prospects of a policy being traced could be significantly improved.

For instance, telling the insurer where your employer was located, may enable the insurer to identify their branch office which dealt with the insurance. Insurers' historical records are often held by intermediaries rather than by the insurers themselves; some intermediaries specialise in dealing with particular types of trades or businesses. So telling the insurer about your employer's business, or about the nature of your injury or disease, may enable the insurer to identify the relevant intermediary.

Another possible problem could be that a relevant policy was held in a name which is not the name of your employer. For instance, you may have worked for a subsidiary company of the main policyholder. A search made by an insurer using your employer's name, might not identify this policy. Insurers appreciate that you may not know the name in which a policy was held, but you should provide any information you can on this. For instance, Companies House records might help in tracing parent company and subsidiary relationships. Or if an employer has been taken over or merged with another organisation, they might help to identify the company which is now responsible for past trading.

---

[7] A claim for compensation should be made against the employer, whose responsibility it is to deal with such claims. The employer will then involve its insurers. They will take over control of the claim, investigate the circumstances and—where there is a liability upon the employer—negotiate a settlement of the claim with the employee or their representative.

[8] See Part 2 and Part 3 of this document.

Providing as much information as you possibly can could therefore help the insurer to help you.

Contacting the right person

A14–11   *Contact an insurer*

The insurance broker who arranged your employer's insurance is not the insurer who provided the insurance policy. Your enquiry needs to be addressed to an insurer.

Which insurer?

- *If you think you know which insurance company or Syndicate at Lloyd's provided the insurance, submit your enquiry directly to them.*

If you know the name of the insurance company, you can get its address from the ABI. Information on how to contact the ABI is at the front of this document. An enquiry to a Lloyd's Syndicate should be sent to:

[Syndicate name]
Lloyd's
One Lime Street,
London EC3M 7HA.

- *If you think the insurance was provided by a Syndicate at Lloyd's but do not know which one, send your enquiry to the Non-Marine Association at Lloyd's (NMA)* whose contact details are at the front of this document.
- *If there are no clues as to who the insurer might have been, submit your enquiry to the Association of British Insurers (ABI),* whose contact details are at the front of this document. They will circulate your request for information to all their members who provide this type of insurance. They will also copy it on your behalf to the Non-Marine Association at Lloyd's, for circulation to relevant Syndicates there.

C. How Insurers Will Deal With Enquiries

A14–12   Most of the information about this is in the ABI and NMA Codes—Parts 2 and 3 of this documetn. These Notes provide additional background.

Insurers' ability to search records

A14–13   Advances in technology mean that insurers now find it simple and cost-effective to maintain permanent policy records, which can be readily searched to identify whether an employers' liability insurance policy was in force at a particular time.

However, when such record keeping systems were developed, it was not always possible to capture data on policies which had lapsed earlier, and some records had already been destroyed. So the database which each insurer has at present, is not necessarily a complete record of the policies they have issued. Progressively, it will become a complete record.

Surviving paper records for earlier periods can be difficult and time-consuming to search effectively: for instance, where they are arranged according to the date when the policy expired, or by policy number.

The situation will vary from insurer to insurer so—as section 4 of the ABI and NMA Codes explains—each will draw up a statement about what historical data they have, and how they can search it. These statements will be made available on request. Historic record statements will be covered in the ABI and NMA Annual Reports on their members' performance under the Code.

Information held by insurance brokers, etc.   **A14–14**
Information which can help to identify a policy may be held by an intermediary—such as an insurance broker—rather than by the insurer. Insurers will make suitable arrangements, so that when they receive a query they can obtain relevant data from intermediaries. The British Insurance Brokers Association (BIBA) will bring this Code to the attention of its members.

D. Independent Review Body

Composition
The Review Body is chaired by the Department of the Environment, Transport   **A14–15**
and the Regions. It has members drawn from the insurance industry, organisations representing employees and employers, and members of the legal profession who specialise in personal injury work and dealing with insurance claims.

Functions
At the end of each year, the Review Body will receive an Annual Report from   **A14–16**
the Association of British Insurers (ABI), giving an overview of all aspects of insurers' performance under the Code during that period. A parallel report will be provided by the Non-Marine Association at Lloyd's (NMA), covering the performance of relevant Lloyd's Syndicates.
Following its consideration of these reports, the Review Body will draw up an Annual Statement commenting on the insurance industry's performance under the Code. DETR will publish the Annual Statement, which will include the Annual Reports from the ABI and NMA.

E. Complaints to DETR

The complaints system
If you need to make a complaint about the performance of an insurer or Syndi-   **A14–17**
cate under the Code, Section 7 in the ABI and NMA Codes (Parts 2 and 3 of this document) explains what to do. Consideration of a complaint by DETR is the final stage of the complaints process.
DETR will only consider a complaint, if

 — in the case of an insurer, the insurer and the Association of British
   Insurers, or
 — in the case of a Lloyd's Syndicate, the Syndicate and Lloyd's Complaints Department,

have first been given the opportunity to resolve it.

Contacting DETR
Complaints should be sent to: **A14–18**
Code of Practice on Tracing EL Insurers,
Health and Safety Sponsorship Division,
Department of the Environment, Transport and the Regions,
Great Minster House,
76 Marsham Street,
London
SW1P 4DR.

Tel: 020 7944 4967 (direct) or 020 7944 3000 (switchboard)

Fax: 0171 890 4979[9] or 020 7944 4979

e-mail: elci@detr.gov.uk

You may wish to contact us for information before sending in a complaint. *But the complaint itself must be submitted in writing.*

How your complaint will be dealt with

A14–19   DETR will acknowledge the complaint within 5 working days of receipt.

DETR will decide if the insurer or Syndicate acted in accordance with the Code or not, on the basis of written evidence from the complainant[10] and the insurer. The complainant should state clearly what aspect of the Code they believe has not been observed, and provide supporting evidence. The insurer or Syndicate will be asked to explain their view of the case and provide relevant supporting evidence.

Where DETR concludes that a complaint is justified

A14–20   It will inform the insurer or Syndicate in writing (with a copy to the ABI or Lloyd's Complaints Department as appropriate), giving the reasons for its decision. DETR will give the insurer or Syndicate one calendar month in which to rectify the situation.

If the insurer or Syndicate does not do so, DETR's report to the Review Body on the complaints it has received that year will highlight the case, and recommend that the Review Body should draw attention to it in its published Annual Statement—naming the insurer or Syndicate concerned.[11]

DETR will inform the complainant of its final decision on their complaint, and the reasons for this.

Where DETR concludes that a complaint is unjustified

A14–21   It will inform the complainant and the relevant insurer or Syndicate (with a copy to the ABI or Lloyd's Complaints Department as appropriate), and give reasons for its conclusion.

F. Sanctions

A14–22   DETR will report to the Review Body on any complaint which it has found to be justified, and where the insurer or Syndicate has failed to provide a remedy within one calendar month of being notified of DETR's view.

DETR will recommend that the Review Body draw attention to the case in its next Annual Statement, and that it name the insurer or Syndicate concerned. The Review Body's Annual Statement will be pubilshed by DETR.

---

[9] Until April 21, 2000.

[10] This can be the potential claimant or their representative.

[11] DETR will report to the Review Body each year on the number of complaints which have been referred to it and their nature, the numbers which were found to be justified, and the numbers which were not justified.

PART 2

ASSOCIATION OF BRITISH INSURERS CODE OF PRACTICE FOR THE TRACING OF
EMPLOYERS' LIABILITY INSURANCE POLICIES

1. Introduction

This Code of Practice applies in respect of potential claims made against   **A14–23**
employers who hold, or may have held, employers' liability insurance at the time of
an injury, or during the period of exposure to a cause of occupational illness or
disease.

The intention of this Code is to:

(i) help current claimants to trace past employers' insurance more
   effectively;
(ii) ensure future claimants (those at work now who may need to claim in
   the future) have access to insurers' details, particularly where the
   employer goes out of business.

The Code is applicable to all members of the Association of British Insurers
("ABI") which transact employers' liability business or have transacted such insurance in previous years.

Guidance Notes on its application, issued by the Department of the Environment, Transport and the Regions, can be found in Part 1 of this document.

2. Procedural Steps to be Taken on an Enquiry Being Made to an Insurer

(i) On receipt of an enquiry from a potential claimant or their representative, it   **A14–24**
will be referred to a central contact point within the Insurer.

(ii) The enquirer must provide the following minimum information for the
Insurer to undertake a search:

— name of employee;
— name and address (including postcode) of employer and/or the policyholder;
— type of injury and when caused, or type of illness/disease and period of
   exposure which caused that illness/disease.

(iii) The Insurer may ask the enquirer for additional information such as:

— whether the employer is still in existence;
— whether the enquirer is aware of the employer's insurers;
— whether enquiries have been made of the employer regarding insurance
   arrangements (including details of any broker involvement).

If the Insurer does ask for such additional information, they will explain that it
is being sought in order to increase the likelihood of a record of insurance being
traced.

(iv) The Insurer will make every practical effort within reasonable bounds to try to establish whether they were on risk at the time of the injury or during the period of exposure.

(v) The Insurer will respond to the enquirer within 20 working days of receipt of the enquiry, irrespective of whether or not any search has found a successful match.

(vi) If—having made extensive enquiries of their own records and exhausted other avenues of enquiry—the Insurer is unable to trace any record of relevant insurance, they will advise the enquirer that the matter will be referred to ABI. The Insurer must advise the enquirer of all steps that it has taken during the course of its search and of all relevant information that has been discovered.

3. Procedural steps to be Taken on an Enquiry Being Referred to ABI

A14–25 (i) On referral of an enquiry to ABI by an Insurer, or on receipt of an enquiry directly from a potential claimant or their representative, a designated contact point at ABI will confirm to the enquirer within 5 working days of receipt of the enquiry that the matter is being dealt with.

(ii) ABI will circulate details of referred and directly received enquiries every 20 working days (by e-mail or fax) to all Insurers participating in this Code, for them to investigate the enquiry in accordance with the procedures set out in Section 2 above. Details will also be sent to the Non-Marine Association at Lloyd's at the same time.

(iii) Each Insurer will respond to ABI within 20 working days of receipt of the e-mail/fax circular, irrespective of whether or not any search has found a successful match.

(iv) When an Insurer(s) has been found, ABI will inform the enquirer within 5 working days of being notified by the Insurer(s), giving the name, address and telephone number of the designated contact at the Insurer(s).

(v) In the event that no Insurer can be traced within 20 working days of receipt of the e-mail/fax circular, ABI will contact the enquirer within 5 working days of being notified by the Insurer(s), explaining all the steps that have been taken, including all Insurers contacted.

4. Record Keeping

(i) Historical Data

A14–26 On becoming a signatory to the Code, each Insurer will make a statement as to the date from and the manner in which they can search historical data.

(ii) Current/Future Data

A14–27 On becoming a signatory to the Code, each Insurer will undertake to record and maintain all current and future policies for a period of 60 years in a form that facilitates ready searches, *i.e.* by name of employer and/or policyholder (after the start date of the Code).

In the event of an Insurer acquiring a new subsidiary, the Insurer must use best endeavours to ensure that all future Employers' Liability records of that subsidiary comply with the terms of the Code.

5. Training

Each Insurer will undertake to train all relevant staff in the procedures for han-   **A14–28**
dling Employers' Liability Code enquiries. All enquiries must be handled in an efficient and courteous manner.

6. Independent Review

(i) The ABI will produce an annual report giving an overview of the perform-   **A14–29**
ance of the Code, including details of complaints received under the complaints
procedure.

(ii) The report will be subject to an independent review. The Review Body will
be chaired by the Department of the Environment, Transport and the Regions
(DETR). Further information about the Review Body is given in *section D of
DETR's Guidance Notes*, which are in *Part 1* of this document.

7. Complaints Procedure

If an enquirer has a complaint about the conduct of a particular Insurer in rela-   **A14–30**
tion to their operation of the Code, this should in the first instance be referred in
writing to that Insurer.

Action by the Insurer
The Insurer must ackowledge a written complaint within 5 working days of   **A14–31**
receipt, giving details of its complaints handling procedure. A definitive response
will be provided within 40 working days.

If the enquirer is not satisfied with the explanation provided

They may refer the complaint in writing to ABI, who will take up the matter
with the company concerned.

Action by ABI
A complaint which is referred to ABI, will be ackowledged within 5 working   **A14–32**
days of receipt. ABI will forward correspondence to the senior management of the
Insurer concerne, for their review and action as appropriate.

If the enquirer is not satisfied with the explanation provided

They may refer the complaint in writing to the Department of the Environment,
Transport and Regions (DETR).

Action by DETR
Information on this stage of the complaints process is given in section E of   **A14–33**
DETR's Guidance Notes, which are in *Part 1* of this document.

8. Sanctions

See section F of DETR's Guidance Notes, which are in Part 1 of this document.   **A14–34**

PART 3

CODE OF PRACTICE FOR UNDERWRITERS AT LLOYD'S: THE NMA CODE FOR THE
TRACING OF RECORDS OF EMPLOYERS' LIABILITY INSURANCES

1. Introduction

A14–35   This Code of Practice applies in respect of potential claims made against employers who hold, or may have held, employers' liability insurance at the time of an injury, or during the period of exposure to a cause of occupational illness or disease. The intention of this Code is to:

> (i)   help current claimants to trace past employers' insurance more effectively;
> (ii) ensure future claimants (those at work now who may need to claim in the future) have access to insurers' details, particularly where the employer goes out of business.

This code is applicable to all Syndicates at Lloyd's which transact employers' liability insurance or which have transacted such insurances in previous years.

Your attention is drawn to the guidance notes in Part 1 of this document, which have been issued by the Department of the Environment, Transport and the Regions.

2. Procedural Steps to be Taken on receipt of an enquiry by a Syndicate

A14–36   (i) On receipt of an enquiry from a potential claimant or their representative, it will be referred to a central contact within the Syndicate.

(ii) The enquirer must provide the folllowing minimum information for the Syndicate to commence a search:

> (a)   name of the employee
> (b)   name of the employer and/or the policyholder (if different)
> (c)   type of injury and when caused or the type of illness/disease and the period of exposure which caused that illness/disease.

(iii) The Syndicate may ask for further informatin or may ask the enquirer to complete an Enquiry Form. In doing so, the Syndicate should explain to the enquirer that this additional information is being requested in order to increase the likelihood of a record being traced.

(iv) The Syndicate will make every effort within reasonable bounds to establish whether it was the insurer on risk at the time of the injury or exposure.

(v) The Syndicate will respond to the enquirer within twenty (20) working days of receipt of the enquiry, irrespective of the result of the search.

(vi) If, after having made extensive enquiries of their own records and exhausted any other avenues of enquiry, the Syndicate is unable to trace any record of a relevant insurance the Syndicate must inform the enquirer and tell the enquirer that the enquiry is being referred to the NMA. In doing so, the Syndicate must tell the enquirer of all steps which were taken during the course of their search and of all relevant information which has been discovered.

3. Procedural Steps to be Taken on referral of an enquiry to the NMA (or on receipt of an enquiry directly by the NMA)

(i) On referral of an enquiry by a Syndicate to the NMA, or on receipt of an enquiry directly by the NMA, a designated contact point at the NMA will confirm to the enquirer within five (5) working days of receipt of the enquiry that their enquiry is being dealt with. **A14–37**

(ii) Each twenty (20) working days, the NMA will circulate details of all referred or received enquiries to all Syndicates participating in this Code who will undertake a search of their records in accordance with the procedures outlined in 2. above. Details will also be sent to the Association of British Insurers.

(iii) Each Syndicate will respond to the NMA within twenty (20) working days of the receipt of the circular, irrespective of the result of the search.

(iv) When a Syndicate is found to be the relevant insurer, the NMA will inform the enquirer within five (5) working days giving the name, address and telephone number of the designated contact at the Syndicate.

(v) In the event that no insurer can be traced within twenty (20) working days of the date of receipt of the circular, the NMA will contact the enquirer within five (5) working days explaining the steps which have been taken.

4. Record Keeping

(i) Historical Data
On becoming a signatory to the Code, each Syndicate will make a statement as to the date from and manner in which they can search historical data. **A14–38**

(ii) Current and Future Data
On becoming a signatory to the Code, each Syndicate will undertake to record and maintain all current and new policies for a period of sixty (60) years in a form which facilitates ready searches (*i.e.* a search by employer's/policyholder's name). **A14–39**

In the event of a Syndicate acquiring the business of another employers' liability insurer, the Syndicate must use its best endeavours to ensure that the records of such business comply with the provisions of this Code.

5. Training

Each Syndicate will undertake to train all relevant staff in the procedures for handling enquiries under the Code. All enquiries must be handled in an efficient and courteous manner. **A14–40**

6. Independent Review

The NMA will produce an annual report giving an overview of the performance of the Code, including details of complaints received under the Complaints procedure. **A14–41**

The report wil be subjet to an independent review. The Review Body will be chaired by the Department of the Environment, Transport and the Regions.

7. Complaints Procedure

A14-42   Any complaint made by an enquirer about the conduct of a particular Syndicate subscribing to the Code should, in the first instance, be referred in writing to that Syndicate. Every Syndicate at Lloyd's is required to have written procedures to enable the prompt and proper handling of complaints.

If it is felt a Syndicate has failed to resolve the matter, the dispute can be referred to Lloyd's Complaints Department.

Correspondence should be addressed to:

> The Manager
> Lloyd's Complaints Department
> Lloyd's
> One Lime Street
> London
> EC3M 7HA

The Lloyd's Complaints Department will acknowledge the complaint within 5 days of receipt, and will initially refer the matter to a senior representative of the Syndicate concerned and allow them a final 14 days to review the matter. Lloyd's Complaints Department can be asked to investigate the matter if it still remains unresolved after that time.

In the unlikely event that the matter remains unresolved after investigation by Lloyd's Complaints Department, the dispute may be referred to the Department of the Environment, Transport and the Regions (DETR). *The Guidance Notes in Part 1E* of this document explain how DETR would deal with such a complaint.

8. Sanctions

A14-43   See the *Guidance Notes in Part 1F* of this document.

ENQUIRY FORM

This form relates to enquiries made under the Code of Practice for the tracing **A14–44**
of records of employers' liability insurances. Before completing this form, please
refer to the Code and the accompanying Guidance Notes which will assist you in
making your enquiry.

You are not obliged to provide this information but you should be aware that by
doing so, the prospects of a record being traced are improved.

This form should be completed as fully as possible. Where you do not know an
answer, leave it blank. Where you know only some of the information requested,
please put down what you do know.

The Guidance Notes accompanying this form, tell you where to send your
enquiry.

1. Information about the Enquirer
Name:

Address
(including
postcode

Postcode: ....

Telephone   Fax
Number: Number:

If you are not the   (*e.g.* Solicitor)
potential claimant,
what is your
relationship to the
potential
claimant?:

2. Information about the Employer (if known)
Name:

Address:
(including
postcode)

Postcode: ....

Whether ceased   Still trading / Ceased trading on   (Complete and/or
trading?   delete as appropriate)

....

If the employer
is/was a subsidiary
company, please
give the name and
address of its parent:

3. Information about the potential Claimant
Full Name:

Age:
....

Period spent working
for the employer:

Type of injury, illness
or disease sustained:

Date injury occurred
or the period of exposure
which caused the illness/
disease:

4. Information about the insurance policy (if known)
Name of the Insurer:

Name of the Policyhoolder
(if different to the Employer)

Policy Number:

The Name and Address of any
intermediary/ies placing the
insurance with the insurer:

Have enquiries already been
made of any Syndicate at
Lloyd's or insurance companies

YES / NO

If Yes, please give details
of who has been approached
and with what result (below or, if
necessary, on a separate sheet)

5. Other Information
Please provide any other information
that you think might assist insurers in
searching for these insurance records

for office use only
reffered by:

APPENDIX 15

THE GENERAL INSURANCE STANDARDS COUNCIL ("GISC") COMMERCIAL CODE

Note: Effective from July 3, 2000. Words in italics are defined terms, in accordance with the GISC Rules. This GISC *Commercial Code* is reproduced with the permission of the General Insurance Standards Council. The original version, and complete Rules, can be found in the GISC website at www.gisc.co.uk or obtained directly from GISC at: 110 Cannon Street, London EC4N 6EU, Tel: 020 7648 7800, Fax: 020 7648 7808, e-mail: enquiries@gisc.co.uk.

INTRODUCTION

Within this *Commercial Code* "*Member*" means a *Member of GISC* (an *Insurer*, *Intermediary* (including broker) or agent), and anyone acting on its behalf, with whom the *Commercial Customer* deals. **A15–01**

CORE PRINCIPLES

In the course of their *General Insurance Activities Members* should: **A15–02**

1.1 act with due skill, care and diligence;

1.2 observe high standards of integrity and deal openly and fairly with their *Commercial Customers*;

1.3 seek from *Commercial Customers* such information about their circumstances and objectives as might reasonably be expected to be relevant in enabling the *Member* to fulfil their responsibilities to them;

1.4 take reasonable steps to give *Commercial Customers* sufficient information in a comprehensible and timely way to enable them to make balanced and informed decisions about their insurance;

1.5 take appropriate steps to safeguard information, money and property held or handled on behalf of *Commercial Customers*;

1.6 conduct their business and organise their affairs in a prudent manner;

1.7 seek to avoid conflicts of interest, but where a confict is unavoidable or does arise, manage it in such a way as to avoid prejudice to any party. *Members* will not unfairly put their own interests above their duty to any *Commercial Customer* for whom they act; and

1.8 handle complaints fairly and promptly.

PRACTICE NOTES

A15–03   **1.** It is *GISC's* intention to promote standards of professional conduct for *Members*. These Practice Notes represent statements of reasonable practice which *Members* will be expected to follow generally in adhering to the Core Principles.

2. A failure on the part of a *Member* to observe the standards set out in these Practice Notes shall not of itself constitute a breach of the *Rules* but any such failure may in disciplinary proceedings be relied upon by *GISC* or any party to the proceedings as tending to establish or to negate any liability which is in question in those proceedings.

MARKETING

A15–04   **3.** *Members* will ensure that all their advertising and promotional material is clear, fair and not misleading.

ARRANGING THE INSURANCE

Commercial Customer relationship

A15–05   **4.** *Members* will advise their *Commercial Customers* of the nature of their service and their relationship with them, in particular, whether they act on behalf of an *Insurer* or act independently on behalf of the *Commercial Customer* as an *Intermediary*. They will also make it clear if they operate as an agent of another *Intermediary*.

5. *Members* will, where it is reasonably practical, confirm in writing instructions to act on behalf of a *Commercial Customer* and this will include appropriate reference to any recommendations made by the *Member* but declined by the *Commercial Customer*.

Commercial Customer requirements

A15–06   **6.** *Members* will take appropriate steps to understand the types of *Commercial Customers* they are dealing with and the extent of their *Commercial Customers'* awareness of risk and *General Insurance Products* and take that knowledge into account in their dealings with them.

7. *Members* will seek from *Commercial Customers* such information about their circumstances and objectives as might reasonably be expected to be relevant in enabling them to identify the *Commercial Customers'* requirements and fulfil their responsibilities to their *Commercial Customers.*

Information about proposed insurance

A15–07   **8.** *Members* will provide adequate information in a comprehensive and timely way to enable *Commercial Customers* to make an informed decision about the

General Insurance Products or *General Insurance Activity*-related services being proposed.

9. If they are acting on behalf of the *Commercial Customer*, *Members* will explain the differences in, and the relative costs of, the types of insurance, which in the opinion of the *Member*, would suit the *Commercial Customers'* needs. In so doing *Members* will take into consideration the knowledge held by their *Commercial Customers* when deciding to what extent it is appropriate for the *Commercial Customers* to have the terms and conditions of a particular insurance explained to them.

10. *Members* will advise *Commercial Customers* of the key features of the insurance proposed, including the essential cover and benefits, any significant or unusual restrictions, exclusions, conditions or obligations, and the period of cover. In so doing, *Members* will take into consideration the knowledge held by their *Commercial Customers* when deciding to what extent it is appropriate for *Commercial Customers* to have the terms and conditions of a particular insurance explained to them.

11. If *Members* are unable to match *Commercial Customers'* requirements they will explain the differences in the insurance proposed.

Advice and recommendations

12. *Members* should only discuss with or advise *Commercial Customers* on matters in which they are knowledgeable and seek or recommend other specialist advice when necessary.

A15–08

13. *Members* will take reasonable steps to advise *Commercial Customers* if any *General Insurance Products* or *General Insurance Activity*-related services being offered or requested are not covered by this *Commercial Code* and any possible risks involved. In so doing, *Members* will take into consideration the knowledge held by their *Commercial Customers* in deciding to what extent such advice may be necessary.

Information about costs and remuneration

14. *Members* will provide details of the costs of each *General Insurance Product* or *General Insurance Activity*-related service offered.

A15–09

15. *Members* will not impose any fees or charges in addition to the premium required by the *Insurer* without first disclosing the amount and purpose of the charge. This will include charges for policy amendments, claims handling or cancellation.

16. *Members* who are acting on behalf of a *Commercial Customer* in arranging their insurance will, on request, or where they are legally obliged to do so, disclose the amount of commission and any other remuneration received for arranging the insurance.

17. *Members* will disclose to *Commercial Customers* any payment they receive for providing to, or securing on behalf of, their *Commercial Customers* any additional *General Insurance Activity*-related services.

Duty of disclosure

A15–10   **18.** *Members* will explain to *Commercial Customers* their duty to disclose all circumstances material to the insurance and the consequences of any failure to make such disclosures, both before the insurance commences and during the policy.

19. *Members* will make it clear to *Commercial Customers* that all answers or statements given on a proposal form, claim form, or any other material document, are the *Commercial Customer's* own responsibility. *Commercial Customers* should always be asked to check the accuracy of information provided.

20. If *Members* believe that any disclosure of material facts by their *Commercial Customers* is not true, fair or complete, they will request their *Commercial Customers* to make the necessary true, fair or complete disclosure, and if this is not forthcoming must consider declining to continue acting on their *Commercial Customer's* behalf.

Quotations

A15–11   **21.** When giving a quotation, *Members* will take due care to ensure its accuracy and their ability to place the insurance at the quoted terms.

Placement

A15–12   **22.** *Members* who act on behalf of *Commercial Customers* when arranging their insurance will use their skill objectively in the best interests of their *Commercial Customers* when choosing *Insurers*.

23. Where two or more *Members* are acting jointly for a *Commercial Customer* when placing an insurance, *Members* will take appropriate steps to see that they and their *Commercial Customers* know their individual responsibilities and duties.

24. *Members* will inform and seek from their *Commercial Customers* written acknowledgement where they are instructed to place an insurance which is contrary to the advice that has been given by the *Member*.

Confirming Cover

A15–13   **25.** *Members* will provide *Commercial Customers* with prompt written confirmation and details of the insurance which has been effected on their behalf.

26. *Members* will identify the Insurer(s) and advise any changes once the contract has commenced at the earliest opportunity.

27. *Members* will forward full policy documentation without avoidable delay where this is not included with the confirmation of cover.

Providing Ongoing Service

A15–14   **28.** *Members* will respond promptly to *Commercial Customers'* queries and correspondence.

29. *Members* will deal promptly with *Commercial Customers* requests for amendments to cover and provide them will full details of any premium or charges to be paid or returned.

30. *Members* will provide written confirmation when amendments are made.

31. *Members* will remit any return premium and charges due to *Commercial Customers* without avoidable delay.

32. *Members* will notify *Commercial Customers* of the renewal or expiry of their policy in time to allow them to consider and arrange any continuing cover they may need.

33. *Members* will remind *Commercial Customers* at renewal of their duty to disclose all circumstances material to the insurance.

34. On expiry or cancellation of the insurance, at the request of the *Commercial Customer*, *Members* will promptly make available all documentation and information to which the *Commercial Customer* is entitled.

CLAIMS

Where *Members* handle claims: **A15–15**

35. *Members* will, on request, give their *Commercial Customers* reasonable guidance in pursuing a claim under their policy.

36. *Members* will handle claims fairly and promptly and keep their *Commercial Customers* informed of progress.

37. *Members* will inform *Commercial Customers* in writing, with an explanation, if they are unable to deal with any part of a claim.

38. *Members* will forward settlement of a claim, without avoidable delay, once it has been agreed.

DOCUMENTATION

39. *Members* will reply promptly or use their best endeavours to obtain a   **A15–16** prompt reply to all correspondence.

40. *Members* will forward documentation without avoidable delay.

41. *Members* should not withhold from their *Commercial Customers* any written evidence or documentation relating to their contracts of insurance without their consent or adequate and justifiable reasons being disclosed in writing and without delay. If *Members* withhold a document from their *Commercial Customers* by way of a lien for monies due from those *Commercial Customers* they should provide advice of this to those *Commercial Customers* in writing at the time that the documents are withheld. If any documentation with withheld *Members* will ensure that *Commercial Customers* receive full details of the insurance cover and any documents to which they are legally entitled.

CONFLICTS OF INTEREST

42. *Members* will seek to avoid conflicts of interest, but where this is unavoid-   **A15–17** able, they will explain the position fully and manage the situation in such a way as to avoid prejudice to any party.

43. *Members* will not put their own interests above their duty to any *Commercial Customers* on whose behalf they act.

CONFIDENTIALITY AND SECURITY

A15–18　　**44.** *Members* will ensure that any information obtained from a *Commercial Customer* wil not be used or disclosed except in the normal course of negotiating, maintaining or renewing insurance for that *Commercial Customer*, unless they have their *Commercial Customer's* consent, or disclosure is made to enable *GISC* to fulfil its regulatory function, or where the *Member* is legally obliged to disclose the information.

45. *Members* will take appropriate steps to ensure the security of any money, documents, other property or information handled or held on behalf of *Commercial Customers*.

COMPLAINTS

A15–19　　**46.** *Members* will provide details of their complaints procedures to *Commercial Customers* and details, if appropriate, of any dispute resolution facility which is available to them.

47. *Members* will handle complaints fairly and promptly.

COMMERCIAL CODE

A15–20　　**48.** *Members* will provide, on request, a copy of this *Commercial Code* to *Commercial Customers* or anyone acting on their behalf.

49. The *Commercial Code* forms part of the *Membership Contract* between *Members* and *GISC* which is governed by English law. Nothing in the *Commercial Code* or in the *Membership Contract* between *Members* and *GISC* will give any person any right to enforce any term of the *Membership Contract* between *Members* and *GISC* (including the *Commercial Code*) which that person would not have had but for the Contracts (Rights of Third Parties) Act 1999.

MORE INFORMATION

A15–21　　**50.** For more information about the *Commercial Code* contact:

General Insurance Standards Council
110 Cannon Street
London
EC4N 6EU
Phone 020 7648 7810
E-mail (general enquiries): enquiries@gisc.co.uk
or access the *GISC* website at:
www.gisc.co.uk

INDEX

Products liability insurance (cont.)
defences, 7–27
generally, 7–22—7–26
builders' duty of care
defences, 7–27
generally, 7–22—7–26
catastrophe, 7–38
cause of injury or damage
introduction, 7–02
loss of profits, 7–02—7–10
conditions
aggregate limit of indemnity, 7–46
generally, 7–45
contractual liability
exclusions, 7–39
fitness for purpose, 7–14—7–17
introduction, 7–11
satisfactory quality, 7–12—7–13
costs, 7–30
employers' liability, 7–40
erectors' duty of care
defences, 7–27
generally, 7–22—7–26
exclusions
catastrophe, 7–38
contractual liability, 7–39
employers' liability, 7–40
product guarantee, 7–34—7–37
professional negligence, 7–41
territorial limits, 7–42—7–44
extensions to cover, 7–30
fitness for purpose
examples, 7–16
generally, 7–14—7–15
hired goods, 7–17
importers, liability of
defences, 7–21
introduction, 7–18
relevant defects, 7–19
strict liability, 7–20
installers' duty of care
defences, 7–27
generally, 7–22—7–26
insured risks
contractual liability, 7–11—7–17
statutory liability, 7–18—7–21
tortious liability, 7–22
legal liability, 7–01
loss of profits, and, 7–02—7–10
manufacturers' duty of care
defences, 7–27

generally, 7–22—7–26
misdescription of insured, 7–31—7–33
own branders, liability of
defences, 7–21
introduction, 7–18
relevant defects, 7–19
strict liability, 7–20
processors' duty of care
defences, 7–27
generally, 7–22—7–26
producers, liability of
defences, 7–21
introduction, 7–18
relevant defects, 7–19
strict liability, 7–20
product guarantee, 7–34—7–37
professional negligence, 7–41
purpose, 7–01
repairers' duty of care
defences, 7–27
generally, 7–22—7–26
retailers duty of care, 7–28—7–29
risks insured
contractual liability, 7–11—7–17
statutory liability, 7–18—7–21
tortious liability, 7–22
satisfactory quality, and
examples, 7–13
generally, 7–12
statutory liability
defences, 7–21
introduction, 7–18
relevant defects, 7–19
strict liability, 7–20
subject matter
cause of injury or damage, 7–02—7–10
legal liability, 7–01
territorial limits, 7–42—7–44
tortious liability
manufacturers, of, 7–22—7–27
retailers, of, 7–28—7–29
unsatisfactory quality, and
examples, 7–13
generally, 7–12
Professional negligence
directors' liability insurance, and, 8–68
products liability insurance, and, 7–41